Lecture Notes in Computer Science　　　8172

Commenced Publication in 1973
Founding and Former Series Editors:
Gerhard Goos, Juris Hartmanis, and Jan van Leeuwen

T0213628

Dang Van Hung   Mizuhito Ogawa (Eds.)

Automated Technology for Verification and Analysis

11th International Symposium, ATVA 2013
Hanoi, Vietnam, October 15-18, 2013
Proceedings

 Springer

Volume Editors

Dang Van Hung
Vietnam National University
University of Engineering and Technology
Xuan Thuy Street, 144
Hanoi, Vietnam
E-mail: dvh@vnu.edu.vn

Mizuhito Ogawa
Japan Advanced Institute of Science and Technology
School of Information Science
1-1 Asahidai
Nomi, Ishikawa 923-1292, Japan
E-mail: mizuhito@jaist.ac.jp

ISSN 0302-9743   e-ISSN 1611-3349
ISBN 978-3-319-02443-1   e-ISBN 978-3-319-02444-8
DOI 10.1007/978-3-319-02444-8
Springer Cham Heidelberg New York Dordrecht London

Library of Congress Control Number: 2013948258

CR Subject Classification (1998): D.2, D.1, F.3, C.2-3, D.3, D.2.4, F.4.1, C.2.4

LNCS Sublibrary: SL 2 – Programming and Software Engineering

Typesetting: Camera-ready by author, data conversion by Scientific Publishing Services, Chennai, India

Printed on acid-free paper

Springer is part of Springer Science+Business Media (www.springer.com)

Preface

This volume contains the invited and contributed papers presented at the 11th International Symposium on Automated Technology for Verification and Analysis (ATVA 2013), held in Hanoi, Vietnam, during October 15–18, 2013. Over the last decade, ATVA has established itself as a premier venue for researchers and practitioners working on both theoretical and practical aspects of automated analysis, verification, and synthesis of computing systems. The symposium also provided a forum for interaction between the regional and international research communities working in these areas. The rich legacy of ATVA continued this year as well, resulting in a very strong technical program.

We received a total of 73 regular submissions and 23 tool submissions, excluding those that were incomplete. The submissions came from 31 different countries spanning five continents. Each submission was reviewed by at least three reviewers, with 295 reviews in total. These were followed by an intensive 10-day online discussion via the EasyChair system. As a result, 27 regular papers, 12 tool papers, and three short papers were finally accepted. This number is slightly higher than in previous years, especially for tool and short papers. Our selection policy for regular papers followed the ATVA tradition, keeping a high scientific quality. For tool and short paper selection, we slightly extended our view to their future possibility and attempts/ideas inspiring participants.

Our program also included three distinguished keynote talks and invited tutorials (prior to technical programs) by Alessandro Cimatti (ITC-IRST), Marta Kwiatkowska (University of Oxford), and Jerome Leroux (LaBRI, University of Bordeaux). The ATVA symposium this year also had the two co-located workshops, Infinity 2013 (co-chaired by Lorenzo Clemente and Lukáš Holik) and TTATT 2013 (chaired by Sebastian Maneth). They extended the scope, interactions, and depth, especially for theoretical views closely related to ATVA.

Many people put in a lot of effort and offered their valuable time to make ATVA 2013 successful. First of all, we would like to thank all of the authors, who worked hard to complete and submit papers to the symposium. Also, we would like to thank the Program Committee members (46 from 16 countries) and 88 external reviewers, who provided detailed reviews for the submissions and online discussions with intense energy and enthusiasm. Without them, a competitive and peer-reviewed international symposium simply cannot take place. We also thank the Steering Committee members for providing guidance on various aspects of planning of the symposium.

The Organizing Committee of the symposium made a tremendous effort in every aspect of the organization of the symposium. We thank all members of the Organizing Committee for their dedication to the success of the symposium. Without their support, we could not even consider hosting the symposium. Last but no least, we give special thanks to Nguyen Ngoc Binh, General Chair of the symposium, for providing helpful guidance whenever it was needed.

The University of Engineering and Technology of the Vietnam National University, Hanoi, the host of the symposium, provided support and facilities for organizing the symposium and its workshops and tutorials. ATVA 2013 was partly sponsored by the National Foundation for Science and Technology Development (NAFOSTED) of Vietnam. We are grateful for their support.

We sincerely hope that the readers find the proceedings of ATVA 2013 informative and rewarding.

October 2013   Dang Van Hung
                                                         Mizuhito Ogawa

Organization

ATVA 2013 was organized by the University of Engineering and Technology of the Vietnam National University, Hanoi (UET-VNU).

Steering Committee

E. Allen Emerson	The University of Texas at Austin, USA
Teruo Higashino	Osaka University, Japan
Oscar H. Ibarra	University of California at Santa Barbara, USA
Insup Lee	University of Pennsylvania, USA
Doron A. Peled	Bar-Ilan University, Israel
Farn Wang	National Taiwan University, Taiwan
Hsu-Chun Yen	National Taiwan University, Taiwan

General Chair

Nguyen Ngoc Binh	UET-VNU, Vietnam

Program Committee

Christel Baier	Technische Universität Dresden, Germany
Jonathan Billington	University of South Australia, Australia
Gianpiero Cabodi	Politecnico di Torino, Italy
Supratik Chakraborty	Indian Institute of Technology, Bombay, India
Wei-Ngan Chin	National University of Singapore, Singapore
Thao Dang	Verimag/CNRS, France
Deepak D'Souza	Indian Institute of Science, Bangalore, India
E.Allen Emerson	The University of Texas at Austin, USA
Martin Fränzle	Carl von Ossietzky Universität Oldenburg, Germany
Laurent Fribourg	ENS Cachan and CNRS, France
Masahiro Fujita	University of Tokyo, Japan
Susanne Graf	Verimag/CNRS, France
Teruo Higashino	Osaka University, Japan
Alan J. Hu	University of British Columbia, Canada
Dang Van Hung (Co-chair)	UET-VNU, Vietnam
Franjo Ivančić	NEC Laboratories America, USA
Jie-Hong Roland Jiang	National Taiwan University, Taiwan
Joost-Pieter Katoen	RWTH Aachen University, Germany
Zurab Khasidashvili	Intel, Israel

Moonzoo Kim	KAIST, Korea
Gerwin Klein	NICTA and UNSW, Australia
Insup Lee	University of Pennsylvania, USA
Xuandong Li	Nanjing University, China
Annabelle McIver	Macquarie University, Australia
Madhavan Mukund	Chennai Mathematical Institute, India
Pham Ngoc-Hung	UET-VNU, Vietnam
Thanh-Binh Nguyen	Danang University of Technology, Vietnam
Viet-Ha Nguyen	UET-VNU, Vietnam
Mizuhito Ogawa (Co-chair)	JAIST, Japan
Doron Peled	Bar-Ilan University, Israel
Thanh-Tho Quan	Ho Chi Minh City University of Technology, Vietnam
Venkatesh R.	Tata Consultancy Services, India
G. Ramalingam	Microsoft Research India, India
Abhik Roychoudhury	National University of Singapore, Singapore
Hiroyuki Seki	Nagoya University, Japan
Martin Steffen	University of Oslo, Norway
Sofiene Tahar	Concordia University, Canada
Hoang Truong	UET-VNU, Vietnam
Mahesh Viswanathan	University of Illinois, Urbana-Champaign, USA
Farn Wang	National Taiwan University, Taiwan
Bow-Yaw Wang	Academia Sinica, Taiwan
Ji Wang	Shangsha Institute of Technology, China
Hsu-Chun Yen	National Taiwan University, Taiwan
Wang Yi	Uppsala University, Sweden
Shoji Yuen	Nagoya University, Japan
Wenhui Zhang	Institute of Software, China

Organizing Committee

Pham Thi Mai Bao	UET-VNU, Vietnam
Thao Dang	VERIMAG/CNRS, France
Pham Ngoc-Hung	UET-VNU, Vietnam
Thanh-Tho Quan	Ho Chi Minh City University of Technology, Vietnam
Van-Khanh To	UET-VNU, Vietnam
Hoang Truong	UET-VNU, Vietnam
Dinh-Hieu Vo	UET-VNU, Vietnam

Additional Reviewers

Étienne André	Abhijeet Banerjee	Xiaojuan Cai
Srivathsan B.	Lei Bu	Franck Cassez
Gogul Balakrishnan	Doron Bustan	Sanjian Chen

Yu-Fang Chen
Pavan Kumar
  Chittimalli
David Cock
Alaeddine Daghar
Pallab Dasgupta
Arnab De
Frank De Boer
Christian Dehnert
Andreas Eggers
Emmanuelle Encrenaz
Lu Feng
Hongfei Fu
Cristian Gherghina
Khalil Ghorbal
Madhu Gopinathan
Eric Goubault
Friedrich Gretz
Ali Habibi
Ernst Moritz Hahn
Matthieu Moy
Kenji Hashimoto
Klaus Havelund
Ghassen Helali
Shin Hong
Johannes Hölzl
Ajith John

Pallavi Joshi
Baekgyu Kim
Yunho Kim
Andrew King
Dileep Kini
Joachim Klein
Pavel Krcal
Shrawan Kumar
Orna Kupferman
Pascale Le Gall
Quang Loc Le
Ton Chanh Le
Joe Leslie-Hurd
Guangyuan Li
Guoqiang Li
Liya Liu
Yang Liu
Carmelo Loiacono
Huan Long
Kumar Madhukar
Daniel Matichuk
Wenrui Meng
Ravindra Metta
Yasuhiko Minamide
Young-Joo Moon
Toby Murray
Viet Yen Nguyen

Bruno Oliveira
Oswaldo Olivo
Marco Palena
Paolo Pasini
Tuan-Hung Pham
Venkatesh Prasad
  Ranganath
Roopsha Samanta
Thomas Sewell
Asankhaya Sharma
Falak Sher
Nishant Sinha
Martin Stigge
Pavle Subotic
Mani Swaminathan
Yoshiaki Takata
Tachio Terauchi
Van-Khanh To
Takashi Tomita
Danilo Vendraminetto
Shaohui Wang
Shengyi Wang
Takuo Watanabe
Zhilin Wu
Aleksandar Zeljić
Pengcheng Zhang

Table of Contents

Tool Papers

Short Papers

Acceleration for Petri Nets

Jérôme Leroux*

LaBRI, Université de Bordeaux, CNRS

Abstract. The reachability problem for Petri nets is a central problem of net theory. The problem is known to be decidable by inductive invariants definable in the Presburger arithmetic. When the reachability set is definable in the Presburger arithmetic, the existence of such an inductive invariant is immediate. However, in this case, the computation of a Presburger formula denoting the reachability set is an open problem. Recently this problem got closed by proving that if the reachability set of a Petri net is definable in the Presburger arithmetic, then the Petri net is flat, i.e. its reachability set can be obtained by runs labeled by words in a bounded language. As a direct consequence, classical algorithms based on acceleration techniques effectively compute a formula in the Presburger arithmetic denoting the reachability set.

1 Introduction

Petri Nets are one of the most popular formal methods for the representation and the analysis of parallel processes [1]. The reachability problem is central since many computational problems (even outside the realm of parallel processes) reduce to this problem. Sacerdote and Tenney provided in [14] a partial proof of decidability of this problem. The proof was completed in 1981 by Mayr [13] and simplified by Kosaraju [8] from [13,14]. Ten years later [9], Lambert provided a further simplified version based on [8]. This last proof still remains difficult and the upper-bound complexity of the corresponding algorithm is just known to be non-primitive recursive. Nowadays, the exact complexity of the reachability problem for Petri nets is still an open-question. Even an Ackermannian upper bound is open (this bound holds for Petri nets with finite reachability sets [2]).

Basically, a Petri net is a pair $(T, \mathbf{c}_{\text{init}})$ where $T \subseteq \mathbb{N}^d \times \mathbb{N}^d$ is a finite set of *transitions*, and $\mathbf{c}_{\text{init}} \in \mathbb{N}^d$ is the *initial configuration*. A vector $\mathbf{c} \in \mathbb{N}^d$ is called a *configuration*. Given a transition $t = (\mathbf{p}, \mathbf{q})$, we introduce the binary relations $\xrightarrow{t}$ over the configurations defined by $\mathbf{x} \xrightarrow{t} \mathbf{y}$ if there exists $\mathbf{v} \in \mathbb{N}^d$ such that $\mathbf{x} = \mathbf{p} + \mathbf{v}$ and $\mathbf{y} = \mathbf{q} + \mathbf{v}$. Notice that in this case $\mathbf{y} - \mathbf{x}$ is the vector $\mathbf{q} - \mathbf{p}$. This vector is called the *displacement* of t, and it is denoted by $\Delta(t)$. Let $\sigma = t_1 \ldots t_k$ be a word of transitions $t_j \in T$. We denote by $\Delta(\sigma) = \sum_{j=1}^{k} \Delta(t_j)$, the *displacement* of σ. We introduce the binary relation $\xrightarrow{\sigma}$ over the configurations defined by $\mathbf{x} \xrightarrow{\sigma} \mathbf{y}$ if there exists a sequence $\mathbf{c}_0, \ldots, \mathbf{c}_k$ of configurations such that $\mathbf{c}_0 = \mathbf{x}$, $\mathbf{c}_k = \mathbf{y}$, and such that $\mathbf{c}_{j-1} \xrightarrow{t_j} \mathbf{c}_j$ for every $1 \leq j \leq k$. A configuration

---

* Work funded by ANR grant REACHARD-ANR-11-BS02-001.

D. Van Hung and M. Ogawa (Eds.): ATVA 2013, LNCS 8172, pp. 1–4, 2013.

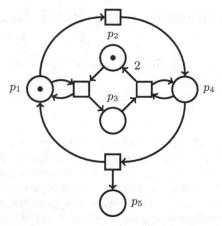

Fig. 1. The Hopcroft and Pansiot net

$\mathbf{c} \in \mathbb{N}^d$ is said to be *reachable* if there exists a word $\sigma \in T^*$ such that $\mathbf{c}_{\text{init}} \xrightarrow{\sigma} \mathbf{c}$. The *reachability set* of a Petri net is the set of reachable configurations.

Example 1.1. The Petri net depicted in Figure 1 was introduced in [7] as an example of Petri net having a reachability set which cannot be defined by a formula in the logic FO $(\mathbb{N}, +)$, called the *Presburger arithmetic*. In fact, the reachability set is equal to:

$$\left\{ (p_1, p_2, p_3, p_4, p_5) \in \mathbb{N}^5 \mid \begin{array}{c} (\; p_1 = 1 \wedge p_4 = 0 \wedge 1 \leq p_2 + p_3 \leq 2^{p_5} \;) \; \vee \\ (\; p_1 = 0 \wedge p_4 = 1 \wedge 1 \leq p_2 + 2p_3 \leq 2^{p_5+1} \;) \end{array} \right\}$$

Recently, in [10], the reachability sets of Petri nets were proved to be *almost semilinear*, a class of sets that extends the class of Presburger sets (the sets definable in FO $(\mathbb{N}, +)$) inspired by the *semilinear sets* [5]. Note that in general reachability sets are not definable in the Presburger arithmetic [7] (see Example 1.1). An application of the almost semilinear sets was provided; a final configuration is not reachable from an initial one if and only if there exists a forward inductive invariant definable in the Presburger arithmetic that contains the initial configuration but not the final one. Since we can decide if a Presburger formula denotes a forward inductive invariant, we deduce that there exist checkable certificates of non-reachability in the Presburger arithmetic. In particular, there exists a simple algorithm for deciding the general Petri net reachability problem based on two semi-algorithms. A first one that tries to prove the reachability by enumerating finite sequences of actions and a second one that tries to prove the non-reachability by enumerating Presburger formulas. Such an algorithm always terminates in theory but in practice an enumeration does not provide an efficient way for deciding the reachability problem. In particular the problem of deciding *efficiently* the reachability problem is still an *open question*.

When the reachability set is definable in the Presburger arithmetic, the existence of checkable certificates of non-reachability in the Presburger arithmetic is immediate since the reachability set is a forward inductive invariant (in fact the most precise one). The problem of deciding if the reachability set of a Petri is definable in the Presburger arithmetic was studied twenty years ago independently by Dirk Hauschildt during his PhD [6] and Jean-Luc Lambert. Unfortunately, these two works were never published. Moreover, from these works, it is difficult to deduce a simple algorithm for computing a Presburger formula denoting the reachability set when such a formula exists.

For the class of *flat* Petri nets [3,12], such a computation can be performed with *accelerations techniques*. A Petri net $(T, \mathbf{c}_{\text{init}})$ is said to be *flat* if there exist some words $\sigma_1, \ldots, \sigma_k \in T^*$ such that for every reachable configuration $\mathbf{c}$, there exists a word $\sigma \in \sigma_1^* \ldots \sigma_k^*$ such that $\mathbf{c}_{\text{init}} \xrightarrow{\sigma} \mathbf{c}$. (A language included in $\sigma_1^* \ldots \sigma_k^*$ is said to be *bounded* [4]). *Acceleration techniques* provide a framework for deciding reachability properties that works well in practice but without termination guaranty in theory. Intuitively, acceleration techniques consist in computing with some symbolic representations transitive closures of sequences of actions. For Petri nets, the Presburger arithmetic is known to be expressive enough for this computation. In fact, denoting by $\xrightarrow{\sigma^*}$ the binary relation $\bigcup_{n \in \mathbb{N}} \xrightarrow{\sigma^n}$ where $\sigma \in T^*$, the following lemma shows that $\xrightarrow{\sigma^*}$ can be denoted by a formula in the Presburger arithmetic.

Lemma 1.2 ([3]). *For every word $\sigma \in T^*$ and $n \geq 1$, we have $\mathbf{x} \xrightarrow{\sigma^n} \mathbf{y}$ if, and only if, the following formula holds:*

$$\exists \mathbf{x}', \mathbf{y}' \quad \mathbf{x} \xrightarrow{\sigma} \mathbf{x}' \wedge \mathbf{y} - \mathbf{x} = n\Delta(\sigma) \wedge \mathbf{y}' \xrightarrow{\sigma} \mathbf{y}$$

As a direct consequence, since the Presburger arithmetic is a decidable logic, the following algorithm can be implemented by denoting the sets $\mathbf{C}$ with Presburger formulas.

> **Acceleration$(T, \mathbf{c}_{\text{init}})$**
> (1) $\mathbf{C} \leftarrow \{\mathbf{c}_{\text{init}}\}$
> (2) **while** there exists $\mathbf{c} \xrightarrow{t} \mathbf{c}'$ with $\mathbf{c} \in \mathbf{C}$, $t \in T$ and $\mathbf{c}' \notin \mathbf{C}$
> (3)   **select** $\sigma \in T^*$
> (4) $\mathbf{C} \leftarrow \{\mathbf{y} \in \mathbb{N}^d \mid \exists \mathbf{c} \in \mathbf{C} \quad \mathbf{c} \xrightarrow{\sigma^*} \mathbf{y}\}$
> (5) **return** $\mathbf{C}$

Naturally, when this algorithm terminates, it returns the reachability set. Moreover, under a fairness condition on line (3), this algorithm terminates on any flat Petri net. Basically, it is sufficient to assume that the infinite sequence of words $\sigma_1, \sigma_1, \ldots$, selected during repeated executions of line (3), contains, as subsequences, all the finite sequences of words in T^*. As a direct consequence flat Petri nets have reachability sets effectively definable in the Presburger arithmetic [12]. Recently, we proved that many classes of Petri nets with known Presburger reachability sets are flat [12], and we conjectured that Petri nets with reachability sets definable in the Presburger arithmetic are flat. In fact, the following theorem shows that the conjecture is true. As a direct consequence, classical tools implementing the previous acceleration algorithms always terminate on the computation of Presburger formulas denoting reachability sets of Petri nets when such a formula exists.

Theorem 1.3 ([11]). *A Petri net is flat if, and only if, its reachability set is definable in the Presburger arithmetic.*

References

1. Esparza, J., Nielsen, M.: Decidability issues for petri nets - a survey. Bulletin of the European Association for Theoretical Computer Science 52, 245–262 (1994)
2. Figueira, D., Figueira, S., Schmitz, S., Schnoebelen, P.: Ackermannian and primitive-recursive bounds with dickson's lemma. In: Proc. of LICS 2011, pp. 269–278. IEEE Computer Society (2011)
3. Fribourg, L.: Petri nets, flat languages and linear arithmetic. In: Alpuente, M. (ed.) Proc. of WFLP 2000, pp. 344–365 (2000)
4. Ginsburg, S., Spanier, E.H.: Bounded regular sets. Proceedings of the American Mathematical Society 17(5), 1043–1049 (1966)
5. Ginsburg, S., Spanier, E.H.: Semigroups, Presburger formulas and languages. Pacific Journal of Mathematics 16(2), 285–296 (1966)
6. Hauschildt, D.: Semilinearity of the Reachability Set is Decidable for Petri Nets. PhD thesis, University of Hamburg (1990)
7. Hopcroft, J.E., Pansiot, J.-J.: On the reachability problem for 5-dimensional vector addition systems. Theoritical Computer Science 8, 135–159 (1979)
8. Rao Kosaraju, S.: Decidability of reachability in vector addition systems (preliminary version). In: Proc. of STOC 1982, pp. 267–281. ACM (1982)
9. Lambert, J.L.: A structure to decide reachability in petri nets. Theoretical Computer Science 99(1), 79–104 (1992)
10. Leroux, J.: The general vector addition system reachability problem by Presburger inductive invariants. In: Proc. of LICS 2009, pp. 4–13. IEEE Computer Society (2009)
11. Leroux, J.: Presburger vector addition systems. In: Proc. LICS 2013, IEEE Computer Society (to appear, 2013)
12. Leroux, J., Sutre, G.: Flat counter automata almost everywhere! In: Peled, D.A., Tsay, Y.-K. (eds.) ATVA 2005. LNCS, vol. 3707, pp. 489–503. Springer, Heidelberg (2005)
13. Mayr, E.W.: An algorithm for the general petri net reachability problem. In: Proc. of STOC 1981, pp. 238–246. ACM (1981)
14. Sacerdote, G.S., Tenney, R.L.: The decidability of the reachability problem for vector addition systems (preliminary version). In: Proc. of STOC 1977, pp. 61–76. ACM (1977)

Automated Verification
and Strategy Synthesis for Probabilistic Systems

Marta Kwiatkowska[1] and David Parker[2]

[1] Department of Computer Science, University of Oxford, UK
[2] School of Computer Science, University of Birmingham, UK

Abstract. Probabilistic model checking is an automated technique to verify whether a probabilistic system, e.g., a distributed network protocol which can exhibit failures, satisfies a temporal logic property, for example, "the minimum probability of the network recovering from a fault in a given time period is above 0.98". Dually, we can also synthesise, from a model and a property specification, a strategy for controlling the system in order to satisfy or optimise the property, but this aspect has received less attention to date. In this paper, we give an overview of methods for automated verification and strategy synthesis for probabilistic systems. Primarily, we focus on the model of Markov decision processes and use property specifications based on probabilistic LTL and expected reward objectives. We also describe how to apply multi-objective model checking to investigate trade-offs between several properties, and extensions to stochastic multi-player games. The paper concludes with a summary of future challenges in this area.

1 Introduction

Probabilistic model checking is an automated technique for verifying quantitative properties of stochastic systems. Like conventional model checking, it uses a systematic exploration and analysis of a system model to verify that certain requirements, specified in temporal logic, are satisfied by the model. In probabilistic model checking, models incorporate information about the likelihood and/or timing of the system's evolution, to represent uncertainty arising from, for example, component failures, unreliable sensors, or randomisation. Commonly used models include Markov chains and Markov decision processes.

Properties to be verified against these models are specified in probabilistic temporal logics such as PCTL, CSL and probabilistic LTL. These capture a variety of quantitative correctness, reliability or performance properties, for example, "the maximum probability of the airbag failing to deploy within 0.02 seconds is at most 10^{-6}". Tool support, in the form of probabilistic model checkers such as PRISM [29] and MRMC [27], has been used to verify quantitative properties of a wide variety of real-life systems, from wireless communication protocols [19], to aerospace designs [9], to DNA circuits [32].

One of the key strengths of probabilistic model checking, in contrast to, for example, approximate analysis techniques based on Monte Carlo simulation, is

D. Van Hung and M. Ogawa (Eds.): ATVA 2013, LNCS 8172, pp. 5–22, 2013.
© Springer International Publishing Switzerland 2013

the ability to analyse quantitative properties in an *exhaustive* manner. A prime example of this is when analysing models that incorporate both probabilistic and nondeterministic behaviour, such as Markov decision processes (MDPs). In an MDP, certain unknown aspects of a system's behaviour, e.g., the scheduling between components executing in parallel, or the instructions issued by a controller at runtime, are modelled as nondeterministic choices. Each possible way of resolving these choices is referred to as a *strategy*. To verify a property ϕ on an MDP $\mathcal{M}$, we check that ϕ holds *for all* possible strategies of $\mathcal{M}$.

Alternatively, we can consider the dual problem of *strategy synthesis*, which finds *some* strategy of $\mathcal{M}$ that satisfies a property ϕ, or which optimises a specified objective. This is more in line with the way that MDPs are used in other fields, such as planning under uncertainty [34], reinforcement learning [42] or optimal control [8]. In the context of probabilistic model checking, the strategy synthesis problem has generally received less attention than the dual problem of verification, despite being solved in essentially the same way. Strategy synthesis, however, has many uses; examples of its application to date include:

(i)   *Robotics.* In recent years, temporal logics such as LTL have grown increasingly popular as a means to specify tasks when synthesising controllers for robots or embedded systems [47]. In the presence of uncertainty, e.g. due to unreliable sensors or actuators, optimal controller synthesis can be performed using MDP model checking techniques [31].

(ii) *Security.* In the context of computer security, model checking has been used to synthesise strategies for malicious attackers, which represent flaws in security systems or protocols. Probability is also often a key ingredient of security; for example, in [41], probabilistic model checking of MDPs was used to generate PIN guessing attacks against hardware security modules.

(iii) *Dynamic power management.* The problem of synthesising optimal (randomised) control strategies to switch between power states in electronic devices can be solved using optimisation problems on MDPs [7] or, alternatively, with multi-objective strategy synthesis for MDPs [21].

In application domains such as these, probabilistic model checking offers various benefits. Firstly, as mentioned above, temporal logics provide an expressive means of formally specifying the goals of, for example, a controller or a malicious attacker. Secondly, thanks to formal specifications for models and properties, rigorous mathematical underpinnings, and the use of exact, exhaustive solution methods, strategy synthesis yields controllers that are guaranteed to be correct (at least with respect to the specified model and property). Such guarantees may be essential in the context of safety-critical systems.

Lastly, advantage can be drawn from the significant body of both past and ongoing work to improve the efficiency and scalability of probabilistic verification and strategy synthesis. This includes methods developed specifically for probabilistic model checking, such as symbolic techniques, abstraction or symmetry reduction, and also advances from other areas of computer science. For example, renewed interest in the area of synthesis for reactive systems has led to

significantly improved methods for generating the automata needed to synthesise strategies for temporal logics such as LTL. Parallels can also be drawn with
verification techniques for timed systems: for example, UPPAAL [33], a model
checker developed for verifying timed automata, has been used to great success
for synthesising solutions to real-time task scheduling problems, and is in many
cases superior to alternative state-of-the-art methods [1].

In this paper, we give an overview of methods for performing verification and
strategy synthesis on probabilistic systems. Our focus is primarily on algorithmic issues: we introduce the basic ideas, illustrate them with examples and then
summarise the techniques required to perform them. For space reasons, we restrict our attention to finite-state models with a discrete notion of time. We also
only consider complete information scenarios, i.e. where the state of the model
is fully observable to the strategy that is controlling it.

Primarily, we describe techniques for Markov decision processes. The first
two sections provide some background material, introduce the strategy synthesis
problem and summarise methods to solve it. In subsequent sections, we describe
extensions to multi-objective verification and stochastic multi-player games. We
conclude the paper with a discussion of some of the important topics of ongoing
and future research in this area.

An extended version of this paper, which includes full details of the algorithms
needed to perform strategy synthesis and additional worked examples, is available as [30]. The examples in both versions of the paper can be run using PRISM
(and its extensions [15]). Accompanying PRISM files are available online [49].

2   Markov Decision Processes

In the majority of this paper, we focus on *Markov decision processes* (MDPs),
which model systems that exhibit both *probabilistic* and *nondeterministic* behaviour. Probability can be used to model *uncertainty* from a variety of sources,
e.g., the unreliable behaviour of an actuator, the failure of a system component
or the use of randomisation to break symmetry.

Nondeterminism, on the other hand, models *unknown* behaviour. Again, this
has many uses, depending on the context. When using an MDP to model and
verify a randomised distributed algorithm or network protocol, nondeterminism
might represent *concurrency* between multiple components operating in parallel,
or *underspecification*, where some parameter or behaviour of the system is only
partially defined. In this paper, where we focus mainly on the problem of strategy
synthesis for MDPs, nondeterminism is more likely to represent the possible
decisions that can be taken by a *controller* of the system.

Formally, we define an MDP as follows.

Definition 1 (Markov decision process). *A* Markov decision process *(MDP)
is a tuple* $\mathcal{M}=(S, \bar{s}, A, \delta_{\mathcal{M}}, Lab)$ *where S is a* finite *set of states, $\bar{s} \in S$ is an
initial state, A is a finite set of* actions, $\delta_{\mathcal{M}} : S{\times}A \rightarrow Dist(S)$ *is a (partial) probabilistic transition function, mapping state-action pairs to probability*

distributions over S, and $Lab : S \rightarrow 2^{AP}$ is a labelling function assigning to each state a set of atomic propositions taken from a set AP.

An MDP models how the state of a system can evolve, starting from an initial state $\bar{s}$. In each state s, there is a choice between a set of enabled actions $A(s) \subseteq A$, where $A(s) \stackrel{\text{def}}{=} \{a \in A \mid \delta_{\mathcal{M}}(s, a)$ is defined$\}$. The choice of an action $a \in A$ is assumed to be nondeterministic. Once selected, a transition to a successor state s' occurs randomly, according to the probability distribution $\delta_{\mathcal{M}}(s, a)$, i.e., the probability that a transition to s' occurs is $\delta_{\mathcal{M}}(s, a)(s')$.

A *path* is a (finite or infinite) sequence of transitions $\pi = s_0 \xrightarrow{a_0} s_1 \xrightarrow{a_1} \cdots$ through MDP $\mathcal{M}$, i.e., where $s_i \in S$, $a_i \in A(s_i)$ and $\delta_{\mathcal{M}}(s_i, a_i)(s_{i+1}) > 0$ for all $i \in \mathbb{N}$. The $(i{+}1)$th state s_i of path π is denoted $\pi(i)$ and, if π is finite, $last(\pi)$ denotes its final state. We write $FPath_{\mathcal{M},s}$ and $IPath_{\mathcal{M},s}$, respectively, for the set of all finite and infinite paths of $\mathcal{M}$ starting in state s, and denote by $FPath_{\mathcal{M}}$ and $IPath_{\mathcal{M}}$ the sets of *all* such paths.

Example 1. Fig. 1 shows an MDP $\mathcal{M}$, which we will use as a running example. It represents a robot moving through terrain that is divided up into a 3×2 grid, with each grid section represented as one state. In each of the 6 states, one or more actions from the set $A = \{north, east, south, west, stuck\}$ are available, which move the robot between grid sections. Due to the presence of obstacles, certain actions are unavailable in some states or probabilistically move the robot to an alternative state. Action *stuck*, in states s_2 and s_3, indicates that the robot is unable to move. In Fig. 1, the probabilistic transition function is drawn as grouped, labelled arrows; where the probability is 1, it is omitted. We also show labels for the states, taken from the set $AP = \{hazard, goal_1, goal_2\}$.

Rewards and Costs. We use *rewards* as a general way of modelling various additional quantitative measures of an MDP. Although the name "reward" suggests a quantity that it is desirable to maximise (e.g., profit), we will often use the same mechanism for *costs*, which would typically be minimised (e.g. energy consumption). In this paper, rewards are values attached to the actions available in each state, and we assume that these rewards are accumulated over time.

Definition 2 (Reward structure). *A* reward structure *for an MDP* $\mathcal{M} = (S, \bar{s}, A, \delta_{\mathcal{M}}, Lab)$ *is a function of the form* $r : S \times A \rightarrow \mathbb{R}_{\geqslant 0}$.

Strategies. We reason about the behaviour of MDPs using *strategies* (which, depending on the context, are also known as *policies*, *adversaries* or *schedulers*). A strategy resolves nondeterminism in an MDP, i.e., it chooses which action (or actions) to take in each state. In general, this choice can depend on the history of the MDP's execution so far and can be randomised.

Definition 3 (Strategy). *A* strategy *of an MDP* $\mathcal{M} = (S, \bar{s}, A, \delta_{\mathcal{M}}, Lab)$ *is a function* $\sigma : FPath_{\mathcal{M}} \rightarrow Dist(A)$ *such that* $\sigma(\pi)(a) > 0$ *only if* $a \in A(last(\pi))$.

We denote by $\Sigma_{\mathcal{M}}$ the set of all strategies of $\mathcal{M}$, but in many cases we can restrict our attention to certain subclasses. In particular, we can classify strategies in terms of their use of *randomisation* and *memory*.

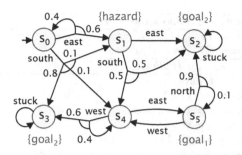

Fig. 1. Running example: an MDP $\mathcal{M}$ representing a robot moving about a 3×2 grid

1. **randomisation**: we say that strategy σ is *deterministic* (or *pure*) if $\sigma(\pi)$ is a point distribution for all $\pi \in FPath_{\mathcal{M}}$, and *randomised* otherwise;
2. **memory**: a strategy σ is *memoryless* if $\sigma(\pi)$ depends only on $last(\pi)$ and *finite-memory* if there are finitely many *modes* such that $\sigma(\pi)$ depends only on $last(\pi)$ and the current mode, which is updated each time an action is performed; otherwise, it is *infinite-memory*.

Under a particular strategy σ of $\mathcal{M}$, all nondeterminism is resolved and the behaviour of $\mathcal{M}$ is fully probabilistic. Formally, we can represent this using an (infinite) *induced discrete-time Markov chain*, whose states are finite paths of $\mathcal{M}$. This leads us, using a standard construction [28], to the definition of a probability measure $Pr^{\sigma}_{\mathcal{M},s}$ over infinite paths $IPath_{\mathcal{M},s}$, capturing the behaviour of $\mathcal{M}$ from state s under strategy σ. We will also use, for a random variable $X : IPath_{\mathcal{M},s} \rightarrow \mathbb{R}_{\geqslant 0}$, the expected value of X from state s in $\mathcal{M}$ under strategy σ, denoted $\mathbb{E}^{\sigma}_{\mathcal{M},s}(X)$. If s is the initial state $\bar{s}$, we omit it and write $Pr^{\sigma}_{\mathcal{M}}$ or $\mathbb{E}^{\sigma}_{\mathcal{M}}$.

3 Strategy Synthesis for MDPs

We now explain the *strategy synthesis* problem for Markov decision processes and give a brief overview of the algorithms that can be used to solve it. From now on, unless stated otherwise, we assume a fixed MDP $\mathcal{M} = (S, \bar{s}, A, \delta_{\mathcal{M}}, Lab)$.

3.1 Property Specification

First, we need a way to formally specify a property of the MDP that we wish to hold under the strategy to be synthesised. We follow the approach usually adopted in probabilistic verification and specify properties using temporal logic. More precisely, we will use a fragment of the property specification language from the PRISM model checker [29], the full version of which subsumes logics such as PCTL, probabilistic LTL, PCTL* and others.

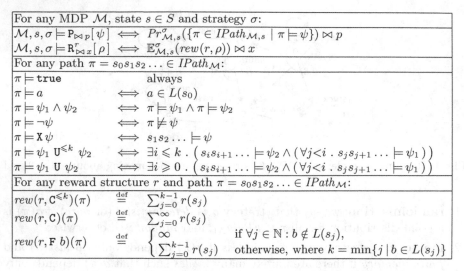

Fig. 2. Inductive definition of the property satisfaction relation $\models$

Definition 4 (Properties and objectives). *For the purposes of this paper, a* property *is a formula ϕ derived from the following grammar:*

$$\phi ::= \mathrm{P}_{\bowtie p}[\psi] \mid \mathrm{R}^r_{\bowtie x}[\rho]$$

$$\psi ::= \mathtt{true} \mid b \mid \psi \wedge \psi \mid \neg\psi \mid \mathrm{X}\,\psi \mid \psi\,\mathrm{U}^{\leqslant k}\,\psi \mid \psi\,\mathrm{U}\,\psi$$

$$\rho ::= \mathrm{C}^{\leqslant k} \mid \mathrm{C} \mid \mathrm{F}\,b$$

where $b \in AP$ is an atomic proposition, $\bowtie \in \{\leqslant, <, \geqslant, >\}$, $p \in [0,1]$, r is a reward structure, $x \in \mathbb{R}_{\geqslant 0}$ and $k \in \mathbb{N}$. We refer to ψ and ρ as objectives.

A property is thus a single instance of either the $\mathrm{P}_{\bowtie p}[\psi]$ operator, which asserts that the probability of a path satisfying (LTL) formula ψ meets the bound $\bowtie p$, or the $\mathrm{R}^r_{\bowtie x}[\rho]$ operator, which asserts that the expected value of a reward objective ρ, using reward structure r, satisfies $\bowtie x$. For now, we forbid multiple occurrences of the P or R operators in the same property,[1] as would typically be permitted when using branching-time probabilistic logics such as PCTL or PCTL* for verification of MDPs. This is because our primary focus in this tutorial is not verification, but strategy synthesis, for which the treatment of branching-time logics is more challenging [4,10].

For an MDP $\mathcal{M}$, state s and strategy σ of $\mathcal{M}$, and property ϕ, we write $\mathcal{M}, s, \sigma \models \phi$ to denote that, when starting from s, and operating under σ, $\mathcal{M}$ satisfies ϕ. Generally, we are interested in the behaviour of $\mathcal{M}$ from its initial state $\bar{s}$, and we write $\mathcal{M}, \sigma \models \phi$ to denote that $\mathcal{M}, \bar{s}, \sigma \models \phi$. A formal definition of the satisfaction relation $\models$ is given in Fig. 2. Below, we identify several key classes of properties and explain them in more detail.

---

[1] We will relax this restriction, for multi-objective strategy synthesis, in Sec. 4.

Probabilistic Reachability. For probabilistic properties $P_{\bowtie p}[\psi]$, a simple but fundamental class of path formulae ψ are "until" formulae of the form $b_1 \, U \, b_2$, where b_1, b_2 are atomic propositions. Intuitively, $b_1 \, U \, b_2$ is true if a b_2-labelled state is eventually reached, whilst passing only through b_1 states. Particularly useful is the derived operator $F \, b \equiv \text{true} \, U \, b$, representing *reachability*, i.e., a b state is eventually reached. Another common derived operator is $G \, b \equiv \neg F \, \neg b$, which captures *invariance*, i.e., that b always remains true. Also useful are step-bounded variants. For example, *step-bounded reachability*, expressed as $F^{\leqslant k} \, b \equiv \text{true} \, U^{\leqslant k} \, b$, means that a b-state is reached within k steps.

Probabilistic LTL. More generally, for the probabilistic properties $P_{\bowtie p}[\psi]$ defined in Defn. 4, ψ can be any formula in the temporal logic LTL. This allows a wide variety of useful properties to be expressed. These include, for example: (i) $G \, F \, b$ (infinitely often b); (ii) $F \, G \, b$ (eventually always b); (iii) $G \, (b_1 \rightarrow X \, b_2)$ (b_2 always immediately follows b_1); and (iv) $G \, (b_1 \rightarrow F \, b_2)$ (b_2 always eventually follows b_1). Notice that, in order to provide convenient syntax for expressing step-bounded reachability (discussed above), we explicitly add a step-bounded until operator $U^{\leqslant k}$. This is not normally included in the syntax of LTL, but does not add to its expressivity (e.g., $b_1 \, U^{\leqslant 2} \, b_2 \equiv b_2 \vee (b_1 \wedge X \, b_2) \vee (b_1 \wedge X \, b_1 \wedge X \, X \, b_2)$).

Reward Properties. As explained in Sec. 2, rewards (or dually, costs) are values assigned to state-action pairs that we assume to be accumulated over time. Properties of the form $R^r_{\bowtie x}[\rho]$ refer to the *expected* accumulated value of a reward structure r. The period of time over which rewards are accumulated is specified by the operator ρ: for the first k steps ($C^{\leqslant k}$), indefinitely (C), or until a state labelled with b is reached ($F \, b$). In the final case, if a b-state is *never* reached, we assume that the accumulated reward is infinite.

3.2 Verification and Strategy Synthesis

Classically, probabilistic model checking is phrased in terms of *verifying* that a model $\mathcal{M}$ satisfies a property ϕ. For an MDP, this means checking that ϕ holds for all possible strategies of $\mathcal{M}$.

Definition 5 (Verification). *The* verification *problem is: given an MDP $\mathcal{M}$ and property ϕ, does $\mathcal{M}, \sigma \models \phi$ hold for all possible strategies $\sigma \in \Sigma_{\mathcal{M}}$?*

In practice, this is closely related to the dual problem of *strategy synthesis*.

Definition 6 (Strategy synthesis). *The* strategy synthesis *problem is: given MDP $\mathcal{M}$ and property ϕ, find, if it exists, a strategy $\sigma \in \Sigma_{\mathcal{M}}$ such that $\mathcal{M}, \sigma \models \phi$.*

Verification and strategy synthesis for a property ϕ on MDP $\mathcal{M}$ can be done in essentially the same way, by computing *optimal values* for either probability or expected reward objectives, defined as follows:

$$Pr^{\min}_{\mathcal{M},s}(\psi) = \inf_{\sigma \in \Sigma_{\mathcal{M}}} \{Pr^{\sigma}_{\mathcal{M},s}(\psi)\} \qquad \mathbb{E}^{\min}_{\mathcal{M},s}(rew(r,\rho)) = \inf_{\sigma \in \Sigma_{\mathcal{M}}} \{\mathbb{E}^{\sigma}_{\mathcal{M},s}(rew(r,\rho))\}$$
$$Pr^{\max}_{\mathcal{M},s}(\psi) = \sup_{\sigma \in \Sigma_{\mathcal{M}}} \{Pr^{\sigma}_{\mathcal{M},s}(\psi)\} \qquad \mathbb{E}^{\max}_{\mathcal{M},s}(rew(r,\rho)) = \sup_{\sigma \in \Sigma_{\mathcal{M}}} \{\mathbb{E}^{\sigma}_{\mathcal{M},s}(rew(r,\rho))\}$$

When s is the initial state $\bar{s}$, we omit the subscript s.

Verifying, for example, property $\phi = P_{\geqslant p}[\psi]$ against $\mathcal{M}$ or, dually, synthesising a strategy for $\phi' = P_{\leqslant p}[\psi]$ can both be done by computing $Pr_{\mathcal{M}}^{\min}(\psi)$. For the former, $\mathcal{M}$ satisfies ϕ if and only if $Pr_{\mathcal{M}}^{\min}(\psi) \geqslant p$. For the latter, there exists a strategy σ satisfying ϕ' if and only if $Pr_{\mathcal{M}}^{\min}(\psi) \leqslant p$, in which case we can take σ to be a corresponding *optimal strategy*, i.e., one that achieves the optimal value. In general, therefore, rather than fix a specific bound p, we often simply aim to compute an optimal value and accompanying optimal strategy. In this case, we adapt the syntax of properties to include *numerical queries*.

Definition 7 (Numerical query). *Let ψ, r and ρ be as specified in Defn. 4. A numerical query takes the form* $P_{\min=?}[\psi]$, $P_{\max=?}[\psi]$, $R_{\min=?}^r[\rho]$ *or* $R_{\max=?}^r[\rho]$ *and yields the optimal value for the probability/reward objective.*

In the rest of this section, we describe how to compute optimal values and strategies for the classes of properties described above. We also explain which class of strategies suffices for optimality in each case (i.e., the smallest class of strategies which is guaranteed to contain an optimal one). This is important both in terms of the tractability of the solution methods, and the size and complexity of the controller that we might wish to construct from the synthesised strategy. As mentioned earlier, an extended version of this paper, available from [49], presents full details of these methods. Coverage of this material can also be found in, for example, [21,5,2] and standard texts on MDPs [6,26,38].

3.3   Strategy Synthesis for Probabilistic Reachability

To synthesise optimal strategies for probabilistic reachability, it suffices to consider *memoryless deterministic* strategies. For this class of properties, and for those covered in the following subsections, the bulk of the work for strategy synthesis actually amounts to computing optimal values. An optimal strategy is extracted either after or during this computation.

Calculating optimal values proceeds in two phases: the first *precomputation* phase performs an analysis of the underlying graph structure of the MDP to identify states for which the probability is 0 or 1; the second performs numerical computation to determine values for the remaining states. The latter can be done using various methods: (i) by solution of a *linear programming* problem; (ii) *policy iteration*, which builds a sequence of strategies (i.e., policies) with increasingly high probabilities until an optimal one is reached; (iii) *value iteration*, which computes increasingly precise approximations to the exact probabilities.

The method used to construct an optimal strategy σ^* depends on how the probabilities were computed. Policy iteration is the simplest case, since a strategy is constructed as part of the algorithm. For the others, minimum probabilities are straightforward – we choose the locally optimal action in each state:

$$\sigma^*(s) = \arg\min\nolimits_{a \in A(s)} \sum\nolimits_{s' \in S} \delta(s, a)(s') \cdot Pr_{\mathcal{M}, s'}^{\min}(F\ b)$$

Maximum probabilities require more care, but simple adapations to precomputation and value iteration algorithms yield an optimal strategy.

For step-bounded reachability, memoryless strategies do not suffice: we need to consider the class of *finite-memory deterministic* strategies. Computation of optimal probabilities (and an optimal strategy) for step-bounded reachability amounts to working backwards through the MDP and determining, at each step, and for each state, which action yields optimal probabilities. In fact, this amounts simply to performing a fixed number of steps of value iteration.

Example 2. We return to the MDP $\mathcal{M}$ from Fig. 1 and synthesise a strategy satisfying the property $P_{\geqslant 0.4}[F\ goal_1]$. To do so, we compute $Pr_{\mathcal{M}}^{max}(F\ goal_1)$, which equals 0.5. This is achieved by the memoryless deterministic strategy that picks *east* in s_0, *south* in s_1 and *east* in s_4 (there is no choice to make in states s_2, s_3 and any action can be taken in s_5, since $goal_1$ has already been reached).

Next, we consider label $goal_2$ and a numerical query $P_{max=?}[F^{\leqslant k}\ goal_2]$ with a step-bounded reachability objective. We find that $Pr_{\mathcal{M}}^{max}(F^{\leqslant k}\ goal_2)$ is 0.8, 0.96 and 0.99 for $k = 1, 2$ and 3, respectively. Taking $k = 3$ as an example, the optimal strategy is deterministic, but finite-memory. For example, if we arrive at state s_4 after 1 step, action *east* is optimal, since it reaches $goal_2$ with probability 0.9. If, on the other hand, we arrive in s_4 after 2 steps, it is better to take *west*, since it would be impossible to reach $goal_2$ within $k - 2 = 1$ steps.

3.4   Strategy Synthesis for Probabilistic LTL

To synthesise an optimal strategy of MDP $\mathcal{M}$ for an LTL formula ψ, we reduce the problem to the simpler case of a reachability property on the product of $\mathcal{M}$ and an ω-automaton representing ψ. Here, we describe the approach of [2], which uses *deterministic Rabin automata* (DRAs) and computes the probability of reaching *accepting end components*. Since the minimum probability of an LTL formula can be expressed as the maximum probability of a negated formula:

$$Pr_{\mathcal{M}}^{min}(\psi) = 1 - Pr_{\mathcal{M}}^{max}(\neg\psi)$$

we only need to consider the computation of maximally optimal probabilities.

A DRA $\mathcal{A}$ with alphabet α represents a set of infinite words $\mathcal{L}(\mathcal{A}) \subseteq \alpha^{\omega}$. For any LTL formula ψ using atomic propositions from AP, we can construct [45,18,5] a DRA $\mathcal{A}_\psi$ with alphabet 2^{AP} that represents it, i.e., such that an infinite path $\pi = s_0 \xrightarrow{a_0} s_1 \xrightarrow{a_1} s_2 \ldots$ of $\mathcal{M}$ satisfies ψ if and only if $Lab(s_0)Lab(s_1)Lab(s_2)\ldots$ is in $\mathcal{L}(\mathcal{A}_\psi)$. We then proceed by building the (synchronous) product $\mathcal{M} \otimes \mathcal{A}_\psi$ of $\mathcal{M}$ and $\mathcal{A}_\psi$. The product is an MDP with state space $S \times Q$, where Q is the set of states of the DRA. We then have:

$$Pr_{\mathcal{M}}^{max}(\psi) = Pr_{\mathcal{M} \otimes \mathcal{A}_\psi}^{max}(F\ acc)$$

where acc is an atomic proposition labelling *accepting end components* of $\mathcal{M} \otimes \mathcal{A}_\psi$. An end component [2] is a strongly connected sub-MDP of $\mathcal{M}$, and whether it is accepting is dictated by the acceptance condition of $\mathcal{A}_\psi$. Computing $Pr_{\mathcal{M}}^{max}(\psi)$ thus reduces to identifying the set of all end components (see, e.g., [2,5]) and calculating the maximum probability of reaching the accepting ones.

To build an optimal strategy maximising the probability of an LTL formula, we need to consider *finite-memory deterministic* strategies. An optimal strategy of this class is constructed in two steps. First, we find a *memoryless* deterministic strategy for the product $\mathcal{M} \otimes \mathcal{A}_\psi$, which maximises the probability of reaching accepting end components (and then stays in those end components, visiting each state infinitely often). Then, we convert this to a finite-memory strategy, with one mode for each state $q \in Q$ of the DRA $\mathcal{A}_\psi$.

Example 3. Again, using the running example (Fig. 1), we synthesise a strategy for the LTL property $\mathrm{P}_{\geqslant 0.05}[(\mathsf{G} \, \neg hazard) \wedge (\mathsf{G} \, \mathsf{F} \, goal_1)]$, which aims to both avoid the *hazard*-labelled state and visit the $goal_1$ state infinitely often. The maximum probability, from the initial state, is 0.1. In fact, for this example, a memoryless strategy suffices for optimality: we choose *south* in state s_0, which leads to state s_4 with probability 0.1. We then remain in states s_4 and s_5 indefinitely by choosing actions *east* and *west*, respectively.

3.5   Strategy Synthesis for Reward Properties

The techniques required to perform strategy synthesis for expected reward properties $\mathrm{R}^r_{\bowtie x}[\rho]$ are, in fact, quite similar to those required for the probabilistic reachability properties, described in Sec. 3.3. For the case where $\rho = \mathsf{F} \, b$, techniques similar to those for $\mathrm{P}_{\bowtie p}[\mathsf{F} \, b]$ are used: first, a graph based analysis of the model (in this case, to identify states of the MDP from which the expected reward is infinite), and then methods such as value iteration or linear programming. The resulting optimal strategy is again memoryless and deterministic.

For the case $\rho = \mathsf{C}$, where rewards are accumulated indefinitely, we need to identify end components containing non-zero rewards, since these can result in the expected reward being infinite. Subsequently, computation is similar to the case of $\rho = \mathsf{F} \, b$ above. For step-bounded properties $\rho = \mathsf{C}^{\leqslant k}$, the situation is similar to probabilities for step-bounded reachability; optimal strategies are deterministic, but may need finite memory, and optimal expected reward values can be computed recursively in k steps.

Example 4. We synthesise an optimal strategy for minimising the number of *moves* that the robot makes (i.e., the number of actions taken in the MDP) before reaching a $goal_2$ state. We use a reward structure *moves* that maps all state-action pairs to 1, and a numerical query $\mathrm{R}^{moves}_{\min=?}[\mathsf{F} \, goal_2]$. This yields the optimal value $\frac{19}{15}$, achieved by the memoryless deterministic strategy that chooses *south*, *east*, *west* and *north* in states s_0, s_1, s_4 and s_5 respectively.

4   Multi-objective Strategy Synthesis

In this section, we describe *multi-objective* strategy synthesis for MDPs, which generates a strategy σ that simultaneously satisfies multiple properties of the kind discussed in the previous section. We first describe the case for LTL properties and then summarise some extensions.

Definition 8 (Multi-objective LTL). *A multi-objective LTL property is a conjunction* $\phi = \mathrm{P}_{\bowtie_1 p_1}[\psi_1] \wedge \cdots \wedge \mathrm{P}_{\bowtie_n p_n}[\psi_n]$ *of probabilistic LTL properties. For MDP* $\mathcal{M}$ *and strategy* σ, $\mathcal{M}, \sigma \models \phi$ *if* $\mathcal{M}, \sigma \models \mathrm{P}_{\bowtie_1 p_1}[\psi_1]$ *for all* $1 \leqslant i \leqslant n$.

An algorithm for multi-objective LTL strategy synthesis was given in [20], although here we describe an adapted version, based on [22], using deterministic Rabin automata. The overall approach is similar to standard (single-objective) LTL strategy synthesis in that it constructs a product automaton and reduces the problem to (multi-objective) reachability.

First, we ensure that all n properties $\mathrm{P}_{\bowtie_i p_i}[\psi_i]$ contain only lower probability bounds $\bowtie \in \{\geqslant, >\}$, by negating LTL formulae as required (e.g., replacing $\mathrm{P}_{<p}[\psi]$ with $\mathrm{P}_{>1-p}[\neg\psi]$). Next, we build a DRA $\mathcal{A}_{\psi_i}$ for each LTL formula ψ_i, and construct the product MDP $\mathcal{M}' = \mathcal{M} \otimes \mathcal{A}_{\psi_1} \otimes \cdots \otimes \mathcal{A}_{\psi_n}$. We then consider each combination $X \subseteq \{1, \ldots, n\}$ of objectives and find the end components of $\mathcal{M}'$ that are accepting for all DRAs $\{\mathcal{A}_i \mid i \in X\}$. We create a special sink state for X in $\mathcal{M}'$ and add transitions from states in the end components to the sink.

The problem then reduces to a multi-objective problem on $\mathcal{M}'$ for n reachability properties $\mathrm{P}_{\bowtie_1 p_1}[\mathrm{F}\ acc_1], \ldots, \mathrm{P}_{\bowtie_n p_n}[\mathrm{F}\ acc_n]$, where acc_i represents the union of, for each set X containing i, the sink states for X. This can be done by solving a linear programming (LP) problem [20].

Optimal strategies for multi-objective LTL may be *finite-memory* and *randomised*. A strategy can be constructed directly from the solution of the LP problem. Like for LTL objectives (in Sec. 3.4), we obtain a memoryless strategy for the product MDP and then convert it to a finite-memory one on $\mathcal{M}$.

We now summarise several useful extensions and improvements.

(i) *Boolean combinations* of LTL objectives (rather than conjunctions, as in Defn. 8) can be handled via a translation to disjunctive normal form [20,22].

(ii) *expected reward objectives* can also be supported, in addition to LTL properties. The LP-based approach sketched above has beeen extended [22] to include reward objectives of the form $\mathrm{R}^r_{\bowtie x}[\mathrm{C}]$. An alternative approach, based on value iteration, rather than LP [23], allows the addition of step-bounded reward objectives $\mathrm{R}^r_{\bowtie x}[\mathrm{C}^{\leqslant k}]$ (and also provides significant gains in efficiency for both classes of properties).

(iii) *numerical multi-objective queries* generalise the numerical queries explained in Defn. 7. For example, rather than synthesising a strategy satisfying property $\mathrm{P}_{\bowtie_1 p_1}[\psi_1] \wedge \mathrm{P}_{\bowtie_2 p_2}[\psi_2]$, we can instead synthesise a strategy that maximises the probability of ψ_1, whilst simultaneously satisfying $\mathrm{P}_{\bowtie_2 p_2}[\psi_2]$. The LP-based methods mentioned above are easily extended to handle numerical queries by adding an objective function to the LP problem.

(iv) *Pareto queries* [23] produce a *Pareto curve* (or an approximation of it) illustrating the trade-off between multiple objectives. For example, if we want to maximise the probabilities of two LTL formulae ψ_1 and ψ_2, the Pareto curve comprises points (p_1, p_2) such that there is a strategy σ with

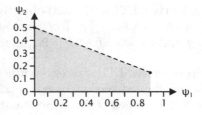

Fig. 3. Pareto curve (dashed line) for maximisation of the probabilities of LTL formulae $\psi_1 = \mathtt{G}\ \neg hazard$ and $\psi_2 = \mathtt{G}\ \mathtt{F}\ goal_1$ (see Ex. 5)

$Pr^\sigma_{\mathcal{M}}(\psi_1) \geqslant p_1$ and $Pr^\sigma_{\mathcal{M}}(\psi_2) \geqslant p_2$, but, if either bound p_1 or p_2 is increased, no strategy exists without decreasing the other bound.

We refer the reader to the references given above for precise details of the algorithms and any restrictions or assumptions that may apply.

Example 5. Previously, in Ex. 3, we synthesised a strategy for the LTL property $\mathtt{P}_{\geqslant 0.05}[\,(\mathtt{G}\ \neg hazard) \wedge (\mathtt{G}\ \mathtt{F}\ goal_1)\,]$ and found that the maximum achievable probability was 0.1. Let us now consider each conjunct of the LTL formula as a separate objective and synthesise a strategy satisfying the multi-objective LTL property $\mathtt{P}_{\geqslant 0.7}[\mathtt{G}\ \neg hazard\,] \wedge \mathtt{P}_{\geqslant 0.2}[\mathtt{G}\ \mathtt{F}\ goal_1\,]$. For convenience, we will abbreviate the objectives to $\psi_1 = \mathtt{G}\ \neg hazard$ and $\psi_2 = \mathtt{G}\ \mathtt{F}\ goal_1$.

Following the procedure outlined at the start of this section, we find that there *is* a strategy satisfying $\mathtt{P}_{\geqslant 0.7}[\psi_1\,] \wedge \mathtt{P}_{\geqslant 0.2}[\psi_2\,]$. To give an example of one such strategy, we consider a numerical multi-objective query that maximises the probability of satisfying ψ_2 whilst satisfying $\mathtt{P}_{\geqslant 0.7}[\psi_1\,]$. The optimal value (maximum probability for ψ_2) is $\frac{41}{180} \approx 0.2278$, which is obtained by a randomised strategy that, in state s_0, picks *east* with probability approximately 0.3226 and *south* with probability approximately 0.6774.

Finally, we also show, in Fig. 3, the Pareto curve obtained when maximising the probabilities of both ψ_1 and ψ_2. The grey shared area shows all points (x, y) for which there is a strategy satisfying $\mathtt{P}_{\geqslant x}[\psi_1\,] \wedge \mathtt{P}_{\geqslant y}[\psi_2\,]$. Points along the top edge of this region, shown as a dashed line in the figure, form the Pareto curve. We also mark, as black circles, points $(Pr^\sigma_{\mathcal{M}}(\psi_1), Pr^\sigma_{\mathcal{M}}(\psi_2))$ for specific *deterministic* strategies of $\mathcal{M}$. The leftmost circle is the strategy described in the first part of Ex. 2, and the rightmost one is the strategy from Ex. 3.

5   Controller Synthesis with Stochastic Games

So far, we have assumed that the nondeterministic choices in the model represent the choices available to a single entity, such as a controller. In many situations, it is important to consider decisions being made by multiple entities, possibly with conflicting objectives. An example is the classic formulation of the *controller synthesis* problem, in which a *controller* makes decisions about how to control, for example, a manufacturing plant, and must respond to nondeterministic behaviour occurring in the *environment* of the plant.

It is natural to model and analyse such systems using game-theoretic methods, which are designed precisely to reason about the strategic decisions of competing agents. From a modelling point of view, we generalise MDPs to *stochastic games*, in which nondeterministic choices are resolved by multiple *players* and the resulting behaviour is probabilistic (MDPs can thus be seen as 1-player stochastic games). We restrict our attention here to *turn-based* (as opposed to *concurrent*) stochastic games, in which a single player is responsible for the nondeterministic choices available in each state. In line with the rest of the paper, we assume finite-state models and total information.

Definition 9 (SMG). *A (turn-based) stochastic multi-player game (SMG) is a tuple $\mathcal{G} = (\Pi, S, (S_i)_{i \in \Pi}, \bar{s}, A, \delta_\mathcal{G}, Lab)$, where $S, \bar{s}, A, \delta_G$ and Lab are as for an MDP, in Defn. 1, Π is a finite set of players and $(S_i)_{i \in \Pi}$ is a partition of S.*

An SMG $\mathcal{G}$ evolves in a similar way to an MDP, except that the nondeterministic choice in each state s is resolved by the player that *controls* that state (the player i for which $s \in S_i$). Like MDPs, we reason about SMGs using strategies, but these are defined separately for each player: a strategy σ_i for player i is a function mapping finite paths ending in a state from S_i to a distribution over actions A. Given strategies $\sigma_1, \ldots, \sigma_k$ for multiple players from Π, we can combine them into a single strategy $\sigma = \sigma_1, \ldots, \sigma_k$. If a strategy σ comprises strategies for all players of the game (sometimes called a *strategy profile*), we can construct, like for an MDP, a probability space $Pr_\mathcal{G}^\sigma$ over the infinite paths of $\mathcal{G}$.

For strategy synthesis on SMGs, we generate strategies either for an individual player, or for a *coalition* $C \subseteq \Pi$ of players. We extend the definition of properties given in Defn. 4 in the style of the logic rPATL [14].

Definition 10 (Multi-player strategy synthesis). *For a property $P_{\bowtie p}[\psi]$ or $R_{\bowtie x}^r[\rho]$ and a coalition $C \subseteq \Pi$ of players, (zero-sum) multi-player strategy synthesis is expressed by a query $\langle\langle C \rangle\rangle P_{\bowtie p}[\psi]$ or $\langle\langle C \rangle\rangle R_{\bowtie x}^r[\rho]$. For example, $\langle\langle C \rangle\rangle P_{\bowtie p}[\psi]$ asks "does there exist a strategy σ_1 for the players in C such that, for all strategies σ_2 for the players $\Pi \backslash C$, we have $Pr_\mathcal{G}^{\sigma_1, \sigma_2}(\psi) \bowtie p$?".*

Intuitively, if $\langle\langle C \rangle\rangle P_{\bowtie p}[\psi]$ is true, then the players in C can collectively *guarantee* that $P_{\bowtie p}[\psi]$ holds, regardless of what the other players do. Like for the other classes of strategy synthesis described in this paper, we can also use numerical queries for stochastic multi-player games. We write, for example, $\langle\langle C \rangle\rangle P_{\max=?}[\psi]$ to denote the maximum probability of ψ that players in C can guarantee, regardless of the actions of the other players.

Multi-player strategy synthesis can be solved using rPATL model checking. Details for the the full logic rPATL (which allows nested operators and includes additional reward operators, but omits $C^{\leq k}$ and C) are given in in [14]. Basically, model checking reduces to the analysis of *zero-sum* properties on a stochastic 2-player game in which player 1 corresponds to C and player 2 to $\Pi \backslash C$. For reachability properties (i.e., $\langle\langle C \rangle\rangle P_{\bowtie p}[F\ b]$), *memoryless deterministic* strategies

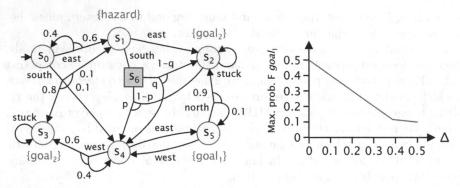

Fig. 4. Left: A stochastic 2-player game modelling an unknown probability interval. Right: The maximum value with which *ctrl* can guarantee reaching $goal_1$ for probability interval $[p, q] = [0.5 - \Delta, 0.5 + \Delta]$. See Ex. 6 for details.

suffice and optimal values and strategies can be computed either with value iteration or strategy iteration [16,17]. For an LTL property ψ, we again reduce the problem to a simpler one on the product of the game $\mathcal{G}$ and a deterministic automaton representing ψ. Unlike MDPs, there is no notion of end components. Instead, we can either use the strategy improvement algorithm of [13] to directly compute probabilities for Rabin objectives, or convert the DRA to a deterministic parity automaton and compute probabilities for parity objectives [12].

Example 6. To give an example of strategy synthesis using stochastic games, we consider a simple extension of the MDP $\mathcal{M}$ from the running example (Fig. 1). We assume that the existing choices in the MDP are made by a player *ctrl*, and we add a second player *env*, which represents nondeterministic aspects of the environment. Recall that transition probabilities in $\mathcal{M}$ model uncertain outcomes of robot actions due to obstacles. For example, when action *south* is taken in state s_1 of $\mathcal{M}$, the MDP only moves in the intended direction (to s_4) with probability 0.5; otherwise, it moves to s_2. Let us now instead assume that this probability (of going to s_4) can vary in some interval $[p, q]$.

Fig. 4 (left) shows how we can model this as a stochastic two-player game.[2] States controlled by player *ctrl* are, as before, shown as circles; those controlled by player *env*, are shown as squares. When action *south* is taken in state s_1, we move to a new state s_6, in which player *env* can choose between two actions, one that leads to s_4 with probability p and one that does so with probability q. Since players are allowed to select actions at random, this means player *env* can effectively cause the transition to occur with any probability in the range $[p, q]$.

In Ex. 2, we computed the maximum probability of reaching $goal_1$ as 0.5. Now, we will consider the maximum probability that *ctrl* can guarantee, regardless of the choices made by *env*, i.e., the maximum probability of reaching $goal_1$,

---

[2] This notion can be captured more cleanly by annotating transitions directly with probability intervals [40], or with more general specifications of uncertainty [39]. Here, we just aim to give a simple illustration of using a stochastic 2-player game.

if the probability of moving to state s_4 after action *south* can be *any* value in $[p, q]$. This is done with the query $\langle\langle ctrl \rangle\rangle P_{\max=?}[F\ goal_1]$. We compute this value for various intervals $[p, q]$ centred around the original value of 0.5, i.e., we let $p = 0.5-\Delta, q = 0.5+\Delta$ and vary Δ. Fig. 4 (right) plots the result. From inspection of the game, we can deduce that the plot corresponds to the function $\min(0.5 - \Delta, 0.15 - 0.1\Delta)$. This means that, if $\Delta \geqslant \frac{7}{18}$ (i.e., if $p \leqslant \frac{1}{9}$), then it is better to switch to the strategy that picks *south* in state s_0, rather than *east*.

6 Challenges and Directions

In this paper, we have given a brief overview of strategy synthesis for probabilistic systems, pointing to some promising application areas, highlighting the benefits that can be derived from existing work on probabilistic verification, and summarising the algorithmic techniques required for a variety of useful strategy synthesis methods. We invite the reader to consult the extended version of this paper [30] for further details.

As noted at the start, the current presentation makes a number of simplifying assumptions. We conclude by reviewing some of the key challenges in the area of strategy synthesis for probabilistic systems.

- *Partial observability.* In this paper, we assumed a *complete information* setting, where the state of the model (and the states of its history) are fully visible when a strategy chooses an action to take. In many situations, this is unrealistic, which could lead to strategies being synthesised that are not feasible in practice. Although fundamental decision problems are undecidable in the context of partial observability [3], practical implementations have been developed for a few cases [11,24] and some tool support exists [36]. Developing efficient methods for useful problem classes is an important challenge.

- *Robustness and uncertainty.* In many potential applications of strategy synthesis, such as the generation of controllers in embedded systems, it may be difficult to formulate a precise model of the stochastic behaviour of the system's environment. Thus, developing appropriate models of uncertainty, and corresponding methods to synthesise strategies that are robust in these environments, is important. We gave a very simple illustration of uncertain probabilistic behaviour in Sec. 5. Developing more sophisticated approaches is an active area of research [46,37].

- *Continuous time and space.* In this paper, we focused on discrete-time probabilistic models. Verification techniques have also been developed for models that incorporate both nondeterminism and continuous notions of time, including probabilistic timed automata [35], interactive Markov chains [25] and Markov automata [43]. Similarly, progress is being made on verification techniques for models with continuous state spaces, and hybrid models that mix both discrete and continuous elements [48,44]. Developing efficient strategy synthesis techniques for such models will bring the benefits of the methods discussed in this paper to a much wider range of application domains.

Acknowledgments. The authors are supported in part by ERC Advanced Grant VERIWARE and EU FP7 project HIERATIC.

References

1. Abdeddaim, Y., Kerbaa, A., Maler, O.: Task graph scheduling using timed automata. In: Proc. IPDPS 2003 (2003)
2. de Alfaro, L.: Formal Verification of Probabilistic Systems. Ph.D. thesis, Stanford University (1997)
3. Baier, C., Bertrand, N., Größer, M.: On decision problems for probabilistic büchi automata. In: Amadio, R.M. (ed.) FOSSACS 2008. LNCS, vol. 4962, pp. 287–301. Springer, Heidelberg (2008)
4. Baier, C., Größer, M., Leucker, M., Bollig, B., Ciesinski, F.: Controller synthesis for probabilistic systems. In: Proc. TCS 2006, pp. 493–5062. Kluwer (2004)
5. Baier, C., Katoen, J.P.: Principles of Model Checking. MIT Press (2008)
6. Bellman, R.: Dynamic Programming. Princeton University Press (1957)
7. Benini, L., Bogliolo, A., Paleologo, G., De Micheli, G.: Policy optimization for dynamic power management. IEEE Trans. CADICS 8(3), 299–316 (2000)
8. Bertsekas, D.: Dynamic Programming and Optimal Control, vol. 1&2. Athena Scientific (1995)
9. Bozzano, M., Cimatti, A., Katoen, J.-P., Nguyen, V.Y., Noll, T., Roveri, M.: The COMPASS approach: Correctness, modelling and performability of aerospace systems. In: Buth, B., Rabe, G., Seyfarth, T. (eds.) SAFECOMP 2009. LNCS, vol. 5775, pp. 173–186. Springer, Heidelberg (2009)
10. Brázdil, T., Brožek, V., Forejt, V., Kučera, A.: Stochastic games with branching-time winning objectives. In: Proc. LICS 2006, pp. 349–358. IEEE CS Press (2006)
11. Černý, P., Chatterjee, K., Henzinger, T.A., Radhakrishna, A., Singh, R.: Quantitative synthesis for concurrent programs. In: Gopalakrishnan, G., Qadeer, S. (eds.) CAV 2011. LNCS, vol. 6806, pp. 243–259. Springer, Heidelberg (2011)
12. Chatterjee, K., Henzinger, T.A.: Strategy improvement and randomized subexponential algorithms for stochastic parity games. In: Durand, B., Thomas, W. (eds.) STACS 2006. LNCS, vol. 3884, pp. 512–523. Springer, Heidelberg (2006)
13. Chatterjee, K., Henzinger, T.A.: Strategy improvement for stochastic rabin and streett games. In: Baier, C., Hermanns, H. (eds.) CONCUR 2006. LNCS, vol. 4137, pp. 375–389. Springer, Heidelberg (2006)
14. Chen, T., Forejt, V., Kwiatkowska, M., Parker, D., Simaitis, A.: Automatic verification of competitive stochastic systems. Formal Methods in System Design 43(1), 61–92 (2013)
15. Chen, T., Forejt, V., Kwiatkowska, M., Parker, D., Simaitis, A.: PRISM-games: A model checker for stochastic multi-player games. In: Piterman, N., Smolka, S.A. (eds.) TACAS 2013. LNCS, vol. 7795, pp. 185–191. Springer, Heidelberg (2013)
16. Condon, A.: The complexity of stochastic games. Information and Computation 96(2), 203–224 (1992)
17. Condon, A.: On algorithms for simple stochastic games. DIMACS Series in Discrete Mathematics and Theoretical Computer Science 13, 51–73 (1993)
18. Daniele, M., Giunchiglia, F., Vardi, M.Y.: Improved automata generation for linear temporal logic. In: Halbwachs, N., Peled, D.A. (eds.) CAV 1999. LNCS, vol. 1633, pp. 249–260. Springer, Heidelberg (1999)

19. Duflot, M., Kwiatkowska, M., Norman, G., Parker, D.: A formal analysis of Bluetooth device discovery. STTT 8(6), 621–632 (2006)
20. Etessami, K., Kwiatkowska, M., Vardi, M., Yannakakis, M.: Multi-objective model checking of Markov decision processes. LMCS 4(4), 1–21 (2008)
21. Forejt, V., Kwiatkowska, M., Norman, G., Parker, D.: Automated verification techniques for probabilistic systems. In: Bernardo, M., Issarny, V. (eds.) SFM 2011. LNCS, vol. 6659, pp. 53–113. Springer, Heidelberg (2011)
22. Forejt, V., Kwiatkowska, M., Norman, G., Parker, D., Qu, H.: Quantitative multi-objective verification for probabilistic systems. In: Abdulla, P.A., Leino, K.R.M. (eds.) TACAS 2011. LNCS, vol. 6605, pp. 112–127. Springer, Heidelberg (2011)
23. Forejt, V., Kwiatkowska, M., Parker, D.: Pareto curves for probabilistic model checking. In: Chakraborty, S., Mukund, M. (eds.) ATVA 2012. LNCS, vol. 7561, pp. 317–332. Springer, Heidelberg (2012)
24. Giro, S., Rabe, M.N.: Verification of partial-information probabilistic systems using counterexample-guided refinements. In: Chakraborty, S., Mukund, M. (eds.) ATVA 2012. LNCS, vol. 7561, pp. 333–348. Springer, Heidelberg (2012)
25. Hermanns, H. (ed.): Interactive Markov Chains and the Quest for Quantified Quality. LNCS, vol. 2428. Springer, Heidelberg (2002)
26. Howard, R.: Dynamic Programming and Markov Processes. The MIT Press (1960)
27. Katoen, J.P., Hahn, E., Hermanns, H., Jansen, D., Zapreev, I.: The ins and outs of the probabilistic model checker MRMC. In: Proc. QEST 2009. IEEE CS Press (2009)
28. Kemeny, J., Snell, J., Knapp, A.: Denumerable Markov Chains, 2nd edn. Springer (1976)
29. Kwiatkowska, M., Norman, G., Parker, D.: PRISM 4.0: Verification of probabilistic real-time systems. In: Gopalakrishnan, G., Qadeer, S. (eds.) CAV 2011. LNCS, vol. 6806, pp. 585–591. Springer, Heidelberg (2011)
30. Kwiatkowska, M., Parker, D.: Automated verification and strategy synthesis for probabilistic systems (extended version) (2013), available from [49]
31. Lahijanian, M., Wasniewski, J., Andersson, S., Belta, C.: Motion planning and control from temporal logic specifications with probabilistic satisfaction guarantees. In: Proc. ICRA 2010, pp. 3227–3232 (2010)
32. Lakin, M., Parker, D., Cardelli, L., Kwiatkowska, M., Phillips, A.: Design and analysis of DNA strand displacement devices using probabilistic model checking. Journal of the Royal Society Interface 9(72), 1470–1485 (2012)
33. Larsen, K., Pettersson, P., Yi, W.: UPPAAL in a nutshell. International Journal on Software Tools for Technology Transfer 1(1-2), 134–152 (1997)
34. Masuam, Kolobov, A.: Planning with Markov Decision Processes: An AI Perspective. Morgan & Claypool (2012)
35. Norman, G., Parker, D., Sproston, J.: Model checking for probabilistic timed automata. Formal Methods in System Design (2012) (to appear)
36. Poupart, P.: Exploiting Structure to Efficiently Solve Large Scale Partially Observable Markov Decision Processes. Ph.D. thesis, University of Toronto (2005)
37. Puggelli, A., Li, W., Sangiovanni-Vincentelli, A.L., Seshia, S.A.: Polynomial-time verification of PCTL properties of MDPs with convex uncertainties. In: Sharygina, N., Veith, H. (eds.) CAV 2013. LNCS, vol. 8044, pp. 527–542. Springer, Heidelberg (2013)
38. Puterman, M.: Markov Decision Processes: Discrete Stochastic Dynamic Programming. John Wiley and Sons (1994)
39. Satia, J., Lave Jr., R.: Markovian decision processes with uncertain transition probabilities. Oper. Res. 21, 728–740 (1970)

40. Sen, K., Viswanathan, M., Agha, G.: Model-checking Markov chains in the presence of uncertainties. In: Hermanns, H., Palsberg, J. (eds.) TACAS 2006. LNCS, vol. 3920, pp. 394–410. Springer, Heidelberg (2006)
41. Steel, G.: Formal analysis of PIN block attacks. Theoretical Computer Science 367(1-2), 257–270 (2006)
42. Sutton, R., Barto, A.: Reinforcement Learning: An Introduction. MIT Press (1998)
43. Timmer, M., Katoen, J.-P., van de Pol, J., Stoelinga, M.I.A.: Efficient modelling and generation of markov automata. In: Koutny, M., Ulidowski, I. (eds.) CONCUR 2012. LNCS, vol. 7454, pp. 364–379. Springer, Heidelberg (2012)
44. Tkachev, I., Abate, A.: Formula-free finite abstractions for linear temporal verification of stochastic hybrid systems. In: Proc. HSCC 2013, pp. 283–292 (2013)
45. Vardi, M., Wolper, P.: Reasoning about infinite computations. Information and Computation 115(1), 1–37 (1994)
46. Wolff, E., Topcu, U., Murray, R.: Robust control of uncertain Markov decision processes with temporal logic specifications. In: Proc. CDC 2012, pp. 3372–3379 (2012)
47. Wongpiromsarn, T., Topcu, U., Murray, R.: Receding horizon temporal logic planning. IEEE Trans. Automat. Contr. 57(11), 2817–2830 (2012)
48. Zhang, L., She, Z., Ratschan, S., Hermanns, H., Hahn, E.M.: Safety verification for probabilistic hybrid systems. Eur. J. Control 18(6), 572–587 (2012)
49. http://www.prismmodelchecker.org/files/stratsynth/

SMT-Based Software Model Checking
Explicit Scheduler, Symbolic Threads

Alessandro Cimatti

Fondazione Bruno Kessler – Irst
cimatti@fbk.eu

In many practical application domains, the software is organized into a set of threads, whose activation is exclusive and controlled by a cooperative scheduling policy: threads execute, without any interruption, until they either terminate or yield the control explicitly to the scheduler.

The formal verification of such software poses significant challenges. On the one side, each thread may have infinite state space, that might require some abstraction. On the other side, the scheduling policy is often important for correctness, and an approach based on abstracting the scheduler may result in loss of precision and false positives. Unfortunately, the translation of the problem into a purely sequential software model checking problem turns out to be highly inefficient for the available technologies.

We discuss a software model checking technique that exploits the intrinsic structure of these programs. Each thread is translated into a separate sequential program and explored symbolically with lazy abstraction [1], while the overall verification is orchestrated by the direct execution of the scheduler. The approach is optimized by filtering the exploration of the scheduler with the integration of partial-order reduction [2]. The technique, called ESST (Explicit Scheduler, Symbolic Threads) [3] has been implemented and experimentally evaluated on a significant set of benchmarks [4]. The results demonstrate that ESST technique is way more effective than software model checking applied to the sequentialized programs, and that partial-order reduction can lead to further performance improvements.

References

1. Henzinger, T.A., Jhala, R., Majumdar, R., Sutre, G.: Lazy abstraction. In: Launchbury, J., Mitchell, J.C. (eds.) POPL, pp. 58–70. ACM (2002)
2. Cimatti, A., Narasamdya, I., Roveri, M.: Boosting lazy abstraction for SystemC with partial order reduction. In: Abdulla, P.A., Leino, K.R.M. (eds.) TACAS 2011. LNCS, vol. 6605, pp. 341–356. Springer, Heidelberg (2011)
3. Cimatti, A., Narasamdya, I., Roveri, M.: Software model checking with explicit scheduler and symbolic threads. Logical Methods in Computer Science 8 (2012)
4. Cimatti, A., Narasamdya, I., Roveri, M.: Software model checking SystemC. IEEE Trans. on CAD of Integrated Circuits and Systems 32, 774–787 (2013)

D. Van Hung and M. Ogawa (Eds.): ATVA 2013, LNCS 8172, p. 23, 2013.
© Springer International Publishing Switzerland 2013

Effective Translation of LTL to Deterministic Rabin Automata: Beyond the (F,G)-Fragment*

Tomáš Babiak, František Blahoudek, Mojmír Křetínský, and Jan Strejček

Faculty of Informatics, Masaryk University, Brno, Czech Republic
{xbabiak, xblahoud, kretinsky, strejcek}@fi.muni.cz

Abstract. Some applications of linear temporal logic (LTL) require to translate formulae of the logic to deterministic ω-automata. There are currently two translators producing deterministic automata: ltl2dstar working for the whole LTL and Rabinizer applicable to LTL(F, G) which is the LTL fragment using only modalities F and G. We present a new translation to deterministic Rabin automata via alternating automata and deterministic transition-based generalized Rabin automata. Our translation applies to a fragment that is strictly larger than LTL(F, G). Experimental results show that our algorithm can produce significantly smaller automata compared to Rabinizer and ltl2dstar, especially for more complex LTL formulae.

1 Introduction

Linear temporal logic (LTL) is a popular formalism for specification of behavioral system properties with major applications in the area of model checking [8,5]. More precisely, LTL is typically used as a human-oriented front-end formalism as LTL formulae are succinct and easy to write and understand. Model checking algorithms usually work with an ω-automaton representing all behaviors violating a given specification formula rather than with the LTL formula directly. Hence, specifications written in the form of LTL formulae are negated and translated to equivalent ω-automata [31]. There has been a lot of attention devoted to translation of LTL to *nondeterministic Büchi automata (NBA)*, see for example [10,11,29,15] and the research in this direction still continues [12,4,2]. However, there are algorithms that need specifications given by *deterministic* ω-automata, for example, those for LTL model checking of probabilistic systems [30,9,5] and those for synthesis of reactive modules for LTL specifications [7,26], for a recent survey see [20]. As *deterministic Büchi automata (DBA)* cannot express all the properties expressible in LTL, one has to choose deterministic automata with different acceptance condition.

There are basically two approaches to translation of LTL to deterministic ω-automata. The first one translates LTL to NBA and then it employs Safra's construction [27] (or some of its variants or alternatives like [23,28]) to transform the NBA into a deterministic automaton. This approach is represented by the

---

* The authors are supported by The Czech Science Foundation, grant P202/12/G061.

D. Van Hung and M. Ogawa (Eds.): ATVA 2013, LNCS 8172, pp. 24–39, 2013.

tool ltl2dstar [16] which uses an improved Safra's construction [17,18] usually in connection with LTL to NBA translator LTL2BA [15]. The main advantage of this approach is its universality: as LTL2BA can translate any LTL formula into an NBA and the Safra's construction can transform any NBA to a *deterministic Rabin automaton (DRA)*, ltl2dstar works for the whole LTL. The main disadvantage is also connected with the universality: the determinization step does not employ the fact that the NBA represents only an LTL definable property. One can easily observe that ltl2dstar produces unnecessarily large automata, especially for formulae with more fairness subformulae.

The second approach is to avoid Safra's construction. As probabilistic modelcheckers deal with linear arithmetic, they do not profit from symbolically represented deterministic automata of [24,22]. A few translations of some simple LTL fragments to DBA have been suggested, for example [1]. Recently, a translation of a significantly larger LTL fragment to DRA has been introduced in [19] and subsequently implemented in the tool Rabinizer [14]. The algorithm builds a *generalized deterministic Rabin automata (GDRA)* directly from a formula. A DRA is then produced by a degeneralization procedure. Rabinizer often produces smaller automata than ltl2dstar. The main disadvantage is that it works for $LTL(F, G)$ only, i.e. the LTL fragment containing only temporal operators *eventually* (F) and *always* (G). Authors of the translation claim that it can be extended to a fragment containing also the operator *next* (X).

In this paper, we present another Safraless translation of an LTL fragment to DRA. The translation is influenced by the successful LTL to NBA translation algorithm LTL2BA [15] and it proceeds in the following three steps:

1. A given LTL formula φ is translated into a *very weak alternating co-Büchi automaton (VWAA)* $\mathcal{A}$ as described in [15]. If φ is an $LTL(F_s, G_s)$ formula, i.e. any formula which makes use of F, G, and their strict variants F_s and G_s as the only temporal operators, then $\mathcal{A}$ satisfies an additional structural condition. We call such automata *may/must alternating automata (MMAA)*.
2. The MMAA $\mathcal{A}$ is translated into a *transition-based generalized deterministic Rabin automaton (TGDRA)* $\mathcal{G}$. The construction of generalized Rabin pairs of $\mathcal{G}$ is inspired by [19].
3. Finally, $\mathcal{G}$ is degeneralized into a (state-based) DRA $\mathcal{D}$.

In summary, our contributions are as follows. First, note that the fragment $LTL(F_s, G_s)$ is strictly more expressive than $LTL(F, G)$. Moreover, it can be shown that our translation works for a fragment even larger than $LTL(F_s, G_s)$ but still smaller than the whole LTL. Second, the translation has a slightly better theoretical bound on the size of produced automata comparing to ltl2dstar, but the same bound as Rabinizer. Experimental results show that, for small formulae, our translation typically produces automata of a smaller or equal size as the other two translators. However, for parametrized formulae, it often produces automata that are significantly smaller. Third, we note that our TGDRA are much smaller than the (state-based) GDRA of [14]. We conjecture that algorithms for model checking of probabilistic system, e.g. those in PRISM [21], can be adapted to work with TGDRA as they are adapted to work with GDRA [6].

2 Preliminaries

This section recalls the notion of linear temporal logic (LTL) [25] and describes the ω-automata used in the following.

Linear Temporal Logic (LTL). The syntax of LTL is defined by

$$\varphi ::= tt \mid a \mid \neg\varphi \mid \varphi \vee \varphi \mid \varphi \wedge \varphi \mid \mathsf{X}\varphi \mid \varphi \mathsf{U}\varphi,$$

where tt stands for *true*, a ranges over a countable set AP of *atomic propositions*, X and U are temporal operators called *next* and *until*, respectively. An *alphabet* is a finite set $\Sigma = 2^{AP'}$, where AP' is a finite subset of AP. An ω-*word* (or simply a *word*) over Σ is an infinite sequence of letters $u = u_0 u_1 u_2 \ldots \in \Sigma^\omega$. By $u_{i..}$ we denote the suffix $u_{i..} = u_i u_{i+1} \ldots$.

We inductively define when a word u *satisfies* a formula φ, written $u \models \varphi$, as follows.

$$
\begin{aligned}
&u \models tt \\
&u \models a && \text{iff } a \in u_0 \\
&u \models \neg\varphi && \text{iff } u \not\models \varphi \\
&u \models \varphi_1 \vee \varphi_2 && \text{iff } u \models \varphi_1 \text{ or } u \models \varphi_2 \\
&u \models \varphi_1 \wedge \varphi_2 && \text{iff } u \models \varphi_1 \text{ and } u \models \varphi_2 \\
&u \models \mathsf{X}\varphi && \text{iff } u_{1..} \models \varphi \\
&u \models \varphi_1 \mathsf{U} \varphi_2 && \text{iff } \exists i \geq 0 . \, (u_{i..} \models \varphi_2 \text{ and } \forall 0 \leq j < i . \, u_{j..} \models \varphi_1)
\end{aligned}
$$

Given an alphabet Σ, a formula φ defines the language $L^\Sigma(\varphi) = \{u \in \Sigma^\omega \mid u \models \varphi\}$. We write $L(\varphi)$ instead of $L^{2^{AP(\varphi)}}(\varphi)$, where $AP(\varphi)$ denotes the set of atomic propositions occurring in the formula φ.

We define derived unary temporal operators *eventually* (F), *always* (G), *strict eventually* ($\mathsf{F_s}$), and *strict always* ($\mathsf{G_s}$) by the following equivalences: $\mathsf{F}\varphi \equiv tt \mathsf{U} \varphi$, $\mathsf{G}\varphi \equiv \neg\mathsf{F}\neg\varphi$, $\mathsf{F_s}\varphi \equiv \mathsf{XF}\varphi$, and $\mathsf{G_s}\varphi \equiv \mathsf{XG}\varphi$.

LTL(F, G) denotes the LTL fragment consisting of formulae built with temporal operators F and G only. The fragment build with temporal operators $\mathsf{F_s}$, $\mathsf{G_s}$, F and G is denoted by LTL($\mathsf{F_s}, \mathsf{G_s}$) as $\mathsf{F}\varphi$ and $\mathsf{G}\varphi$ can be seen as abbreviations for $\varphi \vee \mathsf{F_s}\varphi$ and $\varphi \wedge \mathsf{G_s}\varphi$, respectively. Note that LTL($\mathsf{F_s}, \mathsf{G_s}$) is strictly more expressive than LTL(F, G) as formulae $\mathsf{F_s}a$ and $\mathsf{G_s}a$ cannot be equivalently expressed in LTL(F, G).

An LTL formula is in *positive normal form* if no operator occurs in the scope of any negation. Each LTL($\mathsf{F_s}, \mathsf{G_s}$) formula can be transformed to this form using De Morgan's laws for $\wedge$ and $\vee$ and the equivalences $\neg\mathsf{F_s}\psi \equiv \mathsf{G_s}\neg\psi$, $\neg\mathsf{G_s}\psi \equiv \mathsf{F_s}\neg\psi$, $\neg\mathsf{F}\psi \equiv \mathsf{G}\neg\psi$, and $\neg\mathsf{G}\psi \equiv \mathsf{F}\neg\psi$. We say that a formula is *temporal* if its topmost operator is neither conjunction, nor disjunction (note that a and $\neg a$ are also temporal formulae).

Deterministic Rabin Automata and Their Generalization. A *semiautomaton* is a tuple $\mathcal{T} = (S, \Sigma, \delta, s_I)$, where S is a finite set of *states*, Σ is an alphabet, $s_I \in S$ is the *initial state*, and $\delta \subseteq S \times \Sigma \times S$ is a deterministic *transition relation*, i.e. for each state $s \in S$ and each $\alpha \in \Sigma$, there is at most one state s' such that $(s, \alpha, s') \in \delta$. A triple $(s, \alpha, s') \in \delta$ is called a *transition* from s to s' labelled by α, or an α-transition of s leading to s'. In illustrations, all transitions with the same source state and the same target state are usually depicted by a single edge labelled by a propositional formula ψ over AP representing the corresponding transition labels (e.g. given $\Sigma = 2^{\{a,b\}}$, the formula $\psi = a \vee b$ represents labels $\{a\}, \{a, b\}, \{b\}$).

A *run* of a semiautomaton $\mathcal{T}$ over a word $u = u_0 u_1 \ldots \in \Sigma^\omega$ is an infinite sequence $\sigma = (s_0, u_0, s_1)(s_1, u_1, s_2) \ldots \in \delta^\omega$ of transitions such that $s_0 = s_I$. By $Inf_t(\sigma)$ (resp. $Inf_s(\sigma)$) we denote the set of transitions (resp. states) occurring infinitely often in σ. For each word $u \in \Sigma^\omega$, a semiautomaton has at most one run over u denoted by $\sigma(u)$.

A *deterministic Rabin automaton* (DRA) is a tuple $\mathcal{D} = (S, \Sigma, \delta, s_I, \mathcal{R})$, where (S, Σ, δ, s_I) is a semiautomaton and $\mathcal{R} \subseteq 2^S \times 2^S$ is a finite set of *Rabin pairs*. Runs of $\mathcal{D}$ are runs of the semiautomaton. A run σ *satisfies* a Rabin pair $(K, L) \in \mathcal{R}$ if $Inf_s(\sigma) \cap K = \emptyset$ and $Inf_s(\sigma) \cap L \neq \emptyset$. A run is *accepting* if it satisfies some Rabin pair of $\mathcal{R}$. The language of $\mathcal{D}$ is the set $L(\mathcal{D})$ of all words $u \in \Sigma^\omega$ such that $\sigma(u)$ is accepting.

A *transition-based generalized deterministic Rabin automaton* (TGDRA) is a tuple $\mathcal{G} = (S, \Sigma, \delta, s_I, \mathcal{GR})$, where (S, Σ, δ, s_I) is a semiautomaton and $\mathcal{GR} \subseteq 2^\delta \times 2^{2^\delta}$ is a finite set of *generalized Rabin pairs*. Runs of $\mathcal{G}$ are runs of the semiautomaton. A run σ *satisfies* a generalized Rabin pair $(K, \{L_j\}_{j \in J}) \in \mathcal{GR}$ if $Inf_t(\sigma) \cap K = \emptyset$ and, for each $j \in J$, $Inf_t(\sigma) \cap L_j \neq \emptyset$. A run is *accepting* if it satisfies some generalized Rabin pair of $\mathcal{GR}$. The language of $\mathcal{G}$ is the set $L(\mathcal{G})$ of all words $u \in \Sigma^\omega$ such that $\sigma(u)$ is accepting.

A generalization of DRA called *generalized deterministic Rabin automata* (GDRA) has been considered in [19,14]. The accepting condition of GDRA is a boolean combination (in disjunctive normal form) of Rabin pairs. A run σ is accepting if σ satisfies this condition.

Very Weak Alternating Automata and Their Subclass. A *very weak alternating co-Büchi automaton* (VWAA) $\mathcal{A}$ is a tuple $(S, \Sigma, \delta, I, F)$, where S is a finite set of *states*, subsets $c \subseteq S$ are called *configurations*, Σ is an *alphabet*, $\delta \subseteq S \times \Sigma \times 2^S$ is an *alternating transition relation*, $I \subseteq 2^S$ is a non-empty set of *initial configurations*, $F \subseteq S$ is a set of *co-Büchi accepting states*, and there exists a partial order on S such that, for every transition $(s, \alpha, c) \in \delta$, all the states of c are lower or equal to s.

A triple $(s, \alpha, c) \in \delta$ is called a transition from s to c labelled by α, or an α-transition of s. We say that s is the *source state* and c the *target configuration* of the transition. A transition is *looping* if the target configuration contains the source state, i.e. $s \in c$. A transition is called a *selfloop* if its target configuration contains the source state only, i.e. $c = \{s\}$.

Figure 1(a) shows a VWAA that accepts the language described by the formula $\mathsf{G}(\mathsf{F_s}a \wedge \mathsf{F_s}b) \vee \mathsf{G}b$. Transitions are depicted by branching edges. If a target

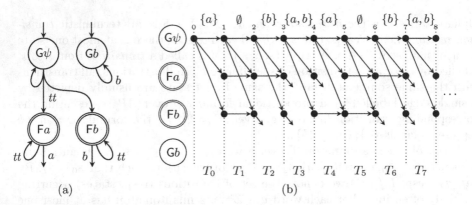

(a)   (b)

Fig. 1. (a) A VWAA (and also MMAA) corresponding to formula $G\psi \vee Gb$, where $\psi = F_s a \wedge F_s b$. (b) An accepting run of the automaton over $(\{a\}\emptyset\{b\}\{a,b\})^\omega$.

configuration is empty, the corresponding edge leads to an empty space. We often depict all transitions with the same source state and the same target configuration by a single edge (as for semiautomata). Each initial configuration is represented by a possibly branching unlabelled edge leading from an empty space to the states of the configuration. Co-Büchi accepting states are double circled.

A *multitransition* T with a label α is a set of transitions with the same label and such that the source states of the transitions are pairwise different. A *source configuration* of T, denoted by $\mathrm{dom}(T)$, is the set of source states of transitions in T. A *target configuration* of T, denoted by $\mathrm{range}(T)$, is the union of target configurations of transitions in T. We define a *multitransition relation* $\Delta \subseteq 2^S \times \Sigma \times 2^S$ as

$$\Delta = \{(\mathrm{dom}(T), \alpha, \mathrm{range}(T)) \mid \text{there exists a multitransition } T \text{ with label } \alpha\}.$$

A *run* ρ of a VWAA $\mathcal{A}$ over a word $w = w_0 w_1 \ldots \in \Sigma^\omega$ is an infinite sequence $\rho = T_0 T_1 \ldots$ of multitransitions of $\mathcal{A}$ such that $\mathrm{dom}(T_0)$ is an initial configuration of $\mathcal{A}$ and, for each $i \geq 0$, T_i is labelled by w_i and $\mathrm{range}(T_i) = \mathrm{dom}(T_{i+1})$.

A run can be represented as a directed acyclic graph (DAG). For example, the DAG of Figure 1(b) represents a run of the VWAA of Figure 1(a). The dotted lines divide the DAG into segments corresponding to multitransitions. Each transition of a multitransition is represented by edges leading across the corresponding segment from the starting state to states of the target configuration. As our alternating automata are very weak, we can order the states in a way that all edges in any DAG go only to the same or a lower row.

An accepting run corresponds to a DAG where each branch contains only finitely many states from F. Formally, the run ρ is *accepting* if it has no suffix where, for some co-Büchi accepting state $f \in F$, each multitransition contains a looping transition from f. The language of $\mathcal{A}$ is the set $L(\mathcal{A}) = \{w \in \Sigma^\omega \mid \mathcal{A} \text{ has an accepting run of over } w\}$. By $Inf_s(\rho)$ we denote the set of states that occur in $\mathrm{dom}(T_i)$ for infinitely many indices i.

Definition 1. *A may/must alternating automaton (MMAA) is a VWAA where each state fits into one of the following three categories:*

1. May-states – *states with a selfloop for each $\alpha \in \Sigma$. A run that enters such a state may wait in the state for an arbitrary number of steps.*
2. Must-states – *every transition of a must-state is looping. A run that enters such a state can never leave it. In other words, the run must stay there.*
3. Loopless states – *states that have no looping transitions and no predecessors. They can appear only in initial configurations (or they are unreachable).*

The automaton of Figure 1(a) is an MMAA with must-states $G\psi, Gb$ and may-states Fa, Fb.

We always assume that the set F of an MMAA coincides with the set of all may-states of the automaton. This assumption is justified by the following observations:

- There are no looping transitions of loopless states. Hence, removing all loopless states from F has no effect on acceptance of any run.
- All transitions leading from must-states are looping. Hence, if a run contains a must-state that is in F, then the run is non-accepting. Removing all must-states in F together with their adjacent transitions from an MMAA has no effect on its accepting runs.
- Every may-state has selfloops for all $\alpha \in \Sigma$. If such a state is not in F, we can always apply these selfloops without violating acceptance of any run. We can also remove these states from all the target configurations of all transitions of an MMAA without affecting its language.

3   Translation of LTL(F_s, G_s) to MMAA

We present the standard translation of LTL to VWAA [15] restricted to the fragment LTL(F_s, G_s). In this section, we treat the transition relation $\delta \subseteq S \times \Sigma \times 2^S$ of a VWAA as a function $\delta : S \times \Sigma \to 2^{2^S}$, where $c \in \delta(s, \alpha)$ means $(s, \alpha, c) \in \delta$. Further, we consider $G\psi$ and $F\psi$ to be subformulae of $G_s\psi$ and $F_s\psi$, respectively. This is justified by equivalences $G_s\psi \equiv XG\psi$ and $F_s\psi \equiv XF\psi$.

Let φ be an LTL(F_s, G_s) formula in positive normal form. An equivalent VWAA is constructed as $\mathcal{A}_\varphi = (Q, \Sigma, \delta, I, F)$, where

- Q is the set of temporal subformulae of φ,
- $\Sigma = 2^{AP(\varphi)}$,
- δ is defined as

$$\delta(tt, \alpha) = \{\emptyset\} \qquad\qquad \delta(a, \alpha) = \{\emptyset\} \text{ if } a \in \alpha, \emptyset \text{ otherwise}$$
$$\delta(\neg tt, \alpha) = \emptyset \qquad\qquad \delta(\neg a, \alpha) = \{\emptyset\} \text{ if } a \notin \alpha, \emptyset \text{ otherwise}$$
$$\delta(G_s\psi, \alpha) = \{\{G\psi\}\} \qquad\qquad \delta(G\psi, \alpha) = \{c \cup \{G\psi\} \mid c \in \overline{\delta}(\psi, \alpha)\}$$
$$\delta(F_s\psi, \alpha) = \{\{F\psi\}\} \qquad\qquad \delta(F\psi, \alpha) = \{\{F\psi\}\} \cup \overline{\delta}(\psi, \alpha), \text{ where}$$

$$\overline{\delta}(\psi, \alpha) = \delta(\psi, \alpha) \text{ if } \psi \text{ is a temporal formula}$$
$$\overline{\delta}(\psi_1 \vee \psi_2, \alpha) = \overline{\delta}(\psi_1, \alpha) \cup \overline{\delta}(\psi_2, \alpha)$$
$$\overline{\delta}(\psi_1 \wedge \psi_2, \alpha) = \{c_1 \cup c_2 \mid c_1 \in \overline{\delta}(\psi_1, \alpha) \text{ and } c_2 \in \overline{\delta}(\psi_2, \alpha)\},$$

– $I = \overline{\varphi}$ where $\overline{\varphi}$ is defined as

$$\overline{\psi} = \{\{\psi\}\} \text{ if } \psi \text{ is a temporal formula}$$
$$\overline{\psi_1 \vee \psi_2} = \overline{\psi_1} \cup \overline{\psi_2}$$
$$\overline{\psi_1 \wedge \psi_2} = \{O_1 \cup O_2 \mid O_1 \in \overline{\psi_1} \text{ and } O_2 \in \overline{\psi_2}\}, \text{ and}$$

– $F \subseteq Q$ is the set of all subformulae of the form $\mathsf{F}\psi$ in Q.

Using the partial order "is a subformula of" on states, one can easily prove that $\mathcal{A}_\varphi$ is a VWAA. Moreover, all the states of the form $\mathsf{G}\psi$ are must-states and all the states of the form $\mathsf{F}\psi$ are may-states. States of other forms are loopless and they are unreachable unless they appear in I. Hence, the constructed automaton is also an MMAA. Figure 1(a) shows an MMAA produced by the translation of formula $\mathsf{G}(\mathsf{F_s}a \wedge \mathsf{F_s}b) \vee \mathsf{G}b$.

In fact, MMAA and LTL($\mathsf{F_s}, \mathsf{G_s}$) are expressively equivalent. The reverse translation can be found in the full version of this paper [3].

4   Translation of MMAA to TGDRA

In this section we present a translation of an MMAA $\mathcal{A} = (S, \Sigma, \delta_\mathcal{A}, I, F)$ with multitransition relation $\Delta_\mathcal{A}$ into an equivalent TGDRA $\mathcal{G}$. At first we build a semiautomaton $\mathcal{T}$ and then we describe the transition based generalized Rabin acceptance condition $\mathcal{GR}$ of $\mathcal{G}$.

4.1   Semiautomaton $\mathcal{T}$

The idea of our seminautomaton construction is straightforward: a run $\sigma(w)$ of the semiautomaton $\mathcal{T}$ tracks all runs of $\mathcal{A}$ over w. More precisely, the state of $\mathcal{T}$ reached after reading a finite input consists of all possible configurations in which $\mathcal{A}$ can be after reading the same input. Hence, states of the semiautomaton are sets of configurations of $\mathcal{A}$ and we call them *macrostates*. We use $f, s, s_1, s_2, \ldots$ to denote states of $\mathcal{A}$ (f stands for an accepting state of F), $c, c_1, c_2, \ldots$ to denote configurations of $\mathcal{A}$, and $m, m_1, m_2, \ldots$ to denote macrostates of $\mathcal{T}$. Further, we use $t, t_1, t_2 \ldots$ to denote the transitions of $\mathcal{A}$, $T, T_0, T_1 \ldots$ to denote multitransitions of $\mathcal{A}$, and $r, r_1, r_2 \ldots$ to denote the transitions of $\mathcal{T}$, which are called *macrotransitions* hereafter.

Formally, we define the *semiautomaton* $\mathcal{T} = (M, \Sigma, \delta_\mathcal{T}, m_I)$ for $\mathcal{A}$ as follows:

– $M \subseteq 2^{2^S}$ is the set *macrostates*, restricted to those reachable from the initial macrostate m_I by $\delta_\mathcal{T}$,
– $(m_1, \alpha, m_2) \in \delta_\mathcal{T}$ iff $m_2 = \bigcup_{c \in m_1} \{c' \mid (c, \alpha, c') \in \Delta_\mathcal{A}\}$, i.e. for each $m_1 \in M$ and $\alpha \in \Sigma$, there is a single macrotransition $(m_1, \alpha, m_2) \in \delta_\mathcal{T}$, where m_2 consists of target configurations of all α-multitransitions leading from configurations in m_1, and
– $m_I = I$ is the *initial macrostate*.

Figure 2 depicts the semiautomaton $\mathcal{T}$ for the MMAA of Figure 1(a). Each row in a macrostate represents one configuration.

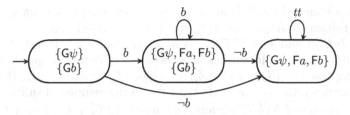

Fig. 2. The semiautomaton $\mathcal{T}$ for the MMAA of Figure 1(a)

4.2 Acceptance Condition $\mathcal{GR}$ of the TGDRA $\mathcal{G}$

For any subset $Z \subseteq S$, $must(Z)$ denotes the set of must-states of Z. An MMAA run ρ is *bounded by* $Z \subseteq S$ iff $Inf_s(\rho) \subseteq Z$ and $must(Inf_s(\rho)) = must(Z)$. For example, the run of Figure 1(b) is bounded by the set $\{G\psi, Fa, Fb\}$.

For any fixed $Z \subseteq S$, we define the set $\mathrm{AC}_Z \subseteq 2^S$ of *allowed configurations* of $\mathcal{A}$ and the set $\mathrm{AT}_Z \subseteq \delta_{\mathcal{T}}$ of *allowed macrotransitions* of $\mathcal{T}$ as follows:

$$\mathrm{AC}_Z = \{c \subseteq Z \mid must(c) = must(Z)\}$$
$$\mathrm{AT}_Z = \{(m_1, \alpha, m_2) \in \delta_{\mathcal{T}} \mid \exists c_1 \in \mathrm{AC}_Z, c_2 \in (m_2 \cap \mathrm{AC}_Z) : (c_1, \alpha, c_2) \in \Delta_{\mathcal{A}}\}^1$$

Clearly, a run ρ of $\mathcal{A}$ is bounded by Z if and only if ρ has a suffix containing only configurations of AC_Z. Let ρ be a run over w with such a suffix. As the semiautomaton $\mathcal{T}$ tracks all runs of $\mathcal{A}$ over a given input, the run $\sigma(w)$ of $\mathcal{T}$ 'covers' also ρ. Hence, $\sigma(w)$ has a suffix where, for each macrotransition (m_i, w_i, m_{i+1}), there exist configurations $c_1 \in m_i \cap \mathrm{AC}_Z$ and $c_2 \in m_{i+1} \cap \mathrm{AC}_Z$ satisfying $(c_1, w_i, c_2) \in \Delta_{\mathcal{A}}$. In other words, $\sigma(w)$ has a suffix containing only macrotransitions of AT_Z. This observation is summarized by the following lemma.

Lemma 1. *If $\mathcal{A}$ has a run over w bounded by Z, then the run $\sigma(w)$ of $\mathcal{T}$ contains a suffix of macrotransitions of AT_Z.*

In fact, the other direction can be proved as well: if $\sigma(w)$ contains a suffix of macrotransitions of AT_Z, then $\mathcal{A}$ has a run over w bounded by Z.

For each $f \in F \cap Z$, we also define the set AT_Z^f as the set of all macrotransitions in AT_Z such that $\mathcal{A}$ contains a non-looping transition of f with the same label and with the target configuration not leaving Z:

$$\mathrm{AT}_Z^f = \{(m_1, \alpha, m_2) \in \mathrm{AT}_Z \mid \exists (f, \alpha, c) \in \delta_{\mathcal{A}} : f \notin c, c \subseteq Z\}$$

Using the sets AT_Z and AT_Z^f, we define one generalized Rabin pair $\mathcal{GR}_Z$ for each subset of states $Z \subseteq S$:

$$\mathcal{GR}_Z = (\delta_{\mathcal{T}} \smallsetminus \mathrm{AT}_Z, \{\mathrm{AT}_Z^f\}_{f \in F \cap Z}) \tag{1}$$

Lemma 2. *If there is an accepting run ρ of $\mathcal{A}$ over w then the run $\sigma(w)$ of $\mathcal{T}$ satisfies $\mathcal{GR}_Z$ for $Z = Inf_s(\rho)$.*

---

[1] A definition of AT_Z with $c_1 \in (m_1 \cap \mathrm{AC}_Z)$ would be more intuitive, but less effective.

Proof. As ρ is bounded by Z, Lemma 1 implies that $\sigma(w)$ has a suffix $r_i r_{i+1} \dots$ of macrotransitions of AT_Z. Thus $Inf_t(\sigma(w)) \cap (\delta_{\mathcal{T}} \smallsetminus \mathrm{AT}_Z) = \emptyset$.

As $Z = Inf_s(\rho)$ and $\rho = T_0 T_1 \dots$ is accepting, for each $f \in F \cap Z$, ρ includes infinitely many multitransitions T_j where $f \in \mathrm{dom}(T_j)$ and T_j contains a non-looping transition $(f, w_j, c) \in \delta_{\mathcal{A}}$ satisfying $f \notin c$ and $c \subseteq Z$. Hence, the corresponding macrotransitions r_j that are also in the mentioned suffix $r_i r_{i+1} \dots$ of $\sigma(w)$ are elements of AT_Z^f. Therefore, $Inf_t(\sigma(w)) \cap \mathrm{AT}_Z^f \neq \emptyset$ for each $f \in F \cap Z$ and $\sigma(w)$ satisfies $\mathcal{GR}_Z$.   □

Lemma 3. *If a run $\sigma(w)$ of $\mathcal{T}$ satisfies $\mathcal{GR}_Z$ then there is an accepting run of $\mathcal{A}$ over w bounded by Z.*

Proof. Let $\sigma(w) = r_0 r_1 \dots$ be a run of $\mathcal{T}$ satisfying $\mathcal{GR}_Z$, i.e. $\sigma(w)$ has a suffix of macrotransitions of AT_Z and $\sigma(w)$ contains infinitely many macrotransitions of AT_Z^f for each $f \in F \cap Z$. Let $r_i = (m_i, w_i, m_{i+1})$ be the first macrotransition of the suffix. The definition of AT_Z implies that there is a configuration $c \in m_{i+1} \cap \mathrm{AC}_Z$. The construction of $\mathcal{T}$ guaranties that there exists a sequence of multitransitions of $\mathcal{A}$ leading to the configuration c. More precisely, there is a sequence $T_0 T_1 \dots T_i$ such that $\mathrm{dom}(T_0)$ is an initial configuration of $\mathcal{A}$, T_j is labelled by w_j for each $0 \le j \le i$, $\mathrm{range}(T_j) = \mathrm{dom}(T_{j+1})$ for each $0 \le j < i$, and $\mathrm{range}(T_i) = c$. We show that this sequence is in fact a prefix of an accepting run of $\mathcal{A}$ over w bounded by Z.

We inductively define a multitransition sequence $T_{i+1} T_{i+2} \dots$ completing this run. The definition uses the suffix $r_{i+1} r_{i+2} \dots$ of $\sigma(w)$. Let us assume that $j > i$ and that $\mathrm{range}(T_{j-1})$ is a configuration of AC_Z. We define T_j to contain one w_j-transition of s for each $s \in \mathrm{range}(T_{j-1})$. Thus we get $\mathrm{dom}(T_j) = \mathrm{range}(T_{j-1})$. As $r_j \in \mathrm{AT}_Z$, there exists a multitransition T' labelled by w_j such that both source and target configurations of T' are in AC_Z. For each must-state $s \in \mathrm{range}(T_{j-1})$, T_j contains the same transition leading from s as contained in T'. For may-states $f \in \mathrm{range}(T_{j-1})$, we have two cases. If $r_j \in \mathrm{AT}_Z^f$, T_j contains a non-looping transition leading from f to some states in Z. The existence of such a transition follows from the definition of AT_Z^f. For the remaining may-states, T_j uses selfloops. Formally, $T_j = \{t_j^s \mid s \in \mathrm{range}(T_{j-1})\}$, where

$$t_j^s = \begin{cases} (s, w_j, c_s) \text{ contained in } T' & \text{if } s \in must(Z) \\ (s, w_j, \{s\}) & \text{if } s \in F \wedge r_j \notin \mathrm{AT}_Z^s \\ (s, w_j, c_s) \text{ where } c_s \subseteq Z, s \notin c_s & \text{if } s \in F \wedge r_j \in \mathrm{AT}_Z^s \end{cases}$$

One can easily check that $range(T_j) \in \mathrm{AC}_Z$ and we continue by building T_{j+1}.

To sum up, the constructed run is bounded by Z. Moreover, T_j contains no looping transition of f whenever $r_j \in \mathrm{AT}_Z^f$. As the run $\sigma(w)$ is accepting, $r_j \in \mathrm{AT}_Z^f$ holds infinitely often for each $f \in F \cap Z$. The constructed run of $\mathcal{A}$ over w is thus accepting.   □

The previous two lemmata give us the following theorem.

Theorem 1. *The TGDRA $\mathcal{G} = (\mathcal{T}, \{\mathcal{GR}_Z \mid Z \subseteq S\})$ is equivalent to $\mathcal{A}$.*

5   Translation of TGDRA to DRA

This section presents a variant of the standard degeneralization procedure. At first we illustrate the idea on a TGDRA $\mathcal{G}' = (M, \Sigma, \delta_T, m_I, \{(K, \{L^j\}_{1 \leq j \leq h})\})$ with one generalized Rabin pair. Recall that a run is accepting if it has a suffix not using macrotransitions of K and using macrotransitions of each L^j infinitely often.

An equivalent DRA $\mathcal{D}'$ consists of $h + 2$ copies of $\mathcal{G}'$. The copies are called *levels*. We start at the level 1. Intuitively, being at a level j for $1 \leq j \leq h$ means that we are waiting for a transition from L^j. Whenever a transition of K appears, we move to the level 0. A transition $r \notin K$ gets us from a level j to the maximal level $l \geq j$ such that $r \in L^{j'}$ for each $j \leq j' < l$. The levels 0 and $h + 1$ have the same transitions (including target levels) as the level 1. A run of $\mathcal{G}'$ is accepting if and only if the corresponding run of $\mathcal{D}'$ visits the level 0 only finitely often and it visits the level $h + 1$ infinitely often.

In general case, we track the levels for all generalized Rabin pair simultaneously. Given a TGDRA $\mathcal{G} = (M, \Sigma, \delta_T, m_I, \{(K_i, \{L_i^j\}_{1 \leq j \leq h_i})\}_{1 \leq i \leq k})$, we construct an equivalent DRA as $\mathcal{D} = (Q, \Sigma, \delta_D, q_i, \{(K_i', L_i')\}_{1 \leq i \leq k})$, where

- $Q = M \times \{0, 1, \ldots, h_1 + 1\} \times \cdots \times \{0, 1, \ldots, h_k + 1\}$,
- $((m, l_1, \ldots, l_k), \alpha, (m', l_1', \ldots, l_k')) \in \delta_D$ iff $r = (m, \alpha, m') \in \delta_T$ and for each $1 \leq i \leq k$ it holds

$$
l_i' = \begin{cases} 0 & \text{if } r \in K_i \\ \max\{l_i \leq l \leq h_i + 1 \mid \forall l_i \leq j < l : r \in L_i^j\} & \text{if } r \notin K_i \wedge 1 \leq l_i \leq h_i \\ \max\{1 \leq l \leq h_i + 1 \mid \forall 1 \leq j < l : r \in L_i^j\} & \text{if } r \notin K_i \wedge l_i \in \{0, h_i + 1\}, \end{cases}
$$

- $q_i = (m_I, 1, \ldots, 1)$,
- $K_i' = \{(m, l_1, \ldots, l_k) \in Q \mid l_i = 0\}$, and
- $L_i' = \{(m, l_1, \ldots, l_k) \in Q \mid l_i = h_i + 1\}$.

6   Complexity

This section discusses the upper bounds of the individual steps of our translation and compares the overall complexity to complexity of the other translations.

Given a formula φ of LTL($\mathsf{F_s}, \mathsf{G_s}$), we produce an MMAA with at most n states, where n is the length of φ. Then we build the TGDRA $\mathcal{G}$ with at most 2^{2^n} states and at most 2^n generalized Rabin pairs. To obtain the DRA $\mathcal{D}$, we multiply the state space by at most $|Z| + 2$ for each generalized Rabin pair $\mathcal{GR}_Z$. The value of $|Z|$ is bounded by n. Altogether, we can derive an upper bound on the number of states of the resulting DRA as

$$
|Q| \leq 2^{2^n} \cdot (n+2)^{2^n} = 2^{2^n} \cdot 2^{2^n \cdot \log_2(n+2)} = 2^{2^n} \cdot 2^{2^{n + \log_2 \log_2(n+2)}} \in 2^{\mathcal{O}(2^{n + \log \log n})},
$$

which is the same bound as in [19], but lower than $2^{\mathcal{O}(2^{n + \log n})}$ of ltl2dstar. It is worth mentioning that the number of states of our TGDRA is bounded by $2^{2^{|\varphi|}}$ while the number of states of the GDRA produced by Rabinizer is bounded by $2^{2^{|\varphi|}} \cdot 2^{AP(\varphi)}$.

7   Simplifications and Translation Improvements

An important aspect of our translation process is simplification of all intermediate results leading to smaller resulting DRA.

We simplify input formulae by reduction rules of LTL3BA, see [4] for more details. Additionally, we rewrite the subformulae of the form $GF\psi$ and $FG\psi$ to equivalent formulae $GF_s\psi$ and $FG_s\psi$ respectively. This preference of strict temporal operators often yields smaller resulting automata.

Alternating automata are simplified in the same way as in LTL2BA: removing unreachable states, merging equivalent states, and removing redundant transitions, see [15] for details.

We improve the translation of an MMAA $\mathcal{A}$ to a TGDRA $\mathcal{G}$ in order to reduce the number of generalized Rabin pairs of $\mathcal{G}$. One can observe that, for any accepting run ρ of $\mathcal{A}$, $Inf_s(\rho)$ contains only states reachable from some must-state. Hence, in the construction of acceptance condition of $\mathcal{G}$ we can consider only subsets Z of states of $\mathcal{A}$ of this form. Further, we omit a subset Z if, for each accepting run over w bounded by Z, there is also an accepting run over w bounded by some $Z' \subseteq Z$. The formal description of subsets Z considered in the construction of the TGDRA $\mathcal{G}$ is described in the full version of this paper [3].

If a run $T_0 T_1 \ldots$ of an MMAA satisfies range$(T_i) = \emptyset$ for some i, then $T_j = \emptyset$ for all $j \geq i$ and the run is accepting. We use this observation to improve the construction of the semiautomaton $\mathcal{T}$ of the TGDRA $\mathcal{G}$: if a macrostate m contains the empty configuration, we remove all other configurations from m.

After we build the TGDRA, we simplify its acceptance condition in three ways (similar optimizations are also performed by Rabinizer).

1. We remove some generalized Rabin pairs $(K_i, \{L_i^j\}_{j \in J_i})$ that cannot be satisfied by any run, in particular when $K_i = \delta_{\mathcal{T}}$ or $L_i^j = \emptyset$ for some $j \in J_i$.
2. We remove L_i^j if there is some $l \in J_i$ such that $L_i^l \subseteq L_i^j$.
3. If the fact that a run ρ satisfies the pair $\mathcal{GR}_Z$ implies that ρ satisfies also some other pair $\mathcal{GR}_{Z'}$, we remove $\mathcal{GR}_Z$.

Finally, we simplify the state spaces of both TGDRA and DRA such that we iteratively merge the equivalent states. Two states of a DRA $\mathcal{D}$ are equivalent if they belong to the same sets of the acceptance condition of $\mathcal{D}$ and, for each α, their α-transitions lead to the same state. Two states of a TGDRA $\mathcal{G}$ are equivalent if, for each α, their α-transitions lead to the same state and belong to the same sets of the acceptance condition of $\mathcal{G}$. Moreover, if the initial state of $\mathcal{D}$ or $\mathcal{G}$ has no selfloop, we check its equivalence to another state regardless of the acceptance condition (note that a membership in acceptance condition sets is irrelevant for states or transitions that are passed at most once by any run).

Of course, we consider only the reachable state space at every step.

8   Beyond LTL(F_s,G_s) Fragment: May/Must in the Limit

The Section 4 shows a translation of MMAA into TGDRA. In fact, our translation can be used for a larger class of very weak alternating automata called *may/must in the limit automata* (limMMAA). A VWAA $\mathcal{B}$ is a limMMAA if $\mathcal{B}$ contains only must-states, states without looping transitions, and co-Büchi accepting states (not exclusively may-states), and each state reachable from a must-state is either a must- or a may-state. Note that each accepting run of a limMMAA has a suffix that contains either only empty configurations, or configurations consisting of must-states and may-states reachable from must-states. Hence, the MMAA to TGDRA translation produces correct results also for limMMAA under an additional condition: generalized Rabin pairs $\mathcal{GR}_Z$ are constructed only for sets Z that contain only must-states and may-states reachable from them.

We can obtain limMMAA by the LTL to VWAA translation of [15] when it is applied to an LTL fragment defined as

$$\varphi ::= \psi \mid \varphi \vee \varphi \mid \varphi \wedge \varphi \mid \mathsf{X}\varphi \mid \varphi \mathsf{U}\varphi,$$

where ψ ranges over LTL($\mathsf{F_s,G_s}$). Note that this fragment is strictly more expressive than LTL($\mathsf{F_s,G_s}$).

9   Experimental Results

We have made an experimental implementation of our translation (referred to as *LTL3DRA*). The translation of LTL to alternating automata is taken from LTL3BA [4]. We compare the automata produced by LTL3DRA to those produced by Rabinizer and `ltl2dstar`. All the experiments are run on a Linux laptop (2.4GHz Intel Core i7, 8GB of RAM) with a timeout set to 5 minutes.

Tables given below (i) compare the sizes of the DRA produced by all the tools and (ii) show the number of states of the generalized automata produced by LTL3DRA and Rabinizer. Note that LTL3DRA uses TGDRA whereas Rabinizer uses (state-based) GDRA, hence the numbers of their states cannot be directly compared. The sizes of DRA are written as $s(r)$, where s is the number of states and r is the number of Rabin pairs. For each formula, the size of the smallest DRA (measured by the number of states and, in the case of equality, by the number of Rabin pairs) is printed in bold.

Table 1 shows the results on formulae from [14] extended with another parametric formula. For the two parametric formulae, we give all the parameter values n for which at least one tool finished before timeout. For all formulae in the table, our experimental implementation generates automata of the same or smaller size as the others. Especially in the case of parametric formulae, the automata produced by LTL3DRA are considerably smaller. We also note that the TGDRA constructed for the formulae are typically very small.

Table 2 shows the results on formulae from SPEC PATTERNS [13] (available online[2]). We only take formulae LTL3DRA is able to work with, i.e. the formulae of the LTL fragment defined in Section 8. The fragment covers 27 out of 55 formulae listed on the web page. The dash sign in Rabinizer's column means

---

[2] http://patterns.projects.cis.ksu.edu/documentation/patterns/ltl.shtml

Table 1. The benchmark from [14] extended by one parametric formula

Formula		LTL3DRA		Rabinizer		ltl2dstar
		DRA	TGDRA	DRA	GDRA	DRA
$G(a \vee Fb)$		3(2)	2	4(2)	5	4(1)
$FGa \vee FGb \vee GFc$		8(3)	1	8(3)	8	8(3)
$F(a \vee b)$		2(1)	2	2(1)	2	2(1)
$GF(a \vee b)$		2(1)	1	2(1)	4	2(1)
$G(a \vee Fa)$		2(1)	1	2(2)	2	2(1)
$G(a \vee b \vee c)$		2(1)	2	2(1)	8	3(1)
$G(a \vee F(b \vee c))$		3(2)	2	4(2)	9	4(1)
$Fa \vee Gb$		3(2)	3	3(2)	3	4(2)
$G(a \vee F(b \wedge c))$		3(2)	2	4(2)	11	4(1)
$FGa \vee GFb$		4(2)	1	4(2)	4	4(2)
$GF(a \vee b) \wedge GF(b \vee c)$		3(1)	1	3(1)	8	7(2)
$(FFa \wedge G\neg a) \vee (GG\neg a \wedge Fa)$		1(0)	1	1(0)	1	1(0)
$GFa \wedge FGb$		3(1)	1	3(1)	4	3(1)
$(GFa \wedge FGb) \vee (FG\neg a \wedge GF\neg b)$		4(2)	1	4(2)	4	5(2)
$FGa \wedge GFa$		2(1)	1	2(1)	2	2(1)
$G(Fa \wedge Fb)$		3(1)	1	3(1)	4	5(1)
$Fa \wedge F\neg a$		4(1)	4	4(1)	4	4(1)
$(G(b \vee GFa) \wedge G(c \vee GF\neg a)) \vee Gb \vee Gc$		12(3)	4	18(4)	18	13(3)
$(G(b \vee FGa) \wedge G(c \vee FG\neg a)) \vee Gb \vee Gc$		4(2)	4	6(3)	18	14(4)
$(F(b \wedge FGa) \vee F(c \wedge FG\neg a)) \wedge Fb \wedge Fc$		5(2)	4	5(2)	18	7(1)
$(F(b \wedge GFa) \vee F(c \wedge GF\neg a)) \wedge Fb \wedge Fc$		5(2)	4	5(2)	18	7(2)
$GF(Fa \vee GFb \vee FG(a \vee b))$		4(3)	1	4(3)	4	14(4)
$FG(Fa \vee GFb \vee FG(a \vee b))$		4(3)	1	4(3)	4	145(9)
$FG(Fa \vee GFb \vee FG(a \vee b) \vee FGb)$		4(3)	1	4(3)	4	145(9)
$\bigwedge_{i=1}^{n}(GFa_i \to GFb_i)$	$n = 1$	4(2)	1	4(2)	4	4(2)
	$n = 2$	18(4)	1	20(4)	16	11324(8)
	$n = 3$	166(8)	1	470(8)	64	timeout
	$n = 4$	7408(16)	1	timeout		timeout
$\bigwedge_{i=1}^{n}(GFa_i \vee FGa_{i+1})$	$n = 1$	4(2)	1	4(2)	4	4(2)
	$n = 2$	10(4)	1	11(4)	8	572(7)
	$n = 3$	36(6)	1	52(6)	16	290046(13)
	$n = 4$	178(9)	1	1288(9)	32	timeout
	$n = 5$	1430(14)	1	timeout		timeout
	$n = 6$	20337(22)	1	timeout		timeout

that Rabinizer cannot handle the corresponding formula as it is not from the LTL(F, G) fragment. For most of the formulae in the table, LTL3DRA produces the smallest DRA. In the remaining cases, the DRA produced by our translation is only slightly bigger than the smallest one. The table also illustrates that LTL3DRA handles many (pseudo)realistic formulae not included in LTL(F, G).

Experimental results for another four parametric formulae are provided in the full version of this paper [3].

Table 2. The benchmark with selected formulae from SPEC PATTERNS. φ_i denotes the i-th formula on the web page.

	LTL3DRA		Rabinizer		ltl2dstar		LTL3DRA		Rabinizer		ltl2dstar
	DRA	TGDRA	DRA	GDRA	DRA		DRA	TGDRA	DRA	GDRA	DRA
φ_2	**4(2)**	4	—		5(2)	φ_{27}	**4(2)**	4	—		5(2)
φ_3	4(2)	3	4(2)	5	**4(1)**	φ_{28}	6(3)	3	8(3)	14	**5(1)**
φ_7	**4(2)**	3	—		**4(2)**	φ_{31}	**4(2)**	4	—		6(2)
φ_8	**3(2)**	3	**3(2)**	5	4(2)	φ_{32}	**5(2)**	5	—		7(2)
φ_{11}	**6(2)**	6	—		10(3)	φ_{33}	**5(2)**	5	—		7(3)
φ_{12}	**8(2)**	8	—		9(2)	φ_{36}	6(3)	4	—		**6(2)**
φ_{13}	**7(3)**	7	—		11(3)	φ_{37}	**6(2)**	6	—		8(3)
φ_{17}	**4(2)**	4	—		5(2)	φ_{38}	7(4)	5	—		**6(3)**
φ_{18}	4(2)	3	4(2)	5	**4(1)**	φ_{41}	**21(3)**	7	—		45(3)
φ_{21}	**4(2)**	3	—		**4(2)**	φ_{42}	**12(2)**	12	—		17(2)
φ_{22}	**4(2)**	4	—		5(2)	φ_{46}	**15(3)**	5	—		20(2)
φ_{23}	5(3)	4	—		**5(3)**	φ_{47}	7(2)	7	—		**6(2)**
φ_{26}	**3(2)**	2	4(2)	5	4(1)	φ_{48}	**14(3)**	6	—		24(2)
						φ_{52}	7(2)	7	—		**6(2)**

10   Conclusion

We present another Safraless translation of an LTL fragment to deterministic Rabin automata (DRA). Our translation employs a new class of *may/must alternating automata*. We prove that the class is expressively equivalent to the LTL($\mathsf{F_s}, \mathsf{G_s}$) fragment. Experimental results show that our translation typically produces DRA of a smaller or equal size as the other two translators of LTL (i.e. Rabinizer and ltl2dstar) and it sometimes produces automata that are significantly smaller.

References

1. Alur, R., Torre, S.L.: Deterministic generators and games for LTL fragments. ACM Trans. Comput. Log. 5(1), 1–25 (2004)
2. Babiak, T., Badie, T., Duret-Lutz, A., Křetínský, M., Strejček, J.: Compositional approach to suspension and other improvements to LTL translation. In: Bartocci, E., Ramakrishnan, C.R. (eds.) SPIN 2013. LNCS, vol. 7976, pp. 81–98. Springer, Heidelberg (2013)
3. Babiak, T., Blahoudek, F., Kretínský, M., Strejcek, J.: Effective translation of LTL to deterministic rabin automata: Beyond the (F,G)-fragment. CoRR, abs/1306.4636 (2013)
4. Babiak, T., Křetínský, M., Řehák, V., Strejček, J.: LTL to Büchi automata translation: Fast and more deterministic. In: Flanagan, C., König, B. (eds.) TACAS 2012. LNCS, vol. 7214, pp. 95–109. Springer, Heidelberg (2012)
5. Baier, C., Katoen, J.-P.: Principles of Model Checking. MIT Press (2008)
6. Chatterjee, K., Gaiser, A., Křetínský, J.: Automata with generalized Rabin pairs for probabilistic model checking and LTL synthesis. In: Sharygina, N., Veith, H. (eds.) CAV 2013. LNCS, vol. 8044, pp. 559–575. Springer, Heidelberg (2013)

7. Church, A.: Logic, arithmetic, and automata. In: Proceedings of the International Congress of Mathematicians, pp. 23–35. Institut Mittag-Leffler (1962)
8. Clarke, E.M., Grumberg, O., Peled, D.A.: Model Checking. MIT Press (1999)
9. Courcoubetis, C., Yannakakis, M.: The complexity of probabilistic verification. J. ACM 42(4), 857–907 (1995)
10. Couvreur, J.-M.: On-the-fly verification of linear temporal logic. In: Wing, J.M., Woodcock, J. (eds.) FM 1999. LNCS, vol. 1708, pp. 253–271. Springer, Heidelberg (1999)
11. Daniele, M., Giunchiglia, F., Vardi, M.Y.: Improved automata generation for linear temporal logic. In: Halbwachs, N., Peled, D.A. (eds.) CAV 1999. LNCS, vol. 1633, pp. 249–260. Springer, Heidelberg (1999)
12. Duret-Lutz, A.: LTL translation improvements in Spot. In: VECoS 2011. Electronic Workshops in Computing. British Computer Society (2011)
13. Dwyer, M.B., Avrunin, G.S., Corbett, J.C.: Patterns in property specifications for finite-state verification. In: ICSE 1999, pp. 411–420. IEEE (1999)
14. Gaiser, A., Křetínský, J., Esparza, J.: Rabinizer: Small deterministic automata for LTL(F,G). In: Chakraborty, S., Mukund, M. (eds.) ATVA 2012. LNCS, vol. 7561, pp. 72–76. Springer, Heidelberg (2012)
15. Gastin, P., Oddoux, D.: Fast LTL to Büchi Automata Translation. In: Berry, G., Comon, H., Finkel, A. (eds.) CAV 2001. LNCS, vol. 2102, pp. 53–65. Springer, Heidelberg (2001)
16. Klein, J.: ltl2dstar – LTL to deterministic Streett and Rabin automata, http://www.ltl2dstar.de
17. Klein, J., Baier, C.: Experiments with deterministic ω-automata for formulas of linear temporal logic. Theor. Comput. Sci. 363(2), 182–195 (2006)
18. Klein, J., Baier, C.: On-the-fly stuttering in the construction of deterministic ω-automata. In: Holub, J., Žďárek, J. (eds.) CIAA 2007. LNCS, vol. 4783, pp. 51–61. Springer, Heidelberg (2007)
19. Křetínský, J., Esparza, J.: Deterministic automata for the (F,G)-fragment of LTL. In: Madhusudan, P., Seshia, S.A. (eds.) CAV 2012. LNCS, vol. 7358, pp. 7–22. Springer, Heidelberg (2012)
20. Kupferman, O.: Recent challenges and ideas in temporal synthesis. In: Bieliková, M., Friedrich, G., Gottlob, G., Katzenbeisser, S., Turán, G. (eds.) SOFSEM 2012. LNCS, vol. 7147, pp. 88–98. Springer, Heidelberg (2012)
21. Kwiatkowska, M., Norman, G., Parker, D.: PRISM 4.0: Verification of probabilistic real-time systems. In: Gopalakrishnan, G., Qadeer, S. (eds.) CAV 2011. LNCS, vol. 6806, pp. 585–591. Springer, Heidelberg (2011)
22. Morgenstern, A., Schneider, K.: From LTL to symbolically represented deterministic automata. In: Logozzo, F., Peled, D.A., Zuck, L.D. (eds.) VMCAI 2008. LNCS, vol. 4905, pp. 279–293. Springer, Heidelberg (2008)
23. Piterman, N.: From nondeterministic Büchi and Streett automata to deterministic parity automata. Logical Methods in Computer Science 3(3) (2007)
24. Piterman, N., Pnueli, A., Sa'ar, Y.: Synthesis of reactive(1) designs. In: Emerson, E.A., Namjoshi, K.S. (eds.) VMCAI 2006. LNCS, vol. 3855, pp. 364–380. Springer, Heidelberg (2006)
25. Pnueli, A.: The temporal logic of programs. In: FOCS 1977, pp. 46–57. IEEE (1977)
26. Pnueli, A., Rosner, R.: On the synthesis of an asynchronous reactive module. In: Ronchi Della Rocca, S., Ausiello, G., Dezani-Ciancaglini, M. (eds.) ICALP 1989. LNCS, vol. 372, pp. 652–671. Springer, Heidelberg (1989)
27. Safra, S.: On the complexity of omega-automata. In: FOCS 1988, pp. 319–327. IEEE Computer Society (1988)

28. Schewe, S.: Tighter bounds for the determinisation of Büchi automata. In: de Alfaro, L. (ed.) FOSSACS 2009. LNCS, vol. 5504, pp. 167–181. Springer, Heidelberg (2009)
29. Somenzi, F., Bloem, R.: Efficient Büchi automata from LTL formulae. In: Emerson, E.A., Sistla, A.P. (eds.) CAV 2000. LNCS, vol. 1855, pp. 248–263. Springer, Heidelberg (2000)
30. Vardi, M.Y.: Automatic verification of probabilistic concurrent finite-state programs. In: FOCS 1985, pp. 327–338. IEEE Computer Society (1985)
31. Vardi, M.Y., Wolper, P.: An automata-theoretic approach to automatic program verification. In: LICS 1986, pp. 332–344. IEEE Computer Society (1986)

Improved Upper and Lower Bounds
for Büchi Disambiguation

Hrishikesh Karmarkar[1], Manas Joglekar[2], and Supratik Chakraborty[1]

[1] Department of Computer Science and Engineering, IIT Bombay
[2] Department of Computer Science, Stanford University

Abstract. We present a new ranking based construction for disambiguating non-deterministic Büchi automata and show that the state complexity tradeoff of the translation is in $O(n \cdot (0.76n)^n)$. This exponentially improves the best upper bound (i.e., $4 \cdot (3n)^n$) known earlier for Büchi disambiguation. We also show that the state complexity tradeoff of translating non-deterministic Büchi automata to strongly unambiguous Büchi automata is in $\Omega((n-1)!)$. This exponentially improves the previously known lower bound (i.e. $\Omega(2^n)$). Finally, we present a new technique to prove the already known exponential lower bound for disambiguating automata over finite or infinite words. Our technique is significantly simpler than earlier techniques based on ranks of matrices used for proving disambiguation lower bounds.

1 Introduction

Unambiguous Büchi automata over infinite words represent an interesting class of automata that are structurally situated between deterministic and non-deterministic Büchi automata, and yet are as expressive as non-deterministic Büchi automata. For notational convenience, we use UBA (respectively, NBA) to denote the class of unambiguous (respectively, non-deterministic) Büchi automata over infinite words in the rest of this paper. The expressive equivalence of UBA and NBA was first shown by Arnold [1], and later re-proven by Carton and Michel [3] and Kahler and Wilke [6]. Bousquet and Löding [2] showed that language equivalence and inclusion checking can be achieved in polynomial time for a sub-class of UBA, called strongly unambiguous Büchi automata (or SUBA), which is expressively equivalent to NBA. In later work [5], two other incomparable sub-classes of UBA were also shown to admit polynomial-time language inclusion and equivalence checking. The class of automata studied by Carton and Michel have also been called *prophetic* automata by others [4]. In a recent work, Preugschat and Wilke [11] have described a framework for characterizing fragments of linear temporal logic (LTL). Their characterization relies heavily on the use of prophetic automata and special Ehrenfeucht-Fraïssé games.

Despite the long history of studies on UBA (including several papers in recent years), important questions about disambiguation still remain open. Notable among these are the exact state complexity trade-offs in translating NBA to language-equivalent UBA or SUBA. The state complexity trade-off question asks

D. Van Hung and M. Ogawa (Eds.): ATVA 2013, LNCS 8172, pp. 40–54, 2013.

"Given an n-state NBA, how many states must a language-equivalent UBA (resp., SUBA) have as a function of n?" The present work attempts to address these questions, and makes the following contributions.

1. We show that the NBA to UBA state complexity trade-off is in $O(n \cdot (0.76n)^n)$. This is exponentially more succinct than the previously known best trade-off of $4 \cdot (3n)^n$ due to Kahler and Wilke [6]. The improved upper-bound is obtained by extending Kupferman and Vardi's ranking function based techniques [9] to the construction of unambiguous automata.
2. We show that the NBA to SUBA state complexity trade-off is in $\Omega((n-1)!)$. This is exponentially larger than the previously known best lower bound of $2^n - 1$ due to Schmidt [13]. The improved lower bound is obtained by a full-automaton technique [14].
3. We present a new technique for proving the already known fact that the NBA to UBA state complexity trade-off is at least $2^n - 1$. Our proof generalizes to all common notions of acceptance for finite and infinite words, and is conceptually simpler than the earlier proof based on ranks of matrices due to Schmidt [13].

2 Notation and Preliminaries

An NBA is a 5-tuple $\mathcal{A} = (\Sigma, Q, Q_0, \delta, F)$, where Σ is a finite alphabet, Q is a finite set of states, $Q_0 \subseteq Q$ is the set of initial states, $\delta : Q \times \Sigma \to 2^Q$ is the state transition relation and $F \subseteq Q$ is a set of accepting or final states. For notational convenience, we often use (with abuse of notation) $\delta(S, a)$ to denote $\bigcup_{q \in S} \delta(q, a)$ for $S \subseteq Q$. Given a word $\alpha \in \Sigma^\omega$ (also called an ω-word), let $\alpha(j)$ denote the jth letter of α. By convention, we say that $\alpha(0)$ is the first letter of α. A run ρ of $\mathcal{A}$ on α is an infinite sequence of states $q_0 q_1 q_2 \ldots$ such that $q_{i+1} \in \delta(q_i, \alpha(i))$ and $q_i \in Q$ for all $i \geq 0$. Given a run ρ of $\mathcal{A}$ on α, let $\rho(j)$ denote the jth state along ρ. The set $inf(\rho)$ is the set of states of $\mathcal{A}$ that appear infinitely often along ρ. A run ρ is called final if $inf(\rho) \cap F \neq \emptyset$; it is called accepting if it is final and $q_0 \in Q_0$. An ω-word α is said to be accepted by NBA $\mathcal{A}$ iff there is an accepting run of $\mathcal{A}$ on α. The set of ω-words accepted by $\mathcal{A}$ is called the language of $\mathcal{A}$ and is denoted $L(\mathcal{A})$. A state q_s of an NBA is called a principal sink if the following conditions hold: (i) q_s is non-final, (ii) every state, including q_s, has an outgoing transition on every $a \in \Sigma$ to q_s, and (iii) q_s has no outgoing transitions to any state other than q_s. It is easy to see that every NBA can be converted to a language-equivalent NBA with a principal sink by adding at most one state. Unless otherwise stated, we assume that all NBAs considered in this paper have a principal sink.

This paper concerns unambiguous and strongly unambiguous Büchi automata. An unambiguous Büchi automaton (UBA) is an NBA that has at most one accepting run for every $\alpha \in \Sigma^\omega$. An NBA is a *strongly unambiguous Büchi automaton* (SUBA) if it has at most one final run for every $\alpha \in \Sigma^\omega$. Clearly, a SUBA is a special kind of UBA.

Given an NBA $\mathcal{A} = (\Sigma, Q, Q_0, \delta, F)$ and an ω-word α, the *run-DAG* of $\mathcal{A}$ on α is a directed acyclic graph, denoted $G_\alpha^{\mathcal{A}}$, with vertices in $Q \times \mathbb{N}$. The vertices of graph $G_\alpha^{\mathcal{A}}$ are defined level-wise as follows. We define *level* 0 of $G_\alpha^{\mathcal{A}}$ to be $L_0 = \{(q, 0) \mid q \in Q_0\}$. For $i \geq 1$, *level* i of $G_\alpha^{\mathcal{A}}$ is defined inductively as $L_i = \{(q, i) \mid \exists (q', i - 1) \in L_{i-1} \text{ such that } q \in \delta(q', \alpha(i - 1))\}$. The run-DAG $G_\alpha^{\mathcal{A}}$ is given by (V, E), where $V = \bigcup_{i \geq 0} L_i$ is the set of vertices and $E = \{((q, i), (q', i+1)) \mid (q, i) \in V, (q', i+1) \in V, q' \in \delta(q, \alpha(i))\}$ is the set of edges. It is easy to see that every path in $G_\alpha^{\mathcal{A}}$ corresponds to a run of $\mathcal{A}$ (from an initial state) on α, and vice versa. We call vertex (q, i) an *F-vertex* (or *final-vertex*) if $q \in F$. Vertex (q, j) is said to be a *successor* of vertex (q, i), or *reachable* from vertex (q, i), if there is a directed path in $G_\alpha^{\mathcal{A}}$ from (q, i) to (q, j). If, in addition, $j = i + 1$, vertex (q, j) is called an *immediate successor* of (q, i). For notational convenience, for every natural number $n \geq 1$, we use $[n]$ to denote the set $\{1, 2, \ldots, n\}$, $[n]^{odd}$ (resp., $[n]^{even}$) to denote the set of odd (resp., even) integers in $[n]$, and $\langle n \rangle$ to denote the set $[n] \cup \{\infty\}$, where $\infty > j$ for all $j \in [n]$.

2.1 Full Rankings

In [9], Kupferman and Vardi showed that given an NBA $\mathcal{A}$ with n states and a word $\alpha \in \Sigma^\omega$, there exists a family of odd ranking functions that assign ranks in $[2n]$ to the vertices of $G_\alpha^{\mathcal{A}}$ such that $\alpha \notin L(\mathcal{A})$ iff all infinite runs of $\mathcal{A}$ on α that start from its initial states get trapped in odd ranks. We extend the notion of odd rankings and define a *full-ranking* of $G_\alpha^{\mathcal{A}} = (V, E)$ as a function $r : V \to \langle 2n \rangle$ that satisfies the following conditions: (i) for every $(q, i) \in V$, if $r((q, i)) \in [2n]^{odd}$ then $q \notin F$, (ii) for every edge $((q, i), (q', i + 1)) \in E$, $r((q', i+1)) \leq r((q, i))$, and (iii) every infinite path in $G_\alpha^{\mathcal{A}}$ eventually gets trapped in a rank in $\{\infty\} \cup [2n]^{odd}$, with at least one path trapped in ∞ iff $w \in L(\mathcal{A})$. The remainder of the discussion in this section closely parallels that in [9,7], where ranking based complementation techniques for NBA were described.

For every $\alpha \in \Sigma^\omega$, we define a unique full-ranking, $r_{\mathcal{A},\alpha}^\star$, of $G_\alpha^{\mathcal{A}}$ along the same lines as the definition of the unique odd ranking $r_{\mathcal{A},\alpha}^{KV}$ in [9,7]. Specifically, we define a sequence of DAGs $G_0 \supseteq G_1 \supseteq \ldots$, where $G_0 = G_\alpha^{\mathcal{A}}$. A vertex v is *finite* in G_i if there are no infinite paths in G_i starting from v, while v is *F-free* in G_i if it is not finite and there is no F-vertex (q, l) that is reachable from v in G_i. The DAGs G_i are now inductively defined as follows.

- For every $i \geq 0$, $G_{2i+1} = G_{2i} \setminus \{(q, l) \mid (q, l) \text{ is finite in } G_{2i}\}$.
- For every $i \geq 0$, if G_{2i+1} has at least one F-free vertex, then $G_{2i+2} = G_{2i+1} \setminus \{(q, l) \mid (q, l) \text{ is F-free in } G_{2i+1}\}$. Otherwise, G_{2i+2} is the empty DAG.

A full-ranking function $r_{\mathcal{A},\alpha}^\star$ can now be defined as follows. For every $i \geq 0$,

- If G_{2i} has at least one finite vertex, then $r_{\mathcal{A},\alpha}^\star((q, l)) = 2i$ for every vertex (q, l) that is finite in G_{2i}. Otherwise, no vertex is ranked $2i$ by $r_{\mathcal{A},\alpha}^\star$.
- If G_{2i+1} has at least one F-free vertex, then $r_{\mathcal{A},\alpha}^\star((q, l)) = 2i + 1$ for every vertex (q, l) that is F-free in G_{2i+1}. Otherwise, $r_{\mathcal{A},\alpha}^\star((q, l)) = \infty$ for every vertex (q, l) in G_{2i+1}.

Using the same arguments as used in [9], it can be shown that if $\mathcal{A}$ has n states, the maximum finite (i.e., non-∞) rank in the range of $r^\star_{\mathcal{A},\alpha}$ is in $[2n]$. In the subsequent discussion, we use FullRankProc to refer to the above "technique" for assigning full-ranks to vertices of a run-DAG.

Analogous to the concept of a *level-ranking* defined in [9], we define a *full-level ranking* as a function $f : Q \to \langle 2n \rangle \cup \{\bot\}$, such that for every $q \in Q$, if $f(q) \in [2n]^{odd}$, then $q \notin F$. Let FL represent the set of all full-level rankings and FL_∞ represent the subset of FL containing only those full-level rankings f such that $f^{-1}(\infty) \neq \emptyset$. Given two full-level rankings g_1 and g_2, and a letter $a \in \Sigma$, g_2 is said to be a *full-cover* of (g_1, a) if for all $q \in Q$ such that $g_1(q) \neq \bot$ and for all $q' \in \delta(q, a)$, $g_2(q') \leq g_1(q)$. A full-ranking r of $G^{\mathcal{A}}_\alpha$ induces a full-level ranking for every level $l \geq 0$ of $G^{\mathcal{A}}_\alpha$ such that all states not in level l of $G^{\mathcal{A}}_\alpha$ are assigned rank $\bot$. It is easy to see that if g and g' are full-level rankings for levels l and $l+1$ respectively, induced by a full-ranking r, then g' is a full-cover of $(g, \alpha(l))$. Let $max\_odd(g)$ (resp., $max\_rank(g)$) denote the highest odd rank (resp., highest rank) in the range of full-level ranking g. A full-level ranking g is said to be *tight* if the following conditions hold: (i) $max\_rank(g)$ is in $[2n]^{odd} \cup \{\infty\}$, and (ii) for all $i \in [2n]^{odd}$ such that $i \leq max\_rank(g)$, there is a state $q \in Q$ with $g(q) = i$.

The ranking $r^\star_{\mathcal{A},\alpha}$ has several interesting properties that collectively characterize it. These are described in Lemma 1. Due to space restrictions, we are unable to include proofs of all lemmas and theorems in the paper. All proofs omitted from the paper can be found in [8].

Lemma 1. *Let* $\mathcal{A} = (\Sigma, Q, Q_0, \delta, F)$ *be an NBA, and* $\alpha \in \Sigma^\omega$. *Let* (q, l) *be a vertex in* $G^{\mathcal{A}}_\alpha$. *For every* $l \in \mathbb{N}$ *and* $q \in Q$, *we have the following.*

1. *There exists a level* $l^* > 0$ *such that all full-level rankings induced by* $r^\star_{\mathcal{A},\alpha}$ *for levels* $l > l^*$ *are tight.*
2. *If* (q, l) *is not an F-vertex or* $r^\star_{\mathcal{A},\alpha}((q, l)) = \infty$, *there exists* $q' \in \delta(q, \alpha(l))$ *such that* $r^\star_{\mathcal{A},\alpha}((q', l+1)) = r^\star_{\mathcal{A},\alpha}((q, l))$.
3. *If* (q, l) *is an F-vertex with rank* $r^\star_{\mathcal{A},\alpha}((q, l)) \in [2n]^{even}$, *there exists a vertex* $(q', l+1)$ *such that* $q' \in \delta(q, \alpha(l))$ *and either* $r^\star_{\mathcal{A},\alpha}((q', l+1)) = r^\star_{\mathcal{A},\alpha}((q, l))$ *or* $r^\star_{\mathcal{A},\alpha}((q', l+1)) = r^\star_{\mathcal{A},\alpha}((q, l)) - 1$.
4. *If* $r^\star_{\mathcal{A},\alpha}((q, l)) \neq \infty$, *there is no* $q' \in \delta(q, \alpha(l))$ *such that* $r^\star_{\mathcal{A},\alpha}((q', l+1)) = \infty$.
5. *If* $r^\star_{\mathcal{A},\alpha}((q, l)) \in [2n]^{even}$, *every path starting from* (q, l) *in* $G^{\mathcal{A}}_\alpha$ *eventually visits a vertex* (q', l') *such that* $1 \leq r^\star_{\mathcal{A},\alpha}((q', l')) < r^\star_{\mathcal{A},\alpha}((q, l))$.
6. *If* $r^\star_{\mathcal{A},\alpha}((q, l)) \in [2n]^{odd}$ *and* $r^\star_{\mathcal{A},\alpha}((q, l)) > 1$, *there exists a* (q', l') *such that* (q', l') *is an F-vertex reachable from* (q, l) *in* $G^{\mathcal{A}}_\alpha$, *and* $r^\star_{\mathcal{A},\alpha}((q', l')) = r^\star_{\mathcal{A},\alpha}((q, l)) - 1$.
7. *If* $r^\star_{\mathcal{A},\alpha}((q, l)) = \infty$, *there exists a* (q', l') *such that* (q', l') *is an F-vertex reachable from* (q, l) *in* $G^{\mathcal{A}}_\alpha$, *and* $r^\star_{\mathcal{A},\alpha}((q', l')) = \infty$.

Properties 2, 3 and 4 in the above Lemma can be checked by examining consecutive levels of the ranked run-DAG; hence these are *local* properties. In contrast, checking properties 5, 6 and 7 requires examining an unbounded fragment of the ranked run-DAG; hence these are *global* properties.

3 Improved Upper Bound by Rank Based Disambiguation

The main contribution of this section is a ranking function based algorithm, called BüchiDisambiguate, that takes as input an NBA $\mathcal{A} = (\Sigma, Q, Q_0, \delta, F)$ with $|Q| = n$, and constructs a UBA $\mathcal{U} = (\Sigma, Z, Z_0, \delta_U, F_U)$ such that (i) $L(\mathcal{U}) = L(\mathcal{A})$, and (ii) $|Z| \in O(n \cdot (0.76n)^n)$. Without loss of generality, we assume that $Q = \{q_0, q_1, \ldots q_{n-1}\}$, $Q_0 = \{q_0\}$ and $q_0 \notin F$. For notational convenience, we use "$\mathcal{A}$-states" (resp., "$\mathcal{U}$-states") to refer to states of $\mathcal{A}$ (resp., states of $\mathcal{U}$) in the following discussion.

3.1 Overview

Drawing motivation from Schewe's work [12], we define a state of $\mathcal{U}$ to be a 4-tuple (f, O, X, i), where $i \in \langle 2n \rangle$, $f : Q \to \langle 2n \rangle \cup \{\bot\}$ is a FL_∞ ranking, and O and X are subsets of Q containing $\mathcal{A}$-states that are ranked i by f and satisfy certain properties. Since every state of $\mathcal{U}$ gives a full-level ranking of $\mathcal{A}$, a run of $\mathcal{U}$ gives an infinite sequence of full-level rankings of $\mathcal{A}$, which can be "stitched" together to potentially obtain a full-ranking of $G_\alpha^{\mathcal{A}}$. The purpose of algorithm BüchiDisambiguate is to define the transitions and final states of $\mathcal{U}$ in such a way that a run of $\mathcal{U}$ on $\alpha \in \Sigma^\omega$ is accepting iff the "stitched" full-ranking of $G_\alpha^{\mathcal{A}}$ obtained from the run is exactly $\mathsf{r}_{\mathcal{A},\alpha}^\star$, as defined in Section 2.1.

Informally, algorithm BüchiDisambiguate works as follows. Suppose $\mathcal{U}$ is in state (f, O, X, i) after reading a finite prefix $\alpha(0) \ldots \alpha(k-1)$ of α. On reading the next letter, i.e. $\alpha(k)$, we want $\mathcal{U}$ to non-deterministically guess the full-level ranking, say f', induced by $\mathsf{r}_{\mathcal{A},\alpha}^\star$ at level $k+1$ of $G_\alpha^{\mathcal{A}}$. Furthermore, every such choice of f' must be a full-cover of $(f, \alpha(k))$ and must satisfy the local properties in Lemma 1. Given f, f' and $\alpha(k)$, the local properties are easy to check, and are used in algorithm BüchiDisambiguate to filter the full-level rankings that can serve as f'. Once a choice of f' has been made, algorithm BüchiDisambiguate uses the O-, X- and i-components of the current state (f, O, X, i) to *uniquely* determine the corresponding components of the next state (f', O', X', i'). In doing so, we use a technique reminiscent of that used by Miyano and Hayashi [10], and subsequently by Schewe [12], to ensure that the global properties in Lemma 1 are satisfied by the sequence of full-level rankings corresponding to an accepting run of $\mathcal{U}$. Note that the choice of f' gives rise to non-determinism in the transition relation of $\mathcal{U}$. However, in every step of the run of $\mathcal{U}$ on α, there is a unique choice of f' that can give rise to $\mathsf{r}_{\mathcal{A},\alpha}^\star$ when the full-level rankings corresponding to the run are "stitched" together.

A closer inspection of Lemma 1 shows that there are two types of global properties: those that relate to *every* path (property 5), and those that relate to *some* path (e.g., properties 6 and 7). Schewe gave a ranking based construction to enforce properties of the first type in the context of Büchi complementation [12]. We use a similar idea here for enforcing property 5. Specifically, suppose $\mathcal{U}$ is in state (f, O, X, i) after reading $\alpha(0) \ldots \alpha(k-1)$, and suppose f' has been chosen as the full-level ranking of level $k+1$ of $G_\alpha^{\mathcal{A}}$. Suppose further that we wish to enforce property 5 for all vertices $(q, k+1)$ in $G_\alpha^{\mathcal{A}}$ where q is assigned an even rank j by f'. To do so, we set i' to j, populate O' with *all* $\mathcal{A}$-states assigned rank j by f', and use the O-components of subsequent $\mathcal{U}$-states along the run to keep track of the successors (in $\mathcal{A}$) of all $\mathcal{A}$-states in O'. During this process, if we encounter an $\mathcal{A}$-state q_k with rank $< j$ in the O-component of a $\mathcal{U}$-state, we know that property 5 is satisfied for all paths ending in q_k. The state q_k is therefore removed from O, and the above process repeated until O becomes empty. The emptiness of O signifies that all paths in $G_\alpha^{\mathcal{A}}$ starting from $\mathcal{A}$-states with rank j at level $k+1$ eventually visit a state with rank $< j$. Once this happens, we reset O to $\emptyset$, choose the next (in cyclic order) even rank i and repeat the above process. Using the same argument as used in [12], it can be shown that a run of $\mathcal{U}$ visits a $\mathcal{U}$-state with $O = \emptyset$ and i set to the smallest even rank infinitely often iff the sequence of full-level rankings corresponding to the run satisfies property 5.

A naive way to adapt the above technique to enforce property 6 (resp., property 7) in Lemma 1 is to choose an odd rank (resp., ∞ rank) $i > 1$, populate O' with *a single non-deterministically chosen* $\mathcal{A}$-state assigned rank i by f', and track *a non-deterministically chosen single successor* of this state in the O-components of $\mathcal{U}$-states along the run until we find an $\mathcal{A}$-state that is final and assigned rank $i-1$ (resp., ∞). The problem with this naive adaptation is that the non-deterministic choice of $\mathcal{A}$-state above may lead to multiple accepting runs of $\mathcal{U}$ on α. This is undesirable, since we want $\mathcal{U}$ to be a UBA. To circumvent this problem, we choose the O-component of the next state, i.e. O' in (f', O', X', i'), deterministically, given the current $\mathcal{U}$-state (f, O, X, i) and $\alpha(k)$. Specifically, for every $\mathcal{A}$-state q_r in O, we find the $\alpha(k)$-successors of q_r in $\mathcal{A}$ that are assigned rank i by f', and choose only one of them, viz. the one with the minimum index, to stay in O'. For notational convenience, for $S \subseteq Q = \{q_0, \ldots q_{n-1}\}$, let $\downarrow S$ denote the singleton set $\{q_i \mid q_i \in S \text{ and } \forall q_j \in S, i \leq j\}$. Then, we have $O' = \bigcup_{q_r \in O} \downarrow \{q_l \mid q_l \in \delta(q_r, \alpha(k)) \text{ and } f'(q_l) = i\}$.

Choosing O' as above has an undesired consequence: not all $\mathcal{A}$-states that are successors (in $\mathcal{A}$) of some state in O and have rank i may be tracked in the O-components of $\mathcal{U}$-states along the run. This may prevent the technique of Schewe [12] from detecting that property 6 (or property 7) is true in the sequence of full-rankings corresponding to a run of $\mathcal{U}$ on α. To rectify this situation, we use the X-component of $\mathcal{U}$-states as follows. We periodically load the X-component with a single $\mathcal{A}$-state from O, which is then removed from O. All successors (in $\mathcal{A}$) of the $\mathcal{A}$-state thus loaded in X are then tracked in the X-components of $\mathcal{U}$-states along the run, until we encounter a final $\mathcal{A}$-state with the desired rank ($i-1$ for property 6, and ∞ for property 7) in X. Once this happens, we empty X, load it with another $\mathcal{A}$-state (specifically, the one with the minimum index) from O, remove this chosen state from O, and repeat the process until both O and X are emptied. When both O and X become empty, we set i to the next rank i' of interest in cyclic order, load O with all $\mathcal{A}$-states assigned rank i', and repeat the entire process. Extending the reasoning used by Schewe in [12], it can be shown that a run of $\mathcal{U}$ visits a $\mathcal{U}$-state with $O = \emptyset, X = \emptyset$ and i set to the smallest rank of interest infinitely often iff the corresponding sequence of full-level rankings satisfies property 6 (or property 7, as the case may be).

3.2 Our Algorithm and Its Analysis

The pseudocode for algorithm BüchiDisambiguate is given below. Note that the checks for global properties are deferred until all full-level rankings have become tight. This is justified by property 1 in Lemma 1. The choice of initial state of $\mathcal{U}$ is motivated by the observation that q_0 is ranked ∞ in the full-level ranking induced by $r^*_{\mathcal{A},\alpha}$ at level 0 of $G^{\mathcal{A}}_\alpha$ iff $\alpha \in L(\mathcal{A})$. Finally, algorithm BüchiDisambiguate implements the following optimization when calculating the next $\mathcal{U}$-state (f', O', X', i') from a given $\mathcal{U}$-state (f, O, X, i) and $a \in \Sigma$: if i is odd or ∞ and if $\delta(X, a)$ intersects O', then X' is reset to $\emptyset$ instead of being populated with $\delta(X, a)$. This is justified because every $\mathcal{A}$-state in O' must eventually have one of its successors (in $\mathcal{A}$) with rank i moved to the X-component of a $\mathcal{U}$-state further down the run, for the run of $\mathcal{U}$ to be accepting.

Algorithm : BüchiDisambiguate
Input: NBA $\mathcal{A} = (\Sigma, Q, Q_0, \delta, F)$
Output: UBA $\mathcal{U} = (\Sigma, Z, Z_0, \delta_U, F_U)$

- States : $Z = \mathsf{FL}_\infty \times 2^Q \times 2^Q \times \langle 2n \rangle$. Furthermore, if $(f, O, X, i) \in Z$, then $O \subseteq Q$, $X \subseteq Q$, and $f \in \mathsf{FL}_\infty$ is such that $\forall q_j \in O \cup X$, $f(q_j) = i$.
- Initial State: $Z_0 = \{(f, O, X, i) \mid f(q_0) = \infty, \ O = X = \emptyset, \ i = 1 \text{ and } \forall q \in Q \, (q \neq q_0 \rightarrow f(q) = \bot)\}$.
- Transitions: For every $(f', O', X', i') \in \delta_U((f, O, X, i), a)$, where $a \in \Sigma$, the following conditions hold.
  1. Let $S = \{q_l \mid f(q_l) \neq \bot\}$. For all $q_j \notin \delta(S, a)$, $f'(q_j) = \bot$.
  2. f' is a full-cover of (f, a).
  3. For all $q_j \in Q$ such that $f(q_j) = \infty$, there is a $q_l \in \delta(q_j, a)$ such that $f'(q_l) = f(q_j)$.
  4. For all $q_j \in Q \setminus F$, there is a $q_l \in \delta(q_j, a)$ such that $f'(q_l) = f(q_j)$.
  5. For all $q_j \in F$ such that $f(q_j) \in [2n]^{even}$, there is a $q_l \in \delta(q_j, a)$ such that either $f'(q_l) = f(q_j)$ or $f'(q_l) = f(q_j) - 1$.
  6. For all $q_j \in Q$ such that $f(q_j) \neq \infty$, there is no $q_l \in \delta(q_j, a)$ such that $f'(q_l) = \infty$.
  7. In addition, O', X' and i' satisfy the following conditions.
     (a) If f is not a tight full-level ranking, then $O' = X' = \emptyset$, $i' = 1$.
     (b) If $O \cup X \neq \emptyset$, then $i' = i$. Furthermore, the following conditions hold. For notational convenience, let $O'' = \bigcup_{q_j \in O} \downarrow \{q_l \mid q_l \in \delta(q_j, a) \wedge f'(q_l) = i\}$ and let $X'' = \{q_l \mid q_l \in \delta(X, a) \wedge f'(q_l) = i\}$.
        i. If $i = 1$, then $O' = X' = \emptyset$.
        ii. If $i \in [2n]^{odd}$ and $i \neq 1$, then
           a. If $X = \emptyset$, then $X' = \downarrow O''$, $O' = O'' \setminus X'$.
           b. Else if $X'' \cap O'' \neq \emptyset$ or $(\exists q_l \in \delta(X, a) \cap F, \ f'(q_l) = (i - 1))$, then $X' = \emptyset$, $O' = O''$.
           c. Else, $X' = X''$, $O' = O''$.
        iii. If $i \in [2n]^{even}$, then $O' = \{q_l \mid q_l \in \delta(O, a) \wedge f'(q_l) = i\}$, $X' = \emptyset$.
        iv. If $i = \infty$, then
           a. If $X = \emptyset$, then $X' = \downarrow O''$, $O' = O'' \setminus X'$.
           b. Else if $X'' \cap O'' \neq \emptyset$ or $X'' \cap F \neq \emptyset$, then $X' = \emptyset$, $O' = O''$.

 c. Else, $X' = X''$, $O' = O''$.
 (c) If $O \cup X = \emptyset$, then $X' = \emptyset$. In addition, the following hold.
   i.   If $(i = 1)$ then $i' = max\_rank(f')$.
         Else if $(i = \infty)$ then $i' = max(\{j \mid \exists q \in Q, f'(q) = j\} \cap [2n])$.
         Else $i' = i - 1$.
   ii. $O' = \{q_l \mid f'(q_l) = i'\}$.
 $- F_U = \{(f, O, X, i) \mid O = X = \emptyset, i = 1, f$ is a tight full-level ranking$\}$.

End Algorithm : BüchiDisambiguate

3.3 Proof of Correctness

Let $\rho = (f_0, O_0, X_0, i_0), (f_1, O_1, X_1, i_1), \ldots$ be an accepting run of the NBA $\mathcal{U}$ constructed using algorithm BüchiDisambiguate. The run ρ *induces* a full-ranking r of $G_\alpha^{\mathcal{A}}$ as follows: for every $i \geq 0$, $r(q, i) = k$ iff $f_i(q) = k$ where $k \in \langle 2n \rangle$. Note that if $f_i(q) = \perp$, then q is not reachable in $\mathcal{A}$ from q_0 after reading $\alpha(0) \ldots \alpha(i - 1)$.

Lemma 2. *For every vertex (q, l) in $G_\alpha^{\mathcal{A}}$, $r((q, l)) = r_{\mathcal{A}, \alpha}^\star((q, l))$.*

Theorem 1. $L(\mathcal{U}) = L(\mathcal{A})$.

Theorem 2. *The automaton $\mathcal{U}$ is unambiguous.*

Proof. Suppose, if possible, there is a word $\alpha \in \Sigma^\omega$ that has two distinct accepting runs ρ_1, ρ_2 in $\mathcal{U}$. By Lemma 2, $r_1((q', l')) = r^\star((q', l')) = r_2((q', l'))$ for every vertex (q', l') in $G_\alpha^{\mathcal{A}}$. Let $(f_{1,l}, O_{1,l}, X_{1,l}, i_{1,l})$ and $(f_{2,l} O_{2,l}, X_{2,l}, i_{2,l})$ be the lth states reached along ρ_1 and ρ_2 respectively. We show below by induction on l that $(f_{1,l}, O_{1,l}, X_{1,l}, i_{1,l}) = (f_{2,l}, O_{2,l}, X_{2,l}, i_{2,l})$ for all $l \geq 0$.

Base Case : By our construction, $O_{1,0} = O_{2,0} = X_{1,0} = X_{2,0} = \emptyset$, $i_{1,0} = i_{2,0} = 1$. Since $r_1((q_0, 0)) = r_2((q_0, 0))$ as well, it follows that $f_{1,0} = f_{2,0}$, and hence $(f_{1,0}, O_{1,0}, X_{1,0}, i_{1,0}) = (f_{2,0}, O_{2,0}, X_{2,0}, i_{2,0})$.

Hypothesis : Assume the claim is true for $l \geq 0$. Hence, $(f_{1,l}, O_{1,l}, X_{1,l}, i_{1,l}) = (f_{2,l}, O_{2,l}, X_{2,l}, i_{2,l})$.

Induction Step : Let $q \in Q$ be such that $(q, l + 1)$ is a vertex in $G_\alpha^{\mathcal{A}}$. Since $r_1((q', l')) = r_2((q', l')) = r_{\mathcal{A}, \alpha}^\star((q', l'))$ for every vertex (q', l') in G_α, it follows that $r_1((q, l+1)) = r^\star((q, l+1)) = r_2((q, l+1))$. This implies $f_{1,l+1}(q) = r^\star((q, l+1)) = f_{2,l+1}(q)$. For every $q' \in Q$ such that $(q', l+1)$ is not in $G_\alpha^{\mathcal{A}}$, by definition of level rankings, $f_{1,l+1}(q') = f_{2,l+1}(q') = \perp$. Hence, $f_{1,l+1}(s) = f_{2,l+1}(s)$ for all $s \in Q$. We thus have the following relations: (i) $f_{1,l+1} = f_{2,l+1}$, and (ii) $(f_{1,l}, O_{1,l}, X_{1,l}, i_{1,l}) = (f_{2,l}, O_{2,l}, X_{2,l}, i_{2,l})$. Since step (7) of algorithm BüchiDisambiguate uniquely determines the values of $O_{k,l+1}, X_{k,l+1}$, $i_{k,l+1}$ from the values of $f_{k,l}, f_{k,l+1}, O_{k,l}, X_{k,l}, i_{k,l}$, for $k \in 1, 2$, it follows that $(f_{1,l+1}, O_{1,l+1}, X_{1,l+1}, i_{1,l+1}) = (f_{2,l+1}, O_{2,l+1}, X_{2,l+1}, i_{2,l+1})$. This completes the inductive step, and we have $(f_{1,l}, O_{1,l}, X_{1,l}, i_{1,l}) = (f_{2,l}, O_{2,l}, X_{2,l}, i_{2,l})$ for all $l \geq 0$. However, this contradicts the assumption that ρ_1 and ρ_2 are distinct runs. Hence, ρ_1 and ρ_2 must be the same run of $\mathcal{U}$.

We have thus shown that for every $\alpha \in \Sigma^\omega$, there is at most one accepting run of $\mathcal{U}$. It follows that $\mathcal{U}$ is unambiguous.   □

Theorem 3. *The number of states of* $\mathcal{U}$ *is in* $O(n \cdot (0.76n)^n)$.

Proof. Every state of $\mathcal{U}$ is a (f, O, X, i) tuple, where f is a full-level ranking. We encode (f, O, X, i) tuples as 3-tuples (p, g, i), where $p \in \{0, 1, 2\}$ and g is a modified ranking function similar to that used in [12,7].

While some states (f, O, X, i) in our construction correspond to tight full-level rankings, others do not. We first use an extension of the idea in [12] to encode (f, O, X, i) with tight full-level ranking f as a tuple (p, g, i), where $g : Q \to \{1, \ldots, r\} \cup \{-1, -2, -3, \infty\}$ and $r = max\_odd(f)$. This is done as follows. For all $q \in Q$ but $q \notin O \cup X$, we let $g(q) = f(q)$. If $q \in O \cup X$ and $f(q) \notin [r]^{odd}$, then we let $g(q) = -1$ and $i = f(q)$. This part of the encoding is similar to that used in [12]. We extend this encoding to consider cases where $q \in O \cup X$ and $f(q) = k \in [r]^{odd}$.

There are three sub-cases to consider: (i) $O \cup X \neq \{q \mid q \in Q \land f(q) = k\}$, (ii) $O \cup X = \{q \mid q \in Q \land f(q) = k\}$ and $O \neq \emptyset$, and (iii) $X = \{q \mid q \in Q \land f(q) = k\}$. In the first case, we let $p = 0$, $i = k$, $g(q) = -2$ for all $q \in O$ and $g(q) = -3$ for all $q \in X$. Since there exists a state $q' \in Q \setminus (O \cup X)$ with rank k, the range of g contains $k \in [r]^{odd}$ in this case. In the second case, we let $p = 1$, $i = k$, $g(q) = k$ for all $q \in O$ and $g(q) = -3$ for all $q \in X$. Finally, in the third case, we let $p = 2$, $i = k$ and $g(q) = k$ for all $q \in X$. Thus, the range of g contains $k \in [r]^{odd}$ in both the second and third cases as well. Note that the component p in (p, g, i) is used only when $i \in [r]^{odd}$. It is now easy to see that g is always onto one of the sets $A_j \cup \{1, 3, \ldots, r\}$, where A_j is a subset of $\{\infty, -1, -2, -3\}$. The total number of functions of each of the above types is $O(tight(n))$. Since $p \in \{0, 1, 2\}$ following Schewe's analysis [12], the total number of (p, g, i) tuples is upper bounded by $O(n \cdot tight(n)) = O(tight(n + 1))$.

Now, let us consider states with non-tight full-level rankings. Our construction ensures that once an odd rank i appears in a full-level ranking g along a run ρ, all subsequent full-level rankings along ρ contain every rank in $\{i, i + 2, \ldots max\_odd(g)\}$. The O, X and i components in states with non-tight full-level ranking are inconsequential; hence we ignore these. Suppose a state with non-tight full-level ranking f contains the odd ranks $\{j, \ldots, i - 2, i\}$, where $1 < j \leq i$, $i = max\_odd(f)$. To encode this state, we first replace f with a level ranking g as follows. For all $k \in \{j, \ldots, i, i + 1\}$ and $q \in Q$, if $f(q) = k$, then $g(q) = k - j + c$, where $c = 0$ if j is even and 1 otherwise. If $f(q) = \infty$, we let $g(q)$ be ∞. Effectively, this transforms f to a tight full-level ranking g by shifting all ranks down by $j - c$. The original state can now be represented as the tuple $(p, g, -(j - c))$. Note that the third component of a state represented as (p, g, i) is always non-negative for states with tight full-level ranking, and always negative for states with non-tight full-level ranking. Hence, there is no ambiguity in decoding the state representation. Clearly, the total no. of states with non-tight full-level rankings is $O(n \cdot tight(n)) = O(tight(n + 1))$. Thus, the total count of all (f, O, X, i) states is in $O(tight(n + 1)) = O(n \cdot tight(n))$, where $tight(n) \approx (0.76n)^n$.   □

4   An Exponentially Improved Lower Bound for NBA-SUBA Translation

In this section, we prove a lower bound for the state complexity trade-off in translating an NBA to a strongly unambiguous Büchi automaton (SUBA). Our proof technique relies on the full automaton technique of Yan [14].

Definition 1 (Full automaton). *A full automaton $\mathcal{A}$ is described by the structure $\mathcal{A} = (\Sigma, Q, I, \delta, F)$ where Q is the set of states, $I \subseteq Q$ is the set of initial states, $\Sigma = 2^{(Q \times Q)}$ is the alphabet and δ is defined as follows: for all $q, q' \in Q, a \in \Sigma, \langle q, a, q' \rangle \in \Delta \Leftrightarrow \langle q, q' \rangle \in a$.*

Thus, a full automaton has a rich alphabet of size $2^{|Q|^2}$, and every automaton with $|Q|$ states has an embedding in a full automaton with the same number of states. An ω-word α over the alphabet Σ of a full automaton corresponds directly to the run-DAG $G_\alpha^{\mathcal{A}}$ of $\mathcal{A}$. Correspondingly, a letter $a \in \Sigma$ represents the section of the run-DAG between two successive levels, and a finite word $w \in \Sigma^*$ represents a finite section of the run-DAG.

For purposes of this section, we focus on a special family of full automata $\mathcal{F} = \{\mathcal{A}_n \mid n \geq 2\}$. Automaton $\mathcal{A}_n$ in this family is given by $\mathcal{A}_n = (\Sigma_n, Q_n, I_n, \delta_n, F_n)$, where $Q_n = \{q_0, \ldots, q_{n-1}, q_n\}$ is a set of $n + 1$ states, $I_n = \{q_0, \ldots q_{n-2}\}$ is the set of initial states, and $F_n = \{q_n\}$ is the singleton set of final states. We define a Q-ranking for $\mathcal{A}_n$ to be a full-level ranking $r : Q_n \to \langle n - 1 \rangle \cup \{\bot\}$ such that (i) r is a tight full-level ranking, (ii) $r(q_n) = \bot$, (iii) $r(q_{n-1}) = \infty$, and (iv) for every $k \in [n - 1]$, $|r^{-1}(k)| = 1$. The total number of Q-rankings of $\mathcal{A}_n$ is easily seen to be $(n - 1)!$.

Let r_1 and r_2 be Q-rankings for $\mathcal{A}_n$. The word $w \in \Sigma_n^*$ is said to be Q-compatible with (r_1, r_2) if the following conditions are satisfied when w is viewed as a finite section of the run-DAG of $\mathcal{A}_n$, and r_1 (resp., r_2) is interpreted as the full-level ranking of states at the first (resp., last) level of w.

- There is no path from the first level to the last level of w that either starts or ends in q_n.
- There is a path from q_i in the first level of w to q_j in the last level of w iff either $r_1(q_i) > r_2(q_j)$, or $r_1(q_i) = r_2(q_j) \in [n - 1]^{odd} \cup \{\infty\}$. Such a path is said to be *final* if it visits q_n; otherwise, it is *non-final*.

Lemma 3. *For every pair (r_1, r_2) of Q-rankings for $\mathcal{A}_n$, there is a word $w \in \Sigma_n^*$ that is Q-compatible with (r_1, r_2).*

Proof sketch: We show how to construct w as the concatenation of three words $w_1, w_2, w_3 \in \Sigma_n^*$. The proof that $w_1.w_2.w_3$ is Q-compatible with (r_1, r_2) follows from their construction, and uses an argument similar to that used in a related proof in [14] (specifically, proof of Lemma 2 in [14]).

The word w_1 is given by $b_1 b_2 b_3 \ldots b_{2n}$, where each $b_i \in \Sigma_n = 2^{(Q_n \times Q_n)}$ is defined as follows. For notational convenience, we use $Id_{non-final}$ below as a shorthand for $\{(q_j, q_j) \mid 0 \leq j < n\}$, i.e. identity transitions for non-final states.

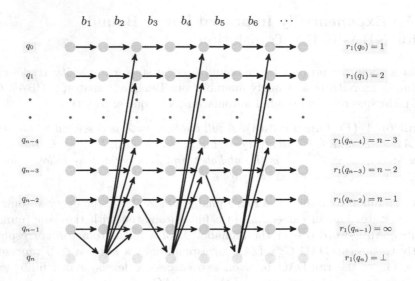

Fig. 1. Construction for w_1

- $b_1 = Id_{non-final} \cup \{(q_{n-1}, q_n)\}$
- $b_2 = Id_{non-final} \cup \{(q_n, q_j) \mid 0 \le j < n\}$
- For $1 \le i \le n-1$, $b_{2i+1} = Id_{non-final} \cup \{(q_j, q_n) \mid r_1(q_j) = n-i\}$ and
  $b_{2i+2} = Id_{non-final} \cup \{(q_n, q_j) \mid r_1(q_j) < n-i\}$

Figure 1 shows the construction for an example word w_1. The word w_2 consists of the single letter of Σ_n given by $\{(q_i, q_j) \mid r_1(q_i) = r_2(q_j) \in [n-1]^{odd} \cup \{\infty\}\}$. The word w_3 is constructed in the same manner as w_1, but with r_2 used in place of r_1.

Lemma 4. *Let r_1, r_2 and r_3 be Q-rankings for A_n. If $w_1 \in \Sigma_n^*$ is Q-compatible with (r_1, r_2) and $w_2 \in \Sigma_n^*$ is Q-compatible with (r_2, r_3), then $w_1 w_2$ is Q-compatible with (r_1, r_3).*

The proof follows from Lemma 3 and mimics the proof of a related result in [14] (specifically, Lemma 3 in [14]).

We now show a factorial lower bound of the NBA to SUBA state complexity trade-off. We make use of the following special class of UBA for this purpose. For notational convenience, we use $L(A^{\{q\}})$ to denote the set of ω-words accepted by an NBA $A = (\Sigma, Q, Q_0, \delta, F)$ starting from state $q \in Q$.

Definition 2 (EUBA). *A UBA $A = (\Sigma, Q, Q_0, \delta, F)$ is called a state-exclusive UBA (EUBA) if for every state $q \in Q$ either $L(A^{\{q\}}) \subseteq L(A)$ or $L(A^{\{q\}}) \subseteq \Sigma^\omega \setminus L(A)$. In other words, all words accepted starting from q are either in the language of A or in its complement.*

Theorem 4. *Every EUBA that is language equivalent to the full automaton A_n has at least $(n-1)!$ states.*

Proof. Let E_n be a EUBA such that $L(E_n) = L(\mathcal{A}_n)$. Let $r_1, r_2, \ldots, r_{n-1!}$ be the Q-rankings for $\mathcal{A}_n$. Repeating this sequence of full-level rankings infinitely many times, we get an infinite sequence of full-level rankings. Let w_i be the word (as constructed in the proof of Lemma 3) that is Q-compatible with (r_i, r_{i+1}), for $i \in [(n-1)! - 1]$. Let w be the infinite word $(w_1 w_2 \ldots w_{(n-1)!-1})^\omega$.

From the construction outlined in the proof of Lemma 3, there is a final path between q_{n-1} (ranked ∞) at the first level of states in w_i to the same state (ranked ∞) at the last level of states in w_i, for every $i \in [(n-1)! - 1]$. The concatenation of these paths gives a path π' that starts from q_{n-1} and visits the final state q_n infinitely often. Note that we cannot have a path in w that starts from any state other than q_{n-1} and visits q_n infinitely often. This is because a visit to q_n from any other state q_j ($\neq q_{n-1}$) with rank k must necessarily be followed by a visit to a state with rank $< k$. Hence, infinitely many visits to q_n will result in infinitely many rank reductions. This is an impossibility since ranks cannot increase along a path. Hence, paths in w starting from every state other than q_{n-1} can visit final states only finitely often.

Since q_{n-1} is not an initial state of $\mathcal{A}_n$, the path π' considered above is not an accepting run of $\mathcal{A}_n$. Hence, $w \notin L(\mathcal{A}_n)$. Let a be the letter in Σ_n that represents only the edge (q_0, q_{n-1}). Hence, the path $q_0 \pi'$ is an accepting run of $\mathcal{A}_n$, and $aw \in L(\mathcal{A}_n)$.

Since $L(E_n) = L(\mathcal{A}_n)$, there must be an accepting run ρ of E_n on aw. Let k be the smallest index such that $\rho(k) \in inf(\rho)$ for all $i \geq k$. Let $T = (n-1)! - 1$, and suppose $|w_i| = s_i$ for all $i \in [T]$, and $s = \sum_{i=1}^{[T]} s_i$. For notational convenience, let us also assume that $s_0 = 0$. Let t be the smallest index such that $t \geq k$ and $t = p.s$ for some integer $p > 0$. Consider the sequence of indices $t + n_0.T + s_0, \ldots t + n_T.T + s_T$, where each $n_i \geq 0$ is such that ρ visits a final state of E_n between consecutive indices in the sequence. If E_n has fewer than $(n-1)!$ states, there must be a state of E_n that repeats in $\rho(t + n_0.T + s_0), \ldots \rho(t + n_T.T + s_T)$. Let $i, j \in \{0, \ldots T\}$ be such that $i < j$ and $\rho(t + n_i.T + s_i) = \rho(t + n_j.T + s_j) = z$, say. Clearly, the run ρ visits a final state of E_n between indices $t + n_i.T + s_i$ and $t + n_j.T + s_j$. Let the segment of the word aw between these two occurrences of z be v. Then, there is a path in E_n from z to itself along v that visits a final state. It follows that $v^\omega \in L(E_n^{\{z\}})$.

We now show that v^ω is also in $L(E_n)$. Consider the two Q-rankings r_i and r_j mentioned above. Clearly, the word v is Q-compatible with (r_i, r_j). Since $r_i \neq r_j$ and both are Q-rankings for $\mathcal{A}_n$, there is a state q_k for $k \in [n-2]$, such that $r_i(q_k) > r_j(q_k)$. By the construction outlined in the proof of Lemma 3, there is a final run along v from state q_k to itself. Since q_k is an initial state of $\mathcal{A}_n$, there exists an accepting run of $\mathcal{A}_n$ on v^ω. Therefore, $v^\omega \in L(\mathcal{A}_n)$; since $L(E_n) = L(\mathcal{A}_n)$, $v^\omega \in L(E_n)$ as well.

Since ρ is an accepting run of E_n, it visits at least one final state of E_n infinitely often. Therefore, there exists a strict suffix w' of w starting from the $(t + n_i.T + s_i)^{th}$ index such that the corresponding run of E_n starting at z sees at least one final state infinitely often. Hence, $w' \in L(E_n^{\{z\}})$. However, the final run of $\mathcal{A}_n$ on w' starts at q_{n-1} since this is the only state ranked ∞ in w. Since q_{n-1} is not an initial state of $\mathcal{A}_n$, $w' \notin L(\mathcal{A}_n)$ and hence $w' \notin L(E_n)$.

Thus, $v^\omega \in L(E_n^{\{z\}})$ and $v^\omega \in L(E_n)$, while $w' \in L(E_n^{\{z\}})$ and $w' \notin L(E_n)$. This contradicts the state-exclusivity property of EUBA. Hence, the number of states of E_n is at least $(n-1)!$. □

Theorem 5. *Every SUBA that is language equivalent to $\mathcal{A}_n$ has at least $(n-1)!$ states.*

Proof. The proof follows from the observation that every SUBA is also a EUBA by definition. □

5   A New Lower Bound Proof for Disambiguation

We now show an exponential lower bound for the NBA-UBA state complexity trade-off. This lower bound was already known from a result due to Schmidt [13]. However, the technique used by Schmidt involves computing ranks of specially constructed matrices. In contrast, our proof uses the full automata technique.

Definition 3 (Trim UBA). *Let $\mathcal{A} = (\Sigma, Q, Q_0, \delta, F)$ be a UBA. $\mathcal{A}$ is trim if $L(\mathcal{A}^{\{q\}}) \neq \emptyset$ for every $q \in Q$.*

Every UBA can be transformed to a language equivalent trim UBA simply by removing states from which no word can be accepted. Let $\mathcal{A}$ be a full automaton with alphabet Σ having 1 initial state, 1 final state, and n other (non-initial and non-final) states. For each non-empty subset S of non-initial and non-final states (there are $2^n - 1$ such subsets), let a_S denote the letter (in Σ) on which we have edges in $\mathcal{A}$ from the initial state to only the states in S. Similarly, let b_S denote the letter on which we have edges in $\mathcal{A}$ from only the states in S to the final state, and also from the final state to itself. It is easy to see that $a_{S_1} b_{S_2}^\omega$ is accepted by $\mathcal{A}$ if and only if $S_1 \cap S_2 \neq \emptyset$. Let D be an unambiguous and trim Büchi automaton accepting the same language as $\mathcal{A}$.

Theorem 6. *The number of states of D is at least $2^n - 1$.*

Proof. For every state q of D, let $\hat{L}(D^{\{q\}})$ denote the set of words of the form b_S^ω accepted by D, starting from q. If s_1 and s_2 are initial states of D, by definition of unambiguous automata, $\hat{L}(D^{\{s_1\}}) \cap \hat{L}(D^{\{s_2\}}) = \emptyset$. Also if any state s in D has paths to two distinct states r_1 and r_2 that are labeled by the same word $l \in \Sigma^*$, then by definition of unambiguous and trim automata, $\hat{L}(D^{\{r_1\}})$ and $\hat{L}(D^{\{r_2\}})$ must be disjoint.

For a set T of states of D, define $\hat{L}(D^T) = \bigcup_{s \in T} \hat{L}(D^{\{s\}})$. If we also have $\hat{L}(D^{\{s_1\}})$ and $\hat{L}(D^{\{s_2\}})$ disjoint for all distinct $s_1, s_2 \in T$, then $\hat{L}(D^T)$ equals the symmetric difference (or xor) of the sets $\hat{L}(D^{\{r\}})$, where r ranges over T. Now for each non-empty set K of the non-initial and non-final states of $\mathcal{A}$, consider the set K_D of states in D that have an edge from an initial state of D on the letter a_K. Then $\hat{L}(D^{K_D})$ is the set of all words of the form b_S^ω, where S is a subset of non-initial and non-final states of $\mathcal{A}$ such that $S \cap K \neq \emptyset$. Let this set of words be called $\Lambda(K)$. Since D is unambiguous, $\Lambda(K)$ can be obtained as the xor of languages $\hat{L}(D^{\{t\}})$, where t ranges over K_D. We will now show that for each non-empty subset S of non-initial and non-final states of $\mathcal{A}$, the set containing only the word b_S^ω can be obtained by xoring appropriate languages $\hat{L}(D^{\{t\}})$. Since there are $2^n - 1$ possible non-empty subsets S, this shows that by xoring appropriate languages $\hat{L}(D^{\{t\}})$, we can get up to $2^{2^n - 1}$ different sets. This, in turn, implies that the number of distinct values taken by t, i.e. number of states in D, is at least $2^n - 1$.

We will prove the above claim by downward induction on the number of states in S. Suppose S is the set of all n non-initial and non-final states of $\mathcal{A}$. Then the set containing only b_S^ω can be obtained by xoring $\Lambda(K)$, where K ranges over all non-empty subsets of non-initial and non-final states of $\mathcal{A}$. This is because b_S^ω occurs in all $2^n - 1$ (i.e, an odd number) languages $\Lambda(K)$, where K ranges over all non-empty subsets of non-initial and non-final states of $\mathcal{A}$. However, for any other non-empty subset S' of non-initial and non-final states of $\mathcal{A}$, $b_{S'}^\omega$ occurs only in those $\Lambda(K)$s where $K \cap S' \neq \emptyset$. The latter is precisely the set of all subsets K excluding those that are disjoint from S', and the number of such subsets is even for $|S'| < n$.

Now suppose we can obtain singleton sets $\{b_S^\omega\}$ for all S with $|S| > t$. Then we can xor every $\Lambda(K)$ suitably with singleton sets containing b_S^ω for $|S| > t$, such that the resulting modified languages $\Lambda'(K)$ do not contain any b_S^ω for $|S| > t$. Now consider any set S of size t. Then take xor of the modified languages $\Lambda'(K)$ obtained above for all non-empty subsets K of S. By definition, b_S^ω occurs in all of these $\Lambda'(K)$, which are odd in count $(2^t - 1)$. For any other set S' of cardinality $\leq t$, its intersection with S is a strict subset of S. The word $b_{S'}^\omega$ doesn't occur in those $\Lambda'(K)$s where K is a non-empty subset of $S \setminus S'$; this, however, is odd in count as $S \setminus S'$ is nonempty. So the sets containing $b_{S'}^\omega$ are even in number.

This proves that all singleton sets containing only b_S^ω can be obtained for all nonempty subset S of non-initial and non-final states of $\mathcal{A}$. As argued above, this implies that D must have at least $2^n - 1$ states. $\qquad\square$

Note that the above proof makes no use of the acceptance condition (i.e. Büchi, Müller, Streett, Rabin, parity, etc.) of the automaton, nor requires the words to be infinite. Hence it works for all acceptance conditions and even for finite words.

6 Conclusion

We now summarize our results on the state complexity trade-off in transforming an NBA to UBA and SUBA. Let $\mathsf{Size}_{NBA:\mathcal{C}}(n)$ denote the worst-case state complexity of an automaton in class $\mathcal{C}$ that accepts the same language as an NBA with n states. Table 1 shows the bounds of obtained from this paper, and compares them with previous best bounds. We propose to work towards closing the complexity gaps further in future.

Table 1. Comparison of state complexity trade-offs

Target class ($\mathcal{C}$)	$\text{Size}_{NBA:\mathcal{C}}(n)$ from this paper		$\text{Size}_{NBA:\mathcal{C}}(n)$ from earlier work	
	Lower bound	Upper bound	Lower bound	Upper bound
UBA	$2^n - 1$ (Thm 6)	$O(n \cdot (0.76n)^n)$ (Thm 3)	$2^n - 1$ [13]	$4 \cdot (3n)^n$ [6]
SUBA	$\Omega((n-1)!)$ (Thm 5)	-	$2^n - 1$ [13]	$O((12n)^n)$ [3]

References

1. Arnold, A.: Rational ω-languages are non-ambiguous. Theor. Comput. Sci. 26, 221–223 (1983)
2. Bousquet, N., Löding, C.: Equivalence and inclusion problem for strongly unambiguous Büchi automata. In: Dediu, A.-H., Fernau, H., Martín-Vide, C. (eds.) LATA 2010. LNCS, vol. 6031, pp. 118–129. Springer, Heidelberg (2010)
3. Carton, O., Michel, M.: Unambiguous Büchi automata. Theor. Comput. Sci. 297, 37–81 (2003)
4. Colcombet, T., Zdanowski, K.: A tight lower bound for determinization of transition labeled Büchi automata. In: Albers, S., Marchetti-Spaccamela, A., Matias, Y., Nikoletseas, S., Thomas, W. (eds.) ICALP 2009, Part II. LNCS, vol. 5556, pp. 151–162. Springer, Heidelberg (2009)
5. Isaak, D., Löding, C.: Efficient inclusion testing for simple classes of unambiguous automata. Inf. Process. Lett. 112(14-15), 578–582 (2012)
6. Kähler, D., Wilke, T.: Complementation, disambiguation, and determinization of Büchi automata unified. In: Aceto, L., Damgård, I., Goldberg, L.A., Halldórsson, M.M., Ingólfsdóttir, A., Walukiewicz, I. (eds.) ICALP 2008, Part I. LNCS, vol. 5125, pp. 724–735. Springer, Heidelberg (2008)
7. Karmarkar, H., Chakraborty, S.: On minimal odd rankings for Büchi complementation. In: Liu, Z., Ravn, A.P. (eds.) ATVA 2009. LNCS, vol. 5799, pp. 228–243. Springer, Heidelberg (2009)
8. Karmarkar, H., Joglekar, M., Chakraborty, S.: Improved upper and lower bounds for Büchi disambiguation. Technical Report TR-13-36, Centre for Formal Design and Verification of Software, IIT Bombay (April 2013), http://www.cfdvs.iitb.ac.in/reports/index.php
9. Kupferman, O., Vardi, M.Y.: Weak alternating automata are not that weak. ACM Transactions on Computational Logic 2(3), 408–429 (2001)
10. Miyano, S., Hayashi, T.: Alternating finite automata on ω-words. Theor. Comput. Sci. 32, 321–330 (1984)
11. Preugschat, S., Wilke, T.: Effective characterizations of simple fragments of temporal logic using prophetic automata. In: Birkedal, L. (ed.) FOSSACS 2012. LNCS, vol. 7213, pp. 135–149. Springer, Heidelberg (2012)
12. Schewe, S.: Büchi complementation made tight. In: Proc. STACS, pp. 661–672 (2009)
13. Schmidt, E.M.: Succinctness of Description of Context-Free, Regular and Unambiguous Language. PhD thesis, Cornell University (1978)
14. Yan, Q.: Lower bounds for complementation of ω-automata via the full automata technique. In: Bugliesi, M., Preneel, B., Sassone, V., Wegener, I. (eds.) ICALP 2006. LNCS, vol. 4052, pp. 589–600. Springer, Heidelberg (2006)

Time-Bounded Reachability for Monotonic Hybrid Automata: Complexity and Fixed Points*

Thomas Brihaye[1], Laurent Doyen[2], Gilles Geeraerts[3], Joel Ouaknine[4],
Jean-Francois Raskin[3], and James Worrell[4]

[1] UMons, Belgium
[2] LSV Cachan, France
[3] ULB, Belgium
[4] Oxford University, UK

Abstract. We study the *time-bounded reachability problem* for *monotonic hybrid automata* (MHA), i.e., rectangular hybrid automata for which the rate of each variable is either always non-negative or always non-positive. In this paper, we revisit the decidability results presented in [5] and show that the problem is NEXPTIME-complete. We also show that we can effectively compute fixed points that characterise the sets of states that are reachable (resp. co-reachable) within T time units from a given state.

1 Introduction

Hybrid systems form a general class of systems that mix *continuous* and *discrete* behaviors. Examples of hybrid systems abound in our everyday life, particularly in applications where an (inherently discrete) computer system interacts with a continuous environment. The need for modeling and analysing hybrid systems is thus obvious.

Hybrid automata are arguably among the most prominent families of models for hybrid systems [7]. Hybrid automata are finite automata (to model the discrete part of the system) augmented with a finite set of real-valued variables (to model the continuous part of the system). The variables evolve with time elapsing, at a rate which is given by a flow that depends on the current location of the automaton. The theory of hybrid automata has been well developed for about two decades, and tools to analyse them are readily available, for instance HYTECH [8,9].

Hybrid automata are thus a class of powerful models, yet their high expressiveness comes at a price, in the sense that the undecidability barrier is rapidly hit. Simple *reachability properties* are undecidable even for the restricted subclass of *stopwatch automata*, where the rate of growth of each variable stays constant in all locations and is restricted to either 0 or 1 (see [10] for a survey).

On the other hand, a recent and successful line of research in the setting of *timed automata* has outlined the benefits of investigating *timed-bounded variants* of classical properties [12,14]. For instance, while *language inclusion* is, in general undecidable for timed automata, it is decidable when considering only executions of *bounded duration*

---

* This work has been partly supported by a grant from the National Bank of Belgium, the ARC project (number AUWB-2010-10/15-UMONS-3), the FRFC project (number 2.4545.11) and a 'Crédit aux chercheurs' of the FRS – F.N.R.S.

D. Van Hung and M. Ogawa (Eds.): ATVA 2013, LNCS 8172, pp. 55–70, 2013.

[14]. Following this line of research, we have recently investigated the decidability of *time-bounded reachability* for rectangular hybrid automata, i.e., whether a given state is reachable by an execution of duration at most **T**, for a given **T** [5]. We have shown that *time-bounded* reachability is *decidable* for *rectangular hybrid automata with non-negative rates* (RHA$^{\geq 0}$), while it is well-known that (plain, time unbounded) reachability is undecidable for this class [10]. We have also shown that the decidability frontier is quite sharp: time-bounded reachability becomes *undecidable* once we allow either diagonal constraints in the guards or a single variable to have both positive and negative rates. The decidability result relies on a so-called *contraction operator* that allows to construct, from any run of duration at most **T** of an RHA$^{\geq 0}$ $\mathcal{H}$, an *equivalent* run that reaches the same state, but whose length (in terms of number of discrete transitions) is *uniformly bounded* by a function F of the size of the automaton $\mathcal{H}$ and the bound **T**. Hence, deciding reachability within **T** time units reduces to exploring runs of bounded lengths only, which is algorithmically feasible [5]. Yet, this yields only a *non-deterministic algorithm with doubly exponential time complexity* for a strict subclass of RHA$^{\geq 0}$, and no lower bound is given.

In the present work, we revisit and extend the results from [5], both from the theoretical and the practical points of view. *First*, we consider the class of *monotonic hybrid automata* (MHA for short) which are rectangular hybrid automata where the rate of each variable is either always non-negative or always non-positive (thus, MHA generalise RHA$^{\geq 0}$). *Second*, we provide a *new contraction operator* that allows to derive a *singly exponential upper bound* on the lengths of the runs that need to be considered, thereby providing an NEXPTIME algorithm for the whole class of MHA. *Third*, we show that this new algorithm is optimal, by establishing a matching lower bound. Hence, *time-bounded reachability for RHA$^{\geq 0}$ is* NEXPTIME-*complete*. *Fourth*, we extend those results towards practical applications, by showing that we can *effectively compute* the set of states that are reachable (resp. co-reachable) within **T** time units, from a given state. Finally, we apply those ideas to two examples of RHA$^{\geq 0}$ for which the classical (time-unbounded) forward and backward fixpoints do not terminate. We manage to compute, using HYTECH, the set of states reachable within **T** time units for values of **T** that are sufficient to prove non-trivial properties of those examples

Note that the missing proofs can be found in the companion technical report [6].

2   Definitions

Let $\mathcal{I}$ be the set of intervals of real numbers with endpoints in $\mathbb{Z} \cup \{-\infty, +\infty\}$. Let X be a set of continuous variables, and let $\dot{X} = \{\dot{x} \mid x \in X\}$ be the set of dotted variables, corresponding to the variables' time derivatives. A *rectangular constraint* over X is an expression of the form $x \in I$ where x belongs to X and I to $\mathcal{I}$. A *diagonal constraint* over X is a constraint of the form $x - y \sim c$ where x, y belong to X, c to $\mathbb{Z}$, and $\sim$ is in $\{<, \leq, =, \geq, >\}$. Finite conjunctions of diagonal and rectangular constraints over X are called *guards*, and over $\dot{X}$ are called *rate constraints*. A guard or rate constraint is *rectangular* if all its constraints are rectangular. We denote by $\mathcal{G}(X)$ and $\mathcal{R}(X)$ respectively the sets of guards and rate constraints over X.

Linear, Rectangular and Singular Hybrid Automata. A *linear hybrid automaton* (LHA) is a tuple $\mathcal{H} = (X, \text{Loc}, \text{Edges}, \text{Rates}, \text{Inv}, \text{Init})$ where $X = \{x_1, \ldots, x_{|X|}\}$ is a finite set of continuous *variables* ; Loc is a finite set of *locations*; Edges $\subseteq$ Loc $\times \mathcal{G}(X) \times 2^X \times$ Loc is a finite set of *edges*; Rates : Loc $\mapsto \mathcal{R}(X)$ assigns to each location a constraint on the *possible variable rates*; Inv : Loc $\mapsto \mathcal{G}(X)$ assigns an *invariant* to each location; and Init $\subseteq$ Loc is a *set of initial locations*. For an edge $e = (\ell, g, Y, \ell')$, we denote by src (e) and trg (e) the locations ℓ and ℓ' respectively, g is called the *guard* of e and Y is the *reset* set of e. In the sequel, we denote by rmax and cmax the maximal constants occurring respectively in the constraints of $\{\text{Rates}(\ell) \mid \ell \in \text{Loc}\}$ and of $\{\text{Rates}(\ell) \mid \ell \in \text{Loc}\} \cup \{g \mid \exists(\ell, g, Y, \ell') \in \text{Edges}\}$.

An LHA has *non-negative rates* if for all variables x, for all locations ℓ, the constraint $\text{Rates}(\ell)$ implies that $\dot{x}$ must be non-negative. A *rectangular hybrid automaton* (RHA) is a linear hybrid automaton in which all guards, rates, and invariants are rectangular. In the case of RHA, we view rate constraints as functions Rates : Loc $\times X \to \mathcal{I}$ that associate with each location ℓ and each variable x an interval of possible rates $\text{Rates}(\ell)(x)$. A *monotonic hybrid automaton* (MHA) is an RHA such that, for all variable x: either $\text{Rates}(\ell, x) \subseteq [0, +\infty)$ in all locations ℓ; or $\text{Rates}(\ell, x) \subseteq (-\infty, 0]$ in all locations ℓ. A *singular hybrid automaton* (SHA) is an RHA such that for all locations ℓ and for all variables x: $\text{Rates}(\ell)(x)$ is a singleton. We note SMHA and RHA$^{\geq 0}$ for *singular* MHA, *non-negative rates* RHA resp. Note that MHA generalises RHA$^{\geq 0}$.

LHA Semantics. A *valuation* of a set of variables X is a function $\nu : X \mapsto \mathbb{R}$. We denote by $\mathbf{0}$ the valuation that assigns 0 to each variable. For a valuation x of X and a guard $g \in \mathcal{G}(X)$, we write $v \models g$ iff v *satisfies* g. Given an LHA $\mathcal{H} = (X, \text{Loc}, \text{Edges}, \text{Rates}, \text{Inv}, \text{Init}, X)$, a *state* of $\mathcal{H}$ is a pair (ℓ, ν), where $\ell \in$ Loc and ν is a valuation of X. The semantics of $\mathcal{H}$ is defined as follows. For a state $s = (\ell, \nu)$ of $\mathcal{H}$, an *edge step* $(\ell, \nu) \xrightarrow{e} (\ell', \nu')$ can occur and change the state to (ℓ', ν') if $e = (\ell, g, Y, \ell') \in$ Edges, $\nu \models g$, $\nu'(x) = \nu(x)$ for all $x \notin Y$, and $\nu'(x) = 0$ for all $x \in Y$; for a time delay $t \in \mathbb{R}^+$, a *continuous time step* $(\ell, \nu) \xrightarrow{t} (\ell, \nu')$ can occur and change the state to (ℓ, ν') if there is a vector $r = (r_1, \ldots r_{|X|})$ such that $r \models \text{Rates}(\ell)$, $\nu' = \nu + (r \cdot t)$, and $\nu + (r \cdot t') \models \text{Inv}(\ell)$ for all $0 \leq t' \leq t$.

A *path* in $\mathcal{H}$ is a finite sequence $e_1, e_2, \ldots, e_n$ of edges such that trg $(e_i) =$ src (e_{i+1}) for all $1 \leq i \leq n - 1$. A *timed path* of $\mathcal{H}$ is a finite sequence of the form $\pi = (t_1, e_1), (t_2, e_2), \ldots, (t_n, e_n)$, such that $e_1, \ldots, e_n$ is a path in $\mathcal{H}$ and $t_i \in \mathbb{R}^+$ for all $0 \leq i \leq n$. For all k, ℓ, we denote by $\pi[k : \ell]$ the maximal portion $(t_i, e_i), (t_{i+1}, e_{i+1}), \ldots, (t_j, e_j)$ of π such that $\{i, i+1, \ldots, j\} \subseteq [k, \ell]$ (note that the interval $[k, \ell]$ could be empty, in which case $\pi[k : \ell]$ would be empty too). Given a timed path $\pi = (t_1, e_1), (t_2, e_2), \ldots, (t_n, e_n)$ of an SHA, we let Effect $(\pi) = \sum_{i=1}^n \text{Rates}(\ell_{i-1}) \cdot t_i$ be the *effect of* π (where $\ell_i =$ src (e_i) for all $1 \leq i \leq n$).

A *run* in $\mathcal{H}$ is a sequence $s_0, (t_1, e_1), s_1, (t_2, e_2), \ldots, (t_n, e_n), s_n$ s.t. (i) (t_1, e_1), $(t_2, e_2), \ldots, (t_n, e_n)$ is a timed path in $\mathcal{H}$, and (ii) for all $0 \leq i < n$, there exists a state s_i' of $\mathcal{H}$ with $s_i \xrightarrow{t_{i+1}} s_i' \xrightarrow{e_{i+1}} s_{i+1}$. Given a run $\rho = s_0, (t_1, e_1), \ldots, s_n$, let first $(\rho) = s_0$, last $(\rho) = s_n$, duration $(\rho) = \sum_{i=1}^n t_i$, and $|\rho| = n + 1$. We say that ρ is $\mathbf{T}$-*time-bounded* (for $\mathbf{T} \in \mathbb{N}$) if duration $(\rho) \leq \mathbf{T}$. Given two runs

$\rho = s_0, (t_1, e_1), \ldots, (t_n, e_n), s_n$ and $\rho' = s'_0, (t'_1, e'_1), \ldots, (t'_k, e'_k), s'_k$ with $s_n = s'_0$, we let $\rho \cdot \rho'$ denote the run $s_0, (t_1, e_1), \ldots, (t_n, e_n), s_n, (t'_1, e'_1), \ldots, (t'_k, e'_k), s'_k$.

Note that a unique timed path $\mathsf{TPath}(\rho) = (t_1, e_1), (t_2, e_2), \ldots, (t_n, e_n)$, is associated with each run $\rho = s_0, (t_1, e_1), s_1, \ldots, (t_n, e_n), s_n$. Hence, we sometimes abuse notation and denote a run ρ with $\mathsf{first}(\rho) = s_0$, $\mathsf{last}(\rho) = s$ and $\mathsf{TPath}(\rho) = \pi$ by $s_0 \xrightarrow{\pi} s$. The converse however is not true: given a timed path π and an initial state s_0, it could be impossible to build a run starting from s_0 and following π because some guards or invariants along π might be violated. However, *when the automaton is singular*, such a run is necessarily unique if it exists, and we denote by $\mathsf{Run}(s_0, \pi)$ the function that returns the unique run ρ such that $\mathsf{first}(\rho) = s_0$ and $\mathsf{TPath}(\rho) = \pi$ if it exists, and $\bot$ otherwise. Note that, when considering an SHA: if $\rho = (\ell_0, \nu_0) \xrightarrow{\pi} (\ell_n, \nu_n)$ is a run, then for all x that is *not reset* along ρ: $\nu_n(x) = \nu_0(x) + \mathsf{Effect}(\pi)(x)$.

Time-Bounded Reachability Problem. While the reachability problem asks whether there is a run reaching a given goal location, we consider only runs with *bounded duration*.

Problem 1 (Time-bounded reachability problem). Given an LHA $\mathcal{H} = (X, \mathsf{Loc}, \mathsf{Edges}, \mathsf{Rates}, \mathsf{Inv}, \mathsf{Init})$, a location $\mathsf{Goal} \in \mathsf{Loc}$ and a time bound $\mathbf{T} \in \mathbb{N}$, the *time-bounded reachability problem* is to decide whether there exists a finite run $\rho = (\ell_0, \mathbf{0}) \xrightarrow{\pi} (\mathsf{Goal}, \cdot)$ of $\mathcal{H}$ with $\ell_0 \in \mathsf{Init}$ and duration$(\rho) \leq \mathbf{T}$.

This problem is decidable [5] for RHA$^{\geq 0}$, but its exact complexity was left open until now. We prove in Section 4 that it is **NExpTime-complete for MHA** . This problem is known to become undecidable either when diagonal constraints are allowed in the guards, or when non-monotonic RHA are considered [5]. In Section 5, we extend these results by showing how to compute a finite and algorithmically manipulable representation of the set of states that are reachable within $\mathbf{T}$ time units.

Let us illustrate, by means of the MHA (actually an RHA$^{\geq 0}$) $\mathcal{H}$ in Fig. 1 (left), the difficulties encountered when computing the reachable states. In this example, one can show that the set of reachable states is not a finite union of polyhedra, see Fig. 1 (right). Moreover, one can observe that the number of bits necessary to encode the states reachable from $(\ell_0, 0, 0)$ grows *linearly* with the length of the run. This example shows that finding an adequate, compact and effective representation (such as regions in the case of Timed Automata [2]) for the set of reachable states of an MHA is not trivial (and, in full generality, impossible because reachability is undecidable for this class). Nevertheless, in Section 5, we show that, for MHA, an effective representation of the set of states that are reachable *within* $\mathbf{T}$ *time units* can be computed.

3   Bounding the Length of Time-Bounded Runs

In this section, we prove the main technical result of the paper. For the sake of clarity, we consider a *singular* MHA $\mathcal{H} = (X, \mathsf{Loc}, \mathsf{Edges}, \mathsf{Rates}, \mathsf{Inv}, \mathsf{Init})$ and explain later why the results extend to general MHA. The result we prove is that '$\mathcal{H}$ *can reach a state s within* $\mathbf{T}$ *time unit iff it can reach s within* $\mathbf{T}$ *time unit by a run of bounded length*, where the bound is *uniform*: it depends only on $\mathbf{T}$ and on the number $|\mathcal{H}|$ of bits

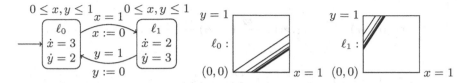

Fig. 1. An MHA with its set of reachable states

necessary to encode $\mathcal{H}$ (with standard encoding for the constants). More precisely, let $F(\mathcal{H}, \mathbf{T}) = 24 \times (\mathbf{T} \times \text{rmax} + 1) \times |X|^2 \times |\text{Loc}|^2 \times (2 \times \text{cmax} + 3)^{2 \times |X|}$. Then:

Theorem 2. *Let $\mathcal{H}$ be an SMHA, $\mathbf{T}$ be a time bound and let s_1 and s_2 be two states of $\mathcal{H}$. Then $\mathcal{H}$ admits a $\mathbf{T}$-time-bounded run ρ with $\text{first}(\rho) = s_1$ and $\text{last}(\rho) = s_2$ iff it admits a $\mathbf{T}$-time-bounded run ρ' s.t. $|\rho'| \leq F(\mathcal{H}, \mathbf{T})$, $\text{first}(\rho') = s_1$ and $\text{last}(\rho') = s_2$.*

This theorem will be used in the next sections to obtain optimal algorithms for deciding time-bounded reachability. Observe that $F(\mathcal{H}, \mathbf{T}) = \mathcal{O}\left(\mathbf{T} \times 2^{|\mathcal{H}|}\right)$. Thus, Theorem 2 says that, to decide $\mathbf{T}$-time-bounded reachability, we only need to consider runs whose length is exponential in the size of the instance $(\mathcal{H}, \mathbf{T})$.

We establish this result in two steps. First, we show that **each time-bounded run can be split into a *bounded* number of so-called type-2 (sub-)runs** (see hereunder for the definitions of type-0, type-1 and type-2 runs). Because of the density of time, we cannot bound the length of those type-2 runs, yet we show that they enjoy properties that allow us to **replace each type-2 run by an equivalent run of bounded length**. By *equivalent* we mean a run that starts and ends in the same states, and has the same duration. Combining the bounds on the number of type-2 runs and on the length of the runs we substitute to the original type-2 runs, we obtain Theorem 2.

Contraction Operator. To obtain the bounded length runs that we substitute to the original type-2 runs, we rely on a *contraction operator*. As this operator is central to our proof we start by describing it intuitively[1]. Let $\rho = (\ell_0, \nu_0), (t_1, e_1), (\ell_1, \nu_1), \ldots, (t_n, e_n), (\ell_n, \nu_n)$ be a run, and let $\pi = \text{TPath}(\rho)$. We *contract* π by looking for a pair of positions $i < j$ s.t. $\ell_i = \ell_j$ (i.e., $\pi[i+1 : j]$ forms a loop) *and* s.t. all locations $\ell_{i+1}, \ell_{i+2}, \ldots, \ell_j$ occur in the prefix $\pi[1 : i]$. An example is the timed path of the run ρ in the top of Fig. 2. Then, the contraction consists, roughly speaking, in *deleting* the portion $\pi[i+1 : j]$ from π, and in *reporting* the delays $t_{i+1}, \ldots, t_{j-1}$ to the other occurrences of $\ell_i, \ldots, \ell_{j-1}$ in π (that exist by hypothesis), see Fig. 2. Obviously, this contraction returns a timed path *with shorter length*. We show (Lemma 7 hereunder) that, by repeatedly applying this contraction, we obtain a timed path $\text{Cnt}^*(\pi)$ whose length is bounded by $|\text{Loc}|^2 + 1$, i.e. a value that does not depend on the length of π.

Now, we can lift the definition of the contraction operator to runs: for a run ρ, $\text{Cnt}(\rho) = \text{Run}(\text{first}(\rho), \text{Cnt}^*(\text{TPath}(\rho)))$. Clearly, there is, in general, no guarantee

---

[1] The definition of this operator is crucial to obtain the NEXPTIME algorithm in Section 4. It differs from the one introduced in [5], which does not allow to obtain an NEXPTIME algorithm.

$$\rho = (\ell_0, \nu_0) \xrightarrow{t_1, e_1} (\ell_1, \nu_1) \xrightarrow{t_2, e_2} (\ell_0, \nu_2) \xrightarrow{t_3, e_3} (\ell_1, \nu_3) \xrightarrow{t_4, e_4} (\ell_2, \nu_4)$$

$$\mathsf{Cnt}\,(\mathsf{TPath}\,(\rho)) = \ell_0 \xrightarrow{t_1 + t_3, e_1} \ell_1 \xrightarrow{t_2 + t_4, e_4} \ell_2$$

Fig. 2. Illustrating the contraction operator

that this contracted run exists, i.e. that $\mathsf{Cnt}\,(\rho) \neq \bot$ (see examples hereunder). However, we will show that, when correctly applied to so-called type-2 runs (see hereunder for the precise definition), $\mathsf{Cnt}\,(\rho)$ produces a genuine run of bounded length that starts and ends in the same states as the original run.

Let us now discuss several concrete examples of this contraction procedure. In all these examples, we assume an MHA with a single variable x whose rate is 1 in all locations, and we consider the run ρ depicted in Fig. 2. We also let $\pi' = \mathsf{Cnt}\,(\mathsf{TPath}\,(\rho))$ and $\rho' = \mathsf{Run}\,((\ell_0, \nu_0), \pi')$ – thus, ρ' could be equal to $\bot$. *First* assume that $\nu_0(x) = 0$, that $t_1 = t_2 = t_3 = t_4 = .1$ and that all edges $e_1, \ldots, e_4$ dot not reset x. In this case, ρ' is a genuine run that reaches $(\ell_2, .4)$. However, as remarked above, there are many cases where either $\rho' = \bot$ or $\rho' \neq \bot$ but does not reach the same state as ρ. Let us observe four of these cases, as they will be used later to justify our constructions.

Case 1. Assume x is never reset along ρ, $\nu_0(x) = 0$, $t_1 = t_3 = 1$ and the guard of e_1 is $x = 1$. Then, $\rho' = \bot$ as $\nu_0(x) + t_1 + t_3 = 2$ and does not satisfy the guard of e_1. Intuitively, the problem occurs because x crosses value 1 along ρ, and the compression reports the delay t_3, occurring *after* x crosses 1 in the original run, to a part where $x \leq 1$ in the original run. To avoid this, we split the run once a variable changes its *region*, where the regions are $[0, 1)$ and all $[a, a], (a, a + 1)$ for $a \geq 1$. Since we consider time-bounded runs, we obtain a *bounded number of sub-runs*. Note that we *do not* split when a variable moves from $[0, 0]$ to $(0, 1)$ or vice-versa, because the density of time allows a variable to be reset and to increase strictly an *unbounded* number of times in any time interval. Hence, this splitting strategy is not sufficient to guarantee that $\mathsf{Cnt}\,(\rho) \neq \bot$ and is equivalent to ρ, as shown by the next three cases, where x is in $[0, 1)$ along ρ.

Case 2. Assume $\rho' \neq \bot$, e_1 resets x, e_2, e_3 and e_4 do not reset x and $t_1 = t_2 = t_3 = t_4 = .1$. Then, $\nu_4(x) = t_2 + t_3 + t_4 = .3$. Observe that $\nu_4(x)$ depends only on the run portion that occurs *after* e_1 because e_1 is the last edge to reset x. On the other hand, ρ' reaches a state (ℓ_2, ν) with $\nu(x) = t_2 + t_4 = .2 \neq \nu_4(x)$, because the contraction *reports, before the last reset (e_1), the delay t_3 that occurs after the last reset in ρ*.

Case 3. Assume $\nu_0(x) = .8$, $t_1 = t_3 = .1$, the guard of e_1 is $x < 1$ and e_1 resets x. Then, $\rho' = \bot$, as $\nu_0(x) + t_1 + t_3 = 1$, which does not satisfy the guard of e_1. Intuitively, the problem occurs because the time delay t_3 that takes place *after the first reset of x* in ρ has been reported *before the first reset of x*.

Case 4. Assume $\nu_0(x) = 0$, $t_1 = 0$, $t_2 = t_3 = t_4 = .1$, e_2, e_3 and e_4 reset x, and the guard of e_1 is $x = 0$. Further assume that that x has just been reset when entering ℓ_0. Then, $\rho' = \bot$, as $\nu_0(x) + t_1 + t_3 = .1$, which does not satisfy the guard of e_1. Intuitively, the problem occurs because, x is null when entering *and* leaving the first occurrence of ℓ_0, while it is null when entering and non-null when leaving the second occurrence of ℓ_0. Thus, the time delay t_3 should not be reported to the first occurrence of ℓ_0. To avoid this, we *label locations* with special *regions* telling us whether x is null when leaving the location (region $\mathbf{0}^=$) or not $(\mathbf{0}^+)$, and we will forbid the contraction operator to report delay from one location to another with different regions.

The actual splitting into type-2 runs proceeds stepwise: we split a run into type-1 runs, then each type-1 in type-2 runs, so that we avoid the pitfalls described above. As explained in the discussion of case 1 above, we first need to track the *regions* of the variables, thanks to the following construction.

Region Labelling. Let $\mathsf{Reg}\,(\mathrm{cmax}) = (\{[a,a],\ (a-1,a)\ |\ a \in \{1,\ldots,\mathrm{cmax}\}\} \cup \{\mathbf{0}^=, \mathbf{0}^+, (\mathrm{cmax}, +\infty)\})$ be the set of *regions*, and further let $\mathsf{Reg}\,(\mathrm{cmax}, X)$ denote the set of all functions $r : X \mapsto \mathsf{Reg}\,(\mathrm{cmax})$ that assign a region to each variable. By abuse of language, we sometimes call *regions* elements of $\mathsf{Reg}\,(\mathrm{cmax}, X)$ too. Remark that the definition of $\mathsf{Reg}\,(\mathrm{cmax}, X)$ differs from the classical regions [2] by the absence of $[0,0]$ which is replaced by two symbols: $\mathbf{0}^=$ and $\mathbf{0}^+$, and by the fact that no information is retained about the relative values of the fractional parts of the variables. The reason of the introduction of the two regions $\mathbf{0}^=$ and $\mathbf{0}^+$ is to avoid the problem occurring in Case 4 above. When testing for membership to a region, $\mathbf{0}^+$ and $\mathbf{0}^=$ should be interpreted as $[0,0]$, i.e., $v \in \mathbf{0}^+$ and $v \in \mathbf{0}^=$ hold iff $v = 0$. Given a valuation ν of the set of variable X, and $r \in \mathsf{Reg}\,(\mathrm{cmax}, X)$, we let $\nu \in r$ iff $\nu(x) \in r(x)$ for all x, and, provided that $\nu > \mathbf{0}$, we denote by $[\nu]$ the (unique) element from $\mathsf{Reg}\,(\mathrm{cmax}, X)$ s.t. $\nu \in [\nu]$. Remark that for all sets of variable X and all maximal constants cmax: $|\mathsf{Reg}\,(\mathrm{cmax}, X)| \leq (2 \times \mathrm{cmax}+3)^{|X|}$. Let r_1 and r_2 be two regions in $\mathsf{Reg}\,(\mathrm{cmax}, X)$, and let $v : X \mapsto \mathbb{R}$ be a function assigning a rate $v(x)$ to each variable x. Then, we say that r_2 *is a time successor of* r_1 *under* v (written $r_1 \leq^v_{\mathrm{ts}} r_2$) iff there are $\nu_1 \in r_1$, $\nu_2 \in r_2$ and a time delay t s.t. $\nu_2 = \nu_1 + t \cdot v$. Remark that, by this definition, we can have $r_1 \leq^v_{\mathrm{ts}} r_2$, $r_1(x) = \mathbf{0}^=$ and $r_2(x) = \mathbf{0}^+$ for some variable x (for instance, if $v(x) = 0$).

Let us now explain how we label the locations of $\mathcal{H}$ by regions. We let $\mathsf{R}\,(\mathcal{H}) = (X, \mathrm{Loc}', \mathrm{Edges}', \mathrm{Rates}', \mathrm{Inv}', \mathrm{Init}')$ be the SMHA where:

- $\mathrm{Loc}' = \mathrm{Loc} \times \mathsf{Reg}\,(\mathrm{cmax}, X)$ and $\mathrm{Init}' = \mathrm{Init} \times \{\mathbf{0}^=, \mathbf{0}^+\}^X$
- for all $(\ell, r) \in \mathrm{Loc}'$: $\mathrm{Rates}'(\ell, r) = \mathrm{Rates}(\ell)$; $\mathrm{Inv}(\ell, r) = \mathrm{Inv}(\ell) \wedge \bigwedge_{x : r(x) = \mathbf{0}^=} x = 0$
- There is an edge $e' = ((\ell, r), g \wedge x \in r'' \wedge g_0, Y, (\ell', r'))$ in Edges' iff there are an edge $e = (\ell, g, Y, \ell')$ in Edges and a region r'' s.t. $r \leq^{\mathrm{Rates}(\ell)}_{\mathrm{ts}} r''$, for all $x \notin Y$: $r'(x) = r''(x)$, for all $x \in Y$: $r'(x) \in \{\mathbf{0}^=, \mathbf{0}^+\}$ and $g_0 = \bigwedge_{x \in X} g_0(x)$ where for all $x \in X$: $g_0(x) = (x = 0)$ if $r(x) = \mathbf{0}^=$; $g_0(x) = (x > 0)$ if $r(x) = \mathbf{0}^+$; and $g_0(x) = \mathbf{true}$ otherwise. In this case, we say that e is the (unique) edge of $\mathcal{H}$ *corresponding* to e'. Symmetrically, e' is the only edge corresponding to e between locations (ℓ, r) and (ℓ', r').

It is easy to see that this construction incurs an exponential blow up in the number of locations, but preserves reachability of states. More precisely, $|\mathrm{Loc}'| \leq |\mathrm{Loc}| \times |\mathsf{Reg}\,(\mathrm{cmax}, X)| = |\mathrm{Loc}| \times (2 \times \mathrm{cmax} + 3)^{|X|}$ and:

Lemma 3. $\mathcal{H}$ *admits a run ρ with* first $(\rho) = (\ell, \nu)$ *and* last $(\rho) = (\ell', \nu')$ *iff there are r and r' s.t.* $\mathsf{R}(\mathcal{H})$ *admits a run ρ' with* first $(\rho') = ((\ell, r), \nu)$, last $(\rho') = ((\ell', r'), \nu')$, duration $(\rho) = $ duration (ρ') *and* $|\rho| = |\rho'|$.

Intuitively, the regions that label locations in $\mathsf{R}(\mathcal{H})$ track the region to which each variable belongs when entering the location. However, in the case where a variable x enters a location with value 0, we also need to remember whether x is still null when crossing the next edge, to avoid the issue with the contraction operator described in case 4 above. This explains the two regions, $\mathbf{0}^=$ and $\mathbf{0}^+$, corresponding to 0. They encode the fact that the variable is null (resp. strictly positive) when leaving the location.

Type-0 and Type-1 Runs. Without loss of generality, we assume that, if a state is reachable, then it is reachable by a run of the same duration which can be split into at most $\mathbf{T} \times \mathrm{rmax} + 1$ portions of duration $< \frac{1}{\mathrm{rmax}}$. In practice, this can be achieved by adding one self-loop on all locations of $\mathsf{R}(\mathcal{H})$, which does not impact time-bounded reachability. Such runs of ρ of $\mathsf{R}(\mathcal{H})$ are called *type-0 runs* and are of the form $\rho = \rho_0 \cdot \rho_1 \cdots \rho_k$ s.t. for all $0 \le i \le k$: duration $(\rho_i) < \frac{1}{\mathrm{rmax}}$. Each ρ_i is called a *type-1 run*. *Intuitively*, each variable will *cross at most one integer value different from 0 in each type 1 run*, because the automaton is *monotonic*. For instance, if $x \in (2, 3)$ at the beginning of a type-1 run, then x can reach $(3, 4)$ along the run, but will never cross 4. However, x could be reset and cross 0 an unbounded number of times because of time density.

Type-2 Runs. Let $\rho = (\ell_0, \nu_0), (t_1, e_1), (\ell_1, \nu_1), \ldots, (t_n, e_n), (\ell_n, \nu_n)$ be a type-1 run s.t. duration $(\rho) \le \mathbf{T}$. Let S_ρ be the set of all $0 < i \le n$ s.t:

$$\exists x \in X : \left(\lfloor \nu_{i-1}(x) \rfloor \ne \lfloor \nu_i(x) \rfloor \right) \text{ or } \left(\lfloor \nu_{i-1}(x) \rfloor > 0 \text{ and } 0 = \langle \nu_{i-1}(x) \rangle < \langle \nu_i(x) \rangle \right)$$

where $\lfloor x \rfloor$ and $\langle x \rangle$ denote respectively the integral and fractional parts of x. Roughly speaking, each transition (t_i, e_i) with $i \in S_\rho$ corresponds to the fact that a variable changes its region, except in the case where the variable moves from 0 to $(0, 1)$ or from $(0, 1)$ to 0: such transitions are not recorded in S_ρ. Since each variable crosses a strictly positive integer value at most once along the *type-1 run* ρ, $|S_\rho|$ can be bounded:

Lemma 4. *For all type-1 run ρ:* $|S_\rho| \le 3 \times |X|$.

Had we recorded in S_ρ the indices of the transitions from (ℓ, ν) to (ℓ', ν') s.t. $\nu(x) = 0$ and $\nu(x) \in (0, 1)$ for some variable x, Lemma 4 would not hold, and we could not bound the size of S_ρ by a value independent from $|\rho|$. Indeed, in any time interval, the density of time allows a variable to be reset and increase an arbitrary number of times.

Let us now explain how we split type-1 runs into type-2 runs. We first consider an example. Consider an RHA with two variables x, y (with rate 1) and one of its runs $\rho = (\ell_0, 2.1, .7) \xrightarrow{.4, e_1} (\ell_1, 2.5, 1.1) \xrightarrow{.1, e_2} (\ell_2, 2.6, 1.2) \xrightarrow{.1, e_3} (\ell_3, 0, 1.3) \xrightarrow{.1, e_4} (\ell_4, .1, 1.4) \xrightarrow{.1, e_5} (\ell_3, 0, 1.5)$, and where e_3 and e_5 reset x. Then $S_\rho = \{1, 3\}$ because y changes its integral part from $(\ell_0, 2.1, .7)$ to $(\ell_1, 2.5, 1.1)$ and x is reset by e_3 and changes its integral part. Also, $\{4, 5\} \cap S_\rho = \emptyset$ as x and y stay resp. in $[0, 1)$ and $(1, 2)$. Then, ρ is split in 5 parts: first $\rho_0 = (\ell_0, 2.1, .7)$; then $\rho'_1 = (\ell_0, 2.1, .7) \xrightarrow{.4, e_1} (\ell_1, 2.5, 1.1)$;

then $\rho_1 = (\ell_1, 2.5, 1.1) \xrightarrow{.1, e_2} (\ell_2, 2.6, 1.2)$; then $\rho_2' = (\ell_2, 2.6, 1.2) \xrightarrow{.1, e_3} (\ell_3, 0, 1.3)$ and $\rho_2 = (\ell_3, 0, 1.3) \xrightarrow{.1, e_4} (\ell_4, .1, 1.4) \xrightarrow{.1, e_5} (\ell_3, 0, 1.5)$.

Formally, assume $\rho = s_0, (t_1, e_1), s_1, \ldots, (t_n, e_n), s_n$, and $S_\rho = \{p_1, \ldots, p_k\}$, with $p_1 \leq p_2 \leq \cdots \leq p_k$. Then, we let $\rho_0, \rho_1, \ldots, \rho_k$ be the sub-runs s.t.: $\rho = \rho_0 \cdot s_{p_1 - 1}, (t_{p_1}, e_{p_1}), s_{p_1} \cdot \rho_1 \cdot s_{p_2 - 1}, (t_{p_2}, e_{p_2}), s_{p_2}, \ldots, s_{p_k - 1}, (t_{p_k}, e_{p_k}), s_{p_k} \cdot \rho_k$. Each ρ_i is called a *type-2 run*, and can be empty. In the example above, ρ_1 and ρ_2 are type-2 runs. The next lemma summarises the properties of this construction:

Lemma 5. *Let ρ be a type-1 run of* R $(\mathcal{H})$ *with duration* $(\rho) \leq$ **T**. *Then, ρ is split into:* $\rho_0 \cdot \rho_1' \cdot \rho_1 \cdot \rho_2' \cdot \rho_2 \cdots \rho_k' \cdot \rho_k$ *where each ρ_i is a type-2 run; $k \leq 3 \times |X|$; $|\rho_i'| = 1$ for all* $1 \leq i \leq k$; *and for all* $1 \leq i \leq k$: $\rho_i = (\ell_0, \nu_0), (t_1, e_1), \ldots, (t_n, e_n), (\ell_n, \nu_n)$ *implies that, for all $x \in X$: (i) either there is $a \in \mathbb{N}^{>0}$ s.t. for all $0 \leq j \leq n$: $\nu_j(x) = a$ and x is not reset along ρ_i; (ii) or for all $0 \leq j \leq n$: $\nu_j(x) \in (a, a+1)$ with $a \in \mathbb{N}^{>0}$ and x is not reset along ρ_i; (iii) or for all $0 \leq j \leq n$: $\nu_j(x) \in [0, 1)$.*

Observe that in the last case (i.e., $x \in [0, 1)$), the number of resets cannot be bounded *a priori*. For the sake of clarity, let us summarise the construction so far:

Lemma 6. *Each type-0 run of* R $(\mathcal{H})$ *can be decomposed into k type-2 runs with $k \leq 3 \times (T \times \text{rmax} + 1) \times |X|$.*

Contraction of Type-2 Runs. We finish the construction by defining formally the contraction operator and establishing its properties. The formal definition follows the intuition sketched at the beginning of the section (see Fig. 2). Let $\pi = (t_1, e_1), (t_2, e_2), \ldots, (t_n, e_n)$ be a timed path, let $\ell_0 = \text{src}(e_1)$, and, for all $1 \leq i \leq n$: $\ell_i = \text{trg}(e_i)$. Assume there are $0 \leq i < j < n$ and a function $h : \{i+1, \ldots, j-1\} \mapsto \{0, \ldots, i-1\}$ s.t. (i) $\ell_i = \ell_j$ and (ii) for all $i < p < j$: $\ell_p = \ell_{h(p)}$. Then, we let Cnt $(\pi) = \ell_0', (t_1', e_1'), \ldots, \ell_m'$ where: (i) $m = n - (j - i)$; (ii) for all $0 \leq p \leq i$: $\ell_p' = \ell_p$; (iii) for all $1 \leq p \leq i$: $e_p' = e_p$ and $t_p' = t_p + \sum_{k \in h^{-1}(p-1)} t_{k+1}$; (iv) $e_{i+1}' = e_{j+1}$; (v) $t_{i+1}' = t_{i+1} + t_{j+1}$; and (vi) for all $i+1 < p \leq m$: $\ell_p' = \ell_{p+j-i}$ and $(t_p', e_p') = (t_{p+j-i}, e_{p+j-i})$.

Then, given a timed path π, we let Cnt$^0 (\pi) = \pi$, Cnt$^i (\pi) = $ Cnt $($Cnt$^{i-1} (\pi))$ for any $i \geq 1$, and Cnt$^* (\pi) = $ Cnt$^k (\pi)$ where k is the least value such that Cnt$^k (\pi) = $ Cnt$^{k+1} (\pi)$. Note that Cnt$^* (\pi)$ always exists since π is finite, and since, for all π: either $|$Cnt $(\pi)| < |\pi|$ or Cnt $(\pi) = \pi$. Moreover, the length of Cnt$^* (\pi)$ is always bounded by a value *that does not depend on* $|\pi|$.

Lemma 7. *For all timed path π: $|$Cnt$^* (\pi)| \leq |\text{Loc}|^2 + 1$.*

Let us now lift the definition of the contraction operator to *runs* of type-2. To this end, we first need to further split type-2 runs into type-3 runs by splitting type-2 runs according to the first and last resets (if they exist) of each variable. Formally, let $s_0, (t_1, e_1), s_1, \ldots, (t_n, e_n), s_n$ be a type-2 run. Assume Y_i is the reset set of e_i, for all $1 \leq i \leq n$. We let $FR_\rho = \{i \mid \exists x \in Y_i \text{ and } \forall 0 \leq j < i : x \notin Y_j\}$ and $LR_\rho = \{i \mid \exists x \in Y_i \text{ and } \forall i < j \leq n : x \notin Y_j\}$ be respectively the set of edge indices where a variable is reset for the first (last) in ρ. Let $R_\rho = FR_\rho \cup LR_\rho$ and assume $R_\rho = \{p(1), p(2), \ldots, p(k)\}$ with $p(1) \leq p(2) \leq \cdots \leq p(k)$. Then, we let

$\rho_0, \rho_1, \ldots, \rho_k$ be the *type-3 runs* making up ρ s.t. $\rho = \rho_0 \cdot s_{p(1)-1}, (t_{p(1)}, e_{p(1)}), s_{p(1)} \cdot$
$\rho_1 \cdots s_{p(k)-1}, (t_{p(k)}, e_{p(k)}), s_{p(k)} \cdot \rho_k$. Note that each type-2 is split into at most
$2 \times |X| + 1$ type-3 runs (i.e., $k \leq 2 \times |X|$). We can now define the contraction of ρ:
$\mathsf{Cnt}(\rho) = \mathsf{Run}\left(\mathsf{first}(\rho), \pi_{\mathsf{Cnt}(\rho)}\right)$, where: $\pi_{\mathsf{Cnt}(\rho)} = \mathsf{Cnt}^*(\mathsf{TPath}(\rho_0)), (t_{p(1)}, e_{p(1)}),$
$\mathsf{Cnt}^*(\mathsf{TPath}(\rho_1)), (t_{p(2)}, e_{p(2)}), \ldots, (t_{p(k)}, e_{p(k)}), \mathsf{Cnt}^*(\mathsf{TPath}(\rho_k))$. Equipped with
this definition, we can show that $\mathsf{Cnt}(\rho)$ is not only of *bounded length*, but is also
equivalent to the original type-2 run ρ, in the following sense:

Proposition 8. *For all type-2 runs* ρ, $\mathsf{Cnt}(\rho) \neq \perp$, $\mathsf{first}(\mathsf{Cnt}(\rho)) = \mathsf{first}(\rho)$,
$\mathsf{last}(\mathsf{Cnt}(\rho)) = \mathsf{last}(\rho)$ *and* $|\mathsf{Cnt}(\rho)| \leq 8 \times |\mathsf{Loc}|^2 \times |X|$.

Proof (sketch). We sketch the proof assuming $\mathcal{H}$ has only one variable x with
non-negative rate (the arguments generalise easily). Let $\rho = (\ell_0, \nu_0) \xrightarrow{t_1, e_1}$
$(\ell_1, \nu_1) \cdots \xrightarrow{t_n, e_n} (\ell_n, \nu_n)$ be a type-2 run, $\pi = \mathsf{TPath}(\rho)$, $\pi' = \mathsf{Cnt}^*(\pi)$ and
$\rho' = \mathsf{Cnt}(\rho)$. Observe that $\mathsf{duration}(\pi') = \mathsf{duration}(\rho)$, and that $\mathsf{Effect}(\pi') = \mathsf{Effect}(\pi)$. Assume *first* that x is never reset along ρ, and that $\nu_0(x) \notin [0, 1)$. Then,
all valuations of x along ρ are in the same interval $[a, a]$ or $(a, a + 1)$ for $a \geq 1$,
by Lemma 5 (thus the issue of case 1 above is ruled out). In this case, all the guards
are still satisfied in π', and $\rho' \neq \perp$. Finally, assuming $\mathsf{last}(\rho') = (\ell_n, \nu'_n)$, we have
$\nu'_n(x) = \nu_0(x) + \mathsf{Effect}(\pi')(x) = \nu_0(x) + \mathsf{Effect}(\pi)(x) = \nu_n(x)$ because x is
not reset along ρ. *Second*, assume x is never reset along ρ and that $\nu_0(x) \in [0, 1)$.
In this case, we have to rule out an additional difficulty. Let k, j be s.t. $k < j$,.
$\nu_j(x) = 0$, $t_{j+1} = 0$, e_{j+1} has guard '$x = 0$' and $t_k > 0$: we must show that
$\ell_k \neq \ell_j$ (otherwise the delay $t_k > 0$ could be 'reported' on ℓ_j, and the guard of e_j
would not be satisfied, this is the problem identified in case 4). $\ell_k \neq \ell_j$ holds be-
cause, by construction of $\mathsf{Reg}(\mathcal{H})$, $\ell_k = (\ell, \mathbf{0}^=)$ and $\ell_j = (\ell', \mathbf{0}^+)$ for some ℓ, ℓ',
because x is null when leaving ℓ_k, but not when leaving ℓ_j. *Third*, assume x is re-
set along ρ, hence x takes values in $[0, 1)$ only along ρ, by Lemma 5. Let j, k be s.t.
$j < k$ and e_j (resp. e_k) is the first (last) edge to reset x along ρ. Then, by definition,
$\pi' = \mathsf{Cnt}^*(\pi[0 : j - 1]), (t_j, e_j), \mathsf{Cnt}^*(\pi[j + 1, k - 1])(t_k, e_k)\mathsf{Cnt}^*(\pi[k + 1, n])$. In
$\mathsf{Cnt}^*(\pi[0 : j - 1])$ and $\mathsf{Cnt}^*(\pi[k + 1, n])$, x is not reset and takes values in $[0, 1)$,
thus $\mathsf{Cnt}^*(\pi[0 : j - 1])$ and $\mathsf{Cnt}^*(\pi[k + 1, n])$ yield genuine runs, by the same arguments as above. If x is reset in $\pi[j + 1, k - 1]$, this is not the first reset along
π, so we avoid the issue of case 2. Thanks to the $\mathbf{0}^+$ and $\mathbf{0}^=$ regions, we are
sure that the '$x = 0$' guards are still satisfied in $\mathsf{Cnt}^*(\pi[j + 1, k - 1])$, so it
yields a genuine run. Thus, $\rho' \neq \perp$. Note however that the value of x after firing
$\mathsf{Cnt}^*(\pi[0 : j - 1]), (t_j, e_j), \mathsf{Cnt}^*(\pi[j + 1, k - 1])$ might not be the same as when firing $\pi[0 : k - 1]$. Yet, this does not prevent from firing e_k. Moreover, the value of x at
the end of the run is preserved (i.e., we avoid the issue of case 3 above): if $\mathsf{last}(\rho') = (\ell_n, \nu'_n)$, then $\nu'_n(x) = \mathsf{Effect}(\mathsf{Cnt}^*(\pi[k + 1, n]))(x)$ (again because x is not reset
along $\pi[k + 1, n]$) with $\mathsf{Effect}(\mathsf{Cnt}^*(\pi[k + 1, n]))(x) = \mathsf{Effect}(\pi[k + 1, n])(x) = \nu_n(x)$. $\square$

We obtain Theorem 1 thanks to Proposition 8, Lemma 6 and the definition of $\mathsf{Reg}(\mathcal{H})$.

Rectangular Rates. Let us now briefly explain how we can adapt the previous construc-
tion to cope with non-singular rates. Let us first notice that for all MHA $\mathcal{H}$, $\mathsf{R}(\mathcal{H})$ is

still well-defined. Then, we adapt the definition of timed path as follows. A timed path is a sequence $(t_1, R_1, e_1) \cdots (t_n, R_n, e_n)$, where each $R_i : X \mapsto \mathbb{R}$ gives the actual rate that was chosen for each variable at the i-th continuous step. It is then straightforward to extend the definitions of Cnt and Effect to take those rates into account and retain the properties needed to prove Theorem 2. More precisely, the contraction of a set of transitions $(t_1, R_1, e_1), \ldots, (t_n, R_n, e_n)$ yields a transition (t, R, e) with $t = \sum_{i=1}^{n} t_i$ and, $R = \frac{\sum_{i=1}^{n} t_i \times R_i}{t}$. Note that we rely on the convexity of the invariants and rates in an RHA to ensure that this construction is correct.

4 Time-Bounded Reachability Is NEXPTIME-Complete

In this section, we establish our main result:

Theorem 9. *Time-bounded reachability for MHA is* NEXPTIME *complete.*

An NEXPTIME *Algorithm.* Recall that an instance of the time-bounded reachability problem is of the form $(\mathcal{H}, \ell, \mathbf{T})$, where $\mathcal{H}$ is an MHA, ℓ is a location, and $\mathbf{T}$ is a time bound (expressed in binary). We establish membership in NEXPTIME by giving a non-deterministic algorithm that runs in time exponential in the size of $(\mathcal{H}, \ell, \mathbf{T})$ in the worst case. The algorithm *guesses* a sequence of edges $\mathcal{E} = e_0 e_1 \ldots e_n$ of $\mathcal{H}$ such that $n+1 \leq F(\mathcal{H}, \mathbf{T})$ and trg $(e_n) = \ell$ and builds a linear constraint $\Phi(\mathcal{E})$, that expresses all the properties that must be satisfied by a run following the sequence of edges $\mathcal{E}$ (see [13] for a detailed explanation on how to build such a constraint). This constraint uses $n + 1$ copies of the variables in X and $n + 1$ variables t_i to model the time elapsing between two consecutive edges, and imposes that the valuations of the variables along the run are consistent with the rates, guards and resets of $\mathcal{H}$. Finally, the algorithm checks whether $\Phi(\mathcal{E})$ is satisfiable and returns 'yes' iff it is the case.

The number of computation steps necessary to build $\Phi(\mathcal{E})$ is, in the worst case, exponential in the size of the instance $(\mathcal{H}, \mathbf{T})$. Moreover, checking satisfiability of $\Phi(\mathcal{E})$ can be done in polynomial time (in the size of the constraint) using classical algorithms to solve linear programs. Clearly this procedure is an NEXPTIME algorithm for solving the time-bounded reachability problem for MHA.

NEXPTIME-*Hardness.* To establish the NEXPTIME-hardness, we encode the membership problem of non-deterministic exponential time Turing machines (NExpTM for short) to time-bounded reachability for SMHA. An NExpTM is a tuple $M = (Q, \Sigma, \Gamma, q_0, \delta, F, \xi)$ where Q is the (nonempty and finite) set of control states, $\Sigma = \{0, 1\}$ is the (finite) input alphabet[2], $\Gamma = \{\sharp, 0, 1\}$ is the (finite) alphabet of the tape, where $\sharp$ is the blank symbol, $q_0 \in Q$ is the initial control state, $\delta \subseteq Q \times \Gamma \times \Gamma \times \{L, R\} \times Q$ is the transition relation, $F \subseteq Q$ is the set of accepting states, and $\xi = \mathcal{O}\left(2^{p(n)}\right)$ (for some polynomial p), is an exponential function to bound the execution length.

A state of M is a triple (q, w_1, w_2), where $q \in Q$, and $w_1, w_2 \in \Gamma^*$ are resp. the content to the left (to the right and below) of the reading head, excluding the trailing sequence of $\sharp$. We rely on the standard semantics for NExpTM: for example,

---

[2] Having $\Sigma = \{0, 1\}$ and $\Gamma = \Sigma \cup \{\sharp\}$ is without loss of generality.

(q_1, a, b, L, q_2) means 'when in q_1 and a is below the head, replace a by b, move the head to the left (L) and go to q_2'. We write $(q, w_1, w_2) \triangleright (q', w_1', w_2')$ when there is a transition from (q, w_1, w_2) to (q', w_1', w_2'). An execution of M on input w is a finite sequence of states $c_0 c_1 \ldots c_n$ such that: (i) $n \leq \xi(|w|)$; (ii) $c_0 = (q_0, \varepsilon, w \cdot \sharp^{\xi(|w|) - |w|})$; and (iii) for all $0 \leq i < n$: $c_i \triangleright c_{i+1}$. It is *accepting* iff $c_n = (q, w_1, w_2)$ with $q \in F$.

Let us show how to encode all executions of M into the executions of an SMHA $\mathcal{H}_M$. We encode the words w_1 and w_2 as pairs of rational values (l_1, c_1) and (l_2, c_2) where $l_i = \frac{1}{2^{|w_i|}}$ encodes the length of the word w_i by a rational number in $[0, 1]$, and c_i encodes w_i as follows. Assume $w_1 = \sigma_0 \sigma_1 \ldots \sigma_n$. Then, we let $c_1 = \mathsf{Val}^{\leftarrow}(w_1) = \sigma_n \cdot \frac{1}{2} + \sigma_{n-1} \cdot \frac{1}{4} + \cdots + \sigma_0 \cdot \frac{1}{2^{n+1}}$. Intuitively, c_1 is the value which is represented in binary by $0.\sigma_n \sigma_{n-1} \cdots \sigma_0$, i.e., w_1 is the binary encoding of the fractional part of c_1 with the most significant bit in the rightmost position. For instance, if $w_1 = 001010$ then $\mathsf{Val}^{\leftarrow}(w_1) = 0 \cdot \frac{1}{2} + 1 \cdot \frac{1}{4} + 0 \cdot \frac{1}{8} + 1 \cdot \frac{1}{16} + 0 \cdot \frac{1}{32} + 0 \cdot \frac{1}{64} = 0.3125$, and so w_1 is encoded as the pair $(\frac{1}{64}, 0.3125)$. Note that we need to remember the actual length of the word w_1 because the function $\mathsf{Val}^{\leftarrow}(\cdot)$ ignores the leading 0's (for instance, $\mathsf{Val}^{\leftarrow}(001010) = \mathsf{Val}^{\leftarrow}(1010)$). Symmetrically, if $w_2 = \sigma_0 \sigma_1 \ldots \sigma_n$, we let $c_2 = \mathsf{Val}^{\rightarrow}(w_2) = \sigma_0 \cdot \frac{1}{2} + \sigma_1 \cdot \frac{1}{4} + \cdots + \sigma_n \cdot \frac{1}{2^{n+1}}$ (i.e., σ_0 is now the most significant bit). Then a state (q, w_1, w_2) of the NExpTM is encoded as follows: the control state q is remembered in the locations of the automaton, and the words w_1, w_2 are stored, using the encoding described above using four variables for the values (l_1, c_1) and (l_2, c_2).

With this encoding in mind, let us list the operations that we must be able to perform to simulate the transitions of the NExpTM. Assume $w_1 = w_0^1 w_1^1 \cdots w_n^1$ and $w_2 = w_0^2 w_2^2 \cdots w_k^2$. To *read the letter under the head* we need to test the value of the bit w_0^2. Clearly, $w_0^2 = 1$ iff $l_2 \leq 1/2$, and $c_2 \geq \frac{1}{2}$; $w_0^2 = 0$ iff $l_2 \leq 1/2$, and $c_2 < \frac{1}{2}$ and $w_0^2 = \sharp$ iff $l_2 = 1$ (which corresponds to $w_2 = \varepsilon$). To *test whether the head is in the leftmost cell of the tape* we must check whether $w_1 = \varepsilon$, i.e. $l_1 = 1$. To *read the letter at the left of the head* (assuming that $w_1 \neq \varepsilon$) we must test the value of the bit w_n^1. Clearly, $w_n^1 = 1$ iff $c_1 \geq \frac{1}{2}$ and $w_n^1 = 0$ iff $c_1 < \frac{1}{2}$.

Then, let us describe the operations that are necessary to update the values on the tape. Clearly, they can be carried out by appending and removing 0's or 1's to the right of w_1 or to the left of w_2. Let us describe how we update c_1 and l_1 to simulate these operations on w_1 (the operations on w_2 can be deduced from this description). We denote by c_1' (resp. l_1') the value of c_1 (l_1) after the simulation of the NExpTM transition. To *append a 1 to the right* of w_1, we let $l_1' = \frac{1}{2} \times l_1$. We let $c_1' = \frac{1}{2}$ if $l_1 = 1$ (i.e. w_1 was empty) and $c_1' = \frac{1}{2} \times c_1 + \frac{1}{2}$ otherwise. To *append a 0 to the right of w_1*, we let $l_1' = \frac{1}{2} \times l_1$ and $c_1' = \frac{1}{2} \times c_1$. To *delete a 0 from the rightmost position of w_1*, we let $l_1' = 2 \times l_1$, $c_1' = 2 \times c_1$. To *delete a 1 from the rightmost position of w_1*, we let $l_1' = 2 \times l_1$, and $c_1' = (c_1 - \frac{1}{2}) \times 2$. In addition, note that we can flip the leftmost bit of w_2 by adding or subtracting $1/2$ from c_2 (this is necessary when updating the value under the head). Thus, the operations that we need to be able to perform on c_1, l_1, c_2 and l_2 are: to multiply by 2, divide by 2, increase by $\frac{1}{2}$ and decrease by $\frac{1}{2}$, while keeping untouched the value of all the other variables. Fig. 3 exhibits four gadgets to perform these operations. Note that these gadgets can be constructed in polynomial time, execute in 1 time unit time and bear only singular rates.

(i)

$$z := 0 \xrightarrow{} \boxed{\substack{\dot{x} = 1 \\ \dot{z} = 1}} \overset{x = 1}{\underset{x := 0}{\longrightarrow}} \boxed{\substack{\dot{x} = 2 \\ \dot{z} = 1}} \xrightarrow{z = 1}$$

$x \le 1$ $z \le 1$

When crossing this edge, $z = 1 - x_0$.

$z = 1/2 + (1 - x_0)$ when crossing this edge

(ii) $z \le 1$

$$z := 0 \xrightarrow{} \boxed{\substack{\dot{x} = 1 \\ \dot{z} = 2}} \xrightarrow{z = 1}$$

(iii) $x \le 1$ $x = 1$ $z \le 1$

$$z := 1/2 \xrightarrow{} \boxed{\substack{\dot{x} = 1 \\ \dot{z} = 1}} \overset{x := 0}{\longrightarrow} \boxed{\substack{\dot{x} = 1 \\ \dot{z} = 1}} \xrightarrow{z = 1}$$

Fig. 3. Gadgets (i) for multiplication by 2, (ii) adding $\frac{1}{2}$ and (iii) subtracting $\frac{1}{2}$. The rates of the $y \notin \{x, z\}$ is 0. Gadget (i) can be modified to divide by 2, by swapping the rates of x and z in the second location. x_0 is the value of x when entering the gadget.

We claim that all transitions of M can be simulated by combining the gadgets in Fig. 3 and the tests described above. For instance, consider the transition: $(q_1, 1, 0, L, q_2)$. It is simulated as follows. First, we check that the reading head is not at the leftmost position of the tape by checking that $l_1 < 1$. Second, we check that the value below the reading head is equal to 1 by testing that $l_2 < 1$ and $c_2 \ge \frac{1}{2}$. Third, we change the value below the reading head from 1 to 0 by subtracting $\frac{1}{2}$ from c_2 using an instance of gadget (iii) in Fig. 3. And finally, we move the head one cell to the left. This is performed by testing the bit on the left of the head, deleting it from w_1 and appending it to the left of w_2, by the operations described above. All other transitions can be simulated similarly. Note that, to simulate one NExpTM transition, we need to perform several tests (that carry out in 0 time units) and to: (i) update the bit under the reading head, which takes 1 time unit with our gadgets; (ii) remove one bit from the right of w_1 (resp. left of w_2), which takes at most 3 time units and (iii) append this bit to the left of w_2 (right of w_1), which takes at most 3 time units. We conclude that each NExpTM transition can be simulate in at most 7 time units. Thus M has an accepting execution on word w (of length at most $\xi(|w|)$ iff $\mathcal{H}_M$ has an execution of duration at most $\mathbf{T} = 7 \cdot \xi(|w|)$ that reaches a location encoding an accepting control state of M. This sets the reduction.

5 Computing All the States Reachable within T Time Units

Let us now show that Theorem 2 (lifted to MHA) implies that, in an MHA, we can compute a *symbolic representation* of the set of states reachable within $\mathbf{T}$ time units. We show, by means of two examples, that this information can be used to verify meaningful properties of MHA, in particular when time-*unbounded* fixed points do not terminate.

Post *and* **Pre.** Let s be a state of an MHA with set of edges Edges. We let $\mathsf{Post}(s) = \{s' \mid \exists e \in \text{Edges}, t \in \mathbb{R}^+ : s \xrightarrow{t, e} s'\}$ and $\mathsf{Pre}(s) = \{s' \mid \exists e \in \text{Edges}, t \in \mathbb{R}^+ : s' \xrightarrow{t, e} s\}$. We further let $\mathsf{Reach}^{\le \mathbf{T}}(s) = \{s' \mid \exists \pi : s \xrightarrow{\pi} s' \wedge \mathsf{duration}(\pi) \le \mathbf{T}\}$, and $\mathsf{coReach}^{\le \mathbf{T}}(s) = \{s' \mid \exists \pi : s' \xrightarrow{\pi} s \wedge \mathsf{duration}(\pi) \le \mathbf{T}\}$ be respectively the set of states that are reachable from s (that can reach s) within $\mathbf{T}$ time units. We extend all those operators to sets of states in the obvious way. Our aim in this section is to compute effective representations of $\mathsf{Reach}^{\leq \mathbf{T}}(s)$ and $\mathsf{coReach}^{\leq \mathbf{T}}(s)$, using fixed points.

Symbolic States. To manipulate potentially infinite sets of MHA states, we need a symbolic representation that is manipulable algorithmically. We rely on the notion of *symbolic states* introduced as an *algebra of regions* in [11]. To manipulate sets of valuations, we use formulas of $(\mathbb{R}, 0, 1, +, \leq)$, i.e. the first-order logic of the reals[3], with the constants 0 and 1, the usual order $\leq$ and addition $+$ [11]. Recall that the satisfiability problem for that logic is decidable [4] and that it admits effective quantifier elimination. Furthermore, all guards of an MHA can be represented by a formula from $(\mathbb{R}, 0, 1, +, \leq)$ ranging over X. Let Ψ be a formula of $(\mathbb{R}, 0, 1, +, \leq)$, and let ν be a valuation of the free variables of Ψ. Then we write $\nu \models \Psi$ iff ν satisfies Ψ, and we let $\llbracket \Psi \rrbracket$ be the set off all valuations ν such that $\nu \models \Psi$. To emphasise the fact that a formula Ψ ranges over the set of variables X, we sometimes denote it by $\Psi(X)$.

Then a *symbolic state* of an MHA $\mathcal{H}$ with set of variables X is a function R mapping each location ℓ of $\mathcal{H}$ to a quantifier free formula of $(\mathbb{R}, 0, 1, +, \leq)$ with free variables in X, representing sets of valuations for the variables in ℓ. Formally, R represents the set of MHA states $\llbracket R \rrbracket = \{(\ell, \nu) \mid \nu \in \llbracket R(\ell) \rrbracket\}$. By abuse of notation, we assume that any formula Φ of $(\mathbb{R}, 0, 1, +, \leq)$ denotes the function f such that $f(\ell) = \Phi$ for all ℓ. Clearly, given symbolic states R_1 and R_2, one can compute symbolic states $R_1 \vee R_2$ and $R_1 \wedge R_2$ representing resp. $\llbracket R_1 \rrbracket \cup \llbracket R_2 \rrbracket$ and $\llbracket R_1 \rrbracket \cap \llbracket R_2 \rrbracket$; and one can test whether $\llbracket R_1 \rrbracket = \llbracket R_2 \rrbracket$ [11]. It is also possible (see details in the appendix) to compute Post and Pre symbolically: we let $\mathsf{post}^\sharp$ and $\mathsf{pre}^\sharp$ be effective operators, returning symbolic states, s.t. for all symbolic states R: $\llbracket \mathsf{post}^\sharp(R) \rrbracket = \mathsf{Post}(\llbracket R \rrbracket)$ and $\llbracket \mathsf{pre}^\sharp(R) \rrbracket = \mathsf{Pre}(\llbracket R \rrbracket)$.

Time-Bounded Forward and Backward Fixpoints. Let $\mathcal{H}$ be an MHA with set of variables X, and let $\mathbf{T} \in \mathbb{N}$ be a time bound. Let us augment $\mathcal{H}$ with a fresh variable t to measure time (hence the rate of t is 1 in all locations, and t is never reset). Let S be a *set of states* of $\mathcal{H}$. Then the sets $\mathsf{Reach}^{\leq \mathbf{T}}(S)$ and $\mathsf{coReach}^{\leq \mathbf{T}}(S)$ can be defined by means of fixed point equations: $\mathsf{Reach}^{\leq \mathbf{T}}(S) = \mu Y \cdot ((S \cup \mathsf{Post}(Y)) \cap \llbracket 0 \leq t \leq \mathbf{T} \rrbracket)$ and $\mathsf{coReach}^{\leq \mathbf{T}}(S) = \mu Y \cdot ((S \cup \mathsf{Pre}(Y)) \cap \llbracket 0 \leq t \leq \mathbf{T} \rrbracket)$. This observation forms the basis of our algorithm for computing symbolic states representing $\mathsf{Reach}^{\leq \mathbf{T}}(\llbracket R \rrbracket)$ and $\mathsf{coReach}^{\leq \mathbf{T}}(\llbracket R \rrbracket)$ for some symbolic state $R(X)$. Let $(F_i)_{i \geq 0}$ and $(B_i)_{i \geq 0}$ be the sequences of symbolic states defined as follows: $F_0 = B_0 = R(X) \wedge (0 \leq t \leq \mathbf{T})$; and for all $i \geq 1$: $F_i = \mathsf{post}^\sharp(F_{i-1}) \wedge (0 \leq t \leq \mathbf{T}) \vee F_{i-1}$ and $B_i = \mathsf{pre}^\sharp(B_{i-1}) \wedge (0 \leq t \leq \mathbf{T}) \vee B_{i-1}$. Note that, for all $i \geq 1$, F_i (resp. B_i) can be computed from F_{i-1} (B_{i-1}).

Proposition 10. *For all MHA $\mathcal{H}$, all symbolic states R and all time bound $\mathbf{T}$, there are k and ℓ such that $0 \leq k, \ell \leq F(\mathcal{H}, \mathbf{T})$, $\llbracket F_k \rrbracket = \llbracket F_{k+1} \rrbracket = \mathsf{Reach}^{\leq \mathbf{T}}(\llbracket R \rrbracket)$ and $\llbracket B_\ell \rrbracket = \llbracket B_{\ell+1} \rrbracket = \mathsf{coReach}^{\leq \mathbf{T}}(\llbracket R \rrbracket)$. Computing F_k and B_ℓ takes at most doubly exponential time.*

By Theorem 9, this deterministic algorithm can be considered optimal (unless NEXP-TIME=EXPTIME). Let us show, by two examples, the usefulness of our approach.

---

[3] In practice, those formulas can be manipulated as finite unions of convex polyhedra for which there exist efficient implementations, see [3] for example.

Example 1: Leaking gas burner With this example, the *time-unbounded* forward fixed-point computation does not terminate, in contrast to the time-bounded fixed-point computation. The gas burner in the example can be either *leaking* or *not leaking*. Leakages are repaired within 1 second, and no leakage can happen in the next 30 seconds after a repair. An MHA modeling this gas burner [1] is given in Fig. 4. Stopwatch y and clock t are

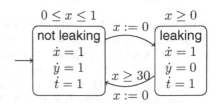

Fig. 4. The leaking gas burner

used resp. to measure the leakage time and the total elapsed time. One can show using *backward* analysis that, in any time interval of at least 60 seconds, the leakage time is at most 5% of the elapsed time [8]. The backward fixpoint is obtained after 7 iterations but the forward does not terminate.

Using forward time-bounded reachability analysis we can prove that, in all time intervals of fixed length $T \geq 60$, the leakage time is at most $\frac{T}{20}$. To prove that this property holds in *all* time intervals, we first compute, using the algorithm described above (see Proposition 10), $\mathsf{Reach}^{\leq 60}(\llbracket R \rrbracket)$, where $\llbracket R \rrbracket = \{(\ell, v) \mid \ell = \text{leaking implies } 0 \leq v(x) \leq 1\}$, i.e. R represents all possible states of the system. HYTECH computes $\mathsf{Reach}^{\leq 60}(\llbracket R \rrbracket)$ after 5 iterations of the forward time-bounded fixpoint. Then, we check that '$t = 60$ implies $y \leq \frac{60}{20} = 3$' holds, in all states of $\mathsf{Reach}^{\leq 60}(\llbracket R \rrbracket)$.

Example 2: bounded invariant Let us come back to the RHA$^{\geq 0}$ of Fig. 1 (left). Notice that all variables have a bounded invariant $[0, 1]$. The forward reachability analysis of HyTech does not terminate here because the set of reachable states is not a finite union of polyhedra, see Fig. 1 (right). Yet, the time-bounded forward fixpoint terminates for all **T** by Proposition 10. This example shows that bounding the variables is not sufficient to obtain termination while performing time-bounded analysis is.

References

1. Alur, R., Courcoubetis, C., Henzinger, T.A., Ho, P.-H.: Hybrid automata: An algorithmic approach to the specification and verification of hybrid systems. In: Grossman, R.L., Ravn, A.P., Rischel, H., Nerode, A. (eds.) HS 1991 and HS 1992. LNCS, vol. 736, Springer, Heidelberg (1993)
2. Alur, R., Dill, D.: A theory of timed automata. TTCS 126(2), 183–235 (1994)
3. Bagnara, R., Hill, P.M., Zaffanella, E.: The parma polyhedra library: Toward a complete set of numerical abstractions for the analysis and verification of hardware and software systems. Sci. Comput. Program. 72(1-2) (2008)
4. Basu, S.: New results on quantifier elimination over real closed fields and applications to constraint databases. J. ACM 46(4) (1999)
5. Brihaye, T., Doyen, L., Geeraerts, G., Ouaknine, J., Raskin, J.-F., Worrell, J.: On reachability for hybrid automata over bounded time. In: Aceto, L., Henzinger, M., Sgall, J. (eds.) ICALP 2011, Part II. LNCS, vol. 6756, pp. 416–427. Springer, Heidelberg (2011)
6. Brihaye, T., Doyen, L., Geeraerts, G., Ouaknine, J., Raskin, J.-F., Worrell, J.: Time-bounded reachability for hybrid automata: Complexity and fixpoints. Technical report CoRR abs/1211.1276, Cornell University Library, arXiv.org (2012),
http://arxiv.org/abs/1211.1276

7. Henzinger, T.A.: The theory of hybrid automata. In: LICS 1996. IEEE Computer Society (1996)
8. Henzinger, T.A., Ho, P.-H., Wong-Toi, H.: A user guide to HYTECH. In: Brinksma, E., Steffen, B., Cleaveland, W.R., Larsen, K.G., Margaria, T. (eds.) TACAS 1995. LNCS, vol. 1019, pp. 41–71. Springer, Heidelberg (1995)
9. Henzinger, T.A., Ho, P.-H., Wong-Toi, H.: Hytech: A model checker for hybrid systems. In: Grumberg, O. (ed.) CAV 1997. LNCS, vol. 1254, pp. 460–463. Springer, Heidelberg (1997)
10. Henzinger, T.A., Kopke, P.W., Puri, A., Varaiya, P.: What's decidable about hybrid automata. JCSS 57(1), 94–124 (1998)
11. Henzinger, T.A., Majumdar, R., Raskin, J.-F.: A classification of symbolic transition systems. ACM Trans. Comput. Log. 6(1), 1–32 (2005)
12. Jenkins, M., Ouaknine, J., Rabinovich, A., Worrell, J.: Alternating timed automata over bounded time. In: LICS 2010. IEEE Computer Society (2010)
13. Jha, S.K., Krogh, B.H., Weimer, J.E., Clarke, E.M.: Reachability for linear hybrid automata using iterative relaxation abstraction. In: Bemporad, A., Bicchi, A., Buttazzo, G. (eds.) HSCC 2007. LNCS, vol. 4416, pp. 287–300. Springer, Heidelberg (2007)
14. Ouaknine, J., Rabinovich, A., Worrell, J.: Time-bounded verification. In: Bravetti, M., Zavattaro, G. (eds.) CONCUR 2009. LNCS, vol. 5710, pp. 496–510. Springer, Heidelberg (2009)

An Automatic Technique for Checking the Simulation of Timed Systems

Elie Fares, Jean-Paul Bodeveix, Mamoun Filali-Amine, and Manuel Garnacho

IRIT, Université de Toulouse

Abstract. In this paper, we suggest an automatic technique for checking the timed weak simulation between timed transition systems. The technique is an observation-based method in which two timed transition systems are composed with a timed observer. A μ-calculus property that captures the timed weak simulation is then verified on the result of the composition. An interesting feature of the suggested technique is that it only relies on an untimed μ-calculus model-checker without any specific algorithm needed to analyze the result of the composition. We also show that our simulation relation supports interesting results concerning the trace inclusion and the preservation of linear properties. Finally, the technique is validated using the FIACRE/TINA toolset.

1 Introduction

The verification of real-time systems plays a major role in the design of highly trusted systems. Yet, the more complex the system in terms of space and time is, the less tractable its verification tends to be. Thus, new techniques have been suggested in order to minimize the verification cost in terms of both space and time [16,13,4]. Among these techniques, refinement is one of the most valuable concepts. Roughly speaking, we say that a concrete system C is a proven refinement of an abstract one A, if each time A is used, C can be used instead.

A wide range of refinement relations and sufficient conditions for refinement exist in the literature [31]. Accordingly, one of the most intuitive relations is trace inclusion. However, the problem of timed trace inclusion for non-deterministic systems has been proven to be undecidable if the timed automata model contains at least two clocks [27]. Since abstract specifications often involve nondeterminism, this solution is clearly not appropriate. Therefore, the need for a condition that implies the trace inclusion has emerged. Timed simulation relations have been introduced as a sufficient condition for trace inclusion [29]. This class of relations is also decidable [29].

In this paper, we study the problem of automatically proving the timed weak simulation between timed transition systems. First, we start by giving a definition of the timed weak simulation and showing that it implies finite trace inclusion which preserves linear safety properties. We also show that the parallel operator of our constrained timed systems (CTTS see Section 2.2) is also monotonic w.r.t our timed simulation. Second, in order to automatically check

D. Van Hung and M. Ogawa (Eds.): ATVA 2013, LNCS 8172, pp. 71–86, 2013.

the timed simulation between systems, we follow a standard technique in model checking which is mostly used in the verification of timed properties. The idea is in fact an observation-based method in which A and C are composed with an observer. The result of their composition is then tested using a μ-calculus property that captures the timed weak simulation definition. We show in this paper that for a given class of systems, the μ-calculus criterion is sound and complete. Furthermore, the approach is validated using the FIACRE/TINA toolset [10,7]. We also show that our technique can be used in real life applications by illustrating it on an industrial-inspired example.

To the best of our knowledge, the use of a μ-calculus property in order to verify the simulation in the timed context is new. Furthermore, following our technique, some of the restrictions that exist in the verification of timed weak simulation are relaxed (see Related Work). Another advantage of our approach is that it is self-contained and relies exclusively on existing model checking tools, which means that no specific algorithm for the simulation verification is given.

The paper is organized as follows. In Section 2, we define our behavioral framework which is based on timed transition systems. In Section 3, we briefly recall the syntax and the semantics of the μ-calculus logic. In Section 4, we give our simulation definition along with its properties. We present in Section 5 the core of our verification technique in which we present the observers along with the μ-calculus property. Afterwards, in Section 6, we discuss the experimental results and give an example of the application of the technique before presenting the related work and concluding the paper in Section 7 and Section 8 respectively.

2   Concrete/Abstract Systems

In this section, we present our considered systems. We start by defining the semantic model (Section 2.1) along with the properties it needs to fulfill for the sake of our simulation verification technique. We then give a finite representation of the semantic model (Section 2.2) and some sufficient conditions that imply the properties given at the semantic level.

2.1   Semantic Model

Definition 1 (Timed Transition System TTS). *Let Δ be a time domain [21], e.g., $\mathbb{R}^+$, L a label set containing the silent action τ, a Timed Transition System TTS [9] is a tuple $\langle Q, Q^0, \rightarrow \rangle$ where Q is a set of states, $Q^0 \subseteq Q$ is the set of initial states, and $\rightarrow$ is a transition relation $\subseteq Q \times (L \cup \Delta) \times Q$. We write $q \xrightarrow{l} q'$ for $(q, l, q') \in \rightarrow$. We require standard properties for $\rightarrow$, namely time determinism, reflexivity, additivity, and continuity as defined in [15].*

We define $q \xrightarrow{a*} q' \triangleq q \xrightarrow{a} q_1 \xrightarrow{a} q_2 \cdots \xrightarrow{a} q'$ and write $q \xrightarrow{ab} q''$ if there exists q' such that $q \xrightarrow{a} q' \xrightarrow{b} q''$ and $q \xrightarrow{b} q''$ for $q \xrightarrow{\tau*b} q'$. We define as well $q \overset{d}{\Longrightarrow}{}^* q' \triangleq \exists q_0 \xrightarrow{\delta_0} q_0' \xrightarrow{\tau} q_1 \xrightarrow{\delta_1} q_1' \xrightarrow{\tau} q_2 \cdots \xrightarrow{\delta_n} q_n'$ such that $\Sigma_{i=0}^n \delta_i = d \wedge q = q_0 \wedge q' = q_n'$ and write $q \overset{d}{\Longrightarrow}{}^+ q'$ when $n > 0$ (there exists at least one τ).

Definition 2 (Timed Trace). *For $\alpha_i \in L - \{\tau\}$ and $\delta_i \in \Delta$, a timed trace is either a finite sequence $((\delta_i \alpha_i)_{i<n})$ or an infinite sequence $((\delta_i \alpha_i)_{i \in \mathbb{N}})$. We denote Tr the set of such traces.*

Definition 3 (TTS Timed Trace). *Given a TTS and I a (finite or infinite) initial segment of $\mathbb{N}$, a timed trace $((\delta_i \alpha_i)_{i \in I})$ is accepted by the TTS if there exists an initial (starting with $q^0 \in Q^0$) TTS execution $((q_i \overset{\delta_i e_i}{\to} q_{i+1})_{i \in I'})$ where I' is an initial segment of $\mathbb{N}$, $e_i \in L$, and every step in the timed execution corresponds to a transition in the TTS and if I' is finite, the last state has no outgoing transition. The trace is then the sequence of labels of the execution after the elimination of τ events and combination of consecutive δ. We denote by $Traces(T)$ the set of traces of T and $Traces_{fin}(T)$ the set of finite prefixes of elements of $Traces(T)$.*

Definition 4 (τ-Divergence). *Given a set of labels L, a TTS $\langle Q, Q^0, \to \rangle$ is τ-divergent if for all $q \in Q$ and for all $\delta \in \Delta$, there exists q' such that $q \overset{\delta}{\Longrightarrow}^* q'$.*

This means that we require that time can always diverge via τ events. Namely, for all d, there always exists a $\tau\delta$ execution that advances to the date d.

Definition 5 (τ Non-Zeno path). *A TTS is said to have a τ Zeno path if it has an infinite time-convergent execution sequence $(\Sigma_{i=0}^{\infty} \delta_i < \infty)$ in which only τ events are executed. A TTS is τ non-Zeno if it does not have such execution sequence, that is all infinite execution sequences of τ actions are time divergent $(\Sigma_{i=0}^{\infty} \delta_i = \infty)$.*

The hypothesis of τ non-Zeno will be used to show inductively that a property is preserved through the elapsing of time interleaved with τ transitions.

Lemma 1 (τ Non-Zenoness Characterization). *We give an induction-based definition of the τ non-Zenoness of a TTS [28]. We denote as $P_\delta(s)$ a property P that holds in a state s at time δ. The TTS is τ non-Zeno iff it satisfies :*

$$\frac{\overbrace{P_0(q_0)}^{(1)} \wedge \left(\begin{array}{l} \forall q \in Q \ \forall \delta_2 < \delta_1, q_0 \overset{\delta_2}{\to} q \wedge P_{\delta_2}(q) \Rightarrow \\ \underbrace{\exists q', q \overset{\delta_1 - \delta_2}{\to} q' \wedge P_{\delta_1}(q')}_{(2)} \vee \overbrace{\exists \delta_3 \in [\delta_2, \delta_1], \exists q', q \overset{\delta_3 - \delta_2}{\Longrightarrow}^+ q' \wedge P_{\delta_3}(q')}^{(3)} \end{array} \right)}{\exists q', q_0 \overset{\delta_1}{\Longrightarrow}^* q' \wedge P_{\delta_1}(q')}$$

The τ non-Zenoness property leads to an induction principle. Here, we say that for a property P to be true in δ, then it is sufficient to show that :

1. P is true at the current instant (1) and,
2. if P is true at a given time, then P must be made true after either a time transition reaching δ (2) or a τ transition (possibly preceded by a delay) (3).

This characterization relies on the fact that time is unbounded ($\forall x \in \Delta, \exists y > x$).

2.2 Constrained Time Transition System (CTTS)

We give the definition of a CTTS which is a syntactic finite representation for the TTS. We also give the properties that need to be satisfied by this finite representation in order to satisfy the assumptions made at the semantic level. A CTTS is close to the abstract model of [20] which introduces the notion of time using time intervals associated to ports.

Definition 6 (Constrained Time Transition System). *Given a set of labels L and the set of intervals $\mathbf{I}$ over the time domain Δ, a CTTS is defined as $\langle Q, Q^0, T, L, \rho : T \to 2^{Q \times Q}, \lambda : T \to L, \iota : T \twoheadrightarrow \mathbf{I}, \rhd \subseteq T \times T \rangle$ where Q denotes the set of states, $Q^0 \subseteq Q$ is the set of initial states, T denotes the set of transitions, ρ maps each transition to a set of state couples (source,target), λ associates each transition with its label, ι associates a time interval to each transition labeled with a τ (the visible events are not constrained) and $\rhd$ denotes a time reset relation between two transitions. We write $t : q \xrightarrow{l} q'$ for $(q, q') \in \rho(t) \wedge l = \lambda(t)$.*

We comment on the reset relation $\rhd$. Each transition of a CTTS is associated to a clock at the semantic level. An enabled transition can be fired when the clock belongs to the time interval of the transition. Whether the firing of a transition resets the clocks of the enabled transitions or not is governed by $\rhd$: if $t \rhd t'$, then the firing of t resets the clock of t'. The intuition behind the reset relation stems from the semantics of Time Petri Nets [9]. Based on the intermediary semantics of Time Petri Nets, $t \rhd t'$ would hold for any pair of transitions sharing an input place. Conversely, based on the atomic semantics, $t \rhd t'$ only holds for $t = t'$. In our model, we explicitly define the $\rhd$ relation for each transition.

CTTS Example. In Fig 1, we show how a CTTS is made out of a FIACRE system (High level). The example shows the intuition behind our choice of representing a transition as set of state pairs. We note in the example that t_0 does not reset the clock of t_1. Otherwise, t_1 would never be fired since its lower bound would never be reached.

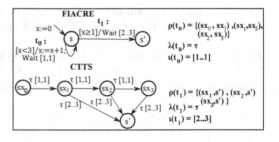

Fig. 1. Example of CTTS

CTTS Semantics. This semantics is defined through three rules: DIS for discrete events, 0-DLY and DLY for time elapse events.

For $(v + \delta)(t) = v(t) + \delta$, $\overleftarrow{I} \triangleq \{x \in \Delta \mid \exists y \in \Delta, x + y \in I\}$ being the downward closure of the interval I and $(q, q') \hookrightarrow t' \triangleq q \notin \mathbf{dom}(\rho(t')) \wedge q' \in \mathbf{dom}(\rho(t'))$ denoting that the transition t' is newly enabled by the transition $q \to q'$, the semantics of a CTTS $\mathcal{T} = \langle Q, Q^0, T, L, \rho, \lambda, \iota, \rhd \rangle$ is defined as a TTS $[\![\mathcal{T}]\!] = \langle Q \times (T \to \Delta), (Q^0 \times \{t : T \mapsto 0\}), \to \rangle$ such that $\to$ is defined as :

$$\frac{t : q \xrightarrow{l} q', \, v(t) \in \iota(t) \wedge \forall t', v'(t') = \begin{cases} 0 & \text{if } (q,q') \hookrightarrow t' \vee t \triangleright t' \\ v(t') & \text{else} \end{cases}}{(q,v) \xrightarrow{l} (q',v')} \text{ D\textsc{is}}$$

$$\frac{}{(q,v) \xrightarrow{0} (q,v)} \text{ 0-D\textsc{ly}} \qquad \frac{\forall t \in T, q \in \mathbf{dom}(\rho(t)) \Rightarrow v(t) + \delta \in \overleftarrow{\iota(t)}}{(q,v) \xrightarrow{\delta} (q,v+\delta)} \text{ D\textsc{ly}}$$

Note that the time properties of the TTS are satisfied by the CTTS semantics.

Definition 7 (CTTS Property Satisfaction). *Given a linear temporal formula φ and a CTTS T, we say that T satisfies φ, denoted by $T \models \varphi$, if $\forall tr, (tr \in Traces(\llbracket T \rrbracket) \Rightarrow tr \models \varphi)$.*

Thus, a CTTS satisfies the property φ if all its traces satisfy φ.

Definition 8 (CTTS Composition). *Given $CTTS_1 = \langle Q_1, Q_1^0, T_1, L, \rho_1, \lambda_1, \iota_1, \triangleright_1 \rangle$, $CTTS_2 = \langle Q_2, Q_2^0, T_2, L, \rho_2, \lambda_2, \iota_2, \triangleright_2 \rangle$ and a set of labels $S \subseteq L$, their composition [1] $CTTS_1 \underset{S}{\|} CTTS_2$ is defined as $\langle Q_1 \times Q_2, Q_1^0 \times Q_2^0, T, L, \rho, \lambda, \iota, \triangleright \rangle$ where T [2] is defined as :*

$$\frac{t_1 : q_1 \xrightarrow{l_1} q_1', \, l_1 \notin S}{t_1 \uparrow_1 : (q_1, q_2) \xrightarrow{l_1} (q_1', q_2)} \text{ I\textsc{nterleaving}}_L \qquad \frac{t_2 : q_2 \xrightarrow{l_2} q_2', \, l_2 \notin S}{t_2 \uparrow_2 : (q_1, q_2) \xrightarrow{l_2} (q_1, q_2')} \text{ I\textsc{nterleaving}}_R$$

$$\frac{t_1 : q_1 \xrightarrow{l} q_1', t_2 : q_2 \xrightarrow{l} q_2', l \in S}{t_1 \odot t_2 : (q_1, q_2) \xrightarrow{l} (q_1', q_2')} \text{ S\textsc{ynchronous}}$$

The visible events are not time constrained. Thus, only the τ events may be associated to time intervals. ι is only defined on τ transitions. The transitions of the resulting CTTS are associated to the same time intervals they had before the application of the composition operation. Formally, this is defined as :

$$\iota(t \uparrow_1) = \iota(t) \text{ if } \lambda(t) = \tau \qquad Time_L \qquad \iota(t \uparrow_2) = \iota(t) \text{ if } \lambda(t) = \tau \qquad Time_R$$

For $t_i, t_i' \in T_i$ and $i = \{1,2\}$, the composition of the clock-reset relation $\triangleright$ is defined as :

$$\frac{t_i \triangleright t_i'}{t_i \uparrow_i \triangleright t_i' \uparrow_i} (1) \qquad \frac{t_i \triangleright t_i'}{t_1 \odot t_2 \triangleright t_i' \uparrow_i} (2) \qquad \frac{t_i \triangleright t_i'}{t_i \uparrow_i \triangleright t_1' \odot t_2'} (3)$$

$$\frac{t_1 \triangleright t_1' \quad t_2 \triangleright t_2'}{t_1 \odot t_2 \triangleright t_1' \odot t_2' \quad t_1 \odot t_2 \triangleright t_1' \odot t_2'} (4)$$

The reset-clock rules mean that if before the composition a transition t resets the clock of another transition t', then after the composition the resulting transition made out of t (either by the *SYNCHRONOUS* rule or by either one of the *INTERLEAVING* rules) will reset the clock of the t' transition.

---

[1] We write $\|$ when S=L and $\|\|$ when $S = \emptyset$.

[2] T is a disjoint union of $T_1 \times T_2 \uplus T_1 \uplus T_2$ with $\odot \uparrow_1 \uparrow_2$ as constructors.

The intuition of the rule (4) is again based on semantics of Time Petri Nets and is illustrated in Fig 2. Consider that the transitions t_1 and t'_1 synchronize with t_2 and t'_2. In this example, t_1 consumes a resource used by t'_1, thus consuming the resource of the composition of t'_1 and t'_2. Consuming a resource in the context of Time Petri Nets is translated to a reset.

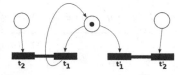

Fig. 2. Reset Composition Rule (4)

Property 1 (Bisimilar States). Given a CTTS T, two states (q, v) and (q, v') in $[T]$ that associate the same valuations (w.r.t v and v') to enabled τ transitions are bisimilar.

This means that the states (q, v) and (q, v') can only differ in the valuation associated to τ transitions that are not enabled in q. However the valuations of clocks associated to transitions labeled by visible events can differ because they are unconstrained. The proof of this property is given in [18].

Definition 9 (1-τ). *A CTTS is called 1-τ if it does not have two successive τ actions. Formally,* $\forall t, t'\ t : q \xrightarrow{\tau} q' \land t' : q' \xrightarrow{l} q'' \Rightarrow l \neq \tau$.

Definition 10 (Upper Closure). *A CTTS is called upper bounded closed if its upper bounded intervals are closed .*

Property 2 (Upper Closure Preservation). Given two upper bounded closed $CTTS_1$ and $CTTS_2$ and a set of synchronization labels S, their composition $CTTS_1 \|_S CTTS_2$ is also upper bounded closed.

3 μ-Calculus

In this section, we present the μ-Calculus logic. The use of this logic is motivated by its ability to naturally express the definition of various notions of untimed simulations [19]. This cannot be done in other logics containing similar operators and quantifiers like CTL [17].

μ-Calculus Syntax. Let Var be a set of variable names, denoted by Z, Y, ...; let Prop be a set of atomic propositions, typically denoted by P, Q,...; and let L be a set of labels, typically denoted by a, b, ... The set of μ-calculus (L_μ) [11] formulas (w.r.t. Var, Prop,L) is defined as $\varphi ::= \top \mid P \mid Z \mid \varphi_1 \land \varphi_2 \mid [a]\varphi \mid \neg\varphi \mid \nu Z.\varphi$. Dual operators are derived, mainly : $\langle a \rangle \varphi \equiv \neg[a]\neg\varphi$ and $\mu Z.\varphi(Z) \equiv \neg\nu Z.\neg\varphi(Z)$. The meaning of $[a]\varphi$ is that φ holds after all a-actions.

μ-Calculus Semantics. The models for the μ-calculus are defined over a structure $\mathfrak{S}$ of the form $\langle S, L, T, v \rangle$ where $\langle S, L, T \rangle$ is a labeled transition system and $v : Prop \rightarrow 2^S$ is a valuation function that maps each atomic proposition $P \in$ Prop to sets of states where P holds. Given a structure $\mathfrak{S}$ and a function $\mathfrak{V} : Var \rightarrow 2^S$ that maps the variables to sets of states in the transition system, the set $\|\varphi\|_{\mathfrak{V}}^{\mathfrak{S}}$ of states satisfying a formula φ is defined as follows :

- $\|\top\|_{\mathfrak{V}}^{\mathfrak{S}} = S$, $\|P\|_{\mathfrak{V}}^{\mathfrak{S}} = v(P)$, $\|X\|_{\mathfrak{V}}^{\mathfrak{S}} = \mathfrak{V}(X)$, $\|\neg\varphi\|_{\mathfrak{V}}^{\mathfrak{S}} = S - \|\varphi\|_{\mathfrak{V}}^{\mathfrak{S}}$.
- $\|\varphi_1 \wedge \varphi_2\|_{\mathfrak{V}}^{\mathfrak{S}} = \|\varphi_1\|_{\mathfrak{V}}^{\mathfrak{S}} \cap \|\varphi_2\|_{\mathfrak{V}}^{\mathfrak{S}}$.
- $\|[a]\varphi\|_{\mathfrak{V}}^{\mathfrak{S}} = \{s \mid \forall t, s \xrightarrow{a} t \Rightarrow t \in \|\varphi\|_{\mathfrak{V}}^{\mathfrak{S}}\}$.
- $\|\nu X.\varphi\|_{\mathfrak{V}}^{\mathfrak{S}} = \bigcup\{Q \in 2^S \mid Q \subseteq \|\varphi\|_{\mathfrak{V}[X \mapsto Q]}^{\mathfrak{S}}\}$ where $\mathfrak{V}[X \mapsto Q]$ is the valuation which maps X to Q and otherwise agrees with $\mathfrak{V}$.

We define the notation $\mathbf{EF}_L P = \mu Z.P \vee \bigvee_{l \in L}\langle l \rangle Z$. This is read as there exists (expressed by $\langle l \rangle$) a finite path labeled by elements of L after which a state is reached where P holds.

4 Timed Weak Simulation and Its Properties

Definition 11 (Timed Weak Simulation). *Given the set of labels L and two TTS $A = \langle Q_a, Q_a^0, \rightarrow_a \rangle$ and $C = \langle Q_c, Q_c^0, \rightarrow_c \rangle$ defined over L, a timed weak simulation between them $\precsim$ is the largest relation such that :*

$$\forall q_c \; q_a, q_c \precsim q_a \Rightarrow$$

E. $\forall q_c', e, q_c \xrightarrow{e}_c q_c' \Rightarrow \exists q_a', q_a \xRightarrow{e}_a q_a' \wedge q_c' \precsim q_a'$ *(Visible Events)*

T. $\forall q_c', q_c \xrightarrow{\tau}_c q_c' \Rightarrow q_c' \precsim q_a$ *(τ Events)*

D. $\forall q_c' \; \delta, q_c \xrightarrow{\delta}_c q_c' \Rightarrow \exists q_a', q_a \xRightarrow{\delta}_a^* q_a' \wedge q_c' \precsim q_a'$ *(Delay)*

We say that $C \precsim A$ if $\forall q_C^0 \in Q_C^0, \exists q_A^0 \in Q_A^0$ such that $(q_C^0, q_A^0) \in \precsim$. We say that a simulation holds between two CTTSs if it holds for their semantics.

Theorem 1 (Trace Inclusion). *Given two CTTSs, A and C, if $C \precsim A$ then $Traces_{fin}(\llbracket C \rrbracket) \subseteq Traces_{fin}(\llbracket A \rrbracket)$.*

The trace inclusion proof is a standard one in the untimed context. Due to the lack of space here, an extension of this proof is given in [18].

Definition 12 (Safety Properties). *A safety property P is defined as a linear time property such that any trace σ where P does not hold contains a bad prefix. Formally, this is defined as follows [8] :*

$$safety(P) \triangleq \forall \sigma \in Tr, \sigma \not\models P \Rightarrow \exists i \text{ such that } \forall \sigma' \in Tr, \sigma_i = \sigma_i' \Rightarrow \sigma' \not\models P$$

where σ_i is the prefix of size i of σ.

Theorem 2 (Property Preservation). *Given two CTTSs A and C, if $C \precsim A$ then any safety linear time property of A is also a property of C.*

Proof. Let P be a safety property such that $A \models P$. We need to prove that $C \models P$. Let $t_c \in Traces(\llbracket C \rrbracket)$. Suppose that $t_c \not\models P$. As P is a safety property, there exists a finite prefix t of t_c such that for all $t' \in Tr$, if t is a prefix of t' then $t' \not\models P$. As t is a prefix of t_c, $t \in Traces_{fin}(\llbracket C \rrbracket)$. As $C \precsim A$, we have $t \in Traces_{fin}(\llbracket A \rrbracket)$. Thus, there exists a $t_a \in Traces(\llbracket A \rrbracket)$ having t as prefix. By choosing $t' = t_a$ we contradict $A \models P$.

The parallel operator is monotonic w.r.t our simulation. Given a component C inside of a composition $C \parallel C_1 \parallel C_2...C_n$ the monotony of $\parallel$ is informally described as : if C is replaced by a component C' such that C' simulates C, then $C' \parallel C_1 \parallel C_2...C_n$ simulates $C \parallel C_1 \parallel C_2...C_n$. This is described as follows :

Theorem 3 (Simulation Compositionality). *Given the CTTSs A_1, A_2, C_1 and C_2 and the set of labels S, we have $C_1 \precsim A_1 \wedge C_2 \precsim A_2 \Rightarrow C_1 \parallel C_2 \underset{S}{\precsim} A_1 \parallel A_2$.*

This proof is made by showing that each transition of $C_1 \underset{S}{\parallel} C_2$ has a corresponding transition in $A_1 \underset{S}{\parallel} A_2$. A complete proof is given in [18].

5   Weak Simulation Verification

5.1   Composing the Abstract/Concrete Systems

Our technique shares its grounds and features with model-checking techniques. Indeed, the first step consists in composing the abstract with the concrete system. Given an abstract CTTS $A = \langle Q_a, Q_a^0, T_a, L, \rho_a, \lambda_a, \iota_a, \triangleright_a \rangle$ and a concrete one $C = \langle Q_c, Q_c^0, T_c, L, \rho_c, \lambda_c, \iota_c, \triangleright_c \rangle$, the two systems are composed after having renamed the events of the two systems by indexing the abstract(resp. concrete) ones by a (resp. c). The composition is thus made asynchronous (Fig. 3) in order to be able to observe all the transitions of the concrete system and verify whether they are simulated by the abstract system. The synchronous

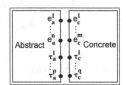

Fig. 3. Systems

composition is not applicable because unmatched concrete transitions may disappear in the product.

5.2   Untimed Weak Simulation Verification

The composition result is analyzed to check the weak simulation between A and C. To do so, the following *Weak Simulation* criterion [19] which corresponds intuitively to the first two rules of the relation $\precsim$ is verified on $A \mid\mid\mid C$:

$$\forall q_a^0 \in Q_a^0 \exists q_c^0 \in Q_c^0, (q_a^0, q_c^0) \models \nu X. \overbrace{\bigwedge_i [e_c^i](\mathbf{EF}_{\tau_a} \langle e_a^i \rangle X)}^{1} \wedge \overbrace{\bigwedge_j [\tau_c^j]X}^{2}$$

(1) means that for each concrete event e_c^i and for each transition labeled by this concrete event e_c^i, there exists a path of a number of abstract local events τ_a that leads eventually to a transition labeled by the abstract event e_a^i such that the target verifies recursively (1) and (2).

(2) means that after each transition labeled with a concrete local event τ_c^j the simulation is maintained.

5.3 Extension to the Timed Context

The already seen property could not be used directly in the timed context since it assumes that concrete and abstract events are composed asynchronously, while the composition of time transitions is necessarily synchronous because time advances at the same rate at the two sides of the composition. Two alternatives are possible. The first is to specify these timing constraints in a timed variant of μ-calculus. The second is to specify the timing aspects with timed observers, to compose the analyzed system with these observers, and to make use of an untimed logic. We follow the second technique. For this purpose, we define two observers (Fig. 4 and 5) :

1. The Control Observer consists in observing the control aspects of the two systems. Namely, for each concrete event, the control observer tries to find a matching abstract event that happens at the same time.
2. The Time Observer models the elapsing of time in the two systems.

In the two observers, the reset relations are empty. This way, the observers never impact the reset relations defined in the abstract and the concrete systems.

Control Observer. The Control Observer is depicted in Fig 4. At the initial state **ok**, the observer synchronizes with either one of the events e_a^i, τ_c^i or e_c^i. When synchronizing with any of e_i^a the observer signals an error (**err** state) since a concrete event is not yet found. When synchronizing with any of τ_c^i the observer maintains the state **ok**. Finally, when synchronizing with the concrete events e_c^i, it tries to match them with the abstract events e_a^i. After a concrete event e_c^i is received, the observer transits to the state **wait**$_i$ meaning that it now awaits for a matching abstract event e_a^i. At this point, the following scenarios may happen :

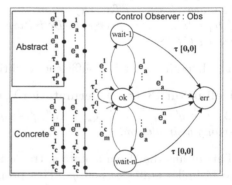

Fig. 4. Control Observer

- A matching abstract event is found and the observer transits back to **ok**.
- The abstract system violates the timing of the concrete system and the observer transits to the state **err**. That is, a matching abstract event is not possible at the same time as the corresponding concrete event. This is modeled by signaling an error in 0 units of time (u.t.). Hence, in case a matching event is found in 0 u.t., we would reach a non-deterministic choice between transiting back to **ok** or also to **err**. The two transitions would then be present in the composition process. This choice is later resolved in the μ-calculus property by searching for a path that satisfies the simulation and thus ignoring the error transition.

Time Observer. The control observer only checks whether two corresponding events could happen simultaneously. However, it mentions nothing about when an elapsing of time occurs. This leads to the definition of an additional observer **Time Observer** (Fig. 5) in which two aspects are modeled. First, at the initial state evt0, only the transitions that are firable in 0 time can occur. This is done by specifying a

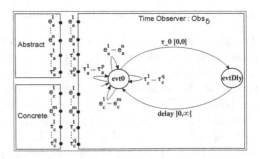

Fig. 5. Time Observer

concurrent choice between a timed event τ_0 constrained with $[0,0]$ and all the events of the abstract and concrete systems. Second, it makes visible the implicit elapsing of time. At the state evtDly, on each elapsing of time, a timed event delay associated with the constraint $]0,\infty[$ is signaled. This event is later used by the μ-calculus property as an time elapsing marker.

Assumption 1 (Concrete/Abstract). *A concrete system is any upper bounded closed CTTS (Definition 10). An abstract system is any τ non-Zeno (Definition 5), τ divergent (Definition 4), 1-τ (Definition 9), upper bounded closed CTTS.*

The hypothesis 1-τ is a sufficient condition for the $\tau - \delta$ permutation property.

Definition 13 ($\tau - \delta$ Permutation). *Given a TTS, for all q q' q_1 $q_2 \in Q, \delta \in \Delta$, $q \xrightarrow{\delta} q' \wedge q \xrightarrow{\tau} q_1 \xrightarrow{\delta} q_2 \Rightarrow \exists q'', q' \xrightarrow{\tau} q'' \wedge q_2 \sim q''$ where $\sim$ denotes the timed strong bisimulation.*

This means that from a state q, transitions τ and δ may be exchanged leading to bisimilar states q_2 and q''. This property is close to the persistency of [26] that says that time cannot suppress the ability to do an action. However, our requirement that $q_2 \sim q''$ is stronger. This property is not true in general since the clocks newly reset at the state q'' have different values at q_2. The 1-τ hypothesis is a sufficient condition on the CTTSs so that the clock differences at q_2 and q'' would not affect the overall execution of the system.

Theorem 4 (1-τ is a sufficient condition for $\tau - \delta$ permutation). *Given a 1-τ CTTS $\mathcal{T}$, its semantics $[\![\mathcal{T}]\!]$ verifies the $\tau - \delta$ permutation.*

The proof of this theorem is given in [18].

Timed Weak Simulation Verification. The check of timed weak simulation consists in a property verified on the composition of the abstract, the concrete and the observers $(A \;|||\; C) \;\|\; (Obs \;\|\; Obs_\delta)$ where Obs is the control observer and Obs_δ is the time observer. The simulation of time transitions consists in verifying whether each delay made by the concrete system can also be made by the abstract one. But unlike the asynchronous composition in the untimed context with which we were able to alternate between the occurrence of the concrete and the abstract events, time is always synchronous in each of A, C and the two observers. Alternating concrete and abstract events does not apply to time transitions. The $TimedWeakSimulation(e_c, e_a, \tau_c, \tau_a)$ criterion is :

$$
\forall q_a^0 \in Q_a^0 \exists q_c^0 \in Q_c^0, (q_a^0, q_c^0, ok, evt0) \models \nu X. \overbrace{Obs\ in\ ok \wedge Obs_\delta\ in\ evt0\ \wedge}^{(1)}
$$
$$
\underbrace{\bigwedge_i [e_c^i](\mathbf{EF}_{\tau_a}\langle e_a^i \rangle X) \wedge \bigwedge_j [\tau_c^j]X}_{(2)Weak\ Simulation} \wedge \overbrace{(\mathbf{EF}_{\tau_a}\langle delay \rangle \top)}^{(3)} \Rightarrow \mathbf{EF}_{\tau_a}(\langle delay \rangle \top \wedge [delay]X)
$$

This property characterizes a set of product states to which the initial state must belong. This set of states is defined over the composition of states of A,C and the two observers. We comment on the *Timed Weak Simulation* criterion :

- (1) denotes the acceptance of a concrete event at current time.
- (2) is the untimed weak simulation criterion.
- (3) denotes that if time can elapse (delay event) in the product via a sequence of τ abstract events -meaning that time can also elapse in the concrete system since the abstract is τ divergent- then time may elapse and for all possible delay events the simulation holds after a number of τ abstract events. In this part of the formula, $\langle delay \rangle \top$ means that in the current state, it is possible to do a transition labeled with the *delay* event.

The proof of the correctness of the μ-calculus criterion w.r.t the mathematical definition of the timed weak simulation is based on the comparison between two relations defined as the largest relations which can also be seen as the greatest fixed points of monotone set functions. The timed weak simulation criterion is correct without the hypothesis $1 - \tau$. This is why we observe τ sequences. However it is not complete. Due to the lack of space, this proof is given in [18]. It has been also formalized and validated in the proof assistant Coq [30]. The complete Coq proof is found at [3].

Discussion on the Assumptions. We discuss our major restrictions :

1. τ non-Zenoness and τ divergence: these two are standard assumptions made on timed systems. In our context, they guarantee the progress of time in the abstract system. This is necessary in our composition-based method because time is always synchronous. Blocking time in the abstract system could result in blocking time in the whole composition and hide concrete delays.
2. No successive τ transitions : permitting τ transitions in A complicates the verification of the timed weak simulation, because in this case, any delay in C can be matched by a series of delays in A separated by τ transitions [12]. Moreover, with our 1-τ restriction, general modeling techniques of real time systems are still permitted. For instance, specifying an upper bound of a global event e is made by a choice between a timed local event τ and the event e. Specifying a lower bound of a global event e is made by a sequential execution of a timed local event τ and e.

6   Experimental Results

The technique is validated using the FIACRE/TINA toolset (Fig 6). The systems and the observers are written in FIACRE (captured here by a CTTS) and the μ-calculus property is verified on the FIACRE model using the model checker TINA. The FIACRE systems are adapted to the input language of

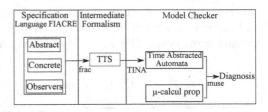

Fig. 6. Approach

TINA thanks to a translation to TTS. TINA generates a time abstracted automaton, that preserves branching properties, on which the μ-calculus property is verified.

6.1   Example of Application

The example is a simplification of an industrial use case that is used to illustrate the BPEL web-services composition language [6].

Abstract and Concrete Modeling. The abstract specification Fig. 7 describes that upon the reception of the purchase request, the process initiates the treatment of the command which takes at most 8 u.t.. Afterwards, either a successful response is sent or the command is simply dropped. A potential refinement of this specification is a composition of three entities (Fig. 8).

Fig. 7. Specification

Upon receiving a purchase order, the management consults the inventory where the stock is checked in 0 to 4 u.t.. In case of availability of the products, the inventory department sends the shipping price to the financial department before sending the result to management. Management then sends

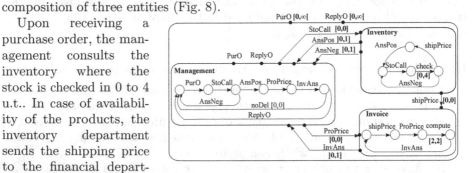

Fig. 8. Purchase Treatment

the products price to the financial department where the final price is computed in 2 u.t.. This price is then given to the management and an immediate response is sent to the customer. The transitions of the abstract/concrete system reset the clocks of all the others.

Simulation Verification. After renaming the events of the systems ($PurO_a$, $ReplyO_a$, $PurO_c$, $ReplyO_c$, ...), they are composed with the two observers. The composition process results in 184 states and 694 transitions. This process is then model checked by an instantiation of the timed weak simulation criterion 5.3 with $e_a = \{PurO_a, ReplyO_a\}$, $e_c = \{PurO_c, ReplyO_c\}$, $\tau_a = \{treat_a\}$ and $\tau_c = \{ShipPrice, ProPrice, InvAns, compute, StoCall, AnsPos, AnsNeg, check, noDel\}$.

The set of states returned by the property contains the initial state of the process. The simulation is then verified. Now suppose that the time interval of compute is changed to $[3, 3]$. In this case, the verification of the μ-calculus property does not hold. This is because the concrete system violates the time allowed by the specification. Finally, the example may be found at [2].

7 Related Work

Even though the study of simulation relations have reached a mature level, timed simulation verification is still an open research subject. Interesting results have been elaborated for different timed formalisms ranging from timed transition systems, to timed automata [5,25], and timed input output automata TIOA [23,14]. However, a less tackled aspect of this research is the automatic verification of timed simulations and especially timed weak simulations. A work which resembles ours appears in [22] in the context of the Uppaal [24] tool. A timed simulation for fully observable and deterministic abstract models is reduced to a reachability problem. This is done via a composition with a testing automaton monitoring whether the behavior of the concrete system is within the bounds of the abstract system and then by checking whether an undesired state is never reached. Compared to this result, we do not restrict our abstract systems to deterministic ones. Furthermore, our abstract systems are not fully observable.

Probably the most complete work is the one of [12,14] which led to the ECDAR tool [1]. In this tool, a timed (weak) simulation verification between two TIOAs is supported. The verification is done via a game-based algorithm between the abstract and the concrete systems [12]. Clearly, a TIOA is different in nature from timed transitions systems regarding its input/output semantics. However, their restriction that the abstract systems does not have any τ actions is relaxed in our technique to no successive τ actions. Moreover, our restriction to upper bounded closed CTTSs can be found in their formalism in the form of restricting the TIOAs states invariants constraints to $clock \leq constant$. Finally, unlike theirs, in our technique no specific algorithm is written to analyze the result of the abstract/concrete composition.

Finally, μ-calculus properties were used as a mechanism to capture and to check simulation relations in the untimed context [19]. The Mec 5 model checker, which handles specifications written in Altarica, embeds the μ-calculus logic as a support for properties verifications on Altarica models. This allows users to check weak/strong simulation and bisimulation relations.

8   Conclusion

We have presented an automatic technique for checking the timed weak simulation between timed transition systems originating from CTTS systems. The technique is based on the idea of composing the analyzed systems with observers and then model check their result using a μ-calculus property which captures the timed weak simulation definition. To the best of our knowledge, this is an original approach. Our criterion is sound and complete for a subclass of timed systems. This, along with all the paper results, have been proven using Coq.

Due to the lack of space and for clarification purposes, we applied our technique on a rather simple, but yet a complete example. For the interested readers, an illustration of the technique is made on a more elaborated example in [18] where the technique is adopted to prove the simulation between FIACRE systems translated from BPEL. The initial process consists of around 7K states and 15K transitions with an execution time of 7 seconds while the product process results in around 290K states and 874K transitions with an execution time of 70 seconds. The verification time of the μ-calculus property is 27 seconds.

On another matter, the specification of the observers and the property is manual for now. However, an automatic generation of these two is obtained directly from the alphabet of the processes..

For our future work, we are currently looking into eliminating the 1-τ restriction. Another complementary work pertains to extending our simulation so that it preserves all linear time properties. Finally, it would be insightful to investigate whether the theoretical results for timed automata can be applied to FIACRE systems (CTTS), or whether our simulation verification technique can be applied to timed automata. Such a study is promising since both CTTS and Timed Automata rely on the same semantical framework.

References

1. http://ecdar.cs.aau.dk/
2. http://www.irit.fr/~Elie.Fares/fiacre/refinement/
3. http://www.irit.fr/~Jean-Paul.Bodeveix/COQ/Refinement/
4. Alur, R., Dang, T., Ivančić, F.: Predicate abstraction for reachability analysis of hybrid systems. ACM Trans. Embed. Comput. Syst. 5(1), 152–199 (2006)
5. Alur, R., Dill, D.L.: A theory of timed automata. Theor. Comput. Sci. 126(2), 183–235 (1994)
6. Alves, A., Arkin, A., Askary, S., Bloch, B., Curbera, F., Goland, Y., Kartha, N., Sterling, König, D., Mehta, V., Thatte, S., van der Rijn, D., Yendluri, P., Yiu, A.: Web Services Business Process Execution Language Version 2.0. OASIS (May 2006)
7. Berthomieu, F.V.B., Ribet, P.-O.: The tool tina – construction of abstract state spaces for petri nets and time petri nets. International Journal of Production Research 42 (2004)
8. Baier, C., Katoen, J.-P.: Principles of Model Checking (Representation and Mind Series). The MIT Press (2008)

9. Bérard, B., Cassez, F., Haddad, S., Lime, D., Roux, O.H.: Comparison of different semantics for time Petri nets. In: Peled, D.A., Tsay, Y.-K. (eds.) ATVA 2005. LNCS, vol. 3707, pp. 293–307. Springer, Heidelberg (2005)
10. Berthomieu, B., Bodeveix, J.-P., Farail, P., Filali, M., Garavel, H., Gaufillet, P., Lang, F., Vernadat, F.: Fiacre: An Intermediate Language for Model Verification in the Topcased Environment. In: ERTS 2008, Toulouse, France (2008)
11. Bradfield, J., Stirling, C.: Modal mu-calculi. In: Handbook of Modal Logic, pp. 721–756. Elsevier (2007)
12. Bulychev, P., Chatain, T., David, A., Larsen, K.G.: Efficient on-the-fly algorithm for checking alternating timed simulation. In: Ouaknine, J., Vaandrager, F.W. (eds.) FORMATS 2009. LNCS, vol. 5813, pp. 73–87. Springer, Heidelberg (2009)
13. Clarke, E.M., Grumberg, O., Long, D.E.: Model checking and abstraction. ACM Trans. Program. Lang. Syst. 16(5), 1512–1542 (1994)
14. David, A., Larsen, K.G., Legay, A., Nyman, U., Wąsowski, A.: Methodologies for specification of real-time systems using timed I/O automata. In: de Boer, F.S., Bonsangue, M.M., Hallerstede, S., Leuschel, M. (eds.) FMCO 2009. LNCS, vol. 6286, pp. 290–310. Springer, Heidelberg (2010)
15. David, A., Larsen, K.G., Legay, A., Nyman, U., Wasowski, A.: Timed I/O automata: a complete specification theory for real-time systems. In: Proc. of HSCC 2010, pp. 91–100. ACM, New York (2010)
16. Dierks, H., Kupferschmid, S., Larsen, K.G.: Automatic abstraction refinement for timed automata. In: Raskin, J.-F., Thiagarajan, P.S. (eds.) FORMATS 2007. LNCS, vol. 4763, pp. 114–129. Springer, Heidelberg (2007)
17. Emerson, E.A.: Model checking and the mu-calculus. DIMACS Series in Discrete Mathematics American Mathematical Society, pp. 185–214. American Mathematical Society (1997)
18. Fares, E., Bodeveix, J.-P., Filali, M.: An automatic technique for checking the simulation of timed systems. Technical Report IRIT/RT–2013-10–FR (January 2013), http://www.irit.fr/~Elie.Fares/PUBLICATIONS/RTIRIT--2013-10--FR.pdf
19. Griffault, A., Vincent, A.: The mec 5 model-checker. In: Alur, R., Peled, D.A. (eds.) CAV 2004. LNCS, vol. 3114, pp. 488–491. Springer, Heidelberg (2004)
20. Henzinger, T., Manna, Z., Pnueli, A.: Timed transition systems. In: de Bakker, J., Huizing, C., de Roever, W., Rozenberg, G. (eds.) REX 1991. LNCS, vol. 600, pp. 226–251. Springer, Heidelberg (1992)
21. Jeffrey, A.S., Schneider, S.A., Vaandrager, F.W.: A comparison of additivity axioms in timed transition systems. Technical report, Amsterdam, The Netherlands, The Netherlands (1993)
22. Jensen, H.E., Guldstr, K., Skou, A.: Scaling up uppaal: Automatic verification of real-time systems using compositionality and abstraction. In: Joseph, M. (ed.) FTRTFT 2000. LNCS, vol. 1926, pp. 19–30. Springer, Heidelberg (2000)
23. Kaynar, D.K., Lynch, N., Segala, R., Vaandrager, F.: The Theory of Timed I/O Automata (Synthesis Lectures in Computer Science) (2006)
24. Larsen, K.G., Pettersson, P., Yi, W.: Uppaal in a nutshell. Int. Journal on Software Tools for Technology Transfer 1, 134–152 (1997)
25. Lynch, N., Vandraager, F.: Forward and backward simulations - part ii: Timing-based systems. Information and Computation 128 (1995)
26. Nicollin, X., Sifakis, J.: An overview and synthesis on timed process algebras. In: Huizing, C., de Bakker, J.W., Rozenberg, G., de Roever, W.-P. (eds.) REX 1991. LNCS, vol. 600, pp. 526–548. Springer, Heidelberg (1992)
27. Ouaknine, J., Worrell, J.: On the language inclusion problem for timed automata: Closing a decidability gap. In: LICS, pp. 54–63. IEEE Computer Society (2004)

28. Schneider, S.: Concurrent and Real Time Systems: The CSP Approach, 1st edn. John Wiley & Sons, Inc., New York (1999)
29. Tasiran, S., Alur, R., Kurshan, R.P., Brayton, R.K.: Verifying abstractions of timed systems. In: Sassone, V., Montanari, U. (eds.) CONCUR 1996. LNCS, vol. 1119, pp. 546–562. Springer, Heidelberg (1996)
30. C. D. Team. The Coq proof assistant reference manual, version 8.2 (August. 2009)
31. van Glabbeek, R.J.: The linear time-branching time spectrum (extended abstract). In: Baeten, J.C.M., Klop, J.W. (eds.) CONCUR 1990. LNCS, vol. 458, pp. 278–297. Springer, Heidelberg (1990)

Synthesis of Bounded Integer Parameters for Parametric Timed Reachability Games[*]

Aleksandra Jovanović, Didier Lime, and Olivier H. Roux

LUNAM Université. École Centrale de Nantes - IRCCyN UMR CNRS 6597
Nantes, France

Abstract. We deal with a parametric version of timed game automata (PGA), where clocks can be compared to parameters, and parameter synthesis. As usual, parametrization leads to undecidability of the most interesting problems, such as reachability game. It is not surprising then that the symbolic exploration of the state-space often does not terminate. It is known that the undecidability remains even when severely restricting the form of the parametric constraints. Since in classical timed automata, real-valued clocks are always compared to integers for all practical purposes, we solve undecidability and termination issues by computing parameters as bounded integers. We give a symbolic algorithm that computes the set of winning states for a given PGA and the corresponding set of bounded integer parameter valuations as symbolic constraints between parameters. We argue the relevance of this approach and demonstrate its practical usability with a small case-study.

1 Introduction

Timed game automata (TGA) [4,15] have become a widely accepted formalism for modeling and analyzing control problems on timed systems. They are essentially timed automata (TA) with the set of actions divided into controllable (used by the controller) and uncontrollable (used by the environment) actions. *Reachability game* for TGA is the problem of determining the strategy for the controller such that, no matter what the environment does, the system ends up in the desired location. Such games are known to be decidable [15]. Introduction of this model is followed by the development of the tool support [5] successfully applied to numerous industrial case studies [9].

This model, however, requires complete knowledge of the systems. Thus, it is difficult to use it in the early design stages when the whole system is not fully characterized. Even when all timing constraints are known, if the environment changes or the system is proven wrong, the whole verification process must be carried out again. Additionally, considering a wide range of values for constants allows for a more flexible and robust design.

Parametric reasoning is, therefore, particularly relevant for timed models, since it allows to the designers to use parameters instead of concrete timing

---

[*] This work was partially funded by the ANR national research program ImpRo (ANR-2010-BLAN-0317).

D. Van Hung and M. Ogawa (Eds.): ATVA 2013, LNCS 8172, pp. 87–101, 2013.

values. This approach, however, leads to the undecidability of the most important questions, such as reachability.

Related Work

Parametric Timed Automata [2], have been introduced as an extension of TA [1], to overcome the limit of checking the correctness of the systems with respect to concrete timing constraints. The central problem for verification purposes, reachability-emptiness, which asks whether there exists a parameter valuation such that the automaton has an accepting run, is undecidable. This naturally lead to the search for a subclasses of the model for which some problems would be decidable. In [11], L/U automata, which use each parameter as either a lower bound or an upper bound on clocks, is proposed. Reachability-emptiness problem is decidable for this model, but the state-space exploration still might not terminate. Decidability of L/U automata is further studied in [6]. The authors give the explicit representation of the set of parameters, when all parameters are integers and of the same type (L-automata and U-automata). In [7], the authors allow parameters both in the model and the property (PTCTL), and they show that the model-checking problem is decidable, in discrete time over a PTA with one parametric clock, if the equality is not allowed in the formulae. A different approach is taken in [3] where the exploration starts from the initial set of parameter values, for which the system is correct, and enlarges the set ensuring that the behaviors of PTA are time-abstract equivalent. They give a conjecture for the termination of the algorithm, being true on the studied examples.

Parametric Timed Game Automata (PGA): In [12], we have introduced an extension of TGA, called parametric timed game automata (PGA) and its subclass for which the reachability-emptiness game, which asks whether there exist a parameter valuation such that a winning strategy exists, is decidable. The subclass is, however, severely restricted in the use of parameters and the symbolic computation [12] of the set of winning states still might not terminate.

Our Contribution. In this paper, we propose an orthogonal restriction scheme that we have introduced in [13] for PTA: since in classical timed game automata, real-valued clocks are always compared to integers for all practical purposes, we solve undecidability and termination issues by computing parameters as bounded integers. We give a symbolic algorithm that computes the set of winning states and the winning strategy for the controller for a given PGA and the corresponding set of parameter valuations as bounded integers. Due to the boundedness of parameters, the termination is ensured, and the resulting set of parameter valuations is given as symbolic constraints between parameters. The symbolic algorithm is based on the computation of the integer hull of the bounded parametric symbolic states. It first computes forward the whole reachable state-space, then propagates backwards the winning states. In order to find the winning states, we extend the well known fixed-point backwards algorithm for solving timed reachability games [15], for the parametric domain. Surprisingly, we do not have to apply an integer hull in the backwards computation, in order to obtain the correct integer solution.

Organization of the Paper. The rest of the paper is organized as follows. Section 2 provides definitions about PGA, the problems we are considering, and recalls some negative decidability results. In Section 3 we first present the algorithm for solving timed games, then we motivate a restriction scheme, introduced in [13] for PTA, and extend the algorithm for the parametric approach and computation of parameters as bounded integers. The practical use of our method is shown with a small case study in Section 4. We conclude with Section 5.

2   Parametric Timed Games

Preliminaries. $\mathbb{R}$ is the set of real numbers ($\mathbb{R}_{\geq 0}$ is the set of non-negative real numbers), $\mathbb{Q}$ the set of rational numbers, and $\mathbb{Z}$ the set of integers. Let $V \subseteq \mathbb{R}$. A V-valuation on some finite set X is a function from X to V. We denote by V^X the set of V-valuations on X.

Let X be a finite set of variables modeling *clocks* and let P be a finite set of *parameters*. A *parametric clock constraint* γ is an expression of the form $\gamma ::= x_i - x_j \frown p \mid x_i \frown p \mid \gamma \wedge \gamma$, where $x_i, x_j \in X$, $\frown \in \{\leq, <\}$, and p is a linear expression of the form $k_0 + k_1 p_1 + ... + k_n p_n$ with $k_0, ... k_n \in \mathbb{Z}$ and $p_1, ... p_n \in P$.

For any parametric clock constraint γ and any parameter valuation v, we note $v(\gamma)$ the constraint obtained by replacing each parameter p_i by its valuation $v(p_i)$. We denote by $G(X, P)$ the set of parametric constraints over X, and $G'(X, P)$ a set of parametric constraints over X of the form $\gamma' ::= x_i \frown p \mid \gamma' \wedge \gamma'$.

For a valuation v on X and $t \in \mathbb{R}_{\geq 0}$, we write $v + t$ for the valuation assigning $v(x) + t$ to each $x \in X$. For $R \subseteq X$, $v[R]$ denotes a valuation assigning 0 to each $x \in R$ and $v(x)$ to each $x \in X \backslash R$. Further, we define the null valuation $\mathbf{0}_X$ on X by $\forall x \in X, \mathbf{0}_X(x) = 0$.

2.1   Parametric Timed Games

Definition 1. *A Parametric Timed Automaton (PTA) is a tuple* $\mathcal{A} = (L, l_0, X, \Sigma, P, E, \mathsf{Inv})$*, where L is a finite set of locations, $l_0 \in L$ is the initial location, X is a finite set of clocks, Σ is a finite alphabet of actions, P is a finite set of parameters, $E \subseteq L \times \Sigma \times G(X, P) \times 2^X \times L$ is a finite set of edges: if $(l, a, \gamma, R, l') \in E$ then there is an edge from l to l' with action a, (parametric) guard γ and set of clocks to reset R, and $\mathsf{Inv} : L \mapsto G'(X, P)$ is a function that assigns a (parametric) invariant to each location.*

For any $\mathbb{Q}$-valuation v on P, the structure $v(\mathcal{A})$ obtained from $\mathcal{A}$ by replacing each constraint γ by $v(\gamma)$ is a *timed automaton* with invariants [1,10]. The behavior of a PTA $\mathcal{A}$ is described by the behavior of all timed automata obtained by considering all possible valuations of parameters.

Definition 2 (Semantics of a PTA). *The concrete semantics of a PTA $\mathcal{A}$ under a parameter valuation v, notation $v(\mathcal{A})$, is the labelled transition system $(Q, q_0, \rightarrow)$ over $\Sigma \cup \mathbb{R}_{\geq 0}$ where:*

- $Q = \{(l, w) \in L \times \mathbb{R}_{\geq 0}^X \mid w(v(\mathsf{Inv}(l)))$ *is true* $\}$
- $q_0 = \{(l_0, \mathbf{0}_X) \in Q\}$
- *delay transition:* $(l, w) \xrightarrow{t} (l, w + t)$ *with* $t \geq 0$, *iff* $\forall t' \in [0, t], (l, w + t') \in Q$
- *action transition:* $(l, w) \xrightarrow{a} (l', w')$ *with* $a \in \Sigma$, *iff* $(l, w), (l', w') \in Q$,
  there exists an edge $(l, a, \gamma, R, l') \in E, w' = w[R]$ *and* $w(v(\gamma))$ *is true.*

A finite run of PTA $\mathcal{A}$, under a parameter valuation v, is a sequence of alternating delay and action transition in the semantics of $v(\mathcal{A})$, $\rho = q_1 a_1 q_2 ... a_{n-1} q_n$, where $\forall i, q_i \in Q, a_i \in \Sigma \cup \mathbb{R}_{\geq 0}$, and $q_i \xrightarrow{a} q_{i+1}$. The last state of ρ is denoted by $last(\rho)$. We denote by $\mathsf{Runs}(v(\mathcal{A}))$ the set of runs starting in the initial state of $v(\mathcal{A})$, and by $\mathsf{Runs}(q, v(\mathcal{A}))$ the set of runs starting in q. A run is maximal if it is either infinite or cannot be extended. A state q is said to be reachable in $\mathcal{A}$ if there exists a finite run $\rho \in \mathsf{Runs}(v(\mathcal{A}))$, such that $last(\rho) = q$.

In [12], we have extended the previous definitions, to obtain a more powerful formalism that allows us to express parametric control problems on timed systems.

Definition 3. *A Parametric (Timed) Game Automaton (PGA) $\mathcal{G}$ is a parametric timed automaton with its set of actions Σ partitioned into controllable (Σ^c) and uncontrollable (Σ^u) actions.*

As for PTA, for any PGA $\mathcal{G}$ and any rational valuation on parameters v, the structure $v(\mathcal{G})$, obtained by replacing each constraint γ by $v(\gamma)$, is a timed game automaton.

In a TGA, two players, a controller and an environment, choose at every instant one of the available actions from their own sets, according to a strategy, and the game progresses. Since the game is symmetric, we give only the definition for the controller playing with actions from Σ^c. At each step, a strategy tells controller to either delay in a location (delay), or to take a particular controllable action.

Definition 4 (Strategy). *A strategy $\mathcal{F}$ over $v(\mathcal{G})$ is a partial function from $\mathsf{Runs}(v(\mathcal{G}))$ to $\Sigma^c \cup \{\mathsf{delay}\}$ such that for every finite run ρ, if $\mathcal{F}(\rho) \in \Sigma^c$ then $last(\rho) \xrightarrow{\mathcal{F}(\rho)} q$ for some state $q = (l, w)$, and if $\mathcal{F}(\rho) = \mathsf{delay}$, then there exists some $d > 0$ such that for all $0 \leq d' \leq d$, there exists some state q such that $last(\rho) \xrightarrow{d'} q$.*

We consider only memory-less strategies, where $\mathcal{F}(\rho)$ only depends on the current $last(\rho)$. Note that the uncontrollable actions cannot be used to reach the desired location, the controller has to be able to reach it by itself.

Outcome defines the restricted behavior of $v(\mathcal{G})$, when the controller plays some strategy $\mathcal{F}$.

Definition 5 (Outcome). *Let $\mathcal{G}$ be a PGA, v be a parameter valuation, and $\mathcal{F}$ be a strategy over $v(\mathcal{G})$. The outcome $\mathsf{Outcome}(q, \mathcal{F})$ of $\mathcal{F}$ from state q is the subset of runs in $\mathsf{Runs}(q, v(\mathcal{G}))$ defined inductively as:*

- *the run with no action $q \in \mathsf{Outcome}(q, \mathcal{F})$*
- *if $\rho \in \mathsf{Outcome}(q, \mathcal{F})$ then $\rho' = \rho \xrightarrow{\delta} q' \in \mathsf{Outcome}(q, \mathcal{F})$ if $\rho' \in \mathsf{Runs}(q, v(\mathcal{G}))$ and one of the following three condition holds:*
  1. *$\delta \in \Sigma^u$,*
  2. *$\delta \in \Sigma^c$ and $\delta = \mathcal{F}(\rho)$,*
  3. *$\delta \in \mathbb{R}_{\geq 0}$ and $\forall 0 \leq \delta' < \delta, \exists q'' \in S$ s.t. $last(\rho) \xrightarrow{\delta'} q'' \wedge \mathcal{F}(\rho \xrightarrow{\delta'} q'') = $ delay.*
- *for an infinite run ρ, $\rho \in \mathsf{Outcome}(q, \mathcal{F})$, if all the finite prefixes of ρ are in $\mathsf{Outcome}(q, \mathcal{F})$.*

As we are interested in reachability games, we consider only the runs in the outcome that are "long enough" to have a chance to reach the goal location: a run $\rho \in \mathsf{Outcome}(q, \mathcal{F})$ is *maximal* if it is either infinite or there is no delay d and no state q' such that $\rho' = \rho \xrightarrow{d} q' \in \mathsf{Outcome}(q, \mathcal{F})$ and $\mathcal{F}(\rho') \in \Sigma^c$ (the only possible actions from $last(\rho)$ are uncontrollable actions). $MaxOut(q, \mathcal{F})$ notes the set of maximal runs for a state q and a strategy $\mathcal{F}$.

Definition 6 (Winning strategy). *Let $\mathcal{G} = (L, l_0, X, \Sigma^c \cup \Sigma^u, P, E, \mathsf{Inv})$ be a PGA and $l_{goal} \in L$. A strategy $\mathcal{F}$ is winning for the location l_{goal} if for all runs $\rho \in MaxOut(q_0, \mathcal{F})$, where $q_0 = (l_0, \mathbf{0}_X)$, there is some state (l_{goal}, w) in ρ.*

Similarly, a state q is winning (for the controller) if it belongs to a run in the outcome of a winning strategy.

We study the problem of *reachability-emptiness game for PGA*, which is the problem of determining whether the set of parameter valuations, such that there exists a strategy for the controller to enforce the system into the desired location, is empty. We are also interested in the corresponding *reachability-synthesis game for PGA*, which is to compute all parameter valuations such that there exists a winning strategy for the controller.

Reachability-emptiness problem for PTA is undecidable, [1]. As PGA extend PTA, the reachability-emptiness game for PGA is also undecidable [12].

3   Integer Parameter Synthesis

Parametrization leads to undecidability of the most important problems. There exist subclasses of PTA [11,6] (resp. PGA [12]) for which the reachability-emptiness (resp. reachability-emptiness game) is decidable, however, they are severely restricted and their practical usability is unclear.

We advocated in [13] for a different restriction scheme for PTA, to search for parameter values as bounded integers. This makes all the problems decidable, since we can enumerate all the possible valuations. Lifting either one of the two assumptions (boundedness or integer) leads to undecidability [13]. The explicit enumeration is not practical, and thus we proposed an efficient symbolic method to find the solution. This has the advantage of giving the set of parameter valuations as symbolic constraints between parameters.

3.1   Computing the Winning States in Parametric Timed Games

We first recall an algorithm from [12] to compute the parameter valuations permitting the existence of a winning strategy for the controller. Due to the associated decidability results, its termination is obviously not guaranteed. For the sake of readability, we present it in a simplified version, closer to an extension of the classical algorithm of [15], in which we first compute forward the whole reachable state-space, then propagate backwards the winning states, instead of interleaving the forward and backward computations as done in [12] as an extension of [8]. There would be no problem in restoring that interleaving in the setting proposed here.

The computation consists of two fixed-points on the state-space of the PGA. To handle these sets of states, we define the notion of parametric symbolic state:

Definition 7 (Parametric symbolic state). *A symbolic state of a parametric timed (game) automaton $\mathcal{G}$, with set of clocks X and set of parameters P, is a pair (l, Z) where l is a location of $\mathcal{A}$ and Z is a set of valuations v on $X \cup P$.*

For the state-space exploration in the parametric domain, we extend the classical operations on valuation sets:

- projection: for any set of states Z, and any set $R \subseteq P \cup X$, $Z_{|R}$ is the projection of Z on R;
- future: $Z^{\nearrow} = \{v' \mid \exists v \in Z \text{ s.t. } v'(x) = v(x) + d, d \geq 0 \text{ if } x \in X; v'(x) = v(x) \text{ if } x \in P\}$
- reset of clocks in set $R \subseteq X$: $Z[R] = \{v[R] \mid v \in Z\}$

We also need the following operators on symbolic states.

- initial symbolic state of the PTA $\mathcal{A} = (L, l_0, \Sigma, X, P, E, \mathsf{Inv})$: $\mathsf{Init}(\mathcal{A}) = (l_0, \{v \in \mathbb{R}^{X \cup P} \mid v_{|X} \in \mathbf{0}_X \cap v_{|P}(\mathsf{Inv}(l_0))_{|X}\})$
- successor by edge $e = (l, a, \gamma, R, l')$: $\mathsf{Succ}((l, Z), e) = (l', (Z \cap \gamma)[R]^{\nearrow} \cap \mathsf{Inv}(l'))$.

We can extend the Succ operator to arbitrary sets of states by defining, for any set of states S and any location l, the subset S^l of S containing the states with location l. S^l is therefore a symbolic state (l, Z) for some set of valuations Z. Then we define $\mathsf{Succ}(S, e)$ as $\mathsf{Succ}(S^l, e)$, with l being the source location of edge e. The reachable state-space of the PGA can be computed by the following fixed-point (when it exists) [13]:

$$S_{n+1} = \mathsf{Init}(\mathcal{A})^{\nearrow} \cup \bigcup_{e \in E} \mathsf{Succ}(S_n, e), \text{ with } S_0 = \emptyset$$

The final fixed-point set is noted S^*. It follows from [11] that all Z are finite unions of convex polyhedra.

In order to compute the winning states, we need a few additional operators:

- past: $v^{\checkmark} = \{v' \mid \exists v \in Z \, s.t. \, v'(x) = v(x) - d, d \geq 0$ if $x \in X; v'(x) = v(x)$ if $x \in P\}$
- inverse reset of clocks in set $R \subseteq X$: $Z[R]^{-1} = \{v', v'(x) = 0$ if $v' \in Z[R] \mid \exists v \in Z$ s.t. $v'(x) = v(x)$ if $x \notin R\}$
- predecessor by edge $e = (l, a, \gamma, R, l')$: $\mathsf{Pred}((l', Z), e) = (l, Z[R]^{-1} \cap \gamma)$.
- controllable (resp. uncontrollable) action predecessors: $\mathsf{cPred}((l', Z))$ (resp. $\mathsf{uPred}((l', Z)))$ is the union of all the predecessors of (l', Z) by some edge with target location l' and labelled by a controllable (resp. an uncontrollable) action.

As before, we extend all these predecessor operators to arbitrary sets of states. We can now define a *safe-timed predecessors* operator $\mathsf{Pred}_t(S_1, S_2) = \{(l, v) \mid \exists d \geq 0$ s.t. $(l, v) \xrightarrow{d} (l, v'), (l, v') \in S_1$ and $Post_{[0,d]}(l, v) \subseteq S^* \backslash S_2\}$, where $Post_{[0,d]}(l, v) = \{(l, v') \in S^* \mid \exists t \in [0, d]$ s.t. $(l, v) \xrightarrow{t} (l, v')\}$.

This corresponds intuitively to the states that can reach S_1 by delay, without going through any state in S_2 along the path.

If we denote by $S_{goal} = \{l_{goal}\} \times \mathbb{R}^X_{\geq 0}$, then the backwards algorithm for solving reachability games is the fixed-point computation of:

$$W_{n+1} = S^* \cap (\mathsf{Pred}_t(W_n \cup \mathsf{cPred}(W_n), \mathsf{uPred}(S^* \backslash W_n)) \cup S_{goal}), \text{ with } W_0 = \emptyset$$

When it exists, the final fixed-point set is noted W^*. We recall the following result from [12]:

Theorem 1 ([12]). *When W^* exists, for any PGA $\mathcal{G}$ and any location l_{goal}, there exists a winning strategy for the controller in $v(\mathcal{G})$, for a parameter valuation v iff $v \in (W^* \cap \mathsf{Init}(\mathcal{G}))_{|P}$.*

The obvious problem with the above approach is that the fixed-point computation of W^* might not terminate. And indeed, already, the fixed-point computation of S^*, the reachable state-space, might not terminate either.

In [13], to solve this problem without restricting the expressiveness of the model too much, we have restricted the problem of parameter synthesis to the search for bounded integer parameters. We wanted to avoid an explicit enumeration of all the possible values of parameters and have therefore proposed a modification of the symbolic computation of S^* that preserves the integer parameter valuations.

The approach is based on the notion of *integer hull*. The integer hull $\mathsf{IntHull}(Z)$ of a convex polyhedron Z in $\mathbb{R}^n$ is the smallest convex subset of Z containing all the elements of Z with integer coordinates. If $\mathsf{Conv}(Z)$ is the smallest convex set containing Z, and $\mathsf{IntVects}(Z)$ the subset of all elements of Z with integer coordinates, then the integer hull of Z is $\mathsf{IntHull}(Z) = \mathsf{Conv}(\mathsf{IntVects}(Z))$. $\mathsf{IntHull}$ is extended to symbolic states as: $\mathsf{IntHull}((l, Z)) = (l, \mathsf{IntHull}(Z))$.

In [13], we have proved that to solve integer parameter synthesis problem it is sufficient to consider the integer hulls of the symbolic states. Therefore, in the standard algorithm for the reachability-synthesis for PTA, we replace all occurrences of the operator Succ with $\mathsf{ISucc}((l, Z), e) = \mathsf{IntHull}(\mathsf{Succ}((l, Z), e))$.

By using the ISucc instead of Succ in the computation of the whole state-space S^* we ensure termination and obtain a subset IS^* of S^* such that $\mathsf{IntVects}(IS^*) = \mathsf{IntVects}(S^*)$, provided we know a bound on the possible values for the parameters and the following assumption holds:

Assumption 1. *Any non-empty symbolic state computed through the Succ operator contains at least one integer point.*

From now on we place ourselves in this setting, and like in [13] we can assume w.l.o.g. that all clocks are bounded by some constant.

3.2   Bounded Integer Parameter Synthesis

In [13], in order to prove the correctness of the algorithm that uses the integer hull, we have relied on the convexity of the symbolic states in the forward computation. However, even if S_1 and S_2 are convex, $\mathsf{Pred}_t(S_1, S_2)$ is not in general. By taking the integer hull of a non-convex set, we could include some integer points that do not belong to the original set. Since we want to preserve the integer points, we define a new operator, an *integer shape*, IntShape. As stated before, any set S produced by the backward computation can be expressed as finite unions of convex polyhedra $\bigcup_i Z_i$. For such a finite union; we define $\mathsf{IntShape}(S) = \bigcup_i \mathsf{IntHull}(Z_i)$. We can now extend the needed backwards operators using the notion of integer shape.

We first extend a predecessor by edge operator (Pred) for the computation of integer parameter valuations, similarly to the extension of Succ operator. For a symbolic state (l, Z) and an edge e, an integer predecessor by an edge e is defined as: $\mathsf{IPred}((l, Z), e) = \mathsf{IntShape}(\mathsf{Pred}((l, Z), e))$.

The following lemma states that the computation of the integer shape of a predecessor of a symbolic state (l, Z), results in the same set as if we would compute the integer shape of a symbolic state (l, Z) at first, and then the integer shape of its predecessor by edge.

Lemma 1. *For any symbolic state (l, Z) and any edge e:*
  $\mathsf{IPred}(\mathsf{IntShape}((l, Z), e)) = \mathsf{IntShape}(\mathsf{Pred}((l, Z), e))$

Proof. We will prove both inclusions:
  1. $\mathsf{IPred}(\mathsf{IntShape}((l, Z)), e) \subseteq \mathsf{IntShape}(\mathsf{Pred}((l, Z), e))$.
Since $\mathsf{IntShape}((l, Z)) \subseteq (l, Z)$ and IntShape and Pred are non-decreasing, the first inclusion holds.
  2. $\mathsf{IPred}(\mathsf{IntShape}((l, Z)), e) \supseteq \mathsf{IntShape}(\mathsf{Pred}((l, Z), e))$.
Let $v \in \mathsf{IntVects}(\mathsf{Pred}((l, Z), e))$. Then $\exists v' \in Z$ s.t. $v \in \mathsf{IntVects}(\mathsf{Pred}((l, \{v'\}), e))$. By definition of Pred we have that $v_{|P} = v'_{|P}$, and therefore $v' \in v_{|P}(Z)$. $v_{|P}$ is an integer vector (since v is) and $v_{|P}(Z)$ is a zone of a classical TA and thus with integer vertices. Therefore $v_{|P}(Z) = \mathsf{IntShape}(v_{|P}(Z))$. Since IntShape is non-decreasing and $v_{|P}(Z) \subseteq Z$ we have $\mathsf{IntShape}(v_{|P}(Z)) \subseteq \mathsf{IntShape}(Z)$, and so $v' \in \mathsf{IntShape}(Z)$ and $v \in \mathsf{IntVects}(\mathsf{Pred}((l, \mathsf{IntShape}(Z)), e))$. Again, since IntShape is non-decreasing, we obtain $\mathsf{IPred}(\mathsf{IntShape}((l, Z)), e) \supseteq \mathsf{IntShape}(\mathsf{Pred}((l, Z), e))$.

We define, in a similar way, an integer controllable (resp. uncontrollable) action predecessors $\mathsf{IcPred}((l, Z)) = \mathsf{IntShape}(\mathsf{cPred}((l, Z)))$ (resp. $\mathsf{IuPred}((l, Z)) = \mathsf{IntShape}(\mathsf{uPred}((l, Z)))$.

Lemma 2. *For any symbolic state* (l, Z)*:*
$\mathsf{IcPred}(\mathsf{IntShape}((l, Z))) = \mathsf{IntShape}(\mathsf{cPred}((l, Z)))$

Proof. Immediate with Lemma 1 from the facts that: $\mathsf{cPred}((l, Z)) = \bigcup_{c \in \Sigma^c} \mathsf{Pred}(\mathsf{IntShape}((l, Z), c)))$ and $\mathsf{IntShape}(S_1, S_2) = \mathsf{IntShape}(S_1) \cup \mathsf{IntShape}(S_2)$ when S_1 and S_2 are finite unions of convex sets.

The same result obviously holds for uPred and we can finally extend this to the safe-timed predecessor operator by $\mathsf{IPred}_t(Z_1, Z_2) = \mathsf{IntShape}(\mathsf{Pred}_t(Z_1, Z_2))$.

Lemma 3. *For any two sets of states* S_1 *and* S_2*:*
$\mathsf{IPred}_t(\mathsf{IntShape}(S_1), \mathsf{IntShape}(S_2)) = \mathsf{IntShape}(\mathsf{Pred}_t(S_1, S_2))$

Proof. Recall that S_1 and S_2 are finite unions of convex polyhedra: $S_1 = \bigcup_i Z_{1i}$ and $S_2 = \bigcup_j Z_{2j}$. By using a result from [8], we then have $\mathsf{Pred}_t(\bigcup_i Z_{1i}, \bigcup_j Z_{2j}) = \bigcup_i \bigcap_j \mathsf{Pred}_t(Z_{1i}, Z_{2j})$. Then for any i, j, with another result from [8], we have: $\mathsf{Pred}_t(Z_{1i}, Z_{2j}) = (Z_{1i}^{\swarrow} \backslash Z_{2j}^{\swarrow}) \cup ((Z_{1i} \cap Z_{2j}^{\swarrow}) \backslash Z_{2j})^{\swarrow}$, because Z_{2j} is convex. What we need to show then is that:
-$\mathsf{IntShape}(Z_1 \cap Z_2) = \mathsf{IntShape}(\mathsf{IntShape}(Z_1) \cap \mathsf{IntShape}(Z_2))$
-$\mathsf{IntShape}(Z_1 \cup Z_2) = \mathsf{IntShape}(\mathsf{IntShape}(Z_1) \cup \mathsf{IntShape}(Z_2))$
-$\mathsf{IntShape}(Z_1^{\swarrow}) = \mathsf{IntShape}(\mathsf{IntShape}(Z_1)^{\swarrow})$
-$\mathsf{IntShape}(Z_1 \backslash Z_2) = \mathsf{IntShape}(\mathsf{IntShape}(Z_1) \backslash \mathsf{IntShape}(Z_2))$
These four results are quite straightforward. Let us just prove the first, the rest being similar.

First remark that Z_1 and Z_2 being convex, integer shapes are actually integer hulls. Second $\mathsf{IntHull}(S) \subseteq S$, for any S and since $\mathsf{IntHull}$ is non-decreasing, $\mathsf{IntHull}(Z_1 \cap Z_2) \supseteq \mathsf{IntHull}(\mathsf{IntHull}(Z_1) \cap \mathsf{IntHull}(Z_2))$.

Now let $v \in \mathsf{IntVects}(\mathsf{IntHull}(Z_1))$ then, by definition, $v \in \mathsf{IntVects}(Z_1)$ and if it also belongs to $\mathsf{IntVects}(\mathsf{IntHull}(Z_1))$ then it is in $\mathsf{IntVects}(Z_1) \cap \mathsf{IntVects}(Z_2)$ or equivalently in $\mathsf{IntVects}(Z_1 \cap Z_2)$ and by taking the convex hull, we have the result.

Now consider the following fixed-point computation:

$$IW_{n+1} = IS^* \cap (\mathsf{IPred}_t(IW_n \cup \mathsf{IcPred}(IW_n), \mathsf{IuPred}(IS^* \backslash IW_n)) \cup S_{goal}), \quad IW_0 = \emptyset$$

Lemma 4. *For a PGA* $\mathcal{G}$*, location* l_{goal}*, and a state* (l, v) *such that* v *is an integer valuation, it holds that for* $\forall i$*, there exist a winning strategy in at most* i *controllable steps from* $(l, v_{|X})$ *in* $v_{|P}(\mathcal{G})$ *iff* $(l, v) \in IW_i$*.*

Proof. We proceed by induction. The property obviously holds for IW_0. Now, suppose it holds for some $n \geq 0$. We first prove the left to right implication. Let (l, v) be a state in IW_{n+1} such that v is an integer point. then $(l, v) \in IS^* \cap (\mathsf{IPred}_t(\mathsf{IntShape}(IW_n \cup \mathsf{cPred}(IW_n)), \mathsf{IntShape}(uPr(IS^* \backslash IW_n))) \cup S_{goal})$.

If $(l, v) \in S_{goal}$ we are done, else, by Lemma 3, we know that $(l, v) \in IS^* \cap$ IntShape(Pred$_t(IW_n) \cup$cPred(IW_n), uPred$(IS^* \setminus IW_n)$) and then in Pred$_t(IW_n) \cup$ cPred(IW_n), uPred$(IS^* \setminus IW_n)$ and we get the result using the correctness of the Pred$_t$ operator and the induction hypothesis.

Now, we prove the right to left implication. If there is a strategy to win in at most $n + 1$ steps, there is one to reach some state (l', v') in one step and win in at most n steps. Then by the induction hypothesis, $(l', v') \in IW_n$ and by the correctness of the Pred$_t$ operator, (l, v) belongs to Pred$_t(IW_n) \cup$ cPred(IW_n), uPred$(IS^* \setminus IW_n)$. Since v is an integer valuation, (l, v) belongs to IntShape(Pred$_t(IW_n) \cup$ cPred(IW_n), uPred$(IS^* \setminus IW_n)$) and we can conclude by Lemma 3.

We now prove that the fixed-point computation IW_n terminates and that its result IW^* is correct and complete.

Theorem 2 (Termination). *For any PGA $\mathcal{G}$ and any desired location l_{goal}, the algorithm terminates.*

Proof. We proved, in [13], that the forward computation of IS^* terminates. When going backwards, each time we apply IPred$_t$ we know that we have added to the winning set of states at least one integer point (otherwise we can terminate). Since there is only a finite number of integer points to add (due to the boundedness of clocks and parameters), the computation terminates.

Theorem 3 (Correctness and completeness). *Let v be an integer parameter valuation. For any PGA $\mathcal{G}$ and any location l_{goal}, upon termination, there exists a winning strategy for the controller in $v(\mathcal{G})$ iff $v \in (IW^* \cap \text{Init}(\mathcal{G}))_{|P}$.*

Proof. We start by proving the right to left implication. Suppose $v \in (IW^* \cap \text{Init}(\mathcal{G}))_{|P}$. Then there exists a state (l_0, v_0) in $IW^* \cap \text{Init}(\mathcal{G})$ such that $v_{0|P} = v$ and $v_{0|X}$ has all coordinates equal to 0. So v_0 is an integer valuation on $X \cup P$ and since it belongs IW^*, it belongs to IW^n for some n. So we can apply Lemma 4 to conclude.

Now, we prove the left to right implication. If there exists a winning strategy for the controller to win in $v(\mathcal{G})$ then it means that it can win within a finite number of controllable steps. Then, by Lemma 4, it means that the state (l_0, v_0) such that $v_{0|P} = v$ and $v_{0|X}$ has all coordinates equal to 0 belongs to IW^n for some n, and therefore to IW^*, which concludes the proof.

3.3   Avoiding Integer Hulls in the Backward Computation

We have shown how we can symbolically compute the bounded integer parameter valuations that permit the controller to win. We will now prove that, surprisingly, we actually do not have to apply an integer hull in the backwards computation, in order to obtain the correct integer solution and ensure termination.

Consider the fixed-point computation corresponding to this setting:

$$IW'_{n+1} = IS^* \cap (\text{Pred}_t(IW'_n \cup \text{cPred}(IW'_n), \text{uPred}(IS^* \setminus IW'_n)) \cup S_{goal}), \quad IW'_0 = \emptyset$$

Let us first show that if this procedure terminates, it is sound and complete.

Theorem 4 (Correctness and completeness). *For any PGA $\mathcal{G}$, a desired location l_{goal}, and an integer parameter valuation v, upon the termination, there exists a winning strategy for the controller in $v(\mathcal{G})$ iff $v \in (IW'^* \cap \mathsf{Init}(\mathcal{G}))_{|P}$.*

Proof. First remark that, for all n, we have $IW_n \subseteq IW'_n \subseteq W_n$, because integer hulls and shapes only remove points. Now, $\mathsf{IntVects}$ is a non-decreasing operator so $\mathsf{IntVects}(IW_n) \subseteq \mathsf{IntVects}(IW'_n) \subseteq \mathsf{IntVects}(W_n)$. By Lemma 3 and correctness of the W_n computation, we know that $\mathsf{IntVects}(IW_n) = \mathsf{IntVects}(W_n)$. So all three sets are equal.

Now, as seen in the proof of Theorem 3, any initial state in $v(\mathcal{G})$ for an integer parameter valuation v certainly has an integer valuation of both clocks and parameters, which permits us to conclude.

Proving the termination is much trickier: we shall construct a new object, that we call *parametric region graph*, that refines the standard region graph for timed automata of [1] with parametric constraints. We therefore further divide the region graph with all the guards from the model and all the constraints defining integer hulls (of the symbolic states) obtained in the forward computation.

A constraint of an integer hull may create a non-integer vertex when intersecting the region graph. For each such vertex, we add constraints that go though the vertex and are parallel to the diagonal constraints of the region graph (added constraints are of the form $x_i - x_j + k = 0$ for all clocks x_i, x_j and $k \in \mathbb{Z}$).

Note that if a constraint of an integer hull intersects a diagonal constraint creating a non-integer vertex, there is already a diagonal constraint going through that vertex. We now give a formal definition of the parametric region graph.

Definition 8 (Parametric regions). *Let m be the maximal value of parametric expressions occurring in the constraints of the PGA (recall that parameters are bounded so it is possible to compute that value). The parametric region graph is constructed in the following way:*

- *the variable-space $\mathbb{R}^{X \cup P}$ is partitioned along the constraints $x \sim k$ and $x - y \sim k$ for all clocks $x, y \in X$, $\sim \in \{<, =, >\}$ and $0 \le k \le m$ (this gives the standard region graph);*
- *for any guard of the automaton and any constraint appearing in the (finite number of) convex polyhedra defining IS^*, $\gamma \sim 0$, we further partition the variable-space, with the constraints $\gamma \sim' 0$ for every $\sim' \in \{<, =, >\}$;*
- *for any (non-integer) vertex of the "pre-regions" defined by the above partition, we further refine the variable-space by constraints of the form $x - y + k \sim 0$, with $\sim \in \{<, =, >\}$ for all clocks $x \ne y$ and $k \in \mathbb{Z}$, going through that vertex.*

Informally, these constraints partition the variable-space $\mathbb{R}^{X \cup P}$ into a finite number of a *parametric regions*, which are either a vertex, a line fragment between two vertices, or a sub-space between line fragments and vertices that does not contain either a line fragment nor a vertex.

Fig. 1 shows a two-dimensional example of the variable-space partitioned into parametric regions. An integer hull obtained in a forward computation is drawn

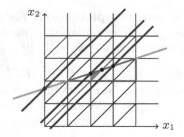

Fig. 1. Parametric region partition

in red. Its side (that does not overlap with the region graph) is extended (in green) as long as it cuts the state-space. Additionally, each non-integer vertex obtained in the intersection of the constraints defining the integer hull and the region graph, has a diagonal constraint that goes through it (in blue). An example of a parametric region is given in gray.

In order to prove the termination when going backwards, we have to show that all the operators preserve the parametric regions.

Lemma 5. *If $(a_i)_i$ and $(b_j)_j$ are finite families of parametric regions then the following sets are a finite union of parametric regions:*

1. $\bigcup_i a_i \cup \bigcup_j b_j$;
2. $\bigcup_i a_i \cap \bigcup_j b_j$;
3. *the complement of $\bigcup_i a_i$;*
4. $(\bigcup_i a_i)^{\swarrow}$;
5. $\mathsf{Pred}((l, \bigcup_i a_i), e)$, *for any location l and edge e;*
6. $\mathsf{Pred}_t(\bigcup_i a_i, \bigcup_j b_j)$.

Proof. The first three are straightforward using the fact that parametric regions are taken from a finite set. The fourth uses the fact that these regions are defined using the diagonal constraints $x - y - k \curvearrowright 0$ going through any vertex. The fifth is immediate. For Pred_t we need to use once again the two results from [8]: $\mathsf{Pred}_t(\bigcup_i a_i, \bigcup_j b_j) = \bigcup_i \bigcap_j \mathsf{Pred}_t(a_i, b_j)$ and $\mathsf{Pred}_t(a_i, b_j) = (a_i^{\swarrow} \backslash b_j^{\swarrow}) \cup ((a_i \cap b_j^{\swarrow}) \backslash b_j)^{\swarrow}$ (if b_j is convex, which is true by definition of the parametric region), which can equivalently be written as: $\mathsf{Pred}_t(a_i, b_j) = (a_i^{\swarrow} \cap \overline{b_j^{\swarrow}}) \cup (a_i \cap b_j^{\swarrow} \cap \overline{b_j})^{\swarrow}$. We can then conclude by using the first four results.

We can now get back to the termination of the IW_n' fixed-point computation:

Theorem 5 (Termination). *For any PGA $\mathcal{G}$ and any desired location l_{goal} the fixed-point computation of IW'^* terminates.*

Proof. Again we know, from [13], that the forward computation of IS^*, using ISucc and for bounded parameters, terminates. By definition of parametric regions, IS^* can be written as a finite union of symbolic states whose associated

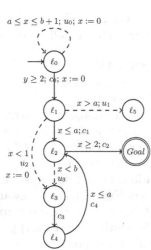

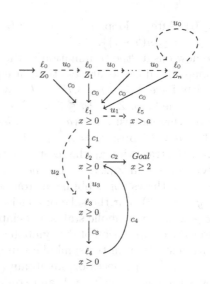

Fig. 2. A Parametric Timed Game Automaton

Fig. 3. Symbolic state graph of PGA of Figure 2

valuations can be represented as finite unions of parametric region. When going backwards using Pred_t, by Lemma 5 we know that parametric regions are preserved. Therefore at each step at least one region is added to the set of winning states (otherwise the fixed-point is reached and we can terminate). Since there is a finite number of parametric regions, the computation must terminate.

3.4 Complexity

As remarked in [13], all of the possible valuations of parameters, that are integer and bounded, can be enumerated in exponential time. Therefore, a problem that is EXPTIME for TGA, the corresponding bounded integer version for PGA is also EXPTIME. The reachability game is EXPTIME-complete for TGA [14], and it is a special case of the reachability-emptiness game for PGA. We can thus conclude that the reachability-emptiness (synthesis) game for PGA is EXPTIME-complete for bounded integer parameters.

4 Example

We consider an extension of the example proposed in [8]. The model has two clocks x and y, controllable (c_i) and uncontrollable (u_i) actions and two parameters a and b. The reachability game consists in finding a strategy for the controller that will eventually end up in the location *Goal*. We will now explain how the algorithm works.

A PGA is given in Figure 2 and its symbolic state graph (graph with nodes (l, Z)) in Figure 3. The initial symbolic state is: (ℓ_0, Z_0) with $Z_0 = \{x = y, x \geq$

$0, y \geq 0\}$. After n loops u_0, we have : (ℓ_0, Z_n) with $Z_n = \{x \geq 0, a \leq b+1, 0 \leq na \leq y - x \leq n(b+1)\}$.

We now ensure the termination in the bounded case. For example, assume all parameters and clocks are less than or equal to 3 (i.e. in each symbolic state we implicitly have $x \leq 3, y \leq 3, a \leq 3, b \leq 3$) then:

  -After one loop: $Z_1 = \{a \leq 3, a \leq b+1, a \leq y - x \leq b+1\}$
  -After three loops: $Z_3 = \{a \leq 1, a \leq b+1, 3a \leq y - x \leq 3(b+1)\}$
  -After $n > 3$ loops: $Z_n = Z_{n+1} = \{a = 0, a \leq b+1, y - x \leq 3\}$

After the transition c_0, the reset of the clock x removes the diagonal constraint involving $y - x$ in $Z_0 \ldots Z_n$ and the new constraints $y \geq 2$ and $y - x \geq 2$ are added. All theses zones obtained from $Z_0 \ldots Z_n$ are included in $(x \geq 0) \wedge (y \geq 2) \wedge (y - x \geq 2)$. For the sake of conciseness, in the sequel, we omit $y \geq 2$ and $y - x \geq 2$ in the symbolic states associated with locations ℓ_1 and its successors.

After the computation of the symbolic states, shown in Figure 3, the backward algorithm starts from the symbolic winning subset $(Goal, x \geq 2)$. By a controllable action (c_2) predecessor, we obtain $(\ell_2, x \geq 2)$. Computing the (timed) past removes the constraint $x \geq 2$, and computing the safe-timed predecessor adds $x \geq b$ in order not to end-up in ℓ_3 by $u3$. The resulting state is $(\ell_2, x \geq b)$. One of the controllable transitions taking us to ℓ_2 is c_4. A controllable action predecessor (c_4) adds a constraint $x \leq a$. A constraint on the parameters derived in this state is $a \geq b$. This contraint is back-propagated to the preceding states. The safe-timed predecessors give us the state $(\ell_4, x \geq 0 \wedge a \geq b)$.

We obtain successively the following sets of winning states: $(\ell_3, x \geq 0 \wedge a \geq b)$, $(\ell_2, (x \geq b) \vee (x \geq 0 \wedge a \geq b))$ and $(\ell_1, (x \leq a) \wedge ((x < 1 \wedge a \geq b) \vee x \geq 1) \wedge ((x \geq b) \vee (x \geq 0 \wedge a \geq b))$. The last one simplifies to $(\ell_1, (x \leq a \wedge a \geq b))$. The constraints are now back-propagated to the states associated with ℓ_0. The constraint $a > 0$ is added in order not to end-up in the symbolic state (ℓ_0, Z_n) by u_0 then the winning states obtained from (ℓ_0, Z_n) is $(\ell_0, \overline{(a \leq b+1) \wedge (a = 0)})$, from (ℓ_0, Z_3) is $(\ell_0, \overline{(a \leq b+1) \wedge (a \leq 1)}) \ldots$ and from (ℓ_0, Z_0) is $(\ell_0, \overline{(a \leq b+1)})$. We finally obtain $(\ell_0, (a \geq b) \wedge ((a > b+1) \vee ((a \leq b+1) \wedge (a > 0))))$. Thus, there exists a winning strategy if and only if $(a \geq b) \wedge ((a > b+1) \vee (a > 0))$.

It is now easy to extract the memory-less winning strategy from the set of winning states as follows: a controllable action predecessor gives us the state from which a corresponding controllable action should be taken, while safe-timed predecessor further gives us the state where we should delay. Thus, a whole winning strategy consists in: delaying in all states $(\ell_0, \{y < 2\})$, doing c_0 in all states $(\ell_0, \{y \geq 2\})$, doing c_1 in all states $(\ell_1, \{x \leq a\})$, delaying in all states $(\ell_2, \{x < 2\})$, doing c_2 in all states $(\ell_2, \{x \geq 2\})$, doing c_3 in all states $(\ell_3, \{x \geq 0\})$, delaying in all states $(\ell_4, \{x < b\})$, doing c_4 in all states $(\ell_4, \{x \geq b \wedge x \leq a\})$.

5   Conclusion

In this paper we have proposed an extension of a method introduced in [13], for the computation of winning states and synthesis of bounded integer parameters for parametric timed game automata. The method is symbolic and it is based on the computation of the integer hull of the bounded parametric symbolic states. In order to find the winning states, we have extended the standard fixed-point backwards algorithm for solving timed reachability games, for the parametric domain. Surprisingly, we do not have to apply an integer hull in the backwards computation, in order to obtain the correct integer solution. In future, we plan to extend this work to other timed models, such as PTA with stopwatches, as well as to look for less restrictive codomains for parameter valuations.

References

1. Alur, R., Dill, D.: A theory of timed automata. Theoretical Computer Science 126(2), 183–235 (1994)
2. Alur, R., Henzinger, T.A., Vardi, M.Y.: Parametric real-time reasoning. In: ACM Symposium on Theory of Computing, pp. 592–601 (1993)
3. André, E., Chatain, T., Encrenaz, E., Fribourg, L.: An inverse method for parametric timed automata. In: RP Workshop on Reachability Problems, vol. 223, pp. 29–46. Liverpool, U.K (2008)
4. Asarin, E., Maler, O., Pnueli, A., Sifakis, J.: Controller synthesis for timed automata. In: Proc. IFAC SSSC. Elsevier (1998)
5. Behrmann, G., Cougnard, A., David, A., Fleury, E., Larsen, K.G., Lime, D.: UPPAAL-tiga: Time for playing games! In: Damm, W., Hermanns, H. (eds.) CAV 2007. LNCS, vol. 4590, pp. 121–125. Springer, Heidelberg (2007)
6. Bozzelli, L., Torre, S.L.: Decision problems for lower/upper bound parametric timed automata. Formal Methods in System Design 35(2), 121–151 (2009)
7. Bruyère, V., Raskin, J.-F.: Real-time model-checking: Parameters everywhere. Logical Methods in Computer Science 3(1), 1–30 (2007)
8. Cassez, F., David, A., Fleury, E., Larsen, K.G., Lime, D.: Efficient on-the-fly algorithms for the analysis of timed games. In: Abadi, M., de Alfaro, L. (eds.) CONCUR 2005. LNCS, vol. 3653, pp. 66–80. Springer, Heidelberg (2005)
9. Cassez, F., Jessen, J.J., Larsen, K.G., Raskin, J.-F., Reynier, P.-A.: Automatic synthesis of robust and optimal controllers – an industrial case study. In: Majumdar, R., Tabuada, P. (eds.) HSCC 2009. LNCS, vol. 5469, pp. 90–104. Springer, Heidelberg (2009)
10. Henzinger, T.A., Nicollin, X., Sifakis, J., Yovine, S.: Symbolic model checking for real-time systems. Inform. and Computation 111(2), 193–244 (1994)
11. Hune, T., Romijn, J., Stoelinga, M., Vaandrager, F.: Linear parametric model checking of timed automata. Journal of Logic and Algebraic Programming 52-53, 183–220 (2002)
12. Jovanović, A., Faucou, S., Lime, D., Roux, O.H.: Real-time control with parametric timed reachability games. In: Proc. of WODES 2012, pp. 323–330. IFAC (October 2012)
13. Jovanović, A., Lime, D., Roux, O.H.: Integer parameter synthesis for timed automata. In: Piterman, N., Smolka, S.A. (eds.) TACAS 2013. LNCS, vol. 7795, pp. 401–415. Springer, Heidelberg (2013)
14. Jurdziński, M., Trivedi, A.: Reachability-time games on timed automata. In: Arge, L., Cachin, C., Jurdziński, T., Tarlecki, A. (eds.) ICALP 2007. LNCS, vol. 4596, pp. 838–849. Springer, Heidelberg (2007)
15. Maler, O., Pnueli, A., Sifakis, J.: On the synthesis of discrete controllers for timed systems. In: Mayr, E.W., Puech, C. (eds.) STACS 1995. LNCS, vol. 900, pp. 229–242. Springer, Heidelberg (1995)

Kleene Algebras and Semimodules
for Energy Problems

Zoltán Ésik[1,*], Uli Fahrenberg[2], Axel Legay[2], and Karin Quaas[3]

[1] University of Szeged, Hungary
[2] Irisa / INRIA Rennes, France
[3] Universität Leipzig, Germany

Abstract. With the purpose of unifying a number of approaches to energy problems found in the literature, we introduce generalized energy automata. These are finite automata whose edges are labeled with energy functions that define how energy levels evolve during transitions. Uncovering a close connection between energy problems and reachability and Büchi acceptance for semiring-weighted automata, we show that these generalized energy problems are decidable. We also provide complexity results for important special cases.

1 Introduction

Energy and *resource management* problems are important in areas such as embedded systems or autonomous systems. They are concerned with the question whether a given system admits infinite schedules during which (1) certain tasks can be repeatedly accomplished and (2) the system never runs out of energy (or other specified resources). Starting with [8], formal modeling and analysis of such problems has recently attracted some attention [7,9,13,16,21,28].

As an example, the left part of Fig. 1 shows a simple model of an electric car, modeled as a weighted timed automaton [4,5]. In the *working* state W, energy is consumed at a rate of 10 energy units per time unit; in the two *recharging* states R_1, R_2, the battery is charged at a rate of 20, respectively 10, energy units per time unit. As the clock c is reset ($c \leftarrow 0$) when entering state W and has guard $c \geq 1$ on outgoing transitions, we ensure that the car always has to be in state W for at least one time unit. Similarly, the system can only transition back from states R_1, R_2 to W if it has spent at most one time unit in these states.

Passing between states W and R_1 requires 4 energy units, while transitioning between W and R_2, and between R_2 to R_1, requires 2 energy units. Altogether, this is intended to model the fact that there are two recharge stations available, one close to work but less powerful, and a more powerful one further away. Now

---

* The reserach of this author is supported by the European Union and co-funded by the European Social Fund. Project title: 'Telemedicine-focused research activities on the field of mathematics, informatics and medical sciences'. Project number: TÁMOP-4.2.2.A-11/1/KONV-2012-0073.

D. Van Hung and M. Ogawa (Eds.): ATVA 2013, LNCS 8172, pp. 102–117, 2013.

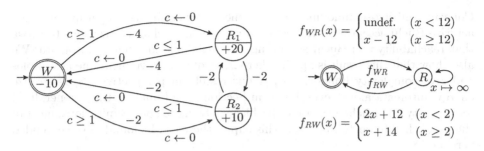

Fig. 1. Simple model of an electric car as a weighted timed automaton (left); the corresponding energy automaton (right)

assume that the initial state W is entered with a given *initial energy* x_0, then the energy problem of this model is as follows: Does there exist an infinite trace which (1) visits W infinitely often and (2) never has an energy level below 0?

This type of energy problems for weighted timed automata is treated in [7], and using a reduction like in [7], our model can be transformed to the *energy automaton* in the right part of Fig. 1. (The reduction is quite complicated and only works for one-clock timed automata; see [7] for details.) It can be shown that the energy problem for the original automaton is equivalent to the following problem in the energy automaton: Given an initial energy x_0, and updating the energy according to the transition label whenever taking a transition, does there exist an infinite run which visits W infinitely often? Remark that the energy update on the transition from R to W is rather complex (in the general case of n recharge stations, the definition of f_{RW} can have up to n branches), and that we need to impose a Büchi condition to enforce visiting W infinitely often.

In this paper we propose a generalization of the energy automata of [7] which also encompasses most other approaches to energy problems. Abstracting the properties of the transition update functions in our example, we define a general notion of *energy functions* which specify how weights change from one system state to another. Noticing that our functional energy automata are semiring-weighted automata in the sense of [17], we uncover a close connection between energy problems and reachability and Büchi problems for weighted automata. More precisely, we show that one-dimensional energy problems can be naturally solved using matrix operations in semirings and semimodules [6, 17, 19, 20].

For reachability, we use only standard results [17], but for Büchi acceptance we have to extend previous work [19, 20] as our semiring is not complete. We thus show that reachability and Büchi acceptance are decidable for energy automata. For the class of *piecewise affine* energy functions, which generalize the functions of Fig. 1 and are important in applications, they are decidable in exponential time.

Structure of the Paper. We introduce our general model of energy automata in Section 2. In Section 3 we show that the set of energy functions forms a star-continuous Kleene algebra, a fact which allows us to give an elegant characterization of reachability in energy automata. We also expose a structure of

Conway semiring-semimodule pair over energy functions which permits to characterize Büchi acceptance. In Section 4 we use these characterizations to prove that reachability and Büchi acceptance are decidable for energy automata. We also show that this result is applicable to most of the above-mentioned examples and give complexity bounds. To put our results in perspective, we generalize energy automata along several axes in Section 5 and analyze these generalized reachability and Büchi acceptance problems. Owing to space limitations, most of the proofs had to be omitted from this paper; these can be found in the extended version [18].

Related Work. A simple class of energy automata is the one of *integer-weighted automata*, where all energy functions are updates of the form $x \mapsto x + k$ for some (positive or negative) integer k. Energy problems on these automata, and their extensions to multiple weights (also called *vector addition systems with states* (VASS)) and games, have been considered *e.g.* in [8,10–14,21]. Our energy automata may hence be considered as a generalization of one-dimensional VASS to arbitrary updates; in the final section of this paper we will also be concerned with multi-dimensional energy automata and games.

Energy problems on *timed automata* [3] have been considered in [7–9,28]. Here timed automata are enriched with integer weights in locations and on transitions (the *weighted timed automata* of [4,5], *cf.* Fig. 1), with the semantics that the weight of a delay in a location is computed by multiplying the length of the delay by the location weight. In [8] it is shown that energy problems for one-clock weighted timed automata without updates on transitions (hence only with weights in locations) can be reduced to energy problems on integer-weighted automata with additive updates.

For one-clock weighted timed automata *with* transition updates, energy problems are shown decidable in [7], using a reduction to energy automata as we use them here. More precisely, each path in the timed automaton in which the clock is not reset is converted to an edge in an energy automaton, labeled with a *piecewise affine* energy function (*cf.* Definition 4). Decidability of the energy problem is then shown using ad-hoc arguments, but can easily be inferred from our general results in the present paper.

Also another class of energy problems on weighted timed automata is considered in [7], in which weights during delays are increasing *exponentially* rather than linearly. These are shown decidable using a reduction to energy automata with *piecewise polynomial* energy functions; again our present framework applies.

We also remark that semigroups acting on a set, or more generally, semiring-semimodule pairs, have been used to describe the infinitary behavior of automata for a long time, see [6,27,31]. In this framework, the infinitary product or omega operation is defined on the semiring and takes its values in the semimodule. Another approach is studied *e.g.* in [26], where the omega operation maps the semiring into itself. It seems to the authors that there is no reasonable definition of an infinitary product or omega operation on energy functions that would again result in an energy function, hence we chose to use the framework of semiring-semimodule pairs.

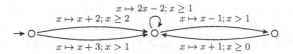

Fig. 2. A simple energy automaton

2 Energy Automata

The transition labels on the energy automata which we consider in the paper, will be functions which model transformations of energy levels between system states. Such transformations have the (natural) properties that below a certain energy level, the transition might be disabled (not enough energy is available to perform the transition), and an increase in input energy always yields at least the same increase in output energy. Thus the following definition.

Definition 1. *An* energy function *is a partial function* $f : \mathbb{R}_{\geq 0} \to \mathbb{R}_{\geq 0}$ *which is defined on a closed interval* $[l_f, \infty[$ *or on an open interval* $]l_f, \infty[$, *for some lower bound* $l_f \geq 0$, *and such that for all* $x_1 \leq x_2$ *for which* f *is defined,*

$$f(x_2) \geq f(x_1) + x_2 - x_1. \tag{$*$}$$

The class of all energy functions is denoted by $\mathcal{F}$.

Thus energy functions are strictly increasing, and in points where they are differentiable, the derivative is at least 1.[1] The inverse functions to energy functions exist, but are generally not energy functions. Energy functions can be *composed*, where it is understood that for a composition $g \circ f$ (to be read from right to left), the interval of definition is $\{x \in \mathbb{R}_{\geq 0} \mid f(x) \text{ and } g(f(x)) \text{ defined}\}$. We will generally omit the symbol $\circ$ and write composition simply as gf.

Definition 2. *An* energy automaton (S, T) *consists of finite sets* S *of states and* $T \subseteq S \times \mathcal{F} \times S$ *of transitions labeled with energy functions.*

We show an example of a simple energy automaton in Fig. 2. Here we use inequalities to give the definition intervals of energy functions.

A finite *path* in an energy automaton is a finite sequence of transitions $\pi = (s_0, f_1, s_1), (s_1, f_2, s_2), \dots, (s_{n-1}, f_n, s_n)$. We use f_π to denote the combined energy function $f_n \cdots f_2 f_1$ of such a finite path. We will also use infinite paths, but note that these generally do not allow for combined energy functions.

A *global state* of an energy automaton is a pair $q = (s, x)$ with $s \in S$ and $x \in \mathbb{R}_{\geq 0}$. A transition between global states is of the form $((s, x), f, (s', x'))$ such that $(s, f, s') \in T$ and $x' = f(x)$. A (finite or infinite) *run* of (S, T) is a path in the graph of global states and transitions.

---

[1] Remark that, in relation to the example in the introduction, the derivative is taken with respect to *energy input*, not *time*. Hence the mapping from input to output energy in state W is indeed an energy function in our sense.

We are ready to state the decision problems with which our main concern will lie. As the input to a decision problem must be in some way finitely representable, we will state them for subclasses $\mathcal{F}' \subseteq \mathcal{F}$ of *computable* energy functions; an $\mathcal{F}'$-automaton is an energy automaton (S, T) with $T \subseteq S \times \mathcal{F}' \times S$.

Problem 1 (Reachability). Given a subset $\mathcal{F}'$ of computable functions, an $\mathcal{F}'$-automaton (S, T), an initial state $s_0 \in S$, a set of accepting states $F \subseteq S$, and a computable initial energy $x_0 \in \mathbb{R}_{\geq 0}$: does there exist a finite run of (S, T) from (s_0, x_0) which ends in a state in F?

Problem 2 (Büchi acceptance). Given a subset $\mathcal{F}'$ of computable functions, an $\mathcal{F}'$-automaton (S, T), an initial state $s_0 \in S$, a set of accepting states $F \subseteq S$, and a computable initial energy $x_0 \in \mathbb{R}_{\geq 0}$: does there exist an infinite run of (S, T) from (s_0, x_0) which visits F infinitely often?

As customary, a run such as in the statements above is said to be accepting. We let $\mathsf{Reach}_{\mathcal{F}'}$ denote the function which maps an $\mathcal{F}'$-automaton together with an initial state, a set of final states, and an initial energy to the Boolean values **ff** or **tt** depending on whether the answer to the concrete reachability problem is negative or positive. $\mathsf{Büchi}_{\mathcal{F}'}$ denotes the similar mapping for Büchi problems.

The special case of Problem 2 with $F = S$ is the question whether there *exists an infinite run* in the given energy automaton. This is what is usually referred to as *energy problems* in the literature; our extension to general Büchi conditions has not been treated before.

3   The Algebra of Energy Functions

In this section we develop an algebraic framework of *star-continuous Kleene algebra* around energy functions which will allow us to solve reachability and Büchi acceptance problems in a generic way. Let $[0, \infty]_{\perp} = \{\perp\} \cup [0, \infty]$ denote the non-negative real numbers together with extra elements $\perp, \infty$, with the standard order on $\mathbb{R}_{\geq 0}$ extended by $\perp < x < \infty$ for all $x \in \mathbb{R}_{\geq 0}$. Also, $\perp + x = \perp - x = \perp$ for all $x \in \mathbb{R}_{\geq 0} \cup \{\infty\}$ and $\infty + x = \infty - x$ for all $x \in \mathbb{R}_{\geq 0}$.

Definition 3. *An* extended energy function *is a mapping* $f : [0, \infty]_{\perp} \to [0, \infty]_{\perp}$, *for which* $f(\perp) = \perp$ *and* $f(x_2) \geq f(x_1) + x_2 - x_1$ *for all* $x_1 \leq x_2$, *as in* (*). *Moreover,* $f(\infty) = \infty$, *unless* $f(x) = \perp$ *for all* $x \in [0, \infty]_{\perp}$. *The class of all* extended energy functions *is denoted* $\mathcal{E}$.

This means, in particular, that $f(x) = \perp$ implies $f(x') = \perp$ for all $x' \leq x$, and $f(x) = \infty$ implies $f(x') = \infty$ for all $x' \geq x$. Hence, except for the extension to ∞, these functions are indeed the same as our energy functions from the previous section. Composition of extended energy functions is defined as before, but needs no more special consideration about its definition interval.

We also define an ordering on $\mathcal{E}$, by $f \leq g$ iff $f(x) \leq g(x)$ for all $x \in [0, \infty]_{\perp}$. We will need three special energy functions, $\perp\!\!\!\perp$, id and $\top$; these are given by $\perp\!\!\!\perp(x) = \perp$, $\mathsf{id}(x) = x$ for $x \in [0, \infty]_{\perp}$, and $\top(\perp) = \perp$, $\top(x) = \infty$ for $x \in [0, \infty]$.

Lemma 1. *With the ordering* $\leq$, $\mathcal{E}$ *is a complete lattice with bottom element* $\perp$ *and top element* $\top$. *The supremum on* $\mathcal{E}$ *is pointwise, i.e.* $(\sup_{i \in I} f_i)(x) = \sup_{i \in I} f_i(x)$ *for any set* I, *all* $f_i \in \mathcal{E}$ *and* $x \in [0, \infty]_\perp$. *Also,* $(\sup_{i \in I} f_i)h = \sup_{i \in I}(f_i h)$ *for all* $h \in \mathcal{E}$.

We denote binary suprema using the symbol $\vee$; hence $f \vee g$, for $f, g \in \mathcal{E}$, is the function $(f \vee g)(x) = \max(f(x), g(x))$.

Lemma 2. $(\mathcal{E}, \vee, \circ, \perp, \mathsf{id})$ *is an idempotent semiring with natural order* $\leq$.

Recall [17] that $\leq$ being natural refers to the fact that $f \leq g$ iff $f \vee g = g$.
For iterating energy functions, we define a unary star operation on $\mathcal{E}$ by

$$f^*(x) = \begin{cases} x & \text{if } f(x) \leq x\,, \\ \infty & \text{if } f(x) > x\,. \end{cases}$$

Lemma 3. *For any* $f \in \mathcal{E}$, *we have* $f^* \in \mathcal{E}$. *Also, for any* $g \in \mathcal{E}$, *there exists* $f \in \mathcal{E}$ *such that* $g = f^*$ *if, and only if, there is* $k \in [0, \infty]_\perp$ *such that* $g(x) = x$ *for all* $x < k$, $g(x) = \infty$ *for all* $x > k$, *and* $g(k) = k$ *or* $g(k) = \infty$.

By Lemma 1, composition right-distributes over arbitrary suprema in $\mathcal{E}$. The following example shows that a similar left distributivity does *not* hold in general, hence $\mathcal{E}$ is *not* a complete semiring the sense of [17]. Let $f_n, g \in \mathcal{E}$ be defined by $f_n(x) = x + 1 - \frac{1}{n}$ for $x \geq 0$, $n \in \mathbb{N}_+$ and $g(x) = x$ for $x \geq 1$. Then $g(\sup_n f_n)(0) = g(\sup_n f_n(0)) = g(1) = 1$, whereas $(\sup_n g f_n)(0) = \sup_n g(f_n(0)) = \sup_n g(1 - \frac{1}{n}) = \perp$.

The next lemma shows a restricted form of left distributivity which holds only for function powers f^n. Note that it implies that $f^* = \sup_n f^n$ for all $f \in \mathcal{E}$, which justifies the definition of f^* above.

Lemma 4. *For any* $f, g \in \mathcal{E}$, $gf^* = \sup_{n \in \mathbb{N}}(gf^n)$.

Proposition 1. *For any* $f, g, h \in \mathcal{E}$, $gf^*h = \sup_{n \in \mathbb{N}}(gf^nh)$. *Hence* $\mathcal{E}$ *is a star-continuous Kleene algebra* [24].

We call a subsemiring $\mathcal{E}' \subseteq \mathcal{E}$ a *subalgebra* if $f^* \in \mathcal{E}'$ for all $f \in \mathcal{E}'$.

It is known [6, 15, 17, 25] that when S is a star-continuous Kleene algebra, then so is any matrix semiring $S^{n \times n}$, for all $n \geq 1$, with the usual sum and product operations. The natural order on $S^{n \times n}$ is pointwise, so that for all $n \times n$ matrices A, B over S, $A \leq B$ iff $A_{i,j} \leq B_{i,j}$ for all i, j. Now a star-continuous Kleene algebra is also a Conway semiring, hence the Conway identities

$$(g \vee f)^* = (g^*f)^*g^* \quad \text{and} \quad (gf)^* = g(fg)^*f \vee \mathsf{id} \tag{1}$$

are satisfied for all $f, g \in \mathcal{E}$. Also, this implies that the matrix semiring $\mathcal{E}^{n \times n}$ is again a Conway semiring, for any $n \geq 1$, with the star operation defined inductively for a matrix

$$M = \begin{bmatrix} a & b \\ c & d \end{bmatrix} \in \mathcal{E}^{n \times n}, \tag{2}$$

where a is $k \times k$ and d is $m \times m$ with $k + m = n$, by

$$M^* = \begin{bmatrix} (a \vee bd^*c)^* & (a \vee bd^*c)^*bd^* \\ (d \vee ca^*b)^*ca^* & (d \vee ca^*b)^* \end{bmatrix} \in \mathcal{E}^{n \times n}. \tag{3}$$

The definition of M^* does not depend on how M is split into parts, and star-continuity implies that for all matrices M, N, O,

$$NM^*O = \sup_{n \in \mathbb{N}}(NM^nO). \tag{4}$$

Note again that this implies that $M^* = \sup_n M^n$ for all matrices M. In a sense, this gives another, inductive definition of the star operation on the matrix semiring; the important property of star-continuous Kleene algebras is, then, that this inductive definition and the one in (3) give rise to the same operation.

We introduce a semimodule $\mathcal{V}$ over $\mathcal{E}$. Let $\mathcal{B} = \{\mathbf{ff}, \mathbf{tt}\}$ be the Boolean algebra, with order $\mathbf{ff} < \mathbf{tt}$, and $\mathcal{V} = \{u : [0, \infty]_\perp \to \mathcal{B} \mid u(\perp) = \mathbf{ff}, x_1 \leq x_2 \Rightarrow u(x_1) \leq u(x_2)\}$. Identifying $\mathbf{ff}$ with $\perp$ and $\mathbf{tt}$ with ∞, we have an embedding of $\mathcal{V}$ into $\mathcal{E}$; note that $\perp, \top \in \mathcal{V}$.

Lemma 5. *With action* $(u, f) \mapsto uf : \mathcal{V} \times \mathcal{E} \to \mathcal{V}$, $\mathcal{V}$ *is a right $\mathcal{E}$-semimodule [20]. Moreover,* $(\sup_{i \in I} u_i)f = \sup_{i \in I}(u_i f)$ *for any set I, all $u_i \in \mathcal{V}$ and $f \in \mathcal{E}$, and* $uf^* = \sup_{n \in \mathbb{N}} uf^n$ *for all $u \in \mathcal{V}$.*

So like the situation for $\mathcal{E}$ (*cf.* Lemmas 1 and 4), the action of $\mathcal{E}$ on $\mathcal{V}$ right-distributes over arbitrary suprema and left-distributes over function powers.

We define an infinitary product operation $\mathcal{E}^\omega \to \mathcal{V}$. Let $f_0, f_1, \ldots$ be an infinite sequence of energy functions and $x_0 \in [0, \infty]_\perp$, and put $x_{n+1} = f_n(x_n)$ for $n \in \mathbb{N}$. Then we define

$$\left(\prod_{i=0}^{\infty} f_i\right)(x_0) = \begin{cases} \mathbf{ff} & \text{if } \exists n \in \mathbb{N} : x_n = \perp, \\ \mathbf{tt} & \text{if } \forall n \in \mathbb{N} : x_n \neq \perp. \end{cases}$$

Note that this product is order-preserving. By the next lemma, it is a conservative extension of the finite product. As $\mathcal{E}$ is not a complete semiring, it follows that $(\mathcal{E}, \mathcal{V})$ is not a complete semiring-semimodule pair in the sense of [20].

Lemma 6. *For all* $f_0, f_1, \ldots \in \mathcal{E}$, $(\prod_{i=1}^{\infty} f_i)f_0 = \prod_{i=0}^{\infty} f_i$. *For all indices* $0 = n_0 \leq n_1 \leq \ldots$, $\prod_{i=0}^{\infty} f_i = \prod_{i=0}^{\infty}(f_{n_{i+1}-1} \cdots f_{n_i})$.

To deal with infinite iterations of energy functions, we define a unary omega operation $\mathcal{E} \to \mathcal{V}$ by

$$f^\omega(x) = \begin{cases} \mathbf{ff} & \text{if } x = \perp \text{ or } f(x) < x, \\ \mathbf{tt} & \text{if } x \neq \perp \text{ and } f(x) \geq x. \end{cases}$$

Note that $f^\omega = \prod_{i=0}^{\infty} f$ for all $f \in \mathcal{E}$.

Proposition 2. $(\mathcal{E}, \mathcal{V})$ *is a Conway semiring-semimodule pair.*

Recall [6] that this means that additionally to the identities (1),

$$(gf)^\omega = (fg)^\omega f \quad \text{and} \quad (f \vee g)^\omega = f^\omega (gf^*)^* \vee (gf^*)^\omega$$

for all $f, g \in \mathcal{E}$. Like for Conway semirings, it implies that the pair $(\mathcal{E}^{n \times n}, \mathcal{V}^n)$ is again a Conway semiring-semimodule pair, for any $n \geq 1$, with the action of $\mathcal{E}^{n \times n}$ on $\mathcal{V}^n$ similar to matrix-vector multiplication using the action of $\mathcal{E}$ on $\mathcal{V}$, and the omega operation $\mathcal{E}^{n \times n} \to \mathcal{V}^n$ given inductively as follows: for $M \in \mathcal{E}^{n \times n}$ with blocks as in (2), define

$$M^\omega = \left[(a \vee bd^*c)^\omega \vee d^\omega c(a \vee bd^*c)^* \quad (d \vee ca^*b)^\omega \vee a^\omega b(d \vee ca^*b)^* \right], \qquad (5)$$
$$M^{\omega_k} = \left[(a \vee bd^*c)^\omega \quad (a \vee bd^*c)^\omega bd^* \right].$$

The definition of M^ω does not depend on how M is split into parts, but the one of M^{ω_k} does (recall that a is a $k \times k$ matrix). It can be shown [6] that (5), and also (3), follow directly from certain general properties of fixed point operations.

4   Decidability

We are now ready to apply the Kleene algebra framework to reachability and Büchi acceptance for energy automata. We first show that it is sufficient to consider energy automata (S, T) with precisely one transition $(s, f, s') \in T$ for each pair of states $s, s' \in S$. This will allow us to consider T as a matrix $S \times S \to \mathcal{E}$ (as is standard in weighted-automata theory [17]).

Lemma 7. *Let $\mathcal{E}' \subseteq \mathcal{E}$ be a subalgebra and (S, T) an $\mathcal{E}'$-automaton. There exists an $\mathcal{E}'$-automaton (S, T') for which $\mathsf{Reach}_{\mathcal{E}'}(S, T) = \mathsf{Reach}_{\mathcal{E}'}(S, T')$ and $\mathsf{Büchi}_{\mathcal{E}'}(S, T) = \mathsf{Büchi}_{\mathcal{E}'}(S, T')$, and in which there is precisely one transition $(s, f, s') \in T'$ for all $s, s' \in S$.*

Hence we may, without loss of generality, view the transitions T of an energy automaton as a matrix $T : S \times S \to \mathcal{E}$. We can also let $S = \{1, \ldots, n\}$ and assume that the set of accepting states is $F = \{1, \ldots, k\}$ for $k \leq n$. Further, we can represent an initial state $s_0 \in S$ by the s_0th unit (column) vector $I^{s_0} \in \{\bot, \mathsf{id}\}^n$, defined by $I_i^{s_0} = \mathsf{id}$ iff $i = s_0$, and F by the (column) vector $F^{\leq k} \in \{\bot, \mathsf{id}\}^n$ given by $F_i^{\leq k} = \mathsf{id}$ iff $i \leq k$. Note that $T \in \mathcal{E}^{n \times n}$ is an $n \times n$-matrix of energy functions; as composition of energy functions is written right-to-left, $T_{ij} \in \mathcal{E}$ is the function on the transition from s_j to s_i.

Theorem 1. *Let $\mathcal{E}' \subseteq \mathcal{E}$ be a subalgebra. For any $\mathcal{E}'$-automaton (S, T) with $S = \{1, \ldots, n\}$, $F = \{1, \ldots, k\}$, $k \leq n$, $s_0 \leq n$, and $x_0 \in \mathbb{R}_{\geq 0}$, we have $\mathsf{Reach}_{\mathcal{E}'}(S, T)(F, s_0, x_0) = \mathsf{tt}$ if, and only if, $_t F^{\leq k} T^* I^{s_0}(x_0) \neq \bot$.*

Proof. Here $_t F^{\leq k}$ denotes the transpose of $F^{\leq k}$. By (4), we have $_t F^{\leq k} T^* I^{s_0} = \sup_n (_t F^{\leq k} T^n I^{s_0})$, so that $_t F^{\leq k} T^* I^{s_0}(x_0) \neq \bot$ iff $_t F^{\leq k} T^n I^{s_0}(x_0) \neq \bot$ for some $n \in \mathbb{N}$, *i.e.* iff there is a finite run from (s_0, x_0) which ends in a state in F. $\qquad \square$

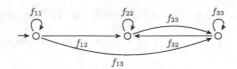

$$f_{11}(x) = \quad x; \quad x \geq 0$$
$$f_{12}(x) = \quad \infty; \quad x > 1$$

$$f_{23}(x) = \begin{cases} x - 1; & 1 < x \leq 2 \\ \infty; & x > 2 \end{cases}$$

$$f_{33}(x) = \begin{cases} x; & x \leq 1 \\ \infty; & x > 1 \end{cases}$$

$$f_{22}(x) = \begin{cases} x; & x \leq 2 \\ \infty; & x > 2 \end{cases}$$

$$f_{32}(x) = \begin{cases} x + 1; & x \leq 1 \\ \infty; & x > 1 \end{cases}$$

$$f_{13}(x) = \quad \infty; \quad x > 1$$

Fig. 3. The closure of the automaton from Fig. 2

Referring back to the example automaton (S, T) from Fig. 2, we display in Fig. 3 the automaton with transition matrix T^*.

Theorem 2. *Let $\mathcal{E}' \subseteq \mathcal{E}$ be a subalgebra. For any $\mathcal{E}'$-automaton (S, T) with $S = \{1, \ldots, n\}$, $F = \{1, \ldots, k\}$, $k \leq n$, $s_0 \leq n$, and $x_0 \in \mathbb{R}_{\geq 0}$, we have $\text{Büchi}_{\mathcal{E}'}(S, T)(F, s_0, x_0) = T^{\omega_k} I^{s_0}(x_0)$.*

Proof. This is a standard result for *complete* semiring-semimodule pairs, *cf.* [20]. Now $(\mathcal{E}, \mathcal{V})$ is not complete, but the properties developed in the previous section allow us to show the result nevertheless. We need to see that for all $M \in \mathcal{E}^{n \times n}$ and $1 \leq i \leq n$,

$$(M^\omega)_i = \sup\{\cdots M_{k_3, k_2} M_{k_2, k_1} M_{k_1, i} : 1 \leq k_1, k_2, \ldots \leq n\},$$

which we shall deduce inductively from (5).

Let $a \in \mathcal{E}^{\ell \times \ell}$, $d \in \mathcal{E}^{m \times m}$, for $\ell + m = n$, and let $i \in \{1, \ldots, \ell\}$. Then the ith component of M^ω is the ith component of $(a \vee bd^*c)^\omega \vee d^\omega c(a \vee bd^*c)^*$. By induction hypothesis, the ith component of $(a \vee bd^*c)^\omega$ is the supremum of all infinite products $(\cdots M_{k_2, k_1} M_{k_1, i})$ such that $1 \leq k_j \leq m$ for an infinite number of indices j, and similarly, the ith component of $d^\omega c(a \vee bd^*c)^*$ is the supremum of all infinite products $(\cdots M_{k_2, k_1} M_{k_1, i})$ such that $1 \leq k_j \leq m$ for a finite number of indices j. Thus, the ith component of $(a \vee bd^*c)^\omega \vee d^\omega c(a \vee bd^*c)^*$ is the supremum of all infinite products $(\cdots M_{k_2, k_1} M_{k_1, i})$. $\square$

We remark that our decision algorithms are *static* in the sense that the matrix expressions can be pre-computed and then re-used to decide reachability and Büchi acceptance for different values x_0 of initial energies.

Using elementary reasoning on infinite paths, we can provide an alternative characterization of Büchi acceptance which does not use the omega operations:

Theorem 3. *Let $\mathcal{E}' \subseteq \mathcal{E}$ be a subalgebra. For any $\mathcal{E}'$-automaton (S, T) with $S = \{1, \ldots, n\}$, $F = \{1, \ldots, k\}$, $k \leq n$, $s_0 \leq n$, and $x_0 \in \mathbb{R}_{\geq 0}$, we have $\text{Büchi}_{\mathcal{E}'}(S, T)(F, s_0, x_0) = \text{tt}$ if, and only if, there exists $j \leq k$ for which*

$$_t I^j T T^* I^j \,_t I^j T^* I^{s_0}(x_0) \geq \,_t I^j T^* I^{s_0}(x_0) \neq \perp.$$

Corollary 1. *For subalgebras $\mathcal{E}' \subseteq \mathcal{E}$ of computable functions in which it is decidable for each $f \in \mathcal{E}'$ whether $f(x) \leq x$, Problems 1 and 2 are decidable. For an energy automaton with n states and m transitions, the decision procedures use $O(m + n^3)$, respectively $O(m + n^4)$, algebra operations.*

Proof. Maxima and compositions of computable functions are again computable, and if it is decidable for each $f \in \mathcal{E}'$ whether $f(x) \leq x$, then also f^* is computable for each $f \in \mathcal{E}'$. Hence all matrix operations used in Lemma 7 and Theorems 1 and 3 are computable. The number of operations necessary in the construction in the proof of Lemma 7 is $O(m)$, and, using *e.g.* the Floyd-Warshall algorithm to compute T^*, $O(n^3)$ operations are necessary to compute ${}_t I^{\leq k} T^* I^{s_0}$.   □

We proceed to identify two important subclasses of computable energy functions, which cover most of the related work mentioned in the introduction, and to give complexity results on their reachability and Büchi acceptance problems. The *integer update functions* in $\mathcal{E}$ are the functions f_k, for $k \in \mathbb{Z}$, given by

$$f_k(x) = \begin{cases} x + k & \text{if } x \geq \max(0, -k), \\ \bot & \text{otherwise}, \end{cases}$$

together with $f_\infty := \top$. These are the update functions usually considered in integer-weighted automata and VASS [8, 10–14, 21]. We have $f_\ell f_k = f_{k+\ell}$ and $f_k \vee f_\ell = f_{\max(k,\ell)}$, and $f_k^* = f_0$ for $k \leq 0$ and $f_k^* = f_\infty$ for $k > 0$, whence the class $\mathcal{E}_{\text{int}}$ of integer update functions forms a subalgebra of $\mathcal{E}$. A function $f_k \in \mathcal{E}_{\text{int}}$ can be represented by the integer k, and algebra operations can then be performed in constant time. Hence Corollary 1 implies the following result.

Theorem 4. *For $\mathcal{E}_{\text{int}}$-automata, Problems 1 and 2 are decidable in PTIME.*

Next we turn our attention to piecewise affine functions as used in Fig. 1.

Definition 4. *A function $f \in \mathcal{E}$ is said to be (rational) piecewise affine if there exist $x_0 < x_1 < \cdots < x_k \in \mathbb{Q}$ such that $f(x) \neq \bot$ iff $x \geq x_0$ or $x > x_0$, $f(x_j) \in \mathbb{Q} \cup \{\bot\}$ for all j, and all restrictions $f_{1]x_j, x_{j+1}[}$ and $f_{1]x_k, \infty[}$ are affine functions $x \mapsto a_j x + b_j$ with $a_j, b_j \in \mathbb{Q}$, $a_j \geq 1$.*

Note that the definition does not make any assertion about continuity at the x_j, but (∗) implies that $\lim_{x \nearrow x_j} f(x) \leq f(x_j) \leq \lim_{x \searrow x_j} f(x)$. A piecewise affine function as above can be represented by its break points $x_0, \ldots, x_k$, the values $f(x_0), \ldots, f(x_k)$, and the numbers $a_0, b_0, \ldots, a_k, b_k$. These functions arise in the reduction used in [7] to show decidability of energy problems for one-clock timed automata with transition updates. The notion of *integer piecewise affine* functions is defined similarly, with all occurrences of $\mathbb{Q}$ above replaced by $\mathbb{Z}$. Fig. 4 shows an example of a piecewise affine function.

The class $\mathcal{E}_{\text{pw}}$ of piecewise affine energy functions forms a subsemiring of $\mathcal{E}$: if $f, g \in \mathcal{E}_{\text{pw}}$ with break points $x_0, \ldots, x_k$, $y_0, \ldots, y_\ell$, respectively, then $f \vee g$ is piecewise affine with break points a subset of $\{x_0, \ldots, x_k, y_0, \ldots, y_\ell\}$, and gf is piecewise affine with break points a subset of $\{x_0, \ldots, x_k, f^{-1}(y_0), \ldots, f^{-1}(y_\ell)\}$.

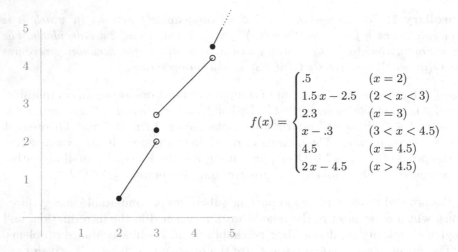

$$f(x) = \begin{cases} .5 & (x = 2) \\ 1.5\,x - 2.5 & (2 < x < 3) \\ 2.3 & (x = 3) \\ x - .3 & (3 < x < 4.5) \\ 4.5 & (x = 4.5) \\ 2\,x - 4.5 & (x > 4.5) \end{cases}$$

Fig. 4. A piecewise affine energy function

Let, for any $k \in \mathbb{Q}$, $g_k^-, g_k^+ : [0, \infty]_\perp \to [0, \infty]_\perp$ be the functions defined by

$$g_k^-(x) = \begin{cases} x & \text{for } x < k, \\ \infty & \text{for } x \geq k, \end{cases} \qquad g_k^+(x) = \begin{cases} x & \text{for } x \leq k, \\ \infty & \text{for } x > k. \end{cases}$$

By Lemma 3 (and noticing that for all $f \in \mathcal{E}_{\mathsf{pw}}$, $\sup\{x \mid f(x) \leq x\}$ is rational), $\mathcal{E}_{\mathsf{pw}}$ completed with the functions g_k^-, g_k^+ forms a subalgebra of $\mathcal{E}$.

Remark that, unlike $\mathcal{E}_{\mathsf{pw}}$, the class $\mathcal{E}_{\mathsf{pwi}}$ of integer piecewise affine functions does *not* form a subsemiring of $\mathcal{E}$, as composites of $\mathcal{E}_{\mathsf{pwi}}$-functions are not necessarily integer piecewise affine. As an example, for the functions $f, g \in \mathcal{E}_{\mathsf{pwi}}$ given by

$$f(x) = 2x, \qquad g(x) = \begin{cases} x + 1; & x < 3, \\ x + 2; & x \geq 3, \end{cases}$$

we have

$$g(f(x)) = \begin{cases} 2x + 1; & x < 1.5, \\ 2x + 2; & x \geq 1.5. \end{cases}$$

which is not integer piecewise affine. Similarly, the class of rational *affine* functions $x \mapsto ax + b$ (without break points) is not closed under maximum, and $\mathcal{E}_{\mathsf{pw}}$ is the semiring generated by rational affine functions.

Theorem 5. *For $\mathcal{E}_{\mathsf{pw}}$-automata, Problems 1 and 2 are decidable in EXPTIME.*

Proof. We need to show that it is decidable for each $f \in \mathcal{E}_{\mathsf{pw}}$ whether $f(x) \leq x$. Let thus f be a piecewise affine function, with representation $(x_0, \ldots, x_k, f(x_0),$ $\ldots, f(x_k), a_0, \ldots, a_k, b_0, \ldots, b_k)$. If $x < x_0$, then $f(x) = \perp \leq x$. If $x = x_j$ for some j, we can simply compare x_j with $f(x_j)$.

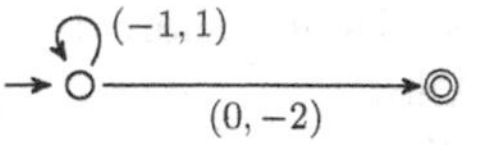

Fig. 5. A simple two-dimensional VASS

Assume now that $x \in \,]x_j, x_{j+1}[$ for some j. If $a_j x_j + b_j \leq x_j$ and $a_j x_{j+1} + b_j \leq x_{j+1}$, then also $f(x) \leq x$ by $(*)$. Likewise, if $a_j x_j + b_j > x_j$ and $a_j x_{j+1} + b_j > x_{j+1}$, then also $f(x) > x$. The case $a_j x_j + b_j > x_j$, $a_j x_{j+1} + b_j \leq x_{j+1}$ cannot occur because of $(*)$, and if $a_j x_j + b_j \leq x_j$ and $a_j x_{j+1} + b_j > x_{j+1}$, then $a_j > 1$, and $f(x) \leq x$ iff $x \leq \frac{b_j}{1 - a_j}$.

For the case $x \in \,]x_k, \infty[$, the arguments are similar: if $a_k x_k + b_k > x_k$, then also $f(x) > x$; if $a_k x_k + b_k \leq x_k$ and $a_k = 1$, then also $f(x) \leq x$, and if $a_k > 1$ in this case, then $f(x) \leq x$ iff $x \leq \frac{b_k}{1 - a_k}$.

Using Corollary 1, we have hence shown decidability. For the complexity claim, we note that all algebra operations in $\mathcal{E}_{\mathsf{pw}}$ can be performed in time linear in the size of the representations of the involved functions. However, the maximum and composition operations may double the size of the representations, hence our procedure may take time $O(2^{m+n^3} p)$ for reachability, and $O(2^{m+n^4} p)$ for Büchi acceptance, for an $\mathcal{E}_{\mathsf{pw}}$-automaton with n states, m transitions, and energy functions of representation length at most p.   □

In the setting of $\mathcal{E}_{\mathsf{pw}}$-automata and their application to one-clock weighted timed automata with transition updates, our Theorem 3 is a generalization of [7, Lemmas 24, 25]. Complexity of the decision procedure was left open in [7]; as the conversion of a one-clock weighted timed automaton to an $\mathcal{E}_{\mathsf{pw}}$-automaton incurs an exponential blowup, we now see that their procedure is doubly-exponential.

Considerations similar to the above show that also the setting of *piecewise polynomial* energy functions allows an application of Theorem 3 to show energy problems on the exponentially weighted timed automata from [7] decidable.

5   Multi-dimensional Energy Automata and Games

Next we turn our attention to several variants of energy automata. We will generally stick to the set $\mathcal{E}_{\mathsf{pwi}}$ of integer piecewise affine energy functions; the fact that $\mathcal{E}_{\mathsf{pwi}}$ is not a subsemiring of $\mathcal{E}$ will not bother us here.

An *n-dimensional integer piecewise affine energy automaton*, or $\mathcal{E}_{\mathsf{pwi}}^n$-*automaton* for short, (S, T), for $n \in \mathbb{N}_+$, consists of finite sets S of states and $T \subseteq S \times \mathcal{E}_{\mathsf{pwi}}^n \times S$ of transitions. A *global state* in such an automaton is a pair $(s, \boldsymbol{x}) \in S \times \mathbb{N}^n$, and *transitions* are of the form $(s, \boldsymbol{x}) \xrightarrow{f} (s', \boldsymbol{x}')$ such that $(s, \boldsymbol{f}, s') \in T$ and $\boldsymbol{x}'(i) = \boldsymbol{f}(i)(\boldsymbol{x}(i))$ for each $i \in \{1, \ldots, n\}$.

For reachability in $\mathcal{E}_{\mathsf{pwi}}^n$-automata (with $n \geq 2$), our algebraic results do not apply. To see this, we refer to the reachability problem in Fig. 5: with initial energy $(1, 1)$, the loop needs to be taken precisely once, but with initial energy

$(2,0)$, one needs to loop twice. Hence there is no static algorithm which can decide reachability for this VASS.

However, we remark that $\mathcal{E}^n_{\mathsf{pwi}}$-automata are *well-structured transition systems* [23], with ordering on global states defined by $(s, \boldsymbol{x}) \preceq (s', \boldsymbol{x}')$ iff $s = s'$ and $\boldsymbol{x}(i) \leq \boldsymbol{x}'(i)$ for each $i = 1, \ldots, n$ (here we also have to assume $x_0 \in \mathbb{N}$). Also, the reachability problem for energy automata is a *control state reachability problem* in the sense of [2]. Decidability of the reachability problem for $\mathcal{E}^n_{\mathsf{pwi}}$-automata thus follows from the decidability of the control state reachability problem for well-structured transition systems [2]. Note that Büchi acceptance is not generally decidable for well-structured transition systems (it is undecidable for lossy counter machines [30]), so our reduction proof does not imply a similar result for Büchi acceptance.

Theorem 6. *The reachability problem for $\mathcal{E}^n_{\mathsf{pwi}}$-automata with $x_0 \in \mathbb{N}$ is decidable.*

Next we show that if the requirement $(*)$ on energy functions, that $f(x_2) \geq f(x_1) + x_2 - x_1$ for each $x_1 \leq x_2$, is lifted, then reachability becomes undecidable from dimension 4. We call such functions *flat* energy functions; remark that we still require them to be strictly increasing, but the derivative, where it exists, may be less than 1. The class of all flat energy functions is denoted $\bar{\mathcal{E}}$ and its restrictions by $\bar{\mathcal{E}}_{\mathsf{pw}}$, $\bar{\mathcal{E}}_{\mathsf{pwi}}$.

Theorem 7. *The reachability problem for $\bar{\mathcal{E}}^4_{\mathsf{pw}}$-automata is undecidable.*

Next we extend our energy automata formalism to (turn based) *reachability games*. Let (S, T) be an n-dimensional energy automaton such that $S = S_A \cup S_B$ forms a partition of S and $T \subseteq (S_A \times \mathcal{E}^n_{\mathsf{pwi}} \times S_B) \cup (S_B \times \mathcal{E}^n_{\mathsf{pwi}} \times S_A)$. Then (S, S_A, S_B, T) induces an n-dimensional *energy game* G. The intuition of the reachability game is that the two players A and B take turns to move along the game graph (S, T), updating energy values at each turn. The goal of player A is to reach a state in F, the goal of player B is to prevent this from happening.

The reachability game is a *coverability game* in the sense of [29]. In general, the reachability game on well-structured transition systems is undecidable [1]. Indeed, the games on VASS considered in [10] are a special case of reachability games on energy automata with integer update functions; their undecidability is shown in [1,10]. It is hence clear that it is undecidable whether player A wins the reachability game in 2-dimensional $\mathcal{E}_{\mathsf{int}}$-automata. As a corollary, we can show that for *flat* energy functions, already one-dimensional reachability games are undecidable.

Theorem 8. *Whether player A wins the reachability game in $\mathcal{E}^2_{\mathsf{int}}$-automata is undecidable.*

Theorem 9. *It is undecidable for $\bar{\mathcal{E}}_{\mathsf{pw}}$-automata whether player A wins the reachability game.*

Proof (sketch). The proof is by reduction from reachability games on 2-dimensional $\mathcal{E}_{\mathsf{int}}$-automata to reachability games on 1-dimensional $\bar{\mathcal{E}}_{\mathsf{pwi}}$-automata. The intuition is that the new energy variable x encodes the two old ones as $x = 2^{x_1}3^{x_2}$, and then transitions in the 2-dimensional game are encoded using gadgets in which the other player may interrupt to demand proof that the required inequalities for x_1 *and* x_2 were satisfied. The energy functions in the so-constructed 1-dimensional automaton are piecewise affine because the original ones were integer updates. The details of the proof are in [18]. □

6 Conclusion

We have in this paper introduced a functional framework for modeling and analyzing energy problems. We have seen that our framework encompasses most existing formal approaches to energy problems, and that it allows an application of the theory of automata over semirings and semimodules to solve reachability and Büchi acceptance problems in a generic way. For the important class of piecewise affine energy functions, we have shown that reachability and Büchi acceptance are PSPACE-hard and decidable in EXPTIME. As our algorithm is static, computations do not have to be repeated in case the initial energy changes. Also, decidability of Büchi acceptance implies that LTL model checking is decidable for energy automata.

In the last part of this paper, we have seen that one quickly comes into trouble with undecidability if the class of energy functions is extended or if two-player games are considered. This can be remedied by considering *approximate* solutions instead, using notions of distances for energy automata akin to the ones in [22] to provide quantitative measures for similar energy behavior.

Another issue that remains to be investigated is reachability and Büchi problems for one-dimensional energy automata with flat energy functions; we plan to do this in future work.

References

1. Abdulla, P.A., Bouajjani, A., d'Orso, J.: Monotonic and downward closed games. J. Log. Comput. 18(1), 153–169 (2008)
2. Abdulla, P.A., Čerāns, K., Jonsson, B., Tsay, Y.-K.: Algorithmic analysis of programs with well quasi-ordered domains. Inf. Comput. 160(1-2), 109–127 (2000)
3. Alur, R., Dill, D.L.: A theory of timed automata. Theor. Comput. Sci. 126(2), 183–235 (1994)
4. Alur, R., La Torre, S., Pappas, G.J.: Optimal paths in weighted timed automata. In: Di Benedetto, M.D., Sangiovanni-Vincentelli, A.L. (eds.) HSCC 2001. LNCS, vol. 2034, pp. 49–62. Springer, Heidelberg (2001)
5. Behrmann, G., Fehnker, A., Hune, T., Larsen, K.G., Pettersson, P., Romijn, J., Vaandrager, F.W.: Minimum-cost reachability for priced timed automata. In: Di Benedetto, M.D., Sangiovanni-Vincentelli, A.L. (eds.) HSCC 2001. LNCS, vol. 2034, pp. 147–161. Springer, Heidelberg (2001)
6. Bloom, S.L., Ésik, Z.: Iteration Theories: The Equational Logic of Iterative Processes. EATCS monographs on theoretical computer science. Springer (1993)

7. Bouyer, P., Fahrenberg, U., Larsen, K.G., Markey, N.: Timed automata with observers under energy constraints. In: HSCC, pp. 61–70 (2010)
8. Bouyer, P., Fahrenberg, U., Larsen, K.G., Markey, N., Srba, J.: Infinite runs in weighted timed automata with energy constraints. In: Cassez, F., Jard, C. (eds.) FORMATS 2008. LNCS, vol. 5215, pp. 33–47. Springer, Heidelberg (2008)
9. Bouyer, P., Larsen, K.G., Markey, N.: Lower-bound constrained runs in weighted timed automata. In: QEST, pp. 128–137 (2012)
10. Brázdil, T., Jančar, P., Kučera, A.: Reachability games on extended vector addition systems with states. In: Abramsky, S., Gavoille, C., Kirchner, C., Meyer auf der Heide, F., Spirakis, P.G. (eds.) ICALP 2010. LNCS, vol. 6199, pp. 478–489. Springer, Heidelberg (2010)
11. Chaloupka, J.: Z-reachability problem for games on 2-dimensional vector addition systems with states is in P. In: Kučera, A., Potapov, I. (eds.) RP 2010. LNCS, vol. 6227, pp. 104–119. Springer, Heidelberg (2010)
12. Chan, T.-H.: The boundedness problem for three-dimensional vector addition systems with states. Inf. Proc. Letters 26(6), 287–289 (1988)
13. Chatterjee, K., Doyen, L.: Energy parity games. In: Abramsky, S., Gavoille, C., Kirchner, C., Meyer auf der Heide, F., Spirakis, P.G. (eds.) ICALP 2010. LNCS, vol. 6199, pp. 599–610. Springer, Heidelberg (2010)
14. Chatterjee, K., Doyen, L., Henzinger, T.A., Raskin, J.-F.: Generalized mean-payoff and energy games. In: FSTTCS, pp. 505–516 (2010)
15. Conway, J.H.: Regular Algebra and Finite Machines. Chapman and Hall (1971)
16. Degorre, A., Doyen, L., Gentilini, R., Raskin, J.-F., Toruńczyk, S.: Energy and mean-payoff games with imperfect information. In: Dawar, A., Veith, H. (eds.) CSL 2010. LNCS, vol. 6247, pp. 260–274. Springer, Heidelberg (2010)
17. Droste, M., Kuich, W., Vogler, H.: Handbook of Weighted Automata. Springer (2009)
18. Ésik, Z., Fahrenberg, U., Legay, A., Quaas, K.: Kleene algebras and semimodules for energy problems. CoRR, abs/1307.0635 (2013), http://arxiv.org/abs/1307.0635
19. Ésik, Z., Kuich, W.: An algebraic generalization of ω-regular languages. In: Fiala, J., Koubek, V., Kratochvíl, J. (eds.) MFCS 2004. LNCS, vol. 3153, pp. 648–659. Springer, Heidelberg (2004)
20. Ésik, Z., Kuich, W.: A semiring-semimodule generalization of ω-regular languages, Parts 1 and 2. J. Aut. Lang. Comb. 10, 203–264 (2005)
21. Fahrenberg, U., Juhl, L., Larsen, K.G., Srba, J.: Energy games in multiweighted automata. In: Cerone, A., Pihlajasaari, P. (eds.) ICTAC 2011. LNCS, vol. 6916, pp. 95–115. Springer, Heidelberg (2011)
22. Fahrenberg, U., Legay, A., Thrane, C.: The quantitative linear-time–branching-time spectrum. In: FSTTCS, pp. 103–114 (2011)
23. Finkel, A., Schnoebelen, P.: Well-structured transition systems everywhere! Theor. Comput. Sci. 256(1-2), 63–92 (2001)
24. Kozen, D.: On Kleene algebras and closed semirings. In: Rovan, B. (ed.) MFCS 1990. LNCS, vol. 452, pp. 26–47. Springer, Heidelberg (1990)
25. Kozen, D.: A completeness theorem for kleene algebras and the algebra of regular events. Inf. Comput. 110(2), 366–390 (1994)
26. Mathieu, V., Desharnais, J.: Verification of pushdown systems using omega algebra with domain. In: MacCaull, W., Winter, M., Düntsch, I. (eds.) RelMiCS 2005. LNCS, vol. 3929, pp. 188–199. Springer, Heidelberg (2006)
27. Perrin, D., Pin, J.-E.: Infinite Words: Automata, Semigroups, Logic and Games. Academic Press (2004)

28. Quaas, K.: On the interval-bound problem for weighted timed automata. In: Dediu, A.-H., Inenaga, S., Martín-Vide, C. (eds.) LATA 2011. LNCS, vol. 6638, pp. 452–464. Springer, Heidelberg (2011)
29. Raskin, J.-F., Samuelides, M., Begin, L.V.: Games for counting abstractions. Electr. Notes Theor. Comput. Sci. 128(6), 69–85 (2005)
30. Schnoebelen, P.: Lossy counter machines decidability cheat sheet. In: Kučera, A., Potapov, I. (eds.) RP 2010. LNCS, vol. 6227, pp. 51–75. Springer, Heidelberg (2010)
31. Wilke, T.: An Eilenberg theorem for infinity-languages. In: Leach Albert, J., Monien, B., Rodríguez-Artalejo, M. (eds.) ICALP 1991. LNCS, vol. 510, pp. 588–599. Springer, Heidelberg (1991)

Looking at Mean-Payoff
and Total-Payoff through Windows

Krishnendu Chatterjee[1],*, Laurent Doyen[2], Mickael Randour[3],**,
and Jean-François Raskin[4],***

[1] IST Austria (Institute of Science and Technology Austria)
[2] LSV - ENS Cachan, France
[3] Computer Science Department, Université de Mons (UMONS), Belgium
[4] Département d'Informatique, Université Libre de Bruxelles (U.L.B.), Belgium

Abstract. We consider two-player games played on weighted directed graphs
with mean-payoff and total-payoff objectives, two classical quantitative objectives. While for single-dimensional games the complexity and memory bounds
for both objectives coincide, we show that in contrast to multi-dimensional mean-
payoff games that are known to be coNP-complete, multi-dimensional total-payoff games are undecidable. We introduce conservative approximations of these
objectives, where the payoff is considered over a local finite window sliding
along a play, instead of the whole play. For single dimension, we show that (i) if
the window size is polynomial, deciding the winner takes polynomial time, and
(ii) the existence of a bounded window can be decided in NP ∩ coNP, and is at
least as hard as solving mean-payoff games. For multiple dimensions, we show
that (i) the problem with fixed window size is EXPTIME-complete, and (ii) there
is no primitive-recursive algorithm to decide the existence of a bounded window.

1 Introduction

Mean-Payoff and Total-Payoff Games. Two-player mean-payoff and total-payoff games are played on finite weighted directed graphs (in which every edge has an integer
weight) with two types of vertices: in player-1 vertices, player 1 chooses the successor vertex from the set of outgoing edges; in player-2 vertices, player 2 does likewise.
The game results in an infinite path through the graph, called a *play*. The mean-payoff
(resp. total-payoff) value of a play is the long-run average (resp. sum) of the edge-
weights along the path. While traditionally games on graphs with ω-regular objectives
have been studied for system analysis, research efforts have recently focused on quantitative extensions to model resource constraints of embedded systems, such as power
consumption, or buffer size [2]. Quantitative games, such as mean-payoff games, are
crucial for the formal analysis of resource-constrained reactive systems. For the analysis of systems with multiple resources, multi-dimension games, where edge weights are
integer vectors, provide the appropriate framework.

* Author supported by Austrian Science Fund (FWF) Grant No P 23499-N23, FWF NFN Grant
  No S11407 (RiSE), ERC Start Grant (279307: Graph Games), Microsoft faculty fellowship.
** Author supported by F.R.S.-FNRS. fellowship.
*** Author supported by ERC Starting Grant (279499: inVEST).

D. Van Hung and M. Ogawa (Eds.): ATVA 2013, LNCS 8172, pp. 118–132, 2013.
© Springer International Publishing Switzerland 2013

Decision Problems. The decision problem for mean-payoff and total-payoff games asks, given a starting vertex, whether player 1 has a strategy that against all strategies of the opponent ensures a play with value at least 0. For both objectives, *memoryless* winning strategies exist for both players (where a memoryless strategy is independent of the past and depends only on the current state) [9,12]. This ensures that the decision problems belong to NP ∩ coNP; and they belong to the intriguing class of problems that are in NP ∩ coNP but whether they are in P (deterministic polynomial time) are long-standing open questions. The study of mean-payoff games has also been extended to multiple dimensions where the problem is shown to be coNP-complete [21,4]. While for one dimension all the results for mean-payoff and total-payoff coincide, our first contribution shows that quite unexpectedly (in contrast to multi-dimensional mean-payoff games) the multi-dimensional total-payoff games are undecidable.

Window Objectives. On the one hand, the complexity of single-dimensional mean-payoff and total-payoff games is a long-standing open problem, and on the other hand, the multi-dimensional problem is undecidable for total-payoff games. In this work, we propose to study variants of these objectives, namely, *bounded window mean-payoff* and *fixed window mean-payoff* objectives. In a bounded window mean-payoff objective instead of the long-run average along the whole play we consider payoffs over a local bounded window sliding along a play, and the objective is that the average weight must be at least zero over every bounded window from some point on. This objective can be seen as a strengthening of the mean-payoff objective (resp. of the total-payoff objective if we require that the window objective is satisfied from the beginning of the play rather than from some point on), i.e., winning for the bounded window mean-payoff objective implies winning for the mean-payoff objective. In the fixed window mean-payoff objective the window length is fixed and given as a parameter. Observe that winning for the fixed window objective implies winning for the bounded window objective.

Attractive Features for Window Objectives. First, they are a strengthening of the mean-payoff objectives and hence provide conservative approximations for mean-payoff objectives. Second, the window variant is very natural to study in system analysis. Mean-payoff objectives require average to satisfy certain threshold in the long-run (or in the limit of the infinite path), whereas the window objectives require to provide guarantee on the average, not in the limit, but within a bounded time, and thus provide better time guarantee than the mean-payoff objectives. Third, the window parameter provides flexibility, as it can be adjusted specific to applications requirement of strong or weak time guarantee for system behaviors. Finally, we will establish that our variant in the single dimension is more computationally tractable, which makes it an attractive alternative to mean-payoff objectives.

Our Contributions. The main contributions of this work (along with the undecidability of multi-dimensional total-payoff games) are as follows:

1. *Single dimension.* For the single-dimensional case we present an algorithm for the fixed window problem that is polynomial in the size of the game graph times the length of the binary encoding of weights times the size of the fixed window. Thus if the window size is polynomial, we have a polynomial-time algorithm. For the bounded window problem we show that the decision problem is in NP ∩ coNP, and at least as hard as solving mean-payoff games. However, winning for mean-payoff

Table 1. Complexity of deciding the winner and memory required, with $|S|$ the number of states of the game (vertices in the graph), V the length of the binary encoding of weights, and l_{max} the window size. New results in bold (h. for hard and c. for complete).

	one-dimension			k-dimension		
	complexity	$\mathcal{P}_1$ mem.	$\mathcal{P}_2$ mem.	complexity	$\mathcal{P}_1$ mem.	$\mathcal{P}_2$ mem.
MP / $\overline{\text{MP}}$	NP∩coNP	mem-less		coNP-c. / NP∩coNP	infinite	mem-less
TP / $\overline{\text{TP}}$	NP∩coNP	mem-less		**undec.** (Thm. 1)	-	-
WMP: fixed polynomial window	**P-c.** (Thm. 2)	mem. req. ≤ **linear**($|S| \cdot l_{max}$) (Thm. 2)		**PSPACE-h.** (Thm. 4) **EXP-easy** (Thm. 4)	**exponential** (Thm. 4)	
WMP: fixed arbitrary window	**P**($|S|, V, l_{max}$) (Thm. 2)			**EXP-c.** (Thm. 4)		
WMP: bounded window problem	**NP∩coNP** (Thm. 3)	**mem-less** (Thm. 3)	**infinite** (Thm. 3)	**NPR-h.** (Thm. 5)	-	-

games does not imply winning for the bounded window mean-payoff objective, i.e., the winning sets for mean-payoff games and bounded window mean-payoff games do not coincide. Moreover, the structure of winning strategies is also very different, e.g., in mean-payoff games both players have memoryless winning strategies, but in bounded window mean-payoff games we show that player 2 requires infinite memory. We also show that if player 1 wins the bounded window mean-payoff objective, then a window of size $(|S| - 1) \cdot (|S| \cdot W + 1)$ is sufficient where S is the state space (the set of vertices of the graph), and W is the largest absolute weight value. Finally, we show that (i) a winning strategy for the bounded window mean-payoff objective ensures that the mean-payoff is at least 0 regardless of the strategy of the opponent, and (ii) a strategy that ensures that the mean-payoff is strictly greater than 0 is winning for the bounded window mean-payoff objective.

2. *Multiple dimensions.* For multiple dimensions, we show that the fixed window problem is EXPTIME-complete (both for arbitrary dimensions with weights in $\{-1, 0, 1\}$ and for two dimensions with arbitrary weights); and if the window size is polynomial, then the problem is PSPACE-hard. For the bounded window problem we show that the problem is non-primitive recursive hard (i.e., there is no primitive recursive algorithm to decide the problem).

3. *Memory requirements.* For all the problems for which we prove decidability we also characterize the memory required by winning strategies.

The relevant results are summarized in Table 1: our results are in bold fonts. In summary, the fixed window problem provides an attractive approximation of the mean-payoff and total-payoff games that we show have better algorithmic complexity. In contrast to the long-standing open problem of mean-payoff games, the one-dimension fixed window problem with polynomial window size can be solved in polynomial time; and in contrast to the undecidability of multi-dimensional total-payoff games, the multi-dimension fixed window problem is EXPTIME-complete.

Related Works. An extended version of this work, including proofs, can be found in [5]. Mean-payoff games have been first studied by Ehrenfeucht and Mycielski in [9] where it is shown that memoryless winning strategies exist for both players. This result entails that the decision problem lies in NP ∩ coNP [17,22], and it was later shown to belong to UP ∩ coUP [15]. Despite many efforts [13,22,19,18,14], no polynomial-time algorithm for the mean-payoff games problem is known so far. Gurvich, Karzanov, Khachivan and Lebedev [13,17] provided the first (exponential) algorithm for mean-payoff games, later extended by Pisaruk [19]. The first pseudo-polynomial-time algorithm for mean-payoff games was given in [22] and was improved in [1]. Lifshits and Pavlov [18] propose an algorithm which is polynomial in the encoding of weights but exponential in the number of vertices of the graph: it is based on a graph decomposition procedure. Bjorklund and Vorobyov [14] present a *randomized* algorithm which is both subexponential and pseudo-polynomial. While all the above works are for single dimension, multi-dimensional mean-payoff games have been studied in [21,4,7]. One-dimension total-payoff games have been studied in [11] where it is shown that memoryless winning strategies exist for both players and the decision problem is in UP ∩ coUP.

2 Multi-dimensional Mean-Payoff and Total-Payoff Objectives

We consider two-player turn-based games and denote the two *players* by P_1 and P_2.

Multi-weighted Two-Player Game Structures. *Multi-weighted two-player game structures* are weighted graphs $G = (S_1, S_2, E, k, w)$ where (*i*) S_1 and S_2 resp. denote the finite sets of vertices, called *states*, belonging to P_1 and P_2, with $S_1 \cap S_2 = \emptyset$ and $S = S_1 \cup S_2$; (*ii*) $E \subseteq S \times S$ is the set of *edges* such that for all $s \in S$, there exists $s' \in S$ with $(s, s') \in E$; (*iii*) $k \in \mathbb{N}$ is the *dimension* of the weight vectors; and (*iv*) $w \colon E \to \mathbb{Z}^k$ is the multi-weight labeling function. When it is clear from the context that a game G is one-dimensional ($k = 1$), we omit k and write it as $G = (S_1, S_2, E, w)$. The game structure G is *one-player* if $S_2 = \emptyset$. We denote by W the largest absolute weight that appears in the game. For complexity issues, we assume that weights are encoded in binary. Hence we differentiate between pseudo-polynomial algorithms (polynomial in W) and truly polynomial algorithms (polynomial in $V = \lceil \log_2 W \rceil$, the number of bits needed to encode the weights).

A *play* in G from an initial state $s_{\text{init}} \in S$ is an infinite sequence of states $\pi = s_0 s_1 s_2 \ldots$ such that $s_0 = s_{\text{init}}$ and $(s_i, s_{i+1}) \in E$ for all $i \geq 0$. The *prefix* up to the n-th state of π is the finite sequence $\pi(n) = s_0 s_1 \ldots s_n$. Let $\text{Last}(\pi(n)) = s_n$ denote the last state of $\pi(n)$. A prefix $\pi(n)$ belongs to P_i, $i \in \{1, 2\}$, if $\text{Last}(\pi(n)) \in S_i$. The set of plays of G is denoted by $\text{Plays}(G)$ and the corresponding set of prefixes is denoted by $\text{Prefs}(G)$. The set of prefixes that belong to P_i is denoted by $\text{Prefs}_i(G)$. The infinite suffix of a play starting in s_n is denoted $\pi(n, \infty)$.

The *total-payoff* of a prefix $\rho = s_0 s_1 \ldots s_n$ is $\text{TP}(\rho) = \sum_{i=0}^{i=n-1} w(s_i, s_{i+1})$, and its *mean-payoff* is $\text{MP}(\rho) = \frac{1}{n} \text{TP}(\rho)$. This is naturally extended to plays by considering the componentwise limit behavior (i.e., limit taken on each dimension). The *infimum (resp. supremum) total-payoff* of a play π is $\underline{\text{TP}}(\pi) = \liminf_{n \to \infty} \text{TP}(\pi(n))$ (resp. $\overline{\text{TP}}(\pi) = \limsup_{n \to \infty} \text{TP}(\pi(n))$). The *infimum (resp. supremum) mean-payoff* of π is $\underline{\text{MP}}(\pi) = \liminf_{n \to \infty} \text{MP}(\pi(n))$ (resp. $\overline{\text{MP}}(\pi) = \limsup_{n \to \infty} \text{MP}(\pi(n))$).

Strategies. A *strategy* for P_i, $i \in \{1, 2\}$, in G is a function $\lambda_i \colon \text{Prefs}_i(G) \to S$ such that $(\text{Last}(\rho), \lambda_i(\rho)) \in E$ for all $\rho \in \text{Prefs}_i(G)$. A strategy λ_i for P_i has *finite-memory* if it can be encoded by a deterministic finite state machine with outputs (Moore machine). It is *memoryless* if it does not depend on history but only on the current state of the game. A play π is said to be *consistent* with a strategy λ_i of $\mathcal{P}_i$ if for all $n \geq 0$ such that $\mathsf{Last}(\pi(n)) \in S_i$, we have $\mathsf{Last}(\pi(n+1)) = \lambda_i(\pi(n))$. Given an initial state $s_{\mathsf{init}} \in S$, and two strategies, λ_1 for $\mathcal{P}_1$ and λ_2 for $\mathcal{P}_2$, the unique play from s_{init} consistent with both strategies is the *outcome* of the game, denoted by $\mathsf{Outcome}_G(s_{\mathsf{init}}, \lambda_1, \lambda_2)$.

Attractors. The *attractor* for $\mathcal{P}_1$ of a set $A \subseteq S$ in G is denoted by $\mathsf{Attr}_G^{\mathcal{P}_1}(A)$ and computed as the fixed point of the sequence $\mathsf{Attr}_G^{\mathcal{P}_1, n+1}(A) = \mathsf{Attr}_G^{\mathcal{P}_1, n}(A) \cup \{s \in S_1 \mid \exists\, (s,t) \in E, t \in \mathsf{Attr}_G^{\mathcal{P}_1, n}(A)\} \cup \{s \in S_2 \mid \forall\, (s,t) \in E, t \in \mathsf{Attr}_G^{\mathcal{P}_1, n}(A)\}$, with $\mathsf{Attr}_G^{\mathcal{P}_1, 0}(A) = A$. The attractor $\mathsf{Attr}_G^{\mathcal{P}_1}(A)$ is exactly the set of states from which $\mathcal{P}_1$ can ensure to reach A no matter what $\mathcal{P}_2$ does. The attractor $\mathsf{Attr}_G^{\mathcal{P}_2}(A)$ for $\mathcal{P}_2$ is defined symmetrically.

Objectives. An *objective* for $\mathcal{P}_1$ in G is a set of plays $\phi \subseteq \mathsf{Plays}(G)$. A play $\pi \in \mathsf{Plays}(G)$ is *winning* for an objective ϕ if $\pi \in \phi$. Given a game G and an initial state $s_{\mathsf{init}} \in S$, a strategy λ_1 of $\mathcal{P}_1$ is winning if $\mathsf{Outcome}_G(s_{\mathsf{init}}, \lambda_1, \lambda_2) \in \phi$ for all strategies λ_2 of $\mathcal{P}_2$. Given a rational threshold vector $v \in \mathbb{Q}^k$, we define the *infimum (resp. supremum) total-payoff (resp. mean-payoff)* objectives as follows:

- $\mathsf{TotalInf}_G(v) = \{\pi \in \mathsf{Plays}(G) \mid \underline{\mathsf{TP}}(\pi) \geq v\}$
- $\mathsf{TotalSup}_G(v) = \{\pi \in \mathsf{Plays}(G) \mid \overline{\mathsf{TP}}(\pi) \geq v\}$
- $\mathsf{MeanInf}_G(v) = \{\pi \in \mathsf{Plays}(G) \mid \underline{\mathsf{MP}}(\pi) \geq v\}$
- $\mathsf{MeanSup}_G(v) = \{\pi \in \mathsf{Plays}(G) \mid \overline{\mathsf{MP}}(\pi) \geq v\}$

Decision Problem. Given a game structure G, an initial state $s_{\mathsf{init}} \in S$, and an inf./sup. total-payoff/mean-payoff objective $\phi \subseteq \mathsf{Plays}(G)$, the *threshold problem* asks to decide if $\mathcal{P}_1$ has a winning strategy for this objective. In one-dimension games, both mean-payoff and total-payoff threshold problems lie in NP∩coNP [11]. In multi-dimension, the mean-payoff threshold problem lies in coNP [21]. In contrast, we show that multi-dimension total-payoff games are undecidable.

Theorem 1. *The threshold problem for infimum and supremum total-payoff objectives is undecidable in multi-dimension games, for five dimensions.*

We reduce the halting problem for two-counter machines to the threshold problem for two-player total-payoff games with five dimensions. Counters take values $(v_1, v_2) \in \mathbb{N}^2$ along an execution, and can be incremented or decremented (if positive). A counter can be tested for equality to zero, and the machine can branch accordingly. We build a game with a sup. (resp. inf.) total-payoff objective of threshold $(0,0,0,0,0)$ for $\mathcal{P}_1$, in which $\mathcal{P}_1$ has to faithfully simulate an execution of the machine, and $\mathcal{P}_2$ can retaliate if he does not. We present gadgets by which $\mathcal{P}_2$ checks that *(a)* the counters are always non-negative, and that *(b)* a zero test is only passed if the value of the counter is really zero. The current value of counters (v_1, v_2) along an execution is encoded as the total sum of weights since the start of the game, $(v_1, -v_1, v_2, -v_2, -v_3)$, with v_3 being the number of steps of the computation. Hence, along a faithful execution, the 1st and 3rd dimensions are always non-negative, while the 2nd, 4th and 5th are always non-positive. To check that counters never go below zero, $\mathcal{P}_2$ is always able to go to an absorbing state with a self-loop of weight $(0,1,1,1,1)$ (resp. $(1,1,0,1,1)$). To check that all zero tests on counter 1 (resp. 2) are faithful, $\mathcal{P}_2$ can branch after a test to an absorbing state with a self-loop of weight $(1,0,1,1,1)$ (resp. $(1,1,1,0,1)$). Using these gadgets, $\mathcal{P}_2$ can punish an unfaithful simulation as he ensures that the sum in the dimension on which $\mathcal{P}_1$ has cheated always stays strictly negative and the outcome is thus losing (it is only the case if $\mathcal{P}_1$ cheats, otherwise all dimensions become non-negative). When an execution halts (with counters equal to zero w.l.o.g.) after a faithful execution, it goes to an absorbing state with weight $(0,0,0,0,1)$, ensuring a winning outcome for $\mathcal{P}_1$ for the total-payoff objective. If an execution does not halt, the 5th dimension stays strictly negative and the outcome is losing.

In multi-weighted total-payoff games, $\mathcal{P}_1$ may need infinite memory. Consider a game with only one state and two self-loops of weights $(1, -2)$ and $(-2, 1)$. For any threshold $v \in \mathbb{Q}^2$, $\mathcal{P}_1$ has an infinite-memory strategy to win the sup. total-payoff objective: alternating between the two loops for longer and longer periods, each time waiting to get back above the threshold in the considered dimension before switching. There exists no finite-memory one as the negative amount to compensate grows boundlessly with each alternation.

3   Window Mean-Payoff: Definition

In one dimension, no polynomial algorithm is known for mean-payoff and total-payoff, and in multi dimensions, total-payoff is undecidable. We introduce the *window mean-payoff objective*, a conservative approximation for which local deviations from the threshold must be compensated in a parametrized number of steps. We consider a *window*, sliding along a play, within which the compensation must happen. Our approach can be applied to mean-payoff and total-payoff objectives. Since we consider *finite* windows, both versions coincide for threshold zero. Hence we present our results for mean-payoff.

Objectives and Decision Problems. Given a multi-weighted two-player game $G = (S_1, S_2, E, k, w)$ and a rational threshold $v \in \mathbb{Q}^k$, we define the following objectives.[1]

– Given $l_{\max} \in \mathbb{N}_0$, the *good window* objective

$$\mathsf{GW}_G(v, l_{\max}) = \left\{ \pi \mid \forall t, 1 \leq t \leq k, \exists l \leq l_{\max}, \frac{1}{l} \sum_{p=0}^{l-1} w\big(e_\pi(p, p+1)\big)(t) \geq v(t) \right\}, \quad (1)$$

where $e_\pi(p, p+1)$ is the edge $(\mathsf{Last}(\pi(p)), \mathsf{Last}(\pi(p+1)))$, requires that for all dimensions, there exists a window starting in the first position and bounded by $l_{\max}$ over which the mean-payoff is at least equal to the threshold.

– Given $l_{\max} \in \mathbb{N}_0$, the *fixed window mean-payoff* objective

$$\mathsf{FixWMP}_G(v, l_{\max}) = \left\{ \pi \mid \exists i \geq 0, \forall j \geq i, \pi(j, \infty) \in \mathsf{GW}_G(v, l_{\max}) \right\} \quad (2)$$

requires that there exists a position i such that in all subsequent positions, good windows bounded by $l_{\max}$ exist.

– The *bounded window mean-payoff* objective

$$\mathsf{BndWMP}_G(v) = \left\{ \pi \mid \exists l_{\max} > 0, \pi \in \mathsf{FixWMP}_G(v, l_{\max}) \right\} \quad (3)$$

asks that there exists a bound $l_{\max}$ such that the play satisfies the fixed objective.

---

[1] For brevity, we omit that $\pi \in \mathsf{Plays}(G)$.

We define *direct* versions of the objectives by fixing $i = 0$ rather than quantifying it existentially. For any $v \in \mathbb{Q}^k$ and $l_{\max} \in \mathbb{N}_0$, the following inclusions are true:

$$\mathsf{DirFixWMP}_G(v, l_{\max}) \subseteq \mathsf{FixWMP}_G(v, l_{\max}) \subseteq \mathsf{BndWMP}_G(v), \qquad (4)$$

$$\mathsf{DirFixWMP}_G(v, l_{\max}) \subseteq \mathsf{DirBndWMP}_G(v) \subseteq \mathsf{BndWMP}_G(v). \qquad (5)$$

The threshold v can be taken equal to $\{0\}^k$ (where $\{0\}^k$ denotes the k-dimension zero vector) w.l.o.g. as we can transform the weight function w to $b \cdot w - a$ for any threshold $\frac{a}{b}$, $a \in \mathbb{Z}^k$, $b \in \mathbb{N}_0 = \mathbb{N} \setminus \{0\}$. Hence, given any variant of the objective, the associated *decision problem* is to decide the existence of a winning strategy for $\mathcal{P}_1$ for threshold $\{0\}^k$. Lastly, for complexity purposes, we make a difference between *polynomial* (in the size of the game) and *arbitrary* (i.e., non-polynomial) window sizes.

Let $\pi = s_0 s_1 s_2 \ldots$ be a play. Fix any dimension $t, 1 \leq t \leq k$. The window from position j to j', $0 \leq j < j'$, is *closed* iff there exists j'', $j < j'' \leq j'$ such that the sum of weights in dimension t over the sequence $s_j \ldots s_{j''}$ is non-negative. Otherwise the window is *open*. Given a position j' in π, a window is still open in j' iff there exists a position $0 \leq j < j'$ such that the window from j to j' is open. Consider any edge (s_i, s_{i+1}) appearing along π. If the edge is non-negative in dimension t, the window starting in i immediately closes. If not, a window opens that must be closed within $l_{\max}$ steps. Consider the *first* position i' such that this window closes, then we have that all intermediary opened windows also get closed by i', that is, for any i'', $i < i'' \leq i'$, the window starting in i'' is closed before or when reaching position i'. Indeed, the sum of weights over the window from i'' to i' is strictly greater than the sum over the window from i to i', which is non-negative. We call this fact the *inductive property of windows*.

Illustration. Consider the game depicted in Fig. 1. It has a unique outcome, and it is winning for the classical mean-payoff objective of threshold 0, as well as for the infimum (resp. supremum) total-payoff objective of threshold -1 (resp. 0). Consider the fixed window mean-payoff objective for threshold 0. If the size of the window is bounded by 1, the play is losing.[2] However, if the window size is at least 2, the play is winning, as in s_3 we close the window in two steps and in s_4 in one step. Notice that by definition of the objective, it is clear that it is also satisfied for all larger sizes.[3] As the fixed window objective is satisfied for size 2, the bounded window objective is also satisfied. On the other hand, if we restrict the objectives to their direct variants, then none is satisfied, as from s_2, no window, no matter how large it is, gets closed.

Consider the game of Fig. 2. Again, the unique strategy of $\mathcal{P}_1$ satisfies the mean-payoff objective for threshold 0. It also ensures value -1 for the infimum and supremum total-payoffs. Consider the strategy of $\mathcal{P}_2$ that takes the self-loop once on the first visit of s_2, twice on the second, and so on. Clearly, it ensures that windows starting in s_1 stay open for longer and longer numbers of steps (we say that $\mathcal{P}_2$ *delays* the closing of the window), hence making the outcome losing for the bounded window objective (and thus the fixed window objective for any $l_{\max} \in \mathbb{N}_0$). This illustrates the added guarantee

---

[2] A window size of one actually requires that all infinitely often visited edges are of non-negative weights.

[3] The existential quantification on the window size l, bounded by $l_{\max}$, is indeed crucial in eq. (1) to ensure monotonicity with increasing maximal window sizes, a desired behavior of the definition for theoretical properties and intuitive use in specifications.

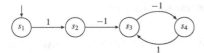

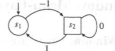

Fig. 1. Fixed window is satisfied for $l_{max} \geq 2$, whereas even direct bounded window is not

Fig. 2. Mean-payoff is satisfied but none of the window objectives is

(compared to mean-payoff) asked by the window objective: in this case, no upper bound can be given on the time needed for a window to close, i.e., on the time needed to get the local sum back to non-negative. Note that P_2 has to go back to s_1 at some point: otherwise, the prefix-independence of the objectives[4] allows P_1 to wait for P_2 to settle on cycling and win. For the direct variants, P_2 has a simpler winning strategy consisting in looping forever, as enforcing one permanently open window is sufficient.

Relation with Classical Objectives. We introduce the bounded window objectives as conservative approximations of mean-payoff and total-payoff in one-dimension games. Indeed, in Lemma 1, we show that winning the bounded window (resp. direct bounded window) objective implies winning the mean-payoff (resp. total-payoff) objective while the reverse implication is only true if a strictly positive mean-payoff (resp. arbitrary high total-payoff) can be ensured.

Lemma 1. *Given a one-dimension game* $G = (S_1, S_2, E, w)$, *the following assertions hold.*

(a) If the answer to the bounded window mean-payoff problem is YES, *then the answer to the mean-payoff threshold problem for threshold zero is also* YES.

(b) If there exists $\varepsilon > 0$ *such that the answer to the mean-payoff threshold problem for threshold* ε *is* YES, *then the answer to the bounded window mean-payoff problem is also* YES.

(c) If the answer to the direct bounded window mean-payoff problem is YES, *then the answer to the supremum total-payoff threshold problem for threshold zero is also* YES.

(d) If the answer to the supremum total-payoff threshold problem is YES *for all integer thresholds (i.e., the total-payoff value is* ∞), *then the answer to the direct bounded window mean-payoff problem is also* YES.

Assertions *(a)* and *(c)* follow from the decomposition of winning plays into bounded windows of non-negative weights. The key idea for assertions *(b)* and *(d)* is that mean-payoff and total-payoff objectives always admit *memoryless* winning strategies, for which the consistent outcomes can be decomposed into *simple cycles* (i.e., with no repeated edge) over which the mean-payoff is at least equal to the threshold and which length is bounded. Hence they correspond to closing windows. Note that strict equivalence with the classical objectives is not verified, as witnessed before (Fig. 2).

---

[4] Fixed and bounded window mean-payoff objectives are prefix-independent: for all $\rho \in$ Prefs(G), $\pi \in$ Plays(G), we have that $\rho \cdot \pi$ is winning if and only if π is winning.

4   Window Mean-Payoff: One-Dimension Games

Fixed Window. Given a game $G = (S_1, S_2, E, w)$ and a window size $l_{max} \in \mathbb{N}_0$, we present an iterative algorithm FWMP (Alg. 1) to compute the winning states of $\mathcal{P}_1$ for the objective $\text{FixWMP}_G(0, l_{max})$. Initially, all states are potentially losing for $\mathcal{P}_1$. The algorithm iteratively declares states to be winning, removes them, and continues the computation on the remaining subgame as follows. In every iteration, *i)* DirectFWMP computes the set W_d of states from which $\mathcal{P}_1$ can win the direct fixed window objective; *ii)* it computes the attractor to W_d; and then proceeds to the next iteration on the remaining subgame (the restriction of G to a subset of states $A \subseteq S$ is denoted $G \downarrow A$). In every iteration, the states of the computed set W_d are obviously winning for the fixed window objective. Thanks to the prefix-independence of the fixed window objective, the attractor to W_d is also winning. Since $\mathcal{P}_2$ must avoid entering this attractor, $\mathcal{P}_2$ must restrict his choices to stay in the subgame, and hence we iterate on the remaining subgame. Thus states removed over all iterations are winning for $\mathcal{P}_1$. The key argument to establish correctness is as follows: when the algorithm stops, the remaining set of states $\overline{W}$ is such that $\mathcal{P}_2$ can ensure to stay in $\overline{W}$ and falsify the direct fixed window objective by forcing the appearance of one open window larger than l_{max}. Since he stays in $\overline{W}$, he can repeatedly use this strategy to falsify the fixed window objective. Thus the remaining set $\overline{W}$ is winning for $\mathcal{P}_2$, and the correctness of the algorithm follows.

Algorithm 1. FWMP(G, l_{max})

Require: $G = (S_1, S_2, E, w)$ and $l_{max} \in \mathbb{N}_0$
Ensure: W is the set of winning states for $\mathcal{P}_1$ for $\text{FixWMP}_G(0, l_{max})$
  $n := 0$; $W := \emptyset$
  repeat
    $W_d^n := \text{DirectFWMP}(G, l_{max})$
    $W_{attr}^n := \text{Attr}_G^{\mathcal{P}_1}(W_d^n)$ {attractor for $\mathcal{P}_1$}
    $W := W \cup W_{attr}^n$; $G := G \downarrow (S \setminus W)$; $n := n+1$
  until $W = S$ or $W_{attr}^{n-1} = \emptyset$
  return W

Algorithm 2. DirectFWMP(G, l_{max})

Require: $G = (S_1, S_2, E, w)$ and $l_{max} \in \mathbb{N}_0$
Ensure: W_d is the set of winning states for $\mathcal{P}_1$ for $\text{DirFixWMP}_G(0, l_{max})$
  $W_{gw} := \text{GoodWin}(G, l_{max})$
  if $W_{gw} = S$ or $W_{gw} = \emptyset$ **then**
    $W_d := W_{gw}$
  else
    $W_d := \text{DirectFWMP}(G \downarrow W_{gw}, l_{max})$
  return W_d

Algorithm 3. GoodWin(G, l_{max})

Require: $G = (S_1, S_2, E, w)$ and $l_{max} \in \mathbb{N}_0$
Ensure: W_{gw} is the set of winning states for $\text{GW}_G(0, l_{max})$
  for all $s \in S$ **do**
    $C_0(s) := 0$
  for all $i \in \{1, \dots, l_{max}\}$ **do**
    for all $s \in S_1$ **do**
      $C_i(s) := \max_{(s,s') \in E} \{w((s,s')) + C_{i-1}(s')\}$
    for all $s \in S_2$ **do**
      $C_i(s) := \min_{(s,s') \in E} \{w((s,s')) + C_{i-1}(s')\}$
  return $W_{gw} := \{s \in S \mid \exists i, 1 \leq i \leq l_{max}, C_i(s) \geq 0\}$

The main idea of algorithm DirectFWMP (Alg. 2) is that to win the direct fixed window objective, $\mathcal{P}_1$ must be able to repeatedly win the good window objective, which consists in ensuring a non-negative sum in at most l_{max} steps. A winning strategy of $\mathcal{P}_1$ in a state s is thus a strategy that enforces a non-negative sum and, *as soon as the sum turns non-negative* (in some state s'), starts doing the same from s'. It is important to start again immediately as it ensures that all suffixes along the path from s to s' also have a non-negative sum thanks to the inductive property. The states from which $\mathcal{P}_1$

can win the good window objective are computed by subroutine GoodWin (Alg. 3): given a state $s \in S$ and a number of steps $i \geq 1$, the value $C_i(s)$ is computed iteratively (from $C_{i-1}(s)$) and represents the best sum that $\mathcal{P}_1$ can ensure from s in exactly i steps. Hence, the set of winning states for $\mathcal{P}_1$ is the set of states for which there exists some i, $1 \leq i \leq l_{max}$ such that $C_i(s) \geq 0$. The construction implies linear bounds (in $|S| \cdot l_{max}$) on the memory needed for both players. We show that the fixed window problem is P-hard even for $l_{max} = 1$ and weights $\{-1, 1\}$ via a simple reduction from reachability games.

Theorem 2. *In two-player one-dimension games, (a) the fixed arbitrary window mean-payoff problem is decidable in time $\mathcal{O}\left(|S|^3 \cdot |E| \cdot l_{max} \cdot V\right)$, with $V = \lceil \log_2 W \rceil$, the length of the binary encoding of weights, and (b) the fixed polynomial window mean-payoff problem is P-complete. In general, both players require memory, and memory of size linear in $|S| \cdot l_{max}$ is sufficient.*

Bounded Window. We establish a $\text{NP} \cap \text{coNP}$ algorithm for bounded window mean-payoff objective using two intermediate results. First, if $\mathcal{P}_1$ has a strategy to win the sup. total-payoff objective, then he wins the good window objective for $l_{max} = (|S| - 1) \cdot (|S| \cdot W + 1)$. Second, if $\mathcal{P}_2$ has a memoryless strategy to ensure that the sup. total-payoff is strictly negative, then all consistent outcomes violate the direct bounded window mean-payoff objective. As a corollary, we obtain that the sets of winning states coincide for objectives $\text{FixWMP}_G(0, l_{max} = (|S| - 1) \cdot (|S| \cdot W + 1))$ and $\text{BndWMP}_G(0)$.

Algorithm 4. $\text{BoundedProblem}(G)$
Require: Game $G = (S_1, S_2, E, w)$
Ensure: W_{bp} is the set of winning states for $\mathcal{P}_1$ for the bounded window mean-payoff problem
$W_{bp} := \emptyset$
$L := \text{UnbOpenWindow}(G)$
while $L \neq S \setminus W_{bp}$ **do**
$\qquad W_{bp} := \text{Attr}_G^{\mathcal{P}_1}(S \setminus L)$
$\qquad L := \text{UnbOpenWindow}\left(G \restriction (S \setminus W_{bp})\right)$
return W_{bp}

Algorithm 5. $\text{UnbOpenWindow}(G)$
Require: Game $G = (S_1, S_2, E, w)$
Ensure: L is the set of states from which $\mathcal{P}_2$ can force a position for which the window never closes
$p := 0$; $L_0 := \emptyset$
repeat
$\qquad L_{p+1} := L_p \cup \text{Attr}_{G \restriction (S \setminus L_p)}^{\mathcal{P}_2}\left(\text{NegSupTP}(G \restriction (S \setminus L_p))\right)$
$\qquad p := p + 1$
until $L_p = L_{p-1}$
return $L := L_p$

Algorithm BoundedProblem (Alg. 4) computes via subroutine UnbOpenWindow the states from which $\mathcal{P}_2$ can force the visit of a position such that the window opening in this position never closes. To prevent $\mathcal{P}_1$ from winning the bounded window problem, $\mathcal{P}_2$ must be able to do so repeatedly as the prefix-independence of the objective otherwise gives the possibility to wait that all such bad positions are encountered before taking the windows into account. Thus, the states that are not in UnbOpenWindow(G), as well as their attractor, are winning for $\mathcal{P}_1$. Since the choices of $\mathcal{P}_2$ are reduced because of the attractor of $\mathcal{P}_1$ being declared winning, we compute in several steps, adding new states to the set of winning states for $\mathcal{P}_1$ up to stabilization. Subroutine UnbOpenWindow (Alg. 5) computes the attractor for $\mathcal{P}_2$ of the set of states from which $\mathcal{P}_2$ can enforce a strictly negative supremum total-payoff. Routine NegSupTP returns this set in $\text{NP} \cap \text{coNP}$ complexity [11]. Again, we compute the fixed point of the sequence as at each iteration, the choices of $\mathcal{P}_1$ are reduced. The main idea of the correctness proof is that from all states in $\overline{W_{bp}}$, $\mathcal{P}_2$ has an infinite-memory winning strategy which is played in rounds, and in round n ensures an open window of size at least n

by playing the total-payoff strategy of $\mathcal{P}_2$ for at most $n \cdot |S|$ steps, and then proceeds to round $(n+1)$ to ensure an open window of size $(n+1)$, and so on. Hence, windows stay open for arbitrary large periods and the bounded window objective is falsified.

The algorithm gives memoryless winning strategies for $\mathcal{P}_1$. The game of Fig. 2 shows that infinite memory is necessary for $\mathcal{P}_2$: he needs to cycle in the zero loop for longer and longer. Mean-payoff games reduce polynomially to bounded window games by simply modifying the weight structure.

Theorem 3. *In two-player one-dimension games, the bounded window mean-payoff problem is in NP∩coNP and at least as hard as mean-payoff games. Memoryless strategies suffice for $\mathcal{P}_1$ and infinite-memory strategies are required for $\mathcal{P}_2$ in general.*

5   Window Mean-Payoff: Multi-dimension Games

Fixed window. Given $G = (S_1, S_2, E, k, w)$ and $l_{\max} \in \mathbb{N}_0$, the fixed window problem is solved in time $\mathcal{O}(|S|^2 \cdot (l_{\max})^{4 \cdot k} \cdot W^{2 \cdot k})$ via reduction to an exponentially larger co-Büchi game (where the objective of $\mathcal{P}_1$ is to avoid visiting a set of bad states infinitely often). Co-Büchi games are solvable in quadratic time [6]. A winning play is such that, starting in some position $i \geq 0$, in all dimensions, all opening windows are closed in at most $l_{\max}$ steps. We keep a counter of the sum over the sequence of edges and as soon as it turns non-negative, we reset the sum counter and start a new sequence. Hence, the reduction is based on accounting for each dimension the current negative sum of weights since the last reset, and the number of steps that remain to achieve a non-negative sum. This accounting is encoded in the states of $G^c = (S_1^c, S_2^c, E^c)$, as from the original state space S, we go to $S \times (\{-l_{\max} \cdot W, \ldots, 0\} \times \{1, \ldots, l_{\max}\})^k$: states of G^c are tuples representing a state of G and the current status of open windows in all dimensions (sum and remaining steps). We add states reached whenever a window reaches its maximum size $l_{\max}$ without closing. We label those as *bad* states. We have one bad state for every state of G. Transitions in G^c are built in order to accurately model the effect of transitions of G on open windows: each time a transition (s, s') in the original game G is taken, the game G^c is updated to a state $(s', (\sigma^1, \tau^1), \ldots, (\sigma^k, \tau^k))$ such that (a) if the current sum becomes positive in some dimension, the corresponding sum counter is reset to zero and the step counter is reset to its maximum value, $l_{\max}$, (b) if the sum is still strictly negative in some dimension and the window for this dimension is not at its maximal size, the sum is updated and the step counter is decreased, and (c) if the sum stays strictly negative and the maximal size is reached in any dimension, the game visits the corresponding bad state and then, all counters are reset for all dimensions and the game continues from the corresponding state $(s', (0, l_{\max}), \ldots, (0, l_{\max}))$. Clearly, a play is winning for the fixed window problem if and only if the corresponding play in G^c is winning for the co-Büchi objective that asks that the set of bad states is not visited infinitely often, as that means that from some point on, all windows close in the required number of steps.

We prove that the fixed *arbitrary* window problem is EXPTIME-hard for $\{-1, 0, 1\}$ weights and arbitrary dimensions via a reduction from the *membership problem for alternating polynomial space Turing machines (APTMs)* [3]. Given an APTM $\mathcal{M}$ and a word $\zeta \in \{0, 1\}^*$, such that the tape contains at most $p(|\zeta|)$ cells, where p is a polynomial function, the membership problem asks to decide if $\mathcal{M}$ accepts ζ. We build a fixed

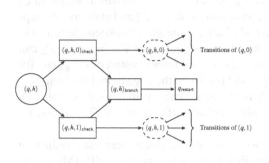

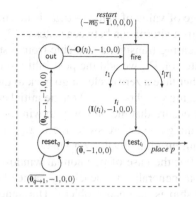

Fig. 3. Gadget ensuring a correct simulation of the APTM on tape cell h

Fig. 4. Gadget simulating an execution of the reset net

arbitrary window game G so that $\mathcal{P}_1$ has to simulate the run of $\mathcal{M}$ on ζ, and $\mathcal{P}_1$ has a winning strategy in G iff the word is accepted. For each tape cell $h \in \{1, 2, \ldots, p(|\zeta|)\}$, we have two dimensions, $(h, 0)$ and $(h, 1)$ such that a sum of weights of value -1 (i.e., an open window) in dimension (h, i), $i \in \{0, 1\}$ encodes that in the current configuration of $\mathcal{M}$, tape cell h contains a bit of value i. In each step of the simulation (Fig. 3), $\mathcal{P}_1$ has to disclose the symbol under the tape head: if in position h, $\mathcal{P}_1$ discloses a 0 (resp. a 1), he obtains a reward 1 in dimension $(h, 0)$ (resp. $(h, 1)$). To ensure that $\mathcal{P}_1$ was faithful, $\mathcal{P}_2$ is then given the choice to either let the simulation continue, or assign a reward 1 in all dimensions except $(h, 0)$ and $(h, 1)$ and then restart the game after looping in a zero self-loop for an arbitrary long time. If $\mathcal{P}_1$ cheats by not disclosing the correct symbol under tape cell h, $\mathcal{P}_2$ can punish him by branching to the restart state and ensuring a sufficiently long open window in the corresponding dimension before restarting (as in Fig. 2). But if $\mathcal{P}_1$ discloses the correct symbol and $\mathcal{P}_2$ still branches, all windows close. In the accepting state, all windows are closed and the game is restarted. The window size l_{max} of the game is function of the existing bound on the length of an accepting run. To force $\mathcal{P}_1$ to go to the accepting state, we add an additional dimension, with weight -1 on the initial edge of the game and weight 1 on reaching the accepting state.

We also prove EXPTIME-hardness for two dimensions and arbitrary weights by establishing a reduction from *countdown games* [16]. A countdown game $\mathcal{C}$ consists of a weighted graph $(\mathcal{S}, \mathcal{T})$, with $\mathcal{S}$ the set of states and $\mathcal{T} \subseteq \mathcal{S} \times \mathbb{N}_0 \times \mathcal{S}$ the transition relation. Configurations are of the form (s, c), $s \in \mathcal{S}$, $c \in \mathbb{N}$. The game starts in an initial configuration (s_{init}, c_0) and transitions from a configuration (s, c) are performed as follows: first $\mathcal{P}_1$ chooses a duration d, $0 < d \leq c$ such that there exists $t = (s, d, s') \in \mathcal{T}$ for some $s' \in \mathcal{S}$, second $\mathcal{P}_2$ chooses a state $s' \in \mathcal{S}$ such that $t = (s, d, s') \in \mathcal{T}$. Then, the game advances to $(s', c - d)$. Terminal configurations are reached whenever no legitimate move is available. If such a configuration is of the form $(s, 0)$, $\mathcal{P}_1$ wins the play. Otherwise, $\mathcal{P}_2$ wins the play. Deciding the winner in countdown games given an initial configuration (s_{init}, c_0) is EXPTIME-complete [16]. Given a countdown game $\mathcal{C}$ and an initial configuration (s_{init}, c_0), we create a game $G = (S_1, S_2, E, k, w)$ with $k = 2$ and a fixed window objective for $l_{max} = 2 \cdot c_0 + 2$. The two dimensions are used to store the value of the countdown counter and its opposite. Each time a duration d is chosen, an edge of value of value $(-d,d)$ is taken. The game simulates the moves available in C: a strict alternation between states of $\mathcal{P}_1$ (representing states of $\mathcal{S}$) and states of $\mathcal{P}_2$ (representing transitions available from a state of $\mathcal{S}$ once a duration has been chosen). On states of $\mathcal{P}_1$, we add the possibility to branch to a state s_{restart} of $\mathcal{P}_2$, in which $\mathcal{P}_2$ can either take a zero cycle, or go back to the initial state and force a restart of the game. By placing weights $(0, -c_0)$ on the initial edge, and $(c_0, 0)$ on the edge branching to s_{restart}, we ensure that the only way to win for $\mathcal{P}_1$ is to accumulate a value exactly equal to c_0 in the game before switching to s_{restart}. This is possible if and only if $\mathcal{P}_1$ can reach a configuration of value zero in C.

For the case of polynomial windows, we prove PSPACE-hardness via a reduction from generalized reachability games [10]. Filling the gap with the EXPTIME membership is an open problem. The generalized reachability objective is a conjunction of reachability objectives: a winning play has to visit a state of each of a series of k reachability sets. If $\mathcal{P}_1$ has a winning strategy in a generalized reachability game $G^r = (S_1^r, S_2^r, E^r)$, then he has one that guarantees visit of all sets within $k \cdot |S^r|$ steps. We create a modified weighted version of the game, $G = (S_1, S_2, E, k, w)$, such that the weights are k-dimension vectors. The game starts by opening a window in all dimensions and the only way for $\mathcal{P}_1$ to close the window in dimension t, $1 \leq t \leq k$ is to reach a state of the t-th reachability set. We modify the game by giving $\mathcal{P}_2$ the ability to close all open windows and restart the game such that the prefix-independence of the fixed window objective cannot help $\mathcal{P}_1$ to win without reaching the target sets. Then, a play is winning in G for the fixed window objective of size $l_{\max} = 2 \cdot k \cdot |S^r|$ if and only if it is winning for the generalized reachability objective in G^r. This reduction also provides exponential lower bounds on memory for both players, while exponential upper bounds follow from the reduction to co-Büchi games.

Theorem 4. *In two-player multi-dimension games, the fixed arbitrary window mean-payoff problem is EXPTIME-complete, and the fixed polynomial window mean-payoff problem is PSPACE-hard. For both players, exponential memory is sufficient and is required in general.*

Bounded Window. We show non-primitive recursive hardness through a reduction from the problem of deciding the existence of an infinite execution in a *marked reset net*, also known as the *termination problem*. Hence, there is no hope for efficient algorithms on the complete class of two-player multi-weighted games. A marked reset net [8] is a Petri net with *reset arcs* together with an initial marking of its places. Reset arcs are special arcs that reset a place (i.e., empty it of all its tokens). The termination problem for reset nets is decidable but non-primitive recursive hard (as follows from [20]).

Given a reset net $\mathcal{N}$ with an initial marking $\overline{m_0} \in \mathbb{N}^{|P|}$ (where P is the set of places of the net), we build a two-player multi-weighted game G with $k = |P| + 3$ dimensions such that $\mathcal{P}_1$ wins the bounded window objective for threshold $\{0\}^k$ if and only if $\mathcal{N}$ does not have an infinite execution from $\overline{m_0}$. A high level description of our reduction is as follows. The structure of the game (Fig. 5) is based on the alternance between two gadgets simulating the net (Fig. 4).[5] Edges are labeled by k-dimension weight vectors

---

[5] $\overline{\mathbf{1}} = (1,\ldots,1)$, $\overline{\mathbf{0}} = (0,\ldots,0)$, and, for $a, b \in \mathbb{Z}$, $p \in P$, the vector $\overline{\mathbf{a}_{p \to b}}$ represents the vector $(a,\ldots,a,b,a,\ldots,a)$ which has value b in dimension p and a in the other dimensions.

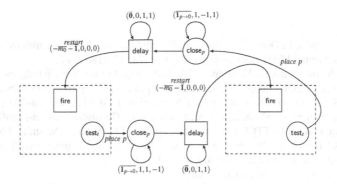

Fig. 5. Careful alternation between gadgets is needed in order for $\mathcal{P}_1$ to win

such that the first $|P|$ dimensions are used to encode the number of tokens in each place. In each gadget, $\mathcal{P}_2$ chooses transitions to simulate an execution of the net. During a faithful simulation, there is always a running open window in all the first $|P|$ dimensions: if place p contains n tokens then the negative sum from the start of the simulation is $-(n+1)$. This is achieved as follows: if a transition t consumes $\mathbf{I}(t)(p)$ tokens from p, then this value is added on the corresponding dimension, and if t produces $\mathbf{O}(t)(p)$ tokens in p, then $\mathbf{O}(t)(p)$ is removed from the corresponding dimension. When a place p is reset, a gadget ensures that dimension p reaches value -1 (the coding of zero tokens). This is thanks to the monotonicity property of reset nets: if $\mathcal{P}_1$ does not simulate a full reset, then the situation gets easier for $\mathcal{P}_2$ as it leaves him more tokens available. If all executions terminate, $\mathcal{P}_2$ has to choose an unfireable transition at some point, consuming unavailable tokens from some place $p \in P$. If so, the window in dimension p closes. After each transition choice of $\mathcal{P}_2$, $\mathcal{P}_1$ can either continue the simulation or branch out of the gadget to close all windows, except in some dimension p of his choice. Then $\mathcal{P}_2$ can arbitrarily extend any still open window in the first $(|P|+1)$ dimensions and restart the game afterwards. Dimension $(|P|+1)$ prevents $\mathcal{P}_1$ from staying forever in a gadget. If an infinite execution exists, $\mathcal{P}_2$ simulates it and never has to choose an unfireable transition. Hence, when $\mathcal{P}_1$ branches out, the window in some dimension p stays open. The last two dimensions force him to alternate between gadgets so that he cannot take profit of the prefix-independence to win after a faithful simulation. So, $\mathcal{P}_2$ can delay the closing of the open window for longer and longer, thus winning the game.

Theorem 5. *In two-player multi-dimension games, the bounded window mean-payoff problem is non-primitive recursive hard.*

The decidability of the bounded window mean-payoff problem remains open.

6   Conclusion

The strong relation between mean-payoff and total-payoff breaks in multi-weighted games as the total-payoff threshold problem becomes undecidable. Window objectives provide conservative approximations with timing guarantees. Some variants prove to be more computationally tractable than the corresponding classical objectives.

References

1. Brim, L., Chaloupka, J., Doyen, L., Gentilini, R., Raskin, J.-F.: Faster algorithms for mean-payoff games. Formal Methods in System Design 38(2), 97–118 (2011)
2. Chakrabarti, A., de Alfaro, L., Henzinger, T.A., Stoelinga, M.: Resource interfaces. In: Alur, R., Lee, I. (eds.) EMSOFT 2003. LNCS, vol. 2855, pp. 117–133. Springer, Heidelberg (2003)
3. Chandra, A.K., Kozen, D., Stockmeyer, L.J.: Alternation. J. ACM 28(1), 114–133 (1981)
4. Chatterjee, K., Doyen, L., Henzinger, T.A., Raskin, J.-F.: Generalized mean-payoff and energy games. In: Proc. of FSTTCS. LIPIcs, vol. 8, pp. 505–516. Schloss Dagstuhl - LZI (2010)
5. Chatterjee, K., Doyen, L., Randour, M., Raskin, J.F.: Looking at mean-payoff and total-payoff through windows. CoRR, abs/1302.4248 (2013), http://arxiv.org/abs/1302.4248
6. Chatterjee, K., Henzinger, M.: An $\mathcal{O}(n^2)$ time algorithm for alternating büchi games. In: Proc. of SODA, pp. 1386–1399. SIAM (2012)
7. Chatterjee, K., Randour, M., Raskin, J.-F.: Strategy synthesis for multi-dimensional quantitative objectives. In: Koutny, M., Ulidowski, I. (eds.) CONCUR 2012. LNCS, vol. 7454, pp. 115–131. Springer, Heidelberg (2012)
8. Dufourd, C., Finkel, A., Schnoebelen, P.: Reset nets between decidability and undecidability. In: Larsen, K.G., Skyum, S., Winskel, G. (eds.) ICALP 1998. LNCS, vol. 1443, pp. 103–115. Springer, Heidelberg (1998)
9. Ehrenfeucht, A., Mycielski, J.: Positional strategies for mean payoff games. Int. Journal of Game Theory 8(2), 109–113 (1979)
10. Fijalkow, N., Horn, F.: The surprizing complexity of generalized reachability games. CoRR, abs/1010.2420 (2010)
11. Gawlitza, T.M., Seidl, H.: Games through nested fixpoints. In: Bouajjani, A., Maler, O. (eds.) CAV 2009. LNCS, vol. 5643, pp. 291–305. Springer, Heidelberg (2009)
12. Gimbert, H., Zielonka, W.: When can you play positionally? In: Fiala, J., Koubek, V., Kratochvíl, J. (eds.) MFCS 2004. LNCS, vol. 3153, pp. 686–697. Springer, Heidelberg (2004)
13. Gurvich, V.A., Karzanov, A.V., Khachivan, L.G.: Cyclic games and an algorithm to find minimax cycle means in directed graphs. USSR Computational Mathematics and Mathematical Physics 28(5), 85–91 (1988)
14. Bjorklund, H., Vorobyov, S.: A combinatorial strongly subexponential strategy improvement algorithm for mean payoff games. Discrete Applied Mathematics 155, 210–229 (2007)
15. Jurdziński, M.: Deciding the winner in parity games is in UP ∩ co-UP. Inf. Process. Lett. 68(3), 119–124 (1998)
16. Jurdziński, M., Sproston, J., Laroussinie, F.: Model checking probabilistic timed automata with one or two clocks. Logical Methods in Computer Science 4(3) (2008)
17. Karzanov, A.V., Lebedev, V.N.: Cyclical games with prohibitions. Math. Program. 60, 277–293 (1993)
18. Lifshits, Y.M., Pavlov, D.S.: Potential theory for mean payoff games. Journal of Mathematical Sciences 145(3), 4967–4974 (2007)
19. Pisaruk, N.N.: Mean cost cyclical games. Mathematics of Operations Research 24(4), 817–828 (1999)
20. Schnoebelen, P.: Verifying lossy channel systems has nonprimitive recursive complexity. Inf. Process. Lett. 83(5), 251–261 (2002)
21. Velner, Y., Rabinovich, A.: Church synthesis problem for noisy input. In: Hofmann, M. (ed.) FOSSACS 2011. LNCS, vol. 6604, pp. 275–289. Springer, Heidelberg (2011)
22. Zwick, U., Paterson, M.: The complexity of mean payoff games on graphs. Theoretical Computer Science 158, 343–359 (1996)

Weighted Safety

Sigal Weiner, Matan Hasson, Orna Kupferman, Eyal Pery, and Zohar Shevach

School of Computer Science and Engineering, Hebrew University, Israel

Abstract. Safety properties, which assert that the system always stays within some allowed region, have been extensively studied and used. In the last years, we see more and more research on quantitative formal methods, where systems and specifications are weighted. We introduce and study safety in the weighted setting. For a value $v \in \mathbb{Q}$, we say that a weighted language $L : \Sigma^* \to \mathbb{Q}$ is v-safe if every word with cost at least v has a prefix all whose extensions have cost at least v. The language L is then weighted safe if L is v-safe for some v.

Given a regular weighted language L, we study the set of values $v \in \mathbb{Q}$ for which L is v-safe. We show that this set need not be closed upwards or downwards and we relate the v-safety of L with the safety of the (Boolean) language of words whose cost in L is at most v. We show that the latter need not be regular but is always context free. Given a deterministic weighted automaton $\mathcal{A}$, we relate the safety of $L(\mathcal{A})$ with the structure of $\mathcal{A}$, and we study the problem of deciding whether $L(\mathcal{A})$ is v-safe for a given v. We also study the weighted safety of $L(\mathcal{A})$ and provide bounds on the minimal value $|v|$ for which a weighted language $L(\mathcal{A})$ is v-safe.

1 Introduction

Of special interest in formal verification are *safety properties*, which assert that the system always stays within some allowed region. The interest in safety started with the quest for natural classes of specifications. The theoretical aspects of safety have been extensively studied [3,18,19,23]. With the growing success and use of formal verification, safety has turned out to be interesting also from a practical point of view [12,14,16]. Indeed, the ability to reason about finite prefixes significantly simplifies both enumerative and symbolic algorithms. In the first, safety circumvents the need to reason about complex ω-regular acceptance conditions. For example, methods for temporal synthesis, program repair, or parametric reasoning are much simpler for safety properties [13,17,22]. In the second, it circumvents the need to reason about cycles, which is significant in both BDD-based and SAT-based methods [6,7]. In addition to a rich literature on safety, researchers have studied additional classes, such as liveness and co-safety properties [3,18].

Traditional formal methods are based on a Boolean satisfaction notion: a reactive system satisfies, or not, a given specification. In the last years, we see more and more research on *quantitative formal methods*, where specifications are multi-valued. Indeed, it is desired to reason about quantitative properties (that is, no longer "is every request eventually acknowledged?" but rather "what is the average waiting time between a request and an acknowledge?") [8,9] and to refine the binary outcome of satisfaction

D. Van Hung and M. Ogawa (Eds.): ATVA 2013, LNCS 8172, pp. 133–147, 2013.
© Springer International Publishing Switzerland 2013

(that is, no longer "is the property satisfied?" but rather "what is the quality, in some predefined scale, in which the specification is satisfied?") [2]. A natural quest that arises is a weighted counterpart to the classes of specifications in the Boolean setting.

In this paper we introduce and study safety in the weighted setting. We focus on finite words and weights in $\mathbb{Q}$. Accordingly, a weighted language is a function $L : \Sigma^* \to \mathbb{Q}$ that assigns to each finite word over the alphabet Σ a cost in $\mathbb{Q}$. We note that weighted languages are defined also with respect to infinite words [9] and our results can be extended to that setting. The study there, however, involves limit behavior, which brings to the picture difficulties that are orthogonal to these we face in the study of safety. We thus focus on finite words. Recall that in the Boolean setting, a language over an alphabet Σ is a set $L \subseteq \Sigma^*$, and L is a safety language if every word not in L has a bad prefix – one that cannot be extended to a word in L. Consider a weighted language $L : \Sigma^* \to \mathbb{Q}$. For $v \in \mathbb{Q}$, we say that L is v-safe if every word whose cost is above v has a bad prefix – one all whose extensions result in words with cost above v. Formally, for all $w \in \Sigma^*$, if $L(w) \geq v$, then w has a prefix x such that for all $y \in \Sigma^*$, we have that $L(x \cdot y) \geq v$. We say that L is *weighted safe* if it is v-safe for some $v \in \mathbb{Q}$.

We describe weighted languages by weighted automata: each transition of the automaton has a cost in $\mathbb{Q}$, the cost of a run is the sum of the costs of the transitions taken along the run, and the cost assigned to a word is the cost of the cheapest run on it. [1] We use WFA and DWFA to abbreviate weighted finite automata and deterministic weighted finite automata, respectively. WFAs and DWFA have been used for the verification of quantitative properties [9], for reasoning about probabilistic systems [5], and for reasoning about the competitive ratio of on-line algorithms [4]. They are also useful in text, speech, and image processing, where the weights of the WFA are used in order to account for the variability of the data and to rank alternative hypotheses [10,20,21].

Recall that a weighted language L is v-safe if each word with cost above v has a prefix that cannot be extended to a word whose cost is below v. The first question we study is a characterization of the *safety zones* of a weighted language. That is, the set $V_L \subseteq \mathbb{Q}$ of values v for which L is v-safe. We show that the safety zones need not be closed upwards or downwards. We relate the safety zones of a weighted language with the structure of a DWFA for it. We use the relation in order to characterize cases in which V_L is empty, namely L is not weighted safe.

For $v \in \mathbb{Z}$, we define the *Boolean v-language* of L, denoted $L_{\downarrow v}$, as the set of all words w for which $L(w) < v$. We show that L and $L_{\downarrow v}$ share the same set of bad prefixes and conclude that L is v-safe iff $L_{\downarrow v}$ is (Boolean) safe. We further show that even when L is given by a DWFA, the language $L_{\downarrow v}$ need not be regular, yet it can always be defined by a pushdown automaton. We show that the regularity of $L_{\downarrow v}$ is independent of v and give a structure-based characterization of *bumpy DWFAs* – these DWFAs $\mathcal{A}$ for which $L(\mathcal{A})_{\downarrow v}$ is regular for all $v \in \mathbb{Q}$. We describe a construction of a DFA for $L(\mathcal{A})_{\downarrow v}$ from a non-bumpy DWFA $\mathcal{A}$, and a PDA for it in cases $\mathcal{A}$ is bumpy. Both constructions involve a polynomial blow-up when the costs in $\mathcal{A}$ are given in

---

[1] In general, weighted automata are defined with respect to an algebraic semiring. We focus on the *tropical* semiring $\langle \mathbb{Q} \cup \{\infty\}, \min, +, \infty, 0 \rangle$, where the sum operator is min (with ∞ being the identity element) and the product operator is + (with 0 being the identity element).

unary. When either v or the costs in $\mathcal{A}$ are given in binary, the construction becomes exponential, and we show matching lower bounds.

We then turn to study the problem of deciding whether the language of a given DWFA is v-safe. While the problem is easy for non-bumpy automata or when $v \leq 0$, the general case for $v > 0$ is very challenging and is our main technical contribution. By definition, a weighted language L is not v-safe if it has a v-*refuter*: a word with cost above v that can be extended to a word whose cost is below v. We show a bound on the length of a shortest v-refuter for a non v-safe language L. For this we show that it is possible to decompose refuters to a base path on which simple cycles are "hanged", where the base path has polynomial length. By carefully reasoning about this decomposition, we are able to use the theory of Frobenius numbers in order to bound the number of used cycles by a polynomial in the DWFA[2]. This enables us to prove that the problem of deciding whether $\mathcal{A}$ is v-safe is co-NP-complete (and is NLOGSPACE-complete when the costs and value are given in unary). We also show that the problem is undecidable for nondeterministic WFAs.

Finally, we study the problem of bounding the minimal value $|v|$ for which the language of a given DWFA is v-safe. We show that if $L(\mathcal{A})$ is weighted safe, then it is v-safe or $(-v)$-safe for $v \geq 0$ that is exponential in $\mathcal{A}$, and we show that the exponential bound is tight. We use this bound to show that the problem of deciding whether a DWFA with costs given in unary is weighted safe is in PSPACE.

Due to the lack of space, some examples and proofs are omitted from this version and can be found in the full version, in the authors' URLs.

2 Preliminaries

2.1 Weighted Finite Automata

A *nondeterministic automaton* (NFA, for short) is $\mathcal{A} = \langle \Sigma, Q, \delta, Q_0, \alpha \rangle$, where Σ is an alphabet, Q is a set of states, $\delta : Q \times \Sigma \to 2^Q$ is a transition relation, $Q_0 \subseteq Q$ is a set of initial states, and $\alpha \subseteq Q$ is a set of accepting states. If for all $q \in Q$ and $\sigma \in \Sigma$ we have that $|\delta(q, \sigma)| \leq 1$, then $\mathcal{A}$ is a *deterministic automaton* (DFA, for short). Given a finite word $w = \sigma_1 \cdot \sigma_2 \cdots \sigma_l \in \Sigma^*$, a run r of $\mathcal{A}$ on w is a sequence $q_0, q_1, \ldots, q_l \in Q^{l+1}$ such that $q_0 \in Q_0$ and for all $0 \leq i \leq l$, we have $q_{i+1} \in \delta(q_i, \sigma_i)$. The run r is *accepting* if $q_l \in \alpha$. A word w is accepted by $\mathcal{A}$ if there is an accepting run of $\mathcal{A}$ on w. Note that a deterministic automaton has at most one run on an input word. The language of $\mathcal{A}$, denoted $L(\mathcal{A})$ is the set of words accepted by $\mathcal{A}$.

The transition function δ induces a relation $\Delta \subseteq Q \times \Sigma \times Q$ such that $\Delta(q, \sigma, q')$ iff $q' \in \delta(q, \sigma)$. A *weighted finite automaton* (WFA, for short) is an NFA augmented with a *cost function* $c : \Delta \to \mathbb{Q}$ that assigns to each transition a cost, which is a rational number. Formally, $\mathcal{A} = \langle \Sigma, Q, \delta, c, Q_0, \alpha \rangle$, where Σ, Q, δ, Q_0, and α are as in an NFA and c is a cost function. The cost of a run r on a word $w = \sigma_1 \cdot \sigma_2 \cdots \sigma_l \in \Sigma^*$ is the cost of the transitions taken along the run. That is, $cost(r, w) = \sum_{i=0}^{l-1} c(q_i, \sigma_i, q_{i+1})$. When clear from the context, we drop the word parameter and refer to $cost(r)$. The

---

[2] For a given set of mutually prime positive integers, their Frobenius number is the greatest integer that cannot be expressed as a linear combination (with nonnegative integer coefficients) of its elements.

cost of a word in $\mathcal{A}$ is the cost of a cheapest accepting run on it. That is, $cost(\mathcal{A}, w) = \min\{cost(r, w) : r$ is an accepting run of $\mathcal{A}$ on $w\}$. If there is no accepting run of $\mathcal{A}$ on w, then $cost(\mathcal{A}, w) = \infty$. We view the language of a WFA $\mathcal{A}$ as a mapping $L(\mathcal{A}) : \Sigma^* \to \mathbb{Q}$, with $L(\mathcal{A})(w) = cost(\mathcal{A}, w)$. We denote by $L_{Bool}(\mathcal{A})$ the Boolean language of all words that have an accepting run in $\mathcal{A}$. When the underlying automaton $\mathcal{A}$ is deterministic, we say that $\mathcal{A}$ is a deterministic WFA (DWFA, for short). Throughout the paper we assume that all WFAs contain only reachable and nonempty states (that is, states from which some word is accepted).

2.2 Boolean and Weighted Safety Languages

Boolean Safety. Consider a Boolean language $L \subseteq \Sigma^*$ over the alphabet Σ. A finite word $x \in \Sigma^*$ is a *bad prefix* for L iff for all $y \in \Sigma^*$, we have $x \cdot y \notin L$. Thus, a bad prefix is a word that cannot be extended to a word in L. A language L is a *safety* language iff every $w \notin L$ has a finite bad prefix. For a safety language L, we denote by $bad\_pref(L)$ the set of all bad prefixes for L.

For a language $L \subseteq \Sigma^*$, let $pref(L)$ denote the set of all prefixes of words in L. It is not hard to prove that L is safe iff $pref(L) = L$. Recall that we assume that DFAs have no empty states. Thus, a DFA $\mathcal{A}_{pref}$ that recognizes $pref(L(\mathcal{A}))$ can be obtained from $\mathcal{A}$ by making all its states accepting. By checking whether $L(\mathcal{A}_{pref}) \subseteq L(\mathcal{A})$, we can thus decide, in NLOGSPACE, whether $L(\mathcal{A})$ is safe.

Weighted Safety. In Boolean safety, once something bad has happened, it cannot be recovered. Lifting the safety definition to weighted languages, we consider "something bad" as a "too high" cost, and the definition is parameterized by a threshold $v \in \mathbb{Q}$ specifying what "too high" is. Thus, a weighted language is v-safe if once a word reaches a cost of v or above, it cannot be extended to a word that costs less than v. Formally, we have the following.

Definition 1. *Consider a weighted language* $L : \Sigma^* \to \mathbb{Q}$ *and a value* $v \in \mathbb{Q}$. *We say that* L *is* v-safe *if for every* $w \in \Sigma^*$, *if* $L(w) \geq v$ *then there is a prefix* x *of* w *such that for all* $y \in \Sigma^*$, *we have that* $L(x \cdot y) \geq v$. *We call such a prefix a* v-bad prefix *for* L.

We say that a weighted language L is *weighted safe* iff L is v-safe for some value $v \in \mathbb{Q}$. Given a DWFA $\mathcal{A}$, we say that $\mathcal{A}$ is v-safe iff $L(\mathcal{A})$ is v-safe. We denote the set of v-bad prefixes of L as $bad\_pref_v(L)$. For all values $c, v \in \mathbb{Q}$, where $c > 0$, we have that a weighted language L is v-safe iff $c \cdot L$ is $(c \cdot v)$-safe, where $c \cdot L$ is obtained from L by multiplying the costs of all words by c. Given a WFA for L, multiplying the costs of all its transitions by c results in a WFA for $c \cdot L$. Accordingly, we assume wlog that our WFAs and weighted languages are over $\mathbb{Z}$.

We define the *safety zones* of L as the set $V_L \subseteq \mathbb{Z}$ that consists of all values $v \in \mathbb{Z}$ for which L is v-safe. Note that once all costs are in $\mathbb{Z}$, we have that L is v-safe for some $v \in \mathbb{R}$ iff it is also $\lceil v \rceil$-safe. Thus, while we only study threshold values in $\mathbb{Z}$, all our results applies also to thresholds in $\mathbb{R}$. Note also that L is weighted-safe iff $V_L \neq \emptyset$.

Remark 1. In the Boolean setting, a language L is *co-safe* if every word in L has a good prefix – one all whose extensions are words in L. Equivalently, the complement of L, namely $\Sigma^* \setminus L$ is safe. Following the same lines (or, equivalently, dualizing our definition of v-safety), we say that a weighted language L is v-co-safe if for every word $w \in \Sigma^*$, if $L(w) \leq v$, then w has a prefix x such that $L(x \cdot y) \leq v$ for all $y \in \Sigma^*$. Equivalently, a weighted language L is v-co-safe iff $(-L)$ is v-safe, where $(-L)$ is obtained from L by negating all costs. For a DWFA $\mathcal{A}$, let $(-\mathcal{A})$ be the DWFA obtained by negating all transition costs in $\mathcal{A}$. It is not hard to see that $L(-\mathcal{A}) = (-L)(\mathcal{A})$, thus $\mathcal{A}$ is v-co-safe iff $(-\mathcal{A})$ is $(-v)$-safe. Consequently, our results on weighted safety are easily extended to weighted co-safety.

3 Observations on Weighted Safety

In this section we study some theoretical aspects of weighted safety. In Sections 4 and 5 we are going to use these observations for deciding v-safety and weighted safety.

3.1 Properties of Weighted Safety

We start by showing that even simple DWFAs may have a complex set of safety zones.

Example 1. Consider the DWFA $\mathcal{A}$ appearing in Figure 1. We show that $V_{L(\mathcal{A})} = (-\infty, -4] \cup \{v : v = 1 \bmod 5\}$. To see this, we consider several cases. First, since all costs in $\mathcal{A}$ are at least -4 then clearly, for $v \leq -4$, we have that $\mathcal{A}$ is v-safe. For every $-3 \leq v \leq 0$, we have that $\mathcal{A}$ is not v-safe, as the word ϵ has cost $0 \geq v$, but it has no v-bad prefix since it can be extended to the word b, with cost $-4 < v$. For $v \geq 1$, consider first the case where $v = 5k + i$ for $1 < i \leq 5$ and some $k \in \mathbb{N}$. Consider the word $x = a^{(k+1)}$. We have that $L(\mathcal{A})(x) = 5(k+1) \geq v$, and that $L(\mathcal{A})(x \cdot b) = 5(k+1) - 4 = 5k + 1 < v$. Thus x can be extended to a word that costs less than v and so has no v-bad prefix. Therefore $\mathcal{A}$ is not v-safe. Now, consider $v = 5k + 1$ for some $k \in \mathbb{N}$. We show that every word x such that $L(\mathcal{A})(x) \geq v$ is a v-bad prefix of itself. If x contains the letter b, then the run on x ends in state q_1, from which there are no reachable negative edges. Thus the cost of any extension of x can only be higher, and so x is a v-bad prefix. Otherwise, x is of the form a^m for some $m \in \mathbb{N}$ such that $L(\mathcal{A})(x) = 5m \geq v = 5k + 1$. Therefore $L(\mathcal{A})(x) \geq v + 4$. But then for any extension $y \in \Sigma^*$ we have that $L(\mathcal{A})(x \cdot y) \geq v + 4 - 4 = v$, thus x is a v-bad prefix. Therefore, $\mathcal{A}$ is v-safe for every $v \geq 1$ of the form $v = 5k + 1$ for some $k \in \mathbb{N}$.

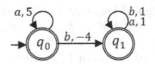

Fig. 1. Simple structure may have complex safety zones

☐

Note that in Example 1 we have seen that $V_L(\mathcal{A})$ contains all values smaller than -4. This is no coincidence. If a weighted language L is v_1-safe for a value $v_1 \leq 0$, then for every $v_2 < v_1$ we have that L is also v_2-safe. Indeed, since $L(\epsilon) = 0 \geq v_1$, then L being v_1-safe implies that all words have cost at least v_1. But then, all words also have cost at least v_2, making L also v_2-safe.

We now relate some properties of a DWFA with its safety zones. We start with relating $V_L(\mathcal{A})$ with the Boolean-safety of $\mathcal{A}$.

Proposition 1. *Consider a DWFA $\mathcal{A}$.*

1. *If $\mathcal{A}$ is not Boolean-safe, then there exists a threshold value $t \in \mathbb{Z}$ such that for every value v such that $v > t$, we have that $\mathcal{A}$ is not v-safe.*
2. *If $\mathcal{A}$ is Boolean-safe, then $\mathcal{A}$ is v-safe for every $v \in \mathbb{Z}$ iff $\mathcal{A}$ has no transition with a negative cost.*

We continue with relating structural properties of $\mathcal{A}$ with its weighted safety.

Proposition 2. *Consider a DWFA $\mathcal{A}$.*

1. *If $\mathcal{A}$ has a negative cycle reachable from a positive reachable cycle or from a non-accepting state, then $\mathcal{A}$ is not weighted-safe.*
2. *If $\mathcal{A}$ is not weighted-safe, then $\mathcal{A}$ contains a negative cycle, and either a positive cycle or a non-accepting state.*

Note that the lack of a negative cycle reachable from a positive cycle or a non-accepting state does not necessarily indicate that the language is weighted-safe. An example for this can be found in the full version.

3.2 From Weighted Safety to Boolean Safety

Given a weighted language $L : \Sigma^* \to \mathbb{Z}$ and a value $v \in \mathbb{Z}$, we define the *Boolean v-language* of L, denoted $L_{\downarrow v}$, as the set of all words w for which $L(w) < v$.

We consider the relation between the v-safety of a weighted language L and the (Boolean) safety of $L_{\downarrow v}$.

Theorem 1. *Given a weighted language $L : \Sigma^* \to \mathbb{Z}$ and a value $v \in \mathbb{Z}$, we have that L is v-safe iff $L_{\downarrow v}$ is safe.*

Proof: We first show that $bad\_pref_v(L) = bad\_pref(L_{\downarrow v})$. By definition, for every $x \in \Sigma^*$ we have that $x \in bad\_pref_v(L)$ iff $L(x \cdot y) \geq v$ for every $y \in \Sigma^*$. This is valid iff $x \cdot y \notin L_{\downarrow v}$ for every $y \in \Sigma^*$, which holds iff $x \in bad\_pref(L_{\downarrow v})$. Thus, $bad\_pref_v(L) = bad\_pref(L_{\downarrow v})$.

Now, by definition, a weighted language L is v-safe iff for every $w \in \Sigma^*$, if $L(w) \geq v$ then w has a prefix $x \in bad\_pref_v(L)$. By the definition of $L_{\downarrow v}$ and since $bad\_pref_v(L) = bad\_pref(L_{\downarrow v})$, this is valid iff every $w \notin L_{\downarrow v}$ has a prefix x such that $x \in bad\_pref(L_{\downarrow v})$. The latter holds iff $L_{\downarrow v}$ is (Boolean) safe. $\qquad\square$

3.3 Regularity of v-Languages

In this section we study the Boolean v-language $L(\mathcal{A})_{\downarrow v}$ of a DWFA $\mathcal{A}$. We show that $L(\mathcal{A})_{\downarrow v}$ need not be regular, characterize the cases where it is regular, and construct a DFA for a regular v-language. We also show that $L(\mathcal{A})_{\downarrow v}$ is context-free and construct a pushdown automaton for it.

We start with two examples showing that $L_{\downarrow v}$ need not be regular.

Example 2. Consider the DWFA $\mathcal{A}$ appearing in Figure 2. One can check that $L(\mathcal{A})$ is not weighted safe. Let $v = 1$. It is easy to see that the cost of every word is less than 1 iff the letter b appears at least as many times as the letter a in it. Therefore, $L(\mathcal{A})_{\downarrow 1} = \{w \in \Sigma^* : \sharp_a(w) \le \sharp_b(w)\}$, which is irregular. □

Example 3. Consider the DWFA $\mathcal{B}$ appearing in Figure 3, and let $v = 1$. One can check $L(\mathcal{B})$ is v-safe for all $v > 0$. It is easy to see that $L(\mathcal{B})_{\downarrow 1} = \{a^n b^m : 1 \le m \le n\}$. Clearly $L(\mathcal{B})_{\downarrow 1}$ is not regular. □

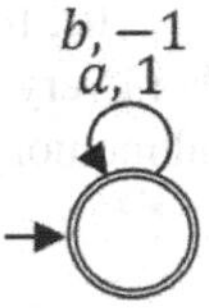

Fig. 2. A non-regular v-language, with $v = 1$, for a not weighted safe language

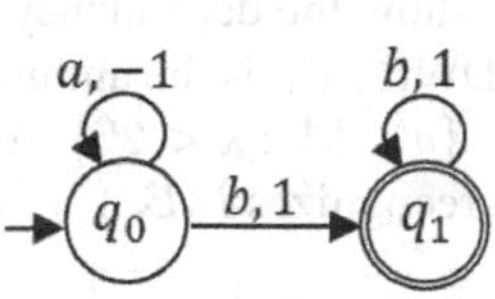

Fig. 3. A non-regular v-language, with $v = 1$, for a weighted safe language

We say an DWFA is *bumpy* if it has a positive cycle reachable from a reachable negative cycle or a negative cycle reachable from a reachable positive cycle.

Note that both $\mathcal{A}$ and $\mathcal{B}$ above are bumpy. This is no coincidence. Once positive and negative cycles are reachable from each other, it is possible to accumulate a cost that is unbounded from above and then reduce it below v or, dually, accumulate an unboundedly low cost and then increase it above v. In such cases, a memory element is required in order to know when the cost is below a value v.

We first show that when $\mathcal{A}$ is not bumpy, we can construct a DFA for $L(\mathcal{A})_{\downarrow v}$.

Theorem 2. *Consider a non-bumpy DWFA $\mathcal{A}$. Let n be the number of states in $\mathcal{A}$ and let M be the maximal absolute cost of a transition in $\mathcal{A}$. Then, for every $v \in \mathbb{Z}$, we can construct a DFA for $L(\mathcal{A})_{\downarrow v}$ with $O(n(nM + v))$ states, and the blow up is tight.*

Proof: Given a DWFA $\mathcal{A} = \langle \Sigma, Q, q_0, \delta, c, \alpha \rangle$ and a value $v \in \mathbb{Z}$, we construct the DFA $\mathcal{A}' = \langle \Sigma, Q', q_0', \delta', \alpha' \rangle$ as follows.

We define the set of *relevant values* of a non-bumpy DWFA to be $Val = \{u : -nM - |v| \le u \le nM + |v|\} \cup \{\top, \bot\}$. To construct $\mathcal{A}'$, we unwind $\mathcal{A}$, augmenting each state with the cost that has been accumulated along the path traversed in order to reach it. Once the cost is not in the relevant values set Val, we use $\top$ or $\bot$ according to the sign of the cost.

Formally, the set of states of $\mathcal{A}'$ is $Q' = Q \times Val$. The initial state is $q_0' = \langle q_0, 0 \rangle$, and the accepting states are $\alpha' = \{\langle s, t \rangle : s \in \alpha$ and $t < v\}$. Given a state $\langle s, t \rangle$ and a letter $\sigma \in \Sigma$, with $q' = \delta(s, \sigma)$, we define $\delta'(\langle s, t \rangle, \sigma) = \langle q', t' \rangle$, where if $t + c(q, \sigma, q') > nM + |v|$ we set $t' = \top$, if $t + c(q, \sigma, q') < -nM - |v|$ we set $t' = \bot$, otherwise $t' = t + c(q, \sigma, q')$.

In order to prove the correctness of the construction, we argue that since $\mathcal{A}$ is not bumpy, then once the cost of a run of $\mathcal{A}$ goes beyond $nM + |v|$ or below $-nM - |v|$, there is no need to maintain it. Note that, by construction, $|Q'| = O(n(nM + v))$ and $|\delta'| = O(|\delta|(nM + v))$.

We now proceed to the lower bound. The number of states in $\mathcal{A}'$ depends on the values M and v. Accordingly, when M or v are given in binary, the construction is exponential. We now show that it is indeed sufficient for one of these two components to be given in binary in order for a DFA that recognizes the v-language to need exponentially many states.

We first show the dependency in v. Consider the family $\langle \mathcal{A}, 2^n \rangle$, for $\Sigma = \{a\}$, where the DWFA $\mathcal{A}$ is the automaton appearing in Figure 4. For every n we have that $L(\mathcal{A})_{\downarrow 2^n} = \{a^k : k < 2^n\}$. This requires exponential memory and therefore a DFA that recognizes $L(\mathcal{A})_{\downarrow v_n}$ is of size at least 2^n.

We now show the dependency in M. Consider the family $\langle \mathcal{B}_n, 0 \rangle$, for $\Sigma = \{a, b\}$, where the DWFA $\mathcal{B}_n$ is the automaton appearing in Figure 5. For every n we have that $L(\mathcal{B}_n)_{\downarrow 0} = \{a^k \cdot b^+ : k < 2^n\}$. Again, this requires exponential memory and therefore a DFA that recognizes $L(\mathcal{B}_n)_{\downarrow u_n}$ is of size at least 2^n.

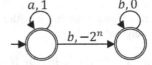

Fig. 4. Lower bound for a binary value   **Fig. 5.** Lower bound for binary costs

$\square$

We now show that bumpiness characterizes the irregularity of the Boolean v-language.

Theorem 3. *A DWFA $\mathcal{A}$ is bumpy iff $L(\mathcal{A})_{\downarrow v}$ is irregular, for all values $v \in \mathbb{Z}$.*

Proof: By Theorem 2, if $\mathcal{A}$ is not bumpy then $L(\mathcal{A})_{\downarrow v}$ is regular. For the other direction, we assume that $L(\mathcal{A})_{\downarrow v}$ is regular and show that $\mathcal{A}$ is not bumpy. Let $\mathcal{D}$ be a DFA that recognizes $L(\mathcal{A})_{\downarrow v}$, and let n be the number of states in $\mathcal{D}$. Assume by way of contradiction that $\mathcal{A}$ is bumpy. Consider the case where there is a path from a positive cycle C_{pos} to a negative cycle C_{neg} (the other case is similar).

The idea is to consider a run over a word that repeats the positive cycle $n + 1$ times, and then repeats the negative cycle enough times for the cost to be less than v. Since the positive cycle is repeated $n + 1$ times, we can pump the positive cycle, increasing the cost of the word while maintaining its acceptance in $\mathcal{D}$, eventually reaching a word that costs more than v and is yet accepted by $\mathcal{D}$, contradicting the fact it recognizes $L(\mathcal{A})_{\downarrow v}$.

$\square$

Note that the regularity of $L(\mathcal{A})_{\downarrow v}$ does not depend on the value v and depends only on the structure of $\mathcal{A}$.

Finally, even though $L(\mathcal{A})_{\downarrow v}$ is not necessarily a regular language, it is always a context-free language, which can be recognized by a PDA. Intuitively, a stack is sufficient as the memory element we previously found lacking. The construction details can be found in the full version.

4   Deciding v-Safety

In this section we solve the problem of deciding, given a DWFA $\mathcal{A}$ and a value $v \in \mathbb{Z}$, whether $\mathcal{A}$ is v-safe. We start with special cases in which the problem is easy. We then show that for nondeterministic WFAs the problem is undecidable, and that when v and the costs of $\mathcal{A}$ are given in binary it is co-NP-hard. We conclude with tight upper bounds, showing the problem is NLOGSPACE-complete (co-NP-complete) when v and the costs in $\mathcal{A}$ are given in unary (respectively, binary).

4.1   Easy Special Cases

In Section 3 we related bumpiness and regularity. We now show that for non-bumpy DWFAs, regularity of the v-language enables an easy v-safety decision procedure.

Theorem 4. *Given a non-bumpy DWFA $\mathcal{A}$ and a value $v \in \mathbb{Z}$, where v and the costs of $\mathcal{A}$ are given in unary, the problem of deciding if $\mathcal{A}$ is v-safe is NLOGSPACE-complete.*

Proof: We start with membership in NLOGSPACE. By Theorem 2, we construct a DFA that recognizes $L(\mathcal{A})_{\downarrow v}$. We then check if $L(\mathcal{A})_{\downarrow v}$ is safe, which holds, by Lemma 1, iff $L(\mathcal{A})$ is v-safe. Since the construction can be done on the fly, and safety checking is in NLOGSPACE, the problem is in NLOGSPACE. Note that since the size of the suggested construction is $O(|\mathcal{A}|(|\mathcal{A}|M + v))$, this can also be done in time $O(|\mathcal{A}|(|\mathcal{A}|M + v))$, where M is the maximal absolute cost of a transition in $\mathcal{A}$. Hardness in NLOGSPACE is easy to prove by a reduction from reachability. $\square$

We continue with the case v is non-positive.

Theorem 5. *Consider a DWFA $\mathcal{A}$ and value $v \leq 0$. Assume that v and the costs in $\mathcal{A}$ are given in unary. The problem of deciding if $\mathcal{A}$ is v-safe is NLOGSPACE-complete.*

Proof: Since $L(\mathcal{A})(\epsilon) = 0$ and $v \leq 0$, we have that $\mathcal{A}$ is v-safe iff the costs of all simple paths (that end in an accepting state) are at least v, and there is no negative reachable cycle. Searching for a simple path with cost less than v or for a reachable negative cycle can clearly be done in NLOGSPACE. Hardness in NLOGSPACE is easy to prove by a reduction from reachability. $\square$

Note that this check can also be performed by the Bellman-Ford algorithm for calculating distances in a graph in time $O(n^3)$, which works for both binary and unary inputs.

4.2   Hardness of the General Case

In this section we show that deciding if a language is v-safe can be hard. Specifically, we show that deciding if a (nondeterministic) WFA is v-safe is undecidable, and that deciding if a DWFA is v-safe when v and the costs are given in binary is co-NP-hard.

Theorem 6. *Let $v \in \mathbb{Z}$. Deciding v-safety for (nondeterministic) WFAs is undecidable.*

Proof: We show a reduction from WFA universality, which is known to be undecidable [1]. The universality problem for WFAs asks, given a WFA $\mathcal{B}$ and a threshold v, whether $\mathcal{B}$ assigns a value that is smaller than v to all words in Σ^*, that is, if $L(\mathcal{B})_{\downarrow v}$ is universal. Given a WFA $\mathcal{B}$ over an alphabet Σ, we construct a WFA $\mathcal{B}'$ over the alphabet $\Sigma' = \Sigma \cup \{\sigma\}$, for $\sigma \notin \Sigma$. The WFA $\mathcal{B}'$ is obtained from $\mathcal{B}$ by adding a new state q', with a $(\tau, -1)$ self-loop for all $\tau \in \Sigma'$, and adding a $(\sigma, 0)$-transition from every state to q'. Thus, for every $x \in \Sigma^*$ and $y \in \Sigma'^*$, we have that $L(\mathcal{B}')(x \cdot \sigma \cdot y) = L(\mathcal{B})(x) - |y|$. We claim that $L(\mathcal{B})$ is universal for threshold v iff $L(\mathcal{B}')$ is v-safe. If $L(\mathcal{B})$ is universal for threshold v then for every word $w \in \Sigma'^*$ we have that $L(\mathcal{B}')(w) < v$, thus $L(\mathcal{B}')$ is clearly v-safe. On the other hand, if $L(\mathcal{B}')$ is not v-safe, there must be a word $w \in \Sigma^*$ for which $v \le L(\mathcal{B}')(w) = L(\mathcal{B})(w)$, thus $w \notin L(\mathcal{B})_{\downarrow v}$ and $L(\mathcal{B})$ is not universal. $\qquad\square$

Theorem 7. *Consider a DWFA $\mathcal{A}$ and $v \in \mathbb{Z}$. Assume that v and the costs in $\mathcal{A}$ are given in binary. The problem of deciding whether $\mathcal{A}$ is v-safe is co-NP-hard.*

Proof: We show that the complementary problem, of deciding whether $\mathcal{A}$ is not v-safe is NP-hard, using a reduction from the (unbounded) knapsack-problem. The input to the problem consists of weights $w_1 \ldots w_k \ge 0$, a required minimal value v, and an allowed total weight $W \ge v$. The goal is decide whether there is an assignment $c_1 \ldots c_k \in \mathbb{N}$ such that $v \le \Sigma_{0 \le i \le l}(c_i w_i) \le W$. The knapsack-problem is NP-complete when the weights are given in binary.

Given an input $w_1 \ldots w_k, v, W$ to the knapsack-problem, we construct the DWFA $\mathcal{A}$ described in Figure 6. In the full version, we prove that there is a legal assignment for this input iff $\mathcal{A}$ is not v-safe. $\qquad\square$

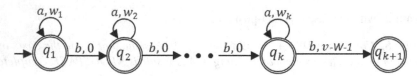

Fig. 6. Lower bound construction for knapsack reduction

4.3   Upper Bound for General Case

In this section we give upper bounds for the general problem of deciding whether a DWFA $\mathcal{A}$ is v-safe for $v > 0$. We show that the problem is NLOGSPACE-complete when the costs in $\mathcal{A}$ and v are given in unary, and co-NP-complete when they are given in binary. Our algorithms are independent of $L(\mathcal{A})_{\downarrow v}$ being regular.

From now on we fix a DWFA $\mathcal{A} = \langle \Sigma, Q, q_0, \delta, c, \alpha \rangle$ and a value $v \in \mathbb{Z}$.

The Small Refuter Property.   We say that a word $x \in \Sigma^*$ is a v-*refuter* for a weighted language $L : \Sigma^* \to \mathbb{Z}$ if it witnesses the fact that L is not v-safe. Formally, $L(x) \ge v$ and there exists a finite word $y \in \Sigma^*$ such that $L(x \cdot y) < v$. We refer to y as an *incriminating tail* for x.

Lemma 1. *Given a weighted language $L : \Sigma^* \to \mathbb{Z}$ and a value $v \in \mathbb{Z}$, we have that L is not v-safe iff L has a v-refuter.*

In order to check whether a language is not v-safe we look for a v-refuter. We show that if $\mathcal{A}$ is not v-safe, it must have a "small" v-refuter, one of polynomial length. The polynomial depends on $|Q|$, v, and the costs of the transitions in $\mathcal{A}$. We first show the existence of a refuter of a certain restricted form, and continue by bounding its length.

Recall that a path in a graph is simple if all the states in it are different. Consider a run r. If the run is simple, then it contains no cycles. Otherwise, r contains cycles. These cycles may be simple or have other cycles "hanged" on them. We decompose the run r into a *base-path* $p = p_1, p_2 \ldots p_k$, which need not be simple, and simple cycles that may be hanged on p. That is, r is of the form $p_1 \ldots p_{i_1} c_1^1 c_1^2 \ldots c_1^{n_1}$ $p_{i_1+1} \ldots p_{i_2} c_2^1 \ldots c_2^{n_2} p_{i_2+1} \ldots p_{i_3} \ldots p_{i_m}$, with $i_m = k$, where each of the c_i^j is a simple cycle. Note that the base-path need not be simple, so r itself may serve as its own base-path. Our goal, however, is to decompose r in a way that would generate base paths of a polynomial length. We refer to the length of the base-path as the size of the decomposition. Lemma 2 below shows how we can, by performing a sequence of rotations on a given refuter, obtain a refuter with a short decomposition.

Lemma 2. *Given a v-refuter x for $L(\mathcal{A})$, there is a v-refuter x' for $L(\mathcal{A})$ with the same incriminating tail as x, such that x' has a decomposition of size $O(|Q|^2)$.*

Assume we are given a refuter with a polynomial base-path. In order to bound its length, it is still required to bound the number of repetitions of the simple cycles in the refuter. Intuitively, a v-refuter tries to reach a cost above v in a way that enables the concatenation of an incriminating tail that reduces the cost below v. As Example 4 below shows, it is sometimes necessary for the intermediate costs of the refuter to go far below v in order to later be able to get closer to v; that is, to get a better *granularity*. Hence, a refuter may need to repeat cycles in a way that may seem redundant.

Example 4. Consider the DWFA $\mathcal{A}$ appearing in Figure 7, and let $v = 1$. One can see that since $v > 0$, the only way for a word to be a 1-refuter for $\mathcal{A}$ is by reaching state q_1 with cost of exactly v. This can be achieved by repeating the -5 transition four times, reaching an intermediate cost of -20, and then repeating the 7 transition three times, reaching an intermediate cost of $1 = v$. Thus, we have to go way below v in order to construct this 1-refuter. It can be verified that there is no shorter refuter. $\square$

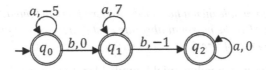

Fig. 7. A 1-refuter should go far below 1

We need to find a bound on how far from v it may be required to go in order to achieve the needed granularity. The cases where all the cycles are positive or negative are easily handled, since they do not stray far from v. The case where the refuter ends in a non-accepting state is simple, since in this case the only target of the refuter is to minimize the cost, thus there is no need to make an effort to get good granularity. The case where there are both negative and positive cycles is more challenging. In this case, as we have seen, the intermediate costs of the refuter may be far below v, indicating cycles are repeated many times. As we now show, the existence of the *Frobenius number*, and the fact the Frobenius number is bounded by a polynomial, enables us to bound the repetitions of cycles by a polynomial.

Given a set of mutually prime numbers, their Frobenius number is the minimal number N such that every $m > N$ can be generated using a linear combination of the given numbers. That is, if $x_1 \ldots x_n$ are mutually prime, and N is their Frobenius number, every number $m > N$ has a set of coefficients $a_1 \ldots a_n$ such that $a_1 x_1 + a_2 x_2 + \cdots + a_n x_n = m$. It is known that $N \leq 2T^2$ where T is the maximal number in the given set [11].

So how does the Frobenius number help us? For intuition, we give the simpler case where the gcd (greatest common deviser) of the positive cycles costs used by r is 1. We denote by N their Frobenius number. We use the base path of r to construct a possibly different run r', which induces a v-refuter, by determining how many times to repeat the cycles of r in r'. We start with the negative cycles, and repeat them until we reach a cost of $t < -N - b$, where b is the cost of the base-path of r. Note that the number of used negative cycles (repetitions included) is at most $|t|$, as each repetition of a negative cycle reduces cost by at least 1. We now repeat the positive cycles until their cost is exactly $|t| + v - b$. By the definition of Frobenius number, the fact $|t| + v - b > N$ implies that we can reach this exact cost. Thus, when reaching the last state of the refuter, the accumulated cost is exactly $b + t + (-t) + v - b = v$. Since each positive cycle adds at least 1 to the cost, we use at most $||t| + v - b|$ positive cycles (including repetitions). We started with a v-refuter, and reached the best possible granularity, ending in the same state as the original refuter. Thus, the constructed run must have an incriminating tail, and so it induces a v-refuter.

Let us consider the length of the generated v-refuter. Let M be the maximal absolute cost of a transition in $\mathcal{A}$, and let W be the maximal absolute cost of a simple cycle in $\mathcal{A}$. Clearly, $W = O(M|Q|)$. Note that N is at most $2W^2$ since we use the Frobenius number on cycle costs, and the maximal absolute cost of a simple cycle is at most W. Also note that $|b|$ is at most $O(M|Q|^2)$, as its cost is the sum of at most $O(|Q|^2)$ edges (indeed, we assume a decomposition of size $O(|Q|^2)$), and edge costs are bounded by M. Hence, we use a polynomial number of negative and positive cycles, and so the generated v-refuter is of a polynomial length.

Lemma 3. *If $\mathcal{A}$ is not v-safe then it has a v-refuter x of length bounded by a polynomial $P(\mathcal{A}, v, M)$, where M is the maximal absolute cost of a transition in $\mathcal{A}$. In addition, x has an incriminating tail of size 1.*

Note that a refuter with a polynomial bounded length also has a polynomial bound on all its intermediate costs.

v-Safety Detection.   We now use the short refuter found above in order to solve the problem of deciding whether a DWFA $\mathcal{A}$ is v-safe for a value $v \in \mathbb{Z}$. We show this problem is NLOGSPACE-complete when both the costs of $\mathcal{A}$ and the value v are given in unary, and is co-NP-complete in the binary case.

Theorem 8. *Consider a DWFA $\mathcal{A}$ and $v \in \mathbb{Z}$. The complexity of the problem of deciding whether $\mathcal{A}$ is v-safe is as follows.*

(i) If v and the costs in $\mathcal{A}$ are given in unary, the problem is NLOGSPACE-complete.
(ii) If v and the costs in $\mathcal{A}$ are given in binary, the problem is co-NP-complete.

Proof: (i) For the upper bound, we describe an algorithm that can be implemented in NLOGSPACE. Let $\widetilde{P}(\mathcal{A}, v, M)$ denote the polynomial bound on all the intermediate costs of the short v-refuter from Lemma 3.

The idea of the algorithm is to use the same construction we have previously used to get a DFA that recognizes $L(\mathcal{A})_{\downarrow v}$, but on the costs range of $Val_{ref} = [-\widetilde{P}(\mathcal{A}, v, M), \widetilde{P}(\mathcal{A}, v, M)] \cup \{\top, \bot\}$, and to check if it is safe. The constructed DFA $\mathcal{A}'$ does not necessarily recognize $L(\mathcal{A})_{\downarrow v}$, but $\mathcal{A}$ is v-safe iff $\mathcal{A}'$ is safe. Intuitively, a v-refuter with intermediate costs in the range of $[-\widetilde{P}(\mathcal{A}, v, M), \widetilde{P}(\mathcal{A}, v, M)]$ clearly induces a witness for the non-safety of $L(\mathcal{A}')$. On the other hand, a minimal witness for the non-safety of $\mathcal{A}'$ must remain in the range $[-\widetilde{P}(\mathcal{A}, v, M), \widetilde{P}(\mathcal{A}, v, M)]$, thus inducing a v-refuter and showing $\mathcal{A}$ is not v-safe.

Given a DWFA $\mathcal{A}$, our algorithm constructs the DFA $\mathcal{A}'$ described above, and accepts iff $\mathcal{A}'$ is safe. Membership in NLOGSPACE follows from an analysis of the size of $\mathcal{A}'$, the fact we can construct it on the fly, and the fact it is possible to check safety of DFAs in NLOGSPACE. Hardness in NLOGSPACE is easy to prove by a reduction from reachability.

(ii) For the lower bound see Theorem 7. For the upper bound, since v and the costs are given in binary, by Lemma 3 we have that $\mathcal{A}$ is not v-safe iff $\mathcal{A}$ has a v-refuter of exponential length with an incriminating tail of size 1. We show that such a refuter has a representation of polynomial length, which can be verified in polynomial time. Therefore, an NP algorithm can guess such a representation, and conclude that $\mathcal{A}$ is not v-safe iff the guessed representation indicates the existence of a v-refuter.

The number of times an exponential sized refuter traverses each transition of $\mathcal{A}$ is at most exponential, and thus can be represented in polynomial space when using binary encoding. We represent a v-refuter as a vector $\bar{t}$ of size $|\delta|$ that associates with each transition in $\mathcal{A}$ the number of times it is traversed in the refuter (in binary), and a single transition $e = (q, \sigma, q')$ with cost c, which is the incriminating tail. To check that $(\bar{t}, e)$ represents a v-refuter we need to verify that $\bar{t}$ represents a legal run r that ends in state q for which $cost(r) \geq v$ and $cost(r) + c < v$. To calculate $cost(r)$ we multiply the weight of each transition with the number of times it was used. To verify that $\bar{t}$ represents a legal run, we check it describes a path from q_0 to q. That is, we verify for every state $s \neq q_0, q$ that the number of s's incoming edges is equal to the number of s's outgoing edges, and that the number of incoming (outgoing, respectively) edges in q (q_0) is bigger (smaller) than the number of outgoing (incoming) edges by 1. It is easy to see the vector $\bar{t}$ represents a legal run from q_0 to q iff these conditions hold.   □

5   Deciding Weighted Safety

In this section we consider the problem of deciding whether a given DWFA $\mathcal{A}$ is weighted safe; that is, whether there exists $v \in \mathbb{Z}$ for which $\mathcal{A}$ is v-safe. We first ask, given a DWFA $\mathcal{A}$ that is weighted safe, how large can the minimal value $|v|$ for which $\mathcal{A}$ is v-safe be (in other words, what is the minimal $c \geq 0$ such that $\mathcal{A}$ is c-safe or $(-c)$-safe). We answer this question with a tight exponential bound for the case the costs in

$\mathcal{A}$ are given in unary. We then use the results of Section 4 to conclude that deciding weighted safety is in PSPACE.

Lemma 4. *Given a DWFA $\mathcal{A}$ with costs given in unary, the minimal value $|v|$ such that $\mathcal{A}$ is v-safe is at most exponential in the number of states of $\mathcal{A}$ and the maximal absolute cost in $\mathcal{A}$. This bound is tight: there is a family of DWFAs with $O(n)$ states where absolute costs are at most n, for which the minimal such value $|v|$ is exponential in n.*

Proof: For the upper bound, assume $\mathcal{A}$ is weighted safe. Let n be the number of states of $\mathcal{A}$ and M the maximal absolute cost of a transition in $\mathcal{A}$. We first consider the simpler case, when $\mathcal{A}$ is v-safe for some non-positive value $v \leq 0$. Since $L(\mathcal{A})(\epsilon) = 0$, the fact $\mathcal{A}$ is v-safe for some non-positive value v implies that $\mathcal{A}$ contains no negative reachable cycle, otherwise ϵ is a v-refuter for every $v \leq 0$. Therefore, the minimal possible cost of a word in $\mathcal{A}$ is at least $-nM$, and so $\mathcal{A}$ is $-nM$-safe.

We now bound from above the minimal positive value $v > 0$ for which $\mathcal{A}$ is v-safe. Let γ be the lcm (least common multiplier) of all the positive simple cycles in $\mathcal{A}$. We have that $\gamma \leq \Pi_{\{c:\mathcal{A} \text{ has a simple cycle of cost } c\}} c \leq (nM)! = O(nM^{nM})$.

Assume that $\mathcal{A}$ is v-safe for some $v > 0$, and let v be the minimal such value. We show that $v = O(nM^{nM})$. If $v \leq \gamma$, we are done. Otherwise, consider $\overline{v} = v - \gamma$. From the minimality of v, it must be the case that $\mathcal{A}$ is not $\overline{v}$-safe. Let $x \in \Sigma^*$ be a $\overline{v}$-refuter, and $y \in \Sigma^*$ be an incriminating tail for x. That is, $L(\mathcal{A})(x) \geq \overline{v}$ but $L(\mathcal{A})(x \cdot y) < \overline{v}$. Let r be the run of $\mathcal{A}$ on x. We consider several cases. First, consider the case where $L(\mathcal{A})(x) \geq v$. By the choice of x and y we have that $L(\mathcal{A})(x \cdot y) < \overline{v} < v$. Therefore, x is also a v-refuter, and so $\mathcal{A}$ is not v-safe, and we have reached a contradiction. Second, consider the case where $L(\mathcal{A})(x) < v$ and r dose not contain a positive cycle. The fact $L(\mathcal{A})(x) < v$ implies that r ends in an accepting state. Thus, since r does not contain a positive cycle, $nM \geq L(\mathcal{A})(x) \geq \overline{v}$. Therefore, $nM \geq v - \gamma$, which implies that $v \leq nM + \gamma = O(nM^{nM})$. Last, consider the case where $L(\mathcal{A})(x) < v$ and r contains a positive cycle. Let c be a cost of a positive cycle in r, and choose $k \in \mathbb{N}$ such that $ck = \gamma$ (such a k exists by the definition of γ). Consider the run r', which is obtained from r by adding k repetitions of the c cycle to r, and let x' be the word traversed along r'. We have that $L(\mathcal{A})(x') = L(\mathcal{A})(x) + \gamma \geq \overline{v} + \gamma = v$, but on the other hand $L(\mathcal{A})(x' \cdot y) = L(\mathcal{A})(x \cdot y) + \gamma < \overline{v} + \gamma = v$. Therefore x' is a v-refuter, with y as an incriminating tail, in contradiction to the fact that $\mathcal{A}$ is v-safe. Thus, the minimal positive value v such that $\mathcal{A}$ is v-safe is at most $O(nM^{nM})$.

The lower-bound proof can be found in the full version.   □

Using Lemma 4 we can decide whether a DWFA $\mathcal{A}$ is weighted safe by going over all values from $-nM$ to the upper bound, which is $O(nM^{nM})$, and checking for each value v whether $\mathcal{A}$ is v-safe. Since encoding of the values is in binary, Theorem 8 *(ii)* implies the following.

Theorem 9. *Consider a DWFA $\mathcal{A}$ with costs given in unary. The problem of deciding whether $\mathcal{A}$ is weighted safe can be solved in PSPACE.*

Acknowledgment. We thank Nati Linial for his help in proving the upper bound in Theorem 8 *(ii)*.

References

1. Almagor, S., Boker, U., Kupferman, O.: What's decidable about weighted automata? In: Bultan, T., Hsiung, P.-A. (eds.) ATVA 2011. LNCS, vol. 6996, pp. 482–491. Springer, Heidelberg (2011)
2. Almagor, S., Boker, U., Kupferman, O.: Formalizing and reasoning about quality. In: Fomin, F.V., Freivalds, R., Kwiatkowska, M., Peleg, D. (eds.) ICALP 2013, Part II. LNCS, vol. 7966, pp. 15–27. Springer, Heidelberg (2013)
3. Alpern, B., Schneider, F.B.: Recognizing safety and liveness. Distributed Computing 2, 117–126 (1987)
4. Aminof, B., Kupferman, O., Lampert, R.: Reasoning about online algorithms with weighted automata. ACM Transactions on Algorithms 6(2) (2010)
5. Baier, C., Bertrand, N.: M Grösser. Probabilistic automata over infinite words: Expressiveness, efficiency, and decidability. In: Proc. 11th DCFS, pp. 3–16 (2006)
6. Biere, A., Cimatti, A., Clarke, E., Zhu, Y.: Symbolic model checking without BDDs. In: Cleaveland, W.R. (ed.) TACAS/ETAPS 1999. LNCS, vol. 1579, pp. 193–207. Springer, Heidelberg (1999)
7. Bloem, R., Gabow, H.N., Somenzi, F.: An algorithm for strongly connected component analysis in $n \log n$ symbolic steps. In: Johnson, S.D., Hunt Jr., W.A. (eds.) FMCAD 2000. LNCS, vol. 1954, pp. 37–54. Springer, Heidelberg (2000)
8. Boker, U., Chatterjee, K., Henzinger, T.A., Kupferman, O.: Temporal specifications with accumulative values. In: Proc. 26th LICS, pp. 43–52 (2011)
9. Chatterjee, K., Doyen, L., Henzinger, T.A.: Quantitative languages. In: Kaminski, M., Martini, S. (eds.) CSL 2008. LNCS, vol. 5213, pp. 385–400. Springer, Heidelberg (2008)
10. Culik, K., Kari, J.: Digital images and formal languages. In: Handbook of Formal Languages, Beyond Words, vol. 3, pp. 599–616 (1997)
11. Erdös, P., Graham, R.L.: On a linear diophantine problem of frobenius. ActaArith 21, 399–408 (1972)
12. Filiot, E., Jin, N., Raskin, J.-F.: An antichain algorithm for LTL realizability. In: Bouajjani, A., Maler, O. (eds.) CAV 2009. LNCS, vol. 5643, pp. 263–277. Springer, Heidelberg (2009)
13. Harel, D., Katz, G., Marron, A., Weiss, G.: Non-intrusive repair of reactive programs. In: ICECCS, pp. 3–12 (2012)
14. Havelund, K., Roşu, G.: Synthesizing monitors for safety properties. In: Katoen, J.-P., Stevens, P. (eds.) TACAS 2002. LNCS, vol. 2280, pp. 342–356. Springer, Heidelberg (2002)
15. Hopcroft, J.E., Ullman, J.D.: Introduction to Automata Theory, Languages, and Computation. Addison-Wesley (1979)
16. Kupferman, O., Vardi, M.Y.: Model checking of safety properties. MFCS 19(3), 291–314 (2001)
17. Kupferman, O., Vardi, M.Y.: Synthesis of trigger properties. In: Clarke, E.M., Voronkov, A. (eds.) LPAR-16 2010. LNCS, vol. 6355, pp. 312–331. Springer, Heidelberg (2010)
18. Manna, Z., Pnueli, A.: The Temporal Logic of Reactive and Concurrent Systems: Specification. Springer (1992)
19. Manna, Z., Pnueli, A.: The Temporal Logic of Reactive and Concurrent Systems: Safety. Springer (1995)
20. Mohri, M.: Finite-state transducers in language and speech processing. Computational Linguistics 23(2), 269–311 (1997)
21. Mohri, M., Pereira, F.C.N., Riley, M.: Weighted finite-state transducers in speech recognition. Computer Speech and Language 16(1), 69–88 (2002)
22. Pnueli, A., Shahar, E.: Liveness and acceleration in parameterized verification. In: Emerson, E.A., Sistla, A.P. (eds.) CAV 2000. LNCS, vol. 1855, pp. 328–343. Springer, Heidelberg (2000)
23. Sistla, A.P.: Safety, liveness and fairness in temporal logic. FAC 6, 495–511 (1994)

A Framework for Ranking Vacuity Results

Shoham Ben-David* and Orna Kupferman

School of Engineering and Computer Science
The Hebrew University, Jerusalem, Israel

Abstract. *Vacuity* detection is a method for finding errors in the model-checking process when the specification is found to hold in the model. Most vacuity algorithms are based on checking the effect of applying mutations on the specification. It has been recognized that vacuity results differ in their significance. While in many cases such results are valued as highly informative, there are also cases where a vacuity result is viewed by users as "interesting to know" at the most, or even as meaningless. As of today, no attempt has been made to formally justify this phenomenon.

We suggest and study a framework for ranking vacuity results, based on the *probability* of the mutated specification to hold on a random computation. For example, two natural mutations of the specification $G(req \rightarrow F ready)$ are $G(\neg req)$ and $GF ready$. It is agreed that vacuity information about satisfying the first mutation is more alarming than information about satisfying the second. Our methodology formally explains this, as the probability of $G(\neg req)$ to hold in a random computation is 0, whereas the probability of $GF ready$ is 1. From a theoretical point of view, we study of the problem of finding the probability of LTL formulas to be satisfied in a random computation and the existence and use of 0/1-laws for fragments of LTL. From a practical point of view, we propose an efficient algorithm for approximating the probability of LTL formulas and provide experimental results demonstrating the usefulness of our approach as well as the suggested algorithm.

1 Introduction

In temporal logic model checking, we verify the correctness of a system with respect to a desired behavior by checking whether a mathematical model of the system satisfies a temporal-logic formula that specifies this behavior [9]. When the formula fails to hold in the model, the model checker returns a counterexample — some erroneous execution of the system [10]. When the formula holds in the system on the other hand, most model-checking tools provide no additional information. While this might seem like a reasonable policy, there has been growing awareness to the need of suspecting the result in the case model checking succeeds, since errors may hide in the modeling of the system or the behavior [19].

---

* Shoham Ben-David is grateful to the Azrieli Foundation for the award of an Azrieli Fellowship.

D. Van Hung and M. Ogawa (Eds.): ATVA 2013, LNCS 8172, pp. 148–162, 2013.

As an example, consider the specification $\varphi = G(req \rightarrow F\,ready)$ ("every request is eventually followed by a ready signal"). One should distinguish between satisfaction of φ in a model in which requests are never sent, and satisfaction in which φ's precondition is sometimes satisfied. Evidently, the first, vacuous, type of satisfaction suggests a suspicious behavior of the model.

In [2], Beer et al. suggested a first formal treatment of vacuity. The definition of vacuity according to [2] is based on mutations applied to the specification, checking whether the model actually satisfies a specification that is stronger than the original one. In the last decade, vacuity detection has attracted significant attention (see [1,4,5,6,8,15,17,18,20] for a partial list).

Different definitions for vacuity exist in the literature and are used in practice. The most commonly used ones are based on the "mutation approach" of [2]. We focus here on its generalization, as defined in [21]. Consider a model M satisfying a specification φ. A subformula ψ of φ *does not affect* (the satisfaction of) φ in M if M satisfies also the (stronger) formula $\varphi[\psi \leftarrow \bot]$, obtained from φ by changing ψ in the most challenging way. Thus, if ψ appears positively in φ, the symbol $\bot$ stands for *false*, and if ψ is negative, then $\bot$ is *true*[1]. We say that M satisfies φ vacuously if φ has a subformula that does not affect φ in M. Consider for example the formula $\varphi = G(req \rightarrow F\,ready)$ described above. In order to check whether the subformula *ready* affects the satisfaction of φ, we model check $\varphi[ready \leftarrow false]$, which is equivalent to $G\neg req$. That is, a model with no requests satisfies φ vacuously. In order to check whether the subformula *req* affects the satisfaction of φ, we model check $\varphi[req \leftarrow true]$. This is equivalent to $GF\,ready$, thus a model with infinitely many *ready* signals satisfies φ vacuously.

In [5], Chechik et al. observe that in many cases, vacuities detected according to the above definition are not considered a problem by the verifier of the system. A similar observation was reported later in [3]. For example consider a specification similar to φ discussed above, describing the desired behavior of a traffic light [5]: $\psi = G(car \rightarrow F\,green)$, stating that whenever a car approaches the traffic light, it will eventually be granted a green light. In many traffic light systems however, a green light is given in a "round robin" manner, granting a green light periodically, whether a car is waiting or not. The mutation $\psi[car \leftarrow \bot] = GF\,green$ is thus satisfied in such a system, causing ψ to be wrongly declared as vacuous. One may argue that ψ is indeed too weak for the traffic light above; we note however, that it is common to have a set of generic formulas which are applied to a variety of systems. A set of formulas for traffic light systems should include ψ and not its mutation $GF\,green$, to accommodate different types of systems.

In this paper we suggest and study a formal framework for ranking vacuity results according to their level of importance. Our goal is to distinguishing between alarming vacuity results that must get the full attention of the verifier,

---

[1] The above definition assumes that ψ appears once in φ, or at least that all its occurrences are of the same polarity; a definition that is independent of this assumption replaces ψ by a universally quantified proposition [1]. Our methodology here applies also to this definition.

and "interesting to know" results that are less important. Earlier work on identifying false alarms in vacuity includes two approaches: In [5], the authors suggest to identify as vacuous only specifications whose satisfaction depend solely on the environment of the system. While such cases should definitely be considered vacuous, we believe that there exist real vacuities that do not fulfill the condition of [5]. In [3], the authors focus on detecting vacuities that are due to *temporal antecedent failure*, claiming that those are never debatable. In fact, already in the original definition of vacuity in [2], not all subformulas of the specification are checked for affecting the satisfaction, as the authors claim that some possibilities do not result in interesting vacuities. No attempt has been made in [2,3] to formally justify this claim or to argue that the classification is exhaustive.

Our framework for ranking vacuity results is based on the *probability* of the mutated specification to hold on a random computation. To see the idea behind the framework, let us consider the mutations $G(\neg req)$ and $GF\,ready$ of the specification φ discussed above. Consider a random computation π. The probabilistic model we assume is that for each atomic proposition p and for each state in π, the probability of p to hold in the state is $\frac{1}{2}$. In this model, the probability of $G(\neg req)$ to hold in a random computation is 0, whereas the probability of $GF\,ready$ to hold is 1. We argue that the lower is the probability of the mutation to hold in a random computation, the higher the vacuity rank should be. In particular, vacuities in which the probability of the mutation is 0, as is the case with $G(\neg req)$, should get the highest rank and vacuities in which the probability is 1, as is the case with $GF(ready)$, should get the lowest rank. Note that we do not claim that low-rank vacuities are not important. In particular, satisfying $GF(ready)$ suggests that the system satisfies some fairness condition that the designer is not aware of.

In Section 4, we give further examples and evidences that our probability-based criteria indeed corresponds to our intuition about the level of importance. In particular, our ranking agrees with, unifies and generalizes the approaches in all earlier work. We also suggest a refinement of the criteria that takes into account the probability of the original specifications, and a refinement of the analysis for the case of invariants. In order to evaluate our ranking framework, we conduct a survey among model-checking users. We describe and discuss the results, which support our framework, in Section 4.

Let us elaborate on our framework and the theoretical and practical challenges it involves. For a specification φ, let $Pr(\varphi)$ denote the probability for φ to be satisfied in a random computation, as formalized above. Glebskii et al. in [16], and later Fagin in [14], proved a 0/1-law for first order logic. That is, for φ in first order logic, the probability of φ to be satisfied in a random model is either 0 or 1. It is not hard to see that a 0/1-law does not hold for LTL. For example, for an atomic proposition p, we have that $Pr(p) = \frac{1}{2}$. We study the problem of finding $Pr(\varphi)$, for φ in LTL, and show that it is PSPACE-complete. The upper bound follows easily from the probabilistic model-checking algorithm of [11]. The algorithm in [11] is complicated. For the case we only want to find out whether $Pr(\varphi) = 0$ or whether $Pr(\varphi) = 1$, we suggest a much simpler algorithm, which analyzes the connected components of a nondeterministic Büchi automaton for φ. The details of the algorithm can be found in the full version of this paper. We also show that large fragments of LTL do respect the 0/1-law. In particular, all invariants (formulas for the form $G\psi$) respect it. Note that for these fragments, our simpler algorithm solves the problem of finding $Pr(\varphi)$.

The high complexity of finding $Pr(\varphi)$ leads us to suggest a heuristic for estimating it in a simple syntax-based bottom-up algorithm. We argue that not only our heuristic often calculates $Pr(\varphi)$ precisely, but that its errors are sometimes welcome. Specifically, we distinguish between two cases in which our heuristic errs. The first is when it returns a probability that is *lower* than $Pr(\varphi)$. In this case, the error is a result of a peculiar structure of the specification, like subformulas that are valid. We are thus happy to declare the specification as one that requires a check, which is indeed the fate of mutations with low probability. The second is when our heuristic returns a probability that is higher than $Pr(\varphi)$. Here, the heuristic may cause real vacuities to get a low rank. We show, however, that these cases are rare. As discussed in Section 4.3, we believe that a framework for ranking vacuity results, and in particular the one suggested here, offers a useful and simple-to-implement upgrade of existing vacuity-checking tools.

The full version of this paper, with more details, can be found in the authors' URLs.

2   Preliminaries

2.1   LTL and Vacuity

For a finite alphabet Σ, an infinite *word* $w = \sigma_0 \cdot \sigma_1 \cdots$ is an infinite sequence of letters from Σ. We use Σ^ω to denote the set of all infinite words over the alphabet Σ. A *language* $L \subseteq \Sigma^\omega$ is a set of words. When $\Sigma = 2^{AP}$, for a set AP of atomic propositions, each infinite word corresponds to a *computation* over AP, usually denoted by π.

The logic *LTL* is a linear temporal logic [22]. LTL formulas describe languages over the alphabet 2^{AP}, and are constructed from a set AP of atomic propositions using the Boolean operators $\neg$ and $\wedge$, and the temporal operators X ("next time") and U ("until"). The semantics of LTL is defined with respect to computations over AP. Typically, computations are given by means of a *Kripke structure* – a state-transition graph in which each state is labeled by a set of atomic propositions true in this state. The Kripke structure models a system, and we also refer to it as "the model". For an LTL formula φ, we use $\mathcal{L}(\varphi)$ to denote the language of φ, namely the set of computations that satisfy φ.

Given a model M and an LTL formula φ, the model-checking problem is to decide whether all the computations of M satisfy φ, denoted $M \models \varphi$. Describing formulas, we use the standard abbreviations $\vee$ and $\rightarrow$ for Boolean operators and F ("eventually") and G ("always") for temporal operators.

Let φ be an LTL formula and ψ an occurrence of a subformula of φ. We say that ψ has a positive polarity in φ if ψ is in the scope of an even number of negations in φ. Dually, ψ has a negative polarity in φ if ψ is in the scope of an odd number of negations in φ. Note that the definition assumes a syntax of LTL with only $\neg, \wedge, X$ and U. In particular, since $\alpha \to \beta$ is equivalent to $\neg\alpha \vee \beta$, the polarity of α there is negative.

Consider a model M and an LTL formula φ. *Vacuity* is a sanity check applied when $M \models \varphi$, aiming to find errors in the modeling of the system or the behavior by M and φ. Most vacuity algorithms proceed by checking whether M also satisfies formulas obtained by strengthening φ.

For a formula φ and an occurrence ψ of a subformula of φ, let $\varphi[\psi \leftarrow \bot]$ denote the formula obtained by replacing ψ by $\bot$ in φ, where $\bot = \textit{false}$ if ψ has a positive polarity in φ, and $\bot = \textit{true}$ otherwise. Consider a model M such that $M \models \varphi$. We say that ψ *does not affect the satisfaction* of φ in M if $M \models \varphi[\psi \leftarrow \bot]$. We use the definition of vacuity given in [21]: the formula φ is *vacuous* in M if there exists a subformula ψ of φ that does not affect the satisfaction of φ in M. Note that the definition of [21] refers to a single occurrence of ψ in φ, and it can be easily extended to multiple occurrences all with the same polarity. A definition that is independent of this assumption replaces ψ by a universally quantified proposition [1]. As we demonstrate in Example 6, our framework here can be extended to the definition in [1].

2.2   The Probabilistic Setting

Given a set of elements S, a *probability distribution* on S is a function $\mu : S \to [0,1]$ such that $\Sigma_{s \in S} \, \mu(s) = 1$. The *support* set of μ, denoted $supp(\mu)$, is the set of all elements s for which $\mu(s) > 0$.

A *finite Markov chain* is a tuple $M = \langle V, p \rangle$, where V is a finite set of states and $p : V \times V \to [0,1]$ is a function. For $v \in V$, let $p_v : V \to [0,1]$ be such that $p_v(u) = p(v,u)$ for all $u \in V$. We require that for all $v \in V$, the function p_v is a probability distribution on V. A *probabilistic labeled structure* is $\mathcal{S} = \langle \Sigma, V, p, p_{init}, \tau \rangle$, where $\langle V, p \rangle$ is a Markov chain, $p_{init} : V \to [0,1]$ is a probability distribution on V that describes the probability of a computation to start in the state, and $\tau : V \to \Sigma$ maps each state to a letter in Σ.

A *path* in a Markov chain M is an infinite sequence $\pi = v_0, v_1, v_2, \ldots$ of vertices. An *event* is a measurable set of paths. Once we add a probability distribution on the starting state of paths, the probabilities of events are uniquely defined.

3   Probability of LTL Properties

3.1   Calculating the Probability

Consider an alphabet Σ. A random word over Σ is a word in which for all indices i, the i-th letter is drown uniformly at random. In particular, when $\Sigma = 2^{AP}$, then a random computation π is such that for each atomic proposition q and for each position in π, the probability of q to hold in the position is

$\frac{1}{2}$. An alternative definition of our probabilistic model is by means of the probabilistic labeled structure $\mathcal{U}_\Sigma$, which generates computations in a uniform distribution. Formally, $\mathcal{U}_\Sigma = \langle \Sigma, \Sigma, p, p_{init}, \tau \rangle$, where for every $\sigma, \sigma' \in \Sigma$, we have $p(\sigma, \sigma') = p_{init}(\sigma) = \frac{1}{|\Sigma|}$, and $\tau(\sigma) = \sigma$. Thus, $\mathcal{U}_\Sigma$ is a clique with a uniform distribution. We define the probability of a language $\mathcal{L} \subseteq \Sigma^\omega$, denoted $Pr(\mathcal{L})$, as the probability of the event $\{\pi : \pi$ is a path in $\mathcal{U}_\Sigma$ that is labeled by a word in $\mathcal{L}\}$. Similarly, for an LTL formula φ, we define $Pr(\varphi)$ as the probability of the event $\{\pi : \pi$ is a path in $\mathcal{U}_{2^{AP}}$ that satisfies $\varphi\}$. For example, the probabilities of Xp, Gp, and Fp are $\frac{1}{2}, 0$, and 1, respectively.

Using $\mathcal{U}_\Sigma$ we can reduce the problem of finding $Pr(\varphi)$ to φ's model checking. Results on probabilistic LTL model checking [11] then imply the upper bound in the theorem below. For the lower bound, we do a generic reduction, and prove hardness already for the easier problem, of deciding whether the probability is 0 or 1.

Theorem 1. *The problem of finding the probability of LTL formulas is PSPACE-complete.*

Proof. Consider an LTL formula φ. The problem of finding $Pr(\varphi)$ can be reduced to LTL probabilistic model checking. In this problem, we are given a probabilistic labeled structure $\mathcal{S}$ and an LTL formula φ, and we find the probability of paths that satisfy φ in $\mathcal{S}$. By definition, model checking φ in $\mathcal{U}_{2^{AP}}$ amounts to finding $Pr(\varphi)$. In [11], Courcoubetis and Yannakakis describe an algorithm for solving LTL probabilistic model checking. The algorithm requires space that is polynomial in the formula and polylogarithmic in the structure, implying a PSPACE complexity for our problem.

For the lower bound, we prove that already the problem of deciding whether the probability of a formula is 0 or 1 is PSPACE-hard. Recall the generic reduction used in the PSPACE-hardness proof for the validity problem of LTL. Given a polynomial space Turing machine and an input x for it, the reduction constructs an LTL formula $\varphi_{T,x}$ that is valid iff T rejects x. The formula $\varphi_{T,x}$ is satisfied in a computation iff the computation does not encode a legal computation of T on x or it encodes a legal yet rejecting computation of T on x. The reduction can be defined so that the encoding of computations of T on x concerns only the prefix of the computation in which a final configuration is reached. Thus, after T reaches a final configuration, all suffixes are considered as legal encodings. We claim that $Pr(\varphi_{T,x}) \in \{0,1\}$ iff T rejects x. First, if T rejects x, then $\varphi_{T,x}$ is valid, so $Pr(\varphi_{T,x}) = 1$. Also, if T accepts x, then the event $\{w : w$ encodes a legal accepting computation of T on $x\}$ has a positive probability – it contains all the words that have the accepting computation of T on x as their prefix. $\square$

First order logic respects the 0/1-law: the probability of a formula to be satisfied in a random model is either 0 or 1 [16,14]. It is not hard to see that a 0/1-law does not hold for LTL. For example, for an atomic proposition p, we have that $Pr(p) = \frac{1}{2}$. We now show that invariants do satisfy the 0/1-law. On the other hand, trigger formulas, which can be viewed as "conditional invariants" do not respect it, even when the condition holds infinitely often. A trigger formula is of the form $r \mapsto \varphi$, where r is a regular expression and φ is an LTL formula. A computation π satisfies the formula $r \mapsto \varphi$ if for every index i, if the prefix $\pi[0, i]$ is in the language of r, then the suffix π^i satisfies φ. We use $\mathcal{L}(r)$ to denote the language of r. For the full definition of trigger formulas and their vacuity see [4].

Theorem 2. *Formulas of the form $G\varphi$ satisfy the $0/1$-law. On the other hand, formulas of the form $r \mapsto \varphi$ need not satisfy the $0/1$-law even when $\mathcal{L}(r)$ is infinite.*

Proof. We start with invariants. Consider a formula $G\varphi$, and let π be a random computation. If $Pr(\varphi) = 1$, then for all suffixes π^i of π, the probability of φ to hold in π^i is 1, thus so is the probability of $G\varphi$ to hold in π. Hence, $Pr(\varphi) = 1$ implies that $Pr(G\varphi) = 1$. Now, if $Pr(\varphi) < 1$, then with probability 1 we have a suffix π^i such that the probability of φ to hold in π^i is strictly less than 1, making the probability of $G\varphi$ to hold in π 0. Hence, $Pr(\varphi) < 1$ implies that $Pr(G\varphi) = 0$.

For triggers, consider the specification $\varphi = req[*]; ack \mapsto Xready$, stating that whenever we have a computation where req is active all the way (from the initial state), followed by ack, then $ready$ must follow one cycle after ack. We show that $0 < Pr(\varphi) < 1$. Note that if both req and ack do not hold in the initial state, then φ holds (since the prefix is false). The probability of this is $\frac{1}{4}$, thus $0 < Pr(\varphi)$. Note further that if req holds on the first state, ack on the second, and $ready$ does not hold on the third state, then φ fails to hold on the computation path. The probability of this is $\frac{1}{8}$; thus $Pr(\varphi) < 1$. $\square$

Recall that the PSPACE algorithm for calculating $Pr(\varphi)$ involves the probabilistic model-checking algorithm of [11], which is complicated. In the full version we describe a much simpler algorithm for the case we only want to find whether $Pr(\varphi) = 0$ or $Pr(\varphi) = 1$. By the lower-bound proof of Theorem 1, this problem is PSPACE-hard too. As we show, however, it can be solved by a simple analysis of the connected components of a nondeterministic automaton for φ.

3.2   A Practical Approach

By Theorem 1, calculating the exact probability of an LTL formula, and even only deciding whether it is 0 or 1, is PSPACE-complete. Moreover, the algorithm of [11] iteratively eliminates the temporal operators in φ, while preserving the probability of its satisfaction, and is complicated to implement. In this section we describe a simple linear-time method for approximating $Pr(\varphi)$. It is based on the syntax of the formula and thus ignores possible dependencies between subformulas. However, it is very easy to calculate, and experiments suggest that the results are accurate in most cases.

Definition 3 (Approximated Probability). *The approximated probability of an LTL formula φ, denoted $Apr(\varphi)$, is defined by induction on the structure of φ as follows.*

- $Apr(false) = 0$
- $Apr(true) = 1$
- $Apr(p) = \frac{1}{2}$
- $Apr(\neg\varphi) = 1 - Apr(\varphi)$
- $Apr(\varphi \wedge \psi) = Apr(\varphi) \cdot Apr(\psi)$
- $Apr(X\varphi) = Apr(\varphi)$
- $Apr(\varphi U \psi) = \begin{cases} 0 & \text{if } Apr(\psi) = 0 \text{ and } Apr(\varphi) = 1 \\ \frac{Apr(\psi)}{1-(1-Apr(\psi))\cdot Apr(\varphi)} & \text{otherwise} \end{cases}$

The calculation of $Apr(\varphi U \psi)$ needs some explanation. We use the fixed-point characterization $\varphi U \psi = \psi \vee [\varphi \wedge X(\varphi U \psi)]$. For calculating probability, we have to make the two disjuncts disjoint, resulting in $\varphi U \psi = \psi \vee [(\neg \psi) \wedge \varphi \wedge X(\varphi U \psi)]$. Accordingly, $Apr(\varphi U \psi) = Apr(\psi) + [(1 - Apr(\psi)) \cdot Apr(\varphi) \cdot Apr(\varphi U \psi)]$. Isolating $Apr(\varphi U \psi)$ results in $Apr(\varphi U \psi) = \frac{Apr(\psi)}{1-(1-Apr(\psi))\cdot Apr(\varphi)}$ as stated in Definition 3. We should be careful with the case the denominator is 0. This happens when $1 = (1 - Apr(\psi)) \cdot Apr(\varphi)$, which can only happen if $Apr(\psi) = 0$ and $Apr(\varphi) = 1$. In such a case we define $Apr(\varphi U \psi)$ to be 0. To see why, note that if the probability of ψ to hold in each state is 0, then its probability to hold on an infinite path is the sum of a countable number of events that each goes to 0, which is 0.

Note that when $Apr(\psi) = 1$ we have $Apr(\varphi U \psi) = 1$ as well. The probability of $\varphi U \psi$ is 1 also in the case where $Apr(\varphi) = 1$ and $Apr(\psi) \neq 0$. This is the case in the abbreviation $F\psi = (true\ U\psi)$, where $Apr(F\psi)$ is 0 if $Apr(\psi) = 0$ and is 1 otherwise. Accordingly, as $G\psi = \neg F \neg \psi$, we have that $Apr(G\psi)$ is 1 if $Apr(\psi) = 1$ and is 0 otherwise. Finally, by applying De-Morgan rules, we have that $Apr(\varphi \vee \psi) = Apr(\varphi) + Apr(\psi) - Apr(\varphi) \cdot Apr(\psi)$.

To see why the approximated probability is not precise, consider for example the specification $p \wedge \neg p$. By definition, $Apr(p \wedge \neg p) = Apr(p) \cdot Apr(\neg p) = \frac{1}{2} \cdot (1 - \frac{1}{2}) = \frac{1}{4}$. On the other hand, $p \wedge \neg p$ is unsatisfiable and thus $Pr(p \wedge \neg p) = 0$. Note that indeed the approximated probability errs only in steps associated with a binary operator where the two subformulas are not independent. In particular, no errors are introduced in steps associated with unary operators. For example, if $Apr(\psi) = Pr(\psi)$, then also $Apr(F\psi) = Pr(F\psi)$. Indeed, if $Pr(\psi) = 0$, then $Pr(F\psi)$ is 0 too, and if $Pr(\psi) > 0$, then ψ eventually holds on a random computation, thus $Pr(F\psi)$ is 1.

Note that if we want to find $Apr(\varphi[\psi \leftarrow \perp])$ for several different subformulas ψ of φ, we can reuse information already calculated for common parts of the formula, as mutations differ from each other only by some subformulas.

3.3   Analyzing the Approximated Probability

The table in Fig. 1 analyzes the different possible relations between the approximated and the precise probabilities. We use γ to stand for a value $0 < \gamma < 1$. For example, Line 3 in the table refers to cases in which the approximated calculation returns the value 0, whereas the precise probability is some $0 < \gamma < 1$. The table also includes examples corresponding to the different cases and some observation about the cases. We elaborate on these observations below.

	$Apr(\varphi)$	$Pr(\varphi)$	Example	Observation
1	0	0	Gq	The approximated probability is precise
2	0	1	$G(p \vee \neg p)$	The approximated probability is helpful
3	0	γ	—	This case is impossible
4	1	0	$F(p \wedge \neg p) \vee Gq$	This case is rare
5	1	1	Fq	The approximated probability is precise
6	1	γ	—	This case is impossible
7	γ	0	$qU(p \wedge \neg p)$	This case is rare
8	γ	1	$(p \vee \neg p)Uq$	The approximated probability is helpful
9	γ	γ	pUq	

Fig. 1. Comparing the approximated probability with the precise probability

We first observe that the approximated probability has only a one-sided error: the approximating algorithm may decide that the probability is γ whereas the precise probability is 0 or 1, but never the other way round. Indeed, γ is introduced to $Apr(\varphi)$ only if some of the subformulas have probability that is not 0 or 1. It follows that the cases described in Lines 3 and 6 are impossible. Other favorable cases are those described in Lines 1 and 5, where the precise and approximated probabilities coincide.

When the approximated probability is not precise, it is due to some relationship between different parts of the formula. As described above, the definition of Apr ignores such a relationship. Consider for example the invariant $G(p \vee \neg p)$. While $Pr(p \vee \neg p) = 1$, we have that $Apr(p \vee \neg p) = \frac{3}{4}$. As a result, while $Pr(G(p \vee \neg p)) = 1$, our approximated algorithm returns $Apr(G(p \vee \neg p)) = 0$. When the approximated probability is lower than the precise probability, as is the case in Lines 2 and 8, we are going to report the vacuity result with a higher rank than it seemingly "deserves". Note that this would rightfully draw the attention of the user to the peculiar structure of the formula. We conclude that when the approximated probability is lower than the precise one, the result we get is more helpful than calculating the precise probability.

The cases where the approximated probability is higher than the real probability, as is the case in Lines 4 and 7, are the least favorable ones, since here too, there is some problem in the formula, but the vacuity result might get a lower ranking than it should. For example, $Pr(F(p \wedge \neg p) \vee Gq) = 0$ but $Apr(F(p \wedge \neg p) \vee Gq) = 1$. Note however, that the subformula causing the discrepancy, $F(p \wedge \neg p)$ in our example, is not the cause of vacuity – the formula holds in the model *in spite of* this odd subformula. Typically, another mutation of the formula, which refers to the odd subformula, would be checked. This latter check would reveal the real problem and would be estimated correctly by our algorithm. In our example, the other check replaces $(p \wedge \neg p)$ with $\perp$, leaving the rest of the formula untouched.

4   Ranking of Vacuity Results

In Section 3 we studied the probability of LTL formulas to hold in a random computation. We suggested algorithms for calculating the probability and estimating it. In this section we suggest several applications of a probability-based criteria for ranking of vacuity results. We focus on three approaches. In all of them, the idea is that the lower the probability of the mutation is, the more alarmed the user should be when it is satisfied.

1. **Simple analysis.** For each mutation φ' that is satisfied in the system, potentially pointing to real vacuity, we find $Pr(\varphi')$ (or an estimation of it). We report to the user only mutations whose probability is below some threshold, given by the user, or we order the mutations according to the probability of their satisfaction, with mutations of low probability being first.
2. **Drop analysis.** For each specification φ and mutation φ' that holds in the system, we find $Pr(\varphi) - Pr(\varphi')$. Note that the mutation is always stronger than the original specification, thus $Pr(\varphi) \geq Pr(\varphi')$ and the drop $Pr(\varphi) - Pr(\varphi') \geq 0$. We proceed as in the simple analysis, with respect to this drop.
3. **Invariants.** Recall that the probability of an invariant to hold on a random computation is equal to 0 or 1. The mutations of invariants are invariants too. Thus, for invariants, which are the vast majority of specifications written in practice, our framework is two-valued and it does not use the full range of values between 0 and 1. We suggest a refinement to our ranking procedure that leads to more accurate results. In the refined procedure, we perform a simple or drop analysis with respect to the invariant itself; that is, the specification without the outermost G. The invariant itself need not have probability 0 or 1.

4.1   Evaluation: Users' Feedback

In order to evaluate our ranking framework, we conducted a survey among model-checking users. The participants, 14 in total, included people from academia that are familiar with LTL model checking, as well as users from industry, mainly from the IBM Haifa laboratory. The participants were asked to rank the vacuity results of 4 typical formulas (we kept the questionnaire short on purpose, to encourage participation). While academic people were hesitant regarding the entire question of a ranking procedure, practical people seemed to have very strong views about the subject. The survey can be found in the full version.

We demonstrate the three approaches described above, and compare our rankings to those given by users.

Example 1. Consider the specification $\varphi_1 = G(a \to Fb)$. We examine two mutations for it, as detailed below.

$$\varphi_1' = \varphi_1[a \leftarrow true] = GFb, \quad \varphi_1'' = \varphi_1[b \leftarrow false] = G\neg a$$

We start with the simple analysis. The probability of each mutation is:

$$Pr(\varphi_1') = 1, \ Pr(\varphi_1'') = 0$$

Hence, if we choose to return only mutations whose probability is below some threshold, we return only $G\neg a$. We proceed to drop analysis. We first calculate $Pr(\varphi_1) = 1$

$$Pr(\varphi_1) - Pr(\varphi_1') = 1 - 1 = 0, \quad Pr(\varphi_1) - Pr(\varphi_1'') = 1 - 0 = 1$$

It follows that the biggest drop is in the mutation $G\neg a$ of φ_1, as before.

We proceed to examine the behavior of the invariant. Note that $\varphi_1 = G\theta_1$ for $\theta_1 = (a \rightarrow Fb)$ Applying the corresponding mutations of the invariant, we have the following.

$$\theta_1' = \theta_1[a \leftarrow true] = Fb, \quad \theta_1'' = \theta_1[b \leftarrow false] = \neg a$$

Calculating probabilities, we get that $Pr(\theta_1') = 1$ and $Pr(\theta_1'') = \frac{1}{2}$. This shows again, in a more refined way, that the mutation GFb is the least interesting one. Combining the invariants with the drop analysis, we take into account the fact that $Pr(\theta_1) = 1$. Accordingly,

$$Pr(\theta_1) - Pr(\theta_1') = 1 - 1 = 0, \quad Pr(\theta_1) - Pr(\theta_1'') = 1 - \frac{1}{2} = \frac{1}{2}$$

This agrees with the order above, with no drop for φ_1' and a drop of $\frac{1}{2}$ for φ_1''. For this example, all three ranking methods agree on the result. In our survey, all practitioners, and a total of 11 out of 14 said that $G\neg a$ was more alarming than GFb. The rest claimed that there was no difference.

Example 2. Consider the specification $\varphi_2 = G(a \rightarrow X(c_1 \vee c_2 \vee \cdots \vee c_m))$. We consider two types of mutations.

- $\varphi_2' = \varphi_2[a \leftarrow true] = GX(c_1 \vee \cdots \vee c_m)$, and
- $\varphi_2'' = \varphi_2[c_1 \leftarrow false] = G(a \rightarrow X(c_2 \vee \cdots \vee c_m))$, and similarly for the other c_i's, with $1 < i \leq m$.

Since the probability of φ_2 is 0, the probability of the mutations is 0 too, suggesting that the simple and drop analysis are not informative. We examine the invariants themselves. Let $\theta_2 = a \rightarrow X(c_1 \vee \cdots \vee c_m)$, and consider the mutations

- $\theta_2' = \theta_2[a \leftarrow true] = X(c_1 \vee \cdots \vee c_m)$, and
- $\theta_2'' = \theta_2[c_1 \leftarrow false] = a \rightarrow X(c_2 \vee \cdots \vee c_m)$.

We have that $Pr(\theta_2) = \frac{2^{m+1}-1}{2^{m+1}}$, whereas $Pr(\theta_2') = Pr(\theta_2'') = \frac{2^m-1}{2^m}$. Thus, the larger m is, the smaller is the drop. This example demonstrates that the probability-based criteria are useful also for the analysis of responsibility and blame studied in the context of coverage in [7].

While we were interested in the probability with respect to m, users presented with the mutations above, commented that the most important mutation is missing. That is, $\varphi_2''' = \varphi_2[(c_2 \vee \cdots \vee c_m) \leftarrow false] = G(\neg a)$. As before, if we set $\theta_2''' = \neg a$, we get that $Pr(\theta_2''') = \frac{1}{2}$, which is significantly less than the other two.

Example 3. Consider the specification $\varphi_3 = G(a \to (bRc))$. The operator R (release) is dual to the Until operator: a computation satisfies bRc if c holds until $b \wedge c$ holds, where possibly $b \wedge c$ never holds, in which case c holds forever. Let $\theta_5 = a \to (bRc)$.

We first note that $Pr(\varphi_3) = 0$. To see this, observe that $Pr(\theta_3) = \frac{5}{6}$. In fact, in this case also $Apr(\theta_3) = \frac{5}{6}$. Indeed, $Apr(a \to (bRc)) = Apr(\neg(a \wedge \neg(bRc))) = 1 - Apr(a) \cdot Apr((\neg b)U(\neg c)) = 1 - \frac{1}{2} \cdot \frac{\frac{2}{3}}{1-(1-\frac{1}{2})\frac{1}{2}} = 1 - \frac{1}{2} \cdot \frac{2}{3} = \frac{5}{6}$. It follows that probabilities of all mutations φ_3' of φ_3 are also 0, and we proceed to analyze the invariants themselves. We consider the following mutations.

- $\theta_3' = \theta_3[a \leftarrow true] = bRc$, so $Pr(\theta_3') = \frac{2}{3}$,
- $\theta_3'' = \theta_3[b \leftarrow false] = a \to Gc$, so $Pr(\theta_3'') = \frac{1}{2}$,
- $\theta_3''' = \theta_3[c \leftarrow false] = \neg a$, so $Pr(\theta_3''') = \frac{1}{2}$.

When presented to the users, the answers were mixed, with no single mutation preferred over the other. This matches again our method, since the difference between the probabilities is not big enough to select one over the other.

Example 4. Consider the specification $\varphi_4 = G(b \to X[1..5](c))$ (where $X[1..5](c)$ stands for $Xc \vee XXc \vee XXXc \vee XXXXc \vee XXXXXc$). Here too, we have that $Pr(\varphi_4) = 0$, and we thus analyze the invariants.

- $\theta_4' = \theta_4[c \leftarrow false] = \neg a$, so $Pr(\theta_4') = \frac{1}{2}$,
- $\theta_4'' = \theta_4[a \leftarrow true] = X[1..5](c)$, so $Pr(\theta_4'') = \frac{31}{32}$,
- $\theta_4''' = \theta_4[XXXXc \leftarrow false] = (b \to X[1..4](c))$, so $Pr(\theta_4''') = \frac{31}{32}$

Our method clearly prefer the first mutation over the other two. The users all agreed with this result.

The following two examples were not part of the survey given to users.

Example 5. Consider the specification $\varphi_5 = GFb_1 \vee GFb_2 \vee ... \vee GFb_m$. For each mutation of the form $\varphi_5' = \varphi_5[b_i \leftarrow false]$ with $1 \leq i \leq m$, we have that $Pr(\varphi_5') = Pr(\varphi_5) = 1$. Also, while φ_5 is not an invariant, it is equivalent to $G\theta_5$, for $\theta_5 = Fb_1 \vee Fb_2 \vee ... \vee Fb_m$. Here too, for each mutation of the form $\theta_4' = \theta_5[b_i \leftarrow false]$, we have that $Pr(\theta_5') = Pr(\theta_5) = 1$. Thus, all approaches lead to the conclusion that mutations of this form are not of big interest.

Example 6. In this example we demonstrate the extension of our framework to the definition of vacuity studied in [1], which handles also subformulas ψ with multiple occurrences, possibly of different polarity. As suggested in [1], such mutations replace ψ by a universally quantified proposition. We also demonstrate how errors in the estimated algorithm may actually be helpful.

Consider the specification $\varphi_6 = idleU(\neg idle \vee err)$. The specification states that eventually we get to a position that is not idle or in which the error signal is active, and until then, all positions are idle. We consider two mutations.

- $\varphi_6' = \varphi_6[err \leftarrow false] = idleU(\neg idle)$,

- $\varphi_6'' = \forall x.\varphi_6[idle \leftarrow x] = \forall x.(xU((\neg x) \vee err))$.

The probability of φ_6 as well as the probability of both mutations is 1. Indeed, φ_6' is equivalent to $F(\neg idle)$ and φ_6'' is equivalent to $F(err)$. This suggests that vacuity detection in this case is not too interesting. Nevertheless, if we examine the approximated analysis of the mutation, we reveal that while $Apr(\varphi_6) = \frac{\frac{3}{4}}{1-(1-\frac{3}{4})\frac{1}{2}} = \frac{6}{7}$, we have that $Apr(\varphi_6') = \frac{\frac{1}{2}}{1-(1-\frac{1}{2})\frac{1}{2}} = \frac{2}{3}$. Thus, the approximated analysis, which ignores the relation between $idle$ and $\neg idle$ shows a drop in the probability. Reporting this to the user is helpful, as φ_6 is *inherently vacuous* [15]: it is equivalent to its mutation $F(\neg idle \vee err)$, obtained by replacing the first occurrence of $idle$ by *true*.

4.2 Evaluation: Statistics

We implemented our approximated probability algorithm and ran it on the formulas listed in the LTL part of the "Property Patterns" project [13]. For each of the 55 formulas (see [12]), we ran our algorithm on the formula itself as well as on all the mutations resulting from replacing one of its subformulas by $\bot$. The number of such mutations ranged between 1 to 20 per formula, totaling over 400 mutations altogether. Note that for formulas from [12], the approximated probability and the precise one agree.

In cases where the formula had an outermost G operation (that is, $\varphi = G(\psi)$), which caused all mutations to have the probability 0, we followed the "Invariants" analysis and omitted the outermost G. Since the analysis of the formula was approximated the runtime of the probability calculations was negligible.

The full list of formulas and mutations along with their probabilities can be found in the full version. In many cases the probability of the mutated formula is not significantly lower than that of the original formula. However, examining those results where the probability decreased significantly or decreased to 0 (while the formula was not equivalent to *false*), we find that many of them correspond to formulas where the left side of an implication is false. Thus, our probabilistic-based approach nicely supports the "antecedent failure" approach.

4.3 Evaluation: Discussion

As discussed in Section 4.1, our probability-based approach usually agrees with the intuition of model-checking users. The main point that came up in the survey and in discussions thereafter is the relation between our probability-based approach and an alternative "antecedent failure" approach, where mutations are considered interesting if they are obtained by replacing right-hand sides of implications by *false*, thus checking whether the implication has been vacuously satisfied. Note that already in the pioneering work about vacuity, which came from the industry [2], the authors suggest to focus on such mutations.

We believe that the two approaches complement each other, and that, as the results in Section 4.2 show, when specifications are cleanly written (note that the antecedent-failure approach is syntax-sensitive), they do coincide. To see this, let us consider the two specifications $\psi_1 = Gp \to Gq$ and $\psi_2 = Fp \to Fq$. In the antecedent-failure approach, the interesting mutations would be $\theta_1 = F\neg p$ for ψ_1 and $\theta_2 = G\neg p$ for ψ_2. In our approach, the interesting mutations would be $\theta_1' = Gq$ for ψ_1 and $\theta_2 = G\neg p$ for ψ_2. Even users that find the antecedent-failure approach satisfying, agree that the ranking of the two mutations in ψ_2, where both approaches coincide, is definite, whereas the ranking for ψ_1, where the approaches do not agree, is debatable.

5   Future Work

We find the probability of LTL formulas to be an interesting question on its own, beyond the application to vacuity ranking. The definition of $Pr(\varphi)$ in the paper, assumes that for each atomic proposition p and for each state in the computation, the probability of p to hold in the state is $\frac{1}{2}$. This corresponds to computations in an infinite-state system and is the standard approach taken in studies of 0/1-laws. Alternatively, one can also study the probability of formulas to hold in computations of finite-state systems. Formally, for integers $k \geq 0$ and $l \geq 1$, let $Pr_{k,l}(\varphi)$ denote the probability that φ holds in a random lasso-shape computation with a prefix of length k and a loop of length l. Here too, the probability of each atomic proposition to hold in a state is $\frac{1}{2}$, yet we have only $k + l$ states to fix an assignment to. So, for example, while $Pr(Gp) = 0$, we have that $Pr_{0,1}(Gp) = \frac{1}{2}$ and $Pr_{0,2}(Gp) = \frac{1}{4}$.

There are several interesting issues in the finite-state approach. First, it may seem obvious that the bigger k and l are, the closer $Pr_{k,l}(\varphi)$ gets to $Pr(\varphi)$. This is, however, not so simple. For example, issues like cycles in φ can cause $Pr_{k,l}(\varphi)$ to be non-monotonic. For example, when φ requires p to hold in exactly all even positions, then $Pr_{0,1}(\varphi) = 0, Pr_{0,2}(\varphi) = \frac{1}{4}, Pr_{0,3}(\varphi) = 0, Pr_{0,1}(\varphi) = \frac{1}{16}$, and so on. It may also seem that, after cleaning the cycle-based issue (for example by restricting attention to formulas without Xs), one can characterize safety and liveness properties by means of the asymptotic behavior of $Pr_{k,l}(\varphi)$. For example, clearly $Pr_{k,l}(Gp)$ goes to 0 as k and l increase, whereas $Pr_{k,l}(Fp)$ goes to 1. Here too, however, the picture is not clean. For example, FGp is a liveness formula, but $Pr_{k,l}(FGp)$ decreases as k and l increase. Finding a characterization of properties that is based on the analysis of $Pr_{k,l}$ is a very interesting question, and we are currently studying it. It should also be noted that, unlike $Pr(\varphi)$, it is possible to estimate $Pr_{k,l}(\varphi)$ using model checking of φ in (sufficiently many) randomly generated lassos.

Acknowledgment. We thank our survey participants, Gadiel Auerbach, Ilan Beer, Hana Chockler, Shahram Esmaeilsabzali, Dana Fisman, Elena Guralnik, Arie Gurfinkel, Tamir Heyman, Alma Juarez-Dominguez, Zarrin Langari, Katia Patkin, Baruch Sterin, Sitvanit Ruah and Julia Rubin, for their time and for their invaluable comments. We thank Moshe Vardi for helpful discussions, and reviewers of an earlier version of this paper for helpful comments and suggestions.

References

1. Armoni, R., Fix, L., Flaisher, A., Grumberg, O., Piterman, N., Tiemeyer, A., Vardi, M.Y.: Enhanced vacuity detection in linear temporal logic. In: Hunt Jr., W.A., Somenzi, F. (eds.) CAV 2003. LNCS, vol. 2725, pp. 368–380. Springer, Heidelberg (2003)
2. Beer, I., Ben-David, S., Eisner, C., Rodeh, Y.: Efficient detection of vacuity in ACTL formulas. Formal Methods in System Design 18(2), 141–162 (2001)
3. Ben-David, S., Fisman, D., Ruah, S.: Temporal antecedent failure: Refining vacuity. In: Caires, L., Vasconcelos, V.T. (eds.) CONCUR 2007. LNCS, vol. 4703, pp. 492–506. Springer, Heidelberg (2007)
4. Bustan, D., Flaisher, A., Grumberg, O., Kupferman, O., Vardi, M.Y.: Regular vacuity. In: Borrione, D., Paul, W. (eds.) CHARME 2005. LNCS, vol. 3725, pp. 191–206. Springer, Heidelberg (2005)
5. Chechik, M., Gheorghiu, M., Gurfinkel, A.: Finding environment guarantees. In: Dwyer, M.B., Lopes, A. (eds.) FASE 2007. LNCS, vol. 4422, pp. 352–367. Springer, Heidelberg (2007)
6. Chockler, H., Gurfinkel, A., Strichman, O.: Beyond vacuity: Towards the strongest passing formula. In: FMCAD, pp. 1–8 (2008)
7. Chockler, H., Halpern, J.Y.: Responsibility and blame: a structural-model approach. In: Proc. 19th IJCAI, pp. 147–153 (2003)
8. Chockler, H., Strichman, O.: Easier and more informative vacuity checks. In: Proc. 5th MEMOCODE, pp. 189–198 (2007)
9. Clarke, E.M., Grumberg, O., Long, D.: Verification tools for finite-state concurrent systems. In: de Bakker, J.W., de Roever, W.-P., Rozenberg, G. (eds.) REX 1993. LNCS, vol. 803, pp. 124–175. Springer, Heidelberg (1994)
10. Clarke, E.M., Grumberg, O., McMillan, K.L., Zhao, X.: Efficient generation of counterexamples and witnesses in symbolic model checking. In: Proc. 32st DAC, pp. 427–432. IEEE Computer Society (1995)
11. Courcoubetis, C., Yannakakis, M.: The complexity of probabilistic verification. J. ACM 42, 857–907 (1995)
12. Dwyer, M.B., Avrunin, G.S., Corbett, J.C.: Property pattern mappings for LTL, http://patterns.projects.cis.ksu.edu/documentation/patterns/ltl.shtml
13. Dwyer, M.B., Avrunin, G.S., Corbett, J.C.: Property specification patterns for finite-state verification. In: FMSP, pp. 7–15 (1998)
14. Fagin, R.: Probabilities in finite models. JSL 41(1), 50–58 (1976)
15. Fisman, D., Kupferman, O., Sheinvald-Faragy, S., Vardi, M.Y.: A framework for inherent vacuity. In: Chockler, H., Hu, A.J. (eds.) HVC 2008. LNCS, vol. 5394, pp. 7–22. Springer, Heidelberg (2009)
16. Glebskii, Y.V., Kogan, D.I., Liogonkii, M.I., Talanov, V.A.: Range and degree of realizability of formulas in the restricted predicate calculus. Kibernetika 2, 17–28 (1969)
17. Gurfinkel, A., Chechik, M.: Extending extended vacuity. In: Hu, A.J., Martin, A.K. (eds.) FMCAD 2004. LNCS, vol. 3312, pp. 306–321. Springer, Heidelberg (2004)
18. Gurfinkel, A., Chechik, M.: How vacuous is vacuous? In: Jensen, K., Podelski, A. (eds.) TACAS 2004. LNCS, vol. 2988, pp. 451–466. Springer, Heidelberg (2004)
19. Kupferman, O.: Sanity checks in formal verification. In: Baier, C., Hermanns, H. (eds.) CONCUR 2006. LNCS, vol. 4137, pp. 37–51. Springer, Heidelberg (2006)
20. Kupferman, O., Li, W., Seshia, S.A.: A theory of mutations with applications to vacuity, coverage, and fault tolerance. In: FMCAD 2008, pp. 1–9 (2008)
21. Kupferman, O., Vardi, M.Y.: Vacuity detection in temporal model checking. STTT 4(2), 224–233 (2003)
22. Pnueli, A.: The temporal logic of programs. In: Proc. 18th FOCS, pp. 46–57 (1977)

Synthesizing Masking Fault-Tolerant Systems from Deontic Specifications

Ramiro Demasi[1], Pablo F. Castro[2,3], Thomas S.E. Maibaum[1], and Nazareno Aguirre[2,3]

[1] Department of Computing and Software, McMaster University, Hamilton, Ontario, Canada
demasira@mcmaster.ca, tom@maibaum.org
[2] Departamento de Computación, FCEFQyN, Universidad Nacional de Río Cuarto, Río Cuarto, Córdoba, Argentina
{pcastro,naguirre}@dc.exa.unrc.edu.ar
[3] Consejo Nacional de Investigaciones Científicas y Técnicas (CONICET), Argentina

Abstract. In this paper, we study the problem of synthesizing fault-tolerant components from specifications, i.e., the problem of automatically constructing a fault-tolerant component implementation from a logical specification of the component, and the system's required level of fault-tolerance. We study a specific level of fault-tolerance: masking tolerance. A system exhibits masking tolerance when both the liveness and the safety properties of the behaviors of the system are preserved under the occurrence of faults. In our approach, the logical specification of components is given in dCTL, a branching time temporal logic with deontic operators, especially designed for fault-tolerant component specification. The synthesis algorithm takes the component specification, and automatically determines whether a component with masking fault-tolerance is realizable, and the maximal set of faults supported for this level of tolerance. Our technique for synthesis is based on capturing masking fault-tolerance via a simulation relation. Furthermore, a combination of an extension of a synthesis algorithm for CTL to cope with dCTL specifications, with simulation algorithms, is defined in order to synthesize masking fault-tolerant implementations.

Keywords: Formal specification, Fault-tolerance, Program synthesis, Temporal logics, Deontic logics, Correctness by construction.

1 Introduction

The increasing demand for highly dependable and constantly available systems has focused attention on providing strong guarantees for software correctness, in particular, for safety critical systems. In this context, a problem that deserves attention is that of capturing *faults*, understood as unexpected events that affect a system, as well as expressing and reasoning about the properties of systems in the presence of faults. Indeed, various researchers have been concerned with formally expressing and reasoning about fault-tolerant behavior, and some formalisms and tools have been proposed for this task [13,4]. Moreover, in formal

D. Van Hung and M. Ogawa (Eds.): ATVA 2013, LNCS 8172, pp. 163–177, 2013.

approaches to fault-tolerance (and in general in formal approaches to software development), it is generally recognized that powerful (semi-)automated analysis techniques are essential for a method to be effectively applicable in practice. Therefore, tools for automated or semi-automated reasoning, such as those based on model checking or automated theorem proving, have been central in many of the above cited works. In this direction, but with less emphasis, approaches for automatically *synthesizing* programs, in particular fault-tolerant ones, have also been studied [1,12,2,5].

In this paper, we study the problem of automatically synthesizing fault-tolerant systems from logical specifications. This work concentrates on a particular kind of fault-tolerance, namely masking tolerance. As stated in [10], the fault tolerance that a system may exhibit can be classified using the liveness and safety properties that the designers want the system to preserve. In masking fault-tolerance, the system must preserve, in the presence of faults, both the safety and the liveness properties of the "fault free" system. More precisely, masking fault-tolerance is usually stated with respect to an observable part of the system or component, its so called *interface*. Essentially, a masking fault-tolerant system ensures that faults are not observable at the system's interface level, and both liveness and safety properties of the system are preserved even when subject to the occurrence of faults.

Our work is strongly related to the approach presented in [2]. The main difference between our approach and that introduced in [2] is that, to specify systems, we use dCTL-, a branching time temporal logic with deontic operators (see Section 2), as opposed to the well established branching time temporal logic CTL used in [2]. More precisely, the logic dCTL- features, besides the CTL temporal operators, deontic operators that allow us to declaratively distinguish the normative (correct, without faults) part of the system from its non-normative (faulty) part. In particular, in our approach faults are declaratively embedded in the logical specification. In our approach, faults are understood as violations to the deontic obligations on the behavior of the system, in contrast with the case of [2] and related works (e.g., [1,12,9]), where faults are given explicitly as part of the behavior model of the system. This leads to some differences in the way in which programs are synthesized. While in [2] a satisfiability algorithm for CTL based on tableau is employed, with faults corresponding to adding states in the tableau, we use instead the deontic specification to produce the faulty states combined with a characterization of masking fault tolerance by means of a simulation relation, in order to "cut out" inappropriate parts of the tableau. Our algorithm then combines a simulation algorithm with an adaptation of tableau based CTL satisfiability to deal with dCTL- specifications. The algorithm is presented in detail in Section 3.

There are some interesting properties that our proposed algorithm enjoys. If the algorithm is able to compute a masking fault tolerant implementation from the system specification, then the implementation produced is *maximal* in the sense that it "removes" the least number of states necessary to achieve the required tolerance. If the algorithm does not compute an implementation, then there are no feasible masking fault tolerant implementations for the specified system. We show that our algorithm is sound, and that it holds the above mentioned kind of strong completeness (it returns a program that is maximal with respect to masking similarity, which as explained later on, implies completeness).

The remainder of the paper is structured as follows. In Section 2 we introduce some notions used throughout the paper. In Section 3, we describe our synthesis method. A practical case study is shown in Section 4. Section 5 reviews some related work. Finally, we discuss some conclusions and directions for further work.

2   Preliminaries

In this section we introduce some concepts that will be necessary throughout the paper. For the sake of brevity, we assume some basic knowledge of model checking; the interested reader may consult [3]. We model fault-tolerant systems by means of *colored Kripke structures*, as introduced in [6]. Given a set of propositional letters $AP = \{p, q, s, \dots\}$, a *colored Kripke structure* is a 5-tuple $\langle S, I, R, L, \mathcal{N} \rangle$, where S is a set of states, $I \subseteq S$ is a set of initial states, $R \subseteq S \times S$ is a transition relation, $L : S \to \wp(AP)$ is a labeling function indicating which propositions are true in each state, and $\mathcal{N} \subseteq S$ is a set of *normal*, or "green" states. The complement of $\mathcal{N}$ is the set of "red", abnormal or faulty states. Arcs leading to abnormal states (i.e., states not in $\mathcal{N}$) can be thought of as faulty transitions, or simply *faults*. Then, normal executions are those transiting only through green states. The set of normal executions is denoted by $\mathcal{NT}$. We assume that in every colored Kripke structure, and for every normal state, there exists at least one successor state that is also normal, and that at least one initial state is green. This guarantees that every system has at least one normal execution, i.e., that $\mathcal{NT} \neq \emptyset$.

As is usual in the definition of temporal operators, we employ the notion of trace. Given a colored Kripke structure $M = \langle S, I, R, L, \mathcal{N} \rangle$, a *trace* is a maximal sequence of states, whose consecutive pairs of states are adjacent with respect to R. When a trace of M starts in an initial state, it is called an *execution* of M, with *partial* executions corresponding to non-maximal sequences of adjacent states starting in an initial state. Given a trace $\sigma = s_0, s_1, s_2, s_3, \dots$, the ith state of σ is denoted by $\sigma[i]$, and the final segment of σ starting in position i is denoted by $\sigma[i..]$. Moreover, we distinguish among the different kinds of outgoing transitions from a state. We denote by $\dashrightarrow$ the restriction of R to faulty transitions, and $\to$ the restriction of R to non-faulty transitions. We define $Post_N(s) = \{s \in S| \ s \to s'\}$ as the set of (immediate) successors of s reachable via non-faulty (or good) transitions; similarly, $Post_F(s) = \{s \in S| \ s \dashrightarrow s'\}$ represents the set of successors of s reachable via faulty arcs. Analogously, we define $Pre_N(s')$ and $Pre_F(s')$ as the set of (immediate) predecessors of s' via normal and faulty transitions, respectively. Moreover, $Post^*(s)$ denotes the states which are reachable from s. Without loss of generality, we assume that every state has a successor [3]. We denote by $\Rightarrow^*$ the transitive closure of $\dashrightarrow \cup \to$.

In order to state properties of systems, we use a fragment of dCTL [6], a branching time temporal logic with deontic operators designed for fault-tolerant system verification. Formulas in this fragment, that we call dCTL-, refer to properties of behaviors of colored Kripke structures, in which a distinction between *normal* and *abnormal* states (and therefore also a distinction between normal and abnormal traces) is made. The logic dCTL is defined over the Computation Tree Logic CTL, with its novel part being the deontic operators $\mathbf{O}(\psi)$ (obligation) and $\mathbf{P}(\psi)$ (permission), which are applied to a certain kind of path formula ψ. The intention of these operators is to capture the notion of *obligation* and *permission* over traces. Intuitively, these operators have the following meaning:

- $\mathbf{O}(\psi)$: property ψ is obliged in every future state, reachable via non-faulty transitions.
- $\mathbf{P}(\psi)$: there exists a normal execution, i.e., not involving faults, starting from the current state and along which ψ holds.

Obligation and permission will enable us to express intended properties which should hold in *all* normal behaviors and *some* normal behaviors, respectively. These deontic operators have an implicit *temporal* character, since ψ is a path formula. Let us present the syntax of dCTL-. Let $AP = \{p_0, p_1, \dots\}$ be a set of atomic propositions. The sets Φ and Ψ of *state formulas* and *path formulas*, respectively, are mutually recursively defined as follows:

$$\Phi ::= p_i \mid \neg\Phi \mid \Phi \to \Phi \mid \mathsf{A}(\Psi) \mid \mathsf{E}(\Psi) \mid \mathbf{O}(\Psi) \mid \mathbf{P}(\Psi)$$
$$\Psi ::= \mathsf{X}\Phi \mid \Phi\,\mathcal{U}\,\Phi \mid \Phi\,\mathcal{W}\,\Phi$$

Other boolean connectives (here, state operators), such as $\wedge$, $\vee$, etc., are defined as usual. Also, traditional temporal operators G and F can be expressed as $\mathsf{G}(\phi) \equiv \phi\,\mathcal{W}\,\bot$, and $\mathsf{F}(\phi) \equiv \top\,\mathcal{U}\,\phi$. The standard boolean operators and the CTL quantifiers A and E have the usual semantics. Now, we formally state the semantics of the logic. We start by defining the relation $\vDash$, formalizing the satisfaction of dCTL- state formulas in colored Kripke structures. For the deontic operators, the definition of $\vDash$ is as follows:

- $M, s \vDash \mathbf{O}(\psi) \Leftrightarrow$ for every $\sigma \in \mathcal{NT}$ such that $\sigma[0] = s$, we have that, for every $i \geq 0$, $M, \sigma[i..] \vDash \psi$.
- $M, s \vDash \mathbf{P}(\psi) \Leftrightarrow$ for some $\sigma \in \mathcal{NT}$ such that $\sigma[0] = s$, we have that, for every $i \geq 0$, $M, \sigma[i..] \vDash \psi$.

For the standard CTL operators, the definition of $\vDash$ is as usual (cf. [3]). We denote by $M \vDash \varphi$ the fact that $M, s \vDash \varphi$ holds for every state s of M, and by $\vDash \varphi$ the fact that $M \vDash \varphi$ for every colored Kripke structure M. Furthermore, the α and β classification of formulas given in [2] for tableau can be extended to our setting. For CTL operators, this is done as in [2]. For the deontic operators we proceed as follows:

- $\mathbf{O}(\varphi\,\mathcal{U}\,\psi)$ is classified as a β formula. In this case: $\beta_1 = O_\psi$ and $\beta_2 = O_\varphi \wedge \mathsf{AXO}(\varphi\,\mathcal{U}\,\psi)$, where O_φ is obtained by substituting in φ any propositional variable p by a fresh variable O_p, and similarly for O_ψ.

- $\mathbf{P}(\varphi\ \mathcal{U}\ \psi)$ is classified as a β formula. In this case: $\beta_1 = O_\psi$ and $\beta_2 = O_\varphi \wedge \mathbf{EXO}(\varphi\,\mathcal{U}\,\psi)$, where O_φ and O_ψ are defined as before.
- $\mathbf{O}(\varphi\ \mathcal{W}\ \psi)$ is classified as a β formula. In this case: $\beta_1 = O_\psi$ and $\beta_2 = O_\varphi \wedge \mathbf{AXO}(\varphi\,\mathcal{W}\,\psi)$, where O_φ and O_ψ are defined as before.
- $\mathbf{P}(\varphi\ \mathcal{W}\ \psi)$ is classified as a β formula. In this case: $\beta_1 = O_\psi$ and $\beta_2 = O_\varphi \wedge \mathbf{EXO}(\varphi\,\mathcal{W}\,\psi)$, where O_φ and O_ψ are defined as before.

This classification of formulas will be essential for the tableau proofs and synthesis algorithm, presented later on in this paper.

Fault-tolerance in characterized in our work via simulation relations. Various detailed notions of fault-tolerance, namely masking, nonmasking and failsafe tolerances, are all defined via appropriate simulation relations, relating a specification of the system (i.e., its fault-free expected behavior) with the fault-tolerant implementation [8]. In this paper, we concentrate on masking fault-tolerance, although synthesis mechanisms for other kinds of fault-tolerance, definable via appropriate simulation relations, are relatively direct. In order to make the paper self contained, let us reproduce here the definition of masking simulation.

Definition 1. *(Masking fault-tolerance) Given two colored Kripke structures $M = \langle S, I, R, L, \mathcal{N} \rangle$ and $M' = \langle S', I', R', L', \mathcal{N}' \rangle$, we say that a relationship $\prec_{Mask}\, \subseteq S \times S'$ is masking fault-tolerant for sublabelings $L_0 \subseteq L$ and $L'_0 \subseteq L'$ iff:*

(A) $\forall s_1 \in I : (\exists s_2 \in I' : s_1 \prec_{Mask} s_2)$ *and* $\forall s_2 \in I' : (\exists s_1 \in I : s_1 \prec_{Mask} s_2)$.
(B) for all $s_1 \prec_{Mask} s_2$ *the following holds:*
   (1) $L_0(s_1) = L'_0(s_2)$.
   (2) if $s'_1 \in Post_N(s_1)$, *then there exists* $s'_2 \in Post(s_2)$ *with* $s'_1 \prec_{Mask} s'_2$.
   (3) if $s'_2 \in Post_N(s_2)$, *then there exists* $s'_1 \in Post_N(s_1)$ *with* $s'_1 \prec_{Mask} s'_2$.
   (4) if $s'_2 \in Post_F(s_2)$, *then either there exists* $s'_1 \in Post_N(s_1)$ *with* $s'_1 \prec_{Mask} s'_2$ *or* $s_1 \prec_{Mask} s'_2$.

Notice that Definition 1 makes use of a sublabeling $L_0 \subseteq L$, whose intention is to capture the *observable* part of the state, that visible from the component's interface. Our approach is in this sense *state based*, as opposed to *event based* approaches where the interface is captured via observable actions/events. Masking fault-tolerance corresponds to the kind of fault-tolerance that completely "masks" faults, not allowing them or their consequences to be observable. Masking fault-tolerance must then preserve both safety and liveness properties of the "fault free" system. For further details, we refer the interested reader to [8].

In the next section, we use the fault-tolerance simulation relation in combination with a CTL synthesis algorithm (extended to cope with dCTL-) in order to automatically construct, from a logical system description, a masking fault-tolerant system. The resulting system is maximal with respect to masking tolerance, in the sense that it "cuts out" the minimal part of the system augmented with faults, to make the resulting program masking tolerant. The synthesized program may not support all original faults, or support faults only when they occur in certain situations, but it is in a sense the most general solution: the "removed" transitions are those that would lead to nonmasking system conditions.

3   The Synthesis Approach

Given a dCTL- specification of a component and a desired level of fault-tolerance
(in this case, masking), our goal is to automatically obtain a fault-tolerant component, with the required level of fault-tolerance. Masking fault-tolerance requires the system augmented with faults to preserve the observable behavior of
the fault-free system, in what concerns both safety and liveness properties. The
interface, in our case, is captured by a subset of the state variables (i.e., a state
sublabeling L_0). The dCTL- system specification involves the use of CTL to describe the system declaratively (including safety and liveness properties of the
system), while the deontic operators of dCTL- allow us to capture *obligations*,
and to indirectly characterize faults as events violating these obligations. Notice
that the deontic specification states what the expected behavior of the system is,
and, indirectly, what the possible faults are. In other words, the possible faults
are not explicitly given, as in other approaches, but stated at the specification
level. We compare our approach with related work in Section 5.

The synthesis process is based on the extraction of a finite behavior model
from a dCTL- specification. This is achieved by constructing a behavior model
that captures the system augmented with faults, and then combining a synthesis
algorithm for dCTL- with a simulation relation that captures masking tolerance,
in order to remove from this model those states and faults that lie outside the
required level of tolerance, i.e., that cannot be masked. The synthesis algorithm
aims at detecting the *maximal* set of faults that can be tolerated (for the required
level of fault-tolerance), and returning a (maximal) program that provides recovery from these faults. Of course, if the resulting system can only deal with
the empty set of faults, then no masking fault-tolerant program is possible, from
the provided specification.

In this paper, we are concerned with the synthesis of a single component.
The approach can be extended to extract several concurrent components from a
specification, by using indexes as done in [2]. We leave this as further work. More
precisely, the problem of synthesis of a fault-tolerant component has as input a
problem specification, a dCTL- formula `problem-spec` of the form `init-spec` ∧
`normal-spec`, where `init-spec` and `normal-spec` can be any dCTL- formula.
From this description, we want to automatically obtain a system that satisfies
`init-spec` ∧ `normal-spec`, while being masking tolerant with respect to the
maximal set of faults obtained from violations of the system obligations.

3.1   The Synthesis Algorithm for Masking Tolerance

Our synthesis algorithm has three phases. The pseudocode of the algorithm
is shown in Figures 1, 2, 3, and 4. It starts by building a tableau (Figure 1),
following the tableau based algorithm for CTL satisfiability. We employ the rules
α and β both for CTL and deontic formulas. That is, we construct a graph $T_N = (d, V_C, V_D, A_{CD}, V_{DC}, L)$, where V_C are called *And*-nodes and V_D are called *Or*-
nodes. The rules used for building the graph (involving also deontic formulas)
allow us to obtain the sub-formulas of the original specification. We stop when all

---

Algorithm 1. Construction of tableau $T_N = (d, V_C, V_D, A_{CD}, V_{DC}, L)$

Require: deontic specification *dSpec*: `init-spec` and `normal-spec`
Ensure: Tableau T_N
 1: Let d be an *Or*-node with label $\{dSpec\}$
 2: $T_N := d$
 3: **repeat**
 4:     Select a node $e \in frontier(T_N)$
 5:     **if** $\exists\, e' \in V_D$ with $L(e) = L(e')$ **then**
 6:         merge e and e'
 7:     **else**
 8:         **for all** $e' \in Succ(e)$ being an *And*-node **do**
 9:             **if** e' is non-faulty **then**
10:                 $Norm := Norm \cup \{e'\}$
11:             **else**
12:                 **if** $\exists e'' \in Succ(e)$ faulty such that $NForm(e') = NForm(e'')$ **then**
13:                     delete(e'')
14:                 **end if**
15:             **end if**
16:         **end for**
17:         attach all $e' \in Succ(e)$ as successors of e and mark e as expanded
18:     **end if**
19:     update V_C, V_D, A_{CD}, V_{DC} appropriately
20: **until** $frontier(T_N) = \emptyset$
21: Apply the deletion rules to T_N
22: Apply Algorithm 2 to check nodes in $Norm$
23: Apply Algorithm 3 to remove and create faulty nodes
24: Apply Algorithm 4 to check the relation of masking and remove nodes.
25: **return** T_N

---

the *frontier* nodes are generated (nodes where no rules can be applied). We then start applying the deletion rules explained in [2], in order to remove inconsistent nodes and nodes containing eventuality formulas that cannot be satisfied. When this process finishes, we obtain a graph similar to that obtained by the tableau method for CTL satisfiability. Regarding deontic operations, we modified the CTL algorithm to cope with these (recall our classification of deontic operators as α and β). *Or*-nodes are expanded following the traditional rules. On the other hand, when a new *And*-node (say x) is created, we check if there is some violation, i.e., if either $O_p \in x$ and $p \notin x$, or $O_{\neg p} \in x$ and $p \in x$, belong to the node. If this is the case, the node is considered faulty (proposition O_p is undestood as: p *should be true*, and when p is false we get a state in which the normal or desirable behavior is not fulfilled). Otherwise, the node is added to $Norm$, the set of normal (non-faulty) states (line 10 of Alg. 1). If there is a faulty node (say e') such that it has the same CTL formulas as a non-faulty node (say e''), e' is deleted, since it is masked by e'' (line 13).

Secondly, the algorithm enters a phase where nodes originating from the specification of the system, that cannot fulfil deontic eventualities, are searched for.

Algorithm 2. Alg. for computing faulty states

Require: Tableau generated by alg. 1
Ensure: All faulty states are identified and removed from $Norm$
1: **repeat**
2:    **if** $\exists x \in V_c$ s.t. $\mathbf{O}(p\,\mathcal{U}\,q)$ and $\exists v : v \in Norm \wedge q \notin v \wedge x \rightarrow^* v$ **then**
3:       $Norm := Norm \backslash \{x\}$
4:    **end if**
5:    **if** $\exists x \in V_c$ s.t. $\mathbf{P}(p\,\mathcal{U}\,q)$ and $\forall v : v \in Norm \wedge q \notin v \wedge x \rightarrow^* v$ **then**
6:       $Norm := Norm \backslash \{x\}$
7:    **end if**
8: **until** $Norm$ does not change

These nodes are marked as faulty, and their treatment is shown in Alg. 2. Thirdly, we inject *faults*. We take each non-faulty state (i.e., each *And*-node) and produce a copy of it which is an *Or*-node. But in order to distinguish it from the other kinds of nodes, we call these *FOr*-nodes (faulty *Or*-nodes). The process for dealing with these states is in Alg. 3. This algorithm consists of an adaptation of the backward simulation algorithm shown in [3]. We use it in order to only generate the nodes that can be masked, and cut out the remaining ones. The generation is performed by applying the indicated operations. If a faulty node that is not masked by any normal state is created, then we move "upwards" in the graph, to appropriately prune the graph to get rid of this unmasked state. After that, since all the faulty nodes that can be masked were generated, we check condition $B.2$ of the masking simulation relation. This step may also lead to cutting out further faulty nodes, namely those which exhibit normal behavior, but that are not part of the correct behavior of the system. Finally, the synthesized program is extracted from the generated tableau. The extraction is as follows. First, a Kripke structure M is obtained from the tableau by unfolding the tableau as explained in [2]. Then, we delete the non propositional formulas from the nodes, and we add new propositional variables to distinguish nodes that have the same formulas, to avoid erroneously collapsing nodes (these extra variables can be seen as variables that indicate different phases of the algorithm; they play the same same role as the shared variables of the algorithm for synthesis introduced in [2]). Then, each transition $s \rightarrow t$ is labeled with the command $A \rightarrow B$ iff A is the conjunction of all variables occurring in s and the negation of those variables that do not appear in s (we assume that the finite alphabet of propositional variables is given). We add $b := \neg b$ if b changes its value from s to t. An example of this is shown in the next section.

Let us state two important properties of the synthesis algorithm, whose proofs are sketched following the proofs of correctness given for the algorithms for CTL satisfiability based on tableau [7,2], and for checking (bi)simulations [3,11].

Theorem 1. *Given a specification S over a set AP of propositional letters, if we obtain a program P by applying the synthesis algorithm over the sublabeling obtained from $AP' \subseteq AP$, then P is a masking tolerant implementation of S, i.e., $P \prec_{Mask} P$ (with respect to AP') and $P \vDash S$.*

Algorithm 3. Computes relations satisfying $B.3$ and $B.4$ of Def. 1

Require: Tableau Generated by SAT
Ensure: $Masks$ and $RemoveL$ satisfy conditions $B.3$ and $B.4$.
1: **for all** s_2 **do**
2:   $Masks(s_2) := \{s_1 \in Norm \mid L_0(s_1) = L_0(s_2)\}$
3:   $RemoveL(s_2) := Norm \backslash Pre_N(Masks(s_2))$ {Note that all the nodes in $Norm$
    are already generated}
4: **end for**
5: **while** $\exists\, s_2' \in S \backslash Norm$ with $RemoveL(s_2') \neq \emptyset$ or there is a unexpanded v Or-node
    do
6:   select s_2' such that $RemoveL(s_2') \neq \emptyset$ or s_2' in $faultySucc(v)$
7:   **for all** $s_1 \in RemoveL(s_2')$ **do**
8:     **for all** $s_2 \in Pre_N(s_2')$ **do**
9:       **if** $s_1 \in Masks(s_2)$ **then**
10:         $Masks(s_2) := Masks(s_2) \backslash \{s_1\}$
11:         **for all** $s \in Pre_N(s_1)$ with $Post_N(s) \cap Masks(s_2) = \emptyset \wedge s \notin Masks(s_2)$
          do
12:           $RemoveL(s_2) := RemoveL(s_2) \cup \{s\}$
13:         **end for**
14:       **end if**
15:     **end for**(* this takes care of the faulty transitions*)
16:     **for all** $s_2 \in Pre_F(s_2')$ **do**
17:       **if** $s_1 \in Masks(s_2) \wedge s_1 \notin Masks(s_2')$ **then**
18:         $Masks(s_2) := Masks(s_2) \backslash \{s_1\}$
19:         **if** $Masks(s_2) = \emptyset$ **then**
20:           delete $DAG[s_2]$
21:           $removeL(s_2) := \emptyset$
22:         **else**
23:           **for all** $s \in Pre_N(s_1)$ with $Post_N(s) \cap Masks(s_2) = \emptyset$ **do**
24:             $RemoveL(s_2) := RemoveL(s_2) \cup \{s\}$
25:           **end for**
26:         **end if**
27:       **end if**
28:     **end for**
29:   **end for**
30:   $RemoveL(s_2') := \emptyset$ and all the FOr-nodes are expanded
31: **end while**

Sketch of Proof. First, we prove that Alg. 3 ensures conditions $B.3$ and $B.4$ of
Def. 1. Then we prove that Alg. 4 ensures condition $B.2$. Notice that, when Alg. 2
starts, all the normative nodes ($Norm$) have been computed. Then, we have the
following invariant of Alg. 3: *(i)* $RemoveL(s_2) = Norm \backslash Pre_N(Masks(s_2))$; *(ii)*
for any relation $\prec_{Mask}$: $\{s_1 \in Norm \mid s_1 \prec_{Mask} s_2\} \subseteq Masks(s_2) \subseteq \{s_2 \in$
$Norm \mid L(s_1) = L(s_2)\}$; and *(iii)* $\forall s_2 \in Masks(s_1)$, either:

- $\exists s_1' \in Post(s_1)$ with $Post_N(s_2) \cap Masks(s_1') = \emptyset \wedge s_1' \notin Masks(s_1)$ and
  $s_2 \in RemoveL(s_1)$,
- $\forall s_1' \in Post(s_1) : Post_N(s_2) \cap Masks(s_1') = \emptyset$

From the last item we obtain that, when $RemoveL(s_1') = \emptyset$ for every s_1', then: $\forall s_1 \in S : \forall s_2 \in Masks(s_1) : \forall s_1' \in Post(s_1) : Post_N(s_2) \cap Masks(s_1') \neq \emptyset \vee s_2 \in Masks(s_1')$. That is, the relation defined as $s_1 \prec_{Mask} s_2$ holds item $B.3$ and $B.4$ of Def. 1.

On the other hand, notice that before executing Alg. 3, all the faulty nodes have been calculated. For this algorithm we have the following invariant: (i) $RemoveR(s_2) = S \backslash Pre(Masked(s_2))$; (ii) for any relation $\prec_{Mask}$: $\{s_2 \in V_C \mid s_1 \prec_{Mask} s_2\} \subseteq Masked(s_1) \subseteq \{s_2 \in V_c \mid L(s_1) = L(s_2)\}$; and (iii) $\forall s_2 \in Masked(s_1)$, either:

- $\exists s_1' \in Post(s_1)$ with $Post(s_2) \cap Masked(s_1') = \emptyset$ and $s_2 \in RemoveL(s_2)$,
- $\forall s_1' \in Post_N(s_1) : Post(s_2) \cap Masked(s_1') = \emptyset$

That is, when $RemoveR(s_1) = \emptyset$, then we have $\forall s_1 \in S : \forall s_2 \in Masked(s_1) : \forall s_1' \in Post_N(s_1) : Post(s_2) \cap Masked(s_1') \neq \emptyset$. Thus, the relation defined as: $s_1 \prec_{Mask} s_2$ iff $s_1 \in Masks(s_2) \wedge s_2 \in Masked(s_1)$ satisfies condition $B.2$ of Def. 1. Since it also satisfies $B.3$ and $B.4$, it is a masking relation. The proof that the obtained structure satisfies the specification can be obtained, for CTL operators, following the proof given in [2]. For the deontic operators notice that all the nodes that do not satisfy the deontic operators are marked as faulty, ensuring that the safety deontic formulas are preserved. We treat deontic eventualities by marking as faulty all the nodes that have unfulfilled deontic eventualities. Thus, both CTL and deontic formulas are satisfied. Termination can be proved by resorting to the approach for proving termination of simulation algorithms (cf. [3]). The only point to note is that the injection of faults finishes at some point since states start repeating.

The definition of masking similarity ensures that the safety and liveness properties of the normal behavior of P are preserved in the presence of faults. If the synthesized program P contains no faults, we conclude that is not possible to synthesize a masking tolerant program supporting faults, from the specification. Moreover, we can prove that the synthesized program is the most general.

Theorem 2. *Given a specification S, if a structure M is obtained by the synthesis algorithm, then for any other structure $M' \vDash S$ such that it is masking and the non-faulty part of M' coincides with that of M, then we have $M' \prec M$, where $\prec$ is the usual notion of simulation with respect to L_0.*

Sketch of Proof. The simulation relation is defined as: (i) if $s \in Norm$, $s' \prec s$ iff $s' \prec_{Mask} s$; (ii) if $s \notin Norm$, $s' \prec s$ iff $Masked(s') \subseteq Masked(s)$, i.e., the M' nodes masked for s' are a subset of those masked by s in M. In order to prove that this relation is a simulation, assume $s \prec t$. If $s \to s'$ and $s' \in Post_N(s)$, by condition $B.3$ of Def. 1 we obtain that there is a $t \to t'$ such that $s' \prec t'$. Otherwise, if $s \to s'$ and $s' \in Post_F(S)$ and s is normative, then the transition matches some part of the specification. Thus, a similar transition is in M and therefore we have $t \to t'$. Now if s' masks any node, the same node has to be masked by t' (otherwise M' would not be masking). Thus, $s' \prec t'$. A similar reasoning can be used when s is faulty.

Algorithm 4. Computes relations that satisfy condition $B.2$ of Def. 1

Require: Colored Kripke structure M
Ensure: Relations $Masked$ and $RemoveR$ satisfy condition $B.2$ of Def. 1
 1: **for all** $s_2 \in \mathcal{F}$ **do**
 2:     $Masked(s_2) := \{s_1 \mid s_2 \in Masks(s_1)\}$
 3:     $RemoveR(s_2) := S \backslash Pre(Masked(s_2))$ {Note that all the faulty and normal states are already generated}
 4: **end for**
 5: **while** $\exists\, s_2' \in \mathcal{F}$ with $RemoveR(s_2') \neq \emptyset$ **do**
 6:     select s_2' such that $RemoveR(s_2') \neq \emptyset$
 7:     **for all** $s_1 \in RemoveR(s_2')$ **do**
 8:         **for all** $s_2 \in Pre(s_2')$ **do**
 9:             **if** $s_1 \in Masked(s_2)$ **then**
10:                 $Masked(s_2) := Masked(s_2) \backslash \{s_1\}$
11:                 **if** $Masks(s_1) \backslash \{s_2\} = \emptyset$ **then**
12:                     delete $DAGG(s_2)$
13:                 **else**
14:                     **for all** $s \in Pre(s_1)$ with $Post(s) \cap Masked(s_2) = \emptyset$ **do**
15:                         $RemoveR(s_2) := RemoveR(s_2) \cup \{s\}$
16:                     **end for**
17:                 **end if**
18:             **end if**
19:         **end for**
20:     **end for**
21:     $RemoveR(s_2') := \emptyset$
22: **end while**

Since the CTL algorithm is complete, if some structure that satisfies the CTL specification exists, then the algorithm produces it, and by Theorem 2 we obtain a program that is masking, and preserves as many faulty states as possible. That is, as a corollary of Theorem 2, the synthesis algorithm is *complete*.

4   An Example: A Memory Cell

Let us consider a memory cell that stores a bit of information and supports reading and writing. A state in this system maintains the current value of the cell ($m = i$, for $i = 0, 1$), writing allows one to change this value, and reading returns the stored value. Evidently, in this system the result of a read operation depends on the value stored in the cell. Some potential faults occur when a bit's value (say 1) unexpectedly loses its charge and it turns into another value (say 0). *Redundancy* can be employed to deal with this situation, using for instance three memory bits instead of one. Also, a variable v, that indicates the value that the user wants to write (i.e., $v = 0$, $v = 1$ or $v = \bot$, the latter being the case in which the system is "idle" with respect to writing) is added to the model.

Writing operations are performed simultaneously on the three bits, whereas a reading returns the value that is repeated at least twice in the memory bits.

Each state in the model is described by variables r_i and w_i which record the last writing operation performed and the actual reading in the state. Each state also has three bits, described by boolean variables c_0, c_1 and c_2. The requirements on this system (init-spec $\wedge$ normal-spec) can be specified in dCTL-, as follows:

(1) $c_0 \leftrightarrow c_1 \wedge c_0 \leftrightarrow c_2$. In the initial state the three bits contain the same value.
(2) $\mathbf{O}((c_0 \wedge c_1 \wedge c_2) \vee (\neg c_0 \wedge \neg c_1 \wedge \neg c_2))$. A safety property of the system: the three bits should coincide.
(3) $\mathbf{O}((r_0 \rightarrow w_0) \wedge (r_1 \rightarrow w_1))$. The value read from the cell ought to coincide with the last writing performed.
(4) $\mathsf{AG}(w_0 \equiv \neg w_1)$. If a zero has been written, then w_1 is false and vice versa.
(5) $\mathsf{AG}(w_0 \; \mathcal{U} \; w_1) \wedge (w_1 \; \mathcal{U} \; w_0)$. Variable w_1 only changes when w_0 becomes true, and vice versa.
(6) $\mathsf{AG}(r_0 \equiv (\neg c_0 \wedge \neg c_1) \vee (\neg c_0 \wedge \neg c_2) \vee (\neg c_1 \wedge \neg c_2))$. The reading of a 0 corresponds to the value read in the majority.
(7) $\mathsf{AG}(r_1 \equiv (c_0 \wedge c_1) \vee (c_0 \wedge c_2) \vee (c_1 \wedge c_2))$. The reading of a 1 corresponds to the value read in the majority.
(8) $\mathsf{AG}(v = 1 \rightarrow \mathsf{AX}(w_1 \wedge v = \bot \wedge c_0 \wedge c_1 \wedge c_2))$. If the user wants to write 1, then in the next step the memory will be setup to one.
(9) $\mathsf{AG}(v = 0 \rightarrow \mathsf{AX}(w_0 \wedge v = \bot \wedge \neg c_0 \wedge \neg c_1 \wedge \neg c_2))$. Similar to the previous, but for 0.
(10) $\mathsf{AG}(v = \bot \rightarrow \mathsf{AX}(v = 1 \vee v = 0 \vee v = \bot))$. At any moment the user may decide to write a value.

Besides these formulas, one may add additional constraints, e.g., indicating that atomic steps (including faults) change bits by one. These constraints are straightforward to capture in CTL.

Let us now illustrate how our synthesis approach works on this example. Fig. 1 shows the partial tableau generated by Alg. 1 for this problem. *And*-nodes and *Or*-nodes are shown as rectangles and rounded corner rectangles, respectively. For the sake of brevity, we put only the relevant information inside each box. Initially, a tableau is built using Alg. 1, employing the rules α and β for CTL and dCTL- formulas until every node in the tableau has at least one successor. The tableau contains a fault injection part, generated from the *And*-node in the second level of the tableau. This *FOr*-node is labeled identically as its *And*-node predecessor. From this *FOr*-node we generate all possible faults from deontic formula violations. Particularly, this node has O_{c_0}, O_{c_1}, and O_{c_2}, deontic propositional variables, expressing that c_0, c_1, and c_2 should be true there, which is the case in this node. Now, we start to consider those cases in which an obligation might be violated. Following Alg. 2, we negate one-by-one these deontic propositional variables and check on-the-fly whether it is possible to mask these faulty states using Alg. 3. We generated three faulty *And*-nodes (for the sake of brevity, just two of them are drawn) from the *FOr*-node with similar information to it except for the new negated propositional variable. The first *FAnd*-node successor introduces $\neg c_0$ violating O_{c_0}. The second and third *FAnd*-nodes introduce $\neg c_1$ and $\neg c_2$ violating O_{c_1} and O_{c_2}, respectively. Every time a new faulty *FAnd*-node is created, we check whether it can be masked. For the

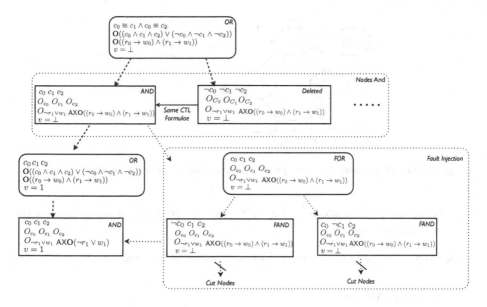

Fig. 1. Partial tableau for a Memory Cell

case of the $FAnd$-node which contains $\neg c_0$ (say f_0), Alg. 3 checks whether this $FAnd$-node can be masked. Similarly for the other $FAnd$-nodes. We continue the process of negating deontic propositional variables from these faulty And-nodes. As a successor of f_0, we obtain the same information of f_0 with $\neg c_1$. Thus, we have that O_{c_0} and O_{c_1} are violated. Our algorithm cuts out these nodes because they cannot be masked. Similar results are obtained for the other combinations. Moreover, for each masked $FAnd$-node f, a (recovery) transition is added from it to each successor of $Masks(f)$ in case that we can reach a normal successor using the rules of the tableau. Notice that faults introduced change a bit and keep the bits unchanged during the recovery process. After that, since all the faulty nodes that can be masked were generated, we check condition $B.2$ of the simulation relation by using Alg. 4. This process may also cut out other faulty nodes: those which exhibit normal behavior which is not the behavior of the correct part of the system. Finally, we are ready to extract the fault-tolerant program from the tableau using the unfolding process (see Section 3). Fig. 2 shows the transition diagram of the program extracted from the structure in Fig. 1. For the sake of simplicity, the program does not include all the masked faults (these are similar to those shown in the program).

This program was generated considering that faults are computed from deontic operators automatically, only considering some basic operations on the data structures of the states (in this case bits). Other approaches [1,12,2] require faults to be given as input of the synthesis, e.g., as special actions specified as guarded commands. Our synthesis method can be straightforwardly adapted to consider fault specifications given by the user, capturing these as CTL formulas. For example, we can add the following formula in the memory cell example:

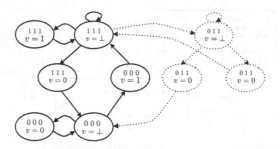

Fig. 2. Part of the fault-tolerant program extracted from the structure in figure 1

(11) $\mathsf{AG}(c_i \wedge v = \bot \rightarrow \mathsf{AX}(v = \bot \wedge \neg c_i))$, for $i = \{0, 1, 2\}$, at some point a bit may lose its charge.

Notice that sentence (11) is covered in our synthesis process.

5   Related Work

Various approaches have been proposed for synthesis of reactive systems from temporal logic specifications. The initial work was presented by Emerson and Clarke [7]. Their synthesis method was based on a decision procedure for checking the satisfiability of a CTL temporal logic specification. With respect to automated synthesis of fault-tolerant systems, Attie, Arora, and Emerson [2] presented an algorithm for synthesizing fault-tolerant programs from CTL specifications, based on a tableau method defined by Emerson and Clarke in [7]. One main difference with our work is that we use deontic operators to distinguish between good and bad system's behavior, while in [2] the abnormal behavior is captured by means of faulty actions. Another difference with our work is that in [2] safety properties only need to hold after faults or through fail-free paths, which implies that the semantics of CTL has to be adapted to cope with this condition. Another important stream of work is presented in [5]. Therein, Unity style programs are developed, the Unity logic is used to specify programs and to state fault-tolerant properties. Moreover, only a finite number of faults are allowed. It is important to notice that a main difference between that work and our approach is that our synthesized programs preserve *all* safety and liveness properties of the non-faulty part of the obtained program, while both [5] and [2] preserve only the properties explicitly stated in the specification.

6   Conclusions

We have presented an approach to synthesizing fault-tolerant components from dCTL- specifications. dCTL- is a branching time temporal logic equipped with deontic operators, which is especially designed for fault-tolerant component specification. We believe this logic is better suited for fault-tolerance specification, and therefore synthesizing fault-tolerant implementations from dCTL- specifications is relevant. In order to capture fault-tolerance, we use an approach based on defining appropriate (bi)simulation relations, describing the relationship that must hold between a system specification and its fault-tolerant implementation. Our mechanism for synthesis is then based on combining decision procedures for the satisfiability of dCTL- temporal formulas, with (bi)simulation algorithms for checking a user required level of fault-tolerance. Here, we have dealt with masking tolerance, but our approach can be extended to other kinds of fault-tolerance, if these are captured via simulation relations.

Acknowledgements. The authors would like to thank the anonymous referees for their helpful comments. This work was partially supported by a Fellowship from IBM Canada, in support of the Automotive Partnership Canada funded project NECSIS; by the Argentinian Agency for Scientific and Technological Promotion (ANPCyT), through grants PICT PAE 2007 No. 2772, PICT 2010 No. 1690 and PICT 2010 No. 2611; and by the MEALS project (EU FP7 programme, grant agreement No. 295261).

References

1. Kulkarni, S.S., Arora, A.: Automating the Addition of Fault-Tolerance. In: Joseph, M. (ed.) FTRTFT 2000. LNCS, vol. 1926, pp. 82–93. Springer, Heidelberg (2000)
2. Attie, P.C., Arora, A., Emerson, E.A.: Synthesis of fault-tolerant concurrent programs. ACM Trans. Program. Lang. Syst. 26(1) (2004)
3. Baier, C., Katoen, J.-P.: Principles of Model Checking. The MIT Press (2008)
4. Bernardeschi, C., Fantechi, A., Gnesi, S.: Model checking fault tolerant systems. Softw. Test., Verif. Reliab. 12(4) (2002)
5. Bonakdarpour, B., Kulkarni, S., Abujarad, F.: Symbolic synthesis of masking fault-tolerant distributed programs. Distributed Computing 25(1) (2012)
6. Castro, P.F., Kilmurray, C., Acosta, A., Aguirre, N.: dCTL: A Branching Time Temporal Logic for Fault-Tolerant System Verification. In: Barthe, G., Pardo, A., Schneider, G. (eds.) SEFM 2011. LNCS, vol. 7041, pp. 106–121. Springer, Heidelberg (2011)
7. Clarke, E.M., Emerson, E.A.: Design and synthesis of synchronization skeletons using branching-time temporal logic. In: Kozen, D. (ed.) Logic of Programs 1981. LNCS, vol. 131, pp. 52–71. Springer, Heidelberg (1982)
8. Demasi, R., Castro, P.F., Maibaum, T.S.E., Aguirre, N.: Characterizing Fault-Tolerant Systems by Means of Simulation Relations. In: Johnsen, E.B., Petre, L. (eds.) IFM 2013. LNCS, vol. 7940, pp. 428–442. Springer, Heidelberg (2013)
9. Ebnenasir, A., Kulkarni, S., Arora, A.: FTSyn: a framework for automatic synthesis of fault-tolerance. STTT 10(5) (2008)
10. Gärtner, F.: Fundamentals of Fault-Tolerant Distributed Computing in Asynchronous Environments. ACM Comput. Surv. 31(1) (1999)
11. Henzinger, M.R., Henzinger, T.A., Kopke, P.W.: Computing Simulations on Finite and Infinite Graphs. In: Proc. of FOCS (1995)
12. Kulkarni, S., Ebnenasir, A.: Automated Synthesis of Multitolerance. In: Proc. of DSN (2004)
13. Lamport, L., Merz, S.: Specifying and Verifying Fault-Tolerant Systems. In: Langmaack, H., de Roever, W.-P., Vytopil, J. (eds.) FTRTFT 1994 and ProCoS 1994. LNCS, vol. 863, pp. 41–76. Springer, Heidelberg (1994)

Verification of a Dynamic Management Protocol for Cloud Applications

Rim Abid[1,3], Gwen Salaün[2,3], Francesco Bongiovanni[1], and Noel De Palma[1]

[1] UJF, Grenoble, France
{Francesco.Bongiovanni,Noel.Depalma}@imag.fr
[2] Grenoble INP, France
[3] Inria Rhône-Alpes, Grenoble, France
{Rim.Abid,Gwen.Salaun}@inria.fr

Abstract. Cloud applications are composed of a set of interconnected software components distributed over several virtual machines. There is a need for protocols that can dynamically reconfigure such distributed applications. In this paper, we present a novel protocol, which is able to resolve dependencies in these applications, by (dis)connecting and starting/stopping components in a specific order. These virtual machines interact through a publish-subscribe communication media and reconfigure themselves upon demand in a decentralised fashion. Designing such protocols is an error-prone task. Therefore, we decided to specify the protocol with the LNT value-passing process algebra and to verify it using the model checking tools available in the CADP toolbox. As a result, the introduction of formal techniques and tools help to deeply revise the protocol, and these improvements have been taken into account in the corresponding Java implementation.

1 Introduction

Cloud computing is a new programming paradigm that emerged a few years ago, which aims at delivering resources and software applications over a network (such as the Internet). Cloud computing leverages hosting platforms based on virtualization and promotes a new software licensing and billing model based on the *pay-per-use* concept. For service providers, this means the opportunity to develop, deploy, and sell cloud applications worldwide without having to invest upfront in expensive IT infrastructure. Cloud applications are distributed applications that run on different virtual machines (*a.k.a.*, Infrastructure as a Service, IaaS). Therefore, to deploy their applications, cloud users need first to instantiate several virtual machines. Moreover, during the application time life, some management operations may be required, such as instantiating new virtual machines, replicating some of them for load balancing purposes, destroying or replacing virtual machines, etc.

Existing protocols [6, 8, 19] mainly focus on self-deployment issues where a model of the application (virtual machines, components, ports, and bindings) to be deployed exists and guides the configuration process. This approach works fine

D. Van Hung and M. Ogawa (Eds.): ATVA 2013, LNCS 8172, pp. 178–192, 2013.

only with specific applications where the application does not need to be changed after deployment. Unfortunately, this is not the case in the cloud, where most applications need to be reconfigured for integrating new requirements, scaling on-demand, or performing failure recovery. Therefore, cloud users need protocols that are not limited to deploying applications but can also work, as automatically as possible, in all the situations where changes have to be applied on to a running application. Such reconfiguration tasks are far from trivial, particularly when some architectural invariants (*e.g.*, a started component cannot be connected to a stopped component) must be preserved at each step of the protocol application.

In this paper, we first present a novel protocol which aims at (re)configuring distributed applications in cloud environments. These applications consist of interconnected software components hosted on several virtual machines (VMs). A deployment manager guides the reconfiguration tasks by instantiating new VMs or destroying existing ones. After instantiation, each VM tries to satisfy its required services (ports) by binding its components to other components providing these services. When a VM receives a destruction request from the deployment manager, that VM unbinds and stops its components. In order to (un)bind/start/stop components, VMs communicate together through a publish-subscribe communication media. As an example, for connecting one component hosted on a VM to another component hosted on another VM, the second VM must send its IP address to the first one for binding purposes.

Designing such protocols is a complicated task because they involve a high degree of parallelism and it is very difficult to anticipate all execution scenarios, which is necessary to avoid unexpected erroneous behaviours in the protocol. Hence, we decided to use formal techniques and tools for ensuring that the protocol satisfies certain key properties. More precisely, we specified the protocol in LOTOS NT (LNT) [4], which is an improved version of LOTOS [11]. The main difference between LOTOS and LNT is that LNT relies on an imperative-like specification language that makes its writing and understanding much simpler. For verification purposes, we used more than 600 hand-crafted examples (application model and reconfiguration scenario) and checked on them 35 identified temporal properties that the protocol must respect during its application. For each example, we generated the Labelled Transition System (LTS) model from the LNT specification and verified all the properties on it using model checking tools available in the CADP toolbox [9].

These verification techniques helped us to improve the protocol. For instance, in an initial version of the protocol, the component start-up/shutdown was guided by a centralised deployment manager. We observed an explosion in terms of states/transitions in the corresponding LTSs, even for simple examples involving few VMs. This was due to an overhead of messages transmitted to and from the deployment manager, which was supposed to keep track of all modifications in each VM to possibly start/stop components. We proposed a decentralised version of the protocol for avoiding this problem, where each VM is in charge of starting and stopping its own components. We also detected a major bug in the VM destruction process. Originally, when it was required to stop a component, it was stopped before the components bound to it. This typically violates some architectural invariants (*e.g.*, a started component cannot be connected to a stopped component) and impedes the robustness level expected from the protocol. We corrected this issue by stopping properly components, which required a deep revision of the protocol. Thus, in the current version of the protocol, when a component must be stopped, it requests to all the components connected to it to unbind and once it is done, it can finally stop.

The rest of this paper is structured as follows. In Section 2, we present the reconfiguration protocol and show how it works on some concrete applications. In Section 3, we present the LNT specification of the protocol and its verification using CADP. We also comment on some experimental results and problems found. We discuss related work in Section 4 and we conclude in Section 5.

2 Dynamic Management Protocol

2.1 Application Model

Distributed applications in the cloud are composed of interconnected software components hosted on virtual machines. A component exports services that it is willing to provide and imports required services. Ports are typed and match when they share the same type, *i.e.*, an import for being satisfied requires an export with the same type. For effectively using a service, a component has to bind its import to an export with the same type. A component can import a service from a component hosted on the same machine (local binding) or hosted on another machine (remote binding). An import can be either mandatory or optional. Unlike optional imports, mandatory imports represent the services required by the component to be functional. A component has two states, started and stopped. Initially a component is in a stopped state. A component can be started when all its mandatory imports are bound to started components. Reversely, a started component must stop when at least one partner component connected to a mandatory import is required to stop.

An example of application model is given in Figure 1. This application consists of two VMs, both hosting two components. We can also see on this figure how imports and exports as well as their optional/mandatory parameter are described, and how bindings can be achieved on ports with the same type.

2.2 Protocol Participants

The management protocol involves three kinds of participants as presented in Figure 2. The deployment manager (DM) guides the application reconfiguration by successively instantiating and destroying VMs. Each VM in the distributed application is equipped with a configuration agent (agent for short in the rest of this paper) that is in charge of (dis)connecting bindings and starting/stopping components upon reception of VM instantiation/destruction reconfiguration operations from the DM. Communications between VMs are carried out thanks

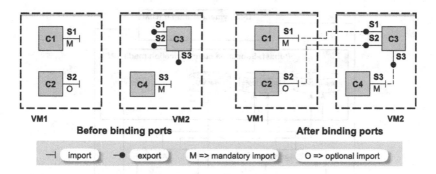

Fig. 1. Example of application model

to a publish-subscribe communication media (PS). The PS is equipped with two topics[1]: (i) an export topic where a component subscribes its imports and publishes its exports, and (ii) an import topic where a component subscribes its exports and publishes its imports (we show in Section 2.3 why this double subscription/publication is required). The PS also contains a list of buffers used to store messages exchanged between agents. When a new VM is instantiated, a buffer for that VM is added to the PS. When an existing machine is destroyed, its buffer is removed from the PS.

2.3 Protocol Description

We now explain how the protocol works and we illustrate with several simple scenarios. Once a VM is instantiated, the agent is in charge of starting all the local components. When a component does not have any import or only optional ones, it can start immediately. Otherwise, each mandatory import requires an export (local or remote) with the same type. The PS is used to resolve compatible dependencies. When an import is bound to an available compatible export, it can be started only after the partner component has been started. The PS is also used to exchange this start-up information between the two VMs involved in a same binding.

Let us focus on two concrete scenarios (Fig. 3) for deploying an application composed of two VMs: in the first scenario we instantiate VM1 and then VM2, whereas they are instantiated in the other way round in the second scenario. These scenarios help to understand how the PS is used for resolving port dependencies and start/stop components.

In the first scenario, when VM1 is instantiated, the Apache component requires a mandatory service whose type is Workers. Therefore, it subscribes to the export topic (1) and then publishes its import to the import topic (2). The PS receives that message from the VM1 agent, checks the import topic, and does not find a provider for the Workers service: the publication message is deleted.

---

[1] A topic is a logical channel where messages are published and subscribers to a topic receive messages published on that topic.

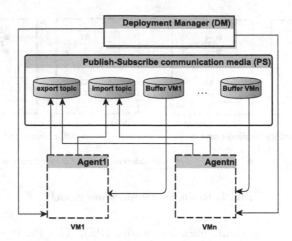

Fig. 2. Protocol participants

VM2 is then instantiated. The Tomcat component does not have any import and can therefore be started immediately (3). It provides an export with type Workers, so it subscribes this export to the import topic (4) and publishes it to the export topic (5). The start-up information is also sent to the PS. The PS receives that message from the VM2 agent, checks and finds that the Apache component hosted on VM1 has required this service (it has subscribed to the export topic). Hence, a message with binding details and Tomcat's state is added to VM1 buffer (6). Upon reception of this message, the Apache component is bound to the Tomcat component (7) and the VM1 agent starts the Apache component (8). The application is fully operational.

In the second scenario, when VM2 is instantiated, the Tomcat component does not have any import and is therefore started immediately (1). It provides an export with type Workers, so it subscribes this export to the import topic (2) and publishes it to the export topic (3). The PS receives that message from the VM2 agent, checks and does not find any component that requires Workers: the publication message is deleted. When VM1 is instantiated, the Apache component requires a mandatory service whose type is Workers. Therefore, it subscribes to the export topic (4) and publishes its import to the import topic (5). The PS receives that message from the VM1 agent, checks the import topic, and finds that Tomcat has provided the Workers service (it has subscribed to the import topic). The PS notifies VM2 that there is an Apache hosted on VM1 that needs Workers (6). VM2 receives the notification message, so it publishes Tomcat's export and state, that is started (7). The PS forwards this information to the VM1 agent (8), and the Apache component can be bound to the Tomcat component (9) and started (10).

Another goal of this protocol is to properly stop components when a VM is destroyed. In that case, all the components hosted on that VM need to be stopped as well as all components bound to them on mandatory imports (components bound on optional imports just need to unbind themselves). If a component does

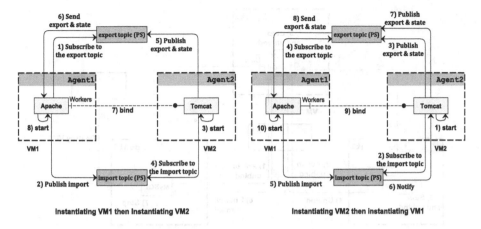

Fig. 3. Examples of VM instantiation scenario

not provide any service (there is no component connected to it), it can immediately stop. Otherwise, it cannot stop before all partner components connected to it have unbound themselves. To do so, the component is unsubscribed from the import topic and then for each export, messages are sent to all components subscribed to that export requiring them to unbind (hence stop if they are bound on mandatory imports). Then the component waits until all components bound to it disconnect and inform the component through the PS. When the component is notified that all components connected to it have effectively unbound, it can stop itself. The component shutdown implies a backward propagation of "ask to unbind" messages and, when this first propagation ends (on components with no exports or only optional imports), a second forward propagation "unbind confirmed" starts to let the components know that the disconnection has been actually achieved.

We present in Figure 4 an example of application containing three VMs where VM3 receives a destruction request from the DM. VM3 hosts the MySQL component that provides a service imported by the Tomcat component, and thus cannot be stopped before Tomcat. Therefore, it unsubscribes from the import topic and sends a message to the PS asking to unbind the Tomcat component. The PS receives this message, transmits it to VM2 hosting Tomcat, that is subscribed to the import topic (1). Once VM2 receives this message, it cannot stop Tomcat because Apache is bound to it. VM2 sends a message to the PS asking to unbind Apache (2). Once VM1 receives the message, Apache does not provide any service so it is immediately stopped and unbound (3). VM2 then receives a message from the PS informing it that Apache has been unbound (4). Tomcat has no component bound to it now, so it is stopped and unbound from MySQL (5). VM3 receives a message from the PS informing it that Tomcat is no longer bound to it (6) and MySQL is finally stopped (7).

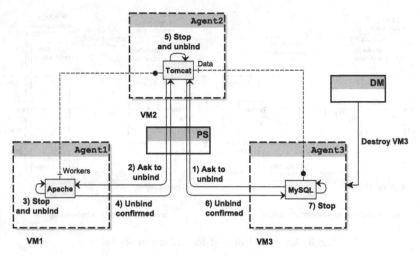

Fig. 4. Example of VM destruction scenario

3   Specification and Verification

We specified the protocol in LNT [4], one of the input languages of CADP [9]. LNT is an improved version of LOTOS. We chose this language because it has the adequate expressiveness for the problem at hand and its user-friendly notation simplifies the specification writing. Moreover, we rely on the state-of-the-art verification tools provided by CADP to check that the protocol works correctly and as expected. CADP is a verification toolbox dedicated to the design, analysis, and verification of asynchronous systems consisting of concurrent processes interacting via message passing. The toolbox contains many tools that can be used to make different analysis such as simulation, model checking, equivalence checking, compositional verification, test case generation, or performance evaluation.

In the rest of this section, we present the specification of the protocol in LNT, its verification using the CADP model checker (Evaluator), some experimental results, and problems detected and corrected during the verification process. It is worth noting that since these techniques and tools work on finite state spaces only, although dynamic reconfiguration may apply infinitely, we use only finite models and scenarios for verification purposes in this section.

3.1   Specification in LNT

The specification can be divided into three parts: data types (200 lines), functions (800 lines), and processes (1,200 lines). Most processes are generated for each input application model[2], because a part of the LNT code depends on the number of VMs and on their identifiers. Therefore, the number of lines for processes

---

[2] We developed an LNT code generator in Python for automating this task.

grows with the number of VMs in the application model. We have given above
the number of lines for an example with three VMs.

Data types are used to describe the application model (VMs, components, ports)
and the communication model (messages, buffers, and topics). We show below a
few examples of data types. An application model (TModel) consists of a set of
virtual machines (TVM). Each VM has an identifier (TID) and a set of components
(TSoftware).

```
type TModel is set of TVM end type
type TVM is tvm (idvm: TID, cs: TSoftware) end type
type TSoftware is set of TComponent end type
```

Functions apply on to data expressions and define all the computations necessary for reconfiguration purposes (*e.g.*, changing the state of a component,
extracting/checking information in import/export topics, adding/retrieving messages from buffers, etc.). Let us show an example of function that aims at removing the oldest message from a FIFO buffer. This function takes as input a
buffer (TBuffer) that is composed of an identifier (TID) and a list of messages
(TMessage). If the buffer is empty, nothing happens. When the buffer is not
empty, the first message is removed.

```
function remove (q: TBUFFER): TBUFFER is
   case q in
      var name:TID, hd: TMessage, tl: TQueue in
         | tbuffer(name,nil)          -> return tbuffer(name,nil)
         | tbuffer(name,cons(hd,tl)) -> return tbuffer(name,tl)
   end case
end function
```

Processes are used to specify the different participants of the protocol (a deployment manager, a publish-subscribe communication media, and an agent per
VM). Each participant is specified as an LNT process and involves two kinds of
actions, that are either interactions with other processes or actions to tag specific
moments of the protocol execution such as the VM instantiation, the effective
binding/unbinding of an import to an export, the component start-up/shutdown,
the destruction of a VM, etc.

   For illustration purposes, we give an example of main process involving three
VMs. This process describes the parallel composition (**par** in LNT followed by
a set of synchronization messages) of the protocol participants. We can see that
all the agents do not interact directly together and evolve independently from
one another. VM agents interact together through the PS. The DM is aware
of the VMs existing in the system (parameter **appli**). Each agent is identified
using the VM name, and the PS is initialised with a buffer per VM and two
topics for imports/exports (ListBuffers). Each process also comes with an
alphabet corresponding to the actions belonging to its behaviour. For instance,
the DM defines actions for VM creation and destruction (INSTANTIATEVMi and

DESTROYVM, resp.). Each agent defines actions for port binding (BINDCOMPO), for starting a component (STARTCOMPO), for stopping a component (STOPCOMPO), etc., as well as interactions with the PS (AGENTtoPSi when sending a message to the PS and PStoAGENTi when receiving a message from it). All these actions are used for analysing the protocol as we will see in the next subsection.

```
process MAIN [INSTANTIATEVM1:any, DESTROYVM:any, STARTCOMPO:any,..] is
   par INSTANTIATEVM1, ..., INSTANTIATEVM3, DESTROYVM in
      DM [INSTANTIATEVM1, ..., INSTANTIATEVM3, DESTROYVM] (appli)
   ||
      par AGENTtoPS1, PStoAGENT3, ... in
         par
            Agent[INSTANTIATEVM1, AGENTtoPS1, PStoAGENT1,
                  DESTROYVM, STARTCOMPO, BINDCOMPO, STOPCOMPO,
                  UNBINDCOMPO] (vm1)
            ||
            Agent[...] (vm2)
            ||
            Agent[...] (vm3)
         end par
      ||
         PS[AGENTtoPS1, ..., PStoAGENT3] (!?ListBuffers)
      end par
   end par
end process
```

3.2   Verification Using CADP

To verify the protocol, we have first identified and specified 35 properties in MCL [15], the temporal logic used in CADP. MCL is an extension of alternation-free μ-calculus with regular expressions, data-based constructs, and fairness operators. We distinguish properties dedicated to start-up scenarios (Prop. 1 and 2 below for instance), destruction scenarios (Prop. 4), and mixed scenarios (Prop. 3). All these properties aim at verifying different parts of the protocol. Some of them focus on the protocol behaviour for checking for example that final objectives are fulfilled (Prop. 1 below) or progress/ordering constraints respected (Prop. 3 and 4). Other properties guarantee that architectural invariants for the application being reconfigured are always satisfied (Prop. 2).

For each application model and reconfiguration scenario taken from our dataset of examples, we generate an LTS by applying the LNT specification to this example and generating all the possible executions using CADP exploration tools. Finally, we use the Evaluator model checker that automatically says whether these properties are verified or not on that LTS. When a bug is detected by model checking tools, it is identified with a counterexample (a sequence of actions violating the property). Let us present some concrete properties verified on the application model presented in Figure 4:

1. All components are eventually started.

   (μX . (< **true** > **true and** [**not** "STARTCOMPO !Apache !VM1"] X))
      and
      . . .
      and
   (μX . (< **true** > **true and** [**not** "STARTCOMPO !MySQL !VM3"] X))

   This property is automatically generated from the application model because it depends on the name of all VMs and components hosted on each VM.

2. A component cannot be started before the component it depends on for mandatory imports.

   [
      true* . "STARTCOMPO !Apache !VM1" .
      true* . "STARTCOMPO !Tomcat !VM2"
   ] **false**

   The Apache component is connected to the Tomcat component on a mandatory import, therefore we will never find a sequence where Apache is started before Tomcat. This property is automatically generated from the application model because it depends on the component and VM names in the application model.

3. There is no sequence where an import (mandatory or optional) is bound twice without an unbind in between.

   [**true*** .
      "BINDCOMPO !Apache !WORKERS" .
      (**not** "UNBINDCOMPO !Apache !VM1")* .
      "BINDCOMPO !Apache !WORKERS"
   ] **false**

   When a component is connected to another component through an import, it cannot be bound again except if it is stopped and unbound before.

4. A component hosted on a VM eventually stops after that VM receives a destruction request from the DM.

   (< **true*** . {DESTROYVM ?vm:String} .
      true* . {STOPCOMPO ?cid:String !vm} > **true**)

   This property does not depend on the application. Parameters can be related in MCL by using variables in action parameters (*e.g.*, vm for the virtual machine identifier). This property shows the data-based features that are available in MCL.

3.3   Experiments

Experiments were conducted on more than 600 hand-crafted examples on a Pentium 4 (2.5GHz, 8GB RAM) running Linux. For each example, the reconfiguration protocol takes as input the application and a specific scenario (a sequence of instantiate/destroy VM operations). The corresponding LTS is generated using CADP exploration tools by enumerating all the possible executions of the system. Finally, the verification tools of the CADP toolbox are called, providing as result a set of diagnostics (true or false) as well as counterexamples if some verifications fail. Let us note that for validating the protocol we used a large variety of examples, ranging from simple ones to pathological models and scenarios in order to check boundary cases.

Table 1 summarizes some of the numbers obtained on illustrative examples of our dataset. The application model used as input to our protocol is characterised using the number of virtual machines (vm), components (co), imports (imp), exports (exp), and reconfiguration operations (op). Then we give the size of the LTS before and after minimization (*wrt.* a strong bisimulation relation). The last column gives the time to execute the whole process (LTS generation and minimization on the one hand, and properties checking on the other).

It is worth observing that the size of LTSs and the time required for generating those LTSs increase with the size of the application, particularly with the number of VMs and the number of ports that can be connected: the more VMs and ports, the more parallelism in the system. Increasing the number of reconfiguration operations yields more complicated scenarios, and this also increases the LTS size and generation time. Let us look at examples 0219, 0222, and 0227 in Table 1 for instance. When we slightly increase the number of components and ports in the application, we see how LTS sizes and analysis time (generation and verification) gradually grow. We can make a similar statement when comparing examples 0227 and 0228. These two examples are exactly the same, but one more reconfiguration is achieved in 0228, resulting in a noticeable grow in the corresponding LTS size and analysis time. Example 0453 shows how this time can take up to several hours. Fortunately, analysing huge systems (with potentially many VMs) is not the most important criterion during the verification of the protocol. Indeed, most issues are usually found on small applications describing pathological reconfiguration cases.

Table 1. Experimental results

	Size					LTS (states/transitions)		Time (m:s)	
	vm	co	imp	exp	op	raw	minimized	LTS gen.	Verif.
0047	2	3	1	2	4	3,489/6,956	836/1,472	0:23	0:15
0219	3	3	2	2	5	28,237/68,255	2,775/6,948	0:35	0:48
0222	3	4	4	4	5	622,592 /1,416,167	10,855/32,901	12:15	2:40
0227	3	6	9	7	5	783,784/1,484,508	15,334/45,812	21:21	3:45
0228	3	6	9	7	6	802,816 / 1,629,118	17,923/54,143	29:25	4:10
0453	4	8	7	5	8	1,643,248 /2,498,564	68,468/227,142	153:12	28:22

3.4 Problems Found

The specification and verification of the protocol using model checking techniques enabled us to revise and improve several parts of the protocol. Beyond correcting several very specific issues in the protocol (*e.g.*, adding some acknowledgement messages after effectively binding ports), we will comment in this section on two important issues we found out during the verification steps and that were corrected in the latest version of the protocol (the one presented in this paper), both in the specification and implementation.

In the initial version of the protocol, the component start-up/shutdown was guided by a centralised DM. More precisely, the DM kept track of the current state (bindings and component states) for each VM. To do so, each VM sends messages to the DM whenever a change is made in its VM, *e.g.*, a stopped component is started. As a consequence, the DM has an overall view of the current state of the system and can send messages to VMs in order to trigger a component start-up/shutdown (when dependencies and other component states permit that). An important drawback of this centralised version is that it induces an overhead of messages transmitted to and from the DM. This was observed during our experiments analysing the size of the corresponding state spaces: some quite simple examples resulted in huge LTSs. This issue was solved by proposing a decentralised version of the protocol, where the DM is not in charge of starting and stopping components any more. This task is delegated to the VM agents. This avoids additional, unnecessary messages exchanged between agents and the DM. The decentralised version of the protocol presents several advantages: more parallelism, better performance in the corresponding implementation of the protocol, and simplification in terms of number of communications (smaller LTSs).

We also detected a major bug in the way VMs are destroyed. Originally, when it was required to stop a component, it was stopped before the components bound to it. Stopping components in this order typically violates the consistency of the component composition and well-formedness architectural invariants. This may result for instance in started components connected to and therefore submitting requests to stopped components. This problem was detected thanks to a property stating that "*a component cannot be started and connected through an import (mandatory or optional) to another component, if that component is not started*". In many cases, we observe that this property was not satisfied, particularly for application models and reconfiguration scenarios requiring to stop components in sequence across several VMs after reception of a VM destruction request. We corrected this issue by stopping properly components. This required a deep revision of the protocol. Thus, in the current version of the protocol, when a component must stop, it requests to all components connected to it to unbind and once it is done, it can finally stop. This implies first a backward propagation along components bound on mandatory imports. Once this first propagation stops, we start a forward propagation during which components are actually stopped and indicate to their partners that they have just stopped and unbound. This double propagation, as presented in Section 2.3, is necessary for preserving the component architecture consistency and for avoiding that started components can keep on using stopped components.

4   Related Work

First of all, let us mention some related papers [10, 5, 16] where are presented languages and configuration protocols for distributed applications in the cloud. [5] adopts a model driven approach with extensions of the Essential Meta-Object Facility (EMOF) abstract syntax to describe a distributed application, its requirements towards the underlying execution platforms, and its architectural constraints (*e.g.*, concerning placement and collocation). The deployment works in a centralised fashion. [16] suggests an extension of SmartFrog [10] that enables an automated and optimised allocation of cloud resources for application deployment. It is based on a declarative description of the available resources and of the components building up a distributed application. Descriptions of architectures and resources are defined using the Distributed Application Description Language. This paper does not give any details concerning the deployment process.

A recent related work [8] presents a system that manages application stack configuration. It provides techniques to configure services across machines according to their dependencies, to deploy components, and to manage the life cycle of installed resources. This work presents some similarities with ours, but [8] does not care about composition consistency issues, that is, their framework does not preserve architectural invariants ensuring for instance that a started component is never connected to a stopped component.

In [12–14, 1, 20, 3, 17], the authors proposed various formal models (Darwin, Wright, etc.) in order to specify dynamic reconfiguration of component-based systems whose architectures can evolve (adding or removing components and connections) at run-time. These techniques are adequate for formally designing dynamic applications. In [12, 14] for instance, the authors show how to formally analyse behavioural models of components using the Labeled Transition System Analyser. Our focus is quite different here, because we work on a protocol whose goal is to automatically achieve these reconfiguration tasks, and to assure that this protocol respects some key properties during its application.

In [6, 7, 19], the authors present a protocol that automates the configuration of distributed applications in cloud environments. In these applications, all elements are known from the beginning (*e.g.*, numbers of VMs and components, bindings among components, etc.). Moreover, this protocol allows one to automate the application deployment, but not to modify the application at run-time. Another related work is [2], where the authors propose a robust reconfiguration protocol for an architectural assembly of software components. This work does not consider the distribution of components across several VMs, but assume they are located on a single VM.

5 Conclusion

We have presented in this paper a protocol for dynamically reconfiguring distributed cloud applications. This protocol enables one to instantiate new VMs and destroy existing VMs. Upon reception of these reconfiguration operations, VM agents connect/disconnect and start/stop components in a defined order for preserving the application consistency, which is quite complicated due to the high parallelism degree of the protocol. Therefore, we have specified and verified this protocol using the LNT specification language and the CADP toolbox, which turned out to be very convenient for modelling and analysing such protocols, see [18] for a discussion about this subject. Model checking techniques were used to verify 35 properties of interest on a large number of application models and reconfiguration scenarios. This helped to improve several parts of the protocol and to detect subtle bugs. In particular, we deeply revise the part of the protocol dedicated to the VM destruction and component shutdown. These issues have also been corrected in the corresponding Java implementation.

As far as future work is concerned, we first plan to add finer-grained reconfiguration operations in order to enable the deployment manager to not only add and remove virtual machines, but also to add and remove components on already deployed VMs. Another perspective aims at extending our protocol for handling VM failures.

Acknowledgements. This work has been supported by the OpenCloudware project (2012-2015), which is funded by the French *Fonds national pour la Société Numérique* (FSN), and is supported by *Pôles* Minalogic, Systematic, and SCS.

References

1. Allen, R., Douence, R., Garlan, D.: Specifying and Analyzing Dynamic Software Architectures. In: Astesiano, E. (ed.) ETAPS 1998 and FASE 1998. LNCS, vol. 1382, pp. 21–37. Springer, Heidelberg (1998)
2. Boyer, F., Gruber, O., Salaün, G.: Specifying and Verifying the SYNERGY Reconfiguration Protocol with LOTOS NT and CADP. In: Butler, M., Schulte, W. (eds.) FM 2011. LNCS, vol. 6664, pp. 103–117. Springer, Heidelberg (2011)
3. Cansado, A., Canal, C., Salaün, G., Cubo, J.: A Formal Framework for Structural Reconfiguration of Components under Behavioural Adaptation. Electr. Notes Theor. Comput. Sci. 263, 95–110 (2010)
4. Champelovier, D., Clerc, X., Garavel, H., Guerte, Y., Powazny, V., Lang, F., Serwe, W., Smeding, G.: Reference Manual of the LOTOS NT to LOTOS Translator (Version 5.4). INRIA/VASY (2011)
5. Chapman, C., Emmerich, W., Galán Márquez, F., Clayman, S., Galis, A.: Software Architecture Definition for On-demand Cloud Provisioning. In: Proc. of HPDC 2010, pp. 61–72. ACM Press (2010)
6. Etchevers, X., Coupaye, T., Boyer, F., de Palma, N.: Self-Configuration of Distributed Applications in the Cloud. In: Proc. of CLOUD 2011, pp. 668–675. IEEE Computer Society (2011)

7. Etchevers, X., Coupaye, T., Boyer, F., De Palma, N., Salaün, G.: Automated Configuration of Legacy Applications in the Cloud. In: Proc. of UCC 2011, pp. 170–177. IEEE Computer Society (2011)
8. Fischer, J., Majumdar, R., Esmaeilsabzali, S.: Engage: A Deployment Management System. In: Proc. of PLDI 2012, pp. 263–274. ACM (2012)
9. Garavel, H., Lang, F., Mateescu, R., Serwe, W.: CADP 2010: A Toolbox for the Construction and Analysis of Distributed Processes. In: Abdulla, P.A., Leino, K.R.M. (eds.) TACAS 2011. LNCS, vol. 6605, pp. 372–387. Springer, Heidelberg (2011)
10. Goldsack, P., Guijarro, J., Loughran, S., Coles, A., Farrell, A., Lain, A., Murray, P., Toft, P.: The SmartFrog Configuration Management Framework. SIGOPS Oper. Syst. Rev. 43(1), 16–25 (2009)
11. ISO/IEC. LOTOS — A Formal Description Technique Based on the Temporal Ordering of Observational Behaviour. International Standard 8807, International Organization for Standardization — Information Processing Systems — Open Systems Interconnection (1989)
12. Kramer, J., Magee, J.: Analysing Dynamic Change in Distributed Software Architectures. IEE Proceedings - Software 145(5), 146–154 (1998)
13. Magee, J., Kramer, J.: Dynamic Structure in Software Architectures. In: Proc. of SIGSOFT FSE 1996, pp. 3–14. ACM (1996)
14. Magee, J., Kramer, J., Giannakopoulou, D.: Behaviour Analysis of Software Architectures. In: Proc. of WICSA 1999. IFIP Conference Proceedings, vol. 140, pp. 35–50. Kluwer (1999)
15. Mateescu, R., Thivolle, D.: A Model Checking Language for Concurrent Value-Passing Systems. In: Cuellar, J., Sere, K. (eds.) FM 2008. LNCS, vol. 5014, pp. 148–164. Springer, Heidelberg (2008)
16. Mirkovic, J., Faber, T., Hsieh, P., Malayandisamu, G., Malavia, R.: DADL: Distributed Application Description Language. USC/ISI Technical Report ISI-TR-664 (2010)
17. Salaün, G.: Generation of Service Wrapper Protocols from Choreography Specifications. In: Proc. of SEFM 2008, pp. 313–322. IEEE Computer Society (2008)
18. Salaün, G., Boyer, F., Coupaye, T., De Palma, N., Etchevers, X., Gruber, O.: An Experience Report on the Verification of Autonomic Protocols in the Cloud. ISSE 9(2), 105–117 (2013)
19. Salaün, G., Etchevers, X., De Palma, N., Boyer, F., Coupaye, T.: Verification of a Self-configuration Protocol for Distributed Applications in the Cloud. In: Proc. of SAC 2012, pp. 1278–1283. ACM Press (2012)
20. Wermelinger, M., Lopes, A., Fiadeiro, J.L.: A Graph Based Architectural (Re)configuration Language. In: Proc. of ESEC / SIGSOFT FSE 2001, pp. 21–32. ACM (2001)

Compact Symbolic Execution*

Jiri Slaby, Jan Strejček, and Marek Trtík

Masaryk University, Brno, Czech Republic
{slaby,strejcek,trtik}@fi.muni.cz

Abstract. We present a generalisation of King's symbolic execution
technique called *compact symbolic execution*. It proceeds in two steps.
First, we analyse cyclic paths in the control flow graph of a given program, independently from the rest of the program. Our goal is to compute
a so called *template* for each such a cyclic path. A template is a declarative parametric description of all possible program states, which may
leave the analysed cyclic path after any number of iterations along it. In
the second step, we execute the program symbolically with the templates
in hand. The result is a *compact* symbolic execution tree. A compact tree
always carry the same information in all its leaves as the corresponding
classic symbolic execution tree. Nevertheless, a compact tree is typically
substantially smaller than the corresponding classic tree. There are even
programs for which compact symbolic execution trees are finite while
classic symbolic execution trees are infinite.

1 Introduction

Symbolic execution [16,13] is a program analysis method originally suggested
for enhanced testing. While testing runs a program on selected input values,
symbolic execution runs the program on symbols that represent arbitrary input
values. As a result, symbolic execution explores all execution paths. On one
hand-side, this means that symbolic execution does not miss any error. On the
other hand-side, symbolic execution applied to real programs hardly ever finishes
as programs typically have a huge (or even infinite) number of execution paths.
This weakness of symbolic execution is known as *path explosion problem*. The
second weakness of symbolic execution comes from the fact that it calls SMT
solvers to decide which program paths are feasible and which are not. The SMT
queries are often formulae of theories that are hard to decide or even undecidable.
Despite the two weaknesses, there are several successful bug-finding tools based
on symbolic execution, for example KLEE [7], EXE [8], PEX [22], or SAGE [11].

This paper introduces the *compact symbolic execution* that partly solves the
path explosion problem. We build on the observation that one of the main sources
of the problem are program cycles. Indeed, many execution paths differ just in
numbers of iterations along program cycles. Hence, before we start symbolic
execution, we detect cyclic paths in the control flow graph of a given program
and we try to find a *template* for each such a cyclic path. A template is a

---

* The authors are supported by The Czech Science Foundation, grant P202/12/G061.

D. Van Hung and M. Ogawa (Eds.): ATVA 2013, LNCS 8172, pp. 193–207, 2013.

declarative parametric description (with a single parameter κ) of all possible program states produced by $\kappa \geq 0$ iterations along the cyclic path followed by any execution step leading outside the cyclic path. The target program locations of such execution steps are called *exits* of the cyclic path.

The compact symbolic execution proceeds just like the classic symbolic execution until we enter a cyclic path for which we have a template. Instead of executing the cyclic path, we can apply the template to jump directly to exits of the cyclic path. At each exit, we obtain a program state with a parameter κ. This parametric program state represents all program states reached by execution paths composed of a particular path to the cycle, κ iterations along the cycle, and the execution step leading to the exit. Symbolic execution then continues from these program states in the classic way again.

Hence, compact symbolic execution reduces the path explosion problem as it explores at once all execution paths that differ only in numbers of iterations along the cyclic paths for which we have templates. As we will see later, a price for this reduction comes in deepening the other weakness of symbolic execution: while SMT queries of standard symbolic execution are always quantifier-free, each application of a template adds one universal quantifier to the SMT queries of compact symbolic execution. Although SMT solvers fail to decide quantified queries significantly more often than queries without quantifiers, our experimental results show that this trade-off is acceptable as compact symbolic execution is able to detect more errors in programs than the classic one. Moreover, future advances in SMT solving can make the disadvantage of compact symbolic execution even smaller.

2   Basic Idea

This section presents basic ideas of compact symbolic execution. To illustrate the ideas, we use a simple program represented by the flowgraph of Figure 1(a). The program implements a standard linear search algorithm. It returns the least index i in the array A such that A[i]=x. If x is not in A at all, then the result is -1. In both cases the result is saved in the variable r. Before we describe the compact symbolic execution, we briefly recall the classic symbolic execution [16].

Classic Symbolic Execution. Symbolic execution runs a program over *symbols* representing arbitrary input values. For each input variable v, we denote a symbol passed to it as $\underline{v}$. A *program state* is a triple (l, θ, φ) consisting of a current program location l in the flowgraph, a *symbolic memory* θ, and a *path condition* φ. θ assigns to each program variable its current symbolic value, i.e. an expression over the symbols. For example, if the first instruction of a program is the assignment i:=2*n+x, then $\theta(\text{i}) = 2\underline{n} + \underline{x}$ after its execution. The path condition φ is a quantifier-free first order logic formula representing a necessary and sufficient condition on symbols to drive the execution along the currently executed path. φ is initially *true* and it can be updated at program branchings. For example, in a location with two out-edges labelled by x>n+5 and x<=n+5, we

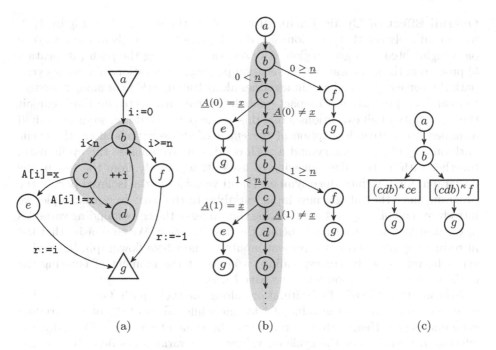

Fig. 1. (a) A flowgraph `linSrch(A,n,x)`. (b) Classic symbolic execution tree of `linSrch`. (c) Compact symbolic execution tree of `linSrch`.

instantiate the conditions with use of the current θ and we check whether the current path condition φ implies their validity. Namely, we ask for validity of implications $\varphi \to \theta(\mathbf{x}) > \theta(\mathbf{n})+5$ and $\varphi \to \theta(\mathbf{x}) \leq \theta(\mathbf{n})+5$. If the first implication is valid, the symbolic execution continues along the first branch. If the second implication is valid, the symbolic execution continues along the second branch. If none of them is valid, it means that we can follow either of the two branches. Hence, the symbolic execution forks in order to execute both branches. In this case, we update the path condition on the first branch to $\varphi \wedge \theta(\mathbf{x}) > \theta(\mathbf{n}) + 5$ and the one on the second branch to $\varphi \wedge \theta(\mathbf{x}) \leq \theta(\mathbf{n}) + 5$. Note that the whole program state is forked into two states in this case.

Due to the forks, symbolic execution is traditionally represented by a tree called *classic symbolic execution tree*. Nodes of the tree are labelled by program states computed during the execution. Edges of the tree correspond to transitions between program states labelling their end nodes. In Figure 1(b), there is a classic symbolic execution tree of the flowgraph from Figure 1(a). For readability of symbolic execution tree figures, nodes are marked only with current program locations instead of full program states. In addition, we label branching edges by instances of the corresponding branching conditions in the flowgraph. These labels allow us to reconstruct the path condition for each node in the tree: it is the conjunction of labels of all edges along the path from the root to the node. Note that contents of symbolic memories are not depicted in the figure.

Overall Effect of Cyclic Paths. If we look at the flowgraph of Figure 1(a), we immediately see that locations b, c, d and edges between them form a cyclic path highlighted by a grey region. All executions entering the path (at location b) proceed in the same way: each execution performs κ iterations along the cyclic path (for some $\kappa \geq 0$) and continues either along the edge (b, f) or along the edges (b, c) and (c, e) to leave it. Compact symbolic execution aims to effectively exploit the uniformity of all executions along this cyclic path. To do so, we need to find a unified declarative description of the *effect* of all executions along the cyclic path on a symbolic memory and a path condition. We analyse the cyclic path, together with all the edges allowing to leave it, separately from the rest of the flowgraph. First we introduce symbols for all variables in the isolated part of the program, since they all are now input variables to the part. In our example, we introduce symbols $\underline{n}, \underline{x}, \underline{i}, \underline{A}$ representing the values of the corresponding variables $\mathtt{n}, \mathtt{x}, \mathtt{i}, \mathtt{A}$ at the entry location b, before the first iteration. We emphasise that the introduced symbols do *not* represent inputs to the whole flowgraph, but rather symbolic values of the corresponding variables at the moment of entering the cyclic path at the location b via the edge (a, b).

Now we study the effect of κ iterations along the cyclic path. One can see that each iteration increases the value of $\mathtt{i}$ by one while values of the other variables keep unchanged. Hence, after κ iterations, the value of $\mathtt{i}$ is $\underline{i} + \kappa$. Formally, the effect of κ iterations of the cycle on values of all variables is described by the following *parametric symbolic memory* $\theta_*[\![\kappa]\!]$ with the parameter κ:

$$\theta_*[\![\kappa]\!](\mathtt{n}) = \underline{n}, \qquad \theta_*[\![\kappa]\!](\mathtt{x}) = \underline{x},$$
$$\theta_*[\![\kappa]\!](\mathtt{i}) = \underline{i} + \kappa, \qquad \theta_*[\![\kappa]\!](\mathtt{A}) = \underline{A}.$$

Further, we formulate a *parametric path condition* $\varphi_*[\![\kappa]\!]$ representing the path condition after κ iterations along the cyclic path. To perform all these κ iterations along the cyclic path, both conditions $\mathtt{i<n}$ and $\mathtt{A[i]!=x}$ along the path have to be valid in each of κ iterations. Therefore, the path condition after κ iterations has the form

$$\underline{i} < \underline{n} \;\wedge\; \underline{A}(\underline{i}) \neq \underline{x} \;\wedge$$
$$\wedge \; \underline{i} + 1 < \underline{n} \;\wedge\; \underline{A}(\underline{i} + 1) \neq \underline{x} \;\wedge$$
$$\vdots$$
$$\wedge \; \underline{i} + (\kappa - 1) < \underline{n} \;\wedge\; \underline{A}(\underline{i} + (\kappa - 1)) \neq \underline{x},$$

where τ-th line, $\tau \in \{0, 1, \ldots, \kappa - 1\}$, consists of two predicates which are instances of the conditions $\mathtt{i<n}$ and $\mathtt{A[i]!=x}$ respectively after τ iterations of the cyclic path, i.e. during the $(\tau + 1)$-st iteration. Unfortunately, the conjunction above is not a first order formula as its length depends on the parameter κ, whose value can be arbitrary. The conjunction can be equivalently expressed by the following universally quantified formula:

$$\forall \tau (0 \leq \tau < \kappa \rightarrow (\underline{i} + \tau < \underline{n} \wedge \underline{A}(\underline{i} + \tau) \neq \underline{x})).$$

If we now add to the formula above the obvious fact that we cannot iterate the cyclic path negative number of times (i.e. $\kappa \geq 0$), we get the resulting parametric path condition $\varphi_*[\![\kappa]\!]$ as

$$\varphi_*[\![\kappa]\!] = \kappa \geq 0 \ \wedge \ \forall \tau (0 \leq \tau < \kappa \rightarrow (\underline{i} + \tau < \underline{n} \ \wedge \ \underline{A}(\underline{i} + \tau) \neq \underline{x})).$$

Finally, we use $\theta_*[\![\kappa]\!]$ and $\varphi_*[\![\kappa]\!]$ to define symbolic memory $\theta_{bf}[\![\kappa]\!]$ and path condition $\varphi_{bf}[\![\kappa]\!]$ describing the effect of κ iterations of the cyclic path followed by leaving it through the edge (b, f), and similarly $\theta_{ce}[\![\kappa]\!], \varphi_{ce}[\![\kappa]\!]$ with the analogous information for leaving the cyclic path through the edge (c, e). As the edges $(b, f), (b, c), (c, e)$ do not modify any variable, we immediately get $\theta_{bf}[\![\kappa]\!] = \theta_{ce}[\![\kappa]\!] = \theta_*[\![\kappa]\!]$. Further, $\varphi_{bf}[\![\kappa]\!]$ and $\varphi_{ce}[\![\kappa]\!]$ are conjunctions of $\varphi_*[\![\kappa]\!]$ with the instances of the conditions on the edge (b, f) or on the edges $(b, c), (c, e)$, respectively. Hence, the path conditions $\varphi_{bf}[\![\kappa]\!], \varphi_{ce}[\![\kappa]\!]$ are defined as follows:

$$\varphi_{bf}[\![\kappa]\!] = \varphi_*[\![\kappa]\!] \ \wedge \ \underline{i} + \kappa \geq \underline{n}$$
$$\varphi_{ce}[\![\kappa]\!] = \varphi_*[\![\kappa]\!] \ \wedge \ \underline{i} + \kappa < \underline{n} \ \wedge \ \underline{A}(\underline{i} + \kappa) = \underline{x}$$

The overall effect of the considered cyclic path with its exit edges is now fully described by a so-called *template* consisting of the entry location b to the cyclic path and two triples $(f, \theta_{bf}[\![\kappa]\!], \varphi_{bf}[\![\kappa]\!])$ and $(e, \theta_{ce}[\![\kappa]\!], \varphi_{ce}[\![\kappa]\!])$, one for each exit edge from the cyclic path. Note that the triples have the same structure and meaning as program states in classic symbolic execution. The only difference is that the triples are parametrised by the parameter κ.

Compact Symbolic Execution. The template is used during *compact symbolic execution* of the program. The execution starts at the location a of the flowgraph. The *compact symbolic execution tree* initially consists of a single node labelled by the initial state $(a, \theta_I, true)$, where θ_I is the initial symbolic memory assigning to each input variable v the corresponding symbol $\underline{v}$. Now we execute the instruction i:=0 of the flowgraph edge (a, b) using the classic symbolic execution. The tree is extended with a single successor node, say u, labelled with a program state (b, θ', φ'). As we have a template for the location b, we can instantiate it instead of executing the original program. The node u gets one successor for each triple of the template. The triple $(f, \theta_{bf}[\![\kappa]\!], \varphi_{bf}[\![\kappa]\!])$ generates a successor node labelled by a program state $(f, \theta'_{bf}[\![\kappa]\!], \varphi'_{bf}[\![\kappa]\!])$. Note that we cannot use $(f, \theta_{bf}[\![\kappa]\!], \varphi_{bf}[\![\kappa]\!])$ directly as $\theta_{bf}[\![\kappa]\!], \varphi_{bf}[\![\kappa]\!]$ describe executions starting just at the entry location b, while $\theta'_{bf}[\![\kappa]\!], \varphi'_{bf}[\![\kappa]\!]$ have to reflect the effect of the executions starting at a. We create $\theta'_{bf}[\![\kappa]\!], \varphi'_{bf}[\![\kappa]\!]$ by composing $\theta_{bf}[\![\kappa]\!], \varphi_{bf}[\![\kappa]\!]$ with θ', φ'. The composition is precisely described in the following section. In our simple program, θ', φ' reflect only the effect of assignment i:=0. Thus, $\theta'_{bf}[\![\kappa]\!]$ and $\varphi'_{bf}[\![\kappa]\!]$ equal to $\theta_{bf}[\![\kappa]\!]$ and $\varphi_{bf}[\![\kappa]\!]$ respectively, where $\underline{i}$ is replaced by 0. The second triple $(e, \theta_{ce}[\![\kappa]\!], \varphi_{ce}[\![\kappa]\!])$ of the template generates the successor node labelled with a program state $(e, \theta'_{ce}[\![\kappa]\!], \varphi'_{ce}[\![\kappa]\!])$ computed analogously using the composition. The symbolic execution then continues from the locations f and e in parallel using the classic symbolic execution. The resulting compact symbolic execution tree is depicted in Figure 1(c). Observe that the two nodes introduced during template instantiation are drawn with different shape than the others. Moreover, labels of these nodes immediately indicate all paths in the flowgraph whose execution is replaced by the application of the template.

If we compare trees at Figures 1(b) and 1(c), we immediately see that the compact tree is much smaller than the classic one. In particular, the infinite path in the classic tree (highlighted by the grey region) does not appear in the compact one. However, both trees keep the same information in all their leaves. For example, the program state of the left leaf of the compact tree contains the following path condition

$$\varphi[\![\kappa]\!] \;=\; \kappa \geq 0 \,\wedge\, \forall \tau (0 \leq \tau < \kappa \,\rightarrow\, (\tau < \underline{n} \wedge \underline{A}(\tau) \neq \underline{x})) \,\wedge\, \kappa < \underline{n} \,\wedge\, \underline{A}(\kappa) = \underline{x}.$$

Let us mark all leaves on the left-hand side of the classic tree as $g_0, g_1, g_2, \ldots$ and let $\varphi_0, \varphi_1, \varphi_2, \ldots$ be the corresponding path conditions (remember, that each φ_i is the conjunction of labels along the corresponding paths in the tree) and check that φ_i is equivalent to $\varphi[\![i]\!]$ for each $i \geq 0$. For example, for $i = 1$ we have

$$\varphi_1 \;=\; 0 < \underline{n} \,\wedge\, \underline{A}(0) \neq \underline{x} \,\wedge\, 1 < \underline{n} \,\wedge\, \underline{A}(1) = \underline{x},$$
$$\varphi[\![1]\!] \;=\; 1 \geq 0 \,\wedge\, \forall \tau (0 \leq \tau < 1 \,\rightarrow\, (\tau < \underline{n} \wedge \underline{A}(\tau) \neq \underline{x})) \,\wedge\, 1 < \underline{n} \,\wedge\, \underline{A}(1) = \underline{x},$$

and hence $\varphi_1 \equiv \varphi[\![1]\!]$. Similarly, each symbolic memory of a node g_i is an instance $\theta[\![i]\!]$ of the parametrized symbolic memory in the left leaf of the compact tree. Analogous relations hold for leafs on the right-hand sides of the compact and the classic symbolic execution trees.

3   Description of the Technique

This section describes the compact symbolic execution in details. For simplicity, we consider only programs represented by a single flowgraph manipulating integer variables and read-only integer arrays. The technique can be extended to handle mutable integer arrays, other data types, and function calls.

3.1   Preliminaries

Besides the terms and notation introduced in the previous section, we use also the following terms and notation.

We write $\theta[\![\kappa]\!]$ to emphasise that κ is the set of parameters appearing in the symbolic memory θ. Similarly, we write $\varphi[\![\kappa]\!]$ to emphasise that κ is the set of parameters with free occurrences in the formula φ. We also write $s[\![\kappa]\!]$ or $(l, \theta, \varphi)[\![\kappa]\!]$, if $s = (l, \theta[\![\kappa]\!], \varphi[\![\kappa]\!])$.

A *valuation* of parameters is a function ν from a finite set of parameters to non-negative integers. By $\theta[\![\nu]\!]$, $\varphi[\![\nu]\!]$, and $s[\![\nu]\!]$ we denote a symbolic memory $\theta[\![\kappa]\!]$, a formula $\varphi[\![\kappa]\!]$, and a program state $s[\![\kappa]\!]$ respectively, where all free occurrences of each $\kappa \in \kappa$ are replaced by $\nu(\kappa)$. If $\kappa = \{\kappa\}$ is a singleton and $\nu(\kappa) = \nu$, we simply write $\theta[\![\kappa]\!], \varphi[\![\kappa]\!], s[\![\kappa]\!]$ instead of $\theta[\![\kappa]\!], \varphi[\![\kappa]\!], s[\![\kappa]\!]$ and $\theta[\![\nu]\!], \varphi[\![\nu]\!], s[\![\nu]\!]$ instead of $\theta[\![\nu]\!], \varphi[\![\nu]\!], s[\![\nu]\!]$.

If θ is a symbolic memory and φ is a formula or a symbolic expression, then $\theta\langle\varphi\rangle$ denotes φ where all occurrences of all symbols $\underline{a}$ are simultaneously replaced by $\theta(\mathsf{a})$, i.e. by the value of the corresponding variable stored in θ.

When θ_1 and θ_2 are two symbolic memories, then $\theta_1 \diamond \theta_2$ is a *composed symbolic memory* satisfying $(\theta_1 \diamond \theta_2)(\mathsf{a}) = \theta_1\langle\theta_2(\mathsf{a})\rangle$ for each variable a. Intuitively, the symbolic memory $\theta_1 \diamond \theta_2$ represents an overall effect of a code with effect θ_1 followed by a code with effect θ_2.

We define *composition of states* $s_1 = (l_1, \theta_1, \varphi_1)$ and $s_2 = (l_2, \theta_2, \varphi_2)$ to be the state $s_1 \diamond s_2 = (l_2, \theta_1 \diamond \theta_2, \varphi_1 \wedge \theta_1\langle\varphi_2\rangle)$. The composed state corresponds to the symbolic state resulting from symbolic execution of the code that produced s_1 immediately followed by the code that produced s_2.

We often use a dot-notation to denote elements of a program state s: $s.l$ denotes its current location, $s.\theta$ denotes its symbolic memory, and $s.\varphi$ denotes its path condition. Further, if u is a node of a symbolic execution tree, then $u.s$ denotes the program state labelling u and we write $u.l$, $u.\theta$, and $u.\varphi$ instead of $(u.s).l$, $(u.s).\theta$, and $(u.s).\varphi$.

Two program states s_1, s_2 are *equivalent*, written $s_1 \equiv s_2$, if $s_1.l = s_2.l$, the formula $s_1.\theta(\mathsf{a}) = s_2.\theta(\mathsf{a})$ holds for each variable a, and the formulae $s_1.\varphi$ and $s_2.\varphi$ are equivalent in the logical sense.

Considered integer programs operate in undecidable theories (like Peano arithmetic). We assume that there is a function $\mathtt{satisfiable}(\varphi)$ that returns SAT if it can prove satisfiability of φ, UNSAT if it can prove unsatisfiability of φ, and UNKNOWN otherwise.

3.2   Templates and Their Computation

We start with a formal definition of *cycle*, i.e. a cyclic path with a specified entry location and exit edges.

Definition 1 (Cycle) *Let (u, e) be an edge of a flowgraph P, $\pi = ewe$ be a cyclic path in P such that ue is not a suffix of π and all nodes in we are pairwise distinct, and let $X = \{(u_1, x_1), \ldots, (u_n, x_n)\}$ be the set of all edges of P that do not belong to the path π, but their start nodes $u_1, \ldots, u_n$ lie on π. Then $C = (\pi, e, X)$ is a cycle in P, the path π is a core of C, e is an entry location of C, all edges in X are exit edges of C, and each location x_i is called an exit location of C.*

We emphasise that the core of a cycle is a cyclic path in a graph sense. Note that a program loop can generate more independent cycles, e.g. if the loop contains interal branching or loop nesting (see [20] for more details).

A template for a cycle (π, e, X) is a pair (e, M), where M is a set containing one parametric program state for each exit edge of the cycle. A template for a given cycle can be computed by Algorithm 1. The algorithm uses a function $\mathtt{executePath}(P, \rho)$ which applies classic symbolic execution to instructions on the path ρ in the program P and returns the resulting symbolic state (u, θ, φ), where u is the last location in ρ.

Algorithm 1. computeTemplate

Input: a program P and a cycle (π, e, X)
Output: a template (e, M) or **null** (if the computation fails)

1 $(e, \theta, \varphi) \longleftarrow$ executePath(P, π)
2 **if** satisfiable$(\varphi) \neq$ SAT **then return null**
3 Set $\theta_*[\![\kappa]\!](a) = \underline{a}$ for each array variable a
4 Set $\theta_*[\![\kappa]\!](a) = \bot$ for each integer variable a
5 **repeat**
6   change $\longleftarrow$ *false*
7   **foreach** integer variable a **do**
8   **if** $\theta_*[\![\kappa]\!](a) = \bot$ **then**
9   **if** $\theta(a) = \underline{a} + c$ for some constant c **then**
10                 $\theta_*[\![\kappa]\!](a) \longleftarrow \underline{a} + \kappa \cdot c$
11   change $\longleftarrow$ *true*
12   **if** $\theta(a) = \underline{a} \cdot c$ for some constant c **then**
13                 $\theta_*[\![\kappa]\!](a) \longleftarrow \underline{a} \cdot c^\kappa$
14   change $\longleftarrow$ *true*
15   **if** $\theta(a) = g$ for some symbolic expression g such
                  that $\theta_*[\![\kappa]\!](b) \neq \bot$ for each symbol $\underline{b}$ in g **then**
16                 $\theta_*[\![\kappa]\!](a) \longleftarrow$ **ite**$(\kappa > 0, \theta_*[\![\kappa - 1]\!]\langle g \rangle, \underline{a})$
17   change $\longleftarrow$ *true*
18 **until** change = *false*
19 **if** $\theta_*[\![\kappa]\!](a) = \bot$ for some variable a **then return null**
20 $\varphi_*[\![\kappa]\!] \longleftarrow \kappa \geq 0 \ \wedge \ \forall \tau (0 \leq \tau < \kappa \implies \theta_*[\![\tau]\!]\langle \varphi \rangle)$
21 $M \longleftarrow \emptyset$
22 **foreach** $(u, x) \in X$ **do**
23   Let ρ be the prefix of π from e to u
24     $(x, \theta, \varphi) \longleftarrow$ executePath$(P, \rho x)$
25   **if** satisfiable$(\varphi) =$ UNKNOWN **then return null**
26   **if** satisfiable$(\varphi) =$ SAT **then**
27         $M \longleftarrow M \cup \{(x, \ \theta_*[\![\kappa]\!] \diamond \theta, \ \varphi_*[\![\kappa]\!] \wedge \theta_*[\![\kappa]\!]\langle \varphi \rangle)\}$
28 **return** (e, M)

The first part of the algorithm (lines 1–20) tries to derive a parametric symbolic memory $\theta_*[\![\kappa]\!]$ and a parametric path condition $\varphi_*[\![\kappa]\!]$, which together describe the symbolic state after κ iterations over the core π of the cycle C, for any $\kappa \geq 0$. Initially, at line 1, we compute the effect of a *single* iteration of the core π and then we check whether the iteration is feasible. If we cannot prove its feasibility, we stop the template computation and return **null**.[1] Otherwise, we get a symbolic state (e, θ, φ), whose elements θ and φ form a basis for the computation of $\theta_*[\![\kappa]\!]$ and $\varphi_*[\![\kappa]\!]$.

---

[1] It is possible that the iteration is feasible and the chosen SMT solver failed to prove it. However, as parametric path conditions of the resulting template are derived from φ, it is highly probable that any application of the template in compact symbolic execution would lead to failures of the SMT solver. Such a template is useless.

We compute $\theta_*[\![\kappa]\!]$ first. As arrays are read-only, we directly set $\theta_*[\![\kappa]\!](\mathsf{a})$ to $\underline{a}$ for each array variable a. For integer variables, we initialise $\theta_*[\![\kappa]\!]$ to an undefined value $\perp$. Then, in the loop at lines 5–18, we try to define $\theta_*[\![\kappa]\!]$ for as many variables as possible. For each variable a, $\theta_*[\![\kappa]\!](\mathsf{a})$ is defined at most once. Hence, the loop terminates after finite number of iterations. The value of $\theta_*[\![\kappa]\!](\mathsf{a})$ is defined according to the content of $\theta(\mathsf{a})$ and known values of $\theta_*[\![\kappa]\!]$. In particular, the conditions at lines 9 and 12 check if the values of a follow an arithmetic or a geometric progression during the iterations. If they do, we can easily express the exact value of a after any κ iterations. Note that the case when the value of a variable is not changed along π at all is a special case of an arithmetic progression ($c = 0$). Obviously, one can add support for other kinds of progression. The condition at line 15 covers the case when each iteration assigns to a an expression containing only variables with known values of $\theta_*[\![\kappa]\!]$. The if-then-else expression $\mathbf{ite}(\kappa > 0, \theta_*[\![\kappa - 1]\!]\langle g \rangle, \underline{a})$ assigned to $\theta_*[\![\kappa]\!](\mathsf{a})$ says that the value of a after $\kappa > 0$ iterations is given by the value of expression g where each symbol $\underline{b}$ represents the value of b at the beginning of the last iteration and thus it must be replaced by $\theta_*[\![\kappa - 1]\!](\mathsf{b})$. The value of a after 0 iterations is obviously unchanged, i.e. $\underline{a}$.

Once we get to line 19, we check whether we succeeded to define $\theta_*[\![\kappa]\!]$ for all variables. If we failed for at least one variable, then we fail to compute a template for C and we return **null**. Otherwise, at line 20 we compute the formula $\varphi_*[\![\kappa]\!]$ in accordance with the intuition provided in Section 2.

The second part of the algorithm (lines 21–28) computes the set M of the resulting template. As we already know from Section 2, we try to compute one element of M for each exit edge $(u, x) \in X$. At line 23 we compute a path ρ from the entry location e to u (along π), where we escape from π to the location x. The path ρx is then symbolically executed. If we fail to decide feasibility of the path, we fail to compute a template. If the path is feasible, we can escape π by taking the exit edge (u, x). Therefore, only in this case we add a new element to M at line 27. The structure of the element follows the intuition given in Section 2.

One can immediately see that the algorithm always terminates. Now we formulate a theorem describing properties of the computed template (e, M). The theorem is crucial for proving soundness and completeness of compact symbolic execution. Roughly speaking, the theorem says that whenever a node u of the symbolic execution tree of a program P satisfies $u.l = e$, then the subtree rooted in u has the property that each branch to a leaf contains a node w such that $w.s$ corresponds to the composition of $u.s$ and a suitable instance of some program state of the template (L1), and vice versa (L2). A proof of the theorem can be found in the full version of this paper [20].

Theorem 1 (Template Properties). *Let T be a classic symbolic execution tree of P and let $\big(e, \{(l_1, \theta_1[\![\kappa]\!], \varphi_1[\![\kappa]\!]), \ldots, (l_n, \theta_n[\![\kappa]\!], \varphi_n[\![\kappa]\!])\}\big)$ be a template for a cycle (π, e, X) in P produced by Algorithm 1. Then the following two properties hold:*

(L1) For each path $\pi = u\omega$ in T leading from a node u satisfying $u.l = e$ to a leaf, there is a node w of ω, an index $i \in \{1, \ldots, n\}$, and an integer $\nu \geq 0$ such that $w.s \equiv u.s \diamond (l_i, \theta_i[\![\nu]\!], \varphi_i[\![\nu]\!])$.

(L2) For each node u of T, an index $i \in \{1, \ldots, n\}$, and an integer $\nu \geq 0$ such that $u.l = e$ and $(u.\varphi \wedge u.\theta\langle\varphi_i[\![\nu]\!]\rangle)$ is satisfiable, there is a successor w of u in T such that $w.s \equiv u.s \diamond (l_i, \theta_i[\![\nu]\!], \varphi_i[\![\nu]\!])$.

3.3   Compact Symbolic Execution

The compact symbolic execution is formally defined by Algorithm 2. If we ignore the lines marked by □, then we get the classic symbolic execution. As we focus on compact symbolic execution, we describe the algorithm with □ lines included. The algorithm gets a program P and a finite set p of templates resulting from analyses of some cycles in P. Lines 1–3 create an initial program state, insert it into a queue Q, and create the root of a symbolic execution tree T labelled by the state.

The queue Q keeps all the program states waiting for their processing in the **repeat-until** loop (lines 4–26). The key part of the loop's body begins at line 9, where we select at most one template of p with entry location matching the actual program location $s.l$. Note that there can be more than one template available at $s.l$ as more cyclic paths can go through the location. We do not put any constraints in the selection strategy. We may for example choose randomly. Also note that we may choose none of the templates (i.e. we select **null**), if there is no template in p for location $s.l$ or even if there are such templates in p. If a template $t = (s.l, M)$ is selected, then we get a fresh parameter (line 12) and replace the original parameter in all tuples of M by the fresh one. This replacement prevents collisions of parameters of already applied templates. The **foreach** loop at lines 14–16 creates a successor state s' for each program state in M. If the template selection at line 9 returns **null**, we proceed to line 18 and compute successor states of the state s by the classic symbolic execution. The successor states with provably satisfiable path conditions are inserted into the queue Q and into the compact symbolic execution tree T in the **foreach** loop at lines 20–22. The successor states with provably unsatisfiable path conditions are ignored as they correspond to infeasible paths. The **foreach** loop at lines 23–25 handles the successor states with path conditions for which we are unable to decide satisfiability; these states are inserted into the resulting tree T as so-called *failed leaves*. A presence of a failed leaf in the resulting tree indicates that applied symbolic execution has failed to explore whole path-space of the executed program. We do not continue computation from these states as there is usually a plethora of other states with provably satisfiable path conditions.

We finish this section by soundness and completeness theorems for compact symbolic execution. We assume that T and T' are classic and compact symbolic execution trees of the program P computed by Algorithm 2 without and with □-lines respectively. The theorems hold on assumption that our **satisfiable**(φ) function never returns UNKNOWN, i.e. neither T nor T' contains failed leaves. Proofs of both theorems can be found in the full version of this paper [20].

Algorithm 2. executeSymbolically

    Input: a program P to be executed

□   and a finite set p of templates computed for cycles in P

    Output: a symbolic execution tree T of P (compact tree in □–version)

1   $s_0 \longleftarrow$ (the starting location of $P, \theta_I, true$)

2   Let Q be a queue of states initially containing only s_0

3   Insert the root node labelled by s_0 to the empty tree T

4   **repeat**

5   Extract the first state s from Q

6   **if** $s.l$ is either an exit from P or an error location **then**

7   **continue**

8      $S \longleftarrow \emptyset$

□ 9 $t \longleftarrow$ chooseTemplate$(s.l, p)$

□10   **if** $t \neq$ **null then**

□11   Let M be the second element of t, i.e. $t = (s.l, M)$

□12 $\kappa \longleftarrow$ getFreshParam$()$

□13   Replace all occurrences of the former parameter in M by κ

□14   **foreach** $(l, \theta[\![\kappa]\!], \varphi[\![\kappa]\!]) \in M$ **do**

□15 $s' \longleftarrow s \diamond (l, \theta[\![\kappa]\!], \varphi[\![\kappa]\!])$

□16   Insert s' into S

□17   **else**   /* apply classic symbolic execution step */

18      $S \longleftarrow$ computeClassicSuccessors(P, s)

19   Let u be the leaf of T whose label is s

20   **foreach** state $s' \in S$ such that satisfiable$(s'.\varphi) =$ SAT **do**

21   Insert s' at the end of Q

22   Insert a new node v labelled with s' and a new edge (u, v) into T

23   **foreach** state $s' \in S$ such that satisfiable$(s'.\varphi) =$ UNKNOWN **do**

24   Insert a new node v labelled with s' and a new edge (u, v) into T

25   Mark the node v in T as a failed leaf

26 **until** Q becomes empty

27 **return** T

Theorem 2 (Soundness). *For each leaf node $e \in T$ there is a leaf node $e' \in T'$ and a valuation ν of parameters in $e'.s$ such that $e.s \equiv e'.s[\![\nu]\!]$.*

Theorem 3 (Completeness). *For each leaf node $e' \in T'$ there is a leaf node $e \in T$ and a valuation ν of parameters in $e'.s$ such that $e.s \equiv e'.s[\![\nu]\!]$.*

Note that in both theorems we discuss only the relation between all *finite* branches of the trees T and T'. Some infinite branches of T (like the one in Figure 1(b)) corresponding to infinite iterations along a cyclic path need not be present in T'. As symbolic execution is typically used to cover as many reachable program locations as possible, missing infinite iterations along cyclic paths can be seen as a feature rather than a drawback.

4   Experimental Results

Implementation. We have implemented both classic and compact symbolic execution in an experimental tool called RUDLA. The tool uses our "library of libraries" called BUGST available at SOURCEFORGE [3]. The sources of RUDLA and all benchmarks mentioned below are available in the same repository. The implementation also uses CLANG 2.9 [4], LLVM 3.1 [5], and Z3 4.3.0 [6].

Evaluation Criteria. We would like to empirically evaluate and compare the effectiveness of the classic and compact symbolic execution in exploration of program paths. Unfortunately, we cannot directly compare explored program paths or nodes in the constructed trees as a path or a node in a compact symbolic execution tree have a different meaning than a path or a node in a classic symbolic execution tree. To compare the techniques, we fix an exploration method of the trees, namely we choose the breadth-first search as indicated in Algorithm 2, and we measure the time needed by each of the techniques to reach a particular location in an analysed program. Note that for compact symbolic execution we also have to fix a strategy for template selection since there can generally be more than one template related to one program location. We always choose randomly between candidate templates.

Benchmarks and Results. We use two collections of benchmarks. The first collection contains 13 programs with a marked target location. As our technique is focused on path explosion caused by loops, all the benchmarks contain typical program loop constructions. There are sequences of loops, nested loops and also loops with internal branching. They are designed to produce a huge number of execution paths. Thus they are challenging for symbolic execution. The target location is chosen to be difficult to reach. The first ten benchmarks have reachable target locations, while the last three do not. For these three benchmarks, all the execution paths must be explored to give an answer.

Experimental results are presented in Table 1. The high numbers of (often infeasible) cycles are due to our translation from LLVM (see [20] for details). We want to highlight the following observations. First, classic symbolic execution was faster only for benchmarks `Hello` and `decode_packets`. Second, the number of states visited by the compact symbolic execution is often several orders of magnitude lower than the number of states visited by the classic one. At the same time we recall that the semantics of a state in classic and compact symbolic execution are different. Finally, presence of quantifiers in path conditions of compact symbolic executions puts high requirements on skills of the SMT solver. This leads to SMT failures, which are not seen in classic symbolic execution.

Algorithm 2 saves SMT failures in the form of failed leaves in the resulting compact symbolic execution tree. Therefore, we may think about subsequent analyses for these leaves. For example, in a failed leaf we may instantiate parameters κ by concrete numbers. The resulting formulae will become quantifier-free and therefore potentially easier for an SMT solver. This way we might be able to explore paths below the failed leaves. But basically, analyses of failed leaves

Table 1. Experimental results of compact and classic symbolic executions. The compact symbolic execution approach is divided into computation of templates and building of compact symbolic execution tree. All the times are in seconds, where 'T/O' identifies exceeding 5 minutes timeout. 'Count' represents the number of computed templates, 'Cycles' shows the number of detected cycles. 'SMTFail' represents the number of failed SMT queries. There was no SMT failure during classic SE of our benchmarks.

Benchmark	Templates			Compact SE			SE	
	Time	Count	Cycles	Time	States	SMTFail	Time	States
hello	12.3	2	126	2.3	187	0	4.5	2262
HW	31.9	4	252	45.4	1048	4	T/O	223823
HWM	48.1	5	336	T/O	5125	24	T/O	162535
matrIR	4.2	4	28	82.9	1234	6	T/O	270737
matrIR_dyn	14.8	5	30	240.5	2472	13	T/O	267636
VM	8.6	6	64	T/O	2274	64	T/O	205577
VMS	4.2	3	32	5.4	466	0	99.8	281263
decode_packets	18.3	5	26	39.9	1276	0	16.3	8992
WinDriver	17.8	5	26	59.2	1370	1	T/O	206903
EQCNT	12.2	3	12	10.6	345	0	T/O	179803
EQCNTex	5.8	4	24	T/O	10581	0	T/O	251061
OneLoop	0.1	1	2	0.1	41	0	T/O	38230
TwoLoops	0.3	2	4	0.1	25	0	T/O	917343
Total time	240			1800			3900	

Table 2. Experimental results of compact and classic symbolic executions on 79 SV-COMP 2013 benchmarks in the category 'loops'. Time is in seconds. For compact SE we provide template computation time plus execution time. 'safe' and 'unsafe' report the numbers of programs where the tool decides unreachability and reachability of a marked error location, respectively (all these answers are correct). 'timeout' presents the number of symbolic executions exceeding 5 minutes. 'unsupported' represents the number of compilation failures plus failures during an analysis. 'points' shows the number of points the tools would get according to the SV-COMP 2013 rules.

	Time	safe	unsafe	timeout	unsupported	points
Compact SE	300+4920	21	25	15	13+5	67
SE	8700	10	27	28	13+1	47

are a topic for our further research. Moreover, as SMT solvers are improving quickly, we may expect that counts of the failures will decrease over time.

The second collection of benchmarks is the whole category 'loops' taken from SV-COMP 2013 (revision 229) [2]. The results are depicted in Table 2.

All the presented experiments were done on a laptop Acer Aspire 5920G (2 × 2GHz, 2GB) running Windows 7 SP1 64-bit.

5   Related Work

The symbolic execution was introduced by King in 1976 [16]. The original concept was generalised in [14] for programs with heap by introducing lazy initialisation of dynamically allocated data structures. The lazy initialisation algorithm was further improved and formally defined in [9]. Another generalisation step was done in [15], where the authors attempt to avoid symbolic execution of library code (called from an analysed program), since such code can be assumed as well defined and properly tested.

In [19,12], the path explosion problem is tackled by focusing on program loops. The information inferred from a loop allows to talk about multiple program paths through that loop. But the goal is to explore classic symbolic execution tree in some effective manner: more interesting paths sooner. Approaches [10,1] share the same goal as the previous ones, but they focus on a computation of function summaries rather than on program loops.

Our goal is completely different: instead of guiding exploration of paths in a classic symbolic execution tree, we build a tree that keeps the same information and contains less nodes. In particular, templates of compact symbolic execution have a different objective than summarisation used in [10,1,12]. While summarisation basically caches results of some finite part of symbolic execution for later fast reuse, our templates are supposed to *replace* potentially infinite parts of symbolic executions by a single node.

Techniques [17,18] group paths of classic symbolic execution tree according to their effect on symbolic values of a priori given output variables, and explore only one path per group. We consider all program variables and we explore all program paths (some of them are explored simultaneously using templates).

Finally, in our previous work [21] we compute a non-trivial necessary condition for reaching a given target location in a given program. In other words, the result of the analysis is a first order logic formula. In the current paper, we focus on a fast exploration of as many execution paths as possible. The technique produces a compact symbolic execution tree. Note that, we do not require any target location, since we do not focus on a program location reachability here. Nevertheless, to achieve our goal, we adopted a part of a technical stuff introduced in [21]. Namely, lines 4–18 of Algorithm 1 are similar to the computation of a so-called iterated memory, which is in [21] an over-approximation of the memory content after several iterations in a program loop. In the current technique, the memory content must always be absolutely precise. Moreover, here we analyse flowgraph cycles while [21] summarises program loops.

6   Conclusion

We have introduced a generalisation of classic symbolic execution, called compact symbolic execution. Before building symbolic execution tree, the compact symbolic execution computes *templates* for cycles of an analysed program. A template is a parametric and declarative description of the overall effect of a related cycle. Our experimental results indicate that the use of templates during the analysis leads to faster exploration of program paths in comparison with the exploration speed of classic symbolic execution. Also a number of symbolic states computed during the program analysis is considerably smaller. On the other hand, compact symbolic execution constructs path conditions with quantifiers, which leads to more failures of SMT queries.

References

1. Anand, S., Godefroid, P., Tillmann, N.: Demand-driven compositional symbolic execution. In: Ramakrishnan, C.R., Rehof, J. (eds.) TACAS 2008. LNCS, vol. 4963, pp. 367–381. Springer, Heidelberg (2008)
2. Beyer, D.: Second competition on software verification. In: Piterman, N., Smolka, S.A. (eds.) TACAS 2013 (ETAPS 2013). LNCS, vol. 7795, pp. 594–609. Springer, Heidelberg (2013)
3. bugst, http://sourceforge.net/projects/bugst
4. clang, http://clang.llvm.org
5. LLVM, http://llvm.org
6. Z3, http://z3.codeplex.com
7. Cadar, C., Dunbar, D., Engler, D.: KLEE: Unassisted and automatic generation of high-coverage tests for complex systems programs. In: OSDI, pp. 209–224. USENIX Association (2008)
8. Cadar, C., Ganesh, V., Pawlowski, P.M., Dill, D.L., Engler, D.R.: EXE: Automatically generating inputs of death. In: CCS, pp. 322–335. ACM (2006)
9. Deng, X., Lee, J., Robby: Efficient and formal generalized symbolic execution. Autom. Softw. Eng. 19(3), 233–301 (2012)
10. Godefroid, P.: Compositional dynamic test generation. In: POPL, pp. 47–54. ACM (2007)
11. Godefroid, P., Levin, M.Y., Molnar, D.A.: Automated whitebox fuzz testing. In: NDSS, pp. 151–166. The Internet Society (2008)
12. Godefroid, P., Luchaup, D.: Automatic partial loop summarization in dynamic test generation. In: ISSTA, pp. 23–33. ACM (2011)
13. Howden, W.E.: Symbolic testing and the DISSECT symbolic evaluation system. IEEE Trans. Software Eng. 3, 266–278 (1977)
14. Khurshid, S., Păsăreanu, C.S., Visser, W.: Generalized symbolic execution for model checking and testing. In: Garavel, H., Hatcliff, J. (eds.) TACAS 2003. LNCS, vol. 2619, pp. 553–568. Springer, Heidelberg (2003)
15. Khurshid, S., Suen, Y.L.: Generalizing symbolic execution to library classes. In: PASTE, pp. 103–110. ACM (2005)
16. King, J.C.: Symbolic execution and program testing. Commun. ACM 19(7), 385–394 (1976)
17. Qi, D., Nguyen, H.D.T., Roychoudhury, A.: Path exploration based on symbolic output. In: ESEC/FSE, pp. 278–288. ACM (2011)
18. Santelices, R.A., Harrold, M.J.: Exploiting program dependencies for scalable multiple-path symbolic execution. In: ISSTA, pp. 195–206. ACM (2010)
19. Saxena, P., Poosankam, P., McCamant, S., Song, D.: Loop-extended symbolic execution on binary programs. In: ISSTA, pp. 225–236. ACM (2009)
20. Slaby, J., Strejček, J., Trtík, M.: Compact Symbolic Execution. CoRR, abs/1201.4715 (2012), http://arxiv.org/abs/1201.4715 Full version of the ATVA 2013 paper
21. Strejček, J., Trtík, M.: Abstracting path conditions. In: ISSTA, pp. 155–165. ACM (2012)
22. Tillmann, N., de Halleux, J.: Pex–white box test generation for.NET. In: Beckert, B., Hähnle, R. (eds.) TAP 2008. LNCS, vol. 4966, pp. 134–153. Springer, Heidelberg (2008)

Multi-threaded Explicit State Space Exploration with State Reconstruction

Sami Evangelista[1], Lars Michael Kristensen[2], and Laure Petrucci[1]

[1] LIPN, CNRS UMR 7030, Université Paris 13, Sorbonne Paris Cité,
99, av. J.-B. Clément, 93430 Villetaneuse, France
[2] Department of Computing, Mathematics, and Physics, Bergen University College,
Nygaardsgaten 112, Postbox 7030, 5020 Bergen, Norway

Abstract. This article introduces a parallel state space exploration algorithm for shared memory multi-core architectures using state compression and state reconstruction to reduce memory consumption. The algorithm proceeds in rounds each consisting of three phases: concurrent expansion of open states, concurrent reduction of potentially new states, and concurrent duplicate detection. An important feature of the algorithm is that it requires little inter-thread synchronisation making it highly scalable. This is confirmed by an experimental evaluation that demonstrates good speed up at a low overhead in workload and with little waiting time caused by synchronisation.

1 Introduction

We consider in this article the problem of explicitly constructing the state space of a system implicitly given through an initial state and a successor function that maps each state to a set of successor states. This is the core operation performed by explicit state model checkers in order to, e.g., verify safety properties and deadlock freedom, and conduct temporal logic model checking. The large number of states combined with the size of each state is a limiting factor for the practical use of standard explicit state space exploration. For complex systems, like software or communication protocols, it is not uncommon that the state vector (the data structure that unambiguously represents a state) consumes up to the order of 100 bytes. One way to overcome this problem is to store only a hash value for each state. This technique is known as *hash compaction* [15] which is an incomplete method in that parts of the state space may not be explored if two states have the same hash value. To guarantee full state space coverage in presence of hash compaction, techniques based on *state reconstruction* [6,14] have been proposed. These techniques reconstruct states from their compressed representation on-demand when comparison of states is required in order to determine whether a newly generated state has been already encountered, i.e. is a duplicate of an already explored state. Clearly, the reconstruction of states implies an increase in exploration time.

One approach [7] to reducing the exploration time in presence of state reconstruction is to delay the duplicate detection and thereby reduce the number of states that needs to be reconstructed. The contribution of this paper is an orthogonal approach in the form of an algorithm that reduces the exploration time by exploiting multiple threads (and multi-core architectures) to perform the reconstruction of states in parallel. In addition,

D. Van Hung and M. Ogawa (Eds.): ATVA 2013, LNCS 8172, pp. 208–223, 2013.

our algorithm processes open states in parallel. The algorithm maintains a *state reconstruction tree* based on which all encountered states can be reconstructed and it proceeds breadth-first in rounds each consisting of three *phases*. In the first phase, the threads traverse the reconstruction tree in order to generate a *frontier set* consisting (in its basic form) of the next breadth-first layer of states. In the second phase, duplicate states in the frontier set are eliminated resulting in a *candidate set* of potentially new states. Finally, in the third phase, threads perform state reconstruction to determine which candidate states are new and such states are then added to the reconstruction tree.

The article is organised as follows. Sect. 2 introduces the basic notations and concepts of transition systems used in order to make our presentation independent of a particular modelling formalism. Sect. 3 gives a high-level overview of the operation of our algorithm by means of a small example, and Sect. 4 provides the formal algorithmic details. An implementation of our algorithm is presented in Sect. 5 together with the findings from an experimental evaluation. Finally, Sect. 6 concludes and discusses further related and future work. The reader is assumed to be familiar with the basic ideas of explicit state space exploration and associated model checking techniques.

2 Background

Let S be a universe of syntactic states and $\mathcal{E}$ a set of events. The system is given through an initial state $s_0 \in S$, a mapping $enab : S \to 2^{\mathcal{E}}$ associating with each state a set of enabled events, and a mapping $succ : S \times \mathcal{E} \to S$ used to generate a successor state from a state and one of its enabled events. State space exploration is concerned with computing the set of states reachable from s_0, i.e. states s such that there exist $e_0, \ldots, e_{n-1} \in \mathcal{E}$, $s_1, \ldots, s_n \in S$ with $s = s_n$ and, for all $i \in \{0, \ldots, n-1\}$: $e_i \in enab(s_i)$ and $succ(s_i, e_i) = s_{i+1}$. For simplicity, we use a function $succ$ to obtain a successor state from a given state and an event. This implies that events are assumed to be deterministic in order to reconstruct a unique state from a sequence of events in the state reconstruction. Many modelling formalisms (including Petri nets) have deterministic transitions (events). As shown in [14], state reconstruction can be extended to handle non-deterministic events.

Algorithm 1(left) gives the basic algorithm for explicit state space exploration. It maintains a set $\mathcal{R}$ of reached states and a set O of currently *open states*. The algorithm iterates until there are no open states. In each iteration, an open state s is selected and *state expansion* is performed by exploring all events enabled in s. Successor states that have not been reached earlier are inserted into $\mathcal{R}$ and O.

State Reconstruction. Earlier [6,14], we have proposed to implement the reachability set $\mathcal{R}$ as a hash table where full state vectors are not stored but each state is instead represented by an integer (hash value) identifying it. The hash table now represents an inverse spanning tree (a state reconstruction tree) rooted in the initial state, and where nodes have references to one parent, each labelled with an event used to generate the full state vector for the node. Figure 1 illustrates state reconstruction. The top of Fig. 1 shows the state space where the upper part of each node is the state vector, the bottom part is its hash value, and the thick edges are edges represented by references in the

Algorithm 1. A basic state space exploration algorithm (left) and a state space exploration algorithm based on delayed duplicate detection (right)

1: $\mathcal{R} := \{s_0\}$	1: $\mathcal{R} := \{s_0\}$; $O := \{s_0\}$; $C := \emptyset$
2: $O := \{s_0\}$	2: **while** $O \neq \emptyset$ **do**
3: **while** $O \neq \emptyset$ **do**	3: **pick** s **in** O ; $O := O \setminus \{s\}$
4: **pick** s **in** O ; $O := O \setminus \{s\}$	4: **for** $e \in enab(s), s' = succ(s,e)$ **do**
5: **for** $e \in enab(s), s' = succ(s,e)$ **do**	5: $C := C \cup \{s'\}$
6: **if** $s' \notin \mathcal{R}$ **then**	6: **if** $O = \emptyset$ **or** *doDuplicateDetection*() **then**
7: $\mathcal{R} := \mathcal{R} \cup \{s'\}$	7: $\mathcal{N} := C \setminus \mathcal{R}$; $C := \emptyset$
8: $O := O \cup \{s'\}$	8: $\mathcal{R} := \mathcal{R} \cup \mathcal{N}$; $O := O \cup \mathcal{N}$

spanning tree. The lower part of Fig. 1 is a linearised graphical representation of the hash table implementing $\mathcal{R}$ where dashed arcs represent references to parents in the reconstruction tree and are labelled by generating events. Note that state vectors appear in the table for the sake of clarity, but they are not stored in memory.

When required, the state vector for a node can be reconstructed by backtracking up to the root (initial) node for which we have the full state vector, and then forward execute the *reconstructing sequence* of events on the path leading from the initial node (state) to the node in question. This is performed each time the algorithm generates a successor state s' from an open state s. As an example, consider Fig. 1 and assume that the algorithm has explored states s_0 to s_3 and is expanding s_4 corresponding to the exploration of the two dotted edges. The expansion of s_4 generates s_2 and s_5 both hashed to 7. To decide whether s_2 is new, we reconstruct all nodes of the reconstruction tree that are also hashed to 7 as these

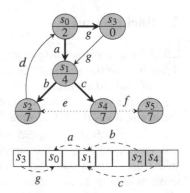

Fig. 1. State reconstruction

could potentially have the same state vector. These correspond to the grey cells of the hash table. For the first cell (s_2), we have to follow references labelled b, a to the initial node (state) and finally execute the reconstruction sequence $a.b$ starting from the initial state. Since this execution produces state s_2, we conclude that executing e from s_4 does not generate a new state. For state s_5, we have to reconstruct s_2 using again $a.b$ as reconstructing sequence, and s_4 using the reconstructing sequence $a.c$. Since $succ(succ(s_0,a),b) \neq s_5$ and $succ(succ(s_0,a),c) \neq s_5$, then s_5 is new and is inserted in the hash table with a reference to its parent s_4 labelled with event f.

Delayed Duplicate Detection. Duplicate detection refers to the the process of checking if a generated state already belongs to the reachability set $\mathcal{R}$ (l. 6 of Alg.1 (left)) and is often the most expensive operation performed by the algorithm in particular in combination with state reconstruction. The principle of *delayed duplicate detection* is that the number of state reconstructions can be reduced if these checks were grouped and performed once. Duplicate detection is delayed because each generated state is not directly looked for in $\mathcal{R}$ but put in a *candidate set* C, and only occasionally is this set compared to $\mathcal{R}$. Algorithm 1 (right) also performs state space exploration but relies on the principle of delayed duplicate detection. New successor states are put in the candidate set C. When the open set is empty or if, for example, the candidate set reaches a specific threshold (l. 6), the algorithm will identify new candidate states (set $\mathcal{N}$) by comparing sets C and $\mathcal{R}$. The resulting set will then be inserted in $\mathcal{R}$ and O as the basic algorithm would have done for individual states. When applied in the context of state reconstruction, delayed duplicate detection allows to group the reconstruction of states and, hence, execute only once the common prefixes of reconstructing sequences [7] and also reduce the number of reconstructions performed. On our example of Fig. 1, the candidate set would contain, after the expansion of s_4, the states s_2 and s_5. Duplicate detection reconstructs s_2 and s_4 together and grouping the execution of reconstructing sequences $a.b$ and $a.c$ allow to execute event a once rather than twice and only reconstruct s_2 once.

3   Algorithm Overview and Example

The primary data structure maintained by our new parallel algorithm is a reconstruction tree as introduced in the previous section representing all encountered states. As a further extension compared to earlier work [6,7,14], we do not use a separate data structure to store open states. Instead, we use the reconstruction tree to also on-the-fly reconstruct open states during exploration which further reduces memory consumption.

Our algorithm proceeds breadth-first in *rounds* where each round explores the next breadth-first search (BFS) level. As depicted in Fig. 2, then each round consists of three *phases*. The first phase uses the current reconstruction tree $\mathcal{T}$ to construct lists of successor states for the currently open states. The second phase merges the lists of successor states to obtain a candidate set C of potentially new states. The third step performs duplicate detection to find new states, i.e. states in C that are not represented in $\mathcal{T}$. Within each phase, all threads cooperate and must synchronise before the algorithm proceeds to the next phase (and hence round). Within each phase, additional synchronisation barriers are employed and represent the only form of synchronisation used by our algorithm. The algorithm proceeds into the next round as long as duplicate detection results in states that are not yet represented by the reconstruction tree.

Below we illustrate the three phases of our algorithm in more detail starting from the partial state space shown in Fig. 3 where the initial state s_0 is assumed to have already been expanded, leading to four new successors s_1, s_2, s_3, and s_4, as shown in Fig. 3. States are stored in the reconstruction tree as a hash value with a reference to their

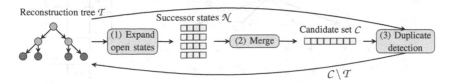

Fig. 2. A round exploring one BFS level in three phases

parent node and the event that was used to generated the state from the parent state. We do not explicitly show this in the figures to improve readability. In the example, two states with the same hash value carry the same name, but are distinguished with primes, e.g. s_4 and s'_4 have different state vectors but are mapped to the same hash value. We denote by $\mathcal{W}$ the number of threads taking part in the exploration of the state space, and assume that each worker is identified by an integer in the range from 0 to $\mathcal{W} - 1$.

Phase 1: Expand Open States. Threads traverse the reconstruction tree using random depth-first search. Randomisation is used in order to break the symmetry between threads and ensure that they can work on different parts of the reconstruction tree.

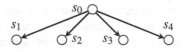

Fig. 3. Initial reconstruction tree

Open states (i.e. leafs at the bottom of the tree) are expanded and their successors put in a *successor lists* structure $\mathcal{N}$ consisting of $\mathcal{W}$ state lists (one per thread). Since each thread w inserts states in the list of the wth slot only, no synchronisation is required. When inserting new states in $\mathcal{N}$, no duplicate detection is performed: each successor state of an open state is inserted at the end of the appropriate list of the structure $\mathcal{N}$ and a state may hence be present in different slots of the array. Considering the example in Fig. 3, then this first step of the algorithm expands the nodes s_1 to s_4 by generating their successors, as depicted by the dotted elements in Fig. 4(left). This phase ends when leaf states have all been expanded (i.e. the current BFS level has been explored) or when the size of structure $\mathcal{N}$ reaches a specific threshold. In the case of four threads, we obtain the successor lists shown in Fig. 4(right). In general, the expansion can be performed concurrently by any number of threads.

Phase 2: Merge. The second phase consists of merging the successor lists of $\mathcal{N}$ into a single set $\mathcal{C}$, hence removing the duplicate successors present in these lists. Merging the states present in the successor lists in Fig. 4(right) results in the candidate states: $s'_4, s_5, s_4, s_6, s_7, s'_3, s_2$. This second phase can be realised using a parallel sort and merge algorithm [9] or hashing on a matrix structure as in our implementation (see Sect. 5).

Phase 3: Duplicate Detection. The last phase removes from $\mathcal{C}$ the states already represented in compressed form in the reconstruction tree. Phase 3 first performs bottom-up tagging (marking) of the nodes to be reconstructed (tagged **R**) and their ancestors (tagged **A**). Considering the example in Fig. 5(a) and the list of candidates from phase

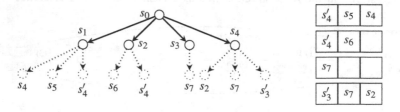

Fig. 4. Phase 1: Expansion of open states (left) and array of successor lists (right)

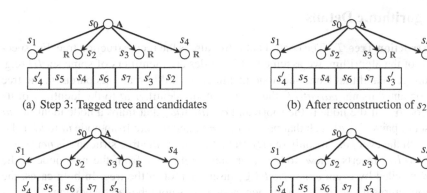

(a) Step 3: Tagged tree and candidates   (b) After reconstruction of s_2

(c) After reconstruction of s_4 (d) After reconstruction of s_3

Fig. 5. Phase 3: Tagging following by state reconstruction and duplicate detection

2: since s'_4 is a candidate, and has the same hash value as s_4, s_4 is marked **R** and its only ancestor, s_0 marked **A**. This is achieved using the references to parent nodes. There is no node in the reconstruction tree with the same hash value as state s_5. Then s_4 is a candidate, and it is already marked in the tree. As soon as a state is encountered already having an identical tag, then tagging stops, and the next candidate is processed. The resulting tagged reconstruction tree is depicted in Fig. 5(a).

Each of the nodes marked **R** must be reconstructed, and each node marked **A** is the ancestor of such a node. Starting from the initial state, the threads perform a random forward traversal of the tree via tagged nodes. Let us assume that from s_0, the branch of s_2 is explored. This latter state is reconstructed from s_0 and the event to s_2. The actual value of state s_2 is compared to the candidate states. Since it is found, s_2 already exists and can be removed from the candidates set. Moreover, the **R** tag is removed from s_2. The resulting tree and candidates set are shown in Fig. 5(b). Next, backtracking is performed since s_0 still has tagged successor states, so, e.g. the branch with s_4 may be explored. When s_4 is reconstructed, the reconstructing thread finds that the state is in the candidates set, so it is removed from it, but s'_4 is kept since, even though it has the same hash value, the actual state is different. The result in shown in Fig. 5(c). Then the process continues, e.g. with state s_3. Finally, as shown in Fig. 5(d), state s_0 has no more tagged successors, and can be untagged, finishing the reconstruction phase. At the end of the exploration, states remaining in C are guaranteed to be new and can thus be inserted in the reconstruction tree. The resulting reconstruction tree for the example is shown in Fig. 6. A new round is now initiated

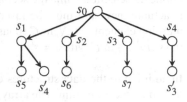

Fig. 6. Updated state tree

on the updated reconstruction tree. To maintain a strict breadth-first search order, the expansion of the new states will occur only when all states of the current BFS level have been expanded. This constraint can be relaxed, but we have chosen to maintain this search order as it guarantees the minimality of reconstruction sequence lengths.

4 Algorithmic Details

Reconstruction Tree $\mathcal{T}$. The central data structure is the reconstruction tree. For specification of the algorithm, we assume that its nodes are identifiers of some set ID (e.g. set of integers) and that from one node identifier its children and its parent in the tree can be obtained using: $parent(id)$ that maps a node identifier id to the identifier of its parent (or to $\perp$ if the node is the root); and $children(id)$ that maps a node identifier id to the set of pairs (id', e) such that $parent(id') = id$ and the arc from node id to id' is labelled with the event e. The only operation that modifies the tree structure is $newNode$. $newNode(id, e)$ inserts a new node and creates a reference from the new node to the node id labelled by event e. $newNode(\perp)$ inserts a root in the tree. In both cases, the operation returns the identifier of the new node that is not labelled by any tag.

Node Tagging. As discussed earlier, nodes are labelled by a set of tags used to prune the traversal of the reconstruction tree. Three operations are used to manipulate tags: $tagged$ (checks whether a node has a specific tag), tag (sets a tag on a node), and $untag$ (removes a tag from a node). Our example from the previous section introduced two tags (**R** and **A**) used during duplicate detection (phase 3). Two additional tags (E_0 and E_1) are used during the expansion phase (phase 1) to tag nodes to expand. The E_0 and E_1 are used in an alternating manner between rounds such that in odd numbered rounds E_0 marks nodes to be expanded and E_1 marks nodes to be expanded in the next (even numbered) round. In an odd numbered round, a node has the E_0 tag if it has children with this same tag or if it corresponds to an open state (in which case it can not have any children yet). Furthermore, the expansion of open states will then create new nodes in the tree having the E_1 tag and also tag nodes on the way up from these new nodes to the root node with E_1. Traversing nodes with the E_0 (resp. E_1) thus leads to open states of the current (next) expansion phase. When a round is completed E_0 and E_1 swap roles. One E tag is not sufficient because nodes can be independently marked for expansion in the current and in the next phase. Note that a node may be simultaneously labelled by several tags.

Successor Lists $\mathcal{N}$ **and Candidate Set** C. The elements of $\mathcal{N}$ and C are triples of the form $S \times ID \times \mathcal{E}$. A triple (s, id, e) represents that state s has been reached from the node id by executing event e on the state corresponding to id. The first item is used during duplicate detection while the second and third items are used in case the candidate state is actually new and must be inserted in the tree using the $newNode$ operation. After merging elements of $\mathcal{N}$ in C (phase 2 of Fig. 2) there cannot be two elements (s, id, e) in (s', id', e') in C with $s = s'$.

In addition to the data structures described above, three shared data structures are required by the algorithm. The array $done$ contains $\mathcal{W}$ booleans indicating which threads have finished their exploration of the current BFS level. It is used to decide when the current BFS level has been completely expanded and threads can move to the next level. An alternating bit r initialised to 0 identifies which tag among E_0 and E_1 is used to indicate nodes that must be explored during the current expansion phase.

Algorithms 2, 3 and 4 contain the pseudo-code of our algorithm. The w subscript of the procedures identify the working thread executing the procedure. Apart from the

---

Algorithm 2. *ParReconstruction*, Initialisation and main worker procedure

1: **algorithm** *ParReconstruction* **is**
2:    *done* := [*false*, . . . , *false*] ; *r* := 0
3:    id_0 := *newNode*($\bot$) ; *tag*(id_0, $\mathbf{E}_0$)
4:    **spawn** *worker*$_0$() $||$ . . . $||$ *worker*$_{\mathcal{W}-1}$()
5: **procedure** *worker*$_w$() **is**
6:    **while** *tagged*(id_0, $\mathbf{E}_r$) **do**
7:       *expandLevel*$_w$()
8:       **if** $w = 0$ **then** $r := \neg r$
9:       barrier()

	Shared Data
$\mathcal{T}$	the state tree initially empty
C	the candidate set initially empty
$\mathcal{N}$	the successor lists initially empty

done	array of $\mathcal{W}$ booleans
r	bit
id_0	identifier of the initial state in $\mathcal{T}$

---

shared data specified in Alg. 2, all other variables are thread local. We have underlined the different barriers that must be executed simultaneously by the $\mathcal{W}$ threads so as to highlight synchronisation points. The variable id_0 is used to store the root node. Thread 0 is the only thread that modifies the values of r and id_0.

Initialisation and Main Worker Procedure (Alg. 2). The main procedure *ParReconstruction* inserts the initial state in the reconstruction tree and records its node identifier in the shared variable id_0. This node is then tagged for expansion and the procedure spawns $\mathcal{W}$ instances of the main worker procedure *worker*$_w$. The loop at l. 6 iterates over all BFS levels expanded using the *expandLevel*$_w$ procedure introduced below. We use the $\mathbf{E}_r$ tag to decide when a thread can terminate. For any node, the tagging procedure guarantees that if a node is tagged with $\mathbf{E}_r$, then so is its parent in the tree. Thus, an untagged root guarantees that no state is tagged for expansion. The barrier at l. 9 is related to duplicate detection as will be discussed shortly. It is the responsibility of thread 0 to swap the r bit before all threads can start processing the next BFS level.

Phase 1: State Expansion (Alg. 3). The expansion procedure *expandLevel*$_w$ expands open states of a BFS level. The working thread w first launches a DFS exploration from the root of the tree using procedure *dfsExpand*$_w$ that is parameterised by the identifier of the visited node in the tree (id) and the corresponding full state vector (s). In case the visited node is a leaf (ll. 12–15), the worker puts all its successors in list $\mathcal{N}[w]$ and enters the duplicate detection phase if this structure reaches a specified threshold. Otherwise (ll. 16–19), the thread picks all children of the node one by one in the random order obtained using the *random* function, and explores those that have the $\mathbf{E}_r$ tag set as these nodes may lead to open states. To maintain the correspondence between nodes and states, procedure *dfsExpand*$_w$ is recursively called (l. 19) with the identifier of the child id' and the state obtained by executing on s the event e labelling the arc from id to id', i.e. the state s' such that $succ(s, e) = s'$. When node id has been processed, the $\mathbf{E}_r$ tag can be removed from it to signal to other threads that this node has been processed.

After the threads have finished exploring the tree, a last duplicate detection is required since successor lists might not be empty (l. 6). Moreover, after exploration, a thread also has to be ready to perform duplicate detection as long as some workers have not yet finished their exploration. These threads may still be feeding successor lists and hence call the duplicate detection procedure (l. 15) that must be executed by all threads. This is where the shared array *done* is used. A thread will keep performing duplicate

---

Algorithm 3. Procedures used during the state expansion phase

1: **procedure** $expandLevel_w()$ **is**
2:   $done[w] :=$ **false**
3:   $dfsExpand_w(id_0, s_0)$
4:   $done[w] :=$ **true**
5:   **do**
6:     $allDone := duplicateDetection_w()$
7:   **while** $\neg allDone$
8: **procedure** $expandState_w(id, s)$ **is**
9:   **for** $e \in enab(s)$ **do**
10:     $append(\mathcal{N}[w], (id, succ(s, e), e))$

11: **procedure** $dfsExpand_w(id, s)$ **is**
12:   **if** $children(id) = \emptyset$ **then**
13:     $expandState_w(id, s)$
14:     **if** $|\sum_x \mathcal{N}[x]| >$ **MemoryLimit then**
15:       $duplicateDetection_w()$
16:   **else**
17:     **for** $(id', e) \in random(children(id))$ **do**
18:       **if** $tagged(id', \mathbf{E}_r)$ **then**
19:         $dfsExpand_w(id', succ(s, e))$
20:   $untag(id, \mathbf{E}_r)$

---

detection until all threads have finished their exploration and executed the assignment at l. 4. Procedure $duplicateDetection_w$ introduced below returns a boolean value specifying if all threads have finished expanding the current level. This check is performed between two barriers (l. 3 of Alg. 4) in a block of statements that does not modify the content of array $done$ to ensure that its outcome will be the same for all threads.

Phases 2 and 3: Merge and Duplicate Detection (Alg. 4). Procedure $duplicate$ $Detection_w$ corresponds to phases 2 and 3 and can be decomposed into four sub-steps. The entry in each sub-step is protected by a barrier. A thread first awaits all its peers to have called the procedure and be waiting at the barrier at l. 2. The parallel merge of successor lists $\mathcal{N}$ in the candidate set C (Phase 2 of Fig. 2) can then take place (l. 2).

Before exploring the reconstruction tree to remove duplicate states from C, all threads first start to mark (with $\mathbf{R}$ and $\mathbf{A}$ tags) the appropriate branches using procedure $tagNodesforDD_w$ (l. 4) in order to avoid reconstructing all states. For efficiency reasons, we assume that the data structure implementing the candidate set can be partitioned in $\mathcal{W}$ classes and that a thread can recover the class it is responsible for using the function $ownedCandidates$ (l. 17). For a candidate state c, the nodes that must be reconstructed are all nodes that have the same hash value as c (ll. 18–21) because these might, after reconstruction, match with c. It is the purpose of the $conflict$ function used at l. 19 to return the identifiers of these nodes. The $tagPath_w$ procedure is used to put a specific tag on a node and all its ancestors. It stops as soon as it reaches the root or a node that already has this tag (in which case all its ancestors also have it).

The reconstruction begins when all threads have finished tagging the branches that need to be explored. The exploration procedure $dfsDD_w$ used to reconstruct states follows the same pattern as procedure $dfsExpand_w$ of Alg. 3. Reconstructed states removed from the candidate set C are those with the $\mathbf{R}$ tag (ll. 23–25) and nodes explored are those with the $\mathbf{A}$ tag (ll. 26–31). In both cases, a processed node is untagged.

All threads must have finished their exploration in order to decide which candidate states are actually new. Thread 0 is then responsible (l. 6) for inserting the new states (those that are still present in C) in the tree using the procedure $insertNodes_w$. Only the last two components of the candidates are required for insertion: the identifier ($parentId$) of the node of which the expansion generated the candidate and the event used to generate it. A new node is then inserted in the tree and the tag $\mathbf{E}_{\neg r}$ is put on all nodes on the path from the initial node to this new node to signify that this node must be

Algorithm 4. Procedures used during merge and duplicate detection phases

1: **procedure** $duplicateDetection_w()$ **is**
2:     $\underline{barrier}()$; $parallelMerge(\mathcal{N}, C)$
3:     $allDone := \wedge_{x \in \{0,...,\mathcal{W}-1\}} done[x]$
4:     $\underline{barrier}()$; $tagNodesForDD_w()$
5:     $\underline{barrier}()$; $dfsDD_w(s_0, id_0)$
6:     $\underline{barrier}()$; **if** $w = 0$ **then** $insertNodes_w()$
7:     **return** $allDone$
8: **procedure** $tagPath_w(id, tag)$ **is**
9:     **while** $id \neq \perp \wedge \neg tagged(id, tag)$ **do**
10:       $tag(id, tag)$
11:       $id := parent(id)$
12: **procedure** $insertNodes_w()$ **is**
13:     **for** $(\_, parentId, e) \in C$ **do**
14:       $id := newNode(parentId, e)$
15:       $tagPath_w(id, \mathbf{E}_{\neg r})$

16: **procedure** $tagNodesForDD_w()$ **is**
17:     **for** $(s, \_, \_) \in ownedCandidates(w)$ **do**
18:       $h := hash(s)$
19:       **for** $id \in conflict(h)$ **do**
20:         $tag(id, \mathbf{R})$
21:         $tagPath_w(parent(id), \mathbf{A})$
22: **procedure** $dfsDD_w(id, s)$ **is**
23:     **if** $tagged(id, \mathbf{R})$ **then**
24:       $removeCandidate(s)$
25:       $untag(id, \mathbf{R})$
26:     **if** $tagged(id, \mathbf{A})$ **then**
27:       **for** $(id', e) \in random(children(id))$ **do**
28:         **if** $tagged(id', \mathbf{A})$
29:         **or** $tagged(id', \mathbf{R})$ **then**
30:         $dfsDD_w(id', succ(s, e))$
31:     $untag(id, \mathbf{A})$

expanded. This insertion step is performed only by thread 0 because the data structure we have chosen for the reconstruction tree does not easily support concurrent insertions although it allows for multiple concurrent read accesses (or node tagging/untagging). Therefore, other threads may proceed to the next expansion step as thread 0 inserts new nodes in the tree. As an extension, this insertion step could also be parallelised. The only situation where other threads have to wait for thread 0 to finish this insertion is when a BFS level has been completely processed, i.e. duplicate detection and insertion was not triggered by a threshold in l. 13 of procedure *dfsExpand*. They will then be waiting at the barrier of procedure *expandLevel$_w$* (l. 7 of Alg. 3).

5 Implementation and Experimental Evaluation

We have integrated our algorithm in the Helena tool [4]. We discuss below the most important implementation aspects and present the results from an experimental evaluation of our algorithm based on the Helena implementation.

Implementation. The implementation uses the pthread library that provides synchronisation barriers. The reconstruction tree $\mathcal{T}$ is implemented as a fixed size hash table using open addressing with linear probing. This allows to support multiple read accesses with a single insertion as performed when thread 0 inserts new nodes in the reconstruction tree while other threads continue their expansion of open states. A main requirement is the possibility to get the parent and children of a node. To reduce the number of pointers and save memory, we represent kinships as linked lists where the parent node stores the identifier (i.e. the slot of the hash table) of its first child in field *fstChild* and each child stores the identifier of the next child in field *next*. Only the last child of the list (identified using a *last* bit set to 1 while the previous children have it set to 0) points with *next* to the parent node. Fig. 7 provides an illustration of this for an example tree. To enumerate the children of a node, we first follow its *fstChild* pointer and then the *next* pointers of its children until the last child with *last* = 1 is met. Recovering the parent of a node is done by following the *next* pointers until the last child is met and then by following the *next* pointer to reach the parent. This means that we cannot get the parent of a node in constant time but this is not a practical problem as the number of children is usually low.

This representation requires $2 \cdot \log_2(|ID|) + 1$ bits per node for the *fstChild* and *next* pointers and the *last* bit. Four more bits are required for tags (R, A, E_0 and E_1) and $\log_2(|\mathcal{E}|)$ bits for the event generating the node from its parent. Hence, a node can be encoded in $2 \cdot \log_2(|ID|) + 5 + \log_2(|\mathcal{E}|)$ bits. To have a representation that is model independent, we encode in each node an event number (the number

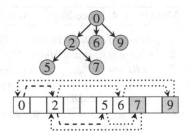

Fig. 7. Implementation of the reconstrunction tree. Dashed lines represent the *fstChild* pointers. Dotted lines represent the *next* pointers. Gray cells identify nodes with *last* = 1.

in the list of enabled events of the parent) rather than the event itself. This requires to recompute enabled events when exploring the tree but leads to significant savings for models such as high-level Petri nets, where events are often complex data structures. We also implemented the fresh successor heuristic [10] that, in our context, forces threads to engage in part of the state tree that no thread is currently visiting. Implementing this heuristic requires two bits per node (one for the expansion step and one for the duplicate detection step) to tag branches where threads are currently engaged.

To avoid concurrent accesses in the successor lists of $\mathcal{N}$, we implemented this data structure as a matrix of size $|\mathcal{W} \times \mathcal{W}|$ where each cell stores a list and using a hash function *hash* on states. During the expansion step, a worker w inserts any new successor state s in the list of cell $(w, hash(s) \mod \mathcal{W})$. During the merging step performed to merge states of successor lists $\mathcal{N}$ into table C, a worker thread $w \in \{0, \ldots, \mathcal{W} - 1\}$ is responsible for moving from $\mathcal{N}$ to C all states s with $hash(s) \mod \mathcal{W} = w$. Thus, during the merging step, it only needs to merge states contained in the list of cells (x, w) for $x \in \{0, \ldots, \mathcal{W} - 1\}$ and because of the use of the hash function no such states can be in a hash conflict with states processed by other threads. Since the expansion and merging steps cannot overlap due to the use of barriers, there cannot be any concurrent insertions or deletions on the lists in $\mathcal{N}$. The candidate set C is also implemented as a fixed size hash table, and a state can only be inserted (if not already present) in a slot l of C such that $l \mod \mathcal{W} = w$. Hence, there cannot be concurrent accesses on a same slot of C during the merging step. During the duplicate detection step occurring right after, the deletion of a state is simply made by swapping a bit in the slot of the deleted state. These choices imply that C can be implemented without locks.

Experimental Setup and Results. We have conducted our experiments on the models of Table 1. The *Time* reported (in seconds) are those obtained with a sequential algorithm, i.e., with a single worker. Helena has its own modelling language for high-level Petri nets and can also analyse automata written in the DVE language, the input language of the DiVinE model checker [1]. We have selected a set of 10 models having

Table 1. Models used for experimental evaluation

Helena models				DVE models			
Model	States	Arcs	Time	Model	States	Arcs	Time
eratosthene	195.3 M	1.252 G	9,689	collision.5	431.9 M	1.644 G	7,570
leader	188.9 M	2.530 G	24,086	firewire-link.3	425.3 M	1.621 G	8,782
neo-election	406.1 M	3.796 G	40,943	iprotocol.8	447.5 M	1.501 G	7,505
peterson	172.1 M	860.7 M	5,105	pub-sub.5	1.153 G	5.447 G	49,395
slotted	189.1 M	1.742 G	12,018	synapse.9	1.675 G	3.291 G	64,842

a set of reachable states ranging from 172 millions (M) to 1.675 billions (G) of states. The memory limit, measured as the maximal number of state vectors the algorithm can keep in memory (in the successor lists and, hence, in the candidate set) was set, for all runs, to one thousandth of the reachable states of the model. We performed our experiments on a 12-core computer with 64 GB of RAM and evaluated our algorithm on each model with 1 to 12 worker threads. Note that, when using a single thread, our algorithm becomes identical to the sequential algorithm of [7] that uses state compression, state reconstruction, and delayed duplicate detection, except for some minor differences on the data structures used, and the implicit representation of the open set.

Our experimental results have been plotted in Fig 8. On the horizontal axis of the three plots is the number of working threads used ranging from 1 to 12. The top plot, entitled *Speed-up*, gives execution times as the ratio of the execution time for 1 thread over the execution time for n threads. The middle plot, entitled *Event execution*, gives the total number of events executed (at any step of the algorithm and by any thread) for n threads relatively to the same number for 1 thread. This measure provides a means to evaluate how good the work is balanced among threads. The bottom plot, *Barrier time*, gives, as a percentage of the total execution time, the time spent by threads at barriers waiting for other threads to join them. It is computed as the average over all threads of the individual barrier times and is reported in percentage of the overall execution time.

Interpretation of Results. The *Speed-up* plot shows a stable speed-up as the number of threads involved increases. As a general trend, Helena models (see Table 1(left)) have better speed-ups than DVE models (see Table 1(right)) considering that Helena models are penalised by a larger redundant work factor (see the *Event execution* plot). We conjecture that this is due to the cost of model operations (computing enabled events, executing events) that are much more costly for high-level Petri nets than for DVE models. Since these operations are purely local and do not need to access shared data structures (the reconstruction tree or the candidate set) they can be more efficiently parallelised. Also note that the algorithm is resilient with respect to the random function we used. We do not provide these results here due to lack of space, but we observed that performance never significantly differed between two runs on the same model.

As expected, the workloads shown by the *Event execution* plot increase with the number of threads but usually following a logarithmic progression. For the four models standing out with a larger amount of redundant work (eratosthene, leader, neo-election and slotted), we see a correlation with the high proportion of arcs of the state space with an average number of arcs per state ranging from 6 up to 13 (see Table 1); and with their state spaces that have diamond like structures. Due to the way nodes are inserted in the reconstruction tree, this automatically increases the proportion of nodes that have no (or few) children nodes in the tree which in turn decreases the potential parallelism. For instance, if two states at the same BFS level have the same successors states, the first state visited among the two will have some successors in the tree whereas the second one will not have any. This situation often occurred for the models mentioned. For these four models we observed that once the exploration completed, the proportion of leaves in the tree reached 65%–70%. For other models, this proportion is around 40%–50%.

The *Barrier time* plot shows that the waiting times remain low with an average (over all runs involving more than 1 thread) of less than 2% of the total exploration time. In the worst case, this time represented around 2.5% of the exploration time (for model synapse.9). Moreover, unlike for event executions, there is no real correlation between the number of working threads and waiting times observed and increasing the number of threads does not seem to have any negative effects in that respect.

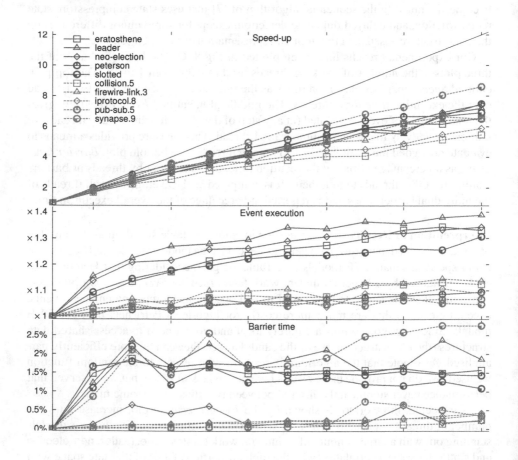

Fig. 8. Experimental results

6   Conclusion and Perspectives

This paper is the logical continuation of previous work based on the principle of state reconstruction that can significantly reduce the memory usage in state space exploration by avoiding the storage of full state vectors of states while maintaining a full coverage of the state space. The foundations of this method have been established in [6,14] and then extended in [7] with the principle of delayed duplicate detection that allows grouping state reconstructions and, hence, saves the redundant executions of shared reconstructing sequences. We also conjectured in [7] that parallelisation could further reduce the cost of duplicate detection. Following this intuition, we developed in this paper an algorithm designed for multi-core processors that preserves previous characteristics in terms of state reconstruction [6,14] and delayed duplicate detection [7].

A main feature of our algorithm is that locks can be avoided by the use of synchronisation barriers separating the different steps of the algorithm. A key property of the algorithm is also that the size of the frontier set can be bounded by a predefined threshold making the memory consumption predictable. A series of experiments done with Helena on a 12-core computer has shown good speed-up with negligible waiting times and a low amount of redundant work (threads that simultaneously engage in the same branch of the tree). The low barrier times show that synchronisation represents a very small overhead which leaves little room for further improvement in that respect. Our observations rather lead us to pursue two directions to further improve the speed-up of our algorithm. First, despite its low memory usage, the data structure we have chosen for the reconstruction tree does not show enough locality. Since the children of a node can be anywhere in the state table due to the hashing mechanism, traversing the tree requires accessing multiple memory areas which in turn means frequent cache misses. It is then relevant to design and experiment with a different data structure that takes better advantage of caching. Second, redundant explorations are still problematic for some models even if the fresh successor heuristic turned out to be quite efficient in that it allowed to reduce the overall workload by a factor of 10–20%. Besides the use of appropriate heuristics, it is also important to address the unbalanced distribution of child nodes (i.e. situations where two states have similar successor states but only one has children in the state tree) that we observed for a few models.

Related Works. Several data structures have been designed for multi-core model checking or reachability analysis: [11,12,13]. All have in common to avoid the use of locks. The approach that seems the closest to ours is the tree database proposed in [12] as it is designed for high scalability while making use of state compression. Speed-ups reported in [12] are clearly better with this tree database structure: the average speed-up on all models of the BEEM database is almost optimal. Nevertheless our algorithm still has some advantages over [12]. First, its memory usage is model independent which is not true for the tree database although, on the average, compression ratios are excellent for BEEM models (around 8 bytes per state [12]). Second, the algorithm of [12] assumes fixed width state vectors, an assumption that does not hold for specification languages such as high-level Petri nets. Last, the support of a delete operation does not seem straightforward in the tree database and hence it is not obvious how to combine it with reduction techniques based on on-the-fly state deletions.

Perspectives. To further assess the scalability of our algorithm a direct practical perspective is to experiment with it with larger models and on massively parallel architectures (e.g. 256-core machines).

The reconstruction tree can be used to check basic properties such as system invariants or to perform offline LTL or CTL model checking. It is relevant to study how our algorithm could serve as a basis for the implementation of on-the-fly LTL algorithms that are compliant with the breadth-first search order, e.g. [3,8]. A last perspective is to study how our algorithm combines with other reduction techniques. The state caching reduction we proposed in [5] maintains a termination detection tree (TD-tree) to keep track of open states. Termination is guaranteed if all states of the TD-tree are kept in memory and these consists of all nodes tagged with E_0 or E_1 in our parallel algorithm. Hence, all other nodes can be safely discarded. For partial order reduction, a breadth-first search compatible solution has been proposed in [2]. For both reductions [2,5] it remains to be investigated how they can be efficiently combined with our algorithm.

References

1. Barnat, J., Brim, L., Češka, M., Ročkai, P.: DiVinE: Parallel Distributed Model Checker. In: HiBi/PDMC 2010, pp. 4–7. IEEE (2010)
2. Bošnački, D., Holzmann, G.J.: Improving Spin's Partial-Order Reduction for Breadth-First Search. In: Godefroid, P. (ed.) SPIN 2005. LNCS, vol. 3639, pp. 91–105. Springer, Heidelberg (2005)
3. Brim, L., Černá, I., Moravec, P., Šimša, J.: Accepting Predecessors Are Better than Back Edges in Distributed LTL Model-Checking. In: Hu, A.J., Martin, A.K. (eds.) FMCAD 2004. LNCS, vol. 3312, pp. 352–366. Springer, Heidelberg (2004)
4. Evangelista, S.: High Level Petri Nets Analysis with Helena. In: Ciardo, G., Darondeau, P. (eds.) ICATPN 2005. LNCS, vol. 3536, pp. 455–464. Springer, Heidelberg (2005)
5. Evangelista, S., Kristensen, L.M.: Search-Order Independent State Caching. In: Jensen, K., Donatelli, S., Koutny, M. (eds.) ToPNoC IV. LNCS, vol. 6550, pp. 21–41. Springer, Heidelberg (2010)
6. Evangelista, S., Pradat-Peyre, J.-F.: Memory Efficient State Space Storage in Explicit Software Model Checking. In: Godefroid, P. (ed.) SPIN 2005. LNCS, vol. 3639, pp. 43–57. Springer, Heidelberg (2005)
7. Evangelista, S., Westergaard, M., Kristensen, L.: The ComBack Method Revisited: Caching Strategies and Extension with Delayed Duplicate Detection. In: Jensen, K., Billington, J., Koutny, M. (eds.) ToPNoC III. LNCS, vol. 5800, pp. 189–215. Springer, Heidelberg (2009)
8. Holzmann, G.J.: Parallelizing the Spin Model Checker. In: Donaldson, A., Parker, D. (eds.) SPIN 2012. LNCS, vol. 7385, pp. 155–171. Springer, Heidelberg (2012)
9. Jaja, J.: Parallel Algorithms. Addisson-Wesley (2002)
10. Laarman, A., van de Pol, J.: Variations on Multi-Core Nested Depth-First Search. In: PDMC 2011, pp. 13–28 (2011), http://arxiv.org/abs/1111.0064v1
11. Laarman, A., van de Pol, J., Weber, M.: Boosting Multi-Core Reachability Performance with Shared Hash Tables. In: FMCAD 2010, pp. 247–255. IEEE (2010)
12. Laarman, A., van de Pol, J., Weber, M.: Parallel Recursive State Compression for Free. In: Groce, A., Musuvathi, M. (eds.) SPIN Workshops 2011. LNCS, vol. 6823, pp. 38–56. Springer, Heidelberg (2011)

13. Saad, R.T., Dal-Zilio, S., Berthomieu, B.: Mixed Shared-Distributed Hash Tables Approaches for Parallel State Space Construction. In: ISPDC, pp. 9–16. IEEE (2011)
14. Westergaard, M., Kristensen, L.M., Brodal, G.S., Arge, L.: The ComBack Method – Extending Hash Compaction with Backtracking. In: Kleijn, J., Yakovlev, A. (eds.) ICATPN 2007. LNCS, vol. 4546, pp. 445–464. Springer, Heidelberg (2007)
15. Wolper, P., Leroy, D.: Reliable Hashing without Collision Detection. In: Courcoubetis, C. (ed.) CAV 1993. LNCS, vol. 697, pp. 59–70. Springer, Heidelberg (1993)

Verification of Heap Manipulating Programs with Ordered Data by Extended Forest Automata

Parosh Aziz Abdulla[1], Lukáš Holík[2], Bengt Jonsson[1], Ondřej Lengál[2],
Cong Quy Trinh[1], and Tomáš Vojnar[2]

[1] Department of Information Technology, Uppsala University, Sweden
[2] FIT, Brno University of Technology, IT4Innovations Centre of Excellence, Czech Republic

Abstract. We present a general framework for verifying programs with complex dynamic linked data structures whose correctness depends on ordering relations between stored data values. The underlying formalism of our framework is that of forest automata (FA), which has previously been developed for verification of heap-manipulating programs. We extend FA by constraints between data elements associated with nodes of the heaps represented by FA, and we present extended versions of all operations needed for using the extended FA in a fully-automated verification approach, based on abstract interpretation. We have implemented our approach as an extension of the Forester tool and successfully applied it to a number of programs dealing with data structures such as various forms of singly- and doubly-linked lists, binary search trees, as well as skip lists.

1 Introduction

Automated verification of programs that manipulate complex dynamic linked data structures is one of the most challenging problems in software verification. The problem becomes even more challenging when program correctness depends on relationships between data values that are stored in the dynamically allocated structures. Such ordering relations on data are central for the operation of many data structures such as search trees, priority queues (based, e.g., on skip lists), key-value stores, or for the correctness of programs that perform sorting and searching, etc. The challenge for automated verification of such programs is to handle *both* infinite sets of reachable heap configurations that have a form of complex graphs *and* the different possible relationships between data values embedded in such graphs, needed, e.g., to establish sortedness properties.

As discussed below in the section on related work, there exist many automated verification techniques, based on different kinds of logics, automata, graphs, or grammars, that handle dynamically allocated pointer structures. Most of these approaches abstract from properties of data stored in dynamically allocated memory cells. The few approaches that can automatically reason about data properties are often limited to specific classes of structures, mostly singly-linked lists (SLLs), and/or are not fully automated (as also discussed in the related work paragraph).

In this paper, we present a general framework for verifying programs with complex dynamic linked data structures whose correctness depends on relations between the stored data values. Our framework is based on the notion of *forest automata* (FA) which

D. Van Hung and M. Ogawa (Eds.): ATVA 2013, LNCS 8172, pp. 224–239, 2013.

has previously been developed for representing sets of reachable configurations of programs with complex dynamic linked data structures [11]. In the FA framework, a heap graph is represented as a composition of tree components. Sets of heap graphs can then be represented by tuples of tree automata (TA). A fully-automated shape analysis framework based on FA, employing the framework of *abstract regular tree model checking* (ARTMC) [7], has been implemented in the Forester tool [13]. This approach has been shown to handle a wide variety of different dynamically allocated data structures with a performance that compares favourably to other state-of-the-art fully-automated tools.

Our extension of the FA framework allows us to represent relationships between data elements stored inside heap structures. This makes it possible to automatically verify programs that depend on relationships between data, such as various search trees, lists, and skip lists [17], and to also verify, e.g., different sorting algorithms. Technically, we express relationships between data elements associated with nodes of the heap graph by two classes of constraints. *Local data constraints* are associated with transitions of TA and capture relationships between data of neighbouring nodes in a heap graph; they can be used, e.g., to represent ordering internal to some structure such as a binary search tree. *Global data constraints* are associated with states of TA and capture relationships between data in distant parts of the heap. In order to obtain a powerful analysis based on such extended FA, the entire analysis machinery must have been redesigned, including a need to develop mechanisms for propagating data constraints through FA, to adapt the abstraction mechanisms of ARTMC, to develop a new inclusion check between extended FAs, and to define extended abstract transformers.

Our verification method analyzes sequential, non-recursive C programs, and automatically discovers memory safety errors, such as invalid dereferences or memory leaks, and provides an over-approximation of the set of reachable program configurations. Functional properties, such as sortedness, can be checked by adding code that checks pre- and post-conditions. Functional properties can also be checked by querying the computed over-approximation of the set of reachable configurations.

We have implemented our approach as an extension of the Forester tool, which is a gcc plug-in analyzing the intermediate representation generated from C programs. We have applied the tool to verification of data properties, notably sortedness, of sequential programs with data structures, such as various forms of singly- and doubly-linked lists (DLLs), possibly cyclic or shared, binary search trees (BSTs), and even 2-level and 3-level skip lists. The verified programs include operations like insertion, deletion, or reversal, and also bubble-sort and insert-sort both on SLLs and DLLs. The experiments confirm that our approach is not only fully automated and rather general, but also quite efficient, outperforming many previously known approaches even though they are not of the same level of automation or generality. In the case of skip lists, our analysis is the first fully-automated shape analysis which is able to handle skip lists. Our previous fully-automated shape analysis, which did not handle ordering relations, could also handle skip lists automatically [13], but only after modifying the code in such a way that the preservation of the shape invariant does not depend on ordering relations.

Related Work. As discussed previously, our approach builds on the fully automated FA-based approach for shape analysis of programs with complex dynamic linked data structures [11,13]. We significantly extend this approach by allowing it to track ordering relations between data values stored inside dynamic linked data structures.

For shape analysis, many other formalisms than FA have been used, including, e.g., separation logic and various related graph formalisms [21,16,8,10], other logics [19,14], automata [7], or graph grammars [12]. Compared with FA, these approaches typically handle less general heap structures (often restricted to various classes of lists) [21,10], they are less automated (requiring the user to specify loop invariants or at least inductive definitions of the involved data structures) [16,8,10,12], or less scalable [7].

Verification of properties depending on the ordering of data stored in SLLs was considered in [5], which translates programs with SLLs to counter automata. A subsequent analysis of these automata allows one to prove memory safety, sortedness, and termination for the original programs. The work is, however, strongly limited to SLLs. In this paper, we get inspired by the way that [5] uses for dealing with ordering relations on data, but we significantly redesign it to be able to track not only ordering between simple list segments but rather general heap shapes described by FA. In order to achieve this, we had to not only propose a suitable way of combining ordering relations with FA, but we also had to significantly modify many of the operations used over FA.

In [1], another approach for verifying data-dependent properties of programs with lists was proposed. However, even this approach is strongly limited to SLLs, and it is also much less efficient than our current approach. In [2], concurrent programs operating on SLLs are analyzed using an adaptation of a transitive closure logic [4], which also tracks simple sortedness properties between data elements.

Verification of properties of programs depending on the data stored in dynamic linked data structures was considered in the context of the TVLA tool [15] as well. Unlike our approach, [15] assumes a fixed set of shape predicates and uses inductive logic programming to learn predicates needed for tracking non-pointer data. The experiments presented in [15] involve verification of sorting and stability properties of several programs on SLLs (merging, reversal, bubble-sort, insert-sort) as well as insertion and deletion in BSTs. We do not handle stability, but for the other properties, our approach is much faster. Moreover, for BSTs, we verify that a node is greater/smaller than all the nodes in its left/right subtrees (not just than the immediate successors as in [15]).

An approach based on separation logic extended with constraints on the data stored inside dynamic linked data structures and capable of handling size, ordering, as well as bag properties was presented in [9]. Using the approach, various programs with SLLs, DLLs, and also AVL trees and red-black trees were verified. The approach, however, requires the user to manually provide inductive shape predicates as well as loop invariants. Later, the need to provide loop invariants was avoided in [18], but a need to manually provide inductive shape predicates remains.

Another work that targets verification of programs with dynamic linked data structures, including properties depending on the data stored in them, is [22]. It generates verification conditions in an undecidable fragment of higher-order logic and discharges them using decision procedures, first-order theorem proving, and interactive theorem proving. To generate the verification conditions, loop invariants are needed. These can either be provided manually or sometimes synthesized semi-automatically using the approach of [20]. The latter approach was successfully applied to several programs with

SLLs, DLLs, trees, trees with parent pointers, and 2-level skip lists. However, for some of them, the user still had to provide some of the needed abstraction predicates.

Several works, including [6], define frameworks for reasoning about pre- and post-conditions of programs with SLLs and data. Decidable fragments, which can express more complex properties on data than we consider, are identified, but the approach does not perform fully automated verification, only checking of pre-post condition pairs.

2   Programs, Graphs, and Forests

We consider sequential non-recursive C programs, operating on a set of variables and the heap, using standard commands and control flow constructs. Variables are either *data variables* or *pointer variables*. Heap cells contain zero or several selector fields and a data field (our framework and implementation extends easily to several data fields). Atomic commands include tests between data variables or fields of heap cells, as well as assignments between data variables, pointer variables, or fields of heap cells. We also support commands for allocation and deallocation of dynamically allocated memory.

Fig. 1 shows an example of a C function insert-ing a new node into a BST (recall that in BSTs, the data value in a node is larger than all the values of its left subtree and smaller than all the values of its right subtree). Variable x descends the BST to find the position at which the node newNode with a new data value d should be inserted.

```
0   Node *insert(Node *root, Data d){
1       Node* newNode = calloc(sizeof(Node));
2       if (!newNode) return NULL;
3       newNode→data = d;
4       if (!root) return newNode;
5       Node *x = root;
6       while (x→data != newNode→data)
7           if (x→data < newNode→data)
8               if (x→right) x = x→right;
9               else x→right = newNode;
10          else
11              if (x→left) x = x→left;
12              else x→left = newNode;
13      if (x != newNode) free(newNode);
14      return root;
15  }
```

Fig. 1. Insertion into a BST

Configurations of the considered programs consist to a large extent of heap-allocated data. A *heap* can be viewed as a (directed) graph whose nodes correspond to allocated memory cells. Each node contains a set of selectors and a data field. Each selector either points to another node, to the value null, or is undefined. The same holds for pointer variables of the program.

We represent graphs as a composition of trees as follows. We first identify the *cut-points* of the graph, i.e., nodes that are either referenced by a pointer variable or by several selectors. We then split the graph into tree components such that each cut-point becomes the root of a tree component. To represent the interconnection of tree components, we introduce a set of *root references*, one for each tree component. After decomposition of the graph, selector fields that point to cut-points in the graph are redirected to point to the corresponding root references. Such a tuple of tree components is called a *forest*. The decomposition of a graph into tree components can be performed canonically as described at the end of Section 3.

Fig. 2(a) shows a possible heap of the program in Fig. 1. Nodes are shown as circles, labeled by their data values. Selectors are shown as edges. Each selector points either to a node or to ⊥ (denoting null). Some nodes are labeled by a pointer variable that points to them. The node with data value 15 is a cut-point since it is referenced by variable x. Fig. 2(b) shows a tree decomposition of the graph into two trees, one rooted at the node referenced by root, and the other rooted at the node pointed by x. The right selector of the root node in the first tree points to root reference $\overline{2}$ ($\overline{i}$ denotes a reference to the i-th tree t_i) to indicate that in the graph, it points to the corresponding cut-point.

Let us now formalize these ideas. We will define graphs as parameterized by a set Γ of selectors and a set Ω of references. Intuitively, the references are the objects that selectors can point to, in addition to other nodes. E.g., when representing heaps, Ω will contain the special value `null`; in tree components, Ω will also include root references.

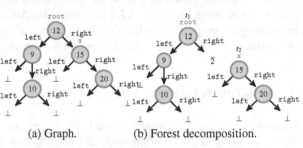

(a) Graph.   (b) Forest decomposition.

Fig. 2. Decomposition of a graph into trees

We use $f : A \rightharpoonup B$ to denote a partial function from A to B (also viewed as a total function $f : A \to (B \cup \{\bot\})$, assuming that $\bot \notin B$). We assume an unbounded data domain $\mathbb{D}$ with a total ordering relation $\preceq$.

Graphs. Let Γ be a finite set of *selectors* and Ω be a finite set of *references*. A *graph g* over $\langle \Gamma, \Omega \rangle$ is a tuple $\langle V_g, next_g, \lambda_g \rangle$ where V_g is a finite set of *nodes* (assuming $V_g \cap \Omega = \emptyset$), $next_g : \Gamma \to (V_g \rightharpoonup (V_g \cup \Omega))$ maps each selector $a \in \Gamma$ to a partial mapping $next_g(a)$ from nodes to nodes and references, and $\lambda_g : (V_g \cup \Omega) \rightharpoonup \mathbb{D}$ is a partial *data labelling* of nodes and references. For a selector $a \in \Gamma$, we use a_g to denote the mapping $next_g(a)$.

Program Semantics. A *heap* over Γ is a graph over $\langle \Gamma, \{\text{null}\} \rangle$ where `null` denotes the null value. A *configuration* of a program with selectors Γ consists of a program control location, a heap g over Γ, and a partial valuation, which maps pointer variables to $V_g \cup \{\text{null}\}$ and data variables to $\mathbb{D}$. For uniformity, data variables will be represented as pointer variables (pointing to nodes that hold the respective data values) so we can further consider pointer variables only. The dynamic behaviour of a program is given by a standard mapping from configurations to their successors, which we omit here.

Forest Representation of Graphs. A graph t is a *tree* if its nodes and selectors (i.e., not references) form a tree with a unique root node, denoted $root(t)$. A *forest* over $\langle \Gamma, \Omega \rangle$ is a sequence $t_1 \cdots t_n$ of trees over $\langle \Gamma, (\Omega \uplus \{\overline{1}, \ldots, \overline{n}\}) \rangle$. The element in $\{\overline{1}, \ldots, \overline{n}\}$ are called *root references* (note that n must be the number of trees in the forest). A forest $t_1 \cdots t_n$ is *composable* if $\lambda_{t_k}(\overline{j}) = \lambda_{t_j}(root(t_j))$ for any k, j, i.e., the data labeling of root references agrees with that of roots. A composable forest $t_1 \cdots t_n$ over $\langle \Gamma, \Omega \rangle$ represents a graph over $\langle \Gamma, \{\text{null}\} \rangle$, denoted $\otimes t_1 \cdots t_n$, obtained by taking the union of the trees of $t_1 \cdots t_n$ (assuming w.l.o.g. that the sets of nodes of the trees are disjoint), and connecting root references with the corresponding roots. Formally, $\otimes t_1 \cdots t_n$ is the graph g defined by (i) $V_g = \cup_{i=1}^{n} V_{t_i}$, and (ii) for $a \in \Gamma$ and $v \in V_{t_k}$, if $a_{t_k}(v) \in \{\overline{1}, \ldots, \overline{n}\}$ then $a_g(v) = root(t_{a_{t_k}(v)})$ else $a_g(v) = a_{t_k}(v)$, and finally (iii) $\lambda_g(v) = \lambda_{t_k}(v)$ for $v \in V_{t_k}$.

3   Forest Automata

A forest automaton is essentially a tuple of tree automata accepting a set of tuples of trees that represents a set of graphs via their forest decomposition.

Tree Automata. A (finite, non-deterministic, top-down) *tree automaton* (TA) over $\langle \Gamma, \Omega \rangle$ extended with data constraints is a triple $A = (Q, q_0, \Delta)$ where Q is a finite set of *states*, $q_0 \in Q$ is the *root state* (or initial state), denoted $root(A)$, and Δ is a set of *transitions*. Each transition is of the form $q \to \bar{a}(q_1, \ldots, q_m) : c$ where $m \geq 0$, $q \in Q$, $q_1, \ldots, q_m \in (Q \cup \Omega)$, $\bar{a} = a^1 \cdots a^m$ is a sequence of different symbols from Γ, and c is a set of *local constraints*. Each local constraint is of the form $0 \sim_{rx} i$ where $\sim \in \{\prec, \preceq, \succ, \succeq, =, \neq\}$, $i \in \{1, \ldots, m\}$, and $x \in \{r, a\}$. Intuitively, a local constraint of the form $0 \sim_{rr} i$ states that the data value of the *root* of every tree t accepted at q is related by $\sim$ with the data value of the *root* of the ith subtree of t accepted at q_i. A local constraint of the form $0 \sim_{ra} i$ states that the data value of the *root* of every tree t accepted at q is related by $\sim$ to the data values of *all* nodes of the i-th subtree of t accepted at q_i.

Let t be a tree over $\langle \Gamma, \Omega \rangle$, and let $A = (Q, q_0, \Delta)$ be a TA over $\langle \Gamma, \Omega \rangle$. A *run* of A over t is a total map $\rho : V_t \to Q$ where $\rho(root(t)) = q_0$ and for each node $v \in V_t$ there is a transition $q \to \bar{a}(q_1, \ldots, q_m) : c$ in Δ with $\bar{a} = a^1 \cdots a^m$ such that (1) $\rho(v) = q$, (2) for all $1 \leq i \leq m$, we have (i) if $q_i \in Q$, then $a_t^i(v) \in V_t$ and $\rho(a_t^i(v)) = q_i$, and (ii) if $q_i \in \Omega$, then $a_t^i(v) = q_i$, and (3) for each constraint in c, the following holds:

- if the constraint is of the form $0 \sim_{rr} i$, then $\lambda_t(v) \sim \lambda_t(a_t^i(v))$, and
- if the constraint is of the form $0 \sim_{ra} i$, then $\lambda_t(v) \sim \lambda_t(w)$ for all nodes w in V_t that are in the subtree of t rooted at $a_t^i(v)$.

We define the *language* of A as $L(A) = \{t \mid \text{there is a run of } A \text{ over } t\}$.

Example 1. BSTs, like the tree labeled by x in Fig. 2, are accepted by the TA with one state q_1, which is also the root state, and the following four transitions:

$q_1 \to$ left,right(q_1, q_1) $: 0 \succ_{ra} 1, 0 \prec_{ra} 2$ $q_1 \to$ left,right(q_1, null) $: 0 \succ_{ra} 1$

$q_1 \to$ left,right$(\text{null}, q_1) : 0 \prec_{ra} 2$ $q_1 \to$ left,right$(\text{null}, \text{null})$

The local constraints of the transitions express that the data value in a node is always greater than the data values of all nodes in its left subtree and less than the data values of all nodes in its right subtree.

A TA that accepts BSTs in which the right selector of the root node points to a root reference, like that labeled by root in Fig. 2, can be obtained from the above TA by adding one more state q_0, which then becomes the root state, and the additional transition $q_0 \to$ left,right$(q_1, \bar{2}) : 0 \succ_{ra} 1, 0 \prec_{rr} 2$ (note that the occurrence of 2 in the root reference $\bar{2}$ is not related with the occurrence of 2 in the local constraint).   □

Forest Automata. A *forest automaton with data constraints* (or simply a forest automaton, FA) over $\langle \Gamma, \Omega \rangle$ is a tuple of the form $F = \langle A_1 \cdots A_n, \varphi \rangle$ where:

- $A_1 \cdots A_n$, with $n \geq 0$, is a sequence of TA over $\langle \Gamma, \Omega \uplus \{\bar{1}, \ldots, \bar{n}\} \rangle$ whose sets of states $Q_1, \ldots, Q_n$ are mutually disjoint.
- φ is a set of *global data constraints* between the states of $A_1 \cdots A_n$, each of the form $q \sim_{rr} q'$ or $q \sim_{ra} q'$ where $q, q' \in \cup_{i=1}^{n} Q_i$, at least one of q, q' is a root state which does not appear on the right-hand side of any transition (i.e., it can accept only the root of a tree), and $\sim \in \{\prec, \preceq, \succ, \succeq, =, \neq\}$. Intuitively, $q \sim_{rr} q'$ says that the data value of any tree node accepted at q is related by $\sim$ to the data value of any tree node accepted at q'. Similarly, $q \sim_{ra} q'$ says that the data value of any tree node accepted at q is related by $\sim$ to the data values of *all* nodes of the trees accepted at q'.

A forest $t_1 \cdots t_n$ over $\langle \Gamma, \Omega \rangle$ is *accepted* by F iff there are runs $\rho_1, \ldots, \rho_n$ such that ρ_i is a run of A_i over t_i for every $1 \leq i \leq n$, and for each global constraint of the form $q \sim_{rx} q'$ where q is a state of some A_i and q' is a state of some A_j, we have

- if $rx = rr$, then $\lambda_{t_i}(v) \sim \lambda_{t_j}(v')$ whenever $\rho_i(v) = q$ and $\rho_j(v') = q'$,
- if $rx = ra$, then $\lambda_{t_i}(v) \sim \lambda_{t_j}(w)$ whenever $\rho_i(v) = q$ and w is in a subtree rooted at some v' with $\rho_j(v') = q'$.

The *language* of F, denoted as $L(F)$, is the set of graphs over $\langle \Gamma, \Omega \rangle$ obtained by applying $\otimes$ on composable forests accepted by F. An FA F over $\langle \Gamma, \{\texttt{null}\} \rangle$ represents a set of heaps H over Γ.

Note that global constraints can imply some local ones, but they cannot in general be replaced by local constraints only. Indeed, global constraints can relate states of different automata as well as states that do not appear in a single transition and hence accept nodes which can be arbitrarily far from each other and unrelated by any sequence of local constraints.

Canonicity. In our analysis, we will represent only *garbage-free* heaps in which all nodes are reachable from some pointer variable by following some sequence of selectors. In practice, this is not a restriction since emergence of garbage is checked for each statement in our analysis; if some garbage arises, an error message can be issued, or the garbage removed. The representation of a garbage-free heap H as $t_1 \cdots t_n$ can be made canonical by assuming a total order on variables and on selectors. Such an ordering induces a canonical ordering of cut-points using a depth-first traversal of H starting from pointer variables, taken in their order, and exploring H according to the order of selectors. The representation of H as $t_1 \cdots t_n$ is called *canonical* iff the roots of the trees in $t_1 \cdots t_n$ are the cut-points of H, and the trees are ordered according to their canonical ordering. An FA $F = \langle A_1 \cdots A_n, \varphi \rangle$ is *canonicity respecting* iff for all $H \in L(F)$, formed as $H = \otimes t_1 \cdots t_n$, the representation $t_1 \cdots t_n$ is canonical. The canonicity respecting form allows us to check inclusion on the sets of heaps represented by FA by checking inclusion component-wise on the languages of the component TA.

4 FA-Based Shape Analysis with Data

Our verification procedure performs a standard abstract interpretation. The concrete domain in our case assigns to each program location a set of pairs $\langle \sigma, H \rangle$ where the *valuation* σ maps every variable to $\texttt{null}$, a node in H, or to an undefined value, and H is a heap representing a memory configuration. On the other hand, the abstract domain maps each program location to a finite set of *abstract configurations*. Each abstract configuration is a pair $\langle \sigma, F \rangle$ where σ maps every variable to $\texttt{null}$, an index of a TA in F, or to an undefined value, and F is an FA representing a set of heaps.

Example 2. The example illustrates an abstract configuration $\langle \sigma, F \rangle$ encoding a single concrete configuration $\langle \sigma, H \rangle$ of the program in Fig. 1. A memory node referenced by newNode is going to be added as the left child of the leaf referenced by x, which is reachable from the root by the sequence of selectors left right. The data values along the path from root to x must be in the proper relations with the data value of newNode, in order for the tree to stay sorted also after the addition. The data value of newNode must be smaller than that of the root (i.e., $q_r \succ_{ra} q_{nN}$), larger than that of its left child (i.e., $q \prec_{ra} q_{nN}$), and smaller than that of x (i.e., $q_x \succ_{ra} q_{nN}$). These relations and also $q \prec_{ra} q_x$ have been accumulated during the tree traversal.   □

The verification starts from an element in the abstract domain that represents the initial program configuration (i.e., it maps the initial program location to an abstract configuration where the heap is empty and the values of all variables are undefined, and maps

$$F = \langle A_1 A_2 A_3, \varphi \rangle$$
$$\sigma(\text{root}) = \overline{1}, \sigma(x) = \overline{2}, \sigma(\text{newNode}) = \overline{3}$$
$$A_1 : \begin{cases} q_r \to \text{left}, \text{right}(q, \text{null}) : 0 \succ_{ra} 1 \\ q \to \text{left}, \text{right}(\text{null}, \overline{2}) : \ 0 \prec_{ra} 2 \end{cases}$$
$$A_2 : q_x \to \text{left}, \text{right}(\text{null}, \text{null})$$
$$A_3 : q_{nN} \to \text{left}, \text{right}(\text{null}, \text{null})$$
$$\varphi = \{ q_r \succ_{ra} q_{nN}, q \prec_{ra} q_{nN}, q_x \succ_{ra} q_{nN}, q \prec_{ra} q_x \}$$

non-initial program locations to an empty set of abstract configurations). The verification then iteratively updates the sets of abstract configurations at each program point until a fixpoint is reached. Each iteration consists of the following steps:

1. The sets of abstract configurations at each program point are updated by abstract transformers corresponding to program statements. At junctions of program paths, we take the unions of the sets produced by the abstract transformers.

2. At junctions that correspond to loop points, the union is followed by a widening operation and a check for language inclusion between sets of FA in order to determine whether a fixpoint has been reached. Prior to checking language inclusion, we normalize the FA, thereby transforming them into the canonicity respecting form.

Our widening operation bounds the size of the TA that occur in abstract configurations. It is based on the framework of *abstract regular (tree) model checking* [7]. The widening is applied to individual TA inside each FA and collapses states which are equivalent w.r.t. certain criteria. More precisely, we collapse TA states q, q' which are equivalent in the sense that they (1) accept trees with the same sets of prefixes of height at most k and (2) occur in isomorphic global data constraints (i.e., $q \sim_{rx} p$ occurs as a global constraint if and only if $q' \sim_{rx} p$ occurs as a global constraint, for any p and x). We use a refinement of this criterion by certain FA-specific requirements, by adapting the refinement described in [13]. Collapsing states may increase the set of trees accepted by a TA, thereby introducing overapproximation into our analysis.

At the beginning of each iteration, the FA to be manipulated are in the saturated form, meaning that they explicitly include all (local and global) data constraints that are consequences of the existing ones. FA can be put into a saturated form by a saturation procedure, which is performed before the normalization procedure. The saturation procedure must also be performed before applying abstract transformers that may remove root states from an FA, such as memory deallocation.

In the following subsections, we provide more detail on some of the major steps of our analysis. Section 4.1 describes the constraint saturation procedure, Section 4.2 describes some representative abstract transformers, Section 4.3 describes normalization, and Section 4.4 describes our check for inclusion.

4.1   Constraint Saturation

In the analysis, we work with FA that are saturated by explicitly adding into them various (local and global) data constraints that are implied by the existing ones. The saturation is based on applying several saturation rules, each of which infers new constraints from the existing ones, until no more rules can be applied. Because of space limitations, we present here only a representative sample of the rules. A complete description of our saturation rules can be found in [3]. Our saturation rules can be structured into the following classes.

- New global constraints can be inferred from existing global constraints by using properties of relations, such as transitivity, reflexivity, or symmetry (when applicable). For instance, from $q \preceq_{rr} q'$ and $q' \prec_{ra} q''$, we infer $q \prec_{ra} q''$ by transitivity.
- New global or local constraints can be inferred by weakening the existing ones. For instance, from $q \prec_{ra} q'$, we infer the weaker constraint $q \preceq_{rr} q'$.
- Each local constraint $0 \prec_{rr} i$ where $q_i \in \Omega$ or q_i has nullary outgoing transitions only can be strengthened to $0 \prec_{ra} i$. The latter applies to global transitions too.
- New local constraints can be inferred from global ones by simply transforming a global constraint into a local constraint whenever the states in a transition are related by a global constraint. For instance, if $q \to \overline{a}(q_1, \ldots, q_m) : c$ is a transition, then from $q \preceq_{rr} q_i$, we infer the local constraint $0 \preceq_{rr} i$ and add it to c.
- If q is a state of a TA A and p is a state of A or another TA of the given FA such that in each sequence of states through which q can be reached from the root state of A there is a state q' such that $p \sim_{ra} q'$, then a constraint $p \sim_{ra} q$ is added as well.
- Whenever there is a TA A_1 with a root state q_0 and a state q such that (i) $q_0 \succeq_{rr} q$, (ii) q has an outgoing transition in whose right-hand side a state q_i appears where q_i is a reference to a TA A_2, and (iii) c includes a constraint $0 \succeq_{rr} i$, then a global constraint $q_0 \succeq_{rr} p_0$ can be added for the root state p_0 of A_2 (likewise for other kinds of relations than $\succeq_{rr}$). Conversely, from $q_0 \succeq_{rr} p_0$ and $q_0 \succeq_{rr} q$, one can derive the local constrain $0 \succeq_{rr} i$.
- Finally, global constraints can be inferred from existing ones by propagating them over local constraints of transitions in which the states of the global constraints occur. Let us illustrate this on a small example. Assume we are given a TA A that has states $\{q_0, q_1, q_2\}$ with q_0 being the root state and the following transitions: $q_0 \to \overline{a}(q_1, q_2) : \{0 \prec_{rr} 1, 0 \prec_{rr} 2\}$, $q_1 \to \overline{a}(\texttt{null}, \texttt{null}) : \emptyset$, and $q_2 \to \overline{a}(\texttt{null}, \texttt{null}) : \emptyset$. Let p be a root state of some TA in an FA in which A appears. There are two ways to propagate global constraints between the states of A, either *downwards* from the root towards leaves or *upwards* from leaves towards the root.
  - In downwards propagation, we can infer $q_2 \succ_{ra} p$ from $q_0 \succeq_{ra} p$, using the local constraint $0 \prec_{rr} 2$.
  - In upwards propagation, we can infer $q_0 \prec_{rr} p$ from $q_2 \prec_{rr} p$, using the local constraint $0 \prec_{rr} 2$.

In more complex situations, a single state may be reached in several different ways. In such cases, propagation of global constraints through local constraints on all transitions arriving to the given state must be considered. If some of the ways how to get to the state does not allow the propagation, it cannot be done. Moreover, since one propagation can enable another one, the propagation must be done iteratively until a fixpoint is reached (for more details, see [3]). Note that the iterative propagation must terminate since the number of constraints that can be used is finite.

4.2 Abstract Transformers

For each operation op in the intermediate representation of the analysed program corresponding to the function f_{op} on concrete configurations $\langle \sigma, H \rangle$, we define an abstract transformer τ_{op} on abstract configurations $\langle \sigma, F \rangle$ such that the result of $\tau_{op}(\langle \sigma, F \rangle)$ denotes the set $\{f_{op}(\langle \sigma, H \rangle) \mid H \in L(F)\}$. The abstract transformer τ_{op} is applied separately for each pair $\langle \sigma, F \rangle$ in an abstract configuration. Note that all our abstract transformers τ_{op} are exact.

Let us present the abstract transformers corresponding to some operations on abstract states of form $\langle \sigma, F \rangle$. For simplicity of presentation, we assume that for all TA A_i in F, (a) the root state of A_i does not appear in the right-hand side of any transition, and (b) it occurs on the left-hand side of exactly one transition. It is easy to see that any TA can be transformed into this form (see [3] for details).

Let us introduce some common notation and operations for the below transformers. We use $A_{\sigma(x)}$ and $A_{\sigma(y)}$ to denote the TA pointed by variables x and y, respectively, and q_x and q_y to denote the root states of these TA. Let $q_y \rightarrow \bar{a}(q_1, \ldots, q_i, \ldots, q_m) : c$ be the unique transition from q_y. We assume that sel is represented by a^i in the sequence $\bar{a} = a^1 \cdots a^m$ so that q_i corresponds to the target of sel. By *splitting* a TA $A_{\sigma(y)}$ at a state q_i for $1 \leq i \leq m$, we mean appending a new TA A_k to F such that A_k is a copy of $A_{\sigma(y)}$ but with q_i as the root state, followed by changing the root transition in $A_{\sigma(y)}$ to $q_y \rightarrow \bar{a}(q_1, \ldots, \bar{k}, \ldots, q_m) : c'$ where c' is obtained from c by replacing any local constraint of the form $0 \sim_{rx} i$ by the global constraint $q_y \sim_{rx} root(A_k)$. Global data constraints are adapted as follows: For each constraint $q \sim_{rx} p$ where q is in $A_{\sigma(y)}$ such that $q \neq q_y$, a new constraint $q' \sim_{rx} p$ is added. Likewise, for each constraint $q \sim_{rx} p$ where p is in $A_{\sigma(y)}$ such that $p \neq q_y$, a new constraint $q \sim_{rx} p'$ is added. Finally, for each constraint of the form $p \sim_{ra} q_y$, a new constraint $p \sim_{ra} root(A_k)$ is added.

Before performing the actual update, we check whether the operation to be performed tries to dereference a pointer to null or to an undefined value, in which case we stop the analysis and report an error. Otherwise, we continue by performing one of the following actions, depending on the particular statement:

x = malloc() We extend F with a new TA A_{new} containing one state and one transition where all selector values are undefined and assign $\sigma(x)$ to the index of A_{new} in F.

x = y->sel If q_i is a root reference (say, j), it is sufficient to change the value of $\sigma(x)$ to j. Otherwise, we split $A_{\sigma(y)}$ at q_i (creating A_k) and assign k to $\sigma(x)$.

y->sel = x If q_i is a state, then we split $A_{\sigma(y)}$ at q_i. Then we put $\overline{\sigma(x)}$ to the i-th position in the right-hand side of the root transition of $A_{\sigma(y)}$; this is done both if q_i is a state and if q_i is a root reference. Any local constraint in c of the form $0 \sim_{rx} i$ which concerns the removed root reference q_i is then removed from c.

y->data = x->data First, we remove any local constraint that involves q_y or a root reference to $A_{\sigma(y)}$. Then, we add a new global constraint $q_y =_{rr} q_x$, and we also keep all global constraints of the form $q' \sim_{rx} q_y$ if $q' \sim_{rr} q_x$ is implied by the constraints obtained after the update.

y->data $\sim$ x->data (where $\sim \in \{\prec, \preceq, \succ, \succeq, =, \neq\}$) First, we execute the saturation procedure in order to infer the strongest constraints between q_y and q_x. Then, if there exists a global constraint $q_y \sim' q_x$ that implies $q_y \sim q_x$ (or its negation), we return *true* (or *false*). Otherwise, we copy $\langle \sigma, F \rangle$ into two abstract configurations: $\langle \sigma, F_{true} \rangle$ for the *true* branch and $\langle \sigma, F_{false} \rangle$ for the *false* branch. Moreover, we extend F_{true} with the global constraint $q_y \sim q_x$ and F_{false} with its negation.

x = y **or** x = NULL We simply update σ accordingly.

free(y) First, we split $A_{\sigma(y)}$ at all states q_j, $1 \leq j \leq m$, that appear in its root transition, then we remove $A_{\sigma(y)}$ from F and set $\sigma(y)$ to undefined. However, to keep all possible data constraints, before removing $A_{\sigma(y)}$, the saturation procedure is executed. After the action is done, every global constraint involving q_y is removed.

x == y This operation is evaluated simply by checking whether $\sigma(x) = \sigma(y)$. If $\sigma(x)$ or $\sigma(y)$ is undefined, we assume both possibilities.

After the update, we check that all TA in F are referenced, either by a variable or from a root reference, otherwise we report emergence of garbage.

4.3 Normalization

Normalization transforms an FA $F = (A_1 \cdots A_n, \varphi)$ into a canonicity respecting FA in three major steps:

1. First, we transform F into a form in which roots of trees of accepted forests correspond to cut-points in a uniform way. In particular, for all $1 \leq i \leq n$ and all accepted forests $t_1 \cdots t_n$, one of the following holds: (a) If the root of t_i is the j-th cut-point in the canonical ordering of an accepted forest, then it is the j-th cut-point in the canonical ordering of all accepted forests. (b) Otherwise the root of t_i is not a cut-point of any of the accepted forests.
2. Then we merge TA so that the roots of trees of accepted forests are cut-points only, which is described in detail below.
3. Finally, we reorder the TA according to the canonical ordering of cut-points (which are roots of the accepted trees).

Our procedure is an augmentation of that in [11] used to normalize FA without data constraints. The difference, which we describe below, is an update of data constraints while performing Step 2.

In order to minimize a possible loss of information encoded by data constraints, Step 2 is preceded by saturation (Section 4.1). Then, for all $1 \leq i \leq n$ such that roots of trees accepted by $A_i = (Q_A, q_A, \Delta_A)$ are not cut-points of the graphs in $L(F)$ and such that there is a TA $B = (Q_B, q_B, \Delta_B)$ that contains a root reference to A_i, Step 2 performs the following. The TA A_i is removed from F, data constraints between q_A and non-root states of F are removed from φ, and A_i is connected to B at the places where B refers to it. In detail, B is replaced by the TA $(Q_A \cup Q_B, q_B, \Delta_{A+B})$ where Δ_{A+B} is constructed from $\Delta_A \cup \Delta_B$ by modifying every transition $q \to \bar{a}(q_1, \ldots, q_m) : c \in \Delta_B$ as follows:

1. all occurrences of $\bar{i}$ among $q_1, \ldots, q_m$ are replaced by q_A, and
2. for all $1 \leq k \leq m$ s.t. q_k can reach $\bar{i}$ by following top-down a sequence of the original rules of Δ_B, the constraint $0 \sim_{ra} k$ is removed from c unless $q_k \sim_{ra} q_A \in \varphi$.

4.4 Checking Language Inclusion

In this section, we describe a reduction of checking language inclusion of FAs with data constraints to checking language inclusion of FAs without data constraints, which can be then performed by the techniques of [11]. We note that "ordinary FAs" correspond to FAs with no global and no local data constraints. Intuitively, an *encoding* of an FA $F = (A_1 \cdots A_n, \varphi)$ with data constraints is an ordinary FA $F^E = (A_1^E \cdots A_n^E, \emptyset)$ where the data constraints are written into symbols of transitions. In detail, each transition $q \to \overline{a}(q_1, \ldots, q_m) : c$ of $A_i, 1 \leq i \leq n$, is in A_i^E replaced by the transition $q \to \langle (a_1, c_1, c_g) \cdots (a_m, c_m, c_g) \rangle (q_1, \ldots, q_m) : \emptyset$ where for $1 \leq j \leq m$, c_j is the subset of c involving j, and c_g encodes the global constraints involving q as follows: for a global constraint $q \sim_{rx} r$ or $r \sim_{rx} q$ where r is the root state of $A_k, 1 \leq k \leq n$, that does not appear within any right-hand side of a rule, c_g contains $0 \sim_{rx} k$ or $k \sim_{rx} 0$, respectively. The language of A_i^E thus consists of trees over the alphabet $\Gamma^E = \Gamma \times \mathbb{C} \times \mathbb{C}$ where $\mathbb{C}$ is the set of constraints of the form $j \sim_{rx} k$ for $j, k \in \mathbb{N}_0$.

Dually, a *decoding* of a forest $t_1 \cdots t_n$ over Γ^E is the set of forests $t_1' \cdots t_n'$ over Γ which arise from $t_1 \cdots t_n$ by (1) removing encoded constraints from the symbols, and (2) choosing data labeling that satisfies the constraints encoded within the symbols of $t_1 \cdots t_n$. Formally, for all $1 \leq i \leq n$, $V_{t_i'} = V_{t_i}$, and for all $a \in \Gamma$, $u, v \in V_{t_i'}$, and $c, c_g \subseteq \mathbb{C}$, we have $(a, c, c_g)_{t_i}(u) = v$ iff: (1) $a_{t_i'}(u) = v$ and (2) for all $1 \leq j \leq n$: if $0 \sim_{rx} j \in c$, then $u \sim_{rx} v$, and if $0 \sim_{rx} j \in c_g$, then $u \sim_{rx} root(t_j)$ (symmetrically for $j \sim_{rx} 0$). The notation $u \sim_{rx} v$ for $u, v \in V_{t'}$ used here has the expected meaning that $\lambda_{t_i'}(u) \sim \lambda_{t_i'}(v)$ and, in case of $x = a$, $\lambda_{t_i'}(u) \sim \lambda_{t_i'}(w)$ for all nodes w in the subtree rooted by v.

The following lemma (proved in [3])assures that encodings of FA are related in the expected way with decodings of forests they accept.

Lemma 1. *The set of forests accepted by an FA F is equal to the union of decodings of forests accepted by F^E.*

A direct consequence of Lemma 1 is that if $L(F_A^E) \subseteq L(F_B^E)$, then $L(F_A) \subseteq L(F_B)$. We can thus use the language inclusion checking procedure of [11] for ordinary FA to safely approximate language inclusion of FA with data constraints.

However, the above implication of inclusions does not hold in the opposite direction, for two reasons. First, constraints of F_B that are strictly weaker than constraints of F_A will be translated into different labels. The labels will then be treated as *incomparable* by the inclusion checking algorithm of [11]. For instance, let $F_A = (A_1, \emptyset)$ where A_1 contains only one transition $\delta_A = q \to a(\overline{1}) : \{0 \prec_{rr} 1\}$ and $F_B = (B_1, \emptyset)$ where B_1 contains only one transition $\delta_B = r \to a(\overline{1}) : \emptyset$. We have that $L(F_A) \subseteq L(F_B)$ (indeed, $L(F_A) = \emptyset$ due to the strict inequality on the root), but $L(F_A^E)$ is incomparable with $L(F_B^E)$. The reason is that δ_A and δ_B are encoded as transitions the symbols of which differ due to different data constraints. The fact that the constraint $\emptyset$ is weaker than the constraint of $0 \prec_{rr} 1$ plays no role. The second source of incompleteness of our inclusion checking procedure is that decodings of some forests accepted by F_A^E and F_B^E may be empty due to inconsistent data constraints. If the set of such inconsistent forests of F_A^E is not included in that of F_B^E, then $L(F_A^E)$ cannot be included in $L(F_B^E)$, but the inclusion $L(F_A) \subseteq L(F_B)$ can still hold since the forests with the empty decodings do not contribute to $L(F_A)$ and $L(F_B)$ (in the sense of Lemma 1).

We do not attempt to resolve the second difficulty since ruling out forests with inconsistent data constraints seems to be complicated, and according to our experiments, it does not seem necessary. On the other hand, we resolve the first difficulty by a quite simple transformation of F_B^E: we pump up the TAs of F_B^E by variants of their transitions which encode stronger data constraints than originals and match the data constraints on transitions of F_A^E. For instance, in our previous example, we wish to add the transition $r \to a(\overline{1}) : \{0 \prec_{rr} 1\}$ to B_1. Notice that this does not change the language of F_B, but makes checking of $L(F_A^E) \subseteq L(F_B^E)$ pass.

Particularly, we call a sequence $\overline{\alpha} = (a_1, c_1, c_g) \cdots (a_m, c_m, c_g) \in (\Gamma^E)^m$ *stronger* than a sequence $\overline{\beta} = (a_1, c_1', c_g') \cdots (a_m, c_m', c_g')$ iff $\bigwedge c_g \implies \bigwedge c_g'$ and for all $1 \leq i \leq m$, $\bigwedge c_i \implies \bigwedge c_i'$. Intuitively, $\overline{\alpha}$ encodes the same sequence of symbols $\overline{a} = a_1 \cdots a_m$ as $\overline{\beta}$ and stronger local and global data constraints than $\overline{\beta}$. We modify F_B^E in such a way that for each transition $r \to \overline{\alpha}(r_1, \ldots, r_m)$ of F_B^E and each transition of F_A^E of the form $q \to \overline{\beta}(q_1, \ldots, q_m)$ where $\overline{\beta}$ is stronger than $\overline{\alpha}$, we add the transition $q \to \overline{\beta}(q_1, \ldots, q_m)$. The modified FA, denoted by $F_B^{E^+}$, accepts the same or more forests than F_B^E (since its TA have more transitions), but the sets of decodings of the accepted forests are the same (since the added transitions encode stronger constraints than the existing transitions). FA $F_B^{E^+}$ can thus be used within language inclusion checking in the place of F_B^E. The checking is still sound, and the chance of missing inclusion is smaller. The following lemma (proved in [3]) summarises soundness of the (approximation of) inclusion check which is implemented in our tool.

Lemma 2. *Given two FAs F_A and F_B, $L(F_A^E) \subseteq L(F_B^{E^+}) \implies L(F_A) \subseteq L(F_B)$*

We note that the same construction is used when checking language inclusion between sets of FAs with data constraints in a combination with the construction of [11] for checking inclusion of sets of ordinary FAs. We also note that for the purpose of checking language inclusion, we need to work with TAs where the tuples $\overline{a}$ of symbols (selectors) on all rules are ordered according to a fixed total ordering of selectors (we use the one from Section 3, used to define canonical forests).

5   Boxes

Forest automata, as defined in Section 3, cannot be used to represent sets of graphs with an unbounded number of cut-points since this would require an unbounded number of TAs within FAs. An example of such a set of graphs is the set of all DLLs of an arbitrary length where each internal node is a cut-point. The solution provided in [11] is to allow FAs to use other nested FAs, called boxes, as symbols to "hide" recurring subgraphs and in this way eliminate cut-points. Here, we give only an informal description of a simplified version of boxes from [11] and of their combination with data constraints. See [3] for details.

A *box* $\square = \langle F_\square, i, o \rangle$ consists of an FA $F_\square = \langle A_1 \cdots A_n, \varphi \rangle$ accompanied with an *input port index* i and an *output port index* o, $1 \leq i, o \leq n$. Boxes can be used as symbols in the alphabet of another FA F. A graph g from $L(F)$ over an alphabet Γ enriched with boxes then represents a set of graphs over Γ obtained by the operation of *unfolding*.

Table 1. Results of the experiments

Example	time	Example	time	Example	time	Example	time
SLL insert	0.06	DLL insert	0.14	BST insert	6.87	SL_2 insert	9.65
SLL delete	0.08	DLL delete	0.38	BST delete	114.00	SL_2 delete	10.14
SLL reverse	0.07	DLL reverse	0.16	BST left rotate	7.35	SL_3 insert	56.99
SLL bubblesort	0.13	DLL bubblesort	0.39	BST right rotate	6.25	SL_3 delete	57.35
SLL insertsort	0.10	DLL insertsort	0.43				

Unfolding replaces an edge with a box label $\Box$ by a graph $g_\Box \in L(F_\Box)$. The node of $g_\Box$ which is the root of a tree accepted by A_i is identified with the source of the replaced edge, and the node of $g_\Box$ which is the root of a tree accepted by A_o is mapped to the target of the edge. The *semantics* of F then consists of all fully unfolded graphs from the language of F. The alphabet of a box itself may also include boxes, however, these boxes are required to form a hierarchy, they cannot be recursively nested.

In a verification run, boxes are automatically inferred using the techniques presented in [13]. Abstraction is combined with *folding*, which substitutes substructures of FAs by TA transitions which use boxes as labels. On the other hand, *unfolding* is required by abstract transformers that refer to nodes or selectors encoded within a box to expose the content of the box by making it a part of the top-level FA.

In order not to loose information stored within data constraints, folding and unfolding require some additional calls of the saturation procedure. When folding, saturation is used to transform global constraints into local ones. Namely, global constraints between the root state of the TA which is to become the input port of a box and the state of the TA which is to become the output port of the box is transformed into a local constraint of the newly introduced transition which uses the box as a label. When unfolding, saturation is used to transform local constraints into global ones. Namely, local constraints between the left-hand side of the transition with the unfolded box and the right-hand side position attached to the unfolded box is transformed to a global constraint between the root states of the TA within the box which correspond to its input and output port.

6   Experimental Results

We have implemented the above presented techniques as an extension of the Forester tool and tested their generality and efficiency on a number of case studies. We considered programs dealing with SLLs, DLLs, BSTs, and skip lists. We verified the original implementation of skip lists that uses the data ordering relation to detect the end of the operated window (as opposed to the implementation handled in [13] which was modified to remove the dependency of the algorithm on sortedness).

Table 1 gives running times in seconds (the average of 10 executions) of the extension of Forester on our case studies. The names of the examples in the table contain the name of the data structure manipulated in the program, which is "SLL" for singly-linked lists, "DLL" for doubly-linked lists, and "BST" for binary search trees. "SL" stands for skip lists where the subscript denotes their level (the total number of next pointers in each cell). All experiments start with a random creation of an instance of the specified structure and end with its disposal. The indicated procedure is performed in between. The "insert" procedure inserts a node into an ordered instance of the structure, at the position given by the data value of the node, "delete" removes the first node with a particular data value, and "reverse" reverses the structure. "Bubblesort" and "insertsort" perform the given sorting algorithm on an unordered instance of the list. "Left rotate" and "right rotate" rotate the BST in the specified direction. Before the disposal of the data structure, we further check that it remained ordered after execution of the operation. Source code of the case studies can be found in [3]. The experiments were run on a machine with the Intel i5 M 480 (2.67 GHz) CPU and 5 GB of RAM.

Compared with works [15,20,5,18], which we consider the closest to our approach, the running times show that our approach is significantly faster. We, however, note that a precise comparison is not easy even with the mentioned works since as discussed in the related work paragraph, they can handle more complex properties on data, but on the other hand, they are less automated or handle less general classes of pointer structures.

7 Conclusion

We have extended the FA-based analysis of heap manipulating programs with a support for reasoning about data stored in dynamic memory. The resulting method allows for verification of pointer programs where the needed inductive invariants combine complex shape properties with constraints over stored data, such as sortedness. The method is fully automatic, quite general, and its efficiency is comparable with other state-of-the-art analyses even though they handle less general classes of programs and/or are less automated. We presented experimental results from verifying programs dealing with variants of (ordered) lists and trees. To the best of our knowledge, our method is the first one to cope fully automatically with a full C implementation of a 3-level skip list.

We conjecture that our method generalises to handle other types of properties in the data domain (e.g., comparing sets of stored values) or other types of constraints (e.g., constraints over lengths of lists or branches in a tree needed to express, e.g., balancedness of a tree). We are currently working on an extension of FA that can express more general classes of shapes (e.g., B+ trees) by allowing recursive nesting of boxes, and employing the CEGAR loop of ARTMC. We also plan to combine the method with techniques to handle concurrency.

Acknowledgement. This work was supported by the Czech Science Foundation (projects P103/10/0306, 13-37876P), the Czech Ministry of Education, Youth, and Sports (project MSM 0021630528), the BUT FIT project FIT-S-12-1, the EU/Czech IT4Innovations Centre of Excellence project CZ.1.05/1.1.00/02.0070, the Swedish Foundation for Strategic Research within the ProFuN project, and by the Swedish Research Council within the UPMARC centre of excellence.

References

1. Abdulla, P.A., Atto, M., Cederberg, J., Ji, R.: Automated Analysis of Data-Dependent Programs with Dynamic Memory. In: Liu, Z., Ravn, A.P. (eds.) ATVA 2009. LNCS, vol. 5799, pp. 197–212. Springer, Heidelberg (2009)

2. Abdulla, P.A., Haziza, F., Holík, L., Jonsson, B., Rezine, A.: An Integrated Specification and Verification Technique for Highly Concurrent Data Structures. In: Piterman, N., Smolka, S.A. (eds.) TACAS 2013. LNCS, vol. 7795, pp. 324–338. Springer, Heidelberg (2013)
3. Abdulla, P.A., Holík, L., Jonsson, B., Lengál, O., Trinh, C.Q., Vojnar, T.: Verification of Heap Manipulating Programs with Ordered Data by Extended Forest Automata. Technical report FIT-TR-2013-02, FIT BUT (2013)
4. Bingham, J., Rakamarić, Z.: A Logic and Decision Procedure for Predicate Abstraction of Heap-Manipulating Programs. In: Emerson, E.A., Namjoshi, K.S. (eds.) VMCAI 2006. LNCS, vol. 3855, pp. 207–221. Springer, Heidelberg (2006)
5. Bouajjani, A., Bozga, M., Habermehl, P., Iosif, R., Moro, P., Vojnar, T.: Programs with Lists Are Counter Automata. Formal Methods in System Design 38(2), 158–192 (2011)
6. Bouajjani, A., Drăgoi, C., Enea, C., Sighireanu, M.: Accurate Invariant Checking for Programs Manipulating Lists and Arrays with Infinite Data. In: Chakraborty, S., Mukund, M. (eds.) ATVA 2012. LNCS, vol. 7561, pp. 167–182. Springer, Heidelberg (2012)
7. Bouajjani, A., Habermehl, P., Rogalewicz, A., Vojnar, T.: Abstract Regular (Tree) Model Checking. Int. Journal on Software Tools for Technology Transfer 14(2), 167–191 (2012)
8. Chang, B.-Y.E., Rival, X., Necula, G.C.: Shape Analysis with Structural Invariant Checkers. In: Riis Nielson, H., Filé, G. (eds.) SAS 2007. LNCS, vol. 4634, pp. 384–401. Springer, Heidelberg (2007)
9. Chin, W.-N., David, C., Nguyen, H., Qin, S.: Automated Verification of Shape, Size and Bag Properties via User-defined Predicates in Separation Logic. Science of Computer Programming 77(9), 1006–1036 (2012)
10. Dudka, K., Peringer, P., Vojnar, T.: Byte-Precise Verification of Low-Level List Manipulation. In: Logozzo, F., Fähndrich, M. (eds.) Static Analysis. LNCS, vol. 7935, pp. 215–237. Springer, Heidelberg (2013)
11. Habermehl, P., Holík, L., Rogalewicz, A., Šimáček, J., Vojnar, T.: Forest Automata for Verification of Heap Manipulation. In: Gopalakrishnan, G., Qadeer, S. (eds.) CAV 2011. LNCS, vol. 6806, pp. 424–440. Springer, Heidelberg (2011)
12. Heinen, J., Noll, T., Rieger, S.: Juggrnaut: Graph Grammar Abstraction for Unbounded Heap Structures. ENTCS, vol. 266 (2010)
13. Holík, L., Lengál, O., Rogalewicz, A., Šimáček, J., Vojnar, T.: Fully Automated Shape Analysis Based on Forest Automata. In: Sharygina, N., Veith, H. (eds.) CAV 2013. LNCS, vol. 8044, pp. 740–755. Springer, Heidelberg (2013), http://arxiv.org/abs/1304.5806
14. Jensen, J., Jørgensen, M., Klarlund, N., Schwartzbach, M.: Automatic Verification of Pointer Programs Using Monadic Second-order Logic. In: Proc. of PLDI 1997. ACM (1997)
15. Loginov, A., Reps, T., Sagiv, M.: Abstraction Refinement via Inductive Learning. In: Etessami, K., Rajamani, S.K. (eds.) CAV 2005. LNCS, vol. 3576, pp. 519–533. Springer, Heidelberg (2005)
16. Magill, S., Tsai, M., Lee, P., Tsay, Y.-K.: A Calculus of Atomic Actions. In: POPL 2010. ACM (2010)
17. Pugh, W.: Skip Lists: A Probabilistic Alternative to Balanced Trees. CACM 33(6) (1990)
18. Qin, S., He, G., Luo, C., Chin, W.-N., Chen, X.: Loop Invariant Synthesis in a Combined Abstract Domain. Journal of Symbolic Computation 50 (2013)
19. Sagiv, S., Reps, T., Wilhelm, R.: Parametric Shape Analysis via 3-valued Logic. TOPLAS 24(3) (2002)
20. Wies, T., Kuncak, V., Zee, K., Podelski, A., Rinard, M.: On Verifying Complex Properties using Symbolic Shape Analysis. In: Proc. of HAV 2007 (2007)
21. Yang, H., Lee, O., Berdine, J., Calcagno, C., Cook, B., Distefano, D., O'Hearn, P.: Scalable Shape Analysis for Systems Code. In: Gupta, A., Malik, S. (eds.) CAV 2008. LNCS, vol. 5123, pp. 385–398. Springer, Heidelberg (2008)
22. Zee, K., Kuncak, V., Rinard, M.: Full Functional Verification of Linked Data Structures. In: Proc. of PLDI 2008. ACM Press (2008)

Integrating Policy Iterations
in Abstract Interpreters*

Pierre Roux[1,2] and Pierre-Loïc Garoche[1]

[1] ONERA – The French Aerospace Lab, Toulouse, France
{pierre.roux,pierre-loic.garoche}@onera.fr
[2] ISAE, University of Toulouse, Toulouse, France

Abstract. Among precise abstract interpretation methods developed during the last decade, policy iterations is one of the most promising. Despite its efficiency, it has not yet seen a broad usage in static analyzers. We believe the main explanation to this restrictive use, beside the novelty of the technique, lies in its lack of integration in the classic abstract domain framework. This prevents an easy integration in existing static analyzers and collaboration with other, already implemented, abstract domains through reduced product. This paper aims at providing a classic abstract domain interface to policy iterations.

Usage of semidefinite programming to infer quadratic invariants on linear systems is one of the most appealing use of policy iteration. Combination with a template generation heuristic, inspired from existing methods from control theory, gives a fully automatic abstract domain to infer quadratic invariants on linear systems with guards. Those systems often constitute the core of embedded control systems and are hard, when not impossible, to analyze with linear abstract domains. The method has been implemented and applied to some benchmark systems, giving good results.

Keywords: abstract interpretation, policy iteration, linear systems with guards, quadratic invariants, ellipsoids, semidefinite programming.

1 Introduction

Classic abstract interpretation based static analysis [8] heavily relies on the so called *widening*. This operator discards some information in order to enforce termination of the analysis. A *narrowing* can then partly recover this lost information. These heuristics often enable a good trade-off between cost and precision of analyses. However, even if impressive improvements were made in the last decade to widening [3,11,21,28, and references therein] and narrowing [22], they do not always guarantee precise results.

Another approach, that appeared in the last decade in the software verification community [7, for instance], is the use of dedicated mathematical solvers like linear or semidefinite programming as a way to solve some kind of problems in a verification setting. This led to the definition of so-called *policy iterations* [1,6,14,15,18,19], as another way to perform overapproximation but trying to achieve better precision than widening-based analyses.

---

* This work has been partially supported by the FNRAE Project CAVALE and the ANR INS Project CAFEIN.

D. Van Hung and M. Ogawa (Eds.): ATVA 2013, LNCS 8172, pp. 240–254, 2013.

However, even if promising, policy iterations have had very little impact on existing tools yet: their use seems orthogonal to the classic use of abstract domains in a Kleene setting, where reduced products allow domains to exchange knowledge about the system during computation.

An explanation to the lack of integration of policy iterations with Kleene-based analyses is that they need to work on a global view of the analyzed system, typically a control flow graph representation of it, while Kleene-based analyzers iterate through program points without providing a global view of the program to the abstract domains. Our solution is mainly to compute this graph while iterating through the program points with a Kleene-based analysis. Once the graph is obtained it can easily be used by policy iterations to compute numerical properties about the program. Those properties can then be exported to other domains through a reduced product. Moreover this new abstract domain can be applied on a strict subset of program variables abstracting other variables by information obtained through reduced product from other domains[1], thus allowing a true interplay between policy iterations and existing abstract domains.

Our proposal has been instantiated on the analysis of linear systems with guards admitting quadratic inductive invariants. These linear systems are widely present in critical embedded systems like aerospace control-command software but are hard to analyze with most abstract domains since they usually do not admit simple linear inductive invariants. The use of our framework enables a fully automatic analysis of such systems, relying on policy iterations with semidefinite programming, while other approaches either impose stronger restrictions on the class of analyzable programs or require more parameters to enable the analysis. It has been implemented and gave significant results.

After a brief policy iteration primer, the paper is organized as follows:

- Section 3 offers an *abstract domain rebuilding the control flow graph* through classic Kleene-based analysis;
- Section 4 enables the *embedding of policy iteration in an abstract domain* based on this computed graph and on template domains;
- in Section 5, we *automatically synthesize meaningful templates* for a specific class of programs: guarded linear systems admitting quadratic invariants.

The paper also provides, in Section 6, experimental results computed using our implementation of the analysis.

2 State of the Art – A Policy Iteration Primer

2.1 A Toy Imperative Language

Throughout this paper, a very classic toy imperative language will be used to illustrate our abstract domains. Figure 1 presents a program in this language.

Syntax. A program of the language is a statement *stm* in the following grammar:

---

[1] As done with expensive relational domains in the abstract interpreter Astrée [9].

$stm ::= stm; stm \mid v := expr \mid v := ?(r, r) \mid \textbf{while } expr \leq r \textbf{ do } stm \textbf{ od}$
$\quad\quad \mid \textbf{if } expr \leq r \textbf{ then } stm \textbf{ else } stm \textbf{ fi}$
$expr ::= v \mid r \mid expr + expr \mid expr - expr \mid expr \times expr$

with $v \in \mathbb{V}$, a set of variables, and $r \in \mathbb{R}$. $?(r_1, r_2)$ represents a random choice of a real number between r_1 and r_2 (useful to simulate inputs).

Collecting Semantics. In the later, we denote by $[\![e]\!](\rho) \in \mathbb{R}$, the usual collecting semantics of an expression e in an environment $\rho : \mathbb{V} \to \mathbb{R}$; and by $[\![s]\!](R) \subseteq (\mathbb{V} \to \mathbb{R})$ the collecting semantics of a statement s for a set of environments $R \subseteq (\mathbb{V} \to \mathbb{R})$.

```
x0 := 0; x1 := 0; x2 := 0;
while −1 ≤ 0 do
    in := ?(−1, 1);
    x0' := x0; x1' := x1; x2' := x2;
    x0 := 0.9379 x0'−0.0381 x1'−0.0414 x2'+0.0237 in;
    x1 := −0.0404 x0'+0.968 x1'−0.0179 x2'+0.0143 in;
    x2 := 0.0142 x0'−0.0197 x1'+0.9823 x2'+0.0077 in;
od
```

Fig. 1. Example of program

It is worth noting that this semantics is given with operations over real numbers $\mathbb{R}$ whereas an actual program would compute using floating point values. This issue will not be addressed in this paper and is left as future work.

2.2 Kleene Iterations with Widening and Narrowing

The previous concrete semantics being non computable, the basic idea of abstract interpretation is to compute a so called abstract semantics. This abstract semantics is designed as a computable overapproximation of the concrete one.

Abstract domains constitute the basic bricks of abstract interpreters. They are given by a complete lattice $\mathcal{D}$, a concretization function $\gamma_{\mathcal{D}} : \mathcal{D} \to 2^{\mathbb{V} \to \mathbb{R}}$ and computable abstract operators $[\![v := e]\!]^\sharp$, $[\![v := ?(r_1, r_2)]\!]^\sharp$ and $[\![e \leq r]\!]^\sharp : \mathcal{D} \to \mathcal{D}$. The concretization function gives a concrete meaning to each abstract value in $\mathcal{D}$ by mapping it to the set of environments it abstracts. The abstract semantics $[\![.]\!]^\sharp$ is then defined by replacing semantics of assignments and guards with the corresponding abstract operator in the equations of the previous section. This abstract semantics can thus be computed, provided fixpoints are reachable after finitely many iterations of loop bodies' semantics. Assuming some soundness hypotheses on the abstract operators, the abstract semantics of a program p can be proved to be an overapproximation of the concrete one, that is $[\![p]\!] \subseteq \gamma_{\mathcal{D}}([\![p]\!]^\sharp)$.

An operator called widening is used to ensure convergence in finitely many iterations by giving up some precision. Some of this lost precision can then be retrieved by descending iterations with a so called narrowing. However, this does not always regain all of it.

Example 1. Analyzing the program of Figure 1 with the intervals domain, we get after a first iteration of the loop $x_0 \in [-0.0237, 0.0237] \wedge x_1 \in [-0.0143, 0.0143] \wedge x_2 \in [-0.0077, 0.0077]$. After a second iteration $x_0 \in [-0.0467, 0.0467] \wedge x_1 \in [-0.0292, 0.0292] \wedge x_2 \in [-0.0158, 0.0158],\ldots$ This does not converge, simply because the program does not admit any invariant in the intervals domain. Unlike the intervals domain, invariants exist in the polyhedra domain. However, classic Kleene iterations with this domain are in practice unable to compute any.

2.3 Policy Iterations

The basic idea of policy[2] iteration is to use numerical optimization tools to compute those bounds that are hard to guess for the widening or to retrieve via narrowing.

Another advantage of the method is to abstract sequences of program instructions like loop bodies "en bloc", avoiding intermediate abstractions which can cause irreversible losses of precision[3].

Template Domains. Policy iteration is performed on so called template domains. Given a finite set $\{t_1, \ldots, t_n\}$ of expressions on variables $\mathbb{V}$, the template domain $\mathcal{T}$ is defined as $\overline{\mathbb{R}}^n = (\mathbb{R} \cup \{-\infty, +\infty\})^n$ and the meaning of an abstract value $(b_1, \ldots, b_n) \in \mathcal{T}$ is the set of environments $\gamma_{\mathcal{T}}(b_1, \ldots, b_n) = \{\rho \in (\mathbb{V} \to \mathbb{R}) \mid [\![t_1]\!](\rho) \le b_1, \ldots, [\![t_n]\!](\rho) \le b_n\}$. In other words, the abstract value $(b_1, \ldots, b_n)$ represents all the environments satisfying all the constraints $t_i \le b_i$.

Indeed, many common abstract domains are template domains. For instance the intervals domain is obtained with templates x_i and $-x_i$ for all variables $x_i \in \mathbb{V}$ and the octagon domain [24] by adding all the $\pm x_i \pm x_j$. The shape of the templates to be considered for policy iteration depends on the optimization tools used. For instance, linear programming [14,16] allows any linear templates whereas quadratic templates can be handled thanks to semidefinite programming and an appropriate relaxation [1,18,19].

Example 2. To bound the variables of the program of Figure 1, we use the quadratic template[4]: $t_1 := 6.2547x_0^2 + 12.1868x_1^2 + 3.8775x_2^2 - 10.61x_0x_1 - 2.4306x_1x_2 + 2.4182x_1x_2$. Templates $t_2 := x_0^2$, $t_3 := x_1^2$ and $t_4 := x_2^2$ are added in order to get bounds on each variable.

System of Equations. While Kleene iterations iterate locally through each construct of the program, policy iterations require a global view on the analyzed program. For that purpose, the whole program is first translated into a system of equations which is later solved.

A first step in deriving those equations from the program is to build its control flow graph.

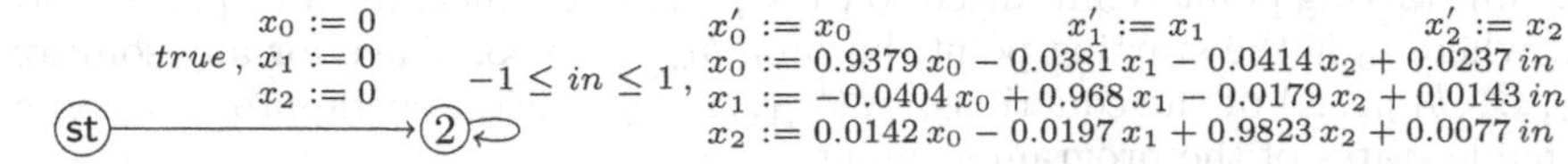

$$
\begin{array}{ll}
& x_0' := x_0 \qquad x_1' := x_1 \qquad x_2' := x_2 \\
x_0 := 0 & x_0 := 0.9379\,x_0 - 0.0381\,x_1 - 0.0414\,x_2 + 0.0237\,in \\
true,\ x_1 := 0 & \quad -1 \le in \le 1, \quad x_1 := -0.0404\,x_0 + 0.968\,x_1 - 0.0179\,x_2 + 0.0143\,in \\
x_2 := 0 & x_2 := 0.0142\,x_0 - 0.0197\,x_1 + 0.9823\,x_2 + 0.0077\,in
\end{array}
$$

(st) ⟶ (2)

Fig. 2. Control flow graph for our running example

Example 3. Figure 2 represents the control flow graph for our running example. Vertex "st" corresponds to the starting point of the program and vertex "2" to the head of the loop. The edge between "st" and "2" reflects the three assignments before the loop and the looping edge on vertex "2" represents the loop body.

---

[2] The word *strategy* is also used in the literature, with equivalent meaning.

[3] This is not illustrated here, one can refer for instance to [17] for more details.

[4] How this template was chosen will be explained later in Section 5.

It is worth noting that, unlike the usual notion of control flow graph with vertices between each single instruction of the program, sequences of instructions are here considered "en bloc" with graph vertices only for starting point and loop heads of the program. This will both improve the precision of the analysis and decrease its cost by avoiding useless intermediate abstractions.

A system of equations is then defined with a variable $b_{i,j}$ for each vertex i of the graph and each template t_j.

Example 4. Here is the system of equations for our running example:

$$
\begin{cases}
b_{1,1} = +\infty \quad\quad b_{1,2} = +\infty \quad\quad b_{1,3} = +\infty \quad\quad b_{1,4} = +\infty \\
b_{2,1} = \max\{0 \mid \mathrm{be}(1)\} \vee \max\{a(t_1) \mid -1 \le in \le 1 \wedge \mathrm{be}(2)\} \\
b_{2,2} = \max\{0 \mid \mathrm{be}(1)\} \vee \max\{a(t_2) \mid -1 \le in \le 1 \wedge \mathrm{be}(2)\} \\
b_{2,3} = \max\{0 \mid \mathrm{be}(1)\} \vee \max\{a(t_3) \mid -1 \le in \le 1 \wedge \mathrm{be}(2)\} \\
b_{2,4} = \max\{0 \mid \mathrm{be}(1)\} \vee \max\{a(t_4) \mid -1 \le in \le 1 \wedge \mathrm{be}(2)\}
\end{cases}
$$

where $\mathrm{be}(i)$ is a shortcut for $t_1 \le b_{i,1} \wedge t_2 \le b_{i,2} \wedge t_3 \le b_{i,3} \wedge t_4 \le b_{i,4}$ and $a(t)$ is the template t in which variable x_0 is replaced by $0.9379\,x_0 - 0.0381\,x_1 - 0.0414\,x_2 + 0.0237\,in$, variable x_1 is replaced by $-0.0404\,x_0 + 0.968\,x_1 - 0.0179\,x_2 + 0.0143\,in$ and variable x_2 is replaced by $0.0142\,x_0 - 0.0197\,x_1 + 0.9823\,x_2 + 0.0077\,in$. The usual maximum on $\mathbb{R}$ is denoted $\vee$.

Each $b_{i,j}$ bounds the template t_j at program point i and is defined in one equation as a maximum over as many terms as incoming edges in i. More precisely, each edge between two vertices v and v' translates to a term in each equation $b_{v',j}$ on the pattern:

$$\max\Big\{a(t_j) \ \Big|\ c \wedge \bigwedge_j t_j \le b_{v,j}\Big\} \quad \text{where} \quad c$$

and a are respectively the constraints and the assignments associated to this edge.

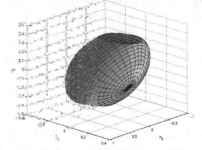

Fig. 3. Invariant for running example

This expresses the maximum value the template t_j can reach in destination vertex v' when applying the assignments a on values satisfying both the constraints c of the edge and the constraints $t_j \le b_{v,j}$ of the initial vertex v. Finally, the program starting point is initialized to $(+\infty, \ldots, +\infty)$, meaning all equations for $b_{i_0,j}$, where i_0 is the starting point, become $b_{i_0,j} = +\infty$. Thus, for any solution $(b_{1,1}, \ldots, b_{1,n}, \ldots)$ of the equations, $\gamma_{\mathcal{T}}(b_{i,1}, \ldots, b_{i,n})$ is an overapproximation of reachable states of the program at point i.

Iterating on Policies. Two different techniques can be found in the literature to compute an overapproximation of the least solution of the previous system of equations (which existence is proved thanks to Knaster-Tarski theorem):

Min-Policy Iteration [1,19] performs descending iterations towards some fixpoint, working in a way similar to the Newton-Raphson method. Iterations are not guaranteed to reach a fixpoint but can be stopped at any time leaving an overapproximation thereof. Moreover, convergence is usually fast.

Max-Policy Iteration [18,19] works in the opposite direction, starting from bottom and iterating computations of greatest fixpoints on so called max-policies until a global fixpoint is reached. The algorithm terminates with a — at least theoretically — precise fixpoint but the user has to wait until the end since intermediate results are not overapproximations of a fixpoint.

In practice, both algorithms compute the same invariant. Min-policies are nonetheless expected to be able to cope with larger systems [19, conclusion].

Example 5. On our running example, policy iterations compute the loop invariant $(1.0029, 0.1795, 0.1136, 0.2757) \in \mathcal{T}$, meaning: $t_1 \leq 1.0029 \wedge t_2 \leq 0.1795 \wedge t_3 \leq 0.1136 \wedge t_4 \leq 0.2757$ or equivalently: $t_1 \leq 1.0029 \wedge |x_0| \leq 0.4236 \wedge |x_1| \leq 0.3371 \wedge |x_2| \leq 0.5251$ (all figures are rounded to the fourth digit). This is a cropped ellipsoid as displayed on Figure 3.

3   An Abstract Control Flow Graph Domain

The previous section stated that policy iterations are able to compute precise fixpoints but require to extract a system of equations from the analyzed program. This fundamentally differs from the classic abstract domain paradigm. Although simply running both kind of analyses in parallel is easy, that would hinder the chances of a tight cooperation between them. The contribution of our work is to define an abstract domain which will gracefully interface both worlds.

This section describes a symbolic abstract domain reconstructing control flow graphs similar to Figure 2. This domain will basically "record" assignments and guards (of if-then-elses conditionals and while loops) in graph edges thanks to the corresponding abstract operators and close loops during widenings.

This will finally be used in the next section to provide an embedding of policy iterations in a classic abstract domain for Kleene iterations.

3.1   Lattice Structure

Definition 1. *Given a set* $\mathbb{V}_{ex}$ *of additional variables* ($\mathbb{V}_{ex} \cap \mathbb{V} = \emptyset$), *we define:*
- $\mathcal{A} := \mathbb{V} \to expr$, *functions from variables to expressions on* $\mathbb{V} \cup \mathbb{V}_{ex}$;
- $\mathcal{C} := expr \to \mathbb{R}$.

Variables $\mathbb{V}_{ex}$ will be used for modeling random inputs, $\mathcal{A}$ for *assignments* and $\mathcal{C}$ for *constraints* (mostly coming from guards). We will later write $x := 2y, y := y + 1$ for instance, to denote the function in $\mathcal{A}$ mapping x to the expression $2 \times y$, y to $y + 1$ and every other variable $z \in \mathbb{V}$ to the expression z. Furthermore id will denote the identity function, mapping every variable $x \in \mathbb{V}$ to the expression x. Regarding constraints, $1 \leq x \leq 2 \wedge y \leq 42$ will represent the function in $\mathcal{C}$ mapping expression x to 2, $-x$ to -1, y to 42 and anything else to $+\infty$. Finally $\perp_{\mathcal{C}}$ is the function in $\mathcal{C}$ mapping every expression to $-\infty$.

Definition 2. *Given a set* V, $\mathsf{st} \in V$ *and* $\mathsf{fi} \in V$ ($\mathsf{fi} \neq \mathsf{st}$) *and denoting* E *the functions* $V \times \mathcal{A} \times V \to \mathcal{C}$, *we define the set of graphs* $\mathcal{G}$ *as:*

$$\mathcal{G} := \{ \top_{\mathcal{G}} \} \cup \left\{ (e, t) \in E \times V \;\middle|\; \begin{array}{l} t \neq \mathsf{st} \wedge \forall v \in V, \forall a \in \mathcal{A}, e(\mathsf{fi}, a, v) = \perp_{\mathcal{C}} \\ \wedge \forall v \in V, \forall a \in \mathcal{A}, t \neq \mathsf{fi} \Rightarrow e(v, a, \mathsf{fi}) = \perp_{\mathcal{C}} \end{array} \right\}.$$

An element of $\mathcal{G}$ (other than $\top_\mathcal{G}$) is a pair (e,t) with e edges of a graph and t a vertex of this graph. t indicates the point of program currently considered by the Kleene iterations, acting like a kind of code pointer on e. The graph e associates to each pair of points v and v' and assignment a the constraint $e(v,a,v')$ to satisfy in order to take this transition and apply assignment a. Among the graph vertices V we distinguish two special vertices: st is the starting point of the program whereas fi will be used as temporary final point. We require two things about fi: that it has no outcoming edge ($\forall v \in V, \forall a \in \mathcal{A}, e(\mathsf{fi},a,v) = \bot_\mathcal{C}$) and that it is used only as current point (if $t \neq \mathsf{fi}$ then fi does not appear in the graph: $\forall v \in V, \forall a \in \mathcal{A}, t \neq \mathsf{fi} \Rightarrow e(v,a,\mathsf{fi}) = \bot_\mathcal{C}$).

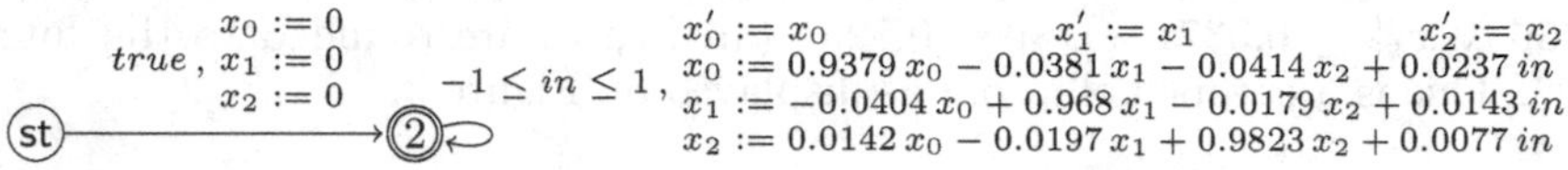

$$\overset{true \,,\ \begin{matrix} x_0 := 0 \\ x_1 := 0 \\ x_2 := 0 \end{matrix}}{\underset{}{\mathsf{st}} \xrightarrow{\hspace{3cm}} \textcircled{2}} \quad -1 \le in \le 1, \begin{matrix} x_0' := x_0 & x_1' := x_1 & x_2' := x_2 \\ x_0 := 0.9379\,x_0 - 0.0381\,x_1 - 0.0414\,x_2 + 0.0237\,in \\ x_1 := -0.0404\,x_0 + 0.968\,x_1 - 0.0179\,x_2 + 0.0143\,in \\ x_2 := 0.0142\,x_0 - 0.0197\,x_1 + 0.9823\,x_2 + 0.0077\,in \end{matrix}$$

Fig. 4. Example of value in $\mathcal{G}$

Example 6. For our running example, the result of Kleene iterations at loop head can be represented as on Figure 4. We chose a graphical representation for edges e, drawing only edges different from $\bot_\mathcal{C}$, while current point t is represented by a doubly circled vertex. More precisely, we draw an edge labeled (c,a) between v_1 and v_2 when $e(v_1,a,v_2) = c \neq \bot_\mathcal{C}$.

An order $\sqsubseteq_\mathcal{G}^\sharp$ on $\mathcal{G}$ is basically[5] defined as the pointwise extension on E of $\sqsubseteq_\mathcal{C}^\sharp$ (itself a pointwise extension of usual order on $\overline{\mathbb{R}}$) for values with the same current point t. A least upper bound $\bigsqcup_\mathcal{G}^\sharp$ is defined likewise, based on the usual max on $\overline{\mathbb{R}}$. This makes $\mathcal{G}$ a complete lattice.

Definition 3 (concretization $\gamma_\mathcal{G}$). *Given a template domain $\mathcal{T}$, the concretization function $\gamma_\mathcal{G} : \mathcal{G} \to 2^{(V \to \mathbb{R})}$ is then defined as $\gamma_\mathcal{G}(\top_\mathcal{G}) = \mathbb{R}^V$ and $\gamma_\mathcal{G}(e,t) = \gamma_\mathcal{T}(b_{t,1},\ldots,b_{t,n})$ with $(b_{v,i})_{v \in V, i \in [\![1,n]\!]}$ the least solution of the system of equations previously defined in Section 2.3.*

This concretization function gives a meaning to abstract values. It can be shown to be monotone ($\forall g, g' \in \mathcal{G}, g \sqsubseteq_\mathcal{G}^\sharp g' \Rightarrow \gamma_\mathcal{G}(g) \subseteq \gamma_\mathcal{G}(g')$). It is also worth noting that, like with any abstract domain, an abstract value $(e,t) \in \mathcal{G}$ overapproximates the reachable state space *at some program point*. The code pointer t is then used to locate this program point in the graph e.

3.2   Abstract Operators

Guards. To compute $[\![p \le r]\!]^\sharp(g)$ for an expression p, a real $r \in \mathbb{R}$ and an abstract value $g \in \mathcal{G}$, we have to distinguish three cases as illustrated on Figure 5:
(a) when $g = \top_\mathcal{G}$, typically at starting point, we return a graph with the code pointer at fi and a unique edge between st and fi labeled with $(p \le r, id)$;
(b) when $g = (e, \mathsf{fi})$, we add the constraint $p \le r$ to all incoming edges of fi;

---

[5] Up to some details later required for the widening.

(c) finally, when $g = (e,t)$ with $t \neq \mathsf{fi}$. we add an edge labeled with $(p \leq r, id)$ between t and fi.

Definition 4. *For any expression p, any real number $r \in \mathbb{R}$ and any abstract value $g \in \mathcal{G}$, $[\![p \leq r]\!]^\sharp(g)$ is defined by case analysis on g:*

$[\![p \leq r]\!]^\sharp(\top_\mathcal{G}) = (e, \mathsf{fi})$ *where e is the following function:*

$$v, a, v' \mapsto p' \mapsto \begin{cases} r & \text{if } (v, a, v') = (\mathsf{st}, id, \mathsf{fi}), p' = p \\ +\infty & \text{if } (v, a, v') = (\mathsf{st}, id, \mathsf{fi}), p' \neq p \; ; \\ -\infty & \text{otherwise} \end{cases}$$

$[\![p \leq r]\!]^\sharp(e, \mathsf{fi}) = (e', \mathsf{fi})$ *where e' is the following function:*

$$v, a, v' \mapsto p' \mapsto \begin{cases} \min(r, e(v, a, v')(p')) & \text{if } v' = \mathsf{fi}, p' = a(p) \\ e(v, a, v')(p') & \text{otherwise} \end{cases} ;$$

$[\![p \leq r]\!]^\sharp(e, t) = (e', \mathsf{fi})$ *where e' is the following function:*

$$v, a, v' \mapsto p' \mapsto \begin{cases} r & \text{if } (v, a, v') = (t, id, \mathsf{fi}), p' = p \\ +\infty & \text{if } (v, a, v') = (t, id, \mathsf{fi}), p' \neq p \; . \\ e(v, a, v')(p') & \text{otherwise} \end{cases}$$

Property 1 (soundness). This abstract operator is sound with respect to the concrete semantics of guards: for all expression p, all real $r \in \mathbb{R}$ and all $g \in \mathcal{G}$, $[\![p \leq r]\!](\gamma_\mathcal{G}(g)) \subseteq \gamma_\mathcal{G}\left([\![p \leq r]\!]^\sharp(g)\right)$.

Assignments. This is very similar to guards, modifying assignments instead of constraints on edges. Soundness property is similar.

Random Assignments. This is a kind of merge between the two previous ones. The variable randomly assigned in range $[r_1, r_2]$ is first assigned to a fresh new variable[6] $x \in \mathbb{V}_{ex}$ which is then constrained by $-x \leq -r_1$ and $x \leq r_2$. A similar soundness property holds.

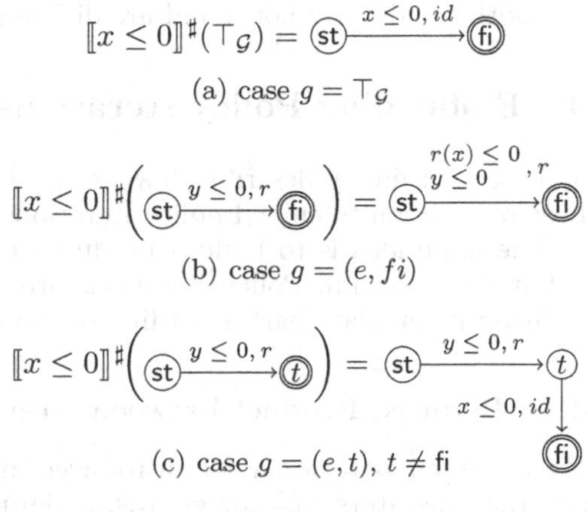

$[\![x \leq 0]\!]^\sharp(\top_\mathcal{G}) = \mathsf{st} \xrightarrow{x \leq 0, id} \mathsf{fi}$

(a) case $g = \top_\mathcal{G}$

$[\![x \leq 0]\!]^\sharp\left(\mathsf{st} \xrightarrow{y \leq 0, r} \mathsf{fi}\right) = \mathsf{st} \xrightarrow[y \leq 0]{r(x) \leq 0} \xrightarrow{, r} \mathsf{fi}$

(b) case $g = (e, fi)$

$[\![x \leq 0]\!]^\sharp\left(\mathsf{st} \xrightarrow{y \leq 0, r} t\right) = \mathsf{st} \xrightarrow{y \leq 0, r} t \xrightarrow{x \leq 0, id} \mathsf{fi}$

(c) case $g = (e, t), t \neq \mathsf{fi}$

Fig. 5. Examples of abstract guards

3.3 Widening

On numerical domains, widening discards information in order to enforce termination of the analysis. This is a source of imprecision. On the contrary, the graphs we are computing are finite objects which can be obtained without introducing imprecision. Thus, the following widening operator only aims at closing loops in graphs.

---

[6] Any variable not appearing in any incoming edge of fi.

None of the abstract operators we have seen up to now introduces new nodes in the graph (other than st and fi). This is done by the widening which plays a key role by introducing new nodes and closing loops on those nodes. Widening is actually the best place to create loops in our abstract control flow graphs since it is usually called at loop heads of programs during analyses[7]. Moreover, in most abstract interpreters, widening is the only indication an abstract domain gets from the presence of loops in the analyzed program.

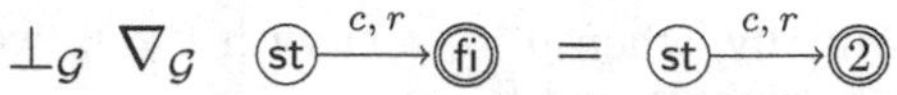

$$\perp_{\mathcal{G}} \; \nabla_{\mathcal{G}} \; \text{(st)} \xrightarrow{c,\,r} \text{(fi)} \;=\; \text{(st)} \xrightarrow{c,\,r} \text{②}$$

(a) both code pointers equal to fi ($\perp_{\mathcal{G}} = (\dot{\perp}_C, \text{fi})$), typical case before entering a loop

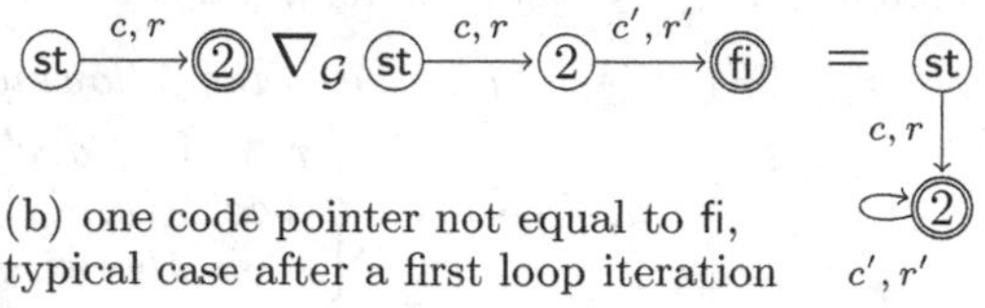

$$\text{(st)} \xrightarrow{c,\,r} \text{②} \; \nabla_{\mathcal{G}} \; \text{(st)} \xrightarrow{c,\,r} \text{②} \xrightarrow{c',\,r'} \text{(fi)} \;=\; \text{(st)}$$

(b) one code pointer not equal to fi, typical case after a first loop iteration

Fig. 6. Widening: introducing new nodes and loops in the control flow graph

To compute the widening $(e, t)\nabla(e', t')$ of two graphs, there are basically three cases to consider:

- both t and t' are equal to fi: in this case, we create a new point t'' and redirect all incoming edges of fi to t'' in both e and e' before computing their join, this is illustrated on Figure 6 (a);
- either t or t' is not fi (or $t = t' \neq$ fi), say $t \neq$ fi: in this case all incoming edges of fi are redirected to t in e' and a pointwise widening is done on each edge, Figure 6 (b);
- both t and t' are not fi and are different: in this case we return $\top_{\mathcal{G}}$.

4   Embedding Policy Iterations into an Abstract Domain

This section finally describes how to use the control flow graph domain of the previous section to embed policy iterations into a classic abstract domain.

The basic idea is to build a product of the control flow graph domain with a template domain. Policy iterations are then performed during widenings to reduce the template part according to the graph part.

4.1   Reduced Product between Graph and Template Domains

First, the template domain $\mathcal{T}$ introduced in Section 2.3 is equipped with dummy abstract operators $[\![.]\!]_{\mathcal{T}}^{\sharp}$ for guards, assignments and random assignments that always return $\top_{\mathcal{T}} = (+\infty, \ldots, +\infty)$. While perfectly useless, those operators are trivially sound.

Definition 5 (policy iterations domain). *We define the domain $\mathcal{P}_i$ as the product $\mathcal{G} \times \mathcal{T}$ of the domain of previous section with the above template domain.*

This means all operations on $\mathcal{P}_i$ are performed component by component. For instance, for (g, β) and $(g', \beta') \in \mathcal{P}_i$, the join $(g, \beta) \sqcup_{\mathcal{P}_i}^{\sharp} (g', \beta')$ is defined as[8]

---

[7] It even *must* be called at least once per loop to ensure convergence of the analyses [4].
[8] The join $\sqcup_{\mathcal{T}}^{\sharp}$ on $\mathcal{T} = \overline{\mathbb{R}}^n$ is simply the pointwise extension of the usual max on $\overline{\mathbb{R}}$.

$(g \sqcup_{\mathcal{G}}^{\sharp} g', \beta \sqcup_{\mathcal{T}}^{\sharp} \beta')$. The concretization function $\gamma_{\mathcal{P}_i} : \mathcal{P}_i \to 2^{V \to \mathbb{R}}$ is the intersection of the concretizations of each component: $\gamma_{\mathcal{P}_i}(g, \beta) = \gamma_{\mathcal{G}}(g) \cap \gamma_{\mathcal{T}}(\beta)$.

At this point, this domain still looks completely useless. But all the policy iteration work will take place during its widening.

Definition 6 (widening of $\mathcal{P}_i$). *We define* $\nabla_{\mathcal{P}_i} : \mathcal{P}_i \times \mathcal{P}_i \to \mathcal{P}_i$ *as:*

$$(g, \beta) \nabla_{\mathcal{P}_i} (g', \beta') = \begin{cases} (g \nabla_{\mathcal{G}} g', \mathrm{PI}(g \nabla_{\mathcal{G}} g')) & \text{if } g' \sqsubseteq_{\mathcal{G}}^{\sharp} g \\ (g \nabla_{\mathcal{G}} g', \top_{\mathcal{T}}) & \text{otherwise} \end{cases}$$

where $\mathrm{PI}(g)$ *is the result of policy iterations applied on graph[9]* g.

The test $g' \sqsubseteq_{\mathcal{G}}^{\sharp} g$ is used to perform policy iterations only when the graph domain has stabilized, thus avoiding potentially costly, and rather useless, computations on yet incomplete graphs.

As usual with reduced products [10], $\nabla_{\mathcal{P}_i}$ is not a widening in the strict acceptation of the term, since it is not greater than the join of $\mathcal{P}_i$. However, it still satisfies the two fundamental following properties:

- it does not break the soundness of the analysis since for all $p, p' \in \mathcal{P}_i$:
  $\gamma_{\mathcal{P}_i}(p \sqcup_{\mathcal{P}_i}^{\sharp} p') \subseteq \gamma_{\mathcal{P}_i}(p \nabla_{\mathcal{P}_i} p')$;
- it ensures termination of the analysis: for all sequences $x \in \mathcal{P}_i^{\mathbb{N}}$, the sequence $y_i = x_i$, $y_{i+1} = y_i \nabla_{\mathcal{P}_i} x_i$ is ultimately stationary.

Equipped with $\nabla_{\mathcal{P}_i}$ as widening operator, $\mathcal{P}_i$ finally offers a classic abstract domain interface to policy iterations.

4.2 Remarks on This Embedding

One may find the previous construction quite complicated and ask why not simply perform policy iterations aside classic Kleene iterations at each loop head. This seemingly simpler approach would however suffer from following drawbacks:

- it is not confined to an abstract domain, breaking the usual abstract interpreter framework [23];
- this would prevent the use of reduced products to exchange information with other domains, since a more static approach would be unable to record those informations on the fly as our graph domain can.

Finally, due to first point, implementation could rapidly become more intricate.

5 Application to Quadratic Invariants on Guarded Linear Systems

Semi-definite programming is a numerical optimization technique allowing by policy iterations to efficiently compute quadratic invariants on linear guarded systems. This short section discusses the interest of such invariants and how to generate adequate templates.

A wide range of today's real-time embedded systems, especially their most critical parts, rely on a control-command computation core. Much, if not most,

---

[9] More precisely on the system of equations introduced in Section 2.3.

of those systems are based on a linear law (lead-lag, LQR or PID controllers, low-pass filters,...). They periodically update their internal state following a matrix expression of the form $x_{k+1} = Ax_k + Bu_k$ in which x_k represents the state of the system at a given time k, matrix A models the system update according to its previous state while matrix B expresses the effect of the bounded input u_k.

On the one hand, analyzing such systems with linear abstract domains often leads at best to a rather costly analysis or at worst to no result at all. For instance, they often do not admit any invariant in the interval domain. On the other hand, control theorists have known for long that such systems are stable if and only if they admit a quadratic invariant (they call them Lyapunov functions [5]). Those invariants take the shape of an ellipsoid as seen on the running example of Section 2. We demonstrated in previous work [26] how good quadratic templates can be computed by adding appropriate constraints to the previous equation.

Actual programs often contain a number of saturations or resets around the linear core. Those guards are well handled by policy iterations.

6   Experimental Results

All the elements presented in this paper have been implemented as a new abstract domain in our static analyzer for Lustre synchronous programs[10].

For the sake of efficiency, policy iterations are performed with floating point computations using the semidefinite programming library CSDP [2]. This usually yields good results but without any formal guarantee about their correctness[11]. Checking that a result is an actual postfixpoint basically amounts, for each term of the equation system, to prove that a given matrix is actually positive definite. This is done by carefully bounding the rounding error on a floating point Cholesky decomposition [27]. Proof of positive definiteness of an $n \times n$ matrix can then be achieved with $O(n^3)$ floating point operations, which in practice induces only a very small overhead to the whole analysis.

Experiments were conducted on a set of stable linear systems. These systems were extracted from [1,13,26]. We have to recall to the reader that those systems, despite their apparent simplicity, do not admit simple linear invariants. Table 1 sums up analysis times for various versions of them, with or without saturations or resets. All computations were performed on an Intel Core2 @ 2.66GHz. It is interesting to notice that we nearly always get better results than [1,26] either thanks to the better templates obtained by solving Lyapunov equations (compared to [1]) or thanks to the extra templates bounding each variable (compared to [26]). Moreover, those quadratic invariants are fully automatically inferred from the analyzed program, while [1] requires the user to supply them. Although [12] may infer better bounds for the first two examples thanks to a kind of unrolling mechanism, Fluctuat [20] and its zonotopes is, to the best of authors' knowledge, the only abstract interpreter that may be able to automatically bound the other examples. This would however be a lot more expensive.

---

[10] Because we had it at hand. This only advocates the versatility of the approach.

[11] Again, we speak here about the soundness of the result (the fixpoint computed) w.r.t. the real semantics of the program and not its floating point one.

Table 1. Result of the experiments: quadratic invariants inference. Column n gives the number of program variables considered for policy iteration. The remaining columns detail the computation time: *templates* corresponds to the quadratic template computation, *iterations* to the actual policy iterations and *check* to the soundness checking. For each example, except the last one, the first line is for the bare linear system, the second for the same system with an added saturation and the third with a reset. $\bot$ indicates failure of the soundness checking.

	n	total (s)	templates (s)	iterations (s)	check (s)
Ex. 1	3	0.47	0.38	0.05	0.01
From [13, slides]	4	1.26	0.70	0.37	$\bot$ (0.00)
	3	0.56	0.41	0.09	0.02
Ex. 2	5	0.70	0.56	0.05	0.02
From [13, slides]	6	1.18	0.57	0.37	0.12
	5	0.82	0.59	0.10	0.04
Ex. 3	3	0.53	0.35	0.13	0.02
Discretized lead-lag	4	1.06	0.36	0.54	0.08
controller	3	0.64	0.35	0.23	0.03
Ex. 4	4	0.66	0.38	0.19	0.03
Linear quadratic gaussian	5	1.33	0.39	0.63	0.14
regulator	4	0.90	0.38	0.38	0.06
Ex. 5	6	1.12	0.66	0.24	0.06
Observer based controller	7	2.59	0.65	1.34	0.26
for a coupled mass system	6	1.39	0.67	0.42	0.11
Ex. 6	6	1.39	0.99	0.17	0.07
Butterworth	7	2.64	1.01	1.05	0.22
low-pass filter	6	1.63	1.00	0.31	0.12
Ex. 7	2	0.35	0.21	0.07	0.01
Dampened oscillator	3	1.25	0.24	0.28	0.09
from [1]	2	0.44	0.23	0.14	0.03
Ex. 8	2	0.36	0.22	0.07	0.01
Harmonic oscillator	3	0.82	0.20	0.44	0.10
from [1]	2	0.44	0.22	0.13	0.03
	6 + 6	2.53	0.67 + 1.00	0.24 + 0.17	0.06 + 0.06
Ex. 5 and 6 chained	12	7.92	4.06	2.00	0.52

The analyzer is released under a GPL license and available along with all examples and results at `http://cavale.enseeiht.fr/policy2013/`.

Example 7. The last line of Table 1 considers two linear systems chained, the output of the first one being used as input by the second one. This program is first analyzed with two policy iteration domains communicating together via reduced product to and from the intervals domain (the two domains do not share any variable). It is worth noting that total analyses time is just the sum of the times needed for the two separate analyses. In comparison, the second analysis with one single domain for the whole program is much more expensive.

7   Related Work

Multiple approaches try to tackle the loss of precision of Kleene iterations. A first line of work concerns recent developments to improve widening [21] and narrowing [22]. However those approaches cannot guarantee to reach the least fixpoint. Furthermore the authors are not aware of any numerical domain able to compute quadratic invariants based on such advanced widening. We recall that the examples presented in the Section 6 do not admit any simple inductive linear invariant.

Policy iteration techniques are another approach. We address the interested reader – beyond our policy iteration primer of Section 2 – to the seminal papers using semidefinite programming: [1,19] for the Min-Policy and [18,19] for the Max-Policy. All those works require appropriate templates for the use of policy iteration, while our instantiation of the framework is fully automatic. Furthermore, they make use of floating point semidefinite programming, but without addressing the soundness issue as we do. They do however acknowledge this fact.

About the integration of policy iterations and classic abstract interpretation, the opposite approach of the current paper has been proposed in [30]. The authors introduced additional transformers in order to extend a numerical abstract domain to its use with policy iterations. Due to this modification of the abstract domain interface, it does not give an embedding of policy iterations in a classic abstract domain as offered in the current paper.

We should also mention alternatives to classic widening, other than policy iterations. These are called acceleration techniques [3,11,28]. They compete with policy iterations but hardly extend to non linear properties.

About the analysis of guarded linear systems, the work [12,13,25] addresses a strict subclass of the programs handled by our tool. However since they rely on some kind of unrolling, they could be more precise for such specific problems. Maximum reachable values (our bounds are usually a few percents larger) can be computed via support functions [29]. However, due to heavy unrolling, only pure linear systems, without guards, are handled and the result is not an inductive invariant.

The generation of quadratic ellipsoid templates was already presented in [26] but this paper did not make use of policy iterations and the approach was only applicable to models of linear systems without if-then-else statements, not on actual program sources.

Last, as already mentioned at the end of Section 3, the work [17] relies on an SMT solver to optimize the policy choice when computing Max-policy iterations. In fact an important system with multiple if-then-else construct will lead to an exponential number of policies. Having an implicit representation and a means to make an efficient choice is then essential. Although this work has only been applied for linear templates, its extension to our framework should be of interest.

8   Conclusion and Future Work

To the author's knowledge this paper presents the *first integration of policy iteration as a fully usable relational abstract domain*. This integration in a Kleene fixpoint is enabled thanks to (i) an *abstract domain* that *rebuilds the control flow graph* and allows the policy iteration algorithm to access a global view of the program as a system of equations; (ii) a method, based on [26], to *synthetize meaningful ellipsoid templates* for a specific class of programs: stable guarded linear systems. This provides a powerful abstract domain able to compute non linear invariants in a fully automatic way, in a manner similar to relational abstractions such as polyhedra.

Reduction between classic domains and our allows both to precisely represent this control flow graph and to inject the result of policy iterations within classic domains. It also enables the use of multiple policy iteration domains; for example when considering sequences of such guarded linear filters as in Example 7.

The experimental results showed that this approach really extends the applicability of Kleene-based abstract interperter to a wider class of systems admitting non linear invariants. When computing our analyzes we only provided the set of variables that have to be analyzed with policy iterations, without any other information like templates.

Finally the issue of floating point semantics should not be forgotten. The introduction of error terms has to be addressed.

Acknowledgments. We deeply thank Éric GOUBAULT, Peter SCHRAMMEL and the anonymous reviewers for useful comments regarding this paper.

References

1. Adjé, A., Gaubert, S., Goubault, E.: Coupling policy iteration with semi-definite relaxation to compute accurate numerical invariants in static analysis. In: Gordon, A.D. (ed.) ESOP 2010. LNCS, vol. 6012, pp. 23–42. Springer, Heidelberg (2010)
2. Borchers, B.: Csdp, a c library for semidefinite programming. Optimization Methods and Software 11(1-4) (1999)
3. Bouissou, O., Seladji, Y., Chapoutot, A.: Acceleration of the abstract fixpoint computation in numerical program analysis. J. Symb. Comput. 47(12) (2012)
4. Bourdoncle, F.: Efficient chaotic iteration strategies with widenings. In: Pottosin, I.V., Bjorner, D., Broy, M. (eds.) FMP&TA 1993. LNCS, vol. 735, pp. 128–141. Springer, Heidelberg (1993)
5. Boyd, S., El Ghaoui, L., Féron, É., Balakrishnan, V.: Linear Matrix Inequalities in System and Control Theory, vol. 15. SIAM, Philadelphia (1994)
6. Costan, A., Gaubert, S., Goubault, E., Martel, M., Putot, S.: A policy iteration algorithm for computing fixed points in static analysis of programs. In: Etessami, K., Rajamani, S.K. (eds.) CAV 2005. LNCS, vol. 3576, pp. 462–475. Springer, Heidelberg (2005)
7. Cousot, P.: Proving program invariance and termination by parametric abstraction, lagrangian relaxation and semidefinite programming. In: Cousot, R. (ed.) VMCAI 2005. LNCS, vol. 3385, pp. 1–24. Springer, Heidelberg (2005)
8. Cousot, P., Cousot, R.: Abstract interpretation: A unified lattice model for static analysis of programs by construction or approximation of fixpoints. In: POPL (1977)
9. Cousot, P., Cousot, R., Feret, J., Mauborgne, L., Miné, A., Rival, X.: Why does astrée scale up? Formal Methods in System Design 35(3), 229–264 (2009)
10. Cousot, P., Cousot, R., Feret, J., Mauborgne, L., Miné, A., Monniaux, D., Rival, X.: Combination of abstractions in the ASTRÉE static analyzer. In: Okada, M., Satoh, I. (eds.) ASIAN 2006. LNCS, vol. 4435, pp. 272–300. Springer, Heidelberg (2008)
11. Feautrier, P., Gonnord, L.: Accelerated invariant generation for c programs with aspic and c2fsm. Electr. Notes Theor. Comput. Sci. 267(2) (2010)

12. Feret, J.: Static analysis of digital filters. In: Schmidt, D. (ed.) ESOP 2004. LNCS, vol. 2986, pp. 33–48. Springer, Heidelberg (2004)
13. Feret, J.: Numerical abstract domains for digital filters. In: International Workshop on Numerical and Symbolic Abstract Domains, NSAD (2005)
14. Gaubert, S., Goubault, E., Taly, A., Zennou, S.: Static analysis by policy iteration on relational domains. In: De Nicola, R. (ed.) ESOP 2007. LNCS, vol. 4421, pp. 237–252. Springer, Heidelberg (2007)
15. Gawlitza, T., Seidl, H.: Precise fixpoint computation through strategy iteration. In: De Nicola, R. (ed.) ESOP 2007. LNCS, vol. 4421, pp. 300–315. Springer, Heidelberg (2007)
16. Gawlitza, T., Seidl, H.: Precise relational invariants through strategy iteration. In: Duparc, J., Henzinger, T.A. (eds.) CSL 2007. LNCS, vol. 4646, pp. 23–40. Springer, Heidelberg (2007)
17. Gawlitza, T.M., Monniaux, D.: Improving strategies via SMT solving. In: Barthe, G. (ed.) ESOP 2011. LNCS, vol. 6602, pp. 236–255. Springer, Heidelberg (2011)
18. Gawlitza, T.M., Seidl, H.: Computing relaxed abstract semantics w.r.t. Quadratic zones precisely. In: Cousot, R., Martel, M. (eds.) SAS 2010. LNCS, vol. 6337, pp. 271–286. Springer, Heidelberg (2010)
19. Gawlitza, T.M., Seidl, H., Adjé, A., Gaubert, S., Goubault, E.: Abstract interpretation meets convex optimization. J. Symb. Comput. 47(12) (2012)
20. Ghorbal, K., Goubault, E., Putot, S.: The zonotope abstract domain taylor1+. In: Bouajjani, A., Maler, O. (eds.) CAV 2009. LNCS, vol. 5643, pp. 627–633. Springer, Heidelberg (2009)
21. Gopan, D., Reps, T.: Lookahead widening. In: Ball, T., Jones, R.B. (eds.) CAV 2006. LNCS, vol. 4144, pp. 452–466. Springer, Heidelberg (2006)
22. Halbwachs, N., Henry, J.: When the decreasing sequence fails. In: Miné, A., Schmidt, D. (eds.) SAS 2012. LNCS, vol. 7460, pp. 198–213. Springer, Heidelberg (2012)
23. Jeannet, B.: Some experience on the software engineering of abstract interpretation tools. Electr. Notes Theor. Comput. Sci. (2) (2010)
24. Miné, A.: The octagon abstract domain. In: AST 2001 in WCRE 2001. IEEE (October 2001)
25. Monniaux, D.: Compositional analysis of floating-point linear numerical filters. In: Etessami, K., Rajamani, S.K. (eds.) CAV 2005. LNCS, vol. 3576, pp. 199–212. Springer, Heidelberg (2005)
26. Roux, P., Jobredeaux, R., Garoche, P.-L., Féron, É.: A generic ellipsoid abstract domain for linear time invariant systems. In: HSCC. ACM (2012)
27. Rump, S.M.: Verification of positive definiteness. BIT Numerical Mathematics 46 (2006)
28. Schrammel, P., Jeannet, B.: Logico-numerical abstract acceleration and application to the verification of data-flow programs. In: Yahav, E. (ed.) SAS 2011. LNCS, vol. 6887, pp. 233–248. Springer, Heidelberg (2011)
29. Seladji, Y., Bouissou, O.: Numerical abstract domain using support functions. In: Brat, G., Rungta, N., Venet, A. (eds.) NFM 2013. LNCS, vol. 7871, pp. 155–169. Springer, Heidelberg (2013)
30. Sotin, P., Jeannet, B., Védrine, F., Goubault, E.: Policy iteration within logico-numerical abstract domains. In: Bultan, T., Hsiung, P.-A. (eds.) ATVA 2011. LNCS, vol. 6996, pp. 290–305. Springer, Heidelberg (2011)

Interpolation Properties
and SAT-Based Model Checking*

Arie Gurfinkel[1], Simone Fulvio Rollini[2], and Natasha Sharygina[2]

[1] Software Engineering Institute, CMU
arie@cmu.edu
[2] Formal Verification Lab, University of Lugano
{simone.fulvio.rollini,natasha.sharygina}@usi.ch

Abstract. Craig interpolation is a widespread method in verification,
with important applications such as Predicate Abstraction, CounterExample Guided Abstraction Refinement and Lazy Abstraction With Interpolants. Most state-of-the-art model checking techniques based on
interpolation require *collections* of interpolants to satisfy particular properties, to which we refer as "collectives"; they do not hold in general
for all interpolation systems and have to be established for each particular system and verification environment. Nevertheless, no systematic
approach exists that correlates the individual interpolation systems and
compares the necessary collectives. This paper proposes a uniform framework, which encompasses (and generalizes) the most common collectives
exploited in verification. We use it for a systematic study of the collectives and of the constraints they pose on propositional interpolation
systems used in SAT-based model checking.

1 Introduction

Craig interpolation is a popular approach in verification [14,13] with notable
applications such as Predicate Abstraction [10], CounterExample Guided Abstraction Refinement (CEGAR) [7], and Lazy Abstraction With Interpolants
(LAWI) [15].

Formally, given two formulae A and B such that $A \wedge B$ is unsatisfiable, a *Craig
interpolant* is a formula I such that A implies I, I is inconsistent with B and
I is defined over the atoms (i.e., propositional variables) common to A and B.
It can be seen as an over-approximation of A that is still inconsistent with B^1.
In model checking applications, A typically encodes some finite program traces,

---

* This material is based upon work funded and supported by the Department of De-
fense under Contract No. FA8721-05-C-0003 with Carnegie Mellon University for the
operation of the Software Engineering Institute, a federally funded research and development center. This material has been approved for public release and unlimited
distribution. DM-0000469.
1 We write $Itp(A \mid B)$ for an interpolant of A and B, and I_A when B is clear from the
context.

D. Van Hung and M. Ogawa (Eds.): ATVA 2013, LNCS 8172, pp. 255–271, 2013.
© Springer International Publishing Switzerland 2013

and B denotes error locations. In this case, an interpolant I represents a set of *safe* states that over-approximate the states reachable in A.

In most verification tasks, a single interpolant, i.e., a single subdivision of constraints into two groups A and B, is not sufficient. For example, consider the refinement problem in CEGAR: given a spurious error trace $\pi = \tau_1, \ldots, \tau_n$, where τ_i is a program statement, find a set of formulae $X_0, \ldots, X_n$ such that $X_0 = \top$, $X_n = \bot$, and for $1 \leq i \leq n$, the Hoare triples $\{X_{i-1}\} \tau_i \{X_i\}$ are valid. The sequence $\{X_i\}$ justifies that the error trace is infeasible and is used to refine the abstraction. The solution is a *sequence* of interpolants $\{I_i\}_{i=1}^n$ such that: $I_i = Itp(\tau_1 \ldots \tau_i \mid \tau_{i+1} \ldots \tau_n)$ and $I_{i-1} \wedge \tau_i \implies I_i$. That is, in addition to requiring that each I_i is an interpolant between the prefix (statements up to position i in the trace) and the suffix (statements following position i), the sequence $\{I_i\}$ of interpolants must be inductive: this property is known as the *path interpolation property* [18].

Other properties (e.g., simultaneous abstraction, interpolation sequence, path-, symmetric-, and tree-interpolation) are used in existing verification frameworks such as IMPACT [15], Whale [1], FunFrog [20] and eVolCheck [21], which implement instances of Predicate Abstraction [9], Lazy Abstraction with Interpolation [15], Interpolation-based Function Summarization [20] and Upgrade Checking [21]. These properties, to which we refer as *collectives* since they concern collections of interpolants, are not satisfied by arbitrary sequences of Craig interpolants and must be established for each interpolation algorithm and verification technique.

This paper performs a systematic study of collectives in verification and identifies the particular constraints they pose on propositional interpolation systems used in SAT-based model checking. The SAT-based approach provides bit-precise reasoning which is essential both in software and hardware applications, e.g., when dealing with pointer arithmetic and overflow. To-date, there exist successful tools which perform SAT-based model checking (such as CBMC[2] and SA-TABS[3]), and which integrate it with interpolation (for example, eVolCheck and FunFrog). However, there is no a framework which would correlate the existing interpolation systems and compare the various collectives. This work addresses the problem and contributes as follows:

Contribution 1: This paper, for the first time, collects, identifies, and uniformly presents the most common collectives imposed on interpolation by existing verification approaches (see §2).

In addition to the issues related to a diversity of interpolation properties, it is often desirable to have flexibility in choosing different algorithms for computing different interpolants in a sequence $\{I_i\}$, rather than using a single interpolation algorithm (or *interpolation system*) Itp_S, as assumed in the path interpolation example above. To guarantee such a flexibility, this paper presents a framework which generalizes the traditional setting consisting of a single interpolation system to allow for sequences, or *families*, of interpolation systems. For example,

---

[2] http://www.cprover.org/cbmc
[3] http://www.cprover.org/satabs

given a family of systems $\mathcal{F} = \{Itp_{S_i}\}_{i=1}^n$, let $I_i = Itp_{S_i}(\tau_1, \ldots \tau_i \mid \tau_{i+1} \ldots \tau_n)$. If the resulting sequence of interpolants $\{I_i\}$ satisfies the condition of path interpolation, we say that the family $\mathcal{F}$ has the path interpolation property.

Families find practical applicability in several contexts[4]. One example is LAWI-style verification, where it is desirable to obtain a path interpolant $\{I_i\}$ with weak interpolants at the beginning (i.e., $I_1, I_2, \ldots$) and strong interpolants at the end (i.e., $\ldots, I_{n-1}, I_n$). This would increase the likelihood of the sequence to be inductive and can be achieved by using a family of systems of different strength. Another example is software Upgrade Checking, where function summaries are computed by interpolation. Different functions in a program could require different levels of abstraction by means of interpolation. A system that generates stronger interpolants can yield a tighter abstraction, more closely reflecting the behavior of the corresponding function. On the other hand, a system that generates weaker interpolants would give an abstraction which is more "tolerant" and is more likely to remain valid when the function is updated.

Contribution 2: This paper systematically studies the collectives and the relationships among them; in particular, it shows that for families of interpolation systems the collectives form a hierarchy, whereas for a single system all but two (i.e., path interpolation and simultaneous abstraction) are equivalent (see §3).

Another issue which this paper deals with is the fact that there exist different approaches for generating interpolants. One is to use specialized algorithms: examples are procedures based on constraint solving (e.g., [19]), machine learning (e.g., [22]), and, even, pure verification algorithms like IC3 [2] and PDR [4] that can be viewed as computing a path interpolation sequence. A second, well-known approach is to extract an interpolant of $A \wedge B$ from a resolution proof of unsatisfiability of $A \wedge B$. Examples are the algorithm by Pudlák [17] (also independently proposed by Huang [8] and by Krajíček [11]), the algorithm by McMillan [12], and the Labeled Interpolation Systems (*LISs*) of D'Silva et al. [3], the latter being the most general version of this approach.

The variety of interpolation algorithms makes it difficult to reason about their properties in a systematic manner. At a low level of representation, the challenge is determined by the complexity of individual algorithms and by the diversity among them, which makes it hard to study them uniformly. On the other hand, at a high level, where the details are hidden, not many interesting results can be obtained. For this reason, this paper adopts a twofold approach, working both at a high and at a low level of representation: at the high level, we give a global view of the entire collection of properties and of their relationships and hierarchy; at the low level, we obtain additional stronger results for concrete interpolation systems. In particular, we first investigate the properties of interpolation systems treating them as black boxes, and then focus on the propositional LISs. In the paper, the results of §3 apply to arbitrary interpolation algorithms, while those of §4 apply to LISs.

---

[4] The notion of families is additionally a useful technical tool to make the discussion and the results more general and easier to compare with the prior work of CAV'12 [18] (which formally defined families for the first time).

Contribution 3: For the first time, this paper gives both sufficient and necessary conditions for a family of LISs and for a single LIS to enjoy each of the collectives. In particular, we show that in case of a single system path interpolation is common to all LISs, while simultaneous abstraction is as strong as all other properties. Concrete applications of our results are also discussed (see §4).

Contribution 4. We developed an interpolating prover, PeRIPLO, implementing the proposed framework as discussed in §5; PeRIPLO is currently employed for solving and interpolation by the FunFrog and eVolcheck tools.

Related Work. To our knowledge, despite interpolation being an important component of verification, no systematic investigation of verification-related requirements for interpolants has been done prior to this paper. One exception is the work by the first two authors [18], that studies a subset of the properties in the context of LISs. This paper significantly extends the results of that work by considering the most common collectives used in verification, at the same time addressing a wider class of interpolation systems. Moreover, for LISs, it provides both the *necessary* and *sufficient* conditions for each property.

2   Interpolation Systems

In this section we introduce the basic notions of interpolation, and then proceed to discuss the collectives. Among several possible styles of presentation, we chose the one that highlights te use of collectives in the context of model checking. We employ the standard convention of identifying conjunctions of formulae with sets of formulae and concatenation with conjunction, whenever convenient. For example, we interchangeably use $\{\phi_1, \dots, \phi_n\}$ and $\phi_1 \cdots \phi_n$ for $\phi_1 \wedge \dots \wedge \phi_n$.

Interpolation System. An *interpolation system* Itp_S is a function that, given an inconsistent $\Phi = \{\phi_1, \phi_2\}$, returns a *Craig's interpolant*, that is a formula $I_{\phi_1,S} = Itp_S(\phi_1 \mid \phi_2)$ such that:

$$\phi_1 \implies I_{\phi_1,S} \qquad I_{\phi_1,S} \wedge \phi_2 \implies \bot \qquad \mathcal{L}_{I_{\phi_1,S}} \subseteq \mathcal{L}_{\phi_1} \cap \mathcal{L}_{\phi_2}$$

where $\mathcal{L}_\phi$ denotes the atoms of a formula ϕ. That is, $I_{\phi_1,S}$ is implied by ϕ_1, is inconsistent with ϕ_2 and is defined over the common language of ϕ_1 and ϕ_2.

For $\Phi = \{\phi_1, \dots, \phi_n\}$, we write $I_{\phi_1 \cdots \phi_i,S}$ to denote $Itp_S(\phi_1 \cdots \phi_i \mid \phi_{i+1} \cdots \phi_n)$. W.l.o.g., we assume that, for any Itp_S and any formula ϕ, $Itp_S(\top \mid \phi) = \top$ and $Itp_S(\phi \mid \top) = \bot$, where we equate the constant true $\top$ with the empty formula. We omit S whenever clear from the context.

An interpolation system Itp is called *symmetric* if for any inconsistent $\Phi = \{\phi_1, \phi_2\}$: $Itp(\phi_1 \mid \phi_2) \iff \overline{Itp(\phi_2 \mid \phi_1)}$ (we use the notation $\overline{\phi}$ for the negation of a formula ϕ).

A sequence $\mathcal{F} = \{Itp_{S_1}, \dots, Itp_{S_n}\}$ of interpolation systems is called a *family*.

Collectives. In the following, we formulate the properties of interpolation systems that are required by existing verification algorithms. Furthermore, we generalize the collectives by presenting them over families of interpolation systems (i.e., we allow the use different systems to generate different interpolants in a sequence). Later, we restrict the properties to the more traditional setting of the singleton families.

n-**Path Interpolation (PI)** was first defined in [9], where it is employed in the refinement phase of CEGAR-based predicate abstraction. It has also appeared in [23] under the name *interpolation-sequence*, where it is used for a specialized interpolation-based hardware verification algorithm.

Formally, a family of $n + 1$ interpolation systems $\{Itp_{S_0}, \ldots, Itp_{S_n}\}$ has the *n-path interpolation* property (n-PI) iff for any inconsistent $\Phi = \{\phi_1, \ldots, \phi_n\}$ and for $0 \le i \le n - 1$ (recall that $I_\top = \top$ and $I_\Phi = \bot$):

$$(I_{\phi_1 \ldots \phi_i, S_i} \wedge \phi_{i+1}) \implies I_{\phi_1 \ldots \phi_{i+1}, S_{i+1}}$$

n-**Generalized Simultaneous Abstraction (GSA)** is the generalization of *simultaneous abstraction*, a property that first appeared, under the name *symmetric interpolation*, in [10], where it is used for approximation of a transition relation for predicate abstraction. We changed the name to avoid confusion with the notion of *symmetric interpolation system* (see above). The reason for generalizing the property will be apparent later.

Formally, a family of $n + 1$ interpolation systems $\{Itp_{S_1}, \ldots, Itp_{S_{n+1}}\}$ has the *n-generalized simultaneous abstraction* property (n-GSA) iff for any inconsistent $\Phi = \{\phi_1, \ldots, \phi_{n+1}\}$:

$$\bigwedge_{i=1}^{n} I_{\phi_i, S_i} \implies I_{\phi_1 \ldots \phi_n, S_{n+1}}$$

The case $n = 2$ is called *Binary GSA (BGSA)*: $I_{\phi_1, S_1} \wedge I_{\phi_2, S_2} \implies I_{\phi_1 \phi_2, S_3}$. If $\phi_{n+1} = \top$, the property is called *n-simultaneous abstraction* (n-SA): $\bigwedge_{i=1}^{n} I_{\phi_i, S_i} \implies \bot (= I_{\phi_1 \ldots \phi_n, S_{n+1}})$ and, if $n = 2$, *binary SA (BSA)*. In n-SA $Itp_{S_{n+1}}$ is irrelevant and is often omitted.

n-**State-Transition Interpolation (STI)** is defined as a combination of PI and SA in a single family of systems. It was introduced in [1] as part of the interprocedural verification algorithm WHALE. Intuitively, the "state" interpolants over-approximate the set of reachable states, and the "transition" interpolants summarize the transition relations (or function bodies). The STI requirement ensures that state over-approximation is "compatible" with the summarization. That is, $\{I_{\phi_1 \ldots \phi_i, S_i}\} I_{\phi_{i+1}, T_{i+1}} \{I_{\phi_1 \ldots \phi_{i+1}, S_{i+1}}\}$ is a valid Hoare triple for each i.

Formally, a family of interpolation systems $\{Itp_{S_0}, \ldots, Itp_{S_n}, Itp_{T_1}, \ldots, Itp_{T_n}\}$ has the *n-state-transition interpolation* property (n-STI) iff for any inconsistent $\Phi = \{\phi_1, \ldots, \phi_n\}$ and for $0 \le i \le n - 1$:

$$(I_{\phi_1 \ldots \phi_i, S_i} \wedge I_{\phi_{i+1}, T_{i+1}}) \implies I_{\phi_1 \ldots \phi_{i+1}, S_{i+1}}$$

T-**Tree Interpolation (TI)** is a generalization of classical interpolation used in model checking applications, in which partitions of an unsatisfiable formula naturally correspond to a tree structure such as call tree or program unwinding. The collective was first introduced by McMillan and Rybalchenko for computing post-fixpoints of a system of Horn clauses (e.g., used in analysis of recursive programs) [16], and is equivalent to the nested-interpolants of [6].

Formally, let $T = (V, E)$ be a tree with n nodes $V = [1, \ldots, n]$. A family of n interpolation systems $\{Itp_{S_1}, \ldots, Itp_{S_n}\}$ has the T-tree interpolation property (T-TI) iff for any inconsistent $\Phi = \{\phi_1, \ldots, \phi_n\}$:

$$\bigwedge_{(i,j) \in E} I_{F_j, S_j} \wedge \phi_i \implies I_{F_i, S_i}$$

where $F_i = \{\phi_j \mid i \sqsubseteq j\}$, and $i \sqsubseteq j$ iff node j is a descendant of node i in T. Notice that for the root i of T, $F_i = \Phi$ and $I_{F_i, S_i} = \bot$.

An interpolation system Itp_S is said to *have a property P* (or, simply, to *have P*), where P is one of the properties defined above, if every family induced by Itp_S has P. For example, Itp_S has GSA iff for every k the family $\{Itp_{S_1}, \ldots, Itp_{S_k}\}$, where $Itp_{S_i} = Itp_S$ for all i, has k-GSA.

3   Collectives of Interpolation Systems

In this section, we study collectives of general interpolation systems, that is, we treat interpolation systems as black-boxes. In section §4 we will extend the study to the implementation-level details of the LISs.

Collectives of Single Systems. We begin by studying the relationships among the various collectives of single interpolation systems.

Theorem 1. *Let Itp_S be an interpolation system. The following are equivalent: Itp_S has BGSA (1), Itp_S has GSA (2), Itp_S has TI (3), Itp_S has STI (4).*

Proof. We show that $1 \to 2$, $2 \to 3$, $3 \to 4$, $4 \to 1$.

$(1 \to 2)$ Assume Itp_S has BGSA. Take any inconsistent $\Phi = \{\phi_1, \ldots, \phi_{n+1}\}$. Then, for $2 \le i \le n$: $(I_{\phi_1 \cdots \phi_{i-1}} \wedge I_{\phi_i}) \Rightarrow I_{\phi_1 \cdots \phi_i}$, which together yield $(\bigwedge_{i=1}^n I_{\phi_i}) \Rightarrow I_{\phi_1 \cdots \phi_n}$. Hence, Itp_S has GSA.

$(2 \to 3)$ Let $T = ([1, \ldots, n], E)$, take any inconsistent $\Phi = \{\phi_1, \ldots, \phi_n\}$. Since Itp_S has GSA: $(\bigwedge_{(i,j) \in E} I_{F_j} \wedge I_{\phi_i}) \Rightarrow I_{F_i}$, and, from the definition of Craig interpolation, $\phi_i \Rightarrow I_{\phi_i}$. Hence, Itp_S has T-TI.

$(3 \to 4)$ Take any inconsistent $\Phi = \{\phi_1, \ldots, \phi_n\}$ and extend it to a Φ' by adding n copies of $\top$ at the end. Define a tree $T_{STI} = ([1, \ldots, 2n], E)$ s.t.: $E = \{(n+i, i) \mid 1 \le i \le n\} \cup \{(n+i, n+i-1) \mid 1 \le i \le n\}$. Then, for $1 \le i \le n$, $F_i = \{\phi_i\}$ and $F_{n+i} = \{\phi_1, \ldots, \phi_i\}$, where F_i is as in the definition of T-TI. By the T-TI property: $(I_{F_{n+i}} \wedge I_{F_{i+1}} \wedge \top) \Rightarrow I_{F_{n+i+1}}$, which is equivalent to STI.

$(4 \to 1)$ Follows from STI being syntactically equivalent to BGSA for $i = 1$.

Theorem 1 has a few simple extensions. First, *GSA* implies *SA* directly from the definitions. Similarly, since $\phi \Rightarrow I_\phi$, STI implies PI. Finally, we conjecture that both SA and PI are strictly weaker than the rest. In §4 (Theorem 16), we show that for LISs, PI is strictly weaker than SA. As for SA, it is equivalent to BGSA in symmetric interpolation systems (Proposition 1 in [5]). But, in the general case, the conjecture remains open.

These results define a hierarchy of collectives which is summarized in Fig. 1, where the edges indicate implications among the collectives. Note that $SA \rightarrow GSA$ holds only for symmetric systems.

In summary, the main contribution in the setting of a single system is the proof that almost all collectives are equivalent and the hierarchy of the collectives collapses. From a practical perspective, this means that McMillan's interpolation system (implemented by most interpolating SMT-solvers) has all of the collective properties, including the recently introduced TI.

Collectives of Families of Systems. Here, we study collectives of families of interpolation systems. We first show that the collectives introduced in §2 directly extend from families to sub-families. Second, we examine the hierarchy of the relationships among the properties. Finally, we conclude by discussing the practical implications of these results.

Collectives of Sub-families. If a family of interpolation systems $\mathcal{F}$ has a property P, then sub-families of $\mathcal{F}$ have P as well. We state this formally for k-STI (since we use it in the proof of Theorem 11); similar statements for the other collectives are discussed in [5] (where all proofs can be found).

Theorem 2. *A family* $\{Itp_{S_0}, \ldots, Itp_{S_n}, Itp_{T_1}, \ldots, Itp_{T_n}\}$ *has n-STI iff for all* $k \leq n$ *the sub-family* $\{Itp_{S_0}, \ldots, Itp_{S_k}\} \cup \{Itp_{T_1}, \ldots, Itp_{T_k}\}$ *has k-STI.*

Relationships among Collectives. We now show the relationships among collectives. First, we note that n-SA and BGSA are equivalent for symmetric interpolation systems. Whenever a family $\mathcal{F} = \{Itp_{S_1}, \ldots, Itp_{S_{n+1}}\}$ has $(n+1)$-SA and $Itp_{S_{n+1}}$ is symmetric, then $\mathcal{F}$ has n-GSA (Proposition 2 in [5], which is the analogue of Proposition 1 for single systems).

In the rest of the section, we delineate the hierarchy of collectives. In particular, we show that T-TI is the most general collective, immediately followed by n-GSA, which is followed by $BGSA$ and n-STI, which are equivalent, and at last by n-SA and n-PI. The first result is that the n-STI property implies both the n-PI and n-SA properties separately:

Theorem 3. *If a family* $\mathcal{F} = \{Itp_{S_0}, \ldots, Itp_{S_n}, Itp_{T_1}, \ldots, Itp_{T_n}\}$ *has n-STI then (1)* $\{Itp_{S_0}, \ldots, Itp_{S_n}\}$ *has n-PI and (2)* $\{Itp_{T_1}, \ldots, Itp_{T_n}\}$ *has n-SA.*

A natural question to ask is whether the converse of Theorem 3 is true. That is, whether the family $\mathcal{F}_1 \cup \mathcal{F}_2$ that combines two arbitrary families $\mathcal{F}_1$ and $\mathcal{F}_2$ that independently enjoy n-PI and n-SA, respectively, has n-STI. We show in §4, Theorem 11, that this is not the case.

As for BGSA, the n-STI property is closely related to it: deciding whether a family $\mathcal{F}$ has n-STI is in fact reducible to deciding whether a collection of sub-families of $\mathcal{F}$ has BGSA.

Theorem 4. *A family* $\mathcal{F} = \{Itp_{S_0}, \ldots, Itp_{S_n}, Itp_{T_1}, \ldots, Itp_{T_n}\}$ *has n-STI iff* $\{Itp_{S_i}, Itp_{T_{i+1}}, Itp_{S_{i+1}}\}$ *has BGSA for all* $0 \leq i \leq n-1$.

From Theorem 4 and Theorem 3 we derive:

Corollary 1. *If there exists a family* $\{Itp_{S_0}, \ldots, Itp_{S_n}\} \cup \{Itp_{T_1}, \ldots, Itp_{T_n}\}$ *s.t.* $\{Itp_{S_i}, Itp_{T_{i+1}}, Itp_{S_{i+1}}\}$ *has BGSA for all* $0 \leq i \leq n-1$, *then* $\{Itp_{T_1}, \ldots, Itp_{T_n}\}$ *has n-SA.*

We now relate T-TI and n-GSA. Note that the need for two theorems with different statements arises from the asymmetry between the two properties: all ϕ_i are abstracted by interpolation in n-GSA, whereas in T-TI a formula is not abstracted, when considering the correspondent parent together with its children.

Theorem 5. *Given a tree* $T = (V, E)$ *if a family* $\mathcal{F} = \{Itp_{S_i}\}_{i \in V}$ *has T-TI, then, for every parent* i_{k+1} *and its children* $i_1, \ldots, i_k$:

1. *If* i_{k+1} *is the root,* $\{Itp_{S_{i_1}}, \ldots, Itp_{S_{i_k}}\}$ *has k-SA.*
2. *Otherwise,* $\{Itp_{S_{i_1}}, \ldots, Itp_{S_{i_k}}, Itp_{S_{i_{k+1}}}\}$ *has k-GSA.*

Theorem 6. *Given a tree* $T = (V, E)$, *a family* $\mathcal{F} = \{Itp_{S_i}\}_{i \in V}$ *has T-TI if, for every node* i_{k+1} *and its children* $i_1, \ldots, i_k$, *there exists* $T_{i_{k+1}}$ *such that:*

1. *If* i_{k+1} *is the root,* $\{Itp_{S_{i_1}}, \ldots, Itp_{S_{i_k}}, Itp_{T_{i_{k+1}}}\}$ *has* $(k+1)$-*SA.*
2. *Otherwise,* $\{Itp_{S_{i_1}}, \ldots, Itp_{T_{i_{k+1}}}, Itp_{S_{i_{k+1}}}\}$ *has* $(k+1)$-*GSA.*

An important observation is that the T-TI property is the most general, in the sense that it realizes any of the other properties, given an appropriate choice of the tree T. We state here (and prove in [5]) that n-GSA and n-STI can be implemented by T-TI for some T^n_{GSA} and T^n_{STI}; the remaining cases can be derived in a similar manner. Note that the converse implications are not necessarily true in general, since the tree interpolation requirement is stronger.

Theorem 7. *If a family* $\mathcal{F} = \{Itp_{S_{n+1}}, Itp_{S_1}, \ldots, Itp_{S_{n+1}}\}$ *has* T^n_{GSA}-*TI, then* $\{Itp_{S_1}, \ldots, Itp_{S_{n+1}}\}$ *has n-GSA.*

Theorem 8. *If a family* $\mathcal{F} = \{Itp_{S_0}, \ldots, Itp_{S_n}\} \cup \{Itp_{T_1}, \ldots, Itp_{T_n}\}$ *has* T^n_{STI}-*TI, then it has n-STI.*

The results of so far (including Theorem 11 of §4) define a hierarchy of collectives which is summarized in Fig. 2. The solid edges indicate direct implication between properties; $SA \rightarrow GSA$ requires symmetry, while $GSA \rightarrow TI$ requires the existence of an additional set of interpolation systems. The dashed edges represent the ability of TI to realize all the other properties for an appropriate tree; only the edges to STI and GSA are shown, the other ones are implicit. The dash-dotted edges represent the sub-family properties.

An immediate application of our results is that they show how to overcome limitations of existing implementations. For example, they enable the trivial construction of tree interpolants in MathSat[5] (currently only available in iZ3) – thus enabling its usability for Upgrade Checking [21] – by reusing existing BGSA-interpolation implementation of MathSat. Similarly, our results enable construction of BGSA and GSA interpolants in iZ3 (currently only available in MathSat) – thus enabling the use of iZ3 in Whale.

---

[5] http://mathsat.fbk.eu/

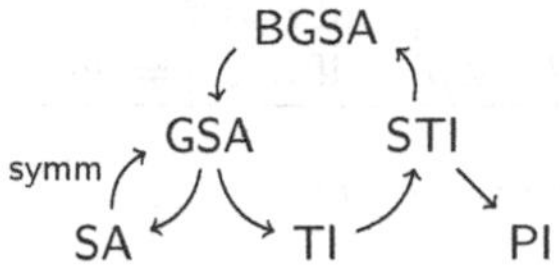

BGSA

symm GSA   STI

SA   TI   PI

Fig. 1. Single systems collectives

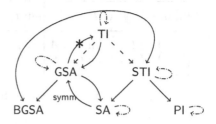

Fig. 2. Families of systems collectives

4   Collectives of Labeled Interpolation Systems

In this section, we move from the abstract level of general interpolation systems
to the implementation level of the propositional Labeled Interpolation Systems.
After introducing and defining LISs, we study collectives of families, then summarize the results for single LISs, also answering the questions left open in §3.
The key results are in Lemmas $1 - 4$. Unfortunately, the proofs are quite technical. For readability, we focus on the main results and their significance and refer
the reader to [5] for full details.

There are several state-of-the art approaches for automatically computing interpolants. The most successful techniques derive an interpolant for $A \wedge B$ from
a resolution proof of the unsatisfiability of the conjunction. Noteworthy examples are the algorithm independently developed by Pudlák [17], Huang [8] and
Krajíček [11], and the one by McMillan [12]. These algorithms are implemented
recursively by initially computing *partial interpolants* for the axioms (leaves of
the proof), and, then, following the proof structure, by computing a partial interpolant for each conclusion from those of the premises. The partial interpolant
of the root of the proof is the interpolant for the formula. In this section, we
review these algorithms following the framework of D'Silva et al. [3].

Resolution Proofs. We assume a *countable set* of propositional variables. A
literal is a variable, either with positive (p) or negative ($\bar{p}$) polarity. A *clause*
C is a finite disjunction of literals; a formula Φ in conjunctive normal form
(CNF) is a finite conjunction of clauses. A *resolution proof of unsatisfiability* (or
refutation) of a formula Φ in CNF is a tree such that the leaves are the clauses of
Φ, the root is the empty clause $\perp$ and the inner nodes are clauses generated via
the *resolution rule* (where $C^+ \vee p$ and $C^- \vee \bar{p}$ are the *antecedents*, $C^+ \vee C^-$ the
resolvent, and p is the *pivot*):

$$\frac{C^+ \vee p \qquad C^- \vee \bar{p}}{C^+ \vee C^-}$$

Labelings and Interpolant Strength. D'Silva et al. [3] generalize the algorithms by Pudlák [17] and McMillan [12] for propositional resolution systems by
introducing the notion of *Labeled Interpolation System* (LIS), focusing on the
concept of *interpolant strength* (a formula ϕ is stronger than ψ when $\phi \Longrightarrow \psi$).

Given a refutation of a formula $A \wedge B$, a variable p can appear as a literal
only in A, only in B or in both; p is respectively said to have *class* A, B or AB.

Leaf:	$C\,[I]$	Inner node:	$\dfrac{C^+ \vee p : \alpha\,[I^+] \qquad C^- \vee \overline{p} : \beta\,[I^-]}{C^+ \vee C^-\,[I]}$
$I = \begin{cases} C \lfloor b & \text{if } C \in A \\ \neg(C \lfloor a) & \text{if } C \in B \end{cases}$			$I = \begin{cases} I^+ \vee I^- & \text{if } \alpha \sqcup \beta = a \\ I^+ \wedge I^- & \text{if } \alpha \sqcup \beta = b \\ (I^+ \vee p) \wedge (I^- \vee \overline{p}) & \text{if } \alpha \sqcup \beta = ab \end{cases}$

Fig. 3. Labeled Interpolation System Itp_L

A *labeling* L is a mapping that assigns a *label* among $\{a, b, ab\}$ independently to each variable in each clause; we assume that no clause has both a literal and its negation, so assigning a label to variables or literals is equivalent. The set of possible labelings is restricted by ensuring that class A variables have label a and class B variables label b; AB variables can be labeled either a, b or ab.

In [3], a *Labeled Interpolation System* (LIS) is defined as a procedure Itp_L (shown in Fig. 3) that, given A, B, a refutation R of $A \wedge B$ and a labeling L, outputs a partial interpolant $I_{A,L}(C) = Itp_L(A \mid B)(C)$ for any clause C in R; this depends on the clause being in A or B (if leaf) and on the label of the pivot associated with the resolution step (if inner node). $I_{A,L} = Itp_L(A \mid B)$ represents the interpolant for $A \wedge B$, that is $Itp_L(A \mid B)(\bot)$. We omit the parameters whenever clear from the context.

In Fig. 3, $C \lfloor \alpha$ denotes the restriction of a clause C to the variables with label α. $p : \alpha$ indicates that variable p has label $\alpha \in \{a, b, ab\}$. By $C[I]$ we represent that clause C has a partial interpolant I. I^+, I^- and I are the partial interpolants respectively associated with the two antecedents and the resolvent of a resolution step: $I^+ = Itp_L(C^+ \vee p)$, $I^- = Itp_L(C^- \vee \overline{p})$, $I = Itp_L(C^+ \vee C^-)$.

A join operator $\sqcup$ allows to determine the label of a pivot p, taking into account that p might have different labels α and β in the two antecedents: $\sqcup$ is defined by $a \sqcup b = ab$, $a \sqcup ab = ab$, $b \sqcup ab = ab$.

The systems corresponding to McMillan and Pudlák's interpolation algorithms are referred to as Itp_M and Itp_P; the system dual to McMillan's is $Itp_{M'}$. Itp_M, Itp_P and $Itp_{M'}$ are obtained as special cases of Itp_L by labeling all the occurrences of AB variables with b, ab and a, respectively (see [3] and [18]).

A total order $\preceq$ is defined over labels as $b \preceq ab \preceq a$, and pointwise extended to a partial order over labelings: $L \preceq L'$ if, for every clause C and variable p in C, $L(p, C) \preceq L'(p, C)$. This allows to directly compare the logical strength of the interpolants produced by two systems. In fact, for any refutation R of a formula $A \wedge B$ and labelings L, L' such that $L \preceq L'$, we have $Itp_L(A, B, R) \implies Itp_{L'}(A, B, R)$ and we say that Itp_L is *stronger* than $Itp_{L'}$ [3].

Since a labeled system Itp_L is uniquely determined by the labeling L, when discussing a family of LISs $\{Itp_{L_1}, \ldots, Itp_{L_n}\}$ we will refer to the correspondent *family of labelings* as $\{L_1, \ldots, L_n\}$.

Labeling Notation. In the previous sections, we saw how the various collectives involve the generation of multiple interpolants from a single inconsistent formula $\Phi = \{\phi_1, \ldots, \phi_n\}$ for different subdivisions of Φ into an A and a B parts; we

Table 1. 3-SA

p in ?	Variable *class, label*		
	ϕ_1 | $\phi_2\phi_3$	ϕ_2 | $\phi_1\phi_3$	ϕ_3 | $\phi_1\phi_2$
ϕ_1	A,a	B,b	B,b
ϕ_2	B,b	A,a	B,b
ϕ_3	B,b	B,b	A,a
$\phi_1\phi_2$	AB,α_1	AB,α_2	B,b
$\phi_2\phi_3$	B,b	AB,β_2	AB,β_3
$\phi_1\phi_3$	AB,γ_1	B,b	AB,γ_3
$\phi_1\phi_2\phi_3$	AB,δ_1	AB,δ_2	AB,δ_3

Table 2. BGSA

p in ?	Variable *class, label*		
	ϕ_1 | $\phi_2\phi_3$	ϕ_2 | $\phi_1\phi_3$	$\phi_1\phi_2$ | ϕ_3
ϕ_1	A,a	B,b	A,a
ϕ_2	B,b	A,a	A,a
ϕ_3	B,b	B,b	B,b
$\phi_1\phi_2$	AB,α_1	AB,α_2	A,a
$\phi_2\phi_3$	B,b	AB,β_2	AB,β_3
$\phi_1\phi_3$	AB,γ_1	B,b	AB,γ_3
$\phi_1\phi_2\phi_3$	AB,δ_1	AB,δ_2	AB,δ_3

refer to these ways of splitting Φ as *configurations*. Remember that a labeling L has freedom in assigning labels only to occurrences of variables of class AB; each configuration identifies these variables.

Since we deal with several configurations at a time, it is useful to separate the variables into *partitions* of Φ depending on whether the variables are local to a ϕ_i or shared, taking into account all possible combinations. For example, Table 1 is the *labeling table* that characterizes 3-SA. Recall that in 3-SA we are given an inconsistent $\Phi = \{\phi_1, \phi_2, \phi_3\}$ and a family of labelings $\{L_1, L_2, L_3\}$ and generate three interpolants $I_{\phi_1,L_1}, I_{\phi_2,L_2}, I_{\phi_3,L_3}$. The labeling L_i is associated with the ith configuration. For example, the table shows that L_1 can independently assign a label from $\{a, b, ab\}$ to each occurrence of each variable shared between ϕ_1 and ϕ_2, ϕ_1 and ϕ_3 or ϕ_1, ϕ_2 and ϕ_3 (as indicated by the presence of $\alpha_1, \gamma_1, \delta_1$).

When talking about an occurrence of a variable p in a certain partition $\phi_{i_1} \cdots \phi_{i_k}$, it is convenient to associate to p and the partition a *labeling vector* $(\eta_{i_1}, \ldots, \eta_{i_k})$, representing the labels assigned to p by $L_{i_1}, \ldots, L_{i_k}$ in configuration $i_1, \ldots, i_k$ (all other labels are fixed). Strength of labeling vectors is compared pointwise, extending the linear order $b \preceq ab \preceq a$ as described earlier.

We reduce the problem of deciding whether a family $\mathcal{F} = \{Itp_{L_1}, \ldots, Itp_{L_n}\}$ has an interpolation property P to showing that all labeling vectors of $\{L_1, \ldots, L_n\}$ satisfy a certain set of *labeling constraints*. For simplicity of presentation, in the rest of the paper we assume that all occurrences of a variable are labeled uniformly. The extension to differently labeled occurrences is straightforward.

Collectives of LISs Families. We derive in the following both *necessary* and *sufficient* conditions for the collectives to hold in the context of LISs families. The practical significance of our results is to identify which LISs satisfy which collectives. In particular, for the first time, we show that not all LISs identified by D'Silva et al. satisfy all collectives. This work provides an essential guide for using interpolant strength results when collectives are required (such as in Upgrade Checking).

We proceed as follows. First, we identify necessary and sufficient labeling constraints to characterize BGSA. Second, we extend them to n-GSA and to n-SA. Third, we exploit the connections between BGSA and n-GSA on one side, and n-STI and T-TI on the other (Theorem 4, Lemma 5, Lemma 6) to derive the labeling constraints both for n-STI and T-TI, thus completing the picture.

BGSA. Let $\Phi = \{\phi_1, \phi_2, \phi_3\}$ be an unsatisfiable formula in CNF, and $\mathcal{F} = \{Itp_{L_1}, Itp_{L_2}, Itp_{L_3}\}$ a family of LISs. We want to identify the restrictions on the labeling vectors of $\{L_1, L_2, L_3\}$ for which $\mathcal{F}$ has BGSA, i.e., $I_{\phi_1, L_1} \wedge I_{\phi_2, L_2} \implies I_{\phi_1\phi_2, L_3}$. We define a set of *BGSA constraints* CC_{BGSA} on labelings as follows. A family of labelings $\{L_1, L_2, L_3\}$ satisfies CC_{BGSA} iff:

$$(\alpha_1, \alpha_2), (\delta_1, \delta_2) \preceq \{(ab, ab), (b, a), (a, b)\}, \beta_2 \preceq \beta_3, \gamma_1 \preceq \gamma_3, \delta_1 \preceq \delta_3, \delta_2 \preceq \delta_3$$

hold for all variables, where α_i, β_i, γ_i and δ_i are as shown in Table 2, the labeling table for *BGSA*. $* \preceq \{*_1, *_2\}$ denotes that $* \preceq *_1$ or $* \preceq *_2$ (both can be true).

We aim to prove that CC_{BGSA} is necessary and sufficient for a family of LISs to have BGSA. On one hand, we claim that, if $\{L_1, L_2, L_3\}$ satisfies CC_{BGSA}, then $\{Itp_{L_1}, Itp_{L_2}, Itp_{L_3}\}$ has BGSA. It is sufficient to prove the thesis for a set of *restricted BGSA constraints* CC^*_{BGSA}, defined as follows:

$$(\alpha_1, \alpha_2), (\delta_1, \delta_2) \in \{(ab, ab), (b, a), (a, b)\}, \beta_2 = \beta_3, \gamma_1 = \gamma_3, \delta_3 = \max\{\delta_1, \delta_2\}$$

Lemma 1. *If $\{L_1, L_2, L_3\}$ satisfies CC^*_{BGSA}, then $\{Itp_{L_1}, Itp_{L_2}, Itp_{L_3}\}$ has BGSA.*

The CC^*_{BGSA} constraints can be relaxed to CC_{BGSA} as shown in [18] (Theorem 2, Lemma 3), due to the connection between partial order on labelings and LISs and strength of the generated interpolants. For example, the constraint $\delta_3 = \max(\delta_1, \delta_2)$ can be relaxed to $\delta_3 \succeq \delta_1, \delta_3 \succeq \delta_2$. This leads to:

Corollary 2. *If $\{L_1, L_2, L_3\}$ satisfies CC_{BGSA}, then $\{Itp_{L_1}, Itp_{L_2}, Itp_{L_3}\}$ has BGSA.*

On the other hand, it holds that the satisfaction of the CC_{BGSA} constraints is necessary for BGSA:

Lemma 2. *If $\{Itp_{L_1}, Itp_{L_2}, Itp_{L_3}\}$ has BGSA, then $\{L_1, L_2, L_3\}$ satisfies CC_{BGSA}.*

Having proved that CC_{BGSA} is both sufficient and necessary, we conclude:

Theorem 9. *A family $\{Itp_{L_1}, Itp_{L_2}, Itp_{L_3}\}$ has BGSA if and only if $\{L_1, L_2, L_3\}$ satisfies CC_{BGSA}.*

n-GSA. After addressing the binary case, we move to defining necessary and sufficient conditions for n-GSA. A family of LISs $\{Itp_{L_1}, \ldots, Itp_{L_{n+1}}\}$ has n-GSA if, for any $\Phi = \{\phi_1, \ldots, \phi_{n+1}\}$, $I_{\Phi_1, L_1} \wedge \cdots \wedge I_{\phi_n, L_n} \implies I_{\phi_1 \ldots \phi_n, L_{n+1}}$, provided Φ is inconsistent. As we defined a set of labeling constraints for BGSA, we now introduce *n-GSA constraints* (CC_{nGSA}) on a family of labelings $\{L_1, \ldots, L_{n+1}\}$; for every variable with labeling vector $(\alpha_{i_1}, \ldots, \alpha_{i_{k+1}})$, $1 \leq k \leq n$, letting $m = i_{k+1}$ if $i_{k+1} \neq n + 1$, $m = i_k$ otherwise:

(1) $(\exists j \in \{i_1, \ldots, i_m\} \, \alpha_j = a) \implies (\forall h \in \{i_1, \ldots, i_m\} \, h \neq j \implies \alpha_h = b)$

(2)   Moreover, if $i_{k+1} = n + 1 : \forall j \in \{i_1, \ldots, i_k\}, \alpha_j \preceq \alpha_{i_{k+1}}$

That is, if a variable is not shared with ϕ_{n+1}, then, if one of the labels is a, all the others must be b; if the variable is shared with ϕ_{n+1}, condition (1) still holds for $(\alpha_{i_1}, \ldots, \alpha_{i_{k-1}})$, and all these labels must be stronger or equal than $\alpha_{i_{k+1}} = \alpha_{n+1}$. We can prove that these constraints are necessary and sufficient for a family of LIS to have n-GSA:

Theorem 10. *A family* $\mathcal{F} = \{Itp_{L_1}, \ldots, Itp_{L_{n+1}}\}$ *has* n-GSA *if and only if* $\{L_1, \ldots, L_{n+1}\}$ *satisfies* CC_{nGSA}.

In [18] (see Setting 1) it is proved that n-SA holds for any family of LISs stronger than Pudlák. Theorem 10 is strictly more general, since it allows for tuples of labels (e.g., $(\alpha_1, \alpha_2) = (a, b)$ or $(\delta_1, \delta_3, \delta_2) = (a, b, b)$) that were not considered in [18]. The constraints for n-SA follow as a special case of CC_{nGSA}:

Corollary 3. *A family* $\mathcal{F} = \{Itp_{L_1}, \ldots, Itp_{L_n}\}$ *has* n-SA *if and only if* $\{L_1, \ldots, L_n\}$ *satisfies* *the* *following* *constraints:* *for* *every* *variable* *with* *labeling* *vector* $(\alpha_{i_1}, \ldots, \alpha_{i_k})$, *for* $2 \leq k \leq n$: $(\exists j \in \{i_1, \ldots, i_k\} \, \alpha_j = a) \implies (\forall h \in \{i_1, \ldots, i_k\} \, h \neq j \implies \alpha_h = b)$.

Moreover, a family that has $(n+1)$-SA also has n-GSA if the last member of the family is Pudlák's system. In fact, from Proposition 2 and Pudlák's system being symmetric (as shown in [8]), it follows that *if a family* $\{Itp_{L_1}, \ldots, Itp_{L_n}, Itp_P\}$ *has* $(n + 1)$-SA, *then it has* n-GSA.

After investigating n-GSA and n-SA, we address two questions which were left open in §3: do n-SA and n-PI imply n-STI? Is the requirement of additional interpolation systems necessary to obtain T-TI from n-GSA? We show here that n-SA and n-PI do not necessarily imply n-STI, and that, for LISs, n-GSA and T-TI are equivalent.

n-STI. Theorem 3 shows that if a family has n-STI, then it has both n-SA and n-PI. We prove that the converse is not necessarily true. First, it is not difficult to show that any family $\{Itp_{L_0}, Itp_{L_1}, Itp_{L_2}\}$ has 2-PI (Proposition 3 in [5]); a second result is that:

Lemma 5. *There exists a family* $\{Itp_{L_0}, Itp_{L_1}, Itp_{L_2}\}$ *that has 2-PI and a family* $\{Itp_{L'_1}, Itp_{L'_2}\}$ *that has 2-SA, but the family* $\{Itp_{L_0}, Itp_{L_1}, Itp_{L_2}, Itp_{L'_1}, Itp_{L'_2}\}$ *does not have 2-STI.*

We obtain the main result applying the STI sub-family property (Theorem 2):

Theorem 11. *There exists a family* $\{Itp_{S_0}, \ldots, Itp_{S_n}\}$ *that has* n-PI, *and a family* $\{Itp_{T_1}, \ldots, Itp_{T_n}\}$ *that has* n-SA, *but the family* $\{Itp_{S_0}, \ldots, Itp_{S_n}\} \cup \{Itp_{T_1}, \ldots, Itp_{T_n}\}$ *does not have* n-STI.

T-TI. The last collective to be studied is T-TI. Theorem 6 shows how T-TI can be obtained by multiple applications of GSA at the level of each parent and its children, provided that we can find an appropriate labeling to generate an interpolant for the parent. We prove here that, in the case of LISs, this requirement is not needed, and derive explicit constraints on labelings for T-TI.

Let us define n-GSA *strengthening* any property derived from n-GSA by not abstracting any of the subformulae ϕ_i, for example $I_{\phi_1, L_1} \wedge \ldots \wedge I_{\phi_{n-1}, L_{n-1}} \wedge \phi_n \implies I_{\phi_1 \ldots \phi_n, L_{n+1}}$; it can be proved that:

Lemma 6. *The set of labeling constraints of any n-GSA strengthening is a subset of constraints of n-GSA.*

From Theorem 6 and Lemma 6, it follows that:

Lemma 7. *Given a tree $T = (V, E)$ a family $\{Itp_{S_i}\}_{i \in V}$ has T-TI if, for every parent i_{k+1} and its children $i_1, \ldots, i_k$, the family of labelings of the $(k+1)$-GSA strengthening obtained by non abstracting the parent satisfies the correspondent subset of $(k+1)$-GSA constraints.*

Note that, in contrast to Theorem 6, in the case of LISs we do not need to ensure the existence of an additional set of interpolation systems to abstract the parents. The symmetry between the necessary and sufficient conditions given by Theorem 6 and Theorem 5 is restored, and we establish:

Theorem 12. *Given a tree $T = (V, E)$ a family $\{Itp_{S_i}\}_{i \in V}$ has T-TI if and only if for every parent i_{k+1} and its children $i_1, \ldots, i_k$, the family of labelings of the $(k+1)$-GSA strengthening obtained by non abstracting the parent satisfies the correspondent subset of $(k+1)$-GSA constraints.*

Alternatively, in the case of LISs, the additional interpolation systems can be constructed explicitly:

Theorem 13. *Any $\mathcal{F} = \{Itp_{L_{i_1}}, \ldots, Itp_{L_{i_k}}, Itp_{L_{n+1}}\}$ s.t. $k < n$ that has an n-GSA strengthening property can be extended to a family that has n-GSA.*

Collectives of Single LISs. In the following, we highlight the fundamental results in the context of single LISs, which represent the most common application of the framework of D'Silva et al. to SAT-based model checking.

First, importantly for practical applications, any LIS satisfies PI:

Theorem 14. *PI holds for all single LISs.*

Second, recall that in §3 we proved that BGSA, STI, TI, GSA are equivalent for single interpolation systems, and that SA $\rightarrow$ BGSA for symmetric ones. We now show that for a single LIS, SA is equivalent to BGSA and that PI is not.

Theorem 15. *If a LIS has SA, then it has BGSA.*

Proof. We show that, for any L, the labeling constraints of SA imply those of BGSA. Refer to Table 2, Table 1, Theorem 10 and Corollary 3. In case of a family $\{L_1, L_2, L_3\}$, the constraints for 3-SA are:

$$(\alpha_1, \alpha_2), (\beta_2, \beta_3), (\gamma_1, \gamma_3) \preceq \{(ab, ab), (b, a), (a, b)\}$$
$$(\delta_1, \delta_2, \delta_3) \preceq \{(ab, ab, ab), (a, b, b), (b, a, b), (b, b, a)\}$$

When $L_1 = L_2 = L_3$, they simplify to $\alpha, \beta, \gamma, \delta \in \{ab, b\}$; this means that, in case of a single LIS, only Pudlák's or stronger systems are allowed. In case of a family $\{L_1, L_2, L_3\}$, the constraints for BGSA are:

$$(\alpha_1, \alpha_2), (\delta_1, \delta_2) \preceq \{(ab, ab), (b, a), (a, b)\}, \beta_2 \preceq \beta_3, \gamma_1 \preceq \gamma_3, \delta_1 \preceq \delta_3, \delta_2 \preceq \delta_3$$

When $L_1 = L_2 = L_3$, they simplify to $\alpha, \delta \in \{ab, b\}$; clearly, the constraints for 3-SA imply those for BGSA, but not vice versa.

Finally, Theorem 14 and Theorem 15 yield:

Theorem 16. *The system $Itp_{M'}$ has PI but does not have BGSA.*

Proof. From the *proof* of Theorem 15: a LIS has the BGSA property iff it is stronger or equal than Pudlák's system. $Itp_{M'}$ is strictly weaker than Itp_P. Thus, it does not have BGSA.

Note that the necessary and sufficient conditions for LISs to support each of the collectives simplify implementing procedures with a given property, or, more importantly from a practical perspective, determine which implementation supports which property.

5   Implementation

We developed an interpolating prover, PeRIPLO[6], which implements the proposed framework. PeRIPLO is, to the best of our knowledge, the first SAT-solver built on MiniSAT 2.2.0 that realizes the Labeled Interpolation Systems of [3] and allows to perform interpolation, path interpolation, generalized simultaneous abstraction, state-transition interpolation and tree interpolation; it also offers proof logging and manipulation routines. The tool has been integrated within the Fun-Frog and eVolCheck verification frameworks, which make use of its solving and interpolation features for SAT-based model checking. In theory, using different partitions of the same formula and different labelings with each partition does not change the algorithmic complexity of LISs (see appendix C in [5]). In our experience, there is no overhead in practice as well.

6   Conclusions

Craig interpolation is a widely used approach in abstraction-based model checking. This paper conducts a systematic investigation of the most common interpolation properties exploited in verification, focusing on the constraints they pose on propositional interpolation systems used in SAT-based model checking.

The paper makes the following contributions. It systematizes and unifies various properties imposed on interpolation by existing verification approaches and proves that for families of interpolation systems the properties form a hierarchy, whereas for a single system all properties except path interpolation and simultaneous abstraction are in fact equivalent. Additionally, it defines and proves both sufficient and necessary conditions for a family of Labeled Interpolation Systems. In particular, it demonstrates that in case of a single system path interpolation is common to all LISs, while simultaneous abstraction is as strong as all other more complex properties. Extending our framework to address interpolation in first order theories is an interesting open problem, and is part of our future work.

---

[6] PeRIPLO is available at `http://verify.inf.usi.ch/periplo.html`

References

1. Albarghouthi, A., Gurfinkel, A., Chechik, M.: WHALE: An Interpolation-Based Algorithm for Inter-procedural Verification. In: Kuncak, V., Rybalchenko, A. (eds.) VMCAI 2012. LNCS, vol. 7148, pp. 39–55. Springer, Heidelberg (2012)
2. Bradley, A.R.: SAT-Based Model Checking without Unrolling. In: Jhala, R., Schmidt, D. (eds.) VMCAI 2011. LNCS, vol. 6538, pp. 70–87. Springer, Heidelberg (2011)
3. D'Silva, V., Kroening, D., Purandare, M., Weissenbacher, G.: Interpolant Strength. In: Barthe, G., Hermenegildo, M. (eds.) VMCAI 2010. LNCS, vol. 5944, pp. 129–145. Springer, Heidelberg (2010)
4. Een, N., Mishchenko, A., Brayton, R.: Efficient Implementation of Property-Directed Reachability. In: FMCAD 2011 (2011)
5. Gurfinkel, A., Rollini, S., Sharygina, N.: Interpolation Properties and SAT-based Model Checking - Extended Version, http://arxiv.org/abs/1212.4650
6. Heizmann, M., Hoenicke, J., Podelski, A.: Nested Interpolants. In: POPL 2010 (2010)
7. Henzinger, T., Jhala, R., Majumdar, R., McMillan, K.: Abstractions from Proofs. In: POPL 2004, pp. 232–244 (2004)
8. Huang, G.: Constructing Craig Interpolation Formulas. In: Li, M., Du, D.-Z. (eds.) COCOON 1995. LNCS, vol. 959, pp. 181–190. Springer, Heidelberg (1995)
9. Jhala, R., McMillan, K.L.: A Practical and Complete Approach to Predicate Refinement. In: Hermanns, H., Palsberg, J. (eds.) TACAS 2006. LNCS, vol. 3920, pp. 459–473. Springer, Heidelberg (2006)
10. Jhala, R., McMillan, K.L.: Interpolant-Based Transition Relation Approximation. In: Etessami, K., Rajamani, S.K. (eds.) CAV 2005. LNCS, vol. 3576, pp. 39–51. Springer, Heidelberg (2005)
11. Krajíček, J.: Interpolation Theorems, Lower Bounds for Proof Systems, and Independence Results for Bounded Arithmetic. J. Symb. Log. 62(2), 457–486 (1997)
12. McMillan, K.L.: An Interpolating Theorem Prover. In: Jensen, K., Podelski, A. (eds.) TACAS 2004. LNCS, vol. 2988, pp. 16–30. Springer, Heidelberg (2004)
13. McMillan, K.L.: Applications of Craig Interpolation to Model Checking. In: Marcinkowski, J., Tarlecki, A. (eds.) CSL 2004. LNCS, vol. 3210, pp. 22–23. Springer, Heidelberg (2004)
14. McMillan, K.L.: Interpolation and SAT-Based Model Checking. In: Hunt Jr., W.A., Somenzi, F. (eds.) CAV 2003. LNCS, vol. 2725, pp. 1–13. Springer, Heidelberg (2003)
15. McMillan, K.L.: Lazy Abstraction with Interpolants. In: Ball, T., Jones, R.B. (eds.) CAV 2006. LNCS, vol. 4144, pp. 123–136. Springer, Heidelberg (2006)
16. McMillan, K.L., Rybalchenko, A.: Solving Constrained Horn Clauses Using Interpolation. Technical Report MSR-TR-2013-6, Microsoft Research (2013)
17. Pudlák, P.: Lower Bounds for Resolution and Cutting Plane Proofs and Monotone Computations. J. Symb. Log. 62(3), 981–998 (1997)
18. Rollini, S.F., Sery, O., Sharygina, N.: Leveraging Interpolant Strength in Model Checking. In: Madhusudan, P., Seshia, S.A. (eds.) CAV 2012. LNCS, vol. 7358, pp. 193–209. Springer, Heidelberg (2012)
19. Rybalchenko, A., Sofronie-Stokkermans, V.: Constraint Solving for Interpolation. In: Cook, B., Podelski, A. (eds.) VMCAI 2007. LNCS, vol. 4349, pp. 346–362. Springer, Heidelberg (2007)

20. Sery, O., Fedyukovich, G., Sharygina, N.: FunFrog: Bounded Model Checking with Interpolation-based Function Summarization. In: Chakraborty, S., Mukund, M. (eds.) ATVA 2012. LNCS, vol. 7561, pp. 203–207. Springer, Heidelberg (2012)
21. Sery, O., Fedyukovich, G., Sharygina, N.: Incremental Upgrade Checking by Means of Interpolation-based Function Summaries. In: FMCAD 2012 (2012)
22. Sharma, R., Nori, A.V., Aiken, A.: Interpolants as Classifiers. In: Madhusudan, P., Seshia, S.A. (eds.) CAV 2012. LNCS, vol. 7358, pp. 71–87. Springer, Heidelberg (2012)
23. Vizel, Y., Grumberg, O.: Interpolation-Sequence Based Model Checking. In: FMCAD 2009, pp. 1–8 (2009)

Analysis of Message Passing Programs
Using SMT-Solvers

Parosh Aziz Abdulla, Mohamed Faouzi Atig, and Jonathan Cederberg

Uppsala University, Sweden

Abstract. We consider message passing programs where processes communicate asynchronously over unbounded channels. The reachability problem for such systems are either undecidable or have very high complexity. In order to achieve efficiency, we consider the *phase-bounded* reachability problem, where each process is allowed to perform a bounded number of *phases* during a run of the system. In a given phase, the process is allowed to perform *send* or *receive* transitions (but not both). We present a uniform framework where the channels are assigned different types of semantics such as *lossy*, *stuttering*, or *unordered*. We show that the framework allows a uniform translation of bounded-phase reachability for each of the above mentioned semantics to the satisfiability of quantifier-free Presburger formulas. This means that we can use the full power of modern SMT-solvers for efficient analysis of our systems. Furthermore, we show that the translation implies that bounded-phase reachability is NP-COMPLETE. Finally, we prove that the problem becomes undecidable if we allow *perfect* channels or push-down processes communicating through (stuttering) lossy channels. We report on the result of applying the prototype on a number of non-trivial examples.

1 Introduction

Programs modeled as message passing processes have a wide range of applications including communication protocols [13,5], programs operating on weak memory models [3,7], WEB service protocols [26], and as semantic models for modern languages such as ERLANG [30] and SCALA [31]. Typically, the processes exchange information asynchronously through a shared unbounded data structure, e.g., counters, multisets, and channels. Despite the increasing popularity of such program models, precise algorithmic analysis is still a major challenge. This is perhaps not without a good reason: it is well known that basic analysis problems (e.g., state reachability) are undecidable for processes communicating via *perfect* FIFO channels [13], even under the assumption that each process is finite-state. Although, checking state reachability becomes decidable for (important) special cases such as *lossy* FIFO channels [1], or *unordered* channels [25], the algorithms have very high complexity (non-primitive recursive for lossy channels [28] and EXPSPACE-HARD for unordered channels [20]).

Given the importance of concurrent software, much research has been devoted in recent years to developing practically useful algorithms. The undecidability and high complexity obstacles are usually addressed by considering different types of over- or under-approximations of system behavior (e.g., [16,4,9,12,26,8,11,10,32,17,15]).

D. Van Hung and M. Ogawa (Eds.): ATVA 2013, LNCS 8172, pp. 272–286, 2013.

One useful approach that has recently been proposed is *context-bounding* [24]. The idea is to only consider computations performing at most some fixed number of context switches between processes. This provides a trade-off between computational complexity and verification coverage: on the one hand, context-bounded verification can be more efficient than unbounded verification; and on the other hand, many concurrency errors, such as data races and atomicity violations, are manifested in executions with few context switches [22].

In this paper, we present a new approach to model checking of concurrent processes that communicate through channels. We introduce a new bounding parameter in the behavior of such systems, namely the number of alternations between *send* operations and *receive* operations performed by each processes. We consider the *bounded-phase* reachability problem, where each process is restricted to performing at most k phases (for some natural number k). A *phase* is a run where the process performs either send or receive operations (but not both). Notice that the bounded-phase restriction does not limit the *number* of sends or receives, and in particular it does not put any restriction on the length of the run. Also, the number of context switches is not limited. We will present a framework and instantiate it for several variants of channel semantics, such as *lossy*, *stuttering*, and *multiset* that allow the messages inside the channels to be lost, duplicated, and re-ordered respectively. One main contribution of this paper is to show that our framework allows to translate (in polynomial time) the bounded-phase reachability problem to the satisfiability of quantifier-free Presburger formulas. This opens the way to leveraging the full power of state-of-the-art SMT-solvers for obtaining a very efficient solution to the bounded-phase reachability problem for all above mentioned models. We perform the translation in two steps. First, we show that bounded-phase reachability can be reduced to (general) reachability under a new restriction, namely that we only consider simple computations. A computation is *simple* if any (local) state of a process appears at most once along the computation. In the second step, we show that simple reachability can be captured by satisfiability of a quantifier-free Presburger formula (that we can then feed to an SMT-solver).

In order to simplify the presentation, we first describe our framework for lossy channel systems LCS. Then, we describe how the method can be modified (in a straightforward manner) to the other channel semantics. Also, as consequence of our translation, we show that bounded-phase reachability for LCS (and the other models) is NP-COMPLETE. This is to be contrasted with the fact that the general reachability problem is not primitive recursive.

Finally, we show undecidability of bounded-phase reachability for several cases, e.g., under the *perfect* channel semantics, or under the *(stuttering) lossy* semantics when one of the processes is allowed to have a (single) stack.

We have implemented our method in a prototype that we have applied on a number of examples with promising results. The examples span several application areas, such as WEB service protocols, communication protocols, and multithreaded programs counters. The prototype and the details of the examples and experimentation are available online (see Section 11).

Related Work. Our work can be seen as a non-trivial extension of bounded-context switches for concurrent shared-memory programs [24] and reversal-bounded analysis for programs manipulating counters [18,16] to the class of message-passing programs.

La Torre et al. [32] propose context-bounded analysis for pushdown processes communicating through perfect channels, where in each context a process is allowed to receive from only one channel (but is allowed to send to all other channels). This implies that, in a context, a process can have an unbounded number of alternations between send and receive modes (which is not allowed in our bounded-phase analysis). However, our bounded-phase analysis allows multiple processes to be active at the same time and each one of them can send or receive to/from all the channels (which is not permitted by context-bounded analysis of [32]).

In [9,4,12] symbolic representations of the contents of the channels have been proposed for analysis of message-passing programs. Our technique does not restrict the content of channels to a class of representable descriptions. Moreover, our reduction to the satisfiability of quantifier-free Presburger formulas allows us to use highly-developed and optimized SMT-solvers.

In [10], the authors consider a different model where the communication is done via Perfect FIFO channels and where "messages/tasks" can be consumed only when the process stack is empty. Although, their proposed bounding scheme is more general than bounding the number of alternations between receive and send operations, their notion leads to undecidability. To obtain decidability, they restrict the number of processor interleavings. We do not do this since we would like to allow any possible shuffle between two processes.

2 Preliminaries

We let $\mathbb{N}$ denote the set of natural numbers. For a natural number n, we define $[n] := \{1, 2, \ldots, n\}$. For a set A, we use $|A|$ to denote its cardinality. For a function $f : A \mapsto B$ from a set A to a set B we use $f[a \leftarrow b]$ to denote the function f' such that $f(a) = b$ and $f'(a') = f(a')$ if $a' \neq a$. We use $[A \mapsto B]$ to denote the set of (total) functions from A to B. For a set A, we let A^* denote the set of finite words over A. We let $|w|$ denote the length of w. We use $w[i]$ to denote the ith element of w, and write $a \in w$ to denote that $w[i] = a$ for some i. For words $w_1 = a_1 a_2 \cdots a_m$ and $w_2 = b_1 b_2 \cdots b_n$, we write $w_1 \preceq w_2$ to denote that there is an injection $h : [m] \mapsto [n]$ such that $i < j$ implies $h(i) < h(j)$ and $a_i = b_{h(i)}$, i.e., w_1 is a (not necessarily contiguous) subword of w_2. We use $w_1 \cdot w_2$ to denote the concatenation of w_1 and w_2, and ε to denote the empty word. For a word $w = a_1 a_2 \cdots a_m$, we use *Stuttering(w)* to denote the set of words defined as $\{a_1^{i_1} a_2^{i_2} \cdots a_m^{i_m} \mid 1 \leq i_1, i_2, \ldots, i_m\}$.

3 Communicating Finite-State Processes

In this section, we introduce finite-state processes communicating through lossy channels. We introduce the notion of processes and the transition system induced by communicating processes, and then consider bounded-phase computations. In the rest of the section, we fix a finite set M of *messages* and a finite set C of *channels*.

Processes. A *process* p is a tuple $\langle Q_p, q_p^{init}, \Delta_p \rangle$ where Q_p is a finite set of *states*, $q_p^{init} \in Q_p$ is the *initial state*, and Δ_p is a finite set of *transitions*. A transition $t \in \Delta_p$ is a triple $\langle q_1, op, q_2 \rangle$ where $q_1, q_2 \in Q_p$ are states, and op is an *operation* of one of the following three forms: (i) $c!m$ sends the message $m \in M$ to channel $c \in C$ (m is appended to the tail of c), (ii) $c?m$ receives the message $m \in M$ from channel $c \in C$ (only enabled if m is at the head of c, and if performed, m is removed from the head of c), (iii) *nop* is the dummy operation (it does not affect the contents of the channels). We define $source(t) := q_1$, $target(t) := q_2$, and $operation(t) := op$. For a state $q \in Q_p$, we define $source^{-1}(q) := \{t | source(t) = q\}$ and define $target^{-1}(q)$ and $operation^{-1}(op)$ similarly. We define Δ_p^{snd} to be the set of transitions in Δ_p whose operations are *send*. We define Δ_p^{rcv} and Δ^{nop} similarly. A sequence $\delta = t_1 t_2 \cdots t_n$ is said to be a *cycle* if (i) $target(t_i) = source(t_{i+1})$ for $i : 1 \leq i < n$, (ii) $target(t_n) = source(t_1)$, and (iii) $t_i \neq t_j$ if $i \neq j$. We say that δ is a q-*loop* if $source(t_1) = q$.

Transition System. We define the transition system induced by processes communicating through lossy channels. A *Lossy Channel System* (LCS for short) consists of a set P of processes. Let process $p \in P$ be of the form $\langle Q_p, q_p^{init}, \Delta_p \rangle$. Define $Q := \cup_{p \in P} Q_p$, $\Delta := \cup_{p \in P} \Delta_p$, $\Delta^{snd} := \cup_{p \in P} \Delta_p^{snd}$, and define Δ^{rcv}, Δ^{nop} similarly. A *state map* is a function $s : P \mapsto Q$ such that $s(p) \in Q_p$, and a *channel map* is a function $\omega : C \mapsto M^*$. We extend the subword ordering $\preceq$ to *channel maps* as follows: Given two *channel maps* $\omega_1 : C \mapsto M^*$ and $\omega_2 : C \mapsto M^*$, we write $\omega_1 \preceq \omega_2$ if and only if $\omega_1(c) \preceq \omega_2(c)$ for all $c \in C$. A *configuration* γ is of the form $\langle s, \omega \rangle$ where s is a state map and ω is a channel map. Intuitively, s defines the states of the processes, while ω defines the contents of the channels. We define a transition relation $\longrightarrow$ on the set of configurations as follows. Consider configurations $\gamma_1 = \langle s_1, \omega_1 \rangle$, $\gamma_2 = \langle s_2, \omega_2 \rangle$, and a transition $t = \langle q_1, op, q_2 \rangle \in \Delta_p$ for some $p \in P$. We write $\gamma_1 \xrightarrow{t} \gamma_2$ to denote that $s_1(p) = q_1$, $s_2 = s_1[p \leftarrow q_2]$, and one of the following three properties is satisfied: (i) $op = c!m$ and $\omega_2 \preceq \omega_1[c \leftarrow m \cdot \omega_1(c)]$, (ii) $op = c?m$ and $\omega_2 \preceq \omega_1[c \leftarrow w]$ where $\omega_1(c) = w \cdot m$, and (iii) $op = nop$ and $\omega_2 \preceq \omega_1$. A computation π (from a configuration γ to a configuration γ') is a sequence $\gamma_0 \xrightarrow{t_1} \gamma_1 \cdots \xrightarrow{t_n} \gamma_n$ such that $\gamma_0 = \gamma$ and $\gamma_n = \gamma'$. In such a case we say that γ' is *reachable* from γ by π. We define the *initial configuration* $\gamma^{init} := \langle s^{init}, \omega^{init} \rangle$, where $s^{init}(p) = q_p^{init}$ for all $p \in P$, and $\omega^{init}(c) = \varepsilon$ for $c \in C$. In other words, the system starts from a configuration where all the processes are in their initial states and where all the channels are empty. A configuration γ is said to be *reachable* if it is reachable from γ^{init}. A state map $s \in [P \mapsto Q]$ is *reachable*, if there is a channel map ω such that $\langle s, \omega \rangle$ is reachable. In the *reachability problem* for the LCS P, we are given a state map $s^{target} \in [P \mapsto Q]$, and we are asked whether s^{target} is reachable.

Bounded-Phase Computations. We introduce bounded-phase computations. From the point of view of any process p, the computation consists of a number of phases where, during a given phase, process p either only performs *send* operations, or only performs *receive* operations (in addition to the dummy operation). Consider a computation $\pi = \gamma_0 \xrightarrow{t_1} \gamma_1 \xrightarrow{t_2} \cdots \xrightarrow{t_n} \gamma_n$. We define $\pi \uparrow := t_1 t_2 \cdots t_n$, i.e., it is the sequence of transitions that occur in π. For a process $p \in P$, we define $\pi \uparrow p$ to be the maximal subword $t_1' t_2' \cdots t_m'$ of $\pi \uparrow$ such that $t_i' \in \Delta_p$ for $i : 1 \leq i \leq m$, i.e., it is the sequence of transitions performed by p in π. Given a sequence of transitions $\delta = t_1 t_2 \cdots t_n \in \Delta_p^*$, we say that δ is a *phase* if either $t_i \in \Delta_p^{snd} \cup \Delta_p^{nop}$ for all $i : 1 \le i \le n$, or $t_i \in \Delta_p^{rcv} \cup \Delta_p^{nop}$ for all $i : 1 \le i \le n$. We define $\sim snd := rcv$, and $\sim rcv := snd$.

A computation π is said to be *k-bounded* with respect to a process p if $\pi \uparrow p = \delta_1 \cdot \delta_2 \cdots \delta_j$ where $j \le k$ and δ_i is a phase for all $i : 1 \le i \le j$. In other words, the transitions performed by p in π form at most k phases. We say that π is *k-bounded* if it is *k-bounded* with respect to all process $p \in P$. For configurations γ and γ', we say that γ' is *k-reachable* from γ if γ' is reachable from γ by a k-bounded computation. (State map) k-reachability is defined in a similar manner to state map reachability (see above). In the *bounded-phase reachability problem*, we are also given a natural number $k \in \mathbb{N}$, and we are asked whether s^{target} is k-reachable. The following theorem follows from the definitions. It shows that k-reachability is an under-approximation of reachability.

Theorem 1. *A state map $s : P \mapsto Q$ is reachable iff s is k-reachable for some $k \in \mathbb{N}$.*

4 Simple Reachability

In this section, we introduce *simple reachability*, i.e., reachability by computations in which a state may occur at most once along the computation. We show that k-reachability is polynomially reducible to simple reachability. We do that in two steps. First, we define *pure* LCS and show that the k-reachability problem for general LCS can be reduced to the reachability problem for pure LCS. Second, for a pure LCS, we derive a new LCS and show that the reachability problem for the former coincides with the simple reachability problem for the latter.

Simple Computations. Consider a set of processes P. Let $p = \langle Q_p, q_p^{init}, \Delta_p \rangle$ for $p \in P$. A sequence of transitions $\delta = t_1 t_2 \cdots t_n \in \Delta_p^*$ is said to be simple if there are no $\delta_1, \delta_2, \delta_3$ such that $\delta = \delta_1 \cdot \delta_2 \cdot \delta_3$ and δ_2 is a q-cycle for some state $q \in Q_p$. In other words, the states appearing along the sequence are all different. A computation π is *simple* if $\pi \uparrow p$ is simple for all $p \in P$. A simple computation then does not visit any state more than once. For configurations γ, γ', we say that γ' is *simply reachable* from γ if γ' is reachable from γ by a simple computation. The *simple reachability problem* is defined in a similar manner to the reachability problem (see Section 3) except that we replace *computations* in the definition by *simple computations*.

Pure LCS. Consider a process $p = \langle Q_p, q_p^{init}, \Delta_p \rangle$. We say that p is *pure* if there is no cycle $t_1 t_1 \cdots t_n$ such that $t_i \in \Delta_p^{snd}$ and $t_j \in \Delta_p^{rcv}$ for some $i \ne j$. In other words, p is pure if there is no cycle (equivalently there is no strongly connected component) in the graph of p that contains both a *send* and a *receive* transition. Notice that this is a syntactic property of the process and it does not depend on the operational semantics. An LCS consisting of a set P of processes is *pure* if all processes $p \in P$ are pure. We will now reduce the k-reachability problem for general LCS to the reachability problem for pure LCS. Suppose that we are given an instance of the k-reachability problem, defined by a set P of processes and a target state map s^{target}. We will derive an equivalent instance of the reachability problem where the given LCS is pure. We do this by transforming each process to a pure one. The idea of the transformation is to make a number of copies of (parts of) the graph of p where each copy contains either transitions in $\Delta_p^{snd} \cup \Delta_p^{nop}$ or transitions in $\Delta_p^{rcv} \cup \Delta_p^{nop}$. Each copy will represent one phase of the computation from the point of view of p. If the next transition of p is consistent with the current "mode" of the phase (i.e., *send* or *receive*) then p will continue in states belonging to the current copy; otherwise it moves to the next one. Let $p = \langle Q_p, q_p^{init}, \Delta_p \rangle$. Define $pure(p) := \langle R_p, r_p^{init}, \Delta_p^R \rangle$, where:

- $R_p := \{r_p^{init}, r_p^{target}\} \cup \{\langle q, m, i \rangle | q \in Q_p \wedge m \in \{snd, rcv\} \wedge 1 \leq i \leq k\}$. In other words, $pure(p)$ has an initial state r_p^{init}, a target state r_p^{target}, together with a set of states each of which is triple. A triple consists of a state q of p, a mode m, and a natural number $i \leq k$. Intuitively, triples containing i are used to simulate the ith phase performed by the process, and the mode m describes whether the process is sending or receiving during the current phase.
- Δ_p^R contains the following transitions:
  - $\langle r_p^{init}, nop, \langle q_p^{init}, m, 1 \rangle \rangle$ for $m \in \{snd, rcv\}$. This corresponds to a transition from the initial state of $pure(p)$ to the initial state of p in its first phase. In the first mode, the process may be either sending or receiving.
  - $\langle \langle q_1, m, i \rangle, op, \langle q_2, m, i \rangle \rangle$ if $t = \langle q_1, op, q_2 \rangle \in \Delta_p^m \cup \Delta_p^{nop}$ for $m \in \{snd, rcv\}$ and $1 \leq i \leq k$. The process performs another transition in the same mode m and therefore it stays in the same phase i.
  - $\langle \langle q_1, m, i \rangle, op, \langle q_2, \sim m, i+1 \rangle \rangle$ if $t = \langle q_1, op, q_2 \rangle \in \Delta_p^{\sim m}$ for $m \in \{snd, rcv\}$ and $1 \leq i < k$. The process performs a transition that violates the current mode m, and hence it moves to the next phase $i+1$.
  - $\langle \langle s^{target}(p), m, i \rangle, nop, r_p^{target} \rangle$ for $m \in \{snd, rcv\}$ and $i : 1 \leq i \leq k$. In its final phase, the process moves from the target state of p to the target state of $pure(p)$. The mode of the final phase may be snd or rcv.

Define $pure(P) := \{pure(p) | p \in P\}$, and define the state map $s_R^{target}(p) := r_p^{target}$ for all $p \in P$. It follows that s_R^{target} is reachable in (the pure LCS) $pure(P)$ iff s^{target} is k-reachable in P, which leads to the following lemma.

Lemma 2. *k-Reachability for* LCS *is polynomially reducible to reachability for pure* LCS.

Saturation. Consider an LCS consisting of a set P of processes. Let $p = \langle Q_p, q_p^{init}, \Delta_p \rangle$ and $q \in Q_p$. We define q^{snd} to be the set of operations of the form $c!m$ such that there is a q-cycle δ and a transition $t \in \delta$ with $operation(t) = c!m$. In other words, it is the set of all *send* operations that appear in cycles visiting q. For a given $k \in \mathbb{N}$, we derive a new LCS through "k-saturating" P as follows. For a process $p \in P$, we derive $sat(p, k)$ from p by adding a number of states and transitions. For each transition $\langle q, op, q' \rangle \in \Delta_p$, with $q^{snd} \neq \emptyset$, we add $k+1$ new states $q_0^{tmp}, q_1^{tmp}, \ldots, q_k^{tmp}$. Furthermore, for each operation $c!m \in q^{snd}$ and each $i : 0 \leq i < k$ we add the transition $\langle q_i^{tmp}, c!m, q_{i+1}^{tmp} \rangle$. Finally, we add the transitions $\langle q, nop, q_0^{tmp} \rangle$ and $\langle q_k^{tmp}, op, q' \rangle$. We define $sat(P, k) := \{sat(p, k) | p \in P\}$, i.e., we k-saturate all the processes in the set P. From the definitions, we notice that $sat(P, k)$ satisfies the following properties. (i) The size $|sat(P,k)|$ of $sat(P,k)$ is polynomial in k and in the size $|P|$ of P (for any appropriate definition of the size $|P|$). This holds since we add at most $k+1$ new states per state of p (more precisely, either $k+1$ states if $q^{snd} \neq \emptyset$, or no states if $q^{snd} = \emptyset$). Also, for each new state the number of added transitions is bounded by $\Sigma_{p \in P} |\Delta_p|$. (ii) If P is pure then $sat(P,k)$ is pure. This follows from the fact that we only add *send* transitions and we add such transitions only from states that are on cycles not containing *receive* transitions. This implies that we will not create any cycles involving both *send* and *receive* transitions. (iii) If P is pure then, for any configurations γ, γ', we have that γ' is reachable from γ in P iff γ' is reachable from γ in $sat(P,k)$. This follows from the fact that for any added sequence of transitions, the *send* operations are already present in existing cycles. Therefore, the effect of the added cycles can be simulated by iterating the existing cycles (possibly) combined with the loss of messages. (iv) For any state mapping s^{target}, we have that s^{target} is reachable in P iff s^{target} is simply reachable in $sat(P, \Sigma_{p \in P} |Q_p|)$. The reason is that effect of performing all the *receive* transitions between the two occurrences of a state q can be simulated by losing messages (by purity of P, none of these transitions can perform a *send* operation). This implies that we need only to consider computations where the number of *receive* transitions is bounded by $\Sigma_{p \in P} |Q_p|$. In turn, this implies that each cycle involving *send* transitions need not be iterated more than $\Sigma_{p \in P} |Q_p|$ times. The result follows from the fact that we add the $(\Sigma_{p \in P} |Q_p|)$-unfolding of all such cycles in the construction of $sat(P, \Sigma_{p \in P} |Q_p|)$. This gives the following lemma.

Lemma 3. *Reachability for pure* LCS *is polynomially reducible to simple reachability for (pure)* LCS.

5   Translation

In this section, we reduce the simple reachability problem for LCS to the problem of checking satisfiability of existential Presburger formulas. Suppose that we are given an instance of the simple reachability problem defined by an LCS consisting of a set P of processes, and a state map s^{target}. We will derive a quantifier-free Presburger formula ϕ such that ϕ is satisfiable iff s^{target} is reachable. For each state and transition in P, we introduce a number of variables that we use to build ϕ. We define ϕ as a conjunction where the conjuncts are divided into four sets, called *indexing*, *traversal*, *simplicity*, and *matching* respectively. Each set of conjuncts is used to describe one aspect of a potential computation reaching s^{target}. For $p \in P$, let $p = \langle Q_p, q_p^{init}, \Delta_p \rangle$. Define Q and Δ as in Section 3.

Indexing. For a state $q \in Q$, we use an "index variable" $\text{index}(q)$. For all pair of states $q, q' \in Q$, ϕ contains $\text{index}(q) \neq \text{index}(q')$, i.e., we assign to each state a unique index.

Traversal. This set of conjuncts ensures that each computation corresponds to a traversal of the graphs of the processes. This is inspired by the construction of an existential Presburger formula for the Parikh image of the language of finite-state automata [29]. To define this group we use the following variables. For each $t \in \Delta$ we use an "occurrence variable" $\text{occ}(t)$ that encodes whether the transition t is executed during the computation or not (1 if *yes* and 0 if *no*). For each state $q \in Q$, we use an "in-flow" variable $\mathtt{in}(q)$ and an "out-flow" variable $\mathtt{out}(q)$ that encode whether state q is entered resp. left during the computation (1 if *yes* and 0 if *no*). The formula ϕ contains the following conjuncts: (i) For each $q \in Q$, ϕ contains $\mathtt{in}(q) = \Sigma_{t \in target^{-1}(q)} \mathtt{occ}(t)$, i.e., q is entered iff exactly one of its ingoing transitions is executed. (ii) For each $q \in Q$, ϕ contains $\mathtt{out}(q) = \Sigma_{t \in source^{-1}(q)} \mathtt{occ}(t)$, i.e., q is left iff exactly one of its outgoing transitions is executed. (iii) For each process $p \in P$, ϕ contains $\mathtt{out}(q_p^{init}) = \mathtt{in}(q_p^{init}) + 1$, i.e., the initial state of a process is left once but not entered. (iv) For each process $p \in P$, ϕ contains $\mathtt{in}(s^{target}(p)) = \mathtt{out}(s^{target}(p)) + 1$, i.e., the target state in a process is entered once but not left. (v) For each process $p \in P$ and each state $q \in Q_p - \{q_p^{init}, s^{target}(p)\}$, ϕ contains $\mathtt{in}(q) = \mathtt{out}(q)$, i.e., all other states are either not visited or both entered once and left once. (vi) For each $q \in Q$, ϕ contains $(\mathtt{in}(q) = 1) \implies \left(\bigvee_{t \in target^{-1}(q)} (\mathtt{occ}(t) = 1) \wedge \mathtt{index}(source(t)) < \mathtt{index}(q) \right)$. The indexing on the states guarantees that the computation corresponds to executing successive edges in the graph of each process p. Each visited state is indexed higher than its (unique) predecessor in the computation. Notice that this means that the order in which states occur in the computation is consistent with the indexing (if q appears before q' then $\mathtt{index}(q) < \mathtt{index}(q')$).

Simplicity. For each $q \in Q$, ϕ contains $\mathtt{in}(q) \leq 1$. Since the computation is simple, each state is visited at most once.

Matching. This set of conjuncts ensures that each *receive* transition is matched by a preceding *send* transitions. More precisely, we will match the occurrence of a *receive* transition by the target state of a corresponding *send* transition as follows. For each transition $t \in \Delta^{rcv}$, we use a "matching" variable $\mathtt{match}(t)$. For each transition $t = \langle q_1, c?m, q_2 \rangle \in \Delta^{rcv}$, ϕ contains

$$(\mathtt{occ}(t) = 1) \implies \left(\bigvee_{t' \in operation^{-1}(c!m)} \left(\begin{array}{c} \mathtt{match}(t) = \mathtt{index}(target(t')) \\ \wedge \\ \mathtt{occ}(t') = 1 \\ \wedge \\ \mathtt{index}(target(t')) < \mathtt{index}(q_2) \end{array} \right) \right)$$

Intuitively, if the *receive* transition t occurs in the computation (i.e., $\mathtt{occ}(t) = 1$), then a matching transition t' occurs (i.e., $\mathtt{occ}(t') = 1$). The matching of t with t' is achieved by requiring that the "matching" variable of t is equal to the index of the target state of t'. Furthermore, t' should occur before t. The latter condition requires that the index of the target state of t (state q_2) is larger than the index of the target state of t'.

Finally, for any pair of *receive* transitions $t, t' \in \Delta^{rcv}$ the formula ϕ contains $(\mathtt{occ}(t) = 1) \wedge (\mathtt{occ}(t') = 1) \wedge (\mathtt{index}(target(t)) < \mathtt{index}(target(t'))) \implies (\mathtt{match}(t) < \mathtt{match}(t'))$. This means that if both t and t' occur (i.e., $\mathtt{occ}(t) = 1$ and $\mathtt{occ}(t') = 1$) and t occurs before t' (the index of the target state of t occurs before the one of t') then the matching *send* transition of t occurs before the matching *send* transition of t'.

The above construction gives the following lemma.

Lemma 4. *Simple reachability for* LCS *is polynomially reducible to the satisfiability of quantifier-free Presburger formulas.*

6 Bounded-Phase Reachability

In this section, we collect the results of the previous sections to prove that k-reachability for LCS is polynomially reducible to the satisfiability of quantifier-free Presburger formulas. The main consequence of this is that it allows the use of advanced tools for SMT-solving for efficient analysis of LCS (see Section 11). Furthermore, we use this result to show an upper bound on the complexity of the k-reachability problem for LCS, namely inclusion in NP. We complete the picture by giving a lower bound which shows that the problem is NP-COMPLETE.

Upper Bound. From Lemma 2, Lemma 3, Lemma 4, we get the following theorem.

Theorem 5. k-*reachability for* LCS *is polynomially reducible to the satisfiability of quantifier-free Presburger formulas.*

Since the latter problem is known to be NP-COMPLETE, we get the following corollary.

Corollary 6. k-*reachability for* LCS *is in* NP.

Lower Bound. We show NP-hardness by a reduction from the Boolean Satisfiability Problem (SAT) (which is known to be NP-COMPLETE [14]). Consider a propositional formula ϕ in conjunctive normal form. We will construct an LCS consisting of a set of processes P. The set P contains (i) one process p_x for each variable x appearing in ϕ, and (ii) one process p_ℓ for each clause ℓ in ϕ. Furthermore, for each variable x, we associate a channel c_x, and two messages $m_x, m_{\bar{x}}$. The finite-state automaton describing the behavior of the process p_x generates traces in the language $(c_x!m_x)^* \cup (c_x!m_{\bar{x}})^*$ from its initial state $q_{p_x}^{init}$ to its unique target state $q_{p_x}^{target}$. Intuitively, the process p_x guesses the assigned value to the variable x by sending a number of copies of the message m_x to the channel c_x if the value assigned to x is *true*, and sending $m_{\bar{x}}$ otherwise. For a clause ℓ, the process p_ℓ contains two states, namely an initial state $q_{p_\ell}^{init}$ and a target state $q_{p_\ell}^{target}$. For any positive (resp. negative) literal x (resp. $\bar{x}$) in ℓ, the process p_ℓ has a transition of the form $\langle q_{p_\ell}^{init}, c_x?m_x, q_{p_\ell}^{target} \rangle$ (resp. $\langle q_{p_\ell}^{init}, c_x?m_{\bar{x}}, q_{p_\ell}^{target} \rangle$). The transition checks if the assigned value to x is *true* (resp. *false*). Define the state map s^{target} such that $s^{target}(p) := q_p^{target}$ for each $p \in P$. It is easy to see that ϕ is satisfiable if and only if s^{target} is 2-reachable. This shows that the k-reachability problem for LCS is NP-HARD for $k \geq 2$. From this and Corollary 6 we get the following theorem.

Theorem 7. k-*reachability for* LCS *is* NP-COMPLETE.

7 Communicating Pushdown Processes

In this section, we define pushdown processes communicating through lossy channels and we show the undecidability of its k-reachability problem. Let M be a finite set of *messages* and C be a finite set of *channels*.

Pushdown Processes. A *pushdown process* p is a tuple $\langle Q_p, q_p^{init}, \Gamma_p, \Delta_p \rangle$ where Q_p is finite set of *states*, $q_p^{init} \in Q_p$ is the *initial state*, Γ_p is the *stack alphabet*, and Δ_p is the set of *pushdown transitions*. A transition $t \in \Delta_p$ is a tuple $\langle q_1, a, op, a', q_2 \rangle$ where $q_1, q_2 \in Q_p$ are states, $a, a' \in \Gamma_p \cup \{\varepsilon\}$ are stack symbols, and op is an *operation* of the form $c!m$, $c?m$, or nop with $m \in M$ and $c \in C$.

Transition System. We define the transition system induced by pushdown processes communicating through lossy channels. A *Lossy Channel Pushdown System* (LCPS for short) consists of a set P of pushdown processes. Let process $p \in P$ be of the form $\langle Q_p, q_p^{init}, \Gamma_p, \Delta_p \rangle$. Define $Q := \cup_{p \in P} Q_p$ and $\Gamma := \cup_{p \in P} \Gamma_p$. A configuration γ is of the form $\langle s, \alpha, \omega \rangle$, where $s : P \mapsto Q$ is a state map such that $s(p) \in Q_p$, $\alpha : P \mapsto \Gamma^*$ is a stack map such that $\alpha(p) \in \Gamma_p^*$, and $\omega : C \mapsto M^*$ is a channel map. Intuitively, α defines the contents of the stacks of the processes, while s and ω have the same meaning as for the case of LCS. We define the initial configuration $\gamma^{init} := \langle s^{init}, \alpha^{init}, \omega^{init} \rangle$ where $s^{init}(p) = q_p^{init}$ and $\alpha^{init}(p) = \varepsilon$ for all $p \in P$, and $\omega^{init}(c) = \varepsilon$ for all $c \in C$ (i.e., the system starts from a configuration where all the processes are in their initial states and where all the stacks and channels are empty).

We define a transition relation $\longrightarrow$ on the set of configurations as follows. Consider configurations $\gamma_1 = \langle s_1, \alpha_1, \omega_1 \rangle$, $\gamma_2 = \langle s_2, \alpha_2, \omega_2 \rangle$, and a transition $t = \langle q_1, a_1, op, a_2, q_2 \rangle \in \Delta_p$ for some $p \in P$. We write $\gamma_1 \overset{t}{\longrightarrow} \gamma_2$ to denote that $s_1(p) = q_1$, $s_2 = s_1[p \leftarrow q_2]$, $\alpha_1(p) = a_1 \cdot u$ for some $u \in \Gamma_p^*$, $\alpha_2 = \alpha_1[p \leftarrow a_2 \cdot u]$ and one of the following properties is satisfied: (i) $op = c!m$ and $\omega_2 \preceq \omega_1[c \leftarrow m \cdot \omega_1(c)]$, (ii) $op = c?m$ and $\omega_2 \preceq \omega_1[c \leftarrow w]$ where $\omega_1(c) = w \cdot m$, (iii) $op = nop$ and $\omega_2 \preceq \omega_1$. The notions of *computations* and *bounded phase computations* are defined in the similar way as for the case of LCS.

Bounded-Phase Reachability Problem. In the following, we show that the (bounded-phase) reachability problem for LCPS is undecidable. The undecidability holds even for the 2-reachability problem for an LCPS that contains only one pushdown process with two lossy channels.

Theorem 8. *k-reachability for LCPS is undecidable.*

8 Stuttering Lossy Channels

In this section, we consider processes communicating through stuttering lossy channels where messages can be both lost and duplicated.

Communicating Finite-State Processes. In the following, we give the model definition for finite-state processes communicating through stuttering lossy channels and show that the bounded-phase reachability problem is NP-COMPLETE. The syntax of the considered system is exactly the same as the one of LCS (described in Section 3). Next, we define the induced transition system. A *Stuttering Lossy Channel System* (SLCS for short) consists of a set P of finite-state processes. Let process $p \in P$ be of the form $\langle Q_p, q_p^{init}, \Delta_p \rangle$. Configurations are defined as for the case of LCS. We define a transition relation $\longrightarrow$ on the set of configurations as follows. Consider configurations $\gamma_1 = \langle s_1, \omega_1 \rangle$, $\gamma_2 = \langle s_2, \omega_2 \rangle$, and a transition $t = \langle q_1, op, q_2 \rangle \in \Delta_p$ for some $p \in P$. We write $\gamma_1 \xrightarrow{t} \gamma_2$ to denote that $s_1(p) = q_1$, $s_2 = s_1[p \leftarrow q_2]$, and that there is $\omega : C \mapsto M^*$ such that $\omega_2(c') \in Stuttering(\omega(c'))$ for all $c' \in C$ and one of the following properties is satisfied: (i) $op = c!m$ and $\omega \preceq \omega_1[c \leftarrow m \cdot \omega_1(c)]$, (ii) $op = c?m$ and $\omega \preceq \omega_1[c \leftarrow w]$ where $\omega_1(c) = w \cdot m$, (iii) $op = nop$ and $\omega \preceq \omega_1$. The notions of *computations* and *bounded phase computations* are defined in the similar way as for the case of LCS. Then, we can show the following theorem.

Theorem 9. *k-reachability for* SLCS *is* NP-COMPLETE.

Communicating Pushdown Processes. We can extend the definition of SLCS to the case where each process is a pushdown as for the case of LCPS (Section 7). This leads to the class of *Stuttering Lossy Channel Pushdown System* (SLCPS).

Theorem 10. *k-reachability problem for* SLCPS *is undecidable.*

9   Unordered Channels

In this section, we consider finite-state processes communicating through unordered lossy channels where messages can be re-ordered.

Communicating Finite-State Processes. In the following, we give the model when the processes are finite-state. finite-state processes. The syntax of the system is the same as the one of LCS (Section 3). Next, we define the induced transition system. An *Unordered Channel System* (UCS for short) consists of a set P of finite-state processes. Let process $p \in P$ be of the form $\langle Q_p, q_p^{init}, \Delta_p \rangle$. Define $Q := \cup_{p \in P} Q_p$. A configuration γ is of the form $\langle s, \omega \rangle$, where $s : P \mapsto Q$ is a state map such that $s(p) \in Q_p$, and $\omega : C \times M \mapsto \mathbb{N}$ is a channel map. Intuitively, ω defines the contents of the channels (i.e., we associate to each message its number of occurrences in each channel). We define the initial configuration $\gamma^{init} := \langle s^{init}, \omega^{init} \rangle$ where $s^{init}(p) = q_p^{init}$ for all $p \in P$, and $\omega^{init}(c, m) = 0$ for all $c \in C$ and $m \in M$ (i.e., the system starts from a configuration where all the processes are in their initial states and where all the channels are empty).

We define a transition relation $\longrightarrow$ on the set of configurations as follows. Consider configurations $\gamma_1 = \langle s_1, \omega_1 \rangle$, $\gamma_2 = \langle s_2, \omega_2 \rangle$, and a transition $t = \langle q_1, op, q_2 \rangle \in \Delta_p$ for some $p \in P$. We write $\gamma_1 \xrightarrow{t} \gamma_2$ to denote that $s_1(p) = q_1$, $s_2 = s_1[p \leftarrow q_2]$, and one of the following three properties is satisfied: (i) $op = c!m$ and $\omega_2 = \omega_1[(c, m) \leftarrow (\omega_1(c, m) + 1)]$, (ii) $op = c?m$, $\omega_1(c, m) \geq 1$ and $\omega_2 = \omega_1[(c, m) \leftarrow (\omega_1(c, m) - 1)]$, or (iii) $op = nop$ and $\omega_2 = \omega_1$. The notions of *computations* and *bounded phase computations* are defined in the similar way as in the case of LCS. Then, we can show the following theorem.

Theorem 11. *k-reachability for* UCS *is* NP-COMPLETE.

Communicating Pushdown Processes. We can extend the definition of UCS to the case where each process is a pushdown as for the case of LCPS (Section 7). This leads to the class of *Unordered Channel Pushdown System* (UCPS for short).

Theorem 12. *k-reachability problem for* UCPS *is* NP-COMPLETE.

10   Perfect Channels

In this section, we consider finite-state processes communicating through perfect channels, and show that the bounded-phase reachability problem is undecidable.

The syntax of the considered system is the same as the one of LCS (described in Section 3). We define the induced transition system. A *Perfect Channel System* (PCS for short) consists of a set P of finite-state processes. Let process $p \in P$ be of the form $\langle Q_p, q_p^{init}, \Delta_p \rangle$. Configurations are defined as for the case of LCS. We define a transition relation $\longrightarrow$ on the set of configurations as follows. Consider configurations $\gamma_1 = \langle s_1, \omega_1 \rangle$, $\gamma_2 = \langle s_2, \omega_2 \rangle$, and a transition $t = \langle q_1, op, q_2 \rangle \in \Delta_p$ for some $p \in P$. We write $\gamma_1 \overset{t}{\longrightarrow} \gamma_2$ to denote that $s_1(p) = q_1$, $s_2 = s_1[p \leftarrow q_2]$, and one of the following properties is satisfied: (i) $op = c!m$ and $\omega_2 = \omega_1[c \leftarrow m \cdot \omega_1(c)]$, (ii) $op = c?m$ and $\omega_2 = \omega_1[c \leftarrow w]$ where $\omega_1(c) = w \cdot m$, (iii) $op = nop$ and $\omega_2 = \omega_1$. The notions of *computations* and *bounded phase computations* are defined in the similar way as for the case of LCS. Then, we can show the following theorem.

Theorem 13. *k-reachability problem for PCS is undecidable.*

11   Experimental Data

We have implemented our technique in a prototype tool called Alternator. The tool is available on GitHub [2], where we also supply the source of all experiments listed below. The tool uses the frontend of the implementation provided by Marques et al in [19], to get XML representations of the protocols from spreadsheets. We have implemented a Python application that, given such an XML representation, builds an SMT-LIB [6] formula as described in Section 5. This SMT-LIB formula can then be given to any SMT solver supporting the SMT-LIB version 2 standard. In our case we use the Z3 solver [21].

We have applied our prototype to a number of different protocols. The results demonstrate the efficiency of our framework. We analyze the web service protocols Subservice Termination Protocol (STP) and Business Agreement with Coordinator Completion (CC). The purpose of these protocols is to ensure that two (or three in the case of STP) processes agree on the global state of the system, as is commonly needed in SOA (Service-Oriented Architecture) frameworks. For more information on these protocols, see [23,19]. By CCv2, we mean the augmented version of the CC protocols that can be found in [23]. Furthermore, we have applied our tool to modified versions of the well-known Alternating Bit Protocol (ABP$_f$) and Sliding Window protocol (SW$_f$) where we have intentionally introduced some errors. The SYNC protocol is a simple protocol requiring perfect channels. The Jingle example [27] is a multimedia session establishment protocol that is used by applications such as Google Talk, Coccinella and Miranda IM.

The results of our analyses can be seen in Table 1. The column "Gen. Time" gives the time that our tool takes to build an SMT-LIB formula. The column "SMT" shows the time that the SMT-solver takes to decide the satisfiability of the generated formula. All times are in seconds. The column "Sem" shows under which channel semantics we have run the examples. Finally the columns "Ph." and "Res" show the number of phases

Table 1. Experimental Results

P	Sem	Gen. Time	SMT	Ph.	Res	P	Sem	Gen. Time	SMT	Ph.	Res
STP	UCS	0.1	0.1	12	U	CC	UCS	0.8	0.2	6	U
STP	SLCS	2.8	38.4	8	S	CC	SLCS	70.8	10.7	2	S
STP	LCS	2.8	13.0	8	S	CC	LCS	70.2	10.1	2	S
CCv2	UCS	1.8	0.8	8	U	ABP$_f$	SLCS	0.5	3.7	4	U
CCv2	SLCS	163.8	26.2	2	S	ABP$_f$	LCS	0.5	5.9	4	U
CCv2	LCS	159.3	24.3	2	S	ABP$_f$	UCS	0.1	0.0	4	U
SW$_f$	SLCS	0.4	0.6	2	U	SYNC	SLCS	0.2	1.3	14	U
SW$_f$	LCS	0.4	0.4	2	U	SYNC	LCS	0.2	2.1	14	U
SW$_f$	UCS	0.0	0.0	2	U	SYNC	UCS	0.2	0.1	14	U
JINGLE	SLCS	18.4	10.8	8	U	JINGLE	LCS	21.2	21.1	8	U

and the result of our analysis. If the result of the analysis is "U" (Unsafe), the number in the "Ph." column is the bound required to prove the result. If the result is "S" (Safe), meaning we did not reach the bad state within the given bound, the number in the "Ph." column is the greatest number of phases that we are able to use without the SMT-solver needing more than 30 s to return an answer. The sizes of the generated automata and the number of assertions fed to the SMT-solver are reported in [2]. More examples and results are also available in [2]. All experiments were performed on a 3.1 GHz Intel Core i5 with 4 GB of RAM.

12   Conclusions and Future Work

We have introduced a new concept for under-approximating the behavior of communicating processes, namely *phase-bounded* computations. We have shown that phase-bounded reachability can be reduced to the satisfiability of logical formulas whose satisfiability can be checked by SMT-solvers, thus yielding an efficient analysis of system behavior. The framework can be instantiated to several classes of channel semantics such as *lossy*, *stuttering*, and *unordered*. The strength of the method is confirmed by results form the application of our prototype on examples from several different application areas. Using the translation, we have also established complexity results for checking bounded reachability on the above classes of systems. Finally, we give undecidability results for the case where the channels are *perfect* and for the case where

Table 2. Decidability/Complexity Results for the Bounded-Reachability

Semantics	Finite-state process	Pushdown process
Lossy	NP-COMPLETE	undecidable
Stuttering Lossy	NP-COMPLETE	undecidable
Unordered	NP-COMPLETE	NP-COMPLETE
Perfect	undecidable	undecidable

the processes are not finite-state with (stuttering) lossy channels. A summary of these results is given in Table 2. While our prototype is already efficient on the considered examples, there is room for several improvements such as minimizing the graphs of processes and the size of the unfolding of processes obtained in the purification step (Section 4) in order to reduce the time that our prototype takes to build an SMT-LIB formula. Also, we are planning to consider systems where the message alphabet is infinite, e.g., ranging over numerical domains.

References

1. Abdulla, P., Jonsson, B.: Undecidable verification problems for programs with unreliable channels. In: Shamir, E., Abiteboul, S. (eds.) ICALP 1994. LNCS, vol. 820, pp. 316–327. Springer, Heidelberg (1994)
2. Abdulla, P.A., Atig, M.F., Cederberg, J.: Alternator - Verifier of programs by bounding mode alternations, https://github.com/it-apv/alternator
3. Abdulla, P.A., Atig, M.F., Chen, Y.-F., Leonardsson, C., Rezine, A.: Counter-example guided fence insertion under TSO. In: Flanagan, C., König, B. (eds.) TACAS 2012. LNCS, vol. 7214, pp. 204–219. Springer, Heidelberg (2012)
4. Abdulla, P.A., Collomb-Annichini, A., Bouajjani, A., Jonsson, B.: Using forward reachability analysis for verification of lossy channel systems. Formal Methods in System Design 25(1), 39–65 (2004)
5. Abdulla, P.A., Jonsson, B.: Verifying programs with unreliable channels. In: Proc. LICS 1993, 8th IEEE Int. Symp. on Logic in Computer Science, pp. 160–170 (1993)
6. Barrett, C., et al.: The smt-lib standard: Version 2.0. Tech. rep. (2010)
7. Atig, M.F., Bouajjani, A., Burckhardt, S., Musuvathi, M.: On the verification problem for weak memory models. In: POPL, pp. 7–18. ACM (2010)
8. Atig, M.F., Bouajjani, A., Touili, T.: On the reachability analysis of acyclic networks of pushdown systems. In: van Breugel, F., Chechik, M. (eds.) CONCUR 2008. LNCS, vol. 5201, pp. 356–371. Springer, Heidelberg (2008)
9. Boigelot, B., Godefroid, P.: Symbolic verification of communication protocols with infinite state spaces using qdds. FMSD 14(3), 237–255 (1999)
10. Bouajjani, A., Emmi, M.: Bounded phase analysis of message-passing programs. In: Flanagan, C., König, B. (eds.) TACAS 2012. LNCS, vol. 7214, pp. 451–465. Springer, Heidelberg (2012)
11. Bouajjani, A., Esparza, J., Touili, T.: A generic approach to the static analysis of concurrent programs with procedures. In: POPL, pp. 62–73. ACM (2003)
12. Bouajjani, A., Habermehl, P.: Symbolic reachability analysis of fifo-channel systems with nonregular sets of configurations. Theor. Comput. Sci. 221(1-2), 211–250 (1999)
13. Brand, D., Zafiropulo, P.: On communicating finite-state machines. J. ACM 30(2), 323–342 (1983)
14. Cook, S.A.: The complexity of theorem-proving procedures. In: STOC, pp. 151–158. ACM (1971)
15. Geeraerts, G., Raskin, J.F., Begin, L.V.: Expand, enlarge and check: New algorithms for the coverability problem of wsts. J. Comput. Syst. Sci. 72(1), 180–203 (2006)
16. Hague, M., Lin, A.W.: Synchronisation- and reversal-bounded analysis of multithreaded programs with counters. In: Madhusudan, P., Seshia, S.A. (eds.) CAV 2012. LNCS, vol. 7358, pp. 260–276. Springer, Heidelberg (2012)
17. Heußner, A., Leroux, J., Muscholl, A., Sutre, G.: Reachability analysis of communicating pushdown systems. Logical Methods in Computer Science 8(3) (2012)

18. Ibarra, O.H.: Reversal-bounded multicounter machines and their decision problems. J. ACM 25(1), 116–133 (1978)
19. Marques Jr., A.P., Ravn, A., Srba, J., Vighio, S.: csv2uppaal, https://github.com/csv2uppaal
20. Lipton, R.: The reachability problem requires exponential time. Technical Report TR 66 (1976)
21. de Moura, L., Bjørner, N.: Z3: An efficient SMT solver. In: Ramakrishnan, C.R., Rehof, J. (eds.) TACAS 2008. LNCS, vol. 4963, pp. 337–340. Springer, Heidelberg (2008)
22. Musuvathi, M., Qadeer, S.: Iterative context bounding for systematic testing of multithreaded programs. In: PLDI, pp. 446–455. ACM (2007)
23. Newcomer, E., Robinson, I. (chairs): Web Services Business Activity Version 1.2 (2009), http://docs.oasis-open.org/ws-tx/wstx-wsba-1.2-spec-os.pdf
24. Qadeer, S., Rehof, J.: Context-bounded model checking of concurrent software. In: Halbwachs, N., Zuck, L.D. (eds.) TACAS 2005. LNCS, vol. 3440, pp. 93–107. Springer, Heidelberg (2005)
25. Rackoff, C.: The covering and boundedness problems for vector addition systems. Theor. Comput. Sci. 6, 223–231 (1978)
26. Ravn, A.P., Srba, J., Vighio, S.: Modelling and verification of web services business activity protocol. In: Abdulla, P.A., Leino, K.R.M. (eds.) TACAS 2011. LNCS, vol. 6605, pp. 357–371. Springer, Heidelberg (2011)
27. Saint-Andre, P.: Jingle: Jabber does multimedia. IEEE MultiMedia 14(1), 90–94 (2007)
28. Schnoebelen, P.: Verifying lossy channel systems has nonprimitive recursive complexity. Information Processing Letters 83(5), 251–261 (2002)
29. Seidl, H., Schwentick, T., Muscholl, A., Habermehl, P.: Counting in trees for free. In: Díaz, J., Karhumäki, J., Lepistö, A., Sannella, D. (eds.) ICALP 2004. LNCS, vol. 3142, pp. 1136–1149. Springer, Heidelberg (2004)
30. The Erlang Programming Language, http://erlang.org
31. The Scala Programming Language, http://scala-lang.org
32. La Torre, S., Madhusudan, P., Parlato, G.: Context-bounded analysis of concurrent queue systems. In: Ramakrishnan, C.R., Rehof, J. (eds.) TACAS 2008. LNCS, vol. 4963, pp. 299–314. Springer, Heidelberg (2008)

An Expressive Framework
for Verifying Deadlock Freedom

Duy-Khanh Le, Wei-Ngan Chin, and Yong-Meng Teo

Department of Computer Science, National University of Singapore
{leduykha,chinwn,teoym}@comp.nus.edu.sg

Abstract. This paper presents an expressive specification and verification framework for ensuring deadlock freedom of shared-memory concurrent programs that manipulate locks. We introduce a novel *delayed lockset checking* technique to guarantee deadlock freedom of programs with interactions between thread and lock operations. With disjunctive formulae, we highlight how an abstraction based on *precise lockset* can be supported in our framework. By combining our technique with locklevels, we form a unified formalism for ensuring deadlock freedom from (1) double lock acquisition, (2) interactions between thread and lock operations, and (3) unordered locking. The proposed framework is general, and can be integrated with existing specification logics such as separation logic. Specifically, we have implemented this framework into a prototype tool, called PARAHIP, to automatically verify deadlock freedom and correctness of concurrent programs against user-supplied specifications.

Keywords: Concurrency, Deadlock, Specification, Verification.

1 Introduction

Concurrent software systems are often complex, error-prone, and require tremendous efforts from programmers to make them work correctly [25]. Over the past decade, verification has been viewed as one of the solutions to this challenging research problem on increasing the quality and reliability of (concurrent) programs, as advocated by Tony Hoare [13]. However, understanding and reasoning about the correctness of concurrent programs is rather complicated due to non-deterministic interleavings of concurrent threads [22]. These interleavings may result in *deadlocks* [6], i.e. states in which each thread in a set blocks waiting for another thread in the set to release a lock or complete its execution. Deadlocks are common defects in software systems. Specifically, in Sun's bug report database at http://bugs.sun.com/, there are approximately 6,500 bug reports out of 198,000 ($\sim$ 3%) containing the keyword "deadlock" [28]. In this paper, we propose an expressive framework for reasoning about the correctness of concurrent programs with a focus on eliminating deadlocks.

Existing verification systems [11,14,23,24] often use *abstract predicates* to represent states of locks. For example, Gotsman et al. [11] use abstract predicate *Locked(x)* to specify that the lock x is owned by the current thread. Hobor

D. Van Hung and M. Ogawa (Eds.): ATVA 2013, LNCS 8172, pp. 287–302, 2013.
© Springer International Publishing Switzerland 2013

et al. [14] use the predicate *hold x R* and CHALICE [23,24] uses *holds(x)* for the same purpose. Intuitively, a lock is owned by a thread if it is in the set of locks already acquired by the thread, i.e. the thread's lockset. Interestingly, although using predicates, previous works [11,14,23,24] formulate their soundness proof using the notion of lockset. Additionally, Haack et al. [12] show that lockset (or rather lockbag) is necessary to reason about Java recursive locks. In retrospect, one can say that lockset has proven to be an important abstraction for verifying concurrent programs that manipulate locks.[1] In this paper, we advocate the use of *precise locksets* for explicitly reasoning about the presence or absence of locks, empowering a more expressive framework for verifying deadlock freedom even in the presence of interactions between thread operations (e.g. fork/join) and lock operations (e.g. acquire/release). Due to the non-deterministic nature of threads, sound reasoning of the interactions between thread and lock operations is non-trivial.

```
1   int running;                    14   void main(){
2   pthread_t thread;               15     running = 0;/*init timer*/
3   mutex_t mutex;                  16     mutex_lock(&mutex);
4                                   17     running = 1;/*start timer*/
5   void* timer(){                  18     pthread_create(&thread,&timer);
6     int state;                    19     mutex_unlock(&mutex);
7     do{                           20     /*begin timed computation*/
8       mutex_lock(&mutex);         21     ...
9       state=running;              22     /*end computation*/
10      mutex_unlock(&mutex);       23     mutex_lock(&mutex);
11      .../*timing*/               24     running = 0;/*stop timer*/
12    }while(state);                25     mutex_unlock(&mutex);
13  }                               26     pthread_join(thread);
                                    27   }
```

Fig. 1. A program with interactions between thread and lock operations

Fig. 1 outlines a simplified[2] C implementation of a timer used in NetBSD operating system's report database [1]. Though rather intricate due to the interactions between lock and thread operations, the program is deadlock-free because the two threads never wait for each other. However, if the programmer does not release the lock before joining (e.g. line 25 is missing or line 25 and 26 are swapped), the interactions will cause a deadlock when the main thread blocks waiting to join the child thread and the child thread also blocks waiting to acquire the mutex being held by the main thread. For larger programs with many (possibly non-deterministic) execution branches, these interactions are not easy to follow [22]. With concurrent programs becoming mainstream in

---

[1] See [21] for detailed comparison between abstract predicates and locksets.
[2] In the original implementation, there is a conditional variable associated with the mutex to more efficiently signal the **timer** thread to start and stop timing. As verifying conditional variables is an orthogonal issue, we have omitted them for simplicity.

this multicore era, we will increasingly require a more comprehensive solution for constructing and verifying these intricate interactions.

In this paper, we propose an expressive verification framework to guarantee deadlock freedom in the presence of such interactions. Our framework has the following innovations:

- *Delayed lockset checking* to help reason about the interactions between thread and lock operations. Unlike the traditional verification approaches [11,12,14,15,23] that check pre-conditions of procedures entirely at fork points, this technique allows lockset constraints in the pre-conditions to be delayed and checked at join points instead. This prevents deadlocks due to the interactions and also permits more programs to be declared as deadlock-free.
- *Precise lockset reasoning*, as opposed to ones based on *abstract predicates* or *approximated locksets*, to ensure that deadlock-free pre-conditions on lock acquisition and release can be guaranteed. Any uncertainty, if any, from static program analysis is simply captured through the use of explicit disjunction.
- *Combining lockset with the concept of locklevels* in the literature [3,23,34] to form an expressive framework for ensuring deadlock freedom, covering various scenarios such as double lock acquisition, interactions between thread and lock operations, and unordered locking.
- A prototype specification and verification system, called PARAHIP, to show that the proposed framework has been successfully integrated with separation logic [32] for reasoning about concurrent programs.

The rest of this paper is organized as follows. Section 2 gives concrete examples that motivate our delayed lockset checking technique and show how precise lockset reasoning can be systematically supported. Section 3 presents our specification logic for verification. Section 4 shows our verification rules and presents our soundness guarantee on deadlock freedom. Section 5 discusses the implementation and experimental results of our prototype tool. Section 6 summarizes related work. Section 7 concludes our paper.

2   Motivation and Proposed Approach

2.1   Precise Lockset Reasoning

As our proposal is language-independent, we have developed a core language (described in Section 3) to capture the basic ideas. In the rest of the paper, we shall express our examples using this core language. In our verification framework, **LS** is a thread-local ghost variable[3] capturing the set of locks held by a thread. Lockset is a verification concept rather than a programming language concept. Using lockset, verification rules for *acquire* and *release* operations on non-recursive (mutex) locks[4] can be defined as follows:

---

[3] Ghost variables are variables used for verification purpose. They do not affect program correctness.

[4] Cannot be acquired more than once; also called non-reentrant locks.

```
void thread()                          void func(lock l1)
  requires LS={} ensures LS'={};         requires l1∉LS ensures LS'=LS;
{                                      {
  lock l1 = new lock();                  //{ l1∉LS ∧ LS'=LS }
  //{ LS'={} }                           acquire(l1);
  acquire(l1);                           //{ l1∉LS ∧ LS'=LS∪{l1} }
  //{ LS'={l1} }                         release(l1);
  func(l1); /*Error*/                    //{ l1∉LS ∧ LS'=LS∪{l1}−{l1} }
  release(l1);                           //{ l1∉LS ∧ LS'=LS }
}                                      }
```

Fig. 2. Deadlock due to double acquisition of a non-recursive lock

```
   acquire(lock x)                    release(lock x)
     requires x∉LS                      requires x∈LS
     ensures LS'=LS∪{x};                ensures LS'=LS−{x};
```

Note that we use *primed notation* to denote updates to variables. The primed version LS' of the variable LS denotes its latest value; the unprimed version LS denotes its old value at the start of the respective procedure call. Using lockset, it is straightforward to prevent the deadlock due to acquiring a non-recursive lock twice in the `thread` code of Fig. 2. In this sequential setting, our verification reports an error because the pre-condition of the callee `func` ($l1∉LS$) cannot be satisfied by the current lockset of the caller ($LS'=\{l1\}$). Additionally, the `release` rule excludes the possibility of releasing a lock more than once.

In each given program, there can be many locking scenarios across different execution branches. Each branch could potentially have a different lockset. The following code fragment shows a simple example where locksets at two branches are $LS'=\{x\}$ and $LS'=\{\}$, which are clearly different:

```
//{ LS'={} }
if (b) { acquire(x);//{ LS'={x} } } else { //{ LS'={} } }
```

For static analysis, we often perform some approximation. For example, one may *over-approximate* on the lockset, by using $LS'=\{x\}$ as the post-state of the above code fragment. However, this approach would fail to detect the definite presence of the lock x for safe release. Another approach is to *under-approximate* on the lockset by using $LS'=\{\}$, but this approach fails to detect the definite absence of the lock for safe acquisition. Thus, one plausible solution is to combine the two approximations by capturing both may-hold and must-hold locksets, simultaneously. However, this approach would be more complex due to the use of two locksets. In this paper, we propose a simpler solution that would mandate the use of *precise locksets* in our verification/analysis. For approximation, we propose to use *disjunctive formulae* to capture uncertainty and also allow program states, other than lockset, to be over-approximated. In the above example, we can ensure precise lockset by using either $b∧LS'=\{x\} ∨ ¬b∧LS'=\{\}$ or even $LS'=\{x\} ∨ LS'=\{\}$ as its post-state, but never $LS'=\{x\}$, since we always ensure

```
void func(lock l1)                  void func(lock l1)
  requires l1∉LS ensures LS'=LS;      requires l1∉LS ensures LS'=LS;
{ acquire(l1); release(l1); }       { acquire(l1); release(l1); }

void main()                         void main()
  requires LS={} ensures LS'={};      requires LS={} ensures LS'={};
{                                   {lock l1 = new lock();
 lock l1 = new lock();               //{ LS'={} }
 //{ LS'={} }                        acquire(l1);
 int id = fork(func,l1);/*DELAY*/    //{ LS'={l1} }
 //{ LS'={} }                        int id = fork(func,l1);/*DELAY*/
 acquire(l1);                        //{ LS'={l1} }
 //{ LS'={l1} }                      release(l1);
 /*Potentially deadlocked when join*/ //{ LS'={} }
 join(id); /*CHECK, error*/          join(id);/*CHECK, ok*/
 release(l1);                        //{ LS'={} }
}                                   }
     (a) Potentially deadlocked          (b) Deadlock-free
```

Fig. 3. Examples of programs exposing interactions between thread and lock operations

that each lockset is precisely captured and never approximated. This principle allows us to support precise reasoning on locksets for verifying deadlock freedom.

2.2   Delayed Lockset Checking

Fig. 3 shows two programs that pose challenges for existing verification systems. The programs are challenging because they express rich interactions between fork/join concurrency and lock operations. The traditional way of verification [11,12,14,15,23] cannot sufficiently handle these scenarios because it performs the check for the pre-condition of the forkee *only* at the *fork point*. This could incorrectly verify the program in Fig. 3a as deadlock-free and reject the deadlock-free program in Fig. 3b. The well-known technique [3,23,34] which requires threads to acquire multiple locks in a specific order to avoid deadlocks could not directly handle complications due to fork/join concurrency. In this paper, we propose *delayed lockset checking* technique that is capable of preventing deadlock scenarios (such as that presented in Fig. 3a) and proving more programs (such as that described in Fig. 3b) to be deadlock-free.

This technique is based on the following observation. At a *fork point*, a verifier is unaware of future operations performed by a main (or parent) thread; the only information it knows of is future locking operations executed by a child thread thanks to the use of *lockset*. For example, a constraint $l1 \notin \mathbf{LS}$ in the pre-condition of a child thread implies that the child thread is going to acquire the lock l1. Therefore, in order to ensure that the child thread will finally be able to acquire the lock (and thus avoid deadlocks), the main thread should not be holding the lock while waiting for the child thread at its *join point*. In other words, *when forking a child thread, lockset constraints in its pre-condition are not checked at the fork point but are delayed to be checked at its join point instead.*

The deadlock in Fig. 3a can be prevented by deferring the lockset constraint $l1 \notin \mathbf{LS}$ of the child thread to its join point. At the join point, the constraint is checked and the verification reports an error because the constraint is unsatisfiable ($\mathbf{LS'} = \{l1\}$ at the join point). Similarly, the program in Fig. 3b is ensured as being deadlock free because the lockset constraint $l1 \notin \mathbf{LS}$ is delayed from the fork point and is satisfiable at the join point ($\mathbf{LS'} = \{\}$). Note that, although main and child threads have different locksets, a constraint $l1 \notin \mathbf{LS}$ in pre-conditions of a child thread indicates its intention to acquire the lock $l1$, hence this constraint can be soundly checked against the lockset of the main thread to prevent deadlocks. Besides, it is unsound to check lockset constraints at any satisfiable points in the middle of the fork point and the join point. For example, in a scenario similar to Fig. 3b, after forking a child thread, the main thread releases the lock. At this point, the lockset constraint is satisfiable. However, the main thread could later acquire the lock again and wait for the child thread to join. This scenario still suffers a potential deadlock. As a result, it is only sound to check delayed lockset constraints at just the join points.

In summary, the main benefit of our *delayed lockset checking* technique is to facilitate more expressive deadlock verification in the presence of interactions between parent/child threads and lock operations.

2.3   Combining Lockset and Locklevel

Another type of deadlocks occurs when threads attempt to acquire the same set of locks in different orders (unordered locking). An example of such a scenario is shown in Fig. 4. Locklevel is a well-known handle to prevent deadlocks due to

```
void main()                        void func(lock l1,lock l2)
  requires LS={}  ensures ...;       requires [waitlevel<l1.mu # l1∉LS∧l2∉LS]
 {lock l1,l2 = new lock();                   ∧ l1.mu<l2.mu
  assume(l1.mu<l2.mu);               ensures ...;
    // { LS'={}∧l1.mu<l2.mu         {
         ∧waitlevel'=0 }                // { waitlevel'<l1.mu ∧ l1.mu<l2.mu
  int id = fork(func,l1,l2);                ∧ LS'=LS }
    // { LS'={}∧l1.mu<l2.mu           acquire(l2);
         ∧waitlevel'=0 }                // { waitlevel'=l2.mu ∧ l1.mu<l2.mu
  acquire(l1);                              ∧ LS'=LS ∪ {l2} }
    // { LS'={l1}∧l1.mu<l2.mu         acquire(l1); /*Error*/
         ∧waitlevel'=l1.mu }           ...
  acquire(l2);                       }
    // { LS'={l1,l2}∧l1.mu<l2.mu
         ∧waitlevel'=l2.mu }
  ...}
```

Fig. 4. A potential deadlock due to unordered locking

unordered locking [3,23,34]. Intuitively, each lock in a program is associated with a ghost field *mu* representing the lock's level. For example, $l1.mu$ denotes the locklevel of lock 11. With it, deadlocks can be prevented indirectly by ensuring that locks are acquired in a strictly increasing order of locklevels. To check that locks are acquired in the specified order, a ghost variable **waitlevel** is used to capture the maximum level currently acquired by a thread, i.e. **waitlevel** is the maximum level among locklevels of all locks in current thread's lockset **LS**. A thread can acquire a lock only if its current waitlevel **waitlevel**' is lower than the lock's level. Using locklevels, the deadlock in Fig. 4 can be prevented. The verification system reports an error when the child thread attempts to acquire lock 11 whose locklevel is lower than the current waitlevel of the child thread.

In the pre-condition of the **func** procedure (Fig. 4), we use the specification $[\omega \# \psi]$ to capture the fact that the waitlevel constraint ω and the lockset constraint ψ are *mutually exclusive*, i.e. the former is checked in sequential settings, while the latter is a check needed to be delayed in concurrent settings. This provides a *single* mechanism for procedure declarations so that each procedure could be either forked as a child thread or invoked as a normal procedure call.

In summary, precise lockset, delayed lockset checking, and locklevel are complementary and combining them is essential to form an expressive framework for verifying various deadlock scenarios such as double acquisition, interactions between fork/join and acquire/release, and unordered locking.

3   A Specification Logic for Deadlock Freedom

In this section, we present a specification logic that can be used to verify deadlock freedom. We show how our approach, based on precise lockset abstraction, can be integrated with the locklevel idea from CHALICE [23]. We also present a specification formalism to unify constraints on lockset, locklevel and waitlevel into a single specification and to allow each procedure to be used internally or as the entry point of a newly-forked thread.

$$
\begin{array}{lll}
P ::= proc^* & \text{Program} \\
proc ::= \textbf{pn}(([\textbf{ref}]\ t\ v)^*)\ spec^*\ \{\ s\ \} & \text{Procedure declaration} \\
spec ::= \textbf{requires}\ \Phi_{pr}\ \textbf{ensures}\ \Phi_{po}; & \text{Pre/Post-conditions} \\
t ::= \textbf{int}\mid\textbf{bool}\mid\textbf{void}\mid\textbf{lock} & \text{Type} \\
\quad\ v = \textbf{fork}(pn,v^*)\mid\textbf{join}(v) & \\
\quad\ \mid\ \textbf{lock}\ v = \textbf{new lock}(v) & \\
s ::= \ \mid\ \textbf{acquire}(v)\mid\textbf{release}(v) & \text{Statement} \\
\quad\ \mid\ s_1; s_2 \mid \textbf{pn}(v^*) \mid \textbf{if}\ e\ \textbf{then}\ s_1\ \textbf{else}\ s_2 & \\
\quad\ \mid\ \ldots & \\
\end{array}
$$

Fig. 5. Programming Language with Annotations and Concurrency

Programming Language. We consider an imperative core language (Fig. 5) with fork/join concurrency for dynamic thread creation and non-recursive locks. The language is relative straightforward; its details are described in [21].

3.1   Integrating Specification with LockLevels

In our specification logic, a lockset variable **LS** captures a set of locks held by the current thread. Like CHALICE [23], each lock in a program has an immutable ghost field mu representing the lock's level. Locklevels are implemented as natural numbers and operators $=$, $<$ and $>$ are used over locklevels. The lowest (bottom) locklevel is denoted as 0. A **waitlevel** variable can be derived from the lockset and locklevels. As a reminder, waitlevel is the maximum level among locklevels of all locks in current thread's lockset **LS**. Levels of locks in a program are strictly positive while a bottom locklevel denotes the waitlevel in case of empty lockset. Using lockset as an abstraction, constraints on waitlevel can be expressed in terms of constraints on lockset and locklevels as follows:

$$\textbf{waitlevel}{<}x \stackrel{\text{def}}{=} (\textbf{LS}{=}\{\}) \Rightarrow 0{<}x) \wedge (\textbf{LS}{\neq}\{\} \Rightarrow \forall v{\in}\textbf{LS} \cdot v.mu{<}x)$$

$$\textbf{waitlevel}{>}x \stackrel{\text{def}}{=} (\textbf{LS}{=}\{\}) \Rightarrow 0{>}x) \wedge (\textbf{LS}{\neq}\{\} \Rightarrow \exists v{\in}\textbf{LS} \cdot v.mu{>}x)$$

$$\textbf{waitlevel}{=}x \stackrel{\text{def}}{=} (\textbf{LS}{=}\{\}) \Rightarrow 0{=}x) \wedge$$
$$(\textbf{LS}{\neq}\{\} \Rightarrow \forall v{\in}\textbf{LS} \cdot v.mu{\leq}x \wedge \exists u{\in}\textbf{LS} \cdot u.mu{=}x)$$

3.2   Specification Formalism

Fig. 6 shows our specification logic. In the specification, Φ is a logic formula in disjunctive normal form. Each disjunct in Φ consists of a thread formula μ for a main (or parent) thread and a list of thread formulae τ (separated by the **and** keyword) to represent child threads. Each disjunct expresses the state

Logic formula Φ	$::= \bigvee(\exists v^* \cdot \mu[(\textbf{and } \tau)^*])$
Main thread formula μ	$::= \ell \wedge \pi$
Child thread formula τ	$::= \textbf{thread}{=}v \wedge \gamma \rightsquigarrow_{\{w^*\}} \pi$
Lock formula ℓ	$::= [\bigwedge \omega \,\#\, \bigwedge \psi]$
Delayed formula γ	$::= \bigvee(\bigwedge \psi \wedge \pi)$
Waitlevel formula ω	$::= \textbf{waitlevel}{=}\alpha^t \mid \textbf{waitlevel}{<}\alpha^t \mid \textbf{waitlevel}{>}\alpha^t$
Lockset formula ψ	$::= v \in \textbf{LS} \mid v \notin \textbf{LS}$
Pure formula π	$::= \alpha \mid \beta \mid \pi_1 \wedge \pi_2 \mid \pi_1 \vee \pi_2 \mid \neg\pi \mid \exists v \cdot \pi \mid \forall v \cdot \pi \mid \textbf{true}$
Set term β^t	$::= \textbf{LS} \mid \{\} \mid \{v\} \mid \beta_1^t \cup \beta_2^t \mid \beta_1^t \cap \beta_2^t \mid \beta_1^t {-} \beta_2^t$
Set formula β	$::= \beta_1^t \sqsubseteq \beta_2^t \mid \beta_1^t = \beta_2^t$
Arithmetic term α^t	$::= k \mid v \mid v.mu \mid k \times \alpha^t \mid \alpha_1^t + \alpha_2^t \mid -\alpha^t$
Arithmetic formula α	$::= \alpha_1^t = \alpha_2^t \mid \alpha_1^t \neq \alpha_2^t \mid \alpha_1^t < \alpha_2^t \mid \alpha_1^t \leq \alpha_2^t$
	$v, w \in$ Variables $k \in$ Integer constants

Fig. 6. Grammar for Specification Language

of the main executing thread μ at a program point and the final states of its child threads τ. A main thread formula μ consists of a lock formula ℓ and a pure formula π. A lock formula ℓ consists of waitlevel formulae ω, and lockset formulae ψ. ω and ψ are self-explanatory.

A lock formula $[\bigwedge\omega \ \# \ \bigwedge\psi]$ presents our mechanism for each procedure's dual use, namely for both sequential and concurrent execution. The formula captures both waitlevel formula $\bigwedge\omega$ and lockset formula $\bigwedge\psi$ that are *mutually exclusive*. The former is checked for sequential procedural calls, while the latter must be delayed and checked at join points of forked threads. We provide both specifications in a unified format to cater to the differences in semantics for both sequential and concurrent computations. In sequential settings, e.g. when invoking a normal procedure call, the pre-condition of a procedure is an assertion that has to be fulfilled by the caller. If one or more constraints about lockset and waitlevel in the pre-condition are not met, verification fails. In concurrent settings and due to the ownership semantics of locks (see §10.1.2 of [4]), each new child thread does not inherit any locks from its parent thread. Hence, it has empty lockset and bottom waitlevel. Thus, constraints on waitlevel need not be checked here. Nevertheless, the constraints on lockset indicate the intention of the child thread and must be "delayed for checking" at its join point instead.

A child thread formula τ represents the final state of a child thread. It consists of a constraint **thread** $= v$ capturing the thread's identifier v, a delayed formula γ, and a pure formula π capturing the thread's post-state (i.e. its effects after finishing its execution). The formula τ denotes the fact that when a child thread with identifier v is joined and its delayed formula γ is satisfied, then its effects π will be visible to the calling thread. The annotation $\leadsto_{\{w^*\}}$ also captures a list of variables w^* that must be passed to the child thread when it is forked.

The formula γ illustrates our support for *delayed lockset checking*. Each disjunct in γ consists of delayed lockset constraints $\bigwedge\psi$ and a pure formula π to more precisely capture additional constraints for the corresponding delayed lockset constraints to hold. At each join point, only disjuncts whose pure formula is satisfied are candidates for delayed lockset checking.

Lastly, a pure formula π consists of standard equality/inequality, Presburger arithmetic and set constraints. Additionally, it is straightforward to enhance our specification logic with permissions to ensure data-race freedom by using separation logic [32] and variables as resource [31]. However, for simplicity of presentation, this paper shall focus on just the framework for deadlock freedom and ignore all issues pertaining to data-races.

For illustration, consider the following logic formula:

$$\exists v1, v2, tid \cdot \ l1{\neq}\textbf{null} \land l1.mu{=}v1 \land v1{>}0 \land l2{\neq}\textbf{null} \land l2.mu{=}v2 \land v2{>}0$$
$$\land \ id{=}tid \land \textbf{LS}'{=}\{l2\} \land b$$
and thread$=tid \land ((l1{\notin}\textbf{LS}' \land b \land l1{\neq}\textbf{null}) \lor (l2{\notin}\textbf{LS}' \land \neg b \land l2{\neq}\textbf{null})) \leadsto_{\{l1,l2,b\}}\textbf{true}$

The formula represents a program state where there are two concurrent threads: a main thread currently holding the lock $l2$ and a child thread with identifier tid. The child thread has a disjunctive delayed formula which precisely captures two locking scenarios: the child thread either acquires the lock $l1$ if the boolean condition on variable b holds or acquires the lock $l2$ if the condition does not hold. Suppose that the main thread is going to join the child thread. The main thread, knowing that b holds, can exclude the deadlock scenario that the child thread potentially attempts to acquire the lock $l2$. Hence it is deadlock-free to join the child thread. Note that due to our assumption on data-race freedom, the boolean condition on variable b is consistent in both threads.

4   Verification Rules

Proof rules for forward verification are presented in Fig. 7. They are formalized using Hoare's triples of the form $\{\Phi_{pr}\}P\{\Phi_{po}\}$: given a program P beginning in a state satisfying the pre-condition Φ_{pr}, if it terminates, it will do so in a state satisfying the post-condition Φ_{po}. In the figure, we only focus on key statements that are related to concurrency and lockset: procedure call, fork/join, conditional, and lock operations. In our framework, each program state $\Delta_\mu[(\textbf{and }\Delta_\tau)^*]$ consists of the current state Δ_μ of a main (or parent) thread and a list of final states Δ_τ of child threads. Here final states of child threads refer to post-states of child threads after they finish execution and their delayed formulae that need to be checked at join points. When joined, the post-state of a child thread will be visible and merged into the state of the main thread if its delayed formula is satisfied. For simplicity of presentation, when discussing the rules for fork/join, we present a program state Δ_μ **and** Δ_τ consisting of two threads (a thread main Δ_μ and a child thread Δ_τ). Additionally, because other rules only affect the main thread, it is sufficient to present only state of the main thread Δ_μ.

In order to invoke a procedure call (**CALL**) in a sequential setting, a main thread should be in a state Δ_μ that can entail the pre-condition Φ_{pr} of the procedure pn. For brevity, we omit the substitutions that link actual and formal parameters of the procedure prior to the entailment. We also omit the treatment of pass-by-ref parameters which can be handled by applying permissions on variables [20,31]. After the entailment, the main thread subsumes the post-condition Φ_{po} of the procedure into its state. Note that the operator $\wedge_{\{w^*,\textbf{LS},\textbf{waitlevel}\}}$ is a "composition with update" operator [29] to capture effects of executing the procedure on its parameters w^*, **LS**, and **waitlevel**.

The auxiliary function $partLS$ is used in concurrent settings to partition a formula into a delayed formula γ (which will be "delayed for checking") and a pure formula π. In case of a disjunctive formula, the corresponding delayed formula is also in a disjunctive form. This is to ensure that deadlock-free preconditions on lock acquisition can be more precisely guaranteed when "delayed checking". The auxiliary function $removeLS$ removes constraints that are related to lockset and waitlevel because they are irrelevant in concurrent settings. The semantics of $removeLS$ is straightforward, hence it is not presented.

The rules for fork and join demonstrate the *delayed lockset checking* technique. A **fork** creates a new thread executing concurrently with the main thread. When forking a new child thread (**FORK**), because lockset and waitlevel are local to each thread, the state of the main thread needs not entail constraints related to waitlevel and lockset in the pre-condition Φ_{pr} of the child thread. However, the main thread should be in a state that can entail the formula π_{pr}. The delayed formula γ_{pr} is delayed for checking at a join point. Afterwards, a new thread Δ_τ with a fresh identifier id carrying the delayed formula γ_{pr} and the post-state π_{po} of the corresponding forked procedure is created. The main thread keeps the identifier of the child thread in its new state Δ_μ^1 via the return value v of the **fork** call. Note that constraints related to lockset and waitlevel in the post-condition Φ_{po} are also omitted (resulted in π_{po}) because they are only local to the child thread and are irrelevant to the context of the main thread after the child thread is joined. Lastly, to guarantee the ownership semantics of locks, the **FORK** rule checks if the forked procedure with an empty lockset in its pre-condition will finally end up with an empty lockset in its post-condition. Alternatively, this check could be done during the verification of each forkable procedure without breaking information hiding at call sites.

Joining a child thread with an identifier v (**JOIN**) requires that the state Δ_μ of the main thread must entail the child thread's delayed formula γ_{pr}. The main

---

$$partLS([\bigwedge\omega \# \bigwedge\psi] \wedge \pi) \stackrel{\text{def}}{=} (\bigwedge\psi \wedge \pi_1, \pi_1) \text{ where } \pi_1 := removeLS(\pi)$$

$$partLS(\Phi_1 \vee \Phi_2) \stackrel{\text{def}}{=} (\gamma_1 \vee \gamma_2, \pi_1 \vee \pi_2)$$
$$\text{where } (\gamma_1, \pi_1) := partLS(\Phi_1) \text{ and } (\gamma_2, \pi_2) := partLS(\Phi_2)$$

$$partLS(\mu \text{ and } \tau) \stackrel{\text{def}}{=} (\pi \text{ and } \tau, \gamma) \text{ where } (\gamma, \pi) := partLS(\mu)$$

AUX

$$\frac{def(pn) := \mathbf{pn}(w^*) \text{ requires } \Phi_{pr} \text{ ensures } \Phi_{po};\ \{\ s\ \} \quad \Delta_\mu \vdash \Phi_{pr}}{\{\Delta_\mu\}\ pn(w^*)\ \{\Delta_\mu \wedge_{\{w^*,\mathbf{LS},\mathbf{waitlevel}\}} \Phi_{po}\}}$$

CALL

$$\frac{\begin{array}{c} def(pn) := \mathbf{pn}(w^*) \text{ requires } \Phi_{pr} \text{ ensures } \Phi_{po};\ \{\ s\ \} \\ (\gamma_{pr}, \pi_{pr}) := partLS(\Phi_{pr}) \qquad (\_, \pi_{po}) := partLS(\Phi_{po}) \\ \Delta_\mu \vdash \pi_{pr} \qquad fresh(id) \qquad \Delta_\mu^1 := \Delta_\mu \wedge_{\{v\}} v'{=}id \\ \Delta_\tau := \mathbf{thread}{=}id \wedge \gamma_{pr} \rightsquigarrow_{\{w^*\}} \pi_{po} \\ \{\Phi_{pr} \wedge \mathbf{LS}{=}\{\}\}\ s\ \{\Phi_{po} \wedge \mathbf{LS}'{=}\{\}\} \end{array}}{\{\Delta_\mu\}\ v := \mathbf{fork}(pn,w^*)\ \{\Delta_\mu^1 \text{ and } \Delta_\tau\}}$$

FORK

$$\frac{\Delta_\mu \vdash \gamma_{pr}}{\{\Delta_\mu \text{ and } \mathbf{thread}{=}v \wedge \gamma_{pr} \rightsquigarrow_{\{w^*\}} \pi_{po}\}\ \mathbf{join}(v)\ \{\Delta_\mu \wedge_{\{w^*\}} \pi_{po}\}}$$

JOIN

$$\frac{\{\Delta_\mu \wedge b\}\ s_1\ \{\Delta_\mu^1\} \qquad \{\Delta_\mu \wedge \neg b\}\ s_2\ \{\Delta_\mu^2\}}{\{\Delta_\mu\}\ \mathbf{if}\ b\ \mathbf{then}\ s_1\ \mathbf{else}\ s_2\ \{\Delta_\mu^1 \vee \Delta_\mu^2\}}$$

COND

$$\frac{fresh(l)}{\{\Delta_\mu\}\ \mathbf{lock}\ l = \mathbf{new\ lock}(v)\ \{\Delta_\mu^1 \wedge l{\neq}\mathbf{null} \wedge l.mu{=}v \wedge l \notin \mathbf{LS}'\}}$$

NEWLOCK

$$\frac{\Delta_\mu \vdash \mathbf{waitlevel}{<}l.mu}{\{\Delta_\mu\}\ \mathbf{acquire}(l)\ \{\Delta_\mu \wedge_{\{\mathbf{LS}\}} \mathbf{LS}'{=}\mathbf{LS} \cup \{l\}\}}$$

ACQUIRE

$$\frac{\Delta_\mu \vdash l \in \mathbf{LS}}{\{\Delta_\mu\}\ \mathbf{release}(l)\ \{\Delta_\mu \wedge_{\{\mathbf{LS}\}} \mathbf{LS}'{=}\mathbf{LS}{-}\{l\}\}}$$

RELEASE

Fig. 7. Forward Verification Rules for Concurrency

thread then merges the post-state of the child thread π_{po} into its state and the child thread disappears from the program state after joined.

The rule for conditionals (COND) illustrates our support for *precise lockset reasoning*. We capture precise lockset by using disjunction in the post-state of the conditional statement. Together with disjunctive delayed formulae supported by the function *partLS* in FORK rule, the use of explicit disjunction in this rule enables more precise reasoning on locksets to ensure deadlock freedom.

Other verification rules are relatively straightforward. The NEWLOCK rule creates a new lock l with a locklevel v. Without specifying a locklevel, a lock is assumed to have an arbitrary non-zero locklevel. We assume that locklevel is immutable during a lock's lifetime. The ACQUIRE rule ensures that locks are acquired in an increasing oder of locklevels (**waitlevel**$<l.mu$). This additionally implies that $l \notin \mathbf{LS}$ (but not vice versa). After acquiring the lock l, it is added to the thread's lockset **LS**. Reversely, a thread must hold a lock ($l \in \mathbf{LS}$) in order to release it (RELEASE). After releasing the lock l, it is removed from the thread's lockset **LS**. The ACQUIRE and RELEASE rules respectively ensure that a lock is not acquired or released more than once. The rest of verification rules used in our framework only operate in sequential settings, therefore they are standard as described in [29].

Theorem 1 (Soundness) *Given a program with a set of procedures P^i and their corresponding pre/post-conditions (Φ^i_{pr}/Φ^i_{po}), if our verifier derives a proof for every procedure P^i, i.e. $\{\Phi^i_{pr}\}P^i\{\Phi^i_{po}\}$ is valid, the program is deadlock-free.*

Proof. Intuitively, for each program state, there is a wait-for graph corresponding to it. We prove that a program that has been successfully verified by our framework will never get stuck due to deadlocks, i.e. there does not exist a state whose wait-for graph contains a cycle. The full proof is given in [21].   □

5   Implementation and Preliminary Comparison

We have implemented our framework into a prototype tool, called PARAHIP[5]. Currently, PARAHIP can automatically verify different deadlock scenarios and several motivating concurrent programs presented in the literature [11,14,15]. In addition, our tool can handle programs with forking of recursive procedures (such as the well-known parallel Fibonacci program) and unbounded number of locks by using shape predicates. We also support intricate nested and non-lexical fork/join concurrency by allowing thread identifiers to be passed between threads. Such a program is outlined in [21].

To demonstrate the expressiveness of our framework, we did a comparison with CHALICE [23,24], a well-known framework for verifying deadlock freedom, in terms of deadlock/deadlock-freedom scenarios that can be proven by the respective frameworks. The benchmark programs cover various scenarios such as

---

[5] The tool is available for both online use and download at
  http://loris-7.ddns.comp.nus.edu.sg/~project/parahip/

Table 1. A comparison between CHALICE and PARAHIP. A tick (✓) indicates that the corresponding scenario can be verified correctly by the respective verification framework. A cross (✗) indicates otherwise. A prefix "disj" indicates that the corresponding scenario requires disjunctive formulae to precisely capture different execution branches.

No	Scenario	CHALICE	PARAHIP	Comments
1	no-deadlock1	✗	✓	CHALICE cannot prove that this program is deadlock-free
2	no-deadlock2	✓	✓	
3	no-deadlock3	✗	✓	CHALICE cannot prove that this program is deadlock-free
4	deadlock1	✗	✓	CHALICE verifies this deadlock scenario as deadlock-free
5	deadlock2	✓	✓	
6	deadlock3	✓	✓	
7	disj-no-deadlock	✓	✓	
8	disj-deadlock	✗	✓	CHALICE verifies this deadlock scenario as deadlock-free
9	ordered-locking	✓	✓	
10	unordered-locking	✓	✓	

double lock acquisition, interactions between thread and lock operations, and unordered locking. One scenario (e.g. double acquisition) is representative of many real-world programs. Therefore, although the scenarios are small, they can be considered as a core benchmark for evaluating expressiveness of deadlock verification systems. The sets of benchmark programs written for both CHALICE and PARAHIP are available for online testing in our project website.

The comparison results are presented in Table 1. Compared with CHALICE, PARAHIP allows more deadlocks to be prevented and also permits more programs to be declared as deadlock-free. The experimental results were very surprising because CHALICE appears unsound. We communicated this issue with CHALICE' developers and confirmed that CHALICE's technical framework is indeed sound but its implementation does not properly consider programs with interactions between thread and lock operations [27]. Due to space limitations, we refer interested readers to [21] and project website for detailed comparison and benchmark programs.

6 Related Work

This section presents related works on specification and verification of deadlock freedom in shared-memory concurrency. Note that our framework currently supports only partial correctness. Hence, we do not consider non-termination due to infinite loops or recursion. Proving (non-)termination [2,7] and livelock freedom [30] is orthogonal to our framework, and could be separately extended.

In the context of concurrency verification, several recent frameworks have been proposed to reason about programs with non-recursive locks and dynamically-created threads [11,14], recursive locks [12], and low-level languages [8], all based on separation logic [32]. However, they focus on verifying partial correctness and ignore the presence of deadlocks. Haack et al. [12] use locksets (but not precise locksets) when verifying partial correctness of concurrent programs manipulating Java recursive locks. However, their approach does not ensure deadlock freedom. VERIFAST [15], a state-of-the-art verifier, also ignores deadlocks when verifying correctness of concurrent programs. CHALICE [23,24], a verification framework based on implicit dynamic frames [33], is capable of preventing deadlocks. Initially, Chalice uses locklevels and is able to prevent deadlocks due to double acquisition and unordered locking [23]. Later development on CHALICE [24] has proposed a technique to prevent deadlocks in programs that use both message passing via channels, and locking. Although it could encode join operations as send/receive over channels, there are programs (such as the program fork-join-as-send-recv in our website) where it is impossible for the encoding to find proper levels assigned to the channels for proving deadlock freedom [27]. Our *delayed lockset checking* technique can enable proving deadlock freedom in the presence of interactions between fork/join and acquire/release based on *precise lockset* as an abstraction. Using the technique, we are able to prove more programs deadlock-free than previous work. We also showed how to incorporate locklevels into our technique to form an expressive framework for specifying and verifying deadlock freedom of concurrent programs.

Besides verification frameworks, there are other approaches to detect or prevent deadlocks in concurrent programs. They can be classified into dynamic and static approaches. There are many systems that detect deadlocks dynamically - see [5,16,26] to name just a few recent works on this topic. Dynamic systems have the advantage that they can check unannotated programs. However, they cannot guarantee the absence of deadlocks due to insufficient test coverage. Static approaches such as those based on static analysis [28,35] and type systems [3,9,10,34] can ensure the absence of certain types of deadlocks. These systems have the advantage that fewer annotations are required. However, they tend to be less expressive than specification logics. Type systems such as [3,34] use locklevels to enforce a locking order while others use lock capabilities [10] and continuation effects [9] to verify programs with no natural ordering on the locks acquired. Nevertheless, existing systems [3,9,10,34] do not ensure the absence of deadlocks due to interactions between thread and lock operations. It is interesting to apply our delayed lockset checking technique to enhance the capability of these type systems.

Deadlock-freedom has also been studied in other contexts, and notably in the setting of message-passing process algebra [17,18,19]. The notion of locklevels in our approach is similar to obligation and capability levels in these type systems [17,18,19]. However, they have only been applied in the context of π-calculus while our framework ensures deadlock freedom for a shared-memory concurrent language with dynamic creation of threads and locks. Although fork/join/acquire/release operations and shared variables could be encoded as send/receive operations over channels, such an encoding would be non-trivial [17,36].

7   Conclusion

In this paper, we presented an expressive deadlock-freedom verification framework for concurrent programs. A novel delayed lockset checking technique is introduced to cover deadlock scenarios due to interactions between thread and lock operations. We described an abstraction based on precise lockset to support verification for deadlock freedom. We then showed how our technique can be integrated with locklevels to form a formalism for verifying different deadlock scenarios such as those due to double acquisition, interactions between thread and lock operations, and unordered locking. Lastly, we implemented the proposed framework into ParaHIP, a prototype verifier based on separation logic reasoning, for specifying and verifying deadlock freedom and partial correctness of concurrent programs.

Acknowledgement. We thank Peter Müller for his insightful discussions about Chalice, and the anonymous reviewers for comments. This work is supported by MOE Project 2009-T2-1-063.

References

1. NetBSD Problem Report 42900, http://gnats.netbsd.org/42900
2. Atig, M.F., Bouajjani, A., Emmi, M., Lal, A.: Detecting Fair Non-termination in Multithreaded Programs. In: Madhusudan, P., Seshia, S.A. (eds.) CAV 2012. LNCS, vol. 7358, pp. 210–226. Springer, Heidelberg (2012)
3. Boyapati, C., Lee, R., Rinard, M.C.: Ownership types for safe programming: preventing data races and deadlocks. In: OOPSLA, pp. 211–230 (2002)
4. Butenhof, D.R.: Programming with POSIX Threads. Addison-Wesley (1997)
5. Cai, Y., Chan, W.K.: MagicFuzzer: Scalable Deadlock Detection for Large-scale Applications. In: ICSE, pp. 606–616 (2012)
6. Coffman, E.G., Elphick, M.J., Shoshani, A.: System Deadlocks. ACM Computing Surveys 3(2), 67–78 (1971)
7. Cook, B., Podelski, A., Rybalchenko, A.: Proving Program Termination. CACM 54(5), 88–98 (2011)
8. Fu, M., Zhang, Y., Li, Y.: Formal Reasoning about Concurrent Assembly Code with Reentrant Locks. In: TASE, pp. 233–240 (2009)
9. Gerakios, P., Papaspyrou, N., Sagonas, K.F.: A Type and Effect System for Deadlock Avoidance in Low-level Languages. In: TLDI, pp. 15–28 (2011)
10. Gordon, C.S., Ernst, M.D., Grossman, D.: Static Lock Capabilities for Deadlock Freedom. In: TLDI, pp. 67–78 (2012)
11. Gotsman, A., Berdine, J., Cook, B., Rinetzky, N., Sagiv, M.: Local Reasoning for Storable Locks and Threads. In: Shao, Z. (ed.) APLAS 2007. LNCS, vol. 4807, pp. 19–37. Springer, Heidelberg (2007)
12. Haack, C., Huisman, M., Hurlin, C.: Reasoning about Java's Reentrant Locks. In: Ramalingam, G. (ed.) APLAS 2008. LNCS, vol. 5356, pp. 171–187. Springer, Heidelberg (2008)
13. Hoare, T.: The Verifying Compiler: A Grand Challenge for Computing Research. JACM 50, 63–69 (2003)
14. Hobor, A., Appel, A.W., Nardelli, F.Z.: Oracle Semantics for Concurrent Separation Logic. In: Drossopoulou, S. (ed.) ESOP 2008. LNCS, vol. 4960, pp. 353–367. Springer, Heidelberg (2008)

15. Jacobs, B., Piessens, F.: Expressive Modular Fine-grained Concurrency Specification. In: POPL, New York, NY, USA, pp. 271–282 (2011)
16. Joshi, P., Naik, M., Sen, K., Gay, D.: An Effective Dynamic Analysis for Detecting Generalized Deadlocks. In: FSE, pp. 327–336 (2010)
17. Kobayashi, N.: Type-based Information Flow Analysis for the Pi-calculus. Acta Informatica 42(4-5), 291–347 (2005)
18. Kobayashi, N.: A New Type System for Deadlock-Free Processes. In: Baier, C., Hermanns, H. (eds.) CONCUR 2006. LNCS, vol. 4137, pp. 233–247. Springer, Heidelberg (2006)
19. Kobayashi, N., Sangiorgi, D.: A Hybrid Type System for Lock-Freedom of Mobile Processes. TOPLAS 32(5) (2010)
20. Le, D.-K., Chin, W.-N., Teo, Y.-M.: Variable Permissions for Concurrency Verification. In: Aoki, T., Taguchi, K. (eds.) ICFEM 2012. LNCS, vol. 7635, pp. 5–21. Springer, Heidelberg (2012)
21. Le, D.K., Chin, W.N., Teo, Y.M.: An Expressive Framework for Verifying Deadlock Freedom. Technical report, National University of Singapore (June 2013), http://loris-7.ddns.comp.nus.edu.sg/~project/parahip/parahip-tr.pdf
22. Lee, E.A.: The Problem with Threads. Computer 39, 33–42 (2006)
23. Leino, K.R.M., Müller, P.: A Basis for Verifying Multi-threaded Programs. In: Castagna, G. (ed.) ESOP 2009. LNCS, vol. 5502, pp. 378–393. Springer, Heidelberg (2009)
24. Leino, K.R.M., Müller, P., Smans, J.: Deadlock-Free Channels and Locks. In: Gordon, A.D. (ed.) ESOP 2010. LNCS, vol. 6012, pp. 407–426. Springer, Heidelberg (2010)
25. Lu, S., Park, S., Seo, E., Zhou, Y.: Learning from Mistakes: A Comprehensive Study on Real World Concurrency Bug Characteristics. In: ASPLOS, New York, NY, USA, pp. 329–339 (2008)
26. Luo, Z.D., Das, R., Qi, Y.: Multicore SDK: A Practical and Efficient Deadlock Detector for Real-World Applications. In: ICST, pp. 309–318 (2011)
27. Müller, P.: Personal communication (March 2013)
28. Naik, M., Park, C.-S., Sen, K., Gay, D.: Effective Static Deadlock Detection. In: ICSE, pp. 386–396 (2009)
29. Nguyen, H.H., David, C., Qin, S.C., Chin, W.-N.: Automated Verification of Shape and Size Properties Via Separation Logic. In: Cook, B., Podelski, A. (eds.) VMCAI 2007. LNCS, vol. 4349, pp. 251–266. Springer, Heidelberg (2007)
30. Ouaknine, J., Palikareva, H., Roscoe, A.W., Worrell, J.: Static Livelock Analysis in CSP. In: Katoen, J.-P., König, B. (eds.) CONCUR 2011. LNCS, vol. 6901, pp. 389–403. Springer, Heidelberg (2011)
31. Parkinson, M., Bornat, R., Calcagno, C.: Variables as Resource in Hoare Logics. In: LICS, Washington, DC, USA, pp. 137–146 (2006)
32. Reynolds, J.: Separation Logic: A Logic for Shared Mutable Data Structures. In: LICS, Copenhagen, Denmark (July 2002)
33. Smans, J., Jacobs, B., Piessens, F.: Implicit Dynamic Frames. In: TOPLAS (2012)
34. Suenaga, K.: Type-Based Deadlock-Freedom Verification for Non-Block-Structured Lock Primitives and Mutable References. In: Ramalingam, G. (ed.) APLAS 2008. LNCS, vol. 5356, pp. 155–170. Springer, Heidelberg (2008)
35. Williams, A., Thies, W., Awasthi, P.: Static Deadlock Detection for Java Libraries. In: Gao, X.-X. (ed.) ECOOP 2005. LNCS, vol. 3586, pp. 602–629. Springer, Heidelberg (2005)
36. Wing, J.M.: FAQ on Pi-calculus. In: Microsoft Internal Memo (2002)

Expected Termination Time in BPA Games

Dominik Wojtczak

University of Liverpool, UK
d.wojtczak@liverpool.ac.uk

Abstract. We consider the problem of computing the value and finding the epsilon-optimal strategies for concurrent Basic Process Algebra games, which is a subclass of two-player infinite-state stochastic games with imperfect information. These games are played on the transition graph of stateless pushdown systems, or equivalently 1-exit recursive state machines, and can model recursive procedural program execution with probabilistic transitions. The objective of one player in these games is to minimise the expected termination time of such a program, while the objective of the other is to maximise it. We show that the quantitative decision questions regarding the value of the game as well as checking whether this value is infinite can be answered in PSPACE. We also show the latter problem to be as hard as the square root sum, whose containment even in the polynomial hierarchy is an open problem since the 1970s. Furthermore, an optimal strategy may require an infinite amount of memory in general, but we show that both player have epsilon-optimal stackless&memoryless strategies (i.e. strategies that do not use memory nor depend on the stack content). Finally, we show how to find such strategies using a strategy improvement algorithm.

1 Introduction

Concurrent games are useful for modelling an interaction of a system with its environment in a distributed setting (see e.g. [25, 22]). At each step of the execution of the system, the controller has to make a decision how it should proceed without the full knowledge about the state of the environment. An optimal strategy for the controller can be used to synthesise a robust system which behaves correctly no matter how the environment changes. This interaction can be modelled as a two-player zero-sum concurrent game where the controller and the environment play against each other. The classical objectives used in this context are qualitative such as a reachability objective [6], i.e. whether the system can reach (almost surely) a particular good state (e.g. terminate the program), a safety objective, i.e. whether the system can (almost surely) stay forever within a particular set of good states, or even more expressive like ω-regular objectives [5]. There is a growing interest in studying quantitative objectives, i.e. trying to find the optimum probability of satisfying a given objective (e.g. [7]) instead of just asking whether it can be done almost surely.

In this paper we study (concurrent) Basic Process Algebra games which can model recursive procedural programs with probabilistic transitions and consider the optimisation problem of their expected total execution time. These games correspond to a subclass of infinite-state zero-sum stochastic games with imperfect information. In previous work we have studied recursive simple stochastic games with positive rewards [9],

D. Van Hung and M. Ogawa (Eds.): ATVA 2013, LNCS 8172, pp. 303–318, 2013.

which are games with perfect-information (also known as turn-based games). These games are essentially played on transition systems of probabilistic pushdown automata. We showed that the problem of deciding whether the optimal expected execution time of a given program equals ∞ is undecidable, but becomes decidable for a 1-exit subclass of that model. This subclass corresponds directly to stateless pushdown systems, a model called Basic Process Algebra for historical reasons. Since we extend the recursive simple stochastic games to an imperfect-information setting, the problems we study in this paper still remain undecidable for concurrent pushdown games, but we show them to be decidable in the BPA setting. The BPA model corresponds directly to stochastic context-free grammars (with leftmost derivation), used in natural language processing (see, e.g. [20]), and branching processes models, which have wide applicability in modelling various physical phenomena, such as nuclear chain reactions, red blood cell formation, population genetics, population migration, epidemic outbreaks and molecular biology (see, e.g. [1] for many examples of branching processes models used in biological systems).

In [10] a monotone system of *polynomial* equations with the $Val(A)$ operator, which returns the value of a one-shot zero-sum game with payoff matrix A, was used for solving the termination probability game in 1-exit recursive concurrent stochastic games. It was showed there that the *least fixed point* solution of that equation system yields the desired probabilities. We study an equivalent model but with the expected termination time objective like in [9]. Here, we show that the value of a BPA game corresponds to the least fixed point solution (over the extended reals) of an associated system of *linear* equations with the Val operator. Just like in [9] we assume that all the rewards in our model are *strictly positive*; an assumption which is essential for our results to work. In this paper we carefully adapt the techniques developed in both of these papers and have to find new techniques to deal with troublesome case of the value of the game being ∞ in order to answer the fundamental quantitative decision questions about our BPA game model. Specifically, we can check in PSPACE whether there exists a strategy of the controller for which no matter what the environment does the expected termination time of the game is $\leq c$. At the same time we show that even the qualitative questions regarding the value of our game, i.e. whether it is $= \infty$, are harder than solving the *square root sum problem*. It is a long standing open problem since the 1970s whether this problem is contained in the polynomial hierarchy.

Finally, our most technical result shows that a (simultaneous) strategy improvement algorithm can be used to find ε-optimal strategies in BPA games. In fact we show that both players have *stackless&memoryless* ε-optimal strategies: randomised strategies that do not depend on the history of the play nor the content of the stack apart from the top stack symbol. It is known that for finite-state concurrent games, explicit probabilistic transitions do not add any power to these games, because the stochastic nature of the games can be simulated by concurrency alone. As we show, this also true in our setting and to simplify the proofs our standard definition of BPA games will not include probabilistic transitions.

Let us now motive our model further by showing how to model and solve the following optimisation problem. Suppose we have a patient infected by bacteria and we have two different antibiotics A1 and A2 which we can use to treat him. A bacterium can be of type T1 or T2 and we assume that it can freely mutate between these two types. The antibiotic Ai kills bacteria of type Ti. If we use A1 against T2 then the bacterium splits into two, and if we use A2 against T1 then the bacterium does not split nor die. We would like to find such a treatment strategy against the disease that no matter how the bacteria mutate the expected time of recovery (i.e. when all bacteria die), which is measured in the number of times the antibiotics are applied, is minimal. We can represent this model using the following BPA game where we set the cost of each pushdown rule to be 1. Player 1 will control the malicious disease and player 2 will be the doctor trying to treat the patient by eradicating all the bacteria.

BACTERIUM($antibiotic\,1, type\,1$) $\rightarrow \epsilon$

BACTERIUM($antibiotic\,1, type\,2$) $\rightarrow$ BACTERIUM BACTERIUM

BACTERIUM($antibiotic\,2, type\,1$) $\rightarrow$ BACTERIUM

BACTERIUM($antibiotic\,2, type\,2$) $\rightarrow \epsilon$

As we will see later, we can calculate the best possible time to recovery by formulating the following fixed point equation system.

$$x_{\text{BACTERIUM}} = Val\left(\begin{bmatrix} 0 & 2 \cdot x_{\text{BACTERIUM}} \\ x_{\text{BACTERIUM}} & 0 \end{bmatrix}\right) + 1$$

We then compute its least fixed point to be $x_{\text{BACTERIUM}} = 3$, which means the expected number of times we have to apply an antibiotic is 3. The optimal treatment is to choose two-thirds of the time antibiotic A1 and one-third of the time choose A2.

Related Work. Stochastic games go back to Shapley [27], who considered finite concurrent stochastic games with (discounted) rewards. See, e.g., [16] for a recent book on stochastic games. Finite-state stochastic games with perfect information were studied by Condon [4]. The qualitative decision problem ("is the game value exactly 1?") was shown to be in P, and the quantitive one ("is this value $\leq c$?") in NP $\cap$ coNP. Two equivalent purely probabilistic recursive models, Recursive Markov chains and probabilistic Pushdown Systems (pPDSs) were introduced in [11] and [8]. These models were extended to the optimization and game setting of (1-exit) recursive Markov decision processes (RMDPs) and (1-exit) recursive simple stochastic games (RSSGs) in [12, 13], and studied further in [2]. The qualitative termination decision problem for 1-exit RMDPs was shown to be in P, and for 1-exit RSSGs in NP $\cap$ coNP ([13]). The quantitative version was shown to be in PSPACE and square root sum hard ([12]).

Concurrent finite-state stochastic games with reachability objectives where studied in [6] and their qualitative decision problems were shown to be in P. The best upper bound on their quantitative questions is PSPACE just like for the more general model of 1-exit RSSGs. Our (simultaneous) strategy improvement algorithms for BPA games is based on the classic Hoffman-Karp algorithm [19]. It was shown in [18] that the same algorithm for the concurrent finite-state games with reachability objectives may require doubly exponential number of steps even to approximate the value of the game within a single bit of precision.

Models related to BPA games have been studied in the operations research under the name of branching Markov decision chains (a controlled version of multi-type branching processes). These are closely related to stochastic context-free grammar model, with non-negative rewards, but simultaneous derivation law. They were studied by Pliska [24] and extensively by Rothblum and co-authors (e.g., [26]). These models are typically restricted to one player setting and require the transition graph to be "transient" to simplify the analysis. We extend the results about these models to the imperfect information setting without making any such auxiliary assumptions.

In [3], the problem of finding a strategy that minimizes the expected number of transitions taken before termination for a given *one-counter Markov decision process* (OC-MDP) was studied. That model is a special subclass of pushdown systems, but is incomparable with BPAs. It was shown there that an ϵ-optimal strategy for the objective of minimizing the expected number of transitions taken before termination can be computed in time linear in $1/\epsilon$ and exponential in the encoding size of the OC-MDP.

Due to the space constraints the details of some of the proofs can only be found in the technical report [28] along with some more examples of BPA games.

2 Background

We will set the notation first. By $\Gamma^{\leq k}$, Γ^*, and Γ^ω, we will denote (respectively) the set of all sequences of letters from some fixed alphabet Γ of length at most k; arbitrary finite length; and infinite length. We represent stacks as such finite sequences and the top stack symbols is the left most symbol in such a sequence.

Let $\mathbb{Z}_n = \{0, \ldots, n-1\}$. Also, $\mathbb{R}_{>0} \stackrel{\text{def}}{=} (0, \infty)$ denotes the positive real numbers, $\mathbb{R}_{>0}^\infty \stackrel{\text{def}}{=} (0, \infty]$ extends this set with ∞ value, and $\mathbb{R}_{\geq 0}^\infty \stackrel{\text{def}}{=} [0, \infty]$ adds further the 0 element. We assume the usual natural total ordering on the extended reals $\mathbb{R}_{\geq 0}^\infty$ and the following usual arithmetic conventions on them: $a \cdot \infty = \infty$, for any $a \in \mathbb{R}_{>0}^\infty$; $0 \cdot \infty = 0$; $a + \infty = \infty$, for any $a \in \mathbb{R}_{\geq 0}^\infty$. This extends naturally to vector and matrix arithmetic over $\mathbb{R}_{\geq 0}^\infty$. We will use capital letter, e.g. A, B, to denote matrices, bold small letters to denote vectors, e.g. $\mathbf{x}, \mathbf{r}$, and non-bold small letter to denote one-dimension variables, e.g. x, y. For a matrix A by $A[i, j]$ we denote the i-th row and j-th column entry of A. Similarly for a vector $\mathbf{x}$ (a string α) by $\mathbf{x}[i]$ ($\alpha[i]$) we denote its i-th entry (letter, respectively). Alternatively, to refer to the i-th element of a vector $\mathbf{x}$ we will also sometimes use $\mathbf{x}_i$. For two vectors $\mathbf{x}, \mathbf{y} \in \mathbb{R}^n$, we write $\mathbf{x} \leq \mathbf{y}$ if $\mathbf{x}[i] \leq \mathbf{y}[i]$ for all $i = 1, \ldots, n$. Similarly for two matrices $A, B \in (\mathbb{R}_{\geq 0}^\infty)^{n \times m}$ we write $A \leq B$ if $A[i, j] \leq B[i, j]$ for all $1 \leq i \leq n, 1 \leq j \leq m$.

For a countable set S, we denote by $\mathcal{D}(S)$ the set of probability distributions over S, i.e. the set of functions $f : S \rightarrow [0, 1]$ such that $\sum_{s \in S} f(s) = 1$. We say that a probability distribution $f \in \mathcal{D}(S)$ is deterministic if there exists $x \in S$ such that $f(x) = 1$. Let $A \in (\mathbb{R}_{\geq 0}^\infty)^{n \times m}$ be a payoff matrix defining a *one-shot zero-sum game* between the *row player* and the *column player*. In such a game the row player picks any distribution $\mathbf{a} \in \mathcal{D}(\mathbb{Z}_n)$ over the rows and the column player picks any distribution over the columns $\mathbf{b} \in \mathcal{D}(\mathbb{Z}_m)$. The payoff to player 1 is defined as $\mathbf{a} A \mathbf{b}^T$, which is the same as the cost incurred by player 2. John von Neumann showed that for any A such a game has a value, i.e. $\sup_{\mathbf{a}} \inf_{\mathbf{b}} \mathbf{a} A \mathbf{b}^T = \inf_{\mathbf{b}} \sup_{\mathbf{a}} \mathbf{a} A \mathbf{b}^T$, which we will denote by $Val(A)$. The optimal *maximin* strategy of player 1 and the optimal *minimax* strategy of player 2 can be computed in poly-time using linear programming (see, e.g. [23]). We are now ready to define our model.

Definition 1. A (concurrent zero-sum) BPA game $\mathcal{G}$ is a tuple $(\Gamma, \Sigma, \delta, r)$ where
- Γ is a finite nonempty *stack alphabet* and its elements are called *stack symbols*,
- Σ is a finite nonempty *action alphabet* and we assume that for every $X \in \Gamma$ we are given two nonempty sets $\Sigma_1(X), \Sigma_2(X) \subseteq \Sigma$ of possible *legal actions* available to player 1 and 2, respectively, when the top stack symbol is X,
- $\delta \colon \Gamma \times \Sigma^2 \to \Gamma^{\leq 2}$ is a *transition function*,
- $r \colon \Gamma \to \mathbb{R}_{>0}$ is a *reward function* mapping each stack symbol to a strictly positive reward to player 1.

Notice that this model naturally captures recursive procedural programs where the transition function corresponds to calling or returning from the execution of a procedure and the reward can be set to the execution time of such a procedure. For computational purposes, we assume that all rewards are rational numbers with numerator and denominator given in binary. When the BPA game $\mathcal{G}$ is clear from the context, for any $X \in \Gamma$ and $a_1, a_2 \in \Sigma$, we will write $X(a_1, a_2)$ to represent $\delta(X, (a_1, a_2))$. We write $X(a_1, \cdot) = \alpha$ if $X(a_1, a_2) = \alpha$ for all $a_2 \in \Sigma_2(X)$; analogously we define $X(\cdot, a_2)$ and $X(\cdot, \cdot)$. For a given BPA $\mathcal{G}$ let $\Gamma_+ \subseteq \Gamma$ be the set of all stack symbols that can increase the stack size, i.e. $\Gamma_+ = \{X : |X(a_1, a_2)| \geq 2 \text{ for some } a_1 \in \Sigma_1(X), a_2 \in \Sigma_2(X)\}$. To simplify some of the proofs, we will require that for all $X \in \Gamma_+$ we have $|\Sigma_1(X)| = |\Sigma_2(X)| = 1$, i.e. the players have a trivial choice for the stack symbols which can increase the size of the stack and each such a symbol increases the stack size by exactly 1. In other words, for all $X \in \Gamma_+$ we effectively have $\delta(X) = YZ$ for some $Y, Z \in \Gamma$. This assumption is without loss of generality, and one can formally show that any BPA game $\mathcal{G}$ has an "essentially equivalent" BPA $\mathcal{G}'$ that satisfies this condition. In fact, we will show in Proposition 3 that even more general models can be effectively reduced to the just given BPA game model.

In the special case $|X(a_1, a_2)| \leq 1$ for all $X \in \Gamma$ and $a_1 \in \Sigma_1(X), a_2 \in \Sigma_2(X)$, a BPA game $\mathcal{G}$ is essentially a finite-state concurrent zero-sum game ([6]) with the expected termination objective. This is because the stack in such a case would always have size 1 until the game terminates when the stack becomes empty and the top stack symbol can be used to simulate the control state of the finite-state game.

Each BPA game $\mathcal{G} = (\Gamma, \Sigma, \delta, r)$ gives rise to $\mathcal{S}_\mathcal{G}$, a concurrent game with a countable number of states. We have that $\mathcal{S}_\mathcal{G} = (V_\mathcal{G}, \Sigma_\mathcal{G}, \delta_\mathcal{G}, r_\mathcal{G})$, where $V_\mathcal{G} = \Gamma^*$ is the countable set of states, $\Sigma_\mathcal{G} = \Sigma$ is the set of actions, $\delta_\mathcal{G} \colon V_\mathcal{G} \times \Sigma_\mathcal{G}^2 \to V_\mathcal{G}$ is the transition function such that for any pair of actions of the players $(a, b) \in \Sigma_\mathcal{G}^2$ we have $\delta_\mathcal{G}(\epsilon, (a, b)) = \epsilon, r_\mathcal{G}(\epsilon) = 0$, and for any stack content $\alpha = X \cdot \beta$ where $X \in \Gamma, \beta \in \Gamma^*$, we have $\delta_\mathcal{G}(\alpha, (a, b)) = \delta(X(a, b)) \cdot \beta$, and finally $r_\mathcal{G}(\alpha) = r(X)$ is the reward function specifying the reward (cost) to player 1 (to player 2) for visiting the state α.

A *play*, π, of the game $\mathcal{S}_\mathcal{G}$ is an infinite sequence $s_0(a_0, b_0)s_1(a_1, b_1) \ldots \in (V_\mathcal{G} \cdot \Sigma_\mathcal{G}^2)^\omega$ such that $\delta_\mathcal{G}(s_j, (a_j, b_j)) = s_{j+1}, a_j \in \Sigma_1(\text{top}(s_j))$ and $b_j \in \Sigma_2(\text{top}(s_j))$ for all $j \in \mathbb{N}$. Any finite prefix of a play is called a *history*. The play π gives rise to an infinite sequence of rewards to player 1 (and an equal infinite sequence of costs to player 2). There are many possible ways of mapping this sequence to player 1's *payoff*. In this paper, we consider the *total accumulated reward* criterion, where the payoff of Player 1 is defined as $\sum_{j=0}^\infty r_\mathcal{G}(s_j)$, and Player 2's payoff is the negation of this value. Clearly, this sum may diverge and because of the assumption that the rewards of all the stack symbols are positive, the sum will be finite if and only if the play π *terminates* by reaching the state ϵ. It is often convenient to designate an *initial* state. An *initialised* game is a tuple $(\mathcal{G}, \alpha)$ where $\mathcal{G}$ is a BPA game and α is an arbitrary sequence of its stack symbols.

Strategies and Strategy Profiles. A *(randomised) strategy* for player i in $\mathcal{S}_\mathcal{G}$ is a mapping $\sigma\colon (V_\mathcal{G} \times \Sigma^2)^* \times V_\mathcal{G} \to \mathcal{D}(\Sigma_\mathcal{G})$ assigning to each possible nonempty history $h \cdot s \in (V_\mathcal{G} \times \Sigma^2)^* \cdot V_\mathcal{G}$ a probability distribution $\sigma(h \cdot s)$ over the set of allowed actions to player i for the stack symbol $\mathrm{top}(s)$, i.e. $\sigma(h \cdot s) \in \mathcal{D}(\Sigma_i(\mathrm{top}(s))$. We write $\sigma(a \mid h \cdot s)$ for the probability assigned to $a \in \Sigma_1(\mathrm{top}(s))$ by the distribution $\sigma(h \cdot s)$. Let Ψ_i denote the set of strategies of player i. A *(randomised) strategy profile of $\mathcal{S}_\mathcal{G}$* is a pair $(\sigma_1, \sigma_2) \in \Psi_1 \times \Psi_2$ of strategies in $\mathcal{S}_\mathcal{G}$, one for each player. A strategy profile induces in a straightforward way a discrete-time Markov chain $\mathcal{M}_\mathcal{G}^{\sigma_1, \sigma_2} = (V_\mathcal{G}', \Delta_\mathcal{G}^{\sigma_1, \sigma_2}, r_\mathcal{G})$, where $V_\mathcal{G}' = (V_\mathcal{G} \times \Sigma^2)^* \times V_\mathcal{G}$ is the set of all histories in $\mathcal{S}_\mathcal{G}$ and the probabilistic transition relation $\Delta_\mathcal{G}^{\sigma_1, \sigma_2}$ consists only of the tuples of the form $(h \cdot s, p, h \cdot s(a_1, a_2) \cdot s')$ where p is the probability of moving from state s to state s' in $\mathcal{S}_\mathcal{G}$ using action profile (a_1, a_2) when the history of the play so far is h. That is $s' = \delta_\mathcal{G}(s, (a_1, a_2))$ and $p = \sigma_1(a_1 \mid hs)\sigma_2(a_2 \mid hs)$. Finally, the reward function $r_\mathcal{G}$ is the same as in $\mathcal{S}_\mathcal{G}$. Any initialised Markov chain $(\mathcal{M}_\mathcal{G}^{\sigma_1, \sigma_2}, \alpha)$ induces a unique probability measure, denoted by $\mathrm{Pr}_{\mathcal{G}, \alpha}^{\sigma_1, \sigma_2}$, assigning a probability to every Borel subset of $(V_\mathcal{G} \times \Sigma^2)^\omega$ (technically a subset of $V_\mathcal{G}'^\omega$ but we can use projection) and also induces the corresponding expectation operator $\mathbb{E}_{\mathcal{G}, \alpha}^{\sigma_1, \sigma_2}$ such that $\mathbb{E}_{\mathcal{G}, \alpha}^{\sigma_1, \sigma_2}(f) = \int f \, \mathrm{d}\mathrm{Pr}_{\mathcal{G}, \alpha}^{\sigma_1, \sigma_2}$ for all Borel measurable functions $f\colon (V_\mathcal{G} \times \Sigma^2)^\omega \to \mathbb{R} \cup \{\pm\infty\}$. We omit writing $\mathcal{G}$ in the subscript if $\mathcal{G}$ is clear from the context.

A strategy σ is called *stackless&memoryless (S&M)* if for each $h \cdot s \in (V_\mathcal{G} \times \Sigma^2)^* \cdot V_\mathcal{G}$ we have $\sigma(h \cdot s) = \sigma(\mathrm{top}(s))$, i.e. the strategy does not depend on the history h, nor the content of the stack apart from the top stack symbol. Such strategies can be specified by a function $\sigma : \Gamma \mapsto \mathcal{D}(\Sigma_\mathcal{G})$. Moreover, a strategy σ is called *deterministic* if it assigns to every history a deterministic distribution. In other words, it can be represented as $\sigma : (V_\mathcal{G} \times \Sigma^2)^* \cdot V_\mathcal{G} \to \Sigma_\mathcal{G}$. A strategy is deterministic stackless&memoryless (DS&M) if it is both S&M and deterministic. Such strategies can be specified by a function $\sigma : \Gamma \mapsto \Sigma_\mathcal{G}$. For a fixed $\mathcal{G}$, there are only finitely many DS&M strategies.

Let $\mathbf{q}_\alpha^{k, \sigma, \tau}$ denote the expected reward in k steps in the initialised Markov chain $(\mathcal{M}_\mathcal{G}^{\sigma, \tau}, \alpha)$. Formally, we could define this at the expectation of the following measurable function on (infinite) paths $f(s_1(a_1, a_2)s_2 \dots) = \sum_{i=1}^k r_\mathcal{G}(s_i)$. When $k = 0$ then of course $\mathbf{q}_\alpha^{0, \sigma, \tau} = 0$ for all α. Clearly the sequence $(\mathbf{q}_\alpha^{k, \sigma, \tau})_{k=0,1,\dots}$ is monotonic and so it converges to some value in $[0, \infty]$. Let $\mathbf{q}_\alpha^{*, \sigma, \tau} = \lim_{k \to \infty} \mathbf{q}_\alpha^{k, \sigma, \tau}$ be that limit, which we will call the *total expected payoff* to player 1 in $\mathcal{M}_\alpha^{\sigma, \tau}$ starting at initial state α. In our BPA games, the aim of player 1 is to maximise this value and the aim of player 2 is to minimise it. Let us define $\mathbf{q}_\alpha^* \stackrel{\mathrm{def}}{=} \sup_{\sigma \in \Psi_1} \inf_{\tau \in \Psi_2} \mathbf{q}_\alpha^{*, \sigma, \tau}$. Also, define $\mathbf{q}_X^{*, \sigma} \stackrel{\mathrm{def}}{=} \inf_{\tau \in \Psi_2} \mathbf{q}_X^{*, \sigma, \tau}$ for all $X \in \Gamma$ and player 1's strategy σ. A game is said to be determined if $\mathbf{q}_\alpha^* = \inf_{\tau \in \Psi_2} \sup_{\sigma \in \Psi_1} \mathbf{q}_\alpha^{*, \sigma, \tau}$ holds. In such a case we would call $\mathbf{q}_\alpha^{*, \sigma, \tau}$ the *value* of the initialised BPA game $(\mathcal{G}, \alpha)$. Intuitively determinacy means that player 1 has a strategy to achieve a payoff arbitrarily "close to" the value of the game no matter what player 2 does, and player 2 has a strategy to prevent him from achieving a "much" higher payoff, which we formalise in the next paragraph. Unlike for the concurrent reachability games [6] or 1-exit recursive concurrent stochastic games with reachability objectives [14], it does not follow directly from general determinacy results of Martin's Blackwell determinacy ([21]) that BPA games are determined, because those results require a Borel payoff function to be bounded, whereas the payoff function in our case is unbounded. Nevertheless, we will show that any BPA game is determined, but also *S&M-determined* which means that the value of the game is the same if a player uses S&M strategy and the other player is allowed to use an arbitrary strategy against it.

If the value $\mathbf{q}^*_\alpha$ is finite, then player 1's strategy σ is called ε-*optimal* if $\inf_\tau \mathbf{q}^{*,\sigma,\tau}_\alpha \geq \mathbf{q}^*_\alpha - \varepsilon$; on the other hand, player 2's strategy τ is ε-optimal if $\sup_\sigma \mathbf{q}^{*,\sigma,\tau}_\alpha \leq \mathbf{q}^*_\alpha + \varepsilon$. However, if the value $\mathbf{q}^*_\alpha = \infty$ then player 1's strategy σ is ε-optimal if $\inf_\tau \mathbf{q}^{*,\sigma,\tau}_\alpha \geq 1/\varepsilon$ (this is a pretty arbitrary choice as we could pick as the r.h.s. any expression which converges to ∞ as ε converges to 0). On the other hand, an arbitrary strategy of player 2 is ε-optimal if $\mathbf{q}^*_\alpha = \infty$. Finally, a strategy is said to be *optimal* if it is 0-optimal (assuming here that $1/0 = \infty$). Straight from the definition, if a game is determined then both players have ε-optimal strategies. There are BPA games where player 1 has no S&M optimal strategy, but has an optimal strategy which uses infinite amount of memory (see [28] for such an example).

We would like to solve the following *quantitative decision problem* for BPA games: Given a BPA game $\mathcal{G}$, an initial state α, and constant c, decide whether $\mathbf{q}^*_\alpha \geq c$. The *qualitative decision problem* would be to check whether $\mathbf{q}^*_\alpha = \infty$. Finally, we would like to find an ε-optimal strategy for each player, which we call the *strategy problem*. The following proposition shows that it suffices to solve the decision problem for initial states $X \in \Gamma$ only as $\mathbf{q}^*_\alpha$ for arbitrary $\alpha \in \Gamma^*$ can be expressed using them.

Proposition 2. $\mathbf{q}^*_\alpha = \sum_{i=1}^{|\alpha|} \mathbf{q}^*_{\alpha[i]}$.

Proof. Proof is by induction on the length of α. For $\alpha = \epsilon$ the empty sum on the r.h.s. is $= 0$ and so is the expected reward $\mathbf{q}^*_\epsilon$ as the game has already terminated. For $\alpha = X$ the statement is trivial. Now let $\alpha = X\beta$, where $\beta \in \Gamma^{\geq 1}$. First, for any pair of strategies σ and τ of player 1 and 2, respectively, for the initialised Markov Chain $\mathcal{M}^{\sigma,\tau}_\alpha$ we define two random variables and two events. Let T be the event that the state β is eventually reached, i.e. the set of all plays from α consistent with (σ, τ) which reach β. Also, let T' be the complement of T. Random variable K is defined as the total accumulated reward of all the states until the β state is reached for the first time, i.e. the stack symbol X is finally removed from the top of the stack, and the value of random variable L is the total accumulated reward thereafter (if the state β is never reached the value of L is assumed to be 0). Straight from this definitions we get $\mathbf{q}^*_\alpha = \sup_\sigma \inf_\tau \mathbb{E}^{\sigma,\tau}_\alpha (K + L) = \sup_\sigma \inf_\tau (\mathbb{E}^{\sigma,\tau}_\alpha K + \mathbb{E}^{\sigma,\tau}_\alpha L) = \sup_\sigma \inf_\tau (\mathbb{E}^{\sigma,\tau}_\alpha(K|T) \cdot \mathrm{Pr}^{\sigma,\tau}_\alpha(T) + \mathbb{E}^{\sigma,\tau}_\alpha(K|T') \cdot \mathrm{Pr}^{\sigma,\tau}_\alpha(T') + \mathbb{E}^{\sigma,\tau}_\alpha(L|T) \cdot \mathrm{Pr}^{\sigma,\tau}_\alpha(T) + \mathbb{E}^{\sigma,\tau}_\alpha(L|T') \cdot \mathrm{Pr}^{\sigma,\tau}_\alpha(T'))$. Now, the event T' consists of all infinite paths of $\mathcal{M}^{\sigma,\tau}_\alpha$ that never reach β so $\mathbb{E}^{\sigma,\tau}_\alpha(L|T') = 0$ and also from the assumption that all rewards are strictly positive we get that $\mathbb{E}^{\sigma,\tau}_\alpha(K|T') = \infty$. Therefore, $\mathbf{q}^*_\alpha = \sup_\sigma \inf_\tau (\mathbb{E}^{\sigma,\tau}_\alpha(K|T) \cdot \mathrm{Pr}^{\sigma,\tau}_\alpha(T) + \infty \cdot \mathrm{Pr}^{\sigma,\tau}_\alpha(T') + \mathbb{E}^{\sigma,\tau}_\alpha(L|T) \cdot \mathrm{Pr}^{\sigma,\tau}_\alpha(T) + 0 \cdot \mathrm{Pr}^{\sigma,\tau}_\alpha(T'))$. We now claim that the last expression is in fact equal to $\sup_\sigma \inf_\tau (\mathbb{E}^{\sigma,\tau}_\alpha(K) + \mathbb{E}^{\sigma,\tau}_\alpha(L|T))$. This is because the equality holds when $\mathrm{Pr}^{\sigma,\tau}_\alpha(T) = 1$ and when it is not the case, then $\mathrm{Pr}^{\sigma,\tau}_\alpha(T') = 1 - \mathrm{Pr}^{\sigma,\tau}_\alpha(T) > 0$ which would imply both of these expressions to be ∞ and again equal.

Now, $\sup_\sigma \inf_\tau (\mathbb{E}_\alpha^{\sigma,\tau} K + \mathbb{E}_\alpha^{\sigma,\tau}(L|T)) = \sup_\sigma \inf_\tau \mathbb{E}_\alpha^{\sigma,\tau} K + \sup_\sigma \inf_\tau \mathbb{E}_\alpha^{\sigma,\tau}(L|T)$, because any pair of player 1's strategies σ_1 and σ_2 that are (ε-)optimal for $\inf_\tau \mathbb{E}_\alpha^{\sigma,\tau} K$ and $\inf_\tau \mathbb{E}_\alpha^{\sigma,\tau}(L|T)$, respectively, can be easily composed into a single strategy σ that is (ε-)optimal for $\inf_\tau (\mathbb{E}_\alpha^{\sigma,\tau} K + \mathbb{E}_\alpha^{\sigma,\tau}(L|T))$ and *vice versa*. Finally, $\sup_\sigma \inf_\tau \mathbb{E}_\alpha^{\sigma,\tau} K = \mathbf{q}_X^*$, because K only accumulates reward from the moment the game reaches β, and the structure of the game between these two moments is isomorphic to a game starting at X. Similarly, $\sup_\sigma \inf_\tau \mathbb{E}_\alpha^{\sigma,\tau}(L|T) = \mathbf{q}_\beta^*$, because the event T implies that the game reaches β at some point, L accumulates reward only from that moment on and the structure of the game from that point on is isomorphic to a game starting at β. Therefore, we showed $\mathbf{q}_\alpha^* = \mathbf{q}_X^* + \mathbf{q}_\beta^*$ for any $\alpha = X\beta$, and by induction $\mathbf{q}_\alpha^* = \sum_{i=1}^{|\alpha|} \mathbf{q}_{\alpha[i]}^*$.   □

Finally, let us examine an extension of BPA games where any given action pair may lead to many possible outcomes each with some fixed probability and the rewards to player 1 not only can depend on the top stack symbol, but also on the action pair.

Proposition 3. *For any* extended BPA game *model $\mathcal{G}$ in which $\delta \colon \Gamma \times \Sigma^2 \to \mathcal{D}(\Gamma^*)$, $r \colon \Gamma \times \Sigma^2 \to \mathbb{R}_{>0}$, there is a BPA game $\mathcal{G}'$ of size polynomial in the size of $\mathcal{G}$ consistent with Definition 1 such that the value of the initialised game $(\mathcal{G}, X)$ for any stack symbol $X \in \Gamma$ is the same as the value of the initialised game $(\mathcal{G}', X)$.*

Let us remark that in the special case of the extended BPA games for which $|\Sigma_1(X)| = 1$ or $|\Sigma_2(X)| = 1$ holds for all $X \in \Gamma$, i.e. only one of the players have a choice for every top stack symbol, the model is essentially the same as 1-exit recursive simple stochastic games with positive rewards [9].

3   Characterisation of the Optimal Values

We now formulate an equation system that will allow us to compute the value $\mathbf{q}_\alpha^*$ of the BPA game $\mathcal{G}$. For each stack symbol $X \in \Gamma$ we have a variable q_X which all together form a vector $\mathbf{q} \in (\mathbb{R}_{\geq 0}^\infty)^\Gamma$. The equation for each variable is given as $q_X = Val(A_X(\mathbf{q})) + r(X)$, where the matrix $A_X(\mathbf{q})$ of dimensions $\Sigma_1(X) \times \Sigma_2(X)$ is defined as follows. For every $(a_1, a_2) \in \Sigma_1(X) \times \Sigma_2(X)$:

- $A_X(\mathbf{q})[a_1, a_2] = 0$ if $X(a_1, a_2) = \epsilon$
- $A_X(\mathbf{q})[a_1, a_2] = q_Y$ if $X(a_1, a_2) = Y$
- $A_X(\mathbf{q})[a_1, a_2] = q_Y + q_Z$ if $X(a_1, a_2) = YZ$ (Recall that in this case $X \in \Gamma_+$ and so this matrix has size 1×1.)

Now, we denote the whole system of equations in a vector form as $\mathbf{q} = P(\mathbf{q})$, where $P \colon (\mathbb{R}_{\geq 0}^\infty)^\Gamma \to (\mathbb{R}_{\geq 0}^\infty)^\Gamma$. Notice that given $\mathbf{q}$ we can compute $P(\mathbf{q})$ in polynomial time by computing all $A_X(\mathbf{q})$-s first and then using one of the polynomial time algorithms for linear programming to solve these one-shot matrix games. Let $\mathbf{0}$ denote the vector whose all entries are equal to 0, and let us define a sequence of vectors $(\mathbf{x}^i)_{i \in \mathbb{N}}$ such that $\mathbf{x}^0 = \mathbf{0}$, $\mathbf{x}^{k+1} = P(\mathbf{x}^k) = P^{k+1}(\mathbf{0})$, for all $k \geq 0$.

Theorem 4. *1. For all $\mathbf{x}' \geq 0$, if $\mathbf{x}' \geq P(\mathbf{x}')$, then $\mathbf{q}^* \leq \mathbf{x}'$.*
2. $\mathbf{q}^* \geq P(\mathbf{q}^*)$.
3. For all stack symbols X

$$\mathbf{q}_X^* \stackrel{\text{def}}{=} \sup_{\sigma \in \Psi_1} \inf_{\tau \in \Psi_2} \mathbf{q}_X^{*;\sigma,\tau} = \inf_{\tau \in \Psi_2} \sup_{\sigma \in \Psi_1} \mathbf{q}_X^{*;\sigma,\tau}.$$

(In other words, these games are determined.)

4. $\mathbf{q}^* = P(\mathbf{q}^*)$.
5. P *is monotone and* $\mathbf{x}^k \leq \mathbf{x}^{k+1}$ *for all* k.
6. *For all* $k \geq 0$, $\mathbf{x}^k \leq \mathbf{q}^*$.
7. $\mathbf{q}^* = \lim_{k \to \infty} \mathbf{x}^k$.

Proof. **1.** Let us denote by τ^* an S&M strategy for player 2 which at any state $\alpha = X\beta$ uses the optimal mixed minimax strategy in the one-shot zero-sum game $A_X(\mathbf{x}')$.

Lemma 5. *For all strategies* $\sigma \in \Psi_1$ *of player 1, and for all* $k \geq 0$, $\mathbf{q}^{k,\sigma,\tau^*} \leq \mathbf{x}'$.

Let $X \in \Gamma$ be any stack symbol. From Lemma 5 for any strategy σ of player 1 we get $\mathbf{q}_X^{*,\sigma,\tau^*} = \lim_{k \to \infty} \mathbf{q}_X^{k,\sigma,\tau^*} \leq \mathbf{x}'_X$, so $\sup_{\sigma \in \Psi_1} \mathbf{q}_X^{*,\sigma,\tau^*} \leq \mathbf{x}'_X$ as well. Therefore

$$\mathbf{q}_X^* = \sup_{\sigma \in \Psi_1} \inf_{\tau \in \Psi_2} \mathbf{q}_X^{*,\sigma,\tau} \leq \inf_{\tau \in \Psi_2} \sup_{\sigma \in \Psi_1} \mathbf{q}_X^{*,\sigma,\tau} \leq \sup_{\sigma \in \Psi_1} \mathbf{q}_X^{*,\sigma,\tau^*} \leq \mathbf{x}'_X \qquad (1)$$

2. For $X \in \Gamma_+$ such that $\delta(X) = YZ$ for some $Y, Z \in \Gamma$, we get $\mathbf{q}_X^* = \mathbf{q}_{YZ}^* + r(X) = \mathbf{q}_Y^* + \mathbf{q}_Z^* + r(X)$ by using Proposition 2. For all other $X \in \Gamma \setminus \Gamma_+$, if $\mathbf{q}_X^* < Val(A_X(\mathbf{q}^*)) + r(X)$, then let us pick any $\varepsilon < Val(A_X(\mathbf{q}^*)) + r(X) - \mathbf{q}_X^*$ and such that $1/\varepsilon \geq \max_{R \in \Gamma: \mathbf{q}_R^* \neq \infty} \mathbf{q}_R^*$. Let player 1 play in the first step its optimal minimax strategy in the one-shot game $A_X(\mathbf{q}^*)$ and if the action pair (a_1, a_2) is chosen in the first step, player 1 plays any ε-optimal strategy from $X(a_1, a_2)$ after that; denote this strategy by σ. Therefore, when player 1 uses strategy σ the value of the game when starting at X is at least $\inf_{\tau \in \Psi_2} \sum_{(a,b) \in \Sigma^2} \sigma(a|X)\tau(b|X)(\mathbf{q}_{X(a,b)}^* - \varepsilon) + r(X) = \inf_{\tau \in \Psi_2} \sum_{(a,b) \in \Sigma^2} \sigma(a|X)\tau(b|X)\mathbf{q}_{X(a,b)}^* + r(X) - \varepsilon$, which is equal to $Val(A_X(\mathbf{q}^*)) + r(X) - \varepsilon$, because σ is optimal in the one-shot game with payoff matrix $A_X(\mathbf{q}^*)$. But from the definition of ε the last expression is larger than $\mathbf{q}_X^*$; a contradiction.

3. In the equation (1) above, choose $\mathbf{x}' = \mathbf{q}^*$. Then for all stack symbols X we get

$$\mathbf{q}_X^* = \sup_{\sigma \in \Psi_1} \inf_{\tau \in \Psi_2} \mathbf{q}_X^{*,\sigma,\tau} \leq \inf_{\tau \in \Psi_2} \sup_{\sigma \in \Psi_1} \mathbf{q}_X^{*,\sigma,\tau} \leq \mathbf{q}_X^*$$

4. For $X \in \Gamma_+$ such that $\delta(X) = YZ$ for some $Y, Z \in \Gamma$, we get $\mathbf{q}_X^* = \mathbf{q}_{YZ}^* + r(X) = \mathbf{q}_Y^* + \mathbf{q}_Z^* + r(X)$ by using Proposition 2. For all other $X \in \Gamma \setminus \Gamma_+$, if $\mathbf{q}_X^* > Val(A_X(\mathbf{q}^*)) + r(X)$, then let us pick any $\varepsilon < \mathbf{q}_X^* - Val(A_X(\mathbf{q}^*)) - r(X)$. Notice, that in the case $\mathbf{q}_X^* = \infty$ the condition $\mathbf{q}_X^* > Val(A_X(\mathbf{q}^*)) + r(X)$ implies that $Val(A_X(\mathbf{q}^*))$ is finite. From (**3.**) we know that player 2 has an ε-optimal strategy from any initial state, because these games are determined. Recall that in the case of a game with ∞ value an ε-optimal strategy for player 2 is a completely arbitrary strategy. Let player 2 play in the first step its optimal minimax strategy in the one-shot game $A_X(\mathbf{q}^*)$ and if the action pair (a_1, a_2) is chosen in the first step, player 2 plays any ε-optimal strategy from $X(a_1, a_2)$ after that; denote this strategy by τ. Notice that in the case $\mathbf{q}_X^*$ is finite, the strategy τ cannot use with positive probability any action b for which there exists an action a of player 1 such that $\mathbf{q}_{X(a,b)}^* = \infty$, because this would imply that $Val(A_X(\mathbf{q}^*)) = \infty$. In other words, $\tau(b|X) = 0$ if $\mathbf{q}_{X(a,b)}^* = \infty$. Therefore, when player 2 uses strategy τ the value of the game when starting at X is at most $\sup_{\sigma \in \Psi_1} \sum_{(a,b) \in \Sigma^2: \tau(b|X) > 0} \sigma(a|X)\tau(b|X)(\mathbf{q}_{X(a,b)}^* + \varepsilon) +$

$r(X) = \sup_{\sigma \in \Psi_1} \sum_{(a,b) \in \Sigma^2} \sigma(a|X)\tau(b|X)\mathbf{q}^*_{X(a,b)} + r(X) + \varepsilon$, which is equal to $Val(A_X(\mathbf{q}^*)) + r(X) + \varepsilon$, because τ is optimal in the one-shot game with payoff matrix $A_X(\mathbf{q}^*)$. But from the definition of ε the last expression is smaller than $\mathbf{q}^*_X$; a contradiction.

5. Notice that $Val(A) \leq Val(B)$ for $A \leq B$, because player 1 reusing the optimal strategy for the zero-sum game with payoff matrix A in the zero-sum game with payoff matrix B guarantees himself a payoff at least as high as for matrix A. Moreover, straight from the definition for every $\mathbf{x} \leq \mathbf{x}'$ we have $A_X(\mathbf{x}) \leq A_X(\mathbf{x}')$, hence we also get in the end $P(\mathbf{x}) \leq P(\mathbf{x}')$. Now, of course $\mathbf{x}^0 = \mathbf{0} \leq \mathbf{x}^1$ so $P(\mathbf{x}^0) \leq P(\mathbf{x}^1)$ and by an easy induction we get $P(\mathbf{x}^k) \leq P(\mathbf{x}^{k+1})$.

6. P is monotonic and $\mathbf{x}^0 = \mathbf{0} \leq \mathbf{q}^*$, so $\mathbf{x}^1 = P(\mathbf{x}^0) \leq P(\mathbf{q}^*) = \mathbf{q}^*$, because as we have just shown $\mathbf{q}^*$ is a fixed point of P. By an easy induction on k we get $\mathbf{x}^k \leq \mathbf{q}^*$ for all k.

7. We know that $\mathbf{x}^* \overset{\text{def}}{=} \lim_{k \to \infty} \mathbf{x}^k$ exists in $[0, \infty]^\Gamma$, because thanks to (**5.**) it is a monotonically non-decreasing sequence and so it has to converge although some of the entries may converge to ∞. In fact we have $\mathbf{x}^* = \lim_{k \to \infty} P^{k+1}(\mathbf{0}) = P(\lim_{k \to \infty} P^k(\mathbf{0}))$, because P is a continuous function. Therefore $\mathbf{x}^*$ is a fixed point of the equation $\mathbf{x} = P(\mathbf{x})$ and so from (**1.**) we have $\mathbf{q}^* \leq \mathbf{x}^*$. Since from (**6.**) $\mathbf{x}^k \leq \mathbf{q}^*$ for all $k \geq 0$, we also have $\lim_{k \to \infty} \mathbf{x}^k \leq \mathbf{q}^*$. Thus $\mathbf{q}^* \leq \mathbf{x}^* \leq \mathbf{q}^*$.

$\square$

From the proof we can derive the following useful fact.

Corollary 6. *In every BPA game, player 2 has an optimal S&M strategy.*

Proof. It is enough to consider the strategy τ^*, in part (**1.**) of Theorem 4, where we let $\mathbf{x}' = \mathbf{q}^*$. Then for any stack symbol $X \in \Gamma$ from equation (1) we get $\mathbf{q}^*_X = \sup_{\sigma \in \Psi_1} \mathbf{q}^{*, \sigma, \tau^*} = \inf_{\tau \in \Psi_2} \sup_{\sigma \in \Psi_1} \mathbf{q}^{*, \sigma, \tau}_X$.

Notice that Theorem 4 gives us a simple iterative algorithm for computing the value of a BPA game. It simply requires to apply P iteratively starting at the $\mathbf{0}$ vector until we reach a solution which does not change much with a further application of P. Of course this is not enough to decide whether a particular value is $\geq c$ or even approximate that value, because it does not allow us to check how close the solution is to the actual value.

4   Decision Procedure

In this section we show how to use the system of equations characterisation of the values of the BPA games to answer the qualitative as well as the quantitative questions regarding their values in PSPACE.

Theorem 7. *Checking whether the value of an initialised BPA game $(\mathcal{G}, \alpha)$ is $\leq c, = c, \geq c$, where c is an arbitrary rational number, or $= \infty$ can be all performed in PSPACE.*

Note that in [9] we showed all of these problems to be in NP∩coNP for turned-based BPA games, and even that they are in P for the one-player case. We now show that these upper bounds are unlikely to hold in the concurrent BPA games setting. Namely, even the qualitative decision problem, i.e. whether the value is $= \infty$, is as hard as the *square root sum problem* (SQRTSUM), an interesting decision problem in numerical computations. Formally, SQRTSUM is defined as follows: Given numbers $d_1, \ldots, d_n, k \in \mathbb{N}$, decide whether $\sum_{i=1}^{n} \sqrt{d_i} \geq k$. In [1] it was shown that SQRTSUM belongs to the fourth level of the *counting hierarchy*, an improvement over the previously known PSPACE upper bound. However, it has been an open question since the 1970s as to whether SQRTSUM falls into the polynomial hierarchy [17, 15]. Hence, showing that the qualitative decision problem for BPA game to be inside the polynomial hierarchy would imply a major breakthrough in understanding the complexity of numerical computations.

Theorem 8. *SQRTSUM is polynomial-time reducible to the quantitative expected termination time decision problem for finite-state concurrent games and the qualitative expected termination time decision problem for BPA games.*

5   Strategy Improvement and SM Determinacy

We now prove S&M-determinacy for BPA games, and we also show that (simultaneous) strategy improvement can be used to compute their values and ε-optimal strategies.

Theorem 9. *We can compute a sequence of S&M strategies $\sigma_0, \sigma_1, \ldots$ for player 1 such that σ_{k+1} can be computed based on σ_k in polynomial time, $\mathbf{q}^{*,\sigma_k} \leq \mathbf{q}^{*,\sigma_{k+1}}$ for all k, and $\lim_{k \to \infty} \mathbf{q}^{*,\sigma_k} = \mathbf{q}^*$. This implies that BPA games are S&M-determined, ε-optimal strategy for player 1 exists for any $\varepsilon > 0$ and can be effectively computed.*

Proof. Recall that $\mathbf{q}_X^{*,\sigma} \overset{\text{def}}{=} \inf_{\tau \in \Psi_2} \mathbf{q}_X^{*,\sigma,\tau}$. Define Ψ_i^{DSM} to be the set of all deterministic S&M strategies for player i and pick any S&M strategy, $\sigma \in \Psi_1^{\text{SM}}$, for player 1. First, note that if $\mathbf{q}^{*,\sigma} = P(\mathbf{q}^{*,\sigma})$ then $\mathbf{q}^{*,\sigma} = \mathbf{q}^*$. This is because, by Theorem 4(I.), $\mathbf{q}^* \leq \mathbf{q}^{*,\sigma}$, and on the other hand, σ is just one strategy for player 1, and hence for every stack symbol $X \in \Gamma$, $\mathbf{q}_X^* = \sup_{\sigma' \in \Psi_1} \mathbf{q}_X^{*,\sigma'} \geq \mathbf{q}_X^{*,\sigma}$. Now for all $X \in \Gamma_+$ we claim that $\mathbf{q}_X^{*,\sigma}$ satisfies its equation in $\mathbf{x} = P(\mathbf{x})$. In other words, $\mathbf{q}_X^{*,\sigma} = \mathbf{q}_Y^{*,\sigma} + \mathbf{q}_Z^{*,\sigma}$, where $\delta(X) = YZ$. This is because once we fix an S&M strategy σ for player 1, the BPA game becomes an extended BPA game, $\mathcal{G}^\sigma$, where only player 2 has no trivial choices and so $\mathbf{q}_{\mathcal{G}^\sigma}^{*,\sigma''} = \mathbf{q}_{\mathcal{G}^\sigma}^*$ for any strategy σ'' of player 1. We can then reduce this game to a BPA game $\mathcal{G}''$ while preserving the expected payoffs from each stack symbol. Finally, applying Proposition 2 to $\mathcal{G}''$ will give us what we need.

Therefore, the equality can fail only for $X \in \Gamma \setminus \Gamma_+$. Notice that $\mathbf{q}_X^{*,\sigma} \leq Val(A_X(\mathbf{q}^{*,\sigma})) + r(X)$, because player 2 can play in his first step starting at vertex X an optimal strategy in the matrix game $A_X(\mathbf{q}^{*,\sigma})$, incurring one-step cost $r(X)$, and thereafter, if some action pair (a_1, a_2) was chosen, play his optimal strategy when starting at $X(a_1, a_2)$, which we showed to exists in Corollary 6. Now, let $\Gamma_{\neq} = (X_1, X_2, \ldots, X_n)$ be the set of all stack symbols (in some fixed order) for which $\mathbf{q}_X^{*,\sigma} < Val(A_X(\mathbf{q}^{*,\sigma})) + r(X)$; and so for any $X \notin \Gamma_{\neq}$ the equality has to hold. Note that obviously $\mathbf{q}_{X_i}^{*,\sigma} \neq \infty$ for all $X_i \in \Gamma_{\neq}$. Now, let $\mathbf{r} = [r(X_1), r(X_2), \ldots, r(X_n)]^T$, $\mathbf{r}^* = [\mathbf{q}_{X_1}^{*,\sigma}, \ldots, \mathbf{q}_{X_n}^{*,\sigma}]^T$ and $\mathbf{r}' = [\mathbf{q}_{X_1}^{*,\sigma'}, \ldots, \mathbf{q}_{X_n}^{*,\sigma'}]^T$.

Consider a revised S&M strategy for player 1, σ', which is identical to σ, except that for each stack symbol $X_i \in \Gamma_{\neq}$ the strategy is changed so that $\sigma'(X_i) \in \mathcal{D}(\Sigma_1(X_i))$

becomes an optimal mixed minimax strategy for player 1 in the one-shot matrix game $A_X(\mathbf{q}^{*,\sigma})$. We will show that switching from σ to σ' will strictly improve player 1's payoff for all stack symbols $X_i \in \Gamma_{\neq}$, and will not reduce its payoff for any other stack symbol.

Now, consider a *parametrized BPA game*, $\mathcal{G}(\mathbf{t})$ where $\mathbf{t} = [t_1, t_2, \ldots, t_n]^T$, which is identical to $\mathcal{G}$, except that we replace the transition function δ for X_i to be $\delta(X_i, a, b) = \varepsilon$ for any $a, b \in \Sigma$ and assign $r(X_i) = t_i$. Fixing the value of $\mathbf{t} \in [0, \infty]^n$ determines a BPA game, $\mathcal{G}(\mathbf{t})$. Note that σ and σ' are still well-defined for $\mathcal{G}(\mathbf{t})$ and define the same strategy, because they differ only for stack symbols $X_i \in \Gamma_{\neq}$ for which the outcome in $\mathcal{G}(\mathbf{t})$ does not depend on the strategy choice. Now, we keep $\mathbf{q}_X^{*,\sigma,\tau}$ to denote $\mathbf{q}_{\mathcal{G},X}^{*,\sigma,\tau}$ and use $\mathbf{q}_{\mathbf{t},X}^{*,\sigma,\tau}$ to denote $\mathbf{q}_{\mathcal{G}(\mathbf{t}),X}^{*,\sigma,\tau}$. Similarly we define $\mathbf{q}_{\mathbf{t},X}^{*,\sigma} = \inf_{\tau \in \Psi_2} \mathbf{q}_{\mathcal{G}(\mathbf{t}),X}^{*,\sigma,\tau}$, which is the infimum of the expected rewards, over all strategies of player 2, when starting at X in $\mathcal{G}(\mathbf{t})$. Observe that $\mathbf{q}_{\mathbf{r}^*,X}^{*,\sigma} = \mathbf{q}_X^{*,\sigma}$ for any $X \in \Gamma$. This is because $\mathcal{G}$ and $\mathcal{G}(\mathbf{t})$ differ only for $X_i \in \Gamma_{\neq}$, the expected payoff for removing $X_i \in \Gamma_{\neq}$ from the top of the stack using σ (against the best strategy of player 2) equals $\mathbf{q}_{X_i}^{*,\sigma}$ in $\mathcal{G}$ and $\mathbf{r}_{X_i}^*$ in $\mathcal{G}(\mathbf{t})$, and these values are the same by the definition of $\mathbf{r}^*$. Also, generalising Proposition 2 we can then get $\mathbf{q}_{\mathbf{t},X_i\beta}^{*,\sigma} = \mathbf{q}_{\mathbf{t},X_i}^{*,\sigma} + \mathbf{q}_{\mathbf{t},\beta}^{*,\sigma}$ for any $\beta \in \Gamma^*$ so the expected payoffs in both of these games do not change if it does not change for any $X_i \in \Gamma_{\neq}$. Similarly we can show $\mathbf{q}_{\mathbf{r}',X}^{*,\sigma'} = \mathbf{q}_X^{*,\sigma'}$. Furthermore, for any $\sigma \in \Psi_1, \tau \in \Psi_2$ if $\mathbf{t}' \geq \mathbf{t}$ then $\mathbf{q}_{\mathbf{t}',X}^{*,\sigma,\tau} \geq \mathbf{q}_{\mathbf{t},X}^{*,\sigma,\tau}$, because increasing the reward for removing the the stack symbols $X_i \in \Gamma_{\neq}$ from the top of the stack can only increase the expected payoff. Lastly, $\mathbf{q}_{\mathbf{t},X}^{*,\sigma,\tau} = \mathbf{q}_{\mathbf{t},X}^{*,\sigma',\tau}$, because σ and σ' differ only for $X_i \in \Gamma_{\neq}$ and in $\mathcal{G}(\mathbf{t})$ these symbols are immediately removed from the top of the stack and have the same reward t_i.

Now, note that for any S&M strategies σ and τ the value of $\mathbf{q}_{\mathbf{t},X}^{*,\sigma,\tau}$ is equal to the expected reward in a BPA process starting at X where neither of the players have nontrivial choices. This can easily be expressed as linear equation system with nonnegative coefficients as follows: $\mathbf{x}_{X_i} = t_i$ for $X_i \in \Gamma_{\neq}$, $\mathbf{x}_X = \mathbf{x}_Y + \mathbf{x}_Z + r(X)$ for $\delta(X) = YZ$ and $\mathbf{x}_X = \sum_{(a,b)\in\Sigma^2} \sigma(a|X)\tau(b|X)\mathbf{x}_{X(a,b)} + r(X)$ for $X \in \Gamma \setminus \Gamma_+$. We can write it down as $\mathbf{x} = R_{\mathbf{t}}(\mathbf{x})$ and observe that it follows from Theorem 4 that $\mathbf{q}_{\mathbf{t},X}^{*,\sigma,\tau} = (\lim_{k\to\infty} R_{\mathbf{t}}^k(\mathbf{0}))_X$. Since operator $R_{\mathbf{t}}$ is linear in $\mathbf{x}$ and variables in $\mathbf{t}$ appear as constants, we can express it as $R_{\mathbf{t}}(\mathbf{x}) = A_{\sigma,\tau}\mathbf{x} + \mathbf{c}(\mathbf{t})$, for some nonnegative matrix $A_{\sigma,\tau}$, and vector $\mathbf{c}(\mathbf{t})$ such that $\mathbf{c}(\mathbf{t})_{X_i} = t_i$ and $\mathbf{c}(\mathbf{t})_X = r(X)$ otherwise. (Notice that for $X_i \in \Gamma_{\neq}$ the X_i-th row vector of $A_{\sigma,\tau}$ has only zero entries.) Simple iteration then shows $\mathbf{q}_{\mathbf{t},X}^{*,\sigma,\tau} = \lim_{k\to\infty} (R_{\mathbf{t}}^k(\mathbf{0}))_X = ((\sum_{k=0}^{\infty} A_{\sigma,\tau}^k)\mathbf{c}(\mathbf{t}))_X$. This implies that $\mathbf{q}_{\mathbf{t},X}^{*,\sigma,\tau}$ is a linear function of $\mathbf{t} \in [0,\infty]^n$ and can be represented as $\mathbf{q}_{\mathbf{t},X}^{*,\sigma,\tau} = \alpha^{X,\tau}\mathbf{t} + \beta^{X,\tau}$, where $\alpha^{X,\tau} = (\alpha_1^{X,\tau}, \alpha_2^{X,\tau}, \ldots, \alpha_n^{X,\tau})$ for some $\alpha_1^{X,\tau}, \ldots, \alpha_n^{X,\tau}, \beta^{X,\tau} \in [0,\infty]$.

For any $\tau \in \Psi_2^{\text{DSM}}$, $\mathbf{b} = (b_1, \ldots, b_n) \in \Sigma^{\Gamma_{\neq}}$ and $\mathbf{t} \geq -\mathbf{r}$, let $\mathbf{g}_{\mathbf{b}}^{\tau}(\mathbf{t}) \in [0,\infty]^{\Gamma_{\neq}}$ be a vector such that

$$\mathbf{g}_{\mathbf{b}}^{\tau}(\mathbf{t})_{X_i} \overset{\text{def}}{=} \sum_{a\in\Sigma} \sigma'(a|X_i)\mathbf{q}_{\mathbf{t}+\mathbf{r},X_i(a,b_i)}^{*,\sigma,\tau} = \sum_{a\in\Sigma} \sigma'(a|X_i)(\alpha^{X_i(a,b_i),\tau}(\mathbf{t}+\mathbf{r}) + \beta^{X_i(a,b_i),\tau})$$

$$= \sum_{a} \sigma'(a|X_i)\alpha^{X_i(a,b_i),\tau} \cdot \mathbf{t} + \sum_{a} \sigma'(a|X_i)(\alpha^{X_i(a,b_i),\tau}\mathbf{r} + \beta^{X_i(a,b_i),\tau})$$

We can write the last expression as $\gamma_{\mathbf{b}}^{X_i,\tau}\mathbf{t} + d_{\mathbf{b}}^{X_i,\tau}$, for some $\gamma_{\mathbf{b}}^{X_i,\tau} \in [0,\infty]^n$, $d_{\mathbf{b}}^{X_i,\tau} \in [0,\infty]$. Note that if $d_{\mathbf{b}}^{X_i,\tau} = 0$ then for all $a \in \Sigma$ such that $\sigma'(a|X_i) > 0$ it has to be $\beta_{\mathbf{b}}^{X_i,\tau} = 0$ and $\boldsymbol{\alpha}_{\mathbf{b}}^{X_i(a,b),\tau} = \mathbf{0}$, because $r(X_i) > 0$ for all i; which also implies $\gamma_{\mathbf{b}}^{X_i,\tau} = 0$. We can now represent $\mathbf{g}^\tau(\mathbf{t})_{\mathbf{b}}$ as $D_{\mathbf{b}}^\tau \mathbf{t} + \mathbf{d}_{\mathbf{b}}^\tau$, where $D_{\mathbf{b}}^\tau$ is the matrix $[\gamma_{\mathbf{b}}^{X_1,\tau}; \gamma_{\mathbf{b}}^{X_2,\tau}; \ldots; \gamma_{\mathbf{b}}^{X_n,\tau}]$ with its X_i-th row equal to $\gamma_{\mathbf{b}}^{X_i,\tau}$ and $\mathbf{d}_{\mathbf{b}}^\tau \in [0,\infty]^{\Gamma_{\neq}}$ consists of all $d_{\mathbf{b}}^{X_i,\tau}$-s. As just shown, the X_i-th row of $D_{\mathbf{b}}^\tau$ consists of only zeroes if $(\mathbf{d}_{\mathbf{b}}^\tau)_{X_i} = 0$.

Now consider the function $\mathbf{f}(\mathbf{t}) = \min_{\mathbf{b}\in\Sigma^{\Gamma_{\neq}}} \min_{\tau\in\Psi_2^{\mathrm{DSM}}} \mathbf{g}_{\mathbf{b}}^\tau(\mathbf{t})$, where the minimum is only over deterministic S&M strategies of player 2. This function is well-defined, because for $\mathcal{G}^\sigma(\mathbf{t}+\mathbf{r})$ where strategy of player 1 is fixed to S&M strategy σ, it follows from Corollary 6 that not only player 2 has a S&M strategy τ^* optimal against σ for every initial state, but also a deterministic one $\tau^* \in \Psi_2^{\mathrm{DSM}}$. In other words, for any other $\tau \in \Psi_2$ we have $\mathbf{q}_{\mathbf{t}+\mathbf{r}}^{*,\sigma,\tau} \geq \mathbf{q}_{\mathbf{t}+\mathbf{r}}^{*,\sigma,\tau^*}$, and so also for any $b \in \Sigma_2(X_i)$ we have $\sum_{a\in\Sigma} \sigma'(a|X_i)\mathbf{q}_{\mathbf{t}+\mathbf{r},X_i(a,b)}^{*,\sigma,\tau} \geq \sum_{a\in\Sigma} \sigma'(a|X_i)\mathbf{q}_{\mathbf{t}+\mathbf{r},X_i(a,b)}^{*,\sigma,\tau^*}$. Finally, notice that the value of $\mathbf{g}_{\mathbf{b}}^\tau(\mathbf{t})_{X_i}$ depends only on b_i, so it suffices for each X_i to find an action $b_i \in \Sigma_2(X_i)$ for which $\mathbf{g}_{\mathbf{b}}^\tau(b_i)_{X_i}$ is minimal. (In fact it suffices to set $b_i = \tau^*(X_i)$).

Lemma 10. *If* $\mathbf{f}(\mathbf{t}) \geq \mathbf{t}$ *for some finite vector* $\mathbf{t}$, *then for any fixed point* $\mathbf{t}^*$ *of* $\mathbf{f}$, $\mathbf{t}^* \geq \mathbf{t}$.

Now notice that for every $X_i \in \Gamma_{\neq}$ we have

$$\mathbf{f}(\mathbf{r}^*-\mathbf{r})_{X_i} = (\min_{\mathbf{b}} \min_{\tau\in\Psi_2^{\mathrm{DSM}}} \mathbf{g}_{\mathbf{b}}^\tau(\mathbf{r}^*-\mathbf{r}))_{X_i} = \min_{\mathbf{b}} \sum_{a\in\Sigma} \sigma'(a|X_i) \min_{\tau\in\Psi_2^{\mathrm{DSM}}} \mathbf{q}_{\mathbf{r}^*,X_i(a,b_i)}^{*,\sigma,\tau}$$

$$= \min_{b_i\in\Sigma} \sum_{a\in\Sigma} \sigma'(a|X_i)\mathbf{q}_{\mathbf{r}^*,X_i(a,b_i)}^{*,\sigma} = \min_{b_i\in\Sigma} \sum_{a\in\Sigma} \sigma'(a|X_i)\mathbf{q}_{X_i(a,b_i)}^{*,\sigma}$$

$$\geq^{(1)} Val(A_{X_i}(\mathbf{q}^{*,\sigma})) > \mathbf{q}_{X_i}^{*,\sigma} - r(X_i) = (\mathbf{r}^*-\mathbf{r})_{X_i}$$

where inequality (1) holds because σ' is an optimal strategy against any strategy of player 2, including the one which picks action b_i with probability 1 as here, in the one-shot game with payoff matrix $A_{X_i}(\mathbf{q}^{*,\sigma})$. Therefore, by Lemma 10, any fixed point of $\mathbf{f}$ has to be greater or equal to $\mathbf{r}^* - \mathbf{r}$. On the other hand

$$\mathbf{f}(\mathbf{r}'-\mathbf{r})_{X_i} = (\min_{\mathbf{b}} \min_{\tau\in\Psi_2^{\mathrm{DSM}}} \mathbf{g}_{\mathbf{b}}^\tau(\mathbf{r}'-\mathbf{r}))_{X_i} = \min_{\mathbf{b}} \sum_{a\in\Sigma} \sigma'(a|X_i)\min_\tau \mathbf{q}_{\mathbf{r}',X_i(a,b_i)}^{*,\sigma,\tau}$$

$$=^{(2)} \min_{\mathbf{b}} \sum_{a\in\Sigma} \sigma'(a|X_i)\mathbf{q}_{\mathbf{r}',X_i(a,b_i)}^{*,\sigma'} = \min_{\mathbf{b}} \sum_{a\in\Sigma} \sigma'(a|X_i)\mathbf{q}_{X_i(a,b_i)}^{*,\sigma'}$$

$$=^{(3)} \min_{\tau\in\Psi_2^{\mathrm{DSM}}} \sum_{(a,b)} \sigma'(a|X_i)\tau(b|X_i)\mathbf{q}_{X_i(a,b)}^{*,\sigma',\tau} = \mathbf{q}_{X_i}^{*,\sigma'} - r(X_i) = (\mathbf{r}'-\mathbf{r})_{X_i}$$

where (2) holds, because $\mathbf{q}_{X,\mathbf{t}}^{*,\sigma} = \mathbf{q}_{X,\mathbf{t}}^{*,\sigma'}$ and (3) holds, because there is an DS&M strategy, τ^*, optimal against σ' in $\mathcal{G}$ and we can map it to an optimal $\mathbf{b}$ by setting $b_i := \tau^*(X_i)$ for all i. Therefore we showed that $\mathbf{r}' - \mathbf{r} \geq \mathbf{r}^* - \mathbf{r}$, i.e. $\mathbf{q}_{X_i}^{*,\sigma'} \geq \mathbf{q}_{X_i}^{*,\sigma}$ for all $X_i \in \Gamma_{\neq}$. On the other hand, for all $X \in \Gamma$ we now have $\mathbf{q}_X^{*,\sigma'} = \mathbf{q}_{\mathbf{r}',X}^{*,\sigma'} \geq \mathbf{q}_{\mathbf{r}^*,X}^{*,\sigma} = \mathbf{q}_{\mathbf{r}^*,X}^{*,\sigma} = \mathbf{q}_X^{*,\sigma}$ so switching to σ' does not decrease player 1's expected payoff for any initial stack symbol. At the same time

$$\mathbf{q}_{X_i}^{*,\sigma} - r(X_i) < Val(A_{X_i}(\mathbf{q}^{*,\sigma})) = \min_{\tau\in\Psi_2^{\mathrm{DSM}}} \sum_{a,b} \sigma'(a|X_i)\tau(b|X_i)\mathbf{q}_{X_i(a,b)}^{*,\sigma}$$

$$\leq \min_{\tau \in \Psi_2^{\mathrm{DSM}}} \sum_{a,b} \sigma'(a|X_i)\tau(b|X_i)\mathbf{q}_{X_i(a,b)}^{*,\sigma'} \leq^{(4)} \min_{\tau \in \Psi_2^{\mathrm{DSM}}} \sum_{a,b} \sigma'(a|X_i)\tau(b|X_i)\mathbf{q}_{X_i(a,b)}^{*,\sigma',\tau}$$

$$= \min_{\tau \in \Psi_2^{\mathrm{DSM}}} \mathbf{q}_{X_i}^{*,\sigma',\tau} - r(X_i) = \mathbf{q}_{X_i}^{*,\sigma'} - r(X_i)$$

where (4) holds because for a fixed τ the value of $\mathbf{q}_{X_i(a,b)}^{*,\sigma',\tau}$ is higher than the minimum over all possible τ. This means that σ' is strictly better than σ for all $X_i \in \Gamma_{\neq}$. Notice that we essentially just showed that for all $X \in \Gamma_{\neq}$ we have $Val(A_X(\mathbf{q}^{*,\sigma})) + r(X) \leq \mathbf{q}_X^{*,\sigma'}$, which can be generalised to all $X \in \Gamma$. Therefore starting at any player 1's S&M strategy $\sigma_0 \in \Psi_1$, we can generate a sequence $\sigma_1, \sigma_2, \ldots$ of S&M strategies with monotonic game values, i.e. $\mathbf{q}^{*,k} \leq \mathbf{q}^{*,k+1}$ for all k, which converges to $\mathbf{q}^*$ at least as fast as the sequence $\mathbf{x}^k := P^k(\mathbf{0})$, i.e. $\mathbf{x}^k \leq \mathbf{q}^{*,\sigma_k}$ for all k. The sequence $\mathbf{q}^{*,\sigma_k}$ converges to $\mathbf{q}^*$, because $\lim_{k\to\infty} \mathbf{x}^k = \mathbf{q}^*$ and clearly $\mathbf{q}^{*,\sigma} \leq \mathbf{q}^*$ for any $\sigma \in \Psi_1$. Now, for any $\varepsilon > 0$ and $X \in \Gamma$ there has to exist some $k(X) > 0$ such that $\mathbf{x}_X^{k(x)} \geq 1/\varepsilon$ if $\mathbf{q}_X^* = \infty$ and $\left|\mathbf{x}_X^{k(X)} - \mathbf{q}_X^*\right| \leq \varepsilon$ if $\mathbf{q}_X^* \neq \infty$. It follows that after $k = \max_{X \in \Gamma} k(X)$ iterations of the strategy improvement we get an S&M strategy σ_k for player 1 which is ε-optimal. This concludes the proof that for any $\varepsilon > 0$ player 1 has an ε-optimal S&M strategy and BPA games are S&M determined.   □

Although we do not provide any bound on the number of steps of the strategy improvement in order to compute an ε-optimal strategy, it is still more likely to compute the value of the game faster in practise than the PSPACE decision procedure given in Section 4. This is because the constants defining the running time of the PSPACE algorithm for deciding the existential theory of the reals are really large. Recently a class of examples was given in [18] of finite-state concurrent games with a reachability objective which shows that the strategy improvement may require doubly exponential number of steps in order to compute the game value with one bit of precision and the usual representation of the strategy which achieves that value requires an exponential number of bits. These examples do not transfer into our total accumulated positive reward model, because the total accumulated reward of all the states in these example games is ∞. In fact, we conjecture that the biggest possible total payoff in our games apart from value ∞ is exponential in the size of the game and so can be represented using polynomial number of bits. This would also imply a PSPACE algorithm for approximating their values using the decision procedure from Section 4.

Acknowledgments. We would like to thank the anonymous reviewers whose comments helped to improve this paper.

References

1. Allender, E., Bürgisser, P., Kjeldgaard-Pedersen, J., Miltersen, P.B.: On the complexity of numerical analysis. SIAM Journal on Computing 38(5), 1987–2006 (2009)
2. Brázdil, T., Brožek, V., Kučera, A., Obdržálek, J.: Qualitative reachability in stochastic BPA games. Information and Computation 209(8), 1160–1183 (2011)

3. Brázdil, T., Kučera, A., Novotný, P., Wojtczak, D.: Minimizing expected termination time in one-counter Markov decision processes. In: Czumaj, A., Mehlhorn, K., Pitts, A., Wattenhofer, R. (eds.) ICALP 2012, Part II. LNCS, vol. 7392, pp. 141–152. Springer, Heidelberg (2012)
4. Condon, A.: The complexity of stochastic games. Inf. & Comp. 96(2), 203–224 (1992)
5. de Alfaro, L., Henzinger, T.A.: Concurrent omega-regular games. In: Proc. of the 15th IEEE Symposium on Logic in Computer Science, pp. 141–154. IEEE Computer Society Press (2000)
6. de Alfaro, L., Henzinger, T.A., Kupferman, O.: Concurrent reachability games. In: Proc. of FOCS 1998, pp. 564–575 (1998)
7. de Alfaro, L., Majumdar, R.: Quantitative solution of omega-regular games. J. Comput. Syst. Sci. 68(2), 374–397 (2004)
8. Esparza, J., Kučera, A., Mayr, R.: Model checking probabilistic pushdown automata. In: Proc. of 19th IEEE LICS 2004 (2004)
9. Etessami, K., Wojtczak, D., Yannakakis, M.: Recursive stochastic games with positive rewards. In: Aceto, L., Damgård, I., Goldberg, L.A., Halldórsson, M.M., Ingólfsdóttir, A., Walukiewicz, I. (eds.) ICALP 2008, Part I. LNCS, vol. 5125, pp. 711–723. Springer, Heidelberg (2008)
10. Etessami, K., Yannakakis, M.: Algorithmic verification of recursive probabilistic state machines. In: Halbwachs, N., Zuck, L.D. (eds.) TACAS 2005. LNCS, vol. 3440, pp. 253–270. Springer, Heidelberg (2005)
11. Etessami, K., Yannakakis, M.: Recursive Markov chains, stochastic grammars, and monotone systems of non-linear equations. In: Diekert, V., Durand, B. (eds.) STACS 2005. LNCS, vol. 3404, pp. 340–352. Springer, Heidelberg (2005)
12. Etessami, K., Yannakakis, M.: Recursive Markov decision processes and recursive stochastic games. In: Caires, L., Italiano, G.F., Monteiro, L., Palamidessi, C., Yung, M. (eds.) ICALP 2005. LNCS, vol. 3580, pp. 891–903. Springer, Heidelberg (2005)
13. Etessami, K., Yannakakis, M.: Efficient qualitative analysis of classes of recursive Markov decision processes and simple stochastic games. In: Durand, B., Thomas, W. (eds.) STACS 2006. LNCS, vol. 3884, pp. 634–645. Springer, Heidelberg (2006)
14. Etessami, K., Yannakakis, M.: Recursive concurrent stochastic games. Logical Methods in Computer Science 4(4) (2008)
15. Etessami, K., Yannakakis, M.: On the complexity of Nash equilibria and other fixed points. SIAM Journal on Computing 39(6), 2531–2597 (2010)
16. Filar, J., Vrieze, K.: Competitive Markov Decision Processes. Springer (1997)
17. Garey, M.R., Graham, R.L., Johnson, D.S.: Some NP-complete geometric problems. In: Proc. of the 8th ACM Symposium on Theory of Computing, STOC 1976, pp. 10–22 (1976)
18. Hansen, K.A., Ibsen-Jensen, R., Miltersen, P.B.: The complexity of solving reachability games using value and strategy iteration. In: Kulikov, A., Vereshchagin, N. (eds.) CSR 2011. LNCS, vol. 6651, pp. 77–90. Springer, Heidelberg (2011)
19. Hoffman, A.J., Karp, R.M.: On nonterminating stochastic games. Management Sci. 12, 359–370 (1966)
20. Manning, C.D., Schütze, H.: Foundations of statistical natural language processing. MIT Press (1999)
21. Martin, D.A.: The Determinacy of Blackwell Games. J. Symb. Logic 63(4), 1565–1581 (1998)
22. Nerode, A., Yakhnis, A., Yakhnis, V.: Concurrent programs as strategies in games. In: Logic from Computer Science. Mathematical Sciences Research Institute Publications, vol. 21, pp. 405–479. Springer, New York (1992)
23. Osborne, M.J., Rubinstein, A.: Course in game theory. MIT Press (1994)

24. Pliska, S.R.: Optimization of multitype branching processes. Management Science 23(2), 117–124 (1976)
25. Pnueli, A., Rosner, R.: On the synthesis of a reactive module. In: Proc. of the 16th Symposium on Principles of Programming Languages, pp. 179–190. ACM (1989)
26. Rothblum, U.G., Whittle, P.: Growth optimality for branching Markov decision chains. Mathematics of Operations Research 7(4), 582–601 (1982)
27. Shapley, L.S.: Stochastic games. Proc. Nat. Acad. Sci. 39, 1095–1100 (1953)
28. Wojtczak, D.: Expected termination time in BPA games. Technical Report ULCS-13-005, University of Liverpool (2013), http://www.csc.liv.ac.uk/research/techreports

Precise Cost Analysis via Local Reasoning

Diego Esteban Alonso-Blas, Puri Arenas, and Samir Genaim

DSIC, Complutense University of Madrid (UCM), Spain

Abstract. The classical approach to static cost analysis is based on first transforming a given program into a set of cost relations, and then solving them into closed-form upper-bounds. The quality of the upper-bounds and the scalability of such cost analysis highly depend on the precision and efficiency of the solving phase. Several techniques for solving cost relations exist, some are efficient but not precise enough, and some are very precise but do not scale to large cost relations. In this paper we explore the gap between these techniques, seeking for ones that are both precise and efficient. In particular, we propose a novel technique that first splits the cost relation into several *atomic* ones, and then uses precise local reasoning for some and less precise but efficient reasoning for others. For the precise local reasoning, we propose several methods that define the cost as a solution of a universally quantified formula. Preliminary experiments demonstrate the effectiveness of our approach.

1 Introduction

Static Cost analysis (a.k.a. resource usage analysis) aims at *statically* determining the amount of resources (e.g., memory, execution steps, etc.) required to execute a given program safely, i.e., without running out of resources. Applications of cost analysis range from detecting performance bottlenecks at the development stage, to providing resource consumption guarantees at runtime.

Several cost analysis frameworks exist [4,13,15,10]. Although different in their underlying techniques, they all report the cost as a closed-form upper-bound function (*UB* for short) in terms of the input parameters. This paper uses the classical approach of Wegbreit [18], in particular its extension for JAVA bytecode [4], where the analysis is carried out in two phases: (1) the input program is transformed into a set of *cost relations* (*CRs* for short) that define its cost; and (2) the *CRs* are solved into *UBs*. While the first phase depends on the programming language in which the program is written [4,11,12,9,17], the second phase is common to all analyses that are based on this approach. In this paper *we focus on the second phase*, i.e., on developing techniques for solving *CRs*. However, we provide enough details to clarify how *CRs* are related to programs.

Example 1. The JAVA class depicted in Fig. 1 implements a dynamic array, where field data is used to store its elements, and field size represents the number of such elements. Method add adds the elements of the array elems to the dynamic array. When the array data is full (L6), it is replaced by a new one of double

D. Van Hung and M. Ogawa (Eds.): ATVA 2013, LNCS 8172, pp. 319–333, 2013.

```
 1 class DynamicArray {                        15   int r;
 2   int[ ] data;                              16   void qsort() {
 3   int size;                                 17     qs(0, size−1);
 4   void add(int[ ] elems) {                  18   }
 5     for (int i=0; i<elems.length; i++) {    19   void qs(int from, int to) {
 6       if (data.length == size) {            20     if (to − from < r)
 7         int[ ] tmp = new int[2*data.length];21       insertionSort(from,to);
 8         copy(tmp,size,data);                22     else {
 9         data = tmp;                         23       int m=partition(from,to);
10       }                                     24       qs(from,m−1);
11       data[size] = elems[i];                25       qs(m+1,to);
12       size++;                               26     }
13     }                                       27   }
14   }                                         28 }
```

$add(e,d,s) = for(e,d,s,i)$	$\varphi_0=\{e\geq0, d\geq0, s\geq0, i=0\}$
$for(e,d,s,i) = 0$	$\varphi_1=\{i\geq e\}$
$for(e,d,s,i) = 2\cdot nat(s) + 2 + for(e,d',s',i')$	$\varphi_2=\{i<e, s=d, d'=2\cdot d, s'=s+1, i'=i+1\}$
$for(e,d,s,i) = 2 + for(e,d,s',i')$	$\varphi_3=\{i<e, d>s, s'=s+1, i'=i+1\}$

$qsort(s,r) = qs(f,t,r)$	$\psi_0 = \{s\geq0, f=0, t=s-1\}$
$qs(f,t,r) = nat(t-f)^2$	$\psi_1 = \{t-f<r, r\geq0\}$
$qs(f,t,r) = nat(t-f) + qs(f,m',r)+$	$\psi_2 = \{t-f\geq r, r\geq0, f\leq m\leq t,$
$\quad qs(m'',t,r)$	$\quad m'=m-1, m''=m+1\}$

Fig. 1. Above, JAVA code of a DynamicArray class. Below, the CRs of the methods

size (L7-9). Methods qsort and qs sort the array using a variation of *Quick Sort*, which resorts to *Insertion Sort* when the segment to be sorted is shorter than a threshold defined by field r. Methods copy, partition, and insertionSort are omitted.

Below the JAVA code we show the corresponding *CRs*, generated using a cost model that counts array accesses. Let us explain the *CR* of method add. Variables e, d, s, and i stand for the lengths of arrays elems and data and the values of size and i. Expression $nat(e)$ is an abbreviation for $\max\{e, 0\}$. The first equation states that the cost of $add(e, d, s)$ is as that of $for(e, d, s, i)$. The constraints on the right impose conditions and relations on the variables. The second equation is for the case of exiting the loop ($i \geq e$). The third one is for the case in which the array is resized. In such case the cost is $2\cdot nat(s)$ (the cost assumed for copy), plus 2 (the accesses at L11), plus the cost of the remaining iterations $for(e, d', s', i')$. Note that $d'=2\cdot d$ states that the size of array data is doubled. The fourth equation describes the case in which the array is not resized. The equations of qsort are defined similarly. We note that $nat(t-f)^2$ and $nat(t-f)$ correspond to the cost of insertionSort and partition respectively. The constraint $f\leq m\leq t$ in ψ_2 is an input-output summary inferred for the value m returned by method partition. Methods add and qsort, respectively, have linear and quadratic worst-case complexity.   □

Early works on cost analysis [11,9] relied on Computer Algebra Systems (CAS) for solving *CRs*. They can only handle cases in which the *CRs* can be transformed into *recurrence equations* (the only valid input for CAS). This, however, is a very limited subset because *CRs* allow using constraints to define complex applicability conditions and relations between the variables. To overcome this limitation, recent works [3,6] have developed dedicated tools for solving *CRs* into *UBs*. They are mostly based on the use of program analysis techniques. These works are our starting point.

The techniques of [3] are based on assuming worst-case behaviour for all loop iterations. It is very efficient and can handle a wide class of *CRs*. To solve the *CR for*, this technique infers that $2+2\cdot\mathsf{nat}(e+s-1)$ is an *UB* on the cost of any iteration of *for*, and it infers that there is at most $\mathsf{nat}(e-i)$ iterations of *for*, from which it concludes that $\mathsf{nat}(e-i)\cdot(2+2\cdot\mathsf{nat}(e+s-1))$ is an *UB* for *CR for*. Note that this is a quadratic *UB* while the actual cost is linear. In the case of qsort, the loss of precision is even bigger. It first infers that $\mathsf{nat}(t-f)^2$ is an *UB* on the cost of each call to qs, and that there are at most $2^{\mathsf{nat}(t-f)}$ of such calls. Then, it concludes that $(t-f)^2\cdot2^{\mathsf{nat}(t-f)}$ is an *UB* for *CR qs*, while the actual cost is quadratic.

The above imprecision issue, among others, was addressed in [6] where precise and novel techniques for solving *CRs* were proposed. They are based on defining the cost as a solution of a corresponding first-order universally quantified formula. This method, as expected, would obtain the most precise *UBs* for the *CRs for* and *qs*, however, it has two major limitations: (1) a template *UB* has to be provided by the user; and (2) the use of a quantifier elimination procedure for real numbers renders the technique impractical.

In this paper we explore the gap between [3] and [6], seeking for solving techniques with efficiency close to [3] and precision close to [6]. Concretely, we develop a novel technique that breaks down the input *CR* into *atomic CRs* of simpler form, solves each of them separately, and then combines the results into an *UB* for the original *CR*. Our main observation is that it is enough to solve few atomic *CRs* precisely, while solving the others as in [3], without affecting the overall precision. We also propose several methods for precisely solving atomic *CRs*, which are based on the idea of specifying the cost using universally quantified formulas as in [6]. However, we do not require the user to provide any template, and, importantly, the generated formulas have almost a linear form for which quantifier elimination can be done efficiently. Our prototype implementation and experiments [1] demonstrate the effectiveness of this approach.

This paper is organised as follows. Sec. 2 provides the required background on *CRs*. Sec. 3 is the technical core of the paper. Sec. 4 describes a prototype implementation and preliminary experiments. Finally, in Sec. 5 we conclude and discuss related work.

2 Cost Relations: Syntax and Semantics

In this section we recall some basic notions related to *CRs* [3]. The sets of real, rational, and integer values are denoted by $\mathbb{R}$, $\mathbb{Q}$, and $\mathbb{Z}$, respectively. $\mathbb{R}^+$, $\mathbb{Q}^+$, and $\mathbb{Z}^+$ denote their non-negative subsets. Variables are denoted by x, y, z, and

w, possibly subscripted. Values from $\mathbb{R}$, $\mathbb{Q}$, and $\mathbb{Z}$ are denoted, respectively, by r, q, and v. A sequence of elements of type t is denoted by $\bar{t}$. The set of variables of t is denoted by $vars(t)$. An assignment $\sigma : \mathcal{V} \mapsto \mathcal{D}$ maps variables from $\mathcal{V}$ to values from $\mathcal{D}$ and $\sigma(\bar{t})$ denotes the replacement of any $x \in vars(\bar{t})$ by $\sigma(x)$.

A *linear expression* has the form $q_0+q_1 \cdot x_1+\cdots+q_n \cdot x_n$. A *linear constraint* has the form $l_1 \le l_2$, $l_1 = l_2$, or $l_1 \ge l_2$, where l_1 and l_2 are linear expressions and $vars(l_1) \cup vars(l_2) \subseteq \mathbb{Z}$. The constraints $l_1 > l_2$ and $l_1 < l_2$ abbreviate $l_1 \ge l_2+1$ and $l_1+1 \le l_2$, respectively. We use φ, ϕ, and ψ, possibly subscripted, to denote conjunctions (often written as sets) of linear constraints. We say that φ is *satisfiable* if there is an assignment σ for $vars(\varphi)$ such that $\sigma(\varphi)$ is true, denoted as $\sigma \models \varphi$. If $\sigma \models \varphi$ for every assignment σ for $vars(\varphi)$ then φ is a *valid* formula.

Definition 1 (cost expression). *A* cost expression e *is defined as:*

$$e ::= q \mid \mathsf{nat}(l) \mid \log_a(1+\mathsf{nat}(l)) \mid a^{\mathsf{nat}(l)}-1 \mid e+e \mid e \cdot e$$

where $q \in \mathbb{Q}^+$, $\mathsf{nat}(l) = \max\{l, 0\}$, $a > 1 \in \mathbb{Z}^+$, *and* l *is a linear expression.*

Note that we use $a^{\mathsf{nat}(l)}-1$, instead of simply $a^{\mathsf{nat}(l)}$, for the sake of simplifying the formal presentation (we explain this after Lemma 3).

Definition 2 (cost relation). *A* cost relation *is a set of* cost equations *of the form* $\langle C(\bar{x}) = e + \sum_{j=1}^{k} D_j(\bar{y}_j), \varphi \rangle$, *where* C *and* D_j *are cost relation symbols.*

Intuitively, a cost equation $\langle C(\bar{x}) = e+\sum_{j=1}^{k} D_j(\bar{y}_j), \varphi \rangle$ states that the cost of $C(\bar{x})$ is e plus the sum of the costs of $D_1(\bar{y}_1), \ldots, D_k(\bar{y}_k)$. The linear constraint φ specifies the values of $\bar{x}$ for which the equation is applicable, and defines relations among the different variables. Since *CRs* usually originate from programs, it is often helpful to think of each *CR* symbol as a (non-deterministic) procedure, in which case we say that C calls $D_1, \ldots, D_k$.

Without loss of generality, in what follows we assume that the input *CR* includes a single *CR* symbol. Namely, in Def. 2 we have $D_j = C$. We call such *CRs stand-alone*. To handle *CRs* with more than one *CR* symbol, we rely on the compositional approach of [3] which we briefly explain next. In a first step, the input *CR* is transformed into a form in which all recursions are direct, i.e. an equation that defines C can either call itself directly, or other *CR* symbols that do not call C (directly or indirectly). In a second step, the *CRs* are solved iteratively, where in each iteration we solve those that do not depend on any other symbols (there must be at least one), and then substitute the result in the calling contexts. In the rest of the paper *CR* refers to a stand-alone *CR*.

To define the cost assigned by C to a concrete input $\bar{v}$, we use evaluation trees. A (possibly infinite) tree will be denoted by $node(r, \langle T_1, \ldots, T_k \rangle)$, where $r \in \mathbb{R}^+$ is the value of the root and $T_1, \ldots, T_k$ are sub-trees.

Definition 3 (evaluation tree). *Given a* CR C *and an input* $\bar{v}$, *we say that* $node(r, \langle T_1, \ldots, T_k \rangle)$ *is an evaluation tree for* $C(\bar{v})$ *iff there exists an equation* $\mathcal{E} \equiv \langle C(\bar{x}) = e+\sum_{j=1}^{k} C(\bar{y}_j), \varphi \rangle$ *and* $\sigma : vars(\mathcal{E}) \mapsto \mathbb{Z}$ *such that: (1)* $\sigma(x_i)=v_i$ *and* $\sigma \models \varphi$; *(2)* $r = \sigma(e)$; *and (3) each* T_i *is an evaluation tree for* $C(\sigma(\bar{y}_i))$.

Intuitively, when viewing C as a procedure, an evaluation tree can be seen as a *recursion tree* where the call $C(\bar{v})$ is evaluated as follows: we pick an equation that defines C and an assignment σ that satisfies the equation's constraints; we evaluate $\sigma(e)$ into r, and we recursively call each $C(\sigma(\bar{y}_i))$. Note that an evaluation tree can be infinite. Note also that $C(\bar{v})$ might have several evaluation trees, due to the nondeterminism induced by choosing an equation for C and a satisfying assignment σ for φ. The set of all evaluation trees for $C(\bar{v})$ is denoted by $Trees(C(\bar{v}))$. The set of all possible costs for $C(\bar{v})$ is then defined as $Answers(C(\bar{v}))=\{\mathsf{Sum}(T) \mid T \in Trees(C(\bar{v}))\}$, where $\mathsf{Sum}(T)$ is the sum of all nodes of T. Our interest is to approximate *CRs* by mean of closed-form *UBs* functions, i.e., functions of the form $f(\bar{x})=e$, where $vars(e) \subseteq \bar{x}$.

Definition 4 (upper bound). *A function $C^+ : \mathbb{Z}^n \mapsto \mathbb{R}^+$ is an UB for a CR C, iff for any input $\bar{v} \in \mathbb{Z}^n$ and cost $r \in Answers(C(\bar{v}))$ we have $C^+(\bar{v}) \geq r$.*

Next we overview the approach of [3] for solving a *CR* into an *UB*. Suppose we have two functions $h(\bar{x})=e_1$ and $g(\bar{x})=e_2$, where e_1 and e_2 are cost expressions, such that for any $T \in Trees(C(\bar{v}))$ the following holds (i) $h(\bar{v})$ is an *UB* on the depth of T; and (ii) $g(\bar{v})$ is an *UB* on the value of any node of T. Now assuming that d is the maximum number of recursive calls in any equation of C, i.e., the maximum branching factor of its evaluation trees, then $C^+(\bar{x})=g(\bar{x})\cdot\mathcal{N}$ where $\mathcal{N}=h(\bar{x})$ if $d = 1$, and $\mathcal{N}=d^{h(\bar{x})}$ if $d>1$. Technically, in [3], $h(\bar{x})$ is computed by inferring a linear *ranking function* [8] that bounds the recursion depth of C, and $g(\bar{x})$ is computed by relying on *linear invariants*.

Example 2. Consider the *CR* for in Fig. 1. The technique of [3] infers $h(e,d,s,i) = \mathsf{nat}(e-i)$ and $g(e,d,s,i) = 2+2\cdot\mathsf{nat}(e+s-1)$. Then, since the branching factor is $d=1$, it reports the *UB* $for^+(e,d,s,i)=\mathsf{nat}(e-i)\cdot(2+2\cdot\mathsf{nat}(e+s-1))$. For *CR* qs, it infers $h(f,t,r)=\mathsf{nat}(t-f)$ and $g(f,t,r)=\mathsf{nat}(t-f)^2$. Then, since the branching factor is $d=2$, it reports the *UB* $qs^+(f,t,r)=\mathsf{nat}(t-f)^2\cdot 2^{\mathsf{nat}(t-f)}$. $\square$

Maximisation procedure. We rely on the technique of [3] that generates $g(\bar{x})$ as we explain next. Let e be the cost expression that is contributed by an equation of C, and let b be a cost sub-expression of e. As explained in Def. 3, when generating the nodes of an evaluation tree $T \in Trees(C(\bar{v}))$, we evaluate $\sigma(e)$ to r. This evaluation requires computing $\sigma(b)$. We call $\sigma(b)$ an instance of b. We reuse the techniques of [3] to infer a cost expression $\hat{b}(\bar{x})$ that satisfies the following: for any input $\bar{v}$, $T \in Trees(C(\bar{v}))$ and any instance $\sigma(b)$ of b in T, we have $\hat{b}(\bar{v}) \geq \sigma(b)$. Intuitively, $\hat{b}(\bar{x})$ is a function that bounds each contribution of b to the total cost. We call $\hat{b}(\bar{x})$ the *maximisation* of b, and, in our implementation, we compute it reusing the components of [3].

3   Solving Cost Relations in Closed-Form Upper-Bounds

In this section we present our approach for solving a *CR* C into an *UB*. We assume that C is defined by m equations of the form $\langle C(\bar{x}) = e_i+\sum_{j=1}^{k_i} C(\bar{y}_{ij}), \varphi_i\rangle$,

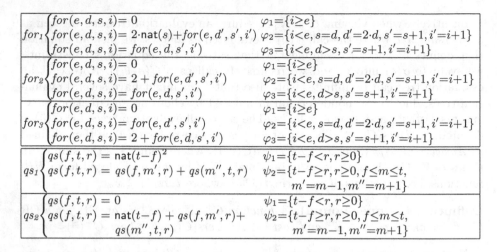

Fig. 2. The sparse *CRs* of *for* and *qs* of Fig. 1

$1 \leq i \leq m$. Our approach is presented in two steps: we reduce the problem of solving C to solving *atomic CRs*, and then we focus on solving atomic *CRs*.

Observe that cost expressions, as in Def. 1, can be normalised into the form $P_1 + \cdots + P_h$, where each P_i is a *product* of cost expressions $b_{i1}, \ldots, b_{ip_i}$ with $b_{ij} \in \{q, \mathsf{nat}(l), \log_a(1+\mathsf{nat}(l)), a^{\mathsf{nat}(l)}-1\}$. For simplicity, since q is non-negative, we assume it is given as $\mathsf{nat}(q)$. We assume that each e_i in C is given in this form. Let $P_C = \{P_1, \ldots, P_t\}$ be the multiset of all non-zero product cost expressions that appear in C (i.e., the products of $e_1, \ldots, e_m$). We define C_i as the *CR* obtained from C by removing all $P_j \in P_C$ with $j \neq i$. Namely, in C_i there is exactly one equation that contributes P_i, the others contribute 0. We call such *CRs sparse* and the equation that includes P_i is called the *main equation*.

Example 3. Consider the *CRs for* and *qs* in Fig. 1. Their products are respectively $P_{for} = \{2 \cdot \mathsf{nat}(s), 2, 2\}$ and $P_{qs} = \{\mathsf{nat}(t-f) \cdot \mathsf{nat}(t-f), \mathsf{nat}(t-f)\}$. Their corresponding sparse *CRs* are depicted in Fig. 2. □

Observation 1 *If $C_i^+(\bar{x})$ is an UB for the sparse CR C_i, for all $1 \leq i \leq t$, then $C^+(\bar{x}) = C_1^+(\bar{x}) + \cdots + C_t^+(\bar{x})$ is an UB for C.*

The above observation explains how an *UB* for C can be obtained from *UBs* for its sparse *CRs* $C_1, \ldots, C_t$. Thus, we can focus on solving sparse *CRs*. We first explain the idea intuitively. Assume that $b_{i1} \cdot b_{i2}$ is the product in the main equation of C_i. Given an arbitrary $T \in \mathit{Trees}(C_i(\bar{v}))$, the cost of each of its nodes is either 0 or an instance of $b_{i1} \cdot b_{i2}$. Let $\sigma_1(b_{i1} \cdot b_{i2}), \ldots, \sigma_h(b_{i1} \cdot b_{i2})$ be the instances of $b_{i1} \cdot b_{i2}$ in $T \in \mathit{Trees}(C_i(\bar{v}))$, then the cost of T is $S = \sum_{j=1}^{h} \sigma_j(b_{i1} \cdot b_{i2})$. As explained in Sec. 2, we can compute a function $\hat{b}_{i1}(\bar{x})$ such that $\hat{b}_{i1}(\bar{v}) \geq \sigma_j(b_{i1})$ for each $1 \leq j \leq h$. Using $\hat{b}_{i1}(\bar{v})$ we bound S as follows:

$$S = \sum_{j=1}^{h} \sigma_j(b_{i1} \cdot b_{i2}) \le \sum_{j=1}^{h} \hat{b}_{i1}(\bar{v}) \cdot \sigma_j(b_{i2}) = \hat{b}_{i1}(\bar{v}) \cdot \sum_{j=1}^{h} \sigma_j(b_{i2})$$

Now assume that we have a function $f^+(\bar{x})$ such that $f^+(\bar{v}) \ge \sum_{j=1}^{h} \sigma_j(b_{i2})$, then $S \le \hat{b}_{i1}(\bar{v}) \cdot f^+(\bar{v})$. Thus, since the above reasoning is done for an arbitrary T, we can conclude that $\hat{b}_{i1}(\bar{x}) \cdot f^+(\bar{x})$ is an UB for C_i. Now to compute $f^+(\bar{x})$, we consider a CR C_{i2} that is obtained from C_i by replacing $b_{i1} \cdot b_{i2}$ by b_{i2}. Clearly, $C_{i2}(\bar{v}) = \sum_{j=1}^{h} \sigma_j(b_{i2})$, and thus any UB for C_{i2} defines a valid $f^+(\bar{x})$. This reduces the problem of solving C_i to that of solving C_{i2}, which is simpler since its main equation includes a basic cost expression. Note that, in a similar way, we could build C_{i1} using $\hat{b}_{i2}(\bar{x})$ and then use it to find an UB for C_i.

Formally, given a sparse CR C_i with a product $b_{i1} \cdots b_{ip_i}$ in its main equation, we define the *atomic CR* C_{ij} as the one obtained from C_i by replacing its product by b_{ij} (i.e., removing all b_{ik} with $k \ne j$).

Example 4. Consider the sparse *CRs* depicted in Fig. 2. The following are possible atomic *CRs* for for_1 and qs_1

for_{12}		qs_{11}	
$for(e,d,s,i)=0$	φ_1	$qs(f,t,r)=\mathsf{nat}(t-f)$	ψ_1
$for(e,d,s,i)=\mathsf{nat}(s)+for(e,d',s',i')$	φ_2	$qs(f,t,r)=qs(f,m',r)+qs(m'',t,r)$	ψ_2
$for(e,d,s,i)=for(e,d,s',i')$	φ_3		

in which $\mathsf{nat}(s)$ and $\mathsf{nat}(t-f)$ are selected as basic cost expressions. *CRs* for_2, for_3 and qs_2 are already atomic. They correspond to for_{21}, for_{31} and qs_{21}. □

Lemma 1. *Let C_i be a sparse CR, $b_{i1} \cdots b_{ip_i}$ the product in its main equation, and C_{ij} an atomic CR of C_i. If $C_{ij}^+(\bar{x})$ is an UB for $C_{ij}(\bar{x})$, then $C_i^+(\bar{x}) = C_{ij}^+(\bar{x}) \cdot \prod_{k \ne j} \hat{b}_{ik}(\bar{x})$ is an UB for C_i.*

The above lemma allows focusing on finding an UB for a single atomic C_{ij} and then combine the result into an UB for C_i. To put this into practice we need to address the following issues: (1) how to select the basic cost expression j from the products in order to build C_{ij}; and (2) how to compute an UB for C_{ij}. In secs. 3.1 and 3.2 we discuss several methods for addressing the second issue. The first issue is discussed later in Sec. 3.4.

Let us first position our approach in the spectrum of related approaches [3,6]. Solving C_i using the techniques of [3] we obtain the UB $(\prod_{k=1}^{p_i} \hat{b}_{ik}(\bar{x})) \cdot \mathcal{N}$. Interestingly, this UB can be explained using our novel view of Lemma 1, which is different from that of [3], as follows: we can consider $\hat{b}_{ij}(\bar{x}) \cdot \mathcal{N}$ as an UB for C_{ij}, and then use it as in Lemma 1 to obtain $(\prod_{k=1}^{p_i} \hat{b}_{ik}(\bar{x})) \cdot \mathcal{N}$. Since, unlike [3], we focus on solving atomic *CRs*, we develop dedicated techniques (i.e., techniques that work only for atomic *CRs*) that are able to obtain an UB far more precise than $\hat{b}_{ij}(\bar{x}) \cdot \mathcal{N}$ (we will usually eliminate the $\mathcal{N}$ factor). Solving C_i using the techniques of [6] requires defining an UB template to be used during the solving process. If C_i does not admit an UB that matches the supplied templates, then this technique will fail. Moreover, using arbitrary templates renders this approach impractical since it is based on the use of quantifier elimination procedure. Our techniques for solving atomic *CRs* are actually inspired by those of [6]. However, since we focus on a simpler form of CRs, we always use linear templates for which the quantifier elimination procedure is efficient. In summary, our approach uses [6] to precisely reason on the *local* cost of a single simple cost expression b_{ij}, and then uses [3] to combine this local cost into an UB for C_i.

To simplify our notation, in what follows, we assume a given atomic CR D with m equations of the form $\langle D(\bar{x}) = e_i + \sum_{j=1}^{k_i} D(\bar{y}_{ij}), \varphi_i \rangle$, where $e_1 = b$ is a basic cost expression, and $e_i = 0$ for all $2 \leq i \leq m$. Note that the main equation of D is the first one. We denote by $\bar{w}_i$ the set of variables in the i-th equation.

3.1 The Tree-Sum Method

We first explain this method for the case in which $b = \mathsf{nat}(l)$, and then we show how to extend it to handle any basic cost expression b. In many cases, in particular in examples that require amortised analysis, the sum of all instances of b in any $T \in Trees(D(\bar{v}))$ can be bounded by a linear expression. Thus, we seek an UB for D of the form $\alpha(\bar{x}) = q_0 + q_1 \cdot x_1 + \cdots + q_n \cdot x_n$, where $q_i \in \mathbb{Q}$. The way we search for $\alpha(\bar{x})$ is based on the use of universally quantified formulas as in [6]. We first define a verification condition which ensures that a given $\alpha(\bar{x})$ is a valid UB for D. Then, using a quantifier elimination procedure, we turn this verification condition into a synthesis procedure that actually infers $\alpha(\bar{x})$.

Lemma 2. *Let* $\alpha(\bar{x}) = q_0 + q_1 \cdot x_1 + \cdots + q_n \cdot x_n$, *and define:*

$$\Psi_1 \triangleq \forall \bar{w}_1 \ : \ \varphi_1 \to \mathsf{nat}(\alpha(\bar{x})) \geq \mathsf{nat}(l) + \sum_{j=1}^{k_1} \mathsf{nat}(\alpha(\bar{y}_{1j}))$$
$$\Psi_2 \triangleq \bigwedge_{i=2}^{m} \forall \bar{w}_i \ : \ \varphi_i \to \mathsf{nat}(\alpha(\bar{x})) \geq \sum_{j=1}^{k_i} \mathsf{nat}(\alpha(\bar{y}_{ij}))$$

If $\Psi_1 \wedge \Psi_2$ *is valid, then* $\mathsf{nat}(\alpha(\bar{x}))$ *is an* UB *for the atomic* CR D.

Intuitively, Ψ_1 requires that $\mathsf{nat}(\alpha(\bar{x}))$ covers the cost of the main equation, i.e., it covers the local cost $\mathsf{nat}(l)$ and the cost of the recursive calls. Similarly, Ψ_2 requires that $\mathsf{nat}(\alpha(\bar{x}))$ covers the cost of the other equations (in this case the local cost is 0). Our main interest is in inferring such $\alpha(\bar{x})$ rather than verifying the correctness of a given one. Turning the verification condition into an inference procedure can be done, using a quantifier elimination procedure, as follows:

1. we generate $\Psi_1 \wedge \Psi_2$ using a *template* function $\alpha(\bar{x})$ in which $q_0, \ldots, q_n$ are variables, i.e., *unknown*;
2. we eliminate the universal quantifiers from $\Psi_1 \wedge \Psi_2$. This results in a set of constraints Θ over the variables $q_0, \ldots, q_n$; and
3. any solution of Θ (i.e., values for $q_0, \ldots, q_n$ that satisfy Θ) defines a valid UB $\mathsf{nat}(\alpha(\bar{x}))$. We simply pick a solution.

Note that if Θ is not satisfiable then there is no $\alpha(\bar{x})$ satisfying $\Psi_1 \wedge \Psi_2$. In such case we say that the Tree-Sum method is not applicable for D. The main subtle point in the above inference procedure is how to eliminate the universal quantifiers, which is computationally expensive in general. However, since the formula $\Psi_1 \wedge \Psi_2$ have a very specific form (almost linear), in Sec. 3.3 we show how this can be done efficiently. For now we just assume the existence of a procedure that implements steps (2) and (3) above.

Example 5. Consider the *CR for*$_{12}$, as defined in Ex. 4, and let $\alpha(e,d,s,i) = q_0+$
$q_1 \cdot e + q_2 \cdot d + q_3 \cdot s + q_4 \cdot i$. The corresponding Ψ_1 and Ψ_2 are:

$$\Psi_1 \triangleq \forall \bar{w}_2 : \varphi_2 \rightarrow \mathsf{nat}(q_0+q_1 \cdot e+q_2 \cdot d+q_3 \cdot s+q_4 \cdot i) \geq \mathsf{nat}(s)+\mathsf{nat}(q_0+q_1 \cdot e+q_2 \cdot d'+q_3 \cdot s'+q_4 \cdot i')$$
$$\Psi_2 \triangleq \forall \bar{w}_3 : \varphi_3 \rightarrow \mathsf{nat}(q_0+q_1 \cdot e+q_2 \cdot d+q_3 \cdot s+q_4 \cdot i) \geq \mathsf{nat}(q_0+q_1 \cdot e+q_2 \cdot d+q_3 \cdot s'+q_4 \cdot i')$$

Solving $\Psi_1 \wedge \Psi_2$, i.e finding values for $q_0, \dots, q_4$, gets $q_0=-2$, $q_1=2$, $q_2=-1$, $q_3=2$,
and $q_4=-2$, which means that $for_{12}^+(e,d,s,i)=\mathsf{nat}(2 \cdot s+2 \cdot e-2 \cdot i-d-2)$ is an *UB*
for *CR for*$_{12}$. Then, to get an *UB* for *CR for*$_1$ we apply Lemma 1 which results in
$for_1^+(e,d,s,i)=2 \cdot \mathsf{nat}(2 \cdot s+2 \cdot e-2 \cdot i-d-2)$. Similarly, generating the formulas for
for_{21} and for_{31} and solving them, we get the *UBs* $for_2^+(e,d,s,i)=\mathsf{nat}(2 \cdot e-2 \cdot i)$
and $for_3^+(e,d,s,i)=\mathsf{nat}(2 \cdot e-2 \cdot i)$. Finally, we can use Obs. 1 to add them in
$for^+(e,d,s,i)=2 \cdot \mathsf{nat}(2 \cdot s+2 \cdot e-2 \cdot i-d-2)+2 \cdot \mathsf{nat}(2 \cdot e-2 \cdot i)$ as *UB* for *for*. Substituting this *UB* in the equation of *add* in Fig. 1, we get the expected linear
bound $add^+(e,d,s) = 2 \cdot \mathsf{nat}(2 \cdot s+2 \cdot e-d-2)+2 \cdot \mathsf{nat}(2 \cdot e)$ for method add.   □

Now we turn to the general case in which b is an arbitrary basic cost ex-
pression, not necessarily $\mathsf{nat}(l)$. In such cases, in addition to $\mathsf{nat}(l)$, b can be
of the form $\log_a(1 + \mathsf{nat}(l))$ or $a^{\mathsf{nat}(l)} - 1$. Recall that when it is $q \in \mathbb{Q}^+$, we
have implicitly assumed it was written as $\mathsf{nat}(q)$. Note that in all cases b has
an embedded $\mathsf{nat}(l)$ expression. Let E be the *CR* obtained from D by replacing
b by its embedded $\mathsf{nat}(l)$. Then the following lemma explains how to obtain an
UB for D from that of E. Computing an *UB* for E is done as above.

Lemma 3. *Let* $\mathsf{nat}(\alpha(\bar{x}))$ *be an* UB *for* E, *and let*

$$D^+(\bar{x}) = \begin{cases} \mathsf{nat}(\alpha(\bar{x})) & b = \mathsf{nat}(l) \\ 1.5 \cdot \mathsf{nat}(\alpha(\bar{x})) & b = \log_a(1 + \mathsf{nat}(l)) \\ a^{\mathsf{nat}(\alpha(\bar{x}))} - 1 & b = a^{\mathsf{nat}(l)} - 1 \end{cases}$$

Then, $D^+(\bar{x})$ *is an* UB *for* D.

It is worth mentioning here the reason for which we use $a^{\mathsf{nat}(l)} - 1$ as a basic
cost expression, instead of $a^{\mathsf{nat}(l)}$. This allows *precisely* lifting the *UB* of E to an
UB of D (in the last case of D^+), which is not possible when using $a^{\mathsf{nat}(l)}$.

Example 6. Let us finish this section by trying to analyse the *CR qs* using the
Tree-Sum method. For qs_{11}, we first generate:

$$\Psi_1 \triangleq \forall \bar{w}_1 : \psi_1 \rightarrow \mathsf{nat}(q_0+q_1 \cdot f+q_2 \cdot t+q_3 \cdot r) \geq \mathsf{nat}(t-f)$$
$$\Psi_2 \triangleq \forall \bar{w}_2 : \psi_2 \rightarrow \mathsf{nat}(q_0+q_1 \cdot f+q_2 \cdot t+q_3 \cdot r) \geq \mathsf{nat}(q_0+q_1 \cdot f+q_2 \cdot m'+q_3 \cdot r)+$$
$$\mathsf{nat}(q_0+q_1 \cdot m''+q_2 \cdot t+q_3 \cdot r)$$

Solving $\Psi_1 \wedge \Psi_2$ results in $q_0 = 0$, $q_1 = -1$, $q_2 = 1$, and $q_3 = 0$. Thus, $\mathsf{nat}(t-f)$ is
an *UB* for qs_{11}. Using Lemma 1, we get $qs_1^+(f,t,r)=\mathsf{nat}(t-f)^2$. Solving qs_{21} with
the Tree-Sum method does not yield any result because the generated formula
is not valid. This is expected since qs_{21} does not have a linear bound. In Sec. 3.2
we develop further methods to handle such cases.   □

3.2   The Level-Sum Method

In this section we describe our method for solving atomic *CRs* that exhibit a *divide and conquer* like behaviour. As we have seen in Ex. 6, the Tree-Sum method fails to handle such examples. We first explain it for the case of $b = \text{nat}(l)$, and then extend it to an arbitrary basic cost expression.

We start with some notation. Given an evaluation tree $T \in Trees(D(\bar{v}))$, a node in T is called *primary* if it is generated by the main equation. Note that the cost of all other nodes in T is 0. The *primary-depth* of a primary node is the number of primary nodes on the path from the root to that node (both included). The primary-depth of T, denoted by $pdepth(T)$, is the maximum among the primary depths of all its primary nodes. The sum of (the cost of) all primary nodes of primary-depth i is denoted by $\text{SumLevel}(T, i)$.

We say that $\text{nat}(\alpha(\bar{x}))$ is an UB *on the primary-depth* of D, if for any input $\bar{v}$ and $T \in Trees(D(\bar{v}))$ we have $\text{nat}(\alpha(\bar{v})) \geq pdepth(T)$. We say that it is an UB *on the Level-Sum* of D, if for any input $\bar{v}$, $T \in Trees(D(\bar{v}))$, and $1 \leq i \leq pdepth(T)$ we have $\text{nat}(\alpha(\bar{v})) \geq \text{SumLevel}(T, i)$.

Lemma 4. *Let* $\text{nat}(\alpha_1(\bar{x}))$ *and* $\text{nat}(\alpha_2(\bar{x}))$ *be UBs on the primary-depth and Level-Sum of D, respectively. Then,* $\text{nat}(\alpha_1(\bar{x})) \cdot \text{nat}(\alpha_2(\bar{x}))$ *is an UB for D.*

The correctness of the above lemma follows from the fact that only primary nodes can have non-zero cost. Intuitively, the above lemma handles divide and conquer examples since, in such examples, the input is distributed between the recursive calls. Thus, the cost of all levels is similar and can be expressed as a linear function on the initial input. Moreover, using the primary-depth, instead of depth, allows ignoring those levels that do not contribute to the cost. Note that the above lemma also reduces the problem of solving D, to that of finding $\text{nat}(\alpha_1(\bar{x}))$ and $\text{nat}(\alpha_2(\bar{x}))$ that bound its primary-depth and Level-Sum. We start with bounding the primary-depth.

Lemma 5. *Let* $\alpha(\bar{x}) = q_0 + q_1 \cdot x_1 + \cdots + q_n \cdot x_n$, *and define:*

$$\Phi_1 \triangleq \begin{cases} \forall \bar{w}_1 \ : \ \varphi_1 & \to \text{nat}(\alpha(\bar{x})) \geq 1 & \text{if } k_1 = 0 \\ \bigwedge_{j=1}^{k_1} \forall \bar{w}_1 \ : \ \varphi_1 \to \text{nat}(\alpha(\bar{x})) \geq 1 + \text{nat}(\alpha(\bar{y}_{1j})) & \text{if } k_1 \geq 1 \end{cases}$$

$$\Phi_2 \triangleq \ \bigwedge_{i=2}^{m} \bigwedge_{j=1}^{k_i} \forall \bar{w}_i \ : \ \varphi_i \to \text{nat}(\alpha(\bar{x})) \geq \text{nat}(\alpha(\bar{y}_{ij}))$$

If $\Phi_1 \wedge \Phi_2$ is valid, then $\text{nat}(\alpha(\bar{x}))$ *is an UB on the primary-depth of D.*

Intuitively, the primary-depth corresponds to the number of applications of the main equation, in a sequence of recursive calls. This is reflected in Φ_1 and Φ_2 as follows. In Φ_1, we treat applications of the main equation. If the main equation is non-recursive, i.e., $k_1 = 0$, then we require that $\text{nat}(\alpha(\bar{x}))$ covers that single application. In case it is recursive, i.e., $k_1 \geq 1$, then we require that $\text{nat}(\alpha(\bar{x}))$ covers that application and further ones that might arise through each recursive call. In Φ_2, we treat applications of other equations. In such case we require that $\text{nat}(\alpha(\bar{x}))$ covers applications of the main equation that might arise through each recursive call. Note that each recursive call is considered separately, since we count primary nodes in each path rather than the whole tree.

It is worth noting that if we apply Φ_1 to all equations instead of only the main one, then $\mathsf{nat}(\alpha(\bar{x}))$ bounds the depth of any evaluation tree rather than the primary-depth. Similar techniques, based on inference of (linear) ranking functions, were used in [3] to bound the depth of the evaluation trees.

Example 7. Applying Lemma 5 to bound the primary-depth of qs_{2_1} (of Ex. 4) results in $\Phi_2 = true$ and Φ_1 as the conjunction of the following formulas:

$$\forall \bar{w}_2 \; : \; \psi_2 \rightarrow \mathsf{nat}(q_0+q_1 \cdot f+q_2 \cdot t+q_3 \cdot r) \geq 1+\mathsf{nat}(q_0+q_1 \cdot f+q_2 \cdot m'+q_3 \cdot r)$$
$$\forall \bar{w}_2 \; : \; \psi_2 \rightarrow \mathsf{nat}(q_0+q_1 \cdot f+q_2 \cdot t+q_3 \cdot r) \geq 1+\mathsf{nat}(q_0+q_1 \cdot m''+q_2 \cdot t+q_3 \cdot r)$$

Both originate from the recursive equation of qs_2. They respectively correspond to the first and second calls. Solving $\Phi_1 \wedge \Phi_2$ results in $q_0 = 1$, $q_1 = -1$, $q_2 = 1$, $q_3 = 0$, which induces the UB $\mathsf{nat}(t-f+1)$ on the primary-depth of qs_{2_1}.   □

Now we turn to bounding the Level-Sum of D.

Lemma 6. *Let* $\alpha(\bar{x}) = q_0+q_1 \cdot x_1+\cdots+q_n \cdot x_n$, *and define:*

$$\Pi_1 \triangleq \forall \bar{w}_1 : \varphi_1 \rightarrow \quad \mathsf{nat}(\alpha(\bar{x})) \geq \mathsf{nat}(l)$$
$$\Pi_2 \triangleq \bigwedge_{i=1}^{m} \forall \bar{w}_i : \varphi_i \rightarrow \quad \mathsf{nat}(\alpha(\bar{x})) \geq \sum_{j=1}^{k_i} \mathsf{nat}(\alpha(\bar{y}_{ij}))$$

If $\Pi_1 \wedge \Pi_2$ *is valid, then* $\mathsf{nat}(\alpha(\bar{x}))$ *is an UB on the Level-Sum of* D.

Intuitively, Π_1 requires that $\mathsf{nat}(\alpha(\bar{x}))$ covers the local cost of the main equation at any level, and Π_2 requires that it also covers the next level. Combining these conditions, and applying inductive reasoning, one can conclude that $\mathsf{nat}(\alpha(\bar{x}))$ is actually an UB on the Level-Sum of D.

Example 8. Consider again qs_{2_1} (of Ex. 4). Its corresponding formulas are:

$$\Pi_1 \triangleq \forall \bar{w}_2 \; : \; \psi_2 \rightarrow \mathsf{nat}(q_0+q_1 \cdot f+q_2 \cdot t+q_3 \cdot r) \geq \mathsf{nat}(t-f)$$
$$\Pi_2 \triangleq \forall \bar{w}_2 \; : \; \psi_2 \rightarrow \mathsf{nat}(q_0+q_1 \cdot f+q_2 \cdot t+q_3 \cdot r) \geq \mathsf{nat}(q_0+q_1 \cdot f+q_2 \cdot m'+q_3 \cdot r)+$$
$$\mathsf{nat}(q_0+q_1 \cdot m''+q_2 \cdot t+q_3 \cdot r)$$

Solving $\Pi_1 \wedge \Pi_2$ results in $q_0=0$, $q_1=-1$, $q_2=1$, $q_3=0$. This induces the bound $\mathsf{nat}(t-f)$ on the Level-Sum. Combining this bound with that in Ex. 7, on the primary depth, we obtain $\mathsf{nat}(t-f) \cdot \mathsf{nat}(t-f+1)$ as an UB for qs_{2_1}, which is also an UB for qs_2. Combining this, using Obs. 1, with the bound of qs_1 computed in Ex. 6, we get $qs^+(f,t,r)=\mathsf{nat}(t-f) \cdot \mathsf{nat}(t-f+1)+\mathsf{nat}(t-f) \cdot \mathsf{nat}(t-f)$. Substituting this UB in the equation of $qsort$ in Fig. 1 we obtain $qsort^+(s,r)=\mathsf{nat}(s-1) \cdot \mathsf{nat}(s)+\mathsf{nat}(s-1) \cdot \mathsf{nat}(s-1)$, which is the expected bound for method qsort.   □

Turning the verification condition to inference procedure, both in Lemma 5 and Lemma 6, is done as we explained in Sec. 3.1. Handling the general case in which b is an arbitrary basic cost expression, is done exactly as the case of Tree-Sum (see Lemma 3). Note that this affects only the UB on the Level-Sum.

Finally, we note that [3] proposed a technique for solving CRs with a divide and conquer behaviour, however, it is limited to cases in which: (1) the cost of all levels is non-increasing; and (2) the cost expression of each equation is linear. Note that, CR qs_1, for example, does not satisfy both conditions.

3.3 Solving the Universally Quantified Formulas

In this section we describe how we solve the universally quantified formulas of Lemma 2, Lemma 5, and Lemma 6. Namely, starting from a template linear function $\alpha(\bar{x}) = q_0 + q_1 \cdot x_1 + \ldots + q_n \cdot x_n$, we find rational values for $q_0, \ldots, q_n$ for which the corresponding formula is valid. Note that our formulas are conjunctions of universally quantified formulas of the following form:

$$\forall \bar{w} : \varphi \to \mathsf{nat}(l_0) \geq q + \mathsf{nat}(l_1) + \ldots + \mathsf{nat}(l_n) \tag{1}$$

where φ defines a closed polyhedron, $q \in \{0, 1\}$, and each l_i is either a linear function over $\bar{w}$, or a template function $\alpha(\bar{x}) = q_0 + q_1 \cdot x_1 + \cdots + q_n \cdot x_n$ such that $\bar{x} \subseteq \bar{w}$ and $q_i \notin \bar{w}$ (i.e., each q_i is existentially quantified). Our goal is to solve these formulas using linear programming (LP) techniques.

Consider a formula as in (1), but without the nat-expressions, i.e., of the form $\forall \bar{w} : \varphi \to l_0 \geq q + l_1 + \ldots + l_n$. It is known that there is a complete algorithm, based on the use of LP [8], able to solve such a formula. Our aim is to transform formulas as (1) to a nat-free as above, and then solve them using this algorithm. Recall that $\mathsf{nat}(l_i) = \max\{l_i, 0\}$. This means that $\mathsf{nat}(l_i)$ can be eliminated by explicitly considering the cases for $l_i \geq 0$ and $l_i \leq 0$ (we use $l_i \geq 0$ and not $l_i > 0$ since in LP constraints must be non-strict). For example, eliminating $\mathsf{nat}(l_0)$ can be done by rewriting (1) as:

$$\forall \bar{w} : \varphi \wedge l_0 \geq 0 \to l_0 \geq q + \mathsf{nat}(l_1) + \ldots + \mathsf{nat}(l_n) \quad \bigwedge$$
$$\forall \bar{w} : \varphi \wedge l_0 \leq 0 \to 0 \geq q + \mathsf{nat}(l_1) + \ldots + \mathsf{nat}(l_n)$$

This process can be applied iteratively to eliminate each $\mathsf{nat}(l_i)$. There is still one problem that prevents us from directly applying the LP techniques: when l_i is a template function, the constraints $l_0 \geq 0$ and $l_0 \leq 0$ are not linear. To overcome this problem, assuming that eliminating the nat-expression results in a formula ξ, we generated ξ' be the by simply removing all non-linear constraints from ξ. Since all non-linear constraints in ξ appear in the left-hand sides of the implications, we observe that $\xi' \to \xi$. This means that we can solve ξ', using the LP based algorithm, instead of ξ. Although we scarify completeness, this approach performs well in practice as demonstrated by our experiments.

3.4 Concluding Remarks

Let us conclude this section describing how all pieces, that have been described so far, connects together to infer an *UB* for C.

Solving CR C. This is as done according to the following steps: (1) generating the sparse *CRs* $C_1, \ldots, C_t$ of C; (2) solving each C_i into an *UB* as described below; and (3) combining these *UBs*, as in Obs. 1, into an *UB* for C.

Solving a sparse CR C_i. This step requires solving, using the methods described in secs. 3.1 and 3.2, one C_{ij} of the corresponding atomic *CR* which might fail for some j and succeed for some others. We iterate over all possible $j=1, \ldots, p_i$, and if all fail then we solve C_i using the approach of [3].

Solving an atomic CR C_{ij}. This is done by trying the methods of secs. 3.1 and 3.2, in this order. Note that in [1] we describe some additional methods.

Table 1. Experimental comparison with PUBS [3]. The times on the right (in secs) correspond to analysing a *CR* that connects all benchmarks together (see Sec. 4).

Entry	$\mathcal{O}(ub)$ – new	$\mathcal{O}(ub)$ – PUBS	Eq	$\mathbf{T}_n$	$\mathbf{T}_p$	Ov
add(a,b,c)	$nat(a)+nat(2a-b+2c)$	$nat(a)\cdot nat(a+c)$	11	0.15	0.11	1.34
qsort(a,b,c)	$nat(a)^2$	$2^{nat(a)}\cdot(nat(a)+nat(b))$	28	0.61	0.27	2.26
sum(a)	$nat(a)$	$2^{nat(a)}\cdot nat(a)$	36	0.88	0.33	2.63
dac(a,b)	$nat(a)^2+nat(a-b)$	$2^{nat(b)}\cdot nat(a)$	45	1.24	0.40	3.13
log(a,b)	$nat(b)+nat(a)\cdot\log(nat(b))$	$nat(b)\cdot nat(a)$	54	1.71	0.47	3.63
once(a,b)	$nat(a)+nat(b)$	$nat(b)\cdot nat(a)$	62	1.98	0.57	3.47
twice(a,b)	$nat(a)+nat(b)$	$nat(b)\cdot nat(a)$	70	2.29	0.69	3.33
full(a,b)	$nat(a)\cdot nat(b)$	$nat(a)\cdot nat(b)^2$	78	2.74	0.84	3.26
eratos(a)	$nat(a)$	$nat(a)^2$	91	3.16	0.94	3.37
peak(a)	$nat(a)$	$nat(a)\cdot\log(nat(a))$	96	3.43	1.01	3.38
stack(a,b,c)	$nat(b)\cdot nat(c)+nat(b)^2$	$nat(c)\cdot nat(b)^2$	107	3.95	1.19	3.32
rotate(a,b)	$nat(a)+nat(b)+nat(a-b)$	$nat(a)\cdot nat(a-b)$	120	4.84	1.62	2.99
maxsum(a,b)	$nat(b)\cdot\log(nat(b))$	$nat(b)^2$	138	7.67	2.12	3.62
mayor(a)	$nat(a)\cdot\log(nat(a))$	$nat(a)\cdot\log(nat(a))$	163	13.21	3.20	4.13
msort(a,b,c,d)	$nat(d-c)\cdot\log(nat(d-c))$	$nat(d-c)^2$	173	13.72	3.81	3.60
mergexp(a)	$nat(a)$	$nat(a)\cdot\log(nat(a))$	187	14.65	4.02	3.65
enque(a,b,c,d)	$nat(c+d)+nat(a+c)$	$nat(c+d)\cdot nat(a+c)$	199	16.34	4.68	3.49
deque(a,b,c)	$nat(a)+nat(c)$	$nat(c)\cdot nat(a)$	208	17.40	4.91	3.55
infinity(a)	$nat(a)$	Failed: No RF	219	18.38	5.07	3.63

4   Implementation and Experiments

We have implemented our techniques as an extension of PUBS [3], the solver used in COSTA [4] for solving *CRs* generated from JAVA programs. This allows us to evaluate our approach directly on JAVA programs. We evaluate accuracy and scalability on a set of benchmarks that we collected from related literature, or were written to demonstrate some powerful features of our approach. Although the programs are not large, they exhibit challenging behaviour for cost analysis. The benchmarks and the implementation are available online [1].

In Table 1 we evaluate the accuracy of our approach by comparing it to PUBS [3]. We applied both approaches on each benchmark using a cost model that measure memory consumption or visits to an specific program point (depending on what was more interesting for each benchmark). Each line includes (from left to right) the entry method and its parameters, the *UB* inferred by our approach and the *UB* inferred by PUBS. For readability, bounds are given in asymptotic form [2]. In all examples our approach obtains *UBs* that are asymptotically more accurate than those obtained by PUBS. Moreover, our *UBs* approach obtains precise asymptotic *UBs*, i.e., they exactly reflect the actual cost.

To analyse scalability, we have merged all our benchmarks into a single program as follows: the benchmark in row i was modified to include a call (in one of its loops) to the program at row $i-1$. This means that the i-th benchmark executes at least i nested loops. The runtime (in seconds) of analysing each such (modifed) benchmark is depicted in columns $\mathbf{T}_n$ (current approach) and

$\mathbf{T}_p$ (PUBS) of Table 1. Columns **Eq** and **Ov** are, respectively, the total number of equations and the overhead $(\mathbf{T}_n/\mathbf{T}_p)$ introduced by our approach.

We have also compared our approach to [6]. For all benchmarks of Table 1, it did not obtain an *UB* within the one minute time limit. This is expected since it is based on a general procedure for real quantifier elimination.

5   Conclusions and Related Work

In this paper we have developed a novel approach for solving *CRs* into precise closed-form *UBs*. It is based on the idea of dividing the *basic cost expressions* of a given *CR C* into two parts: (a) those for which we employ precise reasoning to track their behaviour along the execution; and (b) those for which we simply use their worst case behavior. Then, we show how such different bounds can be combined into an *UB* for *C*. For part (b) we rely on existing techniques [4] to *maximise* cost expressions. For part (a) we first model the contribution of the corresponding cost expressions using universally quantified formulas, and then, a precise *UB* on their costs can be obtain by eliminating the universal quantifiers. Note that while quantifier elimination is a very expensive procedure in general, in our case, since the formulas are of a very specific form, they can be solved efficiently. Our method has been implemented within COSTA [4], and preliminary experiments demonstrate its superiority on previous methods for solving *CRs*.

Related work. The most related works to ours are [4,6] which aim at solving *CRs* into closed-form *UBs*. In Sec. 4 we have seen that, in practice, our approach is more precise than [4] and more efficient than [6]. Detailed discussion on similarities and differences is provided along Sec. 3. Note that although the method described so far is usually more precise than [3], as we have seen in Sec. 4, there are some examples for which the use of the last case of Lemma 3 causes a loss of precision. E.g., replacing $\mathsf{nat}(s)$ by $2^{\mathsf{nat}(s)}$ in for_{12} of Ex. 4, the approach of [3] obtains $\mathsf{nat}(e-i) \cdot 2^{\mathsf{nat}(s+e-1)}$ while we obtain $2^{\mathsf{nat}(2(s+e-i-1)-d)}$. In [5], the techniques of [4] were improved to handle cases in which the cost can be modeled with arithmetic or geometric sequences. This approach is complementary to ours, in the sense that it cannot handle our benchmarks and we cannot handle some of their examples (when basic cost expressions require non-linear bounds).

There are some works that aim at inferring loop bounds on the visits to a given program point [14,19]. They are mostly related to our Lemma 5. These approaches are not limited to linear bounds, however, they cannot handle recursive programs with more than one recursive call. Our techniques can benefit from these approaches when each cost equation has at most one recursive call. Cost analysis techniques that are based on *amortised analysis* [15,16], could, in principle, handle some of our examples when the bounds are polynomial, and the data are over the non-negative integers. Solving *CRs* using template functions and real quantifier elimination has been considered before in [7]. Finally, several cost analysis frameworks [9,11] that are based on generating *CRs* can benefit from our advances in solving *CRs*.

Acknowledgements. This work was funded partially by the projects FP7-ICT-610582, TIN2008-05624, TIN2012-38137, PRI-AIBDE-2011-0900 and S2009TIC-1465. Diego Esteban Alonso-Blas is supported by the PhD scholarship program of the Complutense University.

References

1. Companion Web-Page, http://costa.ls.fi.upm.es/amor/
2. Albert, E., Alonso, D., Arenas, P., Genaim, S., Puebla, G.: Asymptotic Resource Usage Bounds. In: Hu, Z. (ed.) APLAS 2009. LNCS, vol. 5904, pp. 294–310. Springer, Heidelberg (2009)
3. Albert, E., Arenas, P., Genaim, S., Puebla, G.: Closed-Form Upper Bounds in Static Cost Analysis. J. Autom. Reasoning 46(2), 161–203 (2011)
4. Albert, E., Arenas, P., Genaim, S., Puebla, G., Zanardini, D.: Cost Analysis of Object-Oriented Bytecode Programs. Theor. Comput. Sci. 413(1), 142–159 (2012)
5. Albert, E., Genaim, S., Masud, A.N.: On the Inference of Resource Usage Upper and Lower Bounds. ACM Trans. Comput. Log. (to appear, 2013)
6. Alonso-Blas, D.E., Genaim, S.: On the Limits of the Classical Approach to Cost Analysis. In: Miné, A., Schmidt, D. (eds.) SAS 2012. LNCS, vol. 7460, pp. 405–421. Springer, Heidelberg (2012)
7. Anderson, H., Khoo, S.-C., Andrei, Ş., Luca, B.: Calculating Polynomial Runtime Properties. In: Yi, K. (ed.) APLAS 2005. LNCS, vol. 3780, pp. 230–246. Springer, Heidelberg (2005)
8. Bagnara, R., Mesnard, F., Pescetti, A., Zaffanella, E.: A new look at the automatic synthesis of linear ranking functions. Inf. Comput. 215, 47–67 (2012)
9. Benzinger, R.: Automated higher-order complexity analysis. Theor. Comput. Sci. 318(1-2), 79–103 (2004)
10. Danner, N., Paykin, J., Royer, J.S.: A Static Cost Analysis for a Higher-Order Language. In: PLPV, pp. 25–34. ACM (2013)
11. Debray, S.K., Lin, N.: Cost Analysis of Logic Programs. ACM Trans. Program. Lang. Syst. 15(5), 826–875 (1993)
12. Grobauer, B.: Cost Recurrences for DML Programs. In: ICFP, pp. 253–264. ACM (2001)
13. Gulwani, S., Mehra, J.K., Chilimbi, T.M.: SPEED: Precise and Efficient Static Estimation of Program Computational Complexity. In: POPL, pp. 127–139. ACM (2009)
14. Gulwani, S., Zuleger, F.: The Reachability-Bound Problem. In: PLDI, pp. 292–304. ACM (2010)
15. Hoffmann, J., Aehlig, a.K., Hofmannn, M.: Multivariate Amortized Resource Analysis. ACM Trans. Program. Lang. Syst. 34(3), 14:1–14:62 (2012)
16. Simões, H.R., Vasconcelos, P.B., Florido, M., Jost, S., Hammond, K.: Automatic Amortised Analysis of Dynamic Memory Allocation for Lazy Functional Programs. In: ICFP, pp. 165–176. ACM (2012)
17. Vasconcelos, P.B., Hammond, K.: Inferring Cost Equations for Recursive, Polymorphic and Higher-Order Functional Programs. In: Trinder, P., Michaelson, G.J., Peña, R. (eds.) IFL 2003. LNCS, vol. 3145, pp. 86–101. Springer, Heidelberg (2004)
18. Wegbreit, B.: Mechanical Program Analysis. Commun. ACM 18(9), 528–539 (1975)
19. Zuleger, F., Gulwani, S., Sinn, M., Veith, H.: Bound Analysis of Imperative Programs with the Size-Change Abstraction. In: Yahav, E. (ed.) SAS 2011. LNCS, vol. 6887, pp. 280–297. Springer, Heidelberg (2011)

Control Flow Refinement and Symbolic Computation of Average Case Bound

Hong Yi Chen, Supratik Mukhopadhyay, and Zheng Lu

Department of Computer Science
Louisiana State University
Baton Rouge, LA 70803
{hchen11,zlu5}@lsu.edu, supratik@csc.lsu.edu

Abstract. This paper presents a new technique for refining the complex control structure of loops that occur in imperative programs. We first introduce a new way of describing program execution patterns – $(+, \cdot)$-*path expressions*, which is a subset of conventional path expressions with the operators $\vee$ and $*$ eliminated. The programs induced by $(+, \cdot)$-path expressions have no path interleaving or skipping-over inner loops, which are the two main issues that cause impreciseness in program analysis. Our refinement process starts from a conventional path expression $\mathcal{E}$ obtained from the control flow graph, and aims to calculate a finite set of $(+, \cdot)$-path expressions $\{\mathfrak{e}_1, ..., \mathfrak{e}_n\}$ such that the language generated by path expression $\mathcal{E}$ is equivalent to the union of the languages generated by each $(+, \cdot)$-path expressions $\mathfrak{e}_i$. In theory, a conventional path expression can potentially generate an infinite set of $(+, \cdot)$-path expressions. To remedy that, we use abstract interpretation techniques to prune the infeasible paths. In practice, the refinement process usually converges very quickly.

We have applied our method to symbolic computation of average case bound for running time of programs. To our best knowledge it is the first tool that automatically computes average case bounds. Experiments on a set of complex loop benchmarks clearly demonstrate the utility of our tool.

1 Introduction

1.1 Motivation

Automatic analysis of source code has become increasingly common. Formal techniques, such as static analysis using abstract interpretation, are used for verifying termination property and computing running time bounds. Several existing techniques [6,7,17,18,15,12,14] can compute worst case bounds. However, the computation of average case bounds is largely left open.

One of the factors that makes a program difficult to analyze for average case bound is that in different executions of a nested loop the control can skip over different inner loops; in addition different "execution patterns" can interleave with each other to create complex ones.

D. Van Hung and M. Ogawa (Eds.): ATVA 2013, LNCS 8172, pp. 334–348, 2013.

This paper is aimed at developing control flow refinement techniques for automatically computing average case running time bound computation. Given a program P and a joint probability distribution on the program input space, our goal is to compute a symbolic average case bound, i.e., the average running time of the program on the input space. One important question to answer in average case performance analysis is how to reasonably partition the input space into different cases such that the program, roughly, has the "same" behavior within each partition. An important observation is that when there are no interleaving of branches or skipping-over of inner loops, existing worst case bound generators can usually get a very precise bound. Thus we assume that for simple loops the average case performance equals the worst case performance. For complex loops, we can divide the input space using different execution patterns such that there is no interleaving and skipping-over.

Conventional path expressions [26] induced by the control flow graph of a program contain operators $\vee$ and $*$. Consider the example program in Figure 1.

```
assume (x > 0 ∧ x < n)
while (x > 0 ∧ x < n)
    if (m % 2 == 0) x := x - 1;
    else   x := x + 1;
```

```
assume (x > 0 ∧ n > 0 ∧ m > 0)
while (x > n)
    while (x > m ) m := m + 1;
    x := x - 1;
```

Fig. 1. Example 1: Interleaving   **Fig. 2.** Example 2: Skipping-over

Let ρ_1 be the statement in the 'if' branch, ρ_2 be that in the 'else' branch; then the conventional path expression for this loop is $(\rho_1 \vee \rho_2)^+$. If we could partition the input space according to the program behavior in different parts of the input space (or different execution patterns), then we will get $(\rho_1)^+$ and $(\rho_2)^+$. Notice that in order to remove the possibility of interleaving, we use two expressions and without the operator $\vee$. And if we could compute the weakest precondition for each execution pattern, i.e., $m\%2 = 0$ and $m\%2 \neq 0$, respectively, existing worst case bound techniques can generate precise bounds for both cases. Thus we get the following bound.

$$B = \begin{cases} x, & m\%2 = 0 \\ n - x, & m\%2 \neq 0 \end{cases}$$

Given an input (joint) probability distribution, we will be able to compute an average case bound.

Similarly let us look at Example 2 in Figure 2. Let $\rho_1 \triangleq m := m + 1, \rho_2 \triangleq x := x - 1$, conventional path expression will be $(\rho_1^* \rho_2)^*$. If we could express the execution patterns without the $*$ operator, i.e., ϵ, ρ_2^+, and $\rho_1^+ \rho_2^+$, and assuming that we could compute the weakest preconditions, i.e., $x \leq n, x > n \wedge x < m$, and $x > n \wedge x > m$, respectively, existing techniques [5] can generate precise bounds for all the three cases below. Thus we get the following bound.

$$B = \begin{cases} 0 & x \leq n \\ x - n & x > n \wedge x < m \\ 2x - m - n & x > n \wedge x > m \end{cases}$$

From the above two examples, we see that

1. the path expressions without operators $\vee$ and $*$ induce loops without interleaving or skipping over, and such loops are easier to analyze
2. if we can also compute weakest precondition for each $(+, \cdot)$-path expressions, we can then utilize the techniques for computing worst case performance to compute average case performance.

Formally, our refinement process starts from a conventional path expression $\mathcal{E}$ obtained from the control flow graph, and aims to calculate a finite set of $(+, \cdot)$-path expressions $\{e_1, ..., e_n\}$ such that the language generated by the path expression $\mathcal{E}$ is equivalent to the union of the languages generated by each of the $(+, \cdot)$-path expressions e_i.

In theory, a conventional path expression can potentially generate an infinite set of $(+, \cdot)$-path expressions. To remedy that, we use abstract interpretation techniques to prune the infeasible paths. In practice, the refinement process usually converges very quickly. We have applied our method to symbolic computation of "partitions" for average case bound. Experiments on a set of complex loop benchmarks clearly demonstrate the utility of our method.

1.2   Related Work

Control Flow Refinement. The differences between our approach and Gulwani et. al.'s and Balakrishnan et. al.'s control flow refinement approach [6,1] are two-fold. First, their approaches aim at attacking the problem of interleaving for loops of multiple paths, but leaves the issue of skipping-over with nested loops open. Second, our refinement approach generates more abstract execution patterns, which are expressive enough for refinement purpose yet converge easily. Consider the following program snippet for instance, where $*$ denotes a nondeterministic condition.

$$\text{while } (*)\{ \text{ if } (*)S_1 \text{ else } S_2\}$$

Gulwani et. al.'s path expression will expand as follows:

$(S_1 \vee S_2)^* \rightarrow$

$\{\epsilon, S_1^+, S_2^+, S_1^+ S_2(S_1 \vee S_2)^*, S_2^+ S_1(S_1 \vee S_2)^*\} \rightarrow$

$\{\epsilon, S_1^+, S_2^+, S_1^+ S_2, S_1^+ S_2 S_1^+, S_1^+ S_2 S_2^+, S_1^+ S_2 S_1^+ S_2(S_1 \vee S_2)^*,$
$S_1^+ S_2 S_2^+ S_1(S_1 \vee S_2)^*, S_2^+ S_1, S_2^+ S_1 S_1^+, S_2^+ S_1 S_2^+, S_2^+ S_1 S_1^+ S_2(S_1 \vee S_2)^*,$
$S_2^+ S_1 S_2^+ S_1(S_1 \vee S_2)^*\} \rightarrow$

$\cdots$

As one can see, the expansion may never end. However, using our method, there are only 6 $(+, \cdot)$-path expressions we can possibly generate, $i.e.$,

$$\{\epsilon, S_1^+, S_2^+, (S_1^+ S_2^+)^+, (S_2^+ S_1^+)^+, ((S_1^+ S_2^+)^+ S_1^+)^+, ((S_2^+ S_1^+)^+ S_2^+)^+\}$$

Worst Case Performance Analysis. *Symbolic Bound Computation using Recurrence Relation Solving:* Worst case computational complexity [10] of a program or an algorithm is calculated by expressing the complexity function as a system of recurrence relations; combinatorial techniques are then used to solve these relations. Automatic techniques for computing closed-form solutions of recurrence relations are based on rewriting rules [12,14], solving difference equations [15], or symbolic algebra manipulation systems [19].

WCET Analysis: Techniques for worst case execution time (WCET) analysis [17,18] are dependent on the low-level details of the underlying machine; as has been frequently observed, the worst case only occurs on a few pathological inputs. In most practical situation execution time is usually much less.

SPEED: SPEED [4,7,6,5,8] provides a framework for (symbolically) computing the worst case (running time) bounds for structured programs. The key idea is to instrument a program with counters whose values (after the program terminates) encode the bound. Invariant generation techniques are used for statically computing these values symbolically. Gulwani et. al. [6] use control-flow refinement and progress invariants, to compute precise worst case bounds for programs with nested loops. We have already compared our approach with their control flow refinement approach above.

Average Case Performance Analysis. Wegbreit [16] first proposed using static analysis for determining the average case performance of a program. He provided an inductive approach to verify average case performance. In this approach, one has to manually annotate the program with inductive assertions. Hence, it is difficult to fully automate this approach.

2   Path Expressions and Abstract Interpretation

Programs are represented by their control flow graphs (CFG). We assume that the CFG is built from a structured imperative program (without goto-statements). Specifically, each loop is assumed to be reducible, consisting of a single loop head, which dominates all the nodes inside the loop. Edges from the loop nodes back to the head are called back edges. Edges from nodes inside a loop to a node outside are called exit edges. We assume that all exit edges from a loop have a single target. For simplicity of presentation, we consider loops that do not contain function calls. Non-recursive function calls can be handled using standard techniques such as inlining or loop summarization. We start by representations of paths in a CFG using restricted regular expressions.

2.1   Path Expressions

Definition 1 (Regular Expression). *Let Σ be a finite alphabet, a regular expression over Σ is any expression built by applying the following rules.*

1. *ϵ and $\emptyset$ are regular expressions;*
2. *$\forall \alpha \in \Sigma$, α is a regular expression;*
3. *If R_1 and R_2 are regular expressions, then $(R_1 \vee R_2)$, $(R_1 \cdot R_2)$, $(R_1)^+$, and $(R_1)^*$ are also regular expressions.*

Definition 2 (Path Expression). *Let Σ be a finite set of transitions, path expressions are a subset of regular expressions over the alphabet Σ such that*

1. *ϵ is a path expression;*
2. *$\forall \alpha \in \Sigma$, α is a path expression;*
3. *If R_1 and R_2 are path expressions, then $(R_1 \vee R_2)$, $(R_1 \cdot R_2)$, $(R_1)^+$, and $(R_1)^*$ are also path expressions.*

Definition 3 ($(+, \cdot)$-Path Expression). *Let Σ be a finite set of transitions, $(+, \cdot)$-path expressions are a subset of path expressions over the alphabet Σ such that*

1. *ϵ is a $(+, \cdot)$-path expression;*
2. *$\forall \alpha \in \Sigma$, α is a $(\cdot, +)$-path expression;*
3. *If R_1 and R_2 are $(+, \cdot)$-path expressions, then $(R_1 \cdot R_2)$ is a $(+, \cdot)$-path expression;*
4. *If R is $(+, \cdot)$-path expressions, then R^+ is a $(+, \cdot)$-path expression.*

It is conventional to abbreviate $R_1 \cdot R_2$ as $R_1 R_2$.

2.2   Predicate Transformers

Let $\mathcal{S}$ represent the set of all possible states of a program P. The semantics of a transition τ is specified by means of its concrete postcondition, which maps a set $S \subseteq \mathcal{S}$ of states to its concrete postcondition $S' = post_\tau(S)$ representing the set consisting of all states that are reachable starting from some state $s \in S$ and executing the transition τ.

Given a first order predicate ψ on program states, the set of states satisfying ψ is denoted $[\![\psi]\!]$.

Definition 4 (predicate entailment). *Given two first order predicates φ and ψ over the program states, we say that φ entails ψ, denoted by $\varphi \models \psi$, if $[\![\varphi]\!] \subseteq [\![\psi]\!]$*

Definition 5 (Precondition). *Let $\mathcal{S}$ be the set of program states, ψ be a first order predicate over the program states, τ be a transition, then the first order predicate $\psi' = pre_\tau \psi$ denotes the pre-condition of ψ with respect to τ defined as*

$$[\![\psi']\!] = \{s \in S \mid \exists s' \in [\![\psi]\!] \text{ such that } s' \text{ is a state obtained after executing } \tau \text{ from } s\}$$

Definition 6 (Weakest Precondition). *Let S be the set of program states, ψ be a first order predicate over the program states, τ be a transition, then the predicate $\psi' = \tilde{pre}_\tau\psi$ denotes the weakest pre-condition of ψ with respect to τ defined as*

$$[\![\psi']\!] = \{s \in S \mid \forall s' \text{ such that } s' \text{ is the state after executing } \tau \text{ on } s, s' \in [\![\psi]\!]\}$$

Definition 7 (Strongest Postcondition). *Let S be the set of program states, ψ be a first order predicate over the program states, τ be a transition, then the predicate $\psi' = post_\tau\psi$ denotes the post-condition of ψ with respect to τ defined as*

$$[\![\psi']\!] = \{s \in S \mid \exists s' \in [\![\psi]\!] \text{ such that } s \text{ is the state after executing } \tau \text{ on } s'\}$$

3   Methodology Overview

We start with a few definitions.

Definition 8. *A $(+, \cdot)$ algebra $\mathcal{A}$ over a finite nonempty set of generators G is the smallest set closed under the following rules:*

1. *$\epsilon \in \mathcal{A}$*
2. *for each $a \in G, a \in \mathcal{A}$*
3. *if $s_1, s_2 \in \mathcal{A}$, then $(s_1 \cdot s_2) \in \mathcal{A}$*
4. *if $s \in \mathcal{A}$ then $s^+ \in \mathcal{A}$*

Definition 9. *A $(+, \cdot)$ quotient algebra $\mathcal{A}/\sim$ is the congruence closure of a $(+, \cdot)$ algebra $\mathcal{A}$ under the following congruences where $\alpha, s \in \mathcal{A}$:*

1. *$s^{++} \sim s^+$*
2. *$s \cdot s^+ \sim s^+ \cdot s \sim s^+$*
3. *$(\alpha \cdot s)^+ \cdot s \sim (\alpha \cdot s)^+$*
4. *$s \cdot (\alpha \cdot s)^+ \sim (s \cdot \alpha)^+ s$*

Example 1: $G = \{a\}, \mathcal{A}/\sim = \{\epsilon, a^+\} \Rightarrow$ finite
Example 2: $G = \{a, b\}, \mathcal{A}/\sim = \{\epsilon, a^+, b^+, (a^+b^+)^+, (b^+a^+)^+, ((a^+b^+)^+a^+)^+,$
$((b^+a^+)^+b^+)^+\} \Rightarrow$ finite
Example 3: $G = \{a, b, c\}, \mathcal{A}/\sim = \{\epsilon, a^+, b^+, c^+, (a^+b^+)^+, (a^+c^+)^+, (b^+a^+)^+,$
$(b^+c^+)^+, (c^+a^+)^+, (c^+b^+)^+, \ldots\} \Rightarrow$ infinite

Given a transition system corresponding to a program $\mathcal{P}$, we consider the set of generators G to be the set of labels on the transitions. Let $\mathcal{A}/\sim$ be the $(+, \cdot)$-quotient algebra generated by G. We say that $\mathcal{P}$ is the program corresponding to $\mathcal{A}/\sim$. Given a generator a corresponding to a transition with guard given by the constraint g_a (over the variables $\overrightarrow{x}$) and update given by the constraint u_a (over the variables $\overrightarrow{x}$ and $\overrightarrow{x}'$), we define the transition constraint corresponding to a to be $\phi_a = g_a \wedge u_a$.

For $a \in G$, $[\![a]\!] = \phi_a$ is the transition constraint corresponding to a, where the only occurring variables are $\overrightarrow{x}$ and $\overrightarrow{x'}$.

For a constraint ϕ as a pre condition, the strongest post condition with respect to a, $post_a(\phi) = \exists_{-\vec{x}'}\phi \wedge [\![a]\!]$ where the existential quantifier is over all variables but x' (we use this convention whenever we use an existential quantifier). Similarly, for a constraint ϕ as a post condition, the precondition and weakest precondition with respect to a are defined as $pre_a(\phi) = \exists_{-\vec{x}}\phi \wedge [\![a]\!]$ and $\tilde{pre}_a(\phi) = \neg pre_a(\neg\phi)$ respectively. We now extend the definitions of weakest precondition and strongest postcondition to $(+, \cdot)$-quotient algebras.

Definition 10 (Weakest Precondition over a $(+, \cdot)$-quotient algebra). $\tilde{pre}_\alpha(\phi)$ for $\alpha \in \mathcal{A}/_\sim$ and a predicate ϕ is defined by induction as follows:

1. if $\alpha = \epsilon$, $\tilde{pre}_\epsilon(\phi) = \phi$
2. if $\alpha = a$, where $a \in G$, $\tilde{pre}_a(\phi)$ is the weakest pre condition for the transition a with ϕ as the post condition
3. if $\alpha = (s_1 s_2)$, where $s_1, s_2 \in \mathcal{A}/_\sim$, $\tilde{pre}_{(s_1 s_2)}(\phi) = \tilde{pre}_{s_1}(\tilde{pre}_{s_2}(\phi))$
4. if $\alpha = s^+$ for $s \in \mathcal{A}/_\sim$, $\tilde{pre}_{s^+}(\phi) = \mu X.\tilde{pre}_s(X) \vee \tilde{pre}_s(\phi)$ where μX denotes the least fixpoint of the functional $F(X) = \tilde{pre}_s(X) \vee \tilde{pre}_s(\phi)$

Definition 11 (Strongest Postcondition over a $(+, \cdot)$-quotient algebra). $post_\alpha(\phi)$ for $\alpha \in \mathcal{A}/_\sim$ is defined by induction as follows:

1. if $\alpha = \epsilon$, $post_\epsilon(\phi) = \phi$
2. if $\alpha = a$, where $a \in G$, $post_a(\phi)$ is the strongest post condition for the transition a with ϕ as the pre condition
3. if $\alpha = (s_1 s_2)$, where $s_1, s_2 \in \mathcal{A}/_\sim$ $post_{(s_1 s_2)}(\phi) = post_{s_2}(post_{s_1}(\phi))$
4. if $\alpha = s^+$ for $s \in \mathcal{A}/_\sim$, $post_{s^+}(\phi) = \mu X.post_s(X) \vee post_s(\phi)$ where μX denotes the least fixpoint of the functional $F(X) = post_s(X) \vee post_s(\phi)$

Definition 12. For a constraint ϕ and a quotient algebra $\mathcal{A}/_\sim$, $post_{\mathcal{A}/_\sim}(\phi)$ is the set of logical formulas $post_\alpha(\phi)$ such that $post_\alpha(\phi) \nvDash False$ for $\alpha \in \mathcal{A}/_\sim$.

Definition 13 (Symbolic Bound over a $(+, \cdot)$-quotient algebra). Given an element α of a quotient algebra $\mathcal{A}/_\sim$, we define the symbolic bound as follows:

1. if $\alpha = \epsilon$, $bound(\epsilon) = 0$
2. if $\alpha = a$ for $a \in G$, $bound(a) = 1$
3. if $\alpha = (s_1 s_2)$ for $s_1, s_2 \in \mathcal{A}/_\sim$, $bound(s_1 s_2) = bound(s_1) + bound(s_2)$
4. if $\alpha = s^+$ for $s \in \mathcal{A}/_\sim$, $bound(s^+) = $ worst case bound computed by standard bound computation tool [7] for the loop with body s

Let $\mathcal{P}$ be a program with input variables $x_1, \dots x_m$ with variable x_i ranging over domain $\mathcal{D}_i$, we define the input space $\mathcal{I}$ of $\mathcal{P}$ as $\Pi_{i=1}^m \mathcal{D}_i$

Definition 14 (Basis of a $(+, \cdot)$-quotient algebra). Given a quotient algebra $\mathcal{A}/_\sim$, we define its basis as the largest subset $max(\mathcal{A}/_\sim)$ of $\mathcal{A}/_\sim$, such that for each element $\alpha \in max(\mathcal{A}/_\sim)$, $[\![\tilde{pre}_\alpha(\phi)]\!]$ for any post condition ϕ is a subset of the input space $\mathcal{I}$ of the program corresponding to $\mathcal{A}$

Definition 15 (Attributed Algebra). *Given the basis* $max(\mathcal{A}/\sim)$ *of a quotient algebra, we define an attributed algebra* $max^{Att}(\mathcal{A}/\sim)$ *corresponding to* $max(\mathcal{A}/\sim)$ *to be the pair* $\langle max(\mathcal{A}/\sim), \mathcal{M} \rangle$ *where* $\mathcal{M}$ *is a mapping that maps each* $\alpha \in max\mathcal{A}/\sim$ *to the pair* $\langle \tilde{pre}_\alpha, bound(\alpha) \rangle$.

For $max^{Att}(\mathcal{A}/\sim) = \langle max(\mathcal{A}/\sim), \mathcal{M} \rangle$, $\alpha \in max(\mathcal{A}/\sim)$, *and* $\mathcal{M}(\alpha) = \langle \tilde{pre}_\alpha, bound(\alpha) \rangle$, $[\![\tilde{pre}_\alpha(\phi)]\!]$ *for any* ϕ *is a subset of the input space of the program corresponding to* $\mathcal{A}$. *In particular, given the input space true,* $[\![\tilde{pre}_\alpha(post_\alpha(true))]\!]$ *is a subset of the input space of the program corresponding to* $\mathcal{A}$.

Given the basis $max(\mathcal{A}/\sim)$ corresponding to a program, the input space $true$ is partitioned by $\tilde{pre}_\alpha(post_\alpha(true))$ for each $\alpha \in max(\mathcal{A}/\sim)$

Definition 16 (Average Case Bound). *Given an attributed algebra* $max^{Att}(\mathcal{A}/\sim) = \langle max(\mathcal{A}/\sim), \mathcal{M} \rangle$ *and an input joint probability distribution* Pr *on the input space of a program, we define the average case bound as follows:*

$$B_{AVG} = \sum_{\alpha \in max(\mathcal{A}/\sim)} bound(\alpha) \times Pr(\tilde{pre}_\alpha(post_\alpha(true)))$$

where for $\alpha \in max(\mathcal{A}/\sim)$, $\mathcal{M}(\alpha) = \langle \tilde{pre}_\alpha, bound(\alpha) \rangle$

4 Algorithm

We explain the algorithm for control flow refinement with an example. The main procedure is given in Figure 4. We will consider a more complex example in Figure 3a. This program takes 4 integer variables x, y, m, n. If the initial value $x \leq 0$, the outer loop is not executed. If $x > 0 \wedge n \leq 1$, then outer loop is entered but not the inner loop. If $x > 0 \wedge n > 1 \wedge m < 1$, then the inner loop is entered every iteration of the outer loop, and the inner loop always takes the if branch. If $x > 0 \wedge n > 1 \wedge m \geq 1 \wedge x \leq n$, then the inner loop is entered on the first iteration of the outer loop, the inner loop first takes the else branch a few times until $m = 0$, then the inner loop takes if branch until $y \geq n$, after that x gets decreased below 0 and the outer loop terminates. If $x > 0 \wedge n > 1 \wedge m \geq 1 \wedge x > n$, at the first iteration of the outer loop, the inner loop first takes the else branch till $m = 0$ then takes the if branch till $y \geq n$, after that x gets decreased but still greater than 0. At the following iterations of the outer loop, inner loop is still entered but only takes the if branch until y is big enough and $x \leq 0$.

To explain the working of the algorithm, we need a few definitions.

Definition 17 (Set concatenation). *Let* S_1, S_2 *be two sets of regular expressions. We define* $S_1 \cdot S_2 = \{(R_1 \cdot R_2) \mid R_1 \in S_1 \text{ and } R_2 \in S_2\}$.

Definition 18 (Guard).
Given a function GUARD *that assigns a constraint to each element of an alphabet* Σ *we define the function* GD *inductively.*

- GD$(\epsilon) \triangleq \top$.

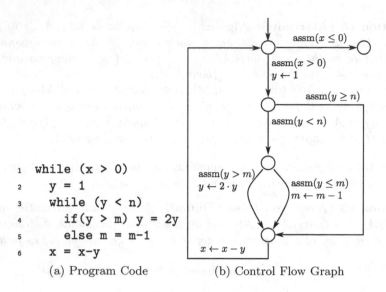

```
1  while (x > 0)
2      y = 1
3      while (y < n)
4          if(y > m) y = 2y
5          else m = m-1
6      x = x-y
```

(a) Program Code   (b) Control Flow Graph

Fig. 3. Example

- If $R \in \Sigma$ then $\mathrm{GD}(R) \triangleq \mathrm{GUARD}(R)$.
- If $R = (R_1 \cdot R_2)$ then $\mathrm{GD}(R) \triangleq \mathrm{GD}(R_1)$.
- If $R = (R_1)^+$ then $\mathrm{GD}(R) \triangleq \mathrm{GD}(R_1)$.

From the CFG in Fig. 3(b) we get the following conventional path expression.

$$R = \rho_1 \vee (\rho_2(\rho_4(\rho_5 \vee \rho_6))^* \rho_3 \rho_7)^+$$

Notice that there is more than one way to generate CFG's and path expressions. Any semantics preserving CFG and path expressions is acceptable for our purpose. Now we execute our algorithm over this input R. The main procedure is Computing_Path (see Figure 4). It initiates by computing a conventional path expression with the same semantics as the input program. It then calls Procedure Closure (Figure 6) and Procedure Gen (Figure 5) to calculate a closure for the breakdown of the expression. Procedure Gen computes the generator set for Procedure Closure to compute a closure upon. It breaks down regular expressions by removing "or" and expressing it as different elements in the generator set. Procedure Closure gradually adds more possible compositions of previously calculated expressions. It recursively builds a set of all possible expressions while considering the constraints imposed by the program. Procedure SAT (Figure 7) helps Procedure Closure to determine when two expressions can be composed. Procedure Reduce (Figure 8) eliminates redundant expressions while generate them. Procedure ReduceTermination (Figure 9) removes expressions that do not belong to the basis as we defined in Def. 14. Procedure Gen and Procedure Closure help to expand the set by adding more elements to the generator set or composing existing expressions to from new expression, while Procedure SAT, Reduce, and ReduceTermination help to prune the set by eliminating infeasible expressions. These procedures work together help us reach a closure. The correctness of the above procedures is given by the following results

Lemma 1. *If procedure Computing_Path (Figure 4) terminates, it returns a set of* $(+, \cdot)$ *expressions*

Theorem 1. *Given a program* $\mathcal{P}$ *with input space* $\mathcal{I}$, *let* $\mathcal{S}$ *be the set of* $(+, \cdot)$ *expressions returned by the procedure Computing_Path (Figure 4) when it terminates. Then*

1. *$\mathcal{S}$ is the basis for the quotient algebra $\mathcal{A}/\sim$ corresponding to $\mathcal{P}$*
2. *For $\alpha, \beta \in \mathcal{S}$, $[\![\tilde{pre}_\alpha(post_\alpha(true))]\!] \cap [\![\tilde{pre}_\beta(post_\alpha(true))]\!] = \emptyset$ and $\bigcup_{\alpha \in \mathcal{S}}[\![\tilde{pre}_\alpha(post_\alpha(true))]\!] = \mathcal{I}$*

procedure Computing_Path
input: a program P
output: a set of path expressions S
begin
  compute a regular expression R from the
  Control Flow Graph of P;
  Return $Closure(Gen(R))$;
end.

Fig. 4. Procedure Computing_Path

procedure Gen
input: regular expression R
output: set of path expressions
begin
  if $R = \emptyset$ return $\emptyset$
  if $R = \epsilon$ return $\{\epsilon\}$
  if $R \in \Sigma$ return $\{R\}$
  if $R = (R_1 \vee R_2)$ return $Gen(R_1) \cup Gen(R_2)$
  if $R = (R_1 \cdot R_2)$ return $Gen(R_1) \cdot Gen(R_2)$
  if $R = (R_1)^*$ return $Closure(Gen(R_1)) \cup \{\epsilon\}$
  if $R = (R_1)^+$ return $Closure(Gen(R_1))$
end.

Fig. 5. Procedure Gen

procedure Closure
input: set of path expressions S
output: set of path expressions
begin
  $S' \leftarrow S$
  do
    $S'' \leftarrow \emptyset$
    for each $R' \in S'$ and $R \in S$
      if SAT(R', R)
        if $R = R'$
          $S'' \leftarrow S'' \cup \{(R)^+\}$
          $S \leftarrow S \setminus \{R\}$
        else
          $S'' \leftarrow S'' \cup \{((R')^+ \cdot (R)^+)\}$
    $S'' \leftarrow Reduce(S'', S)$
    $S \leftarrow S \cup S''$
    $S' \leftarrow S''$
  while S' not empty
  ReduceTermination(S)
  return S
end.

Fig. 6. Procedure Closure

procedure SAT
input: path expressions R_1, R_2
output: bool
begin
  Return $post_{R_1}(\text{GD}(R_1)) \models \text{GD}(R_2)$
end.

Fig. 7. Procedure SAT

procedure Reduce
input: two sets of regular expressions S_1, S_2
output: set of regular expressions
begin
    $T \leftarrow \emptyset$
    $S_2' \leftarrow \emptyset$
    for each $R \in S_2$
        compute the minimal DFA for R and store
it in A
        add A to S_2'
    for each $R \in S_1$
        compute the minimal DFA for R and store
it in A
        if $A \notin S_2'$ then add R to T
    return T
end.

procedure ReduceTermination
input: sets of regular expressions S
output: set of regular expressions
begin
    return S without the expressions for which the
last edge is not an "ending" edge
end.

Fig. 8. Procedure Reduce   **Fig. 9.** Procedure ReduceTermination

After executing the algorithm, we generate a set of 5 $(+, \cdot)$-path expressions. They are

$$\rho_1$$
$$\rho_2(\rho_4\rho_6)^+(\rho_4\rho_5)^+\rho_3\rho_7$$
$$(\rho_2(\rho_4\rho_5)^+\rho_3\rho_7)^+$$
$$(\rho_2\rho_3\rho_7)^+$$
$$(\rho_2(\rho_4\rho_6)^+(\rho_4\rho_5)^+\rho_3\rho_7)^+(\rho_2(\rho_4\rho_5)^+\rho_3\rho_7)^+$$

A closer examination tell us, the 5 expressions match our intuition of different execution patterns when we first analyze the program. These 5 expressions will become 5 cases in our bound computation. Assuming precondition *true*, we generate the post conditions for each of the expressions, then we go backwards to generate the weakest precondition. Post conditions and preconditions are computed using the approach outlined in Section 4. By feeding each expression along with the corresponding weakest precondition to a standard worst case bound tool [7], we get a bound in the following:

$$B = \begin{cases} 0 & x \leq 0 \\ x & x > 0 \wedge n \leq 1 \\ x\log(n^{1/n}) & x > 0 \wedge n > 1 \wedge m < 1 \\ m + \log n & x > 0 \wedge n > 1 \wedge m \geq 1 \wedge x \leq n \\ m + \frac{x}{n}\log n & x > 0 \wedge n > 1 \wedge m \geq 1 \wedge x > n \end{cases}$$

Given an joint probability distribution over the input space, we will be able to compute an average case bound.

5   Experimental Results

In this section we apply our control flow refinement approach to average case bound computation. There are several existing techniques that can compute

Table 1. Experiment results 1

Example	LOC	case #	B_{AVG}
dma_example_spu.c	252	3	$B = \begin{cases} 1, & !(tag = MFC\_TAG\_INVALID) \\ num\_chunks, & i < num\_chunks \wedge control\_block.out\_addr > 0 \\ 1, & control\_block.num\_elements\_per\_spe = 0 \end{cases}$
spe-sum.c	168	20	$B = \begin{cases} 1, & 5\ expressions \\ nbufs, & 15\ expressions \end{cases}$
cpaudio.c	277	2	$B = \begin{cases} n\_frames, & (i < n\_frames - 1) \wedge size\&15 = 1 \\ 1, & (i < n\_frames - 1) \wedge size > 0 \end{cases}$
normalize.c	692	4	$B = \begin{cases} 1, & (size\&15 = 1) \wedge size < 32 \\ 1, & size > 32 \wedge src > 0 \\ n\_frames - 2, & (size\&15 = 1) \wedge size < 32 \wedge \\ & (foralln\_frames, n\_frames > size \times (2^{14})) \wedge \\ & i < n\_frames - 2) \\ n\_frames - 2, & (foralln\_frames, n\_frames > size \times (2^{14})) \wedge \\ & i < n\_frames - 2) \wedge size > 32 \end{cases}$
simple_dma_spu.c	83	4	$B = \begin{cases} 1, & tag_i d = MFC\_TAG\_INVALID \\ 1, & tag_i d \neq MFC\_TAG\_INVALID \\ DATA\_BUFFER\_ENTRIES - 2, & DATA\_BUFFER\_ENTRIES > 2 \wedge \\ & error = 0 \wedge \\ & data[i] = data[i-1] + data[i-2] \\ DATA\_BUFFER\_ENTRIES - 2, & DATA\_BUFFER\_ENTRIES > 2 \wedge \\ & error = 0 \wedge \\ & data[i]! = data[i-1] + data[i-2] \end{cases}$
atomic_add_return_test.c	111	3	$B = \begin{cases} 1, & argp > 1 \\ RETURN\_COUNT - argp, & (argp < RETURN\_COUNT) \wedge argp > 0 \\ (RETURN\_COUNT - argp) \times & (argp < RETURN\_COUNT) \wedge argp > 0 \wedge \\ RETURN\_SZ, & RETURN\_SZ > 0 \end{cases}$
mutex_spu_example.c	112	5	$B = \begin{cases} 1, & LOOP\_COUNT = 0 \wedge mutex > 0 \\ LOOP\_COUNT, & spu\_argv.mutex\_ea > 0 \wedge i < LOOP\_COUNT \wedge \\ & mutex\_unlock(mutex) > 1 \wedge \\ & (mutex\_trylock(mutex) = 0 \\ LOOP\_COUNT, & spu\_argv.mutex\_ea > 0 \wedge i < LOOP\_COUNT \wedge \\ & mutex\_unlock(mutex) > 1 \wedge \\ & (mutex\_trylock(mutex) = 1 \\ LOOP\_COUNT, & spu_a rgv.mutex_e a > 0 \wedge i < LOOP\_COUNT \wedge \\ & (mutex_t rylock(mutex) = 0 \\ LOOP\_COUNT, & spu_a rgv.mutex_e a > 0 \wedge i < LOOP\_COUNT \wedge \\ & (mutex_t rylock(mutex) = 1 \end{cases}$
particle.c	330	4	$B = \begin{cases} 1, & cnt \leq 0 \wedge time \geq END\_OF\_TIME \\ END\_OF\_TIME/dt, & cnt > 0 \wedge time \geq END\_OF\_TIME \\ END\_OF\_TIME/dt, & cnt \leq 0 \wedge time < END\_OF\_TIME \\ (ctx.particles/PARTICLES\_PER\_BLOCK) \times & \\ (END\_OF\_TIME/dt), & cnt > 0 \wedge time < END\_OF\_TIME \end{cases}$
race_condition1.c	78	1	$B = 1$ (NO LOOPS)
ray.c	524	∞	non-terminating

worst case complexity or worst case bound for programs [4] [7] [9] [17] [3]. In our application we use the approach of [4], which develops a counter instrumentation which adds new counter variables at the back edges of loops and computes invariants on each counter variable. A worst case bound is then synthesized in terms of these invariants.

To symbolically compute the average case bound, we take the following two steps:

1. Run the control flow refinement method of Section 4, and return a finite set of $(+, \cdot)$-path expressions, each accompanied with its precondition;
2. Run any method of computing worst case bound on each of the $(+, \cdot)$-path expressions with its preconditions.

Assume that we are provided with a (joint) probability distribution on the set of initial values of the program variables, we are able to compute the average case bound for the program. We provide two sets of experimental results. We first run our method on several benchmarks of C programs [11]. The results are presented in Table 1. Column "Example file" gives the example names; column "LOC" shows the number of lines of code of the corresponding example; column

Table 2. Experiment results 2

Example	B_{WORST}	case #	B_{AVG}

`assume(0 <= id < maxId);`
`int tmp := id+1;`
`while(tmp != id)`
`    if (tmp <= maxId)`
`        tmp := tmp+1;`
`    else`
`        tmp := 0;`
	$maxId + 1$	2	$B = \begin{cases} maxId + 1 & id \neq 0 \\ maxId + 1 & id = 0 \end{cases}$

`assume(0 <= n && 0 <= m && 0 <= N);`
`i := 0;`
`while(i < n)`
`    j := 0;`
`    while(j < m)`
`        j := j+1;`
`        k := i;`
`        while(k < N)`
`            k := K+1;`
`        i := k;`
`    i := i+1;`
	$n + (m \times n) + N$	5	$B = \begin{cases} 0 & n < 1 \\ n & n \geq 1 \wedge m < 1 \\ n \times m & n \geq 1 \wedge m \geq 1 \wedge N < 1 \\ N + m & n \geq 1 \wedge m \geq 1 \wedge N \geq 1 \wedge N \geq n - 1 \\ N + m+ & n \geq 1 \wedge m \geq 1 \wedge N \geq 1 \wedge N < n - 1 \\ (n - N) \times (m - 1) \end{cases}$

`assume (n > 0 && m > 0);`
`v1 := n; v2 := 0;`
`while (v1 > 0)`
`    if (v2 < m)`
`        v2++; v1--;`
`    else`
`        v2 := 0;`
	$\frac{n}{m} + n$	2	$B = \begin{cases} n & v1 \leq m - v2 \\ \frac{n}{m} + n & v1 > m - v2 \end{cases}$

`assume (0 < m < n);`
`i := 0; j := 0;`
`while (i < n)`
`    if (j < m)`
`        j++;`
`    else`
`        j :=0; i++;`
	$n \times m$	1	$B = \{ m \times n \quad true$

`assume (0 < m < n);`
`i := n;`
`while (i > 0)`
`    if (i < m)`
`        i--;`
`    else`
`        i := i - m;`
	$\frac{n}{m} + m$	1	$B = \left\{ \frac{n}{m} + m \quad true \right.$

`assume (0 < m < n);`
`i := m;`
`while (0 < i < n)`
`    if (dir = fwd)`
`        i++;`
`    else`
`        i--;`
	$max(m, n - m)$	2	$B = \begin{cases} n - m & dir = fwd \\ m & dir \neq fwd \end{cases}$

"#" indicates how many $(+, \cdot)$-path expressions we obtain when we calculate the bound; column "Bound" gives the end result of our computation. Notice that except for the last example where the program is not terminating, we are able to find finitely many $(+, \cdot)$-path expressions for all the rest examples. The second set of benchmarks is taken from literature [20,1,7,22,25,23,21]. The results are presented in Table 2. The column titled B_{WORST} shows the worst case complexity for these examples. It can be seen that for all the examples in Table 2, the average case bound is smaller than or equal to the worst one (assuming an arbitrary joint probability distribution).

6   Conclusions

Our first contribution is that we introduced a new concept, $(+, \cdot)$-path expressions, to describe the behavior of execution patterns. Programs induced by $(+, \cdot)$-path expressions have no branch interleaving or inner loop skipping-over. Two main factors that cause impreciseness in control flow analysis.

The second contribution of this paper is that we developed a practical algorithm that takes a conventional path expression and generates a set of equivalent $(+, \cdot)$-path expressions. In theory, the conversion may lead to an infinite set. We leverage the abstract interpretation approach to calculate the weakest precondition and post condition, thus by checking satisfiability, we can prune the infeasible expressions while we generate them. Therefore the algorithm is more likely to converge.

Lastly, we implemented the first automatic prototype that computes average case bounds for C programs. The experiments are clear indication of the utility of our tool. The results are inline with our claim that for most programs in practice we only need finitely many $(+,\cdot)$-path expressions to express different execution patterns and the computation converges very quickly. Also from Table 2, it can be seen that for reasonable joint probability distributions, the average case bound can be less than the worst case one (see the second, third, and the sixth examples in Table 2).

References

1. Balakrishnan, G., Sankaranarayanan, S., Ivančić, F., Gupta, A.: Refining the control structure of loops using static analysis. In: Proceedings of the Seventh ACM International Conference on Embedded Software, EMSOFT 2009, pp. 49–58. ACM, New York (2009)
2. Cousot, P., Cousot, R.: Abstract interpretation: A unified lattice model for static analysis of programs by construction or approximation of fixpoints. In: POPL, pp. 238–252 (1977)
3. Goldsmith, S.F., Aiken, A.S., Wilkerson, D.S.: Measuring empirical computational complexity. In: Proceedings of the the the 6th Joint Meeting of the European Software Engineering Conference and the ACM SIGSOFT Symposium on The Foundations of Software Engineering, ESEC-FSE 2007, pp. 395–404. ACM, New York (2007)
4. Gulavani, B.S., Gulwani, S.: A numerical abstract domain based on expression abstraction and max operator with application in timing analysis. In: Gupta, A., Malik, S. (eds.) CAV 2008. LNCS, vol. 5123, pp. 370–384. Springer, Heidelberg (2008)
5. Gulwani, S.: SPEED: Symbolic complexity bound analysis. In: Bouajjani, A., Maler, O. (eds.) CAV 2009. LNCS, vol. 5643, pp. 51–62. Springer, Heidelberg (2009)
6. Gulwani, S., Jain, S., Koskinen, E.: Control-flow refinement and progress invariants for bound analysis. SIGPLAN Not. 44, 375–385 (2009)
7. Gulwani, S., Mehra, K.K., Chilimbi, T.: Speed: precise and efficient static estimation of program computational complexity. In: Proceedings of the 36th Annual ACM SIGPLAN-SIGACT Symposium on Principles of Programming Languages, POPL 2009, pp. 127–139. ACM, New York (2009)
8. Gulwani, S., Zuleger, F.: The reachability-bound problem. In: PLDI, pp. 292–304 (2010)
9. Healy, C., Sjödin, M., Rustagi, V., Whalley, D., Van Engelen, R.: Supporting timing analysis by automatic bounding of loop iterations. Real-Time Syst. 18, 129–156 (2000)
10. Knuth, D.E.: The Art of Computer Programming, 2nd edn. Fundamental Algorithms, vol. I. Addison-Wesley (1973)
11. Kröning, D.: Cprover benchmarking toolkit, http://www.cprover.org/software/benchmarks/
12. Le Métayer, D.: Ace: An automatic complexity evaluator. ACM Trans. Program. Lang. Syst. 10(2), 248–266 (1988)

13. Podelski, A., Rybalchenko, A.: A complete method for the synthesis of linear ranking functions. In: Steffen, B., Levi, G. (eds.) VMCAI 2004. LNCS, vol. 2937, pp. 239–251. Springer, Heidelberg (2004)
14. Rosendahl, M.: Automatic complexity analysis. In: FPCA, pp. 144–156 (1989)
15. Wegbreit, B.: Mechanical program analysis. Commun. ACM 18(9), 528–539 (1975)
16. Wegbreit, B.: Verifying program performance. J. ACM 23, 691–699 (1976)
17. Wilhelm, R., Engblom, J., Ermedahl, A., Holsti, N., Thesing, S., Whalley, D., Bernat, G., Ferdinand, C., Heckmann, R., Mitra, T., Mueller, F., Puaut, I., Puschner, P., Staschulat, J., Stenström, P.: The worst-case execution time problem—overview of methods and survey of tools. ACM Transactions on Embedded Computing Systems (TECS) 7(3) (2008)
18. Wilhelm, R., Wachter, B.: Abstract interpretation with applications to timing validation. In: Gupta, A., Malik, S. (eds.) CAV 2008. LNCS, vol. 5123, pp. 22–36. Springer, Heidelberg (2008)
19. Wolfram, S.: The Mathematica Book, 5th edn. Wolfram Media, Incorporated (2003)
20. Albert, E., Arenas, P., Genaim, S., Puebla, G.: Automatic inference of upper bounds for recurrence relations in cost analysis. In: Alpuente, M., Vidal, G. (eds.) SAS 2008. LNCS, vol. 5079, pp. 221–237. Springer, Heidelberg (2008)
21. Bradley, A.R., Manna, Z., Sipma, H.B.: Linear ranking with reachability. In: Etessami, K., Rajamani, S.K. (eds.) CAV 2005. LNCS, vol. 3576, pp. 491–504. Springer, Heidelberg (2005)
22. Chen, H.Y., Flur, S., Mukhopadhyay, S.: Termination proofs for linear simple loops. In: Miné, A., Schmidt, D. (eds.) SAS 2012. LNCS, vol. 7460, pp. 422–438. Springer, Heidelberg (2012)
23. Cook, B., Gulwani, S., Lev-ami, T., Rybalchenko, A., Sagiv, M.: Proving conditional termination (2008)
24. Kroening, D., Sharygina, N., Tonetta, S., Tsitovich, A., Wintersteiger, C.M.: Loop summarization using abstract transformers. In: Cha, S(S.), Choi, J.-Y., Kim, M., Lee, I., Viswanathan, M. (eds.) ATVA 2008. LNCS, vol. 5311, pp. 111–125. Springer, Heidelberg (2008)
25. Kroening, D., Sharygina, N., Tsitovich, A., Wintersteiger, C.M.: Termination analysis with compositional transition invariants. In: Touili, T., Cook, B., Jackson, P. (eds.) CAV 2010. LNCS, vol. 6174, pp. 89–103. Springer, Heidelberg (2010)
26. Tarjan, R.E.: Fast algorithms for solving path problems. J. ACM 28, 594–614 (1981)

Termination and Cost Analysis of Loops with Concurrent Interleavings*

Elvira Albert[1], Antonio Flores-Montoya[2], Samir Genaim[1],
and Enrique Martin-Martin[1]

[1] Complutense University of Madrid (UCM), Spain
[2] Technische Universität Darmstadt (TUD), Germany

Abstract. By following a *rely-guarantee* style of reasoning, we present a novel termination analysis for concurrent programs that, in order to prove termination of a considered loop, makes the assumption that the "shared-data that is involved in the termination proof of the loop is modified a finite number of times". In a subsequent step, it proves that this assumption holds in all code whose execution might interleave with such loop. At the core of the analysis, we use a *may-happen-in-parallel* analysis to restrict the set of program points whose execution can interleave with the considered loop. Interestingly, the same kind of reasoning can be applied to infer *upper bounds* on the number of iterations of loops with concurrent interleavings. To the best of our knowledge, this is the first method to automatically bound the cost of such kind of loops.

1 Introduction

We develop new techniques for cost and termination analyses of *concurrent objects*. The *actor*-based paradigm [1] on which concurrent objects are based has evolved as a powerful computational model for defining distributed and concurrent systems. In this paradigm, actors are the universal primitives of concurrent computation: in response to a message, an actor can make local decisions, create more actors, send more messages, and determine how to respond to the next message received. *Concurrent objects* (a.k.a. active objects) [18,19] are actors which communicate via *asynchronous* method calls. Each concurrent object is a monitor and allows at most one *active* task to execute within the object. Scheduling among the tasks of an object is cooperative (or non-preemptive) such that a task has to release the object lock explicitly. Each object has an unbounded set of pending tasks. When the lock of an object is free, any task in the set of pending tasks can grab the lock and start to execute. The synchronization between the caller and the callee methods can be performed when the result is necessary by means of *future variables* [11]. The underlying concurrency model of actor languages forms the basis of the programming languages Erlang [7] and Scala [14] that have gained in popularity, in part due to their support for scalable concurrency. There are also implementations of actor libraries for Java.

* This work was funded partially by the projects FP7-ICT-610582, TIN2008-05624, TIN2012-38137, PRI-AIBDE-2011-0900 and S2009TIC-1465.

D. Van Hung and M. Ogawa (Eds.): ATVA 2013, LNCS 8172, pp. 349–364, 2013.
© Springer International Publishing Switzerland 2013

Termination analysis of concurrent and distributed systems is receiving considerable attention [17,2,9]. The main challenge is in handling *shared-memory* concurrent programs. This is because, when execution interleaves from one task to another, the shared-memory may be modified by the interleaved task. The modifications will affect the behavior of the program and, in particular, can change its termination behavior and its resource consumption. Inspired by the rely-guarantee style of reasoning used for compositional verification [12] and analysis [9] of thread-based concurrent programs, we present a novel termination analysis for concurrent objects which assumes a *property* on the global state in order to prove termination of a loop and, then, proves that this property holds. The property we propose to prove is the *finiteness* of the shared-data involved in the termination proof, i.e., proving that such shared-memory is updated a finite number of times. Our method is based on a circular style of reasoning since the finiteness assumptions are proved by proving termination of the loops in which that shared-memory is modified. Crucial for accuracy is the use of the information inferred by a *may-happen-in-parallel* (MHP) analysis [4], which allows us to restrict the set of program points on which the property has to be proved to those that may actually interleave its execution with the considered loop.

Besides termination, we also are able to apply this style of reasoning in order to infer the resource consumption (or cost) of executing the concurrent program. The results of our termination analysis already provide useful information for cost: if the program is terminating, we know that the size of all data is bounded. Thus, we can give cost bounds in terms of the maximum and/or minimum values that the involved data can reach. Still, we need novel techniques to infer upper bounds on the number of iterations of loops whose execution might interleave with instructions that update the shared memory. We provide a novel approach which is based on the combination of *local* ranking functions (i.e., ranking functions obtained by ignoring the concurrent interleaving behaviors) with upper bounds on the *number of visits* to the instructions which update the shared memory. As in the case of the termination analysis, an auxiliary MHP analysis is used to restrict the set of points whose visits have to be counted to those that indeed may interleave. To the best of our knowledge this is the first approach to infer the cost of loops with concurrent interleavings.

Our analysis has been implemented, and its termination component is already fully integrated in COSTABS [2], a COSt and Termination analyzer for concurrent objects. Experimental evaluation of the termination analysis has been performed on a case study developed by Fredhopper® and several other smaller applications. Preliminary results are promising in both the accuracy and efficiency of the analysis.

The rest of the paper is organized as follows. Sec. 2 contains preliminaries about the language, termination and cost. Sec. 3 and 4 explains the rely-guarantee termination and cost analysis, respectively. Sec. 5 contains the preliminary evaluation of the analyses. Finally, Sec. 6 presents the conclusions and related work.

2   Concurrency Model, Termination and Cost

This section presents the syntax and concurrency model of the concurrent objects language, which is basically the same as [15,2]. A *program* consists of a set of classes, each of them can define a set of fields, and a set of methods. The notation $\bar{T}$ is used as a shorthand for $T_1, ... T_n$, and similarly for other names. The set of types includes the classes and the set of *future* variable types $fut(T)$. *Pure* expressions pu (i.e., functional expressions that do not access the shared memory) and primitive types are standard and omitted. The abstract syntax of class declarations CL, method declarations M, types T, variables V, and statements s is:

$$CL ::= \text{class } C \ \{\bar{T} \ \bar{f}; \bar{M}\} \quad M ::= T \ m(\bar{T} \ \bar{x})\{s; \text{return } p; \} \quad V ::= x \,|\, \text{this}.f$$
$$s ::= s; s \,|\, x = e \,|\, V = x \,|\, \text{await } V? \,|\, \text{if } p \text{ then } s \text{ else } s \,|\, \text{while } p \text{ do } s$$
$$e ::= \text{new } C(\bar{V}) \,|\, V!m(\bar{V}) \,|\, pu \quad T ::= C \,|\, fut(T)$$

As in the actor-model, the main idea is that control and data are encapsulated within the notion of concurrent object. Thus each object encapsulates a *local heap* which stores the data that is *shared* within the object. Fields are always accessed using the **this** object, and any other object can only access such fields through method calls. We assume that every method ends with a **return** instruction. The concurrency model is as follows. Each object has a lock that is shared by all tasks that belong to the object. Data synchronization is by means of future variables: An **await** y? instruction is used to synchronize with the result of executing task $y=x!m(\bar{z})$ such that **await** y? is executed only when the future variable y is available (i.e., the task is finished). In the meantime, the object's lock can be released and some other *pending* task on that object can take it. W.l.o.g, we assume that all methods in a program have different names.

A *program state* St is a set $St = \text{Ob} \cup \text{T}$ where Ob is the set of all created objects, and T is the set of all created tasks. An *object* is a term $ob(o, a, lk)$ where o is the object identifier, a is a mapping from the object fields to their values, and lk the identifier of the *active task* that holds the object's lock or $\perp$ if the object's lock is free. Only one task can be *active* (running) in each object and has its *lock*. All other tasks are *pending* to be executed, or *finished* if they terminated and released the lock. A *task* is a term $tsk(t, m, o, l, s)$ where t is a unique task identifier, m is the method name executing in the task, o identifies the object to which the task belongs, l is a mapping from local (possibly future) variables to their values, and s is the sequence of instructions to be executed or $s = \epsilon(v)$ if the task has terminated and the return value v is available. Created objects and tasks never disappear from the state. Complete semantic rules can be found in the extended version of this paper [5].

Example 1. Figure 1 shows some simple examples which will illustrate different aspects of our analysis. We have an interface Task, and a class TaskQueue which implements a queue of tasks to which one can add a single task using method AddTask or a list of tasks using method AddTasks. The loop that adds the tasks invokes asynchronously method AddTask and then awaits for its termination at

```
1 Class TaskQueue{
2 List<Task> pending=Nil;
3 void AddTask(Task tk){
4 pending= appendright(pending,tk);
5 }
6 void AddTasks(List<Task> list){
7 while (list != Nil) {
8   Task tk = head(list);
9   pending = tail(list);
10  Fut f=this!AddTask(tk);
11  await f?;}
12 }
13 void ConsumeAsync(){
14 while (pending != Nil) {
15  Task tk = head(pending);
16  pending = tail(pending);
17  Fut f=tk!start();}
18 }
19 void ConsumeSync(){
20 while (pending != Nil) {
21  Task tk = head(pending);
22  pending = tail(pending);
23  Fut f=tk!start();
24  await f?;}
25 }} //end class TaskQueue
26 Interface Task {void start();}
```

```
27 //implementations of main methods
28 main1(List<Task> l){
29  TaskQueue q=new TaskQueue();
30  q!AddTasks(l);
31  q!ConsumeAsync();
32 }
33 main2(List<Task> l){
34  TaskQueue q= new TaskQueue();
35  Fut f=q!AddTasks(l);
36  await f?;
37  q!ConsumeSync();
38 }
39 main3(List<Task> l){
40  TaskQueue q= new TaskQueue();
41  q!AddTasks(l);
42  q!ConsumeSync();
43 }
44 main4(List<Task> l){
45  TaskQueue q= new TaskQueue();
46  while (true){
47    Fut x=q!AddTasks(l);
48    Fut y=q!ConsumeSync();
49    await x?;
50    await y?;}
51 }
```

Fig. 1. Simple examples for termination and cost

Line 11 (L11 for short). We use the predefined generic type List<E> with the usual operations appendright to add an element of type <E> to the end of the list, head to get the element in the head of the list and tail to get the remaining elements. These operations are performed on pure data (i.e., data that possibly contains references but does not access the shared memory) and are executed sequentially. The class has two other methods, ConsumeAsync and ConsumeSync, to consume the tasks inside the queue. The former method starts all tasks (L17) concurrently. Instead, method ConsumeSync executes each task synchronously. It releases the processor and waits until the task is finished at L24. In the rightmost column, there are four implementations of main methods which are defined outside the classes. Here we show some execution steps from main3:

$St_1 \equiv \{obj(0, f, 0)\ tsk(0, \mathsf{main3}, 0, l, \mathsf{q=new\ TaskQueue();}...)\} \xrightarrow{new}$

$St_2 \equiv \{obj(0, f, 0)\ obj(1, f_1, \bot)\ tsk(0, \mathsf{main3}, 0, l', \mathsf{q!AddTasks(l);}...)\} \xrightarrow{async-call}$

$St_3 \equiv \{obj(0, f, 0)\ obj(1, f_1, \bot)\ tsk(0, \mathsf{main3}, 0, l', \mathsf{q!ConsumeSync(1);}...)$
$\quad tsk(1, \mathsf{AddTasks}, 1, l'', \mathsf{while(list!= Nil);}...)\} \xrightarrow{async-call}$

$St_4 \equiv \{obj(0, f, 0)\ obj(1, f_1, \bot)\ tsk(0, \mathsf{main3}, 0, l', \mathsf{return;})\ tsk(1, \mathsf{AddTasks}, 1, l'', ...)$
$\quad tsk(2, \mathsf{ConsumeSync}, 1, l''', \mathsf{while(pending!= Nil);}...)\} \xrightarrow{return}\xrightarrow{activate}$

$St_5 \equiv \{obj(0, f, \bot)\ obj(1, f_1, 2)\ tsk(0..)\ tsk(1..)\ tsk(2..)\}$

Observe that the execution of **new** at St_1 creates the object identified by 1. Then, the executions of the asynchronous calls at St_2 and St_3 spawn new tasks on object 1 identified by 1 and 2, respectively. In St_4, we perform two steps, first the execution of task 0 terminates (executes return) and object 0 becomes idle, next object 1 (which was idle) selects task 2 for execution. Note that as scheduling is non-deterministic any of both pending tasks (1 or 2) could have been selected.

2.1   Termination and Cost

Traces take the form $t \equiv St_0 \to^{b_0} \cdots \to^{b_{n-1}} St_n$, where St_0 is an initial state in which only the main method is available and the superscript b_i is the instruction that is executed in the step. A trace is *complete* if it cannot continue from St_n(not taking into account spurious cycles of take-release an object's lock). A trace is *finished* if every task in the configuration $tsk(t, m, o, l, s) \in$ T is finished $s = \epsilon(v))$. If a trace is complete but not finished, the trace must be *deadlocked*. Deadlocks happen when several tasks are awaiting for each other to terminate and remain blocked. Deadlock is different from non-termination, as non-terminating traces keep on consuming instructions. As we have seen, since we have no assumptions on scheduling, from a given state there may be several possible *non-deterministic* execution steps that can be taken. We say that a program is *terminating* if all possible traces from the initial state are complete.

When measuring the cost, different metrics can be considered. A cost model is a function $\mathcal{M} : Ins \mapsto \mathbb{R}^+$ which maps instructions built using the grammar above to positive real numbers and, in this way, it defines the considered metrics. The cost of an execution step is defined as $\mathcal{M}(St \to^b St') = \mathcal{M}(b)$, i.e., the cost of the instruction applied in the step. The cost of a trace is the sum of the costs of all its execution steps. The cost of executing a program is the *maximum* of the costs of all possible traces from the initial state. We aim at inferring an *upper bound* on the cost of executing a program P for the defined cost model, denoted UB_P, which is larger than or equal to that maximum.

Example 2. A cost model that counts the number of instructions is defined as $\mathcal{M}_{inst}(b) = 1$ where b is any instruction of the grammar. A cost model that counts the number of visits to a method m is defined as $\mathcal{M}_{visits\_m}(b) = 1$ if $b = x!m(\bar{z})$ and 0 otherwise. Consider the partial trace of Ex. 1. By applying $\mathcal{M}_{inst}$ we get 4 executed instructions (as the application of ACTIVATE does not involve any instruction) and if we count $\mathcal{M}_{visits\_ConsumSync}$ we obtain 1.

3   Termination Analysis

This section gives first in Sec. 3.1 the intuition behind our method, then it presents the termination algorithm in Sec. 3.2, and finally it provides the results that we need for its application in cost analysis in Sec. 3.3.

3.1 Basic Reasoning

Our starting point is an analysis [2] that infers the termination (and resource consumption) of concurrent programs by losing all information on the shared-memory at "processor release points" (i.e., at the points in which the processor can switch the execution to another task because of an **await** instruction or a method return). Alternatively, instead of losing all information, it can also use monitor invariants (provided by the user) to force some assumptions on the shared-memory. In the latter alternative, the correctness of the analysis depends on the correctness of the provided invariants (the analysis does not infer nor prove them correct). Let us show the kind of problems that [2] can and cannot solve. Consider the first three implementations of main methods:

- main1 creates a TaskQueue q, adds the list of tasks received as input parameter to it, and executes ConsumeAsync. It is not guaranteed that the tasks are added to the queue when ConsumeAsync starts to execute because, as the call at L30 is not synchronized, the processor can be released at L11 and the call at L31 can start to execute. This is not a problem for termination, since ConsumeAsync is executed without releasing the processor. Hence, the method of [2] can prove all methods terminating.
- in main2 the addition of tasks (i.e., the call to AddTasks at L35) is guaranteed to be terminated when ConsumeSync starts to execute due to the use of **await** at L36. However, the difficulty is that ConsumeSync contains a release point. The method of [2] fails to prove termination because at this release point pending is lost. The key is to detect that there are no concurrent interleavings at L24 in this loop by means of an auxiliary MHP analysis.
- main3 has a loop with concurrent interleavings since ConsumeSync is called without waiting for completion of AddTasks. Thus, some tasks can be added to the list of pending tasks in the middle of the execution of ConsumeSync, resulting in a different ordering in which tasks are executed, or even can be added when ConsumeSync has finished and hence start will not be executed at all on them. Proving termination requires developing novel techniques.

Our reasoning is at the level of the strongly connected components (SCCs), denoted $\langle S_1, \ldots, S_n \rangle$, in which the code to be analyzed is split. For each method m, we have an SCC named S_m and for each loop (in the methods) starting at Lx we have an SCC named S_x. The analysis starting from main2 must consider the SCCs: $\langle S_{\text{main2}}, S_{\text{AddTasks}}, S_7, S_{\text{AddTask}}, S_{\text{ConsumeSync}}, S_{20} \rangle$. For simplifying the presentation, we assume that each recursive SCC has a single cut-point (in the corresponding CFG). Moreover, the cut-point is assumed to be the entry of the SCC. In such case, an SCC can be viewed as a simple while loop (i.e., without nested loops) with several possible paths in its body. Nested loops can be transformed into this form, by viewing the inner loops as separate procedures that are called from the outer ones. This, however, cannot be done for complex mutual recursions which are rare in our context. The purpose of this assumption is to simplify the way we count the number of visits to a given program point in Sec. 4.

In order to use the techniques of [2] as a black-box, in what follows, we assume that seq_termin(S, F) is a basic termination analysis procedure that receives an

SCC S and a set of fields F, and works as follows: (1) given a function *fields* that returns the set of fields accessed in the given scope, for any $f \in fields(S) \setminus F$, it adds the instruction $f = *$ at each release point of S; (2) it tries to proves termination of the instrumented code using an off-the-shelf termination analyzer for sequential code; and (3) it returns the result. We assume that seq_termin ignores calls to SCCs transitively invoked from the considered scope S, assumes nothing about their return values, and ignores the instruction **await**.

Observation 1 (finiteness assumption). *If S terminates under the assumption that a set of fields F are not modified at the release points of S, then S also terminates if they are modified a finite number of times.*

The intuition behind our observation is as follows. Since the fields are modified finitely, then we will eventually reach a state from which that state on they are not modified. From that state, we cannot have non-termination since we know that S terminates if the fields are not modified. Moreover, one can construct a lexicographical ranking function [8] that witnesses the termination of S.

Example 3. Consider the following two loops:

$$
S_1 \begin{cases}
\text{52 } \textbf{while (f > 0) \{} \\
\text{53 } \quad \text{x = g();} \\
\text{54 } \quad \textbf{await} \text{ x?;} \\
\text{55 } \quad \text{f}--; \text{ \}} \\
\text{56 }
\end{cases}
\qquad
S_2 \begin{cases}
\text{57 } \textbf{while (m > 0) \{} \\
\text{58 } \quad \text{x = g();} \\
\text{59 } \quad \textbf{await} \text{ x?;} \\
\text{60 } \quad \text{f=*;} \\
\text{61 } \quad \text{m}--; \text{ \}}
\end{cases}
$$

and assume that S_1 and S_2 are the only running processes. Their execution might interleave since both loops have a release point. We let f be a shared variable, m a local variable, and we ignore the behavior of method g. It is easy to see that (a) S_1 terminates under the assumption that f does not change at the release point (L54), and that $RF_1(m, f) = f$ is a ranking function that witnesses its termination; and (b) S_2 terminates without any assumption and $RF_2(m, f) = m$ is a ranking function that witnesses its termination. Since S_2 terminates, we know that f is modified a finite number of times at the release point of S_1 and thus, according to Observation 1, S_1 terminates when running in parallel with S_2. The lexicographical ranking function $RF_3(f, m) = \langle m, f \rangle$ is a witness of the termination of S_1.

3.2   Termination Algorithm

Algorithm 1 presents the main components of our termination algorithm, defined by means of function TERMINATES. The first parameter S is an SCC that we want to prove terminating, and the second one *SSet* includes the SCCs whose termination requires the termination of S. The role of the second parameter is to detect circular dependencies. In order to prove that a program P terminates, we prove that all its SCCs terminate by calling TERMINATES$(S, \emptyset)$ on each one of them. Let us explain the different lines of the algorithm:

Algorithm 1. MHP-based Termination Analysis

1: **function** TERMINATES(S,$SSet$)
2: **if** $S \in SSet$ **then return false**
3: **if** seq_termin($S, \emptyset$) **then return true**
4: $F = $ select_fields(S)
5: **if** (**not** seq_termin(S, F)) **then return false**
6: $RP = $ release_points(S)
7: $MP = $ MHP_pairs(RP)
8: $I = $ field_updates(MP, F)
9: $DepSet = $ extract_sccs(I)
10: **for each** $S' \in DepSet$ **do**
11:   **if** (**not** TERMINATES($S', SSet \cup \{S\}$)) **then return false**
12: **return true**

---

1. At Line 2, if S is in the set *SSet*, then a circular dependency has been detected, i.e., the termination of S depends on the termination of S itself. In such case the algorithm returns **false** (since we cannot handle such cases).
2. At Line 3, it first tries to prove termination of S without any assumption on the fields, i.e., assuming that their values are lost at release points. If it succeeds, then it returns **true**. Otherwise, in the next lines it will try to prove termination w.r.t. some finiteness assumptions on the fields.
3. At Line 4, it selects a set of fields F and, at Line 5, it tries to prove that S terminates when assuming that fields from F keep their values at the release points. If it fails, then it returns **false**. Otherwise, in the next lines it will try to prove that these fields are modified finitely in order to apply Observation 1. The simplest strategy for constructing F (which is the one implemented in our system) is to include all fields used in S. This can also be refined to select only those that might affect the termination of S (using some dependency analysis or heuristics).
4. At this point the algorithm identifies all instructions that might modify a field from F while S is waiting at a release point. This is done as follows: at Line 6 it constructs the set RP of all release points in S; at Line 7 it constructs the set MP of all program points that may run in parallel with program points in RP (this is provided by an auxiliary MHP analysis [4]); and at Line 8 it remains with $I \subseteq MP$ that actually update a field in F.
5. At Line 9, it constructs a set *DepSet* of *all* SCCs that can reach a program point in I, i.e., those SCCs that include a program point from I or can reach one by (transitively) calling a method that includes one. Proving termination of these SCCs guarantees that each instruction in I is executed finitely, and thus the fields in F are updated finitely and the finiteness assumption holds.
6. The loop at Line 10 tries to prove that each SCC in *DepSet* terminates. If it finds one that might not terminate, it returns **false**. In the recursive call S is added to the second parameter in order to detect circular dependencies.
7. If the algorithm reaches Line 12, then S is terminating and returns **true**.

Essentially our approach translates the concurrent program into a sequential setting using the assumptions. To define our proposal, we have focused exclusively on the finiteness assumption because of its wide applicability for proving termination of different forms of loops. Being more general requires a more complex reasoning than when handling other kinds of simpler assumptions. For instance, simpler assumptions (like checking that a field always increases or decreases its value when it is updated) can be easily handled by adding a corresponding test, after Line 8, that checks the assumption holds on the instructions in I.

Example 4. We can now prove termination of both main2 and main3. For main2, the challenge is to prove termination of ConsumeSync and namely of the loop that forms S_{20}. This loop depends on the field pending whose size is decreased at each iteration. However, there is a release point in the loop's body (L24). Thus, we need to guarantee the finiteness assumption on pending at that point. The MHP analysis infers that the only other instruction that updates pending at L4 cannot happen in parallel with the release point. This can be inferred thanks to the use of **await** at L11 and L36. Therefore, the set I at Line 8 of Alg. 1 is empty and TERMINATES returns **true**. In the analysis of main3, when proving termination of $S_{\text{ConsumeSync}}$ we have that L4 can happen in parallel with L24 so we have to prove the *finiteness assumption* recursively. In particular, $DepSet = \{S_{\text{AddTask}}, S_7, S_{\text{AddTasks}}, S_{\text{main3}}\}$. Proving termination of S_7 is done directly by seq_termin as termination of the loop depends only on the non-shared data list. Also, S_{AddTask}, S_{AddTasks} and S_{main3} are proved terminating by seq_termin as they do not contain loops. Thus, pending can only increase up to a certain limit and the termination of $S_{\text{ConsumeSync}}$ and all other scopes can be guaranteed.

We can achieve further precision by replacing extract_sccs by a procedure extract_mhp_sccs which returns all SCCs that can reach a program point in I *and* that can happen in parallel with a release point in RP. A sufficient condition for an SCC to happen in parallel with a point in RP is that its entry point (entry point of while rule) might happen in parallel with a point in RP. The correctness of this enhancement is proved in [5]. The point is that with extract_sccs we could find loops that contain I but cannot iterate at RP. These do not have to be taken into account because during the execution of S they will be stopped in a single iteration and therefore cannot cause unboundedness in S. This happens in the next example.

Example 5. Using extract_mhp_sccs we can prove that ConsumeSync always terminates in the context of main4. This is true because only one instance of AddTasks is running in parallel with ConsumeSync (due to the **await**s at L49 and L50), and AddTasks is terminating. Using extract_sccs, we would detect that L4 is reached from S_{46} and thus, it cannot be proved bounded (due to the **while (true)**). However, the MHP analysis tells us that the **await** in L24 of ConsumeSync can run in parallel with AddTasks but not with S_{46}. This reduces the number of SCC we have to consider (removing S_{46}) and thus we can prove ConsumeSync terminating.

Proving termination of the SCCs given by extract_mhp_sccs guarantees that each instruction in I is executed finitely during the release points RP, and thus the fields in F are updated finitely and the finiteness assumption holds. We assume that `extract_mhp_sccs` is used in what follows. The following theorem ensures the soundness of our approach (the proof is in [5]).

Theorem 1 (soundness). *Given a program P and its set of recursive SCCs SSet. If, $\forall S \in SSet$, TERMINATES$(S, \emptyset)$ returns* ***true***, *then P is terminating.*

3.3   Inferring Field-Boundedness

The termination procedure in Sec. 3 gives us an automatic technique to infer field-boundedness, i.e., knowing that field f has upper and lower bounds on the values that it can take. The *upper* (resp. *lower*) bound of a field f is denoted as f^+ (resp. f^-), and we use f^b to refer to the bounds $[f^-, f^+]$ for f.

Corollary 1. *Consider a field f. If all recursive SCCs that reach a point in which f is updated are terminating, then f is bounded.*

4   Cost Analysis

As for termination, the resource consumption (or cost) of executing a fragment of code can be affected by concurrent interleavings in the loops. Previous work [2] is not able to estimate the cost in these cases. This section proposes new techniques to bound the number of iterations of such loops and thus the cost. This requires to have first proved field-boundedness (Sec. 3.3).

4.1   Cost Analysis of Sequential Programs

Let us first provide an intuitive view of the process of inferring the cost of a program divided in SCCs $S_1, \ldots, S_n$. As an example consider this code:

```
62   main (int n, int m)
63      { int i=0; while (i<n) { i++; s₂; int j=i; while (j<m) {s₁; j++; }}}
```

where s_1 and s_2 represent a sequence of instructions that do not call any other SCC and do not modify the counters. This leads to one SCC for the inner loop S_1 and one SCC for the outer loop S_2. We first consider the SCC which does not call any other scope, S_1. Given a fragment of sequential code s, we can apply the cost model $\mathcal{M}$ to all instructions in s (see Sec. 2.1) and sum the result, denoted as $\mathcal{M}(s)$. Now, an upper bound on the cost of executing the SCC S_1 is $\text{UB}_{S_1} = \#iter * \mathcal{M}(body(S_1))$ where $\#iter$ is an upper bound on the number of loop iterations. For sequential programs [3], a ranking function for the loop soundly approximates $\#iter$ and can be automatically inferred. In this case, $\text{UB}_{S_1} = \text{nat}(m-j+1) * \mathcal{M}(body(S_1))$, where function nat is defined as $\text{nat}(n) = n$ if $n \geq 0$ and 0 otherwise (it is used to avoid having negative costs [3]).

We consider now the general case in which we need to *compose* the cost of different SCCs. The point is that in order to plug the cost that we have already computed for S_1 in its calling SCC S_2, we need to *maximize* it (i.e., compute its worst case cost). Intuitively, the worst case cost is when j is 0 and hence UB_{S_1} becomes $\mathtt{nat}(m+1)*\mathcal{M}(body(S_1))$. Intuitively, maximization works by first inferring an *invariant* that holds between the arguments at the initial call (main method) and at each iteration during the execution. For instance, we infer the invariant $0 \leq j \leq m_0$ which holds in S_1 where m_0 is the initial value for m. Maximizing UB_{S_1} using the invariant results in $\mathtt{nat}(m+1)*\mathcal{M}(body(S_1))$. In what follows, we refer as $\mathtt{max\_init}(e)$ to the maximization of an expression e using such procedure (see [3]) which we simply adopt in this paper. Thus, the upper bound for S_2 is $UB_{S_2} = \#iter*(\mathcal{M}(body(S_2)) + \mathtt{max\_init}(UB_{S_1})) \equiv \mathtt{nat}(n)*(\mathcal{M}(body(S_2)) + \mathtt{nat}(m+1)*\mathcal{M}(body(S_1)))$.

Note that if the considered SCC is not recursive, then we simply apply $\mathcal{M}$ to the sequential instructions and compose the SCCs as above. SCCs with multiple recursive calls (that lead to an exponential complexity) and loops with logarithmic complexity are treated analogously, see [3].

4.2 Basic Reasoning

In order to explain the intuition of our approach, let us first consider the sequential loop in S_1 whose termination behavior has been widely studied by the termination community (we use $*$ to ignore irrelevant code):

$$
S_1 \begin{cases} {}_{64}\,\textbf{while } (\text{f>0})\{ \\ \quad {}_{65}\ \ \text{f}--; \\ \quad {}_{66}\ \ \textbf{if } (*\ \&\ \text{m>0}) \\ \quad {}_{67}\qquad \{ \ \text{m}--; \\ \quad {}_{68}\qquad\quad \text{f}=*; \\ \quad {}_{69}\,\}\} \end{cases}
\qquad
S_2 \begin{cases} {}_{70}\,\textbf{while } (\text{f>0})\{ \\ \quad {}_{71}\ \ \text{f}--; \\ \quad {}_{72}\ \ \textbf{await } *? \\ \quad {}_{73}\,\} \end{cases}
\qquad
S_3 \begin{cases} {}_{74}\,\textbf{while } (\text{m>0})\{ \\ \quad {}_{75}\ \ \text{m}--; \\ \quad {}_{76}\ \ \text{f}=*; \\ \quad {}_{77}\,\} \end{cases}
$$

Our method is inspired by the observation that, provided the **if** statement is executed a finite number of times, an upper bound on the number of iterations of S_1 can be computed as: the maximum number of iterations of the loop ignoring the **if** statement, but assuming that such **if** statement updates the field f with its maximum value, *multiplied* by the maximum number of times that the **if** statement can be executed. Intuitively, we assume that every time the **if** statement is executed the field can be put to its maximum value and thus the loop can be executed the maximum number of times in the next iteration. Hence, $\mathtt{max\_init}(f)*m$ is an upper bound for the loop, and $\mathtt{max\_init}(f) = f^+$ results in the maximum value for field f (see Sec. 3.3).

We propose to apply a similar reasoning to bound the number of iterations of loops with concurrent interleavings. Assume that S_2 and S_3 are the only running processes and that the execution of the instruction at L76 that updates the field may interleave with the **await** in S_2. We have a similar behavior to the leftmost loop, though they are obviously not equivalent. Instead of having an interleaving **if**, we have an interleaving process that updates the field. Our proposal is to first bound the number of times that instruction 76 can be executed. A sound and precise bound is m. Our main observation is that, the upper bound for S_2 is the maximum number of iterations ignoring the **await**, but assuming that at this point f can take its maximum value f^+, multiplied by the maximum number of *visits* to 76. Thus, f^+*m is a sound upper bound. If we have a loop like while (f<0) {f++; await *?}, whose ranking function is $-f$, then the worst case cost occurs when f is set to its minimum value f^-, i.e., max_init$(-f) = f^-$. Therefore, maximizing a ranking function that involves a field f is done by relying on its field bound f^b, and it may result, depending on the case, in f^+ or f^-.

Observation 2 (loop bounds). *An upper bound on the number of iterations of a loop l with interleaving instructions that update fields F is* NITER*(NVISITS+1):

1. *where* NVISITS *is the number of visits to the points in which fields in F are updated and that might interleave their execution with the loop release points;*
2. *and* NITER *is the number of iterations of the loop ignoring the interleavings —maximized w.r.t. the bounds for the fields in F;*

Our analysis relies on the assumption that the number of visits (item 1) is bounded, which has been proved in Corollary 1. Given a bound on the number of loop iterations, the cost is obtained as in the sequential case, i.e., by applying the cost model to the instructions in the loop body and multiplying it by our loop bound. Thus, we only focus now on bounding the number of loop iterations.

4.3   Bounding the Number of Iterations for Loops with Interleavings

Alg. 2 presents two mutually recursive functions which allow us to infer the two items of the observation above. For each SCC S, we assume that after executing Alg. 1 we have the following information: the set RP computed at Line 6, denoted as S_{RP}; the set I computed at Line 8, denoted as S_I; and a (linear) ranking function computed by the seq_termin at Lines 3 and 5, denoted as S_{RF}. If S was proved terminating at Line 3 (i.e., losing the fields), we assume that S_I and S_{RP} are empty. Function NITER receives an SCC S whose number of iterations is to be bounded and a set of SCCs $SSet$ which, as before, is initially empty and allows us to detect cyclic dependencies (Line 2). As the number of SCCs is finite, termination is guaranteed. If the SCC S is not recursive, it simply returns one (Line 3). Otherwise, the number of iterations in the SCC can be bound by the maximization of the local ranking function, multiplied by the maximum number of visits to all the points that update the fields (Line 7) *and* that may happen in parallel with S_{RP} (to this end we pass S_{RP} as parameter to NVISITS). As mentioned in Sec. 4.1, function max_init maximizes the received expression w.r.t. the input parameters of the entry method (often main), and the field bounds f^b are used for maximizing the fields.

Function NVISITS receives a program point p, a set of release points RP, and infers an upper bound on the number of visits to p while the program is waiting at a point of RP. We first compute the multiset of reachable paths to p. Each path is of the form $\langle S_1, \ldots, S_n \rangle$, i.e., it is a sequence of SCCs which reach the program point p. For each of the paths (Line 11), we traverse all the SCCs in the path (Line 13) and multiply the number of iterations of the corresponding

---

Algorithm 2. Bounding the Number of Iterations for Loops with Interleavings

1: **function** NITER($S, SSet$)
2:   **if** $S \in SSet$ **then return false**
3:   **if** S *is not recursive* **then return** 1
4:   $i = 1$;
5:   **for each** $p \in S_I$ **do**
6:     $i = i + $NVISITS$(p, S_{RP}, SSet \cup S)$
7:   **return** max_init$(S_{RF})*i$

8: **function** NVISITS($p, RP, SSet$)
9:   $V_p = 0$;
10:   $P =$ mhp_reachable_paths(p, RP);
11:   **for each** $\langle S_1, \ldots, S_n \rangle$ in P **do**
12:     $V_{aux} = 1$;
13:     **for** $i = 1$ **to** n **do**
14:       $V_{aux} = V_{aux}*$NITER$(S_i, SSet)$
15:     $V_p = V_p + V_{aux}$
16:   **return** V_p

SCC by those of the SCCs already traversed *if* the SCC might happen in parallel with the release points RP. We assume that mhp_reachable_paths gives us only those SCC that may happen in parallel with the release points RP passed as parameters. The number of visits from each of the paths is accumulated to the paths that have been already accounted (Line 15).

Example 6. Let us consider method ConsumeSync invoked from main3. We want to compute NITER$(S_{20}, \emptyset)$. Alg. 1 gives us that the local ranking function is $RF = length(\text{pending})$ and that the program point 4 may happen in parallel with the release point 24 and update the field pending. Hence, we need to compute NVISITS$(4, \{24\}, \{S_{20}\})$. We first compute the reachable paths to 4, which gives us the only element $\langle S_{\text{AddTask}}, S_7, S_{\text{AddTasks}} \rangle$. Note that S_{main3} is not included in the path because its entry point cannot happen in parallel with 24. We start by computing NITER$(S_{\text{AddTask}}, \{S_{20}\})$, since S_{AddTask} is not recursive, we simply return 1 which is multiplied at Line 14 of Alg. 2 by the initial value for V_{aux} (which is 1). The next iteration of the **for** loop at Line 13 invokes NITER$(S_7, \{S_{20}, S_{\text{AddTask}}\})$. In this case, by Alg. 1, we have the local ranking function $length(\text{list})$ and that the set of points at which list is updated is empty. The maximization of $length(\text{list})$ returns it in terms of the initial parameters of main3, i.e., $length(\text{l})$. This value is multiplied at Line 14 by 1 (previous value of V_{aux}). Finally, we compute NITER$(S_{\text{AddTasks}}, \{S_7, S_{20}, S_{\text{AddTask}}\})$ that, as it is not recursive, simply returns 1. The execution of the **for** loop at Line 13 finishes and also the execution of the **for each** loop at Line 11 and we have that NVISITS$(4, \{S_{20}\}) = length(\text{l})$. Thus, we can now finish the computation of NITER$(S_{20}, \emptyset)$ returning $length(\text{pending}^+)$ $*length(\text{l})$. The upper bound for ConsumeSync when invoked from main4 can be obtained in a similar way.

The following theorem ensures the soundness of our approach. The proof can be found in [5].

Theorem 2 (soundness). *Given a recursive SCC S, the execution of* NITER$(S, \emptyset)$ *terminates and returns an upper bound on the number of iterations in S.*

5   Implementation and Preliminary Evaluation

We have implemented the described cost and termination analyses, although currently only the termination component is integrated within COSTABS. Our analysis can be tried online at http://costa.ls.fi.upm.es/costabs by enabling the option *"rely-guarantee termination analysis"*. The cost analysis component will be available for its online use from the same site soon. Given a program and a selection of an entry method from which the analysis will start, the output of the analysis is a description of the SCCs (reachable from the entry) which are terminating. This section aims at performing a preliminary experimental evaluation of the accuracy and performance of our implementation, by comparing our results with those obtained by the previous version of the analyzer which loses all information on the shared-memory. For this purpose, we have analyzed a set of small and medium-sized programs, as well as one industrial case study, the *Replication System*, developed by Fredhopper®. The analyzed code for all examples can be found and tried in the above site.

Regarding the small and medium-sized examples, their number of lines of code ranges from 20 to 100 and the number of SCCs from 5 to 20. Both versions of the analyzer need less than 1 sec. to analyze each program. All terminating loops with concurrent interleavings are reported by our rely-guarantee method, improving the results of the previous analyzer. Our largest experiment is performed on the *Replication System*, a case study that provides search and merchandising IT services to e-Commerce companies, developed within the HATS project (http://www.hats-project.eu/). It has 2100 lines of code and 426 SCCs that need to be analyzed. The previous analyzer needs 2813 sec. and proves 420 SCCs terminating, whereas the rely-guarantee method proves 423 SCCs terminating in only 41 sec. Times are obtained as the arithmetic mean of five runs on a Ubuntu 12.04 32-bit with Intel Core2 Quad CPU Q9550 2.83GHz and 3.4GiB of memory. The efficiency of our rely-guarantee method can be explained because it works modularly at the level the SCCs, instead of analyzing the program globally as the previous analyzer. An inspection of the three additional SCCs that have been proved terminating confirms that they indeed correspond to loops with concurrent interleavings. The reason why a simple analysis that loses the shared-memory could achieve already good results is that the (experienced) developers of the case study were aware of the risks of having loops with concurrent interleavings and they were very much avoided.

6   Conclusions and Related Work

Concurrency adds further difficulty when attempting to prove program termination and inferring resource consumption. The problem is that the analysis must consider all possible interactions between concurrently executing objects. This is challenging because processes interact in subtle ways through fields and future variables. We have proposed novel techniques to prove termination and inferring upper bounds on the number of iterations of loops with such concurrent interleavings. Our analysis benefits from an existing MHP analysis to achieve further precision [4].

Existing methods for proving termination of thread-based programs also apply a rely-guarantee or assume-guarantee style of reasoning [9,17,10]. These methods consider every thread in isolation under assumptions on its environment, thus avoiding to reason about thread interactions directly. Applying this technique to our concurrent setting could be done by assuming a property of the second object while proving the property of the first object, and then assuming the recently proved property of the first object when proving the assumed property of the second object. Although we make assumptions and then prove them, our assumptions are of a different kind, i.e., namely they are assumptions on finiteness of data, no matter on which thread (or object) they are executed. This point makes our work fundamentally different from [9]. We can still apply our method in the presence of dynamically created objects and the number of concurrency units does not need to be known a priori as in [9].

As regards the bounds on loop iterations, to the best of our knowledge, there are no other works that have attempted to infer those bounds for loops with concurrent interleavings before. There are several techniques [13,6,20] for inferring complex loop bounds for (sequential) transition systems. Our basic termination component could benefit from these techniques. Moreover, in principle, a concurrent program could be translated to a transition system that simulates all possible interleavings, which then would allow using these techniques for inferring bounds on loops with concurrent interleaving. However, we expect such translation to be far more complicated that our techniques.

Finally, as in other kinds of analyses, by making the analysis *object-sensitive* (i.e., by distinguishing between different objects of the same class) we can achieve further precision. For instance, if we add to main3 the following two instructions TaskQueue q1=new TaskQueue(); q1!ConsumeSync();. The MHP analysis infers that ConsumeSync can run in parallel with itself. When trying to solve the equations a cyclic dependency is created and both TERMINATES and NITER algorithms terminate returning **false**.

References

1. Agha, G.A.: Actors: A Model of Concurrent Computation in Distributed Systems. MIT Press, Cambridge (1986)
2. Albert, E., Arenas, P., Genaim, S., Gómez-Zamalloa, M., Puebla, G.: Cost Analysis of Concurrent OO programs. In: Yang, H. (ed.) APLAS 2011. LNCS, vol. 7078, pp. 238–254. Springer, Heidelberg (2011)
3. Albert, E., Arenas, P., Genaim, S., Puebla, G.: Closed-Form Upper Bounds in Static Cost Analysis. Journal of Automated Reasoning 46(2), 161–203 (2011)
4. Albert, E., Flores-Montoya, A.E., Genaim, S.: Analysis of May-Happen-in-Parallel in Concurrent Objects. In: Giese, H., Rosu, G. (eds.) FMOODS/FORTE 2012. LNCS, vol. 7273, pp. 35–51. Springer, Heidelberg (2012)

5. Albert, E., Flores-Montoya, A., Genaim, S., Martin-Martin, E.: Termination and Cost Analysis of Loops with Concurrent Interleavings (Extended Version). Technical Report SIC 06/13, Univ. Complutense de Madrid (2013)
6. Alias, C., Darte, A., Feautrier, P., Gonnord, L.: Multi-dimensional rankings, program termination, and complexity bounds of flowchart programs. In: Cousot, R., Martel, M. (eds.) SAS 2010. LNCS, vol. 6337, pp. 117–133. Springer, Heidelberg (2010)
7. Armstrong, J., Virding, R., Wistrom, C., Williams, M.: Concurrent Programming in Erlang. Prentice Hall (1996)
8. Bradley, A.R., Manna, Z., Sipma, H.B.: Linear ranking with reachability. In: Etessami, K., Rajamani, S.K. (eds.) CAV 2005. LNCS, vol. 3576, pp. 491–504. Springer, Heidelberg (2005)
9. Cook, B., Podelski, A., Rybalchenko, A.: Proving Thread Termination. In: Proc. of PLDI 2007, pp. 320–330. ACM (2007)
10. Cook, B., Podelski, A., Rybalchenko, A.: Proving program termination. Commun. ACM 54(5), 88–98 (2011)
11. de Boer, F.S., Clarke, D., Johnsen, E.B.: A Complete Guide to the Future. In: De Nicola, R. (ed.) ESOP 2007. LNCS, vol. 4421, pp. 316–330. Springer, Heidelberg (2007)
12. Flanagan, C., Freund, S.N., Qadeer, S.: Thread-Modular Verification for Shared-Memory Programs. In: Le Métayer, D. (ed.) ESOP 2002. LNCS, vol. 2305, pp. 262–277. Springer, Heidelberg (2002)
13. Gulwani, S., Zuleger, F.: The reachability-bound problem. In: Zorn, B.G., Aiken, A. (eds.) PLDI, pp. 292–304. ACM (2010)
14. Haller, P., Odersky, M.: Scala actors: Unifying thread-based and event-based programming. Theor. Comput. Sci. 410(2-3), 202–220 (2009)
15. Johnsen, E.B., Hähnle, R., Schäfer, J., Schlatte, R., Steffen, M.: ABS: A Core Language for Abstract Behavioral Specification. In: Aichernig, B.K., de Boer, F.S., Bonsangue, M.M. (eds.) FMCO 2010. LNCS, vol. 6957, pp. 142–164. Springer, Heidelberg (2011)
16. Milanova, A., Rountev, A., Ryder, B.G.: Parameterized object sensitivity for points-to analysis for java. ACM Trans. Softw. Eng. Meth. 14, 1–41 (2005)
17. Popeea, C., Rybalchenko, A.: Compositional Termination Proofs for Multi-Threaded Programs. In: Flanagan, C., König, B. (eds.) TACAS 2012. LNCS, vol. 7214, pp. 237–251. Springer, Heidelberg (2012)
18. Schäfer, J., Poetzsch-Heffter, A.: Jcobox: Generalizing Active Objects to Concurrent Components. In: D'Hondt, T. (ed.) ECOOP 2010. LNCS, vol. 6183, pp. 275–299. Springer, Heidelberg (2010)
19. Srinivasan, S., Mycroft, A.: Kilim: Isolation-Typed Actors for Java. In: Vitek, J. (ed.) ECOOP 2008. LNCS, vol. 5142, pp. 104–128. Springer, Heidelberg (2008)
20. Zuleger, F., Gulwani, S., Sinn, M., Veith, H.: Bound analysis of imperative programs with the size-change abstraction. In: Yahav, E. (ed.) SAS 2011. LNCS, vol. 6887, pp. 280–297. Springer, Heidelberg (2011)

Linear Ranking for Linear Lasso Programs*

Matthias Heizmann, Jochen Hoenicke, Jan Leike, and Andreas Podelski

University of Freiburg, Germany

Abstract. The general setting of this work is the constraint-based synthesis of termination arguments. We consider a restricted class of programs called lasso programs. The termination argument for a lasso program is a pair of a ranking function and an invariant. We present the—to the best of our knowledge—first method to synthesize termination arguments for lasso programs that uses linear arithmetic. We prove a completeness theorem. The completeness theorem establishes that, even though we use only linear (as opposed to non-linear) constraint solving, we are able to compute termination arguments in several interesting cases. The key to our method lies in a constraint transformation that replaces a disjunction by a sum.

1 Introduction

Termination is arguably the single most interesting correctness property of a program. Research on proving termination can be divided according to three (interrelated) topics, namely: practical tools [1,9,13,17,18,19,21,22], decidability questions [4,8,25], and constraint-based synthesis of termination arguments [2,3,5,6,7,10,12,14,20,23]. The work in this paper falls under the research on the third topic. The general goal of this research is to investigate how one can derive a constraint from the program text and compute a termination argument (of a restricted form) through the solution of the constraint, i.e., via constraint solving.

In this paper, we present a method for the synthesis of termination arguments for a specific class of programs that we call *lasso programs*. As the name indicates, the control flow graph of a lasso program is of a restricted shape: a *stem* followed by a *loop*.

Lasso programs do not appear as stand-alone programs. Lasso programs appear in practice whenever one needs a finite representation of an infinite path in a control flow graph, for example in (potentially spurious) counterexamples in a termination analysis[13,17,18,19], non-termination analysis[16], stability analysis[11,22], or cost analysis[1,15].

Importantly, the termination argument for a lasso program is a pair of a ranking function and an invariant (the rank must decrease only for states that satisfy the invariant). Figure 1 shows an example of a lasso program.

* This work is supported by the German Research Council (DFG) as part of the Transregional Collaborative Research Center "Automatic Verification and Analysis of Complex Systems" (SFB/TR14 AVACS).

D. Van Hung and M. Ogawa (Eds.): ATVA 2013, LNCS 8172, pp. 365–380, 2013.
© Springer International Publishing Switzerland 2013

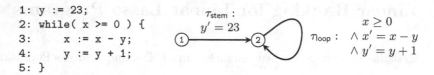

```
1:  y := 23;
2:  while( x >= 0 ) {
3:      x := x - y;
4:      y := y + 1;
5:  }
```

Fig. 1. Example of a lasso program and its formal representation $P_{\mathsf{yPositive}} = (\tau_{\mathsf{stem}}, \tau_{\mathsf{loop}})$. The ranking function defined by $f(x, y) = x$ decreases in transitions from states that satisfy the invariant $y \geq 1$ (the ranking function does not decrease when $y \leq 0$).

The class of lasso programs lies between two classes of programs for which constraint-based methods have been studied extensively. For the first, more specialized class, methods can be based on linear arithmetic constraint solving [2,3,10,12,20]. For the second, more general class, all known methods are based on non-linear arithmetic constraint solving [5,7]. The contribution of our method can be phrased, alternatively, as the generalization of the applicability of the 'linear methods', or as the optimization of the 'non-linear method' to a 'linear method' for a subproblem. The step from 'non-linear' to 'linear' is interesting for principled reasons (non-linear arithmetic constraint solving is undecidable in the case of integers). As we will show the step is also practically interesting.

The reader may wonder how practical tools presently handle the situation where one needs to compute termination arguments for lasso programs. One possibility is to resort to heuristics. For example, instead of computing a termination argument for the lasso program in Figure 1, one would compute the ranking function $f(x) = x$ for the program while(x>=0){x:=x-23;}.

The key to our method is a constraint transformation that replaces a disjunction by a sum. We apply the 'or-to-plus' transformation in the context of Farkas' Lemma. Following [2,5,10,12,20], we apply Farkas' Lemma in order to eliminate the universal quantifiers in the arithmetic constraint whose solution is the termination argument. If we apply Farkas' Lemma to the constraint *after* the 'or-to-plus' transformation, we obtain a *linear* arithmetic constraint.

The effect of the 'or-to-plus' transformation to the constraint is a restriction of its solution space. The restriction seems strong; i.e., in some cases, the solution space becomes empty. We can characterize those cases. In other words, we can characterize when the 'or-to-plus' transformation leads to the loss of an termination argument, and when it does not. The characterization is formulated as a completeness theorem for which we will present the proof. This characterization allows us to establish that, even though we use only linear (as opposed to non-linear) constraint solving, we are able to compute termination arguments in several interesting cases. A possible explanation for this (perhaps initially surprising) fact is that, for synthesis, we are interested in the mere existence of a solution, and the loss of *many* solutions does not necessarily mean the loss of *all* solutions of the constraint.

We have implemented our method and we have used our implementation to illustrate the applicability and the efficiency of our method. Our implementation is available through a web interface, together with a number of example programs (including the ones used in this paper).[1]

2   Preliminaries: Linear Arithmetic

We use x to denote the vector with entries $x_1, \ldots, x_n$, and x^T to denote the transposed vector of x. As usual, the expression $A \cdot x \leq b$ denotes the conjunction of linear constraints $\bigwedge_{j=0}^{m} (\sum_{i=0}^{n} a_{ij} \cdot x_i) \leq b_j$.

We call a relation $\tau(x, x')$ a *linear relation* if τ is defined by a conjunction of linear constraints over the variables x and x', i.e., if there is a matrix A with m rows and $2n$ columns and a vector b of size m such that the following equation holds.

$$\tau(x, x') = \{(x, x') \mid A \cdot \left(\begin{smallmatrix} x \\ x' \end{smallmatrix}\right) \leq b\}$$

We call a function $f(x)$ an *(affine) linear function*, if $f(x)$ is defined by an affine linear term, i.e., there is a vector r^T and a number r_0 such that the following equation holds.

$$f(x) = r^\mathsf{T} \cdot x + r_0.$$

We call a predicate $I(x)$ a *linear predicate*, if $I(x)$ is defined by a linear inequality, i.e., there is a vector s^T and a number s_0 such that following equivalence holds.

$$I(x) = \{x \mid s^\mathsf{T} \cdot x + s_0 \geq 0\}.$$

Farkas' Lemma. We use the affine version of Farkas' Lemma [24] which is also used in [2,5,12,23,20] and states the following. Given

- a satisfiable conjunction of linear constraints $A \cdot x \leq b$
- and a linear constraint $c^\mathsf{T} \cdot x \leq \delta$,

the following equivalence holds.

$$\forall x\ (A \cdot x \leq b \to c^\mathsf{T} \cdot x \leq \delta)\quad \text{iff}\quad \exists \lambda\ (\lambda \geq 0 \wedge \lambda^\mathsf{T} \cdot A = c^\mathsf{T} \wedge \lambda^\mathsf{T} \cdot b \leq \delta)$$

3   Lasso Program

To abstract away from program syntax, we define a lasso program directly by the two relations that generate its execution sequences.

Definition 1 (Lasso Program). *Given a set of states Σ, a lasso program*

$$P = (\tau_{\mathsf{stem}}, \tau_{\mathsf{loop}})$$

is given by the two relations $\tau_{\mathsf{stem}} \subseteq \Sigma \times \Sigma$ and $\tau_{\mathsf{loop}} \subseteq \Sigma \times \Sigma$. We call τ_{stem} the stem of P and τ_{loop} the loop of P.

An execution of the lasso program P is a possibly infinite sequence of states $\sigma_0, \sigma_1, \ldots$ such that

---
[1] http://ultimate.informatik.uni-freiburg.de/LassoRanker

− *the pair of the first two states is an element of the stem, i.e.,*

$$(\sigma_0, \sigma_1) \in \tau_{stem}$$

− *and each other consecutive pair of states is an element of the loop, i.e.,*

$$(\sigma_i, \sigma_{i+1}) \in \tau_{loop} \qquad for\ i = 1, 2, \ldots$$

We call the lasso program P terminating if P has no infinite execution.

We use constraints over primed and unprimed variables to denote a transition relation (see Figure 1).

In order to avoid cumbersome technicalities, we consider only lasso programs that have an execution that contains at least three states. This means we consider only programs where the relational composition of τ_{stem} and τ_{loop} is non-empty, i.e.,

$$\tau_{\text{stem}} \circ \tau_{\text{loop}} \neq \emptyset.$$

Since Turing, a termination argument is based on an ordering which does not allow infinite decreasing chains (such as ordering on the natural numbers). Here, we use the ordering over the set of positive reals which is defined by some value $\delta > 0$, namely

$$a \prec_\delta b \qquad \text{iff} \qquad a \geq 0 \wedge a - b \geq \delta \qquad\qquad a, b \in \mathbb{R}.$$

Ranking Function. We call a function f from the states of the lasso program P into the reals $\mathbb{R}$ a *ranking function* for P if there is a positive number $\delta > 0$ such that for each consecutive pair of states $(\boldsymbol{x}_i, \boldsymbol{x}_{i+1})$ of a loop transition $(i \geq 1)$ in every execution of P

− the value of f is decreasing by at least δ, i.e.,

$$f(\boldsymbol{x}_i) - f(\boldsymbol{x}_{i+1}) \geq \delta,$$

− and the value of f is non-negative, i.e.,

$$f(\boldsymbol{x}_i) \geq 0.$$

If there is a ranking function for the lasso program P, then P is terminating.

Inductive Invariant. We call a state predicate $I(x)$ an *inductive invariant* of the lasso program P if

− the predicate holds after executing the stem, i.e.,

$$\forall \boldsymbol{x} \ \forall \boldsymbol{x}' \quad \tau_{\text{stem}}(\boldsymbol{x}, \boldsymbol{x}') \rightarrow I(x'), \tag{φ_{invStem}}$$

− and if the predicate holds before executing the loop, then the predicate holds afterwards, i.e.,

$$\forall \boldsymbol{x} \ \forall \boldsymbol{x}' \quad I(x) \wedge \tau_{\text{loop}}(\boldsymbol{x}, \boldsymbol{x}') \rightarrow I(x'). \tag{φ_{invLoop}}$$

Ranking Function with Supporting Invariant. We call a pair of a ranking function $f(x)$ and an inductive invariant $I(x)$ of the lasso program P a *ranking function with supporting invariant* if the following holds.

– There exists a positive real number $\delta > 0$ such that, if the inductive invariant holds then an execution of the loop decreases the value of the ranking function by at least δ, i.e.,

$$\exists \delta > 0 \forall x\ \forall x'\quad I(x) \wedge \tau_{\text{loop}}(x, x') \rightarrow f(x) - f(x') \geq \delta. \qquad (\varphi_{\text{rkDecr}})$$

– In states in which the inductive invariant holds and the loop can be executed, the value of the ranking function is non-negative, i.e.,

$$\forall x\ \forall x'\quad I(x) \wedge \tau_{\text{loop}}(x, x') \rightarrow f(x) \geq 0. \qquad (\varphi_{\text{rkBound}})$$

For example, the lasso program depicted in Figure 1 has the ranking function $f(x, y) = x$ with supporting invariant $y \geq 1$.

Linear Lasso Programs. Linear lasso programs. For the remainder of this paper we consider only linear lasso programs, linear ranking functions, and linear inductive invariants which we will define next. The variables of the programs will range over the reals until we come to Section 9 where we turn to programs over integers.

Definition 2 (Linear Lasso Program). *A* linear lasso program

$$P = (\tau_{\text{stem}}, \tau_{\text{loop}})$$

is a lasso program whose states are vectors over the reals, i.e. $\Sigma = \mathbb{R}^n$, *and whose relations* τ_{stem} *and* τ_{loop} *are linear relations.*

We use the expression $A_{\text{stem}} \cdot \binom{x}{x'} \leq b_{\text{stem}}$ to denote the relation τ_{stem} of P. We use the expression $A_{\text{loop}} \cdot \binom{x}{x'} \leq b_{\text{loop}}$ to denote the relation τ_{loop} of P.

Linear Ranking Function. If a ranking function $f : \mathbb{R}^n \rightarrow \mathbb{R}$ is an (affine) linear function, we call f a *linear ranking function*. We use $r_1, \ldots, r_n$ as coefficients of a linear ranking function, r as their vector,

$$f : \mathbb{R}^n \rightarrow \mathbb{R} \qquad f(x) = r^{\mathsf{T}} \cdot x + r_0.$$

Linear Invariant. If an inductive invariant $I(x)$ is a linear predicate, we call I a *linear inductive invariant*. We use $s_1, \ldots, s_n$ as coefficients of the term that defines the linear predicate, s as their vector,

$$I(x) \equiv s^{\mathsf{T}} \cdot x + s_0 \geq 0.$$

4   The Or-to-Plus Method

Our constraint-based method for the synthesis of linear ranking functions for linear lasso programs consists of three main steps:

Step 1. Set up four (universally quantified) constraints whose free variables are the coefficients of a linear ranking function with linear supporting invariant.

Step 2. Apply Farkas' Lemma to the four constraints to obtain equivalent constraints without universal quantification.

Step 3. Obtain solutions for the free variables by linear constraint solving.

The particularity of our four constraints in Step 1 is that the application of Farkas' Lemma in Step 2 yields constraints that are linear.

Instead of presenting our constraints immediately, we derive them in three successive transformations of constraints. We start with the four constraints $(\varphi_{\mathsf{invStem}})$, $(\varphi_{\mathsf{invLoop}})$, $(\varphi_{\mathsf{rkDecr}})$, and $(\varphi_{\mathsf{rkBound}})$. Below, we have rephrased the four constraints for the setting where the ranking function is linear and the supporting invariant is linear. We marked them $(\varphi_1^{\mathrm{BMS}})$, $(\varphi_2^{\mathrm{BMS}})$, $(\varphi_3^{\mathrm{BMS}})$, and $(\varphi_4^{\mathrm{BMS}})$ in reference to Bradley, Manna and Sipma [5] who were the first to use them in the corresponding step of their method.

The Bradley–Manna–Sipma Constraints

for the special case of lasso programs and one linear supporting invariant[2]

$$\forall \boldsymbol{x} \, \forall \boldsymbol{x}' \qquad\qquad \tau_{\mathsf{stem}}(\boldsymbol{x}, \boldsymbol{x}') \to s^{\mathsf{T}} \cdot \boldsymbol{x}' + s_0 \geq 0 \qquad\qquad (\varphi_1^{\mathrm{BMS}})$$

$$\forall \boldsymbol{x} \, \forall \boldsymbol{x}' \quad s^{\mathsf{T}} \cdot \boldsymbol{x} + s_0 \geq 0 \wedge \tau_{\mathsf{loop}}(\boldsymbol{x}, \boldsymbol{x}') \to s^{\mathsf{T}} \cdot \boldsymbol{x}' + s_0 \geq 0 \qquad (\varphi_2^{\mathrm{BMS}})$$

$$\exists \delta > 0 \, \forall \boldsymbol{x} \, \forall \boldsymbol{x}' \quad s^{\mathsf{T}} \cdot \boldsymbol{x} + s_0 \geq 0 \wedge \tau_{\mathsf{loop}}(\boldsymbol{x}, \boldsymbol{x}') \to r^{\mathsf{T}} \cdot \boldsymbol{x} - r^{\mathsf{T}} \cdot \boldsymbol{x}' \geq \delta \qquad (\varphi_3^{\mathrm{BMS}})$$

$$\forall \boldsymbol{x} \, \forall \boldsymbol{x}' \quad s^{\mathsf{T}} \cdot \boldsymbol{x} + s_0 \geq 0 \wedge \tau_{\mathsf{loop}}(\boldsymbol{x}, \boldsymbol{x}') \to r^{\mathsf{T}} \cdot \boldsymbol{x} + r_0 \geq 0 \qquad (\varphi_4^{\mathrm{BMS}})$$

The free variables of $\varphi_1^{\mathrm{BMS}} \wedge \varphi_2^{\mathrm{BMS}} \wedge \varphi_3^{\mathrm{BMS}} \wedge \varphi_4^{\mathrm{BMS}}$ are r, r_0, s, and s_0.

Transformation 1: Move supporting invariant to right-hand side.

We bring the conjunct $s^{\mathsf{T}} \cdot \boldsymbol{x} + s_0 \geq 0$ in three of the four constraints $(\varphi_1^{\mathrm{BMS}})$, $(\varphi_2^{\mathrm{BMS}})$, $(\varphi_3^{\mathrm{BMS}})$, and $(\varphi_4^{\mathrm{BMS}})$ to the right-hand side of the implication, according to the following scheme.

$$\phi_1 \wedge \phi_2 \to \psi \quad \equiv \quad \phi_2 \to \psi \vee \neg \phi_1$$

We obtain the following constraints.

$$\forall \boldsymbol{x} \, \forall \boldsymbol{x}' \quad \tau_{\mathsf{stem}}(\boldsymbol{x}, \boldsymbol{x}') \to s^{\mathsf{T}} \cdot \boldsymbol{x}' + s_0 \geq 0 \qquad\qquad (\psi_1)$$

$$\forall \boldsymbol{x} \, \forall \boldsymbol{x}' \quad \tau_{\mathsf{loop}}(\boldsymbol{x}, \boldsymbol{x}') \to s^{\mathsf{T}} \cdot \boldsymbol{x}' + s_0 \geq 0 \vee -s^{\mathsf{T}} \cdot \boldsymbol{x} - s_0 > 0 \qquad (\psi_2)$$

$$\exists \delta > 0 \, \forall \boldsymbol{x} \, \forall \boldsymbol{x}' \quad \tau_{\mathsf{loop}}(\boldsymbol{x}, \boldsymbol{x}') \to r^{\mathsf{T}} \cdot \boldsymbol{x} - r^{\mathsf{T}} \cdot \boldsymbol{x}' \geq \delta \vee -s^{\mathsf{T}} \cdot \boldsymbol{x} - s_0 > 0 \qquad (\psi_3)$$

$$\forall \boldsymbol{x} \, \forall \boldsymbol{x}' \quad \tau_{\mathsf{loop}}(\boldsymbol{x}, \boldsymbol{x}') \to r^{\mathsf{T}} \cdot \boldsymbol{x} + r_0 \geq 0 \vee -s^{\mathsf{T}} \cdot \boldsymbol{x} - s_0 > 0 \qquad (\psi_4)$$

---

[2] In [5] the authors use more general general constraints that can be used to synthesize lexicographic linear ranking functions together with a conjunction of linear supporting invariants for programs that can also contains disjunctions.

Transformation 2: Drop supporting invariant in fourth constraint. We strengthen the fourth constraint (ψ_4) by removing the disjunct $-s^\mathsf{T} \cdot x - s_0 > 0$. A solution for the strengthened constraint defines a ranking function whose value is bounded from below for all states (and not just those that satisfy the supporting invariant).

Transformation 3: Replace disjunction by sum. We replace the disjunction on the right-hand side of the implication in constraints (ψ_2) and (ψ_3) by a single inequality, according to the scheme below. (It is the disjunction which prevents us from applying Farkas' Lemma to the constraints (ψ_2) and (ψ_3).)

$$m \geq 0 \vee n > 0 \quad \rightsquigarrow \quad m + n \geq 0$$

In the second constraint (ψ_2), we replace the disjunction

$$-s^\mathsf{T} \cdot x - s_0 > 0 \ \vee \ s^\mathsf{T} \cdot x' + s_0 \geq 0$$

by the inequality

$$s^\mathsf{T} \cdot x' + s_0 - s^\mathsf{T} \cdot x - s_0 \geq 0.$$

In the third constraint (ψ_3), we replace the disjunction

$$-s^\mathsf{T} \cdot x - s_0 > 0 \ \vee \ r^\mathsf{T} \cdot x - r^\mathsf{T} \cdot x' \geq \delta$$

by the inequality

$$r^\mathsf{T} \cdot x - r^\mathsf{T} \cdot x' - s^\mathsf{T} \cdot x - s_0 \geq \delta.$$

We obtain the following four constraints.

The Or-to-Plus Constraints

$$\forall x \, \forall x' \quad \tau_{\mathsf{stem}}(x, x') \rightarrow s^\mathsf{T} \cdot x' + s_0 \geq 0 \tag{φ_1}$$

$$\forall x \, \forall x' \quad \tau_{\mathsf{loop}}(x, x') \rightarrow s^\mathsf{T} \cdot x' + s_0 - s^\mathsf{T} \cdot x - s_0 \geq 0 \tag{φ_2}$$

$$\exists \delta > 0 \, \forall x \, \forall x' \quad \tau_{\mathsf{loop}}(x, x') \rightarrow r^\mathsf{T} \cdot x - r^\mathsf{T} \cdot x' - s^\mathsf{T} \cdot x - s_0 \geq \delta \tag{φ_3}$$

$$\forall x \, \forall x' \quad \tau_{\mathsf{loop}}(x, x') \rightarrow r^\mathsf{T} \cdot x + r_0 \geq 0 \tag{φ_4}$$

The free variables of the conjunction $\varphi_1 \wedge \varphi_2 \wedge \varphi_3 \wedge \varphi_4$ are r, r_0, s, and s_0.

Since we consider linear lasso programs, the relations τ_{stem} and τ_{loop} are given as conjunctions of linear constraints.

$$\tau_{\mathsf{stem}}(x, x') \ \equiv \ A_{\mathsf{stem}} \cdot \left(\begin{smallmatrix} x \\ x' \end{smallmatrix}\right) \leq b_{\mathsf{stem}}$$

$$\tau_{\mathsf{loop}}(x, x') \ \equiv \ A_{\mathsf{loop}} \cdot \left(\begin{smallmatrix} x \\ x' \end{smallmatrix}\right) \leq b_{\mathsf{loop}}$$

We have now finished the description for the three transformation steps that lead us to the the or-to-plus constraints. We are now ready to introduce our method.

The Or-to-Plus Method

Input: linear lasso program P.
Output: coefficients r, r_0, s, and s_0 of a linear ranking function with
    linear supporting invariant

1. Set up the or-to-Plus constraints φ_1, φ_2, φ_3, and φ_4 for P.
2. Apply Farkas' Lemma to each constraint.
3. Obtain r, r_0, s, and s_0, by linear constraint solving.

After setting up the four or-to-plus constraints φ_1, φ_2, φ_3, φ_4 in Step 1, we apply Farkas' Lemma to each of the four constraints in Step 2. We obtain four linear constraints. E.g., by applying Farkas' Lemma to the constraint (φ_3) we obtain the following linear constraint.

$$\exists \delta > 0 \quad \exists \boldsymbol{\lambda} \quad \boldsymbol{\lambda} \geq 0 \quad \wedge \quad \boldsymbol{\lambda}^{\mathsf{T}} \cdot A_{\mathsf{loop}} = \left(\begin{smallmatrix} s-r \\ r \end{smallmatrix}\right)^{\mathsf{T}} \quad \wedge \quad \boldsymbol{\lambda}^{\mathsf{T}} \cdot b_{\mathsf{loop}} \leq -\delta - s_0$$

We apply linear constraint solving in Step 3. We obtain a satisfying assignment for the free variables in the resulting constraints. The values obtained for r, r_0, s and s_0 are the coefficients of a linear ranking function $f(x)$ with linear supporting invariant $I(x)$.

The or-to-plus method inherits its soundness from method of Bradley–Manna–Sipma. Step 1 is an equivalence transformation on the Bradley–Manna–Sipma constraints, Step 2 and Step 3 strengthen the constraints, and the application of Farkas' Lemma is an equivalence transformation. Thus, a satisfying assignment of the or-to-plus constraints obtained after the application of Farkas' Lemma is also a satisfying assignment of the Bradley–Manna–Sipma constraints.

5 Completeness of the Or-to-Plus Method

In the tradition of constraint-based synthesis for verification, we will formulate completeness according to the following scheme: the method X applied to a program P in the class Y computes (the coefficients of) a correctness argument of the form Z whenever one exists (i.e., whenever a correctness argument of the form Z exists for the program P). Here, X is the or-to-plus method, Y is the class of lasso programs, and Z is a termination argument consisting of a linear ranking function and an invariant of a form that we we define next.

Definition 3 (Non-decreasing linear inductive invariant). *We call a linear inductive invariant $s^{\mathsf{T}} \cdot x + s_0 \geq 0$ of the lasso program P non-decreasing if the loop implies that the value of the term $s^{\mathsf{T}} \cdot x + s_0$ does not decrease when executing the loop, i.e.,*

$$\tau_{\mathsf{loop}} \rightarrow s^{\mathsf{T}} \cdot x' \geq s^{\mathsf{T}} \cdot x.$$

In Section 6 we give examples which may help to convey some intuition about the meaning of 'non-decreasing', examples of those terminating programs that do have a linear ranking function with a non-decreasing linear supporting invariant, and examples of those that don't.

```
x := y + 42;
while( x >= 0 ) {
    y := 2*y - x;
    x := (y + x) / 2;
}
```

$\tau_{stem} : x' = y + 42 \wedge y' = y$

$\tau_{loop} : x \geq 0 \wedge x' = y \wedge y' = 2y - x$

Fig. 2. Linear lasso program $P_{diff42} = (\tau_{stem}, \tau_{loop})$ that has the linear ranking function $f(x, y) = x$ with linear supporting invariant $x - y \geq 42$.

Theorem 1 (Completeness). *The or-to-plus method applied to the linear lasso program P succeeds and computes the coefficients of a linear ranking function with non-decreasing linear supporting invariant whenever one exists.*

To prove this theorem we use the following lemma.

Lemma 1. *Given are*

(1) satisfiable linear inequalities $A \cdot x \leq b$,
(2) an inequality $g^{\mathsf{T}} \cdot x + g_0 \geq 0$, and
(3) a strict inequality $h^{\mathsf{T}} \cdot x + h_0 > 0$.

If $A \cdot x \leq b$ does not imply the strict inequality (3), but the disjunction of (2) and (3), i.e.

$$\forall x \quad A \cdot x \leq b \rightarrow g^{\mathsf{T}} \cdot x + g_0 \geq 0 \vee h^{\mathsf{T}} \cdot x + h_0 > 0,$$

then there exists a constant $\mu \geq 0$ such that

$$\forall x \quad A \cdot x \leq b \rightarrow (g^{\mathsf{T}} \cdot x + g_0) + \mu \cdot (h^{\mathsf{T}} \cdot x + h_0) \geq 0.$$

Proof (of Lemma 1).

$$\forall x \quad A \cdot x \leq b \rightarrow (g^{\mathsf{T}} \cdot x + g_0 \geq 0 \vee h^{\mathsf{T}} \cdot x + h_0 > 0)$$

is equivalent to

$$\forall x \quad (A \cdot x \leq b \wedge h^{\mathsf{T}} \cdot x + h_0 \leq 0) \rightarrow g^{\mathsf{T}} \cdot x + g_0 \geq 0.$$

By assumption, *(1)* does not imply *(3)*, so $A \cdot x \leq b \wedge h^{\mathsf{T}} \cdot x + h_0 \leq 0$ is satisfiable, and by Farkas' Lemma this formula is equivalent to

$$\exists \mu \geq 0 \, \exists \lambda \geq 0 \quad \mu \cdot h^{\mathsf{T}} + \lambda^{\mathsf{T}} \cdot A = -g^{\mathsf{T}} \wedge \lambda^{\mathsf{T}} \cdot b + \mu \cdot (-h_0) \leq g_0,$$

and thus

$$\exists \mu \geq 0 \, \exists \lambda \geq 0 \quad \lambda^{\mathsf{T}} \cdot A = -(\mu \cdot h^{\mathsf{T}} + g^{\mathsf{T}}) \wedge \lambda^{\mathsf{T}} \cdot b \leq \mu \cdot h_0 + g_0.$$

Because $A \cdot x \leq b$ is satisfiable by assumption, Farkas' Lemma can be applied again to yield

$$\exists \mu \geq 0 \, \forall x \quad A \cdot x \leq b \rightarrow -(\mu \cdot h^{\mathsf{T}} + g^{\mathsf{T}})x \leq \mu \cdot h_0 + g_0. \quad \square$$

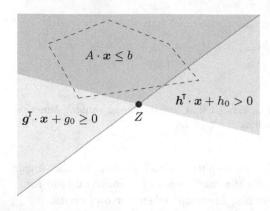

Let $H = \{x \mid g^{\mathsf{T}} \cdot x + g_0 \geq 0\}$, and $H' = \{x \mid h^{\mathsf{T}} \cdot x + h_0 > 0\}$ be half-spaces defined by linear inequalities. A half-space $H_\mu = \{x \mid (g^{\mathsf{T}} \cdot x + g_0) + \mu \cdot (h^{\mathsf{T}} \cdot x + h_0) \geq 0\}$ defined by a weighted sum is a rotation of H around the intersection Z of the boundary of H and the boundary of H'.

If a polyhedron X is contained in the union $H \cup H'$, then there is a half-space H_μ defined by a weighted sum that contains X.

Fig. 3. A geometrical interpretation of Lemma 1

Proof (of Theorem 1). Let $f(x) = \mathring{r}^{\mathsf{T}} \cdot x + \mathring{r}_0$ be a ranking function with non-decreasing supporting invariant $I(x) \equiv \mathring{s}^{\mathsf{T}} \cdot x + \mathring{s}_0 \geq 0$ for the lasso program P. Since executions of our lasso programs comprise at least three states, there can be no supporting invariant that contradicts the loop, i.e.

$$A_{\mathsf{loop}} \cdot \left(\begin{smallmatrix} x \\ x' \end{smallmatrix}\right) \leq b_{\mathsf{loop}} \;\to\; -\mathring{s}^{\mathsf{T}} \cdot x - \mathring{s}_0 > 0 \tag{1}$$

is not valid. From ($\varphi_{\mathsf{rkBound}}$) it follows that

$$\mathring{s}^{\mathsf{T}} \cdot x + \mathring{s}_0 \geq 0 \;\wedge\; A_{\mathsf{loop}} \cdot \left(\begin{smallmatrix} x \\ x' \end{smallmatrix}\right) \leq b_{\mathsf{loop}} \;\to\; \mathring{r}^{\mathsf{T}} \cdot x + \mathring{r}_0 \geq 0,$$

and hence the implication

$$A_{\mathsf{loop}} \cdot \left(\begin{smallmatrix} x \\ x' \end{smallmatrix}\right) \leq b_{\mathsf{loop}} \;\to\; \mathring{r}^{\mathsf{T}} \cdot x + \mathring{r}_0 \geq 0 \;\vee\; -\mathring{s}^{\mathsf{T}} \cdot x - \mathring{s}_0 > 0$$

is valid. By (1) and Lemma 1 there is a $\mu_1 \geq 0$ such that

$$A_{\mathsf{loop}} \cdot \left(\begin{smallmatrix} x \\ x' \end{smallmatrix}\right) \leq b_{\mathsf{loop}} \;\to\; (\mathring{r}^{\mathsf{T}} \cdot x + \mathring{r}_0) + \mu_1 \cdot (-\mathring{s}^{\mathsf{T}} \cdot x - \mathring{s}_0) \geq 0$$

is valid. If we assign $r \mapsto \mathring{r} - \mu_1 \cdot \mathring{s}, r_0 \mapsto \mathring{r}_0 - \mu_1 \cdot \mathring{s}_0$, then ($\varphi_4$) is satisfied.

Because $I(x) \equiv \mathring{s} \cdot x + \mathring{s}_0 \geq 0$ is a non-decreasing invariant,

$$A_{\mathsf{loop}} \cdot \left(\begin{smallmatrix} x \\ x' \end{smallmatrix}\right) \leq b_{\mathsf{loop}} \;\to\; \mathring{s}^{\mathsf{T}} \cdot x' - \mathring{s}^{\mathsf{T}} \cdot x \geq 0,$$

and hence, since $\mu_1 \geq 0$,

$$A_{\mathsf{loop}} \cdot \left(\begin{smallmatrix} x \\ x' \end{smallmatrix}\right) \leq b_{\mathsf{loop}} \;\to\; -\mu_1 \cdot \mathring{s}^{\mathsf{T}} \cdot (x - x') \geq 0. \tag{2}$$

From ($\varphi_{\mathsf{rkDecr}}$) we know that

$$\mathring{s}^{\mathsf{T}} \cdot x + \mathring{s}_0 \geq 0 \;\wedge\; A_{\mathsf{loop}} \cdot \left(\begin{smallmatrix} x \\ x' \end{smallmatrix}\right) \leq b_{\mathsf{loop}} \;\to\; \mathring{r}^{\mathsf{T}} \cdot x - \mathring{r}^{\mathsf{T}} \cdot x' \geq \delta,$$

and hence equivalently

$$A_{\mathsf{loop}} \cdot \left(\begin{smallmatrix} x \\ x' \end{smallmatrix}\right) \leq b_{\mathsf{loop}} \;\to\; \mathring{r}^{\mathsf{T}} \cdot x - \mathring{r}^{\mathsf{T}} \cdot x' \geq \delta \;\vee\; -\mathring{s}^{\mathsf{T}} \cdot x - \mathring{s}_0 > 0.$$

With (2) we obtain validity of the following formula.

$$A_{\text{loop}} \cdot \begin{pmatrix} x \\ x' \end{pmatrix} \leq b_{\text{loop}} \;\rightarrow\; (\mathring{r}^{\mathsf{T}} - \mu_1 \cdot \mathring{s}^{\mathsf{T}}) \cdot (x - x') \geq \delta \;\vee\; -\mathring{s}^{\mathsf{T}} \cdot x - \mathring{s}_0 > 0$$

By (1) and Lemma 1 there exists a $\mu_2 \geq 0$ such that

$$A_{\text{loop}} \cdot \begin{pmatrix} x \\ x' \end{pmatrix} \leq b_{\text{loop}} \;\rightarrow\; (\mathring{r}^{\mathsf{T}} - \mu_1 \cdot \mathring{s}^{\mathsf{T}}) \cdot (x - x') + \mu_2 \cdot (-\mathring{s}^{\mathsf{T}} \cdot x - \mathring{s}_0) > \delta.$$

We pick the assignment $r \mapsto \mathring{r} - \mu_1 \cdot \mathring{s}, r_0 \mapsto \mathring{r}_0 - \mu_1 \cdot \mathring{s}_0, s \mapsto \mu_2 \cdot \mathring{s}, s_0 \mapsto \mu_2 \cdot \mathring{s}_0$, which hence satisfies (φ_3). We already argued that it satisfies (φ_4), and from $\mu_2 \geq 0$ and the fact that $I(x)$ is a non-decreasing inductive invariant it follows that the assignment also satisfies (φ_1) and (φ_2). Hence, the ranking function $(\mathring{r} - \mu_1 \cdot \mathring{s})^{\mathsf{T}} \cdot x + \mathring{r}_0 - \mu_1 \cdot \mathring{s}_0$ with supporting invariant $(\mu_2 \cdot \mathring{s})^{\mathsf{T}} \cdot x + \mu_2 \cdot \mathring{s}_0 \geq 0$ can be found by the or-to-plus method. □

6 Examples

Our three transformations strengthened the Bradley–Manna–Sipma constraints, hence the solution space of the or-to-plus constraints is smaller than the solution space of the Bradley–Manna–Sipma constraints. This can be seen e.g., in the example depicted in Figure 4. The program P_{bound} has the linear

```
y := 23;
while( x >= y ) {
    x := x - 1;
}
```

Fig. 4. Lasso program P_{bound}

ranking function $f(x, y) = x$ with linear supporting invariant $y \geq 23$, but the coefficients of this ranking function and supporting invariant are no solution of the or-to-plus constraints; the constraint φ_4 is violated. Does this mean that our method will not succeed? No, it does not. By Theorem 1, in fact, we do know that the method will succeed. I.e., since we know of some linear ranking function with non-decreasing supporting invariant (in this case, $f(x, y) = x$ and $y \geq 23$), even if it is not a solution, we know that there exists one which is a solution (here, for example, $f(x, y) = x - y$ with the (trivial) supporting invariant $0 \geq 0$).

```
y := 2;
while( x >= 0 ) {
    x := x - y;
    y := (y + 1) / 2;
}
```

Fig. 5. Lasso program P_{zeno}

The prerequisite of Theorem 1 is the existence of a non-decreasing supporting invariant. There are linear lasso programs that have a linear ranking function with linear supporting invariant, but do not have a linear ranking function with a non-decreasing linear supporting invariant. E.g., for the lasso programs depicted in Figure 5 and Figure 6 our or-to-plus method is not able to synthesize a ranking function for these programs.

The linear lasso program P_{zeno} depicted in Figure 5 has the linear ranking function $f(x, y) = x$ with the linear supporting invariant $y \geq 1$. However this inductive invariant is not non-decreasing; while executing the loop the value of the variable y converges to 1 in the following sequence. $2, 1 + \frac{1}{2}, 1 + \frac{1}{4}, 1 + \frac{1}{8}, \ldots$.

The statement `havoc y;` in the lasso program P_{wild} is a nondeterministic assignment to the variable y. The relations τ_{stem} and τ_{loop} of this lasso program are given by the constraints $y' \geq 1$ and $x \geq 0 \;\wedge\; x' = x - y \;\wedge\; y' \geq 1$. P_{wild} has the ranking function $f(x, y) = x$ with the supporting invariant $y \geq 1$, however this inductive invariant is not non-decreasing in each execution of the loop the variable y can get any value greater than or equal to one.

```
assume y >= 1;
while( x >=0 ) {
    x := x - y;
    havoc y;
    assume (y >= 1);
}
```

Fig. 6. Lasso program P_{wild}

The next example shows that nondeterministic updates are no general obstacle for our or-to-plus method. In the linear lasso program P_{array} the loop iterates over an array of positive integers. The index accessed in the next iteration is the sum of the current index, the current entry of the array, and an offset. The relations τ_{stem} and τ_{loop} of this lasso program are given by the constraints $\mathit{offset}' = 1 \;\wedge\; i' = 0$ and $i \leq a.\mathit{length} \;\wedge\; \mathit{curVal}' \geq 0 \;\wedge\; i' = i + \mathit{offset} + \mathit{curVal}'$. The variable curVal which represents the current entry of the array `a[i]` can get any value greater than or equal to one in each loop iteration. The or-to-plus method finds the linear ranking function $f(i, \mathit{offset}) = i - a.\mathit{length}$ with the linear supporting invariant $\mathit{offset} \geq 1$.

```
offset := 1;
i := 0;
while(i<=a.length) {
    assume a[i]>=0;
    i := i + offset + a[i];
}
```

Fig. 7. Lasso program P_{array}

7   Lasso Programs over the Integers

In the preceding sections we considered lasso programs over the reals. In this section we discuss the applicability of the or-to-plus method to linear lasso programs over the integers, i.e., programs where the set of states Σ is a subset of $\mathbb{Z}^n$. We still use real-valued ranking functions. We obtain the constraints for coefficients of a linear ranking function with linear supporting invariant by restricting the range of the universal quantification in the constraints φ_1, φ_2, φ_3, and φ_4 to the integers. E.g., the constraint φ_3 for linear lasso programs over the integers is

$$\exists \delta > 0 \; \forall \boldsymbol{x} \in \mathbb{Z}^n \; \forall \boldsymbol{x}' \in \mathbb{Z}^n \quad \tau_{\mathsf{loop}}(\boldsymbol{x}, \boldsymbol{x}') \to r^{\mathsf{T}} \cdot \boldsymbol{x} - r^{\mathsf{T}} \cdot \boldsymbol{x}' - s^{\mathsf{T}} \cdot \boldsymbol{x} - s_0 \geq \delta$$

where the domain of the coefficients r, r_0, s, and s_0 and the quantified variable δ are the reals. Now, Farkas' lemma is not an equivalence transformation, its application results in weaker formulas. This means the or-to-plus method is still sound, but we loose the completeness result of Theorem 1. An example for this is

```
assume 2*y >= 1;
while( x >= 0 ) {
    x := x - 2*y + 1;
}
```

Fig. 8. Lasso program $P_{\mathsf{nonIntegral1}}$

the program $P_{\mathsf{nonIntegral}}$, depicted in Figure 8 that has the following transition relations.

$$\tau_{\mathsf{stem}} : 2y' \geq 1 \wedge x' = x$$

$$\tau_{\mathsf{loop}} : x \geq 0 \wedge x' = x - 2y + 1 \wedge y' = y;$$

Over integer variables, $P_{\mathsf{nonIntegral1}}$ has the linear ranking function $f(x, y) = x$ with the linear supporting invariant $y \geq 1$. Over real-valued variables, $P_{\mathsf{nonIntegral1}}$ does not terminate. If we add the additional constraint $y' \geq 1$ to τ_{stem}, the programs' semantics over the integers is not changed, but we are able to synthesize a linear ranking function with a linear supporting invariant. Adding this additional constraint gives the constraints a property that we formally define as follows.

Integral constraints. A conjunction of linear constraints $A \cdot x \leq b$ is called *integral* if the set of satisfying assignments over the reals $S := \{r \in \mathbb{R}^n \mid A \cdot r \leq b\}$ coincides with the integer hull of S (the convex hull of all integer vectors in S).

For each conjunction of m linear constraints there is an equivalent conjunction of at most 2^m linear constraints that is integral [24]. We add an additional step to the or-to-plus method in which we make the constraints in the stem transition τ_{stem} and loop transition τ_{loop} integral.

The Or-to-Plus Method (Int)

Input: linear lasso program P with integer variables
Output: coefficients r, r_0, s, and s_0 of linear ranking function with linear supporting invariant

1. Replace τ_{stem} and τ_{loop} by equivalent integral linear constraints.
2. Set up constraints φ_1, φ_2, φ_3, and φ_4 for P.
3. Apply Farkas' Lemma to each constraint.
4. Obtain r, r_0, s, and s_0, by linear constraint solving.

That we find more solutions after making the linear constraints τ_{stem} and τ_{loop} integral is due to the following lemma which was stated in [12]. We present our proof for the purpose of self-containment.

Lemma 2 (Integral version of Farkas' Lemma). *Given a conjunction of linear constraints $A \cdot x \leq b$*

$$\forall x \in \mathbb{Z}^n \ (A \cdot x \leq b \rightarrow c^{\mathsf{T}} \cdot x \leq \delta) \quad \textit{iff} \quad \exists \lambda \ (\lambda \geq 0 \wedge \lambda^{\mathsf{T}} \cdot A = c^{\mathsf{T}} \wedge \lambda^{\mathsf{T}} \cdot b \leq \delta)$$

Proof. We write this statement as a linear programming problem.

$$\textbf{(P)} \qquad \max\{c^{\mathsf{T}} \cdot x \mid A \cdot x \leq b\} \leq \delta$$

Because the constraints $A \cdot x \leq b$ are integral, there is an integral vector $x \in \mathbb{Z}^n$ such that $c^{\mathsf{T}} \cdot x$ is the optimum solution to **(P)**. Thus the optimum over integers is $\leq \delta$ if and only if the optimum of the reals is. The statement now follows from the real version of Farkas' Lemma.   □

However, even if τ_{stem} and τ_{loop} are integral, our method is not complete over the integers. In the completeness proof for the reals we applied Farkas' Lemma to conjunctions of a polyhedron $A \cdot x \leq b$ and an inequality $h^{\mathsf{T}} \cdot x + h_0 \leq 0$. This inequal-

```
assume 2*y >= z;
while( x >= 0 && z == 1 ) {
    x := x - 2*y + 1;
}
```

Fig. 9. Lasso program $P_{\text{nonIntegral2}}$

ity contains free variables, namely the coefficients of the supporting invariant $s^{\mathsf{T}} \cdot x + s_0 \geq 0$. Even if τ_{stem} and τ_{loop} are integral, this conjunction might not be integral and we cannot apply the integer version of Farkas' lemma in this case.

A counterexample to completeness of our integer version of the or-to-plus method is the linear lasso program $P_{\text{nonIntegral2}}$ depicted in Figure 9.

8   Conclusion

We have presented a constraint-based synthesis method for a class of programs that was not investigated before for the synthesis problem. The class is restricted (though less restricted than the widely studied class of simple while programs) but still requires the combined synthesis of not only a ranking function but also an invariant. We have formulated and proven a completeness theorem that gives us an indication on the extent of power of a method that does without nonlinear constraint solving.

We implemented the or-to-plus method as plugin of the ULTIMATE software analysis framework. A version that allows one to 'play around' with lasso programs is available via a web interface at the following URL.

http://ultimate.informatik.uni-freiburg.de/LassoRanker

As mentioned in the introduction, the class of lasso programs is motivated by the fact that they are a natural way (and, it seems, the only way) to represent an (infinite) counterexample path in a control flow graph. It is a topic of future research to explore the different scenarios in practical tools that use a module to find a ranking function and a supporting invariant for a lasso program (e.g., in [1,13,15,16,17,21,22]) and to compare the performance of our— theoretically motivated—synthesis method in comparison with the existing— heuristically motivated—approach used presently in the module.

References

1. Albert, E., Arenas, P., Genaim, S., Puebla, G.: Closed-form upper bounds in static cost analysis. J. Autom. Reasoning 46(2), 161–203 (2011)
2. Bagnara, R., Mesnard, F., Pescetti, A., Zaffanella, E.: A new look at the automatic synthesis of linear ranking functions. Inf. Comput. 215, 47–67 (2012)
3. Ben-Amram, A.M., Genaim, S.: On the linear ranking problem for integer linear-constraint loops. In: POPL (2013)
4. Ben-Amram, A.M., Genaim, S., Masud, A.N.: On the termination of integer loops. In: Kuncak, V., Rybalchenko, A. (eds.) VMCAI 2012. LNCS, vol. 7148, pp. 72–87. Springer, Heidelberg (2012)

5. Bradley, A.R., Manna, Z., Sipma, H.B.: Linear ranking with reachability. In: Etessami, K., Rajamani, S.K. (eds.) CAV 2005. LNCS, vol. 3576, pp. 491–504. Springer, Heidelberg (2005)
6. Bradley, A.R., Manna, Z., Sipma, H.B.: The polyranking principle. In: Caires, L., Italiano, G.F., Monteiro, L., Palamidessi, C., Yung, M. (eds.) ICALP 2005. LNCS, vol. 3580, pp. 1349–1361. Springer, Heidelberg (2005)
7. Bradley, A.R., Manna, Z., Sipma, H.B.: Termination analysis of integer linear loops. In: Abadi, M., de Alfaro, L. (eds.) CONCUR 2005. LNCS, vol. 3653, pp. 488–502. Springer, Heidelberg (2005)
8. Braverman, M.: Termination of integer linear programs. In: Ball, T., Jones, R.B. (eds.) CAV 2006. LNCS, vol. 4144, pp. 372–385. Springer, Heidelberg (2006)
9. Brockschmidt, M., Musiol, R., Otto, C., Giesl, J.: Automated termination proofs for Java programs with cyclic data. In: Madhusudan, P., Seshia, S.A. (eds.) CAV 2012. LNCS, vol. 7358, pp. 105–122. Springer, Heidelberg (2012)
10. Colón, M.A., Sipma, H.B.: Synthesis of linear ranking functions. In: Margaria, T., Yi, W. (eds.) TACAS 2001. LNCS, vol. 2031, pp. 67–81. Springer, Heidelberg (2001)
11. Cook, B., Fisher, J., Krepska, E., Piterman, N.: Proving stabilization of biological systems. In: Jhala, R., Schmidt, D. (eds.) VMCAI 2011. LNCS, vol. 6538, pp. 134–149. Springer, Heidelberg (2011)
12. Cook, B., Kroening, D., Rümmer, P., Wintersteiger, C.M.: Ranking function synthesis for bit-vector relations. Formal Methods in System Design 43(1), 93–120 (2013)
13. Cook, B., Podelski, A., Rybalchenko, A.: Terminator: Beyond safety. In: Ball, T., Jones, R.B. (eds.) CAV 2006. LNCS, vol. 4144, pp. 415–418. Springer, Heidelberg (2006)
14. Cousot, P.: Proving program invariance and termination by parametric abstraction, lagrangian relaxation and semidefinite programming. In: Cousot, R. (ed.) VMCAI 2005. LNCS, vol. 3385, pp. 1–24. Springer, Heidelberg (2005)
15. Gulwani, S., Zuleger, F.: The reachability-bound problem. In: Zorn, B.G., Aiken, A. (eds.) PLDI, pp. 292–304. ACM (2010)
16. Gupta, A., Henzinger, T.A., Majumdar, R., Rybalchenko, A., Xu, R.-G.: Proving non-termination. In: POPL, pp. 147–158 (2008)
17. Harris, W.R., Lal, A., Nori, A.V., Rajamani, S.K.: Alternation for termination. In: Cousot, R., Martel, M. (eds.) SAS 2010. LNCS, vol. 6337, pp. 304–319. Springer, Heidelberg (2010)
18. Kroening, D., Sharygina, N., Tonetta, S., Tsitovich, A., Wintersteiger, C.M.: Loop summarization using abstract transformers. In: Cha, S(S.), Choi, J.-Y., Kim, M., Lee, I., Viswanathan, M. (eds.) ATVA 2008. LNCS, vol. 5311, pp. 111–125. Springer, Heidelberg (2008)
19. Kroening, D., Sharygina, N., Tsitovich, A., Wintersteiger, C.M.: Termination analysis with compositional transition invariants. In: Touili, T., Cook, B., Jackson, P. (eds.) CAV 2010. LNCS, vol. 6174, pp. 89–103. Springer, Heidelberg (2010)
20. Podelski, A., Rybalchenko, A.: A complete method for the synthesis of linear ranking functions. In: Steffen, B., Levi, G. (eds.) VMCAI 2004. LNCS, vol. 2937, pp. 239–251. Springer, Heidelberg (2004)
21. Podelski, A., Rybalchenko, A.: Transition invariants. In: LICS, pp. 32–41 (2004)
22. Podelski, A., Wagner, S.: A sound and complete proof rule for region stability of hybrid systems. In: Bemporad, A., Bicchi, A., Buttazzo, G. (eds.) HSCC 2007. LNCS, vol. 4416, pp. 750–753. Springer, Heidelberg (2007)

23. Rybalchenko, A.: Constraint solving for program verification: Theory and practice by example. In: Touili, T., Cook, B., Jackson, P. (eds.) CAV 2010. LNCS, vol. 6174, pp. 57–71. Springer, Heidelberg (2010)
24. Schrijver, A.: Theory of linear and integer programming. John Wiley & Sons, Inc., New York (1986)
25. Tiwari, A.: Termination of linear programs. In: Alur, R., Peled, D.A. (eds.) CAV 2004. LNCS, vol. 3114, pp. 70–82. Springer, Heidelberg (2004)

Merge and Conquer:
State Merging in Parametric Timed Automata

Étienne André[1], Laurent Fribourg[2], and Romain Soulat[2]

[1] Université Paris 13, Sorbonne Paris Cité, LIPN, F-93430, Villetaneuse, France
[2] LSV, ENS Cachan & CNRS, Cachan, France

Abstract. Parameter synthesis for real-time systems aims at synthesizing dense sets of valuations for the timing requirements, guaranteeing a good behavior. A popular formalism for modeling parameterized real-time systems is parametric timed automata (PTAs). Compacting the state space of PTAs as much as possible is fundamental. We present here a state merging reduction based on convex union, that reduces the state space, but yields an over-approximation of the executable paths. However, we show that it preserves the sets of reachable locations and executable actions. We also show that our merging technique associated with the inverse method, an algorithm for parameter synthesis, preserves locations as well, and outputs larger sets of parameter valuations.

Keywords: Parameter synthesis, state space reduction, real-time systems.

1   Introduction

Ensuring the correctness of critical real-time systems, involving concurrent behaviors and timing requirements, is crucial. Formal verification methods may not always be able to verify full size systems, but they provide designers with an important help during the design phase, in order to detect otherwise costly errors. Formalisms for modeling real-time systems, such as time Petri nets or timed automata (TAs), have been extensively used in the past decades, and led to useful and efficient implementations. Parameter synthesis for real-time systems is a set of techniques aiming at synthesizing dense sets of valuations for the timing requirements of the system. We consider the delays as unknown constants, or *parameters*, and synthesize constraints on these parameters guaranteeing the system correctness; of course, the weaker the constraint (i.e., the larger the set of parameter valuations), the more interesting the result. Parameterizing TAs gives parametric timed automata (PTAs) [2].

A fundamental problem in the exploration of the reachability space in PTAs is to compact as much as possible the generated space of symbolic states. Our first contribution is to introduce a state merging technique based on convex union. Roughly speaking, two states are merged when their discrete part is the same, and the union of their respective continuous part (values of the clocks

D. Van Hung and M. Ogawa (Eds.): ATVA 2013, LNCS 8172, pp. 381–396, 2013.
© Springer International Publishing Switzerland 2013

and parameters) is convex. On the one hand, this technique often considerably reduces the state space. On the other hand, exploring the state space using this technique does not reflect the standard semantics of PTAs: the set of possible paths is an over-approximation of the set of paths in the original PTAs semantics. However, we show that the state space computed using the merging reduction preserves the set of reachable locations and executable actions. That is, the sets of reachable locations and executable actions obtained using the merging reduction are the same as those obtained using the classical semantics.

The inverse method IM [8] is an algorithm that takes advantage of a known reference parameter valuation, and synthesizes a constraint around the reference valuation guaranteeing the same traces as for the reference valuation, i.e., the same time-abstract (or discrete) behavior. Our second contribution is to show that IM equipped with our merging reduction (called IM_{Mrg}) does not preserve traces anymore; however, it preserves locations (i.e., discrete reachability), and outputs a weaker constraint. However, we show that actions are not preserved in the general case. We exhibit a subclass of PTAs, namely backward-deterministic PTA, for which action preservation is guaranteed. Furthermore, we show that IM_{Mrg} outputs a weaker constraint (i.e., a larger set of parameter valuations) than IM, which is interesting.

Our third contribution is to define a new version IM'_{Mrg} of IM_{Mrg} that preserves not only locations but actions too, at the cost of a more restrictive constraint than IM_{Mrg}, but still weaker than IM. Our work is implemented in IMITATOR [4] and shows large state space reductions in many cases, especially for scheduling problems. Finally, and more surprisingly, the time overhead induced by the convexity test is often not significant in the few case studies where the state space is not reduced.

Related Work. In [19], it is shown that, in a network of TAs, all the successor states can be merged together when all the interleavings of actions are possible. However, this result does not extend to the parametric case. In [13,14], it is proposed to replace the union of two states by a unique state when the union of their continuous part (viz., the symbolic clock values) is convex, and the discrete part (viz., the location) is identical. This technique is applied to timed constraints represented in the form of Difference Bound Matrices (DBMs). Our merging technique can be seen as an extension of the technique in [13,14] to the parametric case. This extension is not trivial, and the implementation is necessarily different, since DBMs (in their original form) do not allow the use of parameters. Instead, we implemented our approach in IMITATOR using polyhedra [9].

Remark. This paper is an extension of a "work in progress" paper [5]. In contrast to [5], we formally define the merging operation, and characterize it in the general setting of reachability analysis for PTAs. Furthermore, we rewrite a result from [5] that erroneously stated that the inverse method with merging preserves traces; we show here that it does not, but preserves (at least) the set of locations. We also exhibit a subclass of PTAs for which IM_{Mrg} preserves actions too. We finally define a new version of the inverse method that preserves not only locations but actions as well, for general PTAs.

Outline. We recall preliminaries in Section 2. We define and characterize the merging reduction in Section 3. Section 4 is dedicated to *IM* combined with the merging reduction. We give experiments in Section 5 and conclude in Section 6.

2   Preliminaries

We denote by $\mathbb{N}$, $\mathbb{Q}_+$ and $\mathbb{R}_+$ the sets of non-negative integers, non-negative rational and non-negative real numbers, respectively.

2.1   Clocks, Parameters and Constraints

Throughout this paper, we assume a fixed set $X = \{x_1, \ldots, x_H\}$ of *clocks*. A *clock* is a variable x_i with value in $\mathbb{R}_+$. All clocks evolve linearly at the same rate. A *clock valuation* is a function $w : X \to \mathbb{R}_+^H$. We will often identify a valuation w with the point $(w(x_1), \ldots, w(x_H))$. Given a constant $d \in \mathbb{R}_+$, we use $X + d$ to denote the set $\{x_1 + d, \ldots, x_H + d\}$. Similarly, we write $w + d$ to denote the valuation such that $(w + d)(x) = w(x) + d$ for all $x \in X$.

Throughout this paper, we assume a fixed set $P = \{p_1, \ldots, p_M\}$ of *parameters*, i.e., unknown constants. A *parameter valuation* π is a function $\pi : P \to \mathbb{R}_+^M$. We will often identify a valuation π with the point $(\pi(p_1), \ldots, \pi(p_M))$.

An *inequality* over X and P is $e \prec e'$, where $\prec \in \{<, \le\}$, and e, e' are two linear terms of the form $\sum_{1 \le i \le N} \alpha_i z_i + d$ where $z_i \in X \cup P$, $\alpha_i \in \mathbb{Q}_+$, for $1 \le i \le N$, and $d \in \mathbb{Q}_+$. We define similarly inequalities over X (resp. P). A *constraint* is a conjunction of inequalities. Given an inequality J over the parameters of the form $e < e'$ (respectively $e \le e'$), the *negation* of J, denoted by $\neg J$, is the linear inequality $e' \le e$ (respectively $e' < e$).

We denote by $\mathcal{L}(X)$, $\mathcal{L}(P)$ and $\mathcal{L}(X \cup P)$ the set of all constraints over X, over P, and over X and P respectively. In the sequel, J denotes an inequality over the parameters, $D \in \mathcal{L}(X)$, $K \in \mathcal{L}(P)$, and $C \in \mathcal{L}(X \cup P)$. A constraint over X and P can be interpreted as a set of points in the space $\mathbb{R}^{M+H}$, more precisely as a convex polyhedron.

Given a clock valuation w, $D[w]$ denotes the expression obtained by replacing each clock x in D with $w(x)$. A clock valuation w *satisfies* constraint D (denoted by $w \models D$) if $D[w]$ evaluates to true. Given a parameter valuation π, $C[\pi]$ denotes the constraint over the clocks obtained by replacing each parameter p in C with $\pi(p)$. Likewise, given a clock valuation w, $C[\pi][w]$ denotes the expression obtained by replacing each clock x in $C[\pi]$ with $w(x)$. We say that a parameter valuation π *satisfies* a constraint C, denoted by $\pi \models C$, if the set of clock valuations that satisfy $C[\pi]$ is nonempty. We use the notation $<w, \pi> \models C$ to indicate that $C[\pi][w]$ evaluates to true.

Given two constraints C_1 and C_2, C_1 is said to be *included in* C_2, denoted by $C_1 \subseteq C_2$, if $\forall w, \pi : <w, \pi> \models C_1 \implies <w, \pi> \models C_2$.

A parameter valuation π *satisfies* a constraint K over the parameters, denoted by $\pi \models K$, if the expression obtained by replacing each parameter p in K with $\pi(p)$ evaluates to true. Given K_1 and K_2, K_1 is *included in* K_2, denoted by $K_1 \subseteq K_2$, if $\forall \pi : \pi \models K_1 \Longrightarrow \pi \models K_2$. We consider true as a constraint over the parameters, corresponding to the set of all possible values for P.

We denote by $C{\downarrow}_P$ the constraint over the parameters obtained by projecting C onto the set of parameters, that is after elimination of the clock variables.

Sometimes we will refer to a variable domain X', which is obtained by renaming the variables in X. Explicit renaming of variables is denoted by the substitution operation. Given a constraint C over the clocks and the parameters, we denote by $C_{[X \leftarrow X']}$ the constraint obtained by replacing in C the variables of X with the variables of X'. We sometime write $C(X)$ or $C(X')$ to denote the set of clocks used within C.

We define the *time elapsing* of C, denoted by $C^\uparrow$, as the constraint over X and P obtained from C by delaying an arbitrary amount of time. Formally:

$$C^\uparrow = \Big((C \wedge X' = X + d){\downarrow}_{X' \cup P}\Big)_{[X' \leftarrow X]}$$

where d is a new parameter with values in $\mathbb{R}_+$, and X' is a renamed set of clocks. The inner part of the expression adds the same delay d to all clocks; the projection onto $X' \cup P$ eliminates the original set of clocks X, as well as the variable d; the outer part of the expression renames clocks X' with X.

2.2 Labeled Transition Systems

We introduce below labeled transition systems, which will be used later in this section to define the semantics of PTAs.

Definition 1. *A labeled transition system is a quadruple* $\mathcal{LTS} = (\Sigma, S, S_0, \Rightarrow)$, *with* Σ *a set of symbols,* S *a set of* states, $S_0 \subset S$ *a set of* initial states, *and* $\Rightarrow \in S \times \Sigma \times S$ *a transition relation. We write* $s \overset{a}{\Rightarrow} s'$ *for* $(s, a, s') \in \Rightarrow$. *A run (of length m) of* $\mathcal{LTS}$ *is an alternating sequence of states* $s_i \in S$ *and symbols* $a_i \in \Sigma$ *of the form* $s_0 \overset{a_0}{\Rightarrow} s_1 \overset{a_1}{\Rightarrow} \cdots \overset{a_{m-1}}{\Rightarrow} s_m$, *where* $s_0 \in S_0$. *A state* s_i *is reachable if it belongs to some run* r.

2.3 Parametric Timed Automata

Parametric timed automata are an extension of the class of timed automata to the parametric case, where parameters can be used within guards and invariants in place of constants [2].

Definition 2 (Parametric Timed Automaton). *A parametric timed automaton (PTA)* $\mathcal{A}$ *is a 8-tuple of the form* $\mathcal{A} = (\Sigma, L, l_0, X, P, K, I, \rightarrow)$, *where*

- Σ *is a finite set of actions,*
- L *is a finite set of locations,* $l_0 \in L$ *is the initial location,*

- X is a set of clocks, P is a set of parameters,
- $K \in \mathcal{L}(P)$ is the initial constraint,
- I is the invariant, assigning to every $l \in L$ a constraint $I(l) \in \mathcal{L}(X \cup P)$,
- $\rightarrow$ is a step relation consisting of elements of the form (l, g, a, ρ, l') where $l, l' \in L$ are the source and destination locations, $a \in \Sigma$, $\rho \subseteq X$ is a set of clocks to be reset by the step, and $g \in \mathcal{L}(X \cup P)$ is the step guard.

The constraint K corresponds to the *initial* constraint over the parameters, i.e., a constraint that will be true in all the states of $\mathcal{A}$. For example, in a PTA with two parameters min and max, we may want to constrain min to be always smaller or equal to max, in which case K is defined as $min \leq max$.

Given a PTA $\mathcal{A} = (\Sigma, L, l_0, X, P, K, I, \rightarrow)$, for every parameter valuation π, $\mathcal{A}[\pi]$ denotes the PTA $(\Sigma, L, l_0, X, P, K_\pi, I, \rightarrow)$, where $K_\pi = K \wedge \bigwedge_{i=1}^{M} p_i = \pi(p_i)$. This corresponds to the PTA obtained from $\mathcal{A}$ by substituting every occurrence of a parameter p_i by constant $\pi(p_i)$ in the guards and invariants. Note that $\mathcal{A}[\pi]$ is a non-parametric timed automaton.

In the following, given a PTA $\mathcal{A} = (\Sigma, L, l_0, X, P, K, I, \rightarrow)$ and when clear from the context, we will often denote this PTA by $\mathcal{A}(K)$, in order to emphasize the value of K in $\mathcal{A}$.

The (symbolic) semantics of PTAs relies on the notion of state, i.e., a pair (l, C) where $l \in L$ is a location, and $C \in \mathcal{L}(X \cup P)$ its associated constraint. For each valuation π of P, we may view a state s as the set of pairs (l, w) where w is a clock valuation such that $<w, \pi> \models C$.

A state $s = (l, C)$ of a PTA $\mathcal{A}$ is π-*compatible* if $\pi \models C$. We say that a set of states S_1 is *included* into a set of states S_2, denoted by $S_1 \sqsubseteq S_2$, if $\forall s : s \in S_1 \implies s \in S_2$.

The *initial state* of $\mathcal{A}(K)$ is $s_0 = (l_0, C_0)$, where $C_0 = K \wedge I(l_0) \wedge \bigwedge_{i=1}^{H-1} x_i = x_{i+1}$. In this expression, K is the initial constraint over the parameters, $I(l_0)$ is the invariant of the initial state, and the rest of the expression lets clocks evolve from the same initial value.

The semantics of PTAs is given in the following in the form of an LTS.

Definition 3 (Semantics of PTAs). *Let $\mathcal{A} = (\Sigma, L, l_0, X, P, K, I, \rightarrow)$ be a PTA. The semantics of $\mathcal{A}$ is $\mathcal{LTS}(\mathcal{A}) = (\Sigma, S, S_0, \Rightarrow)$ where*

$$S = \{(l, C) \in L \times \mathcal{L}(X \cup P) \mid C \subseteq I(l)\},$$
$$S_0 = \{s_0\}$$

and a transition $(l, C) \overset{a}{\Rightarrow} (l', C')$ belongs to $\Rightarrow$ if $\exists C'' : (l, C) \overset{a}{\rightarrow} (l', C'') \overset{d}{\rightarrow} (l', C')$, with

- *discrete transitions $(l, C) \overset{a}{\rightarrow} (l', C')$ if there exists $(l, g, a, \rho, l') \in \rightarrow$ and*

$$C' = \left(\left(C(X) \wedge g(X) \wedge X' = \rho(X) \right) \downarrow_{X' \cup P} \wedge I(l')(X') \right)_{[X' \leftarrow X]} \quad and$$

- *delay transitions $(l, C) \overset{d}{\rightarrow} (l, C')$ with $C' = C^\uparrow \wedge I(l)(X)$.*

Let $\mathcal{LTS}(\mathcal{A}) = (\Sigma, S, S_0, \Rightarrow)$. When clear from the context, given $(s_1, a, s_2) \in \Rightarrow$, we write $(s_1 \overset{a}{\Rightarrow} s_2) \in \Rightarrow(\mathcal{A})$.

A *path* of $\mathcal{A}$ is an alternating sequence of states and actions of the form $s_0 \overset{a_0}{\Rightarrow} s_1 \overset{a_1}{\Rightarrow} \cdots \overset{a_{m-1}}{\Rightarrow} s_m$, such that for all $i = 0, \ldots, m-1$, $a_i \in \Sigma$ and $s_i \overset{a_i}{\Rightarrow} s_{i+1} \in \Rightarrow(\mathcal{A})$. The set of all paths of $\mathcal{A}$ is denoted by $Paths(\mathcal{A})$. We define *traces* as time-abstract paths. Given a path $(l_0, C_0) \overset{a_0}{\Rightarrow} (l_1, C_1) \overset{a_1}{\Rightarrow} \cdots \overset{a_{m-1}}{\Rightarrow} (l_m, C_m)$, the corresponding trace is $l_0 \overset{a_0}{\Rightarrow} l_1 \overset{a_1}{\Rightarrow} \cdots \overset{a_{m-1}}{\Rightarrow} l_m$. The set of all traces of $\mathcal{A}$ (or *trace set*) is denoted by $Traces(\mathcal{A})$.

The *Post* operation computes the successors of a state. Formally, $Post_{\mathcal{A}}(s) = \{s' | \exists a \in \Sigma : (s \overset{a}{\Rightarrow} s') \in \Rightarrow(\mathcal{A})\}$. We define $Post^i_{\mathcal{A}}(s)$ as the set of states reachable from a state s_0 in exactly i steps. The *Post* operation extends to a set S of states: $Post_{\mathcal{A}}(S) = \bigcup_{s \in S} Post_{\mathcal{A}}(s)$. And similarly for $Post^i_{\mathcal{A}}(S)$. We write $Post^*_{\mathcal{A}}(S) = \bigcup_{i \geq 0} Post^i_{\mathcal{A}}(S)$.

Given a PTA $\mathcal{A}$ of initial state s_0, we write $Reach^i(\mathcal{A})$ (resp. $Reach^*(\mathcal{A})$) for $Post^i_{\mathcal{A}}(\{s_0\})$ (resp. $Post^*_{\mathcal{A}}(\{s_0\})$). We also define $Locations(\mathcal{A})$ (resp. $Actions(\mathcal{A})$) as the set of locations (resp. actions) reachable (resp. executable) from the initial state of $\mathcal{A}$. We will often use these notations with $\mathcal{A}(K)$ in place of $\mathcal{A}$.

Remark 1. For sake of conciseness, we do not recall the concrete semantics of PTAs here. Our symbolic semantics is commonly used (see, e.g., [17,8]), and it is clear that the sets $Locations(\mathcal{A})$ and $Actions(\mathcal{A})$ are the same for both the symbolic and concrete semantics. $\qquad\square$

2.4   The Inverse Method

The inverse method *IM* is a semi-algorithm (i.e., if it terminates, its result is correct) that takes as input a PTA $\mathcal{A}$ and a reference parameter valuation π, and synthesizes a constraint K over the parameters such that, for all $\pi' \models K$, $\mathcal{A}[\pi]$ and $\mathcal{A}[\pi']$ have the same trace sets [8].

Algorithm 1. Inverse method $IM(\mathcal{A}, \pi)$

---

   input : PTA $\mathcal{A}$ of initial state s_0, parameter valuation π
   output: Constraint K over the parameters

1 $i \leftarrow 0$; $K_c \leftarrow$ true; $S_{new} \leftarrow \{s_0\}$; $S \leftarrow \{\}$
2 **while** true **do**
3   **while** *there are π-incompatible states in S_{new}* **do**
4   Select a π-incompatible state (l, C) of S_{new} (i.e., s.t. $\pi \not\models C$) ;
5   Select a π-incompatible J in $C{\downarrow}_P$ (i.e., s.t. $\pi \not\models J$) ;
6         $K_c \leftarrow K_c \wedge \neg J$; $S \leftarrow \bigcup_{j=0}^{i-1} Post^j_{\mathcal{A}(K_c)}(\{s_0\})$; $S_{new} \leftarrow Post_{\mathcal{A}(K_c)}(S)$;
7   **if** $S_{new} \sqsubseteq S$ **then return** $K \leftarrow \bigcap_{(l,C) \in S} C{\downarrow}_P$
8      $i \leftarrow i+1$; $S \leftarrow S \cup S_{new}$; $S_{new} \leftarrow Post_{\mathcal{A}(K_c)}(S)$

IM, recalled in Algorithm 1, uses 4 variables: an integer i measuring the depth of the state space exploration, the current constraint K_c, the set S of states explored at previous iterations, and a set S_{new} of states explored at the current iteration i. Starting from the initial state s_0, IM iteratively computes reachable states. When a π-incompatible state is found, an incompatible inequality is non-deterministically selected within the projection onto P of the constraint (line 5); its negation is then added to K_c (line 6). The set of reachable states is then updated. When all successor states have already been reached (line 7), IM returns the intersection K of the projection onto P of the constraints associated with all the reachable states. Otherwise, the exploration goes one step further (line 8). Recall from [8] that IM is non-deterministic, and hence its result may be non-complete, i.e., the resulting constraint may not be the weakest constraint guaranteeing the preservation of trace sets.

3 Merging States in Parametric Timed Automata

3.1 Principle

We extend here the notion of merging from [13] to the parametric case.

Definition 4. *Two states $s_1 = (l_1, C_1)$ and (l_2, C_2) are mergeable if $l_1 = l_2$ and $C_1 \cup C_2$ is convex; then, $(l_1, C_1 \cup C_2)$ is their* merging *denoted by $merge(s_1, s_2)$.*

Given a set S of states, $Merge(S)$ denotes the result of applying iteratively the merging of a pair of states of S until no further merging applies, as given in Algorithm 2.

Algorithm 2. Merging a set of states

---

   input : Set S of states
   output: Merged set S of states

1 $Q \leftarrow S$;
2 **while** $\exists (l, C_1), (l, C_2) \in Q$ *such that* $C_1 \neq C_2$ *and* $C_1 \cup C_2$ *is convex* **do**
3    $\lfloor$ $Q \leftarrow Q \setminus \{(l, C_1), (l, C_2)\} \cup \{merge((l, C_1), (l, C_2))\}$;
4 **return** Q

Remark. This process is not deterministic, i.e., the result depends on the order of the iterative merging operations of pairs of states. Consider three states $(l, C_1), (l, C_2), (l, C_3)$ such that $C_1 \cup C_2$ and $C_2 \cup C_3$ are convex, but $C_1 \cup C_3$ is not. This situation is depicted in Fig. 1 with 2 parameter dimensions. In that case, two possible sets of states can result from an application of the merging to these 3 states. That is, either $\{(l, C_1), (l, C_2 \cup C_3)\}$ or $\{(l, C_1 \cup C_2), (l, C_3)\}$.

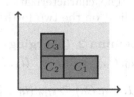

Fig. 1. Non-determinism

3.2   Merging and Reachability

We define below the semantics of PTAs with merging.

Definition 5. *Let* $\mathcal{A} = (\Sigma, L, l_0, X, P, K, I, \rightarrow)$ *be a PTA. The semantics of* $\mathcal{A}$ *with merging is* $\mathcal{LTS}_{Mrg}(\mathcal{A}) = (\Sigma, S, S_0, \Rightarrow_{Mrg})$ *where*

$$S = \{(l, C) \in L \times \mathcal{L}(X \cup P) \mid C \subseteq I(l)\},$$
$$S_0 = \{(l_0, K \wedge I(l_0) \wedge \bigwedge_{i=1}^{H-1} x_i = x_{i+1})\}$$

and a transition $(l, C) \overset{a}{\Rightarrow} (l', C')$ *belongs to* $\Rightarrow_{Mrg}$ *if there exists* $n \in \mathbb{N}$ *such that* $(l, C) \in ReachM^n$, *and* $(l', C') \in ReachM^{n+1}$, *where* $ReachM^n$ *is inductively defined as follows:*

- $ReachM^0 = S_0$, *and*
- $ReachM^{i+1} = Merge(Post_{\mathcal{A}}(ReachM^i))$ *for all* $i \in \mathbb{N}$.

Recall that *Post* is defined using the $\Rightarrow$ relation of $\mathcal{A}$ without merging. Hence the semantics of PTAs with merging iteratively computes states (using the standard transition relation), and merges the new states at each iteration.

Then we define $\Rightarrow_{Mrg}^i$, *PostM*, *ReachM**, *PathsM*, *TracesM*, *LocationsM* and *ActionsM* the same way as $\Rightarrow^i$, *Post*, *Reach**, *Paths*, *Traces*, *Locations* and *Actions*, respectively, by replacing within their respective definition $\Rightarrow$ with $\Rightarrow_{Mrg}$. Observe that, from the definition of $\Rightarrow_{Mrg}$ in Definition 5, *PostM* can be defined as *Post* followed by *Merge*, i.e., *PostM* = *Merge* ∘ *Post*.

3.3   Characterization of the Merging Reduction

The following lemma states that the initial state of any path (hence, including of length 0) of $\mathcal{A}$ without merging is the same for $\mathcal{A}$ with merging.

Lemma 1. *Let* $\mathcal{A}$ *be a PTA. Then* $Reach^0(\mathcal{A}) = ReachM^0(\mathcal{A})$.

Proof. From Definitions 3 and 5.   ∎

The main property preserved by merging states while generating the reachability graph is the preservation of each time-abstract transition, i.e., taken one by one. In other words, for each time-abstract transition $l_1 \overset{a}{\Rightarrow} l_2$ in the graph obtained without merging, there is a corresponding time-abstract transition $l_1 \overset{a}{\Rightarrow} l_2$ in the graph obtained with merging. However, this does not extend to traces.

The characterization of merging will be stated in Theorem 1. This result relies[1] on the two forthcoming lemmas 2 and 3.

Lemma 2 (Merging and reachability ($\Longrightarrow$)). *Let* $\mathcal{A}$ *be a PTA. Let* $(l_0, C_0) \overset{a_0}{\Rightarrow} \ldots \overset{a_{n-1}}{\Rightarrow} (l_n, C_n) \in Paths(\mathcal{A})$. *Then there exist* $C_1', \ldots, C_n'$ *such that:*

1. $(l_0, C_0) \overset{a_0}{\Rightarrow}_{Mrg} (l_0, C_1') \overset{a_1}{\Rightarrow}_{Mrg} \ldots \overset{a_{n-1}}{\Rightarrow}_{Mrg} (l_n, C_n') \in PathsM(\mathcal{A})$, *and*

---

[1] The proofs of all results can be found in [6].

2. $C_i \subseteq C_i'$, for all $1 \leq i \leq n$.

We show in Lemma 3 that the constraint associated to each state in the merged graph is the union of several constraints in the non-merged graph.

Lemma 3 (Merging and reachability ($\Longleftarrow$)). *Let $\mathcal{A}$ be a PTA. For all $n \in \mathbb{N}$, for all $(l, C) \in ReachM^n(\mathcal{A})$, there exist $m \in \mathbb{N}$ and $(l, C_1), \ldots, (l, C_m) \in Reach^*(\mathcal{A})$ such that*

$$C = \bigcup_{1 \leq i \leq m} C_i.$$

We can finally characterize the merging in the following theorem.

Theorem 1 (Merging states in PTAs). *Let $\mathcal{A}$ be a PTA. Then:*

1. *For all $(l_0, C_0) \overset{a_0}{\Rightarrow} \ldots \overset{a_{n-1}}{\Rightarrow} (l_n, C_n) \in Paths(\mathcal{A})$, there exist $C_1', \ldots, C_n'$ such that:*
   (a) $(l_0, C_0) \overset{a_0}{\Rightarrow}_{Mrg} (l_0, C_1') \overset{a_1}{\Rightarrow}_{Mrg} \ldots \overset{a_{n-1}}{\Rightarrow}_{Mrg} (l_n, C_n') \in PathsM(\mathcal{A})$, and
   (b) $C_i \subseteq C_i'$, for all $1 \leq i \leq n$.
2. *For all $(l, C) \in ReachM^*(\mathcal{A})$ there exist $m \in \mathbb{N}$ and $(l, C_1), \ldots, (l, C_m) \in Reach^*(\mathcal{A})$ such that $C = \bigcup_{1 \leq i \leq m} C_i$.*

Proof. From Lemmas 2 and 3. ∎

We can derive several results from Theorem 1.

First, each trace in the non-merged graph exists in the merged graph. (Note that the converse statement does not hold.) Hence, $TracesM(\mathcal{A})$ is an over-approximation of $Traces(\mathcal{A})$.

Corollary 1 (Inclusion of traces). $Traces(\mathcal{A}) \subseteq TracesM(\mathcal{A})$.

We state below that each timed-abstract transition in the non-merged graph exists in the merged graph, and vice versa. (Note that this cannot be generalized to complete traces.)

Corollary 2 (Preservation of time-abstract transitions). *Let $\mathcal{A}$ be a PTA.*

1. *Let $l \overset{a}{\Rightarrow} l' \in Traces(\mathcal{A})$. Then $l \overset{a}{\Rightarrow}_{Mrg} l' \in TracesM(\mathcal{A})$.*
2. *Let $l \overset{a}{\Rightarrow}_{Mrg} l' \in TracesM(\mathcal{A})$. Then $l \overset{a}{\Rightarrow} l' \in Traces(\mathcal{A})$.*

Finally, locations and actions are preserved by the merging reduction.

Corollary 3 (Preservation of locations and actions). *Let $\mathcal{A}$ be a PTA. Then: $Locations(\mathcal{A}) = LocationsM(\mathcal{A})$ and $Actions(\mathcal{A}) = ActionsM(\mathcal{A})$.*

To summarize, computing the set of reachable states using the merging reduction yields an over-approximation of the set of paths. In the original semantics, each trace of $\mathcal{A}(K)$ exists in $\mathcal{A}[\pi]$ for at least one valuation $\pi \models K$; this is not the case anymore with the use of merging, where some traces in $\mathcal{A}(K)$ may not exist for any $\pi \models K$. Nevertheless, both the set of reachable locations and the set of actions are identical to those computed using the original semantics. As a consequence, the merging reduction can be safely used to verify the reachability or the non-reachability of a (set of) location(s), but not to verify more complex properties such as properties on traces (linear-time formulas).

4   The Inverse Method with Merging

4.1   Principle

We extend IM with the merging operation, by merging states within the algorithm, i.e., by replacing within Algorithm 1 all occurrences of $Post$ with $PostM$. (The extension IM_{Mrg} is given in [6].)

Remark 2. In IM_{Mrg}, states are merged *before* the π-compatibility test. Hence, some π-incompatible states may possibly be merged, and hence become π-compatible. As a consequence, less inequalities will be negated and added to K_c, thus giving a weaker output constraint K_{Mrg}. Also note that the addition of merging to IM adds a new reason for non-confluence since the merging process is itself non-deterministic. □

We will see that, in contrast to IM, IM_{Mrg} does not preserve traces. That is, given $\pi, \pi' \models K_{Mrg}$, a trace in $\mathcal{A}[\pi]$ may not exist in $\mathcal{A}[\pi']$, and vice versa.

Example 1. We use here a jobshop example in the setting of parametric schedulability [16], in order to show that the traces are no longer preserved with IM_{Mrg}. This system (modeled by a PTA $\mathcal{A}$) contains 2 machines on which 2 jobs should be performed. The system parameters are d_i (for $i = 1, 2$) that encode the duration of each job. The system actions are js_1 (job 1 starting), jf_1 (job 1 finishing) and similarly for job 2.

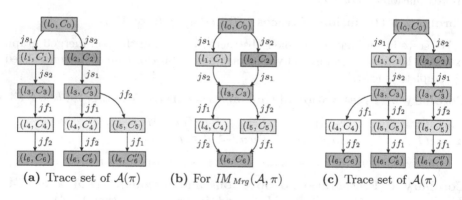

(a) Trace set of $\mathcal{A}(\pi)$ **(b)** For $IM_{Mrg}(\mathcal{A}, \pi)$ **(c)** Trace set of $\mathcal{A}(\pi)$

Fig. 2. Trace sets of $\mathcal{A}$

Consider $\pi = \{d_1 := 1, d_2 := 2\}$. The trace set of $\mathcal{A}[\pi]$ using the standard semantics (Definition 3) is given in Fig. 2a (in the form of a graph). Applying IM to $\mathcal{A}$ and π gives $K = d_2 > d_1$. From the correctness of IM [8], the trace set of $\mathcal{A}[\pi']$, for all $\pi' \models K$, is the same as for $\mathcal{A}[\pi]$. Now, applying IM_{Mrg} to $\mathcal{A}$ and π gives $K_{Mrg} = \text{true}$; the merged trace set is given in Fig. 2b. Then, let $\pi' = \{d_1 := 2, d_2 := 1\}$ be a valuation in K_{Mrg} but outside of K. The trace set of $\mathcal{A}[\pi']$ (using the standard semantics) is given in Fig. 2c. The trace sets of $\mathcal{A}[\pi]$

and $\mathcal{A}[\pi']$ are different: the trace $l_0 \overset{js_2}{\Rightarrow} l_2 \overset{js_1}{\Rightarrow} l_3 \overset{if_1}{\Rightarrow} l_4 \overset{if_2}{\Rightarrow} l_6$ exists in $\mathcal{A}[\pi]$ but not in $\mathcal{A}[\pi']$; the trace $l_0 \overset{js_1}{\Rightarrow} l_1 \overset{js_2}{\Rightarrow} l_3 \overset{if_2}{\Rightarrow} l_5 \overset{if_1}{\Rightarrow} l_6$ exists in $\mathcal{A}[\pi']$ but not in $\mathcal{A}[\pi]$. However, note that the reachable locations and executable actions are the same in these two trace sets. $\qquad\square$

4.2 Preservation of Locations

We will show in Theorem 2 that IM_{Mrg} preserves locations. This result relies on the forthcoming lemma.

Lemma 4. *Suppose* $IM_{Mrg}(\mathcal{A}, \pi)$ *terminates with output* K_{Mrg}. *Then* $\pi \models K_{Mrg}$.

Proof. At the end of IM_{Mrg}, all merged states in S are π-compatible by construction. That is, for all $(l, C) \in S$, we have $\pi \models C{\downarrow}_P$. Since $K_{Mrg} = \bigcap_{(l,C) \in S} C{\downarrow}_P$, then $\pi \models K_{Mrg}$. $\qquad\blacksquare$

Theorem 2. *Suppose* $IM_{Mrg}(\mathcal{A}, \pi)$ *terminates with output* K_{Mrg}. *Then, for all* $\pi' \models K_{Mrg}$, $Locations(\mathcal{A}[\pi]) = Locations(\mathcal{A}[\pi'])$.

Hence, although the trace set is not preserved by IM_{Mrg}, the set of locations is. As a consequence, the reachability and safety properties (based on locations) that are true in $\mathcal{A}[\pi]$ are also true in $\mathcal{A}[\pi']$.

4.3 Preserving Actions

General Case. Although the set of locations is preserved by IM_{Mrg}, the set of actions is not preserved in the general case (in contrast to the reachability analysis with merging). A counterexample is given in [6].

Proposition 1 (Non-preservation of actions). *There exist* $\mathcal{A}$, π *and* π' *such that (1)* $IM_{Mrg}(\mathcal{A}, \pi)$ *terminates with output* K_{Mrg}, *(2)* $\pi' \models K_{Mrg}$, *and (3)* $Actions(\mathcal{A}[\pi]) \neq Actions(\mathcal{A}[\pi'])$.

Not all properties are based on actions. Hence IM_{Mrg} is suitable for systems the correctness of which is expressed using the reachability or the non-reachability of locations. Nevertheless, to be able to handle as well systems the correctness of which is expressed using the (non-)reachability of actions, the rest of this section will be devoted to identifying techniques to preserve actions too.

Backward-Deterministic Parametric Timed Automata. We identify here a subclass of PTAs for which IM_{Mrg} preserves the set of actions. We restrict the model so that, for any location, at most one action is used on its incoming edges. This restriction can be checked syntactically.

Definition 6 (Backward-determinism). *A PTA is* backward-deterministic *if for all* $(l_1, g, a, \rho, l_2), (l'_1, g', a', \rho', l'_2) \in \rightarrow$, *then* $l_2 = l'_2 \Longrightarrow a = a'$.

In a backward-deterministic PTA, if a location is reachable, then its incoming action is executed too. Hence the preservation of the locations by IM_{Mrg} implies the preservation of the actions too.

Proposition 2 (Action preservation). *Let $\mathcal{A}$ be a backward-deterministic PTA. Suppose $IM_{Mrg}(\mathcal{A}, \pi)$ terminates with output K_{Mrg}. Then, for all $\pi' \models K_{Mrg}$, $Actions(\mathcal{A}[\pi]) = Actions(\mathcal{A}[\pi'])$.*

Proof. From Theorem 2 and Definition 6.   ■

This restriction of backward-determinism may be seen as quite strong in practice. Hence, in the following, in order to preserve the set of actions, we propose to modify the algorithm itself rather than restricting the model.

Improvement of the Inverse Method. The non-preservation of the actions by IM_{Mrg} comes from the fact that the states are first merged, and then tested against π-compatibility (see Remark 2). In order to guarantee the action preservation, we propose to first test newly generated states against π-compatibility, and then merge them. Although this modification is only a subtle inversion of two operations in the algorithm, it has consequences on the properties preserved.

We introduce an improved version IM'_{Mrg} of IM_{Mrg} in Algorithm 3, where states are merged after the π-compatibility tests. Technically, the differences with IM_{Mrg} (highlighted using a non-white background) are as follows: (1) the operation to compute the states at the current deepest level i is *Post* instead of *PostM* (lines 9 and 6), and (2) the states are merged *after* the end of the π-incompatibility tests (addition of line 7).

Algorithm 3. Inverse method with merging (variant) $IM'_{Mrg}(\mathcal{A}, \pi)$

---

input : PTA $\mathcal{A}$ of initial state s_0, parameter valuation π
output: Constraint K'_{Mrg} over the parameters

1 $i \leftarrow 0$; $K_c \leftarrow \text{true}$; $S_{new} \leftarrow \{s_0\}$; $S \leftarrow \{\}$
2 **while** true **do**
3   **while** *there are π-incompatible states in S_{new}* **do**
4   Select a π-incompatible state (l, C) of S_{new} (i.e., s.t. $\pi \not\models C$) ;
5   Select a π-incompatible J in $C\!\downarrow_P$ (i.e., s.t. $\pi \not\models J$) ;
6          $K_c \leftarrow K_c \wedge \neg J$; $S \leftarrow \bigcup_{j=0}^{i-1} PostM_{\mathcal{A}(K_c)}^j(\{s_0\})$; $S_{new} \leftarrow Post_{\mathcal{A}(K_c)}(S)$;
7          $S_{new} \leftarrow Merge(S_{new})$
8   **if** $S_{new} \sqsubseteq S$ **then return** $K'_{Mrg} \leftarrow \bigcap_{(l,C) \in S} C\!\downarrow_P$
9      $i \leftarrow i + 1$; $S \leftarrow S \cup S_{new}$; $S_{new} \leftarrow Post_{\mathcal{A}(K_c)}(S)$

Proposition 3. *Suppose $IM(\mathcal{A}, \pi)$, $IM_{Mrg}(\mathcal{A}, \pi)$ and $IM'_{Mrg}(\mathcal{A}, \pi)$ terminate in a deterministic manner with an output K, K_{Mrg} and K'_{Mrg}, respectively. Then, $K \subseteq K'_{Mrg} \subseteq K_{Mrg}$*

Note that IM'_{Mrg} still does not preserve traces; the situation in Fig. 2 is exactly the same for IM'_{Mrg} as for IM_{Mrg}.

Theorem 3. *Suppose $IM'_{Mrg}(\mathcal{A}, \pi)$ terminates with output K'_{Mrg}. Then, for all $\pi' \models K'_{Mrg}$:*

1. $Locations(\mathcal{A}[\pi]) = Locations(\mathcal{A}[\pi'])$, and
2. $Actions(\mathcal{A}[\pi]) = Actions(\mathcal{A}[\pi'])$.

Proof. Preservation of locations follows the same reasoning as for Theorem 2. Preservation of actions is guaranteed by construction of IM'_{Mrg} together with the preservation of locations.　　　　　　　　　　　　　　　　■

5　Experimental Validation

We implemented IM'_{Mrg} in IMITATOR [4], in addition to the classical IM. In [13], the main technique for merging two timed constraints C, C' consists in comparing their convex hull H with their union. If the hull and the union are equal (or alternatively, if $(H \setminus C) \setminus C' = \emptyset$, where $\setminus$ is the operation of *convex difference*), then C and C' are mergeable into H. In [13,14], this technique is specialized to the case where the timed constraints are represented as DBMs. DBMs are not suitable to represent the state space of PTAs; in IMITATOR, polyhedra are used. We implemented the mergeability test using the (costly) operation of convex merging from the Parma Polyhedra Library (PPL) [9].

Table 1 describes experiments comparing the performances and results of IM and IM'_{Mrg}. Column $|X|$ (resp. $|P|$) denotes the number of clocks (resp. parameters) of the PTA. For each algorithm, columns States, Trans., t and Cpl denote the number of states, of transitions the computation time in seconds, and whether the resulting constraint is complete[2], respectively. In the last 3 columns, we compare the results: first, we divide the number of states in IM by the number of states in IM'_{Mrg} and multiply by 100 (hence, a number smaller than 100 denotes an improvement of IM'_{Mrg}); second, we perform the same comparison for the computation time; the last column indicates whether $K = K'_{Mrg}$ or $K \subsetneq K'_{Mrg}$. Experiments were performed on a KUbuntu 12.10 64 bits system running on an Intel Core i7 CPU 2.67GHz with 4 GiB of RAM.

The first 4 models are asynchronous circuits [11,8]. The SIMOP case study is an industrial networked automation system [8]. The next 5 models are common protocols [12,17,8]. The other models are scheduling problems (e.g., [1,10,18]). All models are described and available (with sources and binaries of IMITATOR) on IMITATOR's Web page[3].

From Table 1, we see that IM'_{Mrg} has the following advantages. First, the state space is often reduced (actually, in all but 4 models) compared to IM. This is

---

[2] Whereas IM and IM'_{Mrg} may be non-complete in general, IMITATOR exploits a sufficient (but non-necessary) condition to detect completeness, when possible.
[3] http://www.lsv.ens-cachan.fr/Software/imitator/merging/

Table 1. Comparison between IM and IM'_{Mrg}

Example	$|X|$	$|P|$	IM				IM'_{Mrg}				Comparison		
			States	Trans.	t	Cpl	States	Trans.	t	Cpl	States	t	K
AndOr	4	12	11	11	0.052	√	9	9	0.056	√	82	108	=
Flip-Flop	5	12	11	10	0.060	√	9	9	0.057	√	82	108	=
Latch	8	13	18	17	0.083	?	12	12	0.069	?	67	83	=
SPSMALL	10	26	31	30	0.618	?	31	30	0.613	?	100	99	=
SIMOP	8	7	-	-	OoM	-	172	262	2.52	?	0	0	-
BRP	7	6	429	474	3.50	√	426	473	4.30	√	99	123	=
CSMA/CD	3	3	301	462	0.514	√	300	461	0.574	√	100	112	=
CSMA/CD'	3	3	13,365	14,271	18.3	√	13,365	14,271	25.4	√	100	139	=
RCP	5	6	327	518	0.748	√	115	186	0.684	√	35	91	=
WLAN	2	8	-	-	OoM	-	8,430	15,152	2,137	√	0	0	-
ABT	7	7	63	62	0.344	?	63	62	0.335	?	100	97	=
AM02	3	4	182	215	0.369	√	53	70	0.112	√	29	30	⊊
BB04	6	7	806	827	28.0	?	141	145	3.15	?	17	11	=
CTC	15	21	1,364	1,363	88.9	√	215	264	17.6	√	16	20	=
LA02	3	5	6,290	8,023	751	√	383	533	17.7	√	6.0	2.4	⊊
LPPRC10	4	7	78	102	0.39	?	31	40	0.251	?	40	64	=
M2.4	3	8	1,497	1,844	8.89	√	119	181	0.374	√	7.9	4.2	⊊

particularly interesting for the scheduling problems, with a division of the number of states by a factor of up to 16 (LA02). Also note that two case studies could not even be verified without the merging reduction, due to memory exhaustion ("OoM"). Second, the computation time is almost always reduced when the merging reduction indeed reduces the state space, by a factor of up to 42 (LA02). Third, and more surprisingly (considering the cost of the mergeability test), the overhead induced by the mergeability test often does not yield a significant augmentation of the computation time, even when the merging reduction does not reduce the state space at all; the worst case is +39 % (CSMA/CD'), which remains reasonable. Finally, the constraint output by IM'_{Mrg} is weaker (i.e., corresponds to a larger set of valuations) than IM for some case studies.

6   Final Remarks

We have shown in this paper that (1) a general technique of state merging in PTAs preserves both the reachability and the non-reachability of actions and locations, (2) the integration of this technique into IM often synthesizes a weaker (hence, better) constraint while reducing the computation space, and preserves locations (but neither traces nor actions), and (3) an improved version of IM_{Mrg} preserves not only locations but actions. Experiments with IMITATOR show that the improved procedure IM'_{Mrg} does not only reduce the state space, but is also often faster than the original procedure IM.

As future work, we plan to study the combined integration into IM of the general technique of state merging with variants [7] and optimizations [3] of IM. Regarding the implementation in IMITATOR, we aim at studying the replacement of polyhedra with parametric DBMs [17]; furthermore, the (costly) mergeability test should be optimized so as to improve performance. Finally, we also plan to generalize the merging technique to the hybrid setting [15].

References

1. Abdeddaïm, Y., Maler, O.: Preemptive job-shop scheduling using stopwatch automata. In: Katoen, J.-P., Stevens, P. (eds.) TACAS 2002. LNCS, vol. 2280, pp. 113–126. Springer, Heidelberg (2002)
2. Alur, R., Henzinger, T.A., Vardi, M.Y.: Parametric real-time reasoning. In: STOC, pp. 592–601. ACM (1993)
3. André, É.: Dynamic clock elimination in parametric timed automata. In: *FSFMA*. OpenAccess Series in Informatics, vol. 31, pp. 18–31. Schloss Dagstuhl – Leibniz-Zentrum für Informatik, Dagstuhl Publishing (2013)
4. André, É., Fribourg, L., Kühne, U., Soulat, R.: IMITATOR 2.5: A tool for analyzing robustness in scheduling problems. In: Giannakopoulou, D., Méry, D. (eds.) FM 2012. LNCS, vol. 7436, pp. 33–36. Springer, Heidelberg (2012)
5. André, É., Fribourg, L., Soulat, R.: Enhancing the inverse method with state merging. In: Goodloe, A.E., Person, S. (eds.) NFM 2012. LNCS, vol. 7226, pp. 100–105. Springer, Heidelberg (2012)
6. André, É., Fribourg, L., Soulat, R.: Merge and conquer: State merging in parametric timed automata (report). Research Report LSV-13-11, Laboratoire Spécification et Vérification, ENS Cachan, France (July 2013), http://www.lsv.ens-cachan.fr/Publis/RAPPORTS_LSV/PDF/rr-lsv-2013-11.pdf
7. André, É., Soulat, R.: Synthesis of timing parameters satisfying safety properties. In: Delzanno, G., Potapov, I. (eds.) RP 2011. LNCS, vol. 6945, pp. 31–44. Springer, Heidelberg (2011)
8. André, É., Soulat, R.: The Inverse Method. In: FOCUS Series in Computer Engineering and Information Technology. ISTE Ltd. and John Wiley & Sons Inc. (2013)
9. Bagnara, R., Hill, P.M., Zaffanella, E.: The Parma Polyhedra Library: Toward a complete set of numerical abstractions for the analysis and verification of hardware and software systems. Science of Computer Programming 72(1-2), 3–21 (2008)
10. Bini, E., Buttazzo, G.C.: Schedulability analysis of periodic fixed priority systems. IEEE Transactions on Computers 53(11), 1462–1473 (2004)
11. Clarisó, R., Cortadella, J.: The octahedron abstract domain. Science of Computer Programming 64(1), 115–139 (2007)
12. D'Argenio, P.R., Katoen, J.-P., Ruys, T.C., Tretmans, J.: The bounded retransmission protocol must be on time! In: Brinksma, E. (ed.) TACAS 1997. LNCS, vol. 1217, pp. 416–431. Springer, Heidelberg (1997)
13. David, A.: Merging DBMs efficiently. In: NWPT, pp. 54–56. DIKU, University of Copenhagen (2005)
14. David, A.: Uppaal DBM library programmer's reference (2006), http://people.cs.aau.dk/~adavid/UDBM/manual-061023.pdf
15. Fribourg, L., Kühne, U.: Parametric verification and test coverage for hybrid automata using the inverse method. International Journal of Foundations of Computer Science 24(2), 233–249 (2013)
16. Fribourg, L., Lesens, D., Moro, P., Soulat, R.: Robustness analysis for scheduling problems using the inverse method. In: TIME, pp. 73–80. IEEE Computer Society Press (2012)
17. Hune, T., Romijn, J., Stoelinga, M., Vaandrager, F.W.: Linear parametric model checking of timed automata. Journal of Logic and Algebraic Programming 52-53, 183–220 (2002)

396   É. André, L. Fribourg, and R. Soulat

18. Le, T.T.H., Palopoli, L., Passerone, R., Ramadian, Y., Cimatti, A.: Parametric analysis of distributed firm real-time systems: A case study. In: ETFA, pp. 1–8. IEEE (2010)
19. Salah, R.B., Bozga, M., Maler, O.: On interleaving in timed automata. In: Baier, C., Hermanns, H. (eds.) CONCUR 2006. LNCS, vol. 4137, pp. 465–476. Springer, Heidelberg (2006)

An Automata-Theoretic Approach to Reasoning about Parameterized Systems and Specifications

Orna Grumberg[1], Orna Kupferman[2], and Sarai Sheinvald[2]

[1] Department of Computer Science, The Technion, Haifa 32000, Israel
[2] School of Computer Science and Engineering, Hebrew University, Jerusalem 91904, Israel

Abstract. We introduce *generalized register automata* (GRAs) and study their properties and applications in reasoning about systems and specifications over infinite domains. We show that GRAs can capture both *VLTL* – a logic that extends LTL with variables over infinite domains, and *abstract systems* – finite state systems whose atomic propositions are parameterized by variable over infinite domains. VLTL and abstract systems naturally model and specify infinite-state systems in which the source of infinity is the data domain (c.f., range of processes id, context of messages). Thus, GRAs suggest an automata-theoretic approach for reasoning about such systems. We demonstrate the usefulness of the approach by pushing forward the known border of decidability for the model-checking problem in this setting. From a theoretical point of view, GRAs extend register automata and are related to other formalisms for defining languages over infinite alphabets.

1 Introduction

In model checking, we verify that a system has a desired behavior by checking that a mathematical model of the system satisfies a formal specification of the behavior. Traditionally, the system is modeled by a Kripke structure – a finite-state system whose states are labeled by a finite set of atomic propositions. The specification is a temporal-logic formula over the same set of atomic propositions [3].

When the system is defined over a large data domain or contains many components, its size becomes large or even infinite, and model checking may become intractable. Moreover, standard temporal logic may not be sufficiently expressive for specifying properties of such systems.

In [7], we introduced a novel approach for model checking systems and specifications that suffer from the size problem described above. Our approach extended both the specification formalism and the system model with atomic propositions that are parameterized by variables ranging over some (possibly infinite) domain. We studied the model-checking problem in this setting. While we showed that model checking in the general case is undecidable, we have managed to find interesting fragments of our systems and specification formalisms for which model checking is decidable. Our methods were based on reducing the problem to standard LTL model checking. The reduction was found helpful in some cases, but lacks a rigorous theoretical treatment.

D. Van Hung and M. Ogawa (Eds.): ATVA 2013, LNCS 8172, pp. 397–411, 2013.

In particular, [7] left open the challenge of developing an automata-theoretic approach for this setting.

In this paper we introduce *generalized register automata* (GRAs), a new formalism for defining languages over infinite alphabets. GRAs can naturally model both the systems and specifications of [7]. We define GRAs, study their properties, and show how they not only provide a unified theoretical basis to the results in [7], but also enable strengthening and extending the results there.

We first elaborate on the setting in [7]. In an *abstract system*, our extension of a Kripke structure, every state is labeled by a set of atomic propositions. Some of the atomic propositions may be parameterized by variables that range over an unbounded or an infinite domain. The system also contains constraints on the possible assignments to the variables, and may reset their value during its execution. The *concrete computations* of an abstract system are induced by paths of the abstract system in which variables are assigned concrete values in a way consistent with the constraints and the resets along the path. For instance, if a path of the abstract system starts with $\{send.x\}, \{rec.x\}, \{send.x\}$, and x is a variable over $\mathbb{N}$ that is reset between the second and third state, then a concrete computation induced by the path may start with $\{send.3\}, \{rec.3\}, \{send.5\}$. Evidently, abstract systems are capable of describing communication protocols with unboundedly many processes, systems with interleaved transactions each carrying a unique id, buffers of messages with an infinite domain, and many more.

Our specification formalism, *Variable LTL* (VLTLs), also uses atomic propositions parameterized by variables. For example, the VLTL formula $\forall x.G\,(send.x \rightarrow F\,receive.x)$ states that for every value d in the domain, whenever a message with content d is sent, then a message with content d is eventually received. As another example, the formula $\exists x.G\,F\,\neg idle.x \wedge G\,F\,\neg idle.x$ states that in each computation, there exists at least one process that is both idle and not idle infinitely often. Note that if the domain of messages or process id's is infinite or unknown in advance, then there exist no equivalent LTL formulas for these VLTL formulas.

As described above, in [7] we solved the VLTL model-checking problem for some fragments of the (undecidable) general setting. Our goal here is to suggest an automata-theoretic approach to the problem, hopefully pushing the boundaries of decidable fragments. In the automata-theoretic approach to model checking [15], we represent systems and their specifications by automata on infinite words. Questions such as model checking and satisfiability are then reduced to questions about automata and their languages. Traditional automata are too weak for modeling abstract systems or VLTL formulas, and a formalism that can handle infinite alphabets is needed.

A classical formalism for defining languages with an infinite alphabet is that of *register automata* [8,9]. A nondeterministic register automaton comprises a state machine and a finite set of registers that may store values of the infinite domain. In a transition, the register automaton either guesses some value and stores it in one of the registers (an ϵ-transition), or advances on the input word if the content of register in the transition matches the next input letter.

Our formalism of GRA extends register automata in a way that enables easy modeling of abstract systems and VLTL formulas.[1] Essentially, this involves features that mimic the conjunctions and disjunctions in the logic (that is, the transition function of GRAs is *alternating*), features that mimic the existential and universal quantification of variables (that is, GRAs have two types of ϵ-transitions, one – $\epsilon_\exists$, which guesses and assigns a single value to a register, and one – $\epsilon_\forall$, which assigns all possible values to a register by splitting the run, creating a different copy for every such value), features that mimic the constraints on the variable values (by adding constraints on the content of the registers), and features that make it possible to complement a given GRA by dualization (by closing the components of a transition, namely the branching mode and guards, to dualization).

We formally define GRAs and study their theoretical properties. We show that GRAs are closed under the Boolean operations. Unsurprisingly, their universality and emptiness problems are generally undecidable, yet we point to the fragment in which the GRAs have only a single register, for which nonemptiness is decidable.

We compare GRAs with the formalisms of register automata and data automata [9,2]. We show that GRAs are strictly more expressive than register automata. We describe a translation from deterministic data automata to GRAs and show that there are languages that are accepted by GRAs and not by (nondeterministic) data automata.

We describe a translation of abstract systems and VLTL formulas to GRAs. The translation of a VLTL formula to an equivalent GRA resembles the translation of LTL formulas to nondeterministic Büchi automata [15]. The quantifiers in the formula are handled by a sequence of $\epsilon_\exists$ (for $\exists$ quantifiers) and $\epsilon_\forall$ transitions (for $\forall$ quantifiers).

In [7], we showed that model checking is undecidable already for VLTL formulas with two $\exists$ quantifiers, and is decidable for formulas with only $\forall$ quantifiers. The translation to GRA enables us to complete the picture and show that for the safe fragment of VLTL, model checking of formulas of type $\forall x_1; \forall x_2; \dots \forall x_k; \exists x \varphi$ is decidable. This is a useful fragment, as it captures specifications of the form "for every environment, there exists a value that satisfies φ". As an example, consider the formula $\forall x_1; \exists x_2; G\left((\neg idle.x_1) \rightarrow X(\neg idle.x_2)\right)$, with $x_1 \neq x_2$. This formula states that if there exists some non-idle process, then it will be immediately followed by a different non-idle process, thus ensuring that there is an infinite sequence of non-idle processes. Another example is the formula $\forall x_1; \exists x_2; G\left(((\neg req.x_1) \wedge X req.x_1) \rightarrow X new\_process.x_2\right)$, stating that whenever a request with new content is sent, a new process with a new process id is envoked. Dually, the satisfiability of formulas of the type $\exists x_1; \exists x_2; \dots \exists x_k; \forall x \varphi$ is also decidable. For formulas of the type $\exists x_1; \forall x_2; \varphi$, model checking is again undecidable.

Our upper-bound proofs rely on a reduction to the nonemptiness problem for multi-counter machines. The model-checking complexity in these cases is then non-elementary. Finding a lower bound has the same flavor as finding a lower bound for the nonemptiness of data automata [2], which also uses multi-counter machines to show the decidability of nonemptiness, and is a problem that is still open.

---

[1] We study GRA on finite words. Extending the definition to infinite words is easy and the technical difficulties are orthogonal to these that the setting of infinite alphabets involves. Thus, the results here are restricted to the safe fragment of VLTL.

Related Work. There are quite a few different models and variants of automata over infinite alphabets, differing in their expressive power and decidable properties. A major motivation for such models origins from formal reasoning about XML [13].

Register automata were first introduced in [8]. These were extended in [9] to include ϵ-transitions. In [6], we studied VFA, a sub-type of nondeterministic register automata that can be represented by finite automata and has fragments that are closed under the Boolean operations.

Several types of *alternating register automata* (ARA) have been studied, differing in their expressive power. In [12], the state machine has universal and existential states. The run on a universal state splits into all possible configurations that may follow the current configuration. [12] also studies the two-way model. In [5], the automaton is single-register, and is enriched with the actions *guess* (an ϵ-transition) and *spread* (creating new threads of the run with all data values that appear with some state, starting from another state). For this model, nonemptiness is decidable. In [4], the authors study the relations between LTL with the freeze quantifier (an extension of LTL that is equiped with a register) and single-register alternating register automata.

Another type of automata over infinite alphabets are *data automata* [2]. Data automata are defined over alphabets of the type $\Sigma \times D$, where Σ is finite and D is infinite. Intuitively, Σ is accessed directly, while D can only be tested for equality, and is used for inducing an equivalence relation on the set of positions. Technically, a data automaton consists of two components. The first is a letter-to-letter transducer that runs on the projection of the input word on Σ and generates words over yet another alphabet Γ. The second is a finite automaton that runs on subwords (determined by the equivalence classes) of the word over Γ generated by the transducer. Data automata turn out to be a very expressive model for which nonemptiness is decidable (albeit non-elementary). [10] and [17] study weaker versions of data automata, for which nonemptiness is elementary.

Data automata too have several extensions. Such an extension is *class automata* [1], which were defined for the purpose of studying of XPath. A class automaton behaves almost similarly to a data automaton, but the automaton component processes the entire word that is produced by the transducer (as opposed to processing a subword of it), and it takes special transitions when it reads letters of the class it handles. This modification makes nonemptiness undecidable for this type. Other models limit the structure of the automaton component of class automata [16], or add counters to the different data values [11] to achieve decidable emptiness.

A third type are *pebble automata* and their variants. A pebble automaton [12] places pebbles on the input word in a stack-like manner. The transitions of a pebble automaton compare the letter in the input with the letters in positions marked by the pebbles. Several variants of this model have been studied. For example, [12] studies alternating and two-way pebble automata, and [14] introduces top-view weak pebble automata.

These formalisms are insufficient for our purposes of studying of VLTL and abstract systems – both in terms of expressive power, and in terms of easiness of translation. Our formalism of GRA is designed specifically to deal with this setting, and offers a clean and natural translation and suitable decidable fragments.

2   Preliminaries

Automata on Data Words. *Data words* are words over an infinite alphabet $\Sigma \times D$, where Σ is a finite set to which we refer to as *labels*, and D is an infinite set to which we refer to as *data*.

A *nondeterministic register automaton on data words (NRA)* $\mathcal{A}$ comprises an alphabet $\Sigma \times D$, a set $r = \{r_1, r_2, \ldots r_k\}$ of registers that can contain a value of D each, an initial register assignment $r_\# \in (D \cup \{\#\})^k$ where $\# \notin D$, a set of states Q, an initial state $q_0 \in Q$, a set of accepting states $F \subseteq Q$, and a transition relation $\delta \subseteq Q \times (\Sigma \cup \{\epsilon\}) \times [k] \times Q$, where $[k] = \{1, 2, \ldots, k\}$.

A run on an input word w over $\Sigma \times D$ begins at state q_0, and r_i is assigned $r_\#(i)$ for $1 \leq i \leq k$. Intuitively, when $\mathcal{A}$ is in state q and the next input letter is $\langle a, d \rangle$, if it takes a transition labeled $\langle \epsilon, i \rangle$, then it nondeterministically stores some value in register r_i that is different from the contents of the rest of the registers, and does not advance on the input word. A transition labeled $\langle a, i \rangle$ may be taken if the content of the register r_i is d, in which case $\mathcal{A}$ also advances to the next input letter.

The word w is accepted by $\mathcal{A}$ if there exists a run on w that advances along all of w and reaches an accepting state. The language of $\mathcal{A}$, denoted $\mathcal{L}(\mathcal{A})$, is the set of all words accepted by $\mathcal{A}$.

Data automata [2] are another formalism that handles data words. A data automaton $\mathcal{C}$ is a tuple $\langle \Sigma \times D, \Gamma, A, B \rangle$, where A is a letter-to-letter transducer whose input alphabet is Σ and output alphabet is Γ, and B is an NFA over Γ.

To explain the way a data automaton operates, we begin with some terms and notations. Consider a word $w = \langle a_1, d_1 \rangle \langle a_2, d_2 \rangle \ldots \langle a_n, d_n \rangle$ over $\Sigma \times D$. The *string projection* of w is the word $a_1 a_2 \ldots a_n$. A *class* in w is a maximal set of indices for which the letters in w in these indices share the same data value. For example, in the data word $\langle a, 1 \rangle \langle b, 1 \rangle \langle b, 2 \rangle \langle c, 1 \rangle \langle a, 2 \rangle$, there are two different classes: $\{1, 2, 4\}$ and $\{3, 5\}$. Every class induces a *class word*, a word over Σ that is formed by concatenating the labels of the matching letters of the class in the order in which they appear in w. In the example, the two class words are abc and ba.

Consider a word $w = \langle a_1, d_1 \rangle \langle a_2, d_2 \rangle \ldots \langle a_n, d_n \rangle$ over $\Sigma \times D$. A run of $\mathcal{C}$ on w consists of two parts. First, the transducer A runs on the string projection of w and outputs a word $\gamma_1 \gamma_2 \ldots \gamma_n$ over Γ. If it rejects then the run is rejecting. Otherwise, the automaton B runs on every class word of $\langle \gamma_1, d_1 \rangle \langle \gamma_2, d_2 \rangle \ldots \langle \gamma_n, d_n \rangle$. If B accepts all the class words then the run is accepting, otherwise it is rejecting.

The class of data automata contains the class of register automata, and the emptiness problem for data automata is decidable. However, data automata are not closed under complementation [2].

Abstract Systems and VLTL. In [7], we introduced *variable LTL* (VLTL) and *abstract systems*. For both, the standard formalism of Kripke structures and LTL formulas is extended with a set of variables that enables the computations of the Kripke structure to carry values over some infinite domain D, and the formulas to express properties with respect to these values. More specifically, the standard finite set of atomic propositions AP over which both the systems and the formulas are defined is extended by a finite set of *parameterized atomic propositions* T. The propositions of T are parameterized by variables from a finite set X. These variables are assigned values from D.

An abstract system S is a finite Kripke structure over $AP \cup (T \times X)$. In every transition of S, a subset X' of X may be reset, meaning that the varibles of X' may change their value in the next step. The system S also includes an inequality set E over X. Having $x_i \neq x_j \in E$ means that in every point of the computation, the value assigned to x_i must be different from the value that is assigned to x_j. It holds that for every system S there exists an equivalent system S' over the same set of variables such that the inequality set S' is the full inequality set $\{x_i \neq x_j | x_i, x_j \in X\}$. A *computation* π of S is then an infinite word over $2^{AP \cup (T \times D)}$, induced by some infinite path w (over $2^{AP \cup (T \times X)}$) of S. The D values in π_i are obtained by the assignment to the variables in w_i. These values comply both with E and with the resets that w traverses – the value of a variable does not change as long as it has not been reset.

A VLTL formula is a pair $\langle \varphi, E \rangle$, where $\varphi = Q_1 x_1; Q_2 x_2; \ldots Q_k x_k; \psi$, where $Q_i \in \{\forall, \exists\}$ and x_i is a variable in X for every $1 \leq i \leq k$, where ψ is an LTL formula over $AP \cup (T \times X)$, and E is an inequality set over the variables. The semantics of VLTL is with respect to computations over $2^{AP \cup (T \times D)}$ and assignments to the variables of φ. Intuitively, a computation π satisfies a formula $\exists x; \psi$ (denoted $\pi \models \exists x; \psi$) if there exists some value d that may (w.r.t. E) be assigned to x such that $\pi \models \psi[x \leftarrow d]$ in the LTL sense. Similarly, π satisfies $\forall x; \psi$ if for every value d that may be assigned to x, it holds that $\pi \models \psi[x \leftarrow d]$. For the formal definition, see [7].

We say that a system S *satisfies* a VLTL formula $\langle \varphi, E \rangle$ (denoted $S \models \langle \varphi, E \rangle$), if every computation of S satisfies $\langle \varphi, E \rangle$. The model-checking problem for VLTL and abstract systems is then to decide, given S and $\langle \varphi, E \rangle$, whether $S \models \langle \varphi, E \rangle$. In [7], we showed that this problem is generally undecidable, already for formulas of the type $\exists x_1; \exists x_2; \psi$, where ψ is quantifier free. We showed, however, that model checking is decidable when there are no resets in the system. Further, model checking is decidable also in the case where the VLTL formula contains only $\forall$ quantifiers.

3   Generalized Register Automata

We present a generalization of register automata, called *generalized register automata* (GRA), that allows alternation and dualization of the conditions on the transition. The following details are generalized.

- Recall that in an $\langle \epsilon, i \rangle$ transition, if the automaton stores some value in register r_i, then it must be different from the values in all other registers. We generalize this idea by labeling every ϵ-transition by a Boolean formula over inequalities between the registers (to which we also refer as a *guard*). For the run to continue along an ϵ transition, the register assignment must satisfy the guard condition.
- Recall that in an $\langle \epsilon, i \rangle$ transition, the automaton nondeterministically stores some value in register r_i. We can view this as follows: The run is accepting if there exists some value that is stored in r_i, such that the rest of the run is accepting. We generalize this notion by defining two types of ϵ-transitions: in an $\langle \epsilon_\exists, i \rangle$-transition, the run is accepting if there exists some legal (w.r.t. the guard condition) value that

is stored in r_i, such that the rest of the run is accepting. in an $\langle \epsilon_\forall, i \rangle$ transition, the run is accepting if for every value that is stored in r_i, the rest of the run is accepting.
- In the definition of register automaton, the state machine component is nondeterministic. We generalize this by allowing the state machine to be alternating.

Formally, a *generalized register automaton* (GRA) is a tuple

$$\langle \Sigma \times D, \#, r, r_\#, Q, q_0, \delta, F \rangle,$$

where

- $\Sigma \times D$ is the input alphabet, where Σ is finite and D is infinite,
- $r = \{r(1), r(2), \ldots r(k)\}$ is a finite set of registers,
- $\# \notin \Sigma$ marks an empty register,
- $r_\# \in (\Sigma \cup \{\#\})^k$ is the initial register assignment,
- Q is a finite set of states,
- q_0 is the initial state,
- $F \subseteq Q$ is a set of accepting states, and
- $\delta \subseteq (Q \times \Sigma \times B^+(Q \times [k])) \cup (Q \times \{\epsilon_\exists, \epsilon_\forall\} \times B^+(Q \times G(r) \times [k]))$ where $G(r)$ is the set of guards over inequalities over $\{r(1), r(2), \ldots, r(k)\}$, and B^+ stands for the set of positive Boolean formulas [2].

We describe a run of a GRA on an input word w. Since GRAs are alternating, a run on w is a tree. Each node of the tree holds the following information: the current state, the current register configuration, and the current position in the input word. The root of the tree is labeled $\langle q_0, r_\#, 1 \rangle$.

The sons of a node x labeled $\langle q, \langle d(1) \ldots d(k) \rangle, i \rangle$ are determined by the type of transition that is taken from x: an ϵ-transition (an $\epsilon_\exists$-transition or $\epsilon_\forall$-transition), or a transition that advances on the input word. We describe how the run continues from x for each of these transitions.

In the case of an $\epsilon_\exists$ transition, suppose that $\langle q_1, g_1, k_1 \rangle, \langle q_2, g_2, k_2 \rangle, \ldots \langle q_p, g_p, k_p \rangle$ is a satisfying set for $\delta(q, \epsilon_\exists)$. Then from x, the run can continue by splitting into the son nodes $x_1, x_2, \ldots x_p$. These sons are all located in position i in w (that is, they do not advance on the input word). A branch that leads from x to a son x_j assigns a value to register k_j in a way that agrees with g_j, and moves to state q_j. Therefore, x_j is labeled $\langle q_j, \langle d_j(1), d_j(2) \ldots d_j(k) \rangle, i \rangle$, where $\langle d_j(1), d_j(2) \ldots d_j(k) \rangle$ satisfies g_j, and may differ from $\langle d(1) \ldots d(k) \rangle$ only in the register k_j.

In the case of an $\epsilon_\forall$ transition, again suppose that $\langle q_1, g_1, k_1 \rangle, \ldots \langle q_p, g_p, k_p \rangle$ is a satisfying set for $\delta(q, \epsilon_\forall)$. Then from x, the run continues by splitting into infinitely many son nodes, all located in position i on w. For every $\langle q_j, g_j, k_j \rangle$, the run branches over all values that can be stored in register k_j and satisfy g_j. Thus, for every $\langle q_j, g_j, k_j \rangle$, for every value d that can be stored in register k_j in a way that satisfies g_j, the node x has a son labeled q_j, in position i, whose register assignment is identical to that of x, except for register k_j, which stores the value d.

---

[2] The full definition of GRA also includes the classification of the transitions to "may" and "must" transitions, which allows easy dualization and complementation. For simplicity, and since we do not use these features in our results, we omit them from the definition.

Finally, for a transition that advances on the input word, suppose that $\langle q_1, k_1 \rangle, \ldots$
$\langle q_p, k_p \rangle$ is a satisfying set for $\delta(q, \sigma)$, and that $w_i = \langle a, d \rangle$. Then from x, the run can
continue by splitting into the son nodes $x_1, x_2, \ldots x_p$. These sons are all located in
position $i + 1$ in w (that is, they advance one letter on the input word), and their register
configuration is identical to the register configuration of x. A branch that leads from x
to a son x_j must hold the value d in its register k_j.

In the representation of δ, the registers to be read or written to are paired with the
state the transition leads to. This is essential for alternation. However, to make δ more
convenient to read, for the rest of the paper we represent it similarly to the transition
of NRA whenever possible. Also, in most cases we discuss the guards are uniform
throughout the GRA, and so we omit the guards from the representation, noting them
elsewhere. For example, we represent a transition $\langle q, \epsilon_\exists, \langle s, r_1 \neq r_2, 1 \rangle \vee \langle t, r_1 \neq$
$r_2, 2 \rangle \rangle$, as two transitions from q; one labeled $\langle \epsilon_\exists, 1 \rangle$ leading to s, and one labeled
$\langle \epsilon_\exists, 2 \rangle$ leading to t. Similarly, we represent a transition $\langle q, a, \langle s, 1 \rangle \rangle$ as a transition from
q labeled $\langle a, 1 \rangle$, leading to s.

Example 1. Figure 1 displays the three types of transitions. In (a), an $\epsilon_\exists$ transition
is followed from q with a satisfying set $\langle s, 2 \rangle, \langle t, 2 \rangle$, and $\langle t, 3 \rangle$ (we omit the guard
conditions, that state that the assignment to all registers must be different). The tree
branches accordingly: the leftmost and middle sons are in states s and t, respectively,
reassigning the second register (the middle son reassigns it with the same value it held
before), and the rightmost son is in state t and reassigns the third register.

In (b), an $\epsilon_\forall$ transition is followed from q with a satisfying set $\langle s, 2 \rangle$, and again we
omit the guard condition. Then the run branches into all possible assignments to the
second register, in each path moving to state s.

In (c), the input letter $\langle a, 4 \rangle$ is read on a transition from q with a satisfying set $\langle s, 1 \rangle$
and $\langle t, 2 \rangle$. Then the run splits to two son nodes s and t, where the path to s reads the
value 4 from the first register, and the path to t reads 4 from the second register.

For convenience, we label the edges by the transitions, represented as a transition for
NRA, as we have explained above.

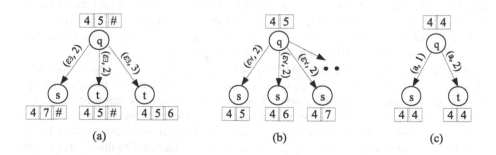

Fig. 1. The three types of transitions (a), (b) and (c)

The run tree is *accepting* if the leaves of all paths of the tree that have read all of w are in an accepting state. Notice that the ϵ-transitions may result in infinite paths that do not advance on the word. Since the definition of acceptance only considers the leaves, these paths are ignored when deciding acceptance. A word w is accepted by a GRA $\mathcal{A}$ if $\mathcal{A}$ has an accepting run tree on w [3].

Example 2. Consider the GRA $\mathcal{A}$ seen in Figure 2. In every transition of $\mathcal{A}$, the guard is $r_1 \neq r_2$, and we omit this detail from Figure 2 for the easiness of reading. The language of $\mathcal{A}$ is the set of all nonempty words over $\{a\} \times D$ in which no data value is repeated. Every run of $\mathcal{A}$ first splits over all values stored in r_1. Then, in every copy, as long as the next input value is different from r_1, the run continues by storing and reading the next value in r_2. The value in r_1 may only be read once and then cannot be read again from state s. Notice that all copies that do not have a value of the input word in their r_1 stay and accept from state r. Figure 2 also includes an accepting run tree on the word $\langle a, 3 \rangle \langle a, 4 \rangle$.

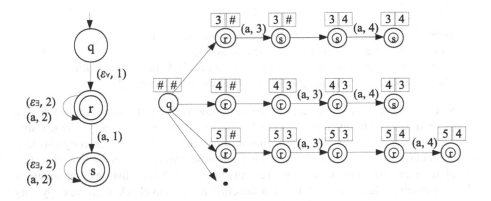

Fig. 2. The GRA $\mathcal{A}$ and an accepting run on the word $\langle a, 3 \rangle \langle a, 4 \rangle$

Since GRAs are a generalization of nondeterministic register automata, we have that every NRA has an equivalent GRA.

Given two GRAs $\mathcal{A}$ and $\mathcal{B}$ with sets of registers r_A and r_B, respectively, we can easily construct GRAs $\mathcal{A} \cup \mathcal{B}$ and $\mathcal{A} \cap \mathcal{B}$ for the languages $\mathcal{L}(\mathcal{A}) \cup \mathcal{L}(\mathcal{B})$ and $\mathcal{L}(\mathcal{A}) \cap \mathcal{L}(\mathcal{B})$, respectively, as follows. For both constructions, the set r of registers is a concatenation of r_A and r_B, and the state machine is the union of the state machines of $\mathcal{A}$ and $\mathcal{B}$, with the addition of a single new initial state q_0. The transition for q_0 in $\mathcal{A} \cup \mathcal{B}$ and in $\mathcal{A} \cap \mathcal{B}$ is defined $\delta(q_0) = \delta_A(q_0^A) \vee \delta_B(q_0^B)$ and $\delta(q_0) = \delta_A(q_0^A) \wedge \delta_B(q_0^B)$, respectively, where

---

[3] We could define Büchi acceptance conditions for infinite words as well in the standard way, in which a run tree is accepting if all of its paths that infinitely often advance on the input word, infinitely often traverse some accepting state. As we have mentioned, in this paper we concentrate on finite words.

$q_0^{\mathcal{A}}$ and $\delta_{\mathcal{A}}$ are the initial state and transition function of $\mathcal{A}$, and similarly for $q_0^{\mathcal{B}}$ and $\delta_{\mathcal{B}}$. That is, the construction for the union and intersection is the standard construction for alternating automata, and the set of registers is obtained by simply concatenating the sets of registers for both automata.

We can reduce PCP (Post's correspondence problem) to both the universality problem and the nonemptiness problem for GRA, and so they are both undecidable. However, given a word w and a GRA $\mathcal{A}$, it is decidable whether $\mathcal{A}$ accepts w. To see why, notice that the precise identity of the data values that do not appear in w and are assigned to the registers during a run does not matter. What matters are only the equality relations between them. Then, we can show that a run tree of $\mathcal{A}$ on w can be simulated by using a bounded number of values (that depends on the the the number of different values in w and the number of registers in $\mathcal{A}$), without using $\epsilon_\forall$-transitions. Further, we can also bound the number of consecutive ϵ-transitions in every path, and so it suffices to check trees of bounded width and bounded length to decide whether $w \in \mathcal{L}(\mathcal{A})$.

Finally, we can show that for the single-register fragment of GRA, the nonemptiness problem is decidable. The next theorem sums up the closure and decidability properties of GRA.

Theorem 1. *1. GRAs are closed under union and intersection.*
2. The membership problem for GRAs is decidable.
3. The nonemptiness and universality problems for GRAs are undecidable.
4. The nonemptiness problem for GRAs with a single register is decidable.

We now proceed to compare data automata to GRA. A deterministic data automaton $\mathcal{C}$ can be translated to an equivalent GRA with two registers r_1, r_2 as follows. Using an $\epsilon_\forall$-transition on r_1, the GRA splits into infinitely many copies. Each copy checks a different class of the input word, where the class is determined by its content of r_1, and simulates a simultaneous run on both the transducer and the automaton components of $\mathcal{C}$; upon reading a letter, if the data is not the class it needs to check, then the copy only advances on the transducer (using r_2 to guess and advance on this data). If the data is the content of r_1, then the copy advances along both the transducer and the automaton. The copy accepts if both the transducer and the automaton reach an accepting state.

In [2], the authors point to a language that cannot be accepted by a data automaton. This language can be accepted by a GRA with three counters. Roughly speaking, a GRA can accept languages of words of the form $w\#w$, and data automata cannot. Therefore, data automata are not stronger than GRA. We leave the precise comparison with data automata open.

Theorem 2. *1. Every deterministic data automaton has an equivalent GRA.*
2. Data automata are not more expressive than GRA.

4   From VLTL and Abstract Systems to GRA

In this section, we show how to translate VLTL formulas and abstract systems to GRAs. Then, we use these constructions to find fragments of VLTL for which the satisfiability and model checking problems are decidable.

Since GRAs are capable of expressing a single value in every letter, we cannot directly express computations in which more than one value appears at a time, and we first concentrate on a restricted type of computations that include a single value in every state. Then, we show how to encode unrestricted computations with restricted ones.

A computation π over $2^{AP \cup (T \times D)}$ is called *restricted* if π_i contains at most one data value for every i.

Let S be an abstract system with k variables and the full inequality set, in which every state contains at most one variable. It is easy to see that this is a sufficient and necessary condition for S to have only restricted computations. An equivalent GRA $\mathcal{A}_S$ is obtained from the structure of S by using k registers, where register r_i holds the data value assigned to the variable x_i. Resets are translated to $\epsilon_\exists$ transitions, and the inequality set is reflected in the guard conditions. All states of $\mathcal{A}_S$ are accepting. Clearly, $\mathcal{L}(\mathcal{A})$ is exactly the set of all concrete computations of S.

Given a VLTL formula $\langle \varphi = Q_1 x_1; Q_2 x_2; \ldots Q_k x_k; \psi, E \rangle$, where $Q_i \in \{\exists, \forall\}$ for every i, where E is an inequality set over the set of variables and where ψ is an LTL formula over $AP \cup (T \times X)$, we construct a GRA $\mathcal{A}_\varphi$ with $k + 1$ registers over $2^{(AP \cup T)} \times D$, whose language is exactly the set of restricted computations that satisfy φ. A letter $\langle s, d \rangle$ represents a set of atomic propositions $s \in 2^{AP \cup T}$, such that the parameterized atomic propositions in s all carry the same value d.

For simplicity, we assume that E states that the value of all variables must be different. A general E can then be handled by the guards in the transitions, requiring that if a set of variables appears in a transition, then they all must carry the same value.

Intuitively, the construction of $\mathcal{A}_\varphi$ relies on the Vardi-Wolper construction for ψ. The variables are handled by a set of $k + 1$ registers, and the quantifiers are translated to an $\epsilon_\exists$-transition for an $\exists$ quantifier, and to an $\epsilon_\forall$-transition for a $\forall$ quantifier.

Thus, the run begins by following a sequence of states and transitions matching the sequence of quantifiers in φ; for every $1 \leq i \leq k$, an occurence of $\exists x_i$ is translated to an $\langle \epsilon_\exists, i \rangle$-transition, and an occurence of $\forall x_i$ is translated to an $\langle \epsilon_\forall, i \rangle$-transition. The inequality set is reflected in the transitions within this sequence, that makes sure that the values stored in registers r_1 through r_k satisfy E. Since we assume that E is the full inequality set, this means that in every copy, every register contains a different value from the other registers. Once the values are stored, in every copy of the run, the registers r_1 through r_k are fixed, while register r_{k+1} handles values in the computation that do not appear in any of the registers.

The NRA component of $\mathcal{A}_\varphi$ then behaves as the automaton for ψ with the following changes.

- Every state may change the value of r_{k+1} to some value different from the values in the rest of the registers, by following self loops labeled $\langle \epsilon_\exists, k + 1 \rangle$.
- Recall that we allow only a single value to appear in every step. However, in the Vardi-Wolper construction the labeling is over $2^{AP \cup (T \times X)}$. We therefore restrict the labels to those that contain a single variable of X.
  Now, consider a transition labeled by a set that contains no variables at all (that is, its set of atomic propositions is $A \subseteq AP$). This means that $a.x$ is set to false for every $a \in T$ and $x \in X$. This can hold if either a does not hold in this step for any value, or if a holds with a value that is different from the values that are assigned

to the variables in X. The register r_{k+1} may hold this value. Therefore, for every $B \subseteq T$, we add to this transition the label $\langle A \cup B, k+1 \rangle$.

The following theorem summarizes this discussion.

Theorem 3.   *1. For every abstract system S with restricted computations there exists a GRA $\mathcal{A}_S$ such that $\mathcal{L}(\mathcal{A}_S)$ is the set of computations of S.*
   2. For every VLTL formula φ there exists a GRA $\mathcal{A}_\varphi$ such that $\mathcal{L}(\mathcal{A}_\varphi)$ is the set of restricted computations that satisfy φ.

We handle unrestricted computations by encoding the content of a single state by a sequence of letters, each carrying a single value. The alphabet is $2^{AP} \cup (T \times D)^4$. Intuitively, a letter of type $\langle t, d \rangle$ represents $t.d$ appearing in the state, and a letter in 2^{AP} represents the set of unparameterized atomic propositions in the state. A sequence that matches a state first lists the unparameterized atomic propositions, and then lists the parameterized atomic propositions, one by one. Thus, when translating an abstract system or a VLTL formula over $X = \{x_1, x_2, \ldots x_k\}$ to a GRA, each label is translated to a sequence of labels in $2^{AP} \cup (T \times [k])$ (or $2^{AP} \cup (T \times [k+1])$ for a VLTL formula).

For model checking purposes, we make sure that: (a) both the system GRA and the VLTL GRA have a uniform representation of each label, which is done listing the content of each state according to some predefined order $<$ on T, and (b) the VLTL GRA is reverse-deterministic (a property that is essential for the decidability of the construction in Theorem 6 below). This is achieved by changing the alphabet of the VLTL GRA to $2^{AP \cup (T \times X)} \times 2^{AP} \cup T \times [k+1]$, where a letter in $2^{AP \cup (T \times X)}$, representing the original label, follows every sequence. When applying the construction in the proof of Theorem 6, we may ignore the letters in $2^{AP \cup (T \times X)}$ for the purposes of the intersection with the abstract system, but consider them for the transition relation.

Example 3. Let $s = \{a.x_1, b.x_1, c.x_2, d\}$ be a state in an abstract system, or a labeling of a transition in the Vardi-Wolper construction for some LTL formula over a set of atomic propositions. Then for the order $a < b < c$, for the case of the abstract system the translation of s to a GRA leads to the sequence of transitions $\{d\}\langle a, 1\rangle\langle b, 1\rangle\langle c, 2\rangle$. In the case of a VLTL formula, this sequence is followed by the letter $\{a.x_1, b.x_1, c.x_2\}$.

We now turn to use the translation of VLTL and abstract systems to GRAs in order identify a new fragment of VLTL for which model checking is decidable. For this, we turn to study a type of GRAs that is relevant for the translation. We define this type of GRA, and show that for GRAs that are a translation of VLTL formulas, nonemptiness is decidable. Further, we prove that this type is also decidable when considering an unary alphabet.

Consider a GRA $\mathcal{A} = \langle \Sigma \times D, \#, \langle r_1, r_2, r_3, \ldots r_k \rangle, \langle \#, \#, \ldots \# \rangle, Q, q_0, \delta, F \rangle$ with the following attributes:

– The guard condition is always the full inequality set.

---

[4] We present the alphabet this way to emphasize that the value attached to the letter in 2^{AP} does not matter.

- From q_0 exits a sequence of states S that assign values to $r_3, r_4, \ldots r_k$ with $\epsilon_\exists$ transitions, followed by a state s_k from which there is an $\epsilon_\forall$ transition that splits over all allowed values in r_1.
- From s_k, the GRA $\mathcal{A}$ behaves as an NRA without returning to the states of S, s_k or q_0.
- The content of the registers r_1 and $r_3 \ldots r_k$ does not change after the initial assignment,
- Every state of the NRA component has a self loop labeled $\langle \epsilon_\exists, 2 \rangle$. So in each step of a run, r_2 may change its content.

We denote GRAs of this type *single-split GRAs*. Recall that both the translation of a deterministic data automaton to a GRA and the GRA of Example 2 yield a single-split GRA with two registers, that is, the $\epsilon_\forall$ transition is taken from the intial state, and from there on the different copies continue their runs as runs of NRA. Moreover, notice that for VLTL formulas of the type $\exists x_1; \exists x_2; \ldots \exists x_k; \forall x; \varphi$ with a full inequality set, their translation to GRA also yields a single-split GRA with $k + 2$ registers.

Theorem 4. *The nonemptiness problem for single-split GRAs is undecidable.*

Nevertheless, there are sub-types of single-split GRAs for which nonemptiness is decidable. The first type are two-register single-split GRAs over an unary alphabet, that is, when $|\Sigma| = 1$.

A second type are *reverse-deterministic single-split GRAs*. An automaton is reverse-deterministic if by reversing its transitions we get a determinisic automaton. A single-split GRA is reverse-deterministic if its NRA component is reverse-deterministic with respect to the labeling of its edges (neglecting $\langle \epsilon_\exists, 2 \rangle$-transitions, that are in self-loops).

A third type of GRAs whose nonemptiness is decidable are GRAs for the intersection of a reverse-deterministic single-split GRA with an NRA.

For both reverse-deterministic single-split GRAs and for their intersection with NRAs, their decidable nonemptiness is essential for our purpose of studying decision problems for VLTL and abstract systems.

Theorem 5. *The nonemptiness problems for single-split GRAs over an unary alphabet, for reverse-deterministic single-split GRAs, and for the interesection of an NRA and a reverse-deterministic single-split GRA are decidable.*

Proof: *(sketch)* For all these types of GRA, we reduce their nonemptiness problem to the nonemptiness problem for multi-counter machines, for which nonemptiness is known to be decidable. Multi-counter machines comprise a state machine and a set of counters. Upon reading a letter, the machine advances on the state machine and increments or decrements some counter. The machine cannot perform zero-checks on the counter, and the run is stuck when it attempts to decrement a counter whose value is zero.

Given a GRA $\mathcal{A}$ of one of these types, the state machine of the multi-counter machine M simulates simultaneous runs on all copies of $\mathcal{A}$ after the $\epsilon_\forall$ split. Every state keeps the set of states of $\mathcal{A}$ in which the various copies are located, and each such state q is paired with a counter that keeps the number of copies that are currently in q. The runs that do not handle a value that is included in the input word all behave similarly, and therefore it suffices to keep a single copy for all of them. Therefore, it suffices to track a finite number of copies. The counters are updated according to the transition relation of $\mathcal{A}$. The run accepts iff all nonempty counters are paired with accepting states.

The challenge in these constructions is to correctly update the counters. In general, since multi-counter machines do not allow zero checks on the counters, it is impossible to unite the content of two counters if the value they hold is unknown. Therefore, if in some transition of the GRA, two different states q and q' may move to the same state state s, updating the counters is impossible. However, we can show that for these three types of GRA, updating the counters is possible.

A single-split GRA over an unary alphabet can be reconstructed in such a way that in every step, the content of two counters is united only if the value of one of them is 1. In case of a reverse-deterministic GRA, no two counters have to be unified during the run.

For the intersection of a reverse-deterministic single-split GRA with an NRA, the challenge in the construction is to ensure that the progress of the single-split GRA agrees with the register assignment in the NRA. To achieve this, some of the states in the single-split GRA are paired with registers of the NRA. When a state q is paired with r_i, this means that one of the copies that is currently in q in the single-split GRA handles the value that is assigned to register r_i in the NRA. When the NRA reassigns a register r_i, a new state may be paired with r_i. Thus, the run progresses legally along both automata.   □

Consider a VLTL formula $\psi = \langle \alpha, E \rangle$ where $\alpha = \exists x_1; \exists x_2; \ldots \exists x_k; \forall x; \varphi$, and E is the full inequality set. Recall from Theorem 3 that ψ can be translated to a single-split GRA $\mathcal{A}_\psi$. Since the Vardi-Wolper construction for φ yields a reverse-deterministic automaton, we have that $\mathcal{A}_\psi$ is a reverse-deterministic single-split GRA. We can check the satisfiability of ψ for finite computations by checking the nonemptiness of $\mathcal{A}_\psi$. According to Theorem 5, this is decidable.

Similarly, recall from Theorem 3 that an abstract system with restricted computations can be translated to an NRA. Given a system and a VLTL formula, we can then decide the model checking problem by checking the nonemptiness of the intersection of the two matching GRAs – for the system, and for the negation of the formula. Consider a VLTL formula $\psi' = \langle \beta, E \rangle$ where $\beta = \forall x_1; \forall x_2; \ldots \forall x_k; \exists x; \varphi$ and E is the full inequality set. Then the negation of β is $\exists x_1; \exists x_2; \ldots \exists x_k; \forall x; \neg\varphi$, again yielding a reverse-deterministic single-split GRA $\mathcal{A}_{\neg\psi'}$ for $\neg\psi'$. According to Theorem 5, it is decidable whether the intersection of $\mathcal{A}_{\neg\psi'}$ with an NRA representing the system is nonempty, proving the decidability of the model-checking problem for this type of VLTL formulas. Therefore, we have the following.

Theorem 6. *Let* $\psi = \langle \alpha, E \rangle$, *where* $\alpha = \exists x_1; \exists x_2; \ldots \exists x_k; \forall x; \varphi$, *for a safety formula* φ, *and where* E *is the full inequality set.*

1. *It is decidable whether* ψ *is satisfiable.*
2. *Let* S *be an abstract system with restricted computations. It is decidable whether* S *satisfies* $\neg\psi$.

5   Discussion

GRAs offer an automata-theoretic approach to VLTL. By reasoning about GRAs, we can work towards closing the gap between the decidable and undecidable fragments and provide a full classification of the model-checking problem for VLTL. Indeed, the proof of undecidability of model checking of VLTL formulas with two $\exists$ quantifiers [7] can be altered to show the undecidability of satisfiability of VLTL formulas with two $\forall$ quantifiers, of satisfiability of VLTL formulas with a $\forall$ followed by an $\exists$ quantifier, and of model checking of VLTL formulas with an $\exists$ followed by a $\forall$ quantifier. Thus, the fragments considered in Theorem 6 complete the picture for the case of safety VLTL formulas. Here, we proved them to be decidable for the safe fragment of LTL. We are optimistic about an extension of our results here to the setting of infinite words and computations, which would lead to further decidable fragments. Finally, GRAs could also provide a framework for studying other formalisms that deal with infinite alphabets, such as XML and its related languages.

References

1. Bojanczyk, M., Lasota, S.: An extension of data automata that captures xpath. Logical Methods in Computer Science 8(1) (2012)
2. Bojanczyk, M., Muscholl, A., Schwentick, T., Segoufin, L., David, C.: Two-variable logic on words with data. In: LICS, pp. 7–16. IEEE Computer Society (2006)
3. Clarke, E.M., Grumberg, O., Peled, D.: Model Checking. MIT Press (1999)
4. Demri, S., Lazic, R.: LTL with the freeze quantifier and register automata. ACM Trans. Comput. Log. 10(3) (2009)
5. Figueira, D.: Alternating register automata on finite words and trees. LMCS 8(1) (2012)
6. Grumberg, O., Kupferman, O., Sheinvald, S.: Variable automata over infinite alphabets. In: Dediu, A.-H., Fernau, H., Martín-Vide, C. (eds.) LATA 2010. LNCS, vol. 6031, pp. 561–572. Springer, Heidelberg (2010)
7. Grumberg, O., Kupferman, O., Sheinvald, S.: Model checking systems and specifications with parameterized atomic propositions. In: Chakraborty, S., Mukund, M. (eds.) ATVA 2012. LNCS, vol. 7561, pp. 122–136. Springer, Heidelberg (2012)
8. Kaminski, M., Francez, N.: Finite-memory automata. TCS 134(2), 329–363 (1994)
9. Kaminski, M., Zeitlin, D.: Finite-memory automata with non-deterministic reassignment. Int. J. Found. Comput. Sci. 21(5), 741–760 (2010)
10. Kara, A., Schwentick, T., Tan, T.: Feasible automata for two-variable logic with successor on data words. In: Dediu, A.-H., Martín-Vide, C. (eds.) LATA 2012. LNCS, vol. 7183, pp. 351–362. Springer, Heidelberg (2012)
11. Manuel, A., Ramanujam, R.: Class counting automata on datawords. Int. J. Found. Comput. Sci. 22(4), 863–882 (2011)
12. Neven, F., Schwentick, T., Vianu, V.: Towards regular languages over infinite alphabets. In: Sgall, J., Pultr, A., Kolman, P. (eds.) MFCS 2001. LNCS, vol. 2136, pp. 560–572. Springer, Heidelberg (2001)
13. Segoufin, L.: Automata and logics for words and trees over an infinite alphabet. In: Ésik, Z. (ed.) CSL 2006. LNCS, vol. 4207, pp. 41–57. Springer, Heidelberg (2006)
14. Tan, T.: Pebble Automata for Data Languages: Separation, Decidability, and Undecidability. PhD thesis, Technion - Computer Science Department (2009)
15. Vardi, M.Y., Wolper, P.: Reasoning about infinite computations. Information and Computation 115(1), 1–37 (1994)
16. Wu, Z.: A decidable extension of data automata. In: GandALF, pp. 116–130 (2011)
17. Wu, Z.: Commutative data automata. In: CSL, pp. 528–542 (2012)

Pushdown Systems with Stack Manipulation

Yuya Uezato and Yasuhiko Minamide

University of Tsukuba
uezato@score.cs.tsukuba.ac.jp,
minamide@cs.tsukuba.ac.jp

Abstract. Pushdown systems are a model of computation equipped with one stack where only the top of the stack is inspected and modified in each step of transitions. Although this is a natural restriction, some extensions of pushdown systems require more general operations on stack: conditional pushdown systems inspect the whole stack contents and discrete timed pushdown systems increment the ages of the whole stack contents.

In this paper, we present a general framework called pushdown systems with transductions (TrPDS) for extending pushdown systems with transitions that modify the whole stack contents with a transducer. Although TrPDS is Turing complete, it is shown that if the closure of transductions appearing in the transitions of a TrPDS is finite, it can be simulated by an ordinary pushdown system and thus the reachability problem is decidable. Both of conditional and discrete timed pushdown systems can be considered as such subclasses of TrPDS.

1 Introduction

The theory of pushdown systems (PDS) has been successfully applied to the verification of recursive programs such as Java programs [4]. The essential result is that the reachability problem of a PDS can be decided efficiently by representing the rational (regular) set of configurations with automata [5,10,8]. Several extensions of PDS have been studied to widen the applications of PDS, and their reachability problems can often be decided by translating them to ordinary pushdown systems.

Esparza et al. introduced pushdown systems with checkpoints that can check the whole stack contents against a rational language [9] to model runtime stack inspection used for security checks. They showed that pushdown systems with checkpoints can be translated into ordinary pushdown systems, and thus the reachability problem is decidable. We call this extension *conditional pushdown systems* in this paper [12].

Abdulla et al. introduced *discrete timed pushdown systems* [2] that combine timed automata [3] and pushdown systems. Stack symbols of a timed pushdown system are extended with the notion of ages, and timed pushdown systems have a transition that increments the ages of all the symbols in the stack. Even with this extension, timed pushdown systems can also be translated into pushdown systems to decide the reachability problem.

D. Van Hung and M. Ogawa (Eds.): ATVA 2013, LNCS 8172, pp. 412–426, 2013.

In this paper, we generalize these extensions and present a general framework called *pushdown systems with transductions* (TrPDS) for extending pushdown systems with transitions that modify the whole stack contents with a finite-state transducer. Transductions are the relations induced by transducers. Since TrPDS is Turing complete in general, we are interested in a *finite* TrPDS where we impose the restriction that the closure of transductions appearing in the transitions of a TrPDS is finite. Both of conditional and timed pushdown systems can be formulated as simple instances of finite TrPDS. We then show that a *finite* TrPDS can be translated into an ordinary PDS by generalizing the construction of Abdulla et al. for timed pushdown systems [2] and the reachability problem of a finite TrPDS is decidable. As a nontrivial example of finite TrPDS, we introduce conditional transformable pushdown systems that can check the whole stack contents against a rational language and modify the whole stack contents by a function from stack symbols to stack symbols.

We also show that the saturation procedure that calculates $\text{pre}^*(C)$ for the rational set of configurations C can be directly extended to finite TrPDS. This is a generalization of the saturation procedure for conditional pushdown systems [14]. A rational set of configurations of finite TrPDS is represented with automata that modify the rest of input by a transduction.

2 Preliminaries

2.1 Transducers

A *transducer* is a structure $(Q, \Gamma, \Delta, I, F)$ where Q is a finite set of states, Γ is a finite set of symbols, $\Delta \subseteq Q \times \Gamma^* \times \Gamma^* \times Q$ is a finite set of transition rules, $I \subseteq Q$ is the set of initial states, and $F \subseteq Q$ is the set of final states.

A computation of a transducer is a sequence of transitions of the following form:

$$p_0 \xrightarrow{w_1/w_1'} p_1 \xrightarrow{w_2/w_2'} \cdots \xrightarrow{w_n/w_n'} p_n$$

where $\langle p_{i-1}, w_i, w_i', p_i \rangle \in \Delta$. When we have the computation above, we write $p_0 \xrightarrow{w_1 \cdots w_n / w_1' \cdots w_n'} p_n$. The language $L(\mathsf{t}) \subseteq \Gamma^* \times \Gamma^*$ of a transducer t is defined as follows:

$$L(\mathsf{t}) = \{\langle w_1, w_2 \rangle \mid q_I \xrightarrow{w_1/w_2} q_f \text{ for some } q_I \in I \text{ and } q_F \in F\}$$

A *letter-to-letter transducer* is a transducer where Δ is restricted to $\Delta \subseteq Q \times \Gamma \times \Gamma \times Q$, i.e., a letter-to-letter transducer is an automaton over $\Gamma \times \Gamma$.

2.2 Transductions

A *transduction* τ over Γ^* is a relation between Γ^* and Γ^*, or a function from Γ^* to $\mathcal{P}(\Gamma^*)$. A transduction τ is a *rational* transduction if there is a transducer t such that $\tau = L(\mathsf{t})$. A transduction τ is a *length-preserving* rational transduction if there is a *letter-to-letter transducer* t such that $\tau = L(\mathsf{t})$.

We write $\mathbf{Transd}_\Gamma$ for the set of all length-preserving rational transductions and use a metavariable t to denote both a transducer and a transduction if there is no danger of confusion. In the rest of this paper, we use the term *transduction* for a length-preserving rational transduction.

The composition of transductions $t_1, t_2 \in \mathbf{Transd}_\Gamma$ is defined as that for relations:

$$t_1 \circ t_2 = \{\langle w, w'' \rangle \mid \langle w, w' \rangle \in t_1, \langle w', w'' \rangle \in t_2\}$$

$\mathbf{Transd}_\Gamma$ is closed under composition and $(\mathbf{Transd}_\Gamma, \circ, \cup, \mathbb{1}, \mathbb{0})$ is a semiring where $\mathbb{1} = \{\langle w, w \rangle \mid w \in \Gamma^*\}$ and $\mathbb{0} = \varnothing$.

By considering $t \in \mathbf{Transd}_\Gamma$ as a rational language over $\Gamma \times \Gamma$, we introduce (left) quotient and nullability $\nu(t)$ defined as follows:

$$
\begin{aligned}
\langle \cdot, \cdot \rangle^{-1} \qquad &: \forall w_1 \in \Gamma^*, w_2 \in \Gamma^{|w_1|}.\mathbf{Transd}_\Gamma \to \mathbf{Transd}_\Gamma \\
\langle \varepsilon, \varepsilon \rangle^{-1} t \;\; &= t \\
\langle \gamma, \gamma' \rangle^{-1} t \;\; &= \{\langle w, w' \rangle \mid \langle \gamma w, \gamma' w' \rangle \in t\} \\
\langle \gamma w, \gamma' w' \rangle^{-1} t &= \langle w, w' \rangle^{-1} (\langle \gamma, \gamma' \rangle^{-1} t)
\end{aligned}
$$

$$
\nu(t) = \begin{cases} \{\varepsilon\} & \langle \varepsilon, \varepsilon \rangle \in t \\ \varnothing & \text{otherwise} \end{cases}
$$

where $\varepsilon \in \Gamma^*$ is the empty string. $\mathbf{Transd}_\Gamma$ is closed under quotient and quotient distributes over composition in the following sense.

Proposition 1. $\langle w_1, w_2 \rangle^{-1}(t_1 \circ t_2) = \displaystyle\bigcup_{w_3 \in \Gamma^{|w_1|}} \left(\langle w_1, w_3 \rangle^{-1} t_1 \circ \langle w_3, w_2 \rangle^{-1} t_2 \right)$

A transduction $t \in \mathbf{Transd}_\Gamma$ can be considered as a function from Γ^* to $\mathcal{P}(\Gamma^*)$. We call this function application *action*, use the postfix notation, and write wt: $wt = \{w' \mid w' \in \Gamma^*, \langle w, w' \rangle \in t\}$.

The action is defined for a language L by $Lt = \displaystyle\bigcup_{w \in L} wt$.

We can also inductively define action by using quotient:

$$\varepsilon t = \nu(t) \qquad (\gamma w)t = \bigcup_{\gamma' \in \Gamma} \left(\gamma' \lhd \left(w \, \langle \gamma, \gamma' \rangle^{-1} t \right) \right)$$

where $w \lhd W = \{ww' \mid w' \in W\}$.

2.3 Pushdown Systems

A pushdown system (PDS) is a structure $\mathcal{P} = (Q, \Gamma, \Delta)$ where Q is a finite set of control locations, Γ is a finite set of stack symbols, and $\Delta \subseteq Q \times (\Gamma^+ \times \Gamma^*) \times Q$ is a finite set of transition rules. For a transition rule $\langle p, \langle w_1, w_2 \rangle, q \rangle \in \Delta$, we write $p \xrightarrow{w_1/w_2} q$. A configuration of PDS $\mathcal{P}$ is a pair $\langle q, w \rangle$ of location $q \in Q$ and string $w \in \Gamma^*$. We write $Conf(\mathcal{P})$ for the set of all configurations $Q \times \Gamma^*$.

We define transition relation $\Rightarrow \subseteq Conf(\mathcal{P}) \times Conf(\mathcal{P})$: $\langle p, w_1 w \rangle \Rightarrow \langle q, w_2 w \rangle$ if $p \xrightarrow{w_1/w_2} q$ and $w \in \Gamma^*$.

We say a PDS $\mathcal{P} = (Q, \Gamma, \Delta)$ is a *standard PDS* if $|w| = 1$ for all $p \xrightarrow{w/w'} q \in \Delta$. It is clear that for a given PDS $\mathcal{P}$ we can construct a standard PDS equivalent to $\mathcal{P}$ by introducing extra states. We use a nonstandard PDS to simplify the construction of PDS for simulating TrPDS.

3   TrPDS : Pushdown Systems with Transductions

TrPDS is an extension of PDS that may modify the whole stack contents by applying a transduction.

A TrPDS is a structure (Q, Γ, T, Δ) where Q is a finite set of control locations, Γ is a finite set of stack symbols, $\Delta \subseteq Q \times (\Gamma \times \Gamma^* \times T) \times Q$ is a finite set of transition rules, and $T \subseteq \mathbf{Transd}_\Gamma$ is a finite set of transductions. For a transition rule $\langle p, \langle \gamma, w, \mathsf{t} \rangle, q \rangle \in \Delta$, we write $p \xrightarrow{\gamma/w|\mathsf{t}} q$ and call the triple "$\gamma/w|\mathsf{t}$" *stack effect*.

A configuration of TrPDS $\mathcal{P}$ is a pair $\langle q, w \rangle$ of location $q \in Q$ and string $w \in \Gamma^*$. We write $Conf(\mathcal{P})$ for the set of all configurations $Q \times \Gamma^*$.

Definition 1 (Labelled transition relation). *We define a labelled transition relation* $\xrightarrow{\delta} \subseteq Conf(\mathcal{P}) \times Conf(\mathcal{P})$: $\langle p, \gamma w' \rangle \xrightarrow{\delta} \langle q, w w'' \rangle$ *if* δ *is* $p \xrightarrow{\gamma/w|\mathsf{t}} q$ *and* $w'' \in w'\mathsf{t}$. *We also write* $c_1 \Rightarrow c_2$ *if* $c_1 \xrightarrow{\delta} c_2$ *for some* $\delta \in \Delta$.

Let us consider an example of a TrPDS and its transitions.

Example 1. Let t be $\langle b, b \rangle^* (\langle a, a \rangle \cup \langle a, b \rangle)^*$. TrPDS $\mathcal{P} = (Q, \Sigma, \{\mathsf{t}, \mathbb{1}\}, \{\delta_1, \delta_2\})$ where $Q = \{q_0, q_1, q_2\}$, $\Sigma = \{a, b\}$, $\delta_1 = q_0 \xrightarrow{a/\varepsilon|\mathsf{t}} q_1$ and $\delta_2 = q_1 \xrightarrow{b/\varepsilon|\mathbb{1}} q_2$. The following are some examples of transitions.

$$\langle q_0, aaa \rangle \xrightarrow{\delta_1} \langle q_1, ba \rangle \xrightarrow{\delta_2} \langle q_2, a \rangle$$
$$\langle q_0, aaa \rangle \xrightarrow{\delta_1} \langle q_1, bb \rangle \xrightarrow{\delta_2} \langle q_2, b \rangle$$

The effect of transition rule $\delta = p \xrightarrow{\sigma} q$ with stack effect σ is captured by the following function $effect_\sigma$ below: $\langle p, w \rangle \xrightarrow{\delta} \langle q, w' \rangle$ iff $w' \in effect_\sigma(w)$.

$$
\begin{aligned}
effect_{\gamma/w|\mathsf{t}} &\quad : \Gamma^* \to \mathcal{P}(\Gamma^*) \\
effect_{\gamma/w|\mathsf{t}}(\varepsilon) &= \varnothing \\
effect_{\gamma/w|\mathsf{t}}(\gamma'w') &= \begin{cases} w \lhd w'\mathsf{t} & \text{if } \gamma' = \gamma \\ \varnothing & \text{otherwise} \end{cases}
\end{aligned}
$$

Definition 2. *The closure* $\langle T \rangle$ *of a transduction set* T *under composition and quotient is inductively defined as follows.*

- $T \subseteq \langle T \rangle$ *and* $\mathbb{0}, \mathbb{1} \in \langle T \rangle$.
- *If* $\mathsf{t}_1, \mathsf{t}_2 \in \langle T \rangle$, *then* $\mathsf{t}_1 \circ \mathsf{t}_2 \in \langle T \rangle$.
- *If* $\mathsf{t} \in \langle T \rangle$, *then* $\langle \gamma, \gamma' \rangle^{-1} \mathsf{t} \in \langle T \rangle$ *for all* $\gamma, \gamma' \in \Gamma$.

Definition 3. *A TrPDS $\mathcal{P}$ over T is called* finite *if $\langle T \rangle$ is finite.*

Example: Conditional Pushdown Systems. A conditional pushdown system is a pushdown system extended with stack inspection [9,12]. A transition rule has the form $\langle p, \langle \gamma, w, L \rangle, q \rangle \in \Delta$ where L is a rational language over stack symbols[1]: it induces the transition relation $\langle p, \gamma w' \rangle \Rightarrow \langle q, ww' \rangle$ if $w' \in L$. The transition can be taken only when $w' \in L$.

Let $\mathcal{L}$ be the finite set of rational languages appearing in transition rules. Here, we define $\langle \mathcal{L} \rangle$ inductively as follows:

- $\mathcal{L} \subseteq \langle \mathcal{L} \rangle$ and $\varnothing, \Gamma^* \in \langle \mathcal{L} \rangle$.
- If $L_1, L_2 \in \langle \mathcal{L} \rangle$, then $L_1 \cap L_2 \in \langle \mathcal{L} \rangle$.
- If $L \in \langle \mathcal{L} \rangle$, then $\gamma^{-1}L \in \langle \mathcal{L} \rangle$ for all $\gamma \in \Gamma$.

The set $\langle \mathcal{L} \rangle$ is finite since quotient distributes over intersection and there are finitely many languages obtained from each rational language with quotient.

For a language L, we define $\widetilde{L} = \{ \langle w, w \rangle \mid w \in L \}$ and then $\widetilde{L}$ is a length-preserving rational transduction for a rational language L. For the composition and the quotient on $\widetilde{L}$, we have the following.

$$\widetilde{L} \circ \widetilde{L'} = \widetilde{L \cap L'} \quad \langle \gamma, \gamma' \rangle^{-1}\widetilde{L} = \begin{cases} \widetilde{\gamma^{-1}L} & \text{if } \gamma = \gamma' \\ 0 & \text{otherwise} \end{cases}$$

Then, a conditional pushdown system over $\mathcal{L}$ can be considered as a *finite* TrPDS over the transduction set $T = \{ \widetilde{L} \mid L \in \mathcal{L} \}$. It is clear that $\langle T \rangle$ is finite since we have $\langle T \rangle = \{ \widetilde{L} \mid L \in \langle \mathcal{L} \rangle \}$ from the properties above.

Example: Transformable Pushdown Systems. A transformable pushdown system is a pushdown system that may modify stack by applying a function over stack symbols. This generalizes the operation of discrete timed pushdown systems [2] that increment the ages of stack symbols. A transition rule has the form $\langle p, \langle \gamma, w, f \rangle, q \rangle \in \Delta$ where f is a function from Γ to Γ: it induces the transition relation $\langle p, \gamma w' \rangle \Rightarrow \langle q, wf(w') \rangle$.

For a given $f \in \Gamma \to \Gamma$, we define a transduction $\widehat{f} = \{ \langle w, f(w) \rangle \mid w \in \Gamma^* \}$. It is clear that $\widehat{f}$ is a length-preserving rational transduction and the following hold.

$$\widehat{f_1} \circ \widehat{f_2} = \widehat{f_2 \circ f_1} \quad \langle \gamma, \gamma' \rangle^{-1}\widehat{f} = \begin{cases} \widehat{f} & \text{if } \gamma' = f(\gamma) \\ 0 & \text{otherwise} \end{cases}$$

Note that $\circ$ in $f_2 \circ f_1$ is the composition of functions, *i.e.*, $f_2 \circ f_1 = \lambda v.f_2(f_1(v))$.

A transformable pushdown system over $\mathcal{F} = \{ f_1, f_2, \ldots, f_n \}$ can be considered as a *finite* TrPDS over $T = \{ \widehat{f_1}, \widehat{f_2}, \ldots, \widehat{f_n} \}$. It is clear that $\langle T \rangle$ is finite because $\langle T \rangle \subseteq \{ \widehat{f} \mid f \in \Gamma \to \Gamma \} \cup \{ 0 \}$.

---

[1] We use the definitions of transition rule and transition relation inspecting whole stack without its top [12] rather than inspecting whole stack [9].

Example: Two-counter Machines. Any two-counter machine without input can be simulated by a TrPDS $\mathcal{P} = (Q, \{0, 1, \lambda\}, \{\eth_0, t_0, \eth_1, t_1\}, \Delta)$. The transduction $\eth_0$ decrements the number of 0's in the stack by replacing the first 0 with λ and the transduction t_0 checks whether stack contains 0 or not. $\eth_1$ and t_1 have the same behaviors for 1's.

Since $\eth_0 \neq \eth_0^2 \neq \cdots \neq \eth_0^n \neq \cdots$, $\mathcal{P}$ is not a finite TrPDS. The reachability problem of two-counter machines is undecidable and thus the reachability problem of TrPDS is undecidable in general. However, we will show that the reachability problem of a *finite* TrPDS is decidable.

4 Construction of PDS from TrPDS

From a given finite TrPDS, we construct a finite PDS by lazily applying a transduction to stack. It is a generalization of the construction introduced by Abdulla et al. [2] for simulating discrete timed pushdown systems. By the construction, we prove that the reachability problem of a finite TrPDS is decidable.

4.1 Construction

For a given TrPDS $\mathcal{P} = (Q, \Gamma, T, \Delta)$, we construct a PDS $\mathcal{P}' = (Q, \Gamma \cup \langle T \rangle, \Delta')$.

Let δ be a transition rule $p \xrightarrow{\gamma/w|t} q \in \Delta$. We have transition $\langle p, \gamma w' \rangle \overset{\delta}{\Rightarrow} \langle q, ww'' \rangle$ in $\mathcal{P}$ for $w'' \in w't$ where the transduction t is applied to the rest of stack w'. In ordinary pushdown systems, we can only modify the top of stack at each transition. Thus, we delay the application of the transduction in $\mathcal{P}'$ by keeping it on stack.

We construct three kinds of transition rules of $\mathcal{P}'$ as follows:

$$APPLY\text{-transition} \quad : p \xrightarrow{\gamma/w\,t} q \in \Delta' \qquad\qquad \text{if } p \xrightarrow{\gamma/w|t} q \in \Delta$$

$$COMPOSE\text{-transition} : p \xrightarrow{t_1 t_2 / t_2 \circ t_1} p \in \Delta' \qquad \text{if } t_1, t_2 \in \langle T \rangle$$

$$UNFOLD\text{-transition} \quad : p \xrightarrow{t\gamma/\gamma'\,\langle\gamma,\gamma'\rangle^{-1}t} p \in \Delta' \text{ if } t \in \langle T \rangle \text{ and } \gamma, \gamma' \in \Gamma$$

With $APPLY$-transition rule, we have transition $\langle p, \gamma w' \rangle \Rightarrow \langle q, wtw' \rangle$ in $\mathcal{P}'$. The application of transduction t is simulated lazily with $COMPOSE$-transition rule and $UNFOLD$-transition rule.

For $\delta \in \Delta$, we have a corresponding $APPLY$-transition rule in Δ' and we write $\overset{\delta}{\Rightarrow}$ for a transition relation obtained from δ. Similarly, we write $\overset{C}{\Rightarrow}$ and $\overset{U}{\Rightarrow}$ for transition relations induced by $COMPOSE$-transition rule and $UNFOLD$-transition rule, respectively. We also write $\langle p, w \rangle \Rightarrow \langle q, w' \rangle$ if $\langle p, w \rangle \overset{\delta}{\Rightarrow} \langle q, w' \rangle$ for some δ, $\langle p, w \rangle \overset{C}{\Rightarrow} \langle q, w' \rangle$, or $\langle p, w \rangle \overset{U}{\Rightarrow} \langle q, w' \rangle$.

For $\delta \in \Delta$, we introduce many-steps transition relation $\overset{\delta}{\Rrightarrow} = \overset{C}{\Rightarrow}{}^* \circ \overset{U}{\Rightarrow}{}^? \circ \overset{\delta}{\Rightarrow}$ in $\mathcal{P}'$ ($\circ$ is used as binary relation composition).

Example 2. The following are the transitions of the constructed PDS that correspond to those in Example 1.

$$\langle q_0, aaa\rangle \overset{\delta_1}{\Rightarrow} \langle q_0, taa\rangle \overset{U}{\Rightarrow} \langle q_0, bt'a\rangle \overset{\delta_2}{\Rightarrow} \langle q_1, \mathbb{1}t'a\rangle \overset{C}{\Rightarrow} \langle q_1, t'a\rangle \overset{U}{\Rightarrow} \langle q_2, a\langle a, a\rangle^{-1}t'\rangle$$
$$\langle q_0, aaa\rangle \overset{\delta_1}{\Rightarrow} \langle q_0, taa\rangle \overset{U}{\Rightarrow} \langle q_0, bt'a\rangle \overset{\delta_2}{\Rightarrow} \langle q_1, \mathbb{1}t'a\rangle \overset{C}{\Rightarrow} \langle q_1, t'a\rangle \overset{U}{\Rightarrow} \langle q_2, b\langle a, b\rangle^{-1}t'\rangle$$

(For the sake of simplicity, we abbreviate $\langle a, b\rangle^{-1}t$ as t'.)

For $\delta = p \overset{\sigma}{\hookrightarrow} q \in \Delta$, we have $\langle p, w\rangle \overset{\delta}{\Rightarrow} \langle q, w'\rangle$ iff $w' \in \mathit{Effect}_\sigma(w)$ where Effect is inductively defined as follows.

$$
\begin{aligned}
\mathit{Effect}_{\gamma/w|t} &\quad : (\Gamma \cup \langle T\rangle)^* \to \mathcal{P}((\Gamma \cup \langle T\rangle)^*) \\
\mathit{Effect}_{\gamma/w|t}(\varepsilon) &= \varnothing \\
\mathit{Effect}_{\gamma/w|t}(t') &= \varnothing \\
\mathit{Effect}_{\gamma/w|t}(\gamma'w') &= \begin{cases} \{w\,t\,w'\} & \text{if } \gamma = \gamma' \\ \varnothing & \text{otherwise} \end{cases} \\
\mathit{Effect}_{\gamma/w|t}(t'\gamma'w') &= \{w\,t\,(\langle\gamma', \gamma\rangle^{-1}t')\,w'\} \\
\mathit{Effect}_{\gamma/w|t}(t_1 t_2 w') &= \mathit{Effect}_{\gamma/w|t}((t_2 \circ t_1)w')
\end{aligned}
$$

4.2   Simulation

To reveal a relation between TrPDS and PDS, we consider the difference in how a transduction is applied to stacks of a TrPDS and a PDS. For a TrPDS, a transduction is applied to its stack immediately. On the other hand, for the PDS constructed from the TrPDS, the corresponding transduction is lazily applied to its stack when the PDS takes transitions that unfold transductions. This difference is reflected in the definitions of $\mathit{effect}_\sigma(w)$ and $\mathit{Effect}_\sigma(w)$.

To relate stacks of a TrPDS and a PDS, we introduce *concretization* to obtain the set of stacks of the TrPDS from a stack of the PDS.

Definition 4 (concretization of stack).

$$
\begin{aligned}
\|\cdot\| &\ : (\Gamma \cup \langle T\rangle)^* \to \mathcal{P}(\Gamma^*) \\
\|\varepsilon\| &= \{\varepsilon\} \\
\|\gamma w\| &= \gamma \triangleleft \|w\| \\
\|tw\| &= \|w\|t
\end{aligned}
$$

The gap between $\mathit{effect}_\sigma(w)$ and $\mathit{Effect}_\sigma(w)$ is filled by applying the concretization of stack.

Lemma 1. *For all stack effect* σ, $\|\mathit{Effect}_\sigma(w)\| = \mathit{effect}_\sigma(\|w\|)$

To establish the simulation, we consider transitions of a set of configurations and define $\mathit{post}_\delta(C)$ for a TrPDS and $\mathit{Post}_\delta(C)$ for a constructed PDS.

$$\mathit{post}_\delta(C) = \{c' \mid c \in C, c \underset{\mathcal{P}}{\overset{\delta}{\Rightarrow}} c'\} \quad \mathit{Post}_\delta(C) = \{c' \mid c \in C, c \underset{\mathcal{P}'}{\overset{\delta}{\Rightarrow}} c'\}$$

Transitions of a set of configurations can be related by extending concretization for configurations.

$$\| \langle p, w \rangle \| = \{ \langle p, w' \rangle \mid w' \in \|w\| \} \qquad \|C\| = \bigcup_{c \in C} \|c\|$$

Theorem 1. *For any set $C \subseteq Q \times (\Gamma \cup \langle T \rangle)^*$, $post_\delta(\|C\|) = \|Post_\delta(C)\|$.*

Proof. Let δ be a transition $p \overset{\sigma}{\hookrightarrow} q$.

$$
\begin{aligned}
\|Post_\delta(C)\| &= \|\{c' \mid c \in C, c \overset{\delta}{\Rightarrow} c'\}\| \\
&= \|\{\langle q, w' \rangle \mid \langle p, w \rangle \in C, w' \in \mathit{Effect}_\sigma(w)\}\| \\
&= \{\langle q, w' \rangle \mid \langle p, w \rangle \in C , w' \in \|\mathit{Effect}_\sigma(w)\|\} \\
&= \{\langle q, w' \rangle \mid \langle p, w \rangle \in C , w' \in \mathit{effect}_\sigma(\|w\|)\} \quad \text{(Lemma 1)} \\
&= \{\langle q, w' \rangle \mid \langle p, w \rangle \in \|C\|, w' \in \mathit{effect}_\sigma(w)\} \\
&= \{c' \mid c \in \|C\|, c \overset{\delta}{\Rightarrow} c'\} = post_\delta(\|C\|)
\end{aligned}
$$

$\square$

We then consider one-step transitions of a set of configurations that may apply any transition rule.

$$post(C) = \bigcup_{\delta \in \Delta} post_\delta(C) \qquad Post(C) = \{c' \mid c \in C, c \underset{\mathcal{P}'}{\Rightarrow} c'\}$$

It should be noted that the definition of $Post(C)$ does not directly correspond to that of $Post_\delta(C)$ because $Post(C)$ captures one-step transitions while $Post_\delta(C)$ captures many-steps transitions. However, we have the following weaker correspondence.

$$Post_\delta(C) \subseteq Post^*(C) \qquad \|Post(C)\| \subseteq \|C \cup \bigcup_{\delta \in \Delta} Post_\delta(C)\|$$

From Theorem 1, for any set $C \subseteq Q \times \Gamma^*$, we have $post_\delta(C) = \|Post_\delta(C)\|$ and obtain the following corollary.

Corollary 1. *For any set $C \subseteq Q \times \Gamma^*$, $post^*(C) = \|Post^*(C)\|$.*

4.3 Computing $Post^*$

In this section, we show the forward reachable set $post^*(C)$ for a rational set of configurations C is rational and effectively computable. Thus, the reachability problem of a finite TrPDS is decidable.

To compute $post^*(C)$, we use Corollary 1 and apply usual (forward) reachability analysis to calculate $Post^*(C)$ [8]. For calculating the concretized set of configurations $\|Post^*(C)\|$, we introduce a tail recursive version of $\|\cdot\|$ as follows:

$$
\begin{aligned}
\| \cdot \|' &: (\Gamma \cup \langle T \rangle)^* \times \langle T \rangle \to \mathcal{P}(\Gamma^*) \\
\|\varepsilon\|'_{\mathfrak{a}} &= \nu(\mathfrak{a}) \\
\|\gamma w\|'_{\mathfrak{a}} &= \bigcup_{\gamma' \in \Gamma} \left(\gamma' \lhd \|w\|'_{\langle \gamma, \gamma' \rangle^{-1} \mathfrak{a}} \right) \\
\|t w\|'_{\mathfrak{a}} &= \|w\|'_{t \circ \mathfrak{a}} \\
\|w\|' &= \|w\|'_{\mathbf{1}}
\end{aligned}
$$

We prove the equivalence of the two versions by induction on w.

Proposition 2. $\|w\|t = \|w\|'_t$.

It should be noted that the function $\|\cdot\|'$ is realized as a transducer [2]. The key of the construction is to consider accumulator $\mathfrak{a}$ as a state of the transducer.

To be exact, we construct the transducer $\mathfrak{c} = (\langle T \rangle, \Gamma, \Delta, I, F)$ where $I = \{\mathbb{1}\}$ and $F = \{\mathfrak{t} \mid \mathfrak{t} \in \langle T \rangle, \nu(\mathfrak{t}) = \{\varepsilon\}\}$.

$$\mathfrak{a} \xrightarrow{\gamma/\gamma'} (\langle \gamma, \gamma' \rangle^{-1} \mathfrak{a}) \in \Delta \qquad \text{for all } \gamma' \in \Gamma$$
$$\mathfrak{a} \xrightarrow{\mathfrak{t}/\varepsilon} (\mathfrak{t} \circ \mathfrak{a}) \in \Delta \qquad \text{for all } \mathfrak{t} \in \langle T \rangle$$

Then, we have $\|w\|' = w\mathfrak{c}$.

For a rational set of configurations C, $Post^*(C)$ is rational from forward reachability analysis. Thus, we can effectively compute $(Post^*(C))\mathfrak{c}$ since it is the image under transducer $\mathfrak{c}$ of rational set $Post^*(C)$.

Finally, we obtain the following theorem.

Theorem 2. *For a rational set of configurations C of a finite TrPDS, $post^*(C)$ is rational and effectively computable.*

5   Conditional Transformable Pushdown Systems

We consider conditional transformable pushdown systems as a nontrivial subclass of finite TrPDS. Such pushdown systems may have both kinds of transition rules of conditional and transformable pushdown systems.

A conditional transformable pushdown system is a TrPDS $(Q, \Gamma, \widetilde{\mathcal{L}} \cup \widehat{\mathcal{F}}, \Delta)$ where $\mathcal{L}$ is a finite set of rational languages over Γ and $\mathcal{F}$ is a finite set of functions over Γ. We show that $\langle \widetilde{\mathcal{L}} \cup \widehat{\mathcal{F}} \rangle$ is finite and thus any conditional transformable pushdown system is a finite TrPDS. Hence, the reachability problem of conditional transformable pushdown systems is decidable.

In order to show that $\langle \widetilde{\mathcal{L}} \cup \widehat{\mathcal{F}} \rangle$ is finite, we introduce a notion of *implementation*. We define an algebra $(U, \bullet, \langle \cdot, \cdot \rangle^{-1})$ which is closed under composition and quotient as follows:

- $\bullet : U \times U \to U$ is a binary operator that corresponds to composition, and
- $\langle \cdot, \cdot \rangle^{-1} : \Gamma \times \Gamma \times U \to U$ is a ternary operator that corresponds to quotient.

Then, we define an *implementation* of a finite transduction set T.

Definition 5 (Implementation of T). *For a given finite transduction set T, we call an algebra $(U, \bullet, \langle \cdot, \cdot \rangle^{-1})$ equipped with functions $F : T \to U$ and $G : U \to$ **Transd**$_\Gamma$ an implementation of T if the following hold:*

- $G \circ F = id$
- $G(\mathfrak{u}_1 \bullet \mathfrak{u}_2) = G(\mathfrak{u}_1) \circ G(\mathfrak{u}_2)$

---

[2] This transducer is not letter-to-letter.

$- G(\langle\gamma,\gamma'\rangle^{-1}\mathfrak{u}) = \langle\gamma,\gamma'\rangle^{-1}G(\mathfrak{u})$

We use the following proposition to show that $\langle T\rangle$ is finite.

Proposition 3. *For a given finite transduction set T, $\langle T\rangle$ is finite if there is a finite implementation of T.*

The following property is the key to the construction of a finite implementation of $\widetilde{\mathcal{L}} \cup \widehat{\mathcal{F}}$.

Proposition 4. *Let $L \subseteq \Gamma^*$ and $h : \Gamma \to \Gamma$. Then, we have $\widehat{h} \circ \widetilde{L} = \widetilde{h^{-1}(L)} \circ \widehat{h}$.*

This property implies any sequence $\widehat{h_1} \circ \widetilde{L_1} \circ \widehat{h_2} \circ \widetilde{L_2} \circ \cdots \circ \widehat{h_i} \circ \widetilde{L_i}$ can be normalized as $(\widetilde{L_1'} \circ \widetilde{L_2'} \circ \cdots \circ \widetilde{L_i'}) \circ (\widehat{h_1} \circ \widehat{h_2} \circ \cdots \circ \widehat{h_i})$. It means that the inspection of the stack can be done before modification.

Based on this property, we define an implementation $\mathcal{I}_T = (\mathcal{C} \times \langle\widehat{\mathcal{F}}\rangle, \bullet, \langle\cdot,\cdot\rangle^{-1})$ with F and G where $\mathcal{C}$ is inductively defined as follows:

- $\mathcal{L} \subseteq \mathcal{C}$ and $\varnothing, \Gamma^* \in \mathcal{C}$.
- If $L_1, L_2 \in \mathcal{C}$, then $L_1 \cap L_2 \in \mathcal{C}$.
- If $L \in \mathcal{C}$ and $\gamma \in \Gamma$, then $\gamma^{-1}L \in \mathcal{C}$.
- If $L \in \mathcal{C}$ and $h \in \mathcal{F}$, then $h^{-1}L \in \mathcal{C}$.

The set $\mathcal{C}$ is finite because $\gamma^{-1}(h^{-1}L) = h^{-1}((h(\gamma))^{-1}L)$, $h^{-1}(g^{-1}(L)) = (g \circ h)^{-1}(L)$, and $h^{-1}(L_1 \cap L_2) = h^{-1}L_1 \cap h^{-1}L_2$.

We define the operators and functions of the implementation as follows:

$$\langle L_1, h_1\rangle \bullet \langle L_2, h_2\rangle = \langle L_1 \cap h_1^{-1}(L_2), h_1 \circ h_2\rangle$$

$$\langle\gamma,\gamma'\rangle^{-1}\langle L, h\rangle = \langle\gamma^{-1}L, \langle\gamma,\gamma'\rangle^{-1}h\rangle$$

$$F(\mathfrak{t}) = \begin{cases} \langle L, \mathbb{1}\rangle & \text{if } \mathfrak{t} \in \widetilde{\mathcal{L}} \text{ and } \mathfrak{t} = \widetilde{L} \\ \langle\Gamma^*, \mathfrak{t}\rangle & \text{otherwise} \end{cases}$$

$$G(\langle L, h\rangle) = \widetilde{L} \circ h$$

With respect to F and G, we need to show that the three conditions of implementations hold: $G \circ F = id$ and $G(\langle\gamma,\gamma'\rangle^{-1}\mathfrak{u}) = \langle\gamma,\gamma'\rangle^{-1}G(\mathfrak{u})$ are easily proved from the definition and we use Proposition 4 to prove $G(\mathfrak{u}_1 \bullet \mathfrak{u}_2) = G(\mathfrak{u}_1) \circ G(\mathfrak{u}_2)$.

Finally, we obtain the following corollary of Theorem 2.

Corollary 2. *For a rational set of configurations C of a conditional transformable pushdown system, $post^*(C)$ is rational and effectively computable.*

6   Saturation Procedure of TrPDS

We extend the saturation procedure of PDS for finite TrPDS which computes the set $pre^*(C)$ backward reachable from a rational set of configurations C [5,10].

First, we review the saturation procedure for ordinary pushdown systems. Then, we extend the saturation procedure for TrPDS based on that for conditional pushdown systems where a rational set of configurations is represented by an automaton with regular lookahead [14]. In particular, we introduce automata with transductions (TrNFA) that apply transductions to the rest of the input and extend the saturation procedure so that it constructs a TrNFA from a given finite TrPDS.

6.1   Saturation Procedure for PDS

We review the ordinary saturation procedure. To simplify our presentation, we first consider the set of configurations backward reachable from a single configuration $\langle q_f, \varepsilon \rangle$. For a given PDS $\mathcal{P} = (Q, \Gamma, \Delta)$, we construct a finite automaton $\mathcal{A}_\omega$ that accepts $pre^*(\langle q_f, \varepsilon \rangle)$ where $q_f \in Q$.

The saturation procedure starts from the initial $\mathcal{P}$-automaton $\mathcal{A}_0$ and iteratively updates $\mathcal{P}$-automaton $\mathcal{A}_i$ into $\mathcal{A}_{i+1}$ until saturation. The saturation procedure is described as follows:

1. Let the initial $\mathcal{P}$-automaton $\mathcal{A}_0$ be $(Q, \Gamma, \varnothing, Q, \{q_f\})$.
2. If $p \xrightarrow{\gamma/w} q \in \Delta$ and $q \xrightarrow[\mathcal{A}_i]{w} p'$, then we obtain $\mathcal{A}_{i+1}$ by adding transition $\langle p, \gamma, p' \rangle$ to $\mathcal{A}_i$.
3. Repeat 2 until saturation.

This procedure always terminates since $Q \times \Gamma \times Q$ is finite, and we obtain a fixed point $\mathcal{P}$-automaton $\mathcal{A}_\omega$.

The constructed $\mathcal{P}$-automaton $\mathcal{A}_\omega$ has the following property and hence we have $L(\mathcal{A}_\omega) = pre^*(\langle q_f, \varepsilon \rangle)$.

Theorem 3. $p \xrightarrow[\mathcal{A}_\omega]{w}{}^* q$ *iff* $\langle p, w \rangle \Rightarrow \langle q, \varepsilon \rangle$.

The saturation procedure above can be used to compute $pre^*(C)$ for a rational set of configurations C. Let $C \subseteq Q \times \Gamma^*$ be a rational set of configurations accepted by $\mathcal{P}$-automaton $B = (P, \Gamma, \Delta', Q, F)$. Without loss of generality, we can assume B has no transition leading to an initial state. We construct new PDS $\mathcal{P}' = (Q \cup P, \Gamma, \Delta'')$ where $\Delta'' = \Delta \cup \{p \xrightarrow{\gamma/\varepsilon} q \mid \langle p, \gamma, q \rangle \in \Delta'\}$.

Then, $pre^*(F \times \{\varepsilon\})$ in PDS $\mathcal{P}'$ is equal to $pre^*(C)$ in PDS $\mathcal{P}$. Hence, we only consider the set of configurations backward reachable from a single configuration with empty stack in the following sections.

6.2   TrNFA

To represent a rational set of configurations of finite TrPDS, we introduce automata with transductions (TrNFA) that apply transductions to the rest of the input.

A TrNFA is a structure $A = (Q, \Sigma, \Delta, T, I, F)$ where Q is a finite set of states, Σ is a finite set of symbols, $\Delta \subseteq Q \times (\Sigma \to \langle\!\langle T \rangle\!\rangle) \times Q$ is a finite set of transition rules, T is a finite set of transductions, $I \subseteq Q$ is a set of initial states, and $F \subseteq Q$ is a set of final states. $\langle\!\langle T \rangle\!\rangle$ is the smallest set S such that $\langle T \rangle \subseteq S$ and S is closed under union $\cup$.

We write $p \xrightarrow{\gamma|t} q$ if $\langle p, \sigma, q \rangle \in \Delta$ and $\sigma(\gamma) = t$. Transition $p \xrightarrow{\gamma|t} q$ means that the automaton consumes γ from input, transforms the rest of input by t, and changes its state from p to q.

Intuitively, the composition of two transitions could be defined as follows:

$$p \xrightarrow{\gamma\gamma''|\langle\gamma'',\gamma'\rangle^{-1} t \circ t'} q \quad \text{if} \quad p \xrightarrow{\gamma|t} r, \ r \xrightarrow{\gamma'|t'} q, \text{ and } \gamma'' \in \Sigma$$

With the above definition, finitely *many* transitions accrue by the composing the two transitions, and then the associativity of the composition of transitions does not hold. On the other hand, we obtain *only one* transition by composing two transitions in usual automata and the associativity of the composition holds.

To deal with this problem, we define product $\otimes$ over $\Sigma^* \to \langle\langle T \rangle\rangle$ and introduce pseudo formal power series semiring $(\mathcal{S}, \otimes, \oplus, 1, 0)$.

Definition 6 (Pseudo formal power series semiring).

$$\mathcal{S} = \Sigma^* \to \langle\langle T \rangle\rangle, \qquad 1 = \lambda w. \begin{cases} \mathbb{1} & \text{if } w = \varepsilon \\ \mathbb{0} & \text{otherwise} \end{cases}, \qquad 0 = \lambda w.\mathbb{0}$$

$$(\sigma_1 \otimes \sigma_2)(w) = \bigcup_{\substack{w = w_1 w_3 \\ |w_3| = |w_2|}} \left(\langle w_3, w_2 \rangle^{-1} \sigma_1(w_1) \circ \sigma_2(w_2) \right)$$

$$(\sigma_1 \oplus \sigma_2)(w) = \sigma_1(w) \cup \sigma_2(w)$$

We define inductively transition relations as follows:

$$p \xrightarrow{1} p$$
$$p \xrightarrow{\sigma} q \qquad \text{if} \quad \langle p, \sigma, q \rangle \in \Delta$$
$$p \xrightarrow{\sigma_1 \otimes \sigma_2} r \qquad \text{if} \quad p \xrightarrow{\sigma_1} q \text{ and } q \xrightarrow{\sigma_2} r$$

The associativity of composition of transitions holds as a result of bundling transitions.

We write $p \xrightarrow{w|t} q$ if $p \xrightarrow{\sigma} q$ and $\sigma(w) = t$, and $p \xrightarrow{w} q$ if $p \xrightarrow{w|t} q$ and $\nu(t) = \{\varepsilon\}$. Even if $p \xrightarrow{w|t} q$, we have a transition from p to q consuming w only when the rest of input is successfully transformed by t. We define the language of automaton : $L(A) = \{w \mid p \xrightarrow{w} q \text{ for some } p \in I, q \in F\}$.

6.3   Computing *pre** of TrPDS

To compute $pre^*(\langle q_f, \varepsilon \rangle)$ of TrPDS $\mathcal{P} = (Q, \Gamma, \Delta, T)$, we start from the initial TrNFA $A_0 = (Q, \Gamma, \Delta', T, Q, \{q_f\})$ where $\Delta' = \{\langle p, \lambda\gamma.\mathbb{0}, q \rangle \mid p, q \in Q\}$.

To construct a TrNFA that accepts $pre^*(\langle q_f, \varepsilon \rangle)$, we extend the saturation rule as follows:

- If $p \xrightarrow{\gamma/w|\mathsf{t}} q \in \Delta$, $q \xrightarrow{w|\mathsf{t}'} p'$ in the current automaton, and $\langle p, \sigma, p' \rangle \in \Delta'$, then we replace $\langle p, \sigma, p' \rangle$ by $\langle p, \sigma \oplus \sigma', p' \rangle$ where $\sigma'(\gamma) = \mathsf{t} \otimes \mathsf{t}'$ and $\sigma'(\gamma') = \mathbb{0}$ if $\gamma \neq \gamma'$.

The saturation procedure always terminates and calculates the fixed point automaton A_ω because $\Sigma \to \langle\!\langle T \rangle\!\rangle$ is finite.

We have the following two lemmas that bridge a computation of TrPDS and a behavior of TrNFA.

Lemma 2. If $\langle p, w \rangle \Rightarrow^* \langle q, \varepsilon \rangle$, then $p \xrightarrow[A_\omega]{w} q$.

Lemma 3. If $p \xrightarrow[A_\omega]{w|\mathsf{t}} q$, then $\langle p, ww' \rangle \Rightarrow^* \langle q, w'' \rangle$ for all $w'' \in w'\mathsf{t}$.

From these lemmas, we have the following theorem that implies $L(A_\omega) = pre^*(\langle q_f, \varepsilon \rangle)$.

Theorem 4. $p \xrightarrow[A_\omega]{w} q$ iff $\langle p, w \rangle \Rightarrow^* \langle q, \varepsilon \rangle$.

6.4 Construction of Automata from TrNFA

We construct a finite automaton A' from a finite TrNFA $A = (S, \Sigma, \Delta, T, I, F)$ to show that pre^* is rational and effectively computable.

The construction is very simple. We construct the finite automaton $A' = (S \times \langle\!\langle T \rangle\!\rangle, \Sigma, \Delta', I \times \{\mathbb{1}\}, F \times \{\mathsf{t} \mid \mathsf{t} \in \langle\!\langle T \rangle\!\rangle, \nu(\mathsf{t}) = \{\varepsilon\}\})$ where each state p_t of A' means that we must apply t to the rest of input. For each $p \xrightarrow{\gamma|\mathsf{t}} q \in \Delta$, we add transition $\left\langle p_\mathsf{u}, \gamma', q_{\langle \gamma', \gamma\mathbb{1} \rangle^{-1}\mathsf{u} \circ \mathsf{t}} \right\rangle$ into Δ' for all $\gamma' \in \Gamma, \mathsf{u} \in \langle\!\langle T \rangle\!\rangle$.

To distinguish transitions of finite automata from those of TrNFA, we write $p_\mathsf{t} \xrightarrow{w} p'_{\mathsf{t}'}$ for transitions of A'. From the definition of A', we have $L(A') = \{w \mid p_\mathbb{1} \xrightarrow{w} q_\mathsf{t}$ and $\nu(\mathsf{t}) = \{\varepsilon\}$ for some $p \in I, q \in F$, and $\mathsf{t} \in \langle\!\langle T \rangle\!\rangle\}$.

Then, we have the following two lemmas: Lemma 4 states that the constructed automaton captures behaviors of TrNFA and Lemma 5 states the other direction.

Lemma 4. If $p \xrightarrow{w|\mathsf{t}} q$, then there exist $\mathsf{t}_1, \mathsf{t}_2, \ldots, \mathsf{t}_n$ such that $p_\mathbb{1} \xrightarrow{w} q_{\mathsf{t}_1}, \ldots,$ $p_\mathbb{1} \xrightarrow{w} q_{\mathsf{t}_n}$ and $\mathsf{t} = \bigcup_{1 \leq i \leq n} \mathsf{t}_i$.

Lemma 5. If $p_\mathbb{1} \xrightarrow{w} q_\mathsf{t}$, then $p \xrightarrow{w|\mathsf{t}'} q$ and $\mathsf{t} \subseteq \mathsf{t}'$ for some t'.

These lemmas imply the equivalence of TrNFA A and the constructed automaton $A' : L(A) = L(A')$. Thus, pre^* is rational and effectively computable.

7 Related Works

Conditional pushdown systems are introduced for the analysis of programs with runtime inspection [9,12]. The second author of this paper recently applied them to formalize a subset of the HTML5 parser specification [14]. A similar extension of pushdown systems is considered in [7] to formulate abstract garbage collection in the control flow analysis of higher-order programs.

We should clarify the relation between discrete timed pushdown systems of Abdulla et al. [2] and transformable pushdown systems in this paper. Stack symbols of a discrete timed pushdown system are equipped with a natural number representing its *age*, and thus stack is a string over $\Gamma \times \mathbb{N}$. However, as the region construction of timed automata [3], it is sufficient to consider $\mathbb{N}_{\leq m} = \{x \mid 0 \leq x \leq m\} \cup \{\omega\}$ where m is the maximum number appearing in conditions of transitions. Then, a discrete timed pushdown system can be considered as a transformable pushdown system. Abdulla et al. [1] also introduced dense timed pushdown systems and showed that the state reachability problem is decidable through the translation to pushdown systems. The idea of the construction is a combination of the region construction and the construction for TrPDS. However, the construction is very involved and it is not clear whether we can clarify the construction by using TrPDS.

We have extended the saturation procedure to compute pre^* for finite TrPDS by introducing TrNFA. This procedure is closely related to the generalized reachability analysis of pushdown systems with indexed weighted domains [13]. It will be possible to refine the pseudo formal power series semiring in this paper to an indexed semiring and consider the saturation procedure as that for weighted pushdown systems.

In regular model checking [6], transitions of a system are modeled by a length-preserving rational transduction. The verification is conducted by computing the transitive closure of a transduction. From a viewpoint of reachability analysis, our approach and regular model checking are similar but we handle push and pop operations that are not represented by length-preserving rational transductions.

8   Conclusion and Future Works

We have introduced a general framework TrPDS to extend pushdown systems with transitions that modify the whole stack contents with a transducer. The class of finite TrPDS generalizes conditional and transformable pushdown systems, and even a combination of the two systems. A finite TrPDS can be simulated by an ordinary pushdown system, and the saturation procedure for computing pre^* can be extended for finite TrPDS.

We only consider manipulations of stack that can be represented with a length-preserving rational transduction. We believe that the framework of TrPDS can be extended for general rational transductions. However, it will be necessary to revise the definition of the closure based on quotient and the representation of transductions must be taken into account.

Most of our results on TrPDS depend on the finiteness of the closure of a transduction set. Thus, it is natural to ask whether it is decidable to check the closure of a transductions set is finite. As far as we know, this problem has not been investigated yet. We have shown that the following problem is undecidable by using undecidability of *uniformly halting problem* [11]:

For a given set T of length-preserving rational transductions, decide whether or not the semigroup generated from $(T, \circ)$ is finite.

However, it seems that this result cannot easily be extended for the closure of a set of transductions in this paper.

References

1. Abdulla, P.A., Atig, M.F., Stenman, J.: Dense-timed pushdown automata. In: LICS 2012, pp. 35–44. IEEE Computer Society (2012)
2. Abdulla, P.A., Atig, M.F., Stenman, J.: The minimal cost reachability problem in priced timed pushdown systems. In: Dediu, A.-H., Martín-Vide, C. (eds.) LATA 2012. LNCS, vol. 7183, pp. 58–69. Springer, Heidelberg (2012)
3. Alur, R., Dill, D.L.: A theory of timed automata. Theoretical Computer Science 126(2), 183–235 (1994)
4. Bouajjani, A., Esparza, J.: Rewriting models of boolean programs. In: Pfenning, F. (ed.) RTA 2006. LNCS, vol. 4098, pp. 136–150. Springer, Heidelberg (2006)
5. Bouajjani, A., Esparza, J., Maler, O.: Reachability analysis of pushdown automata: Application to model-checking. In: Mazurkiewicz, A., Winkowski, J. (eds.) CONCUR 1997. LNCS, vol. 1243, pp. 135–150. Springer, Heidelberg (1997)
6. Bouajjani, A., Jonsson, B., Nilsson, M., Touili, T.: Regular model checking. In: Emerson, E.A., Sistla, A.P. (eds.) CAV 2000. LNCS, vol. 1855, pp. 403–418. Springer, Heidelberg (2000)
7. Earl, C., Sergey, I., Might, M., Van Horn, D.: Introspective pushdown analysis of higher-order programs. In: ICFP 2012, pp. 177–188. ACM (2012)
8. Esparza, J., Hansel, D., Rossmanith, P., Schwoon, S.: Efficient algorithms for model checking pushdown systems. In: Emerson, E.A., Sistla, A.P. (eds.) CAV 2000. LNCS, vol. 1855, pp. 232–247. Springer, Heidelberg (2000)
9. Esparza, J., Kučera, A., Schwoon, S.: Model checking LTL with regular valuations for pushdown systems. Information and Computation 186(2), 355–376 (2003)
10. Finkel, A., Willems, B., Wolper, P.: A direct symbolic approach to model checking pushdown systems. In: INFINITY 1997. ENTCS, vol. 9, pp. 27–37 (1997)
11. Hughes, C.E., Selkow, S.M.: The finite power property for context-free languages. Theoretical Computer Science 15(1), 111–114 (1981)
12. Li, X., Ogawa, M.: Conditional weighted pushdown systems and applications. In: PEPM 2010, pp. 141–150. ACM (2010)
13. Minamide, Y.: Weighted pushdown systems with indexed weight domains. In: Piterman, N., Smolka, S.A. (eds.) TACAS 2013. LNCS, vol. 7795, pp. 230–244. Springer, Heidelberg (2013)
14. Minamide, Y., Mori, S.: Reachability analysis of the HTML5 parser specification and its application to compatibility testing. In: Giannakopoulou, D., Méry, D. (eds.) FM 2012. LNCS, vol. 7436, pp. 293–307. Springer, Heidelberg (2012)

Robustness Analysis of String Transducers*

Roopsha Samanta[1], Jyotirmoy V. Deshmukh[2,**], and Swarat Chaudhuri[3]

[1] University of Texas at Austin
roopsha@cs.utexas.edu
[2] University of Pennsylvania
djy@cis.upenn.edu
[3] Rice University
swarat@rice.edu

Abstract. Many important functions over strings can be represented as finite-state string transducers. In this paper, we present an automata-theoretic technique for algorithmically verifying that such a function is *robust* to uncertainty. A function encoded as a transducer is defined to be robust if for each small (i.e., bounded) change to any input string, the change in the transducer's output is proportional to the change in the input. Changes to input and output strings are quantified using weighted generalizations of the Levenshtein and Manhattan distances over strings. Our main technical contribution is a set of decision procedures based on reducing the problem of robustness verification of a transducer to the problem of checking the emptiness of a reversal-bounded counter machine. The decision procedures under the generalized Manhattan and Levenshtein distance metrics are in PSPACE and EXPSPACE, respectively. For transducers that are Mealy machines, the decision procedures under these metrics are in NLOGSPACE and PSPACE, respectively.

1 Introduction

Many tasks in computing involve the evaluation of functions from strings to strings. Such functions are often naturally represented as finite-state string transducers [12,17,2,21]. For example, inside every compiler is a transducer that maps user-written text to a string over tokens, and authors of web applications routinely write transducers to sanitize user input. Systems for natural language processing use transducers for executing morphological rules, correcting spelling, and processing speech. Many of the string algorithms at the heart of computational biology or image processing are essentially functional transducers.

The transducer representation of functions has been studied thoroughly over the decades, and many decision procedures and expressiveness results about them are known [17,21]. Less well-studied, however, is the behavior of finite-state

---

* This research was partially supported by CCC-CRA Computing Innovation Fellows Project, NSF Award 1162076 and NSF CAREER award 1156059.
** Jyotirmoy Deshmukh is now a researcher at Toyota Technical Center, Gardena, CA.

D. Van Hung and M. Ogawa (Eds.): ATVA 2013, LNCS 8172, pp. 427–441, 2013.

transducers under *uncertain inputs*. The data processed by real-world transducers often contains small amounts of error or uncertainty. The real-world images handled by image processing engines are frequently noisy, DNA strings that transducers in computational biology process may be incomplete or incorrectly sequenced, and text processors must account for wrongly spelled keywords. Clearly, it is desirable that such random noise in the input does not cause a transducer to behave unpredictably. However, this is not mandated by traditional correctness properties: a transducer may have a "correct" execution trace on every individual input, but its output may be highly sensitive to even the minutest perturbation to these inputs.

One way to ensure that a transducer behaves reliably on uncertain inputs is to show that it is *robust*, as formalized in [15,4,6]. Informally, robustness means that small perturbations to the transducer's inputs can only lead to small changes in the corresponding outputs. In this paper, we present an automata-theoretic technique for verifying that a given functional transducer is robust in this sense.

Our definition of robustness of (functional) transducers is inspired by the analytic notion of *Lipschitz continuity*. Recall that a function f over a metric space (let us say with distance metric d) is K-Lipschitz if for all x, y, we have $d(f(x), f(y)) \leq Kd(x, y)$. Intuitively, a Lipschitz function responds proportionally, and hence robustly, to changes in the input. In our model, a transducer is robust if the function encoded by the transducer satisfies a property very similar to Lipschitz-continuity. The one difference between the Lipschitz criterion and ours is that the output of a Lipschitz-continuous function changes proportionally to *every* change to the input, however large. From the modeling point of view, this requirement seems too strong: if the input is noisy beyond a certain point, it makes little sense to constrain the behavior of the output. Accordingly, we define robustness of a transducer $\mathcal{T}$ with respect to a certain threshold B on the amount of input perturbation—given constants B, K and a distance metric d over strings, $\mathcal{T}$ is (B, K)-robust if for all x, y: $d(x, y) \leq B \Rightarrow d(\mathcal{T}(x), \mathcal{T}(y)) \leq Kd(x, y)$.

Our main technical contribution is a set of decision procedures based on reducing the problem of verifying (B, K)-robustness of a transducer to the problem of checking the emptiness of a reversal-bounded counter machine. Naturally, whether a transducer is robust or not depends on the distance metric used. We present decision procedures to verify robustness under two distance metrics that are weighted generalizations of the well-known Manhattan and Levenshtein distances over strings. Our decision procedures under these metrics are in PSPACE and EXPSPACE, respectively. When the transducer in question is restricted to be a Mealy machine, we present simpler decision procedures under these metrics that are in NLOGSPACE and PSPACE, respectively.

The rest of the paper is organized as follows. In Sec. 2, we present our formal models and definitions. In Sec. 3, we present a class of *distance-tracking automata* that are central to our decision procedures, presented in Sec. 4. We conclude with a discussion of related work in Sec. 5.

2   Preliminaries

In this section, we define our transducer models, distance metrics and our notion of robustness. In what follows, we use the following notation. Input strings are typically denoted by lowercase letters s, t etc. and output strings by s', t' etc. We denote the concatenation of strings s and t by $s.t$, the ith character of string s by $s[i]$, the substring $s[i].s[i+1].\ldots.s[j]$ by $s[i,j]$, the length of the string s by $|s|$, and the empty string and empty symbol by ϵ.

Functional Transducers. The transducers considered in this paper may be nondeterministic, but must define functions between regular sets of strings. Formally, a *transduction* R from a finite alphabet Σ to a finite alphabet Γ is an arbitrary subset of $\Sigma^* \times \Gamma^*$. We use $R(s)$ to denote the set $\{t \mid (s,t) \in R\}$. We say that a transduction is *functional* if $\forall s \in \Sigma^*$, $|R(s)| \leq 1$.

A *finite transducer* (FT) is a finite-state device with two tapes: a read-only input tape and a write-only output tape. It scans the input tape from left to right; in each step, it reads an input symbol, nondeterministically chooses its next state, writes a corresponding finite string to the output tape, and advances its reading head by one position to the right. The output of an FT is the string on the output tape if the FT finishes scanning the input tape in some designated final state. Formally, a finite transducer T is a tuple $(Q, \Sigma, \Gamma, q_0, E, F)$ where Q is a finite nonempty set of states, q_0 is the initial state, $E \subseteq Q \times \Sigma \times \Gamma^* \times Q$ is a set of transitions, and F is a set of final states[1].

A run of T on a string $s = s[0]s[1]\ldots s[n]$ is defined in terms of the sequence: $(q_0, w'_0), (q_1, w'_1), \ldots, (q_n, w'_n), (q_{n+1}, \epsilon)$ where for each $i \in [0, n]$, $(q_i, s[i], w'_i, q_{i+1})$ is a transition in E. A run is called accepting if $q_{n+1} \in F$. The output of T along a run is the string $w'_0.w'_1.\ldots.w'_n$ if the run is accepting, and is undefined otherwise. The transduction computed by an FT T is the relation $[\![T]\!] \subseteq \Sigma^* \times \Gamma^*$, where $(s, s') \in [\![T]\!]$ iff there is an accepting run of T on s with s' as the output along that run. T is called *single-valued* or *functional* if $[\![T]\!]$ is functional. Checking if an arbitrary FT is functional can be done in polynomial time [10]. The input language, L, of a functional transducer T is the set $\{s \mid [\![T]\!](s) \text{ is defined}\}$. When viewed as a relation over $\Sigma^* \times \Gamma^*$, $[\![T]\!]$ defines a partial function; however, when viewed as a relation over $L \times \Gamma^*$, $[\![T]\!]$ is a total function.

Mealy Machines. These are deterministic, symbol-to-symbol, functional transducers. The notion of determinism is the standard one, and a symbol-to-symbol transduction means that for every transition of the form (q, a, w', q'), $|w'| = 1$. The input language L of a Mealy machine T is the set Σ^* (i.e., every state is accepting). Thus, the transduction $[\![T]\!] : \Sigma^* \to \Gamma^*$ is a total function.

In what follows, we use the term finite transducers, or simply transducers, to refer to both functional transducers and Mealy machines, and distinguish between them as necessary. As a technicality that simplifies our proofs, we assume

---

[1] Some authors prefer to call this model a *generalized sequential machine*, and define transducers to allow ϵ-transitions, i.e., the transducer can change state without moving the reading head. Note that we disallow ϵ-transitions.

that for all $i > |s|$, $s[i] = \#$, where $\#$ is a special end-of-string symbol not in Σ or Γ.

Distance Metrics. A *metric space* is an ordered pair (M, d), where M is a set and $d : M \times M \to \mathbb{R}$, the distance metric, is a function with the properties: (1) $d(x, y) \geq 0$, (2) $d(x, y) = 0$ iff $x = y$, (3) $\forall x, y : d(x, y) = d(y, x)$, and (4) $\forall x, y, z : d(x, z) \leq d(x, y) + d(y, z)$.

The Hamming distance and Levenshtein distance metrics are often used to measure distances (or similarity) between strings. The Hamming distance, defined for two equal length strings, is the minimum number of symbol substitutions required to transform one string into the other. For strings of unequal length, the Hamming distance is replaced by the Manhattan distance or the L_1-norm that also accounts for the difference in the lengths. The Levenshtein distance between two strings is the minimum number of symbol insertions, deletions and substitutions required to transform one string into the other.

The Hamming/Manhattan and Levenshtein distances only track the number of symbol mismatches, and not the degree of mismatch. For some applications, these distance metrics can be too coarse. Hence, we use distance metrics equipped with integer penalties - *pairwise symbol mismatch penalties* for substitutions and a *gap penalty* for insertions/deletions. We denote by $\mathtt{diff}(a, b)$ the mismatch penalty for substituting symbols a and b, with $\mathtt{diff}(a, b) = 0$ if $a = b$. We require $\mathtt{diff}(a, b)$ to be well-defined when either a or b is $\#$. We denote by α the fixed, non-zero gap penalty for insertion or deletion of a symbol. We now define the weighted extensions of the Manhattan and Levenshtein distances formally.

The generalized Manhattan distance is defined by the following recurrence relations, for $i, j \geq 1$, and $s[0] = t[0] = \epsilon$:

$$d_M(s[0], t[0]) = 0 \quad d_M(s[0,j], t[0,j]) = d_M(s[0,j\text{-}1], t[0,j\text{-}1]) + \mathtt{diff}(s[j], t[j]). \quad (1)$$

The generalized Levenshtein distance is defined by the following recurrence relations, for $i, j \geq 1$, and $s[0] = t[0] = \epsilon$:

$$
\begin{aligned}
d_L(s[0], t[0]) = 0, \qquad & d_L(s[0,i], t[0]) = i\alpha, \qquad d_L(s[0], t[0,j]) = j\alpha \\
d_L(s[0,i], \; t[0,j]) = \min(\; & d_L(s[0,i\text{-}1], \; t[0,j\text{-}1]) + \mathtt{diff}(s[i], \; t[j]), \\
& d_L(s[0,i\text{-}1], \; t[0,j]) + \alpha, \\
& d_L(s[0,i], \; t[0,j\text{-}1]) + \alpha).
\end{aligned} \quad (2)
$$

The first three relations in (2), that involve empty strings, are obvious. The generalized Levenshtein distance between the nonempty prefixes, $s[0, i]$ and $t[0, j]$, is the minimum over the distances corresponding to three possible transformations: (1) optimal (generalized Levenshtein) transformation of $s[0, i\text{-}1]$ into $t[0, j\text{-}1]$ and substitution of $s[i]$ with $t[j]$, with a mismatch penalty of $\mathtt{diff}(s[i], t[j])$, (2) optimal transformation of $s[0, i\text{-}1]$ into $t[0, j]$ and deletion of $s[i]$, with a gap penalty of α, and, (3) optimal transformation of $s[0, i]$ into $t[0, j\text{-}1]$ and insertion of $t[j]$ with a gap penalty of α.

Observe that if $\mathtt{diff}(a, b)$ is defined to be 1 for $a \neq b$ and 0 otherwise, the above definitions correspond to the usual Manhattan and Levenshtein distances, respectively. In our work, $\mathtt{diff}(a, b)$ and α are external parameters provided to the algorithm by the user, and we require that the resulting generalized Manhattan and Levenshtein distances are distance metrics.

Robustness. As explained in Sec. 1, our notion of robustness for finite transducers is an adaptation of the analytic notion of Lipschitz continuity, and is defined with respect to a fixed bound on the amount of input perturbation.

Definition 2.1 (Robust String Transducers). *Given an upper bound B on the input perturbation, a constant K and a distance metric $d : \Sigma^* \times \Sigma^* \cup \Gamma^* \times \Gamma^* \to \mathbb{N}$, a transducer T defined over a regular language $L \subseteq \Sigma^*$, with $[\![T]\!] : L \to \Gamma^*$, is called (B, K)-robust if:*

$$\forall \delta \leq B, \forall s, t \in L: \ d(s,t) = \delta \ \Rightarrow \ d([\![T]\!](s), [\![T]\!](t)) \leq K\delta.$$

3 Distance Tracking Automata

In Sec. 4, we show how to reduce the problem of verifying robustness of finite transducers to the problem of checking emptiness of carefully constructed composite machines. A key component of these constructions are machines that can track the generalized Manhattan or Levenshtein distance between two strings. Our earlier work [18] presents automata constructions for tracking the usual Manhattan and Levenshtein distances. In this section, we first briefly review reversal-bounded counter machines and then adapt our distance tracking automata constructions for the generalized versions of the distance metrics.

3.1 Review: Reversal-Bounded Counter Machines [13,14]

A (one-way, nondeterministic) h-counter machine A is a (one-way, nondeterministic) finite automaton, augmented with h integer counters. Let G be a finite set of integer constants (including 0). In each step, A may read an input symbol, perform a test on the counter values, change state, and increment each counter by some constant $g \in G$. A test on a set of integer counters $Z = \{z_1, \ldots, z_h\}$ is a Boolean combination of tests of the form $z\theta g$, where $z \in Z$, $\theta \in \{\leq, \geq, =, <, >\}$ and $g \in G$. Let T_Z be the set of all such tests on counters in Z.

Formally, A is defined as a tuple $(\Sigma, X, x_0, Z, G, E, F)$ where Σ, X, x_o, F, are the input alphabet, set of states, initial state, and final states respectively. Z is a set of h integer counters, and $E \subseteq X \times (\Sigma \cup \epsilon) \times T_Z \times X \times G^h$ is the transition relation. Each transition $(x, \sigma, t, x', g_1, \ldots, g_h)$ denotes a change of state from x to x' on symbol $\sigma \in \Sigma \cup \epsilon$, with $t \in T_Z$ being the enabling test on the counter values, and $g_k \in G$ being the amount by which the kth counter is incremented.

A configuration μ of a one-way multi-counter machine is defined as the tuple $(x, \sigma, z_1, \ldots, z_h)$, where x is the state of the automaton, σ is a symbol of the input string being read by the automaton and $z_1, \ldots, z_h$ are the values of the counters. We define a move relation $\to_A$ on the configurations: $(x, \sigma, z_1, \ldots, z_h) \to_A (x', \sigma', z_1', \ldots, z_h')$ iff $(x, \sigma, t(z_1, \ldots, z_h), x', g_1, \ldots, g_h) \in E$, where, $t(z_1, \ldots, z_h)$ is $true$, $\forall k: z_k' = z_k + g_k$, and σ' is the next symbol in the input string being read.

A path is an element of $\to_{\mathcal{A}}^\star$, i.e., a path is a finite sequence of configurations $\mu_1, \ldots, \mu_m$ where for all $j : \mu_j \to_{\mathcal{A}} \mu_{j+1}$. A string $s \in \Sigma^\star$ is accepted by $\mathcal{A}$ if $(x_0, s[0], 0, \ldots 0) \to_{\mathcal{A}}^\star (x, s[j], z_1, \ldots, z_h)$, for some $x \in F$ and $j \leq |s|$ (we make no assumptions about $z_1, \ldots, z_h$ in the accepting configuration). The set of strings (language) accepted by $\mathcal{A}$ is denoted $\mathcal{L}(\mathcal{A})$.

In general, multi-counter machines can simulate actions of Turing machines (even with just 2 counters). In [13], the author presents a class of counter machines - *reversal-bounded* counter machines - with efficiently decidable properties. A counter is said to be in the increasing mode between two successive configurations if the counter value is the same or increasing, and in the decreasing mode if the counter value is strictly decreasing. We say that a counter is *r-reversal bounded* if the maximum number of times it changes mode (from increasing to decreasing and vice versa) along *any* path is r. We say that a multi-counter machine $\mathcal{A}$ is r-reversal bounded if each of its counters is at most r-reversal bounded. We denote the class of h-counter, r-reversal-bounded machines by NCM(h, r).

Lemma 3.1. *[11] The nonemptiness problem for $\mathcal{A}$ in class NCM(h, r) can be solved in* NLOGSPACE *in the size of $\mathcal{A}$.*

Recall that for all $i > |s|$, $s[i] = \#$. In what follows, let $\Sigma^\# = \Sigma \cup \{\#\}$.

3.2   Automaton for Tracking Generalized Manhattan Distance

We now define automata $\mathcal{D}_M^{=\delta}$, $\mathcal{D}_M^{>\delta}$ that accept pairs of strings (s, t) such that $d_M(s,t) = \delta$, $d_M(s,t) > \delta$, respectively, where $d_M(s,t)$ is the Manhattan distance between s and t. The automata $\mathcal{D}_M^{=\delta}$, $\mathcal{D}_M^{>\delta}$ are 1-reversal-bounded 1-counter machines (i.e., in NCM(1,1)), and are each defined as a tuple $(\Sigma^\# \times \Sigma^\#, X, x_0, Z, G, E, \{acc\})$, where $(\Sigma^\# \times \Sigma^\#)$ is the input alphabet, $X = \{x_0, x, acc\}$, is a set of three states, x_0 is the initial state, $Z = \{z\}$ is a single 1-reversal-bounded counter, $G = \{\delta, 0\} \cup \bigcup_{a,b \in \Sigma^\#} \{\texttt{diff}(a,b)\}$ is a set of integers, and $\{acc\}$ is the singleton set of final states. The transition relations of $\mathcal{D}_M^{=\delta}$, $\mathcal{D}_M^{>\delta}$ both include the following transitions:

1. An *initialization transition* $(x_0, (\epsilon, \epsilon), true, x, \delta)$ that sets the counter z to δ.
2. Transitions of the form $(x, (a, a), z \geq 0, x, 0)$, for $a \neq \#$, that read a pair of identical, non-# symbols, and leave the state and counter unchanged.
3. Transitions of the form $(x, (a, b), z \geq 0, x, -\texttt{diff}(a,b))$, for $a \neq b$, which read a pair (a, b) of distinct symbols, and decrement the counter z by the corresponding mismatch penalty $\texttt{diff}(a,b)$.
4. Transitions of the form $(acc, (*, *), *, acc, 0)$, which ensure that the machine stays in its final state upon reaching it.

The only difference in the transition relations of $\mathcal{D}_M^{=\delta}$, $\mathcal{D}_M^{>\delta}$ is in their transitions into accepting states. The *accepting transitions* of $\mathcal{D}_M^{=\delta}$ are of the form $(x, (\#, \#), z = 0, acc, 0)$, and move $\mathcal{D}_M^{=\delta}$ to an accepting state upon reading a $(\#, \#)$ pair when the counter value is zero, i.e., when the Manhattan distance between the strings being read is exactly equal to δ. The accepting transitions of

$\mathcal{D}_M^{>\delta}$ are of the form $(x, (*, *), z < 0, acc, 0)$, and move $\mathcal{D}_M^{>\delta}$ to an accepting state whenever the counter value goes below zero, i.e., when the Manhattan distance between the strings being read is greater than δ.

Lemma 3.2. $\mathcal{D}_M^{=\delta}$, $\mathcal{D}_M^{>\delta}$ *accept a pair of strings* (s, t) *iff* $d_M(s, t) = \delta$, $d_M(s, t) > \delta$, *respectively.*

Note: The size of $\mathcal{D}_M^{=\delta}$ or $\mathcal{D}_M^{>\delta}$ is $O(\delta + |\Sigma|^2 \text{MAX}_{\text{diff}_\Sigma})$, where $\text{MAX}_{\text{diff}_\Sigma}$ is the maximum mismatch penalty over Σ.

3.3   Automaton for Tracking Generalized Levenshtein Distance

The standard dynamic programming-based algorithm for computing the Levenshtein distance $d_L(s, t)$ can be extended naturally to compute the generalized Levenshtein distance using the recurrence relations in (2). This algorithm organizes the bottom-up computation of the generalized Levenshtein distance with the help of a table $\mathbf{t}$ of height $|s|$ and width $|t|$. The 0th row and column of $\mathbf{t}$ account for the base case of the recursion. The $\mathbf{t}(i, j)$ entry stores the generalized Levenshtein distance of the strings $s[0, i]$ and $t[0, j]$. In general, the entire table has to be populated in order to compute $d_L(s, t)$. However, when one is only interested in some bounded distance δ, then for every i, it suffices to compute values for the cells from $\mathbf{t}(i, i - \delta)$ to $\mathbf{t}(i, i + \delta)$ [12]. We call this region the δ-*diagonal* of $\mathbf{t}$, and use this observation to construct DFA's $\mathcal{D}_L^{=\delta}$, $\mathcal{D}_L^{>\delta}$ that accept pairs of strings (s, t) such that $d_L(s, t) = \delta$, $d_L(s, t) > \delta$, respectively[2].

In each step, $\mathcal{D}_L^{=\delta}$, $\mathcal{D}_L^{>\delta}$ read a pair of input symbols and change state to mimic the bottom-up edit distance computation by the dynamic programming algorithm. As in the case of Manhattan distance, $\mathcal{D}_L^{=\delta}$, $\mathcal{D}_L^{>\delta}$ are identical, except for their accepting transitions. Formally, $\mathcal{D}_L^{=\delta}$, $\mathcal{D}_L^{>\delta}$ are each defined as a tuple $(\Sigma^\# \times \Sigma^\#, Q, q_0, \Delta, \{acc\})$, where $(\Sigma^\# \times \Sigma^\#)$, Q, q_0, Δ, $\{acc\}$ are the input alphabet, the set of states, the initial state, the transition function and the singleton set of final states respectively. A state is defined as the tuple $(x, y, \mathbf{e})$, where x and y are strings of length at most δ and $\mathbf{e}$ is a vector containing $2\delta + 1$ entries, with values from the set $\{0, 1, \ldots, \delta, \perp, \top\}$. A state of $\mathcal{D}_L^{=\delta}$, $\mathcal{D}_L^{>\delta}$ maintains the invariant that if i symbol pairs have been read, then x, y store the last δ symbols of s, t (i.e., $x = s[i-\delta+1, i]$, $y = t[i-\delta+1, i]$), and the entries in $\mathbf{e}$ correspond to the values stored in $\mathbf{t}(i, i)$ and the cells within the δ-diagonal, above and to the left of $\mathbf{t}(i, i)$. The values in these cells greater than δ are replaced by $\top$. The initial state is $q_0 = (\epsilon, \epsilon, \langle \perp, \ldots, \perp, 0, \perp, \ldots, \perp \rangle)$, where ϵ denotes the empty string, $\perp$ is a special symbol denoting an undefined value, and the value 0 corresponds to entry $\mathbf{t}(0, 0)$. Upon reading the ith input symbol pair, say (a, b), $\mathcal{D}_L^{=\delta}$, $\mathcal{D}_L^{>\delta}$ transition from state $q_{i-1} = (x_{i-1}, y_{i-1}, \mathbf{e}_{i-1})$ to a state $q_i = (x_i, y_i, \mathbf{e}_i)$ such that x_i, y_i are the δ-length suffices of $x_{i-1}.a$, $y_{i-1}.b$, respectively, and $\mathbf{e}_i$ is the appropriate set of entries in the δ-diagonal of $\mathbf{t}$ computed from x_{i-1}, y_{i-1}, $\mathbf{e}_{i-1}$, the

---

[2] The fact that there exists a DFA that accepts string pairs within bounded (generalized) Levenshtein distance from each other follows from results in [8,9]. However, these theorems do not provide a constructive procedure for such an automaton.

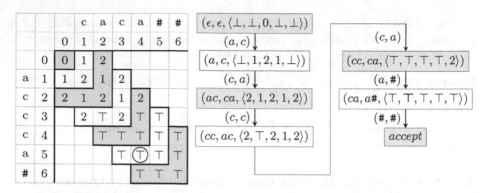

Fig. 3.1. Dynamic programming table emulated by $\mathcal{D}_L^{>2}$. The table **t** filled by the dynamic programming algorithm for $\delta = 2$ is shown to the left, and a computation of $\mathcal{D}_L^{>2}$ on the strings $s = accca$, $t = caca$ is shown to the right. Here, $\Sigma = \{a, b, c\}$, $\text{diff}(a,b) = \text{diff}(b,c) = \text{diff}(a,\#) = 1$, $\text{diff}(a,c) = \text{diff}(b,\#) = 2$, $\text{diff}(c,\#) = 3$ and $\alpha = 1$.

input symbol pair and the relevant mismatch/gap penalties (for more details, see [18]).

Finally, upon reading the symbol $(\#, \#)$ in state $(x, y, \mathbf{e})$, we add transitions to the single accepting state acc in $\mathcal{D}_L^{=\delta}$ (and in $\mathcal{D}_L^{>\delta}$) iff:

- $|s| = |t|$, i.e., x and y do not contain $\#$, and the $(\delta + 1)^{th}$ entry in $\mathbf{e}$ is δ ($\top$ in the case of $\mathcal{D}_L^{>\delta}$), or,
- $|s| = |t| + \ell$, i.e., y contains ℓ $\#$'s, x contains no $\#$, and the $(\delta + 1 - \ell)^{th}$ entry in $\mathbf{e}$ is δ ($\top$ in the case of $\mathcal{D}_L^{>\delta}$), or,
- $|t| = |s| + \ell$, i.e., x contains ℓ $\#$'s, y contains no $\#$, and the $(\delta + 1 + \ell)^{th}$ entry in $\mathbf{e}$ is δ ($\top$ in the case of $\mathcal{D}_L^{>\delta}$).

Upon reaching acc, $\mathcal{D}_L^{=\delta}$, $\mathcal{D}_L^{>\delta}$ remains in it.

Example Run. A run of $\mathcal{D}_L^{>2}$ on the string pair $s = accca$, $t = caca$ that checks if $d_L(s, t) > 2$, is shown in Fig. 3.1. The mismatch and gap penalties are as enumerated in the caption.

The following lemma states the correctness of these constructions. The proof follows from the state-invariants maintained by $\mathcal{D}_L^{=\delta}$, $\mathcal{D}_L^{>\delta}$ and their accepting transitions.

Lemma 3.3. $\mathcal{D}_L^{=\delta}$, $\mathcal{D}_L^{>\delta}$ *accept a pair of strings* (s, t) *iff* $d_L(s, t) = \delta$, $d_L(s, t) > \delta$, *respectively.*

Note: The size of $\mathcal{D}_L^{=\delta}$ or $\mathcal{D}_L^{>\delta}$ is $O((\delta|\Sigma|)^{4\delta})$.

4 Robustness Analysis

From Definition 2.1, it follows that checking (B, K)-robustness of a transducer $\mathcal{T}$ is equivalent to checking if *for each* $\delta \leq B$, $\forall s, t \in L : d(s, t) = \delta \implies$

$d(\llbracket T \rrbracket(s), \llbracket T \rrbracket(t)) \leq K\delta$. Thus, we focus on the problem of checking robustness of a transducer for some *fixed input perturbation* δ. We reduce this problem to checking language emptiness of a product machine $\mathcal{A}^\delta$ constructed from (1) an input automaton $\mathcal{A}_I^\delta$ that accepts a pair of strings (s,t) iff $d(s,t) = \delta$, (2) a pair-transducer $\mathcal{P}$ that transforms input string pairs (s,t) to output string pairs (s',t') according to T, and (3) an output automaton $\mathcal{A}_O^\delta$ that accepts (s',t') iff $d(s',t') > K\delta$. We construct $\mathcal{A}^\delta$ such that T is robust iff for all $\delta \leq B$, the language of $\mathcal{A}^\delta$ is empty.

Later in this section, we present specialized constructions for $\mathcal{A}_I^\delta, \mathcal{A}_O^\delta$ for checking robustness of Mealy machines and functional transducers, with respect to the generalized Manhattan and Levenshtein distances. The definition of the pair-transducer $\mathcal{P}$ is standard in all these scenarios, and hence we present it first. We next define the product machine $\mathcal{A}^\delta$ for two relevant scenarios. Scenario 1 is when $\mathcal{A}_I^\delta$ and $\mathcal{A}_O^\delta$ are both DFAs - as we will see, this scenario presents itself while checking robustness of either type of transducer with respect to the generalized Levenshtein distance. Scenario 2 is when $\mathcal{A}_I^\delta$ and $\mathcal{A}_O^\delta$ are both 1-reversal-bounded counter machines - this scenario presents itself while checking robustness of either type of transducer with respect to the generalized Manhattan distance.

Recall that $\Sigma^\# = \Sigma \cup \{\#\}$. Let $\Gamma^\# = \Gamma \cup \{\#\}$, $\Gamma^{\epsilon,\#} = \Gamma \cup \{\epsilon, \#\}$, $\widetilde{\Sigma} = \Sigma^\# \times \Sigma^\#$ and $\widetilde{\Gamma} = \Gamma^{\epsilon,\#} \times \Gamma^{\epsilon,\#}$.

Pair-Transducer, $\mathcal{P}$. Given a transducer T, the pair-transducer $\mathcal{P}$ reads an input string pair and produces an output string pair according to T. Formally, given $T = (Q, \Sigma, \Gamma, q_0, E, F)$, $\mathcal{P}$ is defined as the tuple $(Q_{\mathcal{P}}, \widetilde{\Sigma}, \widetilde{\Gamma}, q_{0_{\mathcal{P}}}, E_{\mathcal{P}}, F_{\mathcal{P}})$ where $Q_{\mathcal{P}} = Q \times Q$, $q_{0_{\mathcal{P}}} = (q_0, q_0)$, $F_{\mathcal{P}} = F \times F$, and, $E_{\mathcal{P}}$ is the set of all transitions of the form $((q_1, q_2), (a, b), (w', v'), (q_1', q_2'))$ such that $(q_1, a, w', q_1') \in E$ and $(q_2, b, v', q_2') \in E$. While for Mealy machines, in all transitions in $E_{\mathcal{P}}$, w', v' are symbols in $\Gamma \cup \{\#\}$, for arbitrary functional transducers, w', v' may be strings of different lengths, and either or both could be ϵ. We define the function $\llbracket \mathcal{P} \rrbracket$ such that $\llbracket \mathcal{P} \rrbracket(s,t) = (s',t')$ if $\llbracket T \rrbracket(s) = s'$ and $\llbracket T \rrbracket(t) = t'$.

Product Machine, $\mathcal{A}^\delta$. Given input automaton $\mathcal{A}_I^\delta$, pair transducer $\mathcal{P}$ and output automaton $\mathcal{A}_O^\delta$, the product machine $\mathcal{A}^\delta$ is constructed to accept all string pairs (s,t) such that (s,t) is accepted by $\mathcal{A}_I^\delta$ and there exists a string pair (s',t') accepted by $\mathcal{A}_O^\delta$ with $(s',t') = \llbracket \mathcal{P} \rrbracket(s,t)$. Notice that while in each of its transitions, $\mathcal{A}_O^\delta$ can only read a pair of *symbols* at a time, each transition of $\mathcal{P}$ potentially generates a pair of (possibly unequal length) output *strings*. Hence, $\mathcal{A}^\delta$ cannot be constructed as a simple synchronized product.

Scenario 1. Given a DFA input automaton $\mathcal{A}_I^\delta = (Q_I, \widetilde{\Sigma}, q_{0_I}, \Delta_I, F_I)$, pair transducer $\mathcal{P} = (Q_{\mathcal{P}}, \widetilde{\Sigma}, \widetilde{\Gamma}, q_{0_{\mathcal{P}}}, E_{\mathcal{P}}, F_{\mathcal{P}})$ and a DFA output automaton $\mathcal{A}_O^\delta = (Q_O, \widetilde{\Gamma}, q_{0_O}, \Delta_O, F_O)$, $\mathcal{A}^\delta$ is a DFA given by the tuple $(Q, \widetilde{\Sigma}, q_0, \Delta, F)$, where $Q \subseteq Q_I \times Q_{\mathcal{P}} \times Q_O$, $q_0 = (q_{0_I}, q_{0_{\mathcal{P}}}, q_{0_O})$, $F = F_I \times F_{\mathcal{P}} \times F_O$, and E is defined as follows: $\Delta((q_I, q_{\mathcal{P}}, q_O), (a, b)) = (q_I', q_{\mathcal{P}}', q_O')$ iff

1. $\Delta_I(q_I, (a, b)) = q_I'$, and
2. there exist w', v' such that
   (a) $(q_{\mathcal{P}}, (a, b), (w', v'), q_{\mathcal{P}}') \in E_{\mathcal{P}}$, and
   (b) $\Delta_O^*(q_O, (w', v')) = q_O'$.

Scenario 2. For counter machines, one also needs to keep track of the counters. Given input automaton A_I^δ in NCM(h_I,1), of the form $(\widetilde{\Sigma}, X_I, x_{0_I}, Z_I, G_I, E_I, F_I)$, pair transducer $\mathcal{P} = (Q_\mathcal{P}, \widetilde{\Sigma}, \widetilde{\Gamma}, q_{0_\mathcal{P}}, E_\mathcal{P}, F_\mathcal{P})$ and output automaton A_O^δ in class NCM(h_O,1), of the form $(\widetilde{\Gamma}, X_O, x_{0_O}, Z_O, G_O, E_O, F_O)$, A^δ is in NCM(h,1), with $h = h_I + h_O$, and is given by the tuple $(\widetilde{\Sigma}, X, x_0, Z, G, E, F)$, where $X \subseteq X_I \times Q_\mathcal{P} \times X_O$, $x_0 = (x_{0_I}, q_{0_\mathcal{P}}, x_{0_O})$, $Z = Z_I \cup Z_O$, $G = G_I \cup G_O$, $F = F_I \times F_\mathcal{P} \times F_O$, and E is defined as follows:

$$((x_I, q_\mathcal{P}, x_O), (a, b), t, (x_I', q_\mathcal{P}', x_O'), g_{I1}, \ldots, g_{Ih_I}, g_{O1}, \ldots, g_{Oh_O}) \in E \text{ iff}$$

1. $(x_I, (a, b), t_I, x_I', g_{I1}, \ldots, g_{Ih_I}) \in E_I$ with $t \Rightarrow t_I$, and
2. there exist w', v' such that
   (a) $(q_\mathcal{P}, (a, b), (w', v'), q_\mathcal{P}') \in E_\mathcal{P}$, and
   (b) $(x_O, (w'[0], v'[0]), z_{O1}, \ldots, z_{Oh_O}) \to^*_{A_O^\delta} (x_O', (w'[j], v'[\ell]), z_{O1}', \ldots, z_{Oh_O}')$, with $j = |w'| - 1$, $\ell = |v'| - 1$, $t \Rightarrow t_O$ where t_O is the enabling test corresponding to the first move along $\to^*_{A_O^\delta}$ and $\forall k$: $z_{Ok}' = z_{Ok} + g_{Ok}$.

4.1 Mealy Machines

Generalized Manhattan Distance. For a Mealy machine $\mathcal{T}$, it is easy to see from the descriptions of A_I^δ, A_O^δ and from the constructions in Sec. 3.2 that A_I^δ is the same as $\mathcal{D}_M^{=\delta}$ and A_O^δ is essentially the same as $\mathcal{D}_M^{>K\delta}$, with the alphabet being $\widetilde{\Gamma}$. Thus, A_I^δ and A_O^δ are both in NCM(1,1). Let A^δ be the product machine, as defined in *Scenario 2* using A_I^δ, $\mathcal{P}$ and A_O^δ. From Lemma 3.2 and the definition of A^δ, it follows that A^δ accepts all input strings (s, t) such that $d_M(s, t) = \delta$, and there exists $(s', t') = [\![\mathcal{P}]\!](s, t)$ with $d_M(s', t') > K\delta$. Thus, any pair of input strings accepted by A^δ is a witness to the non-robustness of $\mathcal{T}$; equivalently $\mathcal{T}$ is robust iff A^δ is empty for all $\delta \leq B$.

The product machine A^δ is in NCM(2, 1) and its size is polynomial in $size(\mathcal{T})$, δ, K, $|\Sigma|$, $|\Gamma|$ and $\texttt{MAX}_{\texttt{diff}}$, where $\texttt{MAX}_{\texttt{diff}}$ is the maximum mismatch penalty over Σ and Γ. Since, we need to check nonemptiness of A^δ for all $\delta \leq B$, we have the following theorem using Lemma 3.1.

Theorem 4.1. *Robustness verification of a Mealy machine $\mathcal{T}$ with respect to the generalized Manhattan distance can be accomplished in* NLOGSPACE *in* $size(\mathcal{T})$, B, K, $|\Sigma|$, $|\Gamma|$ *and* $\texttt{MAX}_{\texttt{diff}}$ *(maximum mismatch penalty).*

Generalized Levenshtein Distance. For a Mealy machine $\mathcal{T}$, A_I^δ is the same as $\mathcal{D}_L^{=\delta}$ and A_O^δ is the same as $\mathcal{D}_L^{>K\delta}$, with alphabet $\widetilde{\Gamma}$. Thus, A_I^δ and A_O^δ are both DFAs. Let A^δ be a product machine, as defined in *Scenario 1* using A_I^δ, $\mathcal{P}$ and A_O^δ. As before, from Lemma 3.3 and the definition of A^δ, it follows that $\mathcal{T}$ is robust iff A^δ is empty for all $\delta \leq B$.

The size of A^δ is $O(size^2(\mathcal{T})|\Sigma|^{4\delta}(|\Gamma|K)^{4K\delta}\delta^{4\delta(1+K)})$. Since the emptiness of the DFA A^δ can be checked in NLOGSPACE in the size of A^δ, and we need to repeat this for all $\delta \leq B$, we have the following theorem.

Theorem 4.2. *Robustness verification of a Mealy machine $\mathcal{T}$ with respect to the generalized Levenshtein distance can be accomplished in* PSPACE *in* B *and* K.

4.2 Functional Transducers

Checking robustness of functional transducers is more involved than checking robustness of Mealy machines. The main reason is that $\mathcal{P}$ may produce output symbols for two strings in an unsynchronized fashion, i.e., the symbols read by $\mathcal{A}_O^\delta$ may be of the form (a, ϵ) or (ϵ, a). While this does not affect the input automata constructions, the output automata for functional transducers differ from the ones for Mealy machines.

Generalized Manhattan Distance. As stated above, $\mathcal{A}_I^\delta$ is the same as $\mathcal{D}_M^{=\delta}$. The construction of $\mathcal{A}_O^\delta$ is based on the observation that if s', t' are mismatched in $1 + K\delta$ positions, $d_M(s', t')$ is guaranteed to be greater than $K\delta$. Let $\eta = 1 + K\delta$. We define $\mathcal{A}_O^\delta$ to be in class NCM($1 + 2\eta$, 1) with a *distance counter* z and two sets of *position counters* $c_1, \ldots, c_\eta$ and $d_1, \ldots, d_\eta$. The counter z is initialized to $K\delta$ and for all j, position counters c_j, d_j are initialized to hold guesses for η *mismatch positions* in s', t', respectively. In particular, the position counters are initialized such that for all j, $c_j = d_j$, $c_j \geq 0$, and $c_j < c_{j+1}$, thereby ensuring that the counter pairs store η *distinct* position guesses [3]. For notational convenience, we denote the initial position guess stored in the position counter c_j (or d_j) by p_j.

Intuitively, for each j, $\mathcal{A}_O^\delta$ uses its position counters to compare the symbols at the p_j^{th} position of each string. For all j, $\mathcal{A}_O^\delta$ decrements c_j, d_j upon reading a nonempty symbol of s', t', respectively. Thus, $\mathcal{A}_O^\delta$ reads the p_j^{th} symbol of s', t' when $c_j = 0$, $d_j = 0$, respectively. If the p_j^{th} symbols are mismatched symbols a, b, then $\mathcal{A}_O^\delta$ decrements the distance counter z by diff(a, b). Now, recall that the symbol at the p_j^{th} position for one string may arrive before that for the other string. Thus, for instance, c_j may be 0, while d_j is still positive. In this case, $\mathcal{A}_O^\delta$ needs to remember the *earlier* symbol in its state till the *delayed* symbol arrives. Fortunately, $\mathcal{A}_O^\delta$ has to remember at most η symbols corresponding to the η guessed positions. When the delayed symbol at position p_j of the trailing string arrives, i.e. d_j finally becomes 0, $\mathcal{A}_O^\delta$ compares it to the symbol stored in its state and decrements z as needed.

Formally, a state of $\mathcal{A}_O^\delta$ is a tuple of the form (pos, id, vec), where $pos \in [1, \eta]$ is a positive integer (initially 0) that keeps track of the earliest position for which $\mathcal{A}_O^\delta$ is waiting to read symbols of both strings, $id \in \{0, 1, 2\}$ is used to track which of the strings is leading the other, and vec is a η-length vector that stores the symbols of the leading string. Initially, all entries of vec are $\perp$. The invariant maintained by the state is as follows: if $pos = j$, (a) $id = 0$ iff $c_j > 0$, $d_j > 0$ and $vec_j = \perp$, (b) $id = 1$ iff $c_j \leq 0$, $d_j > 0$ and $vec_j = s'[p_j]$, and (c) $id = 2$ iff $c_j > 0$, $d_j \leq 0$ and $vec_j = t'[p_j]$. Thus, if c_j becomes zero while d_j is non-zero, id is set to 1, and vec_j is set to the symbol read, i.e., $s'[p_j]$; when d_j eventually

---

[3] Note that this can be done nondeterministically as follows. First all 2η counters are incremented by 1, and at some nondeterministically chosen point, the machine stops incrementing the c_1, d_1 counters, then at some further point stops incrementing the c_2, d_2 counters, and so on. This ensures that for each j, $c_j = d_j$, and the higher index counters have higher (distinct) values.

becomes zero due to the p_j^{th} symbol of t' being read, then vec_j is set to $\perp$, z is decremented by $\texttt{diff}(s'[p_j], t'[p_j])$ and pos is incremented. The case when the p_j^{th} symbol of t' is output before that of s' is handled symmetrically. $\mathcal{A}_O^\delta$ moves to an accepting state whenever the value in z goes below 0, i.e. $d_M(s', t') > K\delta$, and stays there. $\mathcal{A}_O^\delta$ moves to a special rejecting state if the value in z is nonnegative and either the string pairs or all position guesses are exhausted, i.e., if $\mathcal{A}_O^\delta$ reads a $(\#, \#)$ symbol or if all position counters are negative.

In effect, the construction ensures that if $\mathcal{A}_O^\delta$ accepts a pair of strings (s', t'), then $d_M(s', t') > K\delta$. On the other hand, note that if $d_M(s', t') > K\delta$, then there exists a run of $\mathcal{A}_O^\delta$ in which it correctly guesses some mismatch positions (whose number is at most η) such that their cumulative mismatch penalty exceeds $K\delta$.

Lemma 4.1. *The above $\mathcal{A}_O^\delta$ accepts a pair of strings (s, t) iff $d_M(s, t) > K\delta$.*

Note that the size of $\mathcal{A}_O^\delta$ is $O(\Gamma^{2K\delta})$. Let $\mathcal{A}^\delta$ be a product machine, as defined in *Scenario 2* using $\mathcal{A}_I^\delta$, $\mathcal{P}$ and $\mathcal{A}_O^\delta$. From Lemma 3.2, Lemma 4.1 and the definition of $\mathcal{A}^\delta$, it follows that $\mathcal{T}$ is robust iff $\mathcal{A}^\delta$ is empty for all $\delta \leq B$. $\mathcal{A}^\delta$ is in class $\text{NCM}(2 + 2\eta, 1)$, and its size is $O(size^2(\mathcal{T})(\delta + |\Sigma|^2 \texttt{MAX}_{\texttt{diff}_\Sigma})\Gamma^{2K\delta})$, with $\texttt{MAX}_{\texttt{diff}}$ being the maximum mismatch penalty over Σ. Since we need to repeat this for all $\delta \leq B$, we have the following theorem using Lemma 3.1.

Theorem 4.3. *Robustness verification of a functional transducer $\mathcal{T}$ with respect to the generalized Manhattan distance can be accomplished in PSPACE in B, K.*

Generalized Levenshtein Distance. The input automaton $\mathcal{A}_I^\delta$ is the same as $\mathcal{D}_L^{=\delta}$. In order to track the generalized Levenshtein distance between the unsynchronized output strings generated by $\mathcal{P}$, $\mathcal{A}_O^\delta$ needs to remember substrings of the leading string in its state, and not simply the symbols at possible mismatch positions. A natural question to ask is whether there exists a bound on the length of the substrings that $\mathcal{A}_O^\delta$ needs to remember in its state. We first address this question before defining $\mathcal{A}_O^\delta$.

Consider $\mathcal{A}_I^\delta \otimes \mathcal{P}$, the synchronous product of the input automaton $\mathcal{A}_I^\delta$ and the pair transducer $\mathcal{P}$. Let $\mathcal{T}_{I \otimes \mathcal{P}} = (Q_{I \otimes \mathcal{P}}, \widetilde{\Sigma}, \widetilde{\Gamma}, q_{0_{I \otimes \mathcal{P}}}, E_{I \otimes \mathcal{P}}, F_{I \otimes \mathcal{P}})$ be obtained by *trimming* $\mathcal{A}_I^\delta \otimes \mathcal{P}$, i.e., by removing all states that are not reachable from the initial state or from which no final state is reachable. The set $E_{I \otimes \mathcal{P}}$ of transitions of $\mathcal{T}_{I \otimes \mathcal{P}}$ can be extended in a natural way to the set $E_{I \otimes \mathcal{P}}^*$ of paths of $\mathcal{T}_{I \otimes \mathcal{P}}$. Note that for any path $(q_{0_{I \otimes \mathcal{P}}}, (w, v), (w', v'), q_{f_{I \otimes \mathcal{P}}})$ from the initial state to some final state $q_{f_{I \otimes \mathcal{P}}} \in F_{I \otimes \mathcal{P}}$, $d_L(w, v) = \delta$ and $[\![\mathcal{P}]\!](w, v) = (w', v')$.

We define the *pairwise-delay* of a path π of $\mathcal{T}_{I \otimes \mathcal{P}}$, denoted $pd(\pi)$, as the difference in lengths of its output string labels: for $\pi = (q, (w, v), (w', v'), q')$, $pd(\pi) = \texttt{abs}(|w'| - |v'|)$. $\mathcal{T}_{I \otimes \mathcal{P}}$ is said to have *bounded pairwise-delay* if the pairwise-delay of all its paths is bounded. For $\mathcal{T}_{I \otimes \mathcal{P}}$ with bounded pairwise-delay, we denote the maximum pairwise-delay over all paths of $\mathcal{T}_{I \otimes \mathcal{P}}$ by $\mathcal{D}(\mathcal{T}_{I \otimes \mathcal{P}})$. Let ℓ_{max} be the length of the longest output string in any transition of $\mathcal{T}$, i.e., $\ell_{max} = \max\{|w'| \mid (q, a, w', q') \in E\}$, and let Q_I, Q be the set of states of $\mathcal{A}_I^\delta$, $\mathcal{T}$.

Lemma 4.2. *$\mathcal{T}_{I \otimes \mathcal{P}}$ has bounded pairwise-delay, with $\mathcal{D}(\mathcal{T}_{I \otimes \mathcal{P}}) < |Q|^2 \cdot |Q_I| \ell_{max}$, iff the pairwise-delay of all cyclic paths in $\mathcal{T}_{I \otimes \mathcal{P}}$ is 0.*

Proof. If there is a cyclic path $c = (q, (w, v), (w', v'), q)$ in $\mathcal{T}_{I \otimes \mathcal{P}}$ with $pd(c) \neq 0$, then for n traversals through c, $pd(c^n) = n(pd(c))$, and hence $\mathcal{D}(\mathcal{T}_{I \otimes \mathcal{P}})$ is not bounded. If for all cycles c, $pd(c) = 0$, then for any path π, $pd(\pi) = pd(\pi_{acy})$, where π_{acy} is the acyclic path obtained from π by iteratively removing all cycles from π. Thus, $\mathcal{D}(\mathcal{T}_{I \otimes \mathcal{P}})$ is bounded by the maximum possible pairwise-delay along any acyclic path of $\mathcal{T}_{I \otimes \mathcal{P}}$. This maximum delay is $(|Q_{I \otimes \mathcal{P}}| - 1)\ell_{max}$ and is exhibited along an acyclic path of maximum length $|Q_{I \otimes \mathcal{P}}| - 1$, with the output string pair along each transition being ϵ and a string of length ℓ_{max}. By definition of $\mathcal{T}_{I \otimes \mathcal{P}}$, $|Q_{I \otimes \mathcal{P}}| \leq |Q|^2 \cdot |Q_I|$. The result follows.   □

Corollary 1. *$\mathcal{T}_{I \otimes \mathcal{P}}$ has bounded pairwise-delay iff each simple cycle of $\mathcal{T}_{I \otimes \mathcal{P}}$ is labeled with equal length output strings.*

Lemma 4.3. *If $\mathcal{T}_{I \otimes \mathcal{P}}$ does not have bounded pairwise-delay, $\mathcal{T}$ is non-robust.*

Proof. We exhibit a witness for non-robustness of $\mathcal{T}$. If $\mathcal{T}_{I \otimes \mathcal{P}}$ does not have bounded pairwise-delay, then there is some simple cycle $c : (q, (w_c, v_c), (w_c', v_c'), q)$ in $\mathcal{T}_{I \otimes \mathcal{P}}$ with $|w_c'| \neq |v_c'|$. Consider the paths $\pi_1 = (q_{0_{I \otimes \mathcal{P}}}, (w_1, v_1), (w_1', v_1'), q)$ and $\pi_2 = (q, (w_2, v_2), (w_2', v_2'), q_{f_{I \otimes \mathcal{P}}})$, with $q_{f_{I \otimes \mathcal{P}}} \in F_{I \otimes \mathcal{P}}$. Let us assume that $|w_1'| > |v_1'|, |w_c'| > |v_c'|$ and $|w_2'| > |v_2'|$ (the other cases can be handled similarly). Let $|w_c'| - |v_c'| = l_c$ and $|w_1' . w_2'| - |v_1' . v_2'| = l$.

Then, given δ, K, there exists $n \in \mathbb{N}$ such that $l + nl_c > K\delta$. The witness path π to non-robustness of $\mathcal{T}$ can now be constructed from π_1, followed by n-traversals of c, followed by π_2. By definition of $\mathcal{T}_{I \otimes \mathcal{P}}$, the generalized Levenshtein distance, $d_L(w_1 . (w_c)^n . w_2, v_1 . (v_c)^n . v_2)$, of the input string labels of π, equals δ, and by construction of π, the difference in the lengths, and hence the generalized Levenshtein distance, $d_L(w_1' . (w_c')^n . w_2', v_1' . (v_c')^n . v_2')$ of the output string labels of π exceeds $K\delta$.   □

Lemma 4.2 is helpful in constructing an output automaton $\mathcal{A}_O^\delta$ that accepts a pair of output strings (s', t') iff $d_L(s', t') > K\delta$. The construction of $\mathcal{A}_O^\delta$ is very similar to that of $\mathcal{D}_L^{>K\delta}$, defined over alphabet $\widetilde{\Gamma}$, with one crucial difference. Having read the jth symbol of s', in order to compute all entries in the jth row of the $K\delta$-diagonal in the dynamic programming table, we need to have seen the $(j + K\delta)^{th}$ symbol of t'. However, the maximum delay between s' and t' could be as much as $\mathcal{D}(\mathcal{T}_{I \otimes \mathcal{P}})$ (by Lemma 4.2). Hence, unlike $\mathcal{D}_L^{>K\delta}$, which only needs to remember strings of length $K\delta$ in its state, $\mathcal{A}_O^\delta$ needs to remember strings of length $\mathcal{D}(\mathcal{T}_{I \otimes \mathcal{P}}) + K\delta$ in its state. Thus, a state of $\mathcal{A}_O^\delta$ is a tuple $(x, y, \mathbf{e})$, where x and y are strings of length at most $\mathcal{D}(\mathcal{T}_{I \otimes \mathcal{P}}) + K\delta$, and $\mathbf{e}$ is a vector of length $2K\delta + 1$.

Lemma 4.4. *If $\mathcal{T}_{I \otimes \mathcal{P}}$ has bounded pairwise-delay, $\mathcal{A}_O^\delta$ as described above accepts a pair of strings (s', t') iff $d_L(s', t') > K\delta$.*

Note that $\mathcal{A}_O^\delta$ is a DFA with size $O(|\Gamma|^{4(K\delta + \mathcal{D}(\mathcal{T}_{I \otimes \mathcal{P}}))})$, where $\mathcal{D}(\mathcal{T}_{I \otimes \mathcal{P}})$ is the maximum pairwise-delay of $\mathcal{T}$ and is $O(size^2(\mathcal{T}) |\Sigma|^{4\delta} \delta^{4\delta} \ell_{max})$. Summarizing our robustness checking algorithm for a functional transducer $\mathcal{T}$, we first check if

$\mathcal{T}_{I \otimes \mathcal{P}}$ does not have bounded pairwise-delay. To do this, we check if there exists a simple cycle c in $\mathcal{T}_{I \otimes \mathcal{P}}$ for which $pd(c) \neq 0$. If yes, $\mathcal{T}$ is non-robust by Lemma 4.3. If not, we construct the product machine $\mathcal{A}^\delta$, as defined in *Scenario 1* using $\mathcal{A}_I^\delta$, $\mathcal{P}$ and $\mathcal{A}_O^\delta$. By Lemma 3.3, Lemma 4.4 and the definition of $\mathcal{A}^\delta$, it follows that $\mathcal{T}$, with bounded pairwise-delay, is robust iff $\mathcal{A}^\delta$ is empty for all $\delta \leq B$.

Checking if there exists a simple cycle c in $\mathcal{T}_{I \otimes \mathcal{P}}$ with $pd(c) \neq 0$ can be done in NLOGSPACE in the size of $\mathcal{T}_{I \otimes \mathcal{P}}{}^4$, which is $O(size^2(\mathcal{T})|\varSigma|^{4\delta}\delta^{4\delta})$. Also, the nonemptiness of $\mathcal{A}^\delta$ can be checked in NLOGSPACE in its size, as given by the product of $size(\mathcal{T}_{I \otimes \mathcal{P}})$ and $size(\mathcal{A}_O^\delta)$. Repeating this for all $\delta \leq B$, we have the following theorem.

Theorem 4.4. *Robustness verification of a functional transducer $\mathcal{T}$ with respect to the Levenshtein distance can be accomplished in* EXPSPACE *in B.*

5 Related Work

In prior work [15], [4,5,6] on continuity and robustness analysis, the focus is on checking if the function computed by a program has desirable properties such as Lipschitz continuity. While these papers reason about programs that manipulate numbers, we focus on robustness analysis of programs manipulating strings. As the underlying metric topologies are quite different, the results from prior work and our current approach are complementary.

More recent papers have aimed to develop a notion of robustness for reactive systems. In [19], the authors present polynomial-time algorithms for the analysis and synthesis of robust transducers. Their notion of robustness is one of input-output stability, that bounds the output deviation from disturbance-free behaviour under bounded disturbance, as well as the persistence of the effect of a sporadic disturbance. Also, unlike our distance metrics, their distances are measured using cost functions that map *each* string to a nonnegative integer. In [16,3,1], the authors develop different notions of robustness for reactive systems, with ω-regular specifications, interacting with uncertain environments. In [7], the authors present a polynomial-time algorithm to decide robustness of sequential circuits modeled as Mealy machines, w.r.t. a *common suffix distance* metric. Their notion of robustness also bounds the persistence of the effect of a sporadic disturbance.

In recent work in [18], we studied robustness of networked systems in the presence of channel perturbations. While the automata-theoretic framework employed in [18] is similar to the one proposed here, there are important differences in the system model, robustness definitions and the distance metrics. In [18], we tracked the deviation in the output of a synchronous network of Mealy machines, in the presence of channel perturbations, w.r.t. the (non-weighted) Manhattan and Levenshtein distances. As is evident in this paper, tracking distances and checking robustness for arbitrary functional transducers w.r.t. generalized distance metrics present a new set of challenges.

---

[4] This can be done using a technique similar to the one presented in [20] (Theorem 2.4) for checking nonemptiness of a Büchi automaton.

References

1. Bloem, R., Greimel, K., Henzinger, T.A., Jobstmann, B.: Synthesizing Robust Systems. In: Formal Methods in Computer Aided Design (FMCAD). pp. 85–92 (2009)
2. Bradley, R.K., Holmes, I.: Transducers: An Emerging Probabilistic Framework for Modeling Indels on Trees. Bioinformatics 23(23), 3258–3262 (2007)
3. Černý, P., Henzinger, T.A., Radhakrishna, A.: Simulation Distances. In: Gastin, P., Laroussinie, F. (eds.) CONCUR 2010. LNCS, vol. 6269, pp. 253–268. Springer, Heidelberg (2010)
4. Chaudhuri, S., Gulwani, S., Lublinerman, R.: Continuity Analysis of Programs. In: Principles of Programming Languages (POPL), pp. 57–70 (2010)
5. Chaudhuri, S., Gulwani, S., Lublinerman, R.: Continuity and Robustness of Programs. Communications of the ACM (2012)
6. Chaudhuri, S., Gulwani, S., Lublinerman, R., Navidpour, S.: Proving Programs Robust. In: Foundations of Software Engineering (FSE), pp. 102–112 (2011)
7. Doyen, L., Henzinger, T.A., Legay, A., Ničković, D.: Robustness of Sequential Circuits. In: Application of Concurrency to System Design (ACSD), pp. 77–84 (2010)
8. Eilenberg, S.: Automata, Languages, and Machines, vol. A. Academic Press, New York (1974)
9. Frougny, C., Sakarovitch, J.: Rational Relations with Bounded Delay. In: Jantzen, M., Choffrut, C. (eds.) STACS 1991. LNCS, vol. 480, pp. 50–63. Springer, Heidelberg (1991)
10. Gurari, E., Ibarra, O.: A Note on Finite-valued and Finitely Ambiguous Transducers. Mathematical Systems Theory 16(1), 61–66 (1983)
11. Gurari, E.M., Ibarra, O.H.: The Complexity of Decision Problems for Finite-Turn Multicounter Machines. In: Even, S., Kariv, O. (eds.) ICALP 1981. LNCS, vol. 115, pp. 495–505. Springer, Heidelberg (1981)
12. Gusfield, D.: Algorithms on Strings, Trees, and Sequences. Cambridge University Press (1997)
13. Ibarra, O.H.: Reversal-Bounded Multicounter Machines and Their Decision Problems. Journal of the ACM 25(1), 116–133 (1978)
14. Ibarra, O.H., Su, J., Dang, Z., Bultan, T., Kemmerer, R.A.: Counter Machines: Decidable Properties and Applications to Verification Problems. In: Nielsen, M., Rovan, B. (eds.) MFCS 2000. LNCS, vol. 1893, pp. 426–435. Springer, Heidelberg (2000)
15. Majumdar, R., Saha, I.: Symbolic Robustness Analysis. In: IEEE Real-Time Systems Symposium, pp. 355–363 (2009)
16. Majumdar, R., Render, E., Tabuada, P.: A Theory of Robust Software Synthesis. To appear in ACM Transactions on Embedded Computing Systems
17. Mohri, M.: Finite-state Transducers in Language and Speech Processing. Computational Linguistics 23(2), 269–311 (1997)
18. Samanta, R., Deshmukh, J.V., Chaudhuri, S.: Robustness Analysis of Networked Systems. In: Giacobazzi, R., Berdine, J., Mastroeni, I. (eds.) VMCAI 2013. LNCS, vol. 7737, pp. 229–247. Springer, Heidelberg (2013)
19. Tabuada, P., Balkan, A., Caliskan, S.Y., Shoukry, Y., Majumdar, R.: Input-Output Robustness for Discrete Systems. In: International Conference on Embedded Software (EMSOFT) (2012)
20. Vardi, M.Y., Wolper, P.: Reasoning about Infinite Computations. Information and Computation 115(1), 1–37 (1994)
21. Veanes, M., Hooimeijer, P., Livshits, B., Molnar, D., Bjørner, N.: Symbolic Finite State Transducers: Algorithms and Applications. In: Principles of Programming Languages (POPL), pp. 137–150 (2012)

Manipulating LTL Formulas Using Spot 1.0

Alexandre Duret-Lutz

LRDE, EPITA, Kremlin-Bicêtre, France
adl@lrde.epita.fr

Abstract. We present a collection of command-line tools designed to generate, filter, convert, simplify, lists of Linear-time Temporal Logic formulas. These tools were introduced in the release 1.0 of Spot, and we believe they should be of interest to anybody who has to manipulate LTL formulas. We focus on two tools in particular: ltlfilt, to filter and transform formulas, and ltlcross to cross-check LTL-to-Büchi-Automata translators.

1 Introduction

Spot is a C++ library of model-checking algorithms that has been around for nearly 10 years [5]. It contains algorithms to perform the usual task in the automata-theoretic approach to LTL model checking [13]. So far, and because it is a library, Spot did not provide any convenient access to its features from the command-line. The adventurous user would use some of the programs built for the test-suite of Spot, but these programs were never designed to offer a user-friendly interface.

This situation has changed with the recent release of Spot 1.0: it now installs a collection of command-line tools that give access to many of Spot's features, and allows to combine them with pipes, in the purest Unix tradition. The current tool set (which we describe in this paper) is focused on the handling of linear-time temporal-logic formulae and on its conversion to Büchi automata. The library also includes many algorithms that work on automata, but which are not yet available from the command-line.

We invite the reader to download Spot from http://spot.lip6.fr/ and install it, in order to play with the example commands provided in this paper. In addition to the man pages that are installed along with Spot, a more detailed description of the tools can be read at http://spot.lip6.fr/userdoc/tools.html.

2 Linear-Time Temporal Logic(s)

Spot supports the usual LTL operators: X (next), F (eventually), G (globally), U (until), R (release), W (weak until), and M (strong release). These can be combined with Boolean operators, Boolean constants, and identifiers that represent atomic propositions.

Although there are many tools using LTL, there is no standard syntax for the representation of LTL formulas. For instance the formula G(*request* → F(*grant*)) could be written as [](request => <>(grant)) by Spin [7], [](request --> <>(grant)) by Goal [12], G(request=1 -> F(grant=1) by Wring [10], G i "request" F "grant" by ltl2dstar [8], or even G i p0 F p1 by tools like LBT[1] or Scheck [9] that

---

[1] http://www.tcs.hut.fi/Software/maria/tools/lbt/

D. Van Hung and M. Ogawa (Eds.): ATVA 2013, LNCS 8172, pp. 442–445, 2013.
© Springer International Publishing Switzerland 2013

do not accept arbitrary identifiers as propositions. Spot's tools will write G(request -> F(grant)) by default, but they can read all the above syntaxes, and can write into most of them (the only missing output is Goal, because Goal can already read Spin's syntax).

In addition to LTL operators, we support operators from the linear fragment of the Property Specifications Language (PSL) [1]. These operators connect Semi-Extended Regular Expressions with LTL. A SERE is built using the usual three regular operators, ';' (concatenation), ∪ (union), and ⋆ (Kleene star), but extended with additional operators such as ∩ (intersection), ':' (fusion), and many other operators that are just syntactic sugar over these.[2] The main two PSL operators are:

– {e} □→ f: *any* finite prefix matching the SERE e must trigger the verification of f (any formula using PSL or LTL operators) from the last letter of the prefix, and
– {e} ◇→ f: f must be verified from the last letter of *some* prefix matching e.

Again more syntactic sugar exists on top of these. For instance {e}! is syntactic sugar for {e} ◇→ ⊤: some finite prefix must match the SERE e.

As an example, the PSL formula {(⊤; ⊤)⋆} □→ p states that p should hold every two states, and has no equivalent LTL formula.

3 Tools

Spot installs six command-line tools: randltl is a random LTL/PSL formula generator; ltlfilt is a multi-function LTL/PSL formula filter, able to convert formulas between formats, filter formulas matching certain criteria, and perform some simple syntactic transformations; genltl is a formula generator for various scalable families of LTL formulas; ltl2tgba is a translator from LTL/PSL formulas to different kinds of Büchi automata [4]; ltl2tgta is a translator from LTL/PSL formulas to different kinds of testing automata [2]; and ltlcross is a test-bench for LTL/PSL translators. By lack of space, we only illustrate three of these commands over a few command-line examples.

3.1 ltlfilt and randltl

```
% ltlfilt --safety --relabel=abc --uniq --spin formulas.ltl
```
Reads formulas from file formulas.ltl (one formula per line), retains only those that represent safety properties, renames the atomic propositions occurring in each formula using the letters 'a', 'b', 'c',... suppresses duplicate formulas, and outputs formulas using Spin's syntax. The safety check is automaton-based [3], so "pathological formulas" that represent safety properties without looking so syntactically are also captured.

```
% randltl -n -1 --tree-size=10..15 a b | ltlfilt --simplify --safety |
ltlfilt --invert-match --syntactic-safety --uniq | head -n 10
```
The randltl command generates an unbounded (-n -1) stream of LTL formulas with a tree size between 10 and 15, and using atomic propositions 'a' and 'b'. These formulas are then simplified (using Spot's LTL rewriting rules) and filtered to preserve only safety

---

[2] A complete description of all the supported operators and their semantics can be found in doc/tl/tl.pdf inside the Spot distribution.

formulas; the result is then filtered again to remove all "syntactic safety" formulas, as well as duplicate formulas. The result of these three commands is therefore a stream of pathological safety formulas, from which we only display the first 10 using the standard head command from Unix.

Chaining commands this way to generate random formulas has proven to be a very useful way to generate sets of formulas matching a certain criterion. The following example generates a list of 20 PSL formulas that are not LTL formulas (i.e., they must use PSL operators) and that are equivalent to $a \cup b$.

```
% randltl --psl -n-1 --tree-size=5..10 a b |ltlfilt --invert-match --ltl|
ltlfilt --uniq --equivalent-to 'a U b' | head -n 20
```

Simplification rules are able to transform *some* PSL formulas into LTL formulas. For instance the PSL formula $\{a^\star; b^\star; c\}!$ is equivalent to the LTL formula $a \cup (b \cup c)$. Similarly the PSL formulas $\{a[\rightarrow 2]\} \Box \rightarrow b$, which states that b should hold every time a holds for the second time, can be transformed into $a \mathrel{R} (\bar{a} \vee X(a \mathrel{R} (\bar{a} \vee b)))$.

```
% ltlfilt --simplify -f '{a*;b*;c}!' -f '{a[->2]}[]->b'
a U (b U c)
a R (!a | X(a R (!a | b)))
```

Note that PSL is more expressive than LTL, so not all PSL formulas can be converted into LTL. Currently, we only implements rewriting for *some* straightforward PSL patterns, and these rewriting rules will certainly be improved in the future.

Occasional questions such as "Is $F(\bar{a} \wedge Xa \wedge Xb)$ stutter-invariant?" can also be answered by instructing ltlfilt to match only stutter-invariant formulas:

```
% ltlfilt --stutter-invariant -f 'F(!a & Xa & Xb)'
F(!a & Xa & Xb)
```

Since the formula was output, it is stuttering invariant. Another option, `--remove-x`, can be used to rewrite this formula without the X operator.[3] Other day-to-day questions like "Is formula φ equivalent to formula ψ?" can be answered similarly.

3.2   ltlcross

Spot has used LBTT, the *LTL-to-Büchi Translator Testbench* [11] in its test-suite since its early days. LBTT feeds randomly generated LTL formulae to the configured LTL-to-Büchi translators, and then cross-compares the results of all tools, using several checks to detect possible bugs in implementations, or simply to compare the results from a statistical standpoint. Unfortunately, LBTT is no longer maintained, we have found it quite hard to extend to gather new kinds of statistics, and most importantly it is restricted to LTL. We therefore introduce ltlcross, a reimplementation of LBTT using Spot, with support for PSL formulas.

ltlcross reads a list of formulas from its standard input (usually some output of randltl) or from a file, runs these formulas through several (PSL or) LTL-to-Büchi translators, read the output of these translators (as never claims or in LBTT's syntax) and then performs the same tests as LBTT on the resulting automata.

---

[3] Stutter invariance is actually asserted using automata to test the language equivalence of the input formula and its rewriting without X [6]. Currently this only works for LTL.

The output of `ltlcross` is a CSV or JSON file that contains more statistics about the produced automata. These files are easily post-processed to compute summary table or graphics. A typical invocation would look as follows:

```
% randltl -n 100 a b c | ltlfilt --remove-wm |
ltlcross --csv=out.csv 'ltl2tgba -s %f >%N' 'spin -f %s >%N''lbt <%L >%T'
```

Here 100 random formulas over a, b, and c are produced, the operators W and M are rewritten away by `ltlfilt` (because W and M are not supported by `spin -f` and `lbt`), and finally `ltlcross` uses the resulting formulas with 3 different translators, and gather statistics in `out.csv`.

The invocation of each tool is configured with %-sequences showing how the formula to translate should be passed (e.g., %f, %s, %l are replaced respectively by the formula is Spot's, Spin's, or LBT's syntax, while %F, %S, %L are replaced by the name of a file that contains the formula in these syntaxes) and how to read the result (%T for a filename that will contain output in LBTT's syntax, and %N for a filename that will contain a neverclaim). If any error is detected while running these translators, or when comparing their outputs (we perform the same checks as LBTT), `ltlcross` will report it.

References

1. Property Specification Language Reference Manual v1.1. Accellera (June 2004), http://www.eda.org/vfv/
2. Ben Salem, A.-E., Duret-Lutz, A., Kordon, F.: Model checking using generalized testing automata. In: Jensen, K., van der Aalst, W.M., Ajmone Marsan, M., Franceschinis, G., Kleijn, J., Kristensen, L.M. (eds.) Transactions on Petri Nets and Other Models of Concurrency VI. LNCS, vol. 7400, pp. 94–122. Springer, Heidelberg (2012)
3. Dax, C., Eisinger, J., Klaedtke, F.: Mechanizing the powerset construction for restricted classes of ω-automata. In: Namjoshi, K.S., Yoneda, T., Higashino, T., Okamura, Y. (eds.) ATVA 2007. LNCS, vol. 4762, pp. 223–236. Springer, Heidelberg (2007)
4. Duret-Lutz, A.: LTL translation improvements in Spot. In: Proc. of VECoS 2011. British Computer Society (September 2011), http://ewic.bcs.org/category/15853
5. Duret-Lutz, A., Poitrenaud, D.: SPOT: An Extensible Model Checking Library using Transition-based Generalized Büchi Automata. In: Proc. of MASCOTS 2004, pp. 76–83. IEEE Computer Society Press (October 2004)
6. Etessami, K.: A note on a question of Peled and Wilke regarding stutter-invariant LTL. Information Processing Letters 75(6), 261–263 (2000)
7. Holzmann, G.J.: The Spin Model Checker: Primer and Reference Manual. Addison-Wesley (2003)
8. Klein, J., Baier, C.: Experiments with deterministic ω-automata for formulas of linear temporal logic. Theoretical Computer Science 363(2), 182–195 (2006)
9. Latvala, T.: Efficient model checking of safety properties. In: Ball, T., Rajamani, S.K. (eds.) SPIN 2003. LNCS, vol. 2648, pp. 74–88. Springer, Heidelberg (2003)
10. Somenzi, F., Bloem, R.: Efficient Büchi automata for LTL formulæ. In: Emerson, E.A., Sistla, A.P. (eds.) CAV 2000. LNCS, vol. 1855, pp. 247–263. Springer, Heidelberg (2000)
11. Tauriainen, H., Heljanko, K.: Testing LTL formula translation into Büchi automata. International Journal on Software Tools for Technology Transfer 4(1), 57–70 (2002)
12. Tsay, Y.K., Chen, Y.F., Tsai, M.H., Wu, K.N., Chan, W.C., Luo, C.J., Chang, J.S.: Tool support for learning büchi automata and linear temporal logic. Formal Aspects of Computing 21(3), 259–275 (2009)
13. Vardi, M.Y.: An automata-theoretic approach to linear temporal logic. In: Moller, F., Birtwistle, G. (eds.) Logics for Concurrency. LNCS, vol. 1043, pp. 238–266. Springer, Heidelberg (1996)

Rabinizer 2:
Small Deterministic Automata for LTL∖GU

Jan Křetínský[1,2,*] and Ruslán Ledesma Garza[1,**]

[1] Institut für Informatik, Technische Universität München, Germany
[2] Faculty of Informatics, Masaryk University, Brno, Czech Republic

Abstract. We present a tool that generates automata for LTL(**X**,**F**,**G**,**U**) where **U** does not occur in any **G**-formula (but **F** still can). The tool generates deterministic generalized Rabin automata (DGRA) significantly smaller than deterministic Rabin automata (DRA) generated by state-of-the-art tools. For complex properties such as fairness constraints, the difference is in orders of magnitude. DGRA have been recently shown to be as useful in probabilistic model checking as DRA, hence the difference in size directly translates to a speed up of the model checking procedures.

1 Introduction

Linear temporal logic (LTL) is a very useful and appropriate language for specifying properties of systems. In the verification process that follows the automata-theoretic approach, an LTL formula is first translated to an ω-automaton and then a product of the automaton and the system is constructed and analyzed. The automata used here are typically non-deterministic Büchi automata (NBA) as they recognize all ω-regular languages and thus also LTL languages. However, for two important applications, *deterministic* ω-automata are important: probabilistic model checking and synthesis of reactive modules for LTL specifications. Here deterministic Rabin automata (DRA) are typically used as deterministic Büchi automata are not as expressive as LTL. In order to transform an NBA to a DRA, one needs to employ either Safra's construction (or some other exponential construction). This approach is taken in PRISM [7] a leading probabilistic model checker, which reimplements the optimized Safra's construction of ltl2dstar [4]. However, a straight application of this very general construction often yields unnecessarily large automata and thus also large products, often too large to be analyzed.

In order to circumvent this difficulty, one can focus on fragments of LTL. The most prominent ones are GR(1)—a restricted, but useful fragment of LTL(**X**,**F**,**G**) allowing for fast synthesis—and fragments of LTL(**F**,**G**) as investigated in e.g. [1]. Recently [6], we showed how to construct DRA from LTL(**F**,**G**) directly without NBA. As we argued there, this is an interesting fragment also

---

* The author is supported by the Czech Science Foundation, grant No. P202/12/G061.
** The author is supported by the DFG Graduiertenkolleg 1480 (PUMA).

D. Van Hung and M. Ogawa (Eds.): ATVA 2013, LNCS 8172, pp. 446–451, 2013.

because it can express all complex fairness constraints, which are widely used in verification. We implemented our approach in a tool `Rabinizer` [3] and observed significant improvements, especially for complex formulae: for example, for a conjunction of three fairness constraints `ltl2dstar` produces a DRA with more than a milion states, while `Rabinizer` produces 469 states. Moreover, we introduced a new type of automaton a *deterministic generalized Rabin automaton* (DGRA), which is an intermediate step in our construction, and only has 64 states in the fairness example and only 1 state if transition acceptance is used. In [2], we then show that for probabilistic model checking DGRA are not more difficult to handle than DRA. Hence, without tradeoff, we can use often much smaller DGRA, which are only produced by our construction.

Here, we present a tool `Rabinizer` 2 that extends our method and implements it for LTL$_{\backslash \mathbf{GU}}$ a fragment of LTL($\mathbf{X},\mathbf{F},\mathbf{G},\mathbf{U}$) where $\mathbf{U}$ are not inside $\mathbf{G}$-formulae (but $\mathbf{F}$ still can) in negation normal form. This fragment is not only substantially more complex, but also practically more useful. Indeed, with the unrestricted $\mathbf{X}$-operator, it covers GR(1) and can capture properties describing local structure of systems and is necessary for description of precise sequences of steps. Further, $\mathbf{U}$-operator allows to distinguish paths depending on their initial parts and then we can require different fairness constraints on different paths such as in $wait\mathbf{U}(answer_1 \wedge \phi_1) \vee wait\mathbf{U}(answer_2 \wedge \phi_2)$ where ϕ_1, ϕ_2 are two fairness constraints. As another example, consider patterns for "before": for "absence" we have $\mathbf{F}r \rightarrow (\neg p\mathbf{U}r)$, for "constrained chains" $\mathbf{F}r \rightarrow (p \rightarrow (\neg r\mathbf{U}(s \wedge \neg r \wedge \neg z \wedge \mathbf{X}((\neg r \wedge \neg z)\mathbf{U}t))))\mathbf{U}r$.

Furthermore, as opposed to other tools (including `Rabinizer`), `Rabinizer` 2 can also produce DGRA, which are smaller by orders of magnitude for complex formulae. For instance, for a conjunction of four fairness constraints the constructed DGRA has 256 states, while the directly degeneralized DRA is 20736-*times* bigger [2]. As a result, we not only obtain smaller DRA now for much larger fragment (by degeneralizing the DGRA into DRA), but also the power of DGRA is made available for this fragment allowing for the respective speed up of probabilistic model checking.

The tool can be downloaded and additional materials and proofs found at `http://www.model.in.tum.de/~kretinsk/rabinizer2.html`

2   Algorithm

Let us fix a formula φ of LTL$_{\backslash \mathbf{GU}}$. We construct an automaton $\mathcal{A}(\varphi)$ recognizing models of φ. Details can be found on the tool's webpage. In every step, $\mathcal{A}(\varphi)$ unfolds φ as in [6], now we also define $\mathfrak{Unf}(\psi_1\mathbf{U}\psi_2) = \mathfrak{Unf}(\psi_2) \vee (\mathfrak{Unf}(\psi_1) \wedge \mathbf{X}(\psi_1\mathbf{U}\psi_2))$. Then it

checks whether the letter currently read complies with thus generated requirements, see the example on the right for $\varphi = a\mathbf{U}b$. E.g. reading $\{a\}$ yields requirement $\mathbf{X}(a\mathbf{U}b)$ for the next step, thus in the next step we have $\mathfrak{Unf}(a\mathbf{U}b)$ which is the same as in the initial state, hence we loop.

Some requirements can be checked at a finite time by this unfolding, such as $b\mathbf{U}(a \wedge \mathbf{X}b)$, some cannot, such as $\mathbf{GF}(a \wedge \mathbf{X}b)$. The state space has to monitor the latter requirements (such as the repetitive satisfaction of $a \wedge \mathbf{X}b$) separately. To this end, let $\mathbf{G}_\varphi := \{\mathbf{G}\psi \in \mathrm{sf}(\varphi)\}$ and $\mathbf{F}_\varphi := \{\mathbf{F}\psi \in \mathrm{sf}(\omega) \mid$ for some $\omega \in \mathbf{G}_\varphi\}$ where $\mathrm{sf}(\varphi)$ denotes the set of all subformulae of φ. Then $\mathcal{R}ec := \{\psi \mid \mathbf{G}\psi \in \mathbf{G}_\varphi$ or $\mathbf{F}\psi \in \mathbf{F}_\varphi\}$ is the set of *recurrent* subformulae of φ, whose repeated satisfaction we must check. (Note that no $\mathbf{U}$ occurs in formulae of $\mathcal{R}ec$.) In the case without the $\mathbf{X}$ operator [6,3], such as with $\mathbf{GF}a$, it was sufficient to record the currently read letter in the states of $\mathcal{A}(\varphi)$. Then the acceptance condition checks whether e.g. a is visited infinitely often. Now we could extend this to keep history of the last n letters read where n is the nesting depth of the $\mathbf{X}$ operator in φ. In order to reduce the size of the state space, we rather store equivalence classes thereof. This is realized by automata. For every $\xi \in \mathcal{R}ec$, we have a finite automaton $\mathcal{B}(\xi)$, and $\mathcal{A}(\varphi)$ will keep track of its current states.

Construction of $\mathcal{B}(\xi)$: We define a finite automaton $\mathcal{B}(\xi) = (Q_\xi, i_\xi, \delta_\xi, F_\xi)$ over 2^{Ap} by

- the set of states $Q_\xi = \mathsf{B}^+(\mathrm{sf}(\xi))$, where $\mathsf{B}^+(S)$ is the set of positive Boolean functions over S and $\mathbf{tt}$ and $\mathbf{ff}$,
- the initial state $i_\xi = \xi$,
- the final states F_ξ where each atomic proposition has $\mathbf{F}$ or $\mathbf{G}$ as an ancestor in the syntactic tree (i.e. no atomic propositions are guarded by only $\mathbf{X}$'s and Boolean connectives),
- transition relation δ_ξ is defined by transitions

$$\chi \xrightarrow{\nu} \mathbf{X}^{-1}(\chi[\nu]) \quad \text{for every } \nu \subseteq Ap \text{ and } \chi \notin F$$
$$i \xrightarrow{\nu} i \quad \text{for every } \nu \subseteq Ap$$

where $\chi[\nu]$ is the function χ with $\mathbf{tt}$ and $\mathbf{ff}$ plugged in for atomic propositions according to ν and $\mathbf{X}^{-1}\chi$ strips away the initial $\mathbf{X}$ (whenever there is one) from each formula in the Boolean combination χ. Note that we do not unfold inner $\mathbf{F}$- and $\mathbf{G}$-formulae. See an example for $\xi = a \vee b \vee \mathbf{X}(b \wedge \mathbf{G}a)$ on the right.

Construction of $\mathcal{A}(\varphi)$: The state space has two components. Beside the component keeping track of the input formula, we also keep track of the history for every recurrent formula of $\mathcal{R}ec$. The second component is then a vector of length $|\mathcal{R}ec|$ keeping the current set of states of each $\mathcal{B}(\xi)$. Formally, we define $\mathcal{A}(\varphi) = (Q, i, \delta)$ to be a deterministic finite automaton over $\Sigma = 2^{Ap}$ given by

- set of states $Q = \mathsf{B}^+(\mathrm{sf}(\varphi) \cup \mathbf{X}\mathrm{sf}(\varphi)) \times \prod_{\xi \in \mathcal{R}ec} 2^{Q_\xi}$ where $\mathbf{X}S = \{\mathbf{X}s \mid s \in S\}$,
- the initial state $i = \langle \mathfrak{Unf}(\varphi), (\xi \mapsto \{i_\xi\})_{\xi \in \mathcal{R}ec} \rangle$;
- the transition function δ is defined by transitions

$$\langle \psi, (R_\xi)_{\xi \in \mathcal{R}ec} \rangle \xrightarrow{\nu} \langle \mathfrak{Unf}(\mathbf{X}^{-1}(\psi[\nu])), (\delta_\xi(R_\xi, \nu))_{\xi \in \mathcal{R}ec} \rangle$$

On $\mathcal{A}(\varphi)$ it is possible to define an acceptance condition such that $\mathcal{A}(\varphi)$ recognizes models of φ. The approach is similar to [6], but now we have to take the information of each $\mathcal{B}(\xi)$ into account. We use this information to get look-ahead necessary for evaluating $\mathbf{X}$-requirements in the first component of $\mathcal{A}(\varphi)$. However, since storing complete future look-ahead would be costly, $\mathcal{B}(\xi)$ actually stores the compressed information of past. The acceptance condition allows then for deducing enough information about the future.

Further optimizations include not storing states of each $\mathcal{B}(\xi)$, but only the currently relevant ones. E.g. after reading $\emptyset$ in $\mathbf{GF}a \vee (b \wedge \mathbf{GF}c)$, it is no more interesting to track if c occurs infinitely often. Further, since only the infinite behaviour of $\mathcal{B}(\xi)$ is important and it has acyclic structure (except for the initial states), instead of the initial state we can start in any subset of states. Therefore, we start in a subset that will occur repetitively and we thus omit unnecessary initial transient parts of $\mathcal{A}(\varphi)$.

3   Experimental Results

We compare our tool to `ltl2dstar`, which yields the same automata as its Java reimplementation in PRISM. We consider some formulae on which `ltl2dstar` was originally tested [5], some formulae used in a network monitoring project Liberouter (https://www.liberouter.org/) showing the LTL$_{\backslash \mathbf{GU}}$ fragment is practically very relevant, and several other formulae with more involved structure such as ones containing fairness constraints. For results on the LTL$(\mathbf{F},\mathbf{G})$ subfragment, we refer to [3]. Due to [2], it only makes sense to use DGRA and we thus display the sizes of DGRA for **Rabinizer 2** (except for the more complex cases this, however, coincides with the degeneralized DRA). Here "?" denotes time-out after 30 minutes. For more experiments, see the webpage.

Formula	ltl2d*	R.2
$(\mathbf{F}p)\mathbf{U}(\mathbf{G}q)$	4	3
$(\mathbf{G}p)\mathbf{U}q$	5	5
$\neg(p\mathbf{U}q)$	4	3
$\mathbf{G}(p \to \mathbf{F}q) \wedge ((\mathbf{X}p)\mathbf{U}q) \vee \neg\mathbf{X}(p\mathbf{U}(p \wedge q))$	19	8
$\mathbf{G}(q \vee \mathbf{XG}p) \wedge \mathbf{G}(r \vee \mathbf{XG}\neg p)$	5	14
$((\mathbf{G}(\mathbf{F}(p_1) \wedge \mathbf{F}(\neg p_1)))) \to (\mathbf{G}((p_2 \wedge \mathbf{X}p_2 \wedge \neg p_1 \wedge \mathbf{X}p_1 \to ((p_3) \to \mathbf{X}p_4))))$	11	8
$((p_1 \wedge \mathbf{XG}(\neg p_1)) \wedge (\mathbf{G}((\mathbf{F}p_2) \wedge (\mathbf{F}\neg p_2))) \wedge ((\neg p_2))) \to (((\neg p_2)\mathbf{U}$ $\mathbf{G}(\neg((p_3 \wedge p_4) \vee (p_3 \wedge p_5) \vee (p_3 \wedge p_6) \vee (p_4 \wedge p_5) \vee (p_4 \wedge p_6) \vee (p_5 \wedge p_6)))))$	17	8
$(\mathbf{X}p_1 \wedge \mathbf{G}((\neg p_1 \wedge \mathbf{X}p_1) \to XXp_1) \wedge \mathbf{GF}\neg p_1 \wedge \mathbf{GF}p_2 \wedge \mathbf{GF}\neg p_2) \to$ $(\mathbf{G}(p_3 \wedge p_4 \wedge !p_2 \wedge \mathbf{X}p_2 \to \mathbf{X}(p_1 \vee \mathbf{X}(\neg p_4 \vee p_1))))$	9	7
$\mathbf{F}r \to (p \to (\neg r\mathbf{U}(s \wedge \neg r \wedge \neg z \wedge \mathbf{X}((\neg r \wedge \neg z)\mathbf{U}t))))\mathbf{U}r$	6	5
$((\mathbf{GF}(a \wedge \mathbf{XX}b) \vee \mathbf{FG}b) \wedge \mathbf{FG}(c \vee (\mathbf{X}a \wedge \mathbf{XX}b)))$	353	73
$\mathbf{GF}(\mathbf{XXX}a \wedge \mathbf{XXXX}b) \wedge \mathbf{GF}(b \vee \mathbf{X}c) \wedge \mathbf{GF}(c \wedge \mathbf{XX}a)$	2127	85
$(\mathbf{GF}a \vee \mathbf{FG}b) \wedge (\mathbf{GF}c \vee \mathbf{FG}(d \vee \mathbf{X}e))$	18176	40
$(\mathbf{GF}(a \wedge \mathbf{XX}c) \vee \mathbf{FG}b) \wedge (\mathbf{GF}c \vee \mathbf{FG}(d \vee \mathbf{X}a \wedge \mathbf{XX}b))$	?	142
$a\mathbf{U}b \wedge (\mathbf{GF}a \vee \mathbf{FG}b) \wedge (\mathbf{GF}c \vee \mathbf{FG}d) \vee a\mathbf{U}c \wedge (\mathbf{GF}a \vee \mathbf{FG}d) \wedge (\mathbf{GF}c \vee \mathbf{FG}b)$	?	60

References

1. Alur, R., La Torre, S.: Deterministic generators and games for LTL fragments. ACM Trans. Comput. Log. 5(1), 1–25 (2004)
2. Chatterjee, K., Gaiser, A., Křetínský, J.: Automata with generalized Rabin pairs for probabilistic model checking and LTL synthesis. In: Sharygina, N., Veith, H. (eds.) CAV 2013. LNCS, vol. 8044, pp. 559–575. Springer, Heidelberg (2013)
3. Gaiser, A., Křetínský, J., Esparza, J.: Rabinizer: Small deterministic automata for lTL(F,G). In: Chakraborty, S., Mukund, M. (eds.) ATVA 2012. LNCS, vol. 7561, pp. 72–76. Springer, Heidelberg (2012)
4. Klein, J.: ltl2dstar - LTL to deterministic Streett and Rabin automata, http://www.ltl2dstar.de/
5. Klein, J., Baier, C.: Experiments with deterministic *omega*-automata for formulas of linear temporal logic. Theor. Comput. Sci. 363(2), 182–195 (2006)
6. Křetínský, J., Esparza, J.: Deterministic automata for the (F,G)-fragment of LTL. In: Madhusudan, P., Seshia, S.A. (eds.) CAV 2012. LNCS, vol. 7358, pp. 7–22. Springer, Heidelberg (2012)
7. Kwiatkowska, M., Norman, G., Parker, D.: PRISM 4.0: Verification of probabilistic real-time systems. In: Gopalakrishnan, G., Qadeer, S. (eds.) CAV 2011. LNCS, vol. 6806, pp. 585–591. Springer, Heidelberg (2011)

LTL Model Checking with Neco

Łukasz Fronc[1] and Alexandre Duret-Lutz[2]

[1] IBISC, Université d'Évry/Paris-Saclay
fronc@ibisc.univ-evry.fr
[2] LRDE, EPITA, Kremlin-Bicêtre, France
adl@lrde.epita.fr

Abstract. We introduce `neco-spot`, an LTL model checker for Petri net models. It builds upon Neco, a compiler turning Petri nets into native shared libraries that allows fast on-the-fly exploration of the state-space, and upon Spot, a C++ library of model-checking algorithms. We show the architecture of Neco and explain how it was combined with Spot to build an LTL model checker.

1 Introduction

Neco is a suite of Unix tools to compile high-level Petri net models into shared libraries that can then be used to check reachability properties (building only the set of reachable states), or check any LTL property (synchronizing the reachability graph with a property automaton). It is based on SNAKES, a general Petri net Python library [12], which key feature is the use of arbitrary Python objects as tokens and Python expressions as net annotations. This allows a great amount of expressivity at the cost of slow execution times, Python being an interpreted language. Neco uses this library as a frontend allowing this high degree of expressivity but also notably speeds up the execution, efficiently compiling the models to native libraries. This compilation step allows Neco to compete with state-of-the-art tools [7,10].

Originally, Neco did only reachability analysis. In this paper, we explain how we connected it with the Spot library to perform LTL model checking. Beside presenting Neco, this paper can therefore be seen as presenting a use-case of Spot, showing how to build an LTL model checker for a custom formalism.

2 Architecture of Neco

To perform model-checking, Neco provides three tools: `neco-compile`, `neco-check`, and `neco-spot`. Each of these tools handle a specific task and the whole tool set allows for a simple workflow as presented in Figure 1.

First, `neco-compile` builds an exploration engine (`net.so`) from a high-level Petri net model. The model can be programmatically specified in Python using the SNAKES toolkit [12], specified in the ABCD formalism [11], or provided in PNML format [9]. This step uses model specific information (inferred or provided by the user) to generate optimized data structures and exploration functions on a per-model basis [7,8].

Next, we set up an atomic proposition checker. Because Spot is a general model-checking library, it does not provide a language for atomic propositions. So each tool

D. Van Hung and M. Ogawa (Eds.): ATVA 2013, LNCS 8172, pp. 451–454, 2013.
© Springer International Publishing Switzerland 2013

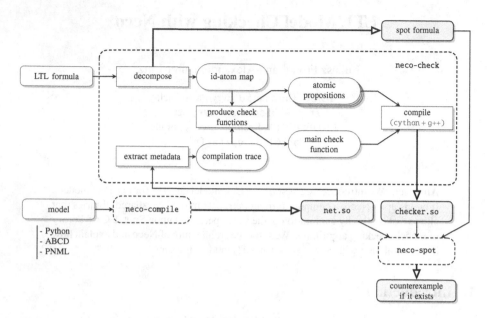

Fig. 1. The architecture of Neco

using Spot has to provide its atomic proposition language, but also functions to check these. This is the role of neco-check tool. It takes a LTL formula as an input, then decomposes it in order to extract atomic propositions. During this step a simplified formula where all atomic propositions were replaced by simple identifiers is produced (spot formula). The tool keeps the track of these atoms using an identifier-atomic proposition map, which can also be used to understand the simplified formula. The exploration engine being model-specific, neco-check cannot make any assumption about the Petri net marking structure or memory layout. Fortunately net.so exports some metadata (compilation trace) about the marking structure that is used by neco-check to generate check functions for each atomic proposition. The last function we produce is a main check function that serves as an interface for the whole module. It returns the value of atomic propositions based on their identifiers and a provided states. All functions generated, we can compile the code producing the shared library checker.so.

The model-checking procedure is performed by the third and last tool: neco-spot. This tool takes as inputs: the LTL formula to check (spot formula), the exploration engine library to build the reachability graph on demand (net.so), and the atomic proposition checker module to check atomic proposition values (checker.so). Then using the Spot library outputs a counterexample if one exists, and builds the whole state space otherwise.

3   Bridge between Neco and Spot

We now describe how we built our LTL model-checking tool, neco-spot, combining Neco's exploration engine with the model-checking algorithms of Spot [4].

Spot handles Transition-based Generalized Büchi Automata (TGBA), which, as the name suggests are Büchi automata with transition-based generalized acceptance conditions. TGBA allows for more compact representation of LTL properties [3], and can be checked for emptiness efficiently [2]. The TGBA is also an abstract C++ class, `tgba`, with an interface that allows on-the-fly exploration. Kripke structures are viewed as a subclass of `tgba` without acceptance sets.

The automata-theoretic approach is implemented by `neco-spot` as follows:

1. A wrapper of `net.so` and `checker.so` that presents the reachability graph of the model as a subclass of Spot's `kripke` class. The interface boils down to three functions: `get_init_state()` returns the initial state, `succ_iter(s)` returns an iterator on the successors of the state s, and `state_condition(s)` returns the valuation of the atomic propositions for the state s. Note that this interface allows an on-the-fly exploration of the state space, computing the results of `succ_iter(s)` and `state_condition(s)` on demand, by simply calling the relevant functions compiled in `net.so` and `checker.so`.

2. The LTL formula is simplified, converted into a TGBA, which is in turn also simplified. All these operations are functions offered by Spot [3].

3. The previous two automata are synchronized using the class `tgba_product` of Spot (another subclass of `tgba`). This synchronous product object is actually constructed in constant time, and delays its computation until it is actually explored.

4. The synchronous product is checked for emptiness using any of the emptiness check algorithms implemented by Spot [4]. It is this emptiness check procedure that will trigger the on-the-fly computation of the product, which will in turn construct the part of the reachability graph that need to be explored.

5. If the product was empty, a counterexample is computed and displayed.

The most important part of the work for building `neco-spot` therefore consisted in implementing the interface for Spot's `kripke` class; the rest is just chaining calls to various algorithms of Spot.

4 Possible Evolutions

There are a couple features of Spot that we do not use in `neco-spot`, and that will constitute some easy extensions.

A first one is the support of the linear fragment of the Property Specification Language [1] (PSL), a superset of LTL. Spot has built-in support for PSL, and all it would require is an extension of Neco's parser of formulas.

A second extension would be to support for weak fairness properties [5] in the model. Currently, `neco-spot` presents its model as an instance of the `kripke` class, which is just a TGBA without acceptance conditions, but it could present the model as a `fair_kripke` where states can be associated to acceptance sets representing weak fairness constraints.

We also plan to add reductions by symmetries [6] which have been already prototyped in Python, but are not available for LTL model checking yet. This would improve both exploration times and state-space sizes, leading to smaller product automata when performing model checking with Spot.

Furthermore, in order to easily debug models, we would like to implement fast simulation within Neco. This would also allow to replay couterexamples provided by `neco-spot`.

5   Availability

Neco is free software. Documentation and installation instructions can be found at

$$\texttt{http://code.google.com/p/neco-net-compiler/.}$$

A test-suite is also supplied.

References

1. Property Specification Language Reference Manual v1.1. Accellera (June 2004), `http://www.eda.org/vfv/`
2. Couvreur, J.-M., Duret-Lutz, A., Poitrenaud, D.: On-the-fly emptiness checks for generalized büchi automata. In: Godefroid, P. (ed.) SPIN 2005. LNCS, vol. 3639, pp. 169–184. Springer, Heidelberg (2005)
3. Duret-Lutz, A.: LTL translation improvements in Spot. In: Proceedings of the 5th International Workshop on Verification and Evaluation of Computer and Communication Systems (VECoS 2011). Electronic Workshops in Computing, British Computer Society, Tunis (2011), `http://ewic.bcs.org/category/15853`
4. Duret-Lutz, A., Poitrenaud, D.: SPOT: An Extensible Model Checking Library using Transition-based Generalized Büchi Automata. In: Proceedings of the 12th IEEE/ACM International Symposium on Modeling, Analysis, and Simulation of Computer and Telecommunication Systems (MASCOTS 2004), pp. 76–83. IEEE Computer Society Press, Volendam (2004)
5. Francez, N.: Fairness. Springer (1986)
6. Fronc, Ł.: Effective marking equivalence checking in systems with dynamic process creation. In: Proceedings of the 14th International Workshop on Verification of Infinite-State Systems (Infinity 2012), Paris. EPTCS (August 2012)
7. Fronc, Ł., Pommereau, F.: Optimizing the compilation of Petri Nets models. In: Proceedings of the Second International Workshop on Scalable and Usable Model Checking for Petri Net and other Models of Concurrency (SUMO 2011), vol. 726. CEUR (2011)
8. Fronc, Ł., Pommereau, F.: Building Petri Nets tools around Neco compiler. In: Proceedings of the International Workshop on Petri Nets and Software Engineering (PNSE 2013), Milano, vol. 989. CEUR (June 2013)
9. Hillah, L., Kindler, E., Kordon, F., Petrucci, L., Trèves, N.: A primer on the Petri Net Markup Language and ISO/IEC 15909-2. In: Proceedings of the 10th International workshop on Practical Use of Colored Petri Nets and the CPN Tools, CPN 2009 (October 2009)
10. Kordon, F., et al.: Raw Report on the Model Checking Contest at Petri Nets 2012. CoRR abs/1209.2382 (2012)
11. Pommereau, F.: Algebras of coloured Petri Nets. LAP LAMBERT Academic Publishing (2010)
12. Pommereau, F.: Quickly prototyping Petri Nets tools with SNAKES. Petri Net Newsletter (October 2008)

Solving Parity Games on the GPU*

Philipp Hoffmann and Michael Luttenberger

Institut für Informatik, Technische Universität München
{hoffmaph,luttenbe}@model.in.tum.de

Abstract. We present our GPU-based implementations of three well-known algorithms for solving parity games. Our implementations are in general faster by a factor of at least two than the corresponding implementations found in the widely known PGSolver collection of solvers. For benchmarking we use several of PGSolver's benchmarks as well as arenas obtained by means of the reduction of the language inclusion problem of nondeterministic Büchi automata to parity games with only three colors [3]. The benchmark suite of http://languageinclusion.org/CONCUR2011 was used in the latter case.

1 Introduction

The term "graphics processing units", short GPUs, was introduced in 1999 by Nvidia when they included hardware on the graphics chip specialized for processing triangles and lighting computations. In the last years, GPUs have constantly gained both computational power and versatility. In particular, GPUs excel at "embarrassingly parallel problems" which can be easily split into a large number of mostly independent parallel tasks, e.g. matrix-vector multiplication. Today, the fastest supercomputers combine both traditional multi-core processors and graphics processing units. Accordingly, there has been an ever growing amount of research on how to take advantage of the computational power of GPUs in general-purpose computing. Recently, Barnat et al. [1] have shown how to take advantage of GPUs in LTL model checking.

In this paper we present GPU-enabled implementations for solving parity games. Solving these games is a problem of great interest because if its applications in model checking as well as synthesis. The algorithms we use are the small-progress-measure (SPM) algorithm by Jurdzinski [5], the recursive algorithm due to Zielonka [9] and a variant of the strategy iteration (SI) algorithms of [2,7,8] described in [6]. We use the GPU for solving, roughly spoken, weighted min-max systems underlying all three algorithms. To our best knowledge, solving parity games using the GPU was not previously studied in literature.

We implemented all three algorithms using the Nvidia specific CUDA tool kit. Implementations using the vendor independent OpenCL framework will be

---

* This work was partially founded by the DFG project "Polynomial Systems on Semirings: Foundations, Algorithms, Applications" and by the DFG Graduiertenkolleg 1480 (PUMA).

D. Van Hung and M. Ogawa (Eds.): ATVA 2013, LNCS 8172, pp. 455–459, 2013.

released at a later point of time; so far we only have a first OpenCL-version of the SI-algorithm. While the CUDA-based implementations make better use of our hardware (but can only be run on Nvidia GPUs) and thus gives a better impression of the attainable speed-up, the advantage of OpenCL, besides being vendor independent, is that it can be executed both on GPUs and also on multi-core CPUs commonly used in todays desktop PCs. This allows us to assess the speedup obtained by moving from the CPU to the GPU.

Furthermore we compare our current implementation to the PGSolver by Friedmann and Lange [4] in order to assess its absolute speed. PGSolver has been in development for several years, therefore we deem it a reasonable choice for evaluating the speed of our own implementation. As benchmarks we use randomly generated arenas, arenas generated from LTL verification, and arenas obtained via the reduction by Etessami et. al. [3] of the language inclusion problem of nondeterministic Büchi automata to parity games.

The current implementations and benchmarks are available at www.model.in.tum.de/tools/gpupg.

2   GPU-Specific Implementation

Due to the page limit, we have to assume that the reader is familiar with parity games and cannot discuss GPU programming in detail. For more informations on the algorithms we refer the reader to the respective articles [5,9,6]; for a general introduction to GPU programming, please see the respective material made available by the Khronos group or by hardware vendors like AMD, Intel, or Nvidia. Very roughly spoken, a modern GPU consists of several multi-processors which act independently of each other; each multi-processor itself processes a large number of "warps" of 32 threads in parallel; all threads of a warp execute the same instruction (or do nothing).

We give a very brief sketch of how we use the GPU: For storing the arena, we use separate arrays for storing attributes like owner, color, etc. The successors are stored similar to the Yale format used for sparse matrices. At the heart of all three algorithms lies the problem of computing the least or greatest solution of min-max systems (over different algebraic structures) which are directly derived from the graph structure underlying the arena (variables correspond to nodes, equations to edges). For instance, computing the usual attractor means to solve a min-max system where every variable takes only values in $\{0, 1\}$. In all three cases the min-max systems can be solved using standard fixed-point iteration. The basic idea common to all three implementations is to implement the fixed-point iteration on the GPU by assigning to each node a thread which re-evaluates its defining equation in each iteration. This approach is advantageous when a lot of variables need to be updated in every iteration, but unprofitable if only a few updates are required. For this reason, we have also experimented with a worklist implementation on the GPU based on the stream compaction methods of the thrust library; but in out experiments the added cost for handling the worklist outranges the benefit of processing less nodes.

3   Evaluation

We have benchmarked our current implementation on several instances of parity games and compared the results to PGSolver (Version 3.3, released January, 19th, 2013). All tests have been run on an Intel Core i7-3820 Processor, currently 280 €, with 16 GB of RAM and a Nvidia GTX660, currently 180 €, with 2 GB of RAM running Windows 7 64bit. To exclude device startup times from our benchmarks, we ran all GPU benchmarks four times, discarded the first and took the average of the remaining three runs.

We apply the following preprocessing steps to the arena before solving them or handing them to PGSolver: We order the nodes in a topological ordering using Tarjan's SCC algorithm as a heuristic to optimize memory access on the GPU. For each of the two players we remove all nodes which the player can win by visiting only nodes controlled by him. For each SCC we further "compact" colors in the obvious way, e.g. if no node uses the color 5, but the colors 4 and 6 are used, we reduce all colors greater than 5 by 2.

We implemented the SI algorithm both in the Nvidia specific CUDA framework and in the vendor independent OpenCL framework. The code is the same up to those changes necessiated by the frameworks. As the CUDA version outperformed the OpenCL version in all benchmarks, we implemented the SPM and the recursive algorithm using only the CUDA framework. For comparison, we ran PGSolver using the solvers corresponding to the SI, the SPM and the recursive algorithm.[1] PGSolver includes lots of (polynomial-time) optimizations and preprocessing steps that already solve parts or in some cases all of the parity game (in these cases all three solvers have nearly identical solving times) before the actual solver is applied. For comparison we also ran the recursive algorithm with disabled preprocessing/optimizations, labelled as "PG Rec (pure)".

To get a rough estimate of the behaviour of the implementation in general we used 100 randomly generated arenas of each of the following types: *Steady random arenas* have 500,000 nodes, 16 colors and in- and outdegree between 2 and 32. *Clustered random arenas* also have 500,000 nodes and 16 colors.[2] Using a timeout of one minute, every solver either solved all arenas (Figure 1 lists the average solving times) or none (denoted by a ∗). For more practical benchmarks, we used the reduction by Etessami et al. [3] of the language inclusion problem of nondeterministic Büchi automata (NBA) – which is at the heart of automata theoretical approach for LTL model checking – to parity games and used the NBAs found on http://languageinclusion.org/CONCUR2011 for benchmarking. These arenas use three colors and their number of nodes ranges between 40,000 and 1,100,000. The benchmark results are summarized in Figure 1. Also included in this table are two instances of PGSolver's elevator (LTL) verification game.

The speedup obtained by our implementations is in most cases quite noticeable: The SI algorithm is faster by a factor 1.5-4 when compared to PGSolver's recursive algorithm (note that PGSolver's SI and SPM had multiple timeouts

---

[1] The parameters for PGSolver are -global {optstratimprov, smallprog, recursive}.

[2] Additional parameters: 2 32 4 4 4 10 20. PGSolver manual offers more information.

	SI				SPM		recursive		
	cuda	ocl (CPU)	ocl (GPU)	PG	cuda	PG	cuda	PG	PG (pure)
clustered	5.84	5.81	5.87	*	*	*	2.31	18.62	18.54
steady	5.40	8.11	5.58	*	*	*	4.12	21.69	32.93
ele_6.txt	0.73	1.85	1.61	0.95	12.03	0.95	0.10	2.00	0.95
ele_7.txt	7.60	20.29	8.63	10.83	559.09	10.81	0.85	16.38	10.81
bakery.fs.pg	0.43	1.11	0.62	2.54	26.55	1.40	0.24	2.95	0.84
bakeryV2.fs.pg	0.22	0.81	0.37	0.69	14.61	0.70	0.13	1.53	0.47
fischer.fs.pg	0.90	1.73	0.96	> 30 min	> 30 min	10.12	0.97	8.24	7.41
fischerV3.fs.pg	0.80	1.70	0.89	2.28	89.19	2.28	0.61	9.22	2.28
fischerV4.fs.pg	0.07	0.62	0.19	0.09	1.77	0.09	0.04	0.44	0.09
mcs.fs.pg	1.02	1.78	1.15	2.84	134.173	2.87	0.62	13.73	2.84
fischerV5.fs.pg	2.59	6.41	2.94	3.56	> 30 min	3.56	0.96	6.63	3.56
philsV4.fs.pg	0.02	0.56	0.06	0.03	2.22	0.03	0.02	0.11	0.03

Fig. 1. Benchmark results. All times in seconds if not stated otherwise.

on arenas which our implementation did solve), the recursive algorithm in some cases reaches a speedup factor of 10. Although the SPM algorithm has the best worst-case upper bound, it performed worst in all of our experiments.

Regarding the question of the advantage of the GPU, in most of our benchmarks the OpenCL version of the SI algorithm performed perceivably better on the GPU than on the quad-core CPU (all cores were used). Future optimizations are certainly possible; an experimental version of our SPM solver containing a better preprocessing including SCC-decomposition on the GPU yielded drastically improved times: for instance, the language inclusion problem "mcs" can now be solved in 7 seconds instead of 134 seconds.

References

1. Barnat, J., Bauch, P., Brim, L., Ceska, M.: Designing fast ltl model checking algorithms for many-core gpus. J. Parallel Distrib. Comput. 72(9), 1083–1097 (2012)
2. Björklund, H., Sandberg, S., Vorobyov, S.: A combinatorial strongly subexponential strategy improvement algorithm for mean payoff games. In: Fiala, J., Koubek, V., Kratochvíl, J. (eds.) MFCS 2004. LNCS, vol. 3153, pp. 673–685. Springer, Heidelberg (2004)
3. Etessami, K., Wilke, T., Schuller, R.A.: Fair simulation relations, parity games, and state space reduction for büchi automata. In: Orejas, F., Spirakis, P.G., van Leeuwen, J. (eds.) ICALP 2001. LNCS, vol. 2076, pp. 694–707. Springer, Heidelberg (2001)
4. Friedmann, O., Lange, M.: The PGSolver collection of parity game solvers. University of Munich (2009), http://www2.tcs.ifi.lmu.de/pgsolver/
5. Jurdziński, M.: Small progress measures for solving parity games. In: Reichel, H., Tison, S. (eds.) STACS 2000. LNCS, vol. 1770, pp. 290–301. Springer, Heidelberg (2000)
6. Luttenberger, M.: Strategy iteration using non-deterministic strategies for solving parity games. Tech. rep., Technische Universität München, Institut für Informatik (April 2008)

7. Schewe, S.: An optimal strategy improvement algorithm for solving parity and payoff games. In: Kaminski, M., Martini, S. (eds.) CSL 2008. LNCS, vol. 5213, pp. 369–384. Springer, Heidelberg (2008)
8. Vöge, J., Jurdziński, M.: A discrete strategy improvement algorithm for solving parity games (Extended abstract). In: Emerson, E.A., Sistla, A.P. (eds.) CAV 2000. LNCS, vol. 1855, Springer, Heidelberg (2000)
9. Zielonka, W.: Infinite games on finitely coloured graphs with applications to automata on infinite trees. Theor. Comput. Sci. 200(1-2), 135–183 (1998)

PYECDAR: Towards Open Source Implementation for Timed Systems

Axel Legay and Louis-Marie Traonouez

INRIA Rennes, France
`firstname.lastname@irisa.fr`

Abstract. PYECDAR is an open source implementation for reasoning on timed systems. PYECDAR's main objective is not efficiency, but rather flexibility to test and implement new results on timed systems.

1 Context

To solve complex problems such as scheduling tasks in embedded applications, the ability to reason on real time is mandatory. It is thus not a surprise that, over the last twenty years, the rigorous design of real-time systems has become a main research topic. Among major successes in the area, one finds the UPPAAL toolset [1] that is promoted by industries, and that has been used to verify complex properties of complex protocols such as the Herschel-Planck, the root contention protocol, or Audio-Control Protocol developed by Philips. Recently, timed tools have been extended to reason not only on the properties of the system, but also on the effects of its interactions with a potentially unknown environment. Tools such as UPPAAL-TIGA do this via game-theory [2]. The code of UPPAAL and related toolsets is not available and their interfaces are fixed in stone. Those choices shall not been seen as drawbacks, but rather as strategic choices for an industrial dissemination. However, from a scientific point of view, this makes it hard for researchers to reuse part of those toolsets to quickly implement and evaluate their new results without sharing them with tool makers.

We present PYECDAR (https://project.inria.fr/pyecdar/) that is a new python implementation of well-known results on timed systems and games. We then show that the tool can be used to implement new results in timed systems. Our main objective with PYECDAR is to offer an open source platform to quickly test new results on timed systems. Of course, this implementation is not as competitive as well-established toolsets, but it is very flexibility and easy to use and extend.

2 The PYECDAR Toolset in a Nutshell

As a foundation to develop new algorithms, PYECDAR offers an implementation of the reachability analysis for timed automata as well as an implementation of the forward algorithm from [2] that is used to solve reachability problem for timed games. Then, the tool offers the implementation of a series of brand new results on timed systems. The first is the timed specification theory from [3] that has been developed to reason on complex systems described as a combination of components. The specifications of

D. Van Hung and M. Ogawa (Eds.): ATVA 2013, LNCS 8172, pp. 460–463, 2013.

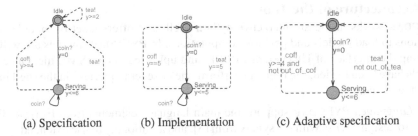

(a) Specification   (b) Implementation   (c) Adaptive specification

Fig. 1. Specifications of timed systems

those components are given by Timed Input/Output Automata (TIOA), where inputs represent behaviors of the environment, and outputs those of the system. The tool is able to 1. decide whether an implementation (e.g. Fig. 1b) conforms to a given specification (e.g. Fig. 1a), decide whether a specification can be implemented (consistency), 3. compare specifications (refinement – timed game), 4. logically/structurally compose two specifications, 5. synthesize a specification from a set of requirements (quotient), and 6. prune states from which the environment has no strategy to avoid bad behaviors (compatibility) – the operation requires the implementation of a timed game. The theory has also been implemented in ECDAR [4]. An advantage of PYECDAR is that its internal data structures can be used to save (and reuse) the result of composing/synthesizing specifications, while the one of ECDAR cannot. Also, PYECDAR can perform compatibility on combined systems while ECDAR cannot.

PYECDAR also offers the implementation of an extension of [5] to decide whether an implementation automaton is robust: i.e. if it remains conform to a specification when its output guards (resp. input) are exceeded (resp. restricted) by some Δ value. The tool can also synthesize the maximal Δ for which the implementation remains robust. The results extend to all the operations of the theory [6]. As an example, implementation of Fig. 1b is robust with respect to specification of Fig. 1a up to $\Delta = 1$. Beyond that point, the perturbations of the output transitions, which is $5 - \Delta \leq y \leq 5 + \Delta$, exceeds the guard $y \geq 4$ and the invariant $y \leq 6$ of the specification. It is worth mentioning that the internal structure of ECDAR does not permit to implement robustness on top of the specification theory. So, albeit the work in [6] is an extension of the one in [3], using ECDAR would require an entirely new implementation. Several robustness theories for timed automata have been implemented in tools such as shrinktech [7], but PYECDAR is the first to offer this feature for a complete specification theory.

Finally, PYECDAR offers the ability to reason on variability [8]. There, the model is an extended timed automata that permits to represent features of both the system and its environment – such features may appear or disappear at runtime. As an example, Fig. 1c represents a specification of the system using two adaptive features for the environment (out_of_tea and out_of_cof). These features may be enabled or disabled at runtime during input transitions, which may restrict the possible behaviors of the system. PYECDAR exploits an extension of timed game algorithms to synthesize e.g., the minimal set of features that are needed by a system so that it verifies a timed CTL property, whatever the environment does. To the best of our knowledge, PYECDAR is the first to offer a timed implementation of such a complex problem in software engineering.

3   Architecture of the Tool

PYECDAR works inside an interactive python shell, and offers a set of modules and fonctions to load models and perform computations. In PYECDAR, models are written by using the interface of UPPAAL or ECDAR, and uploaded via an XML file. Once the models have been loaded, the user can perform one or several queries via the shell in an on-demand manner.

Input Language. PYECDAR supports the main language elements from ECDAR. That allows to design TIOAs with the syntax from [3], and additionaly to use extended syntax elements, like constants and integer variables. See https://project.inria.fr/pyecdar/ for the grammar. TIOAs are specified with the ECDAR interface that is freely available, and then saved in XML. In case of features, Boolean variables are added to the model to witness the presence or absence of each feature. For the internal representation, PYECDAR relies on the UPPAAL DBMs library used to represent the timing constraints of the model and a classical graph-based structure to represent its syntax. Contrary to ECDAR, PYECDAR creates a dedicated structure for each component, including those that are obtained by combining existing ones. ECDAR is rigid and can only represent a new component by a pointer on states of the structures of those that participated to its creation. As a consequence, ECDAR cannot perform composability that consists in removing "bad states". Indeed, since new components do not have their own structure, this operation would eventually remove states of individual components that participated to its creation and hence falsify the design. If features are present, then PYECDAR combines BDDs used to logically represent sets of features on transitions with DBMs (see [8] for details). Finally, PYECDAR also uses polyhedra, with bindings to the Parma Polyhedra Library, to encode parametric constraints in case the user wants to solve a robustness problem.

Queries. PYECDAR offers two types of queries. The first one comes as a set of operators such as composition or quotient to build complex systems from small ones. The second type concerns operational queries such as the one of checking consistency, refinement, robustness, or properties of adaptive systems (see https://project.inria.fr/pyecdar/ for the complete list of queries). Depending on the problem to be solved, PYECDAR outputs different kinds of results. As an example, if the tool is used to synthesize the set of features that allows to satisfy some temporal formula, this set is output as a binary expression. The tool can also be used to determine the winning states for a timed game, which allows to determine if the consistency, compatibility or refinement problems have been solved. Finally, using a counter-example refinement approach (CEGAR), it can compute the maximum perturbation allowed by the system to solve a robustness problem. PYECDAR offers some extra features such as saving TIOAs into a new XML file so that they can be reused in other designs.

Algorithms. 1. PYECDAR implements the on-the-fly safety game algorithm from [2] that is used e.g. to check consistency and refinement. The tool also uses a model transformation to reduce robust consistency/compatibility to consistency/compatibility and hence reuse the former algorithm. 2. The CEGAR algorithm is a parametric extension of the first [9] that allows to compute the maximal delta for which an implementation remains robust. 3. The last algorithms are backward propagation game algorithms [8] that compute the set of features that satisfies a formula for an adaptive system.

4   PYECDAR in Action

We quickly demonstrate how to use PYECDAR. Assume that the models presented in Fig. 1 are saved in an XML file `machine.xml`. We first load the XML file of the first two TIOAs:

```
In [1]: W = pyecdar.loadModel("machine.xml")
In [2]: MS = W.getSpecification("MachineSpec")
In [3]: MI = W.getSpecification("MachineImpl")
```

We check if the implementation of Fig. 1b satisfies the specification in Fig. 1a:

```
In [4]: MI <= MS
Out[4]: True
```

We can then compute the maximum perturbation allowed by the implementation. This applies the CEGAR approach, starting with value 5, and with a confidence 0.1 for the result. The result is computed after 2 iterations and $\Delta = 1$ is returned.

```
In [5]: MI.maxRobSat(MS,5,0.1)
INFO:CEGAR: New game with value 5
INFO:REACH:2 states visited.
INFO:CEGAR: ...game is lost; refining...
INFO:CEGAR: ...refinement result: max=1 min=0 strict: False
INFO:CEGAR: New game with value 1
INFO:REACH:6 states visited.
INFO:CEGAR: ...game is won;
INFO:CEGAR: ...refinement result: max=1 min=1 strict: False
Out[5]: 1.0
```

Other examples, e.g. checking a temporal formula on the adaptive specification of Fig. 1c, are described on https://project.inria.fr/pyecdar/

References

1. Behrmann, G., David, A., Larsen, K.G., Pettersson, P., Yi, W.: Developing uppaal over 15 years. Softw., Pract. Exper. 41, 133–142 (2011)
2. Behrmann, G., Cougnard, A., David, A., Fleury, E., Larsen, K.G., Lime, D.: UPPAAL-tiga: Time for playing games! In: Damm, W., Hermanns, H. (eds.) CAV 2007. LNCS, vol. 4590, pp. 121–125. Springer, Heidelberg (2007)
3. David, A., Larsen, K.G., Legay, A., Nyman, U., Wasowski, A.: Timed i/o automata: a complete specification theory for real-time systems. In: HSCC, pp. 91–100. ACM (2010)
4. David, A., Larsen, K.G., Legay, A., Nyman, U., Wąsowski, A.: ECDAR: An environment for compositional design and analysis of real time systems. In: Bouajjani, A., Chin, W.-N. (eds.) ATVA 2010. LNCS, vol. 6252, pp. 365–370. Springer, Heidelberg (2010)
5. Chatterjee, K., Prabhu, V.S.: Synthesis of memory-efficient "real-time" controllers for safety objectives. In: HSCC, pp. 221–230. ACM (2011)
6. Larsen, K.G., Legay, A., Traonouez, L.-M., Wąsowski, A.: Robust specification of real time components. In: Fahrenberg, U., Tripakis, S. (eds.) FORMATS 2011. LNCS, vol. 6919, pp. 129–144. Springer, Heidelberg (2011)
7. Bouyer, P., Markey, N., Sankur, O.: Robust reachability in timed automata: A game-based approach. In: Czumaj, A., Mehlhorn, K., Pitts, A., Wattenhofer, R. (eds.) ICALP 2012, Part II. LNCS, vol. 7392, pp. 128–140. Springer, Heidelberg (2012)
8. Cordy, M., Legay, A., Schobbens, P.Y., Traonouez, L.M.: A framework for the rigorous design of highly adaptive timed systems. In: Proc. FormaliSE, pp. 64–70. IEEE (2013)
9. Traonouez, L.-M.: A parametric counterexample refinement approach for robust timed specifications. In: FIT. EPTCS, vol. 87, pp. 17–33 (2012)

CCMC: A Conditional CSL Model Checker
for Continuous-Time Markov Chains

Yang Gao[1], Ernst Moritz Hahn[1,2], Naijun Zhan[1], and Lijun Zhang[1,3,4]

[1] State Key Lab. of Comp. Sci., Institute of Software, Chinese Academy of Sciences, China
[2] University of Oxford, United Kingdom
[3] Technical University of Denmark, DTU Compute, Denmark
[4] Saarland University — Computer Science, Germany

Abstract. We present CCMC (Conditional CSL Model Checker), a model checker for continuous-time Markov chains (CTMCs) with respect to properties specified in continuous-time stochastic logic (CSL). Existing CTMC model checkers such as PRISM or MRMC handle only binary CSL until path formulas. CCMC is the first tool that supports algorithms for analyzing multiple until path formulas. Moreover, CCMC supports a recent extension of CSL – conditional CSL – which makes it possible to verify a larger class of properties on CTMC models. Our tool is based on our recent algorithmic advances for CSL, that construct a *stratified* CTMC before performing transient probability analyses. The stratified CTMC is a product obtained from the original CTMC and an automaton extracted from a given formula, aiming to filter out the irrelevant paths and make the computation more efficient.

1 Introduction

Continuous-time Markov chains (CTMCs) play an important role in performance evaluation of networked, distributed and biological systems. The concept of formal verification for CTMCs was introduced by Aziz *et al.* [1]. In their seminal work, continuous-time stochastic logic (CSL) was defined to specify properties of CTMCs. They showed that the model checking problem of CSL over CTMCs, i.e., whether a CTMC satisfies a given CSL property, is decidable. The approach has not yet been implemented, due to the high theoretical complexity. Later, efficient approximation algorithms have been studied by Baier *et al.* [2]. Based on this, several tools have been developed to support CSL model checking, such as PRISM [3] and MRMC [4]. Both of them can only deal with CSL properties with binary until path formulas.

Recently, we have extended the approximation algorithm in [2] to deal with multiple until path formulas [5]. The main idea is to exploit the notion of *stratified* CTMCs, which is a subclass of CTMCs that has the nice feature of allowing one to obtain the desired probability using a sequence of transient probability analyses. First, a deterministic finite automaton (DFA) is constructed for the formula being considered. Then, the product of the CTMC and the DFA is constructed, which is stratified by construction. This product CTMC can then be analyzed efficiently, using standard numerical methods for CTMCs.

D. Van Hung and M. Ogawa (Eds.): ATVA 2013, LNCS 8172, pp. 464–468, 2013.
© Springer International Publishing Switzerland 2013

Moreover, we have proposed an extension of CSL with conditional probabilistic operators [6], and in addition, we allow disjunction and conjunction of path formulas. With conditional CSL, one can for instance formulate the following property: *"The probability is at least* 0.1 *that in the interval* $[10, 20)$ *the number of proteins becomes more than* 5 *and the gene becomes inactive, under the condition that the proteins have increasingly accumulated from* 0 *to k within the same time interval"*, as $\mathcal{P}_{\geq 0.1}(true\ U_{[10,20)}$ $f \wedge g\ |\ f_1\ U_{[10,20)}\ f_2\ U_{[10,20)}\ \cdots f_k)$ where $f, g, f_1, \dots, f_k$ are appropriate atomic propositions.

In this paper, we present the probabilistic model checker **CCMC**, which is based on the recent work in [5,6,7], and supports the multiple until and conditional probabilistic formulas. These formulas allow one to express a richer class of properties for CTMCs, and thus we consider our tool an important complementation of **PRISM** [3] and **MRMC** [4].

2 Logic and Tool Architecture

The syntax of Conditional CSL (CCSL) is given by the following grammar:

$$\Phi := f\ |\ \neg\Phi\ |\ \Phi \wedge \Phi\ |\ \mathcal{P}_{\bowtie p}(\varphi)\ |\ \mathcal{P}_{\bowtie p}(\varphi\ |\ \varphi),\quad \varphi := \varphi \wedge \varphi\ |\ \varphi \vee \varphi\ |\ \Phi_1 U_{I_1} \Phi_2 U_{I_2} \cdots U_{I_{K-1}} \Phi_K$$

where f is an atomic proposition, I_i are non-empty left-closed and right-open intervals on $\mathbb{R}_{\geq 0}$, $\bowtie\ \in \{<, \leq, \geq, >\}$, $0 \leq p \leq 1$, $K > 1$. Φ is called a *state formula*, while φ is called a *path formula*. In particular, **CCMC** supports multiple until path formulas, in contrast to existing model checkers (e.g. [3,4]) which are restricted to binary ones, i.e., $K = 2$.

For the sake of efficiency, **CCMC** was implemented in C/C++ and consists of approximately 5000 lines of code. It has been applied on a number of relevant case studies from diverse areas (performance evaluation, biological models, etc.). **CCMC** is available for Linux with libc6 and GNU Scientific Library 1.15, and is distributed under the GNU General Public License (GPL) Version 3. The binary code, source code and case studies can be downloaded from:

```
http://lcs.ios.ac.cn/~gaoy/CCMC/homepage.xhtml.
```

The architecture and components of **CCMC** are depicted in Fig. 1. The inputs of **CCMC** include the model description files and the property file. The model description files can be written manually or generated by **PRISM**, including a state file and a transition matrix file. They will be loaded, where we use explicit sparse matrix representations. The property file keeps the CCSL properties of interest.

The preprocessing component constructs the stratified CTMC, which is a product obtained from the original

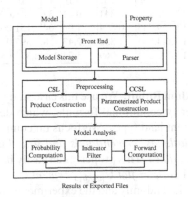

Fig. 1. CCMC Architecture

CTMC and an automaton extracted from the given formula [5]. For CCSL conjunctive path formulas, we need an extended product construction which also takes sub path formulas into account [6].

By the preprocessing procedure, the paths which are irrelevant to the given properties are filtered out and the model analysis component will carry out a forward transient probability computation. The verification results and other information can be visualized or exported into a file.

3 Experiments

In this section, we conduct experiments on some CTMC benchmarks from the PRISM webpage (http://www.prismmodelchecker.org/) and other publications [8]. All experiments were performed on a Linux (Ubuntu 12.10) machine with an Intel(R) Core(TM) i7-2600 processor at 3.40GHz equipped with 3 GB of RAM. Due to space constraints, detailed information about the cases and comparison with MRMC are provided on the CCMC webpage.

PRISM Benchmark Suite. Firstly, we compare our model checker CCMC with PRISM (sparse matrix engine) on verifying benchmark CTMC models. Here we use three models which can be found on the PRISM homepage. The first one is a *cyclic server polling system* [9], the second one is a *workstation cluster* [10], and the third one is an *embedded control system* [11]. We consider binary CSL until formulas, which can also be handled by PRISM. Results and executing time (in seconds) are listed in Table 1. The meaning of parameter N is as on the PRISM homepage. Execution times of CCMC and PRISM for the analyses considered are almost equal.

Table 1. Comparism with PRISM. N and *MAX* are model parameters influencing the number of states.

Polling				Cluster				Embedded			
N	states	PRISM	CCMC	N	states	PRISM	CCMC	*MAX*	states	PRISM	CCMC
8	3,073	0.016	0.01	2	276	0.006	<0.01	5	6,013	0.319	0.16
9	6,913	0.047	0.03	4	820	0.011	<0.01	8	8,548	0.437	0.22
10	15,361	0.077	0.06	8	2,772	0.014	0.01	10	10,238	0.53	0.29
11	33,793	0.161	0.14	16	10,132	0.051	0.03	20	18,688	0.925	0.50
12	73,729	0.341	0.41	32	38,676	0.166	0.11	50	44,038	2.715	1.14
13	159,745	0.804	1.04	64	151,060	0.639	0.45	100	86,288	4.285	2.73
14	344,065	1.853	2.43	128	597,012	2.871	3.09	200	170,788	8.535	6.00
15	737,281	4.069	5.73	256	2,373,652	12.345	19.53	500	424,288	21.649	20.46

Random Robot. We use this case study (revised from [8]) to show the ability of CCMC to verify conditional formula, which describe a robot on a grid with $N \times N$ cells of different land types. We focus on computing the probability that *the robot goes across the flatlands, cementlands and grasslands under the condition that it will get stuck within time t*. This property can easily be expressed by a CCSL formula, that is, $\mathcal{P}_{=?}(\varphi \mid \psi)$ where $\varphi = $ *flat* $U_{[a_1,b_1)}$ *cement* $U_{[a_2,b_2)}$ *grass* and $\psi = $ *true* $U_{[0,t)}$ *trap*. We generate the grid randomly and the experimental results are listed in the left part of Table 2, where $a_1 = 1, a_2 = 1.5, b_1 = 2, b_2 = 3$ and $t = 10$.

Cyclic Server Polling System. We reconsider the Cyclic Server Polling System (CSP) [9] and the CSL property: *what is the probability of finding all the queues full in the whole round when the server serves them within T seconds*, which can be expressed using a multiple until formula: $\mathcal{P}_{=?}(s = 1 \wedge s_1\ U_{[0,T)}\ s = 2 \wedge s_2\ U_{[0,T)} \cdots U_{[0,T)}\ s = k \wedge s_k)$, where $s = 1, \cdots, k$ means the server is at the i-th station, and $s_k = 1$ shows that the k-th station is full. The right part of Table 2 shows the results by fixing $T = 10$.

Table 2. Experimental results

	Random Robot							Cyclic Server Polling System					
N	Before Product		After Product		time(s)	result	N	Before Product		After Product		time(s)	result
	states	transitions	states	transitions				states	transitions	states	transitions		
70	4900	14463	4869	14373	0.07	0.02602991	7	1345	6273	993	3456	<0.01	0.01779250
100	10000	29513	9941	29399	0.14	0.00213756	8	3073	15873	2305	8960	0.02	0.00908245
120	14400	43094	14288	42761	0.22	0.00210038	9	6913	39169	5249	22528	0.03	0.00462759
150	22500	67288	22301	66707	0.39	0.00106487	10	15361	94721	11777	55296	0.11	0.00235415
200	40000	119397	39748	118656	0.98	0.00107120	11	33793	225281	26113	133120	0.33	0.00119605
300	90000	268560	89330	266591	2.42	0.00077518	12	73729	528385	57345	315392	1.22	0.00060700
350	122500	366852	121695	364570	3.36	0.01079894	13	159745	1224750	124929	737280	5.06	0.00030786

Table 2 gives the number of states and transitions of original CTMC and product CTMC for each model. From this table, we can conclude that the product construction decreases the size of CTMCs to be analyzed since it filters out the irrelevant paths w.r.t. the properties to be verified. For Random Robot, the size of product CTMC does not decrease so much, as this depends on the CCSL formula. However, the product construction makes the original CTMC stratified and we need just perform the transient probability analyses at each endpoint of the intervals which occur in the CCSL formula. Thus, the execution time only depends on the size of product CTMC and the number of endpoints.

Remark 1. More recently, Donatelli *et al.* [12] have extended CSL such that path properties can be expressed via a deterministic timed automaton (DTA) with a single clock. Chen *et al.* [8,13] take this approach further and consider DTA specifications with multiple clocks as well. In the Cyclic Server Polling System case study, we compare our approach with the DTA based approach. In [8], a DTA is used to specify the property: *What is the probability that after consulting all queues for one round, the server serves each queue one after the other within T time units?* This property can be separated into two phases and formulated by multiple until formulas. (We remark that DTAs are in general more expressive than CSL specifications.) At each phase, we construct the corresponding product CTMC which reduces the computation work a lot. As a result, we can handle larger models, and the running time is considerably improved.

4   Concluding Remarks

In this work, we have introduced CCMC, a probabilistic model checker for CTMC models. Its effectiveness and efficiency have been demonstrated through the successful analysis of several case studies. As future work, we will extend this work to Continuous-Time Markov Decision Process (CTMDP) models which can model and analyze the systems with both probabilistic and nondeterministic behaviors. We also want to explore the possibility to use symbolic data structures, such as MTBDDs or the one of the PRISM hybrid engine.

Acknowledgement. The authors are supported by NSFC-91118007, NSFC-61061130541 and 2012ZX03039-004. Ernst Moritz Hahn is supported by Chinese Academy of Sciences fellowship for young international scientists, by ERC Advanced Grant VERIWARE. Lijun Zhang is supported IDEA4CPS, the VKR Center of Excellence MT-LAB, the EU FP7-ICT projects MEALS (295261), and the DFG Sonderforschungsbereich AVACS.

References

1. Aziz, A., Sanwal, K., Singhal, V., Brayton, R.: Model-checking continous-time Markov chains. ACM TCL 1(1), 162–170 (2000)
2. Baier, C., Haverkort, B.R., Hermanns, H., Katoen, J.P.: Model-checking algorithms for continuous-time Markov chains. IEEE TSE 29(6), 524–541 (2003)
3. Hinton, A., Kwiatkowska, M., Norman, G., Parker, D.: PRISM: A tool for automatic verification of probabilistic systems. In: Hermanns, H., Palsberg, J. (eds.) TACAS 2006. LNCS, vol. 3920, pp. 441–444. Springer, Heidelberg (2006)
4. Katoen, J.P., Zapreev, I.S., Hahn, E.M., Hermanns, H., Jansen, D.N.: The ins and outs of the probabilistic model checker MRMC. PEVA 68(2), 90–104 (2011)
5. Zhang, L., Jansen, D.N., Nielson, F., Hermanns, H.: Efficient CSL model checking using stratification. LMCS 8(2:17), 1–18 (2012)
6. Gao, Y., Xu, M., Zhan, N., Zhang, L.: Model checking conditional CSL for continuous-time Markov chains. In: IPL, pp. 44–50 (2012)
7. Zhang, L., Jansen, D.N., Nielson, F., Hermanns, H.: Automata-based CSL model checking. In: Aceto, L., Henzinger, M., Sgall, J. (eds.) ICALP 2011, Part II. LNCS, vol. 6756, pp. 271–282. Springer, Heidelberg (2011)
8. Barbot, B., Chen, T., Han, T., Katoen, J.-P., Mereacre, A.: Efficient CTMC model checking of linear real-time objectives. In: Abdulla, P.A., Leino, K.R.M. (eds.) TACAS 2011. LNCS, vol. 6605, pp. 128–142. Springer, Heidelberg (2011)
9. Ibe, O., Trivedi, K.: Stochastic Petri net models of polling systems. IEEE JSAC 8(9), 1649–1657 (1990)
10. Haverkort, B., Hermanns, H., Katoen, J.P.: On the use of model checking techniques for dependability evaluation. In: SRDS, pp. 228–237 (October 2000)
11. Muppala, J., Ciardo, G., Trivedi, K.: Stochastic reward nets for reliability prediction. Communications in Reliability, Maintainability and Serviceability 1(2), 9–20 (1994)
12. Donatelli, S., Haddad, S., Sproston, J.: Model checking timed and stochastic properties with CSL^{TA}. IEEE TSE 35(2), 224–240 (2009)
13. Chen, T., Han, T., Katoen, J.-P., Mereacre, A.: Quantitative model checking of continuous-time Markov chains against timed automata specifications. In: LICS, pp. 309–318. IEEE Comp. Soc. (2009)

NLTOOLBOX: A Library for Reachability Computation of Nonlinear Dynamical Systems

Romain Testylier and Thao Dang

VERIMAG/CNRS, 2 Avenue de Vignate, 38610 Gières, France

Abstract. We describe NLTOOLBOX, a library of data structures and algorithms for reachability computation of nonlinear dynamical systems. It provides the users with an easy way to "program" their own analysis procedures or to solve other problems beyond verification. We illustrate the use of the library for the analysis of a biological model.

1 Introduction

Reachability analysis is a fundamental problem in model checking, program analysis, controller synthesis. This problem was initially motivated by the interest in extending model checking to hybrid systems (comprising both discrete and continuous dynamics). In addition, the behaviors of these systems are often non-deterministic due to various uncertainties which could be inherent or epistemic (such as unknown initial conditions, parameter values, multiple mode switchings). Reachability analysis involves computing the set of all possible trajectories under such uncertainties. There are numerous tools for reachable set computation, such as Checkmate [5], d/dt [1], MPT tool [11], level set toolbox [13] HySAT/iSAT [8], Ariadne [7], SpaceEx [9], Flow* [6]. Compared to the scalability of the existing techniques on linear systems, their scalability on nonlinear systems is much lower, not only because of their inherently higher complexity, but also because they often require sophisticated fine tuning of computation parameters (such as time steps, error tolerance), choice of set representations and exploration strategies. An automatic fine tuning can hardly be efficient for all types of systems, since it cannot include a-priori knowledge that the user possesses and a-posterior knowledge that he could gain from the analysis. It is thus important to provide the user with a possibility of "programming" the analysis process so that he can easily readjust the computation parameters or include exploration intention. For this reason, NLTOOLBOX[1] was designed as a $C++$ library providing an algorithmic infrastructure for reachability computation with which the user can write a simple $C++$ program to develop and explore different exploration strategies or to solve specific analysis problems. Two major functionalities of the library are: reachability analysis of polynomial systems (using the Bernstein expansion technique) and reachability analysis of general nonlinear systems (using hybridization). The latter can be applied directly to continuous-time systems while the former only to discrete-time systems and thus its use

---

[1] http://www-verimag.imag.fr/PEOPLE/Thao.Dang/nltoolboxlib

D. Van Hung and M. Ogawa (Eds.): ATVA 2013, LNCS 8172, pp. 469–473, 2013.

for continuous-time systems requires a system time-discretization. The rest of the paper is organized as follows. We first present the main data structures and algorithms and then illustrate the use of the library on a biological model.

2   Data Structures and Reachability Algorithms

Polytopes defined by constraints are the main set representation, which contains additional constructors for *template polyhedra, hyper-rectangles* and *hyper-octagons*. The library contains a number of set operations needed by reachability analysis, such as inclusion test, affine transformation, set splitting (used for refinement). In the following, we describe only two main reachability algorithms: one is based on hybridization [3] and the other on the Bernstein expansion [4]. The library also includes an algorithm specialized for multi-affine systems [14].

Reachability Algorithm Using the Bernstein Expansion. This algorithm computes the reachable set (represented by template polyhedra) of a discrete-time polynomial systems $x[k+1] = \pi(x[k])$ from an initial polyhedron $P \subset \mathbb{R}^n$. To handle continuous-time systems, the library offers a number of discretization methods. For a given template matrix T, we need to find a vector b such that the image $\pi(P)$ is included in the template polyhedron defined by $Tx \leq b$. To determine b, we formulate an polynomial optimization problems and replace it by a linear program (which can be solved more efficiently) by using affine bound functions. To compute affine bound functions for polynomials, the Bernstein expansion can be used. Indeed, an n-variate polynomial can be represented in the Bernstein basis functions and the coefficients of this representation allow capturing geometric properties of the polynomial and thus obtaining accurate function approximations. However, the Bernstein expansion is valid only inside the unit box $[0, 1]^n$, and to address this problem, we use two methods: (1) oriented-box approximation and (2) rewriting the polynomial using a change of variables. Furthermore, two methods for handling templates are used: the template can be *static* (the polyhedra share the same constant matrix T) or *dynamic* (the matrix T evolves according to a local approximation of the dynamics).

Reachability Algorithm Using Hybridization. The main idea of hybridization is to approximate a nonlinear system $\dot{x} = f(x)$ by a piecewise affine one. We compute an approximation domain (that contains the current reachable set) and an approximate vector field for that domain. When the system leaves the current approximation domain, a new domain is created. Our hybridization algorithm uses simplicial domains and piecewise affine approximate vector fields, which is motivated by many available methods for piecewise affine systems (see for instance [1,5,11,10,9]). In addition, we exploit the curvature of the vector field f to determine large domains with good error bound. To handle resulting piecewise affine systems, the library includes a basic reachability algorithm [1].

Programming an Analysis Procedure. These algorithms were successfully applied to many case studies (in particular a mitochondrial aging model with 9 variables and a model of ongiogenesis with 12 variables) and they were also evaluated using randomly generated systems, which shows that they can handle efficiently systems with up to 10 variables and are among the state-of-the-art computational methods for nonlinear systems (see [3,2]). The goal of this section is to demonstrate the usefulness of NLTOOLBOX by showing how to program with the library to solve a reachability problem. As a working example, we use the Laub-Loomis model [12] for spontaneous oscillations during the aggregation stage of Dictyostelium [12]: $\dot{x} = f(x)$, where the state variable $x = (x_0, \ldots, x_6)$ represents the concentrations of seven proteins, and the derivatives are $f_0 = k_1 x_2 - k_2 x_0$, $f_1 = k_3 x_4 - k_4 x_1$, $f_2 = k_5 x_6 - k_6 x_2 x_1$, $f_3 = k_7 - k_8 x_3 x_2$, $f_4 = k_9 x_0 - k_{10} x_3 x_4$, $f_5 = k_{11} x_0 - k_{12} x_5$, $f_6 = k_{13} x_5 - k_{14} x_6 x_1$. The model has 14 parameters $(k_1, \ldots, k_{14})$. The main steps of an analysis procedure using hybridization is shown in the following (pseudo) C++ program.

```
void Dictyostelium_hybridization() {
    1:    createOctagonalSet(n, r, c, T, b); Hpolyhedron I(n, T, b);
    2:    PointerSystem Sp(n, fp, df, hp);
    3:    ReachHybridization reachHyb(Sp, I, err, dt);
    4:    reachHybridization.reach(nbIter);
    5:    vector<Hpolyhedron> res=reachHyb.getReachabilityResult();
    6:    exporter.save(res, color);
}
```

In line 1 we define the octogonal initial set I, centered at c, with circumradius r. In line 2, we create a dynamical system Sp by specifying the pointers to the functions computing f, the Jacobian matrix of f and the Hessian matrix of f (used to define curvature). In line 3, an instance $reachHyb$ of the class $ReachHybridization$ is created with a desired error bound err and a time step dt. Then, the reachable set is computed for $nbIter$ iterations and stored in res. The final phase (line 6) involves saving the result in a matlab file for visualization

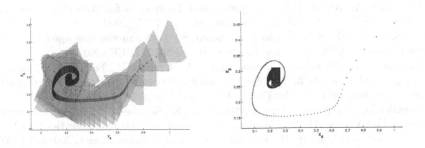

Fig. 1. The reachable sets computed by hybridization (left) and by the Bernstein technique (right). The grey areas in the left figure are the template projections of the hybridization domains.

purposes. It is possible to choose the templates for the viewing projection (by default the box templates are used). To use the Bernstein technique, an instance *reachBern* of the class *ReachPolynomial* can be created. Figure 1 shows the reachability results for the initial octagonal set with circumradius 0.0001 cented at $(1.2, 1.105, 1.5, 2.4, 1.0, 0.1, 0.45)$. For the hybridization method, the time step is 0.007 and the computation time for 4000 iterations is $346.43s$ (on a machine with 2.2 GHz Intel Core 2 Duo Processor). For the Berstein technique, the time step is 0.028, and the computation time for 1000 iterations is $283.46s$. The hybridization technique for this example is less time-efficient but more accurate when the reachable set converges towards the attraction basin.

3   Conclusion

The advantage of the library is twofold. On one hand, it provides the users with an easy way to "program" their own analysis procedures or to use reachability algorithms to solve other problems beyond verification. On the other hand, the library can also be used by other existing tools to increase their scope in terms of problems and methods. NLTOOLBOX is currently being integrated in SpaceEx [9], to extend the applicability of SpaceEx to nonlinear hybrid systems. Our future work includes using the library to for controller synthesis.

References

1. Asarin, E., Bournez, O., Dang, T., Maler, O.: Approximate reachability analysis of piecewise-linear dynamical systems. In: Lynch, N.A., Krogh, B.H. (eds.) HSCC 2000. LNCS, vol. 1790, pp. 20–31. Springer, Heidelberg (2000)
2. Dang, T., Le Guernic, C., Maler, O.: Computing reachable states for nonlinear biological models. Theoretical Computer Science 412(21), 2095–2107 (2011)
3. Dang, T., Testylier, R.: Hybridization domain construction using curvature estimation. In: HSCC 2011. LNCS, pp. 123–132 (2011)
4. Dang, T., Testylier, R.: Reachability analysis for polynomial dynamical systems using the Bernstein expansion. Reliable Computing Journal (2011) ISSN 1573-1340
5. Chutinan, A., Krogh, B.H.: Computational Techniques for Hybrid System Verification. IEEE Trans. on Automatic Control 48, 64–75 (2003)
6. Chen, X., Ábrahám, E., Sankaranarayanan, S.: Taylor model flowpipe construction for non-linear hybrid systems. In: Proc. RTSS 2012. IEEE (2012)
7. Benvenuti, L., Bresolin, D., Casagrande, A., Collins, P., Ferrari, A., Mazzi, E., Sangiovanni-Vincentelli, A., Villa, R.: Reachability computation for hybrid systems with Ariadne. In: Proc. the 17th IFAC World Congress (2008)
8. Fränzle, M., Herde, C., Teige, T., Ratschan, S., Schubert, T.: Efficient Solving of Large Non-Linear Arithmetic Constraint Systems with Complex Boolean Structure. J. on Satisfiability, Boolean Modeling, and Computation 1, 209–236 (2007)
9. Frehse, G., Le Guernic, C., Donzé, A., Cotton, S., Ray, R., Lebeltel, O., Ripado, R., Girard, A., Dang, T., Maler, O.: SpaceEx: Scalable verification of hybrid systems. In: Gopalakrishnan, G., Qadeer, S. (eds.) CAV 2011. LNCS, vol. 6806, pp. 379–395. Springer, Heidelberg (2011)

10. Kurzhanskiy, A., Varaiya, P.: Ellipsoidal Techniques for Reachability Analysis of Discrete-time Linear Systems. IEEE Trans. Automatic Control 52, 26–38 (2007)
11. Kvasnica, M., Grieder, P., Baotić, M., Morari, M.: Multi-Parametric Toolbox (MPT). In: Alur, R., Pappas, G.J. (eds.) HSCC 2004. LNCS, vol. 2993, pp. 448–462. Springer, Heidelberg (2004)
12. Laub, M.T., Loomis, W.F.: A Molecular Network That Produces Spontaneous Oscillations in Excitable Cells of Dictyostelium. Molecular Biology of the Cell 9, 3521–3532 (1998)
13. Mitchell, I.M., Templeton, J.A.: A Toolbox of Hamilton-Jacobi Solvers for Analysis of Nondeterministic Continuous and Hybrid Systems. In: Morari, M., Thiele, L. (eds.) HSCC 2005. LNCS, vol. 3414, pp. 480–494. Springer, Heidelberg (2005)
14. Testylier, R., Dang, T.: Analysis of Parametric Biological Models. In: Workshop on Hybrid Systems and Biology HSB 2012. Springer (2012)

CELL: A Compositional Verification Framework*

Kun Ji[1], Yang Liu[2], Shang-Wei Lin[1], Jun Sun[3], Jin Song Dong[1],
and Truong Khanh Nguyen[1]

[1] National University of Singapore
[2] Nanyang Technological University
[3] Singapore University of Technology and Design

Abstract. This paper presents CELL, a comprehensive and extensible framework for compositional verification of concurrent and real-time systems based on commonly used semantic models. For each semantic model, CELL offers three libraries, i.e., compositional verification paradigms, learning algorithms and model checking methods to support various state-of-the-art compositional verification approaches. With well-defined APIs, the framework could be applied to build customized model checkers. In addition, each library could be used independently for verification and program analysis purposes. We have built three model checkers with CELL. The experimental results show that the performance of these model checkers can offer similar or often better performance compared to the state-of-the-art verification tools.

1 Introduction

Compositional verification technique presents a promising way to alleviate *state explosion problem* associated with model checking via the "divide-and-conquer" strategy. In recent years, a number of approaches have been proposed to conduct compositional verification automatically which are categorized as *learning based assume-guarantee reasoning* (LAGR) [4], *symbolic learning based assume-guarantee reasoning* (SLAGR) [3], *assume-guarantee reasoning by abstraction refinement* (AGAR) [5] and *compositional abstraction refinement* (CAR) [2]. Furthermore, different compositional verification paradigms may work with different learning (or abstraction refinement) algorithms and model checking methods (e.g., symbolic model checking, explicit-state model checking). It is thus desirable to build a framework such that different approaches can be systematically experimented, compared or applied.

In this work, we propose a comprehensive and extensible framework named CELL, which contains various state-of-the-art compositional verification approaches for concurrent and real-time systems based on commonly used semantics models (i.e., *labeled transition system* (LTS) for concurrent systems and *timed transition system* (TTS) [6] for real-time systems). For each semantic model, CELL offers three libraries, i.e., compositional verification paradigms, learning algorithms and model checking methods. Various state-of-the-art compositional verification approaches can be constructed by

---

* This project is supported by project 'IDD11100102' from Singapore University of Technology and Design and by the NAP project in Nanyang Technological University.

D. Van Hung and M. Ogawa (Eds.): ATVA 2013, LNCS 8172, pp. 474–477, 2013.

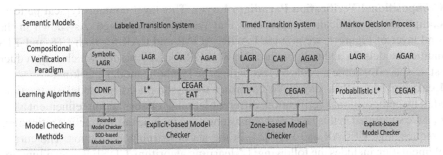

Fig. 1. Design of CELL

combining items from each library. For instance, the compositional verification approach proposed in [4] can be achieved by combining LAGR compositional verification paradigm, the L* learning algorithm and an explicit-based model checking method respectively from the three libraries designed for models whose semantics are LTSs. Currently, CELL provides seven compositional verification paradigms, seven learning algorithms, four model checking methods and ten ways of combinations to perform automatic compositional verifications. In addition, CELL can be extended in multiple ways, e.g., with new semantic models (e.g., Markov Decision Process), new compositional verification paradigms, learning algorithms or model checking methods. Figure 1 shows the overall architecture of CELL. Notice the light-color part shows how CELL can be (and is being) extended to support probabilistic systems.

To the best of our knowledge, CELL is the only stable and publicly available compositional verification framework. CELL is an open source project under LGPL v3 license in the format of dynamic linked library (DLL) with no GUI. We used PAT [7] framework's GUI to develop the three demonstrating model checkers. It is possible to build new model checkers using CELL to conduct the verification tasks.

2 CELL Architecture

CELL's architecture includes four layers. With the defined APIs from the semantic model layer, domain experts are allowed to easily manufacture model checkers with various compositional verification approaches to alleviate the state explosion problem. Furthermore, the APIs of the lower layers are well defined so that they can be used independently for various purposes.

Semantic Model Layer. In this layer, we support commonly used semantic models (i.e., LTS for concurrent systems and TTS for real-time systems). Any modelling language whose semantic model is LTS or TTS can be verified using our framework. In CELL, we assume for systems, which have LTS/TTS semantics, both the system and the property are represented in LTS/TTS[1]. The verification problem is thus reduced to check the language inclusive of the model and whether the model defines a language which is a subset of that of the property.

---

[1] For real-time system, we assume the property is determinizable.

Compositional Verification Paradigm Layer. This layer contains typical patterns of compositional verification approaches that we have categorized. As shown in the second layer of Figure 1, we provide LAGR, AGAR and CAR for both LTS and TTS semantics models. In addition, we provide SLAGR for LTS model, which may reduce the state space for some models by leveraging the symbolic model checking.

Learning Algorithm Layer. To construct the assumptions or model abstractions needed by compositional verification, different learning or abstraction refinement algorithms are supported in this layer. For consistency, we include the abstraction refinement techniques (e.g., CEGAR and EAT [2]) in the set of learning algorithms. The current implementation includes the following: L* learning algorithm, CDNF Boolean function learning algorithm, CEGAR and EAT techniques for concurrent systems, TL* learning algorithm and CEGAR for real-time systems. The basic idea of EAT [2] is to use evolutionary algorithm to generate abstractions, which can increase the probability of finding good abstractions.

Model Checking Method Layer. In this layer, we provide various model checking methods. We provide *explicit-state model checking* and *symbolic model checking* for LTS, and *zone-based model checking* for TTS. For symbolic model checking, we provide both SAT-based bounded model checking and BDD-based model checking.

Under each semantic model, compositional verification paradigms, learning algorithms and model checking methods can be mix-and-match to construct compositional verification approaches. Notice that not every combination is effective. The arrows in Fig. 1 show the relationship. Currently, CELL supports seven different verification approaches for LTS and three for TTS. All these combinations and their features are summarized in our website [1]. A technical report that explains more details about each component in CELL can be also found there.

3   Implementation and Evaluation

CELL is implemented on Microsoft .NET framework via $C\#$ language. Starting from 2011, the latest version 0.3 of CELL has 54K LOC. CELL is a stand-alone library in the format of DLL and can be used by calling its APIs.

To prove the capability of CELL framework, we developed three compositional model checkers adopting the GUI from PAT framework [7]. The model checkers include *CLTS* that is used to verify concurrent systems modelled by finite state machines, *CERA* to verify real-time systems modelled by *event-recording automata* (ERAs) and *CTA* to verify real-time systems modelled by *timed automata* (TAs). It is non-trivial to measure how easy to use CELL. However, we have built those model checkers within one month, which shows that our design is promising. The CELL DLL binary file together with the source code, complete APIs description document, user manual and three aforementioned model checkers are available in [1].

With CLTS and CEAR, we modelled a bunch of concurrent and real-time systems which include the *AIP manufacturing system*, *Dinner Philosopher problems* (DP) and various versions of *flexible manufacturing systems* (FMSs) that differ by complexities for both concurrent and real-time versions (FMS-4 is the most complex one). We did not compare with other model checkers such as NuSMV or Uppaal because of the different modelling languages and supported properties. In addition, it is unfair

Table 1. Running time (in seconds), the number of highest visited locations in all the verification rounds $|L|$, $|P|$ means number of processes and ROM means running out of memory

	LTS		Monolithic		AGAR		LAGR		CAR		SLAGR
Case	$|P|$	Valid?	$|L|$	Time	$|L|$	Time	$|L|$	Time	$|L|$	Time	Time
AIP	10	Yes	104,650	7.86	2,745	0.44	2,745	**0.29**	2,878	0.98	0.90
DP	30	Yes	ROM	ROM	20,824	11.95	20,824	7.03	1,500	**3.32**	11.19
FMS-3	11	Yes	312,064	12.77	1,920	0.11	1,260	**0.08**	20	0.17	0.12
FMS-4	14	Yes	ROM	ROM	24,744	6.93	26,320	2.61	530	0.22	**0.14**
	TTS		Monolithic		AGAR		LAGR		CAR		
FMS-1	6	Yes	212	0.13	36	0.02	36	**0.01**	36	0.02	
FMS-2	10	Yes	97,136	7.49	1,260	0.29	1,260	0.13	1,260	**0.02**	
FMS-3	11	Yes	312,064	23.39	1,920	0.35	1,528	**0.19**	3,936	1.42	
FMS-4	14	Yes	ROM	ROM	24,744	30.93	26,320	**5.13**	24,744	12.81	

to compare with these monolithic model checkers since CELL adopts compositional technique, and NuSMV and Uppaal may have advanced reduction techniques that are not available in CELL. Table 1 shows the verification results. For the concurrent systems, due to the limited space, we show results collected from subset of the verification approaches, which are CEGAR-based AGAR, L*-based LAGR, EAT-based CAR, CDNF-based (with BDD) SLAGR. It can be obversed that all the compositional verification approaches outperform the monolithic approach. CDNF-based SLAGR has better performance since it takes advantages of symbolic model checking. EAT-based CAR outperforms CEGAR-based CAR as EAT can find better abstractions [2]. For the real-time experiments, we show results from all the three approaches, which respectively are CEGAR-based AGAR, TL*-based LAGR and CEGAR-based CAR. Observe that all the compositional verification approaches outperform the monolithic one. More detailed results are available with our technical report [1].

References

1. CELL website, http://www.comp.nus.edu.sg/~pat/cell/
2. EAT: Evolutionary abstraction technique,
   https://sites.google.com/site/shangweilin/eat
3. Chen, Y.-F., Clarke, E.M., Farzan, A., Tsai, M.-H., Tsay, Y.-K., Wang, B.-Y.: Automated assume-guarantee reasoning through implicit learning. In: Touili, T., Cook, B., Jackson, P. (eds.) CAV 2010. LNCS, vol. 6174, pp. 511–526. Springer, Heidelberg (2010)
4. Cobleigh, J.M., Giannakopoulou, D., Păsăreanu, C.S.: Learning assumptions for compositional verification. In: Garavel, H., Hatcliff, J. (eds.) TACAS 2003. LNCS, vol. 2619, pp. 331–346. Springer, Heidelberg (2003)
5. Gheorghiu Bobaru, M., Păsăreanu, C.S., Giannakopoulou, D.: Automated assume-guarantee reasoning by abstraction refinement. In: Gupta, A., Malik, S. (eds.) CAV 2008. LNCS, vol. 5123, pp. 135–148. Springer, Heidelberg (2008)
6. Henzinger, T., Manna, Z., Pnueli, A.: Timed transition systems. In: Huizing, C., de Bakker, J.W., Rozenberg, G., de Roever, W.-P. (eds.) REX 1991. LNCS, vol. 600, pp. 226–251. Springer, Heidelberg (1992)
7. Sun, J., Liu, Y., Dong, J.S., Pang, J.: PAT: Towards flexible verification under fairness. In: Bouajjani, A., Maler, O. (eds.) CAV 2009. LNCS, vol. 5643, pp. 709–714. Springer, Heidelberg (2009)

VCS: A Verifier for Component-Based Systems[*]

Fei He[1,2,3], Liangze Yin[1,2,3], Bow-Yaw Wang[4], Lianyi Zhang[1,2,3],
Guanyu Mu[1,2,3], and Wenrui Meng[1,2,3]

[1] Tsinghua National Laboratory for Information Science and Technology (TNList)
[2] School of Software, Tsinghua University
[3] Key Laboratory for Information System Security, Ministry of Education, China
[4] Academia Sinica, Taiwan

Abstract. This paper presents the VCS verification tool for the BIP modeling language. The tool admits sophisticated interactions specified in BIP models. Particularly, private variables in components can be updated by user-defined interactions. On the verification back-end, the BIP models are formulated as transition systems. Several efficient algorithms are proposed for verification of transition systems on safety properties. Experimental results show very promising performance of VCS. It runs several magnitudes faster than NuSMV for a variety of examples.

1 Introduction

Component-based design has attracted significant interests from both industry and academy. Recent modeling languages such as AADL [1] and BIP [2] offer mechanisms for specifying sophisticated interactions among components. In the BIP language, for instance, components expose their private variables through ports, and the exposed private variables can be updated during user-specified interactions. The feature allows users to specify intricate interactions among components, but also complicates the semantics of the modeling language. Implementing verification tools for the BIP language can be demanding.

VCS [1] is a verification tool for models specified in the BIP language. In contrast to the existing BIP model checker DFINDER [3], VCS allows to specify interactions with data transfer among components. Users are able to fully exploit features of the BIP language in their models. Additionally, the VCS tool verifies properties specified in the Computation Tree Logic (CTL) as well as deadlock freedom on BIP models.

To the best of our knowledge, the VCS tool is the first BIP model checker which admits interactions with data transfer. An efficient SAT-based verification engine is implemented. Experiments show very promising performance of the tool in verification of component-based systems.

[*] This work was supported by the National 973 Plan (No. 2010CB328003), the NSF of China (No. 61272001, 60903030, 91218302), the Chinese National Key Technology R&D Program (No. SQ2012BAJY4052), the NSC 101-2221-E-001-007, and the Tsinghua University Initiative Scientific Research Program.

[1] http://code.google.com/p/bip-vcs/

D. Van Hung and M. Ogawa (Eds.): ATVA 2013, LNCS 8172, pp. 478–481, 2013.

2   Model Representation

The BIP model is defined in a hierarchical way. The model behaviors are described in atomic components. A compound component consists of a collection of (atomic or compound) components and connectors. Each connector can have temporary variables [2] to specify the interactions with data transfer among components. The BIP model is the topmost compound component.

In VCS, each atomic component is encoded as a transition system (X, I, T), where X is a set of variables, I is the initial predicate and T is the transition predicate. Let T^I be the transition predicate related to the internal transitions only. Given a hierarchical BIP model H, the tool first transforms the input model into a flattened BIP model [4]. The flattened BIP model contains only atomic components $A_i = (X_i, I_i, T_i)$ $(1 \leq i \leq N)$ and connectors C_j $(1 \leq j \leq M)$. Let F_j be the symbolic representation of the connector C_j. The hierarchical BIP model H is thus a transition system (X_H, I_H, T_H), where

- $X_H = \bigcup_{i=1}^{N} X_i$;
- $I_H = \bigwedge_{i=1}^{N} I_i$;
- $T_H = \bigvee_{i=1}^{N} (T_i^I \wedge \bigwedge_{k \neq i}(X_k' = X_k)) \vee \bigvee_{j=1}^{M}(F_j \wedge \bigwedge_{k \notin dom(C_j)}(X_k' = X_k))$, where $dom(C_j)$ gives the indices of atomic components in C_j.

3   Verification Algorithms

In traditional settings, the transition systems are interpreted as state machines, and then verified by model checking algorithms (either explicit or symbolic). However, during this interpretation, much useful information implied in the transition system is lost. We propose several efficient techniques to utilize such information to improve the model checking for transition systems.

Macro Step-Based Verification: Given a transition system, we distinguish the set of transitions which may lead the property from true to false, called property-sensitive transitions. Each search step of bounded model checking is extended to a macro step, which consists of exactly one property-sensitive transition and any number of other transitions. Moreover, we employ an algorithm to eliminate all loops among property-sensitive transitions in the model. Then we are able to formulate the model checking problem as a Boolean SAT formula. We call this technique *macro step-based verification.*

Variable Decision Heuristic: We propose in [5] to utilize the structure information hidden in a transition system during model checking. We define a *transition variable* for each transition in the model. During the SAT solving, the transition variable is assigned higher priority than other variables to be chosen as the decision variable. Among the many transition variables, we follow the structure of the transition system to assign their priorities. In such a way, the structure information is utilized to guide the search process of a SAT solver.

---

[2] The current version of DFINDER does not support this feature.

Incremental Verification: The proof for temporal induction [6] consists of two parts: the base case and the induction step. Both parts generate a series of SAT problems. We can exploit the symmetry and similarities in the series for incremental SAT verification. We show that, under certain conditions: (1) conflict clauses can be shared among SAT problems within each sequence; (2) conflict clauses can be shared between these two sequences; (3) after shifting or reversing the time steps, the transformed clauses can also be shared. Compared to existing works, our algorithm explores much bigger degree of clause sharing.

4   Experimental Results

The VCS tool is implemented in C++. All experiments are conducted on a computer with a 2.53GHz Intel Core2 Duo CPU with 2GB memory.

Experimental results for six examples are reported. Three examples are from real systems in industry, including the data processing unit (DPU) used in a space vehicle [7], the gate control system (GCS) used in the stage of LingShan Buddhist Palace in Jiangsu, China [8], and the message transmission protocol (MTP) used in the train communication network. Three examples are originated from public websites or literature, including the ATM system [3], the dining philosophers problem (DPP) [3], and the automatic callback system (ACS) [9].

Note the industrial examples exploit sophisticated interactions among components, they cannot be verified by DFINDER [3]. We chose to use NuSMV(version 2.5.3) to perform the comparison. Two state-of-the-art SAT-based algorithms (*Een-sorensson* and *Zigzag* [6]) implemented in NuSMVare tested. For each model, we test both algorithms and report the better one for NuSMV.

Experimental results are listed in Table 1. In the table, *step* give the steps for standard bounded model checking (including NuSMVand *Std*) to find a bug, while $step_m$ give the steps for our macro step-based verification to find a bug. We observe in all cases the value of $step_m$ is much less than that of *step*. This is reasonable since a macro step may involve several transitions in the model. The VCS tool can be configured with different settings, where *Std* stands for the standard bounded model checking, *Mco* stands for the macro step-based verification, Mco^+ stands for *Mco* plus the incremental verification technique, and Mco^{++} stands for Mco^+ plus the variable decision heuristic. All runtimes are reported in seconds. The label "-" indicates the checker cannot get a conclusive answer in 900 seconds.

For all cases, *Mco*, Mco^+ and Mco^{++} run several magnitudes faster than either *Std* or NuSMV, especially when the problems scale up. For the industrial examples DPU, GCS and MTP, which involve sophisticated behaviors and interactions, Mco^{++} runs fastest. For other examples ACS, ATM and DPP, which contain no local variables, the variable decision heuristic is useless, thus Mco^+ runs fastest.

---

[3] http://www-verimag.imag.fr/DFinder.html?lang=en

Table 1. Experimental Results for Macro-Step Verification

Model	Prop	NuSMV		VCS				
		step	time	$step_m$	Std	Mco	Mco^+	Mco^{++}
DPU	P1	24	2.23	9	1.95	0.52	0.16	**0.1**
DPU	P2	26	2.43	9	2.65	0.7	0.23	**0.08**
DPU	P3	32	5.79	10	7.05	1.07	0.32	**0.17**
GCS	P1	46	7.4	18	28.74	2.05	0.31	**0.22**
GCS	P2	54	28.55	21	127.96	7.63	1.26	**0.42**
MTP	P2	30	-	13	143.92	17.58	13.68	**7.11**
MTP	P3	30	-	13	199.7	18.41	24.37	**4.11**
MTP	P4	33	-	15	199.9	41.03	38.57	**10.32**
MTP	P5	30	-	13	111.19	8.27	4.21	**3.92**
ATM6	P1	13	334.28	6	43.81	0.13	**0.04**	1.83
ATM8	P1	-	-	8	-	1.46	**0.97**	-
ATM10	P1	-	-	10	-	11.13	**11.21**	-
DPP10	P1	10	9.03	10	6.75	1.09	**0.77**	141.85
DPP11	P1	11	61.5	11	29.21	4.11	**2.65**	-
DPP12	P1	12	-	12	152.53	22.6	**18.12**	-
ACS3	P1	24	2.07	6	63.87	0.03	**0.01**	0.04
ACS5	P1	-	-	10	-	0.56	**0.13**	55.85
ACS7	P1	-	-	14	-	4.44	**0.62**	-
ACS9	P1	-	-	18	-	29.9	**9.61**	-

References

1. Feiler, P.H.: The architecture analysis & design language (AADL): An introduction. Technical report, CMU/SEI-2006-TN-011 (2006)
2. Basu, A., Bozga, M., Sifakis, J.: Modeling heterogeneous real-time components in bip. In: SEFM 2006, pp. 3–12. IEEE (2006)
3. Bensalem, S., Bozga, M., Nguyen, T.-H., Sifakis, J.: D-finder: A tool for compositional deadlock detection and verification. In: Bouajjani, A., Maler, O. (eds.) CAV 2009. LNCS, vol. 5643, pp. 614–619. Springer, Heidelberg (2009)
4. Bozga, M., Jaber, M., Sifakis, J.: Source-to-source architecture transformation for performance optimization in bip. IEEE Transactions on Industrial Informatics 5(4), 708–718 (2010)
5. Yin, L., He, F., Gu, M.: Optimizing the sat decision ordering of bounded model checking by structural information. In: Proceedings of the 7th International Symposium on Theoretical Aspects of Software Engineering, TASE (2013)
6. Eén, N., Sorensson, N.: Temporal induction by incremental sat solving. Electronic Notes in Theoretical Computer Science 89(4), 543–560 (2003)
7. Wan, H., Huang, C., Wang, Y., He, F., Gu, M., Chen, R., Marius, B.: Modeling and validation of a data process unit control for space applications. In: Embedded Real Time Software and Systems (2012)
8. Wang, R., Zhou, M., Yin, L., Zhang, L., Gu, M., Sun, J., Bozga, M.: Modeling and validation of plc-controlled system: A case study. Technical report, Tsinghua University (2011)
9. Cha, G., Gu, T.: Formal Analysis and Design of Network Protocols (2003)

SmacC: A Retargetable Symbolic Execution Engine*

Armin Biere[1], Jens Knoop[2], Laura Kovács[3], and Jakob Zwirchmayr[2]

[1] JKU Linz
[2] TU Vienna
[3] Chalmers University of Technology

Abstract. SmacC is a symbolic execution engine for C programs. It can be used for program verification, bounded model checking and generating SMT benchmarks. More recently we also successfully applied SmacC for high-level timing analysis of programs to infer exact loop bounds and safe over-approximations. SmacC uses the logic for bit-vectors with arrays to construct a bit-precise memory-model of a program for path-wise exploration.

1 Introduction

Symbolic execution executes a program by using symbolic instead of concrete data. Typically, the program is analyzed path-wise, i.e. paths are analyzed one-by-one in isolation. Splitting the analysis to focus on single paths can be exploited to track important information about the path under analysis and allows to check properties where other techniques fail, for example as illustrated in Fig. 2(c). However, for whole program analysis the costs of path-wise symbolic execution are often prohibitive because of the so-called path-explosion problem that the number of paths grows exponentially with the number of conditionals in a program. Fortunately, even analyzing only parts of the program, such as focusing on all paths within a certain function, still allows to infer valuable properties and catch subtle errors.

In this paper we present SmacC, a retargetable symbolic execution engine. SmacC is an acronym for *SMT Memory-model and Assertion Checker for C*. Retargebility, a term borrowed form [4] inspired the front-end implementation of SmacC, and refers to its capability of being retargetable to conceptually quite different applications in program analysis. SmacC supports a relevant fragment of (ANSI) C analyzing such programs by path-wise symbolic execution. It derives verification conditions for program statements and expressions, expressed as satisfiability modulo theory (SMT) formulas in the logic of bit-vectors with arrays. This allows bit-precise reasoning about the program, including reasoning about memory accesses and arithmetic overflow. The generated verification conditions precisely capture the memory-model of the program. Proving them to hold guarantees that the supported runtime- and memory-errors cannot occur. Violations in the symbolic representation constitute actual violations.

SmacC can be applied in a number of program analysis settings. The tool can prove absence of runtime-errors if full symbolic coverage is achieved. Further, it allows to

---

* This research is supported by the FP7-ICT Project 288008 T-CREST, the FWF RiSE projects S11408-N23 and S11410-N23, the WWTF PROSEED grant ICT C-050, the FWF grant T425-N23, and the CeTAT project of TU Vienna.

D. Van Hung and M. Ogawa (Eds.): ATVA 2013, LNCS 8172, pp. 482–486, 2013.

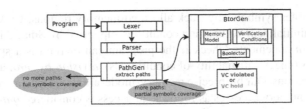

Fig. 1. Architecture of SmacC: path-wise execution leads to *partial symbolic coverage* if there are more paths to be executed. Exhaustive execution of all paths yields *full symbolic coverage*.

perform bounded model checking by exhaustive symbolic execution up to a provided bound. Functional correctness, e.g. equivalence checking, is supported via assertions. Generated verification conditions can be dumped to files and used as SMT benchmarks for testing or performance evaluation of SMT solvers. A new application for SmacC is the high-level worst-case execution time (WCET) analysis of programs. More specifically, the tool finds flow-facts, such as infeasible paths and safe loop bounds, required for successful WCET analysis. We use SmacC in combination with the WCET analysis toolchain r-TuBound [5].

SmacC is implemented in 10Klocs of C and is available at http://www.complang.tuwien.ac.at/jakob/smacc/

2   Tool Architecture

Figure 1 shows the architecture of SmacC. SmacC reads a C program as input file, which is then tokenized (`Lexer`) and parsed to abstract syntax trees according to the C expression grammar (`Parser`). The abstract syntax trees are stored as elements of a code-list. Paths through the program are extracted (`PathGen`) and symbolically executed (`BtorGen`), which consists of updating the symbolic representation of the executed path. This symbolic representation is used to generate verification conditions in form of SMT formulas, which express runtime-safety of statements occurring on the path. We use the SMT solver Boolector [2] for checking these SMT formulas in the quantifier-free logic of bit-vectors with arrays. In the sequel, we overview the main ingredients of SmacC, and refer to [6] and the url for further details.

PathGen. In the path-generation phase, in order to remove loops, the code-list is flattened, by unwinding program loops up to a certain bound. This way, for each program path, a code-list is constructed. Conditionals, which require to split the control-flow, will produce two paths to explore both branches of the condition. Each fully extracted path is then symbolically executed in `BtorGen`.

BtorGen, Memory-Model and Verification Conditions. This step constructs a symbolic SMT representation of the memory used in the program, faithfully covering the semantics of each statement on the program path. Additionally, verification conditions are constructed as SMT formulas. The *program memory* is a collection of symbolic values and modeled by a contiguous array. The memory layout, e.g. the set of declared addresses, is represented by bit-vector variables indexing the memory array. Additional bit-vector variables symbolically track allocated memory regions. Unwritten memory is treated as uninitialized. Verification conditions supported by SmacC include reasoning about *return* statements (check if the program can or returns a specified value), *path conditions* (check satisfiability of conditionals), *division by zero*, and *overflow* of arithmetic operations. Our bit-precise memory-model allows us to construct verification conditions for memory accesses as follows: an access is considered *out-of-allocated* if the address can evaluate to an unallocated array index, i.e. outside the region constrained by *global_beg*, *global_end*, *heap_beg*, *heap_end*, *stack_beg* and *stack_end*.

Output Results. SmacC produces as output a textual report for each statement symbolically executed along all analyzed paths. For each verification condition, the tool reports whether the property is safe or violated on a specific path. If a verification condition is violated on at least one path, then the corresponding property can be violated by an actual run. If the verification condition holds on all paths, then the corresponding program property cannot be violated by any actual run.

3 Applications of SmacC

We have successfully applied SmacC to verify C programs and generate SMT benchmarks using our precise memory-model [6]. We illustrate the bit-precise memory-model and generation and proving of verification conditions using the examples in Fig. 2(a) and (b) below. We also integrated SmacC with r-TuBound to support timing analysis, and show its use on Fig. 2(c). For more details, we refer to the url of our tool.

```
1: int a[4];                 int main () {        int main() {         :1
2: int main () {               int x, y;            int i, flag;        :2
3:   int i;                    if (x > 0) {         for(i=0; i<5; i++)  :3
4:   a[0] = 1;                   y = x * x;           if(i==4 && flag){ :4
5:   for(i=0; i<4; i++)          if (y == 0)            i = 0;          :5
6:     if (a[i] > 0)               assert(0); }}        flag = 0; }}    :6
7:       i = i + 1;                                                     :7
8:   assert(i >= 4); }                                                  :8
```

         (a)   (b)   (c)

Fig. 2. (a) a program with an assertion and a conditional update; (b) a program with a reachable, failing, assertion; (c) SmacC finds the loop bound, CBMC keeps unwinding the loop

Example. The variable declarations in the program of Fig. 2(a) in lines 1 and 3 (a:1,3), result in the following SMT variable declarations, where variables that do not occur in the source are used to track allocated memory: *global_beg*, *global_end*, *heap_beg*, *heap_end*, *stack_beg*, *stack_end*, *mem*, *i*, *x*, *a*, where *mem* is an array and models memory. Symbolic execution of a path tracks declared memory constructing the formula $(a = global\_beg) \land (global\_end = global\_beg + 16) \land (heap\_end = heap\_beg) \land (i = stack\_beg) \land (stack\_end = stack\_beg - 4)$, while $(read(mem[i]) < 0 \ldots 100)$ is the verification condition for the assertion (a:8). The assertion holds for any variable assignment valid on the current path if the conjunction of the formulas is unsatisfiable. Fig. 2(b), taken from [1], illustrates the need for a bit-precise memory-model: both conditions (b:3,5) must evaluate to *true* to reach the failing assertion (b:6). When reasoning about unbounded integers the assertion is unreachable due to unsatisfiable path conditions. SmacC infers overflow for the multiplication and thus a satisfiable path condition guarding the failing assertion, therefore the failing assertion is reachable.

Experiments. We analyzed a *memcopy* and a *stringcopy* implementation for bounded runtime-and memory-safety (with bounded array-size 50, respectively 40), verified the functional correctness of a *palindrome check* and checked equality of two *power-of-3 implementations*. Path-wise verification of the *memcopy* implementation up to bound 50 takes approximately two hours. Functional correctness for the *palindrome check* (bounded by word length 16) exhibits high run-times (4.5h), and complete equality checking of two *power-of-3 implementations* (with 32bit int) times out (10h). Varying the bound of the input problems and dumping a conjunction of the verification conditions thus allows to generate SMT benchmarks with varying runtime.

We also integrated the memory-model of SmacC in r-TuBound and extended verification conditions to express arithmetic properties about conditional updates to the loop counter. This allows us to compute loop bounds in cases where the loop bound computation step of r-TuBound would fail. For example, the loop counter i in Fig. 2(a) is conditionally updated, therefore no safe loop bound can be computed initially. Verifying that the conditional update can never decrease the loop counter allows us to use the constant increment in the loop header to compute a safe over-approximation. For the conditional update $i' = upd(i)$, e.g. i = i + 1 in Fig.2(a), (a:7), we verify that executing it can only increase the loop counter for the next iteration i', i.e. $i' < i$ must be unsatisfiable for arbitrary values of i, as for example in Fig. 2(a) where a loop bound of 4 can be computed using the update i++ (a:5) in the loop header.

Fig. 2(a) illustrates another usage of SmacC for loop bound detection. Here, SmacC is called with an initial loop bound. If it reports that the negation of the loop condition is satisfiable along a path, the bound is increased. Upon termination, no execution of the program exhibits a higher loop bound. The loop counter i in Fig. 2(c) is reset in iteration 5 (c:5), therefore the loop is executed 4 more times. SmacC infers the exact loop bound 9, while a WCET analysis using the model checker CBMC [3] without SmacC does not terminate and keeps unwinding the loop.

4 Conclusion

SmacC has successfully been used in a number of applications, ranging from program verification to high-level WCET analysis. A key feature of SmacC is its bit-precise symbolic execution which enables it to find a number of typical and important program errors and to functionally verify programs via assertions. Verification conditions that exhibit high solving time can be dumped and used as regression and performance tests for SMT solvers. High-level WCET analysis turned out to be a another promising application field of SmacC and we successfully retargeted SmacC and the underlying memory-model towards integration into a WCET analysis toolchain, improving high-level analysis results. Currently, we are working on implementing the memory-model for binaries and extending SmacC with generation of test-inputs guiding actual program executions towards the WCET path. To improve the runtime of SmacC, we also investigate techniques shown effective for symbolic execution, such as query caching.

References

1. Bjørner, N., de Moura, L., Tillmann, N.: Satisfiability Modulo Bit-precise Theories for Program Exploration. In: Proc. of CFV (2008)
2. Brummayer, R., Biere, A.: Boolector: An Efficient SMT Solver for Bit-Vectors and Arrays. In: Kowalewski, S., Philippou, A. (eds.) TACAS 2009. LNCS, vol. 5505, pp. 174–177. Springer, Heidelberg (2009)
3. Clarke, E., Kroning, D., Lerda, F.: A Tool for Checking ANSI-C Programs. In: Jensen, K., Podelski, A. (eds.) TACAS 2004. LNCS, vol. 2988, pp. 168–176. Springer, Heidelberg (2004)
4. Fraser, C., Hanson, D.: lcc, A Retargetable C Compiler for ANSI C. The Benjamin/Cummings Publishing Company, Inc., Redwood City (1995)
5. Knoop, J., Kovács, L., Zwirchmayr, J.: r-TuBound: Loop Bounds for WCET Analysis (Tool Paper). In: Bjørner, N., Voronkov, A. (eds.) LPAR-18 2012. LNCS, vol. 7180, pp. 435–444. Springer, Heidelberg (2012)
6. Zwirchmayr, J.: A Satisfiability Modulo Theories Memory-Model and Assertion Checker for C. Master's thesis, JKU Linz, Austria (2009)

MoTraS: A Tool for Modal Transition Systems and Their Extensions*

Jan Křetínský[1,2] and Salomon Sickert[1]

[1] Institut für Informatik, Technische Universität München, Germany
[2] Faculty of Informatics, Masaryk University, Brno, Czech Republic

Abstract. We present a tool for modal transition systems (MTS), disjunctive MTS and further extensions of MTS supporting also non-deterministic systems. We provide the operations required from specification theories as well as some additional support such as deterministic hull, LTL model checking etc. The tool comes with both graphical and command line interface.

1 Introduction

Due to the ever increasing complexity of software systems and their reuse, component-based design and verification have become crucial. Therefore, having a specification formalism that supports *component-based* development and *stepwise refinement* is very useful. In such a framework, one can start from an initial specification, proceed with a series of small and successive refinements until eventually a specification is reached from which an implementation can be extracted directly. *Modal transition systems* (MTS) [11] is a successful specification formalism satisfying the above requirements.

The formalism of MTS has proven to be useful in practice. Industrial applications are as old as [5] where MTS have been used for an air-traffic system at Heathrow airport. Besides, MTS are advocated as an appropriate base for interface theories in [16] and for product line theories in [13]. Further, MTS based software engineering methodology for design via merging partial descriptions of behaviour has been established in [17].

MTS consist of a set of states and two transition relations. The *must* transitions prescribe which behaviour has to be present in every refinement of the system; the *may* transitions describe the behaviour that is allowed, but need not be realized in the refinements. Over the years, many extensions of MTS have been proposed. While MTS can only specify whether or not a particular transition is required, some extensions equip MTS with more general abilities to describe what *combinations* of transitions are possible. Disjunctive MTS (DMTS) [12,3] can specify that at least one of a given set of transitions is present. One selecting

---

* Jan Křetínský is partially supported by the Czech Science Foundation, project No. P202/12/G061, and Salomon Sickert is partially supported by the DFG project "Polynomial Systems on Semirings: Foundations, Algorithms, Applications".

D. Van Hung and M. Ogawa (Eds.): ATVA 2013, LNCS 8172, pp. 487–491, 2013.

MTS [8] allow to choose exactly one of them. Boolean MTS (BMTS) [4] and expressively equivalent acceptance automata [14] cover all Boolean combinations of transitions. Parametric MTS (PMTS) [4] add parameters on top of it, so that we can also express persistent choices of transitions and relate possible choices in different parts of a system. This way, one can also model hardware dependencies of transitions and systems with prices.

The tool support is so far limited to basic MTS and, moreover, partially limited to deterministic systems. The currently available tools are MTSA (Modal transition system analyzer) [7] and MIO (MIO Workbench) [1]. While MTSA is a tool for MTS, MIO is a tool for modal I/O automata (MIOA) [10,15], which combine MTS and interface automata based on I/O automata. Although MIOA have three types of may and must transitions (input, output, and internal), if we restrict to say only input transitions, the refinement works the same as for MTS, and some other operations, too. Further, there are also tools for loosely related formalisms of I/O automata (with no modalities) such as ECDAR (Environment for Compositional Design and Analysis of Real Time Systems) [6], which supports their timed extension.

In this paper, we present a tool for MTS and DMTS together with partial support of BMTS and PMTS as described below. In the following sections, we describe MoTraS and compare it to the existing tools both with respect to functionality and experimentally. The tool can be downloaded and additional materials found at http://www.model.in.tum.de/~kretinsk/motras.html

2   Functionality

MoTraS comes not only with a graphical user interface, but as opposed to other mentioned tools also with a command line interface, which allows for batch processing. The Netbeans-based GUI offers all the standard components such as a canvas for drawing systems, windows for editing their properties, algorithms menu, possibility to view more systems at once etc. Both the GUI and the independent algorithms package, which contains all data-structures, algorithms and the CLI, are written in Java.

As to the available algorithms, MoTraS supports all operations required for complete specification theories [2] and more. This includes modal refinement checking, parallel composition (for quotient see below), conjunction (or merge) and the related consistency checking and maximal implementation generation, deterministic hull and generalized LTL model checking. This functionality comes for MTS as well as more general DMTS and in all cases also *non-deterministic* systems are supported (in particular, the algorithm for conjunction is now considerably more complex [3]). In contrast, MTSA supports only modal refinement, parallel composition and consistency. It also offers a model checking procedure, which is, unfortunately, fundamentally flawed. This has been shown in [3] from where we adopt the corrected implementation. MIO offers modal refinement, the MIOA parallel composition and conjunction for deterministic systems. On the top, it also offers quotient for deterministic systems. As there are no algorithms for the quotient of non-deterministic MTS, DMTS and BMTS and this question is a subject of current research, we only implement the quotient for deterministic systems as MIO does. Note that both MTSA and MIO can only handle modal systems, not their disjunctive extension. MoTraS supports DMTS as they have more expressive power, and as opposed to (non-deterministic) MTS are rich enough to express solutions to process equations [12] (hence a specification of a missing component in a system can be computed) and are closed under all operations, in particular conjunction (which is necessary for merging views on a system).

Further, on the top of this functionality for MTS and DMTS, we also provide an implementation of a new method for modal refinement checking of BMTS and PMTS [9]. While modal refinement on MTS and DMTS can be decided in polynomial time, on BMTS and PMTS it is higher in the polynomial hierarchy (Π_2 and Π_4, respectively). The new method, however, reduces the refinement problem to a problem directly and efficiently solvable by a QBF solver. Already the preliminary results of [9] show that this solution scales well in the size of the system as well as in the number of parameters, while a direct naive solution is infeasible.

Moreover, we also implement the deterministic hull and the parameter-free hull for BMTS and PMTS, which we recently proposed [9]. This allows to both over- and under-approximate the EXPTIME-complete thorough refinement using the fast modal refinement, now even for the most general class of PMTS.

In order to make the tool easily extensible, we introduced a file format *xmts*, which facilitates textual representation of different extensions of modal transition systems. The description of the format can be found on the web page of the tool. The table below summarizes the functionality: ✓indicates a MoTraS implementation; for the other tools, the name indicates an implementation; "det." denotes a functionality limited to deterministic systems.

Operation	MTS		DMTS	BMTS	PMTS
Parallel composition	MTSA	MIO(MIAO) ✓	✓		
Consistency	MTSA(of 2 systems)	MIO(det.) ✓	✓		
Conjunction		MIO(det.) ✓	✓		
Quotient (det.)		MIO ✓	×		
Generalized LTL	MTSA(incorrect)	✓	✓		
Det./Par. hull		✓	✓	✓	✓
Refinement	MTSA	MIO ✓	✓	✓	✓

3   Experimental Results

We briefly compare the performance of the MTS tools on the algorithm that each of them implements, namely modal refinement of MTS. We compare MoTraS and MTSA on systems with 500 states, see the table on the right (computational times in seconds). We consider systems with different sizes

Size	Structure:	MTSA	MoTraS
Alphabet 2, branching 5	Monolithic:	4.57	2.23
	Clustered:	0.34	0.04
Alphabet 2, branching 10	Monolithic:	6.62	8.75
	Clustered:	5.99	6.73
Alphabet 10, branching 5	Monolithic:	1.46	0.50
	Clustered:	1.54	0.01

of alphabet and branching degrees. We further consider monolithic systems where the transitions are evenly distributed, and systems with several clusters mutually connected with only a few edges. We do not include results for MIO here as there are stack overflows already for systems with <150 states, and for systems with 100 states the time is—despite MIO statistics reporting 0 seconds—actually more than 3 seconds. See the webpage for more details and more experiments.

Although our results are already more than competitive, there are several ways how to further optimize them. The algorithms are implemented using fixed-point-iteration and waiting-queue skeleton classes, which allows for an easy introduction of multi-threading to all algorithms. Due to the independence of elements processing we conjecture the speed up factor will be very close to the number of cores used.

For the QBF-based modal refinement some additional steps were taken to reduce the memory footprint, such as storing the generated formulae in negation-normal-form and using the Tseitin encoding to limit the growth of the formulae while transforming it into CNF, which is required for the QBF solver. An interesting task for the future work is to introduce combined modal refinement checker, which uses the standard modal refinement checker to prune the initial relation before the QBF-based checker is called.

References

1. Bauer, S.S., Mayer, P., Legay, A.: MIO workbench: A tool for compositional design with modal input/Output interfaces. In: Bultan, T., Hsiung, P.-A. (eds.) ATVA 2011. LNCS, vol. 6996, pp. 418–421. Springer, Heidelberg (2011)
2. Bauer, S.S., David, A., Hennicker, R., Larsen, K.G., Legay, A., Nyman, U., Wasowski, A.: Moving from specifications to contracts in component-based design. In: de Lara, J., Zisman, A. (eds.) FASE. LNCS, vol. 7212, pp. 43–58. Springer, Heidelberg (2012)
3. Beneš, N., Černá, I., Křetínský, J.: Modal transition systems: Composition and LTL model checking. In: Bultan, T., Hsiung, P.-A. (eds.) ATVA 2011. LNCS, vol. 6996, pp. 228–242. Springer, Heidelberg (2011)
4. Beneš, N., Křetínský, J., Larsen, K.G., Møller, M.H., Srba, J.: Parametric modal transition systems. In: Bultan, T., Hsiung, P.-A. (eds.) ATVA 2011. LNCS, vol. 6996, pp. 275–289. Springer, Heidelberg (2011)
5. Bruns, G.: An industrial application of modal process logic. Sci. Comput. Program. 29(1-2), 3–22 (1997)
6. David, A., Larsen, K.G., Legay, A., Nyman, U., Wąsowski, A.: ECDAR: An environment for compositional design and analysis of real time systems. In: Bouajjani, A., Chin, W.-N. (eds.) ATVA 2010. LNCS, vol. 6252, pp. 365–370. Springer, Heidelberg (2010)
7. D'Ippolito, N., Fischbein, D., Foster, H., Uchitel, S.: MTSA: Eclipse support for modal transition systems construction, analysis and elaboration. In: ETX, pp. 6–10 (2007)
8. Fecher, H., Schmidt, H.: Comparing disjunctive modal transition systems with an one-selecting variant. J. Log. Algebr. Program. 77(1-2), 20–39 (2008)

9. Křetínský, J., Sickert, S.: On refinements of boolean and parametric modal transition systems. In: Zhu, H. (ed.) ICTAC 2013. LNCS, vol. 8049, pp. 213–230. Springer, Heidelberg (2013)
10. Larsen, K.G., Nyman, U., Wąsowski, A.: Modal I/O automata for interface and product line theories. In: De Nicola, R. (ed.) ESOP 2007. LNCS, vol. 4421, pp. 64–79. Springer, Heidelberg (2007)
11. Larsen, K.G., Thomsen, B.: A modal process logic. In: LICS, pp. 203–210 (1988)
12. Larsen, K.G., Xinxin, L.: Equation solving using modal transition systems. In: LICS, pp. 108–117 (1990)
13. Nyman, U.: Modal Transition Systems as the Basis for Interface Theories and Product Lines. PhD thesis, Institut for Datalogi, Aalborg Universitet (2008)
14. Raclet, J.-B.: Quotient de spécifications pour la réutilisation de composants. PhD thesis, Université de Rennes I (December 2007) (in French)
15. Raclet, J.-B., Badouel, E., Benveniste, A., Caillaud, B., Legay, A., Passerone, R.: A modal interface theory for component-based design. Fundamenta Informaticae 108(1-2), 119–149 (2011)
16. Raclet, J.-B., Badouel, E., Benveniste, A., Caillaud, B., Passerone, R.: Why are modalities good for interface theories? In: ACSD (2009)
17. Uchitel, S., Chechik, M.: Merging partial behavioural models. In: SIGSOFT FSE, pp. 43–52 (2004)

Cunf: A Tool for Unfolding and Verifying Petri Nets with Read Arcs

César Rodríguez and Stefan Schwoon

LSV (ENS Cachan & CNRS & INRIA), France

Abstract. CUNF is a tool for building and analyzing unfoldings of Petri nets with read arcs. An unfolding represents the behaviour of a net by a partial order, effectively coping with the state-explosion problem stemming from the interleaving of concurrent actions. C-net unfoldings can be up to exponentially smaller than Petri net unfoldings, and recent work proposed algorithms for their construction and verification. CUNF is the first implementation of these techniques, it has been carefully engineered and optimized to ensure that the theoretical gains are put into practice.

1 Overview

Petri nets are a model for concurrent, distributed systems. Unfoldings are a well-established technique for verifying properties of Petri nets; their use for this purpose was initially proposed by McMillan [6]. The unfolding of a (Petri) net is another net of acyclic structure that fully represents the state-space (reachable markings) of the first, see, e.g., fig. 1 (c). Because unfoldings represent behaviour by acyclic structures rather than by interleaved actions, they are often exponentially smaller than the state-space of N, and never larger than it.

Recently, the unfolding construction was extended to Petri nets with read arcs, also called *contextual nets* (c-nets) [2]. This extension is partially motivated by the fact that c-net unfoldings can yet again be exponentially smaller than Petri net unfoldings. In this paper, we present CUNF the first tool for constructing and analyzing c-net unfoldings, freely available from [8]. The theoretical basis of the tool was presented in [2, 1, 9].

We assume the reader is familiar to Petri nets [7]. A *c-net* is a Petri net where in addition to the ordinary *arcs* (arrows) between *places* and *transitions*, one may use *read arcs*. Figure 1 (a) shows a c-net, read arcs are the undirected lines; we say that t_2 reads p_4. A *marking* enables t_2 if it puts tokens on places p_1 and p_4; but firing t_2 only consumes the token in p_1, the token in p_4 remains there.

Every c-net can be seen as the marking-equivalent Petri net that results from replacing read arcs for pairs of arcs, as in fig. 1 (a) and (b). Although both nets have the same markings, remark, however, that t_1, t_2 are concurrent in (a), both read p_4 at the same time, but not in (b), as they compete for the token in p_4.

The *unfolding* of a bounded c-net N is another well-defined, finite, *acyclic* c-net $\mathcal{P}_N$, where each place (resp. transition) of $\mathcal{P}_N$ is labelled by a place (resp. transition) of N and such that runs of $\mathcal{P}_N$ are labelled by runs of N.

D. Van Hung and M. Ogawa (Eds.): ATVA 2013, LNCS 8172, pp. 492–495, 2013.

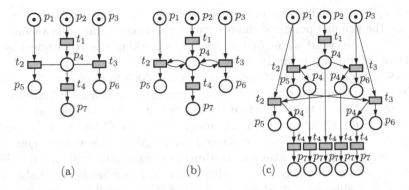

Fig. 1. (a) a c-net; (b) its encoding into a Petri net; (c) unfolding of (b)

The crucial property of $\mathcal{P}_N$ is that for every marking m of N, it contains a marking m' labelled by m.[1] Reachability on N is a PSPACE-complete problem which, however, reduces to an NP-complete problem on $\mathcal{P}_N$. The decreased complexity comes from $\mathcal{P}_N$ being acyclic. Thus, $\mathcal{P}_N$ can be seen as a symbolic representation of the reachable markings of N, particularly compact for concurrent systems.

Abstractly, this explains why c-net unfoldings can be even smaller than plain unfoldings. The unfolding of fig. 1 (a), which is isomorphic to (a), exploits that t_1, t_2 are concurrent and leaves them unmodified. The unfolding of (b), however, need to *unfold* the loops around p_4, explicitly producing all *interleavings* of the reading transitions t_1, t_2 — up to exponentially many of them for n readers.

2   Cunf and Cna's Algorithms and Their Implementation

Our toolset mainly consists of two programs: CUNF constructs unfoldings of 1-safe (places carry 0 or 1 tokens) c-nets, and CNA (Contextual Net Analyser) carries out verification on them.

Unfoldings are built iteratively. CUNF starts with an unfolding prefix containing just a copy of the initial marking of N. This prefix is extended with one *event* (transition), called *possible extension*, yielding a new prefix; this is repeated until the unfolding prefix is big enough to represent all reachable markings of N. Computing the possible extensions is NP-complete, and requires solving (a variant of) the coverability problem for sets of places of the prefix.

CUNF achieves this by a *concurrency relation* on the (enriched) places of the prefix [1]. This relation can be seen as a database that serves to both solve coverability queries and update the relation itself. CUNF spends more than 80% of the time computing the concurrency relation. Efficient computation of the unfolding, thus, almost entirely relies on the efficient computation of this relation, which CUNF implements with adjacency lists. The tool uses around a dozen optimizations for handling these lists, some of them are reported in [1, Sec. 6].

---

[1] The reader acquainted with the literature on unfoldings may have realized that by *unfolding*, or $\mathcal{P}_N$, in this paper we mean the unique, finite, marking-complete branching process one builds from the c-net after fixing a complete adequate order [1].

To keep the unfolding finite, certain enriched events are marked as *cut-offs*, they are the pruning points of the otherwise potentially infinite branches. Intuitively, those are events whose *history* reaches a marking already reached by (the history of) an event previously added, cf. [1].

CUNF is a mature tool that comprises around 4000 lines of C code, carefully profiled and optimized during its 3 years of existence. It is a command-line tool, but comes with scripts to translate the output of graphical c-net editors such as COLOANE [5]. CUNF and CNA are integrated in the COSYVERIF [3] environment, which facilitates its invocation and usage. Also, several c-net generators (Conway's game of life, Dekker's algorithm) are distributed with the tool [8].

CNA inputs unfoldings generated with CUNF and searches for reachable markings of the original c-net that enable no transition (deadlocks) or mark a set of given places (coverability). CNA generates, out of the unfolding, a propositional formula whose models coincide with the (offending) traces searched by the tool. It relies on MINISAT [4] to solve the formula, and displays the trace if it is found. Notice that once the unfolding is built, it can serve to answer multiple queries. Around 10 optimizations for reducing the solving time are implemented. We highlight, e.g., the elimination of *stubborn events* [9], i.e., certain events that negatively impact the performance of MINISAT's unit-propagation; or the reductions of the *asymmetric conflict graph*, see [9]. In our benchmarks, CNA has better accumulated solving time than previously existing verification tools [9], which proves that CNA's algorithms are practical.

3   Experiments and Applications for the Tool

Every c-net can be encoded into an equivalent Petri net. The c-net unfolding can be smaller, but its construction algorithm is more involved. This posed several questions: Are c-net unfoldings smaller than ordinary ones? Can they be computed faster? Is reachability checking practical on c-net unfoldings?

These questions drove our experiments [1,9]. Considerable effort was invested into assuring the efficiency and correctness of the unfolder and analyser. In [1], we applied CUNF to a benchmark of around 100 nets gathered from the unfolding literature, comparing the results to those obtained from other well established Petri-net based tools. Contextual unfolding was significantly *faster* in almost all examples, and *smaller* in roughly half of them. These unfoldings had between 10^2 and 10^5 events; among the larger ones, CUNF unfolded an average rate of 25000 events per second, running on a 2.67GHz CPU.

Table 1 shows some experimental results. For each example, CUNF is run on the c-net and its Petri net encoding, and deadlocked-markings are searched with CNA. Running times, number of events in the unfoldings, and *histories* [1] for c-net unfoldings are shown. The numbers for the plain unfoldings are in fact *ratios* over corresponding numbers in c-net unfolding. C-net unfolding is faster than plain unfolding in 4 cases, and slower in 3. In this 3 cases, however, it is between 14 and 58 times smaller. CNA running times are much smaller than CUNF's ones, so verification seems not to be the bottleneck.

Table 1. Experimental results, see the text for more information

Net		Contextual Unfoldings				Plain Unfoldings		
		CUNF			CNA	CUNF		CNA
Name	Ddlk.	Time	Hist.	Ev.	Time	Time	Ev.	Time
BDS(1)	No	0.10	4210	1830	0.01	4.19	7.05	8.00
BYZ	No	2.36	8044	8044	1.68	1.35	1.83	0.23
FTP	No	16.30	50928	50928	0.06	2.26	1.80	4.19
RW(1,2)	No	0.924	49179	49179	0.01	1.42	1.00	1.50
KEY(4)	Yes	1.32	21742	4754	0.01	0.82	14.64	64.00
DIJ(5)	No	9.89	126240	10702	1.17	0.48	14.04	1.85
DEK(60)	No	4.92	216120	3720	0.03	0.86	58.10	0.43

C-net unfoldings are smaller when the c-nets contain transitions that *concurrently read* common resources, as t_1, t_2 in fig. 1 (a). This happens naturally in several applications. Last two examples of table 1 are models of the Dijkstra's and Dekker's mutual exclusion algorithms where c-net unfoldings exhibit important gains. Recall that in both algorithms, *concurrent processes* need to *read* other processes' state variables, hence the gain. Verification of mutual exclusion protocols, we believe, could be an important application of c-net unfoldings.

Hazard checking in asynchronous circuits (ACs) [6] is another promising application. A network of asynchronous boolean gates can be modelled by a c-net, where each gadget encoding a boolean gate contains many read arcs [9]. Hazards are undesirable behaviours of ACs, whose existence reduces to a coverability question on the c-net [6]. In our experiments, we observed that signal changes in the circuit could propagate in many different orders, which were distinguished by Petri-net unfoldings but not by c-net unfoldings, reducing the unfolding size [9].

References

1. Baldan, P., Bruni, A., Corradini, A., König, B., Rodríguez, C., Schwoon, S.: Efficient unfolding of contextual Petri Nets. Theo. Comp. Sci. 449, 2–22 (2012)
2. Baldan, P., Corradini, A., König, B., Schwoon, S.: McMillan's complete prefix for contextual nets. In: Jensen, K., van der Aalst, W.M.P., Billington, J. (eds.) ToPNoC I. LNCS, vol. 5100, pp. 199–220. Springer, Heidelberg (2008)
3. Cosyverif Project: COSYVERIF http://www.cosyverif.org
4. Eén, N., Sörensson, N.: An extensible SAT-solver. In: Giunchiglia, E., Tacchella, A. (eds.) SAT 2003. LNCS, vol. 2919, pp. 502–518. Springer, Heidelberg (2004)
5. LIP6/MoVe Team: COLOANE, http://coloane.lip6.fr/
6. McMillan, K.L.: Using unfoldings to avoid the state explosion problem in the verification of asynchronous circuits. In: Probst, D.K., von Bochmann, G. (eds.) CAV 1992. LNCS, vol. 663, pp. 164–177. Springer, Heidelberg (1993)
7. Murata, T.: Petri Nets: Properties, analysis and applications. Proc. of the IEEE 77(4), 541–580 (1989)
8. Rodríguez, C.: CUNF, http://www.lsv.ens-cachan.fr/~rodriguez/tools/cunf/
9. Rodríguez, C., Schwoon, S.: Verification of Petri Nets with Read Arcs. In: Koutny, M., Ulidowski, I. (eds.) CONCUR 2012. LNCS, vol. 7454, pp. 471–485. Springer, Heidelberg (2012)

SAT Based Verification of Network Data Planes

Shuyuan Zhang and Sharad Malik

Department of Electrical Engineering, Princeton University, Princeton, NJ
{shuyuanz,sharad}@princeton.edu

Abstract. Formal verification has seen relatively less application in verifying computer networking infrastructure. This is in part due to the lack of clean layers of abstraction that enable design modeling and specification of correctness criteria. However, the recent move towards Software Defined Networking (SDN) provides a clean separation between a centralized control plane and a distributed data plane. This provides an opportunity to formally verify critical data plane properties. In this paper, we present a Boolean Satisfiability (SAT) based framework for data plane modeling and checking of key correctness criteria. This provides greater efficiency and/or greater coverage of properties when compared to other existing approaches.

1 Introduction

Network configuration and management are notoriously difficult due to the size and complexity of the network and it has been shown that 62% of the network downtime is caused by configuration errors [1]. Traditionally this has been addressed through testing [2], however this is increasingly inadequate for the properties of interest and the scale of modern networks. There has been some recent interest in applying formal verification techniques such as model checking, ternary symbolic simulation and SAT-based analysis (discussed in [3]), and this paper takes this significantly forward.

The network is traditionally viewed in two parts: the **Data Plane**, responsible for forwarding and/or modifying packets, and the **Control Plane**, responsible for configuring the data plane. While these are conceptually separate, traditional distributed implementations make it difficult to derive suitable abstractions of these for verification. Recently, there has been a move towards Software Defined Networking (SDN) that provides a clean separation between a centralized control plane and a distributed data plane [4]. This enables deriving a clean abstraction of the data plane and stating the correctness criteria for it.

In this paper we focus on the verification of a given configuration of the data plane, and use the term network to refer to this static view of the data plane. Thus, this verification deals with properties related to the outcome of individual packets through the network. This is of particular interest since any network fault must manifest itself as an undesirable outcome for some packet through the network. We present a SAT-based framework to model this network and verify a set of network properties of interest. Further, the data-plane properties

D. Van Hung and M. Ogawa (Eds.): ATVA 2013, LNCS 8172, pp. 496–505, 2013.

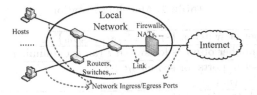

Fig. 1. An illustrative Sketch of a Local Area Network

considered deal with functional correctness related to packets in the network and not performance related such as meeting latency/throughput requirements.

This paper makes the following contributions: First, the SAT-based framework can model diverse network components such as routers, firewalls etc. by customizing a single propositional logic model of a generic switch component. This provides for uniformity in modeling. Second, we show how to model a rich set of network properties as Boolean formulas. This work is the first to cover a broad range of correctness criteria in a single uniform framework. Third, we have demonstrated the practical applicability of this framework through checking the publicly available Stanford network [5] and large synthetic benchmarks.

2   Network Systems: Background

2.1   Network System State

The network components considered here span a variety of devices such as routers, NATs and firewalls. We refer to these devices collectively as **switches** (Figure 1). In this paper, we only focus on the **packet header** (and not payload) since it captures information needed to process the packets. The header may be modified during packet processing in a switch. The network states we are interested in are the rules extracted from the switch data structures such as routing/forwarding tables in routers/switches, Access Control List (ACL) in firewalls, and Translation Table in NAT. Each switch can be modeled as a set of these **rules**. These rules have two fields, one **matching field** which the incoming packets should match against, and one **action field** which specifies what actions will be taken on the matching packets. The matching field is composed of the fields in the packet header, e.g. IP addresses, and is specified using $0, 1, *$, where wildcard $*$ matches both 0 and 1. The action field includes forwarding actions such as: forwarding packets to specific ports, flooding packets (forwarding a copy to all but the incoming ports), and packet rewriting. The **matching chain** consists of a list of strictly prioritized rules and the action for a packet corresponds to the highest priority rule which matches that packet.

We define the **switch state** as the collection of all the extracted rules stored in the switch. The **network state** is the collection of the switch states in all switches. While the controller can change the rules in the switches, we consider a snapshot of a dynamic network for verification. This snapshot has been traditionally difficult to obtain because of the distributed nature of the control and

Table 1. Modeling Notation

S	The set of switches $\{s_1, s_2, \ldots, s_i, \ldots, s_m\}$
$l(i)$	The number of ports for switch i (an even number)
$P(s_i)$	The set of ports for switch s_i: $P(s_i) = \{p_{i,1}, p_{i,2}, \ldots, p_{i,j}, \ldots, p_{i,l(i)}\}$
s_0	The abstraction of the network interface: $P(s_0)$ are the network ingress/egress ports
$type(.)$	The type of port: $type(p_{i,j}) \in \{IN, OUT\}$ (input/output port)
$h_{i,j}$	The value of the packet at port $p_{i,j}$: $h_{i,j} = (h_{i,j,1}, \ldots, h_{i,j,k}, \ldots, h_{i,j,n})$, $h_{i,j,k} \in \{0,1\}$
$valid(h_{i,j})$	The validity bit of a packet
$flag(h_{i,j})$	The flag bit of a packet
$\mathcal{T}_i$	The switch formula relating the input and output port headers
$\mathcal{N}$	The network formula - this is a topology based composition of switch formulas. $\mathcal{N} = \bigwedge_i \mathcal{T}_i$
$\mathcal{P}$	The property violation formula

data planes. *However, the move to SDN with a single centralized controller enables a clean abstraction of the data plane.* Gude argued that changes in the network rules are on the order of tens of events per second for a decent sized network while millions of packets arrive per second [6]. As network rule updates are much slower than the packet arrival rate, the network can be largely regarded as a static system. *Consequently, we assume that the network is stateless as it is fixed during verification and no packet can modify the network state.*

3   Formal Modeling

3.1   Property Violation and Packet Path Trace Counterexample

A key observation of our approach is that property violation can be specified through a counterexample consisting of a single packet and a path that it takes through the network. (This packet and path is referred to as **packet path** for short.) This path starts at a network ingress port and ends at some switch (if the packet is dropped) or at some network egress port (if the packet exits). *This observation is key in developing a SAT-based network and property model that constructs a Boolean formula for which a satisfying assignment is the packet path counterexample. A SAT based solution can only provide for existential quantification and it is convenient that universal or alternating quantification is not needed for any of the properties of interest discussed in Section 3.4.*

3.2   Network and Property Modeling

The network is composed of a set of switches and links. Each switch has a set of bidirectional ports. However, for ease of modeling each port (and link) is replaced by a pair of unidirectional ports (and links). The notation used in network modeling is listed in Table 1. A set of variables $h_{i,j}$ is used to represent the packet at port $p_{i,j}$. Since not all ports will have valid packets, $valid(h_{i,j}) ==$ 1 indicates that a valid packet is at $p_{i,j}$ and $valid(h_{i,j}) == 0$ indicates the absence of a valid packet. The flag bit is used for bookkeeping during packet processing. L is the set of links, where a link connects two ports. $(p_{i,j}, p_{k,l}) \in L$ indicates that $p_{i,j}$ is connected to port $p_{k,l}$ and $type(p_{i,j}) == OUT$ and $type(p_{k,l}) == IN$ and further $(h_{i,j} == h_{k,l})$.

$\mathcal{N}$ represents the consistent assignments to the packet variables for a single packet path through the network. Since $\mathcal{N}$ represents valid packet paths, the packet at only one of the network ingress ports can have its validity bit be 1. Thus, satisfiability of $\mathcal{N} \wedge \mathcal{P}$ indicates property failure and the satisfying assignment provides a packet path counterexample. As part of packet processing, a location may see multiple packets over time. This may happen when multiple packets are created at a switch, e.g., in flooding, and these different packets may arrive at a location at different times, or even when a packet loops through the network and reaches a location twice. However, in $\mathcal{N}$ each network location has only one set of variables representing the packet header. Two important modeling characteristics overcome this inadequacy.

Characteristic 1: The network model ensures that packets do not loop by detecting and blocking looping behavior.

Characteristic 2: The satisfying assignments to $\mathcal{N}$ represent *a single packet path through the network*. Thus, different paths created by packet creation (e.g. flooding) are represented through different satisfying assignments of $\mathcal{N}$.

These modeling characteristics are key in our ability to use a single set of packet variables at each network location to model signals that can take multiple values over time. Section 3.3 describes how these characteristics are achieved.

3.3 Switch Modeling

The switch formula $\mathcal{T}_i$ relates the input and output packet variables at switch i. *Since $\mathcal{N}$ represents valid packet paths, each switch must place at most one valid packet at its output ports* . A switch has the architecture shown in the Figure 2 consisting of three parts: an **input selection module** $(\mathcal{I}_i)$, a **matching chain**$(\mathcal{M}_i)$, and a **output selection module**$(\mathcal{O}_i)$ and $\mathcal{T}_i = \mathcal{I}_i(\{h_{i,j}\}, h_i) \wedge \mathcal{M}_i(h_i, \{h'_{i,k}\}) \wedge \mathcal{O}_i(\{h'_{i,k}\}, \{h_{i,l}\})$. The input selection module selects one of the incoming packets and passes it on as h_i. h_i is then matched against the matching chain, which processes h_i and possibly produces a packet $h'_{i,k}$ for port $p_{i,k}$. The output selection module non-deterministically selects one of the valid packets $h'_{i,k}$ and passes it on to port $p_{i,k}$ and drops all other packets.

Input Selection Module. Since there is only one packet that is allowed to match against the matching table, there are two possibilities.

Case 1: There is at most one valid packet at the input ports. The input selection passes this valid packet, if present, to the matching chain.

Case 2: There are two valid packets at the input ports (it can be shown that there cannot be more than two valid packets at the input ports). Since each

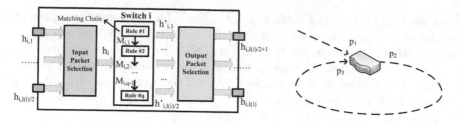

Fig. 2. Switch Overview   **Fig. 3.** Forwarding Loop

switch can place at most one valid packet at its output ports and there is a single valid packet at the network ingress ports, intuitively the only way this can happen is if there is a forwarding loop in the network as illustrated in Figure 3. (This is formally stated in Theorem 1.) In this figure the packet from the ingress port arrives at p_1 and after processing is placed on p_2 and this traverses back to p_3 at the switch. In this case the switch model explicitly blocks this looping packet from further processing. This is accomplished as follows. The flag bit, $flag(h_{i,j})$ indicates if a packet has not yet entered a loop. This bit is set to 1 for packets entering the network. If the input selection module sees two valid packets at the input ports, then the packet entering the loop from outside must have the flag bit 1 (packet at p_1). It selects this packet and sets its flag bit to 0. This packet is then processed by the switch, placed at p_2 from where it traverses to p_3. Since the input selection module sees the flag bit as 0 for the packet at p_3, it recognizes that this packet has looped back and does not select it for processing. Thus, effectively the loop is logically broken at p_3. *This is a key component of the modeling that enables a structural loop to be logically broken and thus satisfy Characteristic 1 highlighted earlier.* This explicit blocking of the looping behavior is justified because once it is detected, the expectation is that this will be removed.

These two cases are reflected by the following formula for $\mathcal{I}_i$: If there is only one port i that has a valid packet, $\mathcal{I}_i = \bigwedge_k (h_{i,k} == \bigvee_{\text{all input ports } j}(h_{i,j,k} \wedge valid(h_{i,j})))$. If there are multiple ports with valid packets, choose the port with flag bit equal to 1, $\mathcal{I}_i = \bigwedge_k (h_{i,k} == \bigvee_j (h_{i,j,k} \wedge valid(h_{i,j}) \wedge flag(h_{i,j})))$.

Matching Chain. $\mathcal{M}_i$ is determined by the matching rules as follows. The matching chain is composed of a chain of prioritized matching rules $R(s_i) = \{r_{i,1}, \ldots, r_{i,q}\}$. Each rule is composed of a matching field, a rewriting field, and a forwarding field i.e., $r_{i,j} = (m_{i,j}, t_{i,j}, F_{i,j})$ ($t_{i,j}$ and $F_{i,j}$ combine to form the action field). $m_{i,j}$ is a ternary array for the matching field and $m_{i,j} = (m_{i,j,1}, \ldots, m_{i,j,n})$, where $m_{i,j,k} \in \{0, 1, *\}$. $t_{i,j}$ is the rewriting field used to specify how the rule transforms the packet. If the rule does not modify the packet, $t_{i,j}(h_i) = h_i$. $F_{i,j}$ is the set of ports that the rules forwards the packet to.

The switch finds the highest priority rule that matches the packet selected by the input selection module and takes the corresponding action for this packet. $M_{i,j}$ indicates if the packet matches rule j. This uses component-wise ternary matching. $M_{i,j} = 1$ iff $(\forall k, k \in [1, n] : \neg(m_{i,j,k} \neq h_{i,k})) \wedge (\forall k, k < j : M_{i,k} == 0) \wedge valid(h_i)$

and $M_{i,j} = 0$ otherwise. $a \neq b$ only when $a == 1 \wedge b == 0$ or $a == 0 \wedge b == 1$. $*$ matches both 0 and 1. Then if $M_{i,j} == 1, \forall k \in F_{i,j} : h'_{i,k} = t_{i,j}(h_i)$, else, $valid(h'_{i,k}) = 0$.

Output Selection Module. $\mathcal{O}_i$ is determined as follows. If more than one output port is specified (e.g. packet flooding), one of $h'_{i,k}$ is non-deterministically selected. This non-determinism is captured in the switch formula through a choice variable C_i, $C(i) \in \{1, l(i)/2\}$. It is this non-determinism that maintains the constraint that there is at most one packet at the switch outputs. This combined with Characteristic 1, provides for Characteristic 2, i.e., the satisfying assignments to $\mathcal{N}$ represent *a single packet path through the network.* Thus, different paths such as those created by packet flooding are represented through different satisfying assignments of $\mathcal{N}$. The packet path is determined by the packet header at the network ingress and the assignment to the choice variables.

The packet at the output ports is determined as follows: $\forall j, type(p_{i,j}) == OUT : h_{i,j} = ($ if $(C_i == j)$ then $h'_{i,j}$ else $0)$, combined with a constraint $(\bigvee_j valid(h_{i,j})) == (\bigvee_j valid(h'_{i,j}))$, which specifies that if there is a valid packet at some $h'_{i,j}$, there must be a valid packet at some output port.

3.4 The Encoding of Properties

The following set of critical data plane properties are considered in this paper:

Reachability. Given a set of packets at network ingress port A (say $h_{0,0}$), we would like to check that every packet in this set reaches network egress port B (say $h_{0,1}$). In $\mathcal{P}$, we constrain $h_{0,0}$ to this set of packets and set $valid(h_{0,0})$ to 1. The validity bits at all other network ingress ports is set to 0, as is $valid(h_{0,1})$. If $\mathcal{N} \wedge \mathcal{P}$ is satisfiable, then the satisfying assignment provides a packet path counterexample of a packet from this set that either got dropped or stuck in a forwarding loop or exited at some other egress port.

Forwarding Loop. The network has a **forwarding loop** if some packet returns to a switch twice and that packet has to be reachable from one of the network's ingress port. From the definition of the input packet selection module in Section 3.3, we intuitively see that for a forwarding loop to be present, there must be two packets entering one switch. One of them must have a flag bit 1 and the other has a flag bit 0. Recall that there is only one packet injected into the network through one of the network ingress ports and that packet has a flag bit set to 1.

The following theorem formally states this condition. The detailed proof has been omitted for brevity.

Theorem 1. (Forwarding Loop Theorem) *There exists a loop if and only if there is some switch i such that there are valid packets at two different input ports $p_{i,j}$ and $p_{i,k}$, i.e.*

$$\exists i, j, k (j \neq k) : (valid(h_{i,j}) == 1) \wedge (valid(h_{i,k}) == 1) \quad (Property \ \mathcal{P})$$

Slice Isolation. Network systems partition resources into different **slices**. A slice can be viewed as a collection of the tuples of packet header and packet locations, such as ports. The **slice isolation** property checks that a packet from one slice does not cross over to another slice. Let s be a switch and $p_{s,1}$ be an input port, $p_{s,2}$ be an output port, and h_1, h_2 be two packets. Let $(h_1, p_{s,1})$ be in Slice 1 and $(h_2, p_{s,2})$ in Slice 2. We need to ensure that h_1 at $p_{s,1}$ is not processed by switch s into h_2 at $p_{s,2}$. While it may seem that this check can be done locally at each switch, this can lead to false positives, i.e., a counterexample $(h_1, p_{s,1})$ may not be reachable if h_1 never presents itself at $p_{s,1}$. Thus, in $\mathcal{P}$ we constrain the *valid* input packet at a switch to be in a different slice from the valid output packet at a switch. The validity of the input packet ensures that this packet can reach s from some network ingress port.

4   Comparison with Related Work

There are several related efforts in the area of formal network/data plane verification. We briefly review them here and place our work relative to them.

There is a set of efforts based on using finite state systems. As in our work, they consider the network state to be fixed, i.e., a snapshot of the dynamic network. However, they consider transitions in the packet state. The packet state is defined as (h, p). The state transitions are determined by the network state, i.e., the rules in the switches. These efforts can further be partitioned into two groups - one based on model checking this finite state system [7,8] and one based on ternary symbolic simulation of this system [5]. The model checking efforts use CTL to model the properties of reachability and absence of forwarding loops and use standard model checkers to check them. In contrast, we avoid the state space analysis involved in model checking through innovative propositional logic network and property modeling.

A key advantage of our approach over ternary symbolic simulation (the *Header Space Analysis* approach) is a uniform framework for checking properties. For example, in order to check forwarding loops, their approach needs to tag each packet with all the ports that it has visited. For large networks this overhead can be substantial. Further, while we uniformly use propositional logic to specify properties, there is no clean formalism for specifying properties in their approach. Overall, the processing of ternary vectors inherits the limitations of a Disjunctive Normal Form (DNF) representation including a possibly exponential growth of packets in going through a prioritized matching chain. [1] While our method does build a Conjunctive Normal Form (CNF) formula, it avoids any size explosion through the standard technique of adding intermediate variables.

The effort that is closest to our work is the *Anteater* project that also encodes the property check as a Boolean formula [9]. However, unlike our model, it does not build a single formula for the network and then check different properties for it. Rather, they build a custom formula for checking the reachability between

---

[1] This is because each matching rule passes down to lower priority rules the set difference of the current set of packets in DNF with what is matched by this rule.

two ports. They also show how a forwarding loop involving a specific switch s can be checked by splitting this switch into two switches s and s' and the checking the reachability of s' from s. Further, for checking loops for the complete network this check needs to be done for each switch separately. Also, like us, they consider single paths, but do so by limiting the method to only simple forwarding, i.e., they do not consider packet creation, which is the difficult case. Thus, the main strength of our approach compared to them is that we provide a uniform framework for modeling the entire network and checking a wide range of properties through a single SAT check per property.

5   Experimental Results

We have implemented a tool called NetSAT based on our approach and conducted a series of experiments to test its efficacy. The first test benchmark used is the publicly available Stanford backbone network [5]. The second set of benchmarks are synthetically generated. In these benchmarks we use the Waxman topology [10]. For each switch in the network, we connect an ingress/egress port to it as the network's input and output. We use depth-first-search on each pair of the network ingress and egress ports to generate the matching rule set for packet forwarding without any header modification. All experiments use Minisat as the SAT solver and run on Ubuntu Linux with kernel 3.2.0 and Intel Xeon processor running at 3.2GHz without using any parallelism.

Stanford Backbone Network: The Stanford network has 16 routers and includes full network complexity (VLAN tags, ACLs, etc.). This expands the rule set to about 15,000 rules and results in a formula with about 6.2 million CNF variables and 32 million CNF clauses. It takes about 100 seconds to return satisfiable for both forwarding loop and reachability checking. It takes about 5 seconds for unsatisfiable cases for reachability checking as in this case the packet gets dropped very quickly as it traverses through the network.

Synthetic Benchmarks: For the synthetic benchmarks, we ran four sets of experiments to study the effect of the total number of rules, total number of switches, and the header size of the packet on the execution time for property checking. The property checked is absence of forwarding loops as this is the more time consuming one (in Experiment 1 we check both forwarding loop and reachability) and we report the run time for the unsatisfiable case as that is the slower case for this benchmark set.

   Experiment 1: We consider two different networks for property checking (reachability and absence of forwarding loops): the first is composed of 50 switches (header width 64 bits) and the second is 100 switches (header width 64 and 160 bits). We increase the number of rules in the network from 100,000 to 2,000,000 with an increment of 100,000 for both networks (Figure 4).

   Experiment 2: For a fixed number of rules (0.5 million and 1 million), we increase the total number of switches from 10 to 200 with an increment of 10 and with a header size of 160 as shown in Figure 5.

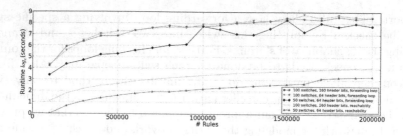

Fig. 4. Increasing the number of rules

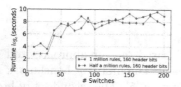

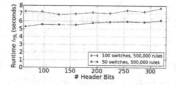

Fig. 5. Increasing the number of switches

Fig. 6. Increasing the size of header

Experiment 3: For a fixed topology (50 and 100 switches) with 500,000 rules stored in the network, we increase the header width from 64 bits to 320 bits as shown in Figure 6.

Experiment 4: For a 200,000-rule-50-switch topology, we divide the network into 50 slices and check if there exist any slices that overlap with each other. The experiment took 47 minutes to finish.

Based on the results of these experiments we make the following observations. Our tool is capable of handling large-sized networks. The 50-switch case in Figure 4 with <1 million rules completes within 10 minutes. The slowest case is checking the 190-switch 1-million-rule 160-header-bit network which took 4.5 hours. Checking reachability is significantly faster than checking forwarding loops (Figure 4) . This is likely because the property formula for reachability checking requires only part of the network. The increase of execution time is mainly caused by the increase in the number of switches and the total number of rules with little effect of the header width (Figure 6). The effect of the number of rules/switches is relatively intuitive since the size of the formula increases with the number of rules/switches. The limited effect of the header width may be due to the fact that we share a lot of packet variables as the network does not modify the header. This could change if this were not the case.

6   Conclusions

We present a propositional logic framework for network data plane modeling and property checking. This framework provides the following advantages: it avoids the state space traversal of model checking based methods, avoids the limitations of a DNF representation inherent in ternary symbolic simulation and provides a clean formalism for stating network properties and constraints that can check a richer set of properties compared to existing approaches. There are key challenges that needed to be overcome in developing this framework. Specifically, networks can have logical loops. This makes it hard to use a propositional logic model as used in combinational networks which deal with a single stable value for each signal. Overcoming these challenges required innovative modeling that took advantage of the typical properties that need to be verified here. Empirically our approach is applicable to real networks, such as the Stanford backbone network. It also compares favorably to the alternate approaches while providing greater property coverage with comparable or better performance.

References

1. Kerravala, Z.: As the value of enterprise networks escalates, so does the need for configuration management. Technical report, Yankee Group (2004)
2. Xie, G., Zhan, J., Maltz, D., Zhang, H., Greenberg, A., Hjalmtysson, G., Rexford, J.: On static reachability analysis of ip networks. In: Proceedings IEEE 24th Annual Joint Conference of the IEEE Computer and Communications Societies, INFOCOM 2005, vol. 3, pp. 2170–2183 (March 2005)
3. Zhang, S., Malik, S., McGeer, R.: Verification of computer switching networks: An overview. In: Chakraborty, S., Mukund, M. (eds.) ATVA 2012. LNCS, vol. 7561, pp. 1–16. Springer, Heidelberg (2012)
4. McKeown, N., Anderson, T., Balakrishnan, H., Parulkar, G., Peterson, L., Rexford, J., Shenker, S., Turner, J.: Openflow: enabling innovation in campus networks. SIGCOMM Comput. Commun. Rev. 38(2), 69–74 (2008)
5. Kazemian, P., Varghese, G., McKeown, N.: Header space analysis: static checking for networks. In: Proceedings of the 9th USENIX Conference on Networked Systems Design and Implementation, NSDI 2012, p. 9. USENIX Association, Berkeley (2012)
6. Gude, N., Koponen, T., Pettit, J., Pfaff, B., Casado, M., McKeown, N., Shenker, S.: Nox: towards an operating system for networks. SIGCOMM Comput. Commun. Rev. 38(3), 105–110 (2008)
7. Al-Shaer, E., Al-Haj, S.: Flowchecker: configuration analysis and verification of federated openflow infrastructures. In: Proceedings of the 3rd ACM Workshop on Assurable and Usable Security Configuration, SafeConfig 2010, pp. 37–44. ACM, New York (2010)
8. Reitblatt, M., Foster, N., Rexford, J., Schlesinger, C., David, W.: Abstractions for network update. SIGCOMM Comput. Commun. Rev. (August 2012)
9. Mai, H., Khurshid, A., Agarwal, R., Caesar, M., Godfrey, P.B., King, S.T.: Debugging the data plane with anteater. In: Proceedings of the ACM SIGCOMM 2011 Conference, SIGCOMM 2011, pp. 290–301. ACM, New York (2011)
10. Waxman, B.: Routing of multipoint connections. IEEE Journal on Selected Areas in Communications 6(9), 1617–1622 (1988)

A Theory for Control-Flow Graph Exploration

Stephan Arlt[1], Philipp Rümmer[2], and Martin Schäf[1]

[1] United Nations University, IIST, Macau S.A.R., China
[2] Uppsala University, Sweden

Abstract. Detection of infeasible code has recently been identified as a scalable and automated technique to locate likely defects in software programs. Given the (acyclic) control-flow graph of a procedure, infeasible code detection depends on an exhaustive search for feasible paths through the graph. A number of encodings of control-flow graphs into logic (understood by theorem provers) have been proposed in the past for this application. In this paper, we compare the performance of these different encodings in terms of runtime and the number of queries processed by the prover. We present a theory of acyclic control-flow as an alternative method of handling control-flow graphs. Such a theory can be built into theorem provers by means of theory plug-ins. Our experiments show that such native handling of control-flow can lead to significant performance gains, compared to previous encodings.

1 Introduction

Recently, attempts are being made to use static verification to prove the presence of *infeasible code* [7,3,14]. Infeasible code refers to statements that cannot occur on any feasible (and complete) control-flow path in a program. Infeasible code detection can be used to detect common coding mistakes like unreachable code, insufficient error handling, or redundant checks whether pointers are well-defined (see [3] for further examples). The benefit of using static verification to prove the presence of bugs instead of their absence is that it can be implemented in a modular and scalable way with a very low rate of false warnings. If a proof exists that a certain statement cannot be executed, most likely this indicates a coding mistake (not necessarily a bug), whereas, if the proof fails, infeasible code detection simply remains silent. That is, while infeasible code detection can miss occurrences of infeasible code (i.e., false negatives), it hardly causes false alarms. Another benefit is that infeasible code detection can be implemented in a modular fashion: if a statement does not have a feasible execution in its containing procedure (regardless of the calling context), then it will not have an execution in its containing program as a whole. Thus, infeasible code detection can be implemented in a modular way on isolated code snippets without risking false alarms (but possibly false negatives).

In order to show that a code fragment (basic block) within a given program is feasible, an execution trace has to be found that contains the fragment. For each code fragment, a formula is constructed whose satisfiability implies the existence

D. Van Hung and M. Ogawa (Eds.): ATVA 2013, LNCS 8172, pp. 506–515, 2013.

of an execution for the considered code fragment. This formula is sent to a theorem prover, which either proves that the fragment in fact has no execution (the formula is unsatisfiable), or computes a model that witnesses the existence of an execution. The construction of execution traces is the main bottleneck of algorithms for checking feasibility.

We present a tighter integration of feasibility checking with the search procedure executed by theorem provers, by defining a *theory of control flow* that is natively implemented and integrated into the prover in the form of a *theory plug-in*. With the help of the theory, we implement a query-optimal algorithm for feasibility checking, similar in spirit to the procedure presented in [3]. The use of a theory plug-in eliminates the need for helper variables to implement the query-optimal algorithm, and generally enables more efficient control-flow exploration; in experiments on real-world Java applications, our new algorithm is more than one order of magnitude faster than the one in [3], and significantly faster than other (encoding-based) algorithms for infeasible code detection that we compared to. We believe that our results make a convincing case for native implementation of decision procedures reasoning about program structure, with implications also for other forms of static analysis, including verification of safety properties and white-box methods to generate test cases.

The *contributions* of this paper are: (i) the definition of a theory of acyclic control flow, and an efficient implementation with the help of a theory plug-in; (ii) a query-optimal algorithm for feasibility checking; and (iii) an experimental evaluation on a set of large Java applications. Our implementation and benchmarks are publicly available.[1]

Related Work. Different approaches have been presented to identify code that does not occur on feasible executions within a given program, such as [6,8,14,3]. In this paper we focus on static verification based approaches to detect infeasible code and on their strategies to explore all paths in a program. In [14] so called *wedges* are identified as a suitable subset of statements that need to be check. In [7] Boolean helper variables are used to render all executions that do not pass a location infeasible. Both approaches are worst-case optimal but neither proposes a strategy to explore the program efficiently.

In [3], integer-typed helper variables are used to enable queries that check for the existence of a feasible path which covers at least n previously uncovered statements. With that, a query-optimal algorithm is possible. We have reimplemented this approach for our experiments.

In [4] a different encoding of the weakest liberal precondition is proposed that also encodes the backward reachability of statements. With this encoding, counterexamples from the theorem prover can be used to identify feasible control-flow paths in a program. Based on this, they present a covering algorithm that uses enabling clauses. They argue that allowing to prover to find a covering strategy is more efficient than forcing it towards a particular strategy. We will also compare with this algorithm in our experiments.

---

[1] http://www.joogie.org

2   A Theory of Acyclic Control-Flow

2.1   Programs and Acyclic Control-Flow Graphs

Throughout this paper, we consider programs written in a simple unstructured language. The language can be seen as a simplified version of Boogie [10]:

$$Program ::= Block^*$$
$$Block ::= label: Stmt^* \textbf{ goto } label^*;$$
$$Stmt ::= VarId := Expr; \mid \textbf{assume } Expr;$$

The semantics of programs is as usual. We focus on the case of *loop-free* (or *acyclic*) programs, and refer to related work for sound approaches to compute, for an arbitrary program P, a loop-free program $P^\#$ that over-approximates the feasible executions of P (e.g., [7,5]). We also assume that programs are upfront transformed to *passive form* [2], which means that assignments are replaced with fresh program variables and **assume** statements. Without loss of generality, it can further be assumed that every block in a program only consists of a single **assume** statement.

Definition 1 (Acyclic Control-Flow Graph). *An acyclic control-flow graph (ACFG) is defined by a tuple (B, E, b_e, b_x), where B is a set of propositional variables representing basic blocks, $E \subseteq B^2$ is an acyclic edge relation, and $\{b_e, b_x\} \subseteq B$ are two nodes such that every node in B is reachable from b_e, and b_x is reachable from every node in B.*

Every passive loop-free program can be represented by an ACFG (B, E, b_e, b_x), together with a function $S : B \to For$ that maps every block variable $b \in B$ (representing a block $l_b :$ **assume** $\phi_b;$ **goto** ...) to the formula $S(b) = \phi_b$.

Definition 2 (Feasible block). *Suppose (B, E, b_e, b_x) is an ACFG, and S a labelling of the blocks as above. A block represented by block variable $b \in B$ is called* feasible *iff there is a set $P = \{b_1, b_2, \ldots, b_n\} \subseteq B$ of nodes such that $b \in P$, $b_1 = b_e$, $b_n = b_x$, for all $i \in \{1, \ldots, n-1\}$ it is the case that $(b_i, b_{i+1}) \in E$, and $\bigwedge_{i=1}^n S(b_i)$ is satisfiable.*

In order to systematically discover feasible blocks, we consider the models of the formula $WLP \wedge b_e$, where:

$$WLP = \bigwedge_{b \in B} \left(b \implies S(b) \wedge SuccConj(b) \right) \tag{1}$$

$$SuccConj(b) = \begin{cases} \bigvee_{(b,b') \in E} b' & \text{if } b \neq b_x \\ true & \text{otherwise} \end{cases}$$

It is easy to see that a block $b \in B$ is feasible iff $WLP \wedge b_e$ has a model that maps b to *true*, and in which the subset $B' \subseteq B$ of block variables that is mapped to *true* is minimal [1]. Hence, a theorem prover can be used to enumerate feasible blocks by repeatedly computing models of the conjunction $WLP \wedge b_e$. While this encoding is correct and practical, for the application of infeasible code detection it can be observed that it tends to provide insufficient guidance to a solver. In particular, when forcing the prover to follow a particular cover strategy (like in [3]), we claim that it is beneficial to assist the prover by providing domain-specific knowledge about the structure of the control-flow graph to be explored; otherwise, the implemented cover strategy can cause a slowdown rather than a speedup, as the prover has to do significantly more internal backtracking [4] in order to accommodate the cover strategy. We present a way of integrating CFG exploration more deeply into the search algorithm used by solvers.

2.2   Acyclic Control-Flow Graphs as a Theory

We want to force a prover to discover paths with many previously uncovered nodes first, and define a particular notion of control-flow path for this purpose:

Definition 3 (k-C-Path). *Suppose (B, E, b_e, b_x) is an ACFG, $C \subseteq B$ is a set of nodes, and $k \in \mathbb{N}$ is an integer. A k-C-path is a set $P = \{b_1, b_2, \ldots, b_n\} \subseteq B$ of nodes such that $b_1 = b_e$, $b_n = b_x$, for all $i \in \{1, \ldots, n-1\}$ it is the case that $(b_i, b_{i+1}) \in E$, and $|P \cap C| \geq k$.*

Since the nodes B of an ACFG are defined to be propositional variables, we can regard an ACFG (together with a set C and an integer k) as a logical theory that restricts the interpretation of B to k-C-paths:

Definition 4 (ACFG theory). *The ACFG theory over (B, E, b_e, b_x), a set $C \subseteq B$, and $k \in \mathbb{N}$ is defined by the following axiom:*

$$\bigvee_{\substack{P \subseteq B \\ a\ k\text{-}\overline{C}\text{-path}}} \left(\bigwedge P \wedge \neg \bigvee (B \setminus P) \right) \tag{2}$$

The ACFG theory can be used to discover feasible blocks in a program, by choosing $C \subseteq B$ as the set of blocks in a program that still have to be covered, and k as some constant determining how many blocks are supposed to be covered simultaneously. Every model of the formula $WLP \wedge b_e$ that also satisfies (2) (i.e., every *model modulo the ACFG theory, with parameters k and C*) represents a feasible k-C-path through the given program.

Clearly, axiom (2) will in general be of exponential size (in the size of the underlying ACFG), and is therefore not a practical way to implement the theory. The next section discusses how an efficient implementation, in the context of a DPLL-based solver, can be achieved by combining a set of smaller logical axioms with a tailor-made constraint propagator.

2.3   Native Implementation of ACFG Theories

We implement a decision procedure for an ACFG theory in two parts:

1. a set of *axioms* that ensure that at least one path from b_e to b_x is selected in every accepted model;
2. a *propagator* (or *theory solver*) that ensures that at most one path is selected in a model, and that this path is a k-C-path.

In the rest of the section, we assume that an ACFG (B, E, b_e, b_x), a set $C \subseteq B$, and a threshold $k \in \mathbb{N}$ have been fixed.

Axioms. The required axioms are simple implications in forward direction, starting at the initial node of the ACFG:

$$\left\{ b_e \right\} \cup \left\{ \left(b \implies \bigvee Succ(b) \right) \mid b \in B \setminus \{b_x\} \right\} \tag{3}$$

where $Succ(b) = \{b' \mid (b, b') \in E\}$ is the set of direct successors of $b \in B$.

In order to satisfy (3), a prover has to assign *true* to variable b_e, and whenever some block variable b is selected (assigned *true*), also one of the successors of b needs to be selected. Consequently, the axioms (3) are satisfied by interpretations of the variables B in which at least one path from b_e to b_x is selected; it is left to the heuristics of the prover which path to pick. However, satisfying interpretations might select multiple paths simultaneously, and they might also contain paths that do not start in the initial node b_e (but end in b_x). Selected paths might moreover not be k-C-paths.

In our context, it can be observed that the axioms (3) are implied by the formula $WLP \wedge b_e$ constructed in Section 2.1. This means that a search for models of $WLP \wedge b_e$ (as done in Section 2.4 below) will automatically satisfy also (3), and it is not necessary to explicitly assert (3) as well.

Propagator. DPLL-style solvers [11] construct models of a given formula (usually modulo a set of background theories) by step-wise extension of partial interpretations, with backtracking being carried out whenever conflicts occur (dead ends in the search space are reached). In the context of an ACFG (B, E, b_e, b_x), this means that at any point during DPLL search there is a subset $B^+ \subseteq B$ of variables that have been assumed to be *true*, and a subset $B^- \subseteq B \setminus B^+$ of variables that have been assumed to be *false*. Other variables $B \setminus (B^+ \cup B^-)$ are unassigned. This means that the search has narrowed down the set of considered k-C-paths to those paths $P \subseteq B$ with $B^+ \subseteq P$ and $B^- \cap P = \emptyset$.

Given such a partial interpretation (B^+, B^-), a tailor-made propagator can infer further information, and thus decide the value of further variables in the remaining set $B \setminus (B^+ \cup B^-)$:

1. most importantly, the propagator can check whether there is at all a k-C-path $P \subseteq B$ with $B^+ \subseteq P$ and $B^- \cap P = \emptyset$. If this is not the case, the assignment (B^+, B^-) is inconsistent, and search has to backtrack.
2. it can be checked whether there are *inevitable nodes*

$$I = \bigcap \{P \subseteq B \mid P \text{ a } k\text{-}C\text{-path with } B^+ \subseteq P, \ B^- \cap P = \emptyset\}$$

that have to visited by every k-C-path that is consistent with the chosen assignment (B^+, B^-). Variables in I can immediately be set to *true*.

3. it can be checked whether there are *unreachable nodes*

$$U = \; B \setminus \bigcup \{P \subseteq B \mid P \text{ a } k\text{-}C\text{-path with } B^+ \subseteq P, \; B^- \cap P = \emptyset\}$$

that are not visited by any k-C-path consistent with the assignment (B^+, B^-). Variables in U can immediately be set to *false*.

Note that the first kind of inference ensures that only satisfying assignments with at most one path are accepted, and only in case the path is a k-C-path. In combination with the axioms (3), this implies that only models representing single k-C-paths are produced. The second and third kind of propagation provide input for further *Boolean constraint propagation,* and ensure that a theorem prover does not spend time exploring parts of the ACFG in which no k-C-paths can exist; in particular, a prover can immediately ignore any implication $b \implies S(b) \wedge SuccConj(b)$ (from (1)) with $b \in U$, and can immediately process the succedent $S(b) \wedge SuccConj(b)$ in case $b \in I$. In comparison with a direct encoding into logic (as in [3]), this provides a degree of look-ahead that can significantly speed up search.

All three types of inference can be performed in linear time in the size of the ACFG (B, E, b_e, b_x) by means of simple dynamic programming.

For our experiments, we implemented an ACFG constraint propagator in form of a *theory plug-in* that is loaded into the Princess theorem prover [13] and initialised with the ACFG (B, E, b_e, b_x), the set $C \subseteq B$, and the threshold $k \in \mathbb{N}$. The theory plug-in monitors the variable assignments made during search, and if possible adds inferred information (about inconsistency of the assignment (B^+, B^-), or the value of the variables in I and U) to the state of the search.

2.4   Infeasibility Checking with ACFG Theories

With the propagator from above, we can now implement a greedy path-cover algorithm for an ACFG on top of an incremental prover, following the idea of [3]: our algorithm *InfCode*, as shown in Algorithm 1, takes a loop-free program P and the associated ACFG (B, E, b_e, b_x), and then repeatedly computes models of the formula $WLP \wedge b_e$ representing terminating executions of P. Such models are constructed modulo the ACFG theory for (B, E, b_e, b_x), with the set C initially set to the set of all nodes B, and k to a sufficiently large number (e.g., the length of a path from b_e to b_x); only models are accepted that represent k-C-paths.

We repeatedly check for the existence of ACFG-models of $WLP \wedge b_e$ using the helper function `checkSat` (line 7). If a model exists, i.e., `checkSat` returns *SAT*, we remove all variables b_i from C that were assigned *true* (line 9); such variables represent blocks on the found k-C-path. We then re-initialize the theory plug-in with the new reduced set C (line 10), and search for further models.

If no k-C-path exists, i.e., `checkSat` returns *UNSAT*, we restart the search for models with $k \leftarrow \lceil k/2 \rceil$ (line 15 and 16). The algorithm terminates if our set C becomes empty and thus all nodes have been covered (line 4), or we do

---

Algorithm 1. *InfCode*: an algorithm to detect infeasible code.

Input: Passive loop-free program P with ACFG $(B, E, entry, exit)$
Output: C: The set of block variables that do not have feasible executions.
begin

    $k \leftarrow$ average path length ;
    $C \leftarrow B$;

    assert($WLP \wedge b_e$);
    restartModelSearch(k, C);

    while $C \neq \{\}$ **do**
        $R \leftarrow$ checkSat ;
        if $R = SAT$ **then**
            $C \leftarrow \{b_i \in C \mid b_i$ is assigned *false* in model$\}$;
            reinitPlugin(C);
        else
            if $k = 1$ **then**
                return C
            end if
            $k \leftarrow \lceil k/2 \rceil$;
            restartModelSearch(k, C);
        end if
    end while
end

---

not find any k-C-path for $k = 1$ (line 10). In that case, all remaining nodes in C cannot occur on a feasible path. A proof is given in [3].

Now let C be a so-called *effectual* subset of B [3]. That is, $C \subseteq B$ is called effectual if it is a minimal set of block variables such that a set of feasible paths that covers all elements in C also covers all elements in B.

Theorem 1. *Given an ACFG (B, E, b_e, b_x) with an unknown set of feasible paths. Let $C \subseteq B$ be an effectual subset of B, and $N(C)$ be the maximum number of elements in C that can occur together on one control-flow path. If K is the size of the smallest set of feasible paths that covers all coverable elements in C, then Algorithm 1 performs at most $O(K \cdot \log(N(C)))$ queries.*

A proof is given in [3]. As shown in [9] and [12] this is a query-optimal solution for the case that the set of feasible paths is unknown. However, the algorithm queries a theorem prover to check for a feasible path with certain properties. This is the most expensive part of the whole algorithm; in previous experiments, which implemented the algorithm with the help of a purely logical encoding and auxiliary variables, this led to the observation that the query-optimal algorithm is in reality slower than theoretically sub-optimal solutions [4]. We hypothesise that the implementation in form of a theory plug-in alleviates this bottleneck; to check if our intuition holds, we compare our algorithm with other approaches on several large-scale programs in the following section.

Table 1. Name, size, and detected infeasible code for the six AUTs in our experiments

Program	LOC	# methods	# inf code
Open eCard	456,220	15,654	26
ArgoUML	156,294	9,981	28
FreeMind	53,737	5,613	10
Joogie	11,401	973	0
Rachota	11,037	1,279	1
TerpWord	6,842	360	3

3 Experiments

We have implemented our approach in Joogie, `http://www.joogie.org`. The Joogie tool takes a Java program as input and computes a loop-free abstraction of this program that can be translated into first-order logic (modulo the theory of arrays, and linear integer arithmetic). Joogie then generates feasibility checks, using four encoding schemes outlined in the next paragraph, and sends the resulting constraints to the theorem prover Princess [13]. For details on this translation and the inserted run-time assertions we refer to [3].

Experimental setup. For the loop-free program provided by Joogie, we compare four ways of detecting infeasible code. **(A)** the method presented in Section 2, implemented using a native theory plug-in, **(B)** an approach that uses enabling clauses to cover at least one new block in each iteration [4], **(C)** an approach that uses blocking clauses to never cover the same path twice [4], and **(D)** an approach that is similar to ours, but uses the solver as a black box and asserts linear inequalities to implement a query-optimal algorithm [3].

Note that all four approaches to detect infeasible code are complete for loop-free Boogie programs. Hence the detection rate is the same for all approaches (and only limited by the abstraction performed by Joogie), and we are only interested in the computation time of each approach.

We evaluate our approach on six open-source applications (AUTs): Open-eCard, a software to support the German eID, a CASE tool called ArgoUML, the mind-mapping tool FreeMind, the time-keeping software Rachota, the word processor TerpWord, and Joogie itself. Joogie applied each infeasible code detection algorithm to each procedure of an AUT individually. That is, Joogie does not perform inter-procedural analysis. Calls to procedures are replaced by non-deterministic assignments to all variables modified by the callee instead. For each procedure, we stop the time spent in the theorem prover process. If the theorem prover takes more than 30 seconds to analyze one procedure, we kill the process with a timeout and continue with the next procedure. All experiments are run on a workstation with 3 GHz CPU, 8 GB RAM, and 640 GB HDD.

Table 1 shows the details of the AUTs including the infeasible code that is found by Joogie. Even though we picked stable releases of each AUT, we could detect infeasible code in all of them besides Joogie. Most of the infeasible code

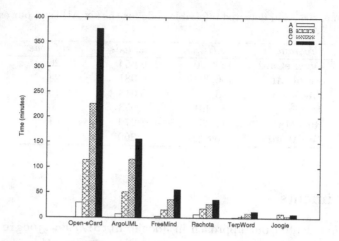

Fig. 1. Total time needed by the four considered algorithms on the six AUTs

found is unreachable, some is caused by `null` checks of objects that have already been accessed (which is actually unreachable), and few cases are reported due to explicit contradictions (e.g., dereferencing a pointer known to be `null`).

Results. Figure 1 shows our experimental results. Our algorithm **A** computed a total $133,330$ queries in 48.26 minutes. Algorithm **B** used $130,059$ queries and 206.20 minutes, algorithm **C** $250,566$ queries and 424.11 minutes, and algorithm **D** $132,976$ queries and 646.21 minutes. The experiments show that our approach is significantly faster on all AUTs than existing approaches. The greedy algorithms **A** and **D** require a similar amount of queries. However, algorithm **D** is significantly slower. This is because **D** forces the prover to restrict it's search to a particular subset of paths by adding linear inequalities which can only be understood by the prover when using the corresponding theory. The algorithms **A**, **B**, **D** require a similar number of queries. Algorithm **C** used significantly more time than **A** and **B**. Apparently, the theorem prover tries to change as few values as possible in each iteration, thus blocking clauses might cause the prover to explore all possible control-flow paths. However, we can see that not restricting the solver results in very fast queries (the smallest time per query).

Threats to validity. We report the expected threats to validity: our AUTs do not represent a statistically significant sample. However, they are real programs, not tailored towards the experiments, and of reasonable size. Another threat is that theorem provers other than Princess might produce different results.

4   Conclusion

We have presented a new algorithm to detect infeasible code. In contrast to previous work, our algorithm deeply integrates with the used theorem prover.

Not treating the theorem prover as a block box not only allows us to avoid additional instrumentation variables, it also enables the theorem prover to search for feasible control-flow paths significantly faster than in previous work. Since the time needed to process individual procedures is comparable to the time required for compilation (in particular type-checking), and since no false alarms are produced, we believe that infeasible code detection can be integrated in an IDE in a non-obtrusive way. With this integration, we will be able to detect infeasible code even before a program is executed. This is also the context in which we expect most occurrences of infeasible code, and a setting in which a large audience of users can be reached, opening a back door to provide programmers with a smooth learning curve towards the use of formal methods.

Acknowledgements. This work is supported by the grant COLAB of the Macao Science and Technology Development Fund, and by Vetenskapsrådet (VR).

References

1. Arlt, S., Liu, Z., Schäf, M.: Reconstructing paths for reachable code. In: ICFEM (to appear, 2013)
2. Barnett, M., Leino, K.R.M.: Weakest-precondition of unstructured programs. SIGSOFT SEN 31 (September 2005)
3. Bertolini, C., Schäf, M., Schweitzer, P.: Infeasible code detection. In: Joshi, R., Müller, P., Podelski, A. (eds.) VSTTE 2012. LNCS, vol. 7152, pp. 310–325. Springer, Heidelberg (2012)
4. Christ, J., Hoenicke, J., Schäf, M.: Towards bounded infeasible code detection. CoRR, abs/1205.6527 (2012)
5. Donaldson, A.F., Haller, L., Kroening, D., Rümmer, P.: Software verification using k-induction. In: Yahav, E. (ed.) SAS. LNCS, vol. 6887, pp. 351–368. Springer, Heidelberg (2011)
6. Engler, D., Chen, D.Y., Hallem, S., Chou, A., Chelf, B.: Bugs as deviant behavior: a general approach to inferring errors in systems code. In: SOSP (2001)
7. Hoenicke, J., Leino, K.R., Podelski, A., Schäf, M., Wies, T.: Doomed program points. FMSD (2010)
8. Hovemeyer, D., Pugh, W.: Finding bugs is easy. In: OOPSLA (2004)
9. Johnson, D.S.: Approximation algorithms for combinatorial problems, vol. 9 (1974)
10. Leino, K.R.M., Rümmer, P.: A polymorphic intermediate verification language: Design and logical encoding. In: Esparza, J., Majumdar, R. (eds.) TACAS 2010. LNCS, vol. 6015, pp. 312–327. Springer, Heidelberg (2010)
11. Nieuwenhuis, R., Oliveras, A., Tinelli, C.: Solving SAT and SAT modulo theories: From an abstract Davis-Putnam-Logemann-Loveland procedure to DPLL(T). Journal of the ACM 53(6) (2006)
12. Raz, R., Safra, S.: A sub-constant error-probability low-degree test, and a sub-constant error-probability PCP characterization of NP. In: STOC (1997)
13. Rümmer, P.: A constraint sequent calculus for first-order logic with linear integer arithmetic. In: Cervesato, I., Veith, H., Voronkov, A. (eds.) LPAR 2008. LNCS (LNAI), vol. 5330, pp. 274–289. Springer, Heidelberg (2008)
14. Tomb, A., Flanagan, C.: Detecting inconsistencies via universal reachability analysis. In: ISSTA

The Quest for Precision: A Layered Approach for Data Race Detection in Static Analysis

Jakob Mund[1,*], Ralf Huuck[2], Ansgar Fehnker[2,3], and Cyrille Artho[4]

[1] Technische Universität München, Munich, Germany
mund@in.tum.de
[2] NICTA, University of New South Wales, Sydney, Australia
ralf.huuck@nicta.com.au
[3] University of the South Pacific, Suva, Fiji
ansgar.fehnker@usp.ac.fj
[4] Research Institute for Secure Systems, AIST, Amagasaki, Japan
c.artho@aist.go.jp

Abstract. Low level data-races in multi-threaded software are hard to detect, especially when requiring exhaustiveness, speed and precision. In this work, we combine ideas from run-time verification, static analysis and model checking to balance the above requirements. In particular, we adopt a well-known dynamic race detection algorithm based on calculating lock sets to static program analysis for achieving exhaustiveness. The resulting data race candidates are in a further step investigated by model checking with respect to a formal threading model to achieve precision. Moreover, we demonstrate the effectiveness of the combined approach by a case study on the open-source TFTP server OPENTFTP, which shows the trade-off between speed and precision in our two-stage analysis.

Keywords: Software verification, static analysis, concurrency, lock sets.

1 Introduction

Modern processors commonly feature multi-core architectures. To fully use such hardware, software for multi-core processors often manages threads in the application code. Such concurrency carries the risk of introducing subtle but serious defects that might show up only sporadically and are extremely hard to debug. Common programming languages such as C provide only basic primitives for concurrency in terms of threading, while at the same time offering only limited tool support for debugging and bug prevention.

In this work we present a new way of detecting data races in embedded source code. We combine ideas from run-time verification, static analysis and software model checking by balancing their strengths and weaknesses. Run-time verification provides a good means to detect certain race conditions, but can only reason over program executions that have actually been observed, limiting coverage. Static analysis is strong in covering all potential execution paths, but is

---

* This work was carried out while visiting NICTA.

D. Van Hung and M. Ogawa (Eds.): ATVA 2013, LNCS 8172, pp. 516–525, 2013.
© Springer International Publishing Switzerland 2013

```
1 int shared_var = 0;      7
2                          8 void *writer() {
3 void *reader() {         9   for(;;) {
4   for(;;) {             10     shared_var = compute();
5     t = shared_var;     11 } }
6 } }
```

Fig. 1. Data Race Example

prone to (over-)approximations leading to false positives. On the other hand, software model checking offers a precise analysis of the program semantics, but with limitations regarding scalability to larger code bases.

We propose a layered approach: In a first step we use a path-sensitive static implementation of the well-known *Eraser* algorithm [15]. Our static version is able to detect data races in C programs with a complete path coverage. While the algorithm is applicable to large-scale software, it is also prone to false positives. Therefore, in a second step we take those data races as *candidates* for a deeper model checking approach. The model checking phase abstracts from non-essential data and instructions and takes the threading model into account.

In this way we avoid to apply traditional software model checking to the full multi-threaded source code, but rather treat its application as a false-positive elimination step on selected code parts only. As a result we obtain a solution that can deal with real software systems, has a higher degree of coverage than run-time verification, but is more precise than traditional static analysis.

This paper is organized as follows: In Section 2 introduces to data races and the objectives of this work, together with related work. We present our two-step analysis approach in Section 3, covering the Eraser lock set analysis and its combination with software model checking. Experimental evaluation is presented in Section 4, followed by our conclusions in Section 5.

2   Data Races in Multi-threaded Programs

Threads are concurrent streams of program execution that can be created, merged and deleted at run-time. Threads might have access to shared resources. A *data race* occurs if two or more threads can simultaneously and non-atomically access a shared resource with at least one access being a write operation.

An example data race is given in Figure 1. A `reader` thread reads a shared variable (lines 3–6); a `writer` thread writes to it (lines 8–11). If these accesses are not synchronized using locks or other coordination mechanisms, then their effects are not well-defined. The update of the writer thread may become visible to other threads immediately or at any time after it has been issued, due to memory caches and other optimizations in modern hardware. Reading `shared_var` may thus yield different results depending on thread scheduling and hardware, which is why it is desirable to avoid data races in concurrent software.

As threads can be created dynamically, the number of threads may be large. The effect of data races may only be visible under a particular interleaving of thread actions at run-time; this makes the detection of data races difficult.

2.1   Scope and Contribution

Like the Eraser algorithm [15] used in run-time verification, we detect low-level data races by finding inconsistent or absent locking of variables shared across threads. Eraser monitors the *lock set* that protects a shared variable during read and write accesses to it. On every access, Eraser computes the intersection of the lock set protecting that variable. If the intersection becomes empty, i. e., there is no single lock consistently protecting a variable, a warning is issued.

Static Eraser Implementation. In this work we introduce a path-sensitive static implementation of Eraser. Unlike run-time verification we consider all paths statically, possibly over-approximating the set of feasible interleavings, but ensuring full coverage. This approach finds all data races but may issue spurious warnings.

Model-checking Thread-Interleaving. We also propose another analysis that is more precise and can reduce false positives from the previous step. The second analysis creates the *thread-interleaving graph* of the program (with limited depth) that captures the call structure of the threads and their termination, as well as the read and write accesses to shared variables. Since the interleaving graph grows exponentially with the number of threads in the program, we restrict it to the *data-race candidates* as identified in the static Eraser approach. We then model-check the thread-interleaving graph for feasible data races. This approach is sound up for a bounded number of threads. Using abstraction we are able to apply this methods to real code as shown in the evaluation in Section 4.

Our approach is based on a thread-interleaving semantics as defined in [12]. This semantics takes into account thread creation, join and cancellation as well as the acquisition and releases of locks. Moreover, it includes the advanced concepts of waiting and signaling that require a view of the global program state and is thus not covered by Eraser or other thread-modular approaches.

2.2   Related Work

Eraser [15] is the classical lock-set based algorithm that approximates potential data races very well, while not having the overhead of more precise but heavyweight approaches based on the happens-before relation [16].

Goldilocks is a newer algorithm that computes data races precisely [7]. To be more accurate than Eraser, Goldilocks requires more elaborate data structures. Furthermore, the precision of Goldilocks depends on its ability to recognize overlapping data of multiple software transactions. That data is readily available and precise when using run-time verification, but is difficult to approximate precisely enough in static analysis, which is why our analysis is based on Eraser.

Other concurrency errors may still exist even in the absence of data races (called low-level data races to compare them with similar concurrency problems).

High-level data races [3] and atomicity violations [2,9] are two types of such problems. High-level data races cover non-atomic accesses to sets of dependent variables (multiple memory locations). Atomicity violations concern the scope during which a lock is held, and thus the use of the data rather than its direct access. These two types of problems have recently been subsumed by the notion of *causality* in data flow, which can cover both accesses to data and its use [6].

Static analysis of such concurrency properties has been attempted in other work, in a static analyzer where the rules are hard-coded in the program [1], and in a framework that is specialized for concurrency properties [11]. In contrast to that tool, we build on top of a general static analysis framework, Goanna [8], that allows flexible rules to express a wide range of different properties.

The second part of our work is closely related to other software model checkers, e. g., Java PathFinder [18] for Java bytecode and Inspect for C source code [19]. The key difference is that these software model checkers execute the full software at run time and explore alternative interleavings by rolling back the system to a previously stored state. This dynamic analysis is much more expensive than our approach, which works on an abstract model of the program.

Software model checkers working on a higher level of abstraction exist as well, such as SLAM, which analyzes device drivers against a given environment model [4], or SATABS, which can analyze programs using a subset of the Pthreads library [5]. In comparison, our work is not limited to certain domains (such as device drivers) and covers the full Pthreads library.

3   A Layered Approach for Static Race Detection

Our layered approach to detect data races first applies static analysis to obtain data race candidates and then applies model checking on those candidates.

3.1   Static Data Race Analysis

A common way to prevent data races is to impose a *locking discipline* that requires any shared (write) variable to be protected by at least one distinct lock among *all* threads. Since each lock can only be held by one thread, data races are effectively prevented.

Eraser [15] monitors the dynamic execution paths of each tread and records for each variable the lock set being held. If the intersection of those lock sets across threads for the same variable is empty, we assume a potential data race.

To achieve the same statically, we propose to check *all program paths* for each thread and then build the same intersection over all threads. Obviously, the static approach is an over-approximation as not all paths might be executable. We use the definition of a *lock set* [15,14] as the mapping of shared variables to its potential set of locks, i. e., $\mathbf{Lockset} : \mathbf{Variables}_\star \rightarrow \wp(\mathbf{Locks}_\star)$. In the following, we show how to compute and check for emptiness of the $\mathbf{Lockset}$.

Algorithm 1. Static implementation of the lock set algorithm.

---

begin

    Lockset$(v) \leftarrow$ **Locks**$_\star$;

    $isReadOnly_v \leftarrow tt$;

    foreach $\pi_i \in$ **Threads**$_\star$ **do**

        $lockstate \longleftarrow$ MFP($Nodes_{\pi_i}$, is_locked);

        foreach $n \in Nodes_{\pi_i}$ **do**

            if n $accesses$ v **then**

                LocalLockset$_{\pi_i}(v) \leftarrow$ **LocalLockset**$_{\pi_i}(v) \cap lockstate(n)$;

                $isReadOnly_v \leftarrow isReadOnly_v \vee (v$ is modified in n);

        Lockset$(v) \leftarrow$ **Lockset**$(v) \cap$ **LocalLockset**$_{\pi_i}(v)$;

Path-Sensitive Lock Set Computation. A thread (procedure) π is defined as a procedure with name pn that occurs in a thread-creation action denoted `create`(θ, pn). Nodes in the control flow graph of π are denoted by **Nodes**$_\pi$. For a given thread π we define a function **is_locked** : **Nodes**$_\pi \times$ **Locks**$_\star \to \mathbb{B}$ that returns for each node n in π and each lock l whether l is held along all paths leading to n by

$$\textbf{is\_locked}(n, l) = \begin{cases} tt & \text{if } n = \textbf{Lock l}, \\ ff & \text{if } n = \textbf{Unlock l}, \\ \forall m \in pred(n) \bigwedge \textbf{is\_locked}(m, l) & \text{otherwise.} \end{cases}$$

Here *pred* denotes the predecessors of a node; the conjunction ensures coverage of all potential paths. This notion captures a standard path-sensitive static program analysis to compute the must-hold locks for each node in a thread.[1] Based on the information about the held locks, the thread-local lock set for each shared variable $v \in$ **Variables**$_\star$ and thread $\pi_i \in$ **Threads**$_\star$ is computed by

$$\textbf{LocalLockset}(v, \pi_i) = \begin{cases} \bigcap_{n \in N_v} \{l' \mid \textbf{is\_locked}(n, l')\} & \text{if } N_v \neq \emptyset \text{ in } \pi_i, \\ \textbf{Locks}_\star & \text{otherwise.} \end{cases}$$

where N_v denotes the set of all nodes of π_i which access variable v. The second case accounts for variables which are not accessed in π_i, mapping them to the set of all locks. Finally, the lock set for a program is the intersection of the lock sets for each thread occurring in a given program, i. e.,

$$\textbf{Lockset}(v) := \bigcap_{\pi_i \in \textbf{Threads}_\star} \textbf{LocalLockset}(v, \pi_i)$$

Our algorithm [12] calculates the lock set using the maximal-fix-point worklist algorithm MFP [10] (see Algorithm 1). If **Lockset**(v) is non-empty for any shared variable v, the program is free of data-races.

---

[1] Modern programming languages like Java support `synchronized` blocks that acquire (resp. release) a lock when entering (resp. exiting) the critical section, enabling path-insensitive approaches [13].

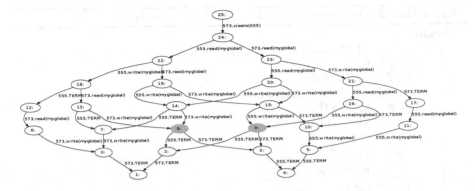

Fig. 2. A labeled transition system generated by applying the threading model. Colored vertices designate states with an imminent data race.

Soundness and Completeness. Under the assumption that shared variables (as well as locks and signals) do not alias, the static lock set algorithm for low-level data race detection presented here is *sound*, hence false negatives (i.e., missed races) are not possible due to the locking discipline.

However, the analysis is *incomplete* as false positives (i.e., spurious warnings) are possible, because the analysis does not consider the *temporal* (also called *happens-before*) relation among events in different threads. Furthermore, warnings may be spurious if data races are avoided by other synchronization primitives like signals, or other more fine-grained accesses of variables [17].

3.2 Model-Checking of the Threading Semantics

While the approach presented in the previous section uses a fast thread-modular analysis, it is also prone to potential false-positives. An alternative precise approach is to use formal semantics for the multi-threading constructs and variable accesses and apply model-checking on the imposed model.

Semantics of Multi-threaded Programs. For model-checking we formalize the essence of multi-threaded program constructs [12], e.g., thread management and lock synchronization, according to structural operational semantics. This results in a labeled transition system, in which a data race happens if for a global state σ there are two threads θ_1, θ_2 and at least one of the threads is write-enabled on a shared variable v, while the other one can read or write to v:

$$datarace(\theta) = enabled(\texttt{write}_v, \theta_1, \sigma) \wedge (enabled(\texttt{write}_v, \theta_2, \sigma) \vee enabled(\texttt{read}_v, \theta_2, \sigma))$$

Using this predicate low-level data races can be detected by checking (on-the-fly) whether there is a path such that a data race can be reached.

An example of such a transition system is shown in Figure 2. Global configurations are numbered nodes; the transition system considers program actions relating to shared variable *myglobal*. Procedure *TERM* denotes successful termination; the number in a label represents the global transition relation (see [12]).

Algorithm 2. On-the-fly reachability checking using BFS.

---

begin
$\quad \Sigma_{worklist} \leftarrow \{\langle \{\theta_{main} \mapsto \Pi(main)\}, \kappa_{\emptyset}, \lambda l.\bot \rangle\};$
$\quad \Sigma_{visited} \leftarrow \emptyset;$
$\quad$ **while** $\Sigma_{worklist} \neq \emptyset$ **do**
$\quad\quad \sigma_{current} \leftarrow dequeue(\Sigma_{worklist});$
$\quad\quad$ **if** $\sigma_{current} \vDash \phi$ **then**
$\quad\quad\quad$ WARN$(\sigma_{current});$
$\quad\quad\quad$ **return** *true*
$\quad\quad$ **foreach** $\sigma' \in \{\sigma' \mid \sigma_{current} \xrightarrow{\theta,a}_G \sigma' \wedge \sigma' \notin \Sigma_{visited}\}$ **do**
$\quad\quad\quad enqueue(\sigma', \Sigma_{worklist});$
$\quad\quad enqueue(\sigma_{current}, \Sigma_{visited});$
$\quad$ **return** *false*

Global states 8 and 9 represent locations at which data races happen, because the two preceding actions in both states are unsynchronized write accesses.

On real systems, model construction potentially results in an exponential blow-up both in the numbers of threads and the number of thread operations. Moreover, thread creation in an (unbounded) loop may yield a possibly unbounded number of threads. In practice, model-checking would use a k-bound to restrict the number of threads that a single thread can create *per local state*.

Our interleaving semantics is a faithful abstraction of the real program by only considering thread-specific concepts and read/writes to shared variables. Mapping a threaded program to this abstraction is a non-trivial task when considering function calls and some subtleties of the POSIX standard.

Implementation. Algorithm 2 checks whether a configuration satisfying a given predicate $\phi : \Sigma \rightarrow \mathbb{B}$ is reachable, and warns if a configuration satisfying ϕ $(\sigma \vDash \phi)$ is found. In this algorithm, the reachable states of the model are not generated *a priori* but during the analysis itself, i.e., on the fly. This happens at the **foreach**-loop where solely the immediate successors of $\sigma_{current}$ are explored.

Unlike Algorithm 1, model checking yields precise diagnostic information. Line numbers shown by WARN substantially facilitate tracking down defects.

The use of a breadth-first-search was motivated by how thread interleaving influences the model. Different interleavings for the termination of threads constitute a large part of the model but are of less interest for race detection.

Soundness and Completeness. Under the assumptions given above, our approach is *sound and complete* up to the fixed thread bound k, i.e., if each program instruction that instantiates a thread is successfully executed at most k times. Imprecision is introduced whenever thread instantiation is nested within loops that exceed the thread bound during execution. In those cases the analysis is neither sound nor complete. Fortunately, such bugs manifest rarely in practice.

3.3 Combining Both Analyses: The Layered Approach

The lock set algorithm is designed for performance, at the cost of possible spurious warnings. Since it is sound, each variable for which the analysis yields a non-empty set of distinct locks protecting it, is regarded as safe. On the other hand, model-checking yields precise results. However, the state-explosion problem often renders (detailed) models of concurrent programs too large for model-checking.

A natural consequence is to use a combined layered approach:

1. The lock set algorithm yields a (global) lock set for each shared variable. Variables with a non-empty lock set are safe.
2. We apply model-checking to the remaining shared variables in isolation. If a data race is reachable, we report that data race.

Step 2 can be thought of as a false-positive elimination for step 1. Note that the lock-set analysis does not worsen the precision of model-checking. It can be formally shown that if a non-empty lock set is found, a data race cannot be detected using the model-checking approach [12].

4 Case Study OpenTFTP

The core ideas of our layered approach have been implemented on top of the industrial-strength analysis tool *Goanna* [8]. Goanna analyzes C/C++ code using static analysis and model checking to detect bugs in large scale code. For our purposes we made use of the fact that the tool can readily produce control flow graphs, allows model generation with custom labels based on syntactic abstraction, and supports a summary-based interprocedural analysis.

However, a number of simplifications were made: The maximum thread creation bound was set to two, a pre-processing heuristics was used to detect the shared variables, and potential aliases as well as dynamic memory allocations were ignored. Moreover, for handling the threading semantics we inlined function calls, which is clearly not scalable, but sufficient for experiments.

The case study was executed on a Mobile Core2Duo Processor (clock freq. 1.83 Ghz, 4 GB of memory) running on Ubuntu Linux 9.10. We measured both the runtime of the multi-threading analyses presented in this paper (T_{MTA}) as well as the complete tool runtime including computation by Goanna (T_{total}).

The TFTP server software OPENTFTP was used as a real-world software example. The size of the program is about 2.5 KLOC, and it features high functional complexity coupled with many multi-threading and synchronization-related constructs. Worker threads handle incoming requests, and shared resources like sockets are protected using mutexes. Furthermore, structured data types (**structs**) are used, whose impact on the precision can be evaluated. Obviously, analysis required an interprocedural setting to obtain meaningful results.

Table 1. Evaluation results on OPENTFTP

Analysis	# Races	Correct/Incorrect	T_{MTA}	T_{total}	$\frac{T_{\mathrm{MTA}}}{T_{total}}$	$\frac{T_{\mathrm{MTA}}}{\#Vars}$	$\frac{T_{\mathrm{MTA}}}{kLOC}$
Lock set	15	4/11 (27 %)	7.58 s	38.63 s	19.6 %	0.47 s	3.03 s
Combined	0	n.a.	131.49 s	153.86 s	85.4 %	8.21 s	51.94 s
Combined*	4	4/0 (100 %)	2176.85 s	2194.36 s	99.2 %	136.05 s	869.69 s

Out of 23 globally defined variables, 16 were identified as potentially shared and written to by at least on concurrent thread. Two distinct threads were identified, one being the main thread while the other is the `processRequest` worker-thread which is started for each incoming request; hence, thread creation is nested inside a loop. The initial run reported a multi-threaded control-flow graph with 2,339 distinct control-states and 3,766 transitions, and data races on 15 out of 16 shared variables.[2] Inspection revealed that the software was not programmed with respect to the POSIX standard, but with respect to some hidden assumptions on Linux, exploiting the fact that concurrently executing threads can release any lock held by any thread. We adjusted our model for this; the modified approach is denoted *Combined**, yielding precise results. Table 1 shows the results for the data race analysis using the lock set algorithm, the combined approach based on the POSIX standard, and the modified model based on the specific implementation on Linux exploited by the software.

5   Conclusion and Future Work

We propose a static implementation of the Eraser lock-set algorithm to detect possible data races in software. This analysis is sound but may result in false warnings. We add a second analysis step that model checks if potential data races detected by the lock-set analysis, can ever occur during program execution. Our two-step analysis takes into account the semantics of the Pthreads library, and is precise at the cost of a higher analysis overhead.

In future work, the performance of the second step could be improved further: As we consider only reachability properties, we could apply a strong partial-order reduction by abstracting from all concrete sequences of actions and considering only all possible global states. Moreover, instead of inlining procedures, some enriched summary information should be sufficient.

Other future work includes the analysis of other concurrency properties, such as deadlocks or high-level data races. Finally, the layered approach presented in this work may be applicable to other properties where fast over-approximations exist, making it be possible to balance speed and precision in a similar way.

Acknowledgments. NICTA is funded by the Australian Government (Department of Broadband, Communications and the Digital Economy) and the Australian Research Council through the ICT Centre of Excellence program.

---

[2] A multi-threaded control-flow graph embeds subgraphs of child threads into calls to `pthread_create`. The states and transitions thus correspond to local states; the number of global states is exponential in the number of local states and threads.

References

1. Artho, C., Biere, A.: Applying static analysis to large-scale, multithreaded Java programs. In: Proc. 13th ASWEC, Canberra, Australia, Canberra, Australia, pp. 68–75. IEEE (2001)
2. Artho, C., Havelund, K., Biere, A.: Using block-local atomicity to detect stale-value concurrency errors. In: Wang, F. (ed.) ATVA 2004. LNCS, vol. 3299, pp. 150–164. Springer, Heidelberg (2004)
3. Artho, C., Havelund, K., Biere, A.: High-level data races. Journal on Software Testing, Verification & Reliability (STVR) 13(4), 220–227 (2003)
4. Ball, T., Majumdar, R., Millstein, T., Rajamani, S.K.: Automatic predicate abstraction of C programs. SIGPLAN Not. 36(5), 203–213 (2001)
5. Clarke, E., Kroning, D., Sharygina, N., Yorav, K.: SATABS: SAT-based predicate abstraction for ANSI-C. In: Halbwachs, N., Zuck, L.D. (eds.) TACAS 2005. LNCS, vol. 3440, pp. 570–574. Springer, Heidelberg (2005)
6. Dias, R.J., Pessanha, V., Lourenço, J.M.: Precise Detection of Atomicity Violations. In: Biere, A., Nahir, A., Vos, T. (eds.) HVC. LNCS, vol. 7857, pp. 8–23. Springer, Heidelberg (2013)
7. Elmas, T., Qadeer, S., Tasiran, S.: Goldilocks: a race and transaction-aware Java runtime. SIGPLAN Not. 42(6), 245–255 (2007)
8. Fehnker, A., Huuck, R., Jayet, P., Lussenburg, M., Rauch, F.: Model checking software at compile time. In: Proc. TASE 2007. IEEE (2007)
9. Flanagan, C., Freund, S., Lifshin, M., Qadeer, S.: Types for atomicity: Static checking and inference for java. ACM Trans. Program. Lang. Syst. 30(4), 1–20 (2008)
10. Knoop, J., Steffen, B., Vollmer, J.: Parallelism for free: Efficient and optimal bitvector analyses for parallel programs. ACM Trans. Progr. Lang. Syst. 18(3), 299 (1996)
11. Loureno, J., Sousa, D., Teixeira, B., Dias, R.: Detecting concurrency anomalies in transactional memory programs. Computer Science and Information Systems 8(2) (April 2011)
12. Mund, J.: Finding Common Defects in Multi-Threaded Programs at Compile Time. PhD thesis, University of Augsburg (2010)
13. Naik, M., Aiken, A., Whaley, J.: Effective static race detection for Java. In: Proc. PLDI 2006, pp. 308–319. ACM (2006)
14. Pratikakis, P., Foster, J., Hicks, M.: LOCKSMITH: context-sensitive correlation analysis for race detection. ACM SIGPLAN Notices 41(6), 320–331 (2006)
15. Savage, S., Burrows, M., Nelson, G., Sobalvarro, P., Anderson, T.: Eraser: A dynamic data race detector for multithreaded programs. ACM Trans. on Computer Systems 15(4), 391–411 (1997)
16. Schonberg, E.: On-the-fly detection of access anomalies. In: Proc. PLDI 1989, pp. 285–297. ACM, New York (1989)
17. Seidl, H., Vojdani, V.: Region analysis for race detection. Static Analysis, 171–187 (2010)
18. Visser, W., Havelund, K., Brat, G., Park, S., Lerda, F.: Model checking programs. Automated Software Engineering Journal 10(2), 203–232 (2003)
19. Wang, C., Yang, Y., Gupta, A., Gopalakrishnan, G.: Dynamic model checking with property driven pruning to detect race conditions. In: Cha, S(S.), Choi, J.-Y., Kim, M., Lee, I., Viswanathan, M. (eds.) ATVA 2008. LNCS, vol. 5311, pp. 126–140. Springer, Heidelberg (2008)

Author Index